THESAURUS LINGUAE GRAECAE

Canon of Greek Authors and Works

THESAURUS LINGUAE GRAECAE

Canon of Greek Authors and Works

THIRD EDITION

Luci Berkowitz
Karl A. Squitier

with technical assistance from
William A. Johnson

New York   Oxford
OXFORD UNIVERSITY PRESS
1990

Oxford University Press

Oxford   New York   Toronto
Delhi   Bombay   Calcutta   Madras   Karachi
Petaling Jaya   Singapore   Hong Kong   Tokyo
Nairobi   Dar es Salaam   Cape Town
Melbourne   Auckland

and associated companies in
Berlin   Ibadan

Published by Oxford University Press, Inc.,
200 Madison Avenue, New York, New York 10016

Oxford is a registered trademark of Oxford University Press

Library of Congress Cataloging-in-Publication Data
Berkowitz, Luci.
Thesaurus Linguae Graecae canon of Greek authors and works
Luci Berkowitz, Karl A. Squitier
with technical assistance from William A. Johnson.
—3rd ed. p. cm. Includes bibliographical references.
ISBN 0-19-506037-7
1. Greek literature—Bibliography.
2. Thesaurus Linguae Graecae Project.
I. Squitier, Karl A.   II. Johnson, William A. (William Allen), 1956– .
III. Title. Z7021.B47 1990 [PA3051] 016.88—dc20
89-49454

2 4 6 8 9 7 5 3 1

Printed in the United States of America
on acid-free paper

CONTENTS

PREFACE TO THE SECOND EDITION

This volume sees the light of day at a juncture at which the Thesaurus Linguae Graecae (TLG), after more than thirteen years of operation, is nearing completion of its computer-based data bank of ancient Greek texts. The prefatory remarks that follow are meant to provide a brief summary of the TLG's history, objectives, and identity.

The latter part of the nineteenth century witnessed an ever-growing desire on the part of classicists for two comprehensive thesauri, one of Greek and one of Latin. To nineteenth-century classicists, the term *thesaurus* denoted a comprehensive lexicon citing and defining all (or essentially all) extant words of a language within a specific chronological framework.

The Thesaurus Linguae Latinae, focusing on approximately nine million words of extant Latin text, was born in the last decade of the 1800s; work on a Thesaurus Linguae Graecae was to commence shortly thereafter. As it happened, human capability was not quite equal to scholarly ambition. By 1905, Hermann Diels, articulating a sentiment shared by most of his colleagues, declared that a TLG was simply an impossible dream. Diels's views on the subject can be found in the 1925 preface to the Liddell, Scott, and Jones *Greek-English Lexicon:*

> Any one who bears in mind the bulk of Greek literature, which is at least 10 times as great [as that of Latin], its dialectical variations, its incredible wealth of forms, the obstinate persistence of the classical speech for thousands of years down to the fall of Constantinople, or, if you will, until the present day: who knows, moreover, that the editions of almost all the Greek classics are entirely unsuited for the purposes of slipping, that for many important writers no critical editions whatever exist: and who considers the state of our collections of fragments and special Lexica, will see that at the present time all the bases upon which a Greek Thesaurus could be erected are lacking.
>
> But even if we were to assume that we possessed such editions and collections from Homer down to Nonnus, or . . . down to Apostolius, and further that they had all been worked over, slipped, or excerpted by a gigantic staff of scholars, and that a great house had preserved and stored the thousands of boxes, whence would come the time, money, and power to sift these millions of slips and to bring Νοῦς into this Chaos?

Sixty-seven years later, the Thesaurus Linguae Graecae was born. Its identity was determined by a conclave of American, Canadian, and European classicists convening at the University of California, Irvine, in late September of 1972. Diels's views were discussed and considered correct—correct, that is, in a 1905 context. But it was now time to reexamine and reconsider sixty-seven-year-old definitions.

The 1972 Thesaurus Linguae Graecae Planning Conference indeed resulted in new definitions and in the acceptance of new methodologies. A thesaurus created in the late twentieth century, it was felt, should take advantage of late-twentieth-century technology. Flexibility, rather than rigidity, should characterize the final product.

In essence, the conference members recommended that the Thesaurus Linguae Graecae should employ computer-assisted data entry rather than manual *Verzettelung* in the process of data collection; that word definition should be one of many pursuits, rather than the principal pursuit, to be supported by such data collection; and that the TLG's product should be organic—that is, readily adaptable to continuing progress in scholarship—rather than static and "frozen" as traditional books and lexica become at the moment of publication. Thus, they created a new definition of the term *thesaurus:* the Greek thesaurus would be not a lexicon, but a computer data bank.

Today, the Thesaurus Linguae Graecae is indeed a data bank of ancient Greek texts allowing for consultation by the broadest possible scholarly audience, and a body of information that, though compiled in the 1970s and 1980s, can readily be adapted to the state of the art of classical scholarship in the future. Ten years ago, computer-assisted research was virtually foreign to our field; a mere handful of classicists sought access to the TLG's resources. Five years later, their number had increased manifold. Today, TLG data-bank texts are being utilized for research and pedagogical purposes at more than a hundred institutions around the United States and abroad, and during the past two years alone more than another hundred individuals or institutions have availed themselves of data and information generated in their behalf by the TLG. This is not the place to enumerate the multiple uses to which TLG data-bank texts are being put. It seems reasonable to predict, however, that five years hence use of the TLG's resources will be commonplace within the field of classics.

By necessity, creation of the TLG data bank entailed consideration of a vast number of ancillary concerns. The 1972 TLG Planning Conference members, for instance, advised the project staff that, when completed, the data bank should reflect all ancient Greek authors and texts extant from the period between Homer and A.D. 600. They did not, however, specify precisely which authors and texts would be involved. By early 1977, the project had sufficiently firm control over the period from Homer to A.D. 200 to complete data entry of the materials falling within this span. Achieving this control necessitated literary-historical and bibliographical research conducted (initially at least) for in-house purposes only.

By early 1977, however, the TLG's activities were also sufficiently well known to occasion requests not only for TLG machine-readable texts (or data generated therefrom) but also for ancillary materials such as the TLG staff's compilation of the literary canon. Between March and August 1977, in an effort to meet requests for information residing in this canon, the project distributed numerous versions of the canon in computer-printout form. In doing so, the project was severely taxed in terms of both staff and financial resources. In December 1977, a more formal *Canon of Greek Authors and Texts between Homer and A.D. 200* was published by a specially created vehicle, TLG Publications, Inc. A total of 250 copies of the *Canon* were produced in December 1977; by April 1978, the *Canon* was out of print. Financial considerations argued against a second printing; furthermore, the TLG staff was now well on its way toward gaining control over the post–A.D. 200 period. TLG Publications, Inc., was placed in a state of dormancy; never meant to function as a publishing house in the first place, the Thesaurus Linguae Graecae could ill afford to let its progress be retarded by publishing tasks far better handled by others.

It was not until 1984 that publication of a second and expanded edition of the *Canon* was considered. Once again, it was decided that the product of TLG literary-historical and bibliographic research, though meant primarily to support only in-house activities (i.e., data-bank creation), should not be denied to the field at large. Furthermore, by early 1985, the number of requests for TLG data-bank texts had grown to a point at which *ad hoc* duplication and dissemination of the blbliographic documentation issued along with TLG text files had reached unmanageable proportions. This volume aims at affording access to the results of thousands of hours of scholarly labor on the part of the TLG's research staff to the broadest possible audience.

There are many who are owed a profound debt of gratitude; in fact, their number is so great as to render comprehensive acknowledgment impossible. It is only proper, however, that the following grateful acknowledgments be made in this preface.

Like every other aspect of the TLG's overall product, this *Canon* is the end result of a massive financial investment sustained by the wisdom and generosity of a large number of private, federal, and institutional TLG supporters. Particular mention must be made of Mr. James C. Gianulias, Dr. Marianne McDonald, the Andrew W. Mellon Foundation, the National Endowment for the Humanities, the David and Lucile Packard Foundation, and the University of California, Irvine.

Next, this printed volume reflects but a small segment of vastly larger amounts of data and information residing both in the TLG data bank and in the electronic version of the TLG *Canon* and constituting a substructure without which the TLG data bank would be unmanageable and unusable. Creation and maintenance of this substructure would have been impossible without complex computing facilities, highly sophisticated software, and other technological support that was not readily available in the general marketplace. Above all in this context, a debt of gratitude is owed to David W. Packard, the creator of the Ibycus computer system, which has been used by the Thesaurus Linguae Graecae since 1980. Without William A. Johnson, neither the electronic nor the printed *Canon* would exist today; his contributions to the design and implementation of both were invaluable.

Finally though perhaps not readily visible, the labor of scores of TLG staff members who devoted their energies to the Thesaurus Linguae Graecae over the past thirteen years is also hidden in this volume. Their contributions are hereby gratefully acknowledged.

University of California, Irvine   THEODORE F. BRUNNER
October 1985   Director, Thesaurus Linguae Graecae

PREFACE TO THE THIRD EDITION

When the previous edition of the *Thesaurus Linguae Graecae Canon* was published in 1986, the TLG was approaching the completion of its data bank of Greek texts deriving from the period between Homer and A.D. 600. By mid-1987, the TLG data bank could be said to contain nearly all pre–A.D. 600 materials, and the project began to shift its focus toward the period between 600 and 1453. At the present juncture, the TLG is concerning itself with scholia to classical authors as well as with later Greek and Byzantine historiography and lexicography. This new edition of the *Canon* reflects the expansion of the TLG data bank in recent years.

Once again, we must acknowledge a profound debt of gratitude to those whose generosity was instrumental in allowing the TLG to grow. The National Endowment for the Humanities has continued to support the project with extensive federal grant funds. Matching for NEH grants was provided by the Annunciation Endowment Foundation, the Axios Foundation for Worthiness, the Costas and Mary Maliotis Charitable Foundation, Marianne McDonald, the David and Lucile Packard Foundation, and numerous private sources. Special thanks are owed to David W. Packard for his continued and multifaceted support of the project, to Athan Anagnostopoulos and Angelo Tsakopoulos for their generous willingness to champion the cause of the TLG, and to the University of California, Irvine, for its firm commitment to one of its major research enterprises.

TFB
January 1990

INTRODUCTION

The *Thesaurus Linguae Graecae Canon of Greek Authors and Works* is a printed version of the literary-historical and bibliographic substructure upon which the Thesaurus Linguae Graecae (TLG) data bank rests.[1] As the data bank grows, the canon also grows.[2] Developed originally as a form of recordkeeping necessary to exercise some measure of control over the thousands of texts that were being converted to machine-readable form, the canon has acquired a character of its own, along with a utility that transcends its functional relationship with the data bank.

Functions of the Canon

In a sense, the canon is designed to function as an electronic aid to the project staff who currently must confront nearly 3,200 authors and more than 9,400 individual pieces of text. It must perform the work of an orderly guide to the authors and works selected for inclusion in the data bank, and it must lend itself to daily maintenance, updating, and correction. Accompanying the name of each author, for instance, are various categories of information that help to distinguish one writer from another, such as author epithets that tradition has preserved to define the essence or character of an individual's literary activity, geographical epithets that identify place of birth or place of domicile during the most productive literary years, date by century in which an author flourished, patronymics, political or religious affiliations, and professional titles. As new information pertaining to authors emerges, it is entered into the canon as supplement or emendation.

As a bibliographic guide to the works of each author, the canon identifies the text editions that have been recommended and endorsed for inclusion in the data bank by the American Philological Association's Advisory Committee on the Thesaurus Linguae Graecae.[3] It also accounts for the emergence of new, improved text editions that may replace older editions already in the data bank. In addition, the canon performs the work of a calculator, tabulating a constantly growing word count, augmented

---

[1] The substance of this introduction is taken from L. Berkowitz and K. A. Squitier, *Thesaurus Linguae Graecae canon of Greek authors and works*, 2nd edn. (New York & Oxford 1986) xi–xxviii. A number of changes were necessitated by five factors: (1) expansion of the data bank during 1986–1989; (2) addition of authors not previously carried on the TLG's roster; (3) inclusion of *addenda* and *corrigenda;* (4) assignment of classification tags to individual works in the TLG data bank; (5) listing of citation systems used for each corrected work.

[2] Henceforth, "canon" will denote the electronic instrument; "*Canon*" will indicate its printed derivative.

[3] The name of this committee was changed in 1980 from APA TLG Advisory Committee to American Philological Association Committee on the Thesaurus Linguae Graecae.

annually by several million words of Greek text. In the process, the canon is also expected to maintain a current record of the status of each text, that is, whether it has simply been converted to machine-readable form or whether it has also been verified and corrected.[4]

The canon is also expected to respond, promptly and efficiently, to questions that draw upon the vast amount of information stored in it. The canon resides in an Ibycus computer system that offers, as one of its many virtues, a means for rapid retrieval of information regarding authors, bibliographic data, status of individual works, word counts, and prosopographical details.

All of these expectations—cataloging, recording, counting, updating, responding quickly and accurately to queries—have been realized even as the canon has continued to grow in size and complexity. In 1977, when the first edition of the *Canon* was published, approximately 20,000,000 words resided in the data bank, and 1,688 authors had been identified. In 1986, a second, revised edition of the *Canon* reflected that the data bank had expanded in size by more than two and a half times in less than a decade: nearly 57,000,000 words were housed in the data bank, and the number of authors had grown to 2,884. With the inclusion of the major scholiastic texts and the beginning of data capture of Byzantine historiography and lexicography, the TLG's holdings have been steadily amplified: at the end of 1989, the data bank consisted of more than 65,000,000 words by 3,165 authors. As both the data bank and the canon have grown considerably during the past triennium, a new edition of the *Canon* again seems appropriate.

Scope of the *Canon*

The scope of this edition extends beyond the original TLG cutoff date of A.D. 600, but with different degrees of completeness along the way. In fact and in practice, the year 600 does not lend itself to either reality or realization. Many authors who antedate 600 are recoverable only by extracting them from the texts of later quoters. Moreover, the addition of scholiastic texts would have been unthinkable without inclusion of the *scholia recentiora* from the Byzantine period. Thus, 600 can no longer limit the TLG's chronological scope for data capture; indeed, that initial terminus has already been exceeded many times.

Inasmuch as the *Canon* is both a reflection of texts already deposited in the data bank and a projection of texts to be added to the data bank, its scope is somewhat broader than the actual contents of the data bank. In this edition of the *Canon*, the scope for each chronological phase is defined as follows:

> *Phase I: Homer to A.D. 200.* Virtually all authors represented by text, whether in independent editions or in quoted form, are listed together with complete bibliographies for all works.

---

[4]The TLG utilizes the services of an overseas contractor for data entry. After conversion into electronic form, the texts are subjected to extensive verification and correction routines by the TLG staff in order to assure a maximum degree of accuracy.

Phase II: 200 to 400. Authors currently represented by text in the data bank are listed together with their bibliographies. Also listed are authors whose works are yet to be added to the data bank. In some instances, the bibliographies cited for such authors are incomplete and the available text editions are not ideal for data entry.[5]

Phase III: 400 to 600. Authors currently represented by text in the data bank are listed together with a bibliography of the specific works that have been converted into machine-readable form.

Phase IV: 600 to 1453. Authors represented by text in the data bank are listed with a bibliography of the specific works that reside in the data bank. Although by no means systematically explored, this period is nonetheless already represented by some of the most important sources for quotations of earlier authors.[6] Also included are the scholia to authors of the classical period,[7] as well as a significant amount of Byzantine historiography and chronography.[8]

Generally, the authors listed in the *Canon* are represented by some form of text that owes its provenance to codices, papyri, inscriptions, or quotations by later authors. There are, however, some authors who are lost except for the testimonia provided by later authors. Although some have been subjected to the challenging but sometimes problematical task of reconstruction, or reconstitution, of their *ipsissima verba*, many others have been consigned to the roster of lost writers. Some of these lost writers have, in fact, been assigned a place in the *Canon*, although there has not been a consistent effort to include every lost author mentioned in the surviving testimonia. The only criterion that has been usefully operative in determining whether a lost author ought to be included has been the fact that the lost author occupies a place in a generic collection of fragments that either is or will be part of the data bank. A lost author may be represented by as little as a title, a list of titles, or a descriptive word that characterizes the literary genre to which the lost writings may have belonged. Entirely omitted from the *Canon*, however, are authors who are known to us only by way of anecdote or through recollected or (ostensibly) reported conversation. Such authors remain lost, and it is the anecdotist whose text resides in the data bank.[9]

[5] For example, Ephraem Syrus, for whom the seventeenth-century Assemani edition (with its numerous ligatures and codical abbreviations) remains the principal available text.

[6] For example, Sophronius (A.D. 6–7), Joannes Damascenus (A.D. 7–8), Photius (A.D. 9), Eustathius Thessalonicensis (A.D. 12).

[7] During 1987–1990, TLG data entry focused upon *scholia vetera* and *scholia recentiora*, whether they were the works of identifiable scholiasts such as Joannes Tzetzes (A.D. 12), Thomas Magister (A.D. 13–14), and Demetrius Triclinius (A.D. 13–14), or of critics and commentators whose names have not survived along with their learned remarks about ancient works of literature.

[8] Especially those authors represented in the original Bonn Corpus, that is, *Corpus scriptorum historiae Byzantinae* (Bonn 1828–1897); for example, Constantinus VII Porphyrogenitus, Georgius Syncellus, Theophanes Confessor, *Theophanes Continuatus*, *Chronicon Paschale*.

[9] The 744 lost works cited in this *Canon* are identifiable by the letters *NQ* (no quotation). For an explanation of codes used to identify the method of transmission of a given work, see pages xxv–xxvii.

Use of the *Canon*

Each author and work in the *Canon* is provided with categories of information that may be useful to scholars interested in history, literary history, and prosopography, as well as to those who simply want to know what editions have been deposited in the data bank. It should be emphasized, however, that the specific categories were devised initially to assist the project staff in quickly locating information about a given author or work. While certain kinds of information may give the appearance of esoterica,[10] the arrangement of the *Canon* should permit even the casual surveyor to locate easily only those items of particular interest.

The categories of information provided for each author listed in this *Canon* are

> TLG Author Number
> Author Name
> Author Epithet
> Date
> Geographical Epithet

The categories of information accompanying each discrete work assigned to an author are

> TLG Work Number
> Work Title
> Text Edition Selected for Data Entry
> Transmission
> Word Count or Word Estimate
> Classification

TLG Author Number. Each author in the canon is assigned a permanent four-digit number meant to permit rapid identification in a computer environment. In the *Canon,* the author number is located in the extreme left-hand margin of the column. An exception is made in the case of authors whose text, if it exists, is to be located elsewhere in the *Canon.* For example, Alcinous, whose name has been transmitted to us as a scribal error for *Albinus* in all of the manuscripts,[11] is cited without an author number of his own[12] but with an appropriate cross-reference, as follows:

ALCINOUS Phil.
Cf. ALBINUS Phil. (0693).

This applies also to authors whose name tradition has been subordinated to the names of works they are supposed to have written, such as

---

[10] For example, author number, work number, word estimate.

[11] Cf. P. Louis, *Albinos: Épitomé* (Paris 1945) xii–xiii.

[12] In the electronic canon, all entries are numbered, including those whose only function is to redirect the user to another entry. These are numbered with the prefix *x*. For example, the entry for Abercius, which cross-refers to the entry for *Epitaphium Abercii*, is numbered x001.

ARCTINUS Epic.
Cf. AETHIOPIS (0683).
Cf. ILIU PERSIS (1445).
Cf. TITANOMACHIA (1737).

as well as to works that once occupied an independent status but are now associated with authors, such as

ANAGRAPHE LINDIA
Cf. TIMACHIDAS Hist. (1732).

and to works that are commonly subsumed into other works, such as

VETUS TESTAMENTUM
Cf. SEPTUAGINTA (0527).

The author number is also an abbreviated way of referring to authors. It is simply easier and more efficient to cite according to the author number 1760 than to the author name *Gaius Suetonius Tranquillus*. Nevertheless, author numbers are more significant to those who interact directly with the computer than to those who consult the *Canon* simply for bibliographic data.[13]

Author Name. Entries in the *Canon* are arranged in alphabetical order according to names of authors and, where authors' names are not known, commonly recognized names of extant treatises, poems, or literary corpora. Names of authors are printed in boldface capital letters, and names of literary works (standing in lieu of authors' names) are given in boldface italic capitals, as follows:

HIPPIAS
HIPPIATRICA
HIPPOCRATES et ***CORPUS HIPPOCRATICUM***
HISTORIA ALEXANDRI MAGNI

Authors with identical names are listed according to the alphabetical priority of their commonly recognized author epithets. For example, the three authors bearing the name *Eudoxus* are listed in the following order:

EUDOXUS Astron.
EUDOXUS Comic.
EUDOXUS Hist.

Authors with identical names and identical epithets are listed in chronological order according to presumed date of authorship. The two authors identified as Alexander Rhet., for example, are distinguished by the supposition that one seems to have flourished during the first century B.C. and the other during the second century A.D. Hence, the earlier author is listed first. When a date cannot even be conjectured, the author is listed last in the chronological order. Thus, the three authors listed as Apollonius Hist. are arranged in the order of their surmised dates: 3 B.C.?, 2 B.C., *Incertum*.

Authors with identical names, identical epithets, and identical dates are cited in

---

[13] The index of authors by author number on pages 407–423 is meant to assist those who consult TLG machine-readable texts and require access to a reference system that quickly translates author numbers into author names.

numerical order of their TLG author numbers. The two writers of comedy who bear the name *Apollodorus,* and who seem to have been contemporaries and were sometimes confused with each other, are listed as follows:

0411 **APOLLODORUS** Comic.
4/3 B.C.: Carystius
0413 **APOLLODORUS** Comic.
4/3 B.C.: Gelous

With the exception of the Pseudo-Auctores Hellenistae and Pseudo-Callisthenes (whose names are alphabetized in the appropriate spot under the letter *P*), names of all authors with the prefix *Pseudo-* are located in the alphabetical position dictated by the second element of the hyphenated name. Thus, *Pseudo-Plutarchus* follows immediately after *Plutarchus*.

Authors whose names are recognized more readily in conjunction with some form of additional descriptive epithet (e.g., place of birth, place of literary activity, patronymic, nickname) are listed after other authors of the same name who are identified only by an author epithet. In the case of such complex names, order is determined by alphabetical sequence of descriptive epithets. Thus, the five Antonii are cited in the following order:

ANTONIUS Epigr.
ANTONIUS Med.
ANTONIUS DIOGENES Scr. Erot.
ANTONIUS JULIANUS Hist.
ANTONIUS MUSA Med.

A descriptive epithet that has become an integral part of an author's identity is printed in boldface capital letters to distinguish it from an epithet frequently used but not universally regarded as inseparable from an author's name. Thus,

DIONYSIUS THRAX   but   **DIONYSIUS Sophista**

Some author names have survived with praenomen, nomen, and cognomen intact. When this is the case, the authors are cited in an alphabetical location determined by their most commonly recognized name. For example, Tiberius Claudius Polybius is cited in the appropriate alphabetical order under the letter *P*; Gaius Suetonius Tranquillus is cited under the letter *S*.

Occasionally, author names are enclosed in angle brackets (< >) or square brackets ([ ]). Angle brackets indicate an author to whom a given work has been assigned, although that person may not be the author of the work in question. For example, the presumed author Ostanes Magus may have no connection to the alchemical fragments assigned to him by Bidez and Cumont.[14] Similarly, Myia Phil., purported to be the daughter of Pythagoras (sixth century B.C.), is also the presumed author of a letter on child care that, despite its archaisms, seems to have been written no earlier than the third century B.C.[15] Their names are thus given as follows:

[14]Cf. J. Bidez and F. Cumont, *Les mages hellénisés,* vol. 1 (Paris 1938; repr. 1973) 173, 198–207.
[15]Cf. H. Thesleff, *An introduction to the Pythagorean writings of the Hellenistic period* (Åbo 1961) 90, 102, 115.

<OSTANES Magus>   and   <MYIA> Phil.

Square brackets enclosing an author's name are intended to question the authenticity of the name; even the existence of the author may be disputed. For instance, *Bacis* seems to have been the name not of an individual author but of an entire class of inspired priests or prophets.[16] And *Linus*, despite the noble parentage the ancient poets have concocted for this much bewailed name, may be nothing more than an eponym for a popular kind of threnody.[17] These names appear as follows:

[BACIS]   and   [LINUS]

In some instances, the identity of one author is linked to another by means of the abbreviation *fiq (fortasse idem qui)*. Adaeus Epigr. and Athenaeus Epigr., for example, are respectively linked to Adaeus Rhet. and Athenaeus Soph. as follows:

ADAEUS Epigr.   and   ATHENAEUS Epigr.
fiq Adaeus Rhet.   fiq Athenaeus Soph.

The notation *fiq* occurs 143 times in the *Canon*, whenever there is reason to suggest that the identities of two separately listed authors may be the same, although there is no conclusive evidence for merging them into one.

Occasionally, it is possible to suggest the name of an author for a work that has been transmitted anonymously. In such instances, the cautious formula *fort(asse) auctore* has been added, as follows:

AEGIMIUS
fort. auctore Cercope vel Hesiodo

In a few instances, the abbreviation *fort.* is used to suggest solutions to the missing pieces in a name. For example, the name fragment *enodorus* is completed as *[Ath]enodorus*, but it might just as reasonably be conceived with other letters initiating the name,[18] hence the following notation:

[ATH]ENODORUS Trag.
fort. [Z]enodorus vel [M]enodorus

Author Epithet. The epithets attached to authors' names are intended to link authors to the kinds of literary activity in which they were primarily engaged.[19] For the most part, author epithets are consistent with traditional usage in literary histories, biographical dictionaries, lexica, and commentaries. The epithets used for authors in this *Canon* are listed in Figure 1.

Occasionally, two or even three epithets may be required to define an author, al-

---

[16] E. Rohde, *Psyche*, vol. 2, 8th edn., trans. W. B. Hillis (New York 1966) 292–293, 314 (n. 58).

[17] Cf. H. J. Rose's article on Linus in *The Oxford classical dictionary (OCD)*, 2nd edn. (Oxford 1970) 611.

[18] B. Snell, *Tragicorum Graecorum fragmenta*, vol. 1 (Göttingen 1971) 309.

[19] Epithets are assigned only to the names of authors. The electronic canon, however, contains a provision for identifying the generic character of literary works that stand in lieu of authors' names. Thus, a scholar seeking all citations of a word or word pattern in epic could expect to find citations not only from writers such as Homer, Hesiod, Apollonius Rhodius, and Nicander but also from writings such as the *Hymni Homerici*, *Titanomachia*, *Aegimius*, and *Cypria*.

Figure 1. List of Epithets Used for Identification of Authors

Alchem(ista)*	Geogr(aphus)	Mimogr(aphus)	Poet(a) Med(icus)
Apol(ogeta)	Geom(etra)	Mus(icus)	Poet(a) Phil(osophus)
Astrol(ogus)	Gnom(ologus)	Myth(ographus)	Poeta
Astron(omus)	Gnost(icus)	Onir(ocriticus)	Polyhist(or)
Attic(ista)	Gramm(aticus)	Orat(or)	Rhet(or)
Biogr(aphus)	Hist(oricus)	Paradox(ographus)	Scr(iptor)
Bucol(icus)	Hymnogr(aphus)	Parodius	Eccl(esiasticus)
Choliamb(ographus)	Iamb(ographus)	Paroemiogr(aphus)	Scr(iptor) Erot(icus)
Chronogr(aphus)	Int(erpres) Vet(eris)	Perieg(eta)	Scr(iptor) Fab(ularum)
Comic(us)	Test(amenti)	Phil(osophus)	Scr(iptor) Rerum
Doxogr(aphus)	Lexicogr(aphus)	Philol(ogus)	Nat(uralium)
Eleg(iacus)	Lyr(icus)	Poet(a) Astrol(ogus)	Soph(ista)
Epic(us)	Math(ematicus)	Poet(a) Christ(ianus)	Tact(icus)
Epigr(ammaticus)	Mech(anicus)	Poet(a) Didac(ticus)	Theol(ogus)
Epist(olographus)	Med(icus)	Poet(a) Ethic(us)	Trag(icus)

*Epithets in the *Canon* are cited in abbreviated form without regard for distinctions in gender or number. The reader is therefore free to supply the correct Latin ending, as in Simonides Lyr(icus) but Sappho Lyr(ica), or Herodotus Med(icus) but Herodotus et Philumenus Med(ici). For ease of reference, the epithets are spelled out here in their masculine singular form only.

though there has been no attempt to reflect every possibility. Aristotle would need at least fifteen different epithets if it were necessary to characterize him in terms of the entire Aristotelian corpus.[20] Yet, no single epithet can be expected to encompass the variety and individuality of the literary works of so polymathic and prolific an author as Aristotle.[21] It is quite in accordance with tradition, however, to permit the epithet *Phil.* to function, albeit imprecisely, in behalf of the entire Aristotelian corpus.

In the case of authors whose literary output cannot be conveniently classified with a traditional epithet, there has been no attempt to impose one artificially. Yet, sometimes it is possible to define the character of unconventional writing with a fairly simple description initiated by the word *Scriptor,* as has been done for Chrysippus Scriptor Rei Coquinariae and Simon Scriptor De Re Equestri. On the other hand, it has sometimes seemed useful to attach an author epithet to a personality who is not usually enrolled in a *repertorium litterarum* but who has left some literary work to posterity. In such cases, an epithet enclosed in angle brackets is meant to suggest that the extant writing falls within the literary genre indicated, although the author in question was not primarily a writer in that genre, or even a writer at all, such as Praxiteles <Epigr.>.

Since epithets do not always characterize accurately and precisely the contents of a writer's literary corpus, a caveat is in order here. Some epithets contain a hint of an intellectual or even religious persuasion rather than the distinctive literary qualities that might suggest a specific genre. For instance, the *gnostici* might be regarded more

[20] In alphabetical order, *astronomus, elegiacus, epistolographus, grammaticus, historicus, lyricus, mathematicus, mechanicus, medicus, onirocriticus, paradoxographus, philosophus, physiognomonicus, rhetor, scriptor naturalium historiarum.*

[21] This inadequacy is rectified by the application of classification tags to discrete works. See "Classification of Works in the TLG Data Bank," pages xxxi–xlix.

properly as *philosophi* or *theologi*, inasmuch as gnosticism implies an attitude rather than a style of writing. Similarly, the *philologi* and *polyhistores* occupy a special place in the history of literature because they seem almost to have made a profession of crossing literary barriers, and their works reflect a wide range of generic writing. In addition, there are forty-five authors who are epithetized simply as *poeta*, without further definition of the specific kind of poetry they wrote. This may be owing to the variety of meters they employed[22] or to the simple fact that certain remnants of poetry defy categorization.[23]

Date. The assignment of dates in the *Canon* is based on a need, realized early in the history of the TLG, to identify the authors and works surviving from the period between Homer and approximately A.D. 200, the first of the four periods that constitute the scope of the project. While neither the TLG staff nor the APA Committee on the TLG imagined that the vexatious questions of chronology could be laid to rest by the assignment of dates, it was apparent that dates could fulfill a useful, albeit limited, function. The scholar who might request a listing of all instances of the word ὕβρις in fifth-century B.C. literature either would have to provide the TLG with a list of the authors whose works should be searched or else would have to rely upon the TLG's ability to provide such a list. The only way the TLG could identify fifth-century B.C. authors who might have used the word ὕβρις would be to have recourse to an already established record of dates. Thus, dates—with all of the imperfections and speculativeness that they imply—have become a fixture of the canon, sometimes functioning as an organizing principle in responding to certain requests for information from the data bank.

Date information in this *Canon* is located immediately beneath author name. Arabic numerals in cardinal form indicate the century of an author's *floruit*.[24] A dash between numerals indicates that the author's *floruit* spans the two centuries. Thus, the date given for Strabo Geogr. is 1 B.C.–A.D. 1, based upon the approximate dates of his sojourns in Rome (44–35 B.C., again ca. 31 B.C., and a third time in 7 B.C.), Egypt (25 until ca. 19 B.C.), and Amasia (ca. 7 B.C. until his death sometime after A.D. 21).[25]

When no firmer evidence can be adduced, a virgule between numerals is used to suggest the earliest and latest possible dates. Thus, the date given for Alciphron Rhet. et Soph. is A.D. 2/3, meaning that the earliest possible date for his letters (though

[22] For example, Ion of Chios, whose poetry seems to have spanned the spectrum from tragedy to comedy, and from lyric to elegiacs and epigrams. Cf. the article on Ion by A. W. Pickard-Cambridge and D. W. Lucas in the *OCD*, 549–550.

[23] For example, Cleomachus of Magnesia who, if he were to be labeled, might best be called κιναιδογράφος. Cf. Pauly-Wissowa 11, 677, #3; H. Lloyd-Jones and P. Parsons, *Supplementum Hellenisticum* (Berlin 1983) 162.

[24] Information regarding dates in the *Canon* is drawn from a variety of sources, including the standard lexica, biographical dictionaries, encyclopedias, and literary histories as well as modern publications that address specific chronological problems. Particularly useful for consultation during the past few years have been *Clavis patrum Graecorum*, 5 vols., ed. M. Geerard and F. Glorie (Turnhout 1974–1987), and *Clavis scriptorum Graecorum et Latinorum*, 4 vols., ed. R. LaRue, G. Vincent, and B. St.-Onge (Trois-Rivières, Québec, 1985).

[25] Cf. E. H. Warmington on Strabo in the *OCD*, 1017.

purportedly written by Athenian fishermen, farmers, parasites, and courtesans of the fourth century B.C.) is the second century and the latest is the third.[26]

When only a *terminus ante quem* is discernible, or at least logically to be assumed, this is indicated by, for instance, *ante* 1 B.C. for Socrates Argivus, an *historicus* whom Jacoby dates "vor Demetrius Magnes."[27] The word *ante*, however, can encompass both antecedence and contemporaneity. Apollonius Med.—the one from Tarsus[28]— is datable only in relation to Galen (who can be dated with certainty to the second century), but whether he was Galen's contemporary or predecessor is indeterminable.

Similarly, a *terminus post quem* is indicated by the word *post* and the appropriate century; the date for Ariston Hist., for instance, is given as *post* 3 B.C.[29]

Question marks have been used with dates that are considered problematical, as for Democritus Epigr. (ante A.D. 3?) and Aristocles Paradox. (3 B.C.?/A.D. 1). When it is simply impossible to suggest a date, the word *Incertum* has been used instead, as for Zenodotus Trag.[30] *Incertum* is also assigned to many of the letters attached to a well-known name, although they were certainly composed later, such as *Chilonis Epistula*, *Cratetis Epistulae*, and *Themistoclis Epistulae*.[31]

Geographical Epithet. Certain authors are distinguished by a descriptive word conjoined to their names and denoting a location.[32] Most authors, however, are recognized by their individual proper names, and geographical epithets are subordinated to their names. In the *Canon*, geographical epithets are positioned after the date and separated from it by a colon.

Obviously, it is impossible to provide an appropriate geographical epithet for every author, although in some cases it is possible to suggest two or three places associated with an author's *floruit*. The inadequacy of geographical epithets lies in their failure to distinguish place of birth from place of literary activity or place of residence in an official or ecclesiastical capacity. For example, the geographical epithets *Antiochenus* and *Constantinopolitanus* in connection with Joannes Chrysostomus Scr. Eccl. do not tell us that the author may have studied rhetoric under Libanius and theology under Diodorus of Tarsus at Antioch or that he was appointed bishop of Constantinople in

---

[26] Cf. the lengthy discourse in A. R. Benner and F. H. Fobes, *Alciphron, Aelian, Philostratus: The letters* (London 1949; repr. 1962) 6–18. Benner and Fobes accept Reich's *terminus post quem* of ca. 170 (p. 14) but insist that a *terminus ante quem* is "still to seek" (p. 18). Cf. also B. Baldwin, "The date of Alciphron," *Hermes* 110 (1982) 253–254, who dates the letters no later than the first decade of the third century.

[27] Cf. *FGrH* #310, vol. 3B, p. 15; also Pauly-Wissowa 4, 2814, #80. Socrates seems to have been included among historiographers by Demetrius Magnes (*FGrH*, vol. 3B, *Kommentar*, p. 37). Cicero recalls that Demetrius Magnes dedicated and sent to Atticus a book entitled Περὶ ὁμονοίας that Cicero himself would now like to read (*Epist. ad Atticum* 11). If this Demetrius Magnes was indeed the author of this Περὶ ὁμονοίας, his contemporaneity with Cicero and Atticus would establish the *terminus ante quem* for Socrates.

[28] Seven medical writers named simply Apollonius are listed. The one in question here is the seventh in order, bearing the TLG author number 0782.

[29] Jacoby dates him "frühestens s. IIIa," *FGrH* #337, vol. 3B, p. 188.

[30] Cf. Snell, *TrGF*, vol. 1, pp. viii, 319, 325.

[31] Cf. Hercher, *Epist. Graec.*, pp. 193, 208–217, 741–762.

[32] For example, Apollonius Rhodius, Diodorus Siculus, Dionysius Thrax.

398.[33] Nor do the three geographical epithets *Antiochenus, Constantinopolitanus,* and *Nicomediensis* in association with Libanius Rhet. et Soph. tell us that he was born (314) and educated in Antioch, that he taught rhetoric in Constantinople for two years (340–342), that he fled "under a cloud" to Nicomedia where his professional tenure lasted five years (344–349), and that he returned to Antioch where he assumed a chair of rhetoric (354) and spent the last three and a half decades of his life.[34]

An effort to be exhaustive in charting the lives and activities of authors in terms of geographical epithets would be doomed to failure in most cases and altogether absurd in many others. What geographical epithets might be cited in connection with a writer as well traveled as, say, Herodotus? The result would be either too unwieldy to be useful for quick consultation or too abbreviated to convey the extent of his travels through the ancient world. In this *Canon,* the only geographical epithets retained for Herodotus are *Halicarnassensis* and *Thurius.* Halicarnassus was his birthplace, and Thurii was the panhellenic foundation he helped to colonize.[35]

Geographical epithets can be especially useful for the purposes of the *Canon* if they are used to distinguish authors of the same name, such as Aeschylus Trag. Atheniensis and Aeschylus Trag. Alexandrinus. But there has not been a systematic effort to include geographical epithets for all authors. Indeed, there is one generic group of authors, the *comici,* for whom the epithet *Atheniensis* might be appropriate, but systematic assignment of geographical epithets remains a task for more leisurely days in the future. In the meantime, those that do appear in this edition are the result of either a fairly firm tradition (including a firm tradition of uncertainty) or a need to distinguish one author from another. There are, moreover, many authors whose geographical connections we can only surmise. When this is the case, the geographical epithet is preceded by the word *fort(asse).* For example, we know a great deal about the places Pausanias Perieg. visited because his *Graeciae descriptio* is a mine of information about geography, topography, and ethnography, but oddly enough we do not know for certain his place of birth. Hence, the most informative geographical epithet that can be attached to his name is *fort. Lydius.*[36] Finally, there are many authors

---

[33]Cf. Sozomenus, *Historia ecclesiastica* 8.2.2–2.3: ἦν δέ τις ἐν Ἀντιοχείᾳ τῇ παρ' Ὀρόντῃ πρεσβύτερος ὄνομα Ἰωάννης, γένος τῶν εὐπατριδῶν, ἀγαθὸς τὸν βίον, λέγειν τε καὶ πείθειν δεινὸς καὶ τοὺς κατ' αὐτὸν ὑπερβάλλων ῥήτορας, ὡς καὶ Λιβάνιος ὁ Σύρος σοφιστὴς ἐμαρτύρησεν· ἡνίκα γὰρ ἔμελλε τελευτᾶν, πυνθανομένων τῶν ἐπιτηδείων, τίς ἀντ' αὐτοῦ ἔσται, λέγεται εἰπεῖν Ἰωάννην, εἰ μὴ Χριστιανοὶ τοῦτον ἐσύλησαν. Although there seems to be no explicit acknowledgment, here or elsewhere, that the Joannes in Libanius's dying statement is Joannes Chrysostomus, there is a long tradition of recognizing Chrysostomus as Libanius's student. See, for instance, Pauly-Wissowa 9, 1812, 25ff.; F. L. Cross, *The Oxford dictionary of the Christian church* (London 1958; repr. 1966) 282–283; and more recently, A.-M. Malingrey, *Palladios: Dialogue sur la vie de Jean Chrysostome,* vol. 1 (Paris 1988) 107, n. 3. Malingrey dates his ordination as bishop of Constantinople to December 15, 397, with formal installation on February 26, 398 (p. 23, n. 1).

[34]Cf. R. Browning on Libanius in the *OCD,* 605–606; also A. F. Norman, *Libanius: Selected works* (London 1969) xxxix–xlv. In fact, some might argue that Atheniensis might be added to the list, inasmuch as Libanius spent four years (336–340) in Athens completing his education; cf. Norman, p. xxxix.

[35]Cf. W. W. How and J. Wells, *A commentary on Herodotus,* vol. 1 (Oxford 1912) 5–9, 16.

[36]But cf. J. G. Frazer, *Pausanias's description of Greece,* vol. 1 (Cambridge 1898) xix, who thinks that, on the basis of internal evidence, "there are good grounds for believing that he was a Lydian," and that it may even be reasonable to surmise that he was born and raised in the area of Mount Sipylus.

whose geographical connections we cannot possibly guess. When this is so, the space allotted for geographical epithets remains blank.

TLG Work Number. Each discrete work ascribed to an author bears a three-digit identification number. This number is located to the left of the work title. Generally, work numbers appear in numerical order, beginning with 001, although there are several lengthy bibliographies for which work numbers appear out of order.[37] The reason for this is that often a work was assigned the next number in sequence when it was selected for data entry, even though its order in a meaningful bibliography may not be reflected by that work number. In fact, in the electronic canon the sequence in a given bibliography is numerical, whereas in the printed *Canon* there has been some consideration for rearrangement of items in certain bibliographies that would otherwise be unwieldy.

In many instances, a work ascribed to an author may not warrant independent status. This is true of the many quotations (whether direct or indirect) or paraphrases (with at least a hint of *ipsissima verba*) that actually reside in the work of other authors, especially compendious medical writers such as Galen, Oribasius, Paul of Aegina, and Aëtius, as well as egregious collectors of quotations such as Athenaeus and Stobaeus. In the case of these works, the first of the three digits in the work number is replaced by an *x*, indicating that the work is not to be found in an independent text edition. For example, the writings of the Alexandrian medical scholar Erasistratus of Ceos (0690) do not survive except in the works of others and are therefore regarded as quoted works. Thus, x01 is the work number for the fragments of Erasistratus that are quoted by Galen, x02 the fragments provided by Pseudo-Galen, and x03 the fragments cited by Oribasius.

Works that are part of a larger collection may or may not warrant consideration as separate works belonging to a given author. Epigrams in the *Anthologia Graeca*, for example, are regarded as though they are independent works assigned to specific authors.[38] For instance, the twenty-eight epigrams attributed to Diogenes Laertius in the *Anthologia Graeca* bear Diogenes' author number 0004 and the work number 002. On the other hand, the sixteen epigrams ascribed to Diogenes Laertius in the *Anthologiae Graecae Appendix* bear the number 0004 x01. Unlike the *Anthologia Graeca*, the *Appendix* (abbreviated *App. Anth.* in the *Canon*) does not lend itself so readily to analysis according to individual authors, but rather breaks naturally into classes of epigrams, such as *Epigrammata sepulcralia* (Book 2), *Epigrammata demonstrativa* (Book 3), and *Epigrammata irrisoria* (Book 5). Other collections, such as *Iambi et elegi Graeci*[39] and the *Supplementum Hellenisticum*,[40] are easily broken into their constituent parts,

---

[37] For example, Aristotle, Galen, Gregory of Nyssa, John Chrysostom, Plutarch, to name only a few. Scholars who work with TLG machine-readable texts may find it useful to consult the index on pages 425–428 for the arrangement of such voluminous bibliographies according to sequential work numbers and *Canon* page on which each work number and its accompanying bibliography are located.

[38] However, the *Anthologia Graeca* has also been given the status of "author" with its own author number (7000).

[39] 2 vols., ed. M. L. West (Oxford 1971–1972).

[40] Ed. H. Lloyd-Jones and P. Parsons (Berlin 1983).

that is to say into the individual authors represented in these collections. The *Anthologiae Graecae Appendix* defies such resolution.

Work Title. The works assigned to each author are designated by their commonly recognized titles (in boldface letters), with a preference for the Latin, or sometimes Latinized, title. Where the title of a work either resists Latinization or is simply better known by its Greek counterpart, the Greek title is retained.

It is not always feasible and is sometimes not possible to assign a title to the remnants of an author's writings beyond the word *Fragmentum* or *Fragmenta*. While the seven surviving plays of Sophocles (0011 001–007), for example, are identified by their familiar Latin titles, the thousand or so Sophoclean fragments, many of which can confidently be assigned to specific lost plays,[41] are called simply *Fragmenta* (0011 008–010). This does not mean that the titles of the lost plays are ignored; titles are deposited in the data bank and are retrievable along with the text of the fragments they govern.

Occasionally, alternative titles of a work are included, especially if both titles seem to have been used interchangeably, as with Anaximenes of Lampsacus (0547), whose work 001 is cited as *Ars rhetorica* vulgo *Rhetorica ad Alexandrum,* or Gregory of Nyssa (2017), whose work 063 is entitled *De spiritu sancto* sive *In pentecosten.*

In general, however, the titles of works are consistent with those found in lexica and biographical dictionaries, as well as in the text editions themselves.

Text Edition Selected for Data Entry. All text editions cited in this *Canon* have been approved by the American Philological Association's Committee on the Thesaurus Linguae Graecae. Obviously, advances in scholarship, and particularly in text editing, necessitate constant reevaluation of previously approved texts, and it is for this reason that all bibliographies in the *Canon* should be regarded as evolving rather than as finally established. The selection of a text is meant to indicate preference based on a number of considerations, including, of course, the scholarly superiority of that text over other editions as well as its relative recency and its availability. Normally, each work is represented in the data bank by a single text edition. Occasionally, there is duplication of text material, especially if a particular work of an author constitutes part of a committee-approved edition but also occupies a place in a generic collection that inhibits subtraction of its parts. For example, Pfeiffer's two-volume edition of the works of Callimachus includes the text of the author's epigrams.[42] These epigrams also constitute part of the *Anthologia Graeca* and cannot reasonably be extracted. As a result, the text of Callimachus's epigrams resides in duplicate in the data bank.[43]

Sometimes it is not possible to adopt a text that merits universal approval from scholars. For many authors, Migne's *Patrologia Graeca (MPG)* is the only available

---

[41] Cf. S. Radt, *Tragicorum Graecorum fragmenta*, vol. 4 (Göttingen 1977) 99–656; West [supra n. 39] vol. 2, pp. 145–146; D. L. Page, *Poetae melici Graeci* (Oxford 1962; repr. with corr. 1967) 380–381.

[42] R. Pfeiffer, *Callimachus*, vol. 2 (Oxford 1953) 80–99.

[43] Cf. Callimachus (0533 003 and 004).

edition. As new editions emerge, the *MPG* text will normally be superseded in the data bank. For example, when data entry of the works of John Chrysostom was begun in the late 1970s, the only accessible editions for the seven homilies *De laudibus sancti Pauli apostoli* were those of Savile (1612–1613) and Montfaucon (1862). The Montfaucon text (via *MPG* 50.473–514) was deposited in the data bank, but it has subsequently been replaced by Piédagnel's new and superior edition.[44]

While one might question the rationale for depositing into the TLG data bank a text that is deemed substandard, one must also realize that the alternative is to perpetuate a lacuna in the data bank that might not be filled by an acceptable edition for many years. For example, new editions in the *Corpus medicorum Graecorum (CMG)* that were conceived as replacements for Kühn's edition of the Galenic corpus do not seem to appear with the regularity that was once expected. Thus, while the TLG has adopted the available *CMG* and other more recent editions for Galen and Pseudo-Galen, more than half of the Galenic corpus still exists only by way of Kühn.[45] By necessity, it was a matter of either adopting the Kühn edition or depositing less than half of the Galenic corpus into the data bank.

Occasionally, a text was available at the time of data entry only in the form of a typescript. If the text subsequently appeared in published form, the bibliographic information cited includes the details associated with the published edition, as well as a note accounting for the discrepancy in pagination that can be expected to occur between typescript and published text.[46]

If the bibliographic details for a given work are found in conjunction with another author, the formula *Cf.* (or *Cf. et*) followed by the author's name and author number (or author + work number) is used. For example, a work that had been traditionally carried as part of the Aristotelian bibliography is now assigned to Anaximenes of Lampsacus. All that remains of it in the bibliography for Aristotle (0086) is the following notation:

    x01 **Rhetorica ad Alexandrum.**
        Cf. ANAXIMENES Hist. et Rhet. (0547 001).

Complete details of the edition used in data entry are carried in the bibliography for Anaximenes (0547) in connection with work 001.[47]

The injunction *Cf. et,* usually found at the end of a bibliographic entry, directs the reader to additional works that ought properly to be considered along with the work in question. Sometimes, this injunction connects works that complement one another,[48] but at other times it may imply a question concerning attribution of a given

---

[44] *Jean Chrysostome: Panégyriques de S. Paul* (Paris 1982) 112–320. Cf. Joannes Chrysostomus (2062 486).

[45] Cf. Galenus (0057) and Pseudo-Galenus (0530).

[46] For example, Galenus (0057 032), where the bibliographic citation reflects De Lacy's edition of *De placitis Hippocratis et Platonis* in the *CMG* series.

[47] That is, M. Fuhrmann, *Anaximenis ars rhetorica* (Leipzig: Teubner, 1966) 1–97.

[48] For example, Euripides (0006), works 023 (*Fragmenta Phaethontis*) and 032 (*Fragmenta Phaethontis incertae sedis*).

work to a given author.[49] For the most part, the reason for the directive becomes apparent when the author name at the end of that directive is consulted.

Generally, abbreviations used in bibliographic citations are those commonly employed for standard sources, such as *AG, App. Anth., FGrH, FHG,* and *MPG.* A list of all bibliographic abbreviations appears on pages lv–lvii. However, in the case of x-works, that is, works that are cited under another author name and are accompanied by a note of cross-reference, abbreviations are used with high frequency to provide a shorthand reference to the precise locus in which the work in question is actually found. The abbreviation in such cases may be understood readily by following the cross-reference to the appropriate entry for author and work, where it is spelled out.

Transmission. Each work title is accompanied by a code or codes identifying the means by which that work has been transmitted to us. These codes, given in abbreviated form at the end of each bibliographic citation, are as follows: *Q*(uotation), *NQ* (no quotation), *Cod*(ex), *Pap*(yrus), *Epigr*(aph).

Q   The abbreviation *Q* is used to identify both direct and indirect quotations. Direct quotations present no problems. In the case of indirect quotations, however, it has been necessary to confront the possibility that we may not be able to say with certainty that an accusative subject was originally a nominative in direct statement or that an infinitive accurately reflects its corresponding finite form. Often, it is simply not feasible or, for that matter, justifiable to attempt to separate *ipsissima verba* from surrounding testimonia, especially when the text in question is prose rather than poetry; in far too many cases, such a separation is at best artificial and at worst misleading. Over the years, the TLG's efforts to isolate *ipsissima verba* have met with exasperation when the fine line between quoter and quoted is stretched so thin as to render a distinction meaningless, if not altogether impossible to achieve. In the end, the line between indirect statement and paraphrase is often so blurred that we are unfortunately but necessarily left with the pitfalls of conjecture, that is to say that the *verba* of a quoted author may be little more than the result of educated guesses.

To be sure, the designation *Q* is an imperfect way of suggesting that a work has been transmitted in the form of a direct statement, an indirect statement, or even a paraphrase. Yet its usefulness perhaps is realized in relation to its counterpart, *NQ.*

NQ   One might argue that an author from whom we have no quotation, whether direct or indirect, is lost and therefore does not merit author status in a *Canon* designed as a record of the surviving works of authors. On

---

[49] For example, the entry for the *Chronicon Olympicum* (fort. auctore Phlegonte), under the Anonymi Historici (FGrH) (1139 019), directs the reader to consider also Publius Aelius Phlegon Paradox. (0585 002–003).

the other hand, there are sometimes testimonia that yield the titles or suggest the content of otherwise lost works. *NQ* is used to designate titles or descriptions of lost works from which not a single word, in either direct or oblique form, can be associated with the author supposed to have written the lost work.

Cod Less problematical are works that have been transmitted by means of the medieval manuscript tradition. If a text editor bases the edition of an author's work on one or more of the codices, the abbreviation *Cod* is assigned to that work, regardless of whether portions of the work are duplicated in and therefore confirmed by papyri.

Pap The abbreviation *Pap* is used for a text that has been transmitted entirely through papyri. *Pap* may designate an author's literary works that, except for the papyri, would otherwise be lost to us;[50] it may also designate the *supplementa* to an existing literary corpus that owes its survival to another means of transmission.[51] *Pap* is not used, however, to designate a text transmitted by the codices if the papyri simply confirm the readings of the manuscripts.

Epigr Similarly, the abbreviation *Epigr* designates a text that has been transmitted through epigraphical remains. It is not used for a text transmitted through other means if the epigraphical evidence merely constitutes confirmed readings.

Sometimes the manner of transmission may be open to argument. For example, a fragment of Alexinus, who belonged to the Megarian school of philosophy,[52] survives in Philodemus's Περὶ ῥητορικῆς.[53] How should the means of transmission of the Alexinus fragment be designated—with *Q* because Philodemus is quoting Alexinus, or with *Pap* because the fragment, irrespective of the fact that it is quoted, is known to us through papyrus alone? It may not be an altogether satisfying solution to suggest, as does the transmission code for Alexinus's *Fragmentum ap. Philodemum* (2607 002), that Alexinus survives—if he survives—on papyrus, without consideration for Philodemus; the alternative, however, is hardly better. Fortunately, no such problem arises in connection with the first work carried under Alexinus (2607 001). A *titulus* (Παιὰν εἰς Κράτερον) is all that Athenaeus associates with Alexinus,[54] thus qualifying for the transmission code *NQ*.

A quandary exists sometimes in connection with fragments preserved in manu-

---

[50] For example, Bacchylides, Hyperides, Menander, Philodemus.

[51] For example, Callimachus, Euripides, Nicander, Pindar.

[52] Cf. J. von Arnim's article on Alexinus in Pauly-Wissowa 1, 1465–1466.

[53] The text, which is part of *P. Herc.* 1674, can be found in S. Sudhaus, *Philodemi volumina rhetorica*, vol. 1 (Leipzig 1892; repr. Amsterdam 1964) 79–80, and in J. von Arnim, "Ein Bruchstück des Alexinos," *Hermes* 28 (1893) 69. K. Döring, *Die Megariker* [*Studien zur antiken Philosophie* 2 (Amsterdam 1972)] 25, carries this fragment as a testimonium for Alexinus.

[54] *Deipn.* 15.696e (= Kaibel, 15.52.9); cf. *Supplementum Hellenisticum*, 16.

scripts, such as those found in the *Catalogus codicum astrologorum Graecorum*.[55] Certain fragments are labeled *Cod* with a measure of confidence;[56] others are designated *Q*, but with less assurance, inasmuch as the fragments represent the reportage of other *astrologi*.[57]

It may be worth mentioning the relative frequency with which each of the transmission codes appears in the *Canon*. The following statistics reflect the number of times each abbreviation is used: $Q = 3,880$; $Cod = 4,421$; $Pap = 1,190$; $NQ = 744$; $Epigr = 123$. These figures, it should be emphasized, do not tally precisely with the total number of works in the data bank, since a single work may owe its survival to more than one means of transmission. When this is the case, multiple codes are cited for the work in question.

Word Count or Word Estimate. Word counts and word estimates constitute information compiled by the TLG staff primarily for in-house purposes. It was felt, however, that the user of the *Canon* might occasionally find this type of statistical information interesting, perhaps even helpful. For this reason, word counts and word estimates, wherever available, have been included in the *Canon*.

Word estimates are determined by random statistical analysis prior to data entry. Word counts are generated electronically after the text has been converted to machine-readable form.

The definition of *word* may be subject to debate among classicists and linguists, but it is quite rigid to a computer. Within the context of the TLG data bank, a word is any aggregate of nonblanks that is separated by one or more blanks.[58] This purely technical definition is rendered even more irksome by the fact that nonblanks may not, even in the minds of the most generous scholars, be words of any conceivable sort, except to a computer. Nonblanks may be symbols peculiar to astrology, mathematics, music, or pharmacology, for which certain sequences of characters are required to represent the articulation of their meaning. Nonblanks may also be sigla of various sorts that are added to the text and are meant to indicate the format of the printed page. The result is that a word count for a given text will usually be somewhat inflated.[59] In the final analysis, word counts are best regarded as relative rather than absolute figures, so that the size of the Galenic corpus (Galen, 2,608,974 words; Pseudo-Galen, 177,005 words) remains more than twice the size of the Aristotelian corpus (1,107,097 words).

All works that have been verified by the TLG computer staff are accompanied by word counts. In addition, many (although by no means all) works not yet in the data bank are accompanied by word estimates. These figures are located after the trans-

---

[55] 12 vols., ed. F. Boll, F. Cumont, W. Kroll, A. Olivieri, and M. A. F. Sangin (Brussels 1898–1936).

[56] For example, Vettius Valens (1764 004).

[57] For example, Vettius Valens (1764 003).

[58] It should be emphasized that this definition was the result of an early decision on the part of the TLG staff. A computer, of course, can be programmed to recognize just about any definition of *word* and to generate word counts accordingly.

[59] Inflated word counts also owe something to the fact that hyphenated words are regarded as multiples rather than parts that can be recombined into a whole.

mission code and are separated from it by a colon. Numbers enclosed in square brackets represent word estimates; numbers without additional sigla signify computer-verified word counts. For example, the word count for Plato's *Symposium* (verified and corrected) is cited as Cod: 17,530. The word estimate for Dictys Cretensis's *Ephemeridos belli Troiani libri* is given as Pap: [634].

Many entries in this *Canon*, although accompanied by detailed bibliographic information, contain no indication of a word estimate. Word estimates are added to the canon each month as specific works are prepared for data entry. Word counts replace word estimates when the works have been returned to the TLG premises and have been verified by the correction staff.

Classification. Classification tags have been assigned to all discrete works in the data bank and, in a few instances, to works yet to be added to the data bank. Although far from settling the complex questions of literary character and literary history, these tags represent a first effort to create organizing principles that might assist the scholar who wishes to search specific categories of Greek literature. In the *Canon*, classification tags are located after the word count or word estimate with an intervening colon. Where no word count or word estimate is provided, classification information follows directly after the transmission code. For a detailed explanation of the use and functions of tags, see "Classification of Works in the TLG Data Bank" on pages xxxi–xlix.

Form of Citation in TLG Texts

The precise form of citation adopted for each text in the TLG data bank is given in the index of citation systems on pages 439–471. Citation systems are presented in work-number order under author names listed alphabetically.

As might be expected, selection of a specific citation system necessitates rejection of other competing forms of citation that may appear to be interlocked in a printed edition. For scholars who consult Ziegler's Teubner text of Plutarch's *Vita Thesei* (0007 001),[60] the presence of multiple citation systems reflecting the Frankfurt editions of 1599 and 1620 (in the outer margin), Sintenis's 1852–1855 editio minor (in the inner margin), and Lindskog's 1914 edition (also in the inner margin), is not an impediment but rather an historical record of discrepant forms of citation. In the TLG's *electronic* version of the text, however, only one citation system, namely the primary system adopted by the editor of the text selected for the TLG data bank, has been retained. The purpose of excluding from the TLG's electronic text what might otherwise be considered a conspectus of textual history is to facilitate reference to the text proper by minimizing potential clutter of citation numbers. Where no obvious or viable method of citation was discernible in a printed source text, the TLG elected to impose its own citation system for the electronic version.[61] In any event, the form

---

[60] *Plutarchi vitae parallelae*, vol. 1.1, 4th edn., ed. K. Ziegler (Leipzig 1969) 1–35.

[61] For example, the partly columnar arrangement of Cassius Dio's *Reliquiae incertae sedis* (0385 009), coupled with a complex provenance of what appear to be three fragments from three remarkably different

of citation provided in this *Canon* is intended as a guide for scholars consulting the specific texts in the TLG data bank; it is not meant to record citation systems used in other editions.

Sample *Canon* Entry

Figure 2 illustrates several categories of information discussed in detail on preceding pages. Obviously, no single entry can exemplify all of the categories of information found in the *Canon*. The sample entry, however, is sufficiently representative to permit the user to recognize easily the major components of other *Canon* entries.

Figure 2. Sample *Canon* Entry

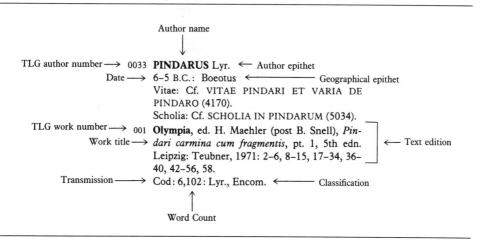

kinds of sources (i.e., Tzetzes' *Scholia in Lycophronis Alexandram*, an anonymous treatise περὶ συντάξεως from Bekker's *Anecdota Graeca*, and a *florilegium* of quotations from Maximus Confessor, Antonius Melissa, and Arsenius) justified the use of fragment, section, and line as a system of citation.

CLASSIFICATION OF WORKS IN THE TLG DATA BANK

Οὐδὲν δὲ κοινόν ἐστιν Ὁμήρῳ καὶ Ἐμπεδοκλεῖ πλὴν τὸ μέτρον, διὸ τὸν μὲν ποιητὴν δίκαιον καλεῖν, τὸν δὲ φυσιολόγον μᾶλλον ἢ ποιητήν.

—ARISTOTLE, *Poetica* 1447b17–20

Homer and Empedocles have nothing in common except their meter, and so it is appropriate to call Homer a *poeta*, but Empedocles a *physiologus* rather than a *poeta*.

Οὐ λανθάνει δ᾽ ἡμᾶς ὅτι τινὲς ἄλλως διαφέρειν τοὺς διαλόγους φασί—λέγουσι γὰρ αὐτῶν τοὺς μὲν δραματικούς, τοὺς δὲ διηγηματικούς, τοὺς δὲ μεικτούς—ἀλλ᾽ ἐκεῖνοι μὲν τραγικῶς μᾶλλον ἢ φιλοσόφως τὴν διαφορὰν τῶν διαλόγων προσωνόμασαν.

—DIOGENES LAERTIUS, *Vitae philosophorum* 3.50

We realize that some people say there are differences in dialogues— for they regard some dialogues as dramatic, others as narrative, and yet others as a combination of the two—but those people have based the name for the difference in dialogues on the fact that they are tragic in mode rather than philosophic.

As the size of the TLG data bank continues to expand, the need to classify its voluminous contents[1] into a comprehensible and manageable system grows ever more urgent. Scholars in search of specific philological, stylistic, or linguistic phenomena likely to be encountered only in certain generic categories of literature should not be required to mine the vast resources of the data bank in their entirety. For example, anyone looking for instances of ἀγκυλόγλωσσος might reasonably expect to locate this word (along with its inflectional forms) in medical writings, but probably not in hymnal poetry.[2] It should, therefore, be possible to limit the scope of the material to be searched and to select only specific portions of the data bank for search purposes.[3]

---

[1] As of December 1989, the data bank contained 3,165 authors, 9,493 discrete literary works, and more than 65,000,000 words.

[2] In fact, there are only six instances of ἀγκυλόγλωσσος in the data bank, all of them in medical literature: Aëtius Med., *Iatricorum liber viii*, 38.1 (bis), 38.7, and *index capitum;* Paulus Med., *Epitomae medicae libri septem*, 6.29.1.1; Oribasius Med., *Collectiones medicae*, 45.16, where Περὶ ἀγκυλογλώσσου (sc. πάθους) is the title of a chapter.

[3] Such selection is possible with appropriate software; the software, however, must be able to analyze each work in the TLG data bank in order to ascertain its precise generic nature.

Until recently, definition of generically related texts in the TLG data bank rested upon specific epithets assigned to authors only. Although useful for comprehending the general character of a given author's literary output,[4] such definition has proved to be too general and therefore inadequate, for it obscures the uniqueness of individual works that do not properly belong to the literary genre suggested by the author's epithet. An obvious case in point is Euripides; his epithet, *Tragicus*, characterizes eighteen of his nineteen extant plays, but does not permit distinction between the *Cyclops*, the one entire surviving satyr play, and the rest of the Euripidean corpus of *tragica*.[5] Similarly, while most would agree that *Philosophus* is an appropriate epithet for Plato, this epithet does not accurately describe Plato's *Epistulae*, which are not of the same character as his philosophical dialogues. And while Callimachus is probably best characterized with the wide-ranging epithet *Philologus*,[6] there is nothing in this epithet that distinguishes his elegiac poems, epigrams, and hymns from the grammatical fragments that survive under his name. In fact, *Philologus* may be an altogether misleading epithet: while it attests to Callimachus's erudition, it does not even hint at the multiple generic categories in which his literary output can be enrolled.[7] Furthermore, while epithets were regularly assigned to authors, works transmitted without benefit of authors' names could not be systematically epithetized.[8]

All of these factors—size of the data bank, the limitations of an author's epithet in relation to the character of that author's individual works, and the growing need to isolate qualitatively related material—have combined to generate a need for classification of the works in the TLG data bank. Ideally, all works listed in the *Canon* would, by now, be classified, were it not for the exigencies of time that have prohibited a concentrated effort to classify every item in every bibliography. Thus, only works already residing in the data bank have been scrutinized for assignment of appropriate classification tags. The majority of works still awaiting data entry have not been examined for the express purpose of classifying them; some, however, have been labeled when it was obvious to what category they belonged by reason of their kindred

---

[4] Cf. comments under "Author Epithet" in the introduction.

[5] There are also fragments of Euripidean satyr plays in A. Nauck, *Tragicorum Graecorum fragmenta* (Leipzig 1889; repr. Hildesheim 1964) 441–443, 453, 474–480, 572–578 (frr. 282–284, 313–315, 371–390, 673–681, 687–695), and B. Snell, *Tragicorum Graecorum fragmenta: Supplementum* (Hildesheim 1964) 6–8, 11 (frr. 282a, 312a, 379a, 386a, 674a).

[6] See A. W. Bulloch's chapter on Hellenistic poetry in *The Cambridge history of classical literature*, vol. 1: *Greek literature*, ed. P. E. Easterling and B. M. W. Knox (Cambridge 1985) 549: "It is often remarked of Callimachus that he was a 'scholar-poet'; in a literal sense this term is accurate. . . ." But see W. Clausen, "The new direction in poetry" in *The Cambridge history of classical literature*, vol. 2: *Latin literature*, ed. E. J. Kenney and W. Clausen (Cambridge 1982) 182: "Callimachus was not a poet and a scholar; he was a poet, or rather could be a poet, because he was a scholar, a γραμματικός, a man whose business was with literature."

[7] Suetonius (*De grammaticis et rhetoribus* 10) tells us that Lucius Ateius Praetextatus, a Latin grammarian, teacher, and scholar, appropriated the epithet *Philologus* for himself (*ad summam Philologus ab semet nominatus*). The eight hundred books he claims to have written might well have added a certain authority to his choice of epithet since his literary output would have covered a vast array of learned subjects: *Philologi appellationem assumpsisse videtur, quia sic ut Eratosthenes, qui primus hoc cognomen sibi vindicavit, multiplici variaque doctrina censebatur* (Suetonius, loc. cit.).

[8] Cf. page xvii, note 19. This does not mean that authorless works were entirely lost to the scholar seeking all samples of a specific genre but that retrieval was cumbersome rather than facile.

Figure 3. List of Tags Used for Classification of Works

Acta	Eleg(iaca)	Jurisprud(entia)	Parod(ica)
Alchem(ica)	Encom(iastica)	Legal(ia)	Paroem(iographa)
Anthol(ogia)	Epic(a)	Lexicogr(apha)	Perieg(esis)
Apocalyp(sis)	Epigr(ammatica)	Liturg(ica)	Phil(osophica)
Apocryph(a)	Epist(olographa)	Lyr(ica)	Physiognom(onica)
Apol(ogetica)	Evangel(ica)	Magica	Poem(a)
Astrol(ogica)	Exeget(ica)	Math(ematica)	Polyhist(orica)
Astron(omica)	Fab(ula)	Mech(anica)	Prophet(ia)
Biogr(apha)	Geogr(apha)	Med(ica)	Pseudepigr(apha)
Bucol(ica)	Gnom(ica)	Metrolog(ica)	Relig(iosa)
Caten(a)	Gramm(atica)	Mim(us)	Rhet(orica)
Chronogr(apha)	Hagiogr(apha)	Mus(ica)	Satura
Comic(a)	Hexametr(ica)	Myth(ographa)	Satyr(a)
Comm(entarius)	Hist(orica)	Narr(atio) Fict(a)	Schol(ia)
Concil(ia)	Homilet(ica)	Nat(uralis) Hist(oria)	Tact(ica)
Coq(uinaria)	Hymn(us)	Onir(ocritica)	Test(imonia)
Dialog(us)	Hypoth(esis)	Orac(ulum)	Theol(ogica)
Doxogr(apha)	Iamb(ica)	Orat(io)	Trag(ica)
Eccl(esiastica)	Invectiv(a)	Paradox(ographa)	Zool(ogica)

relationship to other works. For the most part, however, currently unclassified works will be assigned tags at the time that they are readied for data entry.

The specific tags that have been used in this edition of the *Canon* are listed alphabetically in Figure 3 and are shown categorically in Figure 4. It will be apparent to users of the *Canon* and the data bank that the TLG has, by necessity, modified the scope and definition of certain terms in order to facilitate consultation of the material, as well as to curtail proliferation of categories that might ultimately prove superfluous. Several of the tags used for classification thus require clarification, which the following comments are meant to provide.

Anthol. is used to classify postclassical collections such as the *Anthologia Graeca* (7000 001), *Doctrina Patrum* (7051 001), *Florilegium Cyrillianum* (4147 001), and Stobaeus's *Anthologium* (2037 001). Although other collections of poems or sayings might be construed, in the strictest sense, as anthologies,[9] the tag *Anthol.* is applied, in the *Canon*, only to those works that represent a sizeable potpourri constructed in late antiquity or the Middle Ages from earlier disparate sources.[10]

Apocalyp. defines works that are essentially of a prophetic nature but with a focus clearly directed "towards the end of things and to the destiny of the world in general."[11] Prophecies that look toward the future but without the apocalyptic vision of a grand terminus are labeled *Prophet.*[12]

[9] For example, the psalms and proverbs in the *Septuaginta* (0527 027, 029).

[10] The *Anthologia Graeca*, for instance, consists of sixteen books of epigrams ascribed to authors as early as Homer and as late as the tenth century.

[11] F. L. Cross, *The Oxford dictionary of the Christian church* (London 1958) 67. For example, *Daniel* in the *Septuaginta* (0527 056–057), the *Apocalypsis Joannis* in the *Novum Testamentum* (0031 027).

[12] For example, the books of the Israelite prophets in the *Septuaginta* (0527 036–050, 053).

Figure 4. Schema of the Branches of Greek Literature, Showing Tags Used for Classification of Works

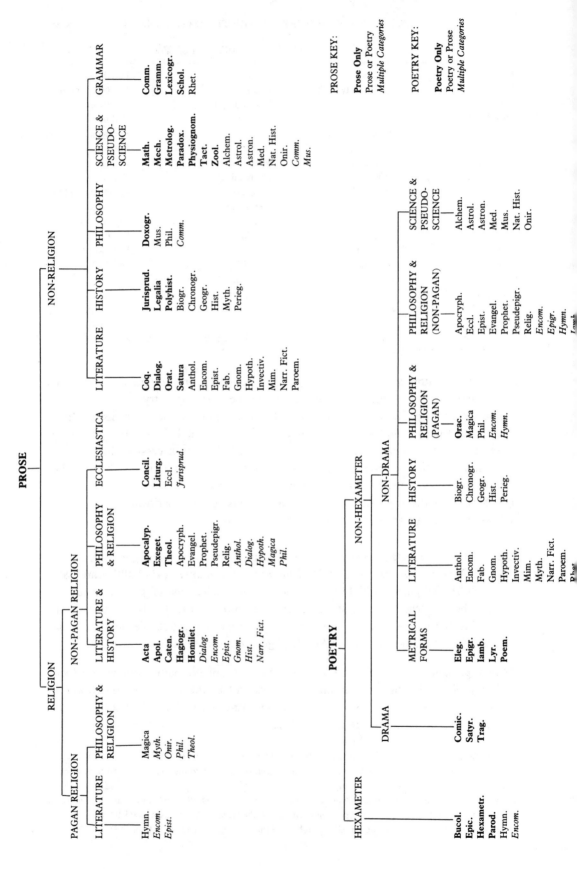

Apocryph. and its sometimes problematical counterpart *Pseudepigr.* can perhaps be best understood in terms of the distinctions articulated by Otto Eissfeldt:

> The books which we normally describe as 'Apocrypha' . . . do not exhaust the number of writings prized as edifying by certain groups within Judaism and then by Christian communities, and hence reckoned in the broader sense as belonging to the Old Testament. The name 'Apocrypha' actually covers only those among them which were taken up into the Greek and Latin Bible. Oriental Church communities—Syriac, Coptic, Armenian, Ethiopic and others—knew other such writings and held them in esteem. These are for the most part preserved not in their original Hebrew or Aramaic or even Greek form, but only in the languages of these Church communities, but in some cases fragments of them in their original language have become known again recently among the Qumrān discoveries. These are usually known by the name 'Pseudepigrapha' and this name is so used here. It is true that it is not really completely appropriate. For on the one hand this name only fits some of the writings for which it is used, namely those which, like Enoch, are actually in circulation 'under a false name', and thus wrongly claim to have been compiled by a man of God of the Old Testament. On the other hand the name could be applied to certain books of the [sc. O.T.] canon and of its appendix the Apocrypha, as for example Dan., Bar., Ep. Jer., Wisd., which purport to derive from Daniel, Baruch, Jeremiah and Solomon respectively, but in fact were composed centuries later by unknown authors.[13]

Since the line of demarcation between apocrypha and pseudepigrapha is not always so clear as one might hope, determining whether works in the TLG data bank are one or the other must be based upon certain other distinctions; these distinctions are, for the most part, pragmatic.

For purposes of classification in the *Canon,* but without consideration for the interests of different groups who might accept or reject certain titles as canonical,[14] the tag *Apocryph.* is used to identify two kinds of works: (1) those that have come down to us as part of the Septuagint but were not part of the traditional Hebrew Bible (i.e., the Old Testament) and (2) those that are generally regarded by Christians as extracanonical in relation to the New Testament.[15] *Pseudepigr.*, on the other

---

[13] O. Eissfeldt, *The Old Testament: An introduction,* trans. P. R. Ackroyd (New York 1965; repr. 1972) 573. Cf. also B. Metzger, *An introduction to the apocrypha* (New York 1957; repr. 1969) 5: "From the point of view of those who approved of these [sc. apocryphal] books, they were 'hidden' or withdrawn from common use because they were regarded as containing mysterious or esoteric lore, too profound to be communicated to any except the initiated. From another point of view, however, it was held that such books deserved to be 'hidden' because they were spurious or heretical. Thus, the term has had an honorable significance as well as a derogatory one, depending upon those who made use of the word."

[14] There is also no consideration of what may be regarded as protocanonical or deuterocanonical. As Metzger [supra n. 13] sums up the confusion: "It is usual among Roman Catholics to apply the term *Apocrypha* to the books which others commonly designate as pseudepigrapha" (6).

[15] To the first group belong works such as *Ecclesiasticus* (0527 034), *Baruch* (0527 050), and *Epistula Jeremiae* (0527 052), to the second *Acta Pauli* (0388 001–005), *Evangelium Mariae* (1369 001–002), and *Apocalypsis apocrypha Joannis* (1158 001–003). The fifteen titles that Metzger [supra n. 13] considers Old Testament apocrypha in the narrowest sense are *Esdras I* and *II, Tobit, Judith,* additions to *Esther, Sapientia Salomonis, Ecclesiasticus, Baruch, Epistula Jeremiae, Oratio Azariae et cantus trium iuvenum, Susanna, Bel et Draco, Oratio Manassis, Machabaeorum I* and *II* (3–4).

hand, has been used for works that belong neither to the Septuagint nor to the Hebrew Bible but that have been transmitted under the name of a Jewish religious thinker.[16] See also *Relig.*

Apol. is applied to works written in defense of the tenets of one religious system against those of another.[17] It is also used of works written in justification of orthodox Christian faith and, implicitly or explicitly, in opposition to heretical beliefs.[18] Pseudo-Justinus Martyr's *Quaestiones Christianorum ad gentiles* (0646 010) and *Quaestiones gentilium ad Christianos* (0646 011) belong, unquestionably, to apologetic literature. Plato's *Apologia Socratis* (0059 002) does not.

Biogr. indicates both biographical and autobiographical writings. Although a case might be made for acknowledging a tradition of autobiographical literature,[19] the *Canon* makes no distinction between Plutarch's biographies of Greeks and Romans in the *Vitae parallelae* (0007 001–066) and Aelius Aristides' reflections on his own religious experiences in the Ἱεροὶ λόγοι (0284 023–028), or between Eusebius's *Vita Constantini* (2018 020) and Gregorius Nazianzenus's *De vita sua* (2022 004). See also *Hagiogr.*

Caten. is restricted to scholiastic comment upon biblical passages and lists of *variae lectiones* to a given *catena* on a biblical passage.[20] On the other hand, the commentaries that individual authors devoted to scriptural texts are classified generally as *Exeget.*,[21] whereas *commenta* derived from *catenae* are tagged as both *Exeget.* and *Caten.*[22] See also *Exeget.* and *Schol.*

Comm. See *Caten.*, *Exeget.*, and *Schol.*

[16] For example, *Apocalypsis Eliae* (1156 001), *Apocalypsis Esdrae* (1157 001–002), *Liber Enoch* (1463 001–002).

[17] For example, Justinus Martyr's *Dialogus cum Tryphone* (0645 003), Josephus's *Contra Apionem* (0526 003), Theodoretus's *Graecarum affectionum curatio* (4089 001).

[18] For example, Gregory of Nyssa's *Refutatio confessionis Eunomii* (2017 031).

[19] Cf. G. Misch, *A history of autobiography in antiquity*, 2 vols., trans. G. Misch and E. W. Dickes (Cambridge, Mass., 1951). Misch (vol. 1, p. 5) recognizes the problems of dismembering autobiography from biography: "In point of fact the body of autobiographical writings, when viewed as a whole, reveals at first a Protean character. This genre of literature defies classification even more stubbornly than do the ordinary forms of creative writing." The main implication of autobiography, Misch notes (p. 7), is that "the person whose life is described is himself the author of the work." See also A. Momigliano, *The development of Greek biography* (Cambridge, Mass., 1971), who, though he is critical of Misch's definition of autobiography as a "history of human self-awareness" (17–18), acknowledges the inseparability of autobiography from biography (11).

[20] The choice of *Caten.* as a classifying tag is consistent with the definition of *catena* in Cross, *ODCC* [supra n. 11]: "a word applied to the Biblical commentaries dating from the 5th cent. onwards, in which the successive verses of the Scriptural text were elucidated by 'chains' of passages derived from previous commentators" (247).

[21] For example, Origenes' *Commentarii in Genesim* (2042 047), Theodoretus's *Interpretatio in xii epistulas sancti Pauli* (4089 030).

[22] For example, some of Didymus Caecus's *Commentarii in Job* (2102 014), Photius's *Commentarii in Matthaeum* (4040 028).

Concil. signifies a miscellany of writings including speeches, letters, rosters, and proceedings of ecumenical councils. In effect, *Concil.* indicates, although it does not always specifically identify, the variety of activities in which delegates to the councils participated.[23] Furthermore, although these writings are generally published together as acts of the councils,[24] there is no separate tag that identifies the precise character of these *acta*.[25]

Dialog. is reserved for literary pieces written in the form of a prose dialogue. It is not used to characterize historiographical prose that incorporates, as part of the historian's technique, dialogue, debate, and diatribe.[26] Nor is it used of compositions that would, by tradition, be regarded as tragedy, comedy, satyr play, mime, or other permutations of drama. Thus, scholars who wish to explore some aspect of *dialogi* in Greek literature will find that the corpus of dialogic writing, as it is defined in the TLG data bank, consists of most of the works of Plato,[27] many of Lucian, some of Plutarch, and isolated works of classical authors such as Xenophon, Aeschines Socraticus, and Philostratus and patristic writers such as Athanasius, Cyril of Alexandria, and Palladius.

[23] The *gesta* at the Council of Ephesus in 431 included individual as well as synodal letters, homilies, apologies, depositions, propositions, petitions, mandates, edicts, prayers, and impeachments.

[24] For example, *Acta conciliorum oecumenicorum* (5000), which includes the acts of the councils at Ephesus in 431 (5000 001–002) and Chalcedon in 451 (5000 003) and of the synods at Constantinople and Jerusalem in 536 (5000 004).

[25] The tag *Acta* is used in its own right, but it is not associated at all with the acts of the councils. Rather it is used exclusively to classify works concerned with the acts of martyrs and saints, for example, *Acta Pauli* (0388 001), *Acta Philippi* (2948 001–004), *Acta Barnabae* (2949 001), *Acta Alexandrinorum* (0300 001).

[26] Diatribe, in its earliest usage, seems to have had none of the philosophical-moral implications that are part of the so-called Cynic-Stoic diatribe. G. Kennedy, *Greek rhetoric under Christian emperors* (Princeton 1983) 240, characterizes diatribe as "the vigorous, informal, philosophical, moral, and sometimes satirical preaching of Cynic and Stoic philosophers throughout the Greek-speaking world." See also A. A. Long in his chapter on post-Aristotelian philosophy in *The Cambridge history of classical literature*, vol. 1 [supra n. 6]: "This term [sc. *diatribe*] has no pejorative sense in Greek; its primary meaning is passage of time, and as early as Plato it can be used for a speech or discourse" (638). J. F. Kindstrand, *Bion of Borysthenes* (Uppsala 1976), considers the concept of diatribe as a "popular philosophical dialexis" a modern notion (97). Drawing upon O. Halbauer, *De diatribis Epicteti* (Diss. Leipzig 1911), Kindstrand dismisses diatribe as a distinct literary form: "It seems that it refers exclusively to the situation in which a teacher is instructing his students, as seen from the students' point of view, and tells us nothing about the content or the style" (ibid.). The question of whether diatribe is a genre or a tactic, a figure of thought or a figure of speech, has been vigorously debated since H. Usener (echoing Diogenes Laertius, *VP* 2.77), *Epicurea* (Berlin 1887; repr. Stuttgart 1966) lxix, applied the term to Bion's writings (of which only the most meager fragments survive): "scilicet postquam Bio Borysthenita sermonibus suis (διατριβαί nomen erat) genus cynicum seueritate risuque mixtum perfecit. . . ." More recently, an entire colloquium was devoted to the nature of diatribe; see G. Kustas, *Diatribe in ancient rhetorical theory* [*Protocol series of the colloquies of the Center for Hermeneutical Studies in Hellenistic and Modern Culture* 22 (Berkeley 1976)] 1–47, with responses, especially that of W. S. Anderson (16–20), who sees the diatribe as "a controlled discourse by a single person" (20). For a critical survey of the study of the diatribe, see S. K. Stowers, *The diatribe and Paul's letter to the Romans* [*SBL Dissertation Series* 57 (Ann Arbor 1981)] 7–78.

[27] In fact, Diogenes Laertius credits Plato with the refinement, if not the invention, of dialogue: δοκεῖ δέ μοι Πλάτων ἀκριβώσας τὸ εἶδος καὶ τὰ πρωτεῖα δικαίως ἂν ὥσπερ τοῦ κάλλους οὕτω καὶ τῆς εὑρέσεως ἀποφέρεσθαι (*VP* 3.48).

Eccl. refers to themes, concerns, and attitudes associated with the Christian church. To a certain extent, *Eccl.* may be regarded as a multipurpose label attached to works that seem to be ecclesiastical in content but that lack characteristics that would permit definition in terms of form.[28] Wherever appropriate, however, *Eccl.* is linked with additional tags that help to narrow the range of generic possibilities.[29] See also *Hist.*, *Relig.*, and *Theol.*

Encom. suggests tone and feeling rather than literary genre. Eulogy, panegyric, *laudationes* of all sorts may be found in either prose or poetry,[30] in orations or homilies,[31] in hexameters, iambics, or lyric meters,[32] in praise of gods or humans,[33] in lighthearted treatises as well as satirical pieces,[34] that is to say, in practically any form within the expanse of Greek literature. Although a less than optimum label because of all that it can embrace, *Encom.* nevertheless creates what may be a useful distinction between the great variety of laudatory literature and the numerous hymns that were (albeit sometimes only ostensibly) composed for religious occasions to celebrate divinities or objects of adoration infused with divine qualities. Thus, the *Hymni Homerici* (0013 001–034) are classified not as *Encom.* but as *Hymn.*, as are the prose hymns of Aristides (0284 001–008, 017–018) and nearly a dozen paeans listed in the *Canon.*[35] At the same time, the expansive nature of *Encom.* obviates a proliferation of categories that might otherwise be needed to account for distinctions between gods and humans, prose and poetry, oration and treatise, religious and secular occasions, to name just a few.[36] See also *Hymn.*

[28] For example, Basil's *Regulae morales* (2040 051), Athanasius's *Petitiones Arianorum* (2035 046), or the second-century *Didache xii apostolorum* (1311 001).

[29] For example, Eusebius's *Historia ecclesiastica* (2018 002) is classified as both *Hist.* and *Eccl.* Similarly, Basil's ascetic sermons (2040 040–042, 044, 046) are characterized as both *Homilet.* and *Eccl.*, and Arethas's *Scholia to Athenagoras* (2130 014) is labeled both *Schol.* and *Eccl.*

[30] For example, Aristides' Πανηγυρικὸς ἐπὶ τῷ ὕδατι ἐν Περγάμῳ (0284 055), Bacchylides' *Epinicia* (0199 001).

[31] For example, Isocrates' *Helenae encomium* (0010 009), Basil's *Homilia in martyrem Julittam* (2040 023).

[32] For example, the anonymous *Encomium ducis Romani* in *P. Flor.* 2.114 (1816 016), the *Laudatio professoris Smyrnaei in universitate Beryti docentis* in *P. Berol.* 10559 A et B (1816 011), Pindar's odes to the victors of the athletic games (0033 001–005).

[33] For example, the anonymous *Mercurius mundi et Hermupolis magnae conditor* in *P. Argent.* 481 (1816 006), *Laudes Theonis gymnasiarchi* (1816 002).

[34] For example, Dio Chrysostomus's *Encomium comae* (0612 002), Synesius's *Calvitii encomium* (2006 006).

[35] That is, Mace(donius) (0202 001), Limenius (0203 001), Aristonous (0204 001), Philodamus (0205 001–002), *Hymni Anonymi* (0742 009), and the *Paeanes* published in the *Collectanea Alexandrina* (1203 001–006). The decision to classify paeans written in lyric meters as *Hymn.* is owing to a suggestion from Malcolm Davies. G. W. Bowersock recommended the use of *Hymn.* also for Aristides' prose celebrations of Zeus, Athena, Poseidon, Dionysus, Heracles, Asclepius, Sarapis, and the Aegean Sea.

[36] Menander of Laodicea, in his Διαίρεσις τῶν ἐπιδεικτικῶν (2586 001), classifies not only the great assortment of hymns to gods (κλητικοί, ἀποπεμπτικοί, φυσικοί, μυθικοί, γενεαλογικοί, πεπλασμένοι, εὐκτικοί, and ἀπευκτικοί) but also the several kinds of encomia that may be delivered in praise of countries, cities, citadels, harbors, and bays. See *Menander Rhetor*, ed. D. A. Russell and N. G. Wilson (Oxford 1981) 7–75.

Exeget. distinguishes writings that interpret the texts of the Old and New Testaments from the numerous commentaries that focus upon secular literature, especially the Platonic and Aristotelian corpora, the medical commentaries of Galen, Alexander of Aphrodisias, and Palladius, and the philological commentaries of Porphyry and Eustathius on Homer. Thus, the Arian theologian Asterius's thirty-one homilies entitled *Commentarii in Psalmos* (2061 001) are classified as *Exeget.*, whereas Olympiodorus's *In Platonis Alcibiadem commentarii* (4019 004) and Simplicius's *In Aristotelis categorias commentarium* (4013 003) are defined as *Comm.* (with the additional tag *Phil.*). Similarly, Galen's *In Hippocratis librum de fracturis commentarii iii* (0057 100) is labeled as both *Comm.* and *Med.*

On the periphery of exegetical literature are several *paraphrases* that warrant classification as either *Exeget.* or *Comm.* according to the religious or secular character of the paraphrased work. Eutecnius's *Paraphrasis in Nicandri Theriaca* (0752 001) is, therefore, characterized as *Comm.* (+ *Med.*), and Themistius's *In libros Aristotelis de anima paraphrasis* (2001 040) is classified as *Comm.* (+ *Phil.*), but Nonnus's *Paraphrasis sancti evangelii Joannei* (2045 002) is labeled *Exeget.* (+ *Evangel.* and *Hexametr.*). See also **Caten.** and **Schol.**

Gramm. does not reside conveniently and exclusively on either side of a line that would categorically divide grammar from rhetoric or even from lexicography.[37] Even though the grammarian Dionysius Thrax (second century B.C.) was quite precise about his own definition of grammar and its constituent parts,[38] the subsequent history of grammatical treatises is not so refined as to detach itself from the rhetorical training of future leaders in Greece and Rome. As Kennedy observes, "Work of grammarians must always be envisioned as going on behind rhetorical theory, though it only rarely is expressly discussed."[39] For purposes of classification, however, *Gramm.* is used to tag those works explicitly entitled *Ars grammatica* or *Fragmenta grammatica*,[40] as well as treatises on prosody, orthography, accentuation, parts of speech, and inflection.[41] See also **Lexicogr.** and **Rhet.**

[37] See G. Kennedy, *The art of persuasion in Greece* (Princeton 1963) 269–270: "A line was usually drawn between the teachings of the grammarian and the more advanced instruction of the rhetorician. The former dealt mostly with the poets and with analysis, the latter concentrated on the orators and on increasingly difficult composition. But in practice the two schools tended to overlap. Some teachers taught both grammar and rhetoric to different classes. . . . Furthermore, grammarians often introduced their students to the first stages of rhetorical composition, the *progymnasmata*."

[38] *Ars grammatica* (*Gramm. Graec.* 1.1, pp. 5–6): Γραμματική ἐστιν ἐμπειρία τῶν παρὰ ποιηταῖς τε καὶ συγγραφεῦσιν ὡς ἐπὶ τὸ πολὺ λεγομένων. Μέρη δὲ αὐτῆς ἐστιν ἕξ· πρῶτον ἀνάγνωσις ἐντριβὴς κατὰ προσῳδίαν, δεύτερον ἐξήγησις κατὰ τοὺς ἐνυπάρχοντας ποιητικοὺς τρόπους, τρίτον γλωσσῶν τε καὶ ἱστοριῶν πρόχειρος ἀπόδοσις, τέταρτον ἐτυμολογίας εὕρεσις, πέμπτον ἀναλογίας ἐκλογισμός, ἕκτον κρίσις ποιημάτων.

[39] Kennedy [supra n. 37] 296.

[40] For example, in addition to Dionysus Thrax's *Ars grammatica* (0063 001), the *Supplementa artis Dionysianae vetusta* (0072 001), and the numerous anonymous *fragmenta grammatica* (0072 003–023) in A. Wouters, *The grammatical papyri from Graeco-Roman Egypt: Contributions to the study of the 'ars grammatica' in antiquity* (Brussels 1979) 49–282.

[41] Hephaestion's *Enchiridion de metris* (1402 001), Herodian's Περὶ ὀρθογραφίας (0087 011), the spurious

Hagiogr., although similar in concept to biography, is used to characterize works whose principal themes are the lives and acts of saints, martyrs, and heroic figures in Judaeo-Christian tradition.[42] A practical distinction between biography and hagiography, for purposes of classification, is that *vitae* assigned a number in *BHG*[43] are regularly tagged as *Hagiogr.* See also ***Biogr.*** and ***Narr. Fict.***

Hexametr. is used of poems (or, more frequently, fragments of poems) that do not immediately betray a generic affiliation with some species of poetry in terms of theme or tone,[44] and if there is insufficient evidence to demonstrate that a single surviving line should be construed as the hexameter part of an elegiac distich.[45] *Hexametr.* is also used in conjunction with other tags to clarify the specific poetic form of a work that belongs more properly to another (usually prose) genre.[46] Finally, it should be noted that the generic tags *Epic.*, *Bucol.*, and *Parod.*, when used to classify a work, indicate an implicit assumption of the hexameter form; the additional tag *Hexametr.* has therefore not been added.

Hist. reflects a variety of subspecialties that fall within the range of Greek historiography.[47] In general, the tag *Hist.* is affixed to the following categories of works: (1) extant *whole* works of the Greek historians;[48] (2) fragments of otherwise lost historical works that may be collected in independent editions;[49] (3) fragments of lost

---

De accentibus assigned to Arcadius (2116 001), Apollonius Dyscolus's *De pronominibus* (0082 001), Theodosius's *Canones isagogici de flexione nominum* (2020 001).

[42] A prominent feature of such lives is a preoccupation with the miraculous, marvelous, and supernatural. See H. Delehaye, *The legends of the saints: An introduction to hagiography*, trans. V. M. Crawford (London 1907), rev. R. J. Schoeck (Notre Dame 1961) 1–11, 50.

[43] *BHG* numbers affixed to texts are located in the right-hand margin of the bibliographical inventories edited by F. Halkin and published in Brussels by the Société des Bollandistes, as follows: (1) *Bibliotheca hagiographica Graeca*, vols. 1–3, 3rd edn. (1957); (2) *Auctarium bibliothecae hagiographicae Graecae* (1969); (3) *Novum auctarium bibliothecae hagiographicae Graecae* (1984).

[44] That is, if it is apparent that a hexameter poem or fragment does not adhere to the usual parameters of epic, hymn, bucolic, parody, or epigram, for example, the hexametric *Orbis descriptio* of Dionysius Perieg. (0084 001); also the fifty-five fragments that are edited together as *Hexametri* (2648 001) in H. Lloyd-Jones and P. Parsons, *Supplementum Hellenisticum* (Berlin 1983) 399–457 (frr. 900–935, 937–956).

[45] For example, a line attributed by Athenaeus to the tragic poet Sthenelus (0315 002): οἶνος καὶ φρονέοντας ἐς ἀφροσύνας ἀναβάλλει, cf. *SH* [supra n. 44] 354 (fr. 736); also a line of Dionysius Iambus (2620 001) preserved by Clement of Alexandria: πόντου μαινομένοιο περιστείνει ἁλυκὴ ζάψ, *SH* 179 (fr. 389).

[46] For example, the *Jusjurandum medicum* (0740 001), classified as both *Med.* and *Hexametr.*

[47] C. Fornara, *The nature of history in ancient Greece and Rome* (Berkeley and Los Angeles 1983) 1, isolates "five basic types of historical writing . . . : genealogy or mythography, ethnography, history, horography or local history, and chronography." Whatever subcategories are embraced by historiography, Fornara emphasizes that history "retained its quite specific definition as the *expositio rerum gestarum*" (3, n. 8), Quintilian's expression for distinguishing between factual historical narrative and the fictitious or realistic but untrue narratives found in tragedy and comedy (*Inst.* 2.4.2).

[48] For example, Thucydides' *Historiae* (0003 001), Josephus's *Antiquitates Judaicae* (0526 001), Herodian's *Ab excessu divi Marci* (0015 001).

[49] For example, the *Excerpta politiarum* of Heraclides Lembus (1407 001), ed. M. Dilts in *Greek, Roman and Byzantine monographs* 5 (Durham, N.C., 1971) 14–40; the various papyrological fragments of the *Hellenica Oxyrhynchia* (0558 001–003), ed. V. Bartoletti (Leipzig 1959) 1–41.

historical works that are edited as part of a generic collection such as *FGrH*, *FHG*, and *HGM;*[50] and (4) works of ecclesiastical writers that focus upon the history of the church.[51] Since ecclesiastical history is not always conjoined with the development of Greek historiography,[52] double labels are provided in order to distinguish the *historiae ecclesiasticae* from secular histories. Thus, scholars who wish to confine their scope of inquiry to church writings will be able to find the material they seek by consulting texts tagged as *Hist.* and *Eccl.*, whereas other histories are labeled simply *Hist.*[53] See also ***Eccl., Myth.***, and ***Narr. Fict.***

Homilet. is used to distinguish *homiliae* (i.e., discourses on religious and moral topics delivered, or written as though they were intended for delivery, to a congregation) from *orationes* (i.e., discourses on secular topics delivered, or intended for delivery, on public occasions, including courtroom trials, legislative assemblies, and funerals). This distinction helps to separate the extant speeches of the ten Attic orators from the thousand or so sermons and homilies ascribed to John Chrysostom.[54] It does not, however, validate the assumption that patristic writers produced only homilies, as the forty-five orations of Gregory of Nazianzus demonstrate.[55]

Hymn., regardless of meter, is assigned to the great variety of hymnal poetry ranging from the *Hymni Homerici* (0013 001–034) and the scraps of poems that appear to

---

[50] *FGrH* = *Die Fragmente der griechischen Historiker*, vols. 1a, 2a–2b, 3a–3c, ed. F. Jacoby (Leiden 1923–1958; repr. 1961–1969); *FHG* = *Fragmenta historicorum Graecorum*, vols. 1–5, ed. K. Müller, T. Müller, and V. Langlois (Paris 1841–1870; vols. 1–4 repr. Frankfurt am Main 1975; vol. 5 repr. Paris 1938 and Frankfurt am Main 1975); *HGM* = *Historici Graeci minores*, vols. 1–2, ed. L. Dindorf (Leipzig 1870–1871).

[51] For example, the several works entitled *Historia ecclesiastica* by Eusebius (2018 002), Evagrius (2733 001), Socrates (2057 001), Sozomenus (2048 001), and Theodoretus (4089 003).

[52] The relationship between ecclesiastical history and the Jewish historical writings of the Old Testament is closer in terms of perspective, materials, and focus than that between either Jewish or ecclesiastical history and Greek historical writing. See, for example, *The Oxford history of the classical world*, ed. J. Boardman, J. Griffin, and O. Murray (Oxford 1986) 186, where Murray observes, "For the Jews history was the record of God's covenant with His chosen people," whereas for the Greeks "history was the record, not of the mercy or wrath of God, but of the great deeds of men." See also A. Momigliano, "Popular religious beliefs and late Roman historians" in *Essays in ancient and modern historiography*, trans. J. Landry and T. J. Cornell (Middletown, Conn., 1977) 145: "The notion of ecclesiastical history implied a new importance being attributed to documentary evidence, a true universal scope both in time and in space, and finally a revolutionary change in contents. Religious beliefs and practices replaced military and political events as the central subject of historiography."

[53] Double and even triple labeling is necessitated, in some instances, by the fact that presumably historical fragments in *FGrH* recur in other generic corpora, such as the collection of philosophical fragments in *Die Fragmente der Vorsokratiker*, vols. 1–2, 6th edn., ed. H. Diels and W. Kranz (Zürich 1951–1952; repr. 1966). Several fragments assigned to Epimenides of Crete (1347 002, 004) are carried in both *FGrH* #457, vol. 3B, pp. 390–394, and Diels-Kranz, vol. 1, pp. 31–37. In both instances, the works are tagged as *Hist., Phil.*, and *Theol.*

[54] Chrysostom's homilies account for 386 works in the TLG data bank.

[55] Gregory's orations are numbered 2022 005–011, 015–052, 054. Seven of these (2022 015, 046–049, 051–052), as Kristoffel Demoen observes in correspondence, were written to commemorate liturgical festivals and therefore constitute a special group.

be samples of dithyramb to the polymetric hymns of Gregory of Nazianzus (2022 059) and the complex *cantica* of Romanus Melodus (2881 001–003, 005). It is also used of the prose hymns of Aelius Aristides (0284 001–008, 017–018). See also ***Encom.***

Hypoth. defines the hypotheses transmitted (for the most part anonymously) as prefixes to Greek tragedies and comedies, as well as the numerous papyrological fragments containing hypotheses and *didascaliae*.[56] Also tagged as *Hypoth.* are Libanius's *argumenta* to the speeches of Demosthenes (2200 007) and the hypotheses of patristic writers to books of the Old and New Testaments.[57] With the exception of the Libanian *argumenta*, the tag *Hypoth.* is generally found in conjunction with (at least) a second tag. Thus, the *Argumenta comica* (0662 006), carried under the heading *Comica Adespota (CGFPR)*, is labeled both *Hypoth.* and *Comic.*, whereas John Chrysostom's *In epistulam ad Romanos* (2062 155) is tagged as *Homilet, Exeget.*, and *Hypoth.*

Lexicogr. characterizes not only the sort of lexicon that takes the form of a glossary or word-list with definitions[58] but also the more extended form of lexicon that incorporates commentary,[59] the literary-biographical-historical encyclopedia,[60] the topically arranged thesaurus that includes vocabularies and lists of synonyms,[61] and the several surviving Attic lexica.[62] Glosses, which are not always easily differentiated from scholiastic comments, are tagged as *Schol.* See also ***Gramm.*** and ***Schol.***

Med. is applied to a wide range of Greek medical writings without distinguishing between human and veterinary medicine. Hippocrates' *De morbis popularibus* (0627 006) and the (mostly fragmented) veterinary treatises that make up the ninth-century *Hippiatrica* (0738 001–010) are all classified as *Med.* Also tagged as *Med.* are writings that deal with antidotes for wounds, bites, and stings,[63] as well as the great many pharmacological prescriptions and formulae that pervade the medical literature.[64]

---

[56] Hypotheses deriving from papyri will be included in a data bank of subliterary papyri, in progress at the University of Michigan under the supervision of Ludwig Koenen.

[57] For example, John Chrysostom's homilies on the Pauline letters, most of which (2062 155–156, 159–160, 163–164, 167–168) have *argumenta* at the beginning.

[58] For example, Hesychius's *Lexicon* (4085 002–003), the *Etymologicum magnum* (4099 001).

[59] For example, Harpocration's *Lexicon in decem oratores Atticos* (1389 001).

[60] For example, *Suda* (9010 001).

[61] For example, Julius Pollux's *Onomasticon* (0542 001).

[62] For example, Aelius Dionysius's Ἀττικὰ ὀνόματα (1323 001), Pausanias's Ἀττικῶν ὀνομάτων συναγωγή (1569 001), Phrynichus's *Praeparatio sophistica* (1608 001) and *Eclogae* (1608 002–004).

[63] For example, Nicander's two hexameter poems, *Theriaca* (0022 001) and *Alexipharmaca* (0022 002).

[64] For example, the remedies for various aches and ailments that others prescribed and Galen collected in his *De compositione medicamentorum secundum locos libri x* (0057 076).

Mus. is used to classify not only theoretical works on music[65] but also musical scales,[66] musical notations,[67] and fragments of music.[68]

Myth. is used, in a fairly restrictive sense, to classify primarily the works of mythographers who produced compendia or interpretations of mythology[69] and secondarily the works of historians (especially the early logographers) who cited myths as evidence in their historical accounts.[70] It does not include the great store of mythology that underlies other literary genres such as epic and tragedy. Thus, Homer's *Iliad* (0012 001) is labeled simply *Epic.*, and Aeschylus's *Prometheus vinctus* (0085 003) is tagged only as *Trag.* See also ***Hist.***

Narr. Fict. is used to categorize a variety of novelistic writings that range from novel or romance to novella, story, tale, and vignette.[71] The term *narratio ficta*, in some respects the most problematical tag because it had no specifically literary significance in antiquity, is the result of an attempt to find a suitable Latin designation for a genre that, in antiquity, had no agreed name either in Latin or in Greek[72] but that now seems to embrace a wide spectrum of themes, motifs, tones, and styles.[73] Thus, *Narr. Fict.* is used in the *Canon* to classify the five extant Greek

---

[65] For example, Aristoxenus's *Elementa harmonica* (0088 001) and *Elementa rhythmica* (0088 002), Aristides Quintilianus's *De musica* (2054 001).

[66] For example, Alypius's *Isagoge musica* (2135 001).

[67] For example, Bacchius Geron's *Isagoge artis musicae* (2136 001).

[68] For example, the *Carmina Delphis inventa* (0362 001) and the few lines that survive of a stasimon from Euripides' *Orestes* (2138 001). Both of these pieces are awaiting data entry, pending a new edition of the *Musici scriptores Graeci* by Jon Solomon.

[69] For example, Apollodorus's *Bibliotheca* (0548 001), Antoninus Liberalis's *Metamorphoseon synagoge* (0651 001), Joannes Pediasimus's *Tractatus de duodecim Herculis laboribus* (2592 001).

[70] For example, Acusilaus (0392 002), Hecataeus (0538 002), Hellanicus (0539 002). For the fragments of the logographers, see *FGrH*, vol. 1a, which Jacoby has subtitled *Genealogie und Mythographie*.

[71] *Narratio*, by itself, may mean "narrative, story, tale" (*Oxford Latin dictionary* s.v.) as early as Terence (*And.* 708–709, where, since the word is set against *verum*, the implication is of something fabricated—as the English word *story* can have that connotation). There is also a rhetorical sense; Quintilian uses *narratio* to mean "statement of fact" in a courtroom case (*Inst.* 3.6.92, 3.9.1; 4.1 passim).

[72] *Narratio ficta* was adopted after profitable discussion with B. P. Reardon. Several other potential tags were considered but rejected as inadequate, inaccurate, or misleading. The traditional term *erotica*, for instance, excludes those works in which the erotic element is subdued or nonexistent, such as the *Life of Apollonius of Tyana*, although they could be called novels on other grounds. A variety of Greek terms is used to characterize narrative fiction; they include διήγημα, δρᾶμα, ἐρωτικαί, ὑποθέσεις, λόγοι, μῦθος, πάθος, πλάσμα, σύνταγμα (see C. Gual, "Le roman grec dans la perspective des genres littéraires" in *Erotica antiqua*, ed. B. P. Reardon [Bangor, Wales, 1977] 99–105). *Narratio ficta* is probably as close as Latin can come to embracing the several kinds of novels that are now recognized as specimens of the genre. For the range of Greco-Roman novels, see T. Hägg, *The novel in antiquity* (Berkeley and Los Angeles 1983).

[73] The literature on the Greek novel is extensive, and often tries to grapple with the question of what constitutes a novel and by what name the form should be called. It may be noted that the question is most acute in English, which possesses the two terms *novel* and *romance;* other modern languages do not share this difficulty: *Roman, roman, romanzo.* There is no very clear distinction between *romance* and *novel.* Hägg

love novels,[74] and also the *Historia Alexandri Magni* (1386 001–020), the biographical novels of Xenophon of Athens and Philostratus,[75] the hagiographical *Vita Barlaam et Joasaph* ascribed to John of Damascus (2934 066), the Pseudo-Clementine romances (1271 004, 006–009, 011–012), a number of religious stories and vignettes associated with the Old Testament,[76] and the several *erotica adespota* (5003 001–004, 006–018) that survive primarily in the form of papyrus fragments.[77]

Nat. Hist. encompasses a broad range of topics such as animal nature and animal behavior,[78] hunting and fishing,[79] horse-breeding and horse-training,[80] colors,[81] stones,[82] plants,[83] rivers,[84] fire,[85] winds,[86] odors,[87] meteorology,[88] and agriculture.[89]

Poem. indicates metrical pieces that do not readily admit generic definition either by reason of meter or in terms of themes and tone. Thus, for example, the eleven-word fragment surviving under the name of Stratonicus (2645 001), and written in a combination of dactylic heptameter catalectic and iambelegus,[90] is tagged as *Poem.;* so are two fragments written in Ionic dimeter *a majore* and carried under Cleomachus (2614 001).[91] Also labeled *Poem.* are lines that appear to be rhythmical but that cannot otherwise be identified, as well as titles that are known, from ancient

---

[supra n. 72] remarks that "both 'romance' and 'novel' can also be used globally, and it seems to me that 'novel' is the more nearly unmarked term of the two, the one less liable to implant prejudice as to the nature of the genre" (4).

[74] That is, Achilles Tatius's *Leucippe et Clitophon* (0532 001), Chariton's *De Chaerea et Callirhoe* (0554 001), Heliodorus's *Aethiopica* (0658 001), Longus's *Daphnis et Chloe* (0561 001), Xenophon's *Ephesiaca* (0641 001).

[75] That is, *Cyropaedia* (0032 007), *Vita Apollonii* (0638 001).

[76] For example, the canonical stories of Esther, Job, and Jonas (0527 019, 032, 041), and the apocryphal books of *Judith, Tobias, Susanna,* and *Bel et Draco* (0527 020, 022, 054–055, 058–059), all of which are also labeled *Relig.*

[77] That is, *Sesonchosis, De Chione, Calligone, Dionysius, Metiochus et Parthenope, Herpyllis, Antheia, Olenius, Tefnut, Tinouphis,* and *Iolaus,* fragments of which were edited by F. Zimmermann, *Griechische Roman-Papyri und verwandte Texte* (Heidelberg 1936). Data entry of these fragments will be based upon a forthcoming new edition by Susan Stephens and John J. Winkler.

[78] For example, Aristotle's *De incessu animalium* (0086 015) and *De motu animalium* (0086 021), both of which are also tagged *Zool.;* Aelian's *De natura animalium* (0545 001), also classified as *Paradox.*

[79] For example, the *Cynegetica* of Oppian of Apamea (0024 001) and the *Halieutica* of Oppian of Anazarbus (0023 001), both of which are also labeled *Epic.*

[80] For example, the *De forma et delectu equorum* of Simon of Athens (2600 001).

[81] For example, Aristotle's *De coloribus* (0086 007).

[82] For example, Pseudo-Dioscorides' *De lapidibus* (1118 003).

[83] For example, Theophrastus's *Historia plantarum* (0093 001) and *De causis plantarum* (0093 002, 014).

[84] For example, the fragmented *De Nilo* of one of the Anonymi Historici (1139 035).

[85] For example, Theophrastus's *De igne* (0093 005).

[86] For example, Aristotle's *De ventorum situ et nominibus* (0086 046).

[87] For example, Theophrastus's *De odoribus* (0093 010, fr. 4).

[88] For example, Aristotle's *Meteorologica* (0086 026).

[89] For example, the tenth-century compilation known as the *Geoponica* (4080 001).

[90] See *Supplementum Hellenisticum* [supra n. 44] xxvi and 354 (fr. 737).

[91] See *Supplementum Hellenisticum* [supra n. 44] xxv and 162 (frr. 341–342).

testimonia, to have signaled poetic content of an otherwise lost poem.[92] To some extent, *Poem.* may be considered a tag used in the last resort when the text at issue is so exceptional that it might well be the sole surviving representative of its category, or when the amount of text is insufficient in size or scope to be assigned with confidence to a suitable category.

Prophet. See **Apocalyp.**

Pseudepigr. See **Apocryph.**

Relig. is used exclusively to designate texts that constitute the basis for the *scripturae sacrae* of Judaeo-Christian tradition. Only the fifty-nine works that constitute the *Septuaginta* (0527 001–059)[93] and the twenty-seven books of the *Novum Testamentum* (0031 001–027) have been so labeled. See also **Apocryph.**

Rhet. is used to classify works concerned with the art, science, theories, and techniques of persuasion, of which oratory is the principal beneficiary.[94] The guidelines that determine whether a work in the *Canon* ought to be categorized as oratory or rhetoric are, for the most part, consistent with Kennedy's definition of rhetoric:

> Rhetoric, defined in the strictest sense, is the art of persuasion as practiced by orators and described by theorists and teachers of speech. That basic meaning may be extended, however, to include the art of all who aim at some kind of attitude change on the part of their audience or readers, and then applied to what I shall call secondary rhetoric: critical or aesthetic theory not directly concerned with persuasion and the technique of works produced under the influence of these critical concepts.[95]

While instances of overlap are likely to be more frequent than examples of clear-cut distinction, an attempt has been made to separate the nearly 250 formal orations in the data bank from the numerous critical essays about oratory and the orators themselves.[96] There are, of course, formally delivered speeches concerned with rhetorical themes and descriptions, and these rhetorical orations are classified as both *Orat.* and *Rhet.*[97] However, the lines are somewhat blurred between what

[92] For example, some of the fragments of Parthenius (0655 003) that Lloyd-Jones and Parsons carry together as *carmina incerti metri* in *Supplementum Hellenisticum* [supra n. 44] 302–306, frr. 627–639. Also, a little poem represented only by its title, Τρίφυλλον, which, according to Athenaeus (*Deip.* 15.685a), is attributed to a certain Demareta (2816 001): καὶ γὰρ εἰς Δημαρέτην ἀναφέρεταί τι ποιημάτιον ὃ ἐπιγράφεται Τρίφυλλον.

[93] The apocryphal books of the *Septuaginta* (i.e., 0527 017, 020–025, 033–034, 050, 052, 054–055, 058–059) are tagged also as *Apocryph.*

[94] See Kennedy's introductory chapter, "The nature of rhetoric," in *The art of persuasion in Greece* [supra n. 37] 3–25.

[95] G. Kennedy, *The art of rhetoric in the Roman world* (Princeton 1972) 3.

[96] For example, Isocrates' extant speeches (0010 001–021) are tagged as *Orat.*, but Dionysius of Halicarnassus's *De Isocrate* (0081 004) is labeled *Rhet.*

[97] For example, Dio Chrysostomus's *Orationes* (0612 001).

constitutes oratorical talk and talk about oratory. The speeches of the ten Attic orators qualify as *Orat.*, whereas the speeches and declamations of the philosophers, orators, and rhetoricians who gained prominence during the so-called second sophistic movement seem to incline toward *Rhet.*[98] *Rhet.* is also applied to works entitled *Ars rhetorica*,[99] as well as to those appearing in various editions of the *Rhetores Graeci*,[100] the several surviving *progymnasmata*,[101] and treatises on a variety of topics relevant to rhetorical training.[102] See also **Gramm.** and **Homilet.**

Schol. is, for the most part, limited to works derived from the *disjecta membra* of otherwise lost commentaries on classical authors.[103] In this edition of the *Canon*, the majority of the scholiastic works (which include glosses as well as *commenta*) are carried under headings beginning with the words *Scholia in*, followed alphabetically by the names of specific authors upon whose works they were written,[104] but a fair number are located under the names of individual authors who wrote comments, interpretations, and glosses.[105] A few are carried under the names of authors upon whose works the scholia were written.[106]

Although on theoretical grounds scholia ought not to be differentiated from the rest of exegetical literature,[107] certain distinctions have been observed in the interest of practicality for this *Canon*. In general, a distinction based upon extent of connected (i.e., running) text determines whether a work is labeled *Schol.* or *Comm.*: extended interpretative works are considered *Comm.*, whereas *disjecta commenta* upon

---

[98] For example, Aelius Aristides (0284 029–039, 045–046, 049–050, 052–054, 056), Maximus of Tyre (0563 001), Philostratus (0638 006, 0652 001, 1600 001), Polemon (1617 001). See Kennedy's chapters entitled "The age of the sophists" and "Greek rhetoricians of the empire" in *The art of rhetoric in the Roman world* [supra n. 95] 553–641.

[99] For example, Anaximenes' *Ars rhetorica* (0547 001).

[100] For example, L. Spengel, 3 vols. (Leipzig 1853–1856; repr. Frankfurt am Main 1966); vol. 1.2, ed. C. Hammer [post Spengel] (Leipzig 1894); C. Walz, 9 vols. in 10 (Stuttgart and Tübingen 1832–1836; repr. Osnabrück 1968).

[101] For example, Hermogenes (0592 001), Libanius (2200 001), Theon (0607 001).

[102] For example, Dionysius of Halicarnassus's *De compositione verborum* (0081 012–013), Herodian's *De figuris* (0087 035) and *De barbarismo et soloecismo* (0087 044), Demetrius's *De elocutione* (0613 001), Suetonius's Περὶ βλασφημιῶν καὶ πόθεν ἑκάστη (1760 001).

[103] There are, to be sure, scholia that survive from commentaries to the works of Christian writers, but these have not yet been systematically examined for the purpose of including them in the TLG data bank.

[104] For example, *Scholia in Aeschylum* (5010), *Scholia in Aratum* (5013).

[105] For example, Joannes Tzetzes, whose scholia and glosses on the plays of Aristophanes are carried under *Scholia in Aristophanem* (4101 035–040, 072, 076, 078), whereas his *Exegesis in Homeri Iliadem* is cited under his own name (9022 002).

[106] For example, the *Scholia ad Bacchylidis carmina* are carried under the name of Bacchylides (0199 007).

[107] There is really no substantive difference between the scholiastic writings and the exegetical works of Arethas, the Byzantine philologist and theologian whose library may have rivaled that of Photius; cf. J. M. Hussey, *The Cambridge medieval history*, vol. 4.2 (Cambridge 1967) 82; H.-G. Beck, *Kirche und theologische Literatur im byzantinischen Reich* (Munich 1959) 591; N. G. Wilson, *Scholars of Byzantium* (London 1983) 120, who suggests that Arethas's library "may have been much smaller than Photius'." Nevertheless, Arethas's *Scholia in Tatianum* is carried under his own name (2130 015), whereas his *Scholia Platonica* is listed, along with the rest of the scholia to Plato, under *Scholia in Platonem* (5035 002).

words, sentences, or passages fall within the parameters of *Schol.*[108] A further distinction is made between *Comm.* and *Exeget.*: commentaries on classical authors are tagged as *Comm.*, whereas commentaries on scriptural texts (although not substantially different except that the subject matter belongs to the realm of Judaeo-Christian tradition) are labeled *Exeget.*[109] If the scholiastic remarks in question do not add up to a commentary, and if they are, moreover, derived from *catenae*, they are classified as both *Exeget.* and *Caten.*[110]

While these distinctions may seem somewhat artificial and arbitrary (especially in view of potential similarities of language and perspective that might warrant conjoining, rather than isolating, the hundreds of works into one category or another), there remains the difference in interests among scholars consulting the TLG data bank: the likelihood that those wishing to explore the large corpus of classical scholia might also wish to wade through hundreds of New Testament *catenae* is slight. On the other hand, the scholar who wishes to do just that may circumscribe the material for investigation in broader terms in order to search through all works that have been classified as *Caten.*, *Comm.*, *Exeget.*, and *Schol.* See also **Caten.** and **Exeget.**

Theol. is used to classify works that can be defined as religious literature insofar as they are concerned primarily with the nature of divinity, the relationship between human and divine, religious doctrine, and other spiritual matters. A distinction is observed, however, between tractates on divine matters and those writings that have become the *scripturae sacrae* in Judaeo-Christian tradition. Another distinction is made between *Theol.* and *Eccl.*, where *Eccl.* characterizes matters of interest to the Christian church but without principal focus upon divinity.[111] Distinction is disregarded entirely, however, in the case of those writings that seem to exhibit both theological and philosophical concerns. The works of Clement of Alexandria, for instance, are specimens of both Christian Platonism and speculative theology,[112] for which the classification tags *Phil.* and *Theol.* together are warranted.[113] Similarly, the *Corpus Hermeticum* (1286 001–022), "those Greek and Latin writings which

[108] For example, Sopater's *Scholia ad Hermogenis status seu artem rhetoricam* (2031 002), with 55,814 words of connected text, is classified as *Comm.* (+ *Rhet.*); in fact, Walz (*Rhet. Graec.* 5) gives the Greek title of this work as Σχόλια (p. iii) as well as Ὑπόμνημα (p. 1). The *Scholia recentiora in Aristophanis Nubes* (5014 005), on the other hand, represents the comments culled from three different sources (i.e., Eustathius, Thomas Magister, and Demetrius Triclinius), justifying the classification *Schol.*

[109] For example, *Scholia in Hippocratis de fracturis* by Palladius Med. (0726 004) is labeled *Comm.* (+ *Med.*); Eusebius's *Commentarius in Isaiam* (2018 019) is classified as *Exeget.*

[110] For example, Asterius of Antioch's *Fragmenta in Psalmos* (2061 002), Ammonius of Alexandria's *Fragmenta in Joannem* (2724 003).

[111] For example, Basil's *De legendis gentilium libris* (2040 002) and John Chrysostom's *Adversus oppugnatores vitae monasticae* (2062 003), both of which are classified as *Eccl.* In fact, *Eccl.* is used of a number of works that, in content, tone, and attitude, reveal their affinity with the literature of the church, yet are not so preoccupied with questions concerning the divine as to require inclusion among *theologica*.

[112] J. Quasten, *Patrology* 2 (Utrecht and Antwerp 1953; repr. 1964) 20: "it is no exaggeration to praise him [sc. Clement] as the founder of speculative theology."

[113] For example, the *Protrepticus* (0555 001) and *Paedagogus* (0555 002).

contain religious or philosophical teachings ascribed to Hermes Trismegistus,"[114] is classified as both *Phil.* and *Theol.* See also ***Eccl.*** and ***Relig.***

While most works in the TLG data bank are accompanied by at least one descriptive classification tag, there are some that do not warrant categorization. The label *Test.* is used primarily to designate testimonia without, however, accounting for the variety of literary genres into which the testimonial statements might fall. Ultimately, testimonia are not overlooked; when they constitute part of a larger work in the data bank, classification tags are assigned to the larger work. As one might expect, the majority of works to which *Test.* is affixed may be found in generic collections of fragments.[115]

Occasionally, a work defies categorization altogether, owing to an insufficient amount of text upon which to base a judgment about its nature.[116] When this is the case, the notation *Ignotum* stands in lieu of a classification tag.

It will be obvious to the user that the classification system adopted for the *Canon* does not always yield neatly to systematic principles and that it does in fact tolerate the coexistence of unrelated categories as though they were members of the same species. While most of the tags are recognizable as traditionally accepted indications of genre or literary form,[117] some are used to characterize content and do not encompass generic criteria that elucidate form.[118] Others characterize, in broad terms, the metrical schemes that dominate the content but without specifying the genre to which the work might belong.[119] Still others emphasize attitude, tone, or persuasion regardless of form and content,[120] while some address only questions of *genuinitas*.[121] Yet others seem to cleave to one side of an invisible line that separates religious material from nonreligious writing.[122]

---

[114] W. Scott and A. S. Ferguson, *Hermetica* 1 (Oxford 1924; repr. London 1968) 1.

[115] For example, *FGrH* [supra n. 50]; Diels-Kranz [supra n. 53].

[116] For example, the eighty-three words in *P. Oxy.* 18.2158, identifiable only as *Fragmenta incerti operis* and perhaps to be ascribed to Philo Judaeus (0018 042). Also the one-word *Fragmentum Eratosthenicum* (0222 010) offers nothing on which to pin a label of any sort; see J. U. Powell, *Collectanea Alexandrina* (Oxford 1925; repr. 1970) 252: "utrum in poematis, an in prosa oratione, non liquet."

[117] For example, *Epic., Comic., Trag.*

[118] For example, *Bucol., Exeget., Math., Med., Nat. Hist.* Bucolic poetry, for instance, shares the dactylic hexameter with epic poetry, hymnal poetry, and parody.

[119] For example, *Hexametr., Iamb., Eleg.* The sometimes fine line between elegy and epigram is crossed if the poem occupies a secure place in a generic collection. All poems in the *Anthologia Graeca* have been labeled *Epigr.* regardless of meter. Elegiac couplets residing in the *Anthologia Lyrica Graeca* but not in the *Anthologia Graeca* are classified as either *Eleg.* or *Epigr.*, depending upon criteria such as theme and tone, as well as definitive statements from surviving testimonia.

[120] For example, *Relig., Satura, Invectiv.* Although many works in Christian literature seem to announce themselves in invective tones, the tag *Invectiv.* has been applied rather sparingly. The majority of *apologiae*, for example, have been labeled *Apol.* but not *Invectiv.*, on the assumption that a defense of one ideology often implies an attack upon another. For invective themes in Greek and Latin literature, see *M. Tulli Ciceronis in L. Calpurnium Pisonem oratio*, ed. R. G. M. Nisbet (Oxford 1961; repr. 1975) 192–198.

[121] For example, *Apocryph., Pseudepigr.*

[122] For example, *Theol.* vs. *Phil., Homilet.* vs. *Orat.*

Quot homines, tot sententiae: perhaps not all decisions made in classifying some 9,740 discrete literary works will meet with universal approval. It should be borne in mind, however, that the TLG's classification effort could not draw upon precedent, that the individual components of Greek literature (like those of any great literary corpus) cannot always be neatly pigeonholed, and that the final classification scheme is intended to serve the broadest possible range of users rather than to acknowledge the specialized (and sometimes necessarily narrow) interests of experts in a given genre. Furthermore, no claim is made that the scheme outlined here is inflexible. As a better understanding is gained of the character that defines specific forms of literature, the present classification system can be supplemented, modified, and refined.

A good case in point is the classification tag *Relig.*, currently used only of the works included in the Septuagint and in the New Testament. The Septuagint, in particular, evokes spirited discussion: some religious scholars argue that there are, within the Septuagint, literary subcategories without parallel in classical literature, which would warrant the adoption of tags peculiar to religious texts.[123] Similarly, some scholars consider the *Historia Alexandri Magni* to be notably different in nature from other accepted specimens of the Greek novel so as to justify replacing *Narr. Fict.* with an altogether different tag.[124] Others believe that a distinction should be made between biography and autobiography rather than to allow the single tag *Biogr.* to encompass both subgenres.

To be sure, such suggestions are valid. By the same token, however, excessive splintering of the corpus of Greek literature would, *ipso facto*, be self-defeating. The purpose of the text-classification effort, after all, has been to create a *reasonable number* of *reasonably sized* text groupings that will permit scholars to consult the TLG data bank selectively. Once the software needed to allow selective consultation has been implemented, actual use of the classification scheme will quickly reveal instances of categories that are too encompassing or too restrictive, thereby requiring modification. Since the classification system, like the TLG data bank itself, is electronic in nature, future modification can be effected with relative ease.

---

[123] For example, law, prophecy, wisdom literature, and folklore (not to be confused with other works to which the tag *Myth.* has been affixed, such as Parthenius's *Narrationes amatoriae* and Apollodorus's *Bibliotheca*).

[124] See Hägg [supra n. 72] who calls the *Historia Alexandri Magni*, in its earliest form, "pseudo-historical" (115) and prefers to regard it as "romanticized biography" rather than "historical novel" (126).

ACKNOWLEDGMENTS

Non omnia possumus omnes. From its very inception in 1972, the Thesaurus Linguae Graecae has had the benefit of a worldwide network of scholars on whom it has been possible to rely for expert guidance and assistance. These individuals have provided us with a special resource in the development and continual refinement of the *Canon.* Certain bibliographies, for example, have been adopted practically wholesale, with only minor adjustments in pagination or the addition of publishers' names. Others have been submitted to the scrutiny of recognized authorities who have helped to hone what may initially have been tentative and unrefined. Still others have been recast to suit the purposes of an electronic repository designed to contain one version, and only one (if possible), of an edited work. To the many scholars who have lent their expertise to this enterprise, a huge debt of gratitude is owed, along with apologies for any unintended deviations from their suggestions. We hope that this *Canon* reflects, more often than it belies, their contributions.

The selection of appropriate texts for inclusion in the data bank has been the primary task of a panel of scholars appointed by the American Philological Association. The first chair of this committee was Professor Douglas C. C. Young (Paddison Professor of Greek, University of North Carolina). Following the death of Professor Young in the autumn of 1973, Lionel Pearson (Professor Emeritus, Stanford University) took the reins and held them until 1980. For brief periods in 1980 and 1981, the committee was chaired by Professor Glen W. Bowersock (Institute for Advanced Study, Princeton University) and Professor David Wiesen (University of Southern California). Thereafter and until 1984, Professor David C. Young (at the time affiliated with our sister campus, the University of California, Santa Barbara) held the post. In early 1985, as the TLG moved closer to the literature of Byzantium, the chairship was passed to Professor Ihor Ševčenko (Harvard University).

Those who have held membership on the committee include Professors Hans-Dieter Betz (University of Chicago), Phillip De Lacy (Emeritus, University of Pennsylvania), Lowell A. Edmunds (Rutgers University), Robert M. Grant (University of Chicago), Christian Habicht (Institute for Advanced Study, Princeton University), Albert Henrichs (Harvard University), Bernard M. W. Knox (formerly Director of the Center for Hellenic Studies), Ludwig Koenen (University of Michigan), Miroslav Marcovich (University of Illinois), Bruce M. Metzger (Princeton Theological Seminary), Jon Mikalson (University of Virginia), John F. Oates (Duke University), David W. Packard (Packard Humanities Institute), Robert Renehan (University of California, Santa Barbara), Kent J. Rigsby (Duke University), John M. Rist (University of Toronto), Catherine Rubincam (University of Toronto), L. G. Westerink (State University of New York, Buffalo), William H. Willis (Duke University), and corresponding member Winfried Buehler (Universität Hamburg).

As we have discovered, some of the most prolific writers in the history of Greek literature are also the most difficult to pin down in terms of precisely what they wrote. In trying to sort out the tangles that seemed to grow along with the Greek corpus, we have had the expertise of others whom we regard as our collaborators.

The bibliographies to Galenus Med. and Pseudo-Galenus Med. were the work of a team led by Dr. Ronald F. Kotrc (formerly affiliated with the Division of Medical History, College of Physicians of Philadelphia), Professor Kenneth R. Walters (Wayne State University), and former TLG Assistant Director David C. Wilson (University of California, Irvine). Professors Phillip De Lacy and Hans Diller (Christian-Albrechts Universität zu Kiel) contributed a number of important suggestions that were incorporated into the Galenic bibliographies.

The bibliography to Hippocrates Med. and the *Corpus Hippocraticum* was a collaborative effort between the TLG and the Projet Hippo, directed by Dr. Gilles Maloney at the Université Laval.

For the bibliography to Hippolytus Scr. Eccl., we benefited from the vast knowledge of Miroslav Marcovich, whose edition of the *Refutatio omnium haeresium* we welcomed for the TLG data bank.

The bibliography to Joannes Chrysostomus Scr. Eccl. was submitted to the careful inspection of Dr. Sever J. Voicu, whose mastery of the Chrysostomic corpus is evident in the *Clavis patrum Graecorum*. His thoughtful suggestions contributed to the development and organization of the works that survive under the name of our most voluminous author.

The bibliography to Philodemus Phil. has proven to be a peculiar thicket of thorns that we have invited many others to explore with us in the hope of seeing some light. Several former TLG staff members helped us to organize the sheer mass of text material Philodemus has generated, among them Renate Gordon, Peter Gimpel, and John Winieski. Many scholars in this country and in Europe supplied us with Philodemian bibliographies of their own. We are especially grateful to Professor Phillip De Lacy; the Norwegian team of Professor Knut Kleve (Universitetet i Oslo), Kjell Gustafson (Universitetet i Oslo), and Jan Songstad (Universitetet i Bergen); Dr. Marcello Gigante (Centro Internazionale per lo Studio dei Papiri Ercolanesi, Naples), whose *Catalogo dei papiri Ercolanesi* provided us with the order of the treatises as well as the proper Greek titles; and Dr. Francesca Longo-Auricchio (Centro Internazionale per lo Studio dei Papiri Ercolanesi), who alerted us to the impending publication of newly edited fragments. Many scholars agreed to review the Philodemus bibliography in its various stages; their suggestions for revision aided us in the selection of appropriate texts and in the rejection of materials that have since been superseded. For this difficult part of our bibliographic work, we benefited from the painstaking scrutiny of Professors Elizabeth Asmis (University of Chicago), David Sider (Fordham University), and especially Albert Henrichs, who challenged us to rethink the purpose and function of a TLG bibliography to Philodemus.

For the bibliography to Origenes Theol., we took advantage of the good will and the learned comments of the Reverend Professor Henry Chadwick (Regius Professor Emeritus of Divinity, Cambridge University).

The bibliography to Proclus Phil. owes its refinement to the detailed criticism and patient guidance extended to us by L. G. Westerink, whose editions of Neoplatonic treatises and commentaries enhance the TLG data bank.

A number of the bibliographies, as well as the names of authors and titles of works, have benefited from our long-standing collaboration with the Spanish team associated with the Greek-Spanish Lexicon at the Instituto Antonio de Nebrija in Madrid. We have shared many of our difficulties and many of our solutions with Professor Francisco Rodriguez Adrados, Dr. Xavier Lopez Facal, and Mr. Aníbal González.

More recently, we have benefited from communication with Father Rodrigue LaRue (Université du Québec à Trois-Rivières), whose contribution to the enormous warehouse of names, titles, and dates appeared in 1985 as the *Clavis scriptorum Graecorum et Latinorum*. The work of Father LaRue and his collaborators provides us with a constant check against flagrant error.

In 1988, when we began the task of classifying works in the data bank, we had to summon the cooperation and the specialized knowledge of scholars around the world. To some we sent bibliographies of individual authors or entire literary genres; to others we addressed specific questions that elicited carefully considered, detailed answers. We were fortunate indeed to have available to us the willing participation and the special expertise of so many, including John P. Adams (briefly our colleague at UC Irvine), Glen Bowersock, John J. Collins (University of Notre Dame), Malcolm Davies (St. John's College, Oxford University), Kristoffel Demoen (Seminarie Byzantinistik RUG, Belgium), Mervin Dilts (New York University), Gerard H. Ettlinger (Fordham University), Paul J. Fedwick (University of St. Michael's College, Toronto), Hans B. Gottschalk (University of Leeds), Jackson P. Hershbell (University of Minnesota), C. P. Jones (University of Toronto), Charles Kannengiesser, s.j. (University of Notre Dame), Robert Kraft (University of Pennsylvania), Hubert Martin, Jr. (University of Kentucky), Alden A. Mosshammer (University of California, San Diego), B. P. Reardon (UC Irvine), Gerasimos Santas (UC Irvine), David Sider, Andreas Spira (Johannes Gutenberg-Universität Mainz), Philip Stadter (University of North Carolina), Susan Stephens (Stanford University), Dana F. Sutton (UC Irvine), Sever Voicu, and John J. Winkler (Stanford University).

Closer to home, we have benefited from daily interaction with our verification and correction staff, whose sharp detective skills have helped us to correct errors of commission and omission. In many ways, they have been our collaborators. Thus, we owe our continuing gratitude to Dr. Douglas Domingo-Forasté, Roberta Frey, and Kathryn Koken who quietly and patiently assisted us whenever we encountered technical difficulties.

Richard Whitaker did the page makeup and prepared the camera-ready copy on an Ibycus system.

Claude Conyers, our gracious editor at Oxford University Press, provided us with numerous suggestions that saved us from skidding into murky waters.

Obviously, a work of this scope cannot be entirely free of faults, for which we ourselves acknowledge responsibility. In the past, we have benefited from suggestions for improvement to which our colleagues have alerted us. Many of their suggestions became *addenda et corrigenda* to the second edition of the *Canon;* these *addenda et corrigenda* have been incorporated into the third edition. It is our hope that scholars who detect other errors will bring them to our attention.

BIBLIOGRAPHIC ABBREVIATIONS

The papyrological abbreviations cited here indicate approved texts for data entry. Generally, papyrological abbreviations are replaced by detailed bibliographic information when the texts are submitted for data entry. Omitted altogether are papyrological abbreviations found within parentheses following the name of a given work or at the end of a bibliographic listing for a work.

AAB	*Abhandlungen der deutschen Akademie der Wissenschaften zu Berlin.* Berlin: Akademie-Verlag, 1944–.
ACO	*Acta conciliorum oecumenicorum*, 3 vols., ed. E. Schwartz. Berlin: De Gruyter, 1924–1940 (repr. 1960–1965).
AG	*Anthologia Graeca*, 4 vols., 2nd edn., ed. H. Beckby. Munich: Heimeran, 1965–1968.
ALG[1]	*Anthologia lyrica Graeca*, vols. 1–2, ed. E. Diehl. Leipzig: Teubner, 1925.
ALG[2]	*Anthologia lyrica Graeca*, vol. 1, fasc. 1–4, 2nd edn., ed. E. Diehl. Leipzig: Teubner, 1936.
ALG[3]	*Anthologia lyrica Graeca*, fasc. 1–3, 3rd edn., ed. E. Diehl. Leipzig: Teubner, 1949–1952.
APAW	*Abhandlungen der königlich preussischen Akademie der Wissenschaften.* Berlin: Reimer, 1815–1944.
App. Anth.	*Epigrammatum anthologia Palatina cum Planudeis et appendice nova*, vol. 3, ed. E. Cougny. Paris: Didot, 1890.
BHG	*Bibliotheca hagiographica Graeca*, vols. 1–3, 3rd edn., ed. F. Halkin. Brussels: Société des Bollandistes, 1957.
BHG[a]	*Auctarium bibliothecae hagiographicae Graecae*, ed. F. Halkin. Brussels: Société des Bollandistes, 1969.
BHG[n]	*Novum auctarium bibliothecae hagiographicae Graecae*, ed. F. Halkin. Brussels: Société des Bollandistes, 1984.
BKP	*Beiträge zur klassischen Philologie.* Meisenheim am Glan: Hain, 1960–.
CA	*Collectanea Alexandrina*, ed. J. U. Powell. Oxford: Clarendon Press, 1925 (repr. 1970).
CAF	*Comicorum Atticorum fragmenta*, 3 vols., ed. T. Kock. Leipzig: Teubner, 1880–1888.
CAG	*Commentaria in Aristotelem Graeca*, 23 vols. + 3 suppl. Berlin: Reimer, 1882–1909.
CGF	*Comicorum Graecorum fragmenta*, vol. 1.1, ed. G. Kaibel in *Poetarum Graecorum fragmenta*, vol. 6.1. Berlin: Weidman, 1899.
CGFPR	*Comicorum Graecorum fragmenta in papyris reperta*, ed. C. Austin. Berlin: De Gruyter, 1973.
CMG	*Corpus medicorum Graecorum.* Leipzig and Berlin: Teubner, 1908–; Berlin: Akademie-Verlag, 1947–.
CPG	*Clavis patrum Graecorum*, 5 vols., ed. M. Geerard and F. Glorie. Turnhout: Brepols, 1974–1987.

CronErc — *Cronache Ercolanesi. Bollettino del Centro internazionale per lo studio dei papiri Ercolanesi.* Naples: Maccharioli, 1971–.

D-K — *Die Fragmente der Vorsokratiker,* 3 vols., 6th edn., ed. H. Diels and W. Kranz. Zürich: Weidmann, 1951–1952 (repr. 1966–1967).

Epist. Graec. — *Epistolographi Graeci,* ed. R. Hercher. Paris: Didot, 1873 (repr. Amsterdam: Hakkert, 1965).

FCG — *Fragmenta comicorum Graecorum,* 5 vols. in 7, ed. A. Meineke. Berlin: Reimer, 1839–1857 (repr. Berlin: De Gruyter, 1970).

FGrH — *Die Fragmente der griechischen Historiker,* 3 vols. in 15, ed. F. Jacoby. Leiden: Brill, 1923–1958 (repr. 1954–1969).

FHG — *Fragmenta historicorum Graecorum,* 5 vols., ed. K. Müller. Paris: Didot, 1841–1870.

Fonti I.2 — *Fonti. Fascicolo ix. Discipline générale antique (iie–ixe s.),* vol. I.2 *(Les canons des synodes particuliers),* ed. P. Joannou. Rome: Tipografia Italo-Orientale "S. Nilo," 1962.

Fonti II — *Fonti. Fascicolo ix. Discipline générale antique (iie–ixe s.),* vol. II *(Les canons des pères grecs),* ed. P. Joannou. Rome: Tipografia Italo-Orientale "S. Nilo," 1963.

GCS — *Die griechischen christlichen Schriftsteller der ersten Jahrhunderte.* Berlin: Akademie-Verlag, 1897–.

GDRK — *Die griechischen Dichterfragmente der römischen Kaiserzeit,* vols. 1, 2nd edn., and 2, ed. E. Heitsch. Göttingen: Vandenhoeck & Ruprecht, 1963–1964.

GGM — *Geographi Graeci minores,* 2 vols. + *tabulae,* ed. K. Müller. Paris: Didot, 1855–1861 (repr. Hildesheim: Olms, 1965).

Gramm. Graec. — *Grammatici Graeci,* 4 vols. in 6, ed. G. Uhlig, A. Hilgard, and A. Lentz. Leipzig: Teubner, 1867–1910 (repr. Hildesheim: Olms, 1965).

HGM — *Historici Graeci minores,* vols. 1–2, ed. L. Dindorf. Leipzig: Teubner, 1870–1871.

IEG — *Iambi et elegi Graeci,* 2 vols., ed. M. L. West. Oxford: Clarendon Press, 1971–1972.

JÖByz — *Jahrbuch der österreichischen Byzantinistik.* Vienna: Verlag der Österreichischen Akademie der Wissenschaften, 1951–.

K — *Claudii Galeni opera,* 20 vols. in 22, ed. C. G. Kühn. Leipzig: Knobloch, 1821–1833 (repr. Hildesheim: Olms, 1964–1965).

MPG — *Patrologiae cursus completus (series Graeca),* 161 vols., ed. J.-P. Migne. Paris: Migne, 1857–1866.

P. Cair. — *Greek papyri. Catalogue général des antiquités égyptiennes du Musée du Caire,* ed. B. P. Grenfell and A. S. Hunt. Oxford: Oxford University Press, 1903.

P. Egerton — *Fragments of an unknown gospel and other early Christian papyri,* ed. H. I. Bell and T. C. Skeat. London: Trustees of the British Museum, 1935.

P. Flor. 3 — *Papiri greco-egizii. Papiri Florentini,* vol. 3: *Documenti e testi letterarii dell'età romana e bizantina,* ed. G. Vitelli. Milan: Hoepli, 1915.

PGM — *Papyri Graecae magicae. Die griechischen Zauberpapyri,* vols. 1–2, 2nd edn., ed. K. Preisendanz and A. Henrichs. Stuttgart: Teubner, 1973–1974.

PGR — *Paradoxographorum Graecorum reliquiae,* ed. A. Giannini. Milan: Istituto Editoriale Italiano, 1965.

P. Hamb. 2 — *Griechische Papyrusurkunden der Hamburger Staats- und Universitätsbibliothek,* vol. 2: *Griechische Papyri der Hamburger Staats- und Universitätsbibliothek mit einigen Stücken aus der Sammlung Hugo Ibscher,* ed B. Snell et al. [Veröffentlichungen aus der Hamburger Staats- und Universitätsbibliothek 4. Hamburg: Augustin, 1954].

P. Lit. Lond. — *Catalogue of the literary papyri in the British Museum,* ed. H. J. M. Milne. London: British Museum, 1927.

PMG — *Poetae melici Graeci,* ed. D. Page. Oxford: Clarendon Press, 1962 (repr. 1967).

P. Oxy. — *The Oxyrhynchus papyri.* London: Egypt Exploration Fund, 1898–1919, and Egypt Exploration Society, 1920–.

P. Rain. 1   *Corpus papyrorum Raineri archiducis Austriae*, vol. 1: *Griechische Texte I. Rechtsurkunden*, ed. C. Wessely. Vienna: Kaiserlich Königliche Hof- und Staatsdruckerei, 1895.

P. Rain. 3   *Corpus papyrorum Raineri archiducis Austriae*, vol. 6.1: *Griechische Texte III*, ed. H. Harrauer and S. M. E. van Lith. Vienna: Hollinek, 1978.

P. Ryl. 1   *Catalogue of the Greek and Latin papyri in the John Rylands Library at Manchester*, vol. 1, ed. A. S. Hunt. Manchester: Manchester University Press, 1911.

P. Ryl. 3   *Catalogue of the Greek and Latin papyri in the John Rylands Library at Manchester*, vol. 3, ed. C. H. Roberts. Manchester: Manchester University Press, 1938.

P. Schubart   *Griechische literarische Papyri*, ed. W. Schubart. Berlin: Akademie-Verlag, 1950.

PSI 13   *Papiri greci e latini (Pubblicazioni della Società Italiana per la ricerca dei papiri greci e latini in Egitto)*, vol. 13, ed. M. Norsa and V. Bartoletti. Florence: Ariani, 1949–1953.

PsVTGr 3   *Pseudepigrapha veteris testamenti Graece 3*, ed. A.-M. Denis. Leiden: Brill, 1970.

PTS   *Patristische Texte und Studien*. Berlin: De Gruyter, 1964–.

RAAN   *Rendiconti dell' Accademia di Archeologia, Lettere e Belle Arti di Napoli*. Naples: L'Arte Tipografica, 1865–.

RFIC   *Rivista di filologia e di istruzione classica*. Turin: Loescher, 1873–.

RhM   *Rheinisches Museum*. Frankfurt: Sauerländer, 1827–.

Savile   Τοῦ ἐν ἁγίοις πατρὸς ἡμῶν Ἰωάννου τοῦ Χρυσοστόμου τῶν εὑρισκομένων τόμος, 8 vols., ed. H. Savile. Eton: Norton, 1612–1613.

SC   *Sources chrétiennes*. Paris: Cerf, 1941–.

SH   *Supplementum Hellenisticum*, ed. H. Lloyd-Jones and P. Parsons. Berlin: De Gruyter, 1983.

SLG   *Supplementum lyricis Graecis*, ed. D. Page. Oxford: Clarendon Press, 1974.

ST   *Studi e Testi*. Vatican City: Biblioteca Apostolica Vaticana, 1900–.

Suppl. Com.   *Supplementum comicum*, ed. J. Demiańczuk. Krakau: Nakładem Akademii, 1912 (repr. Hildesheim: Olms, 1967).

TGF   *Tragicorum Graecorum fragmenta*, ed. A. Nauck. Leipzig: Teubner, 1889 (repr. with *Supplementum*, ed. B. Snell. Hildesheim: Olms, 1964).

TGL   *Thesaurus Graecae Linguae ab H. Stephano constructus*, 8 vols., ed. K. B. Haase, W. and L. Dindorf. Paris: Didot, 1831–1865.

TrGF 1   *Tragicorum Graecorum fragmenta*, vol. 1, ed. B. Snell. Göttingen: Vandenhoeck & Ruprecht, 1971. [= Tragici minores].

TrGF 2   *Tragicorum Graecorum fragmenta*, vol. 2, ed. R. Kannicht and B. Snell. Göttingen: Vandenhoeck & Ruprecht, 1981. [= Fragmenta adespota].

TrGF 3   *Tragicorum Graecorum fragmenta*, vol. 3, ed. S. Radt. Göttingen: Vandenhoeck & Ruprecht, 1985. [= Aeschylus].

TrGF 4   *Tragicorum Graecorum fragmenta*, vol. 4, ed. S. Radt. Göttingen: Vandenhoeck & Ruprecht, 1977. [= Sophocles]

ZKT   *Zeitschrift für katholische Theologie*. Vienna: Herder, 1877–.

CODES AND SIGLA

Category of Information	Siglum	Definition
TLG Author Number	4-digit number	This number is used to identify an author in the TLG data bank.
Author or Work Name	[ ]	Authenticity of the name, or even existence of the author, is questioned.
	< >	Author to whom a given work is attributed may not be the correct author.
	fiq + name	*Fortasse idem qui.* Author might be identified with the name indicated.
	Cf. + name	*Confer.* Extant works are carried under the name of a different author; bibliographic data can be found by consulting the name indicated.
	Cf. et + name	*Confer et.* Additional related information can be found by consulting the name indicated.
Author Epithet	< >	Extant work falls within the literary genre indicated by the epithet, although the author in question was not primarily a writer in the specified genre, or perhaps not primarily a writer.
Date	ante + century	Extant writing may be dated to the century indicated, or earlier.
	post + century	Extant writing may be dated to the century indicated, or later.
	/	Extant writing is dated to either of the two centuries indicated, *or* the two centuries define the earliest or latest range of dates.
	–	Author's writings span the two centuries indicated.
Geographical Epithet	fort. + Latin proper adjective	*Fortasse.* Author might have lived in, or been associated with, the place indicated by the Latin proper adjective.
TLG Work Number	3-digit number	This number is used, in conjunction with the 4-digit author number, to identify a work in the TLG data bank.
Work	[Sp.]	*Spurium.* Authenticity of the work is generally rejected.
	[Dub.]	*Dubium.* Authorship of the work is in doubt.
	Cf.	*Confer.* Bibliographic data for recommended text(s) can be found under the author or author and work indicated.
	Cf. et	*Confer et.* Attribution of extant writings may be questioned; additional bibliographic data may be found under the author or author and work indicated.
	Dup.	*Duplicat.* Text duplicates another edition in the data bank; bibliographic data can also be found under the author and work indicated.
	Dup. partim	*Duplicat partim.* Text partially duplicates another edition in the data bank; bibliographic data can also be found under the author and work indicated.
Transmission	Q	*Quotation.* Work has been transmitted via quotation(s) from a later source.

Category of Information	*Siglum*	*Definition*
	NQ	*No quotation*. Work does not survive; text cited may include testimonia or titles only.
	Cod	*Codex*. Work has been transmitted via manuscript(s).
	Pap	*Papyrus*. Work has been transmitted via papyri.
	Epigr	*Epigraph*. Work has been transmitted via inscription(s).
Classification		For abbreviations used to classify works in the TLG data bank, see pages xxxiii–xxxiv.
Word Count or Word Estimate	[ ]	Number enclosed reflects an estimate only of the work(s) indicated; brackets are removed when word count is verified by computer.
Citation		For citation systems used for texts in the TLG data bank, see pages 439–471.

THESAURUS LINGUAE GRAECAE

Canon of Greek Authors and Works

1883 **ABARIS** Hist.
Incertum: Scythicus
001 **Testimonium**, FGrH #34: 1A:258.
NQ: 29: Test.
002 **Fragmenta**, FGrH #34: 1A:*13–*14 addenda.
fr. 2: *P. Oxy.* 13.1611.
Q, Pap: 138: Hist., Myth.

1891 **ABAS** Hist.
ante A.D. 2
001 **Fragmenta**, FGrH #46: 1A:272.
Q: 148: Hist., Myth.

0754 **ABASCANTUS** Med.
ante A.D. 1: Lugdunensis
x01 **Fragmenta ap. Galenum.**
K13.71, 278; **14**.177.
Cf. GALENUS Med. (0057 076, 078).

ABERCIUS
A.D. 2: Hierapolitanus
Cf. EPITAPHIUM ABERCII (1353).

0115 *ABGARI EPISTULA*
A.D. 1
x01 **Fragmentum ap. Eusebium.**
HE 1.13.6–9.
Cf. EUSEBIUS Scr. Eccl. et Theol. (2018 002).

2473 **ABLABIUS** Hist.
A.D. 5/6?
001 **Testimonium**, FGrH #708: 3C:582.
NQ: 9: Test.
002 **Fragmenta**, FGrH #708: 3C:582–583.
Q: 669: Hist.

4023 **ABLABIUS** Rhet.
A.D. 5
001 **Epigramma**, AG 9.762.
Q: 26: Epigr.

0116 **ABYDENUS** Hist.
A.D. 2?
001 **Fragmenta**, FGrH #685: 3C:399–403, 405–410.
Q: 1,050: Hist.

0755 **ACACIUS** Med.
ante A.D. 1
x01 **Fragmentum ap. Galenum.**
K13.79.
Cf. GALENUS Med. (0057 076).

2064 **ACACIUS** Theol.
A.D. 4: Caesariensis
002 **Fragmenta in epistulam ad Romanos** (in catenis), ed. K. Staab, *Pauluskommentar aus der griechischen Kirche aus Katenenhandschriften gesammelt.* Münster: Aschendorff, 1933: 53–56.
Q: 1,109: Exeget., Caten.

0101 **ACERATUS** Gramm.
A.D. 1
001 **Epigramma**, AG 7.138.
Q: 23: Epigr.

1832 **ACESANDER** Hist.
4?/2 B.C.
001 **Fragmenta**, FGrH #469: 3B:423–425.
Q: 542: Hist.
002 **Fragmentum** (*P. Oxy.* 32.2637), ed. H.J. Mette, "Die 'Kleinen' griechischen Historiker heute," *Lustrum* 21 (1978) 29–30.
fr. 6 bis.
Pap: 83: Hist.

1818 **ACESTODORUS** Hist.
3 B.C.: Megalopolitanus
x01 **Fragmentum.**
FGrH #334, fr. 22.
Cf. ISTER Hist. (1450 002).

1878 **ACESTORIDES** Hist.
Incertum
001 **Testimonia**, FGrH #28: 1A:212–213.
NQ: 254: Test.

0309 **ACHAEUS** Trag.
5 B.C.: Eretriensis
001 **Fragmenta**, ed. B. Snell, *Tragicorum Graecorum fragmenta*, vol. 1. Göttingen: Vandenhoeck & Ruprecht, 1971: 115–128.
frr. 1–5, 6–16a, 17–38, 40–42, 43 (sub 24+43), 44, 47–56.
Q: 475: Trag., Satyr.

0756 **ACHILLAS** Med.
1 B.C./A.D. 1
x01 **Fragmenta ap. Galenum.**
K13.90, 834.
Cf. GALENUS Med. (0057 076, 077).

2133 **ACHILLES TATIUS** Astron.
A.D. 3: fort. Alexandrinus
001 **Isagoga excerpta**, ed. E. Maass, *Commentariorum in Aratum reliquiae.* Berlin: Weidmann, 1898 (repr. 1958): 27–75.
Cod: 12,525: Astron.
x01 **Vita Arati** (olim sub auctore Achille Tatio).
Martin, pp. 6–10.
Cf. VITAE ARATI ET VARIA DE ARATO (4161 002).
x02 Περὶ ἐξηγήσεως (olim sub auctore Achille Tatio).
Martin, pp. 32–34.
Cf. VITAE ARATI ET VARIA DE ARATO (4161 007).

0532 **ACHILLES TATIUS** Scr. Erot.
A.D. 2

001 **Leucippe et Clitophon**, ed. E. Vilborg, *Achilles Tatius. Leucippe and Clitophon.* Stockholm: Almqvist & Wiksell, 1955: 1–161.
Cod: 43,440: Narr. Fict.

0757 **ACHOLIUS** Med.
ante A.D. 6
x01 **Fragmentum ap. Aëtium** (lib. 8).
CMG, vol. 8.2, p. 506.
Cf. AËTIUS Med. (0718 008).

2545 **Gaius ACILIUS** Phil. et Hist.
2 B.C.: Romanus
001 **Testimonia**, FGrH #813: 3C:883–884.
NQ: 125: Test.
002 **Fragmenta**, FGrH #813: 3C:884–887.
Q: 1,049: Hist.

3141 **Georgius ACROPOLITES** Hist.
A.D. 13: Constantinopolitanus
002 **Annales**, ed. A. Heisenberg, *Georgii Acropolitae opera*, vol. 1. Leipzig: Teubner, 1903 (repr. Stuttgart: 1978 (1st edn. corr. P. Wirth)): 3–189.
Cod: 39,604: Hist., Chronogr.
003 **Historia in brevius redacta**, ed. Heisenberg, *op. cit.*, vol. 1, 193–274.
Cod: 16,012: Hist., Chronogr.
005 **Epitaphius in Irenam imperatricem**, ed. Heisenberg, *op. cit.*, vol. 2 (1903; repr. 1978 (1st edn. corr. P. Wirth)): 3–6.
Cod: 715: Encom., Iamb.
006 **In imaginem beatae virginis**, ed. Heisenberg, *op. cit.*, vol. 2, 6–7.
Cod: 116: Iamb.
007 **Praefatio in epistulas Theodori Lascaris**, ed. Heisenberg, *op. cit.*, vol. 2, 7–9.
Cod: 347: Iamb.
008 **Carmen in magnum sabbatum**, ed. Heisenberg, *op. cit.*, vol. 2, 9–11.
Cod: 201: Hymn.
009 **Epitaphius in Joannem Ducam**, ed. Heisenberg, *op. cit.*, vol. 2, 12–29.
Cod: 4,907: Encom.
010 **Contra Latinos**, ed. Heisenberg, *op. cit.*, vol. 2, 30–66.
Orat. 1: pp. 30–45.
Orat. 2: pp. 45–66.
Cod: 10,562: Orat.
011 **Epistula ad Joannem Tornicem**, ed. Heisenberg, *op. cit.*, vol. 2, 67–69.
Cod: 754: Epist.
012 **In Gregorii Nazianzeni sententias**, ed. Heisenberg, *op. cit.*, vol. 2, 70–80.
Cod: 3,048: Phil., Theol., Comm.
013 **Laudatio Petri et Pauli**, ed. Heisenberg, *op. cit.*, vol. 2, 81–111.
Cod: 8,621: Encom.
x01 **Theodori Scutariotae additamenta ad Georgii Acropolitae historiam.**
Heisenberg-Wirth, vol. 1, pp. 277–302.
Cf. THEODORUS Scutariota Hist. (3157 001).

0300 **ACTA ALEXANDRINORUM**
A.D. 2/3
001 **Acta Alexandrinorum**, ed. H. Musurillo, *Acta Alexandrinorum.* Leipzig: Teubner, 1961: 1–72.
De senatu Alexandrinorum (*PSI* 1160): pp. 1–2.
Congressus cum Flacco (*P. Oxy.* 8.1089): pp. 2–5.
Sine titulo (*P. bibl. univ. Giss.* 46): pp. 6–10.
Acta Isidori (recensio A) (*P. Berol.* inv. 7118): pp. 11–13.
Acta Isidori (recensio B) (*P. Lond.* inv. 2785): pp. 14–16.
Acta Isidori (recensio C) (*P. Berol.* inv. 8877): pp. 16–17.
Acta Diogenis (*P. Oxy.* 20.2264): pp. 18–20.
Ingressus triumphalis Vespasiani (*P. Fuad* 8): p. 21.
Acta Hermiae (*P. Harris*): p. 22.
Acta Maximi (*P. Oxy.* 3.471 + *P. Schubart* 42): pp. 22–31.
Acta Hermaisci (*P. Oxy.* 10.1242): pp. 32–35.
Acta Pauli et Antonini (*P. Lond.* inv. 1 + *P. Louvre* 2376bis): pp. 36–43.
Acta Pauli et Antonini (recensio B Alexandrina brevior) (*P. Oxy.* 10.1242): pp. 44–45.
Acta Pauli et Antonini (textus C) (*P. Berol.* 8111): pp. 45–46.
Acta Athenodori (*P. Oxy.* 18.2177): pp. 47–50.
Acta Appiani (*P. Yale* inv. 1536 + *P. Oxy.* 1.33): pp. 51–56.
Fragmenta dubia vel incerta: pp. 56–72.
Pap: 6,800: Acta

2949 **ACTA BARNABAE**
Incertum
001 **Acta Barnabae**, ed. M. Bonnet, *Acta apostolorum apocrypha*, vol. 2.2. Leipzig: Mendelssohn, 1903 (repr. Hildesheim: Olms, 1972): 292–302.
Cod: 2,223: Hagiogr., Acta, Apocryph.

0304 **ACTA ET MARTYRIUM APOLLONII**
A.D. 2/4
001 **Acta et martyrium Apollonii**, ed. H. Musurillo, *The acts of the Christian martyrs.* Oxford: Clarendon Press, 1972: 90–104.
Cod: 1,874: Hagiogr.

2012 **ACTA EUPLI**
post A.D. 4
001 **Acta Eupli**, ed. H. Musurillo, *The acts of the Christian martyrs.* Oxford: Clarendon Press, 1972: 310–312.
Cod: 472: Hagiogr.

0317 **ACTA JOANNIS**
A.D. 2
001 **Acta Joannis**, ed. M. Bonnet, *Acta apostolorum apocrypha*, vol. 2.1. Leipzig: Mendelssohn,

1898 (repr. Hildesheim: Olms, 1972): 151–215.
Cod: 12,788: Acta, Apocryph.

002 **Acta Joannis** (recensio), ed. Bonnet, *op. cit.*, 152–160, 169, 171–179, 203–206, 209–210.
Cod: 2,552: Acta, Apocryph.

0384 *ACTA JUSTINI ET SEPTEM SODALIUM*
A.D. 2/3

001 **Acta Justini et septem sodalium** (recensio A), ed. H. Musurillo, *The acts of the Christian martyrs.* Oxford: Clarendon Press, 1972: 42–46.
Cod: 566: Hagiogr.

002 **Acta Justini et septem sodalium** (recensio B), ed. Musurillo, *op. cit.*, 46–52.
Cod: 840: Hagiogr.

003 **Acta Justini et septem sodalium** (recensio C), ed. Musurillo, *op. cit.*, 54–60.
Cod: 976: Hagiogr.

0388 *ACTA PAULI*
A.D. 2

001 **Acta Pauli**, ed. W. Schubart and C. Schmidt, *Acta Pauli.* Glückstadt: Augustin, 1936: 22–72.
Pap: 3,428: Acta, Apocryph.

002 **Martyrium Pauli**, ed. R.A. Lipsius, *Acta apostolorum apocrypha*, vol. 1. Leipzig: Mendelssohn, 1891 (repr. Hildesheim: Olms, 1972): 104, 106, 108, 110, 112, 114–117.
Cod: 1,252: Hagiogr., Acta, Apocryph.

003 **Pauli et Corinthiorum epistulae** (*P. Bodmer* 10), ed. M. Testuz, *Papyrus Bodmer X–XII.* Geneva: Bibliotheca Bodmeriana, 1959: 30–44.
Pap: 798: Epist., Apocryph.

004 **Acta Pauli et Theclae**, ed. Lipsius, *op. cit.*, 235–271.
Cod: 3,677: Acta, Apocryph.

005 **Acta Pauli et Theclae** (partis finalis recensio e codice G), ed. Lipsius, *op. cit.*, 271–272.
Cod: 735: Acta, Apocryph.

0389 *ACTA PETRI*
A.D. 2

001 **Martyrium Petri**, ed. L. Vouaux, *Les actes de Pierre.* Paris: Letouzey & Ané, 1922: 398–466.
Cod: 2,548: Hagiogr., Acta, Apocryph.

002 **Fragmentum** (*P. Oxy.* 6.849), ed. B.P. Grenfell and A.S. Hunt, *The Oxyrhynchus papyri*, pt. 6. London: Egypt Exploration Fund, 1908: 10.
Pap

2014 *ACTA PHILEAE*
post A.D. 4

001 **Acta Phileae** (*P. Bodmer* 20), ed. H. Musurillo, *The acts of the Christian martyrs.* Oxford: Clarendon Press, 1972: 328–344.
Pap: 1,043: Hagiogr.

2948 *ACTA PHILIPPI*
Incertum

001 **Acta Philippi**, ed. M. Bonnet, *Acta apostolorum apocrypha*, vol. 2.2. Leipzig: Mendelssohn, 1903 (repr. Hildesheim: Olms, 1972): 1–90.
Cod: 16,537: Hagiogr., Acta, Apocryph.

002 **Acta Philippi** (recensio), ed. Bonnet, *op. cit.*, 41–90.
Cod: 3,857: Hagiogr., Acta, Apocryph.

003 **Acta Philippi** (recensio), ed. Bonnet, *op. cit.*, 51–90.
Cod: 3,142: Hagiogr., Acta, Apocryph.

004 **Acta Philippi** (epitome), ed. Bonnet, *op. cit.*, 91–98.
Cod: 2,870: Hagiogr., Acta, Apocryph.

0391 *ACTA SCILLITANORUM MARTYRUM*
A.D. 2–3

001 **Acta Scillitanorum martyrum** *sive* **Passio Sperati et sociorum**, ed. J.A. Robinson, *The passion of S. Perpetua* [*Texts and Studies* 1.2, appendix. Cambridge: Cambridge University Press, 1891 (repr. Nendeln, Liechtenstein: Kraus, 1967)]: 113–117.
Cod: 677: Hagiogr.

2038 *ACTA THOMAE*
A.D. 3

001 **Acta Thomae**, ed. M. Bonnet, *Acta apostolorum apocrypha*, vol. 2.2. Leipzig: Mendelssohn, 1903 (repr. Hildesheim: Olms, 1972): 99–288.
Cod: 29,803: Hagiogr., Acta, Apocryph.

004 **Acta Thomae** (recensio), ed. Bonnet, *op. cit.*, 108–109, 111–145, 251–258, 269–288.
Cod: 4,717: Hagiogr., Acta, Apocryph.

005 **Actorum Thomae consummatio**, ed. Bonnet, *op. cit.*, 289–291.
Cod: 550: Hagiogr., Acta, Apocryph.

006 **Acta Thomae** (e cod. Brit. Mus. add. 10,073), ed. M.R. James, *Apocrypha anecdota II* [*Texts and Studies* 5.1. Cambridge: Cambridge University Press, 1897 (repr. Nendeln, Liechtenstein: Kraus, 1967)]: 28–45.
Cod: Hagiogr., Acta, Apocryph.

002 **Carmen animae** (**De margarita**) (cod. Rom. vallicellanus B 35), ed. P.-H. Poirier, *L'hymne de la perle des actes de Thomas* [*Homo religiosus* 8. Louvain-La-Neuve: Université Catholique de Louvain, 1981]: 352–356.
Dup. partim 2038 001.
Cod: 981: Hymn., Acta, Apocryph.

003 **Carmen animae** (**De margarita**) (paraphrasis Nicetae), ed. Poirier, *op. cit.*, 366–369.
Dup. partim 2038 001.
Cod: 782: Hymn., Acta, Exeget.

2248 *ACTA XANTHIPPAE ET POLYXENAE*
A.D. 3

001 **Acta Xanthippae et Polyxenae** (sub auctore Onesimo), ed. M.R. James, *Apocrypha anecdota* [*Texts and Studies* 2.3. Cambridge: Cambridge

University Press, 1893 (repr. Nendeln, Liechtenstein: Kraus, 1967)]: 58–85.
Cod: Acta, Hagiogr.

0392 **ACUSILAUS** Hist.
5 B.C.: Argivus
001 **Testimonia**, FGrH #2: 1A:47–48.
NQ: 429: Test.
002 **Fragmenta**, FGrH #2: 1A:49–58.
fr. 22: *P. Oxy.* 13.1611.
fr. 45 bis: *P. Giessen* 307.
Q, Pap: 3,012: Hist., Myth.
003 **Testimonia**, ed. H. Diels and W. Kranz, *Die
Fragmente der Vorsokratiker*, vol. 1, 6th edn.
Berlin: Weidmann, 1951 (repr. Dublin: 1966):
52–53.
test. 1–5.
NQ: 148: Test.
004 **Fragmenta**, ed. Diels and Kranz, *op. cit.*, 53–
60.
frr. 1–41.
Q: 1,901: Phil., Theol.

0102 **ADAEUS** Epigr.
fiq Adaeus Rhet.
A.D. 1: Macedo vel Mytilenensis
001 **Epigrammata**, AG **6**.228, 258; **7**.51, 238, 240,
305, 694; **9**.300, 303, 544; **10**.20.
Q: 344: Epigr.

2950 **ADAMANTIUS** Scr. Eccl.
A.D. 4
001 **De recta in deum fide**, ed. W.H. van de Sande
Bakhuyzen, *Der Dialog des Adamantius περὶ
τῆς εἰς θεὸν ὀρθῆς πίστεως* [*Die griechischen
christlichen Schriftsteller* 4. Leipzig: Hinrichs,
1901]: 2–242.
Cod: Dialog.

0731 **ADAMANTIUS Judaeus** Med.
A.D. 4–5: Alexandrinus
001 **Physiognomonica**, ed. R. Foerster, *Scriptores
physiognomonici Graeci et Latini*, vol. 1. Leip-
zig: Teubner, 1893: 297–426.
Cod: 8,233: Med., Physiognom.
002 **De ventis**, ed. V. Rose, *Anecdota Graeca et
Graecolatina*, vol. 1. Berlin: Duemmler, 1864
(repr. Amsterdam: Hakkert, 1963): 29–48.
Cod: 5,757: Nat. Hist.
003 **Physiognomonica** (epitome Matritensis), ed.
Foerster, *op. cit.*, 320–347, 351–359, 386–424.
Cod: Physiognom.
x01 **Fragmenta ap. Oribasium**.
CMG, vol. 6.3, pp. 50, 73, 74, 75, 76, 77.
Cf. ORIBASIUS Med. (0722 004).
x02 **Fragmenta ap. Aëtium** (lib. 15).
Zervos, *Athena* 21, p. 23.
Cf. AËTIUS Med. (0718 015).

2433 ***ADDITAMENTA*** (FGrH)
Varia

001 Οἱ συντεταχότες τὰ Τρωικά, FGrH #48 bis:
1A:*19–*20 addenda.
fr. 1.
Q: 158: Hist., Myth.
002 **De Aeolia**, FGrH #301: 3B:4.
fr. 1.
Q: 58: Hist.
003 **De Argo**, FGrH #311: 3B:20–21.
test. 1–2, frr. 1–2.
Q: 317: Hist.
004 **Anonymi apud Pausaniam de Argo**, FGrH
#314: 3B:22–25.
frr. 1–12.
Q: 1,298: Hist.
005 **De Arcadia**, FGrH #321: 3B:33–34.
frr. 1–3.
fr. 2: Dup. partim AGATHYLLUS Eleg. (2606
001).
Q: 180: Hist., Eleg.
006 **Anonymi apud Pausaniam de Arcadia**, FGrH
#322: 3B:34–40.
frr. 1–37.
Q: 2,932: Hist.
007 **Testimonium de Arcadia** (ap. Plinium, *NH*
8.81), FGrH #320: 3B:33.
NQ: 78: Test.
008 **De Chio**, FGrH #395: 3B:284, 757–758 addenda.
frr. 1–2, 3.
Q: 251: Hist.
010 **De Delo** (excerpta ex oratoribus Atticis) (testimonia et fragmenta), FGrH #401: 3B:293–297.
fr. c10 (Lycurgus): *P. Berol.*
Q, Pap: 1,362: Hist.
011 **De tabulis victorum Olympicorum** (testimonia
et fragmenta), FGrH #416: 3B:309–314.
frr. 1–6.
fr. 6: *IG* 2².2326.
Q, Epigr: 1,595: Hist.
012 **De Euboea**, FGrH #427: 3B:323.
frr. 1–5.
Q: 314: Hist.
013 **De Ithaca**, FGrH #441: 3B:372.
fr. 1.
Q: 52: Hist.
014 **De Creta**, FGrH #468: 3B:404–423.
frr. 1–15.
fr. 15: *Inscr. Cret.* 3.
Q, Epigr: 8,080: Hist.
016 **De Magnesia**, FGrH #482: 3B:445–448.
frr. 1–5.
fr. 1: *Inscr. Magnesia* 46.
fr. 2: *Inscr. Magnesia* 16.
fr. 3: *Inscr. Magnesia* 17.
fr. 4: *Inscr. Magnesia* 20.
fr. 5: *Inscr. Magnesia* 215.
Epigr: 1,126: Hist.
017 **De Malide (Thessaliae)**, FGrH #483: 3B:448.
frr. 1–2.
fr. 1 (inscriptio ex Lamia): *IG* 9.2.62.
fr. 2 (inscriptio ex Lamia): *IG* 9.2.63.
Epigr: 111: Hist.

018 **De Megara**, FGrH #487: 3B:453–455.
frr. 1–13.
Q: 1,233: Hist.

019 **De Mileto**, FGrH #496: 3B:467–469.
frr. 1–9.
Q: 907: Hist.

020 **De Naxo**, FGrH #501: 3B:475–478.
frr. 1–5.
Q: 1,403: Hist.

021 **De Rhodo**, FGrH #533: 3B:514–519.
frr. 1–11.
fr. 2 (auctore Demetrio Poliorcete): *P. Berol.*
inv. 11632.
Q, Pap: 2,519: Hist.

022 **De Samo**, FGrH #545: 3B:527–530.
frr. 1–10.
Q: 1,252: Hist.

023 **De Samothrace**, FGrH #548: 3B:532–535.
frr. 1–6.
fr. 6: *Inscr. Priene* 69.
Q, Epigr: 1,418: Hist.

024 **De Sicyone**, FGrH #551: 3B:536–539.
frr. 1–3.
fr. 1b (= FGrH #105, fr. 2) (fort. auctore Aristotele vel Ephoro vel Menaechmo): *P. Oxy.*
11.1365.
Q, Pap: 1,143: Hist.

025 **De Siphno**, FGrH #553: 3B:539–540.
frr. 1–3.
Q: 347: Hist.

026 **De Sicilia et Magna Graecia**, FGrH #577:
3B:679–688.
frr. 1–17.
fr. 1, Siciliae historia (fort. epitome historiae
Timaei vel argumentum Philisti): *P. Oxy.*
4.665.
fr. 2: *P. Oxy.* saeculi secundi.
Q, Cod, Pap: 3,930: Hist.

027 **De Sparta**, FGrH #596: 3B:719–729.
frr. 1–46.
Q: 4,583: Hist.

028 **De Troezene**, FGrH #607: 3B:739–740.
frr. 1–7.
Q: 508: Hist.

029 **De Aegypto**, FGrH #665: 3C:214–277.
frr. 1–208.
fr. 180 (Calendarium): *P. Hibeh* 1.27.
fr. 194d: *P. Oxy.* 15.1826.
fr. 194d: Dup. partim EROTICA ADESPOTA
(5003 001).
Cf. et 2433 051.
Q, Pap: 21,628: Hist., Narr. Fict.

030 **De Aethiopia**, FGrH #673: 3C:284–337.
frr. 1–166.
Q: 17,922: Hist.

031 **De Arabia**, FGrH #677: 3C:345–350.
frr. 1–8.
Cf. et 2433 052.
Q: 1,651: Hist.

032 **De Armenia**, FGrH #679: 3C:351–356.
frr. 1–4.
Q: 2,308: Hist.

033 **De Persia**, FGrH #696: 3C:534–547.
frr. 1–18, 20–35.
fr. 28: *P. Florent.* (= *PSI* 151).
fr. 28: Dup. EROTICA ADESPOTA (5003 004).
Cf. et 2433 053.
Q, Pap: 4,981: Hist., Narr. Fict.

034 **De Epiro**, FGrH #704: 3C:561–565.
frr. 1–4, 6.
Q: 1,774: Hist.

035 **De Etruria**, FGrH #706: 3C:565–577.
frr. 1–38.
Q: 5,031: Hist.

036 **De India**, FGrH #721: 3C:657–666.
frr. 1–4a, 5a–21.
Q: 3,254: Hist.

037 **De Judaeis**, FGrH #737: 3C:701–713.
frr. 1–15, 17, 19–23.
Q: 5,305: Hist.

038 **De Caria**, FGrH #742: 3C:719–721.
frr. 1–9.
Q: 889: Hist.

039 **De Carthagine**, FGrH #744: 3C:722–727.
frr. 1–12.
Q: 2,544: Hist.

040 **De Cypro**, FGrH #758: 3C:737–741.
frr. 1–13.
fr. 11a: *PSI* 1221.
Q, Pap: 1,437: Hist.

041 **De Libya**, FGrH #764: 3C:745–750.
frr. 1–19.
Q: 1,905: Hist.

042 **De Lydia**, FGrH #768: 3C:759–760.
frr. 1–10.
fr. 3: *P. Oxy.* 15.1802.
Q: 667: Hist.

043 **De Macedonia**, FGrH #776: 3C:771.
frr. 1–2.
fr. 1: *P. Oxy.* 9.1176.
Q, Pap: 233: Hist.

044 **De Parthia**, FGrH #782: 3C:785–788.
frr. 2–6.
Q: 1,102: Hist.

045 **De Phoenicia**, FGrH #794: 3C:825–833.
frr. 1–19.
Q: 2,397: Hist.

046 **De Phrygia**, FGrH #800: 3C:836–839.
frr. 1–6a, 7–13.
Q: 1,006: Hist.

047 **De Roma et de Italia**, FGrH #840: 3C:908–
927.
frr. 1–34, 36–42.
Q: 6,565: Hist.

048 **De Scythia**, FGrH #845: 3C:930–931.
frr. 1–5.
fr. 5: *P. Oxy.* 15.1802.
Q, Pap: 435: Hist.

049 **De Hispania**, FGrH #847: 3C:932–934.
frr. 1–3.
Q: 959: Hist.

050 **De Syria**, FGrH #855: 3C:942.
fr. 1.
Q: 19: Hist.

051 **De Aegypto** (*P. Oxy.* 37.2820), ed. H.J. Mette,
"Die 'Kleinen' griechischen Historiker heute,"
Lustrum 21 (1978) 35–36.
fr. 209.
Cf. et 2433 029.
Pap: 135: Hist.

052 **De Arabia** (*P. Oxy.* 27.2466), ed. Mette, *op.
cit.*, 36.
fr. 9.
Cf. et 2433 031.
Pap: 147: Hist.

053 **De Persia** (fort. auctore Choerilo Samio) (*P.
Oxy.* 37.2814), ed. Mette, *op. cit.*, 37.
fr. 33/34 bis.
Cf. et 2433 033.
Pap: 182: Hist.

2648 *ADESPOTA PAPYRACEA* (SH)
Varia

001 **Hexametri**, ed. H. Lloyd-Jones and P. Parsons,
Supplementum Hellenisticum. Berlin: De Gruyter, 1983: 399–406, 409, 411–417, 419–421,
424–432, 434–437, 439, 441–445, 447–450,
452–457.
frr. 900–935, 937–956.
Pap: 3,537: Hexametr.

002 **Elegiae**, ed. Lloyd-Jones and Parsons, *op. cit.*,
458–459, 461–464, 466–471, 475–479.
frr. 957–970.
Pap: 1,021: Eleg.

003 **Epigrammata**, ed. Lloyd-Jones and Parsons, *op.
cit.*, 482–489, 491, 493–499, 501, 503–505.
frr. 971–988.
Pap: 1,337: Epigr.

004 **Miscellanea**, ed. Lloyd-Jones and Parsons, *op.
cit.*, 506–507, 509–516.
frr. 989–997.
fr. 992: fort. auctore Callimacho.
Pap: 542: Iamb., Hymn., Poem.

0665 **ADRIANUS** Hist.
post 4 B.C.

x01 **De historia Alexandri**.
FGrH #153, fr. 15.
Cf. ANONYMI HISTORICI (FGrH) (1139 007).

0666 **ADRIANUS** Rhet. et Soph.
A.D. 2: Tyrius

001 **Declamatio**, ed. H. Hinck, *Polemonis declamationes quae exstant duae*. Leipzig: Teubner,
1873: 44–45.
Cod: 294: Rhet.

x01 **Declamatio alia**.
Habrich, p. 73, fr. 101.
Cf. IAMBLICHUS Scr. Erot. (1441 001).

x02 **Epigramma dedicatorium**.
App. Anth. 1.241: Cf. ANTHOLOGIAE GRAE-
CAE APPENDIX (7052 001).

0668 *AEGIMIUS*
fort. auctore Cercope vel Hesiodo
6 B.C.?

001 **Aegimius** (fragmenta), ed. G. Kinkel, *Epicorum
Graecorum fragmenta*. Leipzig: Teubner, 1877:
83–85.
frr. 3–5, 7–8.
Q: 81: Epic.

2700 **AELIANUS** Epigr.
post A.D. 2

x01 **Epigrammata demonstrativa**.
App. Anth. 3.111–113: Cf. ANTHOLOGIAE
GRAECAE APPENDIX (7052 003).

0545 **Claudius AELIANUS** Soph.
A.D. 2–3

001 **De natura animalium**, ed. R. Hercher, *Claudii
Aeliani de natura animalium libri xvii, varia
historia, epistolae, fragmenta*, vol. 1. Leipzig:
Teubner, 1864 (repr. Graz: Akademische
Druck- und Verlagsanstalt, 1971): 3–436.
Cod: 107,271: Nat. Hist., Paradox.

002 **Varia historia**, ed. Hercher, *op. cit.*, vol. 2
(1866; repr. 1971): 3–172.
Cod: 39,966: Nat. Hist., Paradox.

003 **Epistulae rusticae**, ed. Hercher, *op. cit.*, vol. 2,
175–185.
Cod: 2,244: Epist.

004 **Fragmenta**, ed. Hercher, *op. cit.*, vol. 2, 189–
283.
Q: 14,065: Nat. Hist., Paradox., Phil.

005 **Titulus**, ed. A. Giannini, *Paradoxographorum
Graecorum reliquiae*. Milan: Istituto Editoriale
Italiano, 1965: 396.
NQ: 4: Paradox.

0546 **AELIANUS** Tact.
A.D. 1–2

001 **Tactica**, ed. H. Köchly and W. Rüstow, *Ascle-
piodotos' Taktik. Aelianos' Theorie der Taktik
[Griechische Kriegsschriftsteller*, vol. 2.1. Leip-
zig: Engelmann, 1855 (repr. Osnabrück: Biblio
Verlag, 1969)]: 218–470.
Cod: 10,913: Tact.

2434 **AELIUS DIUS** Hist.
A.D. 2?

001 **Testimonia**, FGrH #629: 3C:179.
NQ: 78: Test.

002 **Fragmentum**, FGrH #629: 3C:179.
Q: 32: Hist.

0674 **AELIUS PROMOTUS** Med.
A.D. 2: Alexandrinus

x01 **Fragmentum ap. Paulum**.
CMG, vol. 9.1, p. 314.
Cf. PAULUS Med. (0715 001).

0670 **AELIUS PUBLIUS JULIUS** Scr. Eccl.
A.D. 2

x01 **Fragmentum ap. Eusebium.**
HE 5.19.3.
Cf. EUSEBIUS Scr. Eccl. et Theol. (2018 002).

2368 **AELURUS** Hist.
Incertum
001 **Titulus**, FGrH #528: 3B:505.
NQ: Hist.

0103 **AEMILIANUS** Rhet.
A.D. 1: Nicaeanus
001 **Epigrammata**, AG 7.623; 9.218, 756.
Q: 92: Epigr.

2378 **AENEAS** Hist.
Incertum
001 **Fragmentum**, FGrH #543: 3B:527.
Q: 77: Hist.

0753 **AENEAS** Med.
A.D. 1?
x01 **Fragmentum ap. Galenum.**
K12.589.
Cf. GALENUS Med. (0057 076).

4001 **AENEAS** Rhet. et Phil.
A.D. 6: Gazaeus
001 **Theophrastus sive de animarum immortalitate et corporum resurrectione dialogus**, ed. M.E. Colonna, *Enea di Gaza. Teofrasto*. Naples: Iodice, 1958: 1–68.
Cod: Phil., Dialog.
002 **Epistulae**, ed. L. Massa Positano, *Enea di Gaza. Epistole*, 2nd edn. [*Collana di studi greci* 19. Naples: Libreria Scientifica Editrice, 1962]: 39–53.
Cod: Epist.

0058 **AENEAS** Tact.
4 B.C.: Stymphalicus
001 **Poliorcetica**, ed. A. Dain and A.-M. Bon, *Énée le tacticien. Poliorcétique*. Paris: Les Belles Lettres, 1967: 1–91.
Cod: 14,558: Tact.

2413 **AENESIDEMUS** Hist.
Incertum
001 **Fragmenta**, FGrH #600: 3B:731–732.
Q: 159: Hist.

0026 **AESCHINES** Orat.
4 B.C.: Atheniensis
Scholia: Cf. SCHOLIA IN AESCHINEM (5009).
Vitae: Cf. VITAE AESCHINIS (4166).
001 **In Timarchum**, ed. V. Martin and G. de Budé, *Eschine. Discours*, vol. 1. Paris: Les Belles Lettres, 1927 (repr. 1962): 20–86.
Cod: 13,961: Orat.
002 **De falsa legatione**, ed. Martin and de Budé, *op. cit.*, vol. 1, 110–169.
Cod: 12,758: Orat.

003 **In Ctesiphontem**, ed. Martin and de Budé, *op. cit.*, vol. 2 (1928; repr. 1962): 25–117.
Cod: 19,171: Orat.
004 **Epistulae** [Sp.], ed. Martin and de Budé, *op. cit.*, vol. 2, 123–143.
Cod: 4,392: Epist.

0104 **AESCHINES** Rhet.
1 B.C.: Milesius
001 **Epigramma**, AG 6.330.
Q: 30: Epigr.

0673 **AESCHINES SOCRATICUS** Phil.
4 B.C.: Sphettius
001 **Fragmenta**, ed. H. Dittmar, *Aischines von Sphettos. Studien zur Literaturgeschichte der Sokratiker* [*Philologische Untersuchungen*, vol. 21. Berlin: Weidmann, 1912]: 266–281, 283–296.
Alcibiades (frr. 1–5, 7–9, 11).
Axiochus (frr. 12–14).
Aspasia (frr. 15–30, 32–33).
Callias (frr. 34–36).
Miltiades (frr. 37–38).
Rhinon (fr. 39).
Telauges (frr. 40–48).
Fragmenta sedis incertae (frr. 49–58).
Fragmentum dubium (fr. 59).
Q, Cod: 3,836: Phil., Dialog.
002 **Alcibiades** (fragmenta) (*P. Oxy.* 13.1608), ed. B.P. Grenfell and A.S. Hunt, *The Oxyrhynchus papyri*, pt. 13. London: Egypt Exploration Fund, 1919: 91–93.
Pap: Phil., Dialog.
003 **Alcibiades** (fragmentum), *P. Lit. Lond.* 148.
Pap: Phil., Dialog.
x01 **Epistulae.**
Epist. Graec., pp. 618, 619–621, 625–626.
Cf. SOCRATICORUM EPISTULAE (0637 001).

2377 **AESCHRION** Epic.
4 B.C.: Mytilenensis
001 **Testimonium**, FGrH #118 bis: 3B:742 addenda.
NQ: 27: Test.
002 **Fragmenta**, FGrH #118 bis: 3B:742 addenda.
Q: 138: Hist., Poem.

0679 **AESCHRION** Lyr.
fiq Aeschrion Mytilenensis
4 B.C.: Samius
001 **Epigramma**, AG 7.345.
Dup. partim 0679 002 (fr. 4).
Q: 62: Epigr.
002 **Fragmenta et tituli**, ed. H. Lloyd-Jones and P. Parsons, *Supplementum Hellenisticum*. Berlin: De Gruyter, 1983: 1–3.
frr. 1–10.
fr. 4: Dup. 0679 001.
Q: 126: Epigr., Iamb.

0085 AESCHYLUS Trag.
6–5 B.C.: Atheniensis
Scholia et vitae: Cf. SCHOLIA IN AESCHY-
LUM (5010).

001 **Supplices**, ed. G. Murray, *Aeschyli tragoediae*,
2nd edn. Oxford: Clarendon Press, 1955 (repr.
1960): 3–48.
Cod: 5,532: Trag.

002 **Persae**, ed. Murray, *op. cit.*, 53–95.
Cod: 5,647: Trag.

003 **Prometheus vinctus**, ed. Murray, *op. cit.*, 103–
145.
Cod: 6,271: Trag.

004 **Septem contra Thebas**, ed. Murray, *op. cit.*,
155–200.
Cod: 5,631: Trag.

005 **Agamemnon**, ed. Murray, *op. cit.*, 207–274.
Cod: 8,754: Trag.

006 **Choephoroe**, ed. Murray, *op. cit.*, 277–322.
Cod: 5,959: Trag.

007 **Eumenides**, ed. Murray, *op. cit.*, 325–367.
Cod: 5,733: Trag.

008 **Fragmenta**, ed. H.J. Mette, *Die Fragmente der
Tragödien des Aischylos*. Berlin: Akademie-
Verlag, 1959: 1–255.
frr. 1–86, 88–106, 108–127, 128 (= 122), 129–
134, 135 (= 116), 136 (= 408), 137–175, 176
(= 169), 177, 178 (= 116), 179 (= 169), 180–
209, 210 (= 194–195), 211–271a, 273–323a,
325–380, 381 (= 150a–150f), 382–383, 384 (=
116), 385–436, 437 (= 430), 438, 440–458,
459a, 459d, 460–653, 653a (= 78), 654–655,
656 (= 647A/B), 657 (= 207), 658–689, 692–
769.
Q, Pap: 41,448: Trag., Satyr.

009 **Fragmentum**, ed. M.L. West, *Iambi et elegi
Graeci*, vol. 2. Oxford: Clarendon Press, 1972:
29.
fr. 2.
Q: 5: Eleg.

010 **Epigrammata**, AG 7.255; **10**.110.
Q: 44: Epigr.

011 **Fragmenta**, ed. S. Radt, *Tragicorum Graecorum fragmenta*, vol. 3. Göttingen: Vandenhoeck & Ruprecht, 1985: 123–511.
frr. 1–6, 8–10, 12–18, 20–29, 31, 34, 36–45,
46a–c, 47, 47a–c, 53a, 54–72, 73b, 74–75, 75a,
77–88, 90–91, 92a, 93–97, 98–122, 123–134,
135–149, 150–155, 157a, 158–167, 167a, 168–
172, 172a, 174–177, 177a, 179–186, 187–192,
195–196, 198–201, 203–205, 207, 208, 209–
246, 246b–d, 247–259, 259a, 261, 263–293,
295–303, 305–325, 327–332, 332a, 334–339,
339a, 341–342, 346–367, 369–375, 378–379,
381–400, 402–402a, 404, 406, 407a, 408–412,
414–451, 451b–x, 452–454, 456, 458, 460–
462, 465–489 + tituli.
Q, Pap: 8,832: Trag., Satyr.

x01 **Epigramma sepulcrale**.
App. Anth. 2.17: Cf. ANTHOLOGIAE GRAE-
CAE APPENDIX (7052 002).

0321 AESCHYLUS Trag.
3 B.C.?: Alexandrinus

001 **Fragmentum**, ed. B. Snell, *Tragicorum Graecorum fragmenta*, vol. 1. Göttingen: Vandenhoeck & Ruprecht, 1971: 312.
fr. 1.
Q: 15: Trag.

002 **Testimonium**, FGrH #488: 3B:456.
NQ: 28: Test.

003 **Titulus**, ed. H. Lloyd-Jones and P. Parsons,
Supplementum Hellenisticum. Berlin: De Gruyter, 1983: 4.
fr. 13.
NQ: 3: Epic.

1980 AESOPUS Hist.
1 B.C.

001 **Testimonium**, FGrH #187a: 2B:918.
NQ: 16: Test.

002 **Fragmenta**, FGrH #187a: 2B:918–919.
Q: 55: Hist.

0096 AESOPUS Scr. Fab. et *AESOPICA*
6 B.C.
Cf. et VITAE AESOPI (1765).

001 **Paroemiae**, ed. E.L. von Leutsch, *Corpus pa-
roemiographorum Graecorum*, vol. 2. Göt-
tingen: Vandenhoeck & Ruprecht, 1851 (repr.
Hildesheim: Olms, 1958): 228–230.
Dup. partim 0096 017.
Q: 109: Paroem.

002 **Fabulae**, ed. A. Hausrath and H. Hunger, *Corpus fabularum Aesopicarum*, vols. 1.1 & 1.2,
2nd edn. Leipzig: Teubner, 1.1:1970; 1.2:1959:
1.1:1–210; **1.2**:1–116.
Cod: 46,077: Fab.

003 **Fabulae tabulis ceratis Assendelftianis servatae**, ed. Hausrath and Hunger, *op. cit.*, vol. 1.2,
117–119.
Cod: 253: Fab.

004 **Fabulae Dosithei**, ed. Hausrath and Hunger,
op. cit., vol. 1.2, 120–129.
Cod: 1,202: Fab.

005 **Fabulae Libanii**, ed. Hausrath and Hunger, *op.
cit.*, vol. 1.2, 130–132.
Cod: 505: Fab.

006 **Fabulae Aphthonii rhetoris**, ed. Hausrath and
Hunger, *op. cit.*, vol. 1.2, 133–151.
Cod: 2,807: Fab.

007 **Fabulae Themistii rhetoris**, ed. Hausrath and
Hunger, *op. cit.*, vol. 1.2, 152.
Q: 119: Fab.

008 **Fabulae Theophylacti Simocattae scholastici**,
ed. Hausrath and Hunger, *op. cit.*, vol. 1.2,
153–154.
Cod: 392: Fab.

009 **Fabulae Syntipae philosophi**, ed. Hausrath and
Hunger, *op. cit.*, vol. 1.2, 155–183.
Cod: 4,839: Fab.

010 **Fabulae rhetoris anonymi Brancatiani**, ed.
Hausrath and Hunger, *op. cit.*, vol. 1.2, 184–
185.

Cod: 290: Fab.

011 **Fabula Nicephori**, ed. Hausrath and Hunger, *op. cit.*, vol. 1.2, 186.
Cod: 90: Fab.

012 **Fabulae** (*P. Ryl.* 493), ed. Hausrath and Hunger, *op. cit.*, vol. 1.2, 187–189.
Pap: 332: Fab.

013 **Fabulae ap. Dionem Chrysostomum**, ed. Hausrath and Hunger, *op. cit.*, vol. 1.2, 189–190.
Q: 331: Fab.

014 **Epigramma**, AG 10.123.
Q: 47: Epigr.

015 **Fabulae** (dodecasyllabi), ed. E. Chambry, *Aesopi fabulae*. Paris: Les Belles Lettres, 1:1925; 2:1926: 1:43, 48, 56–58, 60, 62–63, 66–67, 85–86, 104, 120–121, 129–130, 134–135, 138, 143–144, 147, 149–151, 153, 160–161, 169–170, 177–178, 192, 199–200, 214, 225, 236, 246–248, 250–252, 255; 2:263–264, 269–270, 272, 287, 289–291, 300–301, 308, 311, 315, 318–320, 323, 327, 331, 337–338, 340, 346, 349–350, 352–353, 357, 359, 361–362, 365–368, 370–371, 375, 379–381, 385, 387–388, 390, 397–400, 402, 406–407, 409–410, 412–413, 419–420, 430, 432, 436, 439–440, 448, 450–451, 455–457, 461–464, 467–468, 475, 478–479, 482–483, 488–489, 501, 510–513, 516, 519–522, 530, 532–533, 536–538, 545–546, 556–557, 561, 564–565.
Fabulae 6, 59, 61, 63, 72, 220, 229, 238, 245, 246, 269, 288, 301, 318, 326, 336, 346, 358, 359.
Fabulae aliter 9, 14, 15, 16, 17, 20, 32, 32 bis, 40, 52, 52 bis, 59, 66, 69, 70, 71, 73, 76, 81, 85, 92, 100, 107, 116, 128, 135, 136, 137, 138, 139, 142, 147, 148, 153, 154, 166, 169, 170, 179, 184, 185, 188, 192, 192 bis, 195, 195 bis, 197, 199, 201, 202, 208, 210, 212, 213, 217, 222, 224, 225, 225 bis, 228, 231, 234, 235, 239, 240, 247, 249, 249 bis, 250, 251, 254, 261, 262, 266, 274, 276, 281, 282, 284, 285, 288, 294, 296, 297, 310, 318, 319, 322, 327, 333, 336, 338, 339, 340, 353, 356.
Cod: 9,602: Fab., Poem.

016 **Sententiae**, ed. B.E. Perry, *Aesopica*, vol. 1. Urbana: University of Illinois Press, 1952: 248–258.
Sententiae 1–5 (e vita): pp. 248–249.
Sententiae 6–22a (dicta e fontibus orta ignotis): pp. 249–253.
Sententiae 23–27 (e fabulis): pp. 253–254.
Sententiae 28–52 (e Joanne Georgide): pp. 254–258.
Q, Cod: 944: Gnom.

017 **Proverbia**, ed. Perry, *op. cit.*, 265–291.
Proverbia 1–143 (proverbiorum sylloge quae inscribitur Αἰσώπου λόγοι): pp. 265–286.
Proverbia 144–179 (proverbiorum sylloge quae inscribitur Αἰσώπου κοσμικαὶ κωμῳδίαι): pp. 287–289.

Proverbia 180–191 (proverbiorum sylloge quae inscribitur παροιμίαι Αἰσώπου): p. 290.
Proverbia 192–200 (e Joanne Georgide): p. 291.
Proverbia 180–191: Dup. partim 0096 001.
Cod: 3,049: Gnom.

0683 ***AETHIOPIS***
fort. auctore Arctino Milesio
7–6 B.C.

001 **Fragmenta**, ed. G. Kinkel, *Epicorum Graecorum fragmenta*, vol. 1. Leipzig: Teubner, 1877: 34–35.
frr. 1, 3.
Q: 71: Epic.

0686 **AETHLIUS** Hist.
5–4 B.C.?: Samius
Cf. et SAMIORUM ANNALES (1657).

001 **Testimonium**, FGrH #536: 3B:521.
NQ: 19: Test.

002 **Fragmenta**, FGrH #536: 3B:521–522.
Q: 267: Hist., Geogr.

0528 **AËTIUS** Doxogr.
A.D. 1/2

001 **De placitis reliquiae** (Stobaei excerpta), ed. H. Diels, *Doxographi Graeci*. Berlin: Reimer, 1879 (repr. De Gruyter, 1965): 275–289, 291–292, 297, 301–383, 386–389, 392–399, 401, 403–411, 414–415, 417–430, 432–435, 438, 440, 442–443.
Q: 12,186: Doxogr.

002 **De placitis reliquiae** (Theodoreti et Nemesii excerpta), ed. Diels, *op. cit.*, 284–289, 292, 307–308, 316, 321–327, 329–331, 341–344, 348–352, 355–357, 362, 386–394, 401–402, 404.
Q: 2,863: Doxogr.

x01 **De placitis reliquiae** (Pseudo-Plutarchi epitome).
Mau, pp. 50–153.
Cf. Pseudo-PLUTARCHUS (0094 003).

0718 **AËTIUS** Med.
A.D. 6: Amidenus

001 **Iatricorum liber i**, ed. A. Olivieri, *Aëtii Amideni libri medicinales i–iv* [*Corpus medicorum Graecorum*, vol. 8.1. Leipzig: Teubner, 1935]: 17–146.
Cod: 34,188: Med.

002 **Iatricorum liber ii**, ed. Olivieri, *CMG* 8.1, 152–255.
Cod: 29,821: Med.

003 **Iatricorum liber iii**, ed. Olivieri, *CMG* 8.1, 260–355.
Cod: 27,696: Med.

004 **Iatricorum liber iv**, ed. Olivieri, *CMG* 8.1, 358–408.
Cod: 14,928: Med.

005 **Iatricorum liber v**, ed. A. Olivieri, *Aëtii Amideni libri medicinales v–viii* [*Corpus medicorum*

Graecorum, vol. 8.2. Berlin: Akademie-Verlag, 1950]: 6–119.
Cod: 33,099: Med.

006 **Iatricorum liber vi**, ed. Olivieri, *CMG* 8.2, 123–249.
Cod: 35,199: Med.

007 **Iatricorum liber vii**, ed. Olivieri, *CMG* 8.2, 253–399.
Cod: 38,757: Med.

008 **Iatricorum liber viii**, ed. Olivieri, *CMG* 8.2, 403–554.
Cod: 41,480: Med.

009 **Iatricorum liber ix**, ed. S. Zervos, "'Αετίου 'Αμιδηνοῦ λόγος ἔνατος," *Athena* 23 (1911) 273–390.
Cod: 35,935: Med.

011 **Iatricorum liber xi**, ed. C. Daremberg and C.É. Ruelle, *Oeuvres de Rufus d'Éphèse*. Paris: Imprimerie Nationale, 1879 (repr. Amsterdam: Hakkert, 1963): 85–126, 568–581.
Cod: 19,197: Med.

012 **Iatricorum liber xii**, ed. G.A. Kostomiris, 'Αετίου λόγος δωδέκατος. Paris: Klincksieck, 1892: 7–131.
Cod: 26,067: Med.

013 **Iatricorum liber xiii**, ed. S. Zervos, "'Αετίου 'Αμιδηνοῦ περὶ δακνόντων ζώων καὶ ἰοβόλων," *Athena* 18 (1906) 264–292.
capita 1–4, 6, 11–13, 15–24, 32, 34–37, 53–56, 58–59 solum.
Cod: 5,072: Med.

015 **Iatricorum liber xv**, ed. S. Zervos, "'Αετίου 'Αμιδηνοῦ λόγος δέκατος πέμπτος," *Athena* 21 (1909) 7–138.
Cod: 26,668: Med.

016 **Iatricorum liber xvi**, ed. S. Zervos, *Gynaekologie des Aëtios*. Leipzig: Fock, 1901: 1–172.
Cod: 40,406: Med.

Sextus Julius AFRICANUS Hist.
Cf. Sextus JULIUS AFRICANUS Hist. (2956).

0687 **AGACLYTUS** Hist.
ante 1 B.C.

001 **Fragmentum**, FGrH #411: 3B:303–304.
Q: 222: Hist.

2605 **AGAMESTOR** Eleg.
ante A.D. 1?: Pharsalius

001 **Fragmentum**, ed. H. Lloyd-Jones and P. Parsons, *Supplementum Hellenisticum*. Berlin: De Gruyter, 1983: 4.
fr. 14.
Q: 27: Eleg.

0761 **AGAPETUS** Med.
ante A.D. 6

x01 **Fragmentum ap. Paulum**.
CMG, vol. 9.1, p. 312.
Cf. PAULUS Med. (0715 001).

x02 **Fragmentum ap. Alexandrum Trallianum**.
Puschmann, vol. 2, p. 529.
Cf. ALEXANDER Med. (0744 003).

0067 **AGATHARCHIDES** Geogr.
2 B.C.: Cnidius

001 **De mari Erythraeo** (excerpta), ed. K. Müller, *Geographi Graeci minores*, vol. 1. Paris: Didot, 1855 (repr. Hildesheim: Olms, 1965): 111–194.
Q: 12,393: Geogr.

002 **Fragmenta**, ed. A. Giannini, *Paradoxographorum Graecorum reliquiae*. Milan: Istituto Editoriale Italiano, 1965: 144–145.
Q: Paradox.

003 **Testimonia**, FGrH #86: 2A:205–206.
NQ: 607: Test.

004 **Fragmenta**, FGrH #86: **2A**:206–222; **3B**:741 addenda.
Q: 6,411: Hist., Geogr.

005 **Fragmenta sedis incertae**, ed. K. Müller, *op. cit.*, vol. 1, 194–195.
Dup. partim 0067 004.
Q: 507: Geogr.

2192 **[AGATHARCHIDES]** Hist.
Incertum: Samius

001 **Fragmenta**, FGrH #284: 3A:162.
Q: 173: Hist.

0090 **AGATHEMERUS** Geogr.
post 1 B.C.

001 **Geographiae informatio**, ed. K. Müller, *Geographi Graeci minores*, vol. 2. Paris: Didot, 1861 (repr. Hildesheim: Olms, 1965): 471–487.
Cod: 2,075: Geogr.

4024 **AGATHIAS Scholasticus** Hist. et Epigr.
A.D. 6: Myrinaeus, Constantinopolitanus

001 **Historiae**, ed. R. Keydell, *Agathiae Myrinaei historiarum libri quinque* [*Corpus fontium historiae Byzantinae* 2. Series Berolinensis. Berlin: De Gruyter, 1967]: 3–197.
Cod: 61,907: Hist.

002 **Epigrammata**, AG 1.34–36; **4**.3; **5**.216, 218, 220, 222, 237, 261, 263, 267, 269, 273, 276, 278, 280, 282, 285, 287, 289, 292, 294, 296–297, 299, 302; **6**.32, 41, 59, 72, 74, 76, 79–80, 167; **7**.204–205, 220, 551–552, 567–569, 572, 574, 578, 583, 589, 593, 596, 602, 612, 614; **9**.152–155, 204, 442, 482, 619, 631, 641–644, 653, 662, 665, 677, 766–769; **10**.14, 64, 66, 68–69; **11**.57, 64, 350, 352, 354, 365, 372, 376, 379, 382; **16**.36, 41, 59, 80, 109, 244, 331–332.
AG 5.241: Cf. PAULUS Silentiarius Poet. Christ. (4039 004).
AG 5.242: Cf. ERATOSTHENES Scholasticus Epigr. (4063 001).
AG 5.305; 6.87: Cf. ANONYMI EPIGRAMMATICI (AG) (0138 001).

AG 7.311: Cf. CALLIMACHUS Philol. (0533 004).

AG 9.344: Cf. Julius LEONIDAS Math. et Astrol. (1457 001).

AG 9.657: Cf. MARIANUS Epigr. (4073 001).
Q: 6,159: Epigr.

x01 **Epigramma demonstrativum** (auctore Agathia vel Pallada).
App. Anth. 3.145(?): Cf. ANTHOLOGIAE GRAECAE APPENDIX (7052 003).
Cf. et PALLADAS Epigr. (2123 x01).

x04 **Scholia in Pausaniae periegesin.**
Spiro, pp. 145–149.
Cf. SCHOLIA IN PAUSANIAM (5033 001).

0675 **AGATHINUS** Med.
A.D. 1

x01 **Fragmenta ap. Galenum.**
K8.749–750, 935–938; **13**.299, 830.
Cf. GALENUS Med. (0057 059, 060, 076, 077).

x02 **Fragmentum ap. Oribasium.**
CMG, vol. 6.1.2, p. 49.
Cf. ORIBASIUS Med. (0722 001).

4248 **AGATHOCLES** Gramm.
fiq Agathocles Hist.
3 B.C.

x01 **Fragmenta grammatica** (fort. auctore Agathocle Hist. vel Agathocle Gramm.).
Montanari, pp. 26–30.
Cf. AGATHOCLES Hist. (0688 004).

0688 **AGATHOCLES** Hist.
fiq Agathocles Gramm.
3 B.C.?: Cyzicenus vel Babylonius

001 **Testimonia,** FGrH #472: 3B:430.
NQ: 71: Test.

002 **Fragmenta,** FGrH #472: 3B:430–433.
Dup. partim 0688 004.
Q: 1,037: Hist.

003 **Fragmentum,** ed. H.J. Mette, "Die 'Kleinen' griechischen Historiker heute," *Lustrum* 21 (1978) 30.
fr. 7 bis.
Q: 29: Hist.

004 **Fragmenta grammatica** (fort. auctore Agathocle Hist. vel Agathocle Gramm.), ed. F. Montanari, *I frammenti dei grammatici Agathokles, Hellanikos, Ptolemaios Epithetes [Sammlung griechischer und lateinischer Grammatiker 7.* Berlin: De Gruyter, 1988]: 26–30.
Dup. partim 0688 002.
Q: Gramm.

2534 **AGATHOCLES** Hist.
Incertum: Samius

001 **Titulus,** FGrH #799: 3C:836.
NQ: Hist.

0762 **AGATHOCLES** Med.
A.D. 1?

x01 **Fragmentum ap. Galenum.**
K13.832.
Cf. GALENUS Med. (0057 077).

4086 **[AGATHODAEMON]** Alchem.
Incertum

001 **Fragmenta,** ed. M. Berthelot, *Collection des anciens alchimistes grecs.* Paris: Steinheil, 1887 (repr. London: Holland Press, 1963): 115, 268–271.
Cod: Alchem.

1775 **Pseudo-AGATHON** Epigr.
Incertum

001 **Epigramma,** ed. E. Diehl, *Anthologia lyrica Graeca,* fasc. 1, 3rd edn. Leipzig: Teubner, 1949: 134.
Q: 13: Epigr.

2535 **AGATHON** Hist.
post 4 B.C.?

001 **Fragmentum,** FGrH #801: 3C:840.
Q: 121: Hist., Perieg.

2566 **[AGATHON]** Hist.
Incertum: Samius

001 **Fragmenta,** FGrH #843: 3C:929.
Q: 199: Hist., Nat. Hist.

0318 **AGATHON** Trag.
5 B.C.

001 **Fragmenta,** ed. B. Snell, *Tragicorum Graecorum fragmenta,* vol. 1. Göttingen: Vandenhoeck & Ruprecht, 1971: 161–168.
frr. 1–9, 11–15, 16a, 18–32, 34.
Q: 302: Trag., Satyr.

2606 **AGATHYLLUS** Eleg.
ante 1 B.C.?: Arcas

001 **Fragmentum,** ed. H. Lloyd-Jones and P. Parsons, *Supplementum Hellenisticum.* Berlin: De Gruyter, 1983: 5.
fr. 15.
Dup. partim ADDITAMENTA (FGrH) (2433 005) (fr. 2).
Q: 22: Eleg.

2555 **AGESILAUS** Hist.
Incertum

001 **Fragmentum,** FGrH #828: 3C:900.
Q: 35: Hist.

0105 **AGIS** Epigr.
3–2 B.C.

001 **Epigramma,** AG 6.152.
Q: 28: Epigr.

0676 **AGLAÏS** Poet. Med.
4 B.C./A.D. 1: Byzantius

001 **Adversus suffusiones incipientes,** ed. U.C.

Bussemaker, *Poetae bucolici et didactici.* Paris: Didot, 1862: 97–98.
Dup. 0676 002.
Cod: 206: Med., Eleg.

002 **Fragmentum**, ed. H. Lloyd-Jones and P. Parsons, *Supplementum Hellenisticum.* Berlin: De Gruyter, 1983: 7–8.
fr. 18.
Dup. 0676 001.
Cod: 179: Med., Eleg.

2345 **AGL(A)OSTHENES** Hist.
4–3 B.C.?
001 **Testimonia**, FGrH #499: 3B:470.
NQ: 65: Test.
002 **Fragmenta**, FGrH #499: 3B:470–473.
Q: 692: Hist.

1776 **AGRAPHA**
Varia
Cf. et FRAGMENTA EVANGELIORUM INCERTORUM (1378 004, 006).
001 **Agrapha**, ed. A. Resch, *Agrapha*, 2nd edn.
[*Texte und Untersuchungen* 30. Leipzig: Hinrichs, 1906]: 23–25, 29–32, 34–37, 39–40, 44–45, 48–65, 67–72, 84–93, 96, 98–100, 102–108, 110–122, 128–132, 136–137, 139, 141, 143, 146–147, 150, 152–153, 161–165, 167–172, 174–185, 188–189, 192–195, 197–199, 204–205, 207–208, 210–211, 214.
Q, Cod, Pap: Apocryph.
002 **Apocrypha**, ed. Resch, *op. cit.*, 215–216, 218–219, 221–222, 224, 227–232, 241, 243, 248, 250, 252–262, 264–269, 271–289.
Q, Cod, Pap: Apocryph.
003 **Logoi**, ed. Resch, *op. cit.*, 295–304, 306–310, 312–317, 320, 322–325, 327–334.
Q, Cod: Apocryph.

0763 **Julius AGRIPPA** Med.
A.D. 2?
x01 **Fragmenta ap. Galenum.**
K13.185, 1030.
Cf. GALENUS Med. (0057 076, 077).

1835 **AGROETAS** Hist.
3/2 B.C.
001 **Fragmenta**, FGrH #762: 3C:743–744.
Q: 400: Hist.

0693 **ALBINUS** Phil.
vel Alcinous
A.D. 2: Smyrnaeus
Scholia: Cf. ARETHAS Philol. et Scr. Eccl. (2130 035).
001 **Epitome doctrinae Platonicae**, ed. P. Louis, *Albinos. Épitomé.* Paris: Les Belles Lettres, 1945: 3–173.
Cod: 13,494: Phil.
002 **Introductio in Platonem**, ed. K.F. Hermann, *Platonis dialogi secundum Thrasylli tetralogias*

dispositi, vol. 6. Leipzig: Teubner, 1853: 147–151.
Cod: 1,444: Phil.

0400 **ALCAEUS** Comic.
4 B.C.
001 **Fragmenta**, ed. T. Kock, *Comicorum Atticorum fragmenta*, vol. 1. Leipzig: Teubner, 1880: 756–764.
frr. 1–3, 6–10, 12–15, 17–27, 29–34, 36, 38–39.
Q: 161: Comic.
002 **Fragmenta**, ed. A. Meineke, *Fragmenta comicorum Graecorum*, vol. 2.2. Berlin: Reimer, 1840 (repr. De Gruyter, 1970): 824–832.
Q: 137: Comic.
003 **Fragmentum**, ed. J. Demiańczuk, *Supplementum comicum.* Krakau: Nakładem Akademii, 1912 (repr. Hildesheim: Olms, 1967): 7.
fr. 1.
Q: 6: Comic.
004 **Fragmentum**, ed. Meineke, *FCG*, vol. 5.1 (1857; repr. 1970): cxxi.
Q: 45: Comic.

0106 **ALCAEUS** Epigr.
3–2 B.C.: Messenius
001 **Epigrammata**, AG 5.10; **6.**218; **7.**1, 5, 55, 247, 412, 429, 495, 536; **9.**518–519, 588; **11.**12; **12.**29–30, 64; **16.**5, 7–8, 196, 226.
AG 6.187: Cf. ALPHEUS Epigr. (0108 001).
AG 7.89: Cf. CALLIMACHUS Philol. (0533 004).
AG 11.53: Cf. ANONYMI EPIGRAMMATICI (AG) (0138 001).
Q: 866: Epigr.

0383 **ALCAEUS** Lyr.
7–6 B.C.: Lesbius
Cf. et SAPPHO et ALCAEUS Lyr. (1815).
Cf. et SAPPHUS vel ALCAEI FRAGMENTA (0387).
001 **Fragmenta**, ed. E. Lobel and D.L. Page, *Poetarum Lesbiorum fragmenta.* Oxford: Clarendon Press, 1955 (repr. 1968 (1st edn. corr.)): 112–116, 118–176, 178–206, 208–286, 290.
frr. 1–424, 439.
Q, Pap: 9,708: Lyr.
002 **Fragmentis addenda**, ed. Lobel and Page, *op. cit.*, 339.
frr. 128a, 304a.
Pap: 17: Lyr.
003 **Fragmenta**, ed. D.L. Page, *Supplementum lyricis Graecis.* Oxford: Clarendon Press, 1974: 77–86.
fr. S262a: *P. Colon.* 2021.
fr. S262b: *P. Oxy.* 21.2303.
fr. S262c: *P. Oxy.* 29.2506.
fr. S262: *P. Colon.* 2021 + *P. Oxy.* 21.2303.
fr. S263: *P. Oxy.* 35.2733.

fr. S264–S272: *P. Oxy.* 35.2734.
Dup. partim 0383 001.
Pap: 695: Lyr.

0764 **ALCAMENES** Med.
ante A.D. 1: Abydenus
x01 **Fragmenta ap. Anonymum Londinensem.**
Iatrica 8.6–10.
Cf. ANONYMUS LONDINENSIS Med. (0643 001).

2285 **ALCETAS** Hist.
3–2 B.C.?
001 **Fragmentum**, FGrH #405: 3B:300.
Q: 70: Hist.

0236 **ALCIBIADES** <Eleg.>
5 B.C.: Atheniensis
001 **Fragmentum**, ed. M.L. West, *Iambi et elegi Graeci*, vol. 2. Oxford: Clarendon Press, 1972: 29.
Q: 16: Eleg.
x01 **Epigramma.**
App. Anth. 5.6b(?) addenda: Cf. ANTHOLO-GIAE GRAECAE APPENDIX (7052 008).
Dup. 0236 001.

0610 **ALCIDAMAS** Rhet.
4 B.C.: Atheniensis
001 **Fragmenta**, ed. L. Radermacher, *Artium scriptores* [Österreichische Akademie der Wissenschaften, Philosoph.-hist. Kl., Sitzungsberichte, Bd. 227, Abh. 3. Vienna: Rohrer, 1951]: 135–147.
Περὶ τῶν τοὺς γραπτοὺς λόγους γραφόντων ἢ περὶ σοφιστῶν (fr. 15): pp. 135–141.
Ὀδυσσεὺς κατὰ Παλαμήδους προδοσίας [Sp.] (fr. 16): pp. 141–147.
Cod: 3,848: Rhet.
002 **Mouseion** (*P. Petrie* 1.25), ed. J.P. Mahaffy, *The Flinders Petrie papyri*, pt. 1 [*Cunningham memoirs* 8. Dublin: Royal Irish Academy, 1891]: 70.
Pap: Rhet.
003 **Mouseion** (fragmentum), *P. Lit. Lond.* 191.
Pap: Rhet.
004 **Vita Homeri** (*P. Mich.* inv. 2754), ed. J.G. Winter, "A new fragment on the life of Homer," *Transactions and Proceedings of the American Philological Association* 56 (1925) 125–126.
Pap: Biogr.

1780 **ALCIMENES** Comic.
Incertum: Atheniensis
001 **Titulus**, ed. T. Kock, *Comicorum Atticorum fragmenta*, vol. 1. Leipzig: Teubner, 1880: 254.
NQ: 2: Comic.
002 **Titulus**, ed. A. Meineke, *Fragmenta comicorum Graecorum*, vol. 1. Berlin: Reimer, 1839 (repr. De Gruyter, 1970): 101.
NQ: 2: Comic.

0765 **ALCIMION** Med.
A.D. 1
Cf. et ALCIMION vel NICOMACHUS Med. (0823).
Cf. et APOLLONIUS et ALCIMION Med. (0810).
x01 **Fragmenta ap. Galenum.**
K13.112, 493, 529, 835, 841, 973.
Cf. GALENUS Med. (0057 076–077).

0823 **ALCIMION vel NICOMACHUS** Med.
A.D. 1?
Cf. et ALCIMION Med. (0765).
x01 **Fragmentum ap. Galenum.**
K13.807.
Cf. GALENUS Med. (0057 077).

0695 **ALCIMUS** Hist.
4 B.C.: Siceliota
001 **Testimonium**, FGrH #560: 3B:570.
Dup. partim ALCIMUS Rhet. (4267 001).
NQ: 17: Test.
002 **Fragmenta**, FGrH #560: 3B:570–574.
fr. 7: *P. Harris* 59.
Q, Pap: 1,374: Hist.

4267 **ALCIMUS** Rhet.
3 B.C.: Atheniensis
001 **Testimonia**, ed. K. Döring, *Die Megariker* [*Studien zur antiken Philosophie* 2. Amsterdam: Grüner, 1972]: 52, 61.
test. 165 (p. 52) = Stilpo (4262 001).
Dup. partim ALCIMUS Hist. (0695 001).
NQ: Test.

ALCINOUS Phil.
Cf. ALBINUS Phil. (0693).

0640 **ALCIPHRON** Rhet. et Soph.
A.D. 2/3
001 **Epistulae**, ed. M.A. Schepers, *Alciphronis rhetoris epistularum libri iv.* Leipzig: Teubner, 1905 (repr. Stuttgart: 1969): 1–155.
Cod: 20,324: Epist.

0766 **ALCMAEON** Phil.
5 B.C.: Crotoniensis
001 **Testimonia**, ed. H. Diels and W. Kranz, *Die Fragmente der Vorsokratiker*, vol. 1, 6th edn. Berlin: Weidmann, 1951 (repr. Dublin: 1966): 210–214.
test. 1–18.
NQ: 1,671: Test.
002 **Fragmenta**, ed. Diels and Kranz, *op. cit.*, 214–216.
frr. 1–5.
Q: 252: Phil.

0696 *ALCMAEONIS*
7 B.C.
001 **Fragmenta**, ed. G. Kinkel, *Epicorum Grae-*

corum fragmenta, vol. 1. Leipzig: Teubner,
1877: 76.
frr. 1–2.
Q: 38: Epic.

0291 **ALCMAN** Lyr.
    7 B.C.: Lacedaemonius
    Scholia: Cf. SCHOLIA IN ALCMANEM (5044).
  001 **Fragmenta**, ed. D.L. Page, *Poetae melici
    Graeci.* Oxford: Clarendon Press, 1962 (repr.
    1967 (1st edn. corr.)): 2–5, 10–38, 41–83, 85–
    87, 89–91.
    frr. 1–10, 12–17, 19–20, 26–32, 34–43, 45–50,
    53–60, 63–65, 68–70, 73–74, 77–98, 100–144,
    146–159, 162, 168–171, 173–174, 177.
    Q, Pap: 3,635: Lyr.
  002 **Fragmenta**, ed. D.L. Page, *Supplementum lyri-
    cis Graecis.* Oxford: Clarendon Press, 1974: 1–
    3.
    frr. S1–S2: *P. Oxy.* 35.2737.
    fr. S3: *P. Oxy.* 37.2801.
    fr. S4: *P. Oxy.* 37.2812.
    fr. S5: *P. Oxy.* 37.2802.
    fr. S1: Dup. partim TERPANDER Lyr. (0299
    002) (fr. S6).
    fr. S1: Dup. partim ION Poeta et Phil. (0308
    004) (fr. S316).
    Pap: 151: Lyr.

0401 **ALEXANDER** Comic.
    1 B.C.
  001 **Fragmenta**, ed. T. Kock, *Comicorum Atti-
    corum fragmenta*, vol. 3. Leipzig: Teubner,
    1888: 372–374.
    frr. 1–6, 9 + titulus.
    Q: 49: Comic.
  002 **Fragmenta**, ed. A. Meineke, *Fragmenta comi-
    corum Graecorum*, vol. 4. Berlin: Reimer, 1841
    (repr. De Gruyter, 1970): 553–555.
    Q: 47: Comic.

0107 **ALEXANDER** Epigr.
    1 B.C.?: Magnes
  001 **Epigramma**, AG 6.182.
    Q: 50: Epigr.

2500 **ALEXANDER** Hist.
    post 4 B.C.?: Chersonensis (Cariae)
  001 **Testimonium**, FGrH #739: 3C:714.
    NQ: 17: Test.

1864 **ALEXANDER** Hist.
    A.D. 1: Myndius
  001 **Fragmenta**, FGrH #25: 1A:189.
    Dup. partim 1864 002.
    Q: 358: Hist., Myth., Geogr., Paradox.
  002 **Fragmenta**, ed. A. Giannini, *Paradoxograph-
    orum Graecorum reliquiae.* Milan: Istituto Edi-
    toriale Italiano, 1965: 164–166.
    Dup. partim 1864 001.
    Dup. partim Cornelius ALEXANDER Polyhist.
    (0697 002).
    Q: Paradox.

0744 **ALEXANDER** Med.
    A.D. 6: Trallianus
  001 **Dedicatio ad Cosman**, ed. T. Puschmann,
    Alexander von Tralles, vol. 1. Vienna: Brau-
    müller, 1878 (repr. Amsterdam: Hakkert,
    1963): 289.
    Cod: 148: Med., Epist.
  002 **De febribus**, ed. Puschmann, *op. cit.*, vol. 1,
    291–439.
    Cod: 20,743: Med.
  003 **Therapeutica**, ed. Puschmann, *op. cit.*, vols. 1
    & 2 (1879; repr. 1963): **1**:441–617; **2**:3–585.
    Cod: 103,803: Med.
  004 **Epistula de lumbricis**, ed. Puschmann, *op. cit.*,
    vol. 2, 587–599.
    Cod: 1,843: Epist., Med.
  005 **De oculis libri tres**, ed. T. Puschmann, *Nach-
    träge zu Alexander Trallianus.* Berlin: Calvary,
    1887 (repr. Amsterdam: Hakkert, 1963): 134–
    178.
    Cod: 6,028: Med.

0732 **ALEXANDER** Phil.
    A.D. 2–3: Aphrodisiensis
  001 **De mixtione**, ed. I. Bruns, *Alexandri Aphro-
    disiensis praeter commentaria scripta minora
    [Commentaria in Aristotelem Graeca*, suppl.
    2.2. Berlin: Reimer, 1892]: 213–238.
    Cod: 10,276: Med., Phil.
  002 **Problemata** (lib. 1–2) [Sp.], ed. J.L. Ideler,
    Physici et medici Graeci minores, vol. 1. Berlin:
    Reimer, 1841 (repr. Amsterdam: Hakkert,
    1963): 3–80.
    Cf. et 0732 017.
    Cod: 24,310: Med., Nat. Hist.
  003 **De febribus** [Sp.], ed. Ideler, *op. cit.*, 81–106.
    Cod: 8,447: Med.
  004 **In Aristotelis metaphysica commentaria**, ed.
    M. Hayduck, *Alexandri Aphrodisiensis in Aris-
    totelis metaphysica commentaria [Commentaria
    in Aristotelem Graeca* 1. Berlin: Reimer, 1891]:
    1–837.
    Lib. A, α, B, Γ, Δ: pp. 1–439.
    Lib. E–N [Sp.]: pp. 440–837.
    Cod: 343,092: Phil., Comm.
  005 **In Aristotelis analyticorum priorum librum i
    commentarium**, ed. M. Wallies, *Alexandri in
    Aristotelis analyticorum priorum librum i* com-
    mentarium [*Commentaria in Aristotelem
    Graeca* 2.1. Berlin: Reimer, 1883]: 1–418.
    Cod: 162,019: Phil., Comm.
  006 **In Aristotelis topicorum libros octo commen-
    taria**, ed. M. Wallies, *Alexandri Aphrodisiensis
    in Aristotelis topicorum libros octo commentaria
    [Commentaria in Aristotelem Graeca* 2.2. Ber-
    lin: Reimer, 1891]: 1–591.
    Cod: 188,697: Phil., Comm.
  007 **In librum de sensu commentarium**, ed. P.
    Wendland, *Alexandri in librum de sensu com-
    mentarium [Commentaria in Aristotelem
    Graeca* 3.1. Berlin: Reimer, 1901]: 1–173.
    Cod: 51,546: Phil., Comm.
  008 **In Aristotelis meteorologicorum libros com-**

mentaria, ed. M. Hayduck, *Alexandri Aphrodisiensis in Aristotelis meteorologicorum libros commentaria* [*Commentaria in Aristotelem Graeca* 3.2. Berlin: Reimer, 1899]: 1–227.
Cod: 85,965: Phil., Comm., Nat. Hist.

010 **De anima**, ed. I. Bruns, *Alexandri Aphrodisiensis praeter commentaria scripta minora* [*Commentaria in Aristotelem Graeca*, suppl. 2.1. Berlin: Reimer, 1887]: 1–100.
Cod: 31,534: Phil., Comm.

011 **De anima libri mantissa** (= **De anima liber alter**) [Sp.], ed. Bruns, *CAG*, suppl. 2.1, 101–186.
Cod: 36,508: Phil., Comm.

012 Ἀπορίαι καὶ λύσεις [Sp.], ed. Bruns, *CAG*, suppl. 2.2, 1–116.
Cod: 43,780: Phil.

013 Ἠθικὰ προβλήματα [Sp.], ed. Bruns, *CAG*, suppl. 2.2, 117–163.
Cod: 18,050: Phil.

014 **De fato**, ed. Bruns, *CAG*, suppl. 2.2, 164–212.
Cod: 16,729: Phil.

015 **In analytica posteriora commentariorum fragmenta**, ed. Wallies, *CAG*, suppl. 2.1, xix–xxii.
Text to be replaced by Moraux edition (cf. 0732 018).
Cod: 1,486: Phil., Comm.

016 **Fragmenta**, ed. P. Moraux, *Alexandre d'Aphrodise*. Paris: Droz, 1942: 207–212, 214, 216–220.
Q: 1,403: Phil.

017 **Problemata** (lib. 3–4) [Sp.], ed. H. Usener, *Alexandri Aphrodisiensis quae feruntur problematorum liber iii et iiii* [*Programm Gymnasium Joachimsthal* (1859)]: 1–37.
Cf. et 0732 002.
Cod: 15,074: Med., Phil.

018 **In analytica posteriora commentariorum fragmenta**, ed. P. Moraux, *Le commentaire d'Alexandre d'Aphrodise aux 'seconds analytiques' d'Aristote* [*Peripatoi. Philologisch-historische Studien zum Aristotelismus* 13. Berlin: De Gruyter, 1979]: 9–13, 16–21, 24, 32–33, 35, 37–39, 42–47, 49, 51–53, 56–61, 64–66, 69, 71–75, 77–78, 81–82, 86–89, 91–93, 95, 97–102, 104–107, 109, 111–112, 114–115, 118–119, 123, 125–127.
Cod: Phil., Comm.

x01 **In Aristotelis sophisticos elenchos commentarius** [Sp.].
Wallies, pp. 1–198.
Cf. MICHAEL Phil. (4034 008).

0697 **Cornelius ALEXANDER** Polyhist.
2–1 B.C.: Milesius

001 **Testimonia**, FGrH #273: 3A:96–97.
NQ: 520: Test.

002 **Fragmenta**, FGrH #273: 3A:97–126.
Dup. partim ALEXANDER Hist. (1864 002).
Q: 7,571: Hist., Paradox.

0698 **ALEXANDER** Rhet.
1 B.C.: Ephesius

002 **Fragmenta et titulus**, ed. H. Lloyd-Jones and P. Parsons, *Supplementum Hellenisticum*. Berlin: De Gruyter, 1983: 10, 12–15.
frr. 20–21, 25–34, 36–38.
Q: 254: Hexametr., Astron., Geogr.

0594 **ALEXANDER** Rhet. et Soph.
A.D. 2

001 Περὶ ῥητορικῶν ἀφορμῶν (fragmenta), ed. L. Spengel, *Rhetores Graeci*, vol. 3. Leipzig: Teubner, 1856 (repr. Frankfurt am Main: Minerva, 1966): 1–6.
Cod: 1,375: Rhet.

002 **De figuris**, ed. Spengel, *op. cit.*, 9–40.
Cod: 7,179: Rhet.

2951 **ALEXANDER** Scr. Eccl.
A.D. 3: Hierosolymitanus

x01 **Epistula ad Antionitas** (ap. Eusebium).
HE 7.2.3.
Cf. EUSEBIUS Scr. Eccl. et Theol. (2018 002).

x02 **Epistula ad ecclesiam Antiochenam** (ap. Eusebium).
HE 7.2.5–8.
Cf. EUSEBIUS Scr. Eccl. et Theol. (2018 002).

x03 **Epistula ad Origenem** (ap. Eusebium).
HE 6.14.8–9.
Cf. EUSEBIUS Scr. Eccl. et Theol. (2018 002).

x04 **Epistula Alexandri et Theoctisti Caesariensis ad Pontianum Romanum** (ap. Eusebium).
HE 6.19.17–18.
Cf. EUSEBIUS Scr. Eccl. et Theol. (2018 002).

2059 **ALEXANDER** Theol.
A.D. 4: Lycopolitanus

001 **Tractatus de placitis Manichaeorum**, ed. A. Brinkmann, *Alexandri Lycopolitani contra Manichaei opiniones disputatio*. Leipzig: Teubner, 1895: 3–40.
Cod: 7,679: Theol.

0216 **ALEXANDER** Trag. et Lyr.
4–3 B.C.: Aetolus

001 **Fragmenta**, ed. J.U. Powell, *Collectanea Alexandrina*. Oxford: Clarendon Press, 1925 (repr. 1970): 121–129.
frr. 1–9, 15, 18 + tituli.
Q: 531: Epic., Eleg., Epigr.

002 **Epigrammata**, AG 7.534, 709; **16**.172.
Dup. 0216 001 (frr. 8–9, 18).
AG 7.507: Cf. SIMONIDES Lyr. (0261 003).
Q: 99: Epigr.

003 **Fragmenta**, ed. B. Snell, *Tragicorum Graecorum fragmenta*, vol. 1. Göttingen: Vandenhoeck & Ruprecht, 1971: 279.
frr. 1–2.
fr. 2: Dup. 0216 001 (fr. 15).
Q: 8: Trag.

0767 **ALEXANDER Philalethes** Med.
A.D. 1: Laodicensis

x01 **Fragmenta ap. Galenum**.
K12.557, 580.
Cf. GALENUS Med. (0057 076).

x02 **Fragmentum ap. Pseudo-Galenum**.
K14.510.
Cf. Pseudo-GALENUS Med. (0530 029).

x03 **Fragmentum ap. Soranum**.
CMG, vol. 4, p. 122.
Cf. SORANUS Med. (0565 001).

ALEXANDER PHORTIUS Gramm.
Incertum
Cf. SCHOLIA IN PINDARUM (5034 005).

0042 *ALEXANDRI MAGNI EPISTULAE*
Incertum
001 **Epistulae**, ed. R. Hercher, *Epistolographi Graeci*. Paris: Didot, 1873 (repr. Amsterdam: Hakkert, 1965): 98–99.
Q: 422: Epist.

2556 **[ALEXARCHUS]** Hist.
Incertum
001 **Fragmentum**, FGrH #829: 3C:900.
Q: 45: Hist.

2607 **ALEXINUS** Phil.
4 B.C.: Eleus, Atheniensis
001 **Titulus**, ed. H. Lloyd-Jones and P. Parsons, *Supplementum Hellenisticum*. Berlin: De Gruyter, 1983: 16.
fr. 40.
Dup. partim 2607 003.
NQ: 4: Encom., Lyr.

002 **Fragmentum** (ap. Philodemum) (*P. Herc.* 1674, col. 44.23–45.30), ed. J. von Arnim, "Ein Bruchstück des Alexinos," *Hermes* 28 (1893) 69.
Dup. partim 2607 003.
Pap: Phil.

003 **Testimonia**, ed. K. Döring, *Die Megariker* [*Studien zur antiken Philosophie* 2. Amsterdam: Grüner, 1972]: 19, 21–27.
test. 63 (p. 19) = Eubulides (4257 001).
test. 73–75, 79–94 (pp. 21–27) = Alexinus.
Dup. partim 2607 001–002.
NQ: Test.

0699 **ALEXION** Gramm.
A.D. 1
001 **Fragmenta**, ed. R. Berndt, *De Charete, Chaeride, Alexione grammaticis eorumque reliquiis*, pt. 2. Königsberg: Hartung, 1906: 4–44.
Q: [4,573]

0402 **ALEXIS** Comic.
4–3 B.C.
001 **Fragmenta**, ed. T. Kock, *Comicorum Atticorum fragmenta*, vol. 2. Leipzig: Teubner, 1884: 297–329, 331–408.
frr. 1–7, 9–30, 32–49, 51–53, 55–66, 68–71, 73–102, 105–128, 130–135, 137–138, 140–150, 152–156, 158–165, 167–183, 185–198, 200–214, 216–299, 301–302, 305–329, 331–343, 345 + tituli.
Q: 7,345: Comic.

002 **Fragmenta**, ed. A. Meineke, *Fragmenta comicorum Graecorum*, vol. 3. Berlin: Reimer, 1840 (repr. De Gruyter, 1970): 382–389, 391–423, 425–440, 442–462, 464–522, 524.
Q: 7,156: Comic.

003 **Fragmentum**, ed. J. Demiańczuk, *Supplementum comicum*. Krakau: Nakładem Akademii, 1912 (repr. Hildesheim: Olms, 1967): 7.
fr. 1.
Q: 3: Comic.

004 **Tituli**, ed. C. Austin, *Comicorum Graecorum fragmenta in papyris reperta*. Berlin: De Gruyter, 1973: 1.
NQ: 4: Comic.

005 **Fragmenta**, ed. Kock, *CAF*, vol. 3 (1888): 744.
frr. 278b, 303b.
Q: 61: Comic.

006 **Fragmenta**, ed. Meineke, *FCG*, vol. 5.1 (1857; repr. 1970): ccx, ccxviii.
Q: 17: Comic.

x01 **Aenigma**.
App. Anth. 7.11: Cf. ANTHOLOGIAE GRAECAE APPENDIX (7052 007).
Dup. partim 0402 002 (p. 493).

0707 **ALEXIS** Hist.
3/2 B.C.: Samius
001 **Fragmenta**, FGrH #539: 3B:522–523.
Q: 203: Hist.

0108 **ALPHEUS** Epigr.
A.D. 1: Mytilenensis
001 **Epigrammata**, AG **6**.187; **7**.237; **9**.90, 95, 97, 100–101, 104, 110, 526; **12**.18; **16**.212.
Q: 434: Epigr.

2135 **ALYPIUS** Mus.
A.D. 3/4?
001 **Isagoge musica**, ed. K. Jan, *Musici scriptores Graeci*. Leipzig: Teubner, 1895 (repr. Hildesheim: Olms, 1962): 367–406.
Cod: Mus.

0758 **AMARANTUS** Gramm.
A.D. 1/2: Alexandrinus
x01 **Fragmenta ap. Galenum**.
K13.84; 14.208.
Cf. GALENUS Med. (0057 076, 078).

0043 *AMASIS EPISTULAE*
Incertum
001 **Epistulae**, ed. R. Hercher, *Epistolographi Graeci*. Paris: Didot, 1873 (repr. Amsterdam: Hakkert, 1965): 100.
Q: 201: Epist.

1777 **AMBROSIUS Rusticus** Med.
ante A.D. 1: Puteolanus

x01 **Fragmenta ap. Galenum.**
K**13**.309–310, 325–326; **14**.184.
Cf. GALENUS Med. (0057 076, 078).

2219 **AMELESAGORAS** Hist.
4–3 B.C.: Atheniensis
001 **Testimonia**, FGrH #330: 3B:162–163.
NQ: 256: Test.
002 **Fragmenta**, FGrH #330: 3B:163–164.
Atthis: fr. 1 [Dub.].
Fragmenta incertae sedis: frr. 2–3.
Q: 297: Hist.

2004 *AMELII EPISTULA*
Incertum
001 **Amelii epistula**, ed. R. Hercher, *Epistolographi Graeci*. Paris: Didot, 1873 (repr. Amsterdam: Hakkert, 1965): 101.
Q: 243: Epist.

1047 **AMERIAS** Gramm.
3 B.C.: Macedonius
001 **Fragmenta**, ed. O. Hoffmann, *Die Makedonen, ihre Sprache und ihr Volkstum*. Göttingen: Vandenhoeck & Ruprecht, 1906: 4–14.
Q: Gramm.

0403 **AMIPSIAS** Comic.
5–4 B.C.
001 **Fragmenta**, ed. T. Kock, *Comicorum Atticorum fragmenta*, vol. 1. Leipzig: Teubner, 1880: 670–678.
frr. 1–5, 7–10, 12–19, 21–26, 29–38.
Q: 250: Comic.
002 **Fragmenta**, ed. A. Meineke, *Fragmenta comicorum Graecorum*, vol. 2.2. Berlin: Reimer, 1840 (repr. De Gruyter, 1970): 701–708, 710–711.
Q: 219: Comic.
003 **Fragmentum**, ed. J. Demiańczuk, *Supplementum comicum*. Krakau: Nakładem Akademii, 1912 (repr. Hildesheim: Olms, 1967): 7.
fr. 1.
Q: 2: Comic.
004 **Tituli**, ed. C. Austin, *Comicorum Graecorum fragmenta in papyris reperta*. Berlin: De Gruyter, 1973: 1.
fr. 1.
Pap: 4: Comic.

0109 **AMMIANUS** Epigr.
A.D. 2
001 **Epigrammata**, AG **9**.573; 11.13–16, 97–98, 102, 146–147, 150, 152, 156–157, 180–181, 188, 209, 221, 226–231, 413.
AG 11.95, 155: Cf. LUCILLIUS Epigr. (1468 001).
AG 11.268: Cf. ANONYMI EPIGRAMMATICI (AG) (0138 001).
AG 16.20: Cf. PALLADAS Epigr. (2123 001).
Q: 565: Epigr.

0110 **AMMONIDES** Epigr.
post 3 B.C.?
001 **Epigramma**, AG 11.201.
Q: 13: Epigr.

0289 **AMMONIUS** Epigr.
A.D. 5
001 **Fragmentum**, ed. E. Heitsch, *Die griechischen Dichterfragmente der römischen Kaiserzeit*, vol. 2. Göttingen: Vandenhoeck & Ruprecht, 1964: 48.
Dup. 0289 002.
Q: 14: Epigr.
002 **Epigramma**, AG 9.827.
Dup. 0289 001.
Q: 21: Epigr.

0708 **<AMMONIUS>** Gramm.
fiq Ammonius Hist.
A.D. 1/2?
Cf. et AMMONIUS Hist. (2254).
001 **De adfinium vocabulorum differentia**, ed. K. Nickau, *Ammonii qui dicitur liber de adfinium vocabulorum differentia*. Leipzig: Teubner, 1966: 1–136.
Cod: 17,755: Lexicogr.
002 **De impropriis**, ed. Nickau, *op. cit.*, 138–153.
Cod: 1,872: Gramm.
x01 **Supplementum glossarum.**
Nickau, pp. 156–159.
Cf. (H)EREN(N)IUS PHILO Hist. et Gramm. (1416 002).

2254 **AMMONIUS** Hist.
fiq Ammonius Gramm.
2 B.C.: fort. Alexandrinus
Cf. et <AMMONIUS> Gramm. (0708).
001 **Testimonia**, FGrH #350: 3B:212–213.
NQ: 70: Test.
002 **Fragmenta**, FGrH #350: 3B:213–214.
Q: 243: Hist.

0709 **AMMONIUS** Hist.
2–1 B.C.?: Atheniensis
001 **Fragmenta**, FGrH #361: 3B:219–220.
Q: 423: Hist.

4016 **AMMONIUS** Phil.
A.D. 5: Alexandrinus
001 **In Porphyrii isagogen sive quinque voces**, ed. A. Busse, *Ammonius in Porphyrii isagogen sive quinque voces* [Commentaria in Aristotelem Graeca 4.3. Berlin: Reimer, 1891]: 1–128.
Cod: 34,396: Phil., Comm.
002 **In Aristotelis categorias commentarius**, ed. A. Busse, *Ammonius in Aristotelis categorias commentarius* [Commentaria in Aristotelem Graeca 4.4. Berlin: Reimer, 1895]: 1–106.
Cod: 28,483: Phil., Comm.
003 **In Aristotelis librum de interpretatione commentarius**, ed. A. Busse, *Ammonius in Aristotelis de interpretatione commentarius* [Com-

mentaria in Aristotelem Graeca 4.5. Berlin:
Reimer, 1897]: 1–272.
Cod: 96,401: Phil., Comm.

004 **In Aristotelis analyticorum priorum librum i
commentarium**, ed. M. Wallies, *Ammonii in
Aristotelis analyticorum priorum librum i com-
mentarium* [*Commentaria in Aristotelem
Graeca* 4.6. Berlin: Reimer, 1899]: 1–36.
Cod: 14,401: Phil., Comm.

005 **In Aristotelis analytica priora** [Sp.], ed.
Wallies, *CAG* 4.6, 37–76.
Cod: 19,720: Phil., Comm.

2724 **AMMONIUS** Scr. Eccl.
A.D. 5–6?: Alexandrinus

001 **Fragmenta in Psalmos** (in catenis), MPG 85:
1361–1364.
Q: Exeget., Caten.

002 **Fragmenta in Danielem** (in catenis), MPG 85:
1364–1381, 1823–1826.
Cf. et 2724 009.
Q: Exeget., Caten.

003 **Fragmenta in Joannem** (in catenis), ed. J.
Reuss, *Johannes-Kommentare aus der griech-
ischen Kirche* [*Texte und Untersuchungen* 89.
Berlin: Akademie-Verlag, 1966]: 196–358.
Q: 22,156: Exeget., Caten.

005 **Fragmenta in Acta apostolorum** (in catenis),
MPG 85: 1524–1608.
Q: Exeget., Caten.

007 **Fragmentum in epistulam Petri i** (in catenis),
MPG 85: 1608–1609.
Q: Exeget., Caten.

008 **Fragmenta in Matthaeum** (in catenis) [Sp.],
MPG 85: 1381–1392.
Q: Exeget., Caten.

009 **Fragmenta in Danielem** (in catenis), ed. M.
Faulhaber, *Die Propheten-Catenen nach röm-
ischen Handschriften* [*Biblische Studien* 4. Frei-
burg im Breisgau: Herder, 1899]: 185–187.
Cf. et 2724 002.
Q: Exeget., Caten.

0768 **AMMONIUS Lithotomus** Med.
ante A.D. 1: Alexandrinus

x01 **Fragmentum ap. Oribasium.**
CMG, vol. 6.2.2, p. 188.
Cf. ORIBASIUS Med. (0722 003).

x02 **Fragmentum ap. Paulum.**
CMG, vol. 9.2, p. 339.
Cf. PAULUS Med. (0715 001).

2445 **AMOMETUS** Hist.
ante 4 B.C.

001 **Testimonium**, FGrH #645: 3C:190.
NQ: 32: Test.

002 **Fragmenta**, FGrH #645: 3C:191.
Q: 200: Hist.

0710 ***AMPHIARAI EXILIUM*** (?)
ante 6 B.C.

001 **Fragmentum**, ed. J.U. Powell, *Collectanea Alexandrina*. Oxford: Clarendon Press, 1925
(repr. 1970): 246.
Q: 22: Epic.

2699 **AMPHICRATES** Rhet.
ante A.D. 2: Atheniensis

x01 **Epigramma demonstrativum.**
App. Anth. 3.99: Cf. ANTHOLOGIAE GRAE-
CAE APPENDIX (7052 003).

2112 **AMPHILOCHIUS** Scr. Eccl.
A.D. 4: Iconiensis

001 **In natalitia domini** (orat. 1), ed. C. Datema,
Amphilochii Iconiensis opera. Turnhout: Bre-
pols, 1978: 5–9.
Cod: 1,520: Homilet.

003 **In occursum domini** (orat. 2), ed. Datema, *op.
cit.*, 37–73.
Cod: 2,374: Homilet.

004 **In Lazarum** (orat. 3), ed. Datema, *op. cit.*, 85–
92.
Cod: 1,320: Homilet.

005 **In mulierem peccatricem** (orat. 4), ed. Datema,
op. cit., 107–126.
Cod: 4,066: Homilet.

006 **In diem sabbati sancti** (orat. 5), ed. Datema,
op. cit., 133–136.
Cod: 818: Homilet.

007 **In illud:** *Pater si possibile est* (orat. 6), ed.
Datema, *op. cit.*, 139–152.
Cod: 3,680: Homilet., Exeget.

008 **De recens baptizatis** (orat. 7), ed. Datema, *op.
cit.*, 155–162.
Cod: 1,626: Homilet.

009 **In Zacchaeum** (orat. 8), ed. Datema, *op. cit.*,
165–171.
Cod: 2,287: Homilet.

010 **In illud:** *Non potest filius a se facere* (orat. 9),
ed. Datema, *op. cit.*, 175–179.
Cod: 1,608: Homilet., Exeget.

011 **Contra haereticos**, ed. Datema, *op. cit.*, 185–
214.
Cod: 10,423: Eccl., Invectiv.

015 **Epistula synodalis**, ed. Datema, *op. cit.*, 219–
221.
Cod: 797: Epist., Eccl.

016 **Fragmenta**, ed. Datema, *op. cit.*, 227–239.
frr. 1–15.
Q, Cod: 2,800: Exeget., Theol., Epist.

017 **Oratio in mesopentecosten** [Sp.], ed. Datema,
op. cit., 251–262.
Cod: 2,235: Homilet.

018 **Fragmenta spuria**, ed. Datema, *op. cit.*, 263–
266.
frr. 1–5.
Q, Cod: 843: Theol., Exeget., Epist.

002 **Iambi ad Seleucum**, ed. E. Oberg, *Amphilochii
Iconiensis iambi ad Seleucum* [*Patristische Texte
und Studien* 9. Berlin: De Gruyter, 1969]: 29–
40.
Cod: 1,937: Iamb., Epist., Eccl.

012 **Oratio in resurrectionem domini** (e cod. Vat. gr. 1936), ed. S. Lilla, "La fonte inedita di un' omelia greca sulla Pasqua," *Byzantion* 40 (1970) 68–73.
Cod: 768: Homilet.

013 **Oratio in resurrectionem domini** (e cod. Vat. gr. 2194), ed. S. Lilla, "Un omelia greca sulla Pasqua," *Byzantion* 38 (1968) 282–284.
Cod: 691: Homilet.

014 **Encomium sancti Basilii Magni**, ed. P.J. Alexander, "The iconoclastic council of St. Sophia (815) and its definition (horos)," *Dumbarton Oaks Papers* 7 (1953) 61.
fr. 22.
Cod: 161: Encom.

026 **Fragmenta**, ed. G. Ficker, *Amphilochiana*. Leipzig: Barth, 1906: 4–5, 10–15.
frr. 1–3, 5–6.
Q: 663: Exeget., Homilet., Theol.

020 **Fragmenta ex tractatu in illud: *Dominus creavit me*** (fr. 4), MPG 39: 101.
Q: 243: Exeget.

021 **In Isaiam** (fr. 5) [Sp.], MPG 39: 101.
Q: 28: Exeget.

022 **In illud: *Solvite templum hoc*** (fr. 9) [Sp.], MPG 39: 105.
Q: 56: Exeget.

019 **Expositio in illud: *De meo accipiet et annuntiabit vobis*** (fr. 13) [Sp.], MPG 39: 109.
Q: 94: Exeget.

023 **Fragmentum xvii** [Sp.], MPG 39: 116.
Q: 157: Exeget.

027 **Fragmentum xix** (ap. Anastasium Sinaïtam, *Viae dux*) [Sp.], MPG 39: 117.
Q: [24]: Exeget.

024 **Fragmentum xx** [Sp.], MPG 39: 117.
Q: 20: Exeget.

025 **Fragmentum xxi** [Sp.], MPG 39: 117.
Q: 33: Exeget.

030 **Vita sancti Basilii Magni**, ed. F. Combefis, *SS. patrum Amphilochii Iconiensis, Methodii Patarensis et Andreae Cretensis opera omnia*. Paris, 1644: 155–225.
Cod: Hagiogr.

031 **Oratio in circumcisionem et in Basilium**, ed. Combefis, *op. cit.*, 10–22.
Cod: Homilet., Encom.

2492 **AMPHINOMUS** Math.
4 B.C.: Colophonius

001 **Doctrina**, ed. F. Lasserre, *De Léodamas de Thasos à Philippe d'Oponte*. Naples: Bibliopolis, 1987: 151–152.
frr. 1–4.
NQ: Test.

2271 **AMPHION** Hist.
1 B.C./A.D. 2?: Thespiensis

001 **Fragmentum**, FGrH #387: 3B:264.
Q: 60: Hist.

0771 **AMPHION** Med.
ante A.D. 2

x01 **Fragmentum ap. Galenum.**
K13.736.
Cf. GALENUS Med. (0057 077).

0404 **AMPHIS** Comic.
4 B.C.

001 **Fragmenta**, ed. T. Kock, *Comicorum Atticorum fragmenta*, vol. 2. Leipzig: Teubner, 1884: 236–250.
frr. 1–23, 25–46, 49–51 + tituli.
Q: 821: Comic.

002 **Fragmenta**, ed. A. Meineke, *Fragmenta comicorum Graecorum*, vol. 3. Berlin: Reimer, 1840 (repr. De Gruyter, 1970): 301–313, 315–319.
Q: 792: Comic.

0711 **AMPHITHEUS** (?) Hist.
3/2 B.C.: Heracleota

001 **Fragmentum**, FGrH #431: 3B:327–328.
Q: 145: Hist.

0223 **AMYCLAS** Phil.
vel Amyntas
4 B.C.: Heracleota (Ponti)

001 **Testimonia**, ed. F. Lasserre, *De Léodamas de Thasos à Philippe d'Oponte*. Naples: Bibliopolis, 1987: 89–90.
test. 1–2, 3b–6.
Cf. et <CLINIAS> Phil. (1277 002).
NQ: Test.

2649 **AMYNTAS** Epigr.
2 B.C.?

001 **Fragmenta** (*P. Oxy.* 4.662 = *P. Lit. Lond.* 61), ed. H. Lloyd-Jones and P. Parsons, *Supplementum Hellenisticum*. Berlin: De Gruyter, 1983: 16–17.
frr. 42–44.
Pap: 120: Epigr.

0712 **AMYNTAS** Hist.
4 B.C.

001 **Fragmenta**, FGrH #122: 2B:627–629.
Q: 617: Hist.

AMYNTAS Phil.
vel Amyclas
4 B.C.: Heracleota (Ponti)
Cf. AMYCLAS Phil. (0223).

1951 **AMYNTIANUS** Hist.
A.D. 2

001 **Testimonium**, FGrH #150: 2B:818.
NQ: 104: Test.

002 **Fragmenta**, FGrH #150: 2B:819.
Q: 93: Hist., Nat. Hist.

0770 **AMYTHAON** Med.
ante A.D. 1

x01 **Fragmenta ap. Galenum.**
K13.976, 983.
Cf. GALENUS Med. (0057 077).

x02 **Fragmentum ap. Oribasium.**
CMG, vol. 6.3, p. 83.
Cf. ORIBASIUS Med. (0722 004).

x03 **Fragmenta ap. Paulum.**
CMG, vol. **9.1**, p. 381; **9.2**, p. 355.
Cf. PAULUS Med. (0715 001).

0037 *ANACHARSIDIS EPISTULAE*
Incertum

001 **Epistulae**, ed. R. Hercher, *Epistolographi Graeci.* Paris: Didot, 1873 (repr. Amsterdam: Hakkert, 1965): 102–105.
Cod: 1,388: Epist.

ANACHARSIS
7–6 B.C.: Scythicus
Cf. <SEPTEM SAPIENTES> (1667 006).
Cf. ANACHARSIDIS EPISTULAE (0037).

0237 **ANACREON** Lyr.
6 B.C.: Teius

001 **Fragmenta**, ed. M.L. West, *Iambi et elegi Graeci*, vol. 2. Oxford: Clarendon Press, 1972: 30–34.
eleg. 1–5, iamb. 1–7.
Q: 115: Eleg., Iamb.

002 **Fragmenta**, ed. D.L. Page, *Poetae melici Graeci.* Oxford: Clarendon Press, 1962 (repr. 1967 (1st edn. corr.)): 172–227, 232, 234.
frr. 1–4, 6–9, 11–98, 100, 102–116, 118, 120–123, 125–126, 128–131, 133–136, 138–142, 156, 160.
Q, Pap: 1,526: Lyr.

003 **Fragmenta**, ed. D.L. Page, *Supplementum lyricis Graecis.* Oxford: Clarendon Press, 1974: 103.
frr. S313a–b, S314.
fr. S313a: Dup. partim 0237 002 (fr. 78).
Q: 11: Lyr.

004 **Epigrammata**, AG **6**.134–145, 346; **7**.160, 226, 263; **9**.715–716; **11**.47–48; **13**.4.
AG 13.4: Dup. partim 0237 002 (fr. 74).
AG 16.388: Cf. JULIANUS <Epigr.> (4050 001).
Q: 412: Epigr.

x01 **Epigramma exhortatorium et supplicatorium.**
App. Anth. 4.9: Cf. ANTHOLOGIAE GRAECAE APPENDIX (7052 004).
Dup. partim 0237 001 (eleg. 2).

0217 **ANACREON Junior** Eleg.
post 4 B.C.?

001 **Fragmentum**, ed. J.U. Powell, *Collectanea Alexandrina.* Oxford: Clarendon Press, 1925 (repr. 1970): 130.
Q: 8: Eleg.

4150 *ANACREONTEA*
A.D. 1?/6
Cf. et SOPHRONIUS Soph., Scr. Eccl. et Epigr. (4042 010).

001 **Anacreontea**, ed. M.L. West, *Carmina Anacreontea.* Leipzig: Teubner, 1984: 1–49.
Q, Cod: 3,917: Iamb.

ANAGRAPHE LINDIA
1 B.C.
Cf. TIMACHIDAS Hist. (1732).

0238 **ANANIUS** Iamb.
6 B.C.

001 **Fragmenta**, ed. M.L. West, *Iambi et elegi Graeci*, vol. 2. Oxford: Clarendon Press, 1972: 34–36.
frr. 1–5.
Q: 135: Iamb.

9005 **ANASTASIUS TRAULUS** Epigr.
Incertum

001 **Epigramma**, AG 15.28.
Q: 91: Epigr.

2577 **ANATOLIUS** Phil. et Math.
A.D. 3: Alexandrinus, Caesariensis

001 Περὶ δεκάδος καὶ τῶν ἐντὸς αὐτῆς ἀριθμῶν, ed. J.L. Heiberg, *Anatolius. Sur les dix premiers nombres.* Macon: Protat, 1901: 5–16.
Cod: Math.

002 **Fragmenta arithmetica** [Sp.], MPG 10: 232–236.
Q: Math.

x01 **De paschate** (fragmenta).
Eusebius, HE 7.32.14–19.
Cf. EUSEBIUS Scr. Eccl. et Theol. (2018 002).

4251 **ANAXAGORAS** Gramm.
3 B.C.: Alexandrinus

001 **Testimonium**, ed. F. Montanari, *I frammenti dei grammatici Agathokles, Hellanikos, Ptolemaios Epithetes* [Sammlung griechischer und lateinischer Grammatiker 7. Berlin: De Gruyter, 1988]: 117–118.
NQ: Test.

0713 **ANAXAGORAS** Phil.
6–5 B.C.: Clazomenius, Atheniensis

001 **Testimonia**, ed. H. Diels and W. Kranz, *Die Fragmente der Vorsokratiker*, vol. 2, 6th edn. Berlin: Weidmann, 1952 (repr. Dublin: 1966): 5–32.
test. 1–117.
NQ: 11,299: Test.

002 **Fragmenta**, ed. Diels and Kranz, *op. cit.*, 32–44.
frr. 1–24.
Q: 2,059: Phil.

2284 **ANAXANDRIDAS** Hist.
3–2 B.C.: Delphicus

001 **Testimonium**, FGrH #404: 3B:298.
NQ: 14: Test.

002 **Fragmenta**, FGrH #404: 3B:298–300.
Q: 472: Hist.

0405 **ANAXANDRIDES** Comic.
4 B.C.
001 **Fragmenta**, ed. T. Kock, *Comicorum Atticorum fragmenta*, vol. 2. Leipzig: Teubner, 1884: 135–153, 155–164.
frr. 1–73, 75–81 + tituli.
Q: 1,585: Comic.
002 **Fragmenta**, ed. A. Meineke, *Fragmenta comicorum Graecorum*, vol. 3. Berlin: Reimer, 1840 (repr. De Gruyter, 1970): 161–177, 179–185, 190–202.
Q: 1,556: Comic.
003 **Fragmentum**, ed. J. Demiańczuk, *Supplementum comicum*. Krakau: Nakładem Akademii, 1912 (repr. Hildesheim: Olms, 1967): 7.
fr. 1.
Q: 2: Comic.
004 **Fragmentum**, ed. C. Austin, *Comicorum Graecorum fragmenta in papyris reperta*. Berlin: De Gruyter, 1973: 2.
fr. 2.
Pap: 7: Comic.
x01 **Epigramma exhortatorium et supplicatorium**.
App. Anth. 4.1: Cf. ANTHOLOGIAE GRAECAE APPENDIX (7052 004).
Dup. partim 0405 002 (p. 169).

0714 **ANAXARCHUS** Phil.
4 B.C.: Abderita
001 **Testimonia**, ed. H. Diels and W. Kranz, *Die Fragmente der Vorsokratiker*, vol. 2, 6th edn. Berlin: Weidmann, 1952 (repr. Dublin: 1966): 235–239.
test. 1–16.
NQ: 1,693: Test.
002 **Fragmenta**, ed. Diels and Kranz, *op. cit.*, 239–240.
frr. 1–2.
Q: 150: Phil.

2210 **ANAXICRATES** Hist.
ante 1 B.C.?
001 **Fragmenta**, FGrH #307: 3B:13–14.
Q: 169: Hist.

0406 **ANAXILAS** Comic.
4 B.C.
001 **Fragmenta**, ed. T. Kock, *Comicorum Atticorum fragmenta*, vol. 2. Leipzig: Teubner, 1884: 264–275.
frr. 1–5, 7–13, 15–25, 27–44 + titulus.
Q: 717: Comic.
002 **Fragmenta**, ed. A. Meineke, *Fragmenta comicorum Graecorum*, vol. 3. Berlin: Reimer, 1840 (repr. De Gruyter, 1970): 341–348, 350–355.
Q: 676: Comic.

0725 **ANAXIMANDER** Phil.
7–6 B.C.: Milesius
001 **Testimonia**, ed. H. Diels and W. Kranz, *Die Fragmente der Vorsokratiker*, vol. 1, 6th edn.

Berlin: Weidmann, 1951 (repr. Dublin: 1966): 81–89.
test. 1–30.
NQ: 3,282: Test.
002 **Fragmenta**, ed. Diels and Kranz, *op. cit.*, 89–90.
frr. 1–6.
Q: 175: Phil.

1120 **ANAXIMANDER Junior** Hist.
4 B.C.: Milesius
001 **Testimonia**, FGrH #9: 1A:159–160.
NQ: 143: Test.
002 **Fragmenta**, FGrH #9: 1A:160–161.
Q: 282: Hist., Myth.

0547 **ANAXIMENES** Hist. et Rhet.
4 B.C.: Lampsacenus
001 **Ars rhetorica** *vulgo* **Rhetorica ad Alexandrum**, ed. M. Fuhrmann, *Anaximenis ars rhetorica*. Leipzig: Teubner, 1966: 1–97.
Cod: 19,010: Rhet.
002 **Testimonia**, FGrH #72: 2A:112–116.
NQ: 1,424: Test.
003 **Fragmenta**, FGrH #72: 2A:116–130.
Q: 4,673: Hist.
x01 **Fragmenta** (*P. Hibeh* 1.15).
FGrH #105, fr. 6.
Cf. ANONYMI HISTORICI (FGrH) (1139 004).

0617 **ANAXIMENES** Phil.
6 B.C.: Milesius
Cf. et ANAXIMENIS MILESII EPISTULAE (1121).
001 **Testimonia**, ed. H. Diels and W. Kranz, *Die Fragmente der Vorsokratiker*, vol. 1, 6th edn. Berlin: Weidmann, 1951 (repr. Dublin: 1966): 90–94.
test. 1–23.
NQ: 1,702: Test.
002 **Fragmenta**, ed. Diels and Kranz, *op. cit.*, 95–96.
frr. 1–3.
Q: 306: Phil.

1121 *ANAXIMENIS MILESII EPISTULAE*
Incertum
001 **Epistulae**, ed. R. Hercher, *Epistolographi Graeci*. Paris: Didot, 1873 (repr. Amsterdam: Hakkert, 1965): 106.
Q: 168: Epist.

0833 **ANAXION** Trag.
Incertum: Mytilenensis
001 **Titulus**, ed. B. Snell, *Tragicorum Graecorum fragmenta*, vol. 1. Göttingen: Vandenhoeck & Ruprecht, 1971: 319.
NQ: 2: Satyr.

0407 **ANAXIPPUS** Comic.
4–3 B.C.

001 **Fragmenta**, ed. T. Kock, *Comicorum Atticorum fragmenta*, vol. 3. Leipzig: Teubner,
1888: 296–301.
frr. 1–8.
Q: 433: Comic.

002 **Fragmenta**, ed. A. Meineke, *Fragmenta comicorum Graecorum*, vol. 4. Berlin: Reimer, 1841
(repr. De Gruyter, 1970): 459–460, 463–466.
Q: 436: Comic.

0027 **ANDOCIDES** Orat.
5–4 B.C.: Atheniensis

001 **De mysteriis**, ed. G. Dalmeyda, *Andocide. Discours*. Paris: Les Belles Lettres, 1930 (repr.
1966): 17–63.
Cod: 10,327: Orat.

002 **De reditu suo**, ed. Dalmeyda, *op. cit.*, 69–77.
Cod: 2,010: Orat.

003 **De pace**, ed. Dalmeyda, *op. cit.*, 87–100.
Cod: 2,772: Orat.

004 **In Alcibiadem** [Sp.], ed. Dalmeyda, *op. cit.*,
113–127.
Cod: 2,855: Orat.

005 **Fragmenta**, ed. Dalmeyda, *op. cit.*, 131–132.
frr. 1–2, 4, 7.
Q: 106: Orat.

2393 **ANDREAS** Hist.
3/2 B.C.?: Panormitanus

001 **Fragmentum**, FGrH #571: 3B:668.
Q: 135: Hist.

0677 **ANDREAS** Med.
3 B.C.: fort. Carystius

x01 **Fragmenta ap. Galenum**.
K13.343, 735, 982; 14.180.
Cf. GALENUS Med. (0057 076–078).

x02 **Fragmentum ap. Aëtium** (lib. 6).
CMG, vol. 8.2, p. 197.
Cf. AËTIUS Med. (0718 006).

x03 **Fragmentum ap. Aëtium** (lib. 9).
Zervos, *Athena* 23, p. 305.
Cf. AËTIUS Med. (0718 009).

x04 **Fragmentum ap. Soranum**.
CMG, vol. 4, p. 131.
Cf. SORANUS Med. (0565 001).

2715 **ANDREAS Libadinarius** Epigr.
Incertum

x01 **Epigramma exhortatorium et supplicatorium**.
App. Anth. 4.114: Cf. ANTHOLOGIAE GRAE-
CAE APPENDIX (7052 004).

2346 **ANDRISCUS** Hist.
4–3 B.C.?

001 **Fragmenta**, FGrH #500: 3B:473–475.
Q: 528: Hist.

2507 **ANDROCLES** Hist.
4 B.C.?

001 **Fragmentum**, FGrH #751: 3C:734.
Q: 70: Hist.

2412 **ANDROETAS** Hist.
4/3 B.C.?: Tenedius

001 **Fragmentum**, FGrH #599: 3B:731.
Q: 82: Hist.

0280 **ANDROMACHUS** Poet. Med.
A.D. 1

001 **Fragmentum**, ed. E. Heitsch, *Die griechischen
Dichterfragmente der römischen Kaiserzeit*, vol.
2. Göttingen: Vandenhoeck & Ruprecht, 1964:
8–15.
Q: 1,045: Eleg., Med.

0772 **ANDROMACHUS Minor** Med.
A.D. 1

x01 **Fragmenta ap. Galenum**.
K12.438; 13.441, 463; 14.42, 73, 106.
Cf. GALENUS Med. (0057 076–078).

x02 **Fragmentum ap. Oribasium**.
CMG, vol. 6.2.2, p. 217.
Cf. ORIBASIUS Med. (0722 003).

x03 **Fragmenta ap. Aëtium** (lib. 8).
CMG, vol. 8.2, pp. 449, 466, 494, 516, 530.
Cf. AËTIUS Med. (0718 008).

x04 **Fragmentum ap. Aëtium** (lib. 9).
Zervos, *Athena* 23, p. 292.
Cf. AËTIUS Med. (0718 009).

x05 **Fragmenta ap. Aëtium** (lib. 15).
Zervos, *Athena* 21, pp. 39, 55.
Cf. AËTIUS Med. (0718 015).

2536 **ANDRON** Geogr.
4 B.C.: Teius

001 **Testimonium**, FGrH #802: 3C:840.
NQ: 8: Test.

002 **Fragmenta**, FGrH #802: 3C:840–841.
Q: 383: Hist., Perieg.

1123 **ANDRON** Hist.
4 B.C.?: Halicarnassensis

001 **Fragmenta**, FGrH #10: 1A:161–165, *9 addenda.
fr. 20: *P. Oxy.* 5.841.
Q: 1,330: Hist., Myth.

2172 **ANDRON** Hist.
2–1 B.C.?: Alexandrinus

001 **Fragmentum**, FGrH #246: 2B:1129.
Q: 122: Hist., Chronogr.

0678 **ANDRON** Med.
1 B.C.

x01 **Fragmentum ap. Galenum**.
K12.830.
Cf. GALENUS Med. (0057 076).

x02 **Fragmenta ap. Oribasium**.
CMG, vol. **6.2.2**, p. 218; **6.3**, p. 495.
Cf. ORIBASIUS Med. (0722 003, 005).

1122 **ANDRON** Paradox.
post 3 B.C.
001 **Fragmentum**, FGrH #360: 3B:218.
Q: 37: Hist.

0111 **ANDRONICUS** Epigr.
3 B.C.?
001 **Epigramma**, AG 7.181.
Q: 26: Epigr.

0773 **ANDRONICUS** Med.
ante A.D. 1
x01 **Fragmentum ap. Galenum.**
K13.114.
Cf. GALENUS Med. (0057 076).

1124 **ANDRONICUS RHODIUS** Phil.
1 B.C.: Rhodius
001 **De passionibus** (lib. 1) [Sp.], ed. X. Kreuttner,
Andronici qui fertur libelli περὶ παθῶν, pt. 1
(De affectibus). Heidelberg: Winter, 1884: 11–
21.
Cod: 959: Phil.
002 **De passionibus** (lib. 2) [Sp.], ed. K. Schuch-
hardt, *Andronici Rhodii qui fertur libelli* περὶ
παθῶν, pt. 2 (De virtutibus et vitiis). Darmstadt: Winter, 1883: 19–31.
Cod: 2,239: Phil.
x01 **Ethicorum Nicomacheorum paraphrasis** (olim
sub auctore Andronico Rhodio).
Heylbut, pp. 1–233.
Cf. ANONYMI IN ARISTOTELIS ETHICA
NICOMACHEA (4033 003).

2867 **Pseudo-ANDRONICUS** Scriptor Catalogi Po-
etarum
Incertum
001 Περὶ τάξεως ποιητῶν (pseudepigraphum a
Constantino Palaeocappa confectum) (e cod.
Paris. 2929), ed. W.J.W. Koster, *Prolegomena
de comoedia. Scholia in Acharnenses, Equites,
Nubes, Scholia in Aristophanem* 1.1A. Gron-
ingen: Bouma, 1975: 115–116.
Cod: Gramm.

1778 **ANDROSTHENES** Perieg.
4 B.C.: Thasius
001 **Testimonia**, FGrH #711: 3C:592–593.
NQ: 126: Test.
002 **Fragmenta**, FGrH #711: 3C:593–596.
Q: 1,263: Hist., Perieg.

1125 **ANDROTION** Hist.
5–4 B.C.: Atheniensis
001 **Testimonia**, FGrH #324: 3B:60–62.
test. 4: *IG*² 2.61.
test. 5: *IG*² 2.216–217.
test. 7: *IG* 12.7, no. 5.
test. 12: *IG*² 2.212.
NQ: 945: Test.
002 **Fragmenta**, FGrH #324: 3B:63–77.
Q: 4,168: Hist.

2703 **ANNA COMNENA** Hist.
A.D. 11–12: Constantinopolitana
001 **Alexias**, ed. B. Leib, *Anna Comnène. Alexiade*,
3 vols. Paris: Les Belles Lettres, 1:1937 (repr.
1967); 2:1943 (repr. 1967); 3:1945: 1:3–168;
2:7–236; 3:7–242.
Vol. 1: lib. 1–4.
Vol. 2: lib. 5–10.
Vol. 3: lib. 11–15.
Cod: 151,330: Hist.
x01 **Epigrammata demonstrativa.**
App. Anth. 3.272, 416(?): Cf. ANTHOLOGIAE
GRAECAE APPENDIX (7052 003).

1127 ***ANONYMA DE MUSICA SCRIPTA BEL-
LERMANNIANA***
Varia
001 **Anonyma de musica scripta Bellermanniana**,
ed. D. Najock, *Anonyma de musica scripta
Bellermanniana*. Leipzig: Teubner, 1975: 1–33.
Cod: 4,863: Mus.

1836 ***ANONYMI AULODIA***
ante A.D. 1
001 **Anonymi aulodia** (*P. Oxy.* 15.1795), ed. D.
Young, *Theognis*. Leipzig: Teubner, 1971:
119–121.
Dup. partim LYRICA ADESPOTA (CA) (0230
001) (CA, pp. 199–200).
Dup. partim SCOLIA ALPHABETICA (0273
001) (GDRK, pp. 38–40).
Pap: 314: Hexametr., Lyr.

1128 ***ANONYMI COMMENTARIUS IN PLATO-
NIS THEAETETUM***
ante A.D. 2
001 **Commentarius in Platonis Theaetetum** (fort.
auctore Eudoro Alexandrino) (*P. Berol.* inv.
9782), ed. H. Diels and W. Schubart, *Anon-
ymer Kommentar zu Platons Theaetet (Papyrus
9782)*. Berlin: Weidmann, 1905: 3–51.
Pap: 12,330: Phil.

0227 ***ANONYMI CURETUM HYMNUS***
4 B.C.
001 **Hymnus Curetum**, ed. J.U. Powell, *Collectanea
Alexandrina*. Oxford: Clarendon Press, 1925
(repr. 1970): 160–161.
Epigr: 209: Lyr., Hymn.

1129 **ANONYMI DE BARBARISMO ET SOLOE-
CISMO** Gramm.
Varia
001 **De barbarismo et soloecismo**, ed. L.C. Valck-
enaer, *Ammonius*. Leipzig: Weigel, 1822: 176–
187.
Dup. partim COMMENTARIA IN DIONYSII
THRACIS ARTEM GRAMMATICAM (4175
005).
Cod: 1,402: Rhet.

002 **De barbarismo et soloecismo**, ed. A. Nauck, *Lexicon Vindobonense.* St. Petersburg: Eggers, 1867 (repr. Hildesheim: Olms, 1965): 290–293.
Cod: 333: Rhet.

2584 *ANONYMI DE COMOEDIA*
A.D. 5?

001 **De comoedia**, ed. G. Kaibel, *Comicorum Graecorum fragmenta*, vol. 1.1 [*Poetarum Graecorum fragmenta*, vol. 6.1. Berlin: Weidmann, 1899]: 6–10.
Cod

2972 *ANONYMI DE TERRAE MOTIBUS*
ante A.D. 11

001 **De terrae motibus**, ed. C. Wachsmuth, *Ioannis Laurentii Lydi liber de ostentis et calendaria Graeca omnia.* Leipzig: Teubner, 1897: 172–175.
Cod: 656: Nat. Hist.

4210 *ANONYMI DE VENTIS*
A.D. 11?

001 **De ventis** (fort. commentarium in librum Aristotelicum de mundo) (olim sub auctore Psello, nunc fort. auctore quodam Constantinopolitano), ed. P. Moraux, "Anecdota Graeca minora ii: Über die Winde," *Zeitschrift für Papyrologie und Epigraphik* 41 (1981) 54–55.
Cod: Nat. Hist.

0138 **ANONYMI EPIGRAMMATICI** (AG)
Varia

001 **Epigrammata**, AG 1.1–18, 21–22, 24–27, 29–32, 37–50, 52–89, 91, 93–98, 100, 102–108, 110–121; **3.**1–19; **5.**2, 11, 26, 50–51, 65, 82–84, 90–91, 95, 98–101, 135, 142, 168, 195b, 200–201, 205, 303–305, 310; **6.**6–8, 21, 23–24, 31, 37, 42, 44–45, 48–49, 51, 87, 169, 171–172, 177, 194, 280, 283–284, 291, 341–344; **7.**2b, 3, 5, 7, 10, 12, 23b, 28, 41–42, 44, 46–48, 53, 56, 61–64, 82–84, 86, 90, 93–94, 119, 125, 128, 131–132, 134–135, 137, 139, 142–144, 148, 151–152, 154–155, 157–158, 169, 179, 221, 224–225, 228, 257, 279, 298, 306, 309–311, 313, 319, 321–325, 327–340, 342–343, 346–347, 350, 352, 356–361, 363, 416, 431, 449, 474, 482–483, 494, 507b, 543–544, 546, 558, 564, 570, 615–619, 621, 626, 667, 671–673, 676, 678, 689–691, 695, 699, 704, 714, 717, 723, 734, 737; **9.**15, 20–21, 31–32, 38, 47–49, 61, 65, 67–68, 74, 105, 108, 115, 115b, 116, 121–122, 124–127, 130–135, 137–138, 141–142, 145–146, 148, 157–160, 162–164, 177, 184–185, 187–191, 194–195, 198–199, 207–213, 252, 317, 325, 328, 357–358, 362, 366, 371–376, 380–384, 386, 388/389, 392, 399, 431, 436, 448–449, 451–480, 483, 492–495, 498–501, 504–505, 510–512, 514–515, 520–525, 527, 529–536, 538–540, 547,
553, 571, 574, 580–585, 589–596, 601, 606–613, 615–618, 621–622, 632, 634–640, 646–647, 655–656, 660, 666, 670–676, 678–680, 682–699, 701–705, 710, 713–714, 725–727, 729, 731, 733, 735–737, 741, 755, 759–761, 779–781, 783–786, 788–789, 799–807, 810–822, 825–826; **10.**3, 9, 12, 30, 33, 39, 43, 106, 108–109, 111–112, 114–116, 118–119, 124b–126; **11.**3, 8, 51–53, 56, 86, 108–109, 125–126, 145, 149, 151, 166, 193, 202–203, 220, 222, 244, 250, 260–262, 267–273, 282, 297–298, 316, 334–339, 342–345, 356, 358–360, 394, 411, 416–417, 420, 425–426, 442; **12.**17, 19, 39–40, 55, 61–62, 66–67, 69, 79, 87–90, 96, 99–100, 103–104, 107, 111–112, 115–116, 123–124, 130, 136, 140, 143, 145, 151–152, 155–156, 160; **13.**13, 15–17; **14.**2–62, 64–96, 100, 102–146, 149–150; **15.**1–8, 10–11, 18–19, 23, 39b, 41–50; **16.**4, 6, 9, 12, 15–19, 21–22, 27–29, 35, 42–48, 53–54, 56, 58, 62–67, 69–74, 78, 83–86, 90–92, 96–102, 105–106, 112, 121–129, 135, 138, 140, 142, 145–146, 151, 156, 159, 162, 168–169, 174–175, 183, 185, 187, 189, 192, 202, 209, 217, 223–224, 227, 229, 246, 249–260, 262–266, 268–269, 271, 274, 279–281, 289, 292–295, 297–304, 309, 311–313, 318–322, 324, 326, 328–330, 335–356, 358–378, 380–387, 387b–387c.
AG 9.137: Cf. et HADRIANUS Imperator (0195 001).
AG 9.388/389: Cf. et TRAJANUS Imperator (1739 001).
Q: 30,584: Epigr.

7056 **ANONYMI EPIGRAMMATICI** (App. Anth.)
Varia

x01 **Epigrammata dedicatoria.**
App. Anth. 1.4–20, 22, 26–83, 85–91, 93–113, 118, 120–128, 130–133, 138–152, 154–158, 162–164, 166, 183, 197–198, 200–240, 243–246, 249–256, 258–262, 265–298, 300–339, 341–372: Cf. ANTHOLOGIAE GRAECAE APPENDIX (7052 001).

x02 **Epigrammata sepulcralia.**
App. Anth. 2.1–3, 7–9, 11–16, 17–21, 27, 29, 31–45, 47–53, 121–123, 125–130, 132–133, 135–153, 155, 157–338, 340–379, 384–490, 492–495, 499–612, 614–624, 626–630, 632–664, 666–746, 748–770: Cf. ANTHOLOGIAE GRAECAE APPENDIX (7052 002).

x03 **Epigrammata demonstrativa.**
App. Anth. 3.2–4, 15–16, 23–26, 30–32, 34, 36–42, 44–46, 49, 53–55, 57–58, 61, 69–70, 73–76, 83–84, 91–94, 100–103, 105, 107–110, 114–119, 121–122, 126–127, 130–131, 133–144, 148–152, 162–165, 167–176, 178, 180–213, 215–240, 242–253, 268–271, 277–283, 286–307, 311–410, 412–415, 417, 419–421: Cf. ANTHOLOGIAE GRAECAE APPENDIX (7052 003).

x04 **Epigrammata exhortatoria et supplicatoria.**
App. Anth. 4.10–11, 18–24, 27–29, 31–32, 37, 41–42, 44, 48–51, 54–73, 76, 78–88, 90–105, 108–110, 112–113, 121–140, 142–143: Cf. ANTHOLOGIAE GRAECAE APPENDIX (7052 004).

x05 **Epigrammata irrisoria.**
App. Anth. 5.7–9, 11–12, 22–24, 26–28, 31–33, 43–47, 50–57, 59–77: Cf. ANTHOLOGIAE GRAECAE APPENDIX (7052 005).

x06 **Oracula.**
App. Anth. 6.238–276, 299–301: Cf. ANTHOLOGIAE GRAECAE APPENDIX (7052 006).

x07 **Aenigmata.**
App. Anth. 7.16–18, 21, 27–33, 46, 81: Cf. ANTHOLOGIAE GRAECAE APPENDIX (7052 007).

3156 ***ANONYMI EXEGESIS IN HESIODI THEOGONIAM***
ante A.D. 15

001 **Exegesis in Hesiodi theogoniam,** ed. H. Flach, *Glossen und Scholien zur hesiodischen Theogonie.* Leipzig: Teubner, 1876 (repr. Osnabrück: Biblio Verlag, 1970): 369–413.
Cod: 11,448: Schol.

2029 ***ANONYMI GEOGRAPHIA IN SPHAERA INTELLIGENDA***
post A.D. 2

001 **Anonymi summaria ratio geographiae in sphaera intelligendae,** ed. K. Müller, *Geographi Graeci minores,* vol. 2. Paris: Didot, 1861 (repr. Hildesheim: Olms, 1965): 488–493.
Cod: 1,979: Geogr.

0092 ***ANONYMI GEOGRAPHIAE EXPOSITIO COMPENDIARIA***
Incertum

001 **Geographiae expositio compendiaria,** ed. K. Müller, *Geographi Graeci minores,* vol. 2. Paris: Didot, 1861 (repr. Hildesheim: Olms, 1965): 494–509.
Cod: 4,413: Geogr.

0072 **ANONYMI GRAMMATICI**
Varia

001 **Supplementa artis Dionysianae vetusta,** ed. G. Uhlig, *Grammatici Graeci,* vol. 1.1. Leipzig: Teubner, 1883 (repr. Hildesheim: Olms, 1965): 105–132.
De prosodiis: pp. 105–114.
Definitio artis: pp. 115–117.
De pedibus et de metro heroico: pp. 117–124.
Tabula flexionum verbi τύπτω: pp. 125–132.
Cf. et DIONYSIUS THRAX Gramm. (0063 001).
Cod: 2,820: Gramm.

003 **Fragmentum grammaticum** (*P. Yale* 1.25 [inv. 446]) (fort. epitome operis Comani), ed. A.

Wouters, *The grammatical papyri from Graeco-Roman Egypt. Contributions to the study of the 'ars grammatica' in antiquity.* Brussels: Paleis der Academiën, 1979: 49–52.
Pap: 342: Gramm.

004 **Fragmentum grammaticum** (*P. Lit. Lond.* 182 = *P. Lond.* 126) (fort. auctore Tryphone Alexandrino), ed. Wouters, *op. cit.,* 67–73.
Pap: 986: Gramm.

005 **Fragmentum grammaticum** (*P. Heid. Siegmann* 197 [inv. 1893]), ed. Wouters, *op. cit.,* 127–129.
Pap: 285: Gramm.

006 **Fragmentum grammaticum** (*PSI* sine numero [inv. 505]), ed. Wouters, *op. cit.,* 136–137.
Pap: 213: Gramm.

007 **Fragmentum grammaticum** (*P. Brooklyn* inv. 47.218.36), ed. Wouters, *op. cit.,* 139–140.
Pap: 87: Gramm.

008 **Fragmentum grammaticum** (*P. Oslo* 2.13), ed. Wouters, *op. cit.,* 143–147.
Pap: 438: Gramm.

009 **Fragmentum grammaticum** (*P. Iand.* 83a [inv. 664]), ed. Wouters, *op. cit.,* 158–159.
Pap: 136: Gramm.

010 **Fragmentum grammaticum** (*P. Harr.* 59 [inv. 172b + 182h]), ed. Wouters, *op. cit.,* 166–169.
Pap: 228: Gramm.

011 **Fragmentum grammaticum** (*P. Heid. Siegmann* 198 [inv. 201a]), ed. Wouters, *op. cit.,* 176–177.
Pap: 123: Gramm.

012 **Fragmentum grammaticum** (*P. Iand.* 5.83 [inv. 555]), ed. Wouters, *op. cit.,* 185.
Pap: 89: Gramm.

013 **Fragmentum grammaticum** (*P. Amh.* 2.21), ed. Wouters, *op. cit.,* 190–191.
Pap: 321: Gramm.

014 **Fragmentum grammaticum** (*P. Ant.* 2.68), ed. Wouters, *op. cit.,* 199–201.
Pap: 163: Gramm.

015 **Fragmentum grammaticum** (*PSI* 7.761), ed. Wouters, *op. cit.,* 205–206.
Pap: 158: Gramm.

016 **Compendium catholicae Herodiani** (*P. Ant.* 2.67), ed. Wouters, *op. cit.,* 217–218.
Pap: 207: Gramm.

017 **Commentarium in anonymi opus** περὶ κλίσεως ὀνομάτων (*P. Oxy.* 15.1801v), ed. Wouters, *op. cit.,* 226–228.
Pap: 177: Gramm.

018 **Compendium Herodiani operis** περὶ κλίσεως ὀνομάτων (*P. Flor.* inv. 3005), ed. Wouters, *op. cit.,* 232–233.
Pap: 128: Gramm.

019 **De participiis** (*P. Rain.* 1.19 [inv. 29772]), ed. Wouters, *op. cit.,* 238–239.
Pap: 76: Gramm.

020 **Fragmentum grammaticum** (*PSI* 7.849), ed. Wouters, *op. cit.,* 255–258.
Pap: 385: Gramm.

021 **Fragmentum grammaticum** (*P. Oxy.* 3.469), ed. Wouters, *op. cit.*, 264–265.
Pap: 116: Gramm.

022 **Fragmentum grammaticum** (*P. Iand.* 1.5 [inv. 2]), ed. Wouters, *op. cit.*, 269–270.
Pap: 180: Gramm.

023 Περὶ Αἰολίδος (?) (fragmentum) (*P. Bouriant* 8 [*P. Sorbonne* inv. 833]), ed. Wouters, *op. cit.*, 276–282.
Pap: 566: Gramm.

x01 Περὶ δυσκλίτων ῥημάτων (*P. Rain.* 3.33A).
Wouters, pp. 243–246.
Cf. HERACLIDES Gramm. (1408 002).

x02 Περὶ προσῳδιῶν.
Hilgard, pp. 150–156.
Cf. COMMENTARIA IN DIONYSII THRACIS ARTEM GRAMMATICAM (4175 004).

1139 **ANONYMI HISTORICI** (FGrH)
Varia

001 **Enchiridion** (*P. Ryl.* 22), FGrH #18: 1A:182–183.
fr. 1.
Pap: 115: Hist., Myth.

002 **Heraclis historia** (*Tabula Albana*) (*IG* 14.1293), FGrH #40: 1A:261–263.
fr. 1.
Epigr: 717: Hist., Myth.

003 **Anonymi ex historiis Polybii**, FGrH #83: 2A:189–191.
test. 1, frr. 1–4.
Q: 711: Hist.

004 **Fragmenta historica**, FGrH #105: 2A:504–507.
frr. 1–8.
fr. 1: *P. Ryl.* 18.
fr. 2: Sicyonis historia (fort. auctore Aristotele vel Ephoro vel Menaechmo), *P. Oxy.* 11.1365.
fr. 3: Epitome historiae Herodoti (fort. auctore Theopompo Chio), *P. Oxy.* 6.857.
fr. 4: (fort. auctore Theopompo Chio), *P. Rain.*
fr. 5: *P. Berol.* inv. 13361.
fr. 6: (fort. auctore Theopompo Chio vel Anaximene Lampsaceno), *P. Hibeh* 1.15.
fr. 7: *P. Oxy.* 6.867.
fr. 8: *P. Oxy.* 7.1014.
Pap: 1,169: Hist.

005 **Alexandri historia** (*P. Oxy.* 15.1798), FGrH #148: 2B:816–818.
frr. 1–6, 44–45.
Cf. et 1139 039–040.
Pap: 480: Hist.

006 **Alexandri historia** (e cod. Sabbaitico 29), FGrH #151: 2B:819–822.
fr. 1.
Cod: 1,109: Hist.

007 **De historia Alexandri**, FGrH #153: 2B:823–828.
frr. 1–15.
fr. 1: *P. Oxy.* 1.13.
fr. 7: *P. Freib.* 7–8.
fr. 8: *P. Oxy.* 2.216.
fr. 9: *P. Berol.* inv. 13044.

fr. 15: Dup. partim ARRIANUS Epic. (2650 001) (fr. 208).
Q, Pap: 2,145: Hist., Epist., Epic.

008 **De historia diadochorum** (epitome Heidelbergensis), FGrH #155: 2B:835–837.
frr. 1–4.
Cod: 691: Hist.

009 **De Pyrrho** (testimonium), FGrH #159: 2B:884.
test. 1.
NQ: 41: Test.

010 **Belli Syrii tertii annales** (*P. Petrie* 2.45; 3.144), FGrH #160: 2B:885–887.
fr. 1.
Pap: 635: Hist.

011 **De Hannibale**, FGrH #180: 2B:907–909.
frr. 1–5.
Q: 957: Hist.

012 **De Marco Aurelio Antonino** (testimonium), FGrH #202: 2B:934.
test. 1.
NQ: 43: Test.

013 **De bello Parthico**, FGrH #203: 2B:934–938.
frr. 1–9.
Q: 1,458: Hist.

014 **Anonymus Corinthius**, FGrH #204: 2B:938–939.
frr. 1–4.
Q: 228: Hist.

015 **Anonymus Milesius**, FGrH #205: 2B:939.
fr. 1.
Q: 125: Hist.

016 **Anonymus philosophus**, FGrH #206: 2B:940.
fr. 1.
Q: 131: Hist.

017 **Chronicon Romanum** (*IG* 14.1297), FGrH #252: 2B:1151–1152.
frr. A-B.
Epigr: 290: Hist., Chronogr.

018 **Chronicon Oxyrhynchi** (*P. Oxy.* 1.12), FGrH #255: 2B:1153–1156.
Pap: 826: Hist., Chronogr.

019 **Chronicon Olympicum** (fort. auctore Phlegonte), FGrH #257a: 2B:1194–1196.
frr. 1–11: *P. Oxy.* 17.2082.
Cf. et Publius Aelius PHLEGON Paradox. (0585 002–003).
Pap: 518: Hist., Chronogr.

020 **Chronicon Archontum** (*P. Oxy.* 13.1613), FGrH #258: 2B:1197.
fr. 1.
Pap: 51: Hist., Chronogr.

021 Εὐμολπιδῶν πάτρια (testimonium), FGrH #355: 3B:217.
test. 1.
NQ: 15: Test.

022 Εὐπατριδῶν πάτρια (fragmentum), FGrH #356: 3B:217.
fr. 1.
Q: 107: Hist.

023 **De sacris Atheniensibus**, FGrH #368: 3B:229–230.

frr. 1–8.
Q: 419: Hist.

024 **Anonymus periegeta** (*P. Hawara* 80/81), FGrH #369: 3B:230–231.
frr. 1–2.
fr. 1: *P. Hawara* 81.
fr. 2: *P. Hawara* 80.
Pap: 265: Hist., Perieg.

025 **De finibus urbis**, FGrH #375: 3B:241.
fr. 1.
Q: 58: Hist., Geogr.

026 **Victores Olympici** (fort. auctore Phlegonte vel Eratosthene) (*P. Oxy.* 2.222), FGrH #415: 3B:307–309.
frr. 1–2.
Cf. et 1139 041.
Pap: 395: Hist.

027 **Chronicon Pergamenum**, FGrH #506: 3B:483–484.
fr. 1: *O. Gr. Inscr. Sel.* 264.
Epigr: 157: Hist., Chronogr.

028 **Anagraphe Sicyonia**, FGrH #550: 3B:536.
frr. 1–2.
Q: 135: Hist.

029 **Anonymus de conditu Hermopolis**, FGrH #637: 3C:184–185.
fr. 1: *P. Strassburg* 481.
Dup. EPICA ADESPOTA (GDRK) (1816 006).
Pap: 524: Hist., Hexametr., Encom.

030 **Apophthegmata Romana**, FGrH #839: 3C: 905–908.
fr. 1.
Dup. Pseudo-CAECILIUS Rhet. (1234 001).
Cod: 866: Hist., Gnom.

031 **De agrimensore Syriae** (fort. auctore Xenophonte quodam), FGrH #849: 3C:935.
fr. 1.
Q: 62: Hist.

032 **Anonymi de imperatore Aureliano**, FGrH #213–215: 2B:944.
Q: 289: Hist.

033 **Anonymus exegeta**, FGrH #352: 3B:214–215.
fr. 1.
Q: 98: Hist.

034 **De Lesbo**, FGrH #479: 3B:443–444.
frr. 1–2.
Q: 364: Hist.

035 **De Nilo**, FGrH #647: 3C:199–203.
frr. 1–3.
Q, Cod: 999: Hist., Nat. Hist.

036 **Scriptores de Athenis**, FGrH #329: 3B:161–162.
frr. 1–8.
Q: 585: Hist.

037 **De Theramene** (*P. Mich.* 5982), ed. H.J. Mette, "Die 'Kleinen' griechischen Historiker heute," *Lustrum* 21 (1978) 11.
FGrH #64 bis.
Pap: 254: Hist.

038 **Philippica** (*P. Ryl.* 3.490), ed. Mette, *op. cit.*, 17–18.

FGrH #115 bis, fr. 1.
Pap: 265: Hist.

039 **Alexandri historia** (*P. Oxy.* 17.2081), ed. Mette, *op. cit.*, 19.
FGrH #148, fr. 55.
Cf. et 1139 005, 040.
Pap: 30: Hist.

040 **Alexandri historia** (*P. Hamb.* 652), ed. Mette, *op. cit.*, 19–20.
FGrH #148 bis.
Cf. et 1139 005, 039.
Pap: 103: Hist.

041 **Victores olympici** (*P. Oxy.* 23.2381), ed. Mette, *op. cit.*, 29.
FGrH #415, fr. 3.
Cf. et 1139 026.
Pap: 39: Hist.

x01 **Epistula cuidam Macedoniae regi** (fort. auctore Hieronymo Cardiano) (*P. Oxy.* 1.13).
FGrH #153, fr. 1.
Cf. ANONYMI HISTORICI (FGrH) (1139 007).

x02 **Dialogus de Alexandri deificatione** (*P. Freib.* 7–8).
FGrH #153, fr. 7.
Cf. ANONYMI HISTORICI (FGrH) (1139 007).

x03 **Anonymus orator** (*P. Oxy.* 2.216).
FGrH #153, fr. 8.
Cf. ANONYMI HISTORICI (FGrH) (1139 007).

x04 **Alexandri Magni historia** (*P. Berol. inv.* 13044).
FGrH #153, fr. 9.
Cf. ANONYMI HISTORICI (FGrH) (1139 007).

0228 *ANONYMI HYMNUS IN DACTYLOS IDAEOS*
ante 4 B.C.

001 **Hymnus in Dactylos Idaeos** (*IG* 12.9.259), ed. J.U. Powell, *Collectanea Alexandrina*. Oxford: Clarendon Press, 1925 (repr. 1970): 171–172.
Epigr: 124: Hymn.

5045 **ANONYMI IN APHTHONIUM**
Varia

001 **Prolegomena in progymnasmata**, ed. H. Rabe, *Prolegomenon sylloge* [*Rhetores Graeci* 14. Leipzig: Teubner, 1931]: 73–80.
Cod: Rhet., Comm.

002 **Prolegomena in progymnasmata** (olim sub auctore Joanne Doxapatre), ed. Rabe, *op. cit.*, 158–170.
Cod: Rhet., Comm.

003 **Commentarium in progymnasmata**, ed. C. Walz, *Rhetores Graeci*, vol. 2. Stuttgart: Cotta, 1835 (repr. Osnabrück: Zeller, 1968): 1–68.
pp. 1–4: Dup. partim RHETORICA ANONYMA (0598 006).
Cod: Rhet., Comm.

004 **Commentarium in progymnasmata**, ed. Walz, *op. cit.*, 565–684.
pp. 682–684: Dup. partim RHETORICA ANONYMA (0598 006).
Cod: Rhet., Comm.

**4191 ANONYMI IN ARISTOTELIS ANALYT-
ICA POSTERIORA**
Varia

001 **Commentarium in analytica posteriora** (fragmentum) (ex editione Aldina), ed. C.A. Brandis, *Aristotelis opera*, vol. 4. Berlin: Reimer,
1836 (repr. De Gruyter, 1961): 203b.
Cod: Phil., Comm.

002 **Commentarium in analytica posteriora** (excerpta e cod. Paris. 1917), ed. Brandis, *op. cit.*,
206b, 216b, 220b nota, 240a–b, 241a.
p. 241a, vv. 1–14: fragmentum est Theodori
Ptochoprodromi.
Cod: Phil., Comm.

**4190 ANONYMI IN ARISTOTELIS ANALYT-
ICA PRIORA**
Varia

001 **Commentarium in analytica priora** (excerpta e
cod. Paris. gr. 1917), ed. C.A. Brandis, *Aristotelis opera*, vol. 4. Berlin: Reimer, 1836 (repr.
De Gruyter, 1961): 143b, 145a, 146a, 150a,
163b, 165b–166a, 188a–b, 189a, 194b, 195a,
195b.
Cod: Phil., Comm.

002 **Commentarium in analytica priora** (excerptum
e cod. Paris. gr. 1918), ed. Brandis, *op. cit.*,
141a.
Cod: Phil., Comm.

003 **Commentarium in analytica priora** (excerpta e
cod. Paris. gr. 1919), ed. Brandis, *op. cit.*, 168a,
171a–b, 175b.
Cod: Phil., Comm.

004 **Commentarium in analytica priora** (excerpta e
cod. Paris. gr. 2061), ed. Brandis, *op. cit.*,
139a–141a, 144a, 146a, 147b–148a, 148b,
151a–b, 154b, 155b, 156b–157b.
Cod: Phil., Comm.

005 **Commentarium in analytica priora** (excerpta e
codd. Paris. gr. 1873 + 1917; Oxon. Bodl. 155
+ Oxon. Nov. Colleg. 230), ed. Brandis, *op.
cit.*, 187a–188a, 189b–190a, 190b, 191a, 191b,
192b–193a, 193b, 194a, 194b, 195b.
Cod: Phil., Comm.

**4026 ANONYMI IN ARISTOTELIS ARTEM
RHETORICAM**
Varia

001 **In Aristotelis artem rhetoricam commentarium**, ed. H. Rabe, *Anonymi et Stephani in
artem rhetoricam commentaria* [*Commentaria
in Aristotelem Graeca* 21.2. Berlin: Reimer,
1896]: 1–262.
Cod: 99,393: Rhet., Comm.

002 **Fragmentum commentarii in Aristotelis rhetorica**, ed. Rabe, *op. cit.*, 323–329.
Cod: 2,098: Rhet., Comm.

003 **Fragmentum paraphrasis in Aristotelis rhetor-
ica**, ed. Rabe, *op. cit.*, 330–334.
= Anonymus περὶ ἐρωτήσεως καὶ ἀποκρίσεως.
Cod: 972: Rhet., Comm.

**4027 ANONYMI IN ARISTOTELIS CATEGOR-
IAS**
Varia

001 **Paraphrasis categoriarum**, ed. M. Hayduck,
Anonymi in Aristotelis categorias paraphrasis
[*Commentaria in Aristotelem Graeca* 23.2. Ber-
lin: Reimer, 1883]: 1–72.
Cod: 32,491: Phil., Comm.

002 **In categorias prolegomena** (e cod. Vat. Urbin.
gr. 35), ed. C.A. Brandis, *Aristotelis opera*, vol.
4. Berlin: Reimer, 1836 (repr. De Gruyter,
1961): 30a–34b.
Cod: Phil., Comm.

003 **Additamenta ad Ammonium in categorias** (e
cod. Paris. 2051) (olim sub auctore Joanne
Philopono), ed. Brandis, *op. cit.*, 46a, 51b.
Cod: Phil., Comm.

004 **Additamenta ad Philoponum in categorias** (e
cod. Marc. 217) (olim sub auctore Ammonio,
nunc fort. auctore Joanne Philopono), ed. A.
Busse, *Philoponi (olim Ammonii) in Aristotelis
categorias commentarium* [*Commentaria in
Aristotelem Graeca* 13.1. Berlin: Reimer, 1898]:
140 (in apparatu ad vv. 6 et 8).
Cod: Phil., Comm.

**4033 ANONYMI IN ARISTOTELIS ETHICA NI-
COMACHEA**
Varia

001 **In ethica Nicomachea ii–v commentaria**, ed. G.
Heylbut, *Eustratii et Michaelis et anonyma in
ethica Nicomachea commentaria* [*Commentaria
in Aristotelem Graeca* 20. Berlin: Reimer,
1892]: 122–255.
Cod: 50,249: Phil., Comm.

002 **In ethica Nicomachea vii commentaria**, ed.
Heylbut, *CAG* 20, 407–460.
Cod: 24,041: Phil., Comm.

003 **In ethica Nicomachea paraphrasis** (pseudepigraphum olim a Constantino Palaeocappa confectum et olim sub auctore Heliodoro Prusensi
vel Andronico Rhodio vel Olympiodoro), ed.
G. Heylbut, *Heliodori in ethica Nicomachea
paraphrasis* [*Commentaria in Aristotelem
Graeca* 19.2. Berlin: Reimer, 1889]: 1–233.
Cod: 100,839: Phil., Comm.

**9004 *ANONYMI IN ARISTOTELIS LIBRUM
ALTERUM ANALYTICORUM POSTERIO-
RUM COMMENTARIUM***
Incertum

001 **Anonymi in analyticorum posteriorum librum
alterum commentarium**, ed. M. Wallies, *Ioannis Philoponi in Aristotelis analytica posteriora commentaria cum anonymo in librum ii*
[*Commentaria in Aristotelem Graeca* 13.3. Berlin: Reimer, 1909]: 547–603.
Cod: 18,396: Phil., Comm.

**4195 ANONYMI IN ARISTOTELIS LIBRUM DE
CAELO**
Varia

001 **Commentarium in librum de caelo** (excerptum e cod. Vat. gr. 499) (olim sub auctore Damascio), ed. C.A. Brandis, *Aristotelis opera*, vol. 4. Berlin: Reimer, 1836 (repr. De Gruyter, 1961): 454a–455a.
Cod: Phil., Comm.

002 **Commentarium in librum de caelo** (fragmentum e codd. Marc. gr. 257 + 263) (olim sub auctore Joanne Philopono), ed. Brandis, *op. cit.*, 467b–468a.
Cod: Phil., Comm.

003 **Commentarium in librum de caelo** (excerpta e cod. Paris. gr. 1853), ed. Brandis, *op. cit.*, 487b, 489a, 491a, 491b, 492b, 495a, 506b, 509a, 518b.
Cod: Phil., Comm.

004 **Commentarium in librum de caelo** (excerpta e cod. Paris. Coislin. 166), ed. Brandis, *op. cit.*, 469b, 470a, 486b, 487a, 487b, 489a, 489b, 491a, 491b, 492a, 493a, 495a, 495b, 497a, 497b, 498a, 504b–505a, 505b, 506b, 507b, 508a, 509a, 511a, 514b, 515b, 516a, 516b, 517b, 518b.
Cod: Phil., Comm.

4165 **ANONYMI IN ARISTOTELIS LIBRUM DE INTERPRETATIONE**
Varia

001 **Commentarium in librum de interpretatione** (e cod. Paris. gr. 2064) (fort. auctore quodam Alexandrino vel Constantinopolitano), ed. L. Tarán, *Anonymous commentary on Aristotle's de interpretatione* [*Beiträge zur klassischen Philologie* 95. Meisenheim am Glan: Hain, 1978]: 1–120.
Cod: 19,773: Comm., Phil.

002 **Commentarium in librum de interpretatione** (= Anonymus Coislinianus) (fragmenta e cod. Coislin. 160), ed. C.A. Brandis, *Aristotelis opera*, vol. 4. Berlin: Reimer, 1836 (repr. De Gruyter, 1961): 93a–94b, 99b nota, 100b nota, 116b nota, 128a nota, 129b nota.
Cod: Comm., Phil.

4032 *ANONYMI IN ARISTOTELIS LIBRUM PRIMUM ANALYTICORUM POSTERIORUM COMMENTARIUM*
A.D. 12?

001 **In primum librum analyticorum posteriorum commentarium**, ed. M. Hayduck, *Eustratii in analyticorum posteriorum librum secundum commentarium* [*Commentaria in Aristotelem Graeca* 21.1. Berlin: Reimer, 1907]: vii–xviii.
Cod: 5,106: Phil., Comm.

4196 **ANONYMI IN ARISTOTELIS METAPHYSICA**
Varia

001 **Commentarium in metaphysica** (excerpta e cod. Paris. gr. 1853), ed. C.A. Brandis, *Aristotelis opera*, vol. 4. Berlin: Reimer, 1836 (repr. De Gruyter, 1961): 526b, 527a, 529b, 530b,

532b, 533a, 533b, 534a, 535b, 537a, 538a, 539a, 540a, 541b–542a, 543b, 544a, 545b, 547b, 549a, 555a nota, 555b nota, 556b, 558a, 578a nota, 589a–b, 590a, 591a–b, 592b, 595a–b, 596b, 602b, 603b, 671a, 673a, 676b, 693b, 701b, 703a, 709b, 712b, 719a, 721b, 724a, 725b, 729b, 730b, 737b, 738a, 739a, 739b, 740a, 740b, 743a, 744a, 747a, 752a, 756a, 758a, 759b, 760a, 764a, 764b, 765a, 766a, 771b, 772b, 774a, 774b, 775a, 776a, 777a, 778a, 778b, 780a, 783a, 783b, 788a, 790a, 798a, 810a, 810b, 811b, 812a, 817a, 817b, 820a.
Cod: Phil., Comm.

002 **Commentarium in metaphysica** (excerpta e cod. Urb. gr. 49), ed. Brandis, *op. cit.*, 520a–b, 522b nota, 524a nota, 532a nota, 533a nota, 533b nota, 534b nota, 539a–b nota, 540a nota, 544b nota, 545a nota, 546a nota.
Cod: Phil., Comm.

003 **Scholion in metaphysica** (excerptum e cod. Coislin. 161 in margine), ed. Brandis, *op. cit.*, 691a.
Cod: Schol.

4194 **ANONYMI IN ARISTOTELIS PHYSICA**
Varia

001 **Commentarium in physica** (excerptum e cod. Vat. gr. 1025), ed. C.A. Brandis, *Aristotelis opera*, vol. 4. Berlin: Reimer, 1836 (repr. De Gruyter, 1961): 322a.
Cod: Phil., Comm.

002 **Commentarium in physica** (excerpta e cod. Vat. gr. 1028), ed. Brandis, *op. cit.*, 322a–b, 329b, 334a–b, 335a, 337b, 338a, 338b, 342b, 343b, 345a–b, 347b, 348a.
Cod: Phil., Comm.

003 **Commentarium in physica** (excerptum e cod. Vat. gr. 1730), ed. Brandis, *op. cit.*, 322b–324a.
Cod: Phil., Comm.

004 **Scholia in physica** (excerpta e cod. Vat. gr. 237), ed. Brandis, *op. cit.*, 369b, 371a, 374b, 378b, 379a, 381a, 381b, 383b, 387a, 393a, 396b–397a, 398b, 400b, 401a, 401b, 404a, 405a, 406b, 408b, 409a, 415b.
Cod: Schol.

006 **Scholion in physica** (excerptum e cod. Paris. gr. 1853 in margine), ed. Brandis, *op. cit.*, 355b.
Cod: Schol.

007 **Commentarium in physica** (excerpta e cod. Paris. gr. 1947), ed. Brandis, *op. cit.*, 334a, 335a, 335b, 339a, 340a, 346a, 349b, 350a, 351b, 355b, 360a, 362a–b, 363b–364a, 366b, 367b.
Cod: Phil., Comm.

4193 **ANONYMI IN ARISTOTELIS SOPHISTICOS ELENCHOS**
Varia

001 **Scholion in sophisticos elenchos** (excerptum e cod. Paris. 1946 in margine), ed. C.A. Brandis,

Aristotelis opera, vol. 4. Berlin: Reimer, 1836 (repr. De Gruyter, 1961): 305a.
Cod: Schol.

007 **Scholia in sophisticos elenchos** (excerpta e codd. Angelicano gr. 42, Paris. gr. 1971) (= commentarium 5), ed. S. Ebbesen, *Commentators and commentaries on Aristotle's sophistici elenchi. A study of post-Aristotelian ancient and medieval writings on fallacies*, vol. 1 [*Corpus Latinum commentariorum in Aristotelem Graecorum. De Wulf-mansion Centre* 7. Leiden: Brill, 1981]: 295–299.
Cf. et 4193 003, 008.
Cod: Schol.

008 **Scholia in sophisticos elenchos** (excerpta e codd. Vat. Reg. gr. 116, Paris. gr. 1845) (= commentaria 3 + 5), ed. Ebbesen, *op. cit.*, vol. 1, 295–299.
Cf. et 4193 003, 007.
Cod: Schol.

009 **Commentarium in sophisticos elenchos** (= Pseudo-Alexander 3) (excerptum e cod. Vat. gr. 244), ed. Ebbesen, *op. cit.*, vol. 1, 316.
Cod: Phil., Comm.

002 **Scholia in sophisticos elenchos** (= commentarium 2), ed. Ebbesen, *op. cit.*, vol. 2 (1981): 27–152.
Cod: Schol.

003 **Scholia in sophisticos elenchos** (excerpta e codd. Hierosol. S. Sepulchri 150, Paris. Coislin. 327, Vat. Reg. gr. 116, Paris. gr. 1845) (= commentarium 3), ed. Ebbesen, *op. cit.*, vol. 2, 200–240.
Cf. et 4193 007, 008.
Cod: Comm.

004 **Scholia in sophisticos elenchos** (excerpta) (= commentarium 1), ed. Ebbesen, *op. cit.*, vol. 2, 241–272.
Cod: Comm.

005 **Concisa traditio modorum sophisticarum importunitatum**, ed. Ebbesen, *op. cit.*, vol. 2, 273–276.
Cod: Epist., Comm.

010 **Commentarium in sophisticos elenchos** (= Anonymus Mutinensis) (excerpta e codd. Mutinensi, busta 1.II.6; Vat. gr. 241; Flor. Laur. 72–75), ed. Ebbesen, *op. cit.*, vol. 2, 307–312.
Cod: Phil., Comm.

012 **In Aristotelis sophisticos elenchos paraphrasis**, ed. M. Hayduck, *Anonymi in Aristotelis sophisticos elenchos paraphrasis* [*Commentaria in Aristotelem Graeca* 23.4. Berlin: Reimer, 1884]: 1–68.
Cod: 29,572: Phil., Comm.

4192 **ANONYMI IN ARISTOTELIS TOPICA**
Varia

001 **Commentarium in topica** (excerptum e cod. Paris. 1843), ed. C.A. Brandis, *Aristotelis opera*, vol. 4. Berlin: Reimer, 1836 (repr. De Gruyter, 1961): 289a.
Cod: Phil., Comm.

002 **Commentarium in topica** (excerpta e cod. Paris. 1845), ed. Brandis, *op. cit.*, 260b, 264a, 272a, 278a, 283b.
Cod: Phil., Comm.

003 **Commentarium in topica** (excerpta e cod. Paris. 1874), ed. Brandis, *op. cit.*, 283b, 288a(?), 292b.
Cod: Phil., Comm.

004 **Commentarium in topica** (excerpta e cod. Paris. 1917), ed. Brandis, *op. cit.*, 260b, 263a, 283b, 285b–286a, 287b, 288a(?), 288b, 291a, 292b, 294b, 295a.
Cod: Phil., Comm.

005 **Commentarium in topica** (excerpta e cod. Paris. 1972), ed. Brandis, *op. cit.*, 283b, 287a, 287b, 292a.
Cod: Phil., Comm.

5024 **ANONYMI IN HERMOGENEM**
Varia

001 **Introductio in prolegomena Hermogenis artis rhetoricae** (fort. auctore Marcellino), ed. C. Walz, *Rhetores Graeci*, vol. 4. Stuttgart: Cotta, 1833 (repr. Osnabrück: Zeller, 1968): 1–38.
Cod: 8,914: Rhet., Comm.
Text to be replaced by Rabe edition (cf. 5024 005).

002 **Prolegomena in librum** περὶ στάσεων (inc. Πολλοὶ πολλὰς τοῦ παρόντος βιβλίου τὰς ἀρχὰς ἐποιήσαντο), ed. H. Rabe, *Prolegomenon sylloge* [*Rhetores Graeci* 14. Leipzig: Teubner, 1931]: 183–228.
Cod: Rhet., Comm.

003 **Excerpta e prolegomenis in librum** περὶ στάσεων (e cod. Paris. 3032, fol. 143r–149r) (inc. Νοῦς μέν ἐστιν ἡ πρώτη ἐπιβολὴ τοῦ πράγματος), ed. Rabe, *op. cit.*, 228–237.
Cod: Rhet., Comm.

004 **Prolegomena in librum** περὶ στάσεων (inc. Εἰ καὶ δόξειεν ἄν τινι παράδοξον τὸ ἐπάγγελμα), ed. Rabe, *op. cit.*, 238–255.
Cod: Rhet., Comm.

005 **Introductio in prolegomena Hermogenis artis rhetoricae** (fort. auctore Marcellino Gramm. et Rhet.), ed. Rabe, *op. cit.*, 258–296.
Cod: Rhet., Comm.

006 **Excerpta e prolegomenis in librum** περὶ στάσεων (e cod. Paris. 3032, fol. 60r–62r) (inc. Δεῖ εἰδέναι, ὅτι Τισίας καὶ Κόραξ), ed. Rabe, *op. cit.*, 296–300.
Cod: Rhet., Comm.

007 **Excerpta e prolegomenis diversis** (e cod. Matr. 4687) (inc. Ὅτι ὅρος λόγου οὗτος), ed. Rabe, *op. cit.*, 300–303.
Cod: Rhet., Comm.

008 **Prolegomena in librum** περὶ στάσεων (inc. Στάσις ἐστὶ φάσις, καθ' ἣν τοῦ πράγματος), ed. Rabe, *op. cit.*, 318–328.
Cod: Rhet., Comm.

009 **Prolegomena in librum** περὶ στάσεων (inc. Ὁ Μινουκιανὸς ὡρίσατο τὴν στάσιν), ed. Rabe, *op. cit.*, 328–336.
Cod: Rhet., Comm.

010 **Prolegomena in artem rhetoricam** (inc. Ἑρμογένην τὸν σοφιστὴν ἤνεγκαν Ταρσοὶ τῆς Κιλικίας), ed. Rabe, *op. cit.*, 336-347.
Cod: Rhet., Comm.

011 **Prolegomena in artem rhetoricam** (excerpta e codd. Marc. 430 + Vat. 900) (inc. Πῶς ἐκάλει ὁ Πλάτων 'πολιτικῆς μορίου εἴδωλον'), ed. Rabe, *op. cit.*, 347-350.
Cod: Rhet., Comm.

012 **Prolegomena in artem rhetoricam** (excerpta e codd. Paris. 1983 + 2977) (inc. Σημείωσαι ὅτι ὁ Ἑρμογένης γένος μὲν ἦν Ταρσεύς), ed. Rabe, *op. cit.*, 351.
Cod: Rhet., Comm.

013 **Prolegomena in librum περὶ ἰδεῶν** (inc. Τὸν πολιτικὸν λόγον δεῖ καὶ τὸ δυνατὸν ἔχειν), ed. Rabe, *op. cit.*, 388-390.
Dup. partim Maximus PLANUDES Polyhist. (4146 008).
Cod: Rhet., Comm.

014 **Περὶ τῆς τάξεως τῶν ἰδεῶν** (inc. Τὸν πολιτικὸν λόγον δεῖ καὶ τὸ δυνατὸν ἔχειν), ed. Rabe, *op. cit.*, 391-393.
Cod: Rhet., Comm.

015 **Prolegomena in librum περὶ ἰδεῶν** (fragmentum e cod. Ambros. 523) (inc. Διὰ τί Περὶ ἰδεῶν, οὐ <Περὶ> χαρακτήρων εἶπεν), ed. Rabe, *op. cit.*, 393.
Cod: Rhet., Comm.

016 **Prolegomena in librum περὶ στάσεων** (inc. Τὴν ῥητορικὴν τέχνην ἄλλοι ἄλλως ὡρίσαντο), ed. Rabe, *op. cit.*, 255-258.
Cod: Rhet., Comm.

017 **Prolegomena in librum περὶ εὑρέσεως** (inc. Διὰ τί τὸ βιβλίον περὶ εὑρέσεως ἔγραψε), ed. Walz, *op. cit.*, vol. 7 (1834; repr. 1968): 55-74.
Cod: Rhet., Comm.

018 **Commentarium in librum περὶ στάσεων** (inc. Ἐδόκει τισὶ χρῆναι τὸν τεχνικὸν εὐθύς), ed. Walz, *op. cit.*, vol. 7, 104-696.
Cod: Rhet., Comm.

019 **Commentarium in librum περὶ εὑρέσεως** (inc. Προοίμιόν ἐστι λόγος παρασκευάζων τὸν ἀκροατήν), ed. Walz, *op. cit.*, vol. 7, 697-860.
Cod: Rhet., Comm.

020 **Commentarium in librum περὶ ἰδεῶν** (inc. Τὸ ἐξῆς οὕτως· τῷ ῥήτορι εἴπερ ἄλλο τι), ed. Walz, *op. cit.*, vol. 7, 861-1087.
Cod: Rhet., Comm.

021 **De figuris in libris περὶ εὑρέσεων et περὶ ἰδεῶν** (inc. Στρογγύλον σχῆμά ἐστι τόδε), ed. Walz, *op. cit.*, vol. 3 (1834; repr. 1968): 704-711.
Cod: Rhet., Comm.

022 **Synopses artis rhetoricae** (excerpta) (inc. Σκοπός ἐστιν ἐν ταῖς στάσεσιν Ἑρμογένει διελεῖν), ed. Walz, *op. cit.*, vol. 3, 461-464.
Synopsis 1 (excerptum e cod. Vat. gr. 1361): pp. 461-463.
Synopsis 2 (excerptum e cod. Vat. gr. 12): pp. 463-464.
Cod: Rhet., Comm.

4171 **ANONYMI IN OPPIANI OPERA**
Incertum

001 **In Oppiani halieutica exegesis** (e cod. Paris. gr. 2735), ed. U.C. Bussemaker, *Scholia et paraphrases in Nicandrum et Oppianum* in *Scholia in Theocritum* (ed. F. Dübner). Paris: Didot, 1849: 364-369.
Cod: Comm.

x01 **Paraphrasis in Oppiani halieutica** (fort. auctore Eutecnio).
Papathomopoulos, pp. 1-29.
Cf. EUTECNIUS Soph. (0752 005).

x02 **Paraphrasis in Oppiani cynegetica** (fort. auctore Eutecnio).
Tüselmann, pp. 8-43.
Cf. EUTECNIUS Soph. (0752 003).

0721 **ANONYMI MEDICI**
Varia

001 **Ὀνομασίαι τῶν κατὰ ἄνθρωπον** (lib. 1), ed. C. Daremberg and C.É. Ruelle, *Oeuvres de Rufus d'Éphèse*. Paris: Imprimerie Nationale, 1879 (repr. Amsterdam: Hakkert, 1963): 233-236.
Cod: 1,452: Med.

002 **Ὀνοματοποιία τῆς ἀνθρώπου φύσεως**, ed. Daremberg and Ruelle, *op. cit.*, 599-600.
Cod: 583: Med.

003 **Περὶ χροιᾶς τοῦ αἵματος τοῦ ἀπὸ φλεβοτομίας ἐκ τῆς ἰατρικῆς τῶν Περσῶν**, ed. J.L. Ideler, *Physici et medici Graeci minores*, vol. 1. Berlin: Reimer, 1841 (repr. Amsterdam: Hakkert, 1963): 293.
Cod: 154: Med.

004 **De generatione et semine**, ed. Ideler, *op. cit.*, vol. 1, 294-296.
Cod: 856: Med.

005 **De corporis hominis natura**, ed. Ideler, *op. cit.*, vol. 1, 301-302.
Cod: 317: Med.

006 **De natura hominis**, ed. Ideler, *op. cit.*, vol. 1, 303-304.
Cod: 562: Med.

007 **Mensium adornatio**, ed. Ideler, *op. cit.*, vol. 1, 421-422.
Cod: 212: Med., Poem.

008 **De duodecim mensium natura**, ed. Ideler, *op. cit.*, vol. 1, 423-429.
Cod: 1,915: Med., Nat. Hist.

009 **De diaeta**, ed. Ideler, *op. cit.*, vol. 2 (1842; repr. 1963): 194-198.
Cod: 1,322: Med.

010 **De alimentis**, ed. Ideler, *op. cit.*, vol. 2, 257-281.
Cod: 6,256: Med.

011 **Περὶ λυκανθρωπίας**, ed. Ideler, *op. cit.*, vol. 2, 282.
Cod: 226: Med.

012 **De urinis secundum Syros**, ed. Ideler, *op. cit.*, vol. 2, 303-304.
Cod: 466: Med.

013 **De urinis secundum Persos**, ed. Ideler, *op. cit.*, vol. 2, 305-306.
Cod: 392: Med.

014 **Commentatio de urinis**, ed. Ideler, *op. cit.*, vol.
2, 307–316.
Cod: 2,748: Med.

015 **De pulsibus**, ed. Ideler, *op. cit.*, vol. 2, 317.
Cod: 118: Med.

016 **De urinis in febribus**, ed. Ideler, *op. cit.*, vol. 2,
323–327.
Cod: 1,440: Med.

017 **De cibis**, ed. F.Z. Ermerins, *Anecdota medica
Graeca*. Leiden: Luchtmans, 1840 (repr. Am-
sterdam: Hakkert, 1963): 225–275.
Cod: 4,148: Med.

020 Περὶ τῆς τῶν πυρετῶν διαφορᾶς, ed. Daremberg and Ruelle, *op. cit.*, 601–610.
Cod: 4,567: Med.

021 Περὶ τροφῶν δυνάμεως, ed. A. Delatte, *Anecdota Atheniensia et alia*, vol. 2. Paris: Droz,
1939: 467–479.
Cod: 3,246: Med.

022 **In aphorismos [Hippocratis]**, ed. H. Flashar,
"Beiträge zur spätantiken Hippokratesdeu-
tung," *Hermes* 90 (1962) 404–405.
Cod: 425: Med.

023 **Physiognomonica**, ed. R. Foerster, *Scriptores
physiognomonici Graeci et Latini*, vol. 2. Leipzig: Teubner, 1893: 225–232.
Cod: 1,225: Med., Physiognom.

024 Ὀνόματα τῶν ἰατρικῶν ἐργαλείων κατὰ στοι-
χεῖα οἷς ἐν ταῖς χειρουργίαις χρώμεθα, ed. F.R.
Dietz, *Severi iatrosophistae de clysteribus liber*
[*Diss. med. Königsberg* (1836)]: 46–48.
Cod: 104: Med.

025 **Fragmenta varia**, ed. R. Fuchs, "Anecdota
medica Graeca," *Rheinisches Museum* 50
(1895) 577–581.
= Anonymus Darembergii.
Cod: 670: Med.

026 Διάγνωσις περὶ τῶν ὀξέων καὶ χρονίων νοσημάτων, ed. R. Fuchs, "Aus Themisons Werk
über die acuten und chronischen Krank-
heiten," *Rheinisches Museum* 58 (1903) 69–
114.
= Anonymus Darembergii.
Cod: 10,567: Med.

027 Περὶ τῆς διαίτης τῶν ιβ΄ μηνῶν (cod. Vindob.
med. gr. 32), ed. A. Garzya, "Diaetetica mi-
nima," Δίπτυχα 2 (1980–1981) 47–49.
Cod: Med.

028 **Pharmacopoeia** *sive* **Iatrosophia** (cod. Par. gr.
2316), ed. I. Oikonomu-Agorastu, *Kritische
Erstausgabe des Rezeptbuchs des cod. Par. gr.
2316, f. 348v–374v* [*Diss. Cologne* (1982)]: 35–
103.
Cod: Med.

x01 **Theriaca** (ap. Galenum).
K14.100–102.
Cf. GALENUS Med. (0057 078).

4037 **ANONYMI PARADOXOGRAPHI**
Varia

001 **De incredibilibus** (excerpta Vaticana), ed. N.

Festa, *Palaephati* περὶ ἀπίστων [*Mythographi
Graeci* 3.2. Leipzig: Teubner, 1902]: 88–99.
Cod: 1,533: Paradox.

002 **Tractatus de mulieribus**, ed. A. Westermann,
Scriptores rerum mirabilium Graeci. Braun-
schweig: Westermann, 1839 (repr. Amsterdam:
Hakkert, 1963): 213–218.
Cod: 1,028: Paradox.

003 Τίνες οἶκοι ἀνάστατοι διὰ γυναῖκας ἐγένοντο,
ed. Westermann, *op. cit.*, 218.
Cod: 73: Paradox.

004 **De fratribus amicis**, ed. Westermann, *op. cit.*,
219.
Cod: 77: Paradox.

005 **De amicis**, ed. Westermann, *op. cit.*, 219–220.
Cod: 70: Paradox.

006 **De Cleobi et Bitone**, ed. Westermann, *op. cit.*,
220.
Cod: 20: Paradox.

007 **De impiis**, ed. Westermann, *op. cit.*, 220–222.
Cod: 293: Paradox.

008 **De transformationibus**, ed. Westermann, *op.
cit.*, 222–223.
Cod: 254: Paradox.

1130 **ANONYMI VALENTINIANI** Theol.
A.D. 2

001 **Fragmenta**, ed. W. Völker, *Quellen zur Ge-
schichte der christlichen Gnosis*. Tübingen:
Mohr, 1932: 60–63, 93–95.
Epistula cuiusdam Valentiniani: pp. 60–63.
Exegesis in Evangelium secundum Joannem:
pp. 93–95.
Q: Epist., Exeget.

1131 **ANONYMUS AD AVIRCIUM MARCEL-
LUM CONTRA CATAPHRYGAS**
A.D. 2–3

001 **Ad Avircium Marcellum contra Cataphrygas**,
ed. M.J. Routh, *Reliquiae sacrae*, vol. 2, 2nd
edn. Oxford: Oxford University Press, 1846
(repr. Hildesheim: Olms, 1974): 183–193.
Q: 1,319: Theol.

1132 **ANONYMUS ALEXANDRI** Phil.
4/3 B.C.

001 **Fragmenta**, ed. H. Thesleff, *The Pythagorean
texts of the Hellenistic period*. Åbo: Åbo Akademi, 1965: 234–237.
Q: 960: Phil.

4168 **ANONYMUS BYZANTINUS IN PORPHY-
RII ISAGOGEN** Phil.
post A.D. 6

001 **Anonymus in Porphyrii isagogen Davidis et
Eliae commentariis usus** (cod. Bodl. [Barocc.]
145) (olim sub auctore Joanne Philopono), ed.
C.A. Brandis, *Aristotelis opera*, vol. 4. Berlin:
Reimer, 1836 (repr. De Gruyter, 1961): 10a–
12b.
Cod: Comm., Phil.

ANONYMUS DE BLEMYOMACHIA
Cf. OLYMPIODORUS Hist. (2590 002).

2117 **ANONYMUS DE METRORUM RATIONE**
A.D. 3
001 **Fragmentum** (*P. Berol.* 9734r), ed. E. Heitsch, *Die griechischen Dichterfragmente der römischen Kaiserzeit*, vol. 1, 2nd edn. Göttingen: Vandenhoeck & Ruprecht, 1963: 204.
Pap: 62: Poem.

4227 **ANONYMUS DE PHILOSOPHIA PLATONICA** Phil.
post A.D. 6: Alexandrinus
001 **Prolegomena philosophiae Platonicae** (fort. auctore Elia, olim sub auctore Olympiodoro), ed. L.G. Westerink, *Anonymous prolegomena to Platonic philosophy*. Amsterdam: North-Holland, 1962: 3–55.
Cod: Phil., Comm.

1813 **ANONYMUS DE PLANTIS AEGYPTIIS**
ante A.D. 2
001 **Fragmentum** (*P. Oxy.* 15.1796), ed. E. Heitsch, *Die griechischen Dichterfragmente der römischen Kaiserzeit*, vol. 1, 2nd edn. Göttingen: Vandenhoeck & Ruprecht, 1963: 203–204.
Pap: 141: Hexametr.

0282 **ANONYMUS DE VIRIBUS HERBARUM**
A.D. 3
001 **Carminis de viribus herbarum fragmentum**, ed. E. Heitsch, *Die griechischen Dichterfragmente der römischen Kaiserzeit*, vol. 2. Göttingen: Vandenhoeck & Ruprecht, 1964: 23–38.
Cod: 1,389: Hexametr., Nat. Hist.

1133 **ANONYMUS DIODORI** Phil.
4 B.C.
001 **Fragmenta**, ed. H. Thesleff, *The Pythagorean texts of the Hellenistic period*. Åbo: Åbo Akademi, 1965: 229–234.
Q: 1,629: Phil.

4005 **ANONYMUS Discipulus Isidori Milesii** Mech.
A.D. 6
Scholia: Cf. SCHOLIA IN EUCLIDEM (5022 001).
001 **Euclidis elementorum qui fertur liber xv**, ed. E.S. Stamatis (post J.L. Heiberg), *Euclidis elementa*, vol. 5.1, 2nd edn. Leipzig: Teubner, 1977: 23–38.
Cf. et EUCLIDES Geom. (1799 001).
Cod: 2,816: Math.

1779 **ANONYMUS EPICUREUS** Phil.
ante A.D. 1
001 **Fragmenta** (*P. Herc.* 176), ed. A. Vogliano, *Epicuri et Epicureorum scripta in Herculanensi-*

bus papyris servata. Berlin: Weidmann, 1928: 23–54.
frr. 1–5.
Pap: 6,496: Phil.
002 **Fragmenta** (ad *P. Herc.* 176 pertinentia), ed. Vogliano, *op. cit.*, 91–96.
frr. 4–34.
Pap: 1,796: Phil.
003 **Vita Philonidis** (*P. Herc.* 1044), ed. W. Crönert, "Der Epikureer Philonides," *Sitzungsberichte der königlich preussischen Akademie der Wissenschaften zu Berlin*, Jahrgang 1900. Berlin: Reimer, 1900: 942–959.
Pap: Biogr.
004 **Fragmenta** (*P. Oxy.* 2.215), ed. W. Schmid, "Chi è l'autore del Pap. 215?," *Miscellanea di studi alessandrini in memoriam di Augusto Rostagni*. Turin: Erasmo, 1963: 40–44.
Pap
x01 **Fragmenta** (*P. Herc.* 346).
Vogliano, pp. 77–89.
Cf. POLYSTRATUS Phil. (1629 002).

1134 **ANONYMUS IAMBLICHI** Phil.
5 B.C.?
001 **Fragmenta**, ed. H. Diels and W. Kranz, *Die Fragmente der Vorsokratiker*, vol. 2, 6th edn. Berlin: Weidmann, 1952 (repr. Dublin: 1966): 400–404.
frr. 1–7.
Q: 1,907: Phil.

4228 **ANONYMUS IN INTRODUCTIONEM ARITHMETICAM NICOMACHI** Math.
A.D. 11?: fort. Constantinopolitanus
001 **Prolegomena in introductionem arithmeticam Nicomachi** (e cod. Paris. gr. 2372), ed. P. Tannery, *Diophanti Alexandrini opera omnia*, vol. 2. Leipzig: Teubner, 1895 (repr. Stuttgart: 1974): 73–77.
Cod: Math., Comm.

ANONYMUS IN MONTANUM
Cf. ANONYMUS AD AVIRCIUM MARCELLUM CONTRA CATAPHRYGAS (1131).

9003 **ANONYMUS LEXICOGRAPHUS**
ante A.D. 12
001 **Fragmenta quattuor apud Eustathium**, ed. H. Erbse, *Untersuchungen zu den attizistischen Lexika* [*Abhandlungen der deutschen Akademie der Wissenschaften zu Berlin*, Philosoph.-hist. Kl. Berlin: Akademie-Verlag, 1950]: 222.
Q: 63: Lexicogr.

0643 **ANONYMUS LONDINENSIS** Med.
A.D. 1
001 **Iatrica** (fort. auctore Menone) (*P. Brit. Mus.* inv. 137), ed. H. Diels, *Anonymi Londinensis ex Aristotelis iatricis Menoniis et aliis medicis*

eclogae [*Commentaria in Aristotelem Graeca*, suppl. 3.1. Berlin: Reimer, 1893]: 1–74.
Pap: 12,579: Med., Phil.
002 **Fragmenta**, ed. Diels, *op. cit.*, 75–76.
Pap: 180: Med., Phil.

4282 **ANONYMUS MANICHAEUS** Biogr.
vel *Mani-Codex*
A.D. 4: Aegyptius
001 Περὶ τῆς γέννης τοῦ σώματος αὐτοῦ (= Codex Manichaicus Coloniensis), ed. L. Koenen and C. Römer, *Der Kölner Mani-Kodex* [*Papyrologica Coloniensia* 14. Cologne: Westdeutscher Verlag, 1988]: 2–118.
Cod: Biogr.

ANONYMUS MUTINENSIS Phil.
A.D. 14/15
Cf. ANONYMI IN ARISTOTELIS SOPHISTICOS ELENCHOS (4193 010).

0799 **ANONYMUS NAUCRATITES** Med.
ante A.D. 2
x01 **Fragmentum ap. Galenum**.
K12.764.
Cf. GALENUS Med. (0057 076).

1119 **ANONYMUS NEAPOLITANUS** Med.
fiq Gaius vel Lycus Neapolitanus
ante A.D. 2
Cf. et GAIUS Med. (0822).
Cf. et LYCUS Med. (0955).
x01 **Fragmenta ap. Galenum**.
K12.746, 751, 752, 755, 763, 986; 13.86, 87, 183, 825, 938, 976, 1020, 1030.
Cf. GALENUS Med. (0057 076, 077).

0800 **ANONYMUS OLYMPIONICES** Med.
ante A.D. 2
x01 **Fragmentum ap. Galenum**.
K12.753.
Cf. GALENUS Med. (0057 076).

ANONYMUS περὶ ἐρωτήσεως καὶ ἀποκρίσεως
Cf. ANONYMI IN ARISTOTELIS ARTEM RHETORICAM (4026 003).

1135 **ANONYMUS PHOTII** Phil.
3/2 B.C.
001 **Fragmenta**, ed. H. Thesleff, *The Pythagorean texts of the Hellenistic period*. Åbo: Åbo Akademi, 1965: 237–242.
Q: 2,008: Phil.

1136 **ANONYMUS PRESBYTER** Scr. Eccl.
A.D. 2?
001 **Fragmentum**, ed. M.J. Routh, *Reliquiae sacrae*, vol. 1, 2nd edn. Oxford: Oxford University Press, 1846 (repr. Hildesheim: Olms, 1974): 385.
Q: 73: Exeget.

1137 **ANONYMUS PYTHAGOREUS** Astrol.
Incertum
001 **De quaternionibus**, ed. S. Weinstock, *Codices Britannici* [*Catalogus codicum astrologorum Graecorum* 9.1. Brussels: Academia, 1951]: 173–179.
Cod: Astrol.

ANONYMUS RHYTHMICUS Mus.
Cf. ARISTOXENUS Mus. (0088 005).

2002 **ANONYMUS SEGUERIANUS** Rhet.
A.D. 3
001 **Ars rhetorica** (olim sub auctore Cornuto), ed. C. Hammer (post L. Spengel), *Rhetores Graeci*, vol. 1. Leipzig: Teubner, 1894: 352–398.
Cod: 9,200: Rhet.

0705 **ANONYMUS SENEX** Med.
ante A.D. 6: Indus
x01 **Fragmentum ap. Aëtium** (lib. 11).
Daremberg-Ruelle, p. 571.
Cf. AËTIUS Med. (0718 011).

1086 **ANONYMUS THEBANUS** Med.
fiq Hierax Thebanus
ante A.D. 2
Cf. et HIERAX Med. (0930).
x01 **Fragmenta ap. Galenum**.
K12.489; 13.739.
Cf. GALENUS Med. (0057 076–077).

ANONYMUS VATICANUS
Cf. PARADOXOGRAPHUS VATICANUS (0582).

0215 **ANTAGORAS** Epic.
3 B.C.: Rhodius
001 **Epigrammata**, ed. J.U. Powell, *Collectanea Alexandrina*. Oxford: Clarendon Press, 1925 (repr. 1970): 120–121.
frr. 1–3 + titulus.
Q: 117: Epigr.
002 **Epigrammata**, AG 7.103; 9.147.
Dup. 0215 001 (frr. 2–3).
Q: 61: Epigr.
x01 **Epigramma demonstrativum**.
App. Anth. 3.60: Cf. ANTHOLOGIAE GRAECAE APPENDIX (7052 003).
Dup. 0215 001 (fr. 1).

2389 **ANTANDER** Hist.
4/3 B.C.?: Syracusanus
001 **Testimonia**, FGrH #565: 3B:580.
NQ: 127: Test.

2322 **ANTENOR** Hist.
ante A.D. 2: Creticus
001 **Testimonia**, FGrH #463: 3B:400–401.
NQ: 52: Test.
002 **Fragmenta**, FGrH #463: 3B:401.
fr. 3: *P. Oxy.* 15.1802.
Q, Pap: 236: Hist.

0775 **ANTHAEUS** Med.
ante A.D. 2
x01 **Fragmentum ap. Galenum**.
K12.764.
Cf. GALENUS Med. (0057 076).

4088 **ANTHEMIUS** Mech. et Math.
A.D. 5–6: Trallianus
003 Περὶ παραδόξων μηχανημάτων, ed. G.L. Huxley, *Anthemius of Tralles. A study in later Greek geometry* [*Greek, Roman and Byzantine monographs* 1. Cambridge, Mass.: Harvard University Press, 1959]: 44–53.
Cod: 2,021: Math., Mech.
005 **Fragmentum mathematicum Bobiense**, ed. Huxley, *op. cit.*, 53–58.
Cod: 1,080: Math.

ANTHIMUS Scr. Eccl.
A.D. 4: Nicomediensis
Cf. MARCELLUS Theol. (2041 002).

7000 *ANTHOLOGIA GRAECA*
Varia
Scholia: Cf. SCHOLIA IN ANTHOLOGIAM GRAECAM (5011).
001 **Anthologia Graeca**, ed. H. Beckby, *Anthologia Graeca*, 4 vols., 2nd edn. Munich: Heimeran, 1–2:1965; 3–4:1968: 1:122–181, 186–210, 218–230, 240–252, 258–436, 444–652; 2:14–438, 448–568; 3:12–468, 474–538, 546–764; 4:12–144, 150–168, 174–248, 258–300, 306–512.
Cod: 139,202: Anthol., Epigr.

7052 *ANTHOLOGIAE GRAECAE APPENDIX*
Varia
001 **Epigrammata dedicatoria**, ed. E. Cougny, *Epigrammatum anthologia Palatina cum Planudeis et appendice nova*, vol. 3. Paris: Didot, 1890: 1–60.
Epigr. 1.1–372.
Q, Epigr: 11,936: Epigr.
002 **Epigrammata sepulcralia**, ed. Cougny, *op. cit.*, 94–224.
Epigr. 2.1–775.
Q, Epigr: 28,595: Epigr.
003 **Epigrammata demonstrativa**, ed. Cougny, *op. cit.*, 287–359.
Epigr. 3.1–422.
Q, Epigr: 14,596: Epigr.
004 **Epigrammata exhortatoria et supplicatoria**, ed. Cougny, *op. cit.*, 390–426.
Epigr. 4.1–143.
Q, Epigr: 7,787: Epigr.
005 **Epigrammata irrisoria**, ed. Cougny, *op. cit.*, 442–457.
Epigr. 5.1–82.
Q, Epigr: 2,880: Epigr.
006 **Oracula**, ed. Cougny, *op. cit.*, 464–533.
Epigr. 6.1–323.
Q, Epigr: 11,748: Epigr.

007 **Problemata et aenigmata**, ed. Cougny, *op. cit.*, 563–578.
Epigr. 7.1–81.
Q, Epigr: 3,128: Epigr.
008 **Addenda**, ed. Cougny, *op. cit.*, 587–602.
Epigr. 1.10b–c, 67b, 86b, 101b, 126b, 128b, 174b, 224b–c, 242b, 249b, 253b, 266b–c, 287b, 292b, 300b, 319b, 329b, 331b, 347b; 2.53b–c, 121b, 131b, 173b–c, 181b, 182b, 198b–e, 242b, 247b, 254b, 255b–c, 257b–c, 320b, 361b, 367b, 371b, 372b–c, 379b, 424b, 447b, 462b, 539b, 641b–c, 671b–d, 680b, 704b, 705b, 712b; 3.66b, 81b, 103b, 115b–c, 138b, 256b–f; 4.62b; 5.6b, 13b, 19b; 6.24b, 30b, 104b, 107; 7.10b.
Q, Epigr: 3,556: Epigr.

0759 **ANTHUS** Med.
ante A.D. 6
x01 **Fragmentum ap. Aëtium** (lib. 12).
Kostomiris, p. 104.
Cf. AËTIUS Med. (0718 012).

1140 **ANTICLIDES** Hist.
3 B.C.: Atheniensis
001 **Testimonia**, FGrH #140: 2B:799.
NQ: 54: Test.
002 **Fragmenta**, FGrH #140: 2B:799–803; 3B:743 addenda.
Q: 1,377: Hist.

1884 **ANTIDAMAS** Hist.
Incertum: Heracleopolitanus
001 **Fragmenta**, FGrH #152: 2B:822–823.
Q: 100: Hist.

0409 **ANTIDOTUS** Comic.
4 B.C.
001 **Fragmenta**, ed. T. Kock, *Comicorum Atticorum fragmenta*, vol. 2. Leipzig: Teubner, 1884: 410–411.
frr. 1–4.
Q: 70: Comic.
002 **Fragmenta**, ed. A. Meineke, *Fragmenta comicorum Graecorum*, vol. 3. Berlin: Reimer, 1840 (repr. De Gruyter, 1970): 528–529.
Q: 72: Comic.

1945 **ANTIGENES** Hist.
ante 3 B.C.
001 **Testimonium**, FGrH #141: 2B:804.
NQ: 14: Test.
002 **Fragmenta**, FGrH #141: 2B:804.
Q: 52: Hist.
003 **Fragmentum**, ed. H.J. Mette, "Die 'Kleinen' griechischen Historiker heute," *Lustrum* 21 (1978) 19.
fr. 3.
Q: 33: Hist.

0139 **ANTIGENES** Lyr.
5 B.C.

x01 **Epigramma.**
AG 13.28.
Cf. BACCHYLIDES Lyr. (0199 009).

0618 *ANTIGONI EPISTULA*
4/3 B.C.
001 **Epistula,** ed. R. Hercher, *Epistolographi Graeci.*
Paris: Didot, 1873 (repr. Amsterdam: Hakkert,
1965): 107.
Q: 105: Epist.

1142 **ANTIGONUS** Astrol.
A.D. 2: Nicaeanus
001 **Imperatoris Hadriani genitura,** ed. W. Kroll,
Codices Vindobonenses [*Catalogus codicum astrologorum Graecorum* 6. Brussels: Lamertin,
1900]: 67–71.
Q: Astrol.

2547 **ANTIGONUS** Hist.
3 B.C.?
001 **Testimonia,** FGrH #816: 3C:892–893.
NQ: 118: Test.
002 **Fragmenta,** FGrH #816: 3C:893.
Q: 100: Hist.

2521 **ANTIGONUS** Hist.
2 B.C.?: Macedo
001 **Fragmentum,** FGrH #775: 3C:770.
Q: 54: Hist., Perieg.

0776 **ANTIGONUS** Med.
ante A.D. 2
x01 **Fragmenta ap. Galenum.**
K12.557–558.
Cf. GALENUS Med. (0057 076).

0568 **ANTIGONUS** Paradox.
3 B.C.: Carystius
001 **Historiarum mirabilium collectio,** ed. A. Giannini, *Paradoxographorum Graecorum reliquiae.*
Milan: Istituto Editoriale Italiano, 1965: 32–
106.
Cod: 6,680: Paradox.
002 **Epigramma,** AG 9.406.
Q: 40: Epigr.
003 **Fragmenta,** ed. Giannini, *op. cit.,* 108–109.
frr. 3–6.
Q: 145: Paradox.
004 **Fragmentum et titulus,** ed. H. Lloyd-Jones and
P. Parsons, *Supplementum Hellenisticum.* Berlin: De Gruyter, 1983: 19–20.
frr. 47, 50.
Q: 20: Epigr.
x01 **Fragmenta** (ap. Paradoxographum Vaticanum
11, 36).
Giannini, PGR, pp. 334, 340.
Cf. PARADOXOGRAPHUS VATICANUS (0582
001).

2173 **ANTILEON** Hist.
2–1 B.C.?

001 **Fragmenta,** FGrH #247: 2B:1130.
Q: 59: Hist., Chronogr.

0239 **ANTIMACHUS** Eleg. et Epic.
5/4 B.C.: Colophonius
001 **Fragmenta,** ed. M.L. West, *Iambi et elegi
Graeci,* vol. 2. Oxford: Clarendon Press, 1972:
38, 40–43.
frr. 57, 66–67, 70, 72–73, 93, 99, 100, 102,
191–192.
Q, Pap: 102: Eleg.
002 **Fragmenta,** ed. B. Wyss, *Antimachi Colophonii
reliquiae.* Berlin: Weidmann, 1936: 1–32, 36–
50, 52–60, 68–72.
frr. 1–11, 15, 19–25, 27–28, 30, 32–37, 39–40,
42–50, 52–54, 57, 66–67, 70–74, 76–79, 82,
84–87, 89–91, 93–94, 96–97, 99–101, 105–
123, 126, 149, 151–152, 154–159.
Dup. partim 0239 004.
Q, Pap: 948: Epic., Eleg., Epigr.
003 **Epigramma,** AG 9.321.
Dup. 0239 002 (fr. 149).
Q: 41: Epigr.
004 **Fragmenta,** ed. H. Lloyd-Jones and P. Parsons,
Supplementum Hellenisticum. Berlin: De Gruyter, 1983: 21–33.
frr. 52–79.
frr. 52–61: *P. Oxy.* 30.2518.
frr. 62–75: *P. Oxy.* 30.2516.
fr. 76: *P. Ant.* 120b.
fr. 78: *P. Herc.* N 1088 ii + N 433 ii.
Dup. partim 0239 002.
Q, Pap: 541: Epic., Poem.

1141 **ANTIMACHUS** Epic.
8 B.C.: Teius
Cf. et EPIGONI (1351).
001 **Fragmentum** [Dub.], ed. J.U. Powell, *Collectanea Alexandrina.* Oxford: Clarendon Press,
1925 (repr. 1970): 247.
fr. 3.
Q: 14: Epic.
002 **Fragmentum,** ed. G. Kinkel, *Epicorum Graecorum fragmenta,* vol. 1. Leipzig: Teubner,
1877: 247.
fr. 1.
Q: 8: Epic.

0044 *ANTIOCHI REGIS EPISTULAE*
Incertum
001 **Epistulae,** ed. R. Hercher, *Epistolographi
Graeci.* Paris: Didot, 1873 (repr. Amsterdam:
Hakkert, 1965): 108–109.
Q: 491: Epist.

1993 **ANTIOCHIANUS** Hist.
A.D. 2
001 **Fragmentum,** FGrH #207: 2B:940.
Q: 74: Hist.

1144 **ANTIOCHUS** Astrol.
1 B.C./A.D. 1: Atheniensis
001 **Fragmenta** (e cod. Florentino 11), ed. A. Olivi-

eri, *Codices Florentini* [*Catalogus codicum astrologorum Graecorum* 1. Brussels: Lamertin, 1898]: 108–113.
Cod: Astrol.

002 **Fragmenta** (e cod. Neapolitano 19), ed. D. Bassi, F. Cumont, A. Martini and A. Olivieri, *Codices Italici* [*Catalogus codicum astrologorum Graecorum* 4. Brussels: Lamertin, 1903]: 154–155.
Cod: Astrol.

003 **Fragmenta** (e cod. Monac. 7), ed. F. Boll, *Codices Germanici* [*Catalogus codicum astrologorum Graecorum* 7. Brussels: Lamertin, 1908]: 107–113, 114–116, 126–128.
Cod: Astrol.

004 **Fragmenta** (e cod. Paris.), ed. P. Boudreaux, *Codices Parisini* [*Catalogus codicum astrologorum Graecorum* 8.3. Brussels: Lamertin, 1912]: 104–119.
Cod: Astrol.

005 **Fragmenta** (e cod. Scorial. 24), ed. K.O. Zuretti, *Codices Hispanienses* [*Catalogus codicum astrologorum Graecorum* 11.2. Brussels: Lamertin, 1934]: 109–114.
Cod: Astrol.

0112 **ANTIOCHUS** Epigr.
A.D. 1–2

001 **Epigrammata**, AG 11.412, 422.
Q: 63: Epigr.

1145 **ANTIOCHUS** Hist.
5 B.C.: Syracusanus

001 **Testimonia**, FGrH #555: 3B:543.
NQ: 123: Test.

002 **Fragmenta**, FGrH #555: 3B:543–551.
Q: 2,335: Hist.

1879 **ANTIOCHUS** Hist.
5 B.C.
Cf. et ANTIOCHUS-PHERECYDES Hist. (2221).

001 **Fragmenta**, FGrH #29: 1A:213–214.
Dup. partim ANTIOCHUS-PHERECYDES Hist. (2221 002).
Q: 157: Hist., Myth.

0778 **ANTIOCHUS** Med.
fiq Paccius Antiochus
A.D. 1?: Romanus
Cf. et PACCIUS ANTIOCHUS Med. (1013).

x01 **Fragmentum ap. Paulum.**
CMG, vol. 9.2, p. 286.
Cf. PAULUS Med. (0715 001).

x02 **Fragmentum ap. Aëtium** (lib. 3).
CMG, vol. 8.1, p. 306.
Cf. AËTIUS Med. (0718 003).

1143 **ANTIOCHUS** Phil.
2–1 B.C.: Ascalonius

001 **Fragmenta**, ed. G. Luck, *Der Akademiker Antiochus*. Bern: Haupt, 1953: 73, 75–82, 85–86, 88, 94.

frr. 1, 2, 7, 12, 13, 15, 18, 23, 31–33, 35–38, 54–55, 58, 65–66, 86.
Q, Pap: 1,184: Phil.

2503 **Publius Anteius ANTIOCHUS** Soph.
A.D. 2/3: Aegaeus

001 **Testimonia**, FGrH #747: 3C:731–732.
test. 2: *Inscr. Argos.*
NQ: 336: Test.

002 **Titulus**, FGrH #747: 3C:732.
NQ: Hist.

0777 **ANTIOCHUS Philometor** <Med.>
vel Antiochus VIII Epiphanes
1 B.C.: Seleuciensis

x01 **Fragmentum ap. Galenum.**
K14.185.
Cf. GALENUS Med. (0057 078).

2221 **ANTIOCHUS-PHERECYDES** Hist.
5 B.C.: Atheniensis
Cf. et ANTIOCHUS Hist. (1879).
Cf. et PHERECYDES Hist. (1584).

001 **Testimonium**, FGrH #333: 3B:166.
Dup. partim PHERECYDES Hist. (1584 001).
NQ: 46: Test.

002 **Fragmenta**, FGrH #333: 3B:166–168.
Dup. partim PHERECYDES Hist. (1584 002).
Dup. partim ANTIOCHUS Hist. (1879 001).
Q: 409: Hist.

0113 **ANTIPATER** Epigr.
2 B.C.: Sidonius

001 **Epigrammata**, AG **6.**10, 14–15, 46, 109, 111, 115, 118, 159–160, 174, 206, 219, 223, 276, 287; **7.**2, 6, 8, 14–15, 23, 26–27, 29–30, 34, 65, 75, 81, 146, 161, 164–165, 172, 209–210, 218, 232, 241, 246, 252, 303, 316, 353, 409, 413, 423–427, 464, 467, 493, 498, 711, 713, 743, 745, 748; **9.**58, 66, 76, 151, 323, 567, 603, 720–724, 728, 790; **10.**2; **12.**97; **16.**133, 167, 176, 178, 220, 296.
AG 6.47, 93; 7.625, 666; 9.93; 16.184: Cf. ANTIPATER Epigr. (0114 001).
AG 6.291; 9.729: Cf. ANONYMI EPIGRAMMATICI (AG) (0138 001).
AG 7.282: Cf. THEODORIDAS Epigr. (1715 001).
AG 7.470: Cf. MELEAGER Epigr. (1492 001).
AG 9.23, 143, 150; 16.131: Cf. ANTIPATER Epigr. (1865 001).
AG 9.25: Cf. LEONIDAS Epigr. (1458 001).
AG 9.45: Cf. STATYLLIUS FLACCUS Epigr. (1694 001).
AG 9.406: Cf. ANTIGONUS Paradox. (0568 002).
AG 9.569: Cf. EMPEDOCLES Poet. Phil. (1342 002).
Q: 3,744: Epigr.

x01 **Epigramma demonstrativum.**
App. Anth. 3.104: Cf. ANTHOLOGIAE GRAECAE APPENDIX (7052 003).

1865 **ANTIPATER** Epigr.
fiq Antipater Sidonius vel Antipater Thessalonicensis
2/1 B.C.?: Sidonius vel Thessalonicensis
Cf. et ANTIPATER Epigr. (0113).
Cf. et ANTIPATER Epigr. (0114).
001 **Epigrammata**, AG **9**.23, 143, 150; **16**.131.
Q: 207: Epigr.

0114 **ANTIPATER** Epigr.
1 B.C.: Thessalonicensis
001 **Epigrammata**, AG **5**.3, 30–31, 109; **6**.47, 93,
198, 208–209, 241, 249, 256, 335; **7**.18, 39,
136, 168, 185, 216, 236, 286–289, 367, 369,
390, 398, 402, 530–531, 625, 629, 637, 639–
640, 666, 692, 705; **9**.3, 10, 26, 46, 59, 72, 77,
82, 92–93, 96, 112, 149, 186, 215, 231, 238,
241, 266, 268–269, 282, 297, 302, 305, 309,
407–408, 417–418, 420–421, 428, 517, 541,
550, 552, 557, 706, 752, 792; **10**.25; **11**.20, 23–
24, 31, 37, 158, 219, 224, 327, 415; **16**.75, 143,
184, 197, 290, 305.
AG 7.138: Cf. ACERATUS Gramm. (0101
001).
AG 7.237; 9.101: Cf. ALPHEUS Epigr. (0108
001).
AG 7.409, 493: Cf. ANTIPATER Epigr. (0113
001).
AG 9.23, 143, 150: Cf. ANTIPATER Epigr.
(1865 001).
AG 9.25, 107: Cf. LEONIDAS Epigr. (1458
001).
AG 9.45: Cf. STATYLLIUS FLACCUS Epigr.
(1694 001).
AG 9.114: Cf. PARMENION Epigr. (1563 001).
AG 11.331: Cf. NICARCHUS II Epigr. (1532
001).
Q: 3,520: Epigr.

1910 **ANTIPATER** Hist.
4 B.C.: Magnes
001 **Testimonium**, FGrH #69: 2A:35–36.
NQ: 246: Test.
002 **Fragmenta**, FGrH #69: 2A:36–37.
Q: 295: Hist.

1929 **ANTIPATER** Hist.
4 B.C.?: Macedo
001 **Testimonium**, FGrH #114: 2B:526.
NQ: 31: Test.

2350 **ANTIPATER** Hist.
2 B.C./A.D. 1
001 **Testimonium**, FGrH #507: 3B:484.
NQ: 22: Test.
002 **Fragmenta**, FGrH #507: 3B:484–485.
Q: 44: Hist.

1997 **ANTIPATER** Hist.
A.D. 2–3: Hierapolitanus
001 **Testimonia**, FGrH #211: 2B:942–943.
NQ: 447: Test.

1898 **ANTIPATER** Hist.
Incertum: Acanthius
001 **Fragmenta**, FGrH #56: 1A:296–297.
Q: 270: Hist., Myth.

0779 **ANTIPATER** Med.
1 B.C.–A.D. 1
Cf. et ANTIPATER et CLEOPHANTUS Med.
(0832).
x01 **Fragmenta ap. Galenum**.
K12.630; **13**.239, 292; **14**.160, 165–167.
Cf. GALENUS Med. (0057 076, 078).

1146 **ANTIPATER** Phil.
2 B.C.: Tarsensis
001 **Testimonia et fragmenta**, ed. J. von Arnim,
Stoicorum veterum fragmenta, vol. 3. Leipzig:
Teubner, 1903 (repr. Stuttgart: 1968): 244–
258.
Testimonia (frr. 1–15): pp. 244–246.
Q: 4,581: Phil.

0832 **ANTIPATER et CLEOPHANTUS** Med.
1 B.C./A.D. 1
Cf. et ANTIPATER Med. (0779).
Cf. et CLEOPHANTUS Med. (0821).
x01 **Fragmenta ap. Galenum**.
K14.108–109.
Cf. GALENUS Med. (0057 078).

0410 **ANTIPHANES** Comic.
4 B.C.
001 **Fragmenta**, ed. T. Kock, *Comicorum Atticorum fragmenta*, vol. 2. Leipzig: Teubner,
1884: 12–20, 22–33, 35–135.
frr. 1–21, 24–29, 31–40, 42–45, 47–50, 52–56,
58–62, 64–98, 100–110, 112–115, 117–169,
171–212, 214–302, 305–324, 327–332, 334 +
tituli.
Q: 7,146: Comic.
002 **Fragmenta**, ed. A. Meineke, *Fragmenta comicorum Graecorum*, vol. 3. Berlin, Berlin: Reimer, 1840 (repr. De Gruyter, 1970): 3–13, 15–
27, 29–30, 32–36, 39–41, 43–59, 61–64, 66–
106, 108–112, 114–126, 128–157.
Q: 6,952: Comic.
003 **Fragmenta**, ed. J. Demiańczuk, *Supplementum
comicum*. Krakau: Nakładem Akademii, 1912
(repr. Hildesheim: Olms, 1967): 8.
frr. 1–2.
fr. 1: *P. Oxy.* 3.427.
Q, Pap: 13: Comic.
004 **Fragmenta**, ed. C. Austin, *Comicorum Graecorum fragmenta in papyris reperta*. Berlin: De
Gruyter, 1973: 2–4.
frr. 3, 9 + tituli.
Pap: 28: Comic.
005 **Fragmenta**, ed. Meineke, *FCG*, vol. 5.1 (1857;
repr. 1970): clxxiii.
Q: 14: Comic.

x01 **Aenigmata.**
App. Anth. 7.7–8: Cf. ANTHOLOGIAE GRAE-
CAE APPENDIX (7052 007).
Dup. partim 0410 002 (p. 112).

0117 **ANTIPHANES** Epigr.
A.D. 1: Macedo vel Megalopolitanus
001 **Epigrammata**, AG **6**.88; **9**.84, 245, 256, 258,
409; **10**.100; **11**.168, 322, 348.
Q: 386: Epigr.

0780 **ANTIPHANES** Med.
2 B.C.: Delius
x01 **Fragmentum ap. Galenum.**
K12.877.
Cf. GALENUS Med. (0057 076).

2253 **ANTIPHANES Junior** Hist.
2 B.C.?
001 **Testimonium**, FGrH #349: 3B:211–212.
NQ: 75: Test.
002 **Fragmenta**, FGrH #349: 3B:212.
Q: 192: Hist.

0118 **ANTIPHILUS** Epigr.
A.D. 1: Byzantius
001 **Epigrammata**, AG **5**.111, 307–308; **6**.95, 97,
199, 250, 252, 257; **7**.141, 175–176, 375, 379,
399, 622, 630, 634–635, 641; **9**.13b–14, 29,
34–35, 71, 73, 86, 156, 178, 192, 222, 242,
263, 277, 294, 298, 306, 310, 404, 413, 415,
546, 549, 551; **10**.17; **11**.66; **16**.136, 147, 333–
334.
AG 5.308: Cf. et PHILODEMUS Phil. (1595
730).
AG 9.123: Cf. Julius LEONIDAS Math. et
Astrol. (1457 001).
AG 9.439: Cf. CRINAGORAS Epigr. (0154
001).
Q: 2,103: Epigr.

0028 **ANTIPHON** Orat.
5 B.C.: Atheniensis
001 **In novercam**, ed. L. Gernet, *Antiphon. Discours.* Paris: Les Belles Lettres, 1923 (repr.
1965): 38–46.
Cod: 1,807: Orat.
002 **Tetralogia 1**, ed. Gernet, *op. cit.*, 53–67.
Cod: 2,580: Orat.
003 **Tetralogia 2**, ed. Gernet, *op. cit.*, 72–84.
Cod: 2,228: Orat.
004 **Tetralogia 3**, ed. Gernet, *op. cit.*, 88–100.
Cod: 2,010: Orat.
005 **De caede Herodis**, ed. Gernet, *op. cit.*, 108–
136.
Cod: 6,508: Orat.
006 **De choreuta**, ed. Gernet, *op. cit.*, 142–157.
Cod: 3,495: Orat.
007 **Fragmenta**, ed. Gernet, *op. cit.*, 164–167.
frr. 1–6.
fr. 3.1: *P. Geneva.*
Q, Pap: 642: Orat., Rhet.

1147 **ANTIPHON** Soph.
5 B.C.: Atheniensis
001 **Fragmenta**, ed. L. Gernet, *Antiphon. Discours.*
Paris: Les Belles Lettres, 1923 (repr. 1965):
176–183.
frr. 1–6, Περὶ τῆς ἀληθείας: pp. 176–179.
frr. 7–9, Περὶ ὁμονοίας: p. 179.
frr. 10–23, Fragmenta incertae sedis: pp. 179–
183.
frr. 4–6: *P. Oxy.* 11.1364, fr. 1.
Dup. partim 1147 003 (fr. 44).
Q, Pap: 1,659: Phil.
002 **Testimonia**, ed. H. Diels and W. Kranz, *Die
Fragmente der Vorsokratiker*, vol. 2, 6th edn.
Berlin: Weidmann, 1952 (repr. Dublin: 1966):
334–337.
test. 1–9.
NQ: 1,310: Test.
003 **Fragmenta**, ed. Diels and Kranz, *op. cit.*, 337–
370.
frr. 1–118.
fr. 44: *P. Oxy.* 11.1364 + 15.1797.
Dup. partim 1147 001.
Q, Pap: 5,062: Phil., Math., Onir.
004 **Fragmenta** (*P. Oxy.* 3.414), ed. B.P. Grenfell
and A.S. Hunt, *The Oxyrhynchus papyri*, pt. 3.
London: Egypt Exploration Fund, 1903: 57–
59.
Pap

0323 **ANTIPHON** Trag.
5–4 B.C.
001 **Fragmenta**, ed. B. Snell, *Tragicorum Graecorum fragmenta*, vol. 1. Göttingen: Vandenhoeck & Ruprecht, 1971: 194–196.
frr. 1–1a, 2–6.
Q: 42: Trag.

2351 **ANTISTHENES** Hist.
3–2 B.C.: Rhodius
001 **Testimonia**, FGrH #508: 3B:485.
NQ: 30: Test.
002 **Fragmenta**, FGrH #508: 3B:485–487.
Q: 768: Hist.

2435 **ANTISTHENES** Hist.
2 B.C./A.D. 1?
x01 **Fragmentum.**
FGrH #655.
Cf. DIONYSIUS Hist. (2446 001).

2313 **ANTISTHENES** Phil.
5–4 B.C.: Atheniensis
001 **Testimonia**, ed. H. Diels and W. Kranz, *Die
Fragmente der Vorsokratiker*, vol. 2, 6th edn.
Berlin: Weidmann, 1952 (repr. Dublin: 1966):
70.
test. 1–3.
NQ: 76: Test.

0591 **ANTISTHENES** Rhet. et Phil.
5–4 B.C.: Atheniensis

Cf. et SOCRATICORUM EPISTULAE (0637).

001 **Declamationes** (fragmenta), ed. F. Caizzi, *Antisthenis fragmenta*. Milan: Istituto Editoriale Cisalpino, 1966: 24–28.
frr. 14–15.
Αἴας ἢ Αἴαντος λόγος (fr. 14): pp. 24–25.
Ὀδυσσεὺς ἢ Ὀδυσσέως λόγος (fr. 15): pp. 26–28.
Cod: 1,462: Rhet.

002 **Fragmenta varia**, ed. Caizzi, *op. cit.*, 29–59.
frr. 16–24b, 25–26, 28–39a, 40a–86, 88–101, 103–110, 111c–121.
Φυσιογνωμονικός (fr. 16): p. 29.
Προτρεπτικός (frr. 17–18d): p. 29.
Κῦρος (frr. 19–21b): p. 30.
Ἡρακλῆς (frr. 22–24b, 25–26, 28): pp. 30–32.
Κῦρος ἢ περὶ βασιλείας vel Ἀλκιβιάδης (frr. 29a–33): pp. 32–34.
Ἀσπασία (frr. 34–35): p. 34.
Σάθων ἢ περὶ τοῦ ἀντιλέγειν (frr. 36–37b): pp. 34–35.
Περὶ παιδείας ἢ περὶ ὀνομάτων (fr. 38): p. 35.
Φυσικός (frr. 39a, 40a–40d): pp. 35–36.
Περὶ οἴνου χρήσεως (fr. 41): p. 37.
Ἀρχέλαος (fr. 42): p. 37.
Πολιτικός (fr. 43): p. 37.
Fragmenta incertae sedis (frr. 44a–86, 88–101, 103–110, 111c–121): pp. 38–59.
Q: 6,757: Rhet., Phil., Physiognom., Dialog.

0119 **ANTISTIUS** <Epigr.>
fiq Antistius Vetus
A.D. 1
001 **Epigrammata**, AG **6**.237; **7**.366; **11**.40; **16**.243.
Q: 157: Epigr.

1149 *ANTONINI PII IMPERATORIS EPISTULA*
A.D. 2
001 **Epistula ad commune Asiae**, ed. J.C.T. Otto, *Corpus apologetarum Christianorum saeculi secundi*, vol. 1. Jena: Mauke, 1876 (repr. Wiesbaden: Sändig, 1969): 244–246.
Cod: 253: Epist.

0931 **ANTONINUS** Med.
ante A.D. 1: Cous
x01 **Fragmenta ap. Galenum.**
K**12**.843–844; **14**.168–169.
Cf. GALENUS Med. (0057 076, 078).

0651 **ANTONINUS LIBERALIS** Myth.
A.D. 2?
001 **Metamorphoseon synagoge**, ed. I. Cazzaniga, *Antoninus Liberalis. Metamorphoseon synagoge*. Milan: Istituto Editoriale Cisalpino, 1962: 12–77.
Cod: 10,585: Myth.

0120 **ANTONIUS** Epigr.
fiq Antonius Thallus
A.D. 1: Argivus

Cf. et Antonius THALLUS Epigr. (1707).

001 **Epigramma**, AG 9.102.
AG 9.103: Cf. MUNDUS MUNATIUS Epigr. (1519 001).
Q: 23: Epigr.

0850 **ANTONIUS** Med.
ante A.D. 1
x01 **Fragmenta ap. Galenum.**
K13.281–282.
Cf. GALENUS Med. (0057 076).

1148 **ANTONIUS DIOGENES** Scr. Erot.
A.D. 1/2
001 Τὰ ὑπὲρ Θούλην ἄπιστα (ap. Photium, *Bibl.* cod. 166), ed. R. Hercher, *Erotici scriptores Graeci*, vol. 1. Leipzig: Teubner, 1858: 233–238.
Q: [2,295]: Narr. Fict.

002 **Fragmentum** (*PSI* 1177), ed. F. Zimmermann, *Griechische Roman-Papyri und verwandte Texte*. Heidelberg: Bilabel, 1936: 85–89.
Pap: Narr. Fict.

003 **Fragmentum** (*P.Oxy.* 42.3012), ed. P. Parsons, *The Oxyrhynchus papyri*, pt. 42. London: Egypt Exploration Society, 1974: 45.
Pap: Narr. Fict.

2478 **ANTONIUS JULIANUS** Hist.
fiq Marcus Antonius Julianus Procurator Judaeae
A.D. 2
001 **Testimonium**, FGrH #735: 3C:700.
NQ: 115: Test.

0669 **ANTONIUS MUSA** Med.
1 B.C./A.D. 1
Cf. et MUSA Med. (0808).
x01 **Fragmenta ap. Galenum.**
K**12**.636, 658, 737–738, 740, 741; **13**.57, 104, 108, 326.
Cf. GALENUS Med. (0057 076).
x02 **Fragmenta ap. Aëtium** (lib. 8).
CMG, vol. 8.2, pp. 491, 544.
Cf. AËTIUS Med. (0718 008).

0749 **ANTYLLUS** Med.
A.D. 2
Cf. et ANTYLLUS et HELIODORUS Med. (0852).
Cf. et ANTYLLUS et POSIDONIUS Med. (0853).
001 Ἐκ τοῦ περὶ κλυσμῶν ὅτι διὰ τρεῖς αἰτίας παραλαμβάνονται, ed. F.R. Dietz, *Severi iatrosophistae de clysteribus liber* [*Diss. med. Königsberg* (1836)]: 43–45.
Cod: 316: Med.
x01 **Fragmenta ap. Oribasium.**
CMG, vol. **6.1.1**, pp. 107, 146, 155, 157, 177, 183, 208, 210, 214, 215, 217, 219, 255, 262, 263; **6.1.2**, pp. 6, 11, 12, 14, 24, 44, 55, 61;

6.2.1, pp. 133, 161, 166, 168, 179, 237; **6.2.2**,
pp. 55, 58, 128; **6.3**, pp. 7, 13, 23, 51.
Cf. ORIBASIUS Med. (0722 001).
x02 **Fragmenta ap. Paulum.**
CMG, vol. 9.2, pp. 70, 347, 394, 397.
Cf. PAULUS Med. (0715 001).
x03 **Fragmenta ap. Aëtium** (lib. 3).
CMG, vol. 8.1, pp. 276, 277.
Cf. AËTIUS Med. (0718 003).
x04 **Fragmenta ap. Aëtium** (lib. 7).
CMG, vol. 8.2, p. 323.
Cf. AËTIUS Med. (0718 007).
x05 **Fragmenta ap. Aëtium** (lib. 9).
Athena 23 (1911) 374.
Cf. AËTIUS Med. (0718 009).

0852 **ANTYLLUS et HELIODORUS** Med.
A.D. 1/2
Cf. et ANTYLLUS Med. (0749).
Cf. et HELIODORUS Med. (0692).
x01 **Fragmenta ap. Oribasium.**
CMG, vol. **6.2.1**, pp. 118–120, 135–142; **6.2.2**,
p. 57.
Cf. ORIBASIUS Med. (0722 001).

0853 **ANTYLLUS et POSIDONIUS** Med.
A.D. 2/5
Cf. et ANTYLLUS Med. (0749).
x01 **Fragmentum ap. Aëtium** (lib. 3).
CMG, vol. 8.1, p. 309.
Cf. AËTIUS Med. (0718 003).

1126 **ANUBION** Poet. Astrol.
A.D. 1
001 **Fragmenta,** *P. Schubart* 15.
Pap
002 **Fragmenta** (e cod. Veneto 7), ed. W. Kroll and
A. Olivieri, *Codices Veneti* [*Catalogus codicum
astrologorum Graecorum* 2. Brussels: Lamertin,
1900]: 202–212.
Cod: Astrol.
003 **Fragmenta** (e cod. Paris. 2417), ed. W. Kroll
and A. Olivieri, *Codices Parisini* [*Catalogus
codicum astrologorum Graecorum* 8.1. Brussels:
Lamertin, 1929]: 147.
Cod: Astrol.

0121 **ANYTE** Epigr.
4 B.C.: Tegeates
001 **Epigrammata,** AG **6.**123, 153, 312; **7.**190, 202,
208, 215, 486, 490, 492, 538, 646, 649, 724;
9.144, 313–314, 745; **16.**228, 231, 291.
AG 6.82: Cf. PAULUS Silentiarius Poet. Christ.
(4039 004).
AG 7.189: Cf. ARISTODICUS Epigr. (0133
001).
AG 7.232: Cf. ANTIPATER Epigr. (0113 001).
AG 7.236: Cf. ANTIPATER Epigr. (0114 001).
AG 7.491: Cf. MNASALCES Epigr. (1513 001).
AG 16.229: Cf. ANONYMI EPIGRAMMATICI
(AG) (0138 001).
Q: 580: Epigr.

1046 **APELLES** Gnost.
A.D. 2: Alexandrinus, Romanus
x01 **Fragmentum** (ap. Origenem, *In Genesim*).
Baehrens, pp. 28–29.
Cf. ORIGENES Theol. (2042 022).

0858 **APELLES** Med.
1 B.C.–A.D. 1
x01 **Fragmentum ap. Galenum.**
K14.148.
Cf. GALENUS Med. (0057 078).

1150 **APHAREUS** Rhet.
4 B.C.: Atheniensis
001 **Epigramma,** ed. E. Diehl, *Anthologia lyrica
Graeca,* fasc. 1, 3rd edn. Leipzig: Teubner,
1949: 114.
Q: 14: Epigr.
002 **Tituli,** ed. B. Snell, *Tragicorum Graecorum
fragmenta,* vol. 1. Göttingen: Vandenhoeck &
Ruprecht, 1971: 239.
NQ: 3: Trag.

0783 **APHRODAS** Med.
ante A.D. 1
Cf. et APHRODAS et MOSCHION Med. (0866).
x01 **Fragmenta ap. Galenum.**
K**12.**695, 878; **13.**94–95, 135–136, 551, 738,
1035; **14.**111–112, 207–208.
Cf. GALENUS Med. (0057 076–078).

0866 **APHRODAS et MOSCHION** Med.
1 B.C./A.D. 1
Cf. et APHRODAS Med. (0783).
Cf. et MOSCHION ὁ διορθωτής Med. (0994).
x01 **Fragmentum ap. Galenum.**
K13.30.
Cf. GALENUS Med. (0057 076).

0760 **APHRODISEUS** Med.
ante A.D. 1
x01 **Fragmentum ap. Galenum.**
K13.1013.
Cf. GALENUS Med. (0057 077).

1151 **APHRODISIUS-EUPHEMIUS** Hist.
post 4 B.C.?: Thespiensis
001 **Fragmentum,** FGrH #386: 3B:263.
Q: 46: Hist.

0784 **APHTHONIUS** Soph.
ante A.D. 4: Romanus
x01 **Fragmentum ap. Oribasium.**
CMG, vol. 6.2.2, p. 246.
Cf. ORIBASIUS Med. (0722 003).

1152 **APION** Gramm.
A.D. 1: Alexandrinus, Oasites
001 **Testimonia,** FGrH #616: 3C:122–126.
NQ: 1,277: Test.
002 **Fragmenta,** FGrH #616: 3C:126–144.
Q: 6,010: Hist.

003 **Fragmenta de glossis Homericis**, ed. A. Ludwich, "Über die homerischen Glossen Apions," *Philologus* **74** (1917) 209–247; **75** (1919) 95–103.
Q: 7,367: Lexicogr.

004 **Fragmenta de glossis Homericis**, ed. S. Neitzel, *Die Fragmente des Grammatikers Dionysios Thrax* [*Sammlung griechischer und lateinischer Grammatiker* 3. Berlin: De Gruyter, 1977]: 213–218, 220–300.
frr. 1–158.
Q: 6,074: Lexicogr.

0769 **APION** Med.
ante A.D. 1
x01 **Fragmentum ap. Galenum.**
K13.856.
Cf. GALENUS Med. (0057 077).

1153 *APOCALYPSIS ADAM*
vel *Testamentum Adam*
A.D. 1?
001 **Νυχθήμερον** (fort. auctore Apollonio Tyanensi), ed. J.A. Robinson, *Texts and Studies* 2.3. Cambridge: Cambridge University Press, 1893 (repr. Nendeln, Liechtenstein: Kraus, 1967): 139–144.
Cod: 486: Apocalyp., Apocryph.

1154 *APOCALYPSIS BARUCH*
ante A.D. 3
001 **Apocalypsis Baruchi Graece** (iii Baruch), ed. J.C. Picard, *Apocalypsis Baruchi Graece* [*Pseudepigrapha veteris testamenti Graece* 2. Leiden: Brill, 1967]: 81–96.
Cod: 3,255: Apocalyp., Pseudepigr.

1156 *APOCALYPSIS ELIAE*
ante A.D. 1
001 **Fragmenta**, ed. A.-M. Denis, *Fragmenta pseudepigraphorum quae supersunt Graeca* [*Pseudepigrapha veteris testamenti Graece* 3. Leiden: Brill, 1970]: 103–104.
Q: 231: Apocalyp., Pseudepigr.

1157 *APOCALYPSIS ESDRAE*
2 B.C./A.D. 2
001 **Apocalypsis Esdrae**, ed. C. Tischendorf, *Apocalypses apocryphae*. Leipzig: Mendelssohn, 1866: 24–33.
Cod: 2,677: Pseudepigr., Apocalyp.

002 **Apocalypsis Esdrae quarta**, ed. A.-M. Denis, *Fragmenta pseudepigraphorum quae supersunt Graeca* [*Pseudepigrapha veteris testamenti Graece* 3. Leiden: Brill, 1970]: 130–132.
Q: 148: Pseudepigr., Apocalyp.

1158 *APOCALYPSIS JOANNIS*
A.D. 2?
001 **Apocalypsis apocrypha Joannis**, ed. C. Tischendorf, *Apocalypses apocryphae*. Leipzig: Mendelssohn, 1866: 70–93.

Cod: 2,961: Apocalyp., Apocryph.

002 **Apocalypsis apocrypha Joannis** (versio altera), ed. F. Nau, "Une deuxième apocalypse apocryphe grecque de saint Jean," *Revue Biblique* 23 (1914) 215–221.
Cod: 1,621: Apocalyp., Apocryph.

003 **Apocalypsis apocrypha Joannis** (versio tertia), ed. A. Vassiliev, *Anecdota Graeco-Byzantina*, vol. 1. Moscow: Imperial University Press, 1893: 317–322.
Cod: 1,916: Apocalyp., Apocryph.

APOCALYPSIS MOSIS
Cf. VITA ADAM et EVAE (1747).

1159 *APOCALYPSIS PETRI*
A.D. 2
001 **Apocalypsis Petri**, ed. E. Klostermann, *Apocrypha I: Reste des Petrusevangeliums, der Petrusapokalypse und des Kerygma Petri*, 2nd edn. [*Kleine Texte* 3. Bonn: Marcus & Weber, 1908]: 8–12.
Cod: [1,634]: Apocalyp., Apocryph.

002 **Kerygma Petri**, ed. Klostermann, *op. cit.*, 12–13.
Q: Apocryph.

2243 *APOCALYPSIS SEDRACH*
Incertum
001 **Apocalypsis Sedrach**, ed. M.R. James, *Apocrypha anecdota* [*Texts and Studies* 2.3. Cambridge: Cambridge University Press, 1893 (repr. Nendeln, Liechtenstein: Kraus, 1967)]: 130–137.
Cod: Apocalyp., Apocryph.

1160 *APOCALYPSIS SOPHONIAE*
ante A.D. 2
001 **Fragmentum**, ed. A.-M. Denis, *Fragmenta pseudepigraphorum quae supersunt Graeca* [*Pseudepigrapha veteris testamenti Graece* 3. Leiden: Brill, 1970]: 129.
Q: 53: Pseudepigr.

1155 *APOCALYPSIS SYRIACA BARUCHI*
vel *II Baruch*
A.D. 1
001 **Fragmentum**, ed. A.-M. Denis, *Fragmenta pseudepigraphorum quae supersunt Graeca* [*Pseudepigrapha veteris testamenti Graece* 3. Leiden: Brill, 1970]: 118–120.
Pap: 234: Pseudepigr., Apocalyp.

1161 *APOCRYPHON EZECHIEL*
Incertum
001 **Fragmenta**, ed. A.-M. Denis, *Fragmenta pseudepigraphorum quae supersunt Graeca* [*Pseudepigrapha veteris testamenti Graece* 3. Leiden: Brill, 1970]: 121–123, 125–127.
Q, Pap: 1,013: Pseudepigr.

1162 **APOLLAS** Hist.
vel Apellas
3 B.C.: Ponticus
001 **Fragmenta**, FGrH #266: 3A:74–75.
Q: 431: Hist.

2074 **APOLLINARIS** Theol.
vel Apollinarius
A.D. 4: Laodicensis
001 **Fides secundum partem**, ed. H. Lietzmann, *Apollinaris von Laodicea und seine Schule*. Tübingen: Mohr, 1904 (repr. Hildesheim: Olms, 1970): 167–185.
Q, Cod: Theol.
002 **De unione corporis et divinitatis in Christo**, ed. Lietzmann, *op. cit.*, 185–193.
Cod: Theol.
003 **De fide et incarnatione contra adversarios**, ed. Lietzmann, *op. cit.*, 194–199.
Cod: Theol.
004 **De unione** (fragmentum), ed. Lietzmann, *op. cit.*, 204.
fr. 2.
Q: Theol.
005 **De incarnatione** (Περὶ σαρκώσεως) (fragmenta), ed. Lietzmann, *op. cit.*, 204–206.
frr. 3–8.
Q: Theol.
028 **De incarnatione** (Περὶ σαρκώσεως ἢ εἰς τὴν παράδοσιν τῆς ἀποτάξεως καὶ τῆς πίστεως) (fragmenta), ed. Lietzmann, *op. cit.*, 206–207.
frr. 9–10.
Q: Theol.
006 **Laudatio Mariae et de incarnatione**, ed. Lietzmann, *op. cit.*, 207–208.
frr. 11–12.
Q: Theol.
007 **Demonstratio de divina incarnatione ad similitudinem hominis** (fragmenta), ed. Lietzmann, *op. cit.*, 208–232.
frr. 13–107.
Q: Theol.
008 **In dei in carne manifestationem** (fragmenta), ed. Lietzmann, *op. cit.*, 232–233.
frr. 108–110.
Q: Theol.
009 **Ad illos qui hominem a verbo assumptum fuisse dicebant** (fragmentum), ed. Lietzmann, *op. cit.*, 233.
fr. 111.
Q: Theol.
010 **Syllogismi** (fragmenta), ed. Lietzmann, *op. cit.*, 233–235.
frr. 112–116.
Q: Theol.
011 **Contra Diodorum ad Heraclium** (fragmenta), ed. Lietzmann, *op. cit.*, 235–236.
frr. 117–120.
Q: Theol.
012 **Ad Diodorum** (Πρὸς Διόδωρον ἢ τὸ κατὰ

κεφάλαιον βιβλίον) (fragmenta), ed. Lietzmann, *op. cit.*, 237–242.
frr. 121–146.
Q: Theol.
013 **Recapitulatio** (fort. epitome), ed. Lietzmann, *op. cit.*, 242–246.
Q: Theol.
014 **Ad Flavianum** (fragmenta), ed. Lietzmann, *op. cit.*, 246–247.
frr. 147–148.
Q: Theol.
015 **Ad Petrum** (fragmentum), ed. Lietzmann, *op. cit.*, 247.
fr. 149.
Q: Theol.
016 **Ad Julianum** (fragmenta), ed. Lietzmann, *op. cit.*, 247–248.
frr. 150–152.
Q: Theol.
017 **Sermones** (fragmenta), ed. Lietzmann, *op. cit.*, 248–249.
frr. 153–156.
Q: Theol., Homilet.
018 **Fragmentum dialogi**, ed. Lietzmann, *op. cit.*, 249.
fr. 157.
Q: Theol., Dialog.
019 **Quod deus in carne Christus** (fragmentum), ed. Lietzmann, *op. cit.*, 249.
fr. 158.
Q: Theol.
020 **Ad Jovianum**, ed. Lietzmann, *op. cit.*, 250–253.
Q: Theol.
021 **Ad Serapionem** (fragmenta), ed. Lietzmann, *op. cit.*, 253–254.
frr. 159–161.
Q: Theol.
022 **Ad Terentium** (fragmenta), ed. Lietzmann, *op. cit.*, 254–255.
frr. 162–163.
Q: Theol.
023 **Ad episcopos Diocaesarienses**, ed. Lietzmann, *op. cit.*, 255–256.
Q: Theol.
024 **Epistula ad Dionysium 1**, ed. Lietzmann, *op. cit.*, 256–262.
Cod: Theol., Epist.
025 **Epistula ad Dionysium 2** (fragmentum), ed. Lietzmann, *op. cit.*, 262.
fr. 164.
Q: Theol., Epist.
026 **Tomus synodalis**, ed. Lietzmann, *op. cit.*, 262–263.
Q: Theol.
027 **Fragmenta ex operibus incertis**, ed. Lietzmann, *op. cit.*, 269–270.
frr. 168–171.
Q: Theol.
030 **Epistula de essentia dei** (epistula Sebastiani), ed. H. de Riedmatten, "La correspondance entre Basile de Césarée et Apollinaire de

Laodicée I," *Journal of Theological Studies*, n.s. 7 (1956) 208–210.
Cod: Epist., Theol.

040 **Fragmenta in Octateuchum et Reges** (in catenis), ed. R. Devreesse, *Les anciens commentateurs grecs de l'Octateuque et des Rois* [*Studi e Testi* 201. Vatican City: Biblioteca Apostolica Vaticana, 1959]: 129–154.
Q: Exeget., Caten.

041 **Fragmenta in Psalmos** (in catenis), ed. E. Mühlenberg, *Psalmenkommentare aus der Katenenüberlieferung*, vol. 1 [*Patristische Texte und Studien* 15. Berlin: De Gruyter, 1975]: 3–118.
Q: 23,432: Exeget., Caten.

031 **Fragmenta in proverbia**, ed. A. Mai, *Nova patrum bibliotheca*, vol. 7.2. Rome, 1854: 76–80.
Q: Exeget.

034 **Fragmenta in Canticum**, MPG 87 bis: 1548–1549, 1552, 1553, 1556, 1581, 1584, 1608, 1662, 1697, 1704, 1708, 1721, 1724, 1749.
Q: Exeget.

033 **Fragmenta in Isaiam**, ed. Mai, *Nova patrum bibliotheca*, vol. 7.2, 128–130.
Q: Exeget.

042 **Fragmenta in Jeremiam** (in catenis), ed. M. Ghisler, *In Ieremiam prophetam commentarii*, vols. 1–2. Lyon: Durand, 1623: 1.54, 55, 84, 160, 298, 427; 2.106, 166, 420, 423, 424, 450, 457, 484, 485, 503, 530, 534, 539, 558, 583, 595, 633, 634, 641, 660, 716, 719, 743, 745, 761, 773, 786, 790, 794, 821, 828, 883.
Q: Exeget., Caten.

043 **Fragmenta in Lamentationes** (in catenis), ed. Ghisler, *op cit.*, vol. 3 (1623): 15, 54.
Q: Exeget., Caten.

032 **Fragmenta in Ezechielem**, ed. Mai, *Nova patrum bibliotheca*, vol. 7.2, 82–91.
Q: Exeget.

035 **Fragmenta in Danielem**, ed. A. Mai, *Scriptorum veterum nova collectio*, vols. 1.2 & 1.3. Rome: Biblioteca Apostolica Vaticana, 1.2:1825; 1.3:1837: **1.2**:161–221; **1.3**:27–56.
Q: Exeget.

037 **Fragmenta in Matthaeum** (in catenis), ed. J. Reuss, *Matthäus-Kommentare aus der griechischen Kirche* [*Texte und Untersuchungen* 61. Berlin: Akademie-Verlag, 1957]: 2–54.
Q: 11,077: Exeget., Caten.

036 **Fragmenta in Lucam**, ed. Mai, *Scriptorum veterum nova collectio*, vol. 1.1 (1825): 179–188.
Q: Exeget.

038 **Fragmenta in Joannem** (in catenis), ed. J. Reuss, *Johannes-Kommentare aus der griechischen Kirche* [*Texte und Untersuchungen* 89. Berlin: Akademie-Verlag, 1966]: 3–64.
Q: 12,749: Exeget., Caten.

044 **Fragmentum in Acta apostolorum** (in catenis), ed. J.A. Cramer, *Catenae Graecorum patrum in*

Novum Testamentum, vol. 3. Oxford: Oxford University Press, 1838: 12.
Q: Exeget., Caten.

039 **Fragmenta in epistulam ad Romanos** (in catenis), ed. K. Staab, *Pauluskommentar aus der griechischen Kirche aus Katenenhandschriften gesammelt*. Münster: Aschendorff, 1933: 57–82.
Q: 8,143: Exeget., Caten.

045 **Fragmenta in epistulas catholicas** (in catenis), ed. Cramer, *op. cit.*, vol. 8 (1844): 11.
Q: Exeget., Caten.

046 **Metaphrasis psalmorum** [Sp.], ed. A. Ludwich, *Apolinarii metaphrasis psalmorum*. Leipzig: Teubner, 1912: 1–304.
Cod: Hexametr., Exeget.

x01 **Epistula ad Basilium 1.**
Courtonne, vol. 3, pp. 222–224 (epist. 362).
Cf. BASILIUS Theol. (2040 004).

x02 **Epistula ad Basilium 2.**
Courtonne, vol. 3, pp. 225–226 (epist. 364).
Cf. BASILIUS Theol. (2040 004).

x03 **In sanctum pascha** (sermones 1–3) (fort. auctore Apollinare Laodicense).
Nautin, vol. 2, pp. 55–75, 77–101, 103–117.
Cf. JOANNES CHRYSOSTOMUS Scr. Eccl. (2062 260–262).

1163 **Claudius APOLLINARIUS** Apol.
vel Apollinaris
A.D. 2: Hierapolitanus

001 **Fragmenta**, ed. J.C.T. Otto, *Corpus apologetarum Christianorum saeculi secundi*, vol. 9. Jena: Mauke, 1872 (repr. Wiesbaden: Sändig, 1969): 486–487.
frr. 1–2: Ex apologia.
frr. 3–4: De pascha.
Q: 216: Apol.

1221 **APOLLINARIUS** Astrol.
A.D. 1–2?

001 **Fragmenta**, ed. C.É. Ruelle, *Codices Parisini* [*Catalogus codicum astrologorum Graecorum* 8.2. Brussels: Lamertin, 1911]: 63, 132.
Q: Astrol.

0122 **APOLLINARIUS** Epigr.
A.D. 2

001 **Epigrammata**, AG 11.399, 421.
Q: 65: Epigr.

0785 **APOLLINARIUS** Med.
ante A.D. 4

x01 **Fragmentum ap. Oribasium.**
CMG, vol. 6.3, p. 98.
Cf. ORIBASIUS Med. (0722 004).

0411 **APOLLODORUS** Comic.
4/3 B.C.: Carystius
Cf. et APOLLODORUS Carystius vel APOLLODORUS Gelous Comic. (0412).

001 **Fragmenta**, ed. T. Kock, *Comicorum Atticorum fragmenta*, vol. 3. Leipzig: Teubner, 1888: 280–288.
frr. 1–13, 23–27.
Q: 366: Comic.

002 **Fragmenta**, ed. A. Meineke, *Fragmenta comicorum Graecorum*, vol. 4. Berlin: Reimer, 1841 (repr. De Gruyter, 1970): 440–442, 444–449.
Q: 354: Comic.

003 **Fragmentum**, ed. J. Demiańczuk, *Supplementum comicum*. Krakau: Nakładem Akademii, 1912 (repr. Hildesheim: Olms, 1967): 9.
fr. 1.
Q: 8: Comic.

004 **Fragmentum**, ed. C. Austin, *Comicorum Graecorum fragmenta in papyris reperta*. Berlin: De Gruyter, 1973: 4.
fr. 10.
Pap: 68: Comic.

0413 **APOLLODORUS** Comic.
4/3 B.C.: Gelous
Cf. et APOLLODORUS Carystius vel APOLLODORUS Gelous Comic. (0412).

001 **Fragmenta**, ed. T. Kock, *Comicorum Atticorum fragmenta*, vol. 3. Leipzig: Teubner, 1888: 278–280.
frr. 1–5 + tituli.
Q: 65: Comic.

002 **Fragmenta**, ed. A. Meineke, *Fragmenta comicorum Graecorum*, vol. 4. Berlin: Reimer, 1841 (repr. De Gruyter, 1970): 438–439.
Q: 56: Comic.

0549 **APOLLODORUS** Gramm.
fiq Apollodorus Myth.
2 B.C.: Atheniensis
Cf. et APOLLODORUS Myth. (0548).

001 **Testimonia**, FGrH #244: **2B**:1022–1025; **3B**:744 addenda.
test. 3: *IG* 2.953.
test. 4: *P. Oxy.* 10.1241.
test. 15 bis: *P. Tebt.*
NQ: 875: Test.

002 **Fragmenta**, FGrH #244: **2B**:1025–1128; **3B**:744 addenda.
fr. 89: *P. Oxy.* 15.1802.
fr. 302 ter: *P. Oxy.* 6.853.
Q: 31,134: Hist., Chronogr., Gramm., Myth.

003 **Fragmenta**, ed. H.J. Mette, "Die 'Kleinen' griechischen Historiker heute," *Lustrum* 21 (1978) 20–22.
frr. 217 bis, 257 bis, 280 bis, 354 bis.
fr. 354 bis: *P. Colon.* 5604.
Q, Pap: 562: Hist.

004 **Fragmenta**, ed. C. Theodoridis, "Vier neue Bruchstücke des Apollodoros von Athen," *Rheinisches Museum*, N.F. 122 (1979) 9–16.
Q

x01 **Bibliotheca**.
Myth. Graec. 1, pp. 1–169.
Cf. APOLLODORUS Myth. (0548 001).

2537 **APOLLODORUS** Hist.
post 4 B.C.?

001 **Fragmentum**, FGrH #803: 3C:842.
Q: 84: Hist.

2295 **APOLLODORUS** Hist.
ante 2 B.C.: Erythraeus

001 **Fragmenta**, FGrH #422: 3B:318.
Q: 127: Hist.

1164 **APOLLODORUS** Hist.
1 B.C.: Artemita

001 **Fragmenta**, FGrH #779: 3C:773–776.
Q: 1,074: Hist.

0365 **APOLLODORUS** Lyr.
6 B.C.: fort. Atheniensis

001 **Fragmentum**, ed. D.L. Page, *Poetae melici Graeci*. Oxford: Clarendon Press, 1962 (repr. 1967 (1st edn. corr.)): 364.
fr. 1.
Q: 9: Lyr.

APOLLODORUS Math.
fiq Apollodorus Cyzicenus
ante A.D. 3
AG 7.119.
Cf. ANONYMI EPIGRAMMATICI (AG) (0138 001).

1165 **APOLLODORUS** Mech.
A.D. 1–2: Damascenus

001 **Poliorcetica**, ed. R. Schneider, *Griechische Poliorketiker* [*Abhandlungen der königlichen Gesellschaft der Wissenschaften zu Göttingen*, Philol.-hist. Kl., N.F. 10, no. 1. Berlin: Weidmann, 1908]: 8–50.
Cod: 5,981: Mech., Tact.

0786 **APOLLODORUS** Med.
3 B.C.: Alexandrinus

x01 **Fragmenta ap. Galenum**.
K14.181, 184.
Cf. GALENUS Med. (0057 078).

x02 **Fragmentum ap. Athenaeum**.
Deipnosophistae 15.681d.
Cf. ATHENAEUS Soph. (0008 001).

0548 **APOLLODORUS** Myth.
fiq Apollodorus Gramm.
A.D. 1/2
Cf. et APOLLODORUS Gramm. (0549).

001 **Bibliotheca**, ed. R. Wagner, *Apollodori bibliotheca. Pediasimi libellus de duodecim Herculis laboribus* [*Mythographi Graeci* 1. Leipzig: Teubner, 1894]: 1–169.
Cod: 28,414: Myth.

2319 **APOLLODORUS** Phil.
5 B.C.: Cyzicenus

001 **Testimonia**, ed. H. Diels and W. Kranz, *Die Fragmente der Vorsokratiker*, vol. 2, 6th edn.

Berlin: Weidmann, 1952 (repr. Dublin: 1966):
246.
test. 1–3.
NQ: 56: Test.

1166 APOLLODORUS Phil.
2 B.C.: Seleuciensis
001 **Fragmenta**, ed. J. von Arnim, *Stoicorum veterum fragmenta*, vol. 3. Leipzig: Teubner,
1903 (repr. Stuttgart: 1968): 259–261.
Q: 819: Phil.

0700 APOLLODORUS Trag.
4 B.C.: Tarsensis
001 **Tituli**, ed. B. Snell, *Tragicorum Graecorum
fragmenta*, vol. 1. Göttingen: Vandenhoeck &
Ruprecht, 1971: 209.
NQ: 6: Trag.

**0412 APOLLODORUS Carystius vel APOLLO-
DORUS Gelous** Comic.
4/3 B.C.
Cf. et APOLLODORUS Comic. (0411).
Cf. et APOLLODORUS Comic. (0413).
001 **Fragmenta**, ed. T. Kock, *Comicorum Atticorum fragmenta*, vol. 3. Leipzig: Teubner,
1888: 288–295.
frr. 1–23, 26.
Q: 441: Comic.
002 **Fragmenta**, ed. Meineke, *Fragmenta comicorum Graecorum*, vol. 4. Berlin: Reimer, 1841
(repr. De Gruyter, 1970): 450–457.
Q: 414: Comic.

APOLLODOTUS Epigr.
AG 7.119.
Cf. ANONYMI EPIGRAMMATICI (AG) (0138
001).

0124 APOLLONIDES Epigr.
A.D. 1: Smyrnaeus
001 **Epigrammata**, AG **6**.105, 238–239; **7**.180, 233,
378, 389, 631, 642, 693, 702, 742; **9**.228, 243–
244, 257, 264–265, 271, 280–281, 287, 296,
408, 422, 791; **10**.19; **11**.25; **16**.49–50, 235,
239.
Q: 1,146: Epigr.

0345 APOLLONIDES Trag.
fiq filius Ardonis
3/2 B.C.
001 **Fragmenta**, ed. B. Snell, *Tragicorum Graecorum fragmenta*, vol. 1. Göttingen: Vandenhoeck & Ruprecht, 1971: 308.
frr. 1–2.
Q: 41: Trag.

2451 APOLLONIDES HORAPIUS Hist.
ante A.D. 2
001 **Fragmenta**, FGrH #661: 3C:212–213.
Q: 308: Hist.

1167 APOLLONIUS Biogr.
A.D. 2?
001 **Vita Aeschinis**, ed. V. Martin and G. de Budé,
Eschine. Discours, vol. 1. Paris: Les Belles
Lettres, 1927 (repr. 1962): 4–6.
Dup. VITAE AESCHINIS (4166 001) (pp. 1–3).
Cod: [864]

0394 APOLLONIUS Comic.
Incertum
001 **Fragmenta**, ed. C. Austin, *Comicorum Graecorum fragmenta in papyris reperta*. Berlin: De
Gruyter, 1973: 5.
frr. 11–12.
Pap: 13: Comic.

0550 APOLLONIUS Geom.
3 B.C.: Pergaeus
001 **Conica**, ed. J.L. Heiberg, *Apollonii Pergaei
quae Graece exstant*, vols. 1–2. Leipzig: Teubner, 1:1891; 2:1893 (repr. Stuttgart: 1974): 1:2–
450; 2:2–96.
Cod: 62,038: Math.
002 **Fragmenta**, ed. Heiberg, *op. cit.*, vol. 2, 101–
139.
Q: Math.

1404 APOLLONIUS Gramm.
2/1 B.C.?
001 **Fragmenta**, ed. R. Berndt, *De Charete, Chaeride, Alexione grammaticis eorumque reliquiis*,
pt. 1. Königsberg: Hartung, 1902: 50–52.
frr. 1–4.
Q: [153]

1170 APOLLONIUS Hist.
3 B.C.?: Aphrodisiensis
001 **Testimonium**, FGrH #740: 3C:714.
NQ: 22: Test.
002 **Fragmenta**, FGrH #740: 3C:715–717.
Q: 625: Hist.

1169 APOLLONIUS Hist.
2 B.C.: Atheniensis
001 **Testimonium**, FGrH #365: 3B:225.
test. 1: *IG*² 2.3487.
NQ: 31: Test.
002 **Fragmenta**, FGrH #365: 3B:225–226.
Q: 295: Hist.

2283 APOLLONIUS Hist.
Incertum
001 **Fragmentum**, FGrH #403: 3B:298.
Q: 37: Hist.

APOLLONIUS Math.
fiq Apollonius Tyanensis
Cf. APOCALYPSIS ADAM (1153 001).

0680 APOLLONIUS Med.
3 B.C.: Memphiticus
Cf. et APOLLONIUS Med. (0741).

x01 **Fragmenta ap. Galenum.**
K8.759, 760–761; **14**.188.
Cf. GALENUS Med. (0057 059, 078).

0741 **APOLLONIUS** Med.
fiq Apollonius Memphiticus
3 B.C.?
Cf. et APOLLONIUS Med. (0680).
x01 **Fragmenta ap. Aëtium** (lib. 6–8).
CMG, vol. 8.2, pp. 223, 230, 238, 353, 375, 451.
Cf. AËTIUS Med. (0718 006–008).

0660 **APOLLONIUS** Med.
1 B.C.: Citiensis
Cf. et APOLLONIUS Med. (0739).
001 **In Hippocratis de articulis commentarius**, ed. J. Kollesch and F. Kudlien, *Apollonios von Kition. Kommentar zu Hippokrates über das Einrenken der Gelenke* [*Corpus medicorum Graecorum*, vol. 11.1.1. Berlin: Akademie-Verlag, 1965]: 10–112.
Cod: 12,505: Med., Comm.

0739 **APOLLONIUS** Med.
fiq Apollonius Citiensis vel Apollonius Pergamenus
1 B.C./A.D. 1?
Cf. et APOLLONIUS Med. (0660).
Cf. et APOLLONIUS Med. (0792).
x01 **Fragmenta ap. Alexandrum Trallianum.**
Puschmann, vol. 1, pp. 559, 561.
Cf. ALEXANDER Med. (0744 003).

0789 **Claudius APOLLONIUS** Med.
A.D. 1
Cf. et APOLLONIUS Archistrator Med. (0747).
x01 **Fragmentum ap. Galenum.**
K14.171–172.
Cf. GALENUS Med. (0057 078).

0792 **APOLLONIUS** Med.
A.D. 1?: Pergamenus
Cf. et APOLLONIUS Med. (0739).
x01 **Fragmenta ap. Oribasium.**
CMG, vol. **6.1.1**, p. 218; **6.2.1**, p. 158; **6.3**, p. 12.
Cf. ORIBASIUS Med. (0722 001, 004).

0782 **APOLLONIUS** Med.
ante A.D. 2: Tarsensis
x01 **Fragmentum ap. Galenum.**
K13.843.
Cf. GALENUS Med. (0057 077).

0569 **APOLLONIUS** Paradox.
2 B.C.?
001 **Historiae mirabiles**, ed. A. Giannini, *Paradoxographorum Graecorum reliquiae*. Milan: Istituto Editoriale Italiano, 1965: 120–142.
Cod: 2,400: Paradox.

0619 **APOLLONIUS** Phil.
A.D. 1: Tyanensis
001 **Apotelesmata** [Sp.], ed. F. Nau, *Patrologia Syriaca* 2 (1907): 1372–1391.
Cod
002 **De horis diei et noctis** (fragmenta e cod. Berol. 26) [Sp.], ed. F. Boll, *Codices Germanici* [*Catalogus codicum astrologorum Graecorum* 7. Brussels: Lamertin, 1908]: 175–181.
Dup. partim 0619 001.
Cod
x01 **Epistulae.**
Kayser, pp. 345–368.
Cf. Flavius PHILOSTRATUS Soph. (0638 002).
x02 **Fragmentum ap. Eusebium.**
Eusebius, *Praep. Ev.* 4.12.
Cf. EUSEBIUS Scr. Eccl. et Theol. (2018 001).
x03 Νυχθήμερον (fort. auctore Apollonio).
Robinson, pp. 139–144.
Cf. APOCALYPSIS ADAM (1153 001).

1171 **APOLLONIUS** Scr. Eccl.
A.D. 2–3: Ephesius
001 **Fragmenta ex libro adversus Cataphrygas seu Montanistas**, ed. M.J. Routh, *Reliquiae sacrae*, vol. 1, 2nd edn. Oxford: Oxford University Press, 1846 (repr. Hildesheim: Olms, 1974): 467–472.
Q: 739: Eccl., Invectiv.

1168 **APOLLONIUS** Soph.
A.D. 1–2
001 **Lexicon Homericum**, ed. I. Bekker, *Apollonii Sophistae lexicon Homericum*. Berlin: Reimer, 1833 (repr. Hildesheim: Olms, 1967): 1–171.
Cod: 41,344: Lexicogr.

0747 **APOLLONIUS Archistrator** Med.
fiq Claudius Apollonius
A.D. 1?
Cf. et Claudius APOLLONIUS Med. (0789).
x01 **Fragmentum ap. Galenum.**
K13.835.
Cf. GALENUS Med. (0057 077).

4259 **APOLLONIUS CRONUS** Phil.
4–3 B.C.: Cyrenaeus, Atheniensis
001 **Testimonia**, ed. K. Döring, *Die Megariker* [*Studien zur antiken Philosophie* 2. Amsterdam: Grüner, 1972]: 28.
test. 96–98 = Diodorus Cronus (0073 001).
NQ: Test.

0082 **APOLLONIUS DYSCOLUS** Gramm.
A.D. 2: Alexandrinus
001 **De pronominibus**, ed. R. Schneider, *Grammatici Graeci*, vol. 2.1. Leipzig: Teubner, 1878 (repr. Hildesheim: Olms, 1965): 3–116.
Cod: 28,064: Gramm.
002 **De adverbiis**, ed. Schneider, *Gramm. Graec.*, vol. 2.1, 119–210.
Cod: 23,861: Gramm.

003 **De conjunctionibus**, ed. Schneider, *Gramm. Graec.*, vol. 2.1, 213–258.
Cod: 15,164: Gramm.

004 **De constructione**, ed. G. Uhlig, *Gramm. Graec.*, vol. 2.2 (1910; repr. 1965): 1–497.
Cod: 63,393: Gramm.

005 **Fragmenta librorum deperditorum**, ed. Schneider, *Gramm. Graec.*, vol. 2.3 (1910; repr. 1965): 1–140.
Q: Gramm.

0810 **APOLLONIUS et ALCIMION** Med.
A.D. 1
Cf. et ALCIMION Med. (0765).

x01 **Fragmentum ap. Galenum.**
K13.31.
Cf. GALENUS Med. (0057 076).

2491 **APOLLONIUS MOLO** Hist.
1 B.C.: Rhodius

001 **Testimonia**, FGrH #728: 3C:687–688.
NQ: 369: Test.

002 **Fragmenta**, FGrH #728: 3C:688–689.
Q: 351: Hist.

0790 **APOLLONIUS MYS** Med.
1 B.C.: Alexandrinus

001 **Fragmentum** (*P. Oxy.* 2.234), ed. B.P. Grenfell and A.S. Hunt, *The Oxyrhynchus papyri*, pt. 2. London: Egypt Exploration Fund, 1899: 135–136.
Pap: Med.

x01 **Fragmenta ap. Galenum.**
K12.475–478, 614–620, 633; **14**.146.
Cf. GALENUS Med. (0057 076, 078).

x02 **Fragmenta ap. Philumenum.**
CMG, vol. 10.1.1, pp. 10, 24, 26, 30, 37.
Cf. PHILUMENUS Med. (0671 001).

x03 **Fragmentum ap. Athenaeum.**
Deipnosophistae 15.688e–689b.
Cf. ATHENAEUS Soph. (0008 001).

APOLLONIUS Opsis Med.
Cf. APOLLONIUS Organicus Med. (0817).
Cf. APOLLONIUS Ther Med. (0791).

0817 **APOLLONIUS Organicus** Med.
fiq Apollonius Opsis
1 B.C.?

x01 **Fragmentum ap. Galenum.**
K13.856.
Cf. GALENUS Med. (0057 077).

0001 **APOLLONIUS RHODIUS** Epic.
3 B.C.: Rhodius
Scholia et vitae: Cf. SCHOLIA IN APOLLO-NIUM RHODIUM (5012).

001 **Argonautica**, ed. H. Fraenkel, *Apollonii Rhodii Argonautica*. Oxford: Clarendon Press, 1961 (repr. 1970 (1st edn. corr.)): 1–242.
Cod: 39,090: Epic.

002 **Fragmenta**, ed. J.U. Powell, *Collectanea Alexandrina*. Oxford: Clarendon Press, 1925 (repr. 1970): 4–8.
frr. 1–2, 5, 7–10, 12–13.
Q: 243: Epic., Epigr.

003 **Epigramma**, AG 11.275.
Dup. 0001 002 (CA, p. 8, fr. 13).
Q: 16: Epigr.

004 **Tituli**, ed. Powell, *op. cit.*, 5–6.
frr. 4, 6.
NQ: Epic.

0791 **APOLLONIUS Ther** Med.
fiq Apollonius Opsis
1 B.C.?

x01 **Fragmentum ap. Oribasium.**
CMG, vol. 6.2.1, p. 282.
Cf. ORIBASIUS Med. (0722 001).

0414 **APOLLOPHANES** Comic.
5–4 B.C.

001 **Fragmenta**, ed. T. Kock, *Comicorum Atticorum fragmenta*, vol. 1. Leipzig: Teubner, 1880: 797–799.
frr. 2–6, 8, 10 + tituli.
Q: 45: Comic.

002 **Fragmenta**, ed. A. Meineke, *Fragmenta comicorum Graecorum*, vol. 2.2. Berlin: Reimer, 1840 (repr. De Gruyter, 1970): 879–881.
Q: 37: Comic.

003 **Fragmentum**, ed. J. Demiańczuk, *Supplementum comicum*. Krakau: Nakładem Akademii, 1912 (repr. Hildesheim: Olms, 1967): 9.
fr. 1.
Q: 5: Comic.

004 **Tituli**, ed. C. Austin, *Comicorum Graecorum fragmenta in papyris reperta*. Berlin: De Gruyter, 1973: 6.
fr. 13.
Pap: 4: Comic.

0794 **APOLLOPHANES** Med.
3 B.C.: Seleuciensis

x01 **Fragmenta ap. Galenum.**
K13.220, 831, 979.
Cf. GALENUS Med. (0057 076–077).

x02 **Fragmentum ap. Oribasium.**
CMG, vol. 6.3, p. 87.
Cf. ORIBASIUS Med. (0722 004).

x03 **Fragmentum ap. Paulum.**
CMG, vol. 9.2, p. 373.
Cf. PAULUS Med. (0715 001).

x04 **Fragmentum ap. Alexandrum Trallianum.**
Puschmann, vol. 2, p. 387.
Cf. ALEXANDER Med. (0744 003).

2168 **APOLLOPHANES** Phil.
3 B.C.

001 **Fragmenta**, ed. J. von Arnim, *Stoicorum veterum fragmenta*, vol. 1. Leipzig: Teubner, 1905 (repr. Stuttgart: 1968): 90.
Q: 171: Phil.

9009 **Michael APOSTOLIUS** Paroemiogr.
  A.D. 15: Constantinopolitanus, Creticus
 001 **Collectio paroemiarum**, ed. E.L. von Leutsch,
  Corpus paroemiographorum Graecorum, vol. 2.
  Göttingen: Vandenhoeck & Ruprecht, 1851
  (repr. Hildesheim: Olms, 1958): 233–744.
  Cod: 56,237: Paroem.

9007 *APPENDIX PROVERBIORUM*
  Incertum
 001 **Appendix proverbiorum**, ed. E.L. von Leutsch
  and F.G. Schneidewin, *Corpus paroemiographorum Graecorum*, vol. 1. Göttingen: Vandenhoeck & Ruprecht, 1839 (repr. Hildesheim:
  Olms, 1965): 379–467.
  Cod: 8,276: Paroem.

0551 **APPIANUS** Hist.
  A.D. 1–2: Alexandrinus
 001 **Prooemium**, ed. P. Viereck, A.G. Roos and E.
  Gabba, *Appiani historia Romana*, vol. 1. Leip-
  zig: Teubner, 1939 (repr. 1962 (1st edn. corr.)):
  1–12.
  Cod: 2,396: Hist.
 002 **Basilica** (fragmenta), ed. Viereck, Roos, and
  Gabba, *op. cit.*, 12–20.
  Q, Cod: 1,411: Hist.
 003 **Italica** (fragmenta), ed. Viereck, Roos, and
  Gabba, *op. cit.*, 20–27.
  Q, Cod: 1,230: Hist.
 004 **Samnitica** (fragmenta), ed. Viereck, Roos, and
  Gabba, *op. cit.*, 27–43.
  Q, Cod: 3,561: Hist.
 005 **Celtica** (fragmenta), ed. Viereck, Roos, and
  Gabba, *op. cit.*, 44–57.
  Q, Cod: 2,321: Hist.
 006 **Sicelica** (fragmenta), ed. Viereck, Roos, and
  Gabba, *op. cit.*, 57–62.
  Q, Cod: 1,019: Hist.
 007 **Iberica**, ed. Viereck, Roos, and Gabba, *op. cit.*,
  62–140.
  Cod: 16,514: Hist.
 008 **Annibaica**, ed. Viereck, Roos, and Gabba, *op.
  cit.*, 141–185.
  Cod: 9,931: Hist.
 009 **Libyca**, ed. Viereck, Roos, and Gabba, *op. cit.*,
  185–304.
  Cod: 25,979: Hist.
 010 **Numidica** (fragmenta), ed. Viereck, Roos, and
  Gabba, *op. cit.*, 305–307.
  Q, Cod: 407: Hist.
 011 **Macedonica** (fragmenta), ed. Viereck, Roos,
  and Gabba, *op. cit.*, 307–326.
  Q, Cod: 3,852: Hist.
 012 **Illyrica**, ed. Viereck, Roos, and Gabba, *op. cit.*,
  326–351.
  Cod: 4,977: Hist.
 013 **Syriaca**, ed. Viereck, Roos, and Gabba, *op. cit.*,
  352–418.
  Cod: 14,027: Hist.
 014 **Mithridatica**, ed. Viereck, Roos, and Gabba, *op.
  cit.*, 418–531.
  Cod: 24,766: Hist.

 015 **Fragmenta historiae Romanae**, ed. Viereck,
  Roos, and Gabba, *op. cit.*, 532–536.
  frr. 2–24.
  Q, Cod: 640: Hist.
 016 **Appiani ad Frontonem epistula**, ed. Viereck,
  Roos, and Gabba, *op. cit.*, 537–538.
  Cod: 330: Epist.
 017 **Bellum civile**, ed. P. Viereck, *Appian's Roman
  history*, vols. 3–4 (ed. H. White). Cambridge,
  Mass.: Harvard University Press, 1913 (repr.
  3:1964; 4:1961): **3**:2–566; **4**:2–616.
  Cod: 120,226: Hist.
 018 **Testimonium**, FGrH #237: 2B:990.
  NQ: 55: Test.

2027 **Valerius APSINES** Rhet.
  A.D. 3: Gadarensis, Atheniensis
 001 **Ars rhetorica**, ed. L. Spengel, *Rhetores Graeci*,
  vol. 1. Leipzig: Teubner, 1856 (repr. Frankfurt
  am Main: Minerva, 1966): 331–406.
  Cod: 19,515: Rhet.
 002 Περὶ τῶν ἐσχηματισμένων προβλημάτων, ed.
  Spengel, *op. cit.*, 407–414.
  Cod: 1,911: Rhet.

1768 **AQUILA** Int. Vet. Test.
  A.D. 2
 001 **Fragmenta**, ed. J. Reider, *An index to Aquila*
  (rev. N. Turner). Leiden: Brill, 1966: passim.
  Q

0795 **AQUILA SECUNDILLA** Med.
  ante A.D. 1
 x01 **Fragmentum ap. Galenum**.
  K13.1031.
  Cf. GALENUS Med. (0057 077).

4035 **ARABIUS** Epigr.
  A.D. 6
 001 **Epigrammata**, AG **9**.667; **16**.39, 144, 148–149,
  225, 314.
  Q: 199: Epigr.

0415 **ARAROS** Comic.
  5–4 B.C.
 001 **Fragmenta**, ed. T. Kock, *Comicorum Atticorum fragmenta*, vol. 2. Leipzig: Teubner,
  1884: 215–219.
  frr. 1–21.
  Q: 115: Comic.
 002 **Fragmenta**, ed. A. Meineke, *Fragmenta comicorum Graecorum*, vol. 3. Berlin: Reimer, 1840
  (repr. De Gruyter, 1970): 273–276.
  Q: 93: Comic.
 003 **Tituli**, ed. C. Austin, *Comicorum Graecorum
  fragmenta in papyris reperta*. Berlin: De Gruyter, 1973: 6.
  fr. 14.
  Pap: 8: Comic.
 004 **Fragmentum**, ed. Kock, *CAF*, vol. 3 (1888):
  738.
  Q: [1]: Comic.

0653 **ARATUS** Epic. et Astron.
4–3 B.C.: Soleus
Vitae: Cf. VITAE ARATI ET VARIA DE
ARATO (4161).
Scholia: Cf. SCHOLIA IN ARATUM (5013).
001 **Phaenomena,** ed. J. Martin, *Arati phaenomena.*
Florence: La Nuova Italia Editrice, 1956: 3–
154.
Cod: 7,866: Epic., Astron.
002 **Fragmentum** (e cod. Vat. gr. 2130), ed. S.
Weinstock, *Codices Romani [Catalogus codicum
astrologorum Graecorum* 5.4. Brussels: Acade-
mia, 1940]: 165–166.
Cf. et 0653 004.
Cod: Astrol.
003 **Epigrammata,** AG 11.437; 12.129.
Q: 51: Epigr.
004 **Fragmentum** (e cod. Matrit. 4616), ed. K.O.
Zuretti, *Codices Hispanienses [Catalogus codi-
cum astrologorum Graecorum* 11.2. Brussels:
Lamertin, 1934]: 133–134.
Cf. et 0653 002.
Cod: Astrol.
005 **Fragmenta et tituli,** ed. H. Lloyd-Jones and P.
Parsons, *Supplementum Hellenisticum.* Berlin:
De Gruyter, 1983: 34–42.
frr. (+ titul.) 83–90, 92–120.
Q: 158: Epic., Astron., Med., Eleg., Epigr.,
Epist., Hymn.

2443 **ARATUS** Hist.
post 4 B.C.?: Cnidius
001 **Testimonium,** FGrH #642: 3C:188.
NQ: 26: Test.

2162 **ARATUS** Hist.
3 B.C.: Sicyonius
001 **Testimonia,** FGrH #231: 2B:974–975.
NQ: 379: Test.
002 **Fragmenta,** FGrH #231: 2B:975–978.
Q: 1,355: Hist.

2116 **ARCADIUS** Gramm.
A.D. 4?: Antiochenus
001 **De accentibus** [Sp.], ed. M. Schmidt, Ἐπιτομὴ
τῆς καθολικῆς προσῳδίας Ἡρωδιανοῦ. Jena:
Mauke, 1860.
Q, Cod: [40,095]: Gramm.

0038 *ARCESILAI EPISTULA*
Incertum
Cf. et ARCESILAUS Phil. (1172).
001 **Epistula,** ed. R. Hercher, *Epistolographi Graeci.*
Paris: Didot, 1873 (repr. Amsterdam: Hakkert,
1965): 131.
Q: 97: Epist.

0520 **ARCESILAUS** Comic.
5 B.C.
001 **Fragmentum,** ed. J. Demiańczuk, *Supplemen-*

tum comicum. Krakau: Nakładem Akademii,
1912 (repr. Hildesheim: Olms, 1967): 10.
fr. 1.
Q: 11: Comic.

1172 **ARCESILAUS** Phil.
vel Arcesilas
4–3 B.C.: Pitanaeus
Cf. et ARCESILAI EPISTULA (0038).
001 **Fragmenta,** ed. H. Lloyd-Jones and P. Parsons,
Supplementum Hellenisticum. Berlin: De Gruy-
ter, 1983: 42–43.
frr. 121–122.
Dup. 1172 x01.
Q: 76: Epigr.
x01 **Epigrammata** (*App. Anth.*).
Epigramma sepulcrale: 2.382.
Epigramma demonstrativum: 3.56.
Dup. 1172 001.
App. Anth. 2.382: Cf. ANTHOLOGIAE GRAE-
CAE APPENDIX (7052 002).
App. Anth. 3.56: Cf. ANTHOLOGIAE GRAE-
CAE APPENDIX (7052 003).

2608 **ARCHEBULUS** Poeta
3 B.C.: Thebaeus vel Theraeus
001 **Fragmentum,** ed. H. Lloyd-Jones and P. Parsons, *Supplementum Hellenisticum.* Berlin: De
Gruyter, 1983: 44.
fr. 124.
Q: 8: Poem.

1173 **ARCHEDEMUS** Phil.
2 B.C.: Tarsensis
001 **Fragmenta,** ed. J. von Arnim, *Stoicorum veterum fragmenta,* vol. 3. Leipzig: Teubner,
1903 (repr. Stuttgart: 1968): 262–264.
Q: 879: Phil.

0416 **ARCHEDICUS** Comic.
4–3 B.C.
001 **Fragmenta,** ed. T. Kock, *Comicorum Atticorum fragmenta,* vol. 3. Leipzig: Teubner,
1888: 276–277.
frr. 1–3.
Q: 171: Comic.
002 **Fragmenta,** ed. A. Meineke, *Fragmenta comicorum Graecorum,* vol. 4. Berlin: Reimer, 1841
(repr. De Gruyter, 1970): 435–437.
Q: 170: Comic.

1935 **ARCHELAUS** Hist.
1 B.C.–A.D. 1: Cappadox
001 **Testimonia,** FGrH #123: 2B:629.
NQ: 38: Test.
002 **Fragmenta,** FGrH #123: 2B:630–631.
fr. 6: *P. Oxy.* 2.218.
Q, Pap: 483: Hist.

0937 **ARCHELAUS** Med.
ante A.D. 1

x01 **Fragmentum ap. Galenum.**
K13.312.
Cf. GALENUS Med. (0057 076).

0570 **ARCHELAUS** Paradox.
3 B.C.: Aegyptius, Chersonesita
001 **Fragmenta**, ed. A. Giannini, *Paradoxographorum Graecorum reliquiae.* Milan: Istituto Editoriale Italiano, 1965: 24–27.
Cod: Paradox.
002 **Epigramma**, AG 16.120.
Q: 33: Epigr.
003 **Fragmenta**, ed. H. Lloyd-Jones and P. Parsons, *Supplementum Hellenisticum.* Berlin: De Gruyter, 1983: 44–45.
frr. 125–129.
Q: 82: Epigr.
x01 **Epigrammata demonstrativa.**
App. Anth. 3.50–52: Cf. ANTHOLOGIAE GRAECAE APPENDIX (7052 003).
Dup. partim 0570 001 (frr. 4–5), 003 (frr. 125–126, 129).

2303 **ARCHELAUS** Phil.
5 B.C.: Milesius, Atheniensis
001 **Testimonia**, ed. H. Diels and W. Kranz, *Die Fragmente der Vorsokratiker*, vol. 2, 6th edn. Berlin: Weidmann, 1952 (repr. Dublin: 1966): 44–47.
test. 1–18.
NQ: 1,170: Test.
002 **Fragmenta**, ed. Diels and Kranz, *op. cit.*, 48.
frr. 1–2.
Q: 184: Phil.

1174 **ARCHEMACHUS** Hist.
3 B.C.?: Euboeus
001 **Fragmenta**, FGrH #424: 3B:319–322.
Q: 637: Hist.

1175 **ARCHESTRATUS** Parodius
4 B.C.: Gelensis vel Syracusanus
001 **Fragmenta**, ed. P. Brandt, *Parodorum epicorum Graecorum et Archestrati reliquiae* [*Corpusculum poesis epicae Graecae Ludibundae*, fasc. 1. Leipzig: Teubner, 1888]: 140–170.
frr. 1–62.
Dup. 1175 002.
Q: 2,616: Parod.
002 **Fragmenta et tituli**, ed. H. Lloyd-Jones and P. Parsons, *Supplementum Hellenisticum.* Berlin: De Gruyter, 1983: 46–74.
frr. (+ titul.) 132–133, 135–140, 142–192.
Dup. 1175 001.
Q: 2,343: Parod.

1115 **ARCHESTRATUS** Trag.
4 B.C.
001 **Titulus**, ed. B. Snell, *Tragicorum Graecorum fragmenta*, vol. 1. Göttingen: Vandenhoeck & Ruprecht, 1971: 239.
NQ: 1: Trag.

0127 **Aulus Licinius ARCHIAS** Epigr.
5 B.C.: Heracleota
001 **Epigramma**, ed. E. Diehl, *Anthologia lyrica Graeca*, fasc. 1, 3rd edn. Leipzig: Teubner, 1949: 111–112.
Q: 25: Epigr.
x01 **Epigramma demonstrativum.**
App. Anth. 3.29: Cf. ANTHOLOGIAE GRAECAE APPENDIX (7052 003).
Dup. 0127 001.

0126 **ARCHIAS** Epigr.
1 B.C.: Antiochenus
001 **Epigrammata**, AG **5.**58–59, 98; **6.**16, 39, 179–181, 192, 195, 207; **7.**68, 140, 147, 165, 191, 213–214, 278, 696; **9.**19, 27, 64, 91, 111, 339, 343, 750; **10.**7–8, 10; **15.**51; **16.**94, 154, 179.
AG 6.194; 9.357: Cf. ANONYMI EPIGRAMMATICI (AG) (0138 001).
AG 7.164: Cf. ANTIPATER Epigr. (0113 001).
AG 9.345–348, 351, 354: Cf. Julius LEONIDAS Math. et Astrol. (1457 001).
Q: 1,425: Epigr.
002 **Testimonium**, FGrH #186: 2B:918.
NQ: 180: Test.

0796 **ARCHIBIUS** Med.
1 B.C.
x01 **Fragmentum ap. Galenum.**
K14.159–160.
Cf. GALENUS Med. (0057 078).

0661 **ARCHIGENES** Med.
A.D. 1–2: Apamensis
Cf. et ARCHIGENES et POSIDONIUS Med. (0869).
001 **Fragmenta**, ed. C. Brescia, *Frammenti medicinali di Archigene.* Naples: Libreria Scientifica, 1955: 9–24.
Περὶ φλεγμονῆς σπληνός: pp. 9–12.
Θεραπεία: pp. 12–14.
Περὶ τῶν ἑλμίνθων γενῶν καὶ πόσαι διαφοραί: pp. 14–20.
Περὶ λειεντερίας: pp. 20–24.
Q: 5,502: Med.
002 **Fragmenta inedita**, ed. G.L. Calabrò, "Frammenti inediti di Archigene," *Bollettino del comitato per la preparazione della edizione nazionale dei classici greci e latini* 9 (1961) 68–72.
Περὶ ἀποστήματος ἐν ἥπατι: pp. 68–69.
Θεραπεία ἡλκωμένου ἥπατος: pp. 69–70.
Περὶ καχεξίας: p. 71.
Κοινὴ δίαιτα πάντων τῶν ὑδρωπικῶν: p. 72.
Q: 1,773: Med.
x01 **Fragmenta ap. Galenum.**
K12.406–410, 432, 443–445, 460–462, 463, 468–469, 533–534, 537–541, 546, 550, 551, 572–573, 576–578, 582, 620–624, 644–646, 655–658, 661–662, 671–673, 675–677, 679–680, 681, 790–803, 807–814, 821–822, 846–847, 855–858, 859–864, 873–877, 954, 969,

972–974, 1000–1002; **13**.167–175, 217–219, 234–236, 254–256, 262–266, 331, 730–734.
Cf. GALENUS Med. (0057 076–077).

x02 **Fragmenta ap. Oribasium.**
CMG **6.1.1**, pp. 247, 250, 296; **6.2.1**, pp. 103, 146, 234, 236, 257; **6.2.2**, pp. 205, 299; **6.3**, pp. 104, 269.
Cf. ORIBASIUS Med. (0722 001, 003–004).

x03 **Fragmenta ap. Paulum.**
CMG **9.1**, pp. 117, 122, 222, 245, 326, 328, 333, 349, 356, 361, 367; **9.2**, pp. 17, 288.
Cf. PAULUS Med. (0715 001).

x04 **Fragmenta ap. Aëtium (lib. 3).**
CMG 8.1, pp. 341–343, 344, 351, 352–355.
Cf. AËTIUS Med. (0718 003).

x05 **Fragmentum ap. Aëtium (lib. 8).**
CMG 8.2, p. 475.
Cf. AËTIUS Med. (0718 008).

x06 **Fragmentum ap. Aëtium (lib. 9).**
Athena 23 (1911) 359–365.
Cf. AËTIUS Med. (0718 009).

x07 **Fragmenta ap. Philumenum.**
CMG 10.1.1, pp. 10, 17, 37, 40.
Cf. PHILUMENUS Med. (0671 001).

x08 **Fragmenta ap. Alexandrum Trallianum.**
Puschmann, vol. 1, pp. 557, 567.
Cf. ALEXANDER Med. (0744 003).

0869 **ARCHIGENES et POSIDONIUS** Med.
A.D. 1–2
Cf. et ARCHIGENES Med. (0661).

x01 **Fragmenta ap. Aëtium (lib. 6).**
CMG, vol. 8.2, pp. 128–141.
Cf. AËTIUS Med. (0718 006).

0232 **ARCHILOCHUS** Iamb. et Eleg.
7 B.C.: Parius

001 **Fragmenta**, ed. M.L. West, *Iambi et elegi Graeci*, vol. 1. Oxford: Clarendon Press, 1971: 1–60, 62, 65–96, 99–100, 102–104, 106–108.
frr. 1–6, 8–32, 34–38, 40–89, 91, 93a, 94–96, 98–166, 168–197, 200–203, 205–239, 242–246, 248–249, 251–258, 260, 262, 268, 276, 279, 282, 296–299, 306–307, 313, 322–331.
Q, Pap, Epigr: 3,675: Eleg., Epigr., Iamb.

002 **Fragmenta lyrica**, ed. D.L. Page, *Supplementum lyricis Graecis*. Oxford: Clarendon Press, 1974: 151–154.
fr. S478a: *P. Colon.* 7511.
fr. S478b: ex Hephaestione, *Enchiridon de metris*.
fr. S478b: Dup. partim 0232 001 (fr. 188).
Pap: 259: Lyr.

003 **Epigrammata**, AG **6**.133; 7.441.
Q: 24: Epigr.

x01 **Epigrammata** (*App. Anth.*).
Epigramma demonstrativum: 3.1.
Epigramma irrisorium: 5.1.
Dup. partim 0232 001 (frr. 2, 5).
App. Anth. 3.1: Cf. ANTHOLOGIAE GRAE-CAE APPENDIX (7052 003).

App. Anth. 5.1: Cf. ANTHOLOGIAE GRAE-CAE APPENDIX (7052 005).

ARCHIMEDES Epigr.
AG 7.50.
Cf. ARCHIMELUS Epigr. (0131 001).

0552 **ARCHIMEDES** Geom.
3 B.C.: Syracusanus

001 **De sphaera et cylindro**, ed. C. Mugler, *Archimède*, vol. 1. Paris: Les Belles Lettres, 1970: 8–131.
Cod: 26,159: Math.

002 **Dimensio circuli**, ed. Mugler, *op. cit.*, vol. 1, 138–143.
Cod: 1,109: Math., Metrolog.

003 **De conoidibus et sphaeroidibus**, ed. Mugler, *op. cit.*, vol. 1, 152–252.
Cod: 23,128: Math.

004 **De lineis spiralibus**, ed. Mugler, *op. cit.*, vol. 2 (1971): 8–74.
Cod: 14,599: Math.

005 **De planorum aequilibriis**, ed. Mugler, *op. cit.*, vol. 2, 80–125.
Cod: 9,170: Math.

006 **Arenarius**, ed. Mugler, *op. cit.*, vol. 2, 134–157.
Cod: 5,113: Math.

007 **Quadratura paraolae**, ed. Mugler, *op. cit.*, vol. 2, 164–195.
Cod: 5,915: Math.

008 **De corporibus fluitantibus**, ed. Mugler, *op. cit.*, vol. 3 (1971): 6–66.
Cod: 8,582: Math.

009 **Stomachion**, ed. Mugler, *op. cit.*, vol. 3, 70–72.
Cod: 453: Math.

010 **Ad Eratosthenem methodus**, ed. Mugler, *op. cit.*, vol. 3, 82–127.
Cod: 9,965: Math.

011 **Liber assumptorum**, ed. Mugler, *op. cit.*, vol. 3, 134–164.
Cod: 3,838: Math.

012 **Problema bovinum**, ed. Mugler, *op. cit.*, vol. 3, 170–173.
Problema [Dub.]: pp. 170–171.
Scholion: pp. 171–173.
Cod: 703: Math., Epigr., Comm.

013 **Fragmenta**, ed. J.L. Heiberg and E. Stamatis, *Archimedis opera omnia cum commentariis Eutocii*, vol. 2. Leipzig: Teubner, 1913 (repr. Stuttgart: 1972): 536–545, 547–554.
De polyedris (frr. 1–3): pp. 536–541.
De mensura circuli (frr. 4–5): p. 542.
Περὶ πλινθίδων καὶ κυλίνδρων (fr. 6): p. 542.
De superficiebus et corporibus irregularibus (frr. 7–8): pp. 543–544.
Appendix libri ii de sphaera et cylindro (fr. 9): p. 544.
Πρὸς Ζεύξιππον (fr. 10): p. 545.
Mechanica (frr. 11–15): pp. 545, 547–548.
Κατοπτρικά (frr. 17–21): pp. 549–551.
Περὶ σφαιροποιίας (fr. 22): pp. 551–554.
De anni magnitudine (fr. 23): p. 554.
Q: 2,882: Math., Mech.

014 **Problema bovinum** [Dub.], ed. H. Lloyd-Jones
and P. Parsons, *Supplementum Hellenisticum.*
Berlin: De Gruyter, 1983: 77–78.
fr. 201.
Dup. partim 0552 012.
Q: 277: Math., Epigr.

x01 **Problema.**
App. Anth. 7.5: Cf. ANTHOLOGIAE GRAE-
CAE APPENDIX (7052 007).
Dup. partim 0552 012.

0131 **ARCHIMELUS** Epigr.
3 B.C.

001 **Epigramma**, AG 7.50.
Q: 37: Epigr.

002 **Fragmentum de Hieronis II navigio**, ed. H.
Lloyd-Jones and P. Parsons, *Supplementum
Hellenisticum.* Berlin: De Gruyter, 1983: 79.
fr. 202.
Q: 116: Epigr.

x01 **Epigramma demonstrativum.**
App. Anth. 3.82: Cf. ANTHOLOGIAE GRAE-
CAE APPENDIX (7052 003).
Dup. 0131 002.

2418 **ARCHINUS** Hist.
post 4 B.C.

001 **Fragmenta**, FGrH #604: 3B:738.
Q: 135: Hist.

0417 **ARCHIPPUS** Comic.
5 B.C.

001 **Fragmenta**, ed. T. Kock, *Comicorum Atticorum fragmenta*, vol. 1. Leipzig: Teubner,
1880: 679–689.
frr. 1–19, 21–27, 29, 31–44, 46–54.
Q: 358: Comic.

002 **Fragmenta**, ed. A. Meineke, *Fragmenta comicorum Graecorum*, vol. 2.2. Berlin: Reimer,
1840 (repr. De Gruyter, 1970): 715–718, 720–
728.
Q: 270: Comic.

003 **Fragmenta**, ed. J. Demiańczuk, *Supplementum
comicum.* Krakau: Nakładem Akademii, 1912
(repr. Hildesheim: Olms, 1967): 10–11.
frr. 1–7.
Q, Cod: 34: Comic.

004 **Tituli**, ed. C. Austin, *Comicorum Graecorum
fragmenta in papyris reperta.* Berlin: De Gruyter, 1973: 6.
fr. 15.
Pap: 6: Comic.

2214 **ARCHITIMUS** Hist.
ante A.D. 2

001 **Fragmentum**, FGrH #315: 3B:25–26.
Q: 252: Hist.

1176 **ARCHYTAS** Epic.
3 B.C.: Amphissensis

001 **Fragmenta**, ed. J.U. Powell, *Collectanea Alex-*

andrina. Oxford: Clarendon Press, 1925 (repr.
1970): 23.
frr. 1–4.
Q: 34: Epic.

0620 **ARCHYTAS** Phil.
4 B.C.: Tarentinus

001 **Testimonia**, ed. H. Diels and W. Kranz, *Die
Fragmente der Vorsokratiker*, vol. 1, 6th edn.
Berlin: Weidmann, 1951 (repr. Dublin: 1966):
421–431.
test. 1–26.
NQ: 3,558: Test.

002 **Fragmenta**, ed. Diels and Kranz, *op. cit.*, 431–
439.
frr. 1–9.
Q: 1,310: Phil., Mus.

1177 **Pseudo-ARCHYTAS** Phil.
Incertum

001 **Fragmenta**, ed. H. Thesleff, *The Pythagorean
texts of the Hellenistic period.* Åbo: Åbo Aka-
demi, 1965: 3–48.
Catholica: pp. 3–8.
De viro bono: pp. 8–15.
De oppositionibus: pp. 15–19.
De principiis: pp. 19–20.
De categoriis: pp. 21–32.
De lege: pp. 33–36.
De intellectu: pp. 36–40.
De natura: p. 40.
De educatione: pp. 40–43.
De sapientia: pp. 43–45.
Epistulae: pp. 45–47.
Fragmenta incertae sedis: pp. 47–48.
Q: 13,025: Phil., Mech., Epist.

ARCTINUS Epic.
7 B.C.?: Milesius
Cf. AETHIOPIS (0683).
Cf. ILIU PERSIS (1445).
Cf. TITANOMACHIA (1737).

1178 **<ARESAS>** Phil.
vel Aesara
3 B.C.

001 **Fragmentum**, ed. H. Thesleff, *The Pythagorean
texts of the Hellenistic period.* Åbo: Åbo Akademi, 1965: 48–50.
Q: 527: Phil.

2193 **[ARETADES]** Hist.
Incertum: Cnidius

001 **Fragmenta**, FGrH #285: 3A:162–163.
Q: 156: Hist.

0719 **ARETAEUS** Med.
A.D. 2

001 **De causis et signis acutorum morborum** (lib.
1), ed. K. Hude, *Aretaeus*, 2nd edn. [*Corpus
medicorum Graecorum*, vol. 2. Berlin:
Akademie-Verlag, 1958]: 3–35.
Cod: 9,771: Med.

002 **De causis et signis acutorum morborum** (lib. 2), ed. Hude, *op. cit.*, 36–90.
Cod: 17,640: Med.

003 **De curatione acutorum morborum libri duo**, ed. Hude, *op. cit.*, 91–143.
Cod: 16,690: Med.

004 **De curatione diuturnorum morborum libri duo**, ed. Hude, *op. cit.*, 144–170.
Cod: 8,269: Med.

2130 **ARETHAS** Philol. et Scr. Eccl.
A.D. 9–10: Patrensis, Constantinopolitanus, Caesariensis (Cappadociae)

001 **Epigrammata**, AG 15.32–34.
Dup. 2130 034 (pp. 137–139).
Q: 229: Epigr.

002 **Fragmenta in epistulam ad Romanos** (in catenis), ed. K. Staab, *Pauluskommentar aus der griechischen Kirche aus Katenenhandschriften gesammelt*. Münster: Aschendorff, 1933: 653–659.
Q: 1,698: Exeget., Caten.

003 **Fragmenta in epistulam i ad Corinthios** (in catenis), ed. Staab, *op. cit.*, 659–660.
Q: 173: Exeget., Caten.

004 **Fragmenta in epistulam ii ad Corinthios** (in catenis), ed. Staab, *op. cit.*, 660–661.
Q: 335: Exeget., Caten.

005 **Fragmentum in epistulam ii ad Thessalonicenses** (in catenis), ed. Staab, *op. cit.*, 661.
Q: 27: Exeget., Caten.

006 **Fragmentum in epistulam i ad Timotheum** (in catenis), ed. Staab, *op. cit.*, 661.
Q: 70: Exeget., Caten.

007 **Fragmentum in epistulam ad Hebraeos** (in catenis), ed. Staab, *op. cit.*, 661.
Q: 42: Exeget., Caten.

008 **Commentarius in Apocalypsin**, ed. J.A. Cramer, *Catenae Graecorum patrum in Novum Testamentum*, vol. 8. Oxford: Oxford University Press, 1840 (repr. Hildesheim: Olms, 1967): 176–496.
Cod: Exeget., Caten.

014 **Scholia in Athenagoram**, ed. O. von Gebhardt, *Der Arethascodex Paris. gr. 451. Zur handschriftlichen Überlieferung der griechischen Apologeten* [*Texte und Untersuchungen* 1.3. Leipzig: Hinrichs, 1883]: 186–196.
Cod: Schol., Eccl.

015 **Scholia in Tatianum** (e cod. Paris. 174), ed. E. Schwartz, *Tatiani oratio ad Graecos* [*Texte und Untersuchungen* 4.1. Leipzig: Hinrichs, 1888]: 44–47.
Cod: Schol., Eccl.

016 **Scholia in Dionem Chrysostomum et Aelium Aristidem** (excerpta), ed. N.A. Bees, "Αἱ ἐπιδρομαὶ τῶν Βουλγάρων ὑπὸ τὸν τζάρον Συμεὼν καὶ τὰ σχετικὰ σχόλια τοῦ Ἀρέθα Καισαρείας," Ἑλληνικά 1 (1928) 337–338.
Scholion in Dionem Chrysostomum, *Oratio de exilio*: p. 337.

Scholion in Aelium Aristidem, Περὶ τοῦ παραφθέγματος: p. 338.
Cod: Schol.

018 **Scholia in Photii quaestiones ad Amphilochium** (e cod. Laur. 449) (fort. auctore Aretha), ed. B. Laourdas, "Τὰ εἰς τὰ Ἀμφιλόχια τοῦ Φωτίου σχόλια τοῦ κώδικος 449 τῆς Λαύρας," Ἑλληνικά 12 (1953) 256–261.
Cod: Schol., Eccl.

019 **Scholia in Photii epistulas** (e cod. Barocc. gr. 217) (fort. auctore Aretha), ed. B. Laourdas, "Τὰ εἰς τὰς ἐπιστολὰς τοῦ Φωτίου σχόλια τοῦ κώδικος Baroccianus Graecus 217," Ἀθηνᾶ 55 (1951) 133–145.
Cod: Schol., Eccl.

032 **Scholia Arethae in Cyrilli apologiam xii anathematismorum contra Theodoretum et in Theodoreti impugnationem**, ed. E. Schwartz, *Acta conciliorum oecumenicorum*, vol. 1.1.6. Berlin: De Gruyter, 1928 (repr. 1960): 112–120, 123–125, 127–128, 130–132, 135, 138–143.
Cod: 1,568: Schol.

035 **Scholia in Albinum** (e cod. Vindob. phil. gr. 314), ed. L.G. Westerink and B. Laourdas, "Scholia by Arethas in Vindob. phil. gr. 314," *Hellenica* 17 (1962) 111–121.
Cod: Schol.

036 **Scholia in Hieroclem Platonicum** (e cod. Vindob. phil. gr. 314), ed. Westerink and Laourdas, *Hellenica* 17, 121–127.
Cod: Schol.

033 **Scripta minora** (praecipue e cod. Mosq. Hist. Mus. gr. 315), ed. L.G. Westerink, *Arethae archiepiscopi Caesariensis scripta minora*, vol. 1. Leipzig: Teubner, 1968: 1–362.
Ἀπολογία τῆς πρὸ τούτου ἐνστάσεως καὶ τῆς αὖθις ἀναχωρήσεως: pp. 1–12.
Ἀπολογία περὶ τῶν αὐτῶν τοῖς ἐπισκόποις: pp. 13–18.
Homilia in Psalmum i: pp. 19–29.
Homilia in Psalmum xxxv: pp. 30–46.
In Armeniorum litteras: pp. 47–58.
Encomium confessorum Edessenorum: pp. 59–74.
In iconomachos: pp. 75–81.
Epitaphius in Euthymium patriarcham: pp. 83–93.
Πρὸς τοὺς ἀπὸ τῆς πολιτείας συναιρουμένους ἀναθέματι καθυποβάλλειν πολυγαμίαν: pp. 94–107.
Πρὸς τὸν οὐκ εἰκότως τὸ ἀπειθὲς ἐπιμεμφόμενον: pp. 108–113.
Πρὸς τοὺς συκοφαντοῦντας ἡμᾶς πολυγαμίαν κηρύσσειν: pp. 114–116.
Πρὸς τοὺς ἐπισκώψαντας τὸ παλίμβολον: pp. 117–119.
Πρὸς τὸν ἀντιγράφειν ἀποθρασυνόμενον: pp. 120–121.
Antirrheticus: pp. 122, 127–177.
Ad Thomam patricium: pp. 178–183.

Πρὸς τοὺς εἰς ἀσάφειαν ἐπισκώψαντας: pp. 186–191.

Ad Plotinum i: pp. 192–193.

Ad Plotinum ii: pp. 194–197.

Πρὸς τοὺς φιλοσκώμμονας ἡμᾶς οἰομένους: pp. 198–199.

Χοιροσφάκτης ἢ Μισογόης: pp. 200–212.

Ad Cosmam magistrum i: pp. 213–215.

Ad Stephanum i: pp. 216–220.

Ἰουλιανοῦ ἐκ τῶν κατὰ τῶν ἁγίων εὐαγγελίων τοῦ Χριστοῦ λήρων καὶ τούτων ἀνατροπή: pp. 221–225.

Apologeticus: pp. 226–232.

Epistula ad ameram Damascenum: pp. 233–245.

De episcopis sedem mutantibus: pp. 246–251.

Ad Stephanum patriarcham: pp. 252–256.

Ad Leonem imperatorem i: pp. 257–259.

Ad Cosmam magistrum ii: pp. 260–264.

Ad Romanum imperatorem: pp. 265–266.

Ad Nicetam scholasticum: pp. 267–270.

Τοῖς ἀπειθέσιν ἐκ παρακοπῆς Ἰουδαίοις ἐν διαλέξεως τύπῳ: pp. 271–278.

Ad Theophilum quaestorem: pp. 279–281.

In Gregorii Nysseni vitam Gregorii thaumaturgi: pp. 283–284.

Ad Gregorium metropolitam Ephesi i: pp. 285–289.

Ad Gregorium metropolitam Ephesi ii: pp. 290–293.

Ad Stephanum ii: p. 294.

Ad Stephanum iii: pp. 296–297.

Ad Eustathium Sidensem de mutatione sedum: pp. 298–301.

Ad Petrum metropolitam Sardium: pp. 302–303.

Ad Leonem imperatorem ii: p. 304.

Ad Demetrium metropolitam Heracleensem: p. 305.

Ad Nicetam Paphlagonem scholasticum i: pp. 306–311.

Ad Nicetam Paphlagonem scholasticum ii: pp. 312–314.

Ad Nicetam Paphlagonem scholasticum iii: pp. 315–319.

Ad Joannem nepotem Orestis domestici numerorum i: p. 320.

Ad Joannem nepotem Orestis domestici numerorum ii: pp. 321–322.

Ad Nicephorum monachum: p. 323.

Ad Stephanum amanuensem: pp. 324–326.

Aporiae: pp. 327–330.

Aporia: pp. 331–332.

Scholion ad Luciani Jovem tragoedum 47–49: pp. 333–336.

Scholion ad Luciani Jovem tragoedum 38: pp. 337–339.

Tractatus ad Nicetam: pp. 340, 342–362.

Cod: Apol., Eccl., Encom., Epist., Exeget., Homilet., Orat., Rhet., Schol.

034 **Scripta minora** (e variis codicibus), ed. Westerink, *Arethae scripta minora*, vol. 2 (1972): 1–139.

Oratio ad Leonem imperatorem: pp. 1–7.

Oratio in ecclesia Sanctae Sophiae habita: pp. 7–10.

Oratio in festo consecrationis ecclesiae Sancti Lazari: pp. 11–16.

Professio fidei suae synodo tradita: pp. 17–22.

Oratio in festo Sancti Eliae i: pp. 23–30.

Oratio celebrans victoriam ex Saracenis Euphratis accolis partam: pp. 31–34.

Oratio in festo luminum: pp. 35–38.

Oratio ad Nicolaum patriarcham in festo orthodoxiae: pp. 39–42.

Oratio in festo Sancti Eliae ii: pp. 43–48.

Epistula ad Nicolaum patriarcham: pp. 49–55.

Epistula ad Leonem data quarto matrimonio iam contracto: pp. 56–63.

Libellus de tetragamia, pars i: pp. 64–76.

Libellus de tetragamia, pars ii cum specie epistulae ad Leonem: pp. 77–93.

Epistula ad Stephanum a secretis data: pp. 94–104.

Epistula ad Leonem de matrimoniis: pp. 105–107.

Epistula ad Leonem scripta Euthymio ad patriarchatum provecto: pp. 108–111.

Epistula ad Leonem conscripta post reditum: p. 112.

Extrema pars epistulae ad synodum datae: pp. 113–114.

Responsio Arethae criminibus Nicolai: pp. 122–131.

Responsio Arethae Nicolaitis poscentibus ut sed Caesariensi cedat: pp. 132–133.

Epistula ad synodum de delicto eorum qui sine ordinatione munera sacerdotis obeunt: pp. 134–136.

Epigramma inscriptum sepulcro sororis (= AG 15.32): p. 137.

Epigramma adscriptum prope sepulcrum (= AG 15.33): p. 138.

Epigramma sepulcrale ad Febroniam monacham (= AG 15.34): p. 139. Epigrammata (pp. 137–139): Dup. 2130 001.

Cod: Epigr., Epist., Homilet., Orat., Schol.

037 **Miscellanea** (*sub titulo* Ἡ Σπευσίππου διαίρεσις) (e cod. Vindob. phil. gr. 314), ed. Westerink and Laourdas, *Hellenica* 17, 127–131.

Cod: Phil., Theol., Gramm.

x01 **Scholion ad Eunapii historiam** (ap. Constantinum Porphyrogenitum, *De sententiis*). Boissevain, pp. 81–82.
Cf. CONSTANTINUS VII PORPHYROGENITUS Imperator (3023 004).

x02 **Scholia in Lucianum.**
Rabe, pp. 1–285.
Cf. SCHOLIA IN LUCIANUM (5029 001).

x03 **Scholia in Platonem.**
Greene, pp. 417–480.
Cf. SCHOLIA IN PLATONEM (5035 002).

x04 **Scholia in Clementis Alexandrini protrepticum et paedagogum.**
Stählin & Treu, vol. 1, pp. 295–340.
Cf. SCHOLIA IN CLEMENTEM ALEXANDRI-NUM (5048 001).

x05 **Scholion in Justinum Martyrem.**
Cramer, vol. 8, p. 361.
Cf. 2130 008.

x06 **Scholia in Eusebii praeparationem evangelicam.**
Mras, GCS 43.1 & 43.2, passim (in apparatu).
Cf. SCHOLIA IN EUSEBIUM (5049 001).

0132 **Marcus ARGENTARIUS** Rhet. et Epigr.
1 B.C.–A.D. 1

001 **Epigrammata**, AG 5.16, 32, 63, 89, 102, 104–105, 110, 113, 116, 118, 127–128; **6**.201, 246, 248, 333; **7**.364, 374, 384, 395, 403; **9**.87, 161, 221, 229, 246, 270, 286, 554, 732; **10**.4, 18; **11**.26, 28, 320; **16**.241.
AG 6.246: Cf. et PHILODEMUS Phil. (1595 730).
AG 9.733: Cf. ANONYMI EPIGRAMMATICI (AG) (0138 001).
Q: 1,405: Epigr.

4237 **Joannes ARGYROPULUS** Gramm.
A.D. 15: Constantinopolitanus, Pataviensis, Florentinus, Romanus

001 **Prolegomena in Aphthonii progymnasmata**, ed. H. Rabe, *Prolegomenon sylloge* [*Rhetores Graeci* 14. Leipzig: Teubner, 1931]: 156–158.
Cod: Rhet., Comm.

2215 **AR(I)AETHUS** Hist.
ante 2 B.C.?: Tegeates

001 **Fragmenta**, FGrH #316: 3B:26–30.
Q: 1,075: Hist.

1179 **<ARIMNESTUS>** Phil.
4–3 B.C.?

001 **Fragmentum**, ed. H. Thesleff, *The Pythagorean texts of the Hellenistic period*. Åbo: Åbo Akademi, 1965: 51.
Q: 61: Phil.

2658 **ARION** Lyr.
7 B.C.: Methymnaeus

x01 **Fragmentum.**
PMG, p. 507.
Cf. LYRICA ADESPOTA (PMG) (0297 001).

x02 **Epigramma dedicatorium.**
App. Anth. 1.3(?): Cf. ANTHOLOGIAE GRAE-CAE APPENDIX (7052 001).

0378 **ARIPHRON** Lyr.
4 B.C.: Sicyonius

001 **Fragmentum**, ed. D.L. Page, *Poetae melici Graeci*. Oxford: Clarendon Press, 1962 (repr. 1967 (1st edn. corr.)): 422.
fr. 1.
Q: 63: Lyr., Encom.

x01 **Epigramma exhortatorium et supplicatorium.**
App. Anth. 4.30: Cf. ANTHOLOGIAE GRAE-CAE APPENDIX (7052 004).
Dup. 0378 001.

4000 **ARISTAENETUS** Epist.
A.D. 5: Nicaeensis

001 **Epistulae**, ed. O. Mazal, *Aristaeneti epistularum libri ii*. Stuttgart: Teubner, 1971: 1–100.
Cod: 15,539: Epist.

2519 **ARISTAENETUS** Hist.
post 4 B.C.?

001 **Fragmentum**, FGrH #771: 3C:766.
Q: 50: Hist.

2429 **ARISTAENETUS** Hist.
A.D. 2/3?: fort. Byzantius

001 **Testimonia**, FGrH #623: 3C:158.
NQ: 55: Test.

002 **Fragmentum**, FGrH #623: 3C:158.
Q: 110: Hist.

1180 **<ARISTAEUS>** Phil.
3–2 B.C.?

001 **Fragmenta**, ed. H. Thesleff, *The Pythagorean texts of the Hellenistic period*. Åbo: Åbo Akademi, 1965: 52–53.
Q: 322: Phil.

0418 **ARISTAGORAS** Comic.
5 B.C.?

001 **Fragmenta**, ed. T. Kock, *Comicorum Atticorum fragmenta*, vol. 1. Leipzig: Teubner, 1880: 710–711.
frr. 1–7.
Q: 38: Comic.

002 **Fragmenta**, ed. A. Meineke, *Fragmenta comicorum Graecorum*, vol. 2.2. Berlin: Reimer, 1840 (repr. De Gruyter, 1970): 761.
Q: 32: Comic.

1190 **ARISTAGORAS** Hist.
4 B.C.: fort. Milesius

001 **Testimonia**, FGrH #608: 3C:2.
NQ: 70: Test.

002 **Fragmenta**, FGrH #608: 3C:3–5.
Q: 536: Hist.

1181 **ARISTARCHUS** Astron.
4–3 B.C.: Samius

001 **De magnitudinibus et distantiis solis et lunae**, ed. T. Heath, *Aristarchus of Samos, the ancient Copernicus*. Oxford: Clarendon Press, 1913 (repr. 1966): 352–410.
Cod: 7,098: Astron.

2290 **ARISTARCHUS** Hist.
A.D. 1–2?: Eleus

001 **Fragmentum**, FGrH #412: 3B:304.
Q: 141: Hist.

0798 **ARISTARCHUS** Med.
ante A.D. 1 : Tarsensis
x01 **Fragmentum ap. Galenum.**
K13.824–825.
Cf. GALENUS Med. (0057 077).

0871 **ARISTARCHUS** Med.
fiq Aristus Aristarchus
ante A.D. 2
Cf. et Aristus ARISTARCHUS Med. (0878).
x01 **Fragmentum ap. Galenum.**
K12.818.
Cf. GALENUS Med. (0057 076).

0878 **Aristus ARISTARCHUS** Med.
ante A.D. 2
x01 **Fragmentum ap. Galenum.**
K13.103–104.
Cf. GALENUS Med. (0057 076).
x02 **Fragmentum ap. Aëtium** (lib. 8).
CMG, vol. 8.2, p. 537.
Cf. AËTIUS Med. (0718 008).

1767 **ARISTARCHUS** Philol.
3–2 B.C. : Samothracenus
001 **Fragmenta**, ed. A. Ludwich, *Aristarchs Homerische Textkritik nach den Fragmenten des Didymos*, 2 vols. Leipzig: Teubner, 1:1884; 2:1885 (repr. Hildesheim: Olms, 1971): 1:175–631; 2:passim.
Q
002 **Fragmenta**, ed. K. Lehrs, *De Aristarchi studiis Homericis*. Leipzig: Hirzel, 1882 (repr. Hildesheim: Olms, 1964): passim.
Q

0306 **ARISTARCHUS** Trag.
5 B.C. : Tegeates
001 **Fragmenta**, ed. B. Snell, *Tragicorum Graecorum fragmenta*, vol. 1. Göttingen: Vandenhoeck & Ruprecht, 1971: 89–92.
frr. 1–6.
fr. 1a: *P. Petrie* 2.49b.
Q, Pap : 118 : Trag.

1183 *ARISTEAE EPISTULA*
3 B.C./A.D. 1
001 **Aristeae epistula ad Philocratem**, ed. A. Pelletier, *Lettre d'Aristée à Philocrate* [*Sources chrétiennes* 89. Paris: Cerf, 1962]: 100–240.
Cod : 13,573 : Epist.

1182 **[ARISTEAS]** Epic.
6 B.C. : Proconnesius
001 **Fragmenta**, ed. G. Kinkel, *Epicorum Graecorum fragmenta*, vol. 1. Leipzig: Teubner, 1877: 245.
frr. 1–4.
Dup. partim 1182 002.
Q : 77 : Epic.
002 **Fragmenta**, ed. J.D.P. Bolton, *Aristeas of Pro-*

connesus. Oxford: Clarendon Press, 1962: 207–214.
Dup. partim 1182 001.
Q
003 **Testimonia**, FGrH #35: 1A:259, *14–*15 addenda.
NQ : 424 : Test.

2488 **ARISTEAS Judaeus** Hist.
2–1 B.C.
001 **Fragmentum**, FGrH #725: 3C:680.
Q : 216 : Hist.

0305 **ARISTIAS** Trag.
5 B.C.
001 **Fragmenta**, ed. B. Snell, *Tragicorum Graecorum fragmenta*, vol. 1. Göttingen: Vandenhoeck & Ruprecht, 1971: 85–87.
frr. 1–8.
Q : 61 : Trag., Satyr.

1184 **ARISTIDES** Apol.
A.D. 2 : Atheniensis
001 **Fragmenta** (*P. Oxy.* 15.1778), ed. C. Vona, *L'apologia di Aristide*. Rome: Facultas Theologica Pontificii Athenaei Lateranensis, 1950: 115.
Pap : 135 : Apol.
002 **Fragmenta** (*P. Lond.* 2486), ed. Vona, *op. cit.*, 116–117.
Pap : 357 : Apol.
003 **Fragmenta**, ed. Vona, *op. cit.*, 117–126.
Q : 3,065 : Apol.

2342 **ARISTIDES** Hist.
2–1 B.C. : fort. Milesius
001 **Testimonia**, FGrH #495: 3B:466.
NQ : 69 : Test.
002 **Fragmentum**, FGrH #495: 3B:466.
Q : 23 : Hist.

1185 **ARISTIDES** Hist.
ante A.D. 1?
001 **Fragmenta**, FGrH #444: 3B:374–376.
Q : 289 : Hist.

2194 **[ARISTIDES]** Hist.
Incertum : Milesius
001 **Fragmenta**, FGrH #286: 3A:163–168.
Q : 1,586 : Hist.

4268 **ARISTIDES** Phil.
4 B.C. : Atheniensis
001 **Testimonium**, ed. K. Döring, *Die Megariker* [*Studien zur antiken Philosophie* 2. Amsterdam: Grüner, 1972]: 52, 61.
test. 164a = Stilpo (4262 001).
NQ : Test.

0284 **Aelius ARISTIDES** Rhet.
A.D. 2 : Mysius

58 ARISTIDES

Scholia: Cf. SCHOLIA IN AELIUM ARISTI-
DEM (5008).

001 Εἰς Δία, ed. W. Dindorf, *Aristides*, vol. 1.
Leipzig: Reimer, 1829 (repr. Hildesheim:
Olms, 1964): 1-11.
Cod: 2,065: Hymn.

002 Ἀθηνᾶ, ed. Dindorf, *op. cit.*, vol. 1, 12-28.
Cod: 2,314: Hymn.

003 Ἰσθμικὸς εἰς Ποσειδῶνα, ed. Dindorf, *op. cit.*,
vol. 1, 29-46.
Cod: 3,493: Hymn.

004 Διόνυσος, ed. Dindorf, *op. cit.*, vol. 1, 47-52.
Cod: 789: Hymn.

005 Ἡρακλῆς, ed. Dindorf, *op. cit.*, vol. 1, 53-62.
Cod: 1,534: Hymn.

006 Λαλιὰ εἰς Ἀσκληπιόν, ed. Dindorf, *op. cit.*,
vol. 1, 63-70.
Cod: 1,240: Hymn.

007 Ἀσκληπιάδαι, ed. Dindorf, *op. cit.*, vol. 1, 71-
80.
Cod: 1,565: Hymn.

008 Εἰς τὸν Σάραπιν, ed. Dindorf, *op. cit.*, vol. 1,
81-97.
Cod: 2,669: Hymn.

009 Εἰς βασιλέα [Sp.], ed. Dindorf, *op. cit.*, vol. 1,
98-112.
Cod: 2,982: Orat.

010 Ἀπελλᾶ γενεθλιακός, ed. Dindorf, *op. cit.*, vol.
1, 113-125.
Cod: 2,142: Orat.

011 Εἰς Ἐτεωνέα ἐπικήδειος, ed. Dindorf, *op. cit.*,
vol. 1, 126-133.
Cod: 1,325: Orat.

012 Ἐπὶ Ἀλεξάνδρῳ ἐπιτάφιος, ed. Dindorf, *op.
cit.*, vol. 1, 134-149.
Cod: 2,803: Orat.

013 Παναθηναϊκός, ed. Dindorf, *op. cit.*, vol. 1,
150-320.
Cod: 29,523: Orat., Encom.

014 Ῥώμης ἐγκώμιον, ed. Dindorf, *op. cit.*, vol. 1,
321-370.
Cod: 8,679: Orat., Encom.

015 Σμυρναϊκὸς πολιτικός, ed. Dindorf, *op. cit.*, vol.
1, 371-381.
Cod: 1,922: Orat.

016 Πανηγυρικὸς ἐν Κυζίκῳ περὶ τοῦ ναοῦ, ed.
Dindorf, *op. cit.*, vol. 1, 382-400.
Cod: 3,327: Orat., Encom.

017 Εἰς τὸ Αἰγαῖον πέλαγος, ed. Dindorf, *op. cit.*,
vol. 1, 401-407.
Cod: 1,203: Hymn.

018 Εἰς τὸ φρέαρ τοῦ Ἀσκληπιοῦ, ed. Dindorf, *op.
cit.*, vol. 1, 408-414.
Cod: 1,287: Hymn.

019 Ἐλευσίνιος, ed. Dindorf, *op. cit.*, vol. 1, 415-
423.
Cod: 1,044: Orat.

020 Μονῳδία ἐπὶ Σμύρνῃ, ed. Dindorf, *op. cit.*, vol.
1, 424-428.
Cod: 745: Orat.

021 Παλινῳδία ἐπὶ Σμύρνῃ καὶ τῷ ταύτης ἀνοι-
κισμῷ, ed. Dindorf, *op. cit.*, vol. 1, 429-438.
Cod: 1,734: Orat.

022 Προσφωνητικὸς Σμυρναϊκός, ed. Dindorf, *op.
cit.*, vol. 1, 439-444.
Cod: 1,137: Orat.

023 Ἱεροὶ λόγοι α΄, ed. Dindorf, *op. cit.*, vol. 1,
445-464.
Cod: 5,331: Med., Onir., Biogr.

024 Ἱεροὶ λόγοι β΄, ed. Dindorf, *op. cit.*, vol. 1,
465-487.
Cod: 5,858: Med., Onir., Biogr.

025 Ἱεροὶ λόγοι γ΄, ed. Dindorf, *op. cit.*, vol. 1,
488-501.
Cod: 3,548: Med., Onir., Biogr.

026 Ἱεροὶ λόγοι δ΄, ed. Dindorf, *op. cit.*, vol. 1,
502-533.
Cod: 8,137: Med., Onir., Biogr.

027 Ἱεροὶ λόγοι ε΄, ed. Dindorf, *op. cit.*, vol. 1,
534-550.
Cod: 4,546: Med., Onir., Biogr.

028 Ἱεροὶ λόγοι ϛ΄, ed. Dindorf, *op. cit.*, vol. 1, 551.
Cod: 132: Med., Onir., Biogr.

029 Περὶ τοῦ πέμπειν βοήθειαν τοῖς ἐν Σικελίᾳ, ed.
Dindorf, *op. cit.*, vol. 1, 552-570.
Cod: 3,906: Rhet.

030 Εἰς τὸ ἐναντίον, ed. Dindorf, *op. cit.*, vol. 1,
571-590.
Cod: 4,562: Rhet.

031 Ὑπὲρ τῆς πρὸς Λακεδαιμονίους εἰρήνης, ed.
Dindorf, *op. cit.*, vol. 1, 591-600.
Cod: 2,411: Rhet.

032 Ὑπὲρ τῆς πρὸς Ἀθηναίους εἰρήνης, ed. Dindorf, *op. cit.*, vol. 1, 601-609.
Cod: 2,060: Rhet.

033 Λευκτρικὸς α΄ (ὑπὲρ Λακεδαιμονίων πρῶτος),
ed. Dindorf, *op. cit.*, vol. 1, 611-641.
Cod: 5,903: Rhet.

034 Λευκτρικὸς β΄ (ὑπὲρ Θηβαίων πρῶτος), ed.
Dindorf, *op. cit.*, vol. 1, 642-670.
Cod: 6,171: Rhet.

035 Λευκτρικὸς γ΄ (ὑπὲρ Λακεδαιμονίων δεύτερος),
ed. Dindorf, *op. cit.*, vol. 1, 671-683.
Cod: 2,692: Rhet.

036 Λευκτρικὸς δ΄ (ὑπὲρ Θηβαίων δεύτερος), ed.
Dindorf, *op. cit.*, vol. 1, 684-695.
Cod: 2,533: Rhet.

037 Λευκτρικὸς ε΄ (ὑπὲρ μηδετέροις βοηθεῖν), ed.
Dindorf, *op. cit.*, vol. 1, 696-710.
Cod: 3,297: Rhet.

038 Συμμαχικὸς α΄, ed. Dindorf, *op. cit.*, vol. 1,
711-731.
Cod: 4,069: Rhet.

039 Συμμαχικὸς β΄ (πρὸς Θηβαίους περὶ τῆς συμ-
μαχίας), ed. Dindorf, *op. cit.*, vol. 1, 732-750.
Cod: 4,275: Rhet.

040 Συμβουλευτικὸς περὶ τοῦ μὴ δεῖν κωμῳδεῖν, ed.
Dindorf, *op. cit.*, vol. 1, 751-761.
Cod: 2,184: Orat.

041 Ἐπιστολὴ περὶ Σμύρνης, ed. Dindorf, *op. cit.*,
vol. 1, 762-767.
Cod: 1,230: Epist.

042 Περὶ ὁμονοίας ταῖς πόλεσιν, ed. Dindorf, *op. cit.*, vol. 1, 768–796.
Cod: 6,621: Orat.

043 Ῥοδιακός [Sp.], ed. Dindorf, *op. cit.*, vol. 1, 797–823.
Cod: 5,399: Orat.

044 Ῥοδίοις περὶ ὁμονοίας, ed. Dindorf, *op. cit.*, vol. 1, 824–844.
Cod: 4,467: Orat.

045 Πρὸς Πλάτωνα περὶ ῥητορικῆς, ed. Dindorf, *op. cit.*, vol. 2 (1829; repr. 1964): 1–155.
Cod: 31,045: Rhet.

046 Πρὸς Πλάτωνα ὑπὲρ τῶν τεττάρων, ed. Dindorf, *op. cit.*, vol. 2, 156–414.
Cod: 54,080: Rhet.

047 Πρὸς Καπίτωνα, ed. Dindorf, *op. cit.*, vol. 2, 415–436.
Cod: 4,437: Orat.

048 Αἰγύπτιος, ed. Dindorf, *op. cit.*, vol. 2, 437–490.
Cod: 11,116: Orat.

049 Περὶ τοῦ παραφθέγματος, ed. Dindorf, *op. cit.*, vol. 2, 491–542.
Cod: 11,476: Rhet.

050 Κατὰ τῶν ἐξορχουμένων, ed. Dindorf, *op. cit.*, vol. 2, 543–570.
Cod: 4,201: Orat., Rhet.

051 Πρὸς τοὺς αἰτιωμένους ὅτι μὴ μελετῴη, ed. Dindorf, *op. cit.*, vol. 2, 571–583.
Cod: 2,319: Orat.

052 Πρεσβευτικὸς πρὸς Ἀχιλλέα, ed. Dindorf, *op. cit.*, vol. 2, 584–608.
Cod: 3,542: Rhet.

053 Πρὸς Δημοσθένη περὶ ἀτελείας, ed. Dindorf, *op. cit.*, vol. 2, 609–641.
Cod: 9,257: Rhet.

054 Πρὸς Λεπτίνην ὑπὲρ ἀτελείας, ed. Dindorf, *op. cit.*, vol. 2, 651–706.
Cod: 11,262: Rhet.

055 Πανηγυρικὸς ἐπὶ τῷ ὕδατι ἐν Περγάμῳ, ed. Dindorf, *op. cit.*, vol. 2, 707–709.
Cod: 375: Orat., Encom.

056 **Ars rhetorica** [Sp.], ed. L. Spengel, *Rhetores Graeci*, vol. 2. Leipzig: Teubner, 1854 (repr. Frankfurt am Main: Minerva, 1966): 459–554.
Cod: 23,686: Rhet.

057 **Fragmenta poetica**, ed. E. Heitsch, *Die griechischen Dichterfragmente der römischen Kaiserzeit*, vol. 2. Göttingen: Vandenhoeck & Ruprecht, 1964: 41–42.
frr. 1–5.
Q: 52: Hexametr., Eleg., Hymn.

x01 **Epigramma dedicatorium**.
App. Anth. 1.257: Cf. ANTHOLOGIAE GRAECAE APPENDIX (7052 001).

x02 **Prolegomena in Aristidem**.
Cf. SOPATER Rhet. (2031 004).

2054 **ARISTIDES QUINTILIANUS** Mus.
A.D. 3
Scholia: Cf. SCHOLIA IN ARISTIDEM QUINTILIANUM (5047).

001 **De musica**, ed. R.P. Winnington-Ingram, *Aristidis Quintiliani de musica libri tres*. Leipzig: Teubner, 1963: 1–134.
Cod: 31,551: Mus.

2352 **ARISTION** Hist.
Incertum
001 **Titulus**, FGrH #509: 3B:487.
NQ: Hist.

0801 **ARISTION** Med.
A.D. 1: Alexandrinus
x01 **Fragmentum ap. Oribasium**.
CMG, vol. 6.2.2, p. 35.
Cf. ORIBASIUS Med. (0722 001).

ARISTIPPI EPISTULAE
Epist. Graec., pp. 617–619, 622, 628–629.
Cf. SOCRATICORUM EPISTULAE (0637 001).

2513 **ARISTIPPUS** Hist.
4 B.C.: Cyrenaeus
001 **Testimonium**, FGrH #759: 3C:741.
NQ: 60: Test.

2216 **ARISTIPPUS** Hist.
ante 2 B.C.
001 **Testimonium**, FGrH #317: 3B:30.
NQ: 48: Test.
002 **Fragmenta**, FGrH #317: 3B:30–31.
Q: 156: Hist.

1187 **ARISTOBULUS** Hist.
4 B.C.: Cassandreus
001 **Testimonia**, FGrH #139: 2B:769.
NQ: 173: Test.
002 **Fragmenta**, FGrH #139: **2B**:769–799; **3B**:743 addenda.
Q: 11,612: Hist.

2557 **[ARISTOBULUS]** Hist.
Incertum
001 **Fragmentum**, FGrH #830: 3C:900.
Q: 85: Hist.

1186 **ARISTOBULUS Judaeus** Phil.
2 B.C.: Alexandrinus
001 **Fragmenta**, ed. A.-M. Denis, *Fragmenta pseudepigraphorum quae supersunt Graeca [Pseudepigrapha veteris testamenti Graece* 3. Leiden: Brill, 1970]: 217–228.
Q: 2,208: Phil., Exeget.

2405 **ARISTOCLES** Hist.
ante 1 B.C.
001 **Titulus**, FGrH #586: 3B:701.
NQ: Hist.

2302 **ARISTOCLES** Hist.
vel Aristoteles
fiq Aristocles Myth. vel Aristocles Paradox.
ante A.D. 2

Cf. et ARISTOCLES Myth. (1882).
Cf. et ARISTOCLES Paradox. (0571).

001 **Fragmenta**, FGrH #436: 3B:368–369.
Dup. partim ARISTOCLES Paradox. (0571 002).
Dup. partim ARISTOCLES Myth. (1882 002).
Q: 324: Hist., Epigr.

2453 **ARISTOCLES** Hist.
A.D. 2: Messenius

001 **Testimonium**, FGrH #664: 3C:214.
NQ: 38: Test.

0802 **ARISTOCLES** Med.
ante A.D. 1

x01 **Fragmenta ap. Galenum**.
K12.936; **13**.205, 977.
Cf. GALENUS Med. (0057 076–077).

1882 **ARISTOCLES** Myth.
fiq Aristocles Hist. vel Aristocles Paradox.
1 B.C.?
Cf. et ARISTOCLES Hist. (2302).
Cf. et ARISTOCLES Paradox. (0571).

001 **Testimonium**, FGrH #33: 1A:257.
NQ: 16: Test.

002 **Fragmenta**, FGrH #33: 1A:257–258.
Dup. partim ARISTOCLES Paradox. (0571 002).
Dup. partim ARISTOCLES Hist. (2302 001).
Q: 377: Hist., Myth., Paradox.

0571 **ARISTOCLES** Paradox.
fiq Aristocles Hist. vel Aristocles Myth.
3 B.C.?/A.D. 1
Cf. et ARISTOCLES Hist. (2302).
Cf. et ARISTOCLES Myth. (1882).

001 **Testimonium**, ed. A. Giannini, *Paradoxographorum Graecorum reliquiae*. Milan: Istituto Editoriale Italiano, 1965: 390.
NQ: Test.

002 **Fragmenta**, ed. Giannini, *op. cit.*, 390–391.
frr. 1–3.
Dup. partim 0571 004.
Dup. partim ARISTOCLES Hist. (2302 001).
Q: Paradox., Epigr.

003 **Fragmenta**, FGrH #831: 3C:901.
Q: 233: Hist., Nat. Hist., Paradox.

004 **Fragmentum**, ed. H. Lloyd-Jones and P. Parsons, *Supplementum Hellenisticum*. Berlin: De Gruyter, 1983: 80–81.
fr. 206.
Dup. partim 0571 002.
Dup. partim ARISTOCLES Hist. (2302 001).
Q: 62: Epigr.

x01 **Epigramma exhortatorium et supplicatorium**.
App. Anth. 4.45: Cf. ANTHOLOGIAE GRAECAE APPENDIX (7052 004).
Dup. partim 0571 002 (fr. 2), 004 (fr. 206).
Dup. partim ARISTOCLES Hist. (2302 001) (fr. 2).

1188 **ARISTOCLES** Phil.
A.D. 2: Messanius

001 **Fragmenta**, ed. H. Heiland, *Aristoclis Messenii reliquiae*. Giessen: Meyer, 1925: 23–42, 45–89.
Q: 9,092: Phil.

0803 **ARISTOCRATES** Gramm.
A.D. 1?

x01 **Fragmenta ap. Galenum**.
K12.878, 879.
Cf. GALENUS Med. (0057 076).

1189 **ARISTOCRATES** Hist.
1 B.C.–A.D. 1: Lacedaemonius

001 **Testimonium**, FGrH #591: 3B:705.
NQ: 8: Test.

002 **Fragmenta**, FGrH #591: 3B:705–706.
Q: 491: Hist.

2659 **ARISTOCREON** Epigr.
3 B.C.

x01 **Epigramma dedicatorium**.
App. Anth. 1.129: Cf. ANTHOLOGIAE GRAECAE APPENDIX (7052 001).

2455 **ARISTOCREON** Hist.
3 B.C.?

001 **Testimonia**, FGrH #667: 3C:279.
NQ: 34: Test.

002 **Fragmenta**, FGrH #667: 3C:279–280.
Q: 283: Hist.

2341 **ARISTOCRITUS** Hist.
3 B.C.?: fort. Milesius

001 **Testimonia**, FGrH #493: 3B:464.
NQ: 33: Test.

002 **Fragmenta**, FGrH #493: 3B:464–465.
Q: 437: Hist.

2148 **ARISTODEMUS** Hist.
post 4 B.C./a. A.D. 2

001 **Fragmenta**, FGrH #104: 2A:493–503.
fr. 1: Cod. Paris. suppl. gr. 607.
Q, Cod: 3,136: Hist.

002 **Fragmentum** (*P. Oxy*. 27.2469), ed. H.J. Mette, "Die 'Kleinen' griechischen Historiker heute," *Lustrum* 21 (1978) 15–16.
fr. 1b.
Pap: 158: Hist.

2292 **ARISTODEMUS** Hist.
2 B.C.?: Eleus

001 **Fragmenta**, FGrH #414: 3B:306–307.
Q: 95: Hist.

2269 **ARISTODEMUS** Hist. et Gramm.
2 B.C.: Thebanus, Alexandrinus

001 **Fragmenta**, FGrH #383: 3B:258–261.
Q: 1,023: Hist., Gramm.

1875 **ARISTODEMUS** Myth. et Hist.
1 B.C.: Nyssensis

001 **Fragmenta**, FGrH #22: 1A:186.
Q: 172: Hist., Myth.

0133 **ARISTODICUS** Epigr.
3 B.C.: Rhodius
001 **Epigrammata**, AG 7.189, 473.
Q: 49: Epigr.

1885 **ARISTODICUS** Hist.
ante 1 B.C.
001 **Fragmentum**, FGrH #36: 1A:259.
Q: 22: Hist., Myth.

1191 **<ARISTOMBROTUS>** Phil.
4 B.C.?
001 **Fragmentum**, ed. H. Thesleff, *The Pythagorean texts of the Hellenistic period*. Åbo: Åbo Akademi, 1965: 53–54.
Q: 125: Phil.

0419 **ARISTOMENES** Comic.
5–4 B.C.
001 **Fragmenta**, ed. T. Kock, *Comicorum Atticorum fragmenta*, vol. 1. Leipzig: Teubner, 1880: 690–693.
frr. 1–15 + tituli.
Q: 94: Comic.
002 **Fragmenta**, ed. A. Meineke, *Fragmenta comicorum Graecorum*, vol. 2.2. Berlin: Reimer, 1840 (repr. De Gruyter, 1970): 730–734.
Q: 68: Comic.
003 **Tituli**, ed. C. Austin, *Comicorum Graecorum fragmenta in papyris reperta*. Berlin: De Gruyter, 1973: 7.
fr. 16.
Pap: 4: Comic.

2261 **ARISTOMENES** Hist.
A.D. 2: Atheniensis
001 **Testimonium**, FGrH #364: 3B:225.
NQ: 31: Test.
002 **Fragmenta**, FGrH #364: 3B:225.
Q: 76: Hist.

1992 **ARISTON** Apol.
A.D. 2: Pellaeus
001 **Fragmenta**, FGrH #201: 2B:933–934.
Dup. partim 1992 002.
Q: 601: Hist.
002 **Disputatio Jasonis et Papisci** (fragmenta), ed. J.C.T. Otto, *Corpus apologetarum Christianorum saeculi secundi*, vol. 9. Jena: Mauke, 1872 (repr. Wiesbaden: Sändig, 1969): 356–357.
Dup. partim 1992 001.
Q

0134 **ARISTON** Epigr.
3/1 B.C.
001 **Epigrammata**, AG 6.303, 306; 7.457.
AG 9.77: Cf. ANTIPATER Epigr. (0114 001).
Q: 150: Epigr.

2223 **ARISTON** Hist.
post 3 B.C.
001 **Fragmentum**, FGrH #337: 3B:188.
Q: 118: Hist.

1192 **ARISTON** Phil.
3 B.C.: Ceus
001 **Fragmenta**, ed. F. Wehrli, *Lykon und Ariston von Keos* [*Die Schule des Aristoteles*, vol. 6, 2nd edn. Basel: Schwabe, 1968]: 32–44.
Scripta: frr. 9, 11.
Περὶ τοῦ κουφίζειν ὑπερηφανίας: frr. 13.1–13.7.
Characterismos: frr. 14.1–16.
Περὶ τῶν ἐρωτικῶν ὁμοίων: frr. 17–24.
Politica. Legalia. Educatio: frr. 25–26.
Vitae philosophorum: frr. 28–32.
Lycon: fr. 33.
Paradoxographica: frr. 34a, 34c.
Q, Pap: 3,336: Phil., Paradox.

1193 **ARISTON** Phil.
3 B.C.: Chius
001 **Testimonia et fragmenta**, ed. J. von Arnim, *Stoicorum veterum fragmenta*, vol. 1. Leipzig: Teubner, 1903 (repr. Stuttgart: 1968): 75–90.
frr. 333–403.
Dup. partim 1193 002 (frr. 204–205).
Q: 5,008: Phil., Doxogr., Hexametr.
002 **Fragmenta**, ed. H. Lloyd-Jones and P. Parsons, *Supplementum Hellenisticum*. Berlin: De Gruyter, 1983: 80.
frr. 204–205.
Dup. partim 1193 001 (frr. 343, 346).
Q: 15: Hexametr.
x01 **Epigramma demonstrativum**.
Dup. partim 1193 001 (frr. 343–344), 002 (fr. 204).
App. Anth. 3.62(?): Cf. ANTHOLOGIAE GRAECAE APPENDIX (7052 003).

2587 **ARISTON** Phil.
3/2 B.C.: Cous
001 **Fragmenta rhetorica**, ed. F. Wehrli, *Hieronymos von Rhodos. Kritolaos und seine Schüler* [*Die Schule des Aristoteles*, vol. 10, 2nd edn. Basel: Schwabe, 1969]: 79–80.
frr. 2–4.
Q, Pap: 143: Rhet.

2447 **ARISTON** Phil.
1 B.C.: Alexandrinus
001 **Testimonium**, FGrH #649: 3C:203–204.
NQ: 88: Test.
002 **Fragmenta**, ed. I. Mariotti, *Aristone d'Alessandria*. Bologna: Patron, 1966: 11–19.
Q

1194 **ARISTONICUS** Gramm.
1 B.C.–A.D. 1: Alexandrinus
001 **De signis Odysseae**, ed. O. Carnuth, *Aristonici*

περὶ σημείων Ὀδυσσείας reliquiae emendatiores. Leipzig: Hirzel, 1869: 3–164.
Q: 36,510: Gramm.

002 **De signis Iliadis**, ed. L. Friedländer, *Aristonici περὶ σημείων Ἰλιάδος reliquiae emendatiores.* Göttingen: Dieterich, 1853 (repr. Amsterdam: Hakkert, 1965): 39–350.
Q: 93,323: Gramm.

003 **Testimonia**, FGrH #53 & #633: **1A**:295; **3C**:182.
NQ: 142: Test.

004 **Fragmentum**, FGrH #633: 3C:182.
Q: 103: Hist.

1899 **ARISTONICUS** Hist.
ante A.D. 2: Tarentinus
001 **Fragmenta**, FGrH #57: 1A:297.
Q: 149: Hist., Myth.

0204 **ARISTONOUS** Lyr.
3 B.C.: Corinthius
001 **Paean in Apollinem**, ed. J.U. Powell, *Collectanea Alexandrina.* Oxford: Clarendon Press, 1925 (repr. 1970): 162–164.
Epigr: 180: Lyr., Hymn.

002 **Hymnus in Vestam**, ed. Powell, *op. cit.*, 164–165.
Epigr: 71: Lyr., Hymn.

0420 **ARISTONYMUS** Comic.
5–4 B.C.
001 **Fragmenta**, ed. T. Kock, *Comicorum Atticorum fragmenta*, vol. 1. Leipzig: Teubner, 1880: 668–669.
frr. 1–3, 5–9.
Q: 40: Comic.

002 **Fragmenta**, ed. A. Meineke, *Fragmenta comicorum Graecorum*, vol. 2.2. Berlin: Reimer, 1840 (repr. De Gruyter, 1970): 698–699.
Q: 26: Comic.

1195 **ARISTONYMUS** Gnom.
Incertum
x01 **Fragmenta ap. Stobaeum.**
Anth. **III**.1.96, 97; 4.105; 10.49, 50, 51; 13.41; 14.9; 21.7; 23.7; 38.36; **IV**.31d.111; 33.29; 35.33; 40.19a; 42.14; 46.21, 22, 23.
Cf. Joannes STOBAEUS (2037 001).

2353 **ARISTONYMUS** Hist.
Incertum
001 **Titulus**, FGrH #510: 3B:487.
NQ: Hist.

0019 **ARISTOPHANES** Comic.
5–4 B.C.: Atheniensis
Vitae: Cf. VITAE ARISTOPHANIS (4158).
Scholia: Cf. SCHOLIA IN ARISTOPHANEM (5014).
001 **Acharnenses**, ed. V. Coulon and M. van Daele, *Aristophane*, vol. 1. Paris: Les Belles

Lettres, 1923 (repr. 1967 (1st edn. corr.)): 12–66.
Cod: 7,819: Comic.

002 **Equites**, ed. Coulon and van Daele, *op. cit.*, vol. 1, 80–141.
Cod: 9,765: Comic.

003 **Nubes**, ed. K.J. Dover, *Aristophanes. Clouds.* Oxford: Clarendon Press, 1968 (repr. 1970): 7–88.
Cod: 10,463: Comic.

004 **Vespae**, ed. D.M. MacDowell, *Aristophanes. Wasps.* Oxford: Clarendon Press, 1971: 48–122.
Cod: 10,560: Comic.

005 **Pax**, ed. Coulon and van Daele, *op. cit.*, vol. 2 (1924; repr. 1969 (1st edn. corr.)): 99–156.
Cod: 8,796: Comic.

006 **Aves**, ed. Coulon and van Daele, *op. cit.*, vol. 3 (1928; repr. 1967 (1st edn. corr.)): 23–108.
Cod: 11,613: Comic.

007 **Lysistrata**, ed. Coulon and van Daele, *op. cit.*, vol. 3, 119–177.
Cod: 8,853: Comic.

008 **Thesmophoriazusae**, ed. Coulon and van Daele, *op. cit.*, vol. 4 (1928; repr. 1967 (1st edn. corr.)): 17–71.
Cod: 7,977: Comic.

009 **Ranae**, ed. Coulon and van Daele, *op. cit.*, vol. 4, 85–157.
Cod: 10,108: Comic.

010 **Ecclesiazusae**, ed. R.G. Ussher, *Aristophanes. Ecclesiazusae.* Oxford: Clarendon Press, 1973: 5–69.
Cod: 8,444: Comic.

011 **Plutus**, ed. Coulon and van Daele, *op. cit.*, vol. 5 (1930; repr. 1963 (1st edn. corr.)): 89–147.
Cod: 8,864: Comic.

012 **Fragmenta**, ed. J.M. Edmonds, *The fragments of Attic comedy*, vol. 1. Leiden: Brill, 1957: 572–580, 584–676, 680–766, 782–788.
frr. 1–11, 18–31, 41–55a, 63–84, 100–111, 125–142, 149–154, 155a–161, 163–168, 184–192, 198–228, 244a–258, 266–274, 278–283, 286–288, 294–307, 318–335, 345–351, 356–367, 376–380, 387–395, 400–405, 407–417, 430–437, 442, 451–455, 461–467, 471–483, 488–507, 528–531, 534–536, 542–552, 558–561, 566–569, 579–640, 642–660, 662–664, 668–670, 672–699, 897–900b, 901b–904a, 912–914.
Q, Pap: 5,054: Comic.

013 **Fragmenta**, ed. T. Kock, *Comicorum Atticorum fragmenta*, vol. 1. Leipzig: Teubner, 1880: 392–439, 441–474, 477–536, 538–562, 564–599.
frr. 1–11, 14–69, 71–85, 87–89, 91–98, 100–111, 117–159, 161–164, 166–167, 171–198, 200–208, 210–228, 234–259, 262–273, 275–283, 285–288, 292–307, 310–338, 340–349, 352–366, 368–395, 397–430, 432–437, 440–467, 469–507, 509–522, 524–537, 541–543,

545–552, 558–563, 566–569, 575–578, 580–640, 642, 644–699, 708–724, 726–915, 920–951, 959.
Q: 5,050: Comic.

014 **Fragmenta**, ed. A. Meineke, *Fragmenta comicorum Graecorum*, vol. 2.2. Berlin: Reimer, 1840 (repr. De Gruyter, 1970): 940, 944–949, 953–959, 961–966, 972, 974–977, 979–983, 985–991, 994–1002, 1004–1005, 1007–1011, 1014–1016, 1018–1020, 1026–1031, 1033, 1037–1044, 1047–1063, 1065–1066, 1068, 1070–1074, 1076–1079, 1082–1086, 1088, 1092–1094, 1096, 1098–1101, 1103–1111, 1113, 1118–1124, 1126–1144, 1146–1154, 1158–1161, 1163–1165, 1167–1173, 1175–1201.
Q: 4,294: Comic.

015 **Fragmenta**, ed. J. Demiańczuk, *Supplementum comicum*. Krakau: Nakładem Akademii, 1912 (repr. Hildesheim: Olms, 1967): 11–27.
frr. 1–60.
Q, Pap: 324: Comic.

016 **Fragmenta**, ed. C. Austin, *Comicorum Graecorum fragmenta in papyris reperta*. Berlin: De Gruyter, 1973: 7–32.
frr. 17–18, 56–66 + tituli.
Pap: 1,379: Comic.

017 **Fragmenta**, ed. Kock, *CAF*, vol. 3 (1888): 724–726.
frr. 344b, 644b, 645b, 676b, 692b, 739b, 899b, 900b, 901b, 902b.
Q: 73: Comic.

018 **Fragmenta**, ed. Meineke, *FCG*, vol. 5.1 (1857; repr. 1970): cxxxiii, cxxxix–cxli, cxlvii, cliii–cliv, clviii.
Q: 126: Comic.

x01 **Oracula ficta.**
App. Anth. 6.277–290: Cf. ANTHOLOGIAE GRAECAE APPENDIX (7052 006).
Dup. partim 0019 002, 005–006.

0644 **ARISTOPHANES** Gramm.
3–2 B.C.: Byzantius

001 **Aristophanis historiae animalium epitome subjunctis Aeliani Timothei aliorumque eclogis**, ed. S.P. Lambros, *Excerptorum Constantini de natura animalium libri duo. Aristophanis historiae animalium epitome* [*Commentaria in Aristotelem Graeca*, suppl. 1.1. Berlin: Reimer, 1885]: 1–154.
Cod: 38,513: Nat. Hist., Paradox.

002 **Nomina aetatum** (fragmentum Parisinum), ed. A. Nauck, *Aristophanis Byzantii grammatici Alexandrini fragmenta*, 2nd edn. Halle: Lippert & Schmid, 1848 (repr. Hildesheim: Olms, 1963): 79–81.
Dup. partim 0644 011.
Cod: 367: Gramm., Lexicogr.

003 **Fragmenta**, ed. Nauck, *op. cit.*, 87–88, 99–102, 104, 111–112, 128–131, 133, 137–138, 143,

146, 149, 151–152, 159, 163–173, 175, 178–179, 181–184, 186–189, 191, 193–197, 200–207, 210–229, 231–234.
frr. 1–101.
Dup. partim 0644 010.
Q, Cod: 5,946: Gramm., Lexicogr.

004 **Paroemiae** (fragmenta), ed. Nauck, *op. cit.*, 236–241.
frr. 1–13.
Q: 474: Paroem.

005 **Commentaria in Callimachi pinaces** (fragmenta), ed. Nauck, *op. cit.*, 247, 249–251.
frr. 1, 3–8.
Q: 381: Gramm.

006 **Ceteri Aristophanis libri** (fragmenta), ed. Nauck, *op. cit.*, 264, 271, 273–277, 279–282.
frr. 1–7.
Q: 628: Gramm.

007 **Argumenta fabularum Aristophani tributa** (fragmenta), ed. Nauck, *op. cit.*, 256–263.
frr. 1–11.
Dup. partim SCHOLIA IN ARISTOPHANEM (5014 001–002, 007–009, 013–014).
Q: 868: Gramm.

008 **Testimonia**, FGrH #347: 3B:209–210.
NQ: 140: Test.

009 **Fragmenta**, FGrH #347: 3B:210.
Q: 125: Hist.

010 **De suspectis apud veteres verbis** (fragmenta), ed. E. Miller, "Opuscles divers," *Lexica Graeca Minora* (ed. L. Latte & H. Erbse). Hildesheim: Olms, 1965: 273–274.
Dup. partim 0644 003.
Q: 135: Lexicogr.

011 **Nomina aetatum** (fragmenta), ed. Miller, *op. cit.*, 274–280.
Dup. partim 0644 002.
Q: 1,380: Lexicogr.

012 **Fragmenta**, ed. W.J. Slater, *Aristophanis Byzantii fragmenta* [*Sammlung griechischer und lateinischer Grammatiker* 6. Berlin: De Gruyter, 1986]: 5–203.
Q, Cod, Pap: Gramm.

x01 **Epigrammata demonstrativa.**
App. Anth. 3.85–90: Cf. ANTHOLOGIAE GRAECAE APPENDIX (7052 003).

1196 **ARISTOPHANES** Hist.
4 B.C.: Boeotus

001 **Testimonia**, FGrH #379: 3B:247.
NQ: 29: Test.

002 **Fragmenta**, FGrH #379: 3B:247–249.
Q: 484: Hist.

003 **Fragmentum** (*P. Oxy.* 27.2463), ed. H.J. Mette, "Die 'Kleinen' griechischen Historiker heute," *Lustrum* 21 (1978) 27.
fr. 2 bis.
Pap: 92: Hist.

0421 **ARISTOPHON** Comic.
4 B.C.

001 **Fragmenta**, ed. T. Kock, *Comicorum Atti-corum fragmenta*, vol. 2. Leipzig: Teubner, 1884: 276–281.
frr. 1–15.
Q: 463: Comic.

002 **Fragmenta**, ed. A. Meineke, *Fragmenta comicorum Graecorum*, vol. 3. Berlin: Reimer, 1840 (repr. De Gruyter, 1970): 356–364.
Q: 460: Comic.

003 **Fragmenta**, ed. R. Kassel and C. Austin, *Poetae comici Graeci*, vol. 4. Berlin: De Gruyter, 1983: 1–11.
frr. 1–2, 4–15.
Q: Comic.

2296 **ARISTOTELES** Hist.
4 B.C.?: Chalcidensis
001 **Testimonium**, FGrH #423: 3B:319.
NQ: 61: Test.
002 **Fragmenta**, FGrH #423: 3B:319.
Q: 117: Hist.

0086 **ARISTOTELES** Phil. et *CORPUS ARISTO-TELICUM*
4 B.C.: Stagirites, Pellaeus, Atheniensis
Scholia: Cf. SCHOLIA IN ARISTOTELEM (5015).
001 **Analytica priora et posteriora**, ed. W.D. Ross, *Aristotelis analytica priora et posteriora*. Oxford: Clarendon Press, 1964 (repr. 1968): 3–183 (24a10–31b38, 71a1–100b17).
Cod: 61,800: Phil.

002 **De anima**, ed. W.D. Ross, *Aristotle. De anima*. Oxford: Clarendon Press, 1961 (repr. 1967): 402a1–435b25.
Cod: 21,477: Phil.

052 **De anima** (codicis E fragmenta recensionis a vulgata diversae), ed. Ross, *De anima*, appendix 1 (412a3–424b18).
fr. 1: 412a3–412a12.
fr. 2: 414b13–416a9.
fr. 3: 421a5–422a24.
fr. 4: 423b8–424b18.
Cod: 2,466: Phil.

053 **De anima** (codicis P lectiones quae valde a lectionibus ceterorum codicum distant), ed. Ross, *De anima*, appendix 2 (412b10–423b8).
fr. 1: 412b10–412b23a.
fr. 2: 413a3–414a15.
fr. 3: 420b5–420b10.
fr. 4: 421a1–421a6.
fr. 5: 422b32–423b8.
Cod: 1,450: Phil.

003 Ἀθηναίων πολιτεία, ed. H. Oppermann, *Aristotelis Ἀθηναίων πολιτεία*. Leipzig: Teubner, 1928 (repr. Stuttgart: 1968): 1–98.
Pap: 16,828: Phil., Hist.

004 **De audibilibus**, ed. I. Bekker, *Aristotelis opera*, vol. 2, 2nd edn. Berlin: Reimer, 1831 (repr. De Gruyter, 1960): 800a1–804b39.
Cod: 3,612: Nat. Hist.

005 **De caelo**, ed. P. Moraux, *Aristote. Du ciel*.

Paris: Les Belles Lettres, 1965: 1–154 (268a1–313b22).
Cod: 30,719: Nat. Hist., Phil.

006 **Categoriae**, ed. L. Minio-Paluello, *Aristotelis categoriae et liber de interpretatione*. Oxford: Clarendon Press, 1949 (repr. 1966): 3–45 (1a1–15b32).
Cod: 10,537: Phil.

007 **De coloribus**, ed. Bekker, *op. cit.*, 791a1–799b20.
Cod: 5,193: Nat. Hist.

008 **De divinatione per somnum**, ed. W.D. Ross, *Aristotle. Parva naturalia*. Oxford: Clarendon Press, 1955 (repr. 1970): 462b12–464b18a.
Cod: 1,260: Phil., Onir.

011 **Epistulae**, ed. R. Hercher, *Epistolographi Graeci*. Paris: Didot, 1873 (repr. Amsterdam: Hakkert, 1965): 172–174.
Cod: 832: Epist.

009 **Ethica Eudemia**, ed. F. Susemihl, [*Aristotelis ethica Eudemia*]. Leipzig: Teubner, 1884 (repr. Amsterdam: Hakkert, 1967): 1–123 (1214a1–1249b25).
Cod: 27,112: Phil.

010 **Ethica Nicomachea**, ed. I. Bywater, *Aristotelis ethica Nicomachea*. Oxford: Clarendon Press, 1894 (repr. 1962): 1–224 (1094a1–1181b23).
Cod: 58,040: Phil.

012 **De generatione animalium**, ed. H.J. Drossaart Lulofs, *Aristotelis de generatione animalium*. Oxford: Clarendon Press, 1965 (repr. 1972): 1–204 (715a1–789b20).
Cod: 52,022: Nat. Hist., Zool., Phil.

013 **De generatione et corruptione**, ed. C. Mugler, *Aristote. De la génération et de la corruption*. Paris: Les Belles Lettres, 1966: 1–74 (314a1–338b19).
Cod: 16,849: Nat. Hist., Phil.

014 **Historia animalium**, ed. P. Louis, *Aristote. Histoire des animaux*, vols. 1–3. Paris: Les Belles Lettres, 1:1964; 2:1968; 3:1969: **1**:1–157; **2**:1–155; **3**:1–145, 156–175.
Lib. 1–4 (486a5–538b23): vol. 1.
Lib. 5–7 (538b28–588a12): vol. 2.
Lib. 8–10 (588a16–633b8, 633b12–638b36): vol. 3.
Cod: 97,577: Nat. Hist., Zool.

015 **De incessu animalium**, ed. W. Jaeger, *Aristotelis de animalium motione et de animalium incessu. Ps.-Aristotelis de spiritu libellus*. Leipzig: Teubner, 1913: 21–47 (704a4–714b23).
Cod: 6,592: Nat. Hist., Zool.

016 **De insomniis**, ed. Ross, *Parva naturalia*, 458a33–462b11.
Cod: 2,511: Phil.

017 **De interpretatione**, ed. Minio-Paluello, *op. cit.*, 49–72 (16a1–24b9).
Cod: 6,201: Phil.

018 **De juventute et senectute + De vita et morte**, ed. Ross, *Parva naturalia*, 467b10–470b5.
Cf. et 0086 037 (De respiratione).
Cod: 1,911: Nat. Hist., Phil.

019 **De lineis insecabilibus**, ed. Bekker, *op. cit.*, 968a1–972b33.
Cod: 3,035: Math.

020 **De longitudine et brevitate vitae**, ed. Ross, *Parva naturalia*, 464b19–467b9.
Cod: 1,842: Nat. Hist., Phil.

022 **Magna moralia**, ed. F. Susemihl, *Aristotle*, vol. 18 (ed. G.C. Armstrong). Cambridge, Mass.: Harvard University Press, 1935 (repr. 1969): 446–684 (1181a23–1213b30).
Cod: 24,131: Phil.

023 **Mechanica**, ed. Bekker, *op. cit.*, 847a11–858b31.
Cod: 8,621: Mech.

024 **De memoria et reminiscentia**, ed. Ross, *Parva naturalia*, 449b4–453b11.
Cod: 2,589: Phil.

025 **Metaphysica**, ed. W.D. Ross, *Aristotle's metaphysics*, 2 vols. Oxford: Clarendon Press, 1924 (repr. 1970 [of 1953 corr. edn.]): 1:980a21–1028a6; 2:1028a10–1093b29.
Cod: 80,635: Phil.

026 **Meteorologica**, ed. F.H. Fobes, *Aristotelis meteorologicorum libri quattuor*. Cambridge, Mass.: Harvard University Press, 1919 (repr. Hildesheim: Olms, 1967): 338a20–390b22.
Cod: 34,820: Nat. Hist., Phil.

027 **Mirabilium auscultationes**, ed. Bekker, *op. cit.*, 830a5–847b10.
Cod: 9,483: Paradox.

021 **De motu animalium**, ed. Jaeger, *op. cit.*, 3–18 (698a1–704b2).
Cod: 4,253: Nat. Hist., Zool.

028 **De mundo**, ed. W.L. Lorimer, *Aristotelis qui fertur libellus de mundo*. Paris: Les Belles Lettres, 1933: 47–103 (391a1–401b29).
Cod: 6,738: Phil.

029 **Oeconomica**, ed. B.A. van Groningen and A. Wartelle, *Aristote. Économique*. Paris: Les Belles Lettres, 1968: 1–35 (1343a1–1353b27).
Cod: 6,491: Phil.

030 **De partibus animalium**, ed. P. Louis, *Aristote. Les parties des animaux*. Paris: Les Belles Lettres, 1956: 1–166 (639a1–697b30).
Cod: 39,595: Nat. Hist., Phil.

031 **Physica**, ed. W.D. Ross, *Aristotelis physica*. Oxford: Clarendon Press, 1950 (repr. 1966 (1st edn. corr.)): 184a10–267b26.
Cod: 57,057: Nat. Hist., Phil.

054 **Physicorum libri octavi textus alter** (post 267b26), ed. Ross, *Aristotelis physica*, 241b24–248b28.
Cod: 2,484: Nat. Hist., Phil.

032 **Physiognomonica**, ed. Bekker, *op. cit.*, 805a1–814b8.
Cod: 6,014: Physiognom.

034 **Poetica**, ed. R. Kassel, *Aristotelis de arte poetica liber*. Oxford: Clarendon Press, 1965 (repr. 1968 [of 1966 corr. edn.]): 3–49 (1447a8–1462b19).
Cod: 10,549: Phil., Rhet.

035 **Politica**, ed. W.D. Ross, *Aristotelis politica*. Oxford: Clarendon Press, 1957 (repr. 1964): 1–269 (1252a1–1342b34).
Cod: 67,723: Phil.

036 **Problemata**, ed. Bekker, *op. cit.*, 859a1–967b27.
Cod: 76,106: Gramm., Math., Med., Mus., Nat. Hist., Phil.

033 **Protrepticus**, ed. I. Düring, *Aristotle's protrepticus*. Stockholm: Almqvist & Wiksell, 1961: 46–92.
Q, Pap: 6,196: Phil.

037 **De respiratione**, ed. Ross, *Parva naturalia*, 470b6–480b30.
Cf. et 0086 018 (De juventute et senectute + De vita et morte).
Cod: 6,275: Nat. Hist., Phil.

038 **Rhetorica**, ed. W.D. Ross, *Aristotelis ars rhetorica*. Oxford: Clarendon Press, 1959 (repr. 1964): 1–191 (1354a1–1420a8).
Cod: 44,373: Phil., Rhet.

041 **De sensu et sensibilibus**, ed. Ross, *Parva naturalia*, 436a1–480b30.
Cod: 8,130: Phil.

042 **De somno et vigilia**, ed. Ross, *Parva naturalia*, 453b11–458a32.
Cod: 3,099: Phil.

040 **Sophistici elenchi**, ed. W.D. Ross, *Aristotelis topica et sophistici elenchi*. Oxford: Clarendon Press, 1958 (repr. 1970 (1st edn. corr.)): 190–251 (164a20–184b8).
Cod: 14,649: Phil.

043 **De spiritu**, ed. Jaeger, *op. cit.*, 51–64 (481a1–486b4).
Cod: 3,577: Phil., Nat. Hist.

044 **Topica**, ed. Ross, *Aristotelis topica et sophistici elenchi*, 1–189 (100a18–164b19).
Cod: 45,655: Phil.

046 **De ventorum situ et nominibus**, ed. Bekker, *op. cit.*, 973a1–973b25.
Cod: 452: Nat. Hist.

045 **De virtutibus et vitiis**, ed. Bekker, *op. cit.*, 1249a26–1251b37.
Cod: 1,554: Phil.

047 **De Xenophane, de Zenone, de Gorgia**, ed. Bekker, *op. cit.*, 974a1–980b21.
De Xenophane: 974a1–977a11.
De Zenone: 977a13–979a9.
De Gorgia: 979a11–980b21.
Cod: 4,984: Phil.

048 **Divisiones Aristoteleae**, ed. H. Mutschmann, *Divisiones quae vulgo dicuntur Aristoteleae*. Leipzig: Teubner, 1906: 1–66.
Q, Cod: 10,005: Phil.

049 **Fragmenta**, ed. M.L. West, *Iambi et elegi Graeci*, vol. 2. Oxford: Clarendon Press, 1972: 44–45.
frr. 672–673.
Q: 53: Eleg.

050 **Fragmentum**, ed. D.L. Page, *Poetae melici*

Graeci. Oxford: Clarendon Press, 1962 (repr. 1967 (1st edn. corr.)): 444.
fr. 1.
Q: 94: Lyr., Hymn.

051 **Fragmenta varia**, ed. V. Rose, *Aristotelis qui ferebantur librorum fragmenta.* Leipzig: Teubner, 1886 (repr. Stuttgart: 1967): 23–425.
Dialogi (testimonia + frr. 1–111): pp. 23–104.
Logica (testimonia + frr. 112–124): pp. 105–114.
Rhetorica et poetica (testimonia + frr. 125–179): pp. 114–137.
Ethica (frr. 180–184): pp. 137–147.
Philosophica (frr. 185–208): pp. 148–167.
Physica (testimonia + frr. 209–278): pp. 167–214.
Zoica (testimonia + frr. 279–380): pp. 215–257.
Historica (testimonia + frr. 381–644): pp. 258–407.
Orationes et epistulae (testimonia + frr. 645–670): pp. 407–421.
Carmina (frr. 671–675): pp. 421–423.
Dubia (frr. 676–680): pp. 424–425.
Q: 88,480: Phil., Rhet., Hist., Nat. Hist., Dialog., Poem., Orat., Encom., Epist.

055 **Testimonia**, FGrH #646: 3C:192–193.
Dup. 0086 051 (frr. 246–247).
NQ: 654: Test.

056 **Fragmenta**, FGrH #646: 3C:194–199.
Dup. 0086 051 (fr. 248).
Q: 1,712: Hist., Nat. Hist.

x01 **Rhetorica ad Alexandrum.**
Cf. ANAXIMENES Hist. et Rhet. (0547 001).

x02 **Sicyonis historia** (*P. Oxy.* 11.1365).
FGrH #551, fr. 1b (= FGrH #105, fr. 2).
Cf. ADDITAMENTA (FGrH) (2433 024).
Cf. ANONYMI HISTORICI (FGrH) (1139 004).

x03 **Epigramma.**
AG 7.145.
Cf. ASCLEPIADES Epigr. (0137 001).

x04 **Epigrammata** (*App. Anth.*).
Epigrammata sepulcralia: 2.54–120(?).
Epigrammata demonstrativa: 3.47–48(?).
App. Anth. 2.54–120(?): Cf. ANTHOLOGIAE GRAECAE APPENDIX (7052 002).
App. Anth. 3.47–48(?): Cf. ANTHOLOGIAE GRAECAE APPENDIX (7052 003).

2562 **ARISTOTHEUS** Hist.
2 B.C.: Troezenius

001 **Testimonium**, FGrH #835: 3C:903.
NQ: 57: Test.

0241 **ARISTOXENUS** <Comic.>
7/6 B.C.: Selinuntius

002 **Fragmentum**, ed. M.L. West, *Iambi et elegi Graeci*, vol. 2. Oxford: Clarendon Press, 1972: 45.
Dup. 0241 003.
Q: [8]: Comic.

003 **Fragmentum**, ed. G. Kaibel, *Comicorum Graecorum fragmenta*, vol. 1.1 [*Poetarum Graecorum fragmenta*, vol. 6.1. Berlin: Weidmann, 1899]: 87.
Dup. 0241 002.
Q: 9: Comic.

0806 **ARISTOXENUS** Med.
1 B.C.–A.D. 1
x01 **Fragmenta ap. Galenum.**
K8.734, 746–747.
Cf. GALENUS Med. (0057 059).

0088 **ARISTOXENUS** Mus.
4 B.C.: Tarentinus

001 **Elementa harmonica**, ed. R. da Rios, *Aristoxeni elementa harmonica.* Rome: Polygraphica, 1954: 5–92.
Cod: 14,788: Mus.

002 **Elementa rhythmica** (lib. 1), ed. G.B. Pighi, *Aristoxeni rhythmica.* Bologna: Patron, 1959: 15–16.
Q: 376: Mus.

003 **Elementa rhythmica** (lib. 2), ed. Pighi, *op. cit.*, 17–26.
Q, Cod: 2,553: Mus.

004 **Fragmenta Parisina** (e cod. bibl. imp. Par. 3027), ed. Pighi, *op. cit.*, 27–28.
Cod: 466: Mus.

005 **Fragmentum** (*P. Oxy.* 1.9), ed. Pighi, *op. cit.*, 29–32.
Pap: 594: Mus.

006 **Fragmenta**, ed. F. Wehrli, *Aristoxenos* [*Die Schule des Aristoteles*, vol. 2, 2nd edn. Basel: Schwabe, 1967]: 10–41.
Πυθαγόρου βίος. Περὶ Πυθαγόρου καὶ τῶν γνωρίμων αὐτοῦ: frr. 11a–20a, 22–25.
Περὶ τοῦ Πυθαγορικοῦ βίου: frr. 26–32.
Πυθαγορικαὶ ἀποφάσεις: frr. 33–41.
Παιδευτικοὶ νόμοι. Πολιτικοὶ νόμοι. Μαντινέων ἔθη. Μαντινέων ἐγκώμιον: frr. 42a–45.1.
᾽Αρχύτα βίος: frr. 47–48, 50.
Σωκράτους βίος: frr. 51–60.
Πλάτωνος βίος: frr. 61–62, 64–65b, 66–68.
Περὶ μουσικῆς. Μουσικὴ ἀκρόασις. Πραξιδαμάντεια. Περὶ μελοποιίας: frr. 69d–69e, 70, 73–91.1, 93.
Περὶ ὀργάνων. Περὶ αὐλῶν. Περὶ αὐλητῶν. Περὶ αὐλῶν τρήσεως: frr. 94–102.
Περὶ χορῶν. Περὶ τραγικῆς ὀρχήσεως. Συγκρίσεις: frr. 103–112.
Περὶ τραγωδοποιῶν: frr. 113–116.
Τελέστου βίος: fr. 117.
Σύμμικτα συμποτικά: frr. 122–127.
῾Υπομνήματα et fragmenta incertae sedis: frr. 128–139.
Q, Pap: 9,598: Phil., Biogr., Mus.

1946 **ARISTUS** Hist.
3 B.C.: Salaminius (Cypri)
001 **Testimonia**, FGrH #143: 2B:812.
NQ: 68: Test.

002 **Fragmenta**, FGrH #143: 2B:812–813.
Q: 249: Hist.

2668 **ARIUS** Epic.
Incertum
x01 **Epigramma dedicatorium.**
App. Anth. 1.192: Cf. ANTHOLOGIAE GRAE-
CAE APPENDIX (7052 001).

0947 **Lecanius ARIUS** Med.
A.D. 1: Tarsensis
x01 **Fragmenta ap. Galenum.**
K12.829; **13**.247–248, 840.
Cf. GALENUS Med. (0057 076–077).

0529 **ARIUS DIDYMUS** Doxogr.
1 B.C.
001 **Physica** (fragmenta), ed. H. Diels, *Doxographi
Graeci.* Berlin: Reimer, 1879 (repr. De Gruyter, 1965): 447–472.
frr. 1–40.
Q: 8,354: Doxogr.
002 **Liber de philosophorum sectis** (epitome ap.
Stobaeum), ed. F.W.A. Mullach, *Fragmenta
philosophorum Graecorum*, vol. 2. Paris: Didot,
1867 (repr. Aalen: Scientia, 1968): 53–101.
Q: 21,272: Phil.

0360 **ARMENIDAS** Hist.
5 B.C.
001 **Fragmenta**, FGrH #378: 3B:245–247.
Q: 488: Hist.

0807 **ARRHABIANUS** Med.
ante A.D. 2
x01 **Fragmentum ap. Galenum.**
K13.83–84.
Cf. GALENUS Med. (0057 076).

1798 **ARRIANUS** Astron.
2 B.C.
x01 **Fragmentum ap. Stobaeum.**
Anth. I.28.2.
Cf. Joannes STOBAEUS (2037 001).

2650 **ARRIANUS** Epic.
2 B.C.
001 **Fragmentum et tituli**, ed. H. Lloyd-Jones and
P. Parsons, *Supplementum Hellenisticum.* Berlin: De Gruyter, 1983: 81–82.
frr. (+ titul.) 207–211.
Dup. partim ANONYMI HISTORICI (FGrH)
1139 007 (FGrH #153, fr. 15).
Q: 25: Epic., Encom.

2669 **ARRIANUS** Epigr.
Incertum
x01 **Epigramma dedicatorium.**
App. Anth. 1.193: Cf. ANTHOLOGIAE GRAE-
CAE APPENDIX (7052 001).

0074 **Flavius ARRIANUS** Hist. et Phil.
A.D. 1–2: Bithynius
001 **Alexandri anabasis**, ed. A.G. Roos and G.
Wirth, *Flavii Arriani quae exstant omnia*, vol.
1. Leipzig: Teubner, 1967 (1st edn. corr.): 1–
390.
Cod: 80,714: Hist.
002 **Historia Indica**, ed. Roos and Wirth, *op. cit.*,
vol. 2 (1968; (1st edn. corr.)): 1–73.
Cod: 14,423: Hist.
003 **Cynegeticus**, ed. Roos and Wirth, *op. cit.*, vol.
2, 74–102.
Cod: 6,254: Hist.
004 **Periplus ponti Euxini**, ed. Roos and Wirth, *op.
cit.*, vol. 2, 103–128.
Cod: 4,510: Hist., Geogr.
005 **Tactica**, ed. Roos and Wirth, *op. cit.*, vol. 2,
129–176.
Cod: 9,460: Tact.
006 **Acies contra Alanos**, ed. Roos and Wirth, *op.
cit.*, vol. 2, 177–185.
Cod: 1,338: Hist.
007 **Fragmenta de rebus physicis**, ed. Roos and
Wirth, *op. cit.*, vol. 2, 186–195.
Q: 1,832: Nat. Hist.
008 **Epistula ad Lucium Gellium**, ed. Roos and
Wirth, *op. cit.*, vol. 2, 196.
Dup. EPICTETUS Phil. (0557 006).
Cod: 205: Epist.
009 **Bithynicorum fragmenta**, ed. Roos and Wirth,
op. cit., vol. 2, 198–223.
Q: 4,604: Hist.
010 **Parthicorum fragmenta**, ed. Roos and Wirth,
op. cit., vol. 2, 224–252.
Cf. et 0074 015.
Q: 3,527: Hist.
011 **Historia successorum Alexandri** (fragmenta ap.
Photium, *Bibl.* cod. 92), ed. Roos and Wirth,
op. cit., vol. 2, 253–286.
Cf. et 0074 016.
Q: 4,662: Hist.
012 **Fragmentum ex historia Alanica** (?), ed. Roos
and Wirth, *op. cit.*, vol. 2, 286.
Q: 82: Hist.
013 **Fragmenta incerta** (utrum e Parthicis an ex
historia successorum Alexandri desumpta sint),
ed. Roos and Wirth, *op. cit.*, vol. 2, 287–290.
Q: 572: Hist.
014 **Fragmentum** (*PSI* 1284), ed. Roos and Wirth,
op. cit., vol. 2, 323–324.
Pap: 173: Hist.
015 **Parthicorum fragmenta** (ap. Joannem Lydum
et Syncellum), ed. Roos and Wirth, *op. cit.*, vol.
2, 224–226.
Cf. et 0074 010.
Q: 145: Hist.
016 **Historia successorum Alexandri** (fragmenta ap.
Photium, *Bibl.* cod. 82), ed. Roos and Wirth,
op. cit., vol. 2, 253–258.
Cf. et 0074 011.
Q: 478: Hist.

017 **Testimonia**, FGrH #156: 2B:837–840.
NQ: 774: Test.

018 **Fragmenta**, FGrH #156: 2B:840–883.
Q, Cod: 13,165: Hist.

x01 **Dissertationes ab Arriano digestae.**
Schenkl, pp. 7–454.
Cf. EPICTETUS Phil. (0557 001).

x02 **Dissertationum Epictetearum sive ab Arriano sive ab aliis digestarum fragmenta.**
Schenkl, pp. 455–460, 462–475.
Cf. EPICTETUS Phil. (0557 003).

x03 **Periplus maris Erythraei.**
GGM, vol. 1, pp. 257–305.
Cf. PERIPLUS MARIS ERYTHRAEI (0071 001).

x04 **Periplus ponti Euxini.**
GGM, vol. 1, pp. 402–423.
Cf. PERIPLUS PONTI EUXINI (0075 001).

9018 **ARSENIUS** Paroemiogr.
vel Aristobulus Apostolius
A.D. 15–16: Monembasiensis

001 **Apophthegmata**, ed. E.L. von Leutsch, *Corpus paroemiographorum Graecorum*, vol. 2. Göttingen: Vandenhoeck & Ruprecht, 1851 (repr. Hildesheim: Olms, 1958): 240–744.
Cod: 23,377: Paroem.

2489 **ARTAPANUS Judaeus** Hist.
2 B.C.: fort. Alexandrinus

001 **Fragmenta**, FGrH #726: 3C:680–686.
Q: 1,964: Hist.

2463 **ARTAVASDES** Hist.
1 B.C.: Armenius

001 **Testimonium**, FGrH #678: 3C:350.
NQ: 64: Test.

0045 ***ARTAXERXIS EPISTULAE***
Incertum

001 **Epistulae**, ed. R. Hercher, *Epistolographi Graeci*. Paris: Didot, 1873 (repr. Amsterdam: Hakkert, 1965): 175–176.
Q: 654: Epist.

2651 **ARTEMIDORUS** Eleg.
ante 2 B.C.

001 **Tituli**, ed. H. Lloyd-Jones and P. Parsons, *Supplementum Hellenisticum*. Berlin: De Gruyter, 1983: 82.
frr. 213–214.
NQ: 5: Astron., Eleg.

0080 **ARTEMIDORUS** Geogr.
2 B.C.: Ephesius

002 **Fragmentum**, FGrH #438: 3B:371.
Q: 19: Hist.

x01 **Geographia.**
GGM, vol. 1, pp. 574–576.
Cf. MARCIANUS Geogr. (4003 003).

0135 **ARTEMIDORUS** Gramm.
1 B.C.: Tarsensis

002 **Epigramma**, AG 9.205.
Q: 16: Epigr.

x01 **Fragmenta ap. Athenaeum.**
Deipnosophistae 4.182d; 14.663d–e.
Cf. ATHENAEUS Soph. (0008 001).

2472 **ARTEMIDORUS** Hist.
ante A.D. 1?: Ascalonius

001 **Testimonium**, FGrH #698: 3C:552.
NQ: 25: Test.

0553 **ARTEMIDORUS** Onir.
A.D. 2: Daldianus

001 **Onirocriticon**, ed. R.A. Pack, *Artemidori Daldiani onirocriticon libri v.* Leipzig: Teubner, 1963: 1–324.
Cod: 66,405: Onir.

0809 **ARTEMIDORUS CAPITO** Med.
A.D. 2

x01 **Fragmentum ap. Galenum.**
K15.22 in CMG, vol. 5.9.1, p. 13.
Cf. GALENUS Med. (0057 085).

0136 **ARTEMON** Epigr.
3 B.C.: Atheniensis

001 **Epigrammata**, AG 12.55, 124.
Q: 88: Epigr.

1197 **ARTEMON** Gramm.
fiq Artemon Pergamenus Hist.
2/1 B.C.?: Cassandrensis

001 **Fragmenta**, FHG 4: 342–343.
frr. 9–14.
Q

2307 **ARTEMON** Hist.
4 B.C.?: Clazomeneus

001 **Fragmenta**, FGrH #443: 3B:374.
Q: 72: Hist., Geogr.

2392 **ARTEMON** Hist.
2 B.C.: Pergamenus

001 **Testimonia**, FGrH #569: 3B:661–662.
NQ: 75: Test.

002 **Fragmenta**, FGrH #569: 3B:662–663.
Q: 591: Hist.

ASCENSIO ISAIAE
Cf. MARTYRIUM ET ASCENSIO ISAIAE (1483).

0137 **ASCLEPIADES** Epigr.
3 B.C.: Samius

001 **Epigrammata**, AG 5.7, 64, 85, 145, 150, 153, 158, 161–162, 164, 167, 169, 181, 185, 189, 194, 202–203, 207, 209–210; **6.**308; **7.**11, 145, 217, 284, 500; **9.**63–64, 752; **12.**36, 46, 50, 75, 77, 105, 135, 153, 161–163, 166; **13.**23; **16.**68, 120.

AG 7.12; 12.17: Cf. ANONYMI EPIGRAM-
MATICI (AG) (0138 001).
AG 13.29: Cf. NICAENETUS Epic. (0218 002).
Q: 1,533: Epigr.

002 **Fragmenta**, ed. H. Lloyd-Jones and P. Parsons,
Supplementum Hellenisticum. Berlin: De Gruyter, 1983: 83–84.
frr. 215–217, 219.
Q: 21: Iamb.

x01 **Epigrammata dedicatoria.**
App. Anth. 1.167–176: Cf. ANTHOLOGIAE
GRAECAE APPENDIX (7052 001).

2224 **ASCLEPIADES** Gramm.
3–2 B.C.?: Nicaeanus, Alexandrinus
001 **Testimonia**, FGrH #339: 3B:195–196.
NQ: 104: Test.
002 **Fragmenta**, FGrH #339: 3B:196.
Q: 158: Hist.

1955 **ASCLEPIADES** Hist.
4–3 B.C.
001 **Fragmentum**, FGrH #157: 2B:883.
Q: 44: Hist.

1198 **ASCLEPIADES** Hist.
3 B.C.?: Cyprius
001 **Fragmentum**, FGrH #752: 3C:735.
Q: 265: Hist.

2430 **ASCLEPIADES** Hist.
A.D. 5: Aegyptius
001 **Testimonium**, FGrH #624: 3C:158–159.
NQ: 224: Test.
002 **Fragmenta**, FGrH #624: 3C:159–160.
Q: 266: Hist.

1199 **ASCLEPIADES** Hist. et Gramm.
1 B.C.: Myrleanus
001 **Testimonia**, FGrH #697: 3C:548.
NQ: 169: Test.
002 **Fragmenta**, FGrH #697: 3C:548–551.
Q: 985: Hist., Perieg.

2423 **ASCLEPIADES** Hist. et Gramm.
1 B.C.–A.D. 1?: Mendesicus
001 **Fragmenta**, FGrH #617: 3C:144–145.
Q: 137: Hist.

0811 **ASCLEPIADES** Med.
1 B.C.: Bithynius
x01 **Fragmenta ap. Galenum.**
K3.446–467 in Helmreich, vol. 1, pp. 340–
341.
Cf. GALENUS Med. (0057 017).
x02 **Fragmentum ap. Galenum.**
K8.757.
Cf. GALENUS Med. (0057 059).
x03 **Praecepta salubria.**
Bussemaker, pp. 132–134.
Cf. PRAECEPTA SALUBRIA (0663 001).

1200 **ASCLEPIADES** Myth.
4 B.C.: Tragilensis
001 **Testimonia**, FGrH #12: 1A:166.
NQ: 89: Test.
002 **Fragmenta**, FGrH #12: 1A:166–176.
Q: 3,209: Hist., Myth.

0229 **ASCLEPIADES** Phil.
4 B.C.
001 **Testimonium**, ed. F. Lasserre, *De Léodamas de
Thasos à Philippe d'Oponte*. Naples: Bibliopolis, 1987: 113.
NQ: Test.
002 **Memoranda** (titulus), ed. Lasserre, *op. cit.*, 113.
Pap: Phil.

0681 **ASCLEPIADES Pharmacion** Med.
vel Asclepiades Junior
A.D. 1
x01 **Fragmenta ap. Galenum.**
K12.378–1007; **13**.1–361, 442–1058; **14**.1–209.
Cf. GALENUS Med. (0057 076–078).
x02 **Fragmenta ap. Aëtium** (lib. 5–8).
CMG, vol. 8.2, pp. 68, 155, 156, 201, 370, 371,
391, 449, 496, 513, 530.
Cf. AËTIUS Med. (0718 005–008).
x03 **Fragmenta ap. Aëtium** (lib. 9).
Zervos, *Athena* 23, pp. 283, 288, 295, 335.
Cf. AËTIUS Med. (0718 009).
x04 **Fragmenta ap. Aëtium** (lib. 12).
Kostomiris, pp. 22, 26, 61, 62, 103, 105.
Cf. AËTIUS Med. (0718 012).
x05 **Fragmentum ap. Aëtium** (lib. 13).
Zervos, *Athena* 18, p. 279.
Cf. AËTIUS Med. (0718 013).
x06 **Fragmenta ap. Aëtium** (lib. 15).
Zervos, *Athena* 21, pp. 58, 67, 91.
Cf. AËTIUS Med. (0718 015).
x07 **Fragmenta ap. Aëtium** (lib. 16).
Zervos, *Gynaekologie des Aëtios*, pp. 57, 141,
156.
Cf. AËTIUS Med. (0718 016).
x08 **Fragmentum ap. Hippiatrica.**
Oder & Hoppe, vol. 2, p. 211.
Cf. HIPPIATRICA (0738 006).

0556 **ASCLEPIODOTUS** Tact.
1 B.C.
001 **Tactica**, ed. C.H. Oldfather and W.A. Oldfather, *Aeneas Tacticus, Asclepiodotus, Onasander*. Cambridge, Mass.: Harvard University
Press, 1923 (repr. 1962): 244–332.
Cod: 7,002: Tact.

0812 **ASCLEPIUS** Med.
A.D. 1?
Cf. et ASCLEPIUS et MACHAON Med. (0879).
x01 **Fragmentum ap. Galenum.**
K13.841.
Cf. GALENUS Med. (0057 077).

x02 **Fragmentum ap. Paulum.**
CMG, vol. 9.2, p. 326.
Cf. PAULUS Med. (0715 001).

4018 **ASCLEPIUS** Phil.
A.D. 6: Trallianus
001 **In Aristotelis metaphysicorum libros A-Z commentaria**, ed. M. Hayduck, *Asclepii in Aristotelis metaphysicorum libros A-Z commentaria* [*Commentaria in Aristotelem Graeca* 6.2. Berlin: Reimer, 1888]: 1-452.
Cod: 179,809: Phil., Comm.
002 **Commentaria in Nicomachi Geraseni Pythagorei introductionem arithmeticam**, ed. L. Tarán, *Asclepius of Tralles. Commentary to Nicomachus' introduction to arithmetic* [*Transactions of the American Philosophical Society*, N.S. 59.4. Philadelphia: American Philosophical Society, 1969]: 24-72.
Cod

0879 **ASCLEPIUS et MACHAON** Med.
A.D. 1?
Cf. et ASCLEPIUS Med. (0812).
x01 **Fragmentum ap. Galenum.**
K12.774.
Cf. GALENUS Med. (0057 076).

2122 **Gaius ASINIUS QUADRATUS** Hist.
A.D. 3?
001 **Epigramma**, AG 7.312.
Q: 27: Epigr.
002 **Testimonia**, FGrH #97: 2A:447-448.
NQ: 97: Test.
003 **Fragmenta**, FGrH #97: 2A:448-451.
Q: 760: Hist.

0242 **ASIUS** Epic. et Eleg.
6 B.C.?: Samius
001 **Fragmentum**, ed. M.L. West, *Iambi et elegi Graeci*, vol. 2. Oxford: Clarendon Press, 1972: 46.
Q: 21: Eleg.
002 **Fragmenta**, ed. G. Kinkel, *Epicorum Graecorum fragmenta*, vol. 1. Leipzig: Teubner, 1877: 203, 205-206.
frr. 1-2, 8, 10, 13.
Q: 96: Epic.
x01 **Epigramma irrisorium.**
App. Anth. 5.2: Cf. ANTHOLOGIAE GRAECAE APPENDIX (7052 005).
Dup. 0242 001.

2609 **ASOPODORUS** Iamb.
4/3 B.C.?: Phliasius
001 **Tituli**, ed. H. Lloyd-Jones and P. Parsons, *Supplementum Hellenisticum*. Berlin: De Gruyter, 1983: 84.
frr. 222-223.
NQ: 7: Iamb.

2711 **ASPASIA** <Epigr.>
5 B.C.: Milesia

x01 **Epigrammata** (*App. Anth.*).
Epigramma exhortatorium et supplicatorium: 4.17.
Epigramma irrisorium: 5.6.
App. Anth. 4.17(?): Cf. ANTHOLOGIAE GRAECAE APPENDIX (7052 004).
App. Anth. 5.6(?): Cf. ANTHOLOGIAE GRAECAE APPENDIX (7052 005).

2529 **ASPASIUS** Hist.
A.D. 2: Byblius
001 **Testimonium**, FGrH #792: 3C:825.
NQ: 30: Test.
002 **Titulus**, FGrH #792: 3C:825.
NQ: Hist.

2530 **ASPASIUS** Hist.
Incertum: Tyrius
001 **Testimonium**, FGrH #793: 3C:825.
NQ: 23: Test.
002 **Tituli**, FGrH #793: 3C:825.
NQ: Hist.

0813 **ASPASIUS** Med.
ante A.D. 1
x01 **Fragmentum ap. Galenum.**
K13.302.
Cf. GALENUS Med. (0057 076).

0615 **ASPASIUS** Phil.
A.D. 2
001 **In ethica Nichomachea commentaria**, ed. G. Heylbut, *Aspasii in ethica Nicomachea quae supersunt commentaria* [*Commentaria in Aristotelem Graeca* 19.1. Berlin: Reimer, 1889]: 1-186.
Cod: 72,111: Phil., Comm.

1201 *ASSUMPTIO MOSIS*
vel *Testamentum Mosis*
A.D. 1
001 **Fragmenta**, ed. A.-M. Denis, *Fragmenta pseudepigraphorum quae supersunt Graeca* [*Pseudepigrapha veteris testamenti Graece* 3. Leiden: Brill, 1970]: 63-67.
Q: 416: Apocalyp., Pseudepigr.

0814 **ASTERIUS** Med.
ante A.D. 6
x01 **Fragmentum ap. Aëtium** (lib. 7).
CMG, vol. 8.2, p. 398.
Cf. AËTIUS Med. (0718 007).

2060 **ASTERIUS** Scr. Eccl.
A.D. 4-5: Amasenus
001 **Homiliae 1-14**, ed. C. Datema, *Asterius of Amasea. Homilies i-xiv*. Leiden: Brill, 1970: 7-15, 17-24, 27-37, 39-43, 45-52, 59-64, 71-78, 85-106, 115, 117, 119, 121, 123, 125, 127, 135-146, 153-155, 165-173, 183-194, 205-219.
Cod: 42,717: Homilet., Encom.

002 **Homilia 9** (ex Symeone Metaphraste), ed. Datema, *op. cit.*, 114, 116, 118, 120, 122, 124, 126.
Cod: 1,673: Homilet., Encom.

003 **Homiliae 15–16**, ed. A. Bretz, *Studien und Texte zu Asterios von Amaseia* [*Texte und Untersuchungen* 40.1 (1914)]: 107–121.
Cod: Homilet.

004 **Homilia in bonum Samaritanum**, MPG 104: 204–208.
Q: Homilet.

005 **Homilia in Zacchaeum**, MPG 104: 209.
Q: Homilet.

006 **Homilia in servum centurionis**, MPG 104: 213–216.
Q: Homilet.

007 **Homilia in Jairum et in mulierem sanguinis profluvio labentem**, MPG 104: 221–224.
Q: Homilet.

2061 **ASTERIUS Sophista** Scr. Eccl.
A.D. 4: Antiochenus

001 **Commentarii in Psalmos** (homiliae 31), ed. M. Richard, *Asterii sophistae commentariorum in Psalmos quae supersunt* [*Symbolae Osloenses*, fasc. suppl. 16. Oslo: Brøgger, 1956]: 3–245.
Cod: 61,092: Homilet., Exeget.

002 **Fragmenta in Psalmos** (in catenis), ed. Richard, *op. cit.*, 249–273.
Q: 5,594: Exeget., Caten.

003 **Syntagmation** (fragmenta), ed. G. Bardy, *Recherches sur saint Lucien d'Antioche et son école*. Paris: Beauchesne, 1936: 341–348.
Q

004 **Epistula**, ed. Bardy, *op. cit.*, 348–354.
Q: Epist.

2642 **<ASTRAMPSYCHUS Magus>** Onir.
ante 4 B.C.

001 **Onirocrita**, ed. N. Rigalt, *Artemidorus*. Paris, 1603.
Cod

002 **Oracula**, ed. R. Hercher, *Astrampsychi oraculorum decades ciii* [*Programm Gymnasium Joachimsthal* (1863)]: 1–48.
Dup. partim 2642 003.
Cod

003 **Sortes**, ed. G.M. Browne, *The papyri of the Sortes Astrampsychi*. Meisenheim am Glan: Hain, 1974: 18–20, 32–35, 44–51.
P. Oxy. 12.1477: pp. 18–20.
P. Oxy. 38.2832: pp. 32–35.
P. Oxy. 38.2833: pp. 44–51.
Dup. partim 2642 002.
Pap

x01 Φιλτροκατάδεσμος (*P. Brit. Mus.* 122).
PGM, vol. 2, pp. 45–50.
Cf. MAGICA (5002 001).

0325 **ASTYDAMAS** Trag.
fort. Astydamas Major vel Astydamas Minor
4 B.C.: Atheniensis

001 **Fragmenta**, ed. B. Snell, *Tragicorum Graecorum fragmenta*, vol. 1. Göttingen: Vandenhoeck & Ruprecht, 1971: 200–207.
frr. 1–1a, 1c–9.
fr. 1h: *P. Hibeh* 2.174.
fr. 1i: *P. Amh.* 2.10.
fr. 2a: *P. Strassb.* W.G. 304.2.
Q, Pap: 444: Trag., Satyr.

x01 **Epigramma demonstrativum.**
App. Anth. 3.43: Cf. ANTHOLOGIAE GRAECAE APPENDIX (7052 003).

1202 **<ATHAMAS>** Phil.
3 B.C.?

001 **Fragmentum**, ed. H. Thesleff, *The Pythagorean texts of the Hellenistic period*. Åbo: Åbo Akademi, 1965: 54.
Q: 63: Phil.

2035 **ATHANASIUS** Theol.
A.D. 4: Alexandrinus

001 **Contra gentes**, ed. R.W. Thomson, *Athanasius. Contra gentes and de incarnatione*. Oxford: Clarendon Press, 1971: 2–132.
Cod: 18,284: Apol.

002 **De incarnatione verbi**, ed. C. Kannengiesser, *Sur l'incarnation du verbe* [*Sources chrétiennes* 199. Paris: Cerf, 1973]: 258–468.
Cod: 20,263: Theol.

003 **De decretis Nicaenae synodi**, ed. H.G. Opitz, *Athanasius Werke*, vol. 2.1. Berlin: De Gruyter, 1940: 1–45.
Epistula Eusebii Caesariensis ad ecclesiam suam: pp. 28–31.
Depositio Arii: p. 31.
Epistula Alexandri Alexandrini: pp. 31–35.
Epistula synodi Nicaenae ad ecclesiam Alexandriae: pp. 35–36.
Symbolum Nicaenum: pp. 36–37.
Epistula Constantini imperatoris ad ecclesiam Alexandriae: p. 37.
Epistula Constantini imperatoris ad episcopos et populos: pp. 37–38.
Epistula Constantini imperatoris ad Arium et socios: pp. 38–43.
Epistula Constantini imperatoris ad ecclesiam Nicomediae: pp. 43–45.
Epistula Constantini imperatoris ad Theodotum Laodicensem: p. 45.
Cod: 20,507: Concil., Epist.

004 **De sententia Dionysii**, ed. Opitz, *op. cit.*, 46–67.
Cod: 7,347: Epist.

005 **Apologia contra Arianos** *sive* **Apologia secunda**, ed. Opitz, *op. cit.*, 87–168.
Epistula synodi Alexandriae: pp. 89–101.
Epistula Julii episcopi Romae: pp. 102–113.
Epistula synodi Sardicensis ad Alexandrinos: pp. 115–118.
Epistula synodalis synodi Sardicensis: pp. 119–132.
Epistula Constantii imperatoris ad Athanasium: p. 132.

Epistula secunda Constantii imperatoris: pp. 132–133.

Epistula tertia Constantii imperatoris: p. 133.

Epistula Julii episcopi Romae ad Alexandrinos: pp. 133–134.

Epistula Constantii imperatoris ad episcopos et presbyteros catholicae ecclesiae: p. 135.

Epistula secunda Constantii imperatoris ad populos catholicae ecclesiae: pp. 135–136.

Epistula Constantii imperatoris de abolendis quae contra Athanasium acta fuerant: p. 136.

Epistula synodi Hierosolymitanae: pp. 136–137.

Epistula Ursacii et Valentis ad Julium papam: p. 138.

Epistula Ursacii et Valentis ad Athanasium: p. 138.

Pars epistulae Constantini: p. 140.

Epistula Constantini imperatoris ad populum Alexandriae: pp. 141–142.

Epistula Ischyrae ad Athanasium: pp. 143–144.

Epistula Alexandri Thessalonicensis ad Athanasium: p. 145.

Pinnes presbyter ad fratrem Joannem: pp. 145–146.

Constantinus imperator ad Athanasium: pp. 146–147.

Arsenius episcopus ad Athanasium: pp. 147–148.

Constantinus ad Joannem: p. 148.

Breviarium a Meletio datum Alexandro episcopo: pp. 149–151.

Presbyteri et diaconi ecclesiae Alexandrinae ad synodum Tyriam: pp. 152–153.

Presbyteri et diaconi qui in Mareote sunt ad synodum Tyriam: pp. 153–155.

Presbyteri et diaconi qui in Mareote ad Philagrium praefectum: pp. 155–156.

Episcopi Aegyptii ad episcopos Tyri congregatos: pp. 156–157.

Epistula prima episcopi Aegyptii ad Flavium Dionysium comitem: pp. 158–159.

Epistula secunda episcopi Aegyptii ad Flavium Dionysium comitem: pp. 159–160.

Alexander Thessalonicensis ad Dionysium: pp. 160–161.

Dionysius comes ad Eusebianos: p. 161.

Epistula synodi Hierosolymitanae: pp. 162–163.

Flavius Himerius ad exactorem Mareotae: p. 164.

Constantinus imperator ad episcopos qui Tyrum convenere: pp. 164–165.

Constantinus imperator ad ecclesiam Alexandrinam: pp. 166–168.

Cod: 26,491: Concil., Eccl., Epist.

006 **Epistula encyclica**, ed. Opitz, *op. cit.*, 169–177.
Cod: 2,783: Epist.

007 **Epistula ad Serapionem de morte Arii**, ed. Opitz, *op. cit.*, 178–180.
Cod: 947: Epist.

008 **Epistula ad monachos**, ed. Opitz, *op. cit.*, 181–182.
Cod: 637: Epist.

009 **Historia Arianorum**, ed. Opitz, *op. cit.*, 183–230.

Epistula Constantii imperatoris Nestorio praefecto: p. 195.

Constantius imperator ad Athanasium: p. 196.

Hosius Constantio imperatori: pp. 207–209.

Contestatio secunda: pp. 228–230.

Cod: 18,489: Hist., Eccl., Epist.

010 **De synodis Arimini in Italia et Seleuciae in Isauria**, ed. Opitz, *op. cit.*, 231–278.

Fidei formula synodi Sirmiensis: pp. 235–236.

Epistula synodi Ariminensis: pp. 237–238.

Decretum synodi Ariminensis (fragmentum): pp. 238–239.

Blasphemiae Arii: pp. 242–243.

Arius ad Alexandrum: pp. 243–244.

Epistula synodi Hierosolymitanae: pp. 247–248.

Epistula synodi Antiochenae ad Julium episcopum Romae: pp. 248–249.

Formula altera: pp. 249–250.

Formula tertia Theophronii Tyanensis: p. 250.

Formula quarta: p. 251.

Ἔκθεσις μακρόστιχος: pp. 251–254.

Ἔκθεσις Sirmiensis (anno 351): pp. 254–256.

Ἔκθεσις Sirmiensis (anno 357): pp. 256–257.

Ἔκθεσις Seleuciensis: pp. 257–258.

Ἔκθεσις Constantinopolitana: pp. 258–259.

Constantius imperator ad episcopos qui Ariminium convenere: pp. 277–278.

Episcopi ad imperatorem: p. 278.

Cod: 19,971: Epist.

011 **Apologia ad Constantium imperatorem**, ed. J.-M. Szymusiak, *Athanase d'Alexandrie. Apologie à l'empereur Constance. Apologie pour sa fuite* [*Sources chrétiennes* 56. Paris: Cerf, 1958]: 88–132.

Epistula Constantii imperatoris ad Alexandrinos: pp. 122–124.

Epistula Constantii imperatoris ad Aizanam et Sazanam: pp. 125–126.

Cod: 8,617: Apol., Epist.

012 **Apologia de fuga sua**, ed. Szymusiak, *op. cit.*, 133–167.
Cod: 6,093: Apol.

013 **Epistula ad Amun**, FONTI II: 63–71.
Cod: 1,010: Epist.

014 **Epistula festalis xxxix** (fragmentum in collectione canonum), FONTI II: 71–76.
Cod: 643: Epist.

015 **Epistula ad Rufinianum**, FONTI II: 76–80.
Cod: 519: Epist.

016 **De non participando divinis mysteriis sine discrimine** [Sp.], FONTI II: 82–84.
Cod: 264: Eccl.

017 **In illud: *Profecti in pagum invenietis pullum alligatum*** [Sp.], ed. H. Nordberg, *Athanasiana*

I [*Commentationes humanarum litterarum*
30.2. Helsinki: Centraltryckeriet, 1962]: 1–19.
Cod: 2,865: Homilet., Exeget.

018 **Homilia in illud: *Ite in castellum*** [Sp.], ed.
Nordberg, *op. cit.*, 20–28.
Cod: 2,148: Homilet., Exeget.

019 **Homilia in illud: *Euntem autem illo*** [Sp.], ed.
Nordberg, *op. cit.*, 29–41.
Cod: 2,759: Homilet., Exeget.

020 **Sermo in ramos palmarum** [Sp.], ed. Nordberg,
op. cit., 42–45.
Cod: 735: Homilet.

021 **Homilia de jejunio et de passione Christi** [Sp.],
ed. Nordberg, *op. cit.*, 46–48.
Cod: 588: Homilet.

023 **Sermo major de fide** [Sp.], ed. E. Schwartz,
"Der s.g. sermo maior de fide des Athanasius,"
*Sitzungsberichte der bayerischen Akademie der
Wissenschaften*, Philosoph.-philol. und hist. Kl.
6 (1925) 5–37.
Cod: 7,622: Homilet.

024 **Quaestio 136 e quaestionibus ad Antiochum
ducem** (e cod. Paris. 635) [Sp.], ed. W. Dindorf, *Athanasii Alexandrini praecepta ad Antiochum*. Leipzig: Weigel, 1857: vii–ix.
Cf. et 2035 077.
Cod: 353: Theol.

025 **Quaestio 136 e quaestionibus ad Antiochum
ducem** (e cod. Guelferbytano-Gudiano 51)
[Sp.], ed. Dindorf, *op. cit.*, vii–ix.
Cf. et 2035 077.
Cod: 323: Theol.

026 **Doctrina ad Antiochum ducem** [Sp.], ed. Dindorf, *op. cit.*, 3–39.
Cod: 9,590: Theol.

027 **De sancta trinitate** (dialogi 2 & 4) [Sp.], ed. C.
Bizer, *Studien zu pseudathanasianischen Dia-
logen der Orthodoxos und Aëtios* [*Diss. Bonn*
(1970)]: 80–126, 307–334.
Cf. et 2035 109.
Cod: 9,044: Theol., Dialog.

028 **Epistula ad imperatorem Jovianum** [Sp.], ed.
Bizer, *op. cit.*, 299–301.
Cod: 206: Epist.

029 **De virginitate** [Sp.], ed. E.F. von der Goltz,
Λόγος σωτηρίας πρὸς τὴν παρθένον [*Texte und
Untersuchungen* N.F. 14. Leipzig: Hinrichs,
1905]: 35–60.
Cod: 5,992: Eccl.

030 **Commentarius de templo Athenarum** [Sp.], ed.
A. Delatte, "Le déclin de la légende des vii
sages et les prophéties théosophiques," *Musée
Belge* 27 (1923) 107–111.
Cf. et 2035 032.
Cod: 860: Apol.

031 **Sermo major** (collatio cod. Laurentiani gr.
4.23) [Sp.], ed. Nordberg, *op. cit.*, 57–71.
Cod: 3,338: Homilet.

032 **Commentarius de templo Athenarum** (cod.
Bodleianus Roe 5) [Sp.], ed. A. von Premer-
stein, "Ein pseudo-athanasianischer Traktat
mit apokryphen Philosophensprüchen im Co-

dex Bodleianus Roe 5," Εἰς μνήμην Σπυρίδωνος Λάμπρου. Athens: Hestia, 1935: 183–
186.
Cf. et 2035 030.
Cod: 600: Apol.

033 **Epistula ad Liberium** [Sp.], ed. M. Tetz, "Zur
Theologie des Markell von Ankyra III," *Zeit-
schrift für Kirchengeschichte* 83 (1972) 152.
Cod: 377: Epist.

034 **Dialogus Athanasii et Zacchaei** [Sp.], ed. F.C.
Conybeare, *The dialogues of Athanasius and
Zacchaeus and of Timothy and Aquila*. Oxford:
Clarendon Press, 1898: 1–63.
Cod: 9,494: Eccl., Dialog.

035 **De morbo et valetudine** (fragmenta), ed. F.
Diekamp, *Analecta patristica* [*Orientalia Chris-
tiana analecta* 117. Rome: Pont. Institutum
Orientalium Studiorum, 1938 (repr. 1962)]: 5–
8.
Cod: 1,038: Eccl.

036 **Oratio in resurrectionem et in recens baptizatos** [Sp.], ed. M. Aubineau, "Une homélie
pascale attribuée à S. Athanase d'Alexandrie
dans le Sinaiticus gr. 492," *Zetesis (Festschrift
E. de Strycker)*. Antwerp: De Nederlandsche
Boekhandel, 1973: 670–674.
Cod: 816: Homilet.

037 **De fallacia diaboli** (= Homilia in diabolum)
[Sp.], ed. R.P. Casey, "An early homily on the
devil ascribed to Athanasius of Alexandria,"
Journal of Theological Studies 36 (1935) 4–10.
Cod: 2,650: Homilet.

038 **Sermo exhortatorius** [Sp.] (e cod. Paris. gr.
769), ed. F. Nau, "Notes sur diverses homélies
pseudépigraphiques, sur les oeuvres attribuées
à Eusèbe d'Alexandrie et sur un nouveau
manuscrit de la chaîne *contra severianos*," *Revue de l'Orient chrétien* 13 (1908) 418–420.
Cod: 527: Homilet.

039 **In illud: *Omnia mihi tradita sunt*,** MPG 25:
208–220.
Cod: 2,257: Homilet., Exeget.

040 **Epistula ad Dracontium**, MPG 25: 524–533.
Cod: 1,968: Epist.

041 **Epistula ad episcopos Aegypti et Libyae**, MPG
25: 537–593.
Epistula = Fragmentum contra Macedonianos:
cf. et 2035 054 (MPG 26.1313b–1313c).
Cod: 8,221: Epist.

042 **Orationes tres contra Arianos**, MPG 26: 12–
468.
Cod: 79,419: Orat., Theol.

043 **Epistulae quattuor ad Serapionem**, MPG 26:
529–648b.
Cod: 20,835: Epist., Theol.

044 **In illud: *Qui dixerit verbum in filium*,** MPG
26: 648c–676.
Cod: 4,693: Exeget.

045 **Tomus ad Antiochenos**, MPG 26: 796–809.
Cod: 2,334: Epist., Theol.

046 **Petitiones Arianorum**, MPG 26: 820–824.
Cod: 786: Eccl.

047 **Vita Antonii**, MPG 26: 835–976b.
Cod: 19,169: Hagiogr.

049 **Epistula ad Afros episcopos**, MPG 26: 1029–1048.
Cod: 3,656: Epist.

050 **Epistula ad Adelphium**, MPG 26: 1072–1084.
Cod: 2,268: Epist.

051 **Epistula ad Maximum**, MPG 26: 1085–1089.
Cod: 1,010: Epist.

052 **Epistula ad Joannem et Antiochum presbyteros**, MPG 26: 1165–1168b.
Cod: 212: Epist.

053 **Epistula ad Palladium**, MPG 26: 1168b–1169.
Cod: 267: Epist.

054 **Fragmenta varia**, MPG 26: 1224, 1233–1249, 1252–1260, 1293b–1296c, 1313b–1313c, 1320–1325.
Contra Valentinum: col. 1224.
De exemplo ex natura hominis allato: coll. 1233–1237c.
Fragmenta sermonis majoris de fide (ex Theodoreti eraniste): coll. 1237d–1240c.
Fragmentum de incarnatione contra Apollinarium: col. 1244d.
Fragmentum orationis quartae contra Arianos et fragmentum epistulae ad Adelphium: col. 1245a–b.
Fragmentum ex Joanne Damasceno de duabus in Christo voluntatibus: col. 1249a.
Fragmentum de mortuis in domino ex Joannis Damasceni oratione de defunctis: col. 1249a.
Fragmentum quod vocatur εἰς τοὺς κοιμηθέντας παναρμονίῳ λόγῳ ex Joannis Damasceni oratione de defunctis: col. 1249b.
Fragmentum ex interpretatione in Matthaeum: coll. 1252–1253a.
In illud: *Laudate dominum de terra, dracones et omnes abyssi*: col. 1256b–c.
Fragmentum e sermone contra haereses: coll. 1256d–1257a.
Fragmentum e cod. Vaticano 392: col. 1257c.
Fragmentum epistulae dogmaticae ad Antiochenos: col. 1260a.
Fragmentum historicum primum: col. 1293b.
Fragmentum historicum alterum: coll. 1293c–1296b.
Fragmentum contra Macedonianos: col. 1313b–c: cf. et 2035 041 (MPG 25.560–561).
Fragmentum de amuletis: col. 1320a–b.
Fragmenta quaedam alia, coll. 1320b–1325d.
Q, Cod: 4,729: Theol., Epist., Exeget.

055 **Epistula ad monachos**, MPG 26: 1185–1188.
Cf. et 2035 120.
Cod: 250: Epist.

056 **Sermo de patientia** [Sp.], MPG 26: 1297–1309.
Cod: 2,720: Homilet.

057 **Scholia in Acta** (fort. ex libris *Contra Novatianos*), MPG 26: 1316–1317.
Q: 547: Exeget., Theol.

058 **De azymis** [Sp.], MPG 26: 1328–1332.
Cod: 958: Eccl.

059 **Epistula ad Marcellinum de interpretatione Psalmorum**, MPG 27: 12–45.
Cod: 8,118: Epist., Exeget.

060 **Argumentum in Psalmos** [Sp.], MPG 27: 56–60.
Cod: 821: Hypoth.

061 **Expositiones in Psalmos**, MPG 27: 60–545, 548–589.
Cod: 104,276: Exeget.

062 **Scholia in cantica canticorum**, MPG 27: 1348–1349.
Q: 280: Exeget.

063 **Homilia in Canticum canticorum** [Sp.], MPG 27: 1349–1361.
Cod: 2,522: Homilet., Exeget.

064 **Testimonia e scriptura (de communi essentia patris et filii et spiritus sancti)** [Sp.], MPG 28: 29–80.
Cod: 9,866: Theol.

065 **Epistula catholica** [Sp.], MPG 28: 81–84.
Cod: 492: Epist.

066 **Refutatio hypocriseos Meletii et Eusebii** [Sp.], MPG 28: 85–88.
Cod: 622: Theol.

067 **Contra Sabellianos** [Sp.], MPG 28: 96–121.
Cod: 4,914: Theol.

068 **De sabbatis et circumcisione** [Sp.], MPG 28: 133–141.
Cod: 1,826: Exeget.

069 **Homilia de semente** [Sp.], MPG 28: 144–168.
Cod: 5,375: Homilet.

070 **Homilia de passione et cruce domini** [Sp.], MPG 28: 185–249.
Cf. et 2035 125.
Cod: 12,729: Homilet.

071 **Synopsis scripturae sacrae** [Sp.], MPG 28: 284–437.
Cod: 32,990: Exeget.

072 **Disputatio contra Arium** [Sp.], MPG 28: 440–501.
Cod: 13,141: Theol.

073 **Sermo contra omnes haereses** [Sp.], MPG 28: 501–524.
Cod: 3,778: Theol.

074 **Historia de Melchisedech** [Sp.], MPG 28: 525–529.
Cod: 1,228: Exeget.

075 **Liber de definitionibus** [Sp.], MPG 28: 533–553.
Cod: 4,576: Theol.

076 **Sermo ad Antiochum ducem** [Sp.], MPG 28: 589–597.
Dup. partim MAXIMUS CONFESSOR Theol. et Poeta (2892 044).
Cod: 1,940: Homilet.

077 **Quaestiones ad Antiochum ducem** [Sp.], MPG 28: 597–700.
Cf. et 2035 024, 025, 111.
Cod: 20,206: Theol.

078 **Quaestiones in evangelia** [Sp.], MPG 28: 700–708.
Q: 1,615: Exeget.

079 **Fragmentum sermonis de imaginibus** [Sp.], MPG 28: 709.
Cod: 351: Homilet., Theol.

080 **Quaestiones in scripturam sacram** [Sp.], MPG 28: 712–773.
Cod: 12,451: Exeget.

081 **Quaestiones aliae** [Sp.], MPG 28: 773–796.
Cod: 4,991: Theol.

082 **Narratio de cruce seu imagine Berytensi** [Sp.], MPG 28: 797–812.
Recensio e codd. Colbert.: col. 797–805.
Recensio e cod. Pal. vet.: col. 805–812.
Cod: 3,255: Homilet.

083 **Sermo contra Latinos** [Sp.], MPG 28: 824–832.
Cod: 1,883: Homilet.

084 **Vitae monasticae institutio** [Sp.], MPG 28: 845–849.
Cod: 779: Eccl.

085 **Epistulae ad Castorem** [Sp.], MPG 28: 849–905.
Cod: 11,750: Epist.

086 **In nativitatem praecursoris** [Sp.], MPG 28: 905–913.
Cod: 1,746: Homilet.

087 **Sermo in annuntiationem deiparae** [Sp.], MPG 28: 917–940.
Cod: 4,947: Homilet.

088 **Sermo de descriptione deiparae** [Sp.], MPG 28: 944–957.
Cod: 2,868: Homilet.

089 **Sermo in nativitatem Christi** [Sp.], MPG 28: 960–972.
Cod: 2,717: Homilet.

090 **Homilia in occursum domini** [Sp.], MPG 28: 973–1000.
Cod: 5,484: Homilet.

091 **In caecum a nativitate** [Sp.], MPG 28: 1001–1024.
Cod: 4,509: Homilet.

094 **Homilia in sanctos patres et prophetas** [Sp.], MPG 28: 1061–1073.
Cod: 2,207: Homilet.

109 **De sancta trinitate** (dialogi 1, 3, 5) [Sp.], MPG 28: 1116–1173a, 1201c–1249b, 1265c–1285b.
Cf. et 2035 027.
Cod: 26,460: Theol., Dialog.

099 **Dialogi duo contra Macedonianos** [Sp.], MPG 28: 1292–1337.
Cod: 10,701: Theol., Dialog.

100 **Syntagma ad quendam politicum** [Sp.], MPG 28: 1396–1408.
Cod: 2,997: Phil., Theol.

101 **Sermo pro iis qui saeculo renuntiarunt** [Sp.], MPG 28: 1409–1420.
Cod: 2,440: Homilet.

102 **Doctrina ad monachos** [Sp.], MPG 28: 1421–1425.
Cod: 1,280: Eccl.

103 **De corpore et anima** [Sp.], MPG 28: 1432–1433.
Cod: 550: Phil., Theol.

104 **Vita sanctae Syncleticae** [Sp.], MPG 28: 1488–1557.
Cod: 14,644: Hagiogr.

105 **Epistula ad episcopum Persarum** [Sp.], MPG 28: 1565–1568.
Cod: 593: Epist.

106 **Symbolum "quicumque"** [Sp.], MPG 28: 1581–1592.
Cod: 2,528: Theol.

107 **De trinitate** [Sp.], MPG 28: 1604–1605.
Cod: 499: Theol.

108 **Recensio definitionum** (ap. Anastasium Sinaïtam, *Viae dux*) [Sp.], MPG 89: 52–88.
Q

110 **Epistula ad Epictetum**, ed. G. Ludwig, *Athanasii epistula ad Epictetum* [*Diss. Jena* (1911)]: 3–18.
Cod: 3,323: Epist.

111 **Quaestio cxii ad Antiochum ducem in collectione canonum**, FONTI II: 80–82.
Cf. et 2035 077.
Cod: 196: Theol.

112 **Epistula prima ad Orsisium**, ed. F. Halkin, *Sancti Pachomii vitae Graecae* [*Subsidia hagiographica* 19. Brussels: Société des Bollandistes, 1932]: 91.
Q: Epist.

113 **Epistula altera ad Orsisium**, ed. Halkin, *op. cit.*, 95–96.
Q: Epist.

114 **Narratio Athanasii** (ap. epistulam Ammonis), ed. Halkin, *op. cit.*, 119–120.
Q

115 **Scholia in Job**, MPG 27: 1344–1348.
Dup. partim 2035 116.
Cod: 917: Exeget.

116 **Scholia in Job** (e cod. Vat. Pii II), ed. J.B. Pitra, *Analecta sacra et classica spicilegio Solesmensi* 5. Paris: Roger & Chernowitz, 1888: 21–26.
Dup. partim 2035 115.
Q: 1,336: Exeget.

117 **Oratio quarta contra Arianos** [Sp.], ed. A. Stegmann, *Die pseudoathanasianische 'IVte Rede gegen die Arianer' als 'κατὰ Ἀρειανῶν λόγος' ein Apollinarisgut*. Rottenburg: Bader, 1917: 43–87.
Cod: 11,093: Orat., Theol.

118 **Syntagma ad monachos** (e cod. Vossiano gr., fol. 46) [Sp.], ed. P. Batiffol, *Studia patristica. Études d'ancienne littérature chrétienne*, fasc. 2. Paris: Leroux, 1890: 121–128.
Cf. et 2035 127.
Cod: 1,890: Eccl.

119 **Epistula ad Jovianum**, MPG 26: 813–820.
Cod: 835: Epist.

120 **Epistula ad monachos**, ed. G. de Jerphanion, "La vraie teneur d'un texte de saint Athanase rétablie par l'épigraphie: l'epistula ad monachos," *Recherches de science religieuse* 20 (1930) textus post 540.
Cf. et 2035 055.
Epigr: 217: Epist.

121 **Epistula ad Epiphanium** (fragmentum ap.
Chronicon paschale), MPG 26: 1257–1260.
Q: 121: Epist.

122 **Homilia in illud:** *Nunc anima mea turbata est*
(fragmenta), MPG 26: 1240–1244.
Q: 811: Homilet., Exeget.

123 **Epistula ad Eupsychium** (fragmenta), MPG 26:
1245–1248.
Q: 274: Epist.

124 **De incarnatione contra Apollinarium libri ii**
[Sp.], MPG 26: 1093–1165.
Cod: 12,436: Theol.

125 **Homilia de passione et cruce domini** (addita-
menta), MPG 28: 249.
Cf. et 2035 070.
Cod: 310: Homilet.

126 **Didascalia cccxviii patrum Nicaenorum** [Sp.],
MPG 28: 1637–1644.
Cod: 2,812: Theol., Eccl.

127 **Syntagma ad monachos** (e cod. Vat. gr. 733)
[Sp.], ed. P. Batiffol, *op. cit.*, 121–128.
Cf. et 2035 118.
Cod: 1,026: Eccl.

x01 **Epistulae festales** (ap. Cosmam Indicopleus-
tem).
Wolska-Conus, vol. 3, pp. 241–253.
Cf. COSMAS INDICOPLEUSTES Geogr. (4061
002).

x02 **Epistula exhortatoria ad virgines** (ap. Theodoretum Cyrrhensem).
HE 2.14.13 (GCS 44.127–128).
Cf. THEODORETUS Scr. Eccl. et Theol. (4089
003).

x03 **Fragmentum de fide** (in *Doctrina patrum*).
Diekamp, p. 11 (fr. 4).
Cf. DOCTRINA PATRUM (7051 001).

x04 **Subscriptio Paulini Antiocheni.**
Tomus ad Antiochenos (MPG 26.809).
Cf. 2035 045.

x05 **Expositio fidei.**
Athanasiana I, pp. 49–56.
Cf. MARCELLUS Theol. (2041 004).

x06 **Interpretatio in symbolum** [Sp.].
ACO 1.1.7, p. 66.
Cf. CONCILIA OECUMENICA (ACO) (5000
001).

x07 **Homilia in feriam v et in proditionem Judae**
[Sp.].
MPG 28.1048–1053.
Cf. BASILIUS Scr. Eccl. (2800 007).

x08 **Homilia in passionem domini et in parasceve**
[Sp.].
MPG 28.1053–1061.
Cf. BASILIUS Scr. Eccl. (2800 008).

x09 **Homilia in sanctum pascha** [Sp.].
MPG 28.1073–1081.
Cf. BASILIUS Scr. Eccl. (2800 003).

x10 **Homilia in sanctum pascha et in recens illu-
minatos** [Sp.].
MPG 28.1081–1092.
Cf. BASILIUS Scr. Eccl. (2800 004).

x11 **Homilia in assumptionem domini** [Sp.].
MPG 28.1092–1100.

Cf. BASILIUS Scr. Eccl. (2800 005).

x12 **Homilia in sanctum Andream** [Sp.].
MPG 28.1101–1108.
Cf. BASILIUS Scr. Eccl. (2800 006).

2207 **ATHANIDAS** Hist.
3 B.C.?

001 **Fragmentum,** FGrH #303: 3B:5–6.
Q: 392: Hist.

2387 **ATHANIS** Hist.
vel Athanas
4 B.C.: Syracusanus

001 **Testimonia,** FGrH #562: 3B:576.
NQ: 78: Test.

002 **Fragmenta,** FGrH #562: 3B:576–577.
Q: 171: Hist.

2379 **ATHENACON** Hist.
4 B.C.?

001 **Testimonium,** FGrH #546: 3B:530.
NQ: 14: Test.

002 **Fragmenta,** FGrH #546: 3B:531–532.
Q: 357: Hist.

0141 **ATHENAEUS** Epigr.
fiq Athenaeus Soph.
A.D. 2–3?
Cf. et ATHENAEUS Soph. (0008).

002 **Epigramma,** AG 9.496.
Dup. partim 0141 003 (fr. 226).
Q: 41: Epigr.

003 **Fragmenta,** ed. H. Lloyd-Jones and P. Parsons,
Supplementum Hellenisticum. Berlin: De Gruyter, 1983: 85.
frr. 225–226.
fr. 226: Dup. 0141 002.
Q: 90: Epigr.

x01 **Epigramma exhortatorium et supplicatorium.**
App. Anth. 4.43: Cf. ANTHOLOGIAE GRAE-
CAE APPENDIX (7052 004).
Dup. partim 0141 003 (fr. 225).

ATHENAEUS Geogr.
Cf. HERACLIDES Criticus Perieg. (1405 001).

2465 **ATHENAEUS** Hist.
1 B.C.?

001 **Fragmentum,** FGrH #681: 3C:398.
Q: 158: Hist.

2220 **ATHENAEUS** Math. et Phil.
4 B.C.: Cyzicenus

001 **Testimonium,** ed. F. Lasserre, *De Léodamas de
Thasos à Philippe d'Oponte.* Naples: Biblio-
polis, 1987: 137.
NQ: Test.

1204 **ATHENAEUS** Mech.
1 B.C.?

001 **De machinis,** ed. R. Schneider, *Griechische
Poliorketiker*, vol. 1 [*Abhandlungen der könig-*

lichen Gesellschaft der Wissenschaften zu Göttingen, Philol.-hist. Kl., N.F. 12, no. 5. Berlin: Weidmann, 1912]: 8–36.
Cod: 3,667: Mech.

0682 **ATHENAEUS** Med.
A.D. 1: Attalensis
x01 **Fragmenta ap. Galenum.**
K8.757; 13.296.
Cf. GALENUS Med. (0057 059, 076).
x02 **Fragmentum ap. Pseudo-Galenum.**
K19.356.
Cf. Pseudo-GALENUS Med. (0530 041).
x03 **Fragmenta ap. Oribasium.**
CMG, vol. 6.1.1, pp. 7, 11, 12; 6.1.2, pp. 8, 12; 6.2.2, pp. 99, 105, 106, 112, 115, 138, 146.
Cf. ORIBASIUS Med. (0722 001–002).
x04 **Fragmentum ap. Aëtium** (lib. 3).
CMG, vol. 8.1, p. 332.
Cf. AËTIUS Med. (0718 003).

0008 **ATHENAEUS** Soph.
fiq Athenaeus Epigr.
A.D. 2–3: Naucratites
Cf. et ATHENAEUS Epigr. (0141).
001 **Deipnosophistae**, ed. G. Kaibel, *Athenaei Naucratitae deipnosophistarum libri xv*, 3 vols. Leipzig: Teubner, 1–2:1887; 3:1890 (repr. Stuttgart: 1–2:1965; 3:1966): 1:1–491; 2:1–498; 3:1–560.
Cod: 288,522: Polyhist.
002 **Fragmentum**, FGrH #166: 2B:891–892.
Q: 246: Hist.
003 **Deipnosophistae** (epitome), ed. S.P. Peppink, *Athenaei dipnosophistarum epitome*, vols. 2.1–2.2. Leiden: Brill, 2.1:1937; 2.2:1939: 2.1:3–174; 2.2:3–162.
Cod: 130,340: Polyhist.
004 **Deipnosophistae** (apparatus criticus), ed. Kaibel, *op. cit.*, 1, 1–491; 2, 1–498; 3, 1–560.
App: 89,169: Polyhist.
005 **Deipnosophistarum epitome** (apparatus criticus), ed. Peppink, *op. cit.*, 2.1, xxiii–xxxii; 2.2, xi–xvi.
App: 4,094: Polyhist.

1205 **ATHENAGORAS** Apol.
A.D. 2: Atheniensis
Scholia: Cf. ARETHAS Philol. et Scr. Eccl. (2130 014).
001 **Legatio**, ed. W.R. Schoedel, *Athenagoras. Legatio and de resurrectione*. Oxford: Clarendon Press, 1972: 2–86.
Cod: 11,646: Apol.
002 **De resurrectione**, ed. Schoedel, *op. cit.*, 88–148.
Cod: 9,134: Phil., Theol.

0422 **ATHENIO** Comic.
3 B.C.
001 **Fragmentum**, ed. T. Kock, *Comicorum Atti-*

corum fragmenta, vol. 3. Leipzig: Teubner, 1888: 369–370.
fr. 1.
Q: 281: Comic.
002 **Fragmentum**, ed. A. Meineke, *Fragmenta comicorum Graecorum*, vol. 4. Berlin: Reimer, 1841 (repr. De Gruyter, 1970): 557–558.
Q: 284: Comic.

ATHENODORUS Epigr.
AG 7.494.
Cf. ANONYMI EPIGRAMMATICI (AG) (0138 001).

1206 **ATHENODORUS** Phil.
1 B.C.: Tarsensis
001 **Testimonia**, FGrH #746: 3C:729.
NQ: 269: Test.
002 **Fragmenta**, FGrH #746: 3C:729–731.
Q: 548: Hist.

0621 **[ATH]ENODORUS** Trag.
fort. [Z]enodorus vel [M]enodorus
2 B.C.
001 **Titulus**, ed. B. Snell, *Tragicorum Graecorum fragmenta*, vol. 1. Göttingen: Vandenhoeck & Ruprecht, 1971: 309.
NQ: 1: Trag.

0815 **ATIMETRUS** Med.
ante A.D. 2
x01 **Fragmentum ap. Galenum.**
K12.771.
Cf. GALENUS Med. (0057 076).

1212 *ATRIDARUM REDITUS*
post 7 B.C.
Cf. et NOSTOI (1541).
001 **Fragmentum**, ed. J.U. Powell, *Collectanea Alexandrina*. Oxford: Clarendon Press, 1925 (repr. 1970): 246.
Q: 10: Epic.

1207 **ATTALUS** Math. et Astron.
2 B.C.: Rhodius
001 **Fragmenta Aratea**, ed. E. Maass, *Commentariorum in Aratum reliquiae*. Berlin: Weidmann, 1898 (repr. 1958): 3–24.
frr. 1–28.
Q: 5,568: Astron., Comm.

1982 **Titus Pomponius ATTICUS** Hist.
2–1 B.C.: Romanus
001 **Testimonia**, FGrH #189: 2B:923.
NQ: 112: Test.

1208 **ATTICUS** Phil.
A.D. 2
001 **Fragmenta**, ed. J. Baudry, *Atticos. Fragments de son oeuvre*. Paris: Les Belles Lettres, 1931: 1–33.
frr. 2, 4–9, 12–13.
Q: 5,889: Phil.

2505 **Cnaeus AUFIDIUS** Hist.
2–1 B.C.: Romanus
001 **Testimonium**, FGrH #814: 3C:887.
NQ: 51: Test.
002 **Fragmentum**, FGrH #814: 3C:887.
Q: 95: Hist.

1782 **AUGEAS** Comic.
fiq Augias vel Agias
Incertum: Atheniensis
001 **Fragmentum**, ed. A. Meineke, *Fragmenta comicorum Graecorum*, vol. 1. Berlin: Reimer, 1839 (repr. De Gruyter, 1970): 416.
Q: 9: Comic.
002 **Tituli**, ed. Meineke, *op. cit.*, 416.
NQ: 16: Comic.

3000 **AUGUSTUS Imperator**
1 B.C.–A.D. 1: Romanus
001 **Laudatio funebris in Agrippam** (*P. Cologne* inv. 4722 + 4701), ed. M. Gronewald, "Ein neues Fragment der Laudatio funebris des Augustus auf Agrippa," *Zeitschrift für Papyrologie und Epigraphik* 52 (1983) 61.
Pap: Encom.
x01 **Res gestae** (monumentum Anycranum).
Volkmann, *Kleine Texte* 29–30.
Cf. RES GESTAE DIVI AUGUSTI (1068 001).

2727 **AULICALAMUS** Epigr.
fiq Theodorus Aulicalamus
A.D. 12?
x01 **Aenigmata**.
App. Anth. 7.79–80: Cf. ANTHOLOGIAE GRAECAE APPENDIX (7052 007).

2643 **Decimus Magnus AUSONIUS** Gramm. et Rhet.
A.D. 4: Burdigalensis
001 **Epistulae**, ed. R. Peiper, *Decimi Magni Ausonii Burdigalensis opuscula*. Leipzig: Teubner, 1886 (repr. Stuttgart: 1976): 232–236.
Cod: Epist.
002 **Epigrammata**, ed. Peiper, *op. cit.*, 316, 318, 330–331, 333.
Cod: Epigr.
x01 **Epigrammata** (*App. Anth.*).
Epigrammata demonstrativa: 3.153–156.
Epigrammata irrisoria: 5.48–49.
Dup. 2643 002.
App. Anth. 3.153–156: Cf. ANTHOLOGIAE GRAECAE APPENDIX (7052 003).
App. Anth. 5.48–49: Cf. ANTHOLOGIAE GRAECAE APPENDIX (7052 005).

2205 **AUTESION** Hist.
3–2 B.C.?
001 **Fragmenta**, FGrH #298: 3B:1.
Q: 55: Hist.
002 **Fragmenta**, ed. H.J. Mette, "Die 'Kleinen'

griechischen Historiker heute," *Lustrum* 21 (1978) 25.
fr. 2a–b.
fr. 2a: *P. Oxy.* 26.2442.
Q, Pap: 95: Hist.

2175 **<AUTOCHARIS>** Hist.
Incertum
001 **Fragmentum**, FGrH #249: 2B:1130.
Q: 41: Hist., Chronogr.

1209 **AUTOCLIDES** Hist.
3 B.C.?
001 **Fragmenta**, FGrH #353: 3B:215–216.
fr. 6: *P. Oxy.* 15.1802.
Q, Pap: 384: Hist.

0423 **AUTOCRATES** Comic.
5–4 B.C.
001 **Fragmenta**, ed. T. Kock, *Comicorum Atticorum fragmenta*, vol. 1. Leipzig: Teubner, 1880: 806.
frr. 1, 3.
Q: 39: Comic.
002 **Fragmenta**, ed. A. Meineke, *Fragmenta comicorum Graecorum*, vol. 2.2. Berlin: Reimer, 1840 (repr. De Gruyter, 1970): 891–892.
Q: 42: Comic.
003 **Titulus**, ed. C. Austin, *Comicorum Graecorum fragmenta in papyris reperta*. Berlin: De Gruyter, 1973: 33.
fr. 67.
Pap: 3: Comic.

2204 **AUTOCRATES** Hist.
3–2 B.C.?
001 **Fragmenta**, FGrH #297: 3B:1.
Q: 48: Hist.

1210 **AUTOLYCUS** Astron.
4 B.C.: Pitanaeus
001 **De sphaera quae movetur**, ed. J. Mogenet, *Autolycus de Pitane*. Louvain: Université de Louvain, 1950: 195–213.
Cod: 4,497: Astron.
002 **De ortibus et occasibus**, ed. Mogenet, *op. cit.*, 214–258.
Cod: 10,498: Astron.

0140 **AUTOMEDON** Epigr.
A.D. 1: Cyzicenus
001 **Epigrammata**, AG 5.129; 7.534; 10.23; 11.29, 46, 50, 319, 324–326, 346, 361; 12.34.
Q: 565: Epigr.

0424 **AXIONICUS** Comic.
4 B.C.
001 **Fragmenta**, ed. T. Kock, *Comicorum Atticorum fragmenta*, vol. 2. Leipzig: Teubner, 1884: 411–416.
frr. 1–10.
Q: 316: Comic.

002 **Fragmenta**, ed. A. Meineke, *Fragmenta comi-corum Graecorum*, vol. 3. Berlin: Reimer, 1840 (repr. De Gruyter, 1970): 530–536.
Q: 289: Comic.

003 **Fragmentum**, ed. Meineke, *FCG*, vol. 5.1 (1857; repr. 1970): ccxviii.
Q: 20: Comic.

AXIOPISTUS Poet. Ethic.
CGFPR, p. 79 (fr. 86).
Cf. EPICHARMUS Comic. et PSEUDEPI-CHARMEA (0521 005).

0774 **AXIORIUS** Med.
ante A.D. 2
x01 **Fragmentum ap. Galenum.**
K12.841.
Cf. GALENUS Med. (0057 076).

0818 **AZANITES** Med.
1 B.C.?
x01 **Fragmentum ap. Galenum.**
K13.784.
Cf. GALENUS Med. (0057 077).
x02 **Fragmentum ap. Paulum.**
CMG, vol. 9.2, p. 376.
Cf. PAULUS Med. (0715 001).

0614 **Valerius BABRIUS** Scr. Fab.
A.D. 2
001 **Mythiambi Aesopici**, ed. B.E. Perry, *Babrius and Phaedrus*. Cambridge, Mass.: Harvard University Press, 1965: 2–186.
Cod: 10,934: Fab.

4249 **BACCHIADAS** Epigr.
5 B.C.?: Sicyonius
x01 **Epigramma** (ap. Athenaeum).
Deipnosophistae 14.629a.
Cf. ATHENAEUS Soph. (0008 001).

0819 **BACCHIUS** Med.
3–2 B.C.: Tanagraeus
x01 **Fragmentum ap. Galenum.**
K13.987.
Cf. GALENUS Med. (0057 077).
x02 **Fragmentum ap. Pseudo-Galenum.**
K19.408.
Cf. Pseudo-GALENUS Med. (0530 041).

2136 **BACCHIUS GERON** Mus.
A.D. 3–4
001 **Isagoge artis musicae**, ed. K. Jan, *Musici scrip-tores Graeci*. Leipzig: Teubner, 1895 (repr. Hildesheim: Olms, 1962): 292–316.
Cod: Mus.

0199 **BACCHYLIDES** Lyr.
5 B.C.: Ceus
001 **Epinicia**, ed. H. Maehler (post B. Snell), *Bac-chylidis carmina cum fragmentis*, 10th edn. Leipzig: Teubner, 1970: 1–51.
Pap: 4,043: Lyr., Encom.

002 **Dithyrambi**, ed. Maehler, *op. cit.*, 52–56, 59–67, 69–72.
Pap: 1,312: Lyr.

003 **Dithyramborum vel epinicorum fragmenta**, ed. Maehler, *op. cit.*, 72–81.
Pap: 514: Lyr., Encom.

004 **Fragmenta**, ed. Maehler, *op. cit.*, 82–87, 89–109, 111.
Q, Pap: 1,373: Lyr., Encom., Hymn.

005 **Fragmenta dubia**, ed. Maehler, *op. cit.*, 111–120.
Q, Pap: 548: Lyr.

006 **Epigrammata**, ed. Maehler, *op. cit.*, 121.
Dup. partim 0199 009.
Q: 45: Epigr.

007 **Scholia ad Bacchylidis carmina** (*P. Oxy.* 23.2367), ed. Maehler, *op. cit.*, 122–127.
Pap: 284: Comm.

008 **Scholia ad dithyrambos** (*P. Oxy.* 23.2368), ed. Maehler, *op. cit.*, 128–129.
Pap: 160: Comm.

009 **Epigrammata**, AG **6**.53, 313; **13**.28.
Dup. partim 0199 006.
Q: 126: Epigr.

0142 **[BACIS]**
5 B.C.: Eleus
001 **Epigrammata**, AG 14.97–99.
Q: 88: Epigr.

1932 **BAETO** Hist.
post 4 B.C.
001 **Testimonia**, FGrH #119: 2B:622.
NQ: 89: Test.
002 **Fragmenta**, FGrH #119: 2B:623–626.
Q: 1,279: Hist.

1211 **BALAGRUS** Hist.
2 B.C.
001 **Testimonium**, FGrH #773: 3C:767.
NQ: 7: Test.
002 **Fragmenta**, FGrH #773: 3C:767.
Q: 79: Hist.

1213 **Julia BALBILLA** Lyr.
A.D. 2
001 **Epigrammata**, ed. G. Kaibel, *Epigrammata Graeca ex lapidibus conlecta*. Berlin: Reimer, 1878: 414–417.
frr. 988–992.
Epigr: 372: Epigr.
x01 **Epigrammata dedicatoria.**
App. Anth. 1.177–180, 181(?): Cf. ANTHO-LOGIAE GRAECAE APPENDIX (7052 001).
Dup. 1213 001.

1215 **BALBILLUS** Astrol.
vel Barbillus
A.D. 1: Ephesius

001 **Fragmenta**, ed. W. Kroll and A. Olivieri, *Co-dices Parisini* [*Catalogus codicum astrologorum Graecorum* 8.3. Brussels: Lamertin, 1912]: 103–104.
Cod: [550]: Astrol.

002 **Fragmenta**, ed. P. Boudreaux, *Codices Parisini* [*Catalogus codicum astrologorum Graecorum* 8.4. Brussels: Lamertin, 1921]: 233–238.
Cod: Astrol.

0820 **BAPHULLUS vel HERAS** Med.
ante A.D. 1
Cf. et HERAS Med. (0917).

x01 **Fragmentum ap. Galenum.**
K14.173.
Cf. GALENUS Med. (0057 078).

4051 **Joannes BARBUCALLUS** Gramm.
A.D. 6: Berytensis

001 **Epigrammata**, AG **6**.55; **7**.555–555b; **9**.425–427, 628–629; **16**.38, 218–219, 327.
Q: 291: Epigr.

1214 **BARDESANES** Gnost.
A.D. 2–3: Edessenus

001 **Fragmenta**, FGrH #719: 3C:643–656.
Q: 2,827: Hist.

3159 **BARLAAM** Theol. et Math.
A.D. 13–14: Calabrius, Constantinopolitanus

001 **Paraphrasis in Euclidis elementorum librum secundum**, ed. E.S. Stamatis (post J.L. Heiberg), *Euclidis opera omnia*, vol. 5.2, 2nd edn. Leipzig: Teubner, 1977: 351–362.
Cod: Math., Comm.

BARLAAM ET JOASAPH
Incertum
Cf. JOANNES DAMASCENUS Theol. et Scr. Eccl. (2934 066).

1216 *BARNABAE EPISTULA*
A.D. 1/2

001 **Barnabae epistula**, ed. R.A. Kraft, *Épître de Barnabé* [*Sources chrétiennes* 172. Paris: Cerf, 1971]: 72–218.
Cod: 7,057: Epist., Theol.

1217 **BASILIDES** Gnost.
A.D. 2

001 **Fragmenta**, ed. W. Völker, *Quellen zur Geschichte der christlichen Gnosis*. Tübingen: Mohr, 1932: 40–41.
Q

2398 **BASILIDES** Phil.
fiq Basilides Scythopolitanus
ante A.D. 3

001 **Fragmentum**, ed. J. von Arnim, *Stoicorum veterum fragmenta*, vol. 3. Leipzig: Teubner, 1903 (repr. Stuttgart: 1968): 268.
Q: 40: Phil.

1218 **BASILIS** Hist.
3/2 B.C.

001 **Testimonia**, FGrH #718: 3C:642.
NQ: 101: Test.

002 **Fragmenta**, FGrH #718: 3C:642.
Q: 61: Hist.

2084 **BASILIUS** Scr. Eccl.
A.D. 4: Ancyranus

001 **De virginitate**, MPG 30: 669–809.
Cod

x01 **Epistula synodica.**
Epiphanius, *Haer.* 73.
Cf. EPIPHANIUS Scr. Eccl. (2021 002).

x02 **Basilii ac Georgii Laodiceni et sociorum professio.**
Epiphanius, *Haer.* 73.
Cf. EPIPHANIUS Scr. Eccl. (2021 002).

2800 **BASILIUS** Scr. Eccl.
A.D. 5: Seleuciensis, Isauricus

002 **Sermones xli**, MPG 85: 28–474.
In illud: *In principio creavit deus coelum et terram* (orat. 1): coll. 28–37.
In Adam (orat. 2): coll. 37–49.
In Adam (orat. 3): coll. 49–61.
In Cain et Abel (orat. 4): coll. 61–76.
In Noe (orat. 5): coll. 76–84.
In Noe (orat. 6): coll. 84–101.
In Abraham (orat. 7): coll. 101–112.
In Josephum (orat. 8): coll. 112–125.
In Moysen (orat. 9): coll. 128–137.
In Elisaeum et Sunamitidem (orat. 10): coll. 137–148.
In Eliam (orat. 11): coll. 148–157.
In Jonam (orat. 12): coll. 157–172.
In Jonam (orat. 13): coll. 172–181.
In Davidis historiam (orat. 14): coll. 181–192.
In Davidem (orat. 15): coll. 192–204.
In Davidem (orat. 16): coll. 204–216.
In Davidem (orat. 17): coll. 216–225.
In Herodiadem (orat. 18): coll. 225–236.
In centurionem (orat. 19): coll. 236–245.
In Chananaeam (orat. 20): coll. 245–253.
In claudum ad portam Speciosam sedentem (orat. 21): coll. 253–264.
In illud: *Navigabant simul cum Jesu discipuli et ecce tempestas magna* (orat. 22): coll. 264–269.
De arreptivo (orat. 23): coll. 269–277.
In illud: *Dic ut sedeant hi duo filii mei, unus ad dexteram tuam et unus ad sinistram tuam* (orat. 24): coll. 277–288.
In illud: *Quem me dicunt homines esse filium hominis?* (orat. 25): coll. 288–297.
In illud: *Ego sum pastor bonus* (orat. 26): coll. 300–308.
In Olympia (orat. 27): coll. 308–316.
In illud: *Nisi conversi fueritis et efficiamini sicut parvuli, non intrabitis in regnum coelorum* (orat. 28): coll. 316–325.
In illud: *Venite ad me, omnes, qui laboratis et*

onerati estis, et ego reficiam vos (orat. 29): coll. 325–332.

In illud: *Venite post me, faciam vos fieri piscatores hominum* (orat. 30): coll. 332–337.

In illud: *Ecce ascendimus Hierosolymam, et filius hominis tradetur in manus peccatorum* (orat. 31): coll. 337–349.

In illud: *Pater, si possibile est, transeat a me calix iste* (orat. 32): coll. 349–360.

In quinquies mille homines quinque panibus pastos (orat. 33): coll. 360–365.

In illud: *Tu es qui venturus es, an alium exspectamus?* (orat. 34): coll. 365–373.

In Publicanum et Pharisaeum (orat. 35): coll. 373–384.

In duos evangelii caecos (orat. 36): coll. 384–388.

De infantibus in Bethleem ab Herode sublatis (orat. 37): coll. 388–400.

Contra Judaeos de salvatoris adventu demonstratio (orat. 38) [Sp.]: coll. 400–425.

In sanctae deiparae annuntiationem (orat. 39) [Sp.]: coll. 425–452.

In transfigurationem (orat. 40): coll. 452–461.

Laudatio promartyris Stephani (orat. 41) [Sp.]: coll. 461–473.

Cod

003 **Homilia in sanctum pascha**, MPG 28: 1073–1081.
Cod: 1,444: Homilet.

004 **Homilia in sanctum pascha et in recens illuminatos**, MPG 28: 1081–1092.
Cod: 1,804: Homilet.

005 **Homilia in assumptionem domini**, MPG 28: 1092–1100.
Cod: 1,784: Homilet.

006 **Homilia in sanctum Andream**, MPG 28: 1101–1108.
Cod: 1,446: Homilet., Hagiogr., Encom.

007 **Homilia in feriam v et in proditionem Judae**, MPG 28: 1048–1053.
Cod: 1,228: Homilet.

008 **Homilia in passionem domini**, MPG 28: 1053–1061.
Cod: 1,385: Homilet.

009 **Homilia in Lazarum**, ed. T.P. Camelot, "Une homélie inédite de Basile de Séleucie," *Mélanges A.M. Desrousseaux*. Paris: Hachette, 1937: 35–48.
Cod: Homilet.

010 **Homilia in resurrectionem domini**, ed. M. Aubineau, *Homélie pascales* [*Sources chrétiennes* 187. Paris: Cerf, 1972]: 169–277.
Cod: Homilet.

011 **Homilia in pentecosten**, ed. B. Marx, *Procliana. Untersuchungen über den homiletischen Nachlass des Patriarchen Proklos von Konstantinopel* [*Münsterische Beiträge zur Theologie* 23. Münster: Aschendorff, 1940]: 100–102.
Cod: Homilet.

012 **Homilia in pentecosten**, MPG 52: 809–812.
Cod: 1,240: Homilet.

017 **Fragmentum in Genesim 22.13**, ed. R. Dev-

reesse, *Les anciens commentateurs de l'Octateuque et des Rois* [*Studi e Testi* 201. Vatican City: Biblioteca Apostolica Vaticana, 1959]: 182.
Q: Exeget.

018 **De vita et miraculis sanctae Theclae libri ii** [Sp.], ed. G. Dagron, *Vie et miracles de s. Thècle* [*Subsidia hagiographica* 62. Brussels: Société des Bollandistes, 1978]].
Cod: Hagiogr.

2040 **BASILIUS** Theol.
A.D. 4: Caesariensis (Cappadociae)

001 **Homiliae in hexaemeron**, ed. S. Giet, *Basile de Césarée. Homélies sur l'hexaéméron*, 2nd edn. [*Sources chrétiennes* 26 bis. Paris: Cerf, 1968]: 86–522.
Cod: 35,834: Homilet., Exeget.

002 **De legendis gentilium libris**, ed. F. Boulenger, *Saint Basile. Aux jeunes gens sur la manière de tirer profit des lettres Helléniques*. Paris: Les Belles Lettres, 1935 (repr. 1965): 41–61.
Cod: 4,762: Eccl.

003 **De spiritu sancto**, ed. B. Pruche, *Basile de Césarée. Sur le Saint-Esprit*, 2nd edn. [*Sources chrétiennes* 17 bis. Paris: Cerf, 1968]: 250–530.
Cod: 26,309: Theol.

004 **Epistulae**, ed. Y. Courtonne, *Saint Basile. Lettres*, 3 vols. Paris: Les Belles Lettres, 1:1957; 2:1961; 3:1966: 1:3–219; 2:1–218; 3:1–229.
Epist. 1–100: vol. 1.
Epist. 101–218: vol. 2.
Epist. 219–366: vol. 3.
Cod: 137,631: Epist.

005 **Epistulae tres**, ed. S.Y. Rudberg, *Études sur la tradition manuscrite de saint Basile*. Lund: Håkan Ohlssons Boktryckeri, 1953: 156–168, 195–200, 205–207.
Epist. 2: Dup. 2040 004 (Courtonne, vol. 1, pp. 5–13).
Epist. 150: Dup. 2040 004 (Courtonne, vol. 2, pp. 71–75).
Epist. 173: Dup. 2040 004 (Courtonne, vol. 2, pp. 108–109).
Cod: 3,150: Epist.

006 **Homilia in illud: *Attende tibi ipsi***, ed. S.Y. Rudberg, *L'homélie de Basile de Césarée sur le mot 'observe-toi toi-même'*. Stockholm: Almqvist & Wiksell, 1962: 23–37.
Cod: 3,508: Homilet.

007 **Homilia in illud: *Destruam horrea mea***, ed. Y. Courtonne, *Saint Basile. Homélies sur la richesse*. Paris: Didot, 1935: 15–37.
Cod: 2,958: Homilet.

008 **Homilia in divites**, ed. Courtonne, *Homélies sur la richesse*, 39–71.
Cod: 4,323: Homilet.

009 **Enarratio in prophetam Isaiam** [Dub.], ed. P. Trevisan, *San Basilio. Commento al profeta Isaia*, 2 vols. Turin: Societa Editrice Internazionale, 1939: 1:3–397; 2:3–575.
Cod: 97,762: Exeget.

010 **Expositio fidei Nicaenae** [Sp.], ed. G.L. Hahn,
*Bibliothek der Symbole und Glaubensregeln der
alten Kirche*, 3rd edn. Breslau: Morgenstern,
1897: 308–310.
Cod: 376: Theol.

011 **Homilia in aquas** [Sp.], ed. S. Costanza, *Ps.-
Basilii εἰς τὰ ὕδατα καὶ εἰς τὸ ἅγιον βάπτισμα.*
Messina: Peloritana Editrice, 1967: 39–44.
Cod: 930: Homilet.

012 **Homilia de virginitate** [Sp.], ed. D. Amand and
M.C. Moons, "Une curieuse homélie grecque
inédite sur la virginité adressée aux pères de
famille," *Revue Bénédictine* 63 (1953) 35–69.
Cod: 3,275: Homilet.

013 **De spiritu** [Sp.], ed. P. Henry, *Études plotin-
iennes I. Les états du texte de Plotin.* Paris:
Brouwer, 1938: 185–196.
Cod: 952: Theol.

018 **Homiliae super Psalmos**, MPG 29: 209–494.
Cod: 53,031: Homilet.

019 **Adversus Eunomium** (libri 5), MPG 29: 497–
669, 672–768.
Lib. 1–3: col. 497–669.
Lib. 4–5 [Sp.]: col. 672–768.
Cod: 47,346: Theol.

020 **De jejunio** (homilia 1), MPG 31: 164–184.
Cod: 3,498: Homilet.

021 **De jejunio** (homilia 2), MPG 31: 185–197.
Cod: 2,388: Homilet.

022 **Homilia de gratiarum actione**, MPG 31: 217–
237.
Cod: 3,357: Homilet.

023 **Homilia in martyrem Julittam**, MPG 31: 237–
261.
Cod: 4,335: Homilet., Encom., Hagiogr.

024 **Homilia dicta tempore famis et siccitatis**, MPG
31: 304–328.
Cod: 4,344: Homilet.

025 **Quod deus non est auctor malorum**, MPG 31:
329–353.
Cod: 4,646: Homilet.

026 **Homilia adversus eos qui irascuntur**, MPG 31:
353–372.
Cod: 3,381: Homilet.

027 **Homilia de invidia**, MPG 31: 372–385.
Cod: 2,735: Homilet.

028 **Homilia in principium proverbiorum**, MPG 31:
385–424.
Cod: 6,703: Homilet., Exeget.

029 **Homilia exhortatoria ad sanctum baptisma**,
MPG 31: 424–444.
Cod: 3,878: Homilet.

030 **In ebriosos**, MPG 31: 444–464.
Cod: 3,297: Homilet.

031 **De fide**, MPG 31: 464–472.
Cod: 1,399: Homilet.

032 **In illud: *In principio erat verbum***, MPG 31:
472–481.
Cod: 1,998: Homilet., Exeget.

033 **In Barlaam martyrem** [Sp.], MPG 31: 484–489.
Cod: 1,020: Homilet., Encom., Hagiogr.

034 **In Gordium martyrem**, MPG 31: 489–508.
Cod: 3,208: Homilet., Encom., Hagiogr.

035 **In quadraginta martyres Sebastenses**, MPG 31:
508–525.
Cod: 2,831: Homilet., Encom., Hagiogr.

036 **De humilitate**, MPG 31: 525–540.
Cod: 2,624: Homilet.

037 **Quod rebus mundanis adhaerendum non sit**,
MPG 31: 540–564.
Cod: 4,742: Homilet.

038 **In Mamantem martyrem**, MPG 31: 589–600.
Cod: 1,865: Homilet., Encom., Hagiogr.

039 **Contra Sabellianos et Arium et Anomoeos**,
MPG 31: 600–617.
Cod: 3,486: Homilet.

040 **Sermo 10 (praevia institutio ascetica)** [Dub.],
MPG 31: 620–625.
Cod: 1,068: Homilet., Eccl.

041 **Sermo 11 (sermo asceticus et exhortatio de
renuntiatione mundi)** [Dub.], MPG 31: 625–
648.
Cod: 3,826: Homilet., Eccl.

042 **Sermo 12 (de ascetica disciplina)** [Dub.], MPG
31: 648–652.
Cod: 736: Homilet., Eccl.

043 **Prologus 7 (de judicio dei)**, MPG 31: 653–676.
Cod: 4,323: Eccl.

044 **Sermo 13 (sermo asceticus)** [Dub.], MPG 31:
869–881.
Cod: 2,159: Homilet., Eccl.

045 **Prologus 8 (de fide)**, MPG 31: 676–692.
Cod: 2,823: Eccl.

046 **Prologus 5 (sermo asceticus)** [Dub.], MPG 31:
881–888.
Cod: 1,479: Homilet., Eccl.

047 **Prologus 4 (prooemium in asceticum magnum)**, MPG 31: 889–901.
Cod: 2,064: Eccl.

048 **Asceticon magnum *sive* Quaestiones** (regulae
fusius tractatae), MPG 31: 901–1052.
Cod: 24,682: Eccl.

049 **Prologus 3 (prooemium in regulas brevius
tractatas)**, MPG 31: 1080.
Cod: 215: Eccl.

050 **Asceticon magnum *sive* Quaestiones** (regulae
brevius tractatae), MPG 31: 1052–1305.
Cod: 38,881: Eccl.

051 **Regulae morales**, MPG 31: 692–869.
Cod: 30,629: Eccl.

052 **De baptismo libri duo**, MPG 31: 1513–1628.
Cod: 22,009: Eccl.

053 **In Psalmum 28** (homilia 2) [Sp.], MPG 30: 72–
81.
Cod: 1,848: Homilet.

054 **Homilia in Psalmum 37** [Sp.], MPG 30: 81–
104.
Cod: 4,159: Homilet.

055 **Homilia in Psalmum 115**, MPG 30: 104–116.
Cod: 2,172: Homilet.

056 **Homilia in Psalmum 132** [Sp.], MPG 30: 116–
117.
Cod: 455: Homilet.

057 **Homilia de spiritu sancto** [Sp.], MPG 31:
1429–1437.
Cod: 1,790: Homilet.

058 **Homilia dicta in Lacisis,** MPG 31: 1437–1457.
Cod: 3,605: Homilet.

059 **In sanctam Christi generationem,** MPG 31: 1457–1476.
Cod: 3,135: Homilet.

060 **Homilia de paenitentia** [Sp.] (sub auctore Eusebio Emeseno), MPG 31: 1476–1488.
Dup. EUSEBIUS Scr. Eccl. (4124 003).
Cod: 2,537: Homilet.

061 **Adversus eos qui per calumniam dicunt dici a nobis tres deos,** MPG 31: 1488–1496.
Cod: 1,585: Homilet., Theol.

062 **Homilia in illud: Ne dederis somnum oculis tuis** [Sp.], MPG 31: 1497–1508.
Cod: 1,886: Homilet., Exeget.

063 **De jejunio** (homilia 3) [Sp.], MPG 31: 1508–1509.
Cod: 554: Homilet.

064 **Orationes** *sive* **Exorcismi** [Sp.], MPG 31: 1677–1684.
Cod: 1,359: Liturg.

065 **Poenae in monachos delinquentes** (epitimia 24) [Dub.], MPG 31: 1305–1308.
Cod: 355: Eccl.

066 **Epitimia in canonicas** (epitimia 25) [Dub.], MPG 31: 1313–1316.
Cod: 307: Eccl.

067 **Epitimia** (epitimia 26) [Sp.], MPG 31: 1308–1313.
Cod: 895: Eccl.

068 **Consolatoria ad aegrotum** [Sp.] (sub auctore Proclo), MPG 31: 1713–1722.
Cod: 1,437: Homilet.

069 **Homilia de misericordia et judicio** [Sp.], MPG 31: 1705–1714.
Cod: 1,360: Homilet.

070 **Sermo ob sacerdotum instructionem** (recensio brevior) [Sp.], MPG 31: 1685–1688.
Cod: 372: Eccl., Liturg.

071 **Liturgia** (recensio brevior vetusta), MPG 31: 1629–1656.
Cod: 5,378: Liturg.

072 **Sermo de contubernalibus** [Sp.], MPG 30: 812–828.
Cod: 3,214: Eccl.

073 **Oratio pro inimicis et amicis** [Sp.], MPG 31: 1685.
Cod: 247: Liturg.

074 **Constitutiones asceticae** [Sp.], MPG 31: 1320–1428.
Cod: 18,846: Eccl.

075 **Sermones de moribus a Symeone Metaphrasta collecti,** MPG 32: 1116–1381.
Cod: 51,476: Homilet., Anthol.

076 **Sermo ob sacerdotum instructionem** (recensio fusior) [Sp.], FONTI II: 187–191.
Cod: Liturg., Eccl.

077 **Liturgia** (recensio longior Byzantina) [Sp.], ed. F.E. Brightman, *Liturgies eastern and western*, vol. 1. Oxford: Clarendon Press, 1896: 309–345.
Cod: Liturg.

078 **Prologus 6** (prooemium ad *Hypotyposin*), ed.

J. Gribomont, *Histoire du texte des ascétiques de S. Basile* [*Bibliothèque du Muséon* 32. Louvain: Université de Louvain, 1953]: 279–282.
Cod: Eccl.

079 **Sermo 14 (De fide)** [Sp.], ed. Gribomont, *op. cit.*, 314–316.
Cod: Eccl.

080 **Sermo 15 (De vita monastica)** (excerptum) [Sp.], ed. Gribomont, *op. cit.*, 317–319.
Cod: Eccl.

081 **Sermo 16 (De calumnia)** [Sp.], ed. Gribomont, *op. cit.*, 320.
Cod: Eccl.

082 **Canon 96 (De haereticis)** (fragmentum), FONTI II: 63–71.
Cod: Eccl.

083 **Scholia in Job** (in catenis, typus II), ed. P. Young, *Catena Graecorum patrum in beatum Iob, collectore Niceta Heraclea metropolita, Graece nunc primum edita et Latine versa.* London, 1637.
Q: Exeget., Caten.

084 **Scholion in Danielem** (in catenis), ed. A. Mai, *Scriptorum veterum nova collectio*, vol. 1.2. Rome: Biblioteca Apostolica Vaticana, 1825.
Q: Exeget., Caten.

086 **Scholia in Matthaeum** (in catenis, typus C: catena Nicetae), ed. B. Corderius, *Symbolarum in Matthaeum tomus alter, quo continetur catena patrum Graecorum triginta collectore Niceta episcopo Serrarum.* Toulouse, 1647.
Q: Exeget., Caten.

087 **Scholia in Matthaeum** (in catenis, typus D), ed. P. Possinus, *Symbolarum in Matthaeum tomus prior exhibens catenam Graecorum patrum unius et viginti.* Toulouse, 1648.
Q: Exeget., Caten.

088 **Scholia in Lucam** (in catenis, typus F: catena Nicetae), ed. Mai, *op. cit.*, vol. 9 (1837).
Q: Exeget., Caten.

090 **Scholia in Joannem** (in catenis, typus F), ed. B. Corderius, *Catena patrum Graecorum in S. Johannem.* Antwerp, 1630.
Q: Exeget., Caten.

x01 **Aenigma.**
App. Anth. 7.24: Cf. ANTHOLOGIAE GRAECAE APPENDIX (7052 007).

x02 **Scholia in Matthaeum** (in catenis, typus A: catena integra).
Cramer, vol. 1.
Cf. CATENAE (Novum Testamentum) (4102 001).

x03 **Scholia in Joannem** (in catenis, typus A: catena integra).
Cramer, vol. 2.
Cf. CATENAE (Novum Testamentum) (4102 005).

x04 **Scholia in Acta** (catena Andreae).
Cramer, vol. 3.
Cf. CATENAE (Novum Testamentum) (4102 008).

x05 **Scholia in Pauli epistulas** (in catenis, typus Vaticanus).

Cramer, vols. 4–5.
Cf. CATENAE (Novum Testamentum) (4102
010–014).

x06 **Scholia in Pauli epistulas** (in catenis, typus
Monacensis).
Cramer, vol. 4.
Cf. CATENAE (Novum Testamentum) (4102
011).

x07 **Scholia in Pauli epistulas** (in catenis, typus
Parisinus).
Cramer, vols. 6–7.
Cf. CATENAE (Novum Testamentum) (4102
019–024, 034–038).

x08 **Scholia in Pauli epistulas** (catena Nicetae).
Cramer, vol. 7.
Cf. CATENAE (Novum Testamentum) (4102
039).

x09 **Scholia in epistulas catholicas** (catena Andreae).
Cramer, vol. 8.
Cf. CATENAE (Novum Testamentum) (4102
040–046).

x10 **Contra Eunomii opinionem** (fragmentum ex
Aëtio) (in *Doctrina patrum*).
Diekamp, pp. 88–89 (fr. 8).
Cf. DOCTRINA PATRUM (7051 001).

2726 **BASILIUS Megalomytes** Epigr.
Incertum
x01 **Aenigmata.**
App. Anth. 7.47–78: Cf. ANTHOLOGIAE
GRAECAE APPENDIX (7052 007).

0941 **Julius BASSUS** Med.
fiq Tullius Bassus
1 B.C.–A.D. 1
x01 **Fragmenta ap. Galenum.**
K13.60, 278, 280–281, 1017–1018, 1033.
Cf. GALENUS Med. (0057 076–077).
x02 **Fragmentum ap. Oribasium.**
CMG, vol. 6.3, p. 98.
Cf. ORIBASIUS Med. (0722 004).
x03 **Fragmentum ap. Aëtium** (lib. 7).
CMG, vol. 8.2, p. 355.
Cf. AËTIUS Med. (0718 007).
x04 **Fragmentum ap. Aëtium** (lib. 12).
Kostomiris, p. 103.
Cf. AËTIUS Med. (0718 012).

0781 **Pomponius BASSUS** <Med.>
A.D. 1/2?
x01 **Fragmentum ap. Galenum.**
K12.781–782.
Cf. GALENUS Med. (0057 076).

0425 **BATO** Comic.
3 B.C.
001 **Fragmenta,** ed. T. Kock, *Comicorum Atticorum fragmenta*, vol. 3. Leipzig: Teubner,
1888: 326–329.
frr. 1–5, 7.
Q: 366: Comic.
002 **Fragmenta,** ed. A. Meineke, *Fragmenta comi-*

corum Graecorum, vol. 4. Berlin: Reimer, 1841
(repr. De Gruyter, 1970): 499–504.
Q: 369: Comic.

1219 **BATO** Hist. et Rhet.
2 B.C.: Sinopensis
001 **Testimonia,** FGrH #268: 3A:77.
NQ: 76: Test.
002 **Fragmenta,** FGrH #268: 3A:77–79.
Q: 805: Hist.

1220 ***BATRACHOMYOMACHIA***
2/1 B.C.
Scholia: Cf. Manuel MOSCHOPULUS Gramm.
(9025 002–003).
001 **Batrachomyomachia,** ed. T.W. Allen, *Homeri
opera,* vol. 5. Oxford: Clarendon Press, 1912
(repr. 1969): 168–183.
Cod: 1,888: Parod.
002 **Batrachomyomachia** (prosodia Byzantina), ed.
Allen, *op. cit.,* 170, 172–173, 176, 178–182.
Cod: 288: Parod.

2152 **BEMARCHIUS** Hist.
A.D. 4: Caesariensis (Cappadociae)
001 **Testimonia,** FGrH #220: 2B:950.
NQ: 118: Test.

1222 **BEROS(S)US** Hist. et Astrol.
4–3 B.C.: Babylonius
001 **Testimonia,** FGrH #680: 3C:364–367.
NQ: 662: Test.
002 **Fragmenta,** FGrH #680: 3C:367–397.
Q: 4,710: Hist.

Pseudo-BEROSSUS Hist.
Incertum: Cous
Cf. BEROS(S)US Hist. (1222).

0144 **BESANTINUS** Poeta
A.D. 2
Scholia: Cf. SCHOLIA IN THEOCRITUM
(5038 001).
Scholia: Cf. Manuel HOLOBOLUS Rhet. (4065
001).
001 **Epigrammata,** AG 9.118; 15.25.
AG 9.119: Cf. PALLADAS Epigr. (2123 001).
AG 15.27: Cf. SIMIAS Gramm. (0211 002).
Q: 134: Epigr.

0145 **BIANOR** Epigr.
1 B.C.–A.D. 1: Bithynius
001 **Epigrammata,** AG 7.49, 387–388, 396, 644,
671; 9.223, 227, 259, 272–273, 278, 295, 308,
423, 548; 10.22, 101; 11.248, 364; 16.276.
AG 9.252: Cf. ANONYMI EPIGRAMMATICI
(AG) (0138 001).
Q: 763: Epigr.

1223 **BIAS** <Phil.>
6 B.C.: Prienaeus
Cf. et <SEPTEM SAPIENTES> (1667).
001 **Fragmentum,** ed. T. Bergk, *Poetae lyrici*

Graeci, vol. 3, 4th edn. Leipzig: Teubner, 1882: 199.
Q: 20: Lyr.

002 **Testimonium**, FGrH #439: 3B:371.
NQ: 18: Test.

0036 **BION** Bucol.
2 B.C.: Smyrnaeus

001 **Epitaphius Adonis**, ed. A.S.F. Gow, *Bucolici Graeci*. Oxford: Clarendon Press, 1952 (repr. 1969): 153–157.
Cod: 728: Bucol.

002 **Epithalamium Achillis et Deidameiae** [Sp.], ed. Gow, *op. cit.*, 157–158.
Cod: 240: Bucol.

003 **Fragmenta**, ed. Gow, *op. cit.*, 159–165.
Q: 868: Bucol.

1871 **BION** Hist.
4 B.C.: Proconnensis

001 **Testimonia**, FGrH #14, #332: 1A:177; 3B:165.
NQ: 151: Test.

002 **Fragmenta**, FGrH #14, #332: 1A:177; 3B:166.
Q: 261: Hist., Myth.

1225 **BION** Hist.
3 B.C.?: Soleus

001 **Testimonia**, FGrH #668: 3B:280.
NQ: 69: Test.

002 **Fragmenta**, FGrH #668: 3B:280–282.
Q: 387: Hist.

1224 **BION** Phil.
3 B.C.: Borysthenius

001 **Fragmenta**, ed. J.F. Kindstrand, *Bion of Borysthenes*. Uppsala: Uppsala University Press, 1976: 113–130.
frr. 1–32, 34–43b, 45–68, 70–71, 73–81.
frr. 26a–26b: *P. Herc.* 1055.
Dup. partim 1224 002 (frr. 227–228).
Q, Pap: 3,536: Phil., Parod.

002 **Fragmenta**, ed. H. Lloyd-Jones and P. Parsons, *Supplementum Hellenisticum*. Berlin: De Gruyter, 1983: 86.
frr. 227–228.
Dup. partim 1224 001 (frr. 7, 15).
Q: 33: Parod.

2153 **BION** Phil. et Math.
4 B.C.: Abderita

001 **Testimonia**, ed. H. Diels and W. Kranz, *Die Fragmente der Vorsokratiker*, vol. 2, 6th edn. Berlin: Weidmann, 1952 (repr. Dublin: 1966): 251.
test. 1–2.
NQ: 143: Test.

1919 **BION** Rhet.
2/1 B.C.?

001 **Testimonium**, FGrH #89: 2A:324.
NQ: 31: Test.

002 **Fragmentum**, FGrH #89: 2A:324.
Q: 167: Hist.

1792 **BIOTTUS** Comic.
post 2 B.C.

001 **Tituli**, ed. T. Kock, *Comicorum Atticorum fragmenta*, vol. 3. Leipzig: Teubner, 1888: 366.
NQ: 3: Comic.

0348 **BIOTUS** Trag.
fiq Biottus Comic.
2 B.C.?

001 **Fragmentum**, ed. B. Snell, *Tragicorum Graecorum fragmenta*, vol. 1. Göttingen: Vandenhoeck & Ruprecht, 1971: 319.
fr. 1.
Q: 15: Trag.

1226 **BITON** Mech.
3/2 B.C.

001 Κατασκευαὶ πολεμικῶν ὀργάνων καὶ καταπαλτικῶν, ed. A. Rehm and E. Schramm, *Bitons Bau von Belagerungsmaschinen und Geschützen* [*Abhandlungen der bayerischen Akademie der Wissenschaften*, Philosoph.-hist. Abt., N.F. 2. Munich: Oldenbourg, 1929]: 9–28.
Cod: 2,491: Mech.

1227 **BLAESUS** Comic.
2/1 B.C.?: Capreensis

001 **Fragmentum**, ed. G. Kaibel, *Comicorum Graecorum fragmenta*, vol. 1.1 [*Poetarum Graecorum fragmenta*, vol. 6.1. Berlin: Weidmann, 1899]: 191.
fr. 2 + tituli.
Q: 9: Comic.

0787 **BLASTUS** Med.
vel Blostus
ante A.D. 1

x01 **Fragmenta ap. Galenum**.
K13.17, 19, 20.
Cf. GALENUS Med. (0057 076).

1228 **[BOEO]** Epic.
fiq [Boeus]
4 B.C.?
Cf. et [BOEUS] Epic. (1229).

001 **Fragmenta**, ed. J.U. Powell, *Collectanea Alexandrina*. Oxford: Clarendon Press, 1925 (repr. 1970): 24.
frr. 1–2.
Q: 25: Epic.

0146 **BOETHUS** Epigr.
1 B.C.–A.D. 1: Tarsensis

001 **Epigramma**, AG 9.248.
Q: 41: Epigr.

002 **Titulus**, ed. H. Lloyd-Jones and P. Parsons, *Supplementum Hellenisticum*. Berlin: De Gruyter, 1983: 87.
fr. 232.
NQ: 5: Epigr.

1986 **BOETHUS** Hist.
1 B.C.: Tarsensis
001 **Testimonium**, FGrH #194: 2B:928.
NQ: 140: Test.

2397 **BOETHUS** Phil.
1 B.C.: Sidonius
001 **Fragmenta**, ed. J. von Arnim, *Stoicorum veterum fragmenta*, vol. 3. Leipzig: Teubner,
1903 (repr. Stuttgart: 1968): 265–267.
Q: 723: Phil.

1229 **[BOEUS]** Epic.
fiq [Boeo]
4 B.C.?
Cf. et [BOEO] Epic. (1228).
001 **Fragmentum**, ed. J.U. Powell, *Collectanea Alexandrina*. Oxford: Clarendon Press, 1925
(repr. 1970): 24–25.
Q: 82: Epic.

2230 **BOÏDAS** Phil.
5 B.C.
001 **Testimonium**, ed. H. Diels and W. Kranz, *Die
Fragmente der Vorsokratiker*, vol. 2, 6th edn.
Berlin: Weidmann, 1952 (repr. Dublin: 1966):
376.
NQ: 50: Test.

2610 **BOISCUS** Iamb.
ante A.D. 4: Cyzicenus
001 **Fragmentum**, ed. H. Lloyd-Jones and P. Parsons, *Supplementum Hellenisticum*. Berlin: De
Gruyter, 1983: 87.
fr. 233.
Q: 16: Epigr.
x01 **Epigramma dedicatorium**.
App. Anth. 1.92: Cf. ANTHOLOGIAE GRAE-
CAE APPENDIX (7052 001).
Dup. 2610 001.

1306 **BOLUS** Phil.
vel Pseudo-Democritus
3 B.C.: Mendesicus
001 Περὶ συμπαθειῶν καὶ ἀντιπαθειῶν, ed. W. Gemoll, *Nepualii fragmentum περὶ τῶν κατὰ
ἀντιπάθειαν καὶ συμπάθειαν et Democriti περὶ
συμπαθειῶν καὶ ἀντιπαθειῶν* [*Städtisches Realprogymnasium zu Striegau* (1884)]: 3–6.
Cod
002 **Physica et mystica**, ed. M. Berthelot, *Collection
des anciens alchimistes grecs*. Paris: Steinheil,
1887 (repr. London: Holland Press, 1963): 41–
53.
Cod
003 **Ad Leucippem**, ed. Berthelot, *op. cit.*, 53–56.
Cod
004 **Testimonia**, FGrH #263: 3A:8–9.
NQ: 357: Test.
005 **Fragmenta**, FGrH #263: 3A:9–10.
Q: 353: Hist.

006 **Testimonium**, ed. H. Diels and W. Kranz, *Die
Fragmente der Vorsokratiker*, vol. 2, 6th edn.
Berlin: Weidmann, 1952 (repr. Dublin: 1966):
251.
NQ: 45: Test.
008 **Fragmentum**, ed. A. Giannini, *Paradoxograph-
orum Graecorum reliquiae*. Milan: Istituto Edi-
toriale Italiano, 1965: 377.
Q
x01 **Fragmenta**.
D-K, vol. 2, pp. 211–221.
Cf. DEMOCRITUS Phil. (1304 002) (fr. 300).

1900 **BOTRYAS** Hist.
ante A.D. 2: Myndius
001 **Fragmentum**, FGrH #58: 1A:297.
Q: 23: Hist., Myth.

1230 **<BROTINUS>** Phil.
vel Brontinus
3/2 B.C.: Metapontinus
001 **Fragmentum**, ed. H. Thesleff, *The Pythagorean
texts of the Hellenistic period*. Åbo: Åbo Akademi, 1965: 55.
Q: 127: Phil.
002 **Testimonia**, ed. H. Diels and W. Kranz, *Die
Fragmente der Vorsokratiker*, vol. 1, 6th edn.
Berlin: Weidmann, 1951 (repr. Dublin: 1966):
106–107.
test. 1–5.
Dup. partim 1230 001.
NQ: 233: Test.

1803 ***BRUTI EPISTULAE***
post 1 B.C.
Cf. et MITHRIDATIS EPISTULA (0039).
001 **Epistulae**, ed. R. Hercher, *Epistolographi
Graeci*. Paris: Didot, 1873 (repr. Amsterdam:
Hakkert, 1965): 178–191.
Cod: 3,973: Epist.

1231 **<BRYSON>** Phil.
3 B.C.?
001 **Fragmentum**, ed. H. Thesleff, *The Pythagorean
texts of the Hellenistic period*. Åbo: Åbo Akademi, 1965: 56–57.
Q: 220: Phil.

4276 **BRYSON** Phil. et Soph.
4 B.C.: Heracleota (Ponti), Atheniensis
001 **Testimonia**, ed. K. Döring, *Die Megariker
[Studien zur antiken Philosophie* 2. Amsterdam: Grüner, 1972]: 11, 19, 57, 62–67.
test. 34, 63, 189, 202–210c, 211.
test. 34 (p. 11) = Euclides (4247 001).
test. 63 (p. 19) = Eubulides (4257 001).
test. 189 (p. 57) = Stilpo (4262 001).
test. 202–210c (pp. 62–67) = Bryson.
test. 211 (p. 67) = Polyxenus (4277 001).
NQ: Test.

1559 ***BUCOLICUM***
ante A.D. 3
001 **Fragmentum bucolicum: Pan et Echo** (*P. Vindob.* 29801), ed. E. Heitsch, *Die griechischen Dichterfragmente der römischen Kaiserzeit*, vol. 1, 2nd edn. Göttingen: Vandenhoeck & Ruprecht, 1963: 56–58.
Pap: 304: Bucol.

1032 **BUPHANTUS** Med.
ante A.D. 6
x01 **Fragmentum ap. Alexandrum Trallianum.**
Puschmann, vol. 2, p. 577.
Cf. ALEXANDER Med. (0744 003).

2611 **BUTAS** Eleg.
1 B.C.: Romanus
001 **Fragmentum**, ed. H. Lloyd-Jones and P. Parsons, *Supplementum Hellenisticum*. Berlin: De Gruyter, 1983: 88.
fr. 234.
Q: 15: Eleg.

1232 **<BUTHERUS>** Phil.
4 B.C.?: Cyzicenus
001 **Fragmentum**, ed. H. Thesleff, *The Pythagorean texts of the Hellenistic period*. Åbo: Åbo Akademi, 1965: 59.
Q: 164: Phil.

2448 **BUTORIDAS** Hist.
2 B.C./A.D. 1?
x01 **Fragmentum.**
FGrH #654.
Cf. DIONYSIUS Hist. (2446 001).

2338 **CADMUS** Hist.
6/5 B.C.: Milesius
001 **Testimonia**, FGrH #489: 3B:456–457.
NQ: 342: Test.
002 **Fragmentum**, FGrH #489: 3B:457.
Q: 57: Hist.

2222 **CADMUS Junior** Hist.
Incertum: Milesius
001 **Testimonium**, FGrH #335: 3B:187.
NQ: 30: Test.

2612 **CAECALUS** (?) Epic.
ante A.D. 2: Argivus
001 **Titulus**, ed. H. Lloyd-Jones and P. Parsons, *Supplementum Hellenisticum*. Berlin: De Gruyter, 1983: 89.
fr. 237.
NQ: 2: Epic.

2664 **CAECILIA** Epigr.
A.D. 2: Trebulana
x01 **Epigrammata dedicatoria.**
App. Anth. 1.184–185: Cf. ANTHOLOGIAE GRAECAE APPENDIX (7052 001).

1233 **CAECILIUS** Rhet.
A.D. 2: Calactinus
001 **Fragmenta**, ed. E. Ofenloch, *Caecilii Calactini fragmenta*. Leipzig: Teubner, 1907 (repr. Stuttgart: 1967): 2–205.
Q: [409]
002 **Testimonia**, FGrH #183: 2B:911.
NQ: 154: Test.
003 **Fragmenta**, FGrH #183: 2B:911–912.
Q: 142: Hist.

1234 **Pseudo-CAECILIUS** Rhet.
Incertum
001 **Apophthegmata Romana**, ed. E. Ofenloch, *Caecilii Calactini fragmenta*. Leipzig: Teubner, 1907 (repr. Stuttgart: 1967): 206–210.
Dup. ANONYMI HISTORICI (FGrH) (1139 030).
Cod: Gnom.

2484 **[CAEMARON]** Hist.
Incertum
001 **Fragmentum**, FGrH #720: 3C:656–657.
Q: 92: Hist.

0040 ***CALANI EPISTULA***
Incertum
001 **Epistula**, ed. R. Hercher, *Epistolographi Graeci*. Paris: Didot, 1873 (repr. Amsterdam: Hakkert, 1965): 192.
Q: 97: Epist.

0147 **CALLEAS** Epigr.
vel Callias
Incertum: Argivus
001 **Epigramma**, AG 11.232.
Q: 29: Epigr.

CALLENIUS Epigr.
AG 9.46.
Cf. ANTIPATER Epigr. (0114 001).

0426 **CALLIAS** Comic.
5 B.C.
001 **Fragmenta**, ed. T. Kock, *Comicorum Atticorum fragmenta*, vol. 1. Leipzig: Teubner, 1880: 693–699.
frr. 1, 3–8, 10–13, 16–30 + tituli.
Q: 142: Comic.
002 **Fragmenta**, ed. A. Meineke, *Fragmenta comicorum Graecorum*, vol. 2.2. Berlin: Reimer, 1840 (repr. De Gruyter, 1970): 735–741.
Q: 104: Comic.
003 **Fragmenta**, ed. J. Demiańczuk, *Supplementum comicum*. Krakau: Nakładem Akademii, 1912 (repr. Hildesheim: Olms, 1967): 27–28.
frr. 1–3.
Q: 32: Comic.
004 **Titulus**, ed. C. Austin, *Comicorum Graecorum fragmenta in papyris reperta*. Berlin: De Gruyter, 1973: 33.
NQ: 2: Comic.

005 **Fragmenta**, ed. Meineke, *FCG*, vol. 5.1 (1857; repr. 1970): cxiii.
Q: 8: Comic.

1235 **CALLIAS** Hist.
4–3 B.C.: Syracusanus
001 **Testimonia**, FGrH #564: 3B:577–578.
NQ: 118: Test.
002 **Fragmenta**, FGrH #564: 3B:578–580.
Q: 664: Hist.

1238 **CALLICRATES** Astrol.
Incertum
001 **Fragmenta**, ed. W. Kroll and A. Olivieri, *Codices Parisini* [*Catalogus codicum astrologorum Graecorum* 8.3. Brussels: Lamertin, 1912]: 102–103.
Q: [121]: Astrol.

1783 **CALLICRATES** Comic.
Incertum
001 **Titulus**, ed. T. Kock, *Comicorum Atticorum fragmenta*, vol. 2. Leipzig: Teubner, 1884: 416.
NQ: 2: Comic.
002 **Titulus**, ed. A. Meineke, *Fragmenta comicorum Graecorum*, vol. 1. Berlin: Reimer, 1839 (repr. De Gruyter, 1970): 418.
NQ: 2: Comic.

1940 **CALLICRATES** Hist.
A.D. 3–4?: Tyrius
001 **Fragmentum**, FGrH #213: 2B:944–945.
Q: 310: Hist.

1236 **CALLICRATES-MENECLES** Perieg.
2/1 B.C.
001 **Fragmenta**, FGrH #370: 3B:231–233.
Q: 293: Hist., Perieg.

1237 **<CALLICRATIDAS>** Phil.
3 B.C.?
001 **Fragmenta**, ed. H. Thesleff, *The Pythagorean texts of the Hellenistic period*. Åbo: Åbo Akademi, 1965: 103–107.
Q: 1,272: Phil.

0148 **CALLICTER** Epigr.
vel Cillactor
A.D. 1/2
001 **Epigrammata**, AG 5.29, 45; 11.2, 5–6, 118–122, 333.
AG 5.31: Cf. ANTIPATER Epigr. (0114 001).
Q: 197: Epigr.

0533 **CALLIMACHUS** Philol.
4–3 B.C.: Cyrenaeus
Scholia: Cf. SCHOLIA IN CALLIMACHUM (5016).
001 **Fragmenta**, ed. R. Pfeiffer, *Callimachus*, vol. 1. Oxford: Clarendon Press, 1949: 1–2, 4–6, 8–10, 12, 14–16, 18, 20–30, 32–37, 39, 41–46, 48–58, 60–104, 106–109, 111–112, 114, 116,

118, 120, 122, 124–159, 161–162, 164, 166–226, 229–272, 274–306, 308–327, 330–338, 354–399, 401–402, 406–429, 431–437, 440–452, 454, 456, 458–486, 489–492, 495.
Aetia (frr. 1–7, 10–12, 15, 17–28, 30, 32–33, 37, 41, 43–46, 48–49, 51, 55, 57–59, 61, 63–70, 72–87, 90–98, 100–106, 108, 110, 112–184, 186).
Iambi (frr. 191–216, 218–225).
Lyrica (frr. 226–229).
Hecala (frr. 230–236, 238–248, 251, 253–263, 265–289, 291–295, 298–305, 309–315, 317–348, 350–351, 353–377).
Carmina epica et elegiaca minora (frr. 378–380, 383–392).
Epigrammatum fragmenta (frr. 393–395, 398–401).
Fragmenta grammatica (fr. 407).
Fragmenta incertae sedis (frr. 467–472, 474–477, 480–500, 502, 504–512, 514–520, 522–536, 538–540, 544, 546–557, 560–562, 567, 571–575, 586–588, 590–593, 597, 599, 601–608, 610–613, 617–621, 623, 625–631, 633–639, 644–648, 650–652, 654–659, 668–677, 680–683, 686–691, 694–695, 700–701, 705, 713–716, 719, 721, 724–725).
Fragmenta incerti auctoris (frr. 726–732, 734–740, 742–776, 778–782, 784–788, 799–803, 805–807, 813–814).
Dup. partim 0533 005.
Q, Pap: 12,481: Eleg., Iamb., Lyr., Epic., Epigr., Gramm.
002 **Hymni**, ed. Pfeiffer, *op. cit.*, vol. 2 (1953): 1–40.
Hymn. 1, In Jovem: pp. 1–5.
Hymn. 2, In Apollinem: pp. 5–9.
Hymn. 3, In Dianam: pp. 9–18.
Hymn. 4, In Delum: pp. 18–29.
Hymn. 5, In lavacrum Palladis: pp. 30–34.
Hymn. 6, In Cererem: pp. 35–40.
Cod: 7,443: Hymn.
003 **Epigrammata**, ed. Pfeiffer, *op. cit.*, vol. 2, 80–99.
Epigr. 1–63.
Dup. 0533 004.
Q: 1,984: Epigr.
004 **Epigrammata**, AG 5.6, 23, 146; 6.121, 146–150, 301, 310–311, 347, 351; 7.80, 89, 170, 271–272, 277, 317–318, 344b, 415, 447, 451, 453–454, 458–460, 471, 517–525, 725, 728; 9.336, 507, 565–566; 11.362; 12.43, 51, 71, 73, 102, 118, 134, 139, 148–150, 230; 13.7, 9–10, 24–25.
Dup. 0533 003.
AG 7.320: Cf. HEGESIPPUS Epigr. (1396 001).
AG 7.729: Cf. TYMNES Epigr. (1744 001).
AG 9.67: Cf. ANONYMI EPIGRAMMATICI (AG) (0138 001).
Q: 2,066: Epigr.
005 **Fragmenta et titulus**, ed. H. Lloyd-Jones and P. Parsons, *Supplementum Hellenisticum*. Berlin: De Gruyter, 1983: 89–90, 92–98, 101–110,

117–119, 122–127, 131–132, 134–143.
frr. (+ titul.) 238–255, 257–265, 267–268,
271–276, 280–283, 285–298, 300–308.
frr. 238–249: *P. Ant.* 3.113.
fr. 249a: *P. Berol.* inv. 17057.
frr. 250–251: *P. Oxy.* 17.2079 + 18.2167.
frr. 252–253: *P. Sorb.* inv. 2248.
frr. 254–265: *P. Oxy.* 18.2173 + *P. Lille* 76,
78–79, 82, 84, 111c + *P. Oxy.* 18.2170.
frr. 271–274: *P. Ant.* 3.114.
fr. 276: *P. Oxy.* 1.14 + *P. Mich.* inv. 4761c +
P. Oxy. 19.2221.
fr. 280: *P. Oxy.* 37.2823.
frr. 282–283: *P. Oxy.* 30.2529.
fr. 285: *PSI* 2.133.
frr. 286–287: *P. Oxy.* 23.2376 + 23.2377.
fr. 288: *P. Rain.* 6 (= tabula Vindobonensis) +
P. Oxy. 19.2217 + *P. Oxy.* 24.2398 + *P. Oxy.*
25.2437.
frr. 290–291: *P. Oxy.* 30, p. 91 (novum *P. Oxy.*
20.2258 fragmentum).
fr. 296: *P. Oxy.* 23.2375.
fr. 297: *P. Ticinensis* 1.
fr. 298: *P. Ant.* 2.60.
fr. 307: *P. Herc.* 243 ii.
fr. 308: *P. Herc.* 243 vii.
Dup. partim 0533 001.
Cf. et ADESPOTA PAPYRACEA (SH) (2648
004, fr. 992).
Pap: 2,867: Eleg., Iamb., Epic., Gramm.
x01 **Epigrammata** (*App. Anth.*).
Epigramma dedicatorium: 1.114.
Epigrammata demonstrativa: 3.63–66.
Epigrammata irrisoria: 5.19; Addenda 5.19b.
App. Anth. 1.114: Cf. ANTHOLOGIAE GRAE-
CAE APPENDIX (7052 001).
App. Anth. 3.63–66: Cf. ANTHOLOGIAE
GRAECAE APPENDIX (7052 003).
App. Anth. 5.19: Cf. ANTHOLOGIAE GRAE-
CAE APPENDIX (7052 005).
App. Anth. 5.19b: Cf. ANTHOLOGIAE GRAE-
CAE APPENDIX (7052 008).
x02 **Fragmentum papyraceum** (*P. Mich.* inv. 3499)
(fort. auctore Callimacho).
SH, p. 511, fr. 992.
Cf. ADESPOTA PAPYRACEA (SH) (2648 004).

2613 **CALLIMACHUS Junior** Epic.
3 B.C.: Cyrenaeus
001 **Titulus**, ed. H. Lloyd-Jones and P. Parsons,
Supplementum Hellenisticum. Berlin: De Gruyter, 1983: 144.
fr. 309.
NQ: 3: Epic.

1996 **CALLIMORPHUS** Med.
A.D. 2
001 **Fragmenta**, FGrH #210: 2B:941–942.
Q: 169: Hist.

0824 **CALLINICUS** Med.
ante A.D. 1

x01 **Fragmentum ap. Galenum.**
K13.984.
Cf. GALENUS Med. (0057 077).

2189 **CALLINICUS** Soph.
A.D. 3: Petraeus
001 **Testimonia**, FGrH #281: 3A:159–160.
NQ: 201: Test.
002 **Fragmenta**, FGrH #281: 3A:160–161.
Q, Cod: 354: Hist.
003 Εἰς τὰ πάτρια Ῥώμης, ed. H. Hinck, *Polemonis
declamationes quae exstant duae.* Leipzig:
Teubner, 1873: 43–44.
Cod: Rhet.

0243 **CALLINUS** Eleg.
7 B.C.: Ephesius
001 **Fragmenta**, ed. M.L. West, *Iambi et elegi
Graeci*, vol. 2. Oxford: Clarendon Press, 1972:
47–49.
frr. 1–2a, 4–5a.
Q: 168: Eleg.

2218 **CALLIPHON et DEMOCEDES** Med. et Phil.
6 B.C.: Cnidius (Calliphon), Crotoniensis
(Democedes)
001 **Testimonia**, ed. H. Diels and W. Kranz, *Die
Fragmente der Vorsokratiker*, vol. 1, 6th edn.
Berlin: Weidmann, 1951 (repr. Dublin: 1966):
110–112.
test. 1–3.
NQ: 795: Test.

0427 <**CALLIPPUS**> Comic.
Incertum: Atheniensis
001 **Fragmenta**, ed. T. Kock, *Comicorum Atticorum fragmenta*, vol. 3. Leipzig: Teubner,
1888: 378–379.
frr. 1–2.
fr. 1: Dup. CALLIMACHUS Philol. (0533 001)
(fr. 227, vv. 5–7).
Q: 18: Comic.
002 **Fragmentum**, ed. A. Meineke, *Fragmenta
comicorum Graecorum*, vol. 4. Berlin: Reimer,
1841 (repr. De Gruyter, 1970): 561.
Dup. CALLIMACHUS Philol. (0533 001, fr.
227, vv. 5–7).
Q: 16: Comic.

2270 **CALLIPPUS** Hist.
ante A.D. 2: Corinthius
001 **Fragmenta**, FGrH #385: 3B:263.
Q: 206: Hist.

0534 **CALLISTHENES** Hist.
4 B.C.: Olynthius
001 **Testimonia**, FGrH #124: 2B:631–639; 3B:743
addenda.
test. 23: *Inscr. Delphi.*
test. 33 bis: *P. Zenon* 60.
NQ: 3,009: Test.

002 **Fragmenta**, FGrH #124: **2B**:639–657; **3B**:743
addenda.
fr. 55: *P. Oxy.* 2.222.
Q, Pap: 6,255: Hist., Perieg., Gnom.

003 **Testimonium et fragmentum**, ed. H.J. Mette,
"Die 'Kleinen' griechischen Historiker heute,"
Lustrum 21 (1978) 18–19.
test. 37: *P. Mich.* 1316.
fr. 32 bis.
Q, Pap: 164: Hist.

2199 **[CALLISTHENES]** Hist.
Incertum: Sybarita
001 **Fragmenta**, FGrH #291: 3A:175.
Q: 161: Hist.

2155 **CALLISTION** Hist.
A.D. 4
001 **Testimonia**, FGrH #223: 2B:951.
NQ: 20: Test.
002 **Fragmentum**, FGrH #223: 2B:951.
Q: 44: Hist.

2252 **CALLISTRATUS** Gramm.
2 B.C.: Alexandrinus
001 **Fragmenta**, FGrH #348: 3B:210–211.
Q: 263: Hist.

1239 **Domitius CALLISTRATUS** Hist.
1 B.C.?
001 **Fragmenta**, FGrH #433: 3B:334–336.
Q: 677: Hist.

4091 **CALLISTRATUS** Soph.
A.D. 4
001 **Statuarum descriptiones**, ed. K. Schenkl and
A. Reisch, *Philostrati minoris imagines et Cal-
listrati descriptiones*. Leipzig: Teubner, 1902:
45–72.
Cod

1845 **CALLISTRATUS** Trag.
5 B.C.
001 **Tituli**, ed. B. Snell, *Tragicorum Graecorum
fragmenta*, vol. 1. Göttingen: Vandenhoeck &
Ruprecht, 1971: 155.
NQ: 8: Trag.

1240 **CALLIXENUS** Hist.
2 B.C.: Rhodius
001 **Testimonia**, FGrH #627: 3C:161.
NQ: 60: Test.
002 **Fragmenta**, FGrH #627: 3C:161–178.
Q: 4,681: Hist.

3015 **Joannes CAMENIATES** Hist.
vel Joannes Caminiates
A.D. 9–10: Thessalonicensis
001 **De expugnatione Thessalonicae**, ed. G. Böh-
lig, *Ioannis Caminiatae de expugnatione Thessalonicae* [*Corpus fontium historiae Byzantinae 4.

Series Berolinensis. Berlin: De Gruyter, 1973]:
3–68.
Cod: 23,382: Hist.

2504 **CANDIDUS** Hist.
A.D. 5: Isauricus
001 **Testimonium**, FGrH #748: 3C:732.
NQ: 73: Test.
002 **Fragmenta**, FHG 4: 135–137.
Q: Hist.

0942 **CANDIDUS** <Med.>
ante A.D. 2
x01 **Fragmentum ap. Galenum**.
K13.926.
Cf. GALENUS Med. (0057 077).
x02 **Fragmentum ap. Aëtium** (lib. 7).
CMG, vol. 8.2, p. 393.
Cf. AËTIUS Med. (0718 007).

1242 *CANON LIBRORUM*
A.D. 2
001 **Canon librorum**, ed. J.P. Audet, "A Hebrew-
Aramaic list of books of the Old Testament in
Greek transcription," *Journal of Theological
Studies*, n.s. 1 (1950) 138.
Cod

0428 **CANTHARUS** Comic.
5 B.C.
001 **Fragmenta**, ed. T. Kock, *Comicorum Atticorum fragmenta*, vol. 1. Leipzig: Teubner,
1880: 764–766.
frr. 1–8, 10 + tituli.
Q: 37: Comic.
002 **Fragmenta**, ed. A. Meineke, *Fragmenta comicorum Graecorum*, vol. 2.2. Berlin: Reimer,
1840 (repr. De Gruyter, 1970): 835–836.
Q: 30: Comic.
003 **Fragmenta**, ed. J. Demiańczuk, *Supplementum
comicum*. Krakau: Nakładem Akademii, 1912
(repr. Hildesheim: Olms, 1967): 28–29.
frr. 1–3.
Q: 12: Comic.
004 **Titulus**, ed. C. Austin, *Comicorum Graecorum
fragmenta in papyris reperta*. Berlin: De Gruyter, 1973: 33.
NQ: 2: Comic.

2138 *CANTICUM EURIPIDIS*
ante 3 B.C.
001 **Ex Orestis stasimo i** (*P. Vindob.* 2315), ed. K.
Jan, *Musici scriptores Graeci*. Leipzig: Teubner,
1895 (repr. Hildesheim: Olms, 1962): 430.
Cf. et EURIPIDES Trag. (0006 016).
Pap: Mus.

0276 *CANTUS LUGUBRIS*
ante A.D. 2
001 **Fragmentum** (*P. Brit. Mus.* 2103), ed. E.
Heitsch, *Die griechischen Dichterfragmente der
römischen Kaiserzeit*, vol. 1, 2nd edn. Göt-

tingen: Vandenhoeck & Ruprecht, 1963: 43–44.
Pap: 113: Lyr.

0149 CAPITO Epigr.
Incertum
001 **Epigramma**, AG 5.67.
Q: 14: Epigr.

2506 CAPITO Hist.
A.D. 5/6?: Lycius
001 **Testimonium**, FGrH #750: 3C:733.
NQ: 24: Test.
002 **Fragmenta**, FGrH #750: 3C:733–734.
Q: 256: Hist.

CARCINUS Epic.
Incertum: Naupactous
Cf. CARMEN NAUPACTIUM (1241).

0310 CARCINUS Trag.
5 B.C.
001 **Fragmentum**, ed. B. Snell, *Tragicorum Graecorum fragmenta*, vol. 1. Göttingen: Vandenhoeck & Ruprecht, 1971: 131.
frr. 1–2.
Q: 14: Trag.

0327 CARCINUS Junior Trag.
4 B.C.
001 **Fragmenta**, ed. B. Snell, *Tragicorum Graecorum fragmenta*, vol. 1. Göttingen: Vandenhoeck & Ruprecht, 1971: 210–215.
frr. 1–10.
Q: 221: Trag., Satyr.

0286 *CARMEN ASTROLOGICUM*
A.D. 4?
001 **Fragmentum**, ed. E. Heitsch, *Die griechischen Dichterfragmente der römischen Kaiserzeit*, vol. 2. Göttingen: Vandenhoeck & Ruprecht, 1964: 43–44.
Q: 97: Hexametr., Astrol.

CARMEN AUREUM
Cf. <PYTHAGORAS> Phil. (0632 001).

1241 *CARMEN NAUPACTIUM*
fort. auctore Carcino Naupactoo
Incertum
001 **Fragmenta**, ed. G. Kinkel, *Epicorum Graecorum fragmenta*, vol. 1. Leipzig: Teubner, 1877: 198–200.
frr. 1–2, 7–8.
Q: 60: Epic.

0296 *CARMINA CONVIVIALIA* (PMG)
Varia
001 **Fragmenta**, ed. D.L. Page, *Poetae melici Graeci*. Oxford: Clarendon Press, 1962 (repr. 1967 (1st edn. corr.)): 472–482.
frr. 1–31, 33–34.
Q, Pap: 630: Lyr.

0362 *CARMINA DELPHIS INVENTA*
A.D. 1–2
001 **Carmina Delphis inventa**, ed. K. Jan, *Musici scriptores Graeci*. Leipzig: Teubner, 1895 (repr. Hildesheim: Olms, 1962): 434–448.
Epigr: Mus.

2988 *CARMINA EPIGRAPHICA*
8–5 B.C.
001 **Carmina**, ed. P.A. Hansen, *Carmina epigraphica Graeca saeculorum viii–v a. Chr. n.* [*Texte und Kommentare* 12. Berlin: De Gruyter, 1983]: 1–259.
Epigr: Epigr., Poem.

0295 *CARMINA POPULARIA* (PMG)
Varia
001 **Fragmenta**, ed. D.L. Page, *Poetae melici Graeci*. Oxford: Clarendon Press, 1962 (repr. 1967 (1st edn. corr.)): 450–470.
frr. 1–12, 14–17, 19–37.
Q, Pap: 566: Lyr., Encom.

1333 CARNEADES Phil.
3–2 B.C.: Cyrenaeus
001 **Testimonia et fragmenta**, ed. B. Wisniewski, *Karneades. Fragmente. Text und Kommentar* [*Archiwum filologiczne* 24. Breslau: Narodowy, 1970]: 15–35, 37–47, 50–56, 63, 74–79, 84, 90–91.
Q: Phil.

1244 CARNEISCUS Phil.
3/2 B.C.
001 **Fragmenta**, ed. W. Crönert, *Kolotes und Menedemos*. Leipzig: Avenarius, 1906 (repr. Amsterdam: Hakkert, 1965): 69–71.
Pap

0150 CARPHYLLIDES Epigr.
3 B.C.
001 **Epigrammata**, AG 7.260; 9.52.
Q: 87: Epigr.

1245 CARYSTIUS Hist.
2 B.C.: Pergamenus
001 **Fragmenta**, FHG 4: 356–359.
frr. 1–19.
Q: Hist.

1822 Julius CASSIANUS Gnost.
A.D. 2
x01 **Fragmentum ap. Clementem Alexandrinum**. Stählin-Früchtel-Treu, vol. 2, p. 238.
Cf. CLEMENS ALEXANDRINUS Theol. (0555 004).

1806 CASSIUS Med.
fiq Cassius Dionysius Uticensis
1 B.C.
x01 **Fragmentum ap. Hippiatrica**.

Oder & Hoppe, vol. 1, pp. 41–42.
Cf. HIPPIATRICA (0738 001).

0385 **CASSIUS DIO** Hist.
vel Cassius Dio Cocceianus
A.D. 2–3: Nicaeensis

001 **Historiae Romanae**, ed. U.P. Boissevain, *Cassii Dionis Cocceiani historiarum Romanarum quae supersunt*, 3 vols. Berlin: Weidmann, 1:1895; 2:1898; 3:1901 (repr. 1955): 1:1–4, 6–20, 23, 25–27, 30–38, 40–49, 51–65, 69–70, 76–81, 83–88, 90–133, 135, 137–139, 141–149, 153–155, 157–161, 163, 165–168, 172, 174–185, 187, 190–199, 201–204, 206–208, 210–217, 219–224, 227–229, 234, 237–241, 243–245, 251, 253–267, 269–278, 280, 286–288, 290, 292, 295–302, 309–311, 313–314, 318, 321–355, 360–539; 2:1–556, 558–690; 3:1–161, 164–279, 282–476.
Q, Cod: 380,976: Hist.

002 **Historiae Romanae** (versio 1 in volumine 1), ed. Boissevain, *op. cit.*, vol. 1, 1–37, 39–95, 97–98, 100–108, 110, 113–191, 194–320, 345.
Q: 58,416: Hist.

003 **Historiae Romanae** (versio 1 in volumine 2), ed. Boissevain, *op. cit.*, vol. 2, 647–648, 660.
Q: 123: Hist.

004 **Historiae Romanae** (versio 1 in volumine 3), ed. Boissevain, *op. cit.*, vol. 3, 7–8, 10, 12, 17–21, 27, 51–52, 85–86, 89–99, 103, 105–106, 108–110, 113, 116, 122–123, 154–156, 169–170, 177, 189, 193–195, 214–215, 245, 247–249, 253, 256, 262–265, 267–268, 270–271, 284, 292, 298, 303, 310, 315, 319, 322, 324, 345–346, 367, 375–377, 381–382, 384–385, 390–391, 470.
Q: 4,294: Hist.

005 **Historiae Romanae** (versio 2 in volumine 1), ed. Boissevain, *op. cit.*, vol. 1, 1–8, 13–14, 28–29, 51–52, 55–57, 72, 74–75, 87–89, 160, 170, 183, 189, 219–220, 223, 232–233, 235, 251–252, 275, 293, 307–308.
Q: 1,990: Hist.

006 **Historiae Romanae** (versio 2 in volumine 2), ed. Boissevain, *op. cit.*, vol. 2, 647–649, 660.
Q: 392: Hist.

007 **Historiae Romanae** (versio 2 in volumine 3), ed. Boissevain, *op. cit.*, vol. 3, 19, 27, 51, 86–90, 92, 96–99, 177, 270–271, 390–391.
Q: 857: Hist.

008 **Historiae Romanae** (versio 3 in volumine 1), ed. Boissevain, *op. cit.*, vol. 1, 72–74.
Q: 100: Hist.

009 **Reliquiae incertae sedis**, ed. Boissevain, *op. cit.*, vol. 1, 356–358.
Q: 492: Hist.

010 **Historiae Romanae** (Xiphilini epitome), ed. Boissevain, *op. cit.*, vol. 3, 479–730.
Cod: 111,057: Hist.

011 **Historiae Romanae** (Petri Patricii excerpta Va-

ticana sive Maiana), ed. Boissevain, *op. cit.*, vol. 3, 731–749.
Q: 4,408: Hist.

012 **Historiae Romanae** (excerpta Planudea), ed. Boissevain, *op. cit.*, vol. 3, 749–750.
Q: 216: Hist.

013 **Historiae Romanae** (Joannis Antiocheni excerpta e Dione derivata), ed. Boissevain, *op. cit.*, vol. 3, 750–762.
Q: 4,954: Hist.

014 **Historiae Romanae** (excerpta Salmasiana), ed. Boissevain, *op. cit.*, vol. 3, 763–766.
Q: 1,665: Hist.

015 **Historiae Romanae** (excerpta Constantiniana cum Dionis verbis composita), ed. Boissevain, *op. cit.*, vol. 3, 767–775.
Q: 1,601: Hist.

016 **Historiae Romanae** (ap. Photium, *Bibl.* cod. 71), ed. Boissevain, *op. cit.*, vol. 3, 775–776.
Q: 287: Hist.

017 **Testimonia**, FGrH #707: 3C:577–578.
NQ: 136: Test.

018 **Fragmenta**, FGrH #707: 3C:578–581.
Q: 1,139: Hist.

0733 **CASSIUS Iatrosophista** Med.
A.D. 2–3

001 **Quaestiones medicae et problemata physica**, ed. J.L. Ideler, *Physici et medici Graeci minores*, vol. 1. Berlin: Reimer, 1841 (repr. Amsterdam: Hakkert, 1963): 144–167.
Cod: 7,180: Med., Nat. Hist.

1246 **CASTOR** Rhet.
1 B.C.: Rhodius

001 **Testimonia**, FGrH #250: 2B:1130–1131.
NQ: 114: Test.

002 **Fragmenta**, FGrH #250: 2B:1132–1133, 1135, 1137, 1143–1145.
Q: 1,324: Hist., Chronogr.

x01 **De metris rhetoricis** [Sp.].
Studemund, pp. 13–26.
Cf. LACHARES Soph. (2937 001).

0382 **CASTORION** Lyr.
4 B.C.: Soleus

001 **Fragmentum**, ed. D.L. Page, *Poetae melici Graeci*. Oxford: Clarendon Press, 1962 (repr. 1967 (1st edn. corr.)): 447.
fr. 1.
Dup. partim 0382 002 (fr. 312).
Q: 10: Lyr.

002 **Fragmenta**, ed. H. Lloyd-Jones and P. Parsons, *Supplementum Hellenisticum*. Berlin: De Gruyter, 1983: 144–145.
frr. 310, 312.
fr. 312: Dup. 0382 001.
Q: 45: Hymn., Lyr.

0826 **CASTUS** Med.
A.D. 1?

x01 **Fragmenta ap. Galenum.**
K13.739, 1037.
Cf. GALENUS Med. (0057 077).

4102 *CATENAE (Novum Testamentum)*
post A.D. 5
001 **Catena in Matthaeum** (catena integra) (e cod.
Paris. Coislin. gr. 23), ed. J.A. Cramer, *Catenae
Graecorum patrum in Novum Testamentum*,
vol. 1. Oxford: Oxford University Press, 1840
(repr. Hildesheim: Olms, 1967): 1–257.
Cod: 78,438: Caten.
002 **Catena in Marcum** (recensio ii) (e codd. Oxon.
Bodl. Laud. 33 + Paris. Coislin. 23 + Paris. gr.
178), ed. Cramer, *op. cit.*, vol. 1, 261–447.
Cod: 52,679: Caten.
003 **Supplementum et varietas lectionis ad commentarium Chrysostomi in evangelium sancti
Matthaei** (e cod. Oxon. Bodl. Auct. T.1.4), ed.
Cramer, *op. cit.*, vol. 1, 449–496.
Cf. et 4102 001.
Cod: 14,134: Caten.
004 **Catena in Lucam** (typus B) (e codd. Paris.
Coislin. 23 + Oxon. Bodl. Misc. 182), ed. Cramer, *op. cit.*, vol. 2 (1841; repr. 1967): 3–174.
Cod: 51,308: Caten.
005 **Catena in Joannem** (catena integra) (e codd.
Paris. Coislin. 23 + Oxon. Bodl. Auct. T.1.4),
ed. Cramer, *op. cit.*, vol. 2, 177–413.
Cod: 75,703: Caten.
006 **Supplementum et varietas lectionis ad ca-
tenam in evangelium sancti Lucae** (e cod.
Oxon. Bodl. Laud. 33), ed. Cramer, *op. cit.*,
vol. 2, 415–430.
Cf. et 4102 004.
Cod: 4,197: Caten.
007 **Supplementum et varietas lectionis ad catenam in evangelium sancti Joannis** (e cod.
Bodl. B.), ed. Cramer, *op. cit.*, vol. 2, 431–450.
Cf. et 4102 005.
Cod: 5,259: Caten.
008 **Catena in Acta** (catena Andreae) (e cod. Oxon.
coll. nov. 58), ed. Cramer, *op. cit.*, vol. 3 (1838;
repr. 1967): 1–424.
Cod: 101,182: Caten.
010 **Catena in epistulam ad Romanos** (typus Vaticanus) (e cod. Oxon. Bodl. Auct. E.2.20 [=
Misc. 48]), ed. Cramer, *op. cit.*, vol. 4 (1844;
repr. 1967): 1–162.
Cf. et 4102 011.
Cod: 49,702: Caten.
011 **Catena in epistulam ad Romanos** (typus Monacensis) (e cod. Monac. gr. 412), ed. Cramer, *op.
cit.*, vol. 4, 163–529.
Cf. et 4102 010.
Cod: 116,658: Caten.
012 **Catena in epistulam i ad Corinthios** (typus Vaticanus) (e cod. Paris. gr. 227), ed. Cramer, *op.
cit.*, vol. 5 (1841; repr. 1967): 1–344.
Cod: 106,993: Caten.
013 **Catena in epistulam ii ad Corinthios** (catena

Pseudo-Oecumenii) (e cod. Paris. gr. 223), ed.
Cramer, *op. cit.*, vol. 5, 345–444.
Cod: 25,764: Caten.
014 **Catena in epistulam ii ad Corinthios** (catena
Pseudo-Oecumenii) (e cod. Paris. gr. 216), ed.
Cramer, *op. cit.*, vol. 5, 445–459.
Cod: 4,173: Caten.
015 **Supplementum et varietas lectionis ad epistulam i ad Corinthios** (catena Pseudo-Oecumenii) (e cod. Bodl. Auct. T.1.7 [= Misc.
185]), ed. Cramer, *op. cit.*, vol. 5, 460–469.
Cod: 2,290: Caten.
016 **Supplementum et varietas lectionis ad epistulam ii ad Corinthios** (catena Pseudo-Oecumenii) (e cod. Bodl. Auct. T.1.7 [= Misc.
185]), ed. Cramer, *op. cit.*, vol. 5, 469–477.
Cod: 2,060: Caten.
017 **Supplementum et varietas lectionis ad epistulam i ad Corinthios** (catena Pseudo-Oecumenii) (e cod. Oxon. Bodl. Roe 16), ed. Cramer, *op. cit.*, vol. 5, 477–478.
Cod: 375: Caten.
018 **Supplementum et varietas lectionis ad epistulam ii ad Corinthios** (catena Pseudo-Oecumenii) (e cod. Oxon. Bodl. Roe 16), ed. Cramer, *op. cit.*, vol. 5, 479.
Cod: 159: Caten.
019 **Catena in epistulam ad Galatas** (typus Parisinus) (e cod. Coislin. 204), ed. Cramer, vol. 6
(1842; repr. 1967): 1–95.
Cod: 27,845: Caten.
020 **Catena in epistulam ad Ephesios** (typus Parisinus) (e cod. Coislin. 204), ed. Cramer, *op.
cit.*, vol. 6, 96–225.
Cod: 39,498: Caten.
021 **Catena in epistulam ad Philippenses** (typus
Parisinus) (e cod. Coislin. 204), ed. Cramer,
op. cit., vol. 6, 226–290.
Cod: 18,940: Caten.
022 **Catena in epistulam ad Colossenses** (typus
Parisinus) (e cod. Coislin. 204), ed. Cramer,
op. cit., vol. 6, 291–340.
Cod: 14,054: Caten.
023 **Catena in epistulam i ad Thessalonicenses**
(typus Parisinus) (e cod. Coislin. 204), ed. Cramer, *op. cit.*, vol. 6, 341–375.
Cod: 9,834: Caten.
024 **Catena in epistulam ii ad Thessalonicenses**
(typus Parisinus) (e cod. Coislin. 204), ed. Cramer, *op. cit.*, vol. 6, 376–398.
Cod: 5,997: Caten.
025 **Supplementum et varietas lectionis in epistulam ad Galatas** (catena Pseudo-Oecumenii)
(e cod. Bodl. Auct. T.1.7 [= Misc. 185]), ed.
Cramer, *op. cit.*, vol. 6, 399–402.
Cod: 900: Caten.
026 **Supplementum et varietas lectionis in epistulam ad Ephesios** (catena Pseudo-Oecumenii)
(e cod. Bodl. Auct. T.1.7 [= Misc. 185]), ed.
Cramer, *op. cit.*, vol. 6, 402–406.
Cod: 1,028: Caten.
027 **Supplementum et varietas lectionis in epis-

tulam i ad Thessalonicenses (catena Pseudo-Oecumenii) (e cod. Bodl. Auct. T.1.7 [= Misc. 185]), ed. Cramer, *op. cit.*, vol. 6, 406–410.
Cod: 1,087: Caten.

028 **Supplementum et varietas lectionis in epistulam ad Galatas** (catena Pseudo-Oecumenii) (e cod. Oxon. Bodl. Roe 16), ed. Cramer, *op. cit.*, vol. 6, 410–411.
Cod: 239: Caten.

029 **Supplementum et varietas lectionis in epistulam ad Ephesios** (catena Pseudo-Oecumenii) (e cod. Oxon. Bodl. Roe 16), ed. Cramer, *op. cit.*, vol. 6, 411–412.
Cod: 188: Caten.

030 **Supplementum et varietas lectionis in epistulam ad Philippenses** (catena Pseudo-Oecumenii) (e cod. Oxon. Bodl. Roe 16), ed. Cramer, *op. cit.*, vol. 6, 412.
Cod: 79: Caten.

031 **Supplementum et varietas lectionis in epistulam ad Colossenses** (catena Pseudo-Oecumenii) (e cod. Oxon. Bodl. Roe 16), ed. Cramer, *op. cit.*, vol. 6, 412.
Cod: 22: Caten.

032 **Supplementum et varietas lectionis in epistulam i ad Thessalonicenses** (catena Pseudo-Oecumenii) (e cod. Oxon. Bodl. Roe 16), ed. Cramer, *op. cit.*, vol. 6, 412.
Cod: 42: Caten.

033 **Supplementum et varietas lectionis in epistulam ii ad Thessalonicenses** (catena Pseudo-Oecumenii) (e cod. Oxon. Bodl. Roe 16), ed. Cramer, *op. cit.*, vol. 6, 413.
Cod: 62: Caten.

034 **Catena in epistulam i ad Timotheum** (e cod. Paris. Coislin. 204), ed. Cramer, *op. cit.*, vol. 7 (1843; repr. 1967): 1–51.
Cod: Caten.

035 **Catena in epistulam ii ad Timotheum** (e cod. Paris. Coislin. 204), ed. Cramer, *op. cit.*, vol. 7, 52–82.
Cod: Caten.

036 **Catena in epistulam ad Titum** (e cod. Paris. Coislin. 204), ed. Cramer, *op. cit.*, vol. 7, 83–100.
Cod: Caten.

037 **Catena in epistulam ad Philemonem** (e cod. Paris. Coislin. 204), ed. Cramer, *op. cit.*, vol. 7, 101–111.
Cod: Caten.

038 **Catena in epistulam ad Hebraeos** (e cod. Paris. Coislin. 204), ed. Cramer, *op. cit.*, vol. 7, 112–278.
Cod: Caten.

039 **Catena in epistulam ad Hebraeos** (catena Nicetae) (e cod. Paris. gr. 238), ed. Cramer, *op. cit.*, vol. 7, 279–598.
Cod: Caten.

040 **Catena in epistulam Jacobi** (catena Andreae) (e cod. Oxon. coll. nov. 58), ed. Cramer, *op. cit.*, vol. 8 (1840; repr. 1967): 1–40.
Cod: Caten.

041 **Catena in epistulam Petri i** (catena Andreae) (e cod. Oxon. coll. nov. 58), ed. Cramer, *op. cit.*, vol. 8, 41–83.
Cod: Caten.

042 **Catena in epistulam Petri ii** (catena Andreae) (e cod. Oxon. coll. nov. 58), ed. Cramer, *op. cit.*, vol. 8, 84–104.
Cod: Caten.

043 **Catena in epistulam Joannis i** (catena Andreae) (e cod. Oxon. coll. nov. 58), ed. Cramer, *op. cit.*, vol. 8, 105–145.
Cod: Caten.

044 **Catena in epistulam Joannis ii** (catena Andreae) (e cod. Oxon. coll. nov. 58), ed. Cramer, *op. cit.*, vol. 8, 146–148.
Cod: Caten.

045 **Catena in epistulam Joannis iii** (catena Andreae) (e cod. Oxon. coll. nov. 58), ed. Cramer, *op. cit.*, vol. 8, 149–152.
Cod: Caten.

046 **Catena in epistulam Juda** (catena Andreae) (e cod. Oxon. coll. nov. 58), ed. Cramer, *op. cit.*, vol. 8, 153–170.
Cod: Caten.

x01 **Prooemium Pseudo-Oecumenii in Apocalypsin commentarii** (e cod. Coislin. 224).
Cramer, vol. 8, pp. 173–175.
Cf. Pseudo-OECUMENIUS Scr. Eccl. (4154 001).

x02 **Commentarius in Apocalypsin.**
Cramer, vol. 8, pp. 176–496.
Cf. ARETHAS Philol. et Scr. Eccl. (2130 008).

x03 **Commentarius in Apocalypsin** (Pseudo-Oecumenii) (e cod. Coislin. 224).
Cramer, vol. 8, pp. 497–582.
Cf. Pseudo-OECUMENIUS Scr. Eccl. (4154 002).

2661 **CATILIUS** Epigr.
post A.D. 1
x01 **Epigrammata dedicatoria.**
App. Anth. 1.159–161: Cf. ANTHOLOGIAE GRAECAE APPENDIX (7052 001).

2672 **CATULLINUS** Epigr.
Incertum
x01 **Epigramma dedicatorium.**
App. Anth. 1.196: Cf. ANTHOLOGIAE GRAECAE APPENDIX (7052 001).

2666 **CATULUS** Epigr.
Incertum
x01 **Epigramma dedicatorium.**
App. Anth. 1.189: Cf. ANTHOLOGIAE GRAECAE APPENDIX (7052 001).

1887 **CAUCALUS** Rhet.
4 B.C.: Chius
001 **Fragmenta**, FGrH #38: 1A:259–260.
Q: 70: Hist., Myth., Encom.

1247 **<CEBES>** Phil.
   A.D. 1
001 **Cebetis tabula**, ed. C. Praechter, *Cebetis tabula*.
   Leipzig: Teubner, 1893: 1–34.
   Cod: 4,836: Phil.

2662 **CELSUS** Epigr.
   3 B.C.
x01 **Epigramma dedicatorium**.
   App. Anth. 1.165: Cf. ANTHOLOGIAE GRAE-
   CAE APPENDIX (7052 001).

1248 **CELSUS** Phil.
   A.D. 2
001 **Ἀληθὴς λόγος**, ed. R. Bader, *Der Ἀληθὴς
   λόγος des Kelsos* [*Tübinger Beiträge zur Alter-
   tumswissenschaft* 33. Stuttgart: Kohlhammer,
   1940]: 39–216.
   Q: 23,564: Phil.

1249 **CEPHALION** Hist. et Rhet.
   A.D. 2
001 **Testimonia**, FGrH #93: 2A:436–437.
   NQ: 397: Test.
002 **Fragmenta**, FGrH #93: 2A:438–445.
   Q: 2,266: Hist.

0429 **CEPHISODORUS** Comic.
   5–4 B.C.
001 **Fragmenta**, ed. T. Kock, *Comicorum Atticorum fragmenta*, vol. 1. Leipzig: Teubner,
   1880: 800–802.
   frr. 1, 3–4, 7–9, 11–12 + titulus.
   Q: 90: Comic.
002 **Fragmenta**, ed. A. Meineke, *Fragmenta comicorum Graecorum*, vol. 2.2. Berlin: Reimer,
   1840 (repr. De Gruyter, 1970): 883–886.
   Q: 90: Comic.

1927 **CEPHISODORUS** Hist.
   4 B.C.: Atheniensis vel Thebanus
001 **Fragmenta**, FGrH #112: 2B:524.
   Q: 101: Hist.

0827 **CEPHISOPHON** Med.
   ante A.D. 4
x01 **Fragmentum ap. Oribasium**.
   CMG, vol. 6.2.1, p. 215.
   Cf. ORIBASIUS Med. (0722 003).

1250 **CERCIDAS** Iamb.
   3 B.C.: Megalopolitanus
   Cf. et CHOLIAMBICA ADESPOTA (ALG)
   (1797).
001 **Fragmenta**, ed. J.U. Powell, *Collectanea Alexandrina*. Oxford: Clarendon Press, 1925 (repr.
   1970): 202–218.
   frr. 1–18.
   fr. 17: *P. Lond.* 2.155.
   fr. 18: *P. Heidelb.* inv. 310.
   Q, Pap: 1,202: Iamb.

CERCOPS Epic.
   6 B.C.?: Milesius
   Cf. AEGIMIUS (0668).

2286 **CERCOPS** Phil.
   6 B.C.: Milesius
001 **Testimonium**, ed. H. Diels and W. Kranz, *Die
   Fragmente der Vorsokratiker*, vol. 1, 6th edn.
   Berlin: Weidmann, 1951 (repr. Dublin: 1966):
   105–106.
   NQ: 98: Test.

0151 **CEREALIUS** Epigr.
   A.D. 1/2?
001 **Epigrammata**, AG 11.129, 144.
   Q: 71: Epigr.

1252 ***CERTAMEN HOMERI ET HESIODI***
   3 B.C./A.D. 2
   Cf. et VITAE HOMERI (1805).
001 **Certamen Homeri et Hesiodi** (*P. Petrie* 25),
   ed. T.W. Allen, *Homeri opera*, vol. 5. Oxford:
   Clarendon Press, 1912 (repr. 1969): 225.
   Pap: 198: Narr. Fict.
002 **Certamen Homeri et Hesiodi**, ed. Allen, *op.
   cit.*, 225–238.
   Cod: 2,449: Narr. Fict.

0152 **CHAEREMON** Epigr.
   3 B.C.
001 **Epigrammata**, AG 7.469, 720–721.
   Q: 53: Epigr.

2424 **CHAEREMON** Hist. et Phil.
   A.D. 1: Alexandrinus
001 **Testimonia**, FGrH #618: 3C:145–146.
   NQ: 259: Test.
002 **Fragmenta**, FGrH #618: 3C:146–153.
   Q: 2,436: Hist.

0328 **CHAEREMON** Trag.
   4 B.C.
001 **Fragmenta**, ed. B. Snell, *Tragicorum Graecorum fragmenta*, vol. 1. Göttingen: Vandenhoeck & Ruprecht, 1971: 216–226.
   frr. 1, 2–9, 10–12, 13–14b, 15–33, 35–39, 41–
   42.
   fr. 14b: *P. Hibeh* 2.224.
   Q, Pap: 503: Trag.

1795 **CHAERION** Comic.
   Incertum
001 **Titulus**, ed. T. Kock, *Comicorum Atticorum
   fragmenta*, vol. 3. Leipzig: Teubner, 1888: 366.
   NQ: 3: Comic.

1253 **CHAERIS** Gramm.
   2 B.C.
001 **Fragmenta**, ed. R. Berndt, *De Charete, Chaeride, Alexione grammaticis eorumque reliquiis*,
   pt. 1. Königsberg: Hartung, 1902: 31–46.
   Q: Gramm.

1251 **CHAMAELEON** Phil.
　4–3 B.C.: Heracleota
001 **Fragmenta**, ed. F. Wehrli, *Phainias von Eresos. Chamaileon. Praxiphanes* [*Die Schule des Aristoteles*, vol. 9, 2nd edn. Basel: Schwabe, 1957]: 49–63.
　Περὶ θεῶν: frr. 2a–2b.
　Προτρεπτικός: frr. 3–6.
　Περὶ ἡδονῆς: frr. 7–8.
　Περὶ μέθης: frr. 9–13.
　Homerica. Περὶ Ἰλιάδος. Περὶ Ὀδυσσείας: frr. 14–22.
　Περὶ Ἀλκμᾶνος: frr. 24–25.
　Περὶ Σαπφοῦς: frr. 26–27.
　Περὶ Στησιχόρου: frr. 28–29.1.
　Περὶ Λάσου: fr. 30.
　Περὶ Πινδάρου: frr. 31–32b.
　Περὶ Σιμωνίδου: frr. 33–35.
　Περὶ Ἀνακρέοντος: fr. 36.
　Περὶ Σατύρων: frr. 37a–37c.
　Περὶ Θέσπιδος: fr. 38.
　Περὶ Αἰσχύλου: frr. 39–42.
　Περὶ κωμῳδίας: frr. 43–44.
　Fragmenta incertae sedis: frr. 45–46.
　Q, Pap: 4,081: Phil., Gramm.
002 **Fragmenta**, ed. H.J. Mette, "Die 'Kleinen' griechischen Historiker heute," *Lustrum* 21 (1978) 41.
　frr. 28 bis, 32c.
　fr. 28 bis: *P. Oxy.* 29.2506.
　fr. 32c: *P. Oxy.* 26.2451.
　Pap: 124: Hist.

1254 **CHARAX** Hist.
　A.D. 2?: Pergamenus
001 **Testimonia**, FGrH #103: 2A:482–483.
　NQ: 175: Test.
002 **Fragmenta**, FGrH #103: **2A**:483–493; **3B**:741–742 addenda.
　Q: 2,714: Hist.

1256 **CHARES** Gnom.
　4/3 B.C.
001 **Sententiae**, ed. S. Jaekel, *Menandri sententiae.* Leipzig: Teubner, 1964: 26–30.
　fr. 1: *P. Heidelb.* inv. 434.
　Dup. 1256 002.
　Q, Pap: 211: Gnom., Iamb.
002 **Sententiae**, ed. D. Young (post E. Diehl), *Theognis.* Leipzig: Teubner, 1971: 113–118.
　fr. 2: *P. Heidelb.* inv. 434.
　Dup. 1256 001.
　Q, Pap: 244: Gnom., Iamb.

1850 **CHARES** Gramm.
　1 B.C.: Alexandrinus
001 **Fragmenta**, ed. R. Berndt, *De Charete, Chaeride, Alexione grammaticis eorumque reliquiis*, pt. 1. Königsberg: Hartung, 1902: 18–22.
　frr. 1–5.
　Q: Gramm.

1255 **CHARES** Hist.
　4 B.C.: Mytilenensis
001 **Testimonia**, FGrH #125: 2B:657–658.
　NQ: 60: Test.
002 **Fragmenta**, FGrH #125: 2B:658–665.
　Q: 2,292: Hist.

2263 **CHARICLES** Hist.
　ante A.D. 3
001 **Fragmentum**, FGrH #367: 3B:229.
　Q: 46: Hist.

0788 **CHARICLES** Med.
　A.D. 1
x01 **Fragmenta ap. Galenum.**
　K13.94, 109, 282, 329.
　Cf. GALENUS Med. (0057 076).

0430 **CHARICLIDES** Comic.
　Incertum
001 **Fragmentum**, ed. T. Kock, *Comicorum Atticorum fragmenta*, vol. 3. Leipzig: Teubner, 1888: 393–394.
　fr. 1.
　Q: 10: Comic.
002 **Fragmentum**, ed. A. Meineke, *Fragmenta comicorum Graecorum*, vol. 4. Berlin: Reimer, 1841 (repr. De Gruyter, 1970): 556.
　Q: 9: Comic.

1257 **CHARINUS** Choliamb.
　1 B.C.?
002 **Fragmentum**, ed. H. Lloyd-Jones and P. Parsons, *Supplementum Hellenisticum.* Berlin: De Gruyter, 1983: 146.
　fr. 313.
　Q: 22: Iamb.

0828 **CHARITON** Med.
　ante A.D. 1
x01 **Fragmentum ap. Galenum.**
　K14.180.
　Cf. GALENUS Med. (0057 078).

0554 **CHARITON** Scr. Erot.
　A.D. 2?: Aphrodisiensis
001 **De Chaerea et Callirhoe**, ed. W.E. Blake, *Charitonis Aphrodisiensis de Chaerea et Callirhoe amatoriarum narrationum libri octo.* Oxford: Clarendon Press, 1938: 1–127.
　Cod: 35,523: Narr. Fict.

0829 **CHARIXENES** Med.
　A.D. 1
x01 **Fragmenta ap. Galenum.**
　K12.635, 638, 685; 13.48, 49, 50, 82–83, 102, 108–109.
　Cf. GALENUS Med. (0057 076).
x02 **Fragmentum ap. Aëtium** (lib. 8).
　CMG, vol. 8.2, p. 492.
　Cf. AËTIUS Med. (0718 008).

1258 **CHARON** Hist.
5 B.C.: Lampsacenus
001 **Testimonia**, FGrH #262 & #687b: **3A**:1-2; **3C**:414-415.
NQ: 247: Test.
002 **Fragmenta**, FGrH #262 & #687b: **3A**:2-8; **3C**:415-416.
Q: 2,322: Hist.

2421 **CHARON** Hist.
post 4 B.C.?: Naucratites
001 **Testimonium**, FGrH #612: 3C:120.
NQ: 34: Test.

1259 **<CHARONDAS Nomographus>** <Phil.>
4/2 B.C.: Cataneus
001 **Fragmentum**, ed. H. Thesleff, *The Pythagorean texts of the Hellenistic period.* Åbo: Åbo Akademi, 1965: 60-63.
Q: 870: Phil.

1260 **CHERSIAS** Epic.
6 B.C.
001 **Fragmentum**, ed. G. Kinkel, *Epicorum Graecorum fragmenta*, vol. 1. Leipzig: Teubner, 1877: 207.
Q: 13: Epic.
x01 **Epigramma**.
AG 7.54: Cf. MNASALCES Epigr. (1513 001).

2209 **CHERSIPHRON-METAGENES** Hist.
6 B.C.?
001 **Testimonium**, FGrH #420: 3B:316.
NQ: 21: Test.

1261 **CHILON** <Phil.>
6 B.C.
Cf. et CHILONIS EPISTULA (0386).
Cf. et <SEPTEM SAPIENTES> (1667).
001 **Fragmentum**, ed. T. Bergk, *Poetae lyrici Graeci*, vol. 3. Leipzig: Teubner, 1882: 199.
Q: Lyr.

0386 *CHILONIS EPISTULA*
Incertum
Cf. et CHILON <Phil.> (1261).
001 **Epistula**, ed. R. Hercher, *Epistolographi Graeci.* Paris: Didot, 1873 (repr. Amsterdam: Hakkert, 1965): 193.
Q: 35: Epist.

CHION <Epist.>
4 B.C.: Heracleensis
Cf. CHIONIS EPISTULAE (0041).

0431 **CHIONIDES** Comic.
5 B.C.
001 **Fragmenta**, ed. T. Kock, *Comicorum Atticorum fragmenta*, vol. 1. Leipzig: Teubner, 1880: 4-6.
frr. 1-6, 8 + tituli.
Q: 68: Comic.

002 **Fragmenta**, ed. A. Meineke, *Fragmenta comicorum Graecorum*, vol. 2.1. Berlin: Reimer, 1839 (repr. De Gruyter, 1970): 5-7.
Q: 57: Comic.
003 **Fragmentum**, ed. Meineke, *FCG*, vol. 5.1 (1857; repr. 1970): 14.
Q: 6: Comic.

0041 *CHIONIS EPISTULAE*
A.D. 1
001 **Epistulae**, ed. R. Hercher, *Epistolographi Graeci.* Paris: Didot, 1873 (repr. Amsterdam: Hakkert, 1965): 194-206.
Text to be replaced by Düring edition (cf. 0041 002).
Cod: 4,953: Epist., Narr. Fict.
002 **Epistulae**, ed. I. Düring, *Chion of Heraclea. A novel in letters.* Göteborg: Wettergren & Kerbers, 1951 (repr. New York: Arno, 1979): 44-78.
Cod: Epist., Narr. Fict.

2689 **CHIRISOPHUS** Epigr.
A.D. 2
x01 **Epigramma sepulcrale**.
App. Anth. 2.631: Cf. ANTHOLOGIAE GRAECAE APPENDIX (7052 002).

1263 **CHOERILUS** Epic.
5 B.C.: Samius
001 **Tituli** (*P. Oxy.* 11.1399), ed. J.U. Powell, *Collectanea Alexandrina.* Oxford: Clarendon Press, 1925 (repr. 1970): 250.
Dup. partim 1263 003.
Pap: 4: Epic.
002 **Fragmenta**, ed. G. Kinkel, *Epicorum Graecorum fragmenta*, vol. 1. Leipzig: Teubner, 1877: 266-271.
frr. 1-4, 6-10.
Dup. partim 1263 003-004.
Q: 166: Epic.
003 **Fragmenta et tituli**, ed. H. Lloyd-Jones and P. Parsons, *Supplementum Hellenisticum.* Berlin: De Gruyter, 1983: 146-151.
frr. 314, 316-320, 322-324.
frr. 314, 324: *P. Oxy.* 11.1399.
Dup. 1263 001-002.
Q, Pap: 153: Epic.
004 **Fragmenta dubia** (fort. auctore Choerilo Iasensi), ed. Lloyd-Jones and Parsons, *op. cit.,* 152.
frr. 329-330.
Dup. partim 1263 002.
Q: 26: Epic.
x01 **Epigrammata**.
AG 7.325; 16.27: Cf. ANONYMI EPIGRAMMATICI (AG) (0138 001).
x02 **De Persia** (fort. auctore Choerilo Samio) (*P. Oxy.* 37.2814).
Cf. ADDITAMENTA (FGrH) (2433 053).

1262 CHOERILUS Epic.
4 B.C.: Iasensis
Cf. et CHOERILUS Epic. (1263 004).
001 **Fragmentum,** ed. G. Kinkel, *Epicorum Grae-*
corum fragmenta, vol. 1. Leipzig: Teubner,
1877: 309.
Dup. partim 1262 002 (fr. 335).
Q: 56: Epigr.
002 **Fragmentum et titulus,** ed. H. Lloyd-Jones and
P. Parsons, *Supplementum Hellenisticum.* Ber-
lin: De Gruyter, 1983: 154–155.
frr. 334–335.
Dup. partim 1262 001.
Q: 62: Epigr.
x01 **Epigramma sepulcrale.**
App. Anth. 2.130(?): Cf. ANTHOLOGIAE
GRAECAE APPENDIX (7052 002).
Dup. 1262 001–002.

0302 CHOERILUS Trag.
5 B.C.: Atheniensis
001 **Fragmenta,** ed. B. Snell, *Tragicorum Grae-*
corum fragmenta, vol. 1. Göttingen: Vandenhoeck & Ruprecht, 1971: 67–68.
frr. 1–3.
Q: 33: Trag., Epic.

4093 Georgius CHOEROBOSCUS Gramm.
A.D. 5/9: Constantinopolitanus
001 **Prolegomena et scholia in Theodosii Alexan-**
drini canones isagogicos de flexione nominum,
ed. A. Hilgard, *Grammatici Graeci,* vol. 4.1.
Leipzig: Teubner, 1894 (repr. Hildesheim:
Olms, 1965): 103–417.
Cod: 123,678: Gramm., Comm.
002 **Prolegomena et scholia in Theodosii Alexan-**
drini canones isagogicos de flexione verborum,
ed. Hilgard, *Gramm. Graec.,* vol. 4.2 (1894;
repr. 1965): 1–371.
Cod: 135,911: Gramm., Comm.

1797 CHOLIAMBICA ADESPOTA (ALG)
3 B.C.?
001 **Anonymus in turpilucrum** (fort. auctore Cer-
cida), ed. E. Diehl, *Anthologia lyrica Graeca,*
fasc. 3, 3rd edn. Leipzig: Teubner, 1952: 131–
136.
Dup. partim CERCIDAS Iamb. (1250 001).
Pap: 500: Iamb.
002 **Fragmenta choliambica,** ed. Diehl, *op. cit.,*
139–140.
Q: 59: Iamb.

CHOLIAMBICA ADESPOTA (CA)
CA, p. 190.
Cf. LYRICA ADESPOTA (CA) (0230 001).

1267 CHRISTI EPISTULA
Incertum
x01 **Fragmentum ap. Eusebium.**
HE 1.13.10.
Cf. EUSEBIUS Scr. Eccl. et Theol. (2018 002).

2119 CHRISTODORUS Epic.
A.D. 5–6: Coptites
001 **Fragmenta,** ed. E. Heitsch, *Die griechischen*
Dichterfragmente der römischen Kaiserzeit, vol.
2. Göttingen: Vandenhoeck & Ruprecht, 1964:
48.
frr. 1–2.
Dup. partim 2119 004.
Q: 20: Epic.
002 **Epigrammata,** AG **2**; **7**.697–698.
Q: 2,719: Epigr.
003 **Testimonium,** FGrH #283: 3A:161.
NQ: 72: Test.
004 **Fragmentum,** FGrH #283: 3A:161.
Dup. partim 2119 001.
Q: 35: Hist., Epic.

4007 CHRISTOPHORUS Rhet.
fiq Christophorus Mytilenensis Poeta
post A.D. 11
001 **Commentarium in Hermogenis librum** περὶ
στάσεων (excerpta e cod. Messanensi S. Salv.
119), ed. H. Rabe, "De Christophori commentario in Hermogenis librum περὶ στάσεων,"
Rheinisches Museum **50** (1895) 243–249; **54**
(1899) 633.
Q: Rhet., Comm.

2371 CHRONICON PASCHALE
vel *Chronicon Alexandrinum* vel *Chronicon*
Constantinopolitanum vel *Fasti Siculi*
A.D. 7
001 **Chronicon paschale,** ed. L. Dindorf, *Chronicon*
paschale, vol. 1 [*Corpus scriptorum historiae*
Byzantinae. Bonn: Weber, 1832]: 3–737.
Cod: 126,707: Hist., Chronogr.

2195 [CHRYSERMUS] Hist.
Incertum: Corinthius
001 **Fragmenta,** FGrH #287: 3A:168–170.
Q: 558: Hist., Nat. Hist.

0830 CHRYSERMUS Med.
1 B.C.
x01 **Fragmenta ap. Galenum.**
K**8**.741; **13**.243.
Cf. GALENUS Med. (0057, 059, 076).

1922 CHRYSERUS Hist.
A.D. 2
001 **Testimonium,** FGrH #96: 2A:446.
NQ: 35: Test.
002 **Fragmentum,** FGrH #96: 2A:447.
Q: 273: Hist.

2559 [CHRYSIPPUS] Hist.
Incertum
001 **Fragmentum,** FGrH #832: 3C:901–902.
Q: 57: Hist.

0831 CHRYSIPPUS Med.
4 B.C.: fort. Cnidius

x01 **Fragmentum ap. Rufum.**
Daremberg-Ruelle, pp. 6–7.
Cf. RUFUS Med. (0564 001).

1264 **CHRYSIPPUS** Phil.
3 B.C.: Soleus
001 **Fragmenta logica et physica,** ed. J. von Arnim,
Stoicorum veterum fragmenta, vol. 2. Leipzig:
Teubner, 1903 (repr. Stuttgart: 1968): 1–348.
Testimonia (frr. 1–12): pp. 1–4.
Scripta (frr. 13–34): pp. 4–12.
Prolegomena philosophiae (frr. 35–44): pp.
15–17.
Logica (frr. 45–51): pp. 18–20.
De cognitione doctrina (frr. 52–121): pp. 21–
37.
Dialectica (frr. 122–287): pp. 38–94.
De rhetorica (frr. 288–298): pp. 95–96.
Λογικὰ ζητήματα (fr. 298a): pp. 96–110.
Physicae doctrinae fundamenta (frr. 299–521):
pp. 111–166.
De mundo (frr. 522–645): pp. 167–194.
De caelestibus et meteoris (frr. 646–707): pp.
195–203.
De animalibus et plantis (frr. 708–772): pp.
204–216.
De anima hominis (frr. 773–911): pp. 217–
263.
De fato (frr. 912–1007): pp. 264–298.
De natura deorum (frr. 1008–1105): pp. 299–
321.
De providentia et natura artifice (frr. 1106–
1186): pp. 322–341.
De divinatione (frr. 1187–1216): pp. 342–348.
Dup. partim 1264 006.
Q, Pap: 129,854: Phil., Rhet., Nat. Hist.
002 **Fragmenta moralia,** ed. von Arnim, *op. cit.,*
vol. 3 (1903; repr. 1968): 3–191.
Testimonium (fr. 1): p. 3.
De fine bonorum (frr. 2–67): pp. 3–16.
De bonis et malis (frr. 68–116): pp. 17–27.
De indifferentibus (frr. 117–168): pp. 28–39.
De appetitu et selectione (frr. 169–196): pp.
40–47.
De virtute (frr. 197–307): pp. 48–75.
De jure et lege (frr. 308–376): pp. 76–91.
De affectibus (frr. 377–490): pp. 92–133.
De actionibus (frr. 491–543): pp. 134–145.
De sapiente et insipiente (frr. 544–684): pp.
146–171.
Vitae agendae praecepta (frr. 685–768): pp.
172–191.
Q, Pap: 71,607: Phil.
003 **Fragmenta quae ad explicationem carminum
Homericorum pertinent,** ed. von Arnim, *op.
cit.,* vol. 3, 192–193.
frr. 769–777.
Q: 320: Comm.
004 **Fragmenta ad singulos libros relata,** ed. von
Arnim, *op. cit.,* vol. 3, 194–200, 202–204.
tractatus 9–10, 12, 17, 25, 28, 45, 47, 57.
Dup. partim 1264 005 (fr. 338).
Q: 1,931: Phil., Epigr.

005 **Fragmenta poetica,** ed. H. Lloyd-Jones and P.
Parsons, *Supplementum Hellenisticum.* Berlin:
De Gruyter, 1983: 158.
frr. 336–338.
Dup. partim 1264 004 (p. 200).
Q: 56: Iamb., Hexametr., Epigr.
006 **Fragmenta** (*P. Herc.* 307), ed. L. Marrone,
"Nuove letture nel P. Herc. 307 (questioni
logiche di Crisippo)," *Cronache Ercolanesi* 12
(1982) 15–18.
Dup. partim 1264 001 (fr. 298a).
Pap: Phil., Rhet.
007 **Fragmentum,** ed. J. Mansfeld, "Techne: a new
fragment of Chrysippus," *Greek, Roman and
Byzantine studies* 24 (1983) 57.
Q: Phil., Rhet.
x01 **Epigramma sepulcrale.**
App. Anth. 2.131?: Cf. ANTHOLOGIAE
GRAECAE APPENDIX (7052 002).
Dup. 1264 005 (fr. 338).

1265 **CHRYSIPPUS** Scriptor Rei Coquinariae
A.D. 1: Tyanensis
x01 **Fragmentum ap. Athenaeum.**
Deipnosophistae 14.647c–648a.
Cf. ATHENAEUS Soph. (0008 001).

9008 **Macarius CHRYSOCEPHALUS** Paroemiogr.
A.D. 14: Philadelphius
001 **Paroemiae,** ed. E.L. von Leutsch, *Corpus paroemiographorum Graecorum,* vol. 2. Göttingen:
Vandenhoeck & Ruprecht, 1851 (repr. Hildesheim: Olms, 1958): 135–227.
Cod: 8,146: Paroem.

2165 **Marcus Tullius CICERO** Orat.
2–1 B.C.: Arpinius
001 **Testimonia,** FGrH #235 & #648: **2B:**987;
3C:203.
NQ: 199: Test.
002 **Fragmenta,** FGrH #235: **2B:**987–988.
Q: 286: Hist.

CINAETHON Epic.
7 B.C.?: Lacedaemonius
Cf. ILIAS PARVA (1444).
Cf. OEDIPODEA (1547).

2543 **Lucius CINCIUS ALIMENTUS** Hist.
3 B.C.: Romanus
001 **Testimonia,** FGrH #810: **3C:**876–877.
NQ: 431: Test.
002 **Fragmenta,** FGrH #810: **3C:**877–880.
Q: 995: Hist.

2417 **CINEAS** Rhet.
4/3 B.C.?: Thessalius
001 **Testimonia,** FGrH #603: **3B:**736–737.
NQ: 177: Test.
002 **Fragmenta,** FGrH #603: **3B:**737.
Q: 162: Hist.

0375 **CINESIAS** Lyr.
5-4 B.C.: Atheniensis
001 **Fragmentum**, ed. D.L. Page, *Poetae melici Graeci*. Oxford: Clarendon Press, 1962 (repr. 1967 (1st edn. corr.)): 398.
fr. 2.
Q: 2: Lyr.
002 **Titulus**, ed. Page, *op. cit.*, 398.
fr. 1.
NQ: 2: Lyr.

4057 **CLAUDIANUS** Epigr.
A.D. 5-6?
001 **Epigrammata**, AG 1.19-20; **9**.139.
Q: 125: Epigr.

4056 **Claudius CLAUDIANUS** Poeta
A.D. 4-5: Alexandrinus, Romanus
001 **Epigrammata**, AG **5**.86; **9**.140, 753-754.
Q: 76: Epigr.
002 **Testimonia**, FGrH #282: 3A:161.
NQ: 30: Test.

1268 **CLAUDIUS** Hist.
A.D. 1?: Iolaus
001 **Fragmenta**, FGrH #788: 3C:800-801.
Q: 358: Hist.

1971 **CLAUDIUS EUSTHENIUS** Hist.
A.D. 4?
001 **Fragmentum**, FGrH #218: 2B:948.
Q: 34: Hist.

2184 **CLAUDIUS Imperator**
1 B.C.-A.D. 1: Romanus
001 **Testimonia**, FGrH #276: 3A:155-156.
NQ: 317: Test.
002 **Fragmenta**, FGrH #276: 3A:156-157.
Q: 307: Hist.

0332 **CLEAENETUS** Trag.
4 B.C.
001 **Fragmenta**, ed. B. Snell, *Tragicorum Graecorum fragmenta*, vol. 1. Göttingen: Vandenhoeck & Ruprecht, 1971: 251.
frr. 1-2.
Q: 18: Trag.

1269 **CLEANTHES** Phil.
4-3 B.C.: Assius
001 **Fragmenta**, ed. J.U. Powell, *Collectanea Alexandrina*. Oxford: Clarendon Press, 1925 (repr. 1970): 227-231.
frr. 1-10.
Q: 490: Hymn., Hexametr., Iamb.
002 **Testimonia et fragmenta**, ed. J. von Arnim, *Stoicorum veterum fragmenta*, vol. 1. Leipzig: Teubner, 1903 (repr. Stuttgart: 1968): 103-137.
Testimonia (frr. 463-480): pp. 103-106.
Scripta (fr. 481): pp. 106-108.
Placita (fr. 482): p. 108.

Logica et rhetorica (frr. 483-492): pp. 108-110.
Physica et theologica (frr. 493-551): pp. 110-125.
Moralia (frr. 552-619): pp. 125-137.
Q: 9,944: Phil., Rhet., Doxogr., Gnom., Hexametr., Iamb.
x01 **Epigrammata exhortatoria et supplicatoria.**
App. Anth. 4.34-35: Cf. ANTHOLOGIAE GRAECAE APPENDIX (7052 004).
Dup. partim 1269 001 (fr. 2).

0432 **CLEARCHUS** Comic.
4 B.C.
001 **Fragmenta**, ed. T. Kock, *Comicorum Atticorum fragmenta*, vol. 2. Leipzig: Teubner, 1884: 408-410.
frr. 1-5.
Q: 104: Comic.
002 **Fragmenta**, ed. A. Meineke, *Fragmenta comicorum Graecorum*, vol. 4. Berlin: Reimer, 1841 (repr. De Gruyter, 1970): 562-564.
Q: 106: Comic.

2730 **CLEARCHUS** Epigr.
Incertum
x01 **Aenigma.**
App. Anth. 7.15: Cf. ANTHOLOGIAE GRAECAE APPENDIX (7052 007).

1270 **CLEARCHUS** Phil.
4-3 B.C.: Soleus
001 **Fragmenta**, ed. F. Wehrli, *Klearchos [Die Schule des Aristoteles*, vol. 3, 2nd edn. Basel: Schwabe, 1969]: 9-40.
Περὶ τῶν ἐν τῇ Πλάτωνος πολιτείᾳ μαθηματικῶς εἰρημένων: frr. 3-4.
Περὶ ὕπνου: frr. 5-9.
᾿Αρκεσίλαος: frr. 11-12.
Περὶ παιδείας: frr. 13-16.
Περὶ φιλίας: frr. 17-18.
Γεργίθιος: frr. 19-20.
Erotica: frr. 21-35.
Περὶ τοῦ πανικοῦ: fr. 36.
Περὶ βίων: frr. 37-62.
Proverbia: frr. 63-83.
Aenigmata: frr. 85-95b.
Optica (?): fr. 96.
De luna: fr. 97.
Περὶ θινῶν: fr. 98.
Lithica: fr. 99.
Botanica: fr. 100.
Περὶ τῶν ἐνύδρων. Περὶ νάρκης: frr. 101-105.
Περὶ σκελετῶν: frr. 106-110.
Dubia et spuria: frr. 111-115 (fr. 113 = Tactica).
Q: 10,499: Phil., Nat. Hist., Paroem.

2147 **CLEMENS** Hist.
Incertum
001 **Testimonium**, FGrH #102: 2A:482.
NQ: 21: Test.

0834 Flavius CLEMENS <Med.>
A.D. 1?

x01 **Fragmentum ap. Galenum.**
K13.1026.
Cf. GALENUS Med. (0057 077).

0555 CLEMENS ALEXANDRINUS Theol.
A.D. 2-3: Alexandrinus
Scholia: Cf. SCHOLIA IN CLEMENTEM
ALEXANDRINUM (5048).

001 **Protrepticus**, ed. C. Mondésert, *Clément d'Alexandrie. Le protreptique*, 2nd edn. [*Sources chrétiennes* 2. Paris: Cerf, 1949]: 52–193.
Cod: 23,716: Phil., Theol.

002 **Paedagogus**, ed. H.-I. Marrou, M. Harl, C. Mondésert and C. Matray, *Clement d'Alexandrie. Le pédagogue*, 3 vols. [*Sources chrétiennes* 70, 108, 158. Paris: Cerf, 1:1960; 2:1965; 3:1970]: 1:108–294; 2:10–242; 3:12–190.
Cod: 57,864: Phil., Theol.

003 **Hymnus Christi servatoris**, ed. C. Mondésert and C. Matray, *Clément d'Alexandrie. Le pédagogue*, vol. 3 [*Sources chrétiennes* 158. Paris: Cerf, 1970]: 192–202.
Cod: 150: Hymn.

004 **Stromata**, ed. O. Stählin, L. Früchtel and U. Treu, *Clemens Alexandrinus*, vols. 2, 3rd edn. & 3, 2nd edn. [*Die griechischen christlichen Schriftsteller* 52(15), 17. Berlin: Akademie-Verlag, 2:1960; 3:1970]: 2:3–518; 3:3–102.
Cod: 166,077: Phil., Theol.

005 **Eclogae propheticae**, ed. Stählin, Früchtel and Treu, *op. cit.*, vol. 3, 137–155.
Cod: 5,098: Phil., Theol.

006 **Quis dives salvetur**, ed. Stählin, Früchtel, and Treu, *op. cit.*, vol. 3, 159–191.
Cod: 9,411: Homilet.

007 **Excerpta ex Theodoto**, ed. F. Sagnard, *Clément d'Alexandrie. Extraits de Théodote*, 2nd edn. [*Sources chrétiennes* 23. Paris: Cerf, 1948 (repr. 1970)]: 52–212.
Cod: 7,691: Theol.

008 **Fragmenta**, ed. Stählin, Früchtel and Treu, *op. cit.*, vol. 3, 195–202, 212, 216–230.
Hypotheses (frr. 1–23): pp. 195–202.
In epistula Joannis prima (fr. 24): p. 212.
De pascha (frr. 25–26, 28–35): pp. 216–218.
Κανὼν ἐκκλησιαστικὸς ἢ πρὸς τοὺς ἰουδαΐζοντας (fr. 36): pp. 218–219.
Περὶ προνοίας (frr. 37–43): pp. 219–221.
Ὁ προτρεπτικὸς εἰς ὑπομονὴν ἢ πρὸς τοὺς νεωστὶ βεβαπτισμένους (fr. 44): pp. 221–223.
Epistulae (frr. 45–47): pp. 223–224.
Fragmenta incertae sedis (frr. 48–49, 51–68, 70–74): pp. 224–230.
fr. 44: Dup. partim GREGORIUS NAZIANZENUS Theol. (2022 066).
fr. 44: Dup. partim Pseudo-MACARIUS Scr. Eccl. (2109 001) (sermo 62).
fr. 44: Dup. partim MAXIMUS CONFESSOR Theol. et Poeta (2892 081).

Q, Cod: 5,959: Exeget., Homilet., Epist., Hypoth.

1271 CLEMENS ROMANUS Theol. et *CLEMENTINA*
A.D. 1: Romanus

001 **Epistula i ad Corinthios**, ed. A. Jaubert, *Clément de Rome. Épître aux Corinthiens* [*Sources chrétiennes* 167. Paris: Cerf, 1971]: 98–204.
Cod: 10,302: Epist.

002 **Epistula ii ad Corinthios** [Sp.], ed. K. Bihlmeyer and W. Schneemelcher (post F.X. Funk), *Die apostolischen Väter*, 3rd edn. Tübingen: Mohr, 1970: 71–81.
Cod: 3,161: Epist.

003 **Epistula Petri ad Jacobum** [Sp.], ed. B. Rehm, J. Irmscher and F. Paschke, *Die Pseudoklementinen I. Homilien*, 2nd edn. [*Die griechischen christlichen Schriftsteller* 42. Berlin: Akademie-Verlag, 1969]: 1–2.
Cod: 510: Epist.

004 **Contestatio** [Sp.], ed. Rehm, Irmscher, and Paschke, *op. cit.*, 2–4.
Cod: 677: Narr. Fict.

005 **Epistula Clementis ad Jacobum** [Sp.], ed. Rehm, Irmscher, and Paschke, *op. cit.*, 5–22.
Cod: 2,563: Epist.

006 **Homiliae** [Sp.], ed. Rehm, Irmscher, and Paschke, *op. cit.*, 23–281.
Cod: 72,713: Narr. Fict.

007 **Recognitiones** [Sp.], ed. B. Rehm and F. Paschke, *Die Pseudoklementinen II. Rekognitionen* [*Die griechischen christlichen Schriftsteller* 51. Berlin: Akademie-Verlag, 1965]: 64, 116, 152, 225–226, 234–237, 242–244, 267, 268, 330–334, 342–344.
Q: 1,687: Narr. Fict.

008 **Recognitiones** (ex Eusebio) [Sp.], ed. Rehm and Paschke, *op. cit.*, 270, 272, 274, 276, 278, 280, 282, 284, 286, 288, 290, 292, 294, 296, 298, 300, 302, 304, 306, 308, 310, 312, 314, 316.
Q: 1,795: Narr. Fict.

009 **Recognitiones** (e Pseudo-Caesario) [Sp.], ed. Rehm and Paschke, *op. cit.*, 271, 273, 275, 277, 279, 281, 283, 287, 289, 291, 293, 295, 297, 299, 301, 303, 307, 309.
Q: 1,239: Narr. Fict.

010 **Epistulae de virginitate** [Sp.], ed. F.X. Funk and F. Diekamp, *Patres apostolici*, vol. 2, 3rd edn. Tübingen: Laupp, 1913: 1–45.
Q: 2,254: Epist.

011 **Pseudo-Clementina** (epitome altera auctore Symeone Metaphrasta) [Sp.], ed. A.R.M. Dressel, *Clementinorum epitomae duae*, 2nd edn. Leipzig: Hinrichs, 1873: 2–118.
Cod: 25,983: Narr. Fict.

012 **Pseudo-Clementina** (epitome de gestis Petri praemetaphrastica) [Sp.], ed. Dressel, *op. cit.*, 122–232.
Cod: 26,605: Narr. Fict.

0622 **CLEOBULI EPISTULA**
Incertum
Cf. et CLEOBULUS Lyr. et Epigr. (1274).
001 **Epistula**, ed. R. Hercher, *Epistolographi Graeci*.
Paris: Didot, 1873 (repr. Amsterdam: Hakkert,
1965): 207.
Q: 37: Epist.

0244 **CLEOBULINA** Scriptor Aenigmatum
6 B.C.: Lindia
001 **Fragmenta**, ed. M.L. West, *Iambi et elegi
Graeci*, vol. 2. Oxford: Clarendon Press, 1972:
50–51.
frr. 1–3.
Q: 38: Eleg.
x01 **Epigramma**.
AG 14.101: Cf. CLEOBULUS Lyr. et Epigr.
(1274 002).
x02 **Epigramma exhortatorium et supplicatorium**.
App. Anth. 4.8: Cf. ANTHOLOGIAE GRAE-
CAE APPENDIX (7052 004).
Dup. partim 0244 001 (fr. 2).

1274 **CLEOBULUS** Lyr. et Epigr.
7–6 B.C.: Lindius
Cf. et CLEOBULI EPISTULA (0622).
Cf. et CLEOBULINA Scriptor Aenigmatum
(0244).
Cf. et <SEPTEM SAPIENTES> (1667).
001 **Fragmenta**, ed. T. Bergk, *Poetae lyrici Graeci*,
vol. 3, 4th edn. Leipzig: Teubner, 1882: 201–
202.
frr. 1–2.
Q: 52: Lyr., Epigr.
002 **Epigrammata**, AG 7.153; 14.101.
Dup. partim 1274 001.
Q: 65: Epigr.

0835 **CLEOBULUS** Med.
ante A.D. 2
x01 **Fragmentum ap. Galenum**.
K13.854.
Cf. GALENUS Med. (0057 077).

2490 **CLEODEMUS-MALCHUS** Hist.
vel Cleodemus vel Malchus
ante 2 B.C.
001 **Fragmentum**, FGrH #727: 3C:686–687.
Q: 196: Hist.

2614 **CLEOMACHUS** Poeta
ante A.D. 2: Magnes
001 **Fragmenta**, ed. H. Lloyd-Jones and P. Parsons,
Supplementum Hellenisticum. Berlin: De Gruyter, 1983: 162.
frr. 341–342.
Q: 13: Poem.

1272 **CLEOMEDES** Astron.
A.D. 2
001 **De motu circulari corporum caelestium**, ed. H.
Ziegler, *Cleomedis de motu circulari corporum*

caelestium libri duo. Leipzig: Teubner, 1891:
2–228.
Cod: 24,880: Astron.

0900 **CLEOMENES** Lyr.
5 B.C.: Rheginus
001 **Titulus**, ed. D.L. Page, *Poetae melici Graeci*.
Oxford: Clarendon Press, 1962 (repr. 1967 (1st
edn. corr.)): 442.
fr. 1.
NQ: 2: Lyr., Hymn.

2411 **CLEOMENES III Rex Lacedaemonis** Hist.
3 B.C.: Lacedaemonius
001 **Fragmentum**, FGrH #598: 3B:730–731.
Q: 377: Hist.

1273 **CLEON** Eleg.
4 B.C.: Siculus vel Curiensis
001 **Fragmentum**, ed. E. Diehl, *Anthologia lyrica
Graeca*, fasc. 1, 3rd edn. Leipzig: Teubner,
1949: 128.
Dup. partim 1273 002 (fr. 340).
Q: 12: Eleg.
002 **Fragmenta et titulus**, ed. H. Lloyd-Jones and
P. Parsons, *Supplementum Hellenisticum*. Berlin: De Gruyter, 1983: 159–161.
frr. 339–340.
fr. 339a: *P. Mich.* inv. 1316.
Dup. partim 1273 001.
Q, Pap: 222: Eleg., Epic., Comm.

0836 **CLEON** Med.
1 B.C.?
x01 **Fragmenta ap. Oribasium**.
CMG, vol. 6.3, pp. 102, 104.
Cf. ORIBASIUS Med. (0722 004).
x02 **Fragmentum ap. Paulum**.
CMG, vol. 9.2, p. 342.
Cf. PAULUS Med. (0715 001).
x03 **Fragmentum ap. Aëtium** (lib. 7).
CMG, vol. 8.2, p. 375.
Cf. AËTIUS Med. (0718 007).

0837 **CLEONIACUS** Med.
vel Cloniacus
ante A.D. 2
x01 **Fragmentum ap. Galenum**.
K13.987–988.
Cf. GALENUS Med. (0057 077).

0361 **CLEONIDES** Mus.
A.D. 2
001 **Introductio harmonica**, ed. H. Menge, *Euclidis
opera omnia*, vol. 8. Leipzig: Teubner, 1916:
186–222.
Cod: 3,791: Mus.

0684 **CLEOPATRA VII PHILOPATOR** <Med.>
1 B.C.
x01 **Fragmenta ap. Galenum**.
K12.403–405, 432–434, 492–493.
Cf. GALENUS Med. (0057 076).

x02 **Fragmentum ap. Pseudo-Galenum.**
K19.767–771, ed. Hultsch, vol. 1, pp. 233–236.
Cf. Pseudo-GALENUS Med. (0530 022).

x03 **Fragmentum ap. Aëtium** (lib. 8).
CMG, vol. 8.2, p. 408.
Cf. AËTIUS Med. (0718 008).

0821 **CLEOPHANTUS** Med.
1 B.C.
Cf. et ANTIPATER et CLEOPHANTUS Med.
(0832).

x01 **Fragmenta ap. Galenum.**
K13.262, 310, 985.
Cf. GALENUS Med. (0057 076–077).

x02 **Fragmenta ap. Soranum.**
CMG, vol. 4, pp. 129–130.
Cf. SORANUS Med. (0565 001).

1087 **CLEOPHON** Trag.
4 B.C.: Atheniensis

001 **Tituli,** ed. B. Snell, *Tragicorum Graecorum
fragmenta,* vol. 1. Göttingen: Vandenhoeck &
Ruprecht, 1971: 247.
NQ: 11: Trag.

1275 **CLEOSTRATUS** Poet. Phil.
6 B.C.: Tenedius

001 **Testimonia,** ed. H. Diels and W. Kranz, *Die
Fragmente der Vorsokratiker,* vol. 1, 6th edn.
Berlin: Weidmann, 1951 (repr. Dublin: 1966):
41.
test. 1–4.
NQ: 140: Test.

002 **Fragmenta,** ed. Diels and Kranz, *op. cit.,* 41–
42.
fr. 1–4.
Q: 130: Astron., Phil., Hexametr.

1276 **CLIDEMUS** Hist.
vel Clitodemus
4 B.C.: Atheniensis

001 **Testimonia,** FGrH #323: 3B:51.
NQ: 117: Test.

002 **Fragmenta,** FGrH #323: 3B:51–60, 757 addenda.
Q: 2,699: Hist.

2305 **CLIDEMUS** Phil.
5 B.C.: Atheniensis

001 **Testimonia,** ed. H. Diels and W. Kranz, *Die
Fragmente der Vorsokratiker,* vol. 2, 6th edn.
Berlin: Weidmann, 1952 (repr. Dublin: 1966):
50.
test. 1–6.
NQ: 324: Test.

2441 **CLINIAS** Hist.
3 B.C.?

001 **Testimonium,** FGrH #819: 3C:894.
NQ: 46: Test.

1277 **<CLINIAS>** Phil.
4 B.C.: Tarentinus

001 **Fragmenta,** ed. H. Thesleff, *The Pythagorean
texts of the Hellenistic period.* Åbo: Åbo Akademi, 1965: 108.
Q: 292: Phil., Math.

002 **Testimonia,** ed. H. Diels and W. Kranz, *Die
Fragmente der Vorsokratiker,* vol. 1, 6th edn.
Berlin: Weidmann, 1951 (repr. Dublin: 1966):
443–444.
test. 1–6: auctores alii nominantur Prorus et
Amyclas.
NQ: 201: Test.

4256 **CLINOMACHUS** Phil.
4 B.C.?: Thurius, Atheniensis

001 **Testimonium,** ed. K. Döring, *Die Megariker
[Studien zur antiken Philosophie* 2. Amsterdam: Grüner, 1972]: 11, 12, 13, 15, 62.
test. 32a, 34, 35, 40, 49, 203b.
test. 32a, 34, 35, 40 (pp. 11–13) = Euclides
(4247 001).
test. 49 (p. 15) = Clinomachus.
test. 203b (p. 62) = Bryson (4276 001).
NQ: Test.

1278 **CLITARCHUS** Gnom.
Incertum

001 **Sententiae,** ed. H. Chadwick, *The sentences of
Sextus.* Cambridge: Cambridge University
Press, 1959: 76–83.
Cod: 1,199: Gnom.

1279 **CLITARCHUS** Hist.
fiq Clitarchus Phil.
4 B.C.: Alexandrinus

001 **Testimonia,** FGrH #137: 2B:741–743.
Dup. partim CLITARCHUS Phil. (4273 001)
(test. 164a).
NQ: 537: Test.

002 **Fragmenta,** FGrH #137: 2B:743–752.
fr. 32: *P. Oxy.* 2.218.
Q, Pap: 2,925: Hist.

4273 **CLITARCHUS** Phil.
fiq Clitarchus Hist.
4 B.C.: Atheniensis

001 **Testimonium,** ed. K. Döring, *Die Megariker
[Studien zur antiken Philosophie* 2. Amsterdam: Grüner, 1972]: 52, 61.
test. 164a = Stilpo (4262 001).
Dup. partim CLITARCHUS Hist. (1279 001)
(test. 3).
NQ: Test.

1280 **CLITOMACHUS** Phil.
2 B.C.

x01 **Fragmenta ap. Stobaeum.**
Anth. III.7.55; **IV.**34.67; 41.29.
Cf. Joannes STOBAEUS (2037 001).

2190 **[CLITONYMUS]** Hist.
Incertum

001 **Fragmenta,** FGrH #292: 3A:176.
Q: 196: Hist., Nat. Hist.

1281 **[CLITOPHON]** Hist.
Incertum: Rhodius
001 **Fragmenta**, FGrH #293: 3A:176–177.
Q: 335: Hist., Nat. Hist.

1282 **CLYTUS** Hist.
4 B.C.: Milesius
001 **Fragmenta**, FGrH #490: 3B:457–458.
Q: 289: Hist.

4244 **COCONDRIUS** Rhet.
Incertum
001 Περὶ τρόπων, ed. L. Spengel, *Rhetores Graeci*,
vol. 3. Leipzig: Teubner, 1856 (repr. Frankfurt
am Main: Minerva, 1966): 230–243.
Cod: Rhet.

0838 **CODAMUS vel NICOMEDES Rex Bithyniae**
<Med.>
ante A.D. 2
x01 **Fragmentum ap. Galenum.**
K13.929.
Cf. GALENUS Med. (0057 077).

0839 **CODIUS TUCUS** Med.
ante 1 B.C.?
x01 **Fragmentum ap. Galenum.**
K14.147.
Cf. GALENUS Med. (0057 078).

4081 **COLLUTHUS** Epic.
A.D. 5: Lycopolitanus
001 **Raptio Helenae**, ed. A.W. Mair, *Oppian, Colluthus, Tryphiodorus*. Cambridge, Mass.: Harvard University Press, 1928 (repr. 1963): 542–
570.
Cod: 2,346: Epic.

1283 **COLOTES** Phil.
4–3 B.C.: Lampsacenus
001 **Fragmenta**, ed. W. Crönert, *Kolotes und Menedemos*. Leipzig: Avenarius, 1906 (repr. Amsterdam: Hakkert, 1965): 5–7, 163–170.
Pap: Phil.

1841 **COMANUS** Gramm.
2 B.C.: Naucratites
001 **Fragmenta**, ed. A.R. Dyck, *The fragments of
Comanus of Naucratis [Sammlung griechischer
und lateinischer Grammatiker* 7. Berlin: De
Gruyter, 1988]: 233–261.
Q, Pap: Gramm.
x01 **Fragmentum grammaticum** (*P. Yale* 1.25 [inv.
446]) (fort. epitome operis Comani).
Wouters, pp. 49–52.
Cf. ANONYMI GRAMMATICI (0072 003).

1284 **COMARCHUS** Hist.
3 B.C.?
001 **Fragmentum**, FGrH #410: 3B:303.
Q: 118: Hist.

2632 **COMARIUS** Alchem.
vel Comerius
A.D. 1?
001 **De lapide philosophorum** (fragmenta), ed. M.
Berthelot, *Collection des anciens alchimistes
grecs*. Paris: Steinheil, 1887 (repr. London:
Holland Press, 1963): 289–299.
Cod: Alchem.

4058 **COMETAS Chartularius** Epigr.
fiq Cometas Grammaticus
fiq Cometas Scholasticus
A.D. 6?
Cf. et COMETAS Grammaticus Epigr. (4059).
Cf. et COMETAS Scholasticus Epigr. (4060).
001 **Epigrammata**, AG 5.265; 9.586.
Q: 78: Epigr.

4059 **COMETAS Grammaticus** Epigr.
fiq Cometas Chartularius
fiq Cometas Scholasticus
A.D. 9
Cf. et COMETAS Chartularius Epigr. (4058).
Cf. et COMETAS Scholasticus Epigr. (4060).
001 **Epigrammata**, AG 15.36–38, 40.
Q: 463: Epigr.

4060 **COMETAS Scholasticus** Epigr.
fiq Cometas Chartularius
fiq Cometas Grammaticus
A.D. 9
Cf. et COMETAS Chartularius Epigr. (4058).
Cf. et COMETAS Grammaticus Epigr. (4059).
001 **Epigramma**, AG 9.597.
Q: 54: Epigr.

0408 *COMICA ADESPOTA* (CAF)
Varia
001 **Fragmenta incertorum poetarum**, ed. T. Kock,
Comicorum Atticorum fragmenta, vol. 3. Leipzig: Teubner, 1888: 397–418, 420–425, 428–
462, 464–547, 553–632, 635–641.
frr. 1–6, 8–23, 25–26, 29–42, 44–57, 61–62,
70–75, 77–102, 104–110, 114–187, 189–298,
310–311, 314–336, 338–621, 625–634, 636–
781, 783–793, 823–824, 827–1059, 1066–
1211, 1213–1220, 1222–1250, 1253–1327,
1329–1331, 1345–1382.
fr. 104: *P. Didot*.
Q, Pap: 7,586: Comic.
002 **Fragmenta**, ed. Kock, *op. cit.*, 754–755.
frr. 352a, 570b–c, 675b, 698b, 743b, 1300b.
Q: 42: Comic.

0662 *COMICA ADESPOTA* (CGFPR)
Varia
001 **Adespota Doriensium comoediae**, ed. C. Austin, *Comicorum Graecorum fragmenta in papyris reperta*. Berlin: De Gruyter, 1973: 219–
220.
frr. 223–224.
Pap: 190: Comic.

002 **Adespota veteris comoediae**, ed. Austin, *op. cit.*, 221–238.
frr. 225–238.
Pap: 1,438: Comic.

003 **Adespota novae comoediae**, ed. Austin, *op. cit.*, 240–243, 245, 247–251, 253–275, 277–313.
frr. 239–242, 244–286.
Pap: 6,350: Comic.

004 **Excerpta, florilegia et sententiae**, ed. Austin, *op. cit.*, 314–333.
frr. 289–319.
Pap: 1,388: Comic., Gnom., Gramm.

005 **Argumenta metrica**, ed. Austin, *op. cit.*, 337.
fr. 339.
Pap: 162: Comic., Hypoth.

006 **Argumenta comica**, ed. Austin, *op. cit.*, 338–339.
frr. 340–341.
Pap: 125: Comic., Hypoth.

007 Λέξεις κωμικαί, ed. Austin, *op. cit.*, 339–343.
frr. 342–343.
Pap: 372: Comic., Lexicogr.

008 Κωμῳδούμενοι, ed. Austin, *op. cit.*, 344.
fr. 344.
Pap: 27: Comic., Gramm.

009 **Dubia**, ed. Austin, *op. cit.*, 345–368.
frr. 345–368.
Pap: 1,717: Comic., Satyr.

0602 *COMICA ADESPOTA* (FCG)
Varia

001 **Fragmenta comicorum anonymorum**, ed. A. Meineke, *Fragmenta comicorum Graecorum*, vol. 4. Berlin: Reimer, 1841 (repr. De Gruyter, 1970): 599–616, 618–630, 638, 645–655, 657–664, 667–679, 683–700.
frr. 1–13, 15–19b, 20b–27b, 27d–29, 31–42, 43b, 47–55, 57–63, 65–67, 71–73a, 74–75, 76b–79, 83–84, 89, 92–94, 95b–98, 100–101, 103, 132, 164, 167, 172, 174–175, 179, 182–188, 194–200, 202–206, 209, 216, 219–220, 222, 228, 235–236, 239–242, 245, 247–248, 253, 264, 280–282, 284–295a, 296a–307, 309b–311, 322, 326–327, 329–336, 339–341, 343a–372, 374–377, 379–383.
Q: 2,160: Comic.

002 **Fragmenta**, ed. Meineke, *FCG*, vol. 5.1 (1857; repr. 1970): cccliii, ccclix–ccclxii, ccclxiv–ccclxvi, ccclxviii, ccclxx, ccclxxiv, ccclxxvi, 118, 122–123.
Q: 276: Comic.

0659 *COMICA ADESPOTA* (Suppl. Com.)
Varia

001 **Adespota veteris comoediae**, ed. J. Demiańczuk, *Supplementum comicum*. Krakau: Nakładem Akademii, 1912 (repr. Hildesheim: Olms, 1967): 89–95.
frr. 1–12b.
fr. 4: *P. Amh.* 2.13.
fr. 5: *P. Oxy.* 2.212.
fr. 12: *P. Oxy.* 1.12.

fr. 12a: *P. Oxy.* 9.1176 (fr. 39, col. 16, vv. 6 sqq.).
fr. 12b: *P. Oxy.* 9.1176 (col. 4, vv. 1–15).
Q, Pap: 345: Comic.

002 **Adespota novae comoediae**, ed. Demiańczuk, *op. cit.*, 95–114.
frr. 13–26.
fr. 14: *P. Argent.* 53.
fr. 15: *P. Berol.* inv. 9941.
fr. 16: *P. Hibeh* 1.5.
frr. 17–20: *P. Sorbonne* inv. 72.
fr. 21: *P. Hibeh* 1.6.
frr. 22–23: *P. Sorbonne* inv. 72.
fr. 24: *P. Oxy.* 1.10.
fr. 25: *P. Oxy.* 1.11.
fr. 25a: *P. Oxy.* 9.1176 (col. 5, vv. 12 sqq.).
fr. 26: *P. Flinders Petrie* 4.1.
Q, Pap: 2,192: Comic.

003 **Fragmenta incertae comoediae**, ed. Demiańczuk, *op. cit.*, 114–121.
frr. 27–53.
fr. 39: *P. Oxy.* 4.677.
fr. 40: *P. Oxy.* 6.863.
Q, Pap: 209: Comic.

004 **Adespota dubia**, ed. Demiańczuk, *op. cit.*, 121–122.
frr. 54–59.
Q, Pap: 33: Comic.

005 **Fragmentum incerti poetae Dorici**, ed. Demiańczuk, *op. cit.*, 126.
fr. 1: *P. Oxy.* 9.1176 (col. 17, vv. 10–13).
Pap: 8: Comic.

4175 *COMMENTARIA IN DIONYSII THRACIS ARTEM GRAMMATICAM*
Varia

001 **Prolegomena Vossiana**, ed. A. Hilgard, *Grammatici Graeci*, vol. 1.3. Leipzig: Teubner, 1901 (repr. Hildesheim: Olms, 1965): 1–10.
Cod: Gramm., Comm.

002 **Commentarius** (sub auctore Melampode vel Diomede), ed. Hilgard, *op. cit.*, 10–67.
Cod: Gramm., Comm.

003 **Commentarius** (sub auctore Heliodoro), ed. Hilgard, *op. cit.*, 67–106.
Cod: Gramm., Comm.

004 **Scholia Vaticana** (partim excerpta ex Georgio Choerobosco, Georgio quodam, Porphyrio, Melampode, Stephano, Diomede), ed. Hilgard, *op. cit.*, 106–292.
Anonymi Περὶ προσῳδιῶν: pp. 150–156.
Cod: Gramm., Comm.

005 **Scholia Marciana** (partim excerpta ex Heliodoro, Tryphone, Diomede, Stephano, Georgio Choerobosco, Gregorio Corinthio), ed. Hilgard, *op. cit.*, 292–442.
Tryphonis de tropis (p. 302): Dup. partim TRYPHON II Gramm. (1763 001).
De barbarismo et soloecismo (pp. 304–305): Dup. partim ANONYMI DE BARBARISMO ET SOLOECISMO Gramm. (1129 001).
Cod: Gramm., Comm.

006 **Scholia Londinensia** (partim excerpta ex Heliodoro), ed. Hilgard, *op. cit.*, 442–565.
Cod: Gramm., Comm.

007 **Commentariolus Byzantinus**, ed. Hilgard, *op. cit.*, 565–586.
Cod: Gramm., Comm.

5000 *CONCILIA OECUMENICA* (ACO)
Varia

001 **Concilium universale Ephesenum anno 431**, ed. E. Schwartz, *Acta conciliorum oecumenicorum*, vol. 1.1.1–1.1.7. Berlin: De Gruyter, 1.1.1 (1927; repr. 1965); 1.1.2–1.1.3 (1927); 1.1.4 (1928); 1.1.5 (1927); 1.1.6 (1928; repr. 1960); 1.1.7 (1929; repr. 1962): **1.1.1**:3–121; **1.1.2**:3–104; **1.1.3**:3–101; **1.1.4**:3–67; **1.1.5**:3–136; **1.1.6**:3–162; **1.1.7**:3–167, 171–174.
Cod: 350,313: Concil., Theol., Epist., Homilet.

002 **Concilium universale Ephesenum anno 431**, ed. Schwartz, *op. cit.*, vol. 1.5.1 (1924–1925; repr. 1963): 219–231.
Cod: 6,018: Concil., Theol., Exeget.

003 **Concilium universale Chalcedonense anno 451**, ed. Schwartz, *op. cit.*, vol. 2.1.1–2.1.2 (1933; repr. 1962); 2.1.3 (1935; repr. 1965): **2.1.1**:3–32, 35–52, 55–196; **2.1.2**:3–42, 45–65, 69–163; **2.1.3**:3–136.
Cod: 161,939: Concil., Theol., Epist.

004 **Synodus Constantinopolitana et Hierosolymitana anno 536**, ed. Schwartz, *op. cit.*, vol. 3 (1940; repr. 1965): 3–214, 217–231.
Cod: 88,001: Concil., Theol., Epist.

1285 **CONON** Hist.
1 B.C.–A.D. 1

001 **Testimonia**, FGrH #26: 1A:190, *12 addenda.
NQ: 169: Test.

002 **Fragmenta**, FGrH #26: 1A:190–211.
Q: 7,689: Hist., Myth.

9014 **CONSTANTINUS** <Epigr.>
A.D. 9–10: Rhodius

001 **Epigrammata**, AG 15.15–17.
Q: 127: Epigr.

9015 **CONSTANTINUS** Gramm.
A.D. 9–10: Sicelius

001 **Epigramma**, AG 15.13.
Q: 31: Epigr.

0840 **CONSTANTINUS** Med.
ante A.D. 6

x01 **Fragmentum ap. Paulum**.
CMG, vol. 9.2, p. 327.
Cf. PAULUS Med. (0715 001).

x02 **Fragmentum ap. Aëtium** (lib. 6).
CMG, vol. 8.2, p. 197.
Cf. AËTIUS Med. (0718 006).

2736 **CONSTANTINUS I Imperator**
vel Constantinus Magnus
A.D. 3–4: Constantinopolitanus

x01 **Oratio ad coetum sanctorum** [Dub.].
Heikel, GCS 7, pp. 151–192.
Cf. EUSEBIUS Scr. Eccl. et Theol. (2018 021).

3023 **CONSTANTINUS VII PORPHYROGENITUS Imperator**
A.D. 10: Constantinopolitanus

001 **De legationibus**, ed. C. de Boor, *Excerpta historica iussu imp. Constantini Porphyrogeniti confecta, vol. 1: excerpta de legationibus*, pts. 1–2. Berlin: Weidmann, 1903: **1.1**:1–227; **1.2**:229–599.
Excerpta de legationibus Romanorum ad gentes: vol. 1.1, pp. 1–227.
Excerpta de legationibus gentium ad Romanos: vol. 1.2, pp. 229–599.
Cod: 181,447: Hist.

002 **De virtutibus et vitiis**, ed. T. Büttner-Wobst and A.G. Roos, *Excerpta historica iussu imp. Constantini Porphyrogeniti confecta, vol. 2: excerpta de virtutibus et vitiis*, pts. 1 & 2. Berlin: Weidmann, 2.1:1906; 2.2:1910: **2.1**:1–361; **2.2**:1–407.
Cod: 198,753: Hist.

003 **De insidiis**, ed. C. de Boor, *Excerpta historica iussu imp. Constantini Porphyrogeniti confecta, vol. 3: excerpta de insidiis*. Berlin: Weidmann, 1905: 1–228.
Cod: 70,698: Hist.

004 **De sententiis**, ed. U.P. Boissevain, *Excerpta historica iussu imp. Constantini Porphyrogeniti confecta, vol. 4: excerpta de sententiis*. Berlin: Weidmann, 1906: 1–452.
Cod: 111,095: Hist.

005 **De strategematibus** (olim sub auctore Herone Byzantio), ed. R. Schneider, *Griechische Poliorketiker* [Abhandlungen der königlichen Gesellschaft der Wissenschaften zu Göttingen, Philol.-hist. Kl., N.F. 11, no. 1. Berlin: Weidmann, 1908]: 4–80.
Cod: Tact.

008 **De administrando imperio**, ed. G. Moravcsik, *Constantine Porphyrogenitus. De administrando imperio*, 2nd edn. [Corpus fontium historiae Byzantinae 1 (= Dumbarton Oaks Texts 1). Washington, D.C.: Dumbarton Oaks, 1967]: 44–286.
Cod: 40,512: Hist.

009 **De thematibus**, ed. A. Pertusi, *Costantino Porfirogenito. De thematibus* [Studi e Testi 160. Vatican City: Biblioteca Apostolica Vaticana, 1952]: 59–100.
Cod: 9,703: Hist.

010 **De cerimoniis aulae Byzantinae** (lib. 1.84–2.56), ed. J.J. Reiske, *Constantini Porphyrogeniti imperatoris de cerimoniis aulae Byzantinae libri duo*, vol. 1 [Corpus scriptorum historiae Byzantinae. Bonn: Weber, 1829]: 386–807.
Lib. 1.84–97: pp. 386–443.
Appendix ad librum primum (= Τὰ βασιλικὰ ταξείδια): pp. 444–508.
Pinax ad librum secundum: pp. 509–515.

Praefatio ad librum secundum: pp. 516–517.
Lib. 2: pp. 518–807 (Cletorologion = pp. 702–791).
Cf. et 3023 011.
Cod: 76,780: Hist.

011 **De cerimoniis aulae Byzantinae** (lib. 1.1–92), ed. A. Vogt, *Le livre des cérémonies*, vols. 1–2. Paris: Les Belles Lettres, 1:1935; 2:1939 (repr. 1967): 1:1–179; 2:1–187.
Vol. 1 = lib. 1.1–46 (= Reiske 1.1–37).
Vol. 2 = lib. 1.47–92 (= Reiske 1.38–83).
Cf. et 3023 010.
Cod: 78,095: Hist.

006 **De contionibus militaribus**, ed. R. Vári, "Zum historischen Exzerptenwerke des Konstantinos Porphyrogennetos," *Byzantinische Zeitschrift* 17 (1908) 78–84.
Cod: Hist.

013 **Narratio de imagine Edessena**, ed. E. von Dobschütz, *Christusbilder. Untersuchungen zur christlichen Legende* [*Texte und Untersuchungen*, N.F. 3. Leipzig: Hinrichs, 1899]: 39**–85** (Beilage II).
Cod: Eccl.

014 **Oratio de translatione Chrysostomi**, ed. K.J. Dyobuniotes, "Λόγος ἀνέκδοτος εἰς τὴν ἀνακομιδὴν τοῦ λειψάνου Ἰωάννου τοῦ Χρυσοστόμου," Ἐπιστημονικὴ ἐπετηρὶς θεολογικῆς σχολῆς τοῦ Ἀθήνησι Πανεπιστημίου 1 (1925) 306–319.
Cod: Orat., Encom.

016 **Preces liturgicae** (cantica Constantini et Leonis Sapientis), MPG 107: 300–307.
Exaposteilaria sunt Constantini.
Matutina sunt Leonis.
Dup. partim 3023 017.
Cod: Hymn.

017 **Exaposteilaria** (e cod. Monac. 205), ed. W. Christ and M. Paranikas, *Anthologia Graeca carminum Christianorum*. Leipzig: Teubner, 1871 (repr. Hildesheim: Olms, 1963): 110–112.
Dup. partim 3023 016.
Cod: Hymn.

019 **Oratio ad milites**, ed. H. Ahrweiler, "Un discours inédit de Constantin VII Porphyrogénète," *Travaux et mémoires* 2 (1967) 397–399.
Cod: 1,146: Orat.

025 **Leonis et Constantini delectus legum compendiarius** [Sp.], MPG 113: 453–549.
Cod: Jurisprud.

026 **Novellae constitutiones**, ed. J. Zepos and P. Zepos (post C.E. Zachariä von Lingenthal), *Jus Graecoromanum*, vol. 1 [*Novellae et aureae bullae imperatorum post Justinianum*]. Athens: Fexis, 1931 (repr. Aalen: Scientia, 1962): 193–239.
Cod: Jurisprud.

x02 **Geoponica**.
Beckh, pp. 1–529.
Cf. GEOPONICA (4080 001).

x03 **Strategicon**.
Mihăescu, pp. 28–380.

Cf. Pseudo-MAURICIUS Tact. (3075 001).

x05 Τὰ βασιλικὰ ταξείδια.
Reiske, vol. 1, pp. 455–508.
Cf. 3023 010.

x06 **Cletorologion** (sub auctore Philotheo).
Reiske, vol. 1, pp. 702–791.
Cf. 3023 010.

x07 **Epistulae ad Theodorum**.
Darrouzès, pp. 317–318, 320, 321–322, 323–324, 327, 328–329, 330–331, 332.
Cf. THEODORUS Epist. (3158 001).

x08 **Historia de vita et rebus gestis Basilii Inclyti imperatoris**.
Bekker, pp. 211–353.
Cf. THEOPHANES CONTINUATUS (4153 001).

x09 **Epistula in translatione Gregorii Nazianzeni** (olim sub auctore Constantino, nunc sub auctore Theodoro Daphnopate).
Darrouzès & Westerink, pp. 143–145 (epist. 11).
Cf. THEODORUS DAPHNOPATES Scr. Eccl. et Hist. (3123 001).

9013 **CONSTANTINUS CEPHALAS** <Epigr.>
A.D. 9–10
001 **Epigramma**, AG 5.1.
Q: 16: Epigr.

0271 *CONVENTUS AVIUM*
ante A.D. 2/3
001 **Fragmentum** (*P. Cairo* inv. 67860), ed. E. Heitsch, *Die griechischen Dichterfragmente der römischen Kaiserzeit*, vol. 1, 2nd edn. Göttingen: Vandenhoeck & Ruprecht, 1963: 34.
Pap: 31: Lyr.

0294 **CORINNA** Lyr.
5/3 B.C.?: Tanagraea
001 **Fragmenta**, ed. D.L. Page, *Poetae melici Graeci*. Oxford: Clarendon Press, 1962 (repr. 1967 (1st edn. corr.)): 326–331, 333–339, 341–357.
frr. 1–2, 4–11, 13–14, 16, 21–28, 31–32, 34, 36–41.
Q, Pap: 1,871: Lyr.

CORISCUS Phil.
4 B.C.: Scepsius
Cf. ERASTUS et CORISCUS Phil. (0226).

0841 **CORNELIUS** Med.
ante A.D. 2
x01 **Fragmentum ap. Galenum**.
K13.292.
Cf. GALENUS Med. (0057 076).

1842 **CORNELIUS** Scr. Eccl.
A.D. 3: Romanus
x01 **Epistula ad Fabianum Antiochenum** (fragmenta).
Eusebius, HE 6.43.5–43.20.
Cf. EUSEBIUS Scr. Eccl. et Theol. (2018 002).

0153 **CORNELIUS LONG(IN)US** Epigr.
A.D. 1?

001 **Epigrammata**, AG 6.191; **16**.117.
Q: 86: Epigr.

0654 **Lucius Annaeus CORNUTUS** Phil.
A.D. 1: Romanus

002 **De natura deorum**, ed. C. Lang, *Cornuti theologiae Graecae compendium*. Leipzig: Teubner, 1881: 1–76.
Cod: 12,578: Phil.

003 **Fragmenta**, ed. R. Reppe, *De L. Annaeo Cornuto*. Leipzig: Noske, 1906: 76–83.
Q: [500]

x01 **Ars rhetorica** (olim sub auctore Cornuto).
Hammer, vol. 1, pp. 352–398.
Cf. ANONYMUS SEGUERIANUS Rhet. (2002 001).

1286 *CORPUS HERMETICUM*
vel *Hermetica*
A.D. 2?/4

001 **Poimandres**, ed. A.D. Nock and A.-J. Festugière, *Corpus Hermeticum*, vol. 1. Paris: Les Belles Lettres, 1946 (repr. 1972): 7–19.
Cod: 2,240: Phil., Theol.

002 **Dialogus** (sine titulo), ed. Nock and Festugière, *op. cit.*, vol. 1, 32–39.
Cod: 1,309: Phil., Theol., Dialog.

003 **Hieros logos**, ed. Nock and Festugière, *op. cit.*, vol. 1, 44–46.
Cod: 341: Phil., Theol.

004 Πρὸς Τὰτ ὁ κρατὴρ ἢ μονάς, ed. Nock and Festugière, *op. cit.*, vol. 1, 49–53.
Cod: 903: Phil., Theol.

005 Πρὸς Τὰτ υἱὸν ὅτι ἀφανὴς θεὸς φανερώτατός ἐστιν, ed. Nock and Festugière, *op. cit.*, vol. 1, 60–65.
Cod: 1,096: Phil., Theol.

006 Ὅτι ἐν μόνῳ τῷ θεῷ τὸ ἀγαθόν ἐστιν, ἀλλαχόθι δὲ οὐδαμοῦ, ed. Nock and Festugière, *op. cit.*, vol. 1, 72–76.
Cod: 758: Phil., Theol.

007 Ὅτι μέγιστον κακὸν ἐν ἀνθρώποις ἡ περὶ τοῦ θεοῦ ἀγνωσία, ed. Nock and Festugière, *op. cit.*, vol. 1, 81–82.
Cod: 244: Phil., Theol.

008 Ὅτι οὐδὲν τῶν ὄντων ἀπόλλυται, ἀλλὰ τὰς μεταβολὰς ἀπωλείας καὶ θανάτους πλανώμενοι λέγουσιν, ed. Nock and Festugière, *op. cit.*, vol. 1, 87–89.
Cod: 473: Phil., Theol.

009 Περὶ νοήσεως καὶ αἰσθήσεως. [ὅτι ἐν μόνῳ τῷ θεῷ τὸ καλὸν καὶ ἀγαθόν ἐστιν, ἀλλαχόθι δὲ οὐδαμοῦ], ed. Nock and Festugière, *op. cit.*, vol. 1, 96–100.
Cod: 983: Phil., Theol.

010 Κλείς, ed. Nock and Festugière, *op. cit.*, vol. 1, 113–126.
Cod: 2,422: Phil., Theol.

011 Νοῦς πρὸς Ἑρμῆν, ed. Nock and Festugière, *op. cit.*, vol. 1, 147–157.
Cod: 2,208: Phil., Theol.

012 Περὶ νοῦ κοινοῦ πρὸς Τάτ, ed. Nock and Festugière, *op. cit.*, vol. 1, 174–183.
Cod: 2,078: Phil., Theol.

013 Πρὸς τὸν υἱὸν Τὰτ ἐν ὄρει λόγος ἀπόκρυφος, περὶ παλιγγενεσίας καὶ σιγῆς ἐπαγγελίας, ed. Nock and Festugière, *op. cit.*, vol. 2 (1946; repr. 1973): 200–209.
Cod: 1,802: Phil., Theol.

014 Ἀσκληπιῷ εὖ φρονεῖν, ed. Nock and Festugière, *op. cit.*, vol. 2, 222–226.
Cod: 825: Phil., Theol.

016 Ὅροι Ἀσκληπιοῦ πρὸς Ἄμμωνα βασιλέα, ed. Nock and Festugière, *op. cit.*, vol. 2, 231–238.
Cod: 1,308: Phil., Theol.

017 **Dialogus** (sine titulo), ed. Nock and Festugière, *op. cit.*, vol. 2, 244.
Cod: 129: Phil., Theol., Dialog.

018 Περὶ τῆς ὑπὸ τοῦ πάθους τοῦ σώματος ἐμποδιζομένης ψυχῆς, ed. Nock and Festugière, *op. cit.*, vol. 2, 248–255.
Cod: 1,337: Phil., Theol.

019 **Asclepius** (verba Graeca solum), ed. Nock and Festugière, *op. cit.*, vol. 2, 304, 305, 308, 312, 313, 315, 316, 317, 318, 319, 349, 350, 351.
Q: 39: Phil., Theol.

020 **Fragmenta**, ed. Nock and Festugière, *op. cit.*, vols. 3–4 (1954; repr. 1972): **3**:2–8, 13–14, 17–18, 21–27, 30–31, 34–39, 44, 47–48, 51–58, 61, 64–67, 72–73, 76–77, 80–83, 86–87, 90–91; **4**:1–22, 52–58, 68–72, 80–88, 97–99.
Q: 16,456: Phil., Theol.

021 **Fragmenta varia** (verba Graeca solum), ed. Nock and Festugière, *op. cit.*, vol. 4, 105, 106, 110, 111, 113, 114, 126, 128, 129–135, 137–143.
frr. 3a, 4a–b, 10, 11a, 12a, 14–15, 23–36.
Q: 917: Phil., Theol.

022 Ἐκ τοῦ ὕμνου πρὸς τὸν παντοκράτορα (fragmentum), ed. Nock and Festugière, *op. cit.*, vol. 4, 147.
Q: 107: Phil., Theol., Hymn.

023 **Fragmenta hermetica** (*P. Vindob.* 29456 + 29828), ed. J.-P. Mahé, "Fragments hermétiques dans les papyri Vindobonenses Graecae 29456 rº et 29828 rº," *Mémorial André-Jean Festugière. Antiquité païenne et chrétienne*. Geneva: Cramer, 1984: 53–55.
Pap: Phil., Theol.

x01 **Epigrammata** (*App. Anth.*).
Epigramma demonstrativum: 3.147.
Epigramma exhortatorium et supplicatorium: 4.47.
App. Anth. 3.147(?): Cf. ANTHOLOGIAE GRAECAE APPENDIX (7052 003).
App. Anth. 4.47(?): Cf. ANTHOLOGIAE GRAECAE APPENDIX (7052 004).
App. Anth. 3.147: Cf. et THEON Math. (2033 x03).

x02 **De deo** (fort. auctore Philone) (*P. Berol.* inv. 17027).
Stahlschmidt, pp. 162–165.
Cf. PHILO JUDAEUS Phil. (0018 041).

4061 COSMAS INDICOPLEUSTES Geogr.
A.D. 6: Alexandrinus
001 **Epigramma**, AG 16.114.
Q: 16: Epigr.
002 **Topographia Christiana**, ed. W. Wolska-Conus, *Cosmas Indicopleustès. Topographie chrétienne*, 3 vols. [*Sources chrétiennes* 141, 159, 197. Paris: Cerf, 1:1968; 2:1970; 3:1973]: 1:255–569: **2**:13–373; **3**:13–381.
Cod: 89,224: Geogr., Theol.

1287 CRANTOR Phil.
4–3 B.C.: Soleus
001 **Fragmenta**, ed. F.W.A. Mullach, *Fragmenta philosophorum Graecorum*, vol. 3. Paris: Didot, 1881 (repr. Aalen: Scientia, 1968): 139–143, 145–152.
frr. 1–16.
Dup. partim 1287 002 (frr. 345–346).
Q: 1,631: Phil., Iamb.
002 **Fragmenta et titulus**, ed. H. Lloyd-Jones and P. Parsons, *Supplementum Hellenisticum*. Berlin: De Gruyter, 1983: 163.
frr. 344–346.
Dup. partim 1287 001 (frr. 14–15).
Q: 36: Iamb.

CRATERI EPISTULA
ante A.D. 1
Cf. ANONYMI HISTORICI (FGrH) (1139 007, fr. 2).

1288 CRATERUS Hist.
4–3 B.C.: Macedo
001 **Testimonia**, FGrH #342: 3B:199.
NQ: 151: Test.
002 **Fragmenta**, FGrH #342: 3B:199–205.
Q: 1,657: Hist.

0842 CRATERUS Med.
1 B.C.
x01 **Fragmentum ap. Galenum**.
K13.96.
Cf. GALENUS Med. (0057 076).

0433 CRATES Comic.
5 B.C.: Atheniensis
001 **Fragmenta**, ed. T. Kock, *Comicorum Atticorum fragmenta*, vol. 1. Leipzig: Teubner, 1880: 130–144.
frr. 1–17, 19–24, 26–37, 39–51, 53–56 + tituli.
Q: 444: Comic.
002 **Fragmenta**, ed. A. Meineke, *Fragmenta comicorum Graecorum*, vol. 2.1. Berlin: Reimer, 1839 (repr. De Gruyter, 1970): 233–249.
Q: 402: Comic.

003 **Fragmenta**, ed. J. Demiańczuk, *Supplementum comicum*. Krakau: Nakładem Akademii, 1912 (repr. Hildesheim: Olms, 1967): 29–30.
frr. 1–6.
Q: 33: Comic.
004 **Fragmentum**, ed. C. Austin, *Comicorum Graecorum fragmenta in papyris reperta*. Berlin: De Gruyter, 1973: 34.
fr. 68.
Pap: 32: Comic.
005 **Fragmenta**, ed. Meineke, *FCG*, vol. 5.1 (1857; repr. 1970): xlix.
Q: 12: Comic.

1290 CRATES Gramm.
2 B.C.: Mallotes
001 **Epigramma**, AG 1.218.
Q: 27: Epigr.
002 **Sphairopoiia**, ed. H.J. Mette, *Sphairopoiia*. Munich: Beck, 1936: 113–298.
Q

1289 CRATES Hist.
1 B.C.: Atheniensis
001 **Fragmenta**, FGrH #362: 3B:220–224.
Q: 1,122: Hist.

0336 CRATES Poet. Phil.
4–3 B.C.: Thebanus
Cf. et CRATETIS EPISTULAE (0623).
001 **Fragmentum**, ed. B. Snell, *Tragicorum Graecorum fragmenta*, vol. 1. Göttingen: Vandenhoeck & Ruprecht, 1971: 259.
Dup. partim 0336 002 (fr. 15), 004 (fr. 364).
Q: 20: Trag.
002 **Fragmenta**, ed. E. Diehl, *Anthologia lyrica Graeca*, fasc. 1, 3rd edn. Leipzig: Teubner, 1949: 120–126.
frr. 1–21.
Dup. partim 0336 001, 003, 004, x01.
Q: 449: Eleg., Hexametr., Trag.
003 **Epigrammata**, AG 7.326; **9**.497; **10**.104.
Dup. partim 0336 002 (fr. 2), 004 (fr. 361).
AG 9.359: Cf. POSIDIPPUS Epigr. (1632 001).
AG 9.359: Cf. PLATO Comic. (0497 001).
Q: 62: Epigr.
004 **Fragmenta et titulus**, ed. H. Lloyd-Jones and P. Parsons, *Supplementum Hellenisticum*. Berlin: De Gruyter, 1983: 164–172.
frr. 347–349, 351–368.
Dup. partim 0336 001–003, x01.
Q: 434: Epic., Eleg., Hexametr., Epigr., Iamb., Trag.
x01 **Epigrammata** (*App. Anth.*).
Epigramma exhortatorium et supplicatorium: 4.33.
Epigrammata irrisoria: 5.13, 13b.
Dup. partim 0336 002 (fr. 1), 004 (fr. 359).
App. Anth. 4.33: Cf. ANTHOLOGIAE GRAECAE APPENDIX (7052 004).
App. Anth. 5.13, 13b: Cf. ANTHOLOGIAE GRAECAE APPENDIX (7052 005).

0623 **CRATETIS EPISTULAE**
Incertum
Cf. et CRATES Poet. Phil. (0336).
001 **Epistulae**, ed. R. Hercher, *Epistolographi Graeci*. Paris: Didot, 1873 (repr. Amsterdam: Hakkert, 1965): 208–217.
Cod: 3,124: Epist.

0657 **CRATEUAS** Med.
2–1 B.C.
001 **Fragmenta**, ed. M. Wellmann, *Pedanii Dioscuridis Anazarbei de materia medica libri quinque*, vol. 3. Berlin: Weidmann, 1914 (repr. 1958): 144–146.
Cod: 508: Med.

0434 **CRATINUS** Comic.
5 B.C.
001 **Fragmenta**, ed. T. Kock, *Comicorum Atticorum fragmenta*, vol. 1. Leipzig: Teubner, 1880: 11–17, 19–21, 23–30, 32–43, 45, 47–109, 113–130.
frr. 1–10, 15–17, 21–30, 36–58, 65–66, 69–74, 76–82, 85–87, 90–98, 100, 107–116, 120–129, 131–132, 135–148, 152–154, 157–170, 172, 175, 177–179, 181–199, 205–209, 211, 213–214, 218–222, 224–225, 227–229, 231–241, 244–246, 249–260, 264–265, 268–269, 271–307, 309–325, 327, 342–343, 346–347, 352–353, 355–361, 365–367, 369–462 + tituli.
Q: 2,424: Comic.
002 **Fragmenta**, ed. A. Meineke, *Fragmenta comicorum Graecorum*, vol. 2.1. Berlin: Reimer, 1839 (repr. De Gruyter, 1970): 15–20, 22, 26–27, 29–31, 33–44, 46–49, 51, 53, 56–57, 60–64, 67–69, 72–75, 77, 80, 82, 84–90, 92–105, 107–111, 113, 116–119, 122–127, 129–130, 132–133, 135–137, 141–142, 144–157, 161–167, 172, 174, 176–179, 181–187, 189, 192, 194–195, 198, 202, 206, 210–212, 215, 217–218, 221–222, 225–226, 230–232.
Q: 2,175: Comic.
003 **Fragmenta**, ed. J. Demiańczuk, *Supplementum comicum*. Krakau: Nakładem Akademii, 1912 (repr. Hildesheim: Olms, 1967): 30–31, 33–39.
frr. 1–29.
Q: 151: Comic.
004 **Fragmenta**, ed. C. Austin, *Comicorum Graecorum fragmenta in papyris reperta*. Berlin: De Gruyter, 1973: 34–40, 42–49.
frr. 69–76 + tituli.
Pap: 988: Comic.
005 **Fragmenta**, ed. Kock, *CAF*, vol. 3 (1888): 713.
frr. 389b, 459b.
Q: 7: Comic.
006 **Fragmenta**, ed. Meineke, *FCG*, vol. 5.1 (1857; repr. 1970): xlviii.
Q: 37: Comic.

0435 **CRATINUS Junior** Comic.
4 B.C.
001 **Fragmenta**, ed. T. Kock, *Comicorum Atti-*

corum fragmenta, vol. 2. Leipzig: Teubner, 1884: 289–293.
frr. 1–2, 4–5, 7–14 + titulus.
Q: 207: Comic.
002 **Fragmenta**, ed. A. Meineke, *Fragmenta comicorum Graecorum*, vol. 3. Berlin: Reimer, 1840 (repr. De Gruyter, 1970): 374–379.
Q: 205: Comic.

1907 **CRATIPPUS** Hist.
1 B.C.?: Atheniensis
Cf. et HELLENICA (0558).
001 **Testimonia**, FGrH #64: 2A:13–14.
NQ: 192: Test.
002 **Fragmenta**, FGrH #64: 2A:14–15.
Q: 438: Hist.

0843 **CRATIPPUS** Med.
1 B.C.
x01 **Fragmenta ap. Galenum**.
K12.959; **14**.170.
Cf. GALENUS Med. (0057 076, 078).

2291 **CRATYLUS** Phil.
5–4 B.C.: Atheniensis
001 **Testimonia**, ed. H. Diels and W. Kranz, *Die Fragmente der Vorsokratiker*, vol. 2, 6th edn. Berlin: Weidmann, 1952 (repr. Dublin: 1966): 69–70.
test. 1–5.
NQ: 404: Test.

2508 **CREON** Hist.
4 B.C.?
001 **Fragmentum**, FGrH #753: 3C:735–736.
Q: 58: Hist.

CREOPHYLUS Epic.
Incertum: Samius vel Chius
Cf. OECHALIAE HALOSIS (1546).

1291 **CREOPHYLUS** Hist.
5–4 B.C.?: Ephesius
001 **Fragmenta**, FGrH #417: 3B:314–315.
fr. 2: *Inscr. Priene* 37.
Q, Epigr: 477: Hist.

1994 **CREPEREIUS CALPURNIANUS** Hist.
A.D. 2: Pompeiopolitanus
001 **Fragmenta**, FGrH #208: 2B:940–941.
Q: 188: Hist.

0154 **CRINAGORAS** Epigr.
1 B.C./A.D. 1: Mytilenensis
001 **Epigrammata**, AG 5.108, 119; **6**.100, 161, 227, 229, 232, 242, 244, 253, 261, 345, 350; **7**.371, 376, 380, 401, 628, 633, 636, 638, 643, 645, 741; **9**.81, 224, 234–235, 239, 276, 283–284, 291, 419, 429–430, 439, 513, 516, 542, 545, 555, 559–560, 562; **10**.24; **11**.42; **16**.40, 61, 199, 273.

AG 7.744: Cf. DIOGENES LAERTIUS Biogr. (0004 002).
AG 9.65: Cf. ANONYMI EPIGRAMMATICI (AG) (0138 001).
Q: 1,899: Epigr.

1293 **CRINIS** Phil.
2 B.C.
001 **Fragmenta**, ed. J. von Arnim, *Stoicorum veterum fragmenta*, vol. 3. Leipzig: Teubner, 1903 (repr. Stuttgart: 1968): 268–269.
Q: 319: Phil.

0844 **CRISPUS** Med.
A.D. 1
x01 **Fragmenta ap. Galenum**.
K12.831; **13**.67, 841, 984.
Cf. GALENUS Med. (0057 076–077).

0319 **CRITIAS** Phil., Trag. et Eleg.
5 B.C.: Atheniensis
001 **Fragmenta**, ed. B. Snell, *Tragicorum Graecorum fragmenta*, vol. 1. Göttingen: Vandenhoeck & Ruprecht, 1971: 171–184.
frr. 1–14, 16–19, 21–25.
frr. 5, 7–9: *P. Oxy.* 17.2078.
Q, Pap: 956: Trag., Satyr.
002 **Fragmenta**, ed. M.L. West, *Iambi et elegi Graeci*, vol. 2. Oxford: Clarendon Press, 1972: 52–56.
frr. B2, 4–9.
Q: 342: Eleg.
003 **Testimonia**, ed. H. Diels and W. Kranz, *Die Fragmente der Vorsokratiker*, vol. 2, 6th edn. Berlin: Weidmann, 1952 (repr. Dublin: 1966): 371–375.
test. 1–23.
NQ: 2,017: Test.
004 **Fragmenta**, ed. Diels and Kranz, *op. cit.*, 375–399.
frr. 1–75.
Q: 3,715: Phil., Hexametr., Eleg., Trag., Satyr., Gnom.

0436 **CRITO** Comic.
2 B.C.
001 **Fragmenta**, ed. T. Kock, *Comicorum Atticorum fragmenta*, vol. 3. Leipzig: Teubner, 1888: 354.
frr. 1–3 + titulus.
Q: 55: Comic.
002 **Fragmenta**, ed. A. Meineke, *Fragmenta comicorum Graecorum*, vol. 4. Berlin: Reimer, 1841 (repr. De Gruyter, 1970): 537–538.
Q: 55: Comic.

1867 **CRITO** Hist.
fiq Titus Statilius Crito Med.
A.D. 1–2: Pieriota
Cf. et Titus Statilius CRITO Med. (0685).

001 **Testimonia**, FGrH #200, #277: **2B**:931; **3A**:157; **3B**:743–744 addenda.
NQ: 112: Test.
002 **Fragmenta**, FGrH #200: 2B:931–932.
Q: 269: Hist.

0685 **Titus Statilius CRITO** Med.
fiq Crito Pieriota Hist.
A.D. 1–2
Cf. et CRITO et HERODOTUS Med. (0882).
Cf. et CRITO Hist. (1867).
x01 **Fragmenta ap. Galenum**.
K**12**.401–402, 435–439, 453–454, 458, 483–492, 587–588, 659–660, 817, 825–826, 827–829, 830–831, 880–881, 933–935, 953–954, 987–988, 991–992; **13**.35–37, 38–39, 257–258, 515–516, 708–716, 786–796, 797–798, 800–801, 863–864, 869–870, 877–880, 883–884, 903–905, 1040–1041; **14**.103–105.
Cf. GALENUS Med. (0057 076–078).
x02 **Fragmentum ap. Oribasium**.
CMG, vol. 6.3, p. 73.
Cf. ORIBASIUS Med. (0722 004).
x03 **Fragmenta ap. Paulum**.
CMG, vol. **9.1**, pp. 130, 328; **9.2**, p. 326.
Cf. PAULUS Med. (0715 001).
x04 **Fragmentum ap. Aëtium** (lib. 4).
CMG, vol. 8.1, p. 369.
Cf. AËTIUS Med. (0718 004).
x05 **Fragmenta ap. Aëtium** (lib. 6, 8).
CMG, vol. 8.2, pp. 201, 405, 419.
Cf. AËTIUS Med. (0718 006, 008).
x06 **Fragmentum ap. Aëtium** (lib. 15).
Zervos, *Athena* 21, pp. 103–105.
Cf. AËTIUS Med. (0718 015).

1292 **CRITO** Phil.
3 B.C.: Argivus
001 **Fragmentum**, ed. H. Thesleff, *The Pythagorean texts of the Hellenistic period*. Åbo: Åbo Akademi, 1965: 109.
Q: 145: Phil.

0882 **CRITO et HERODOTUS** Med.
A.D. 1–2
Cf. et Titus Statilius CRITO Med. (0685).
Cf. et HERODOTUS Med. (0926).
x01 **Fragmentum ap. Aëtium** (lib. 15).
Zervos, *Athena* 21, p. 61.
Cf. AËTIUS Med. (0718 015).

3147 **Michael CRITOBULUS** Hist.
vel Critopulus
A.D. 15: Imbrius
001 **Precatio**, ed. D.R. Reinsch, *Critobuli Imbriotae historiae* [Corpus fontium historiae Byzantinae 22. Series Berolinensis. Berlin: De Gruyter, 1983]: 12*–15*.
Cod: Eccl.
002 **Poema**, ed. Reinsch, *op. cit.*, 16*.
Cod: Poem.

003 **Epistula ad Mechemet II**, ed. Reinsch, *op. cit.*,
3–9.
Cod: Epist.

004 **Historiae**, ed. Reinsch, *op. cit.*, 11–207.
Cod: Hist.

1295 **CRITODEMUS** Astrol.
3 B.C.

001 **Fragmenta**, ed. W. Kroll, *Codices Romani [Ca-*
talogus codicum astrologorum Graecorum 5.2.
Brussels: Lamertin, 1906]: 52–53, 113, 120–
121.
Q

002 **Fragmenta**, ed. F. Cumont, *Codices Parisini*
[*Catalogus codicum astrologorum Graecorum*
8.1. Brussels: Lamertin, 1929]: 257–261.
Q

003 **Fragmenta**, ed. P. Boudreaux, *Codices Parisini*
[*Catalogus codicum astrologorum Graecorum*
8.3. Brussels: Lamertin, 1912]: 102.
Q

x01 **Fragmenta ap. Vettium Valentem.**
Kroll, pp. 142–144.
Cf. VETTIUS VALENS Astrol. (1764 001).

2552 **CRITOLAUS** Hist.
ante 1 B.C.

001 **Fragmenta**, FGrH #823: 3C:896–897.
Q: 329: Hist.

1294 **CRITOLAUS** Phil.
2 B.C.: Phaselinus

001 **Fragmenta**, ed. F. Wehrli, *Hieronymos von*
Rhodos. Kritolaos und seine Schüler [Die Schule
des Aristoteles, vol. 10, 2nd edn. Basel:
Schwabe, 1969]: 51–58.
Cosmologica: frr. 12–16.
Ethica: frr. 19–20, 24.
Rhetorica: frr. 26–32, 34–39.
Fragmenta dubia: frr. 40a–40c.
Q, Pap: 1,549: Phil., Rhet.

0437 **CROBYLUS** Comic.
4 B.C.

001 **Fragmenta**, ed. T. Kock, *Comicorum Atti-*
corum fragmenta, vol. 3. Leipzig: Teubner,
1888: 379–382.
frr. 1–10.
Q: 159: Comic.

002 **Fragmenta**, ed. A. Meineke, *Fragmenta comi-*
corum Graecorum, vol. 4. Berlin: Reimer, 1841
(repr. De Gruyter, 1970): 565–569.
Q: 161: Comic.

0845 **CTESIAS** Hist. et Med.
5–4 B.C.: Cnidius

001 **Testimonia**, FGrH #688: 3C:416–420.
NQ: 1,494: Test.

002 **Fragmenta**, FGrH #688: 3C:420–517.
fr. 8b: *P. Oxy.* 22.2330.
Q, Pap: 31,306: Hist., Perieg., Nat. Hist., Med.

003 **Fragmentum** (*P. Oxy.* 24.2389), ed. H.J.
Mette, "Die 'Kleinen' griechischen Historiker
heute," *Lustrum* 21 (1978) 36.
fr. 66 bis.
Pap: 51: Hist.

2201 **[CTESIPHON]** Hist.
Incertum

001 **Fragmenta**, FGrH #294: 3A:177–178.
Q: 244: Hist., Nat. Hist.

0846 **CTESIPHON** Med.
1 B.C.

x01 **Fragmenta ap. Galenum.**
K13.927, 936.
Cf. GALENUS Med. (0057 077).

2567 **CTESIPPUS** Hist.
Incertum

001 **Fragmentum**, FGrH #844: 3C:929–930.
Q: 123: Hist.

0368 **CYDIAS** Lyr.
6/5 B.C.: Hermioneus

001 **Fragmentum**, ed. D.L. Page, *Poetae melici*
Graeci. Oxford: Clarendon Press, 1962 (repr.
1967 (1st edn. corr.)): 370.
fr. 1.
Q: 9: Lyr.

0156 **CYLLENIUS** Epigr.
A.D. 1

001 **Epigrammata**, AG 9.4, 33.
AG 9.35: Cf. ANTIPHILUS Epigr. (0118 001).
AG 9.46: Cf. ANTIPATER Epigr. (0114 001).
Q: 53: Epigr.

2154 **CYLLENIUS** Hist.
A.D. 4

001 **Testimonium**, FGrH #222: 2B:950–951.
NQ: 79: Test.

1296 *CYPRIA*
fort. auctore Hegesia vel Stasino
7–6 B.C.?

001 **Fragmenta**, ed. T.W. Allen, *Homeri opera*, vol.
5. Oxford: Clarendon Press, 1912 (repr. 1969):
118–120, 122–125.
frr. 1, 4–7, 11, 13, 16, 23–25.
Q: Epic.

1482 *CYRANIDES*
fort. auctoribus Cyrano et Harpocratione
ante A.D. 1/2
Cf. et HARPOCRATIONIS EPISTULA (0691).

001 **Cyranides**, ed. D. Kaimakis, *Die Kyraniden.*
Meisenheim am Glan: Hain, 1976: 14–18, 21–
28, 30–37, 39–42, 44–47, 49–50, 52–58, 60–
90, 92–96, 98–267, 269–310.
Cod: 36,514: Magica, Nat. Hist.

2877 **CYRILLUS** Biogr.
A.D. 6: Scythopolitanus
001 **Vita Euthymii**, ed. E. Schwartz, *Kyrillos von Skythopolis* [*Texte und Untersuchungen* 49.2. Leipzig: Hinrichs, 1939]: 3–85.
Cod: 21,284: Hagiogr.
002 **Vita Sabae**, ed. Schwartz, *op. cit.*, 85–200.
Cod: 29,189: Hagiogr.
003 **Vita Joannis Hesychastae**, ed. Schwartz, *op. cit.*, 201–222.
Cod: 5,494: Hagiogr.
004 **Vita Cyriaci**, ed. Schwartz, *op. cit.*, 222–235.
Cod: 3,777: Hagiogr.
005 **Vita Theodosii**, ed. Schwartz, *op. cit.*, 235–241.
Cod: 1,464: Hagiogr.
006 **Vita Theognii**, ed. Schwartz, *op. cit.*, 241–243.
Cod: 640: Hagiogr.
007 **Vita Abramii**, ed. Schwartz, *op. cit.*, 243–247.
Cod: 1,114: Hagiogr.
008 **Vita Gerasimi** [Sp.], ed. A. Papadopoulos-Kerameus, Ἀνάλεκτα Ἱεροσολυμιτικῆς σταχυολογίας, vol. 4. St. Petersburg: Kirschbaum, 1897 (repr. Brussels: Culture et Civilisation, 1963): 175–184.
Cod: 2,291: Hagiogr.

0157 **CYRILLUS** Epigr.
1 B.C./A.D. 1
001 **Epigramma**, AG 9.369.
Q: 16: Epigr.

2110 **CYRILLUS** Scr. Eccl.
A.D. 4: Hierosolymitanus
001 **Procatechesis**, ed. W.C. Reischl and J. Rupp, *Cyrilli Hierosolymorum archiepiscopi opera quae supersunt omnia*, vol. 1. Munich: Lentner, 1848 (repr. Hildesheim: Olms, 1967): 1–26.
Cod: 2,648: Homilet.
002 **Mystagogiae 1–5** [Sp.], ed. A. Piédagnel and P. Paris, *Cyrille de Jérusalem. Catéchèses mystagogiques* [*Sources chrétiennes* 126. Paris: Cerf, 1966]: 82–174.
Cod: 5,633: Homilet.
003 **Catecheses ad illuminandos 1–18**, ed. Reischl and Rupp, *op. cit.*, vols. 1 & 2 (1860; repr. 1967): 1:28–320; 2:2–342.
Cod: 75,549: Homilet.
004 **Additamentum ad catechesis illuminandorum sextae decimae caput tertium**, ed. Reischl and Rupp, *op. cit.*, vol. 2, 248–249.
Cod: 324: Homilet.
005 **Tituli catechesium**, ed. Reischl and Rupp, *op. cit.*, vol. 2, 396–398.
Cod: 605: Homilet.
006 **Homilia in paralyticum juxta piscinam jacentem**, ed. Reischl and Rupp, *op. cit.*, vol. 2, 405–426.
Cod: 2,661: Homilet.
007 **Homilia in occursum domini** [Sp.], ed. Reischl and Rupp, *op. cit.*, vol. 2, 444–456.
Cod: 1,966: Homilet.

008 **Homilia aquae in vinum conversae** (fragmenta) [Sp.], ed. F. Diekamp, *Doctrina patrum de incarnatione verbi*. Münster: Aschendorff, 1907: 92–93.
Q: 161: Homilet.
009 **Homilia in illud**: *Ego vado ad patrem meum* (fragmenta) [Sp.], ed. F. Diekamp, *Analecta patristica* [*Orientalia Christiana analecta* 117. Rome: Pont. Institutum Orientalium Studiorum, 1938 (repr. 1962)]: 10.
Q: 79: Homilet., Exeget.
010 **Suppositarum Cyrilli et Julii pontificis epistularum compendium** [Sp.], MPG 33: 1208–1209.
Cod: 375: Epist., Eccl.
011 **Catechesis ad illuminandos 2** (exemplar alterum), MPG 33: 409–424.
Cod: 2,773: Homilet.
012 **Catechesis ad illuminandos 2** (e cod. Paris. 409), ed. J.B. Pitra, *Iuris ecclesiastici Graecorum historia et monumenta*, vol. 2. Rome: Congregatio de Propaganda Fide, 1868: 291–292.
Cod: Homilet.
013 **Epistula ad Constantium imperatorem**, ed. E. Bihain, "L'épître de Cyrille de Jérusalem à Constance sur la vision de la Croix," *Byzantion* 43 (1973) 286–291.
Cod: Epist.

4090 **CYRILLUS** Theol.
A.D. 4–5: Alexandrinus
001 **Commentarius in xii prophetas minores**, ed. P.E. Pusey, *Sancti patris nostri Cyrilli archiepiscopi Alexandrini in xii prophetas*, 2 vols. Oxford: Clarendon Press, 1868 (repr. Brussels: Culture et Civilisation, 1965): 1:1–740; 2:1–626.
Cod: 311,212: Exeget.
002 **Commentarii in Joannem**, ed. P.E. Pusey, *Sancti patris nostri Cyrilli archiepiscopi Alexandrini in D. Joannis evangelium*, 3 vols. Oxford: Clarendon Press, 1872 (repr. Brussels: Culture et Civilisation, 1965): 1:1–728; 2:1–737; 3:1–171.
Cf. et 4090 031.
Cod: 400,944: Exeget.
003 **Fragmenta in sancti Pauli epistulam ad Romanos**, ed. Pusey, *In Joannis evangelium*, vol. 3, 173–248.
Cod: 18,393: Exeget.
004 **Fragmenta in sancti Pauli epistulam i ad Corinthios**, ed. Pusey, *In Joannis evangelium*, vol. 3, 249–318.
Cod: 15,724: Exeget.
005 **Fragmenta in sancti Pauli epistulam ii ad Corinthios**, ed. Pusey, *In Joannis evangelium*, vol. 3, 320–360.
Cod: 9,225: Exeget.
006 **Fragmenta in sancti Pauli epistulam ad Hebraeos**, ed. Pusey, *In Joannis evangelium*, vol. 3, 362–423.
Cod: 14,389: Exeget.

008 **Fragmenta homiliae de uno filio**, ed. Pusey, *In Joannis evangelium*, vol. 3, 452–454.
fr. 1.
Q: 670: Homilet., Theol.

009 **Fragmenta homiliae quod unus est Christus**, ed. Pusey, *In Joannis evangelium*, vol. 3, 455–458.
fr. 2.
Q: 956: Homilet., Theol.

010 **Quod homo non deiferus** (homilia diversa 20) (fragmenta), ed. Pusey, *In Joannis evangelium*, vol. 3, 459–460.
fr. 3.
Q: 367: Homilet., Theol.

011 **Sermo ad Alexandrinos** (fragmentum), ed. Pusey, *In Joannis evangelium*, vol. 3, 460–461.
fr. 4.
Q: 251: Homilet.

012 **Homiliarum incertarum fragmenta**, ed. Pusey, *In Joannis evangelium*, vol. 3, 461–468, 470–475.
frr. 5–11, 13–15.
Q: 3,024: Homilet.

013 **Fragmenta homiliae de die novissima**, ed. Pusey, *In Joannis evangelium*, vol. 3, 469.
fr. 12.
Q: 178: Homilet.

014 **Fragmenta ex libro contra Diodorum Tarsensem**, ed. Pusey, *In Joannis evangelium*, vol. 3, 492–497.
Cod: 840: Theol., Apol.

015 **Fragmenta ex libro ii contra Theodorum Mopsuestenum**, ed. Pusey, *In Joannis evangelium*, vol. 3, 511–513.
Cod: 329: Theol., Apol.

016 **Fragmenta ex libro iii contra Theodorum Mopsuestenum**, ed. Pusey, *In Joannis evangelium*, vol. 3, 525–526.
Cod: 170: Theol., Apol.

017 **Sermo prosphoneticus ad Alexandrinos de fide** (homilia diversa 21) (fragmenta), ed. Pusey, *In Joannis evangelium*, vol. 3, 538–541.
Cod: 374: Homilet., Theol.

018 **Adversus eos qui negant offerendum esse pro defunctis**, ed. Pusey, *In Joannis evangelium*, vol. 3, 541–544.
Q: 627: Theol.

019 **Quaestio ad Cyrillum** (e tractatu de dogmatum solutione), ed. Pusey, *In Joannis evangelium*, vol. 3, 547–548.
Cod: 561: Theol.

020 **Solutiones** (e tractatu de dogmatum solutione), ed. Pusey, *In Joannis evangelium*, vol. 3, 549–566.
Cod: 3,627: Theol.

021 **Responsiones ad Tiberium diaconum sociosque suos**, ed. Pusey, *In Joannis evangelium*, vol. 3, 577–602.
Cod: 5,145: Theol.

022 **Ad Calosyrium** (epistula 83), ed. Pusey, *In Joannis evangelium*, vol. 3, 603–607.
Cod: 831: Epist., Theol.

023 **De sancta trinitate dialogi i-vii**, ed. G.M. de Durand, *Cyrille d'Alexandrie. Dialogues sur la Trinité*, 3 vols. [*Sources chrétiennes* 231, 237, 246. Paris: Cerf, 1:1976; 2:1977; 3:1978]: 1:126–354; 2:10–384; 3:10–226.
Cod: 101,001: Theol., Dialog.

026 **De incarnatione unigeniti**, ed. G.M. de Durand, *Cyrille d'Alexandrie. Deux dialogues christologiques* [*Sources chrétiennes* 97. Paris: Cerf, 1964]: 188–300.
Cod: 12,933: Theol., Dialog.

027 **Quod unus sit Christus**, ed. de Durand, *SC* 97, 302–514.
Cod: 23,016: Theol., Dialog.

029 **Commentarii in Matthaeum** (in catenis), ed. J. Reuss, *Matthäus-Kommentare aus der griechischen Kirche* [*Texte und Untersuchungen* 61. Berlin: Akademie-Verlag, 1957]: 153–269.
Cf. et 4090 x92.
Q: 25,632: Exeget., Caten.

030 **Commentarii in Lucam**, ed. J. Sickenberger, *Fragmente der Homilien des Cyrill von Alexandrien zum Lukasevangelium* [*Texte und Untersuchungen* 34. Leipzig: Hinrichs, 1909]: 76–107.
Q: [7,938]: Homilet., Exeget.

031 **Commentarii in Joannem** (additamenta), ed. J. Reuss, *Johannes-Kommentare aus der griechischen Kirche* [*Texte und Untersuchungen* 89. Berlin: Akademie-Verlag, 1966]: 188–195.
Cf. et 4090 002.
Q: 1,843: Exeget.

095 **Fragmenta in Acta apostolorum et in epistulas catholicas**, MPG 74: 757–773, 1008–1024.
Q: [3,534]: Homilet., Exeget.

096 **De adoratione et cultu in spiritu et veritate**, MPG 68: 132–1125.
Cod: 212,635: Exeget.

097 **Glaphyra in Pentateuchum**, MPG 69: 9–677.
Cod: 151,248: Exeget.

098 **Fragmenta duo in Numeros**, MPG 69: 641.
Q: 113: Exeget.

099 **Fragmenta in libros Regum**, MPG 69: 680–697.
Q: 3,156: Exeget.

100 **Expositio in Psalmos**, MPG 69: 717–1273.
Dup. partim 4090 125.
Cod: 111,663: Exeget.

101 **Fragmentum in Proverbia**, MPG 69: 1277.
Q: 72: Exeget.

102 **Fragmenta in Canticum canticorum**, MPG 69: 1277–1293.
Q: 2,779: Exeget.

103 **Commentarius in Isaiam prophetam**, MPG 70: 9–1449.
Cod: 320,709: Exeget.

104 **Fragmenta in Jeremiam** (in catenis), MPG 70: 1452–1457.
Q: 1,116: Exeget., Caten.

105 **Fragmentum in librum Baruch** (in catenis), MPG 70: 1457.
Q: 111: Exeget., Caten.

106 **Fragmenta in Ezechielem** (in catenis), MPG 70: 1457–1460.
Q: 519: Exeget., Caten.

107 **Fragmenta in Danielem** (in catenis), MPG 70: 1461.
Q: 158: Exeget., Caten.

108 **Commentarii in Lucam** (in catenis), MPG 72: 476–949.
Q: 99,418: Exeget., Caten.

109 **Thesaurus de sancta consubstantiali trinitate,** MPG 75: 9–656.
Cf. et 4090 130.
Cod: 134,452: Theol.

110 **Dialogus cum Nestorio** [Sp.], MPG 76: 249–256.
Cod: 972: Theol., Dialog.

111 **Contra Julianum imperatorem,** MPG 76: 504–1057.
Cf. et 4090 139–142, 144, 175–176.
Cod: 121,642: Apol.

112 **De synagogae defectu** (fragmentum) [Sp.], MPG 76: 1421–1424.
Q: 277: Exeget.

114 **Ad Xystum episcopum Romae** (epistula 53) (fragmentum), MPG 77: 285–288.
Q: 70: Epist.

115 **Ad Optimum episcopum** (epistula 80), MPG 77: 365–372.
Dup. partim BASILIUS Theol. (2040 004) (epist. 260).
Q: 1,320: Epist., Exeget.

116 **Commentarii in Lucam** (homilia 51) (= **In transfigurationem** [homilia diversa 9]), MPG 77: 1009–1016.
Cod: 1,403: Homilet., Exeget.

117 **Encomium in sanctam Mariam deiparam** (homilia diversa 11), MPG 77: 1029–1040.
Cod: 2,153: Homilet., Encom.

118 **Commentarii in Lucam** (homilia 3 et 4) (= **In occursum domini** [homilia diversa 12]), MPG 77: 1040–1049.
Cod: 2,131: Homilet., Exeget.

119 **De exitu animi** (homilia diversa 14), MPG 77: 1072–1089.
Cod: 4,093: Homilet.

120 **In parabolam vineae** (homilia diversa 17), MPG 77: 1096–1100.
Cod: 773: Homilet., Exeget.

121 **Fragmenta de translatione reliquiarum martyrum Cyri et Joannis** (homilia diversa 18), MPG 77: 1100–1105.
Cod: 871: Homilet., Hagiogr.

122 **Sermo de obitu sanctorum trium puerorum** (fragmenta) [Sp.], MPG 77: 1117.
Cod: 238: Homilet.

123 **De sancta trinitate** [Sp.], MPG 77: 1120–1173.
Cod: 11,868: Theol.

124 **Collectio dictorum veteris testamenti** [Sp.], MPG 77: 1176–1289.
Cod: 24,090: Exeget.

125 **Expositio in Psalmos** (prooemium), ed. G. Mercati, *Osservazioni a Proemi del Salterio di Origene, Ippolito, Eusebio, Cirillo Alessandrino e altri, con frammenti inediti* [*Studi e Testi* 142. Vatican City: Biblioteca Apostolica Vaticana, 1948]: 140–144.
Dup. partim 4090 100.
Cod: [1,299]: Exeget.

126 **Fragmentum in Psalmum 1.5**, ed. G. Mercati, *Alla ricerca dei nomi degli "altri" traduttori nelle Omilie sui Salmi di S. Giovanni Crisostomo e variazioni su alcune catene del Salterio* [*Studi e Testi* 158. Vatican City: Biblioteca Apostolica Vaticana, 1952]: 186.
Cod: [100]: Exeget.

127 **Fragmentum in Psalmum 2.7**, ed. Mercati, *ST* 142, 144.
Cod: [271]: Exeget.

129 **Fragmentum in sancti Pauli epistulam i ad Corinthios**, ed. M. Richard, "Le florilège du Cod. Vatopédi 236 sur le corruptible et l'incorruptible," *Muséon* 86 (1973) 262.
fr. 21.
Cod: [103]: Exeget.

130 **Thesaurus de sancta et consubstantiali trinitate** (additamenta), ed. J.B. Pitra, *Analecta sacra et classica spicilegio Solesmensi parata*, vol. 5.1. Paris: Roger & Chernowitz, 1888: 38–41.
Cf. et 4090 109.
Cod: [1,616]: Theol.

135 **Solutiones** (fragmentum e tractatu de dogmatum solutione), ed. G. Mercati, *Un nuovo frammento del "de dogmatum solutione" di S. Cirillo Alessandrino* in *Varia sacra* [*Studi e Testi* 11. Rome: Tipografia Vaticana, 1903]: 85–86.
Cod: Theol.

139 **Contra Julianum imperatorem** (fragmentum apud Aretham Caesariensem), ed. K.J. Neumann, "Ein neues Bruchstück aus Kaiser Julians Büchern gegen die Christen," *Theologische Literatur Zeitung* 24 (1899) 298–304.
Cf. et 4090 111, 140–142, 144, 175–176.
Q: Apol.

140 **Contra Julianum imperatorem** (fragmentum e libro xiv apud Joannem Thessalonicensem), ed. A. Brinkmann, "Klassische Reminiscenzen," *Rheinisches Museum* 60 (1905) 632.
Cf. et 4090 111, 139, 141–142, 144, 175–176.
Q: Apol.

141 **Contra Julianum imperatorem** (Cyrillus Plotinum citans), ed. P. Henry, *Les états du texte de Plotin*. Paris: Brouwer, 1938: 71–74, 125–140, 170.
Cf. et 4090 111, 139–140, 142, 144, 175–176.
Q: Apol.

142 **Contra Julianum imperatorem** (Cyrillus Hermen Trismegistum citans), ed. A.D. Nock and A.J. Festugière, *Corpus Hermeticum*, vol. 4. Paris: Cerf, 1954: 126–142.
frr. 23–35.
Dup. partim CORPUS HERMETICUM (1286 021).

Cf. et 4090 111, 139–141, 144, 175–176.
Q: Apol.

144 **Contra Julianum imperatorem** (fragmenta), ed.
F. Diekamp, *Analecta patristica* [*Orientalia Christiana analecta* 117. Rome: Pont. Institutum Orientalium Studiorum, 1938 (repr. 1962)]: 228–229.
Cf. et 4090 111, 139–142, 175–176.
Q: Apol.

148 **Oratio in ascensionem domini**, ed. C. Datema, "Une homélie inédite sur l'ascension," *Byzantion* 44 (1974) 126–137.
Cod: [3,233]: Homilet., Theol.

149 **Homilia habita in ecclesia Cyrini** (fragmentum), ed. Richard, *Muséon* 86, 262.
fr. 27.
Cod: [90]: Homilet.

162 **Epistula canonica ad Domnum** (epistula 78),
FONTI II: 276–281.
Q: [600]: Epist.

163 **Ad episcopos qui sunt in Libya et Pentapoli** (epistula 79), FONTI II: 281–284.
Q: [309]: Epist.

165 **Ad Carthaginiense concilium** (epistula 85),
FONTI I.2: 422–424.
Q: [187]: Epist.

166 **Epistula ad Theodosium imperatorem** (fragmenta), ed. M. Richard, "Deux lettres perdues de Cyrille d'Alexandrie," *Opera minora* 2. Turnhout: Brepols, 1977: 274–275.
Q: Epist.

167 **Epistula ad Photium presbyterum** (fragmentum), ed. Richard, *Opera minora* 2, 275.
Cod: [24]: Epist.

170 **Fragmentum incertum papyraceum** (*P. Johnson*), ed. J.W. Barns, "Literary texts from the Fayum," *Classical Quarterly* 43 (1949) 5–8.
Pap: [230]: Apol.

171 **Fragmenta in Job** (in catenis, typus II), ed. P. Young, *Catena Graecorum patrum in beatum Iob, collectore Niceta Heraclea metropolita, Graece nunc primum edita et Latine versa*, 2nd edn. Venice, 1792.
Q: Exeget., Caten.

172 **Commentarii in Lucam** (in catenis), ed. Reuss, *Matthäus-Kommentare*, 153–269 (passim et in apparatu).
Cf. 4090 029 (textus in scholiis in Matthaeum).
Q: Exeget., Caten.

175 **Contra Julianum imperatorem** (fragmenta),
MPG 76: 1057–1064.
Cf. et 4090 111, 139–142, 144, 176.
Q: Apol.

176 **Contra Julianum** (lib. 1–2), ed. P. Burguière and P. Évieux, *Cyrille d'Alexandrie. Contre Julien, tome 1: livres 1 et 2* [*Sources chrétiennes* 322. Paris: Cerf, 1985]: 100–318.
Dup. partim 4090 111.
Cf. et 4090 111, 139–142, 144, 175.
Cod: Apol.

x01 **Ad monachos Aegypti** (epistula 1).
ACO 1.1.1, pp. 10–23.
Cf. CONCILIA OECUMENICA (ACO) (5000 001).

x02 **Ad Nestorium** (epistula 2).
ACO 1.1.1, pp. 23–25.
Cf. CONCILIA OECUMENICA (ACO) (5000 001).

x04 **Ad Nestorium** (epistula 4).
ACO 1.1.1, pp. 25–28 (= ACO 2.1.1, pp. 104–106).
Cf. CONCILIA OECUMENICA (ACO) (5000 001, 003).

x05 **Ad Nestorium** (una cum synodo Alexandrina) (epistula 17).
ACO 1.1.1, pp. 33–42.
Cf. CONCILIA OECUMENICA (ACO) (5000 001).

x06 **Oratio ad Theodosium imperatorem de recta fide.**
ACO 1.1.1, pp. 42–72.
Cf. CONCILIA OECUMENICA (ACO) (5000 001).

x07 **Ad Joannem Antiochenum** (epistula 13).
ACO 1.1.1, pp. 92–93.
Cf. CONCILIA OECUMENICA (ACO) (5000 001).

x08 **Ad Juvenalem Hierosolymitanum** (epistula 16).
ACO 1.1.1, pp. 96–98.
Cf. CONCILIA OECUMENICA (ACO) (5000 001).

x09 **Ad Acacium Beroeensem** (epistula 14).
ACO 1.1.1, pp. 98–99.
Cf. CONCILIA OECUMENICA (ACO) (5000 001).

x10 **Ad quendam Nestorii studiosum** (epistula 9).
ACO 1.1.1, p. 108.
Cf. CONCILIA OECUMENICA (ACO) (5000 001).

x11 **Ad vituperatores** (epistula 8).
ACO 1.1.1, p. 109.
Cf. CONCILIA OECUMENICA (ACO) (5000 001).

x12 **Ad apocrisiarios Constantinopoli constitutos** (epistula 10).
ACO 1.1.1, pp. 110–112.
Cf. CONCILIA OECUMENICA (ACO) (5000 001).

x13 **Ad clerum populumque Constantinopolitanum** (una cum synodo Alexandrina) (epistula 18).
ACO 1.1.1, pp. 113–114.
Cf. CONCILIA OECUMENICA (ACO) (5000 001).

x14 **Ad clerum populumque Alexandrinum** (epistula 20).
ACO 1.1.1, p. 116.
Cf. CONCILIA OECUMENICA (ACO) (5000 001).

x15 **Ad clerum populumque Alexandrinum** (epistula 21).
ACO 1.1.1, p. 117.

Cf. CONCILIA OECUMENICA (ACO) (5000 001).

x16 **Ad clerum populumque Alexandrinum** (epistula 24).
ACO 1.1.1, pp. 117–118.
Cf. CONCILIA OECUMENICA (ACO) (5000 001).

x17 **Ad clerum populumque Alexandrinum** (epistula 25).
ACO 1.1.1, pp. 118–119.
Cf. CONCILIA OECUMENICA (ACO) (5000 001).

x18 **Ad Comarium et Potamonem episcopos et Dalmatium archimandritam et Timotheum et Eulogium presbyteros** (epistula 23).
ACO 1.1.2, pp. 66–68.
Cf. CONCILIA OECUMENICA (ACO) (5000 001).

x19 **Ad patres monachorum** (epistula 26).
ACO 1.1.2, pp. 69–70.
Cf. CONCILIA OECUMENICA (ACO) (5000 001).

x20 **Ephesi dicta deposito Nestorio** (homilia diversa 5).
ACO 1.1.2, pp. 92–94.
Cf. CONCILIA OECUMENICA (ACO) (5000 001).

x21 **Ephesi habita in basilica sancti Joannis evangelistae** (homilia diversa 2).
ACO 1.1.2, pp. 94–96.
Cf. CONCILIA OECUMENICA (ACO) (5000 001).

x22 **Ephesi habita, valde pulchra** (homilia diversa 1).
ACO 1.1.2, pp. 96–98.
Cf. CONCILIA OECUMENICA (ACO) (5000 001).

x23 **Ephesi dicta in Joannem Antiochenum** (homilia diversa 6).
ACO 1.1.2, pp. 98–100.
Cf. CONCILIA OECUMENICA (ACO) (5000 001).

x24 **Ephesi dicta priusquam a comite comprehenderetur** (homilia diversa 7).
ACO 1.1.2, pp. 100–102.
Cf. CONCILIA OECUMENICA (ACO) (5000 001).

x25 **De Maria deipara in Nestorium** (homilia diversa 4).
ACO 1.1.2, pp. 102–104.
Cf. CONCILIA OECUMENICA (ACO) (5000 001).

x26 **Libellus Cyrilli et Memnonis Ephesini ad concilium Ephesinum.**
ACO 1.1.3, pp. 16–17.
Cf. CONCILIA OECUMENICA (ACO) (5000 001).

x27 **Ad clerum populumque Constantinopolitanum** (epistula 27).
ACO 1.1.3, pp. 45–46.
Cf. CONCILIA OECUMENICA (ACO) (5000 001).

x28 **Ad Theopemptum, Potamonem et Danielem episcopos** (epistula 28).
ACO 1.1.3, pp. 50–51.
Cf. CONCILIA OECUMENICA (ACO) (5000 001).

x29 **Ad Maximianum Constantinopolitanum** (epistula 31).
ACO 1.1.3, p. 72.
Cf. CONCILIA OECUMENICA (ACO) (5000 001).

x30 **Apologeticus ad Theodosium imperatorem.**
ACO 1.1.3, pp. 75–90.
Cf. CONCILIA OECUMENICA (ACO) (5000 001).

x31 **Ad Valerianum episcopum Iconii** (epistula 50).
ACO 1.1.3, pp. 90–101.
Cf. CONCILIA OECUMENICA (ACO) (5000 001).

x32 **De Paulo Emeseno** (homilia diversa 3).
ACO 1.1.4, pp. 14–15.
Cf. CONCILIA OECUMENICA (ACO) (5000 001).

x33 **Ad Joannem Antiochenum** (de pace) (epistula 39).
ACO 1.1.4, pp. 15–20 (= ACO 2.1.1, pp. 107–111).
Cf. CONCILIA OECUMENICA (ACO) (5000 001, 003).

x34 **Ad Acacium Melitenum** (epistula 40).
ACO 1.1.4, pp. 20–31.
Cf. CONCILIA OECUMENICA (ACO) (5000 001).

x35 **Ad Dynatum episcopum Nicopolis** (epistula 48).
ACO 1.1.4, pp. 31–32.
Cf. CONCILIA OECUMENICA (ACO) (5000 001).

x36 **Ad Maximianum Constantinopolitanum** (epistula 49).
ACO 1.1.4, p. 34.
Cf. CONCILIA OECUMENICA (ACO) (5000 001).

x37 **Commonitorium ad Eulogium presbyterum** (epistula 44).
ACO 1.1.4, pp. 35–37.
Cf. CONCILIA OECUMENICA (ACO) (5000 001).

x38 **Ad Joannem Antiochenum et synodum Antiochenum** (epistula 67).
ACO 1.1.4, pp. 37–39.
Cf. CONCILIA OECUMENICA (ACO) (5000 001).

x39 **Ad Acacium episcopum Scythopolis** (epistula 41).
ACO 1.1.4, pp. 40–48.
Cf. CONCILIA OECUMENICA (ACO) (5000 001).

x40 **Ad Anastasium, Alexandrum, Martinianum, Joannem, Paregorium presbyteros et Maximum diaconum ceterosque monachos orientales** (epistula 55).
ACO 1.1.4, pp. 49–61.

Cf. CONCILIA OECUMENICA (ACO) (5000 001).

x41 **Expositio et interrogatio de incarnatione verbi dei filii patris** [Sp.].
ACO 1.1.5, pp. 3–6.
Cf. CONCILIA OECUMENICA (ACO) (5000 001).

x42 **Ad Caelestinum papam** (epistula 11).
ACO 1.1.5, pp. 10–12.
Cf. CONCILIA OECUMENICA (ACO) (5000 001).

x43 **Ad monachos Constantinopolitanos** (una cum synodo Alexandrina) (epistula 19).
ACO 1.1.5, pp. 12–13.
Cf. CONCILIA OECUMENICA (ACO) (5000 001).

x44 **Explanatio xii capitulorum.**
ACO 1.1.5, pp. 15–25.
Cf. CONCILIA OECUMENICA (ACO) (5000 001).

x45 **Oratio ad Pulcheriam et Eudociam augustas de fide.**
ACO 1.1.5, pp. 26–61.
Cf. CONCILIA OECUMENICA (ACO) (5000 001).

x46 **Oratio ad Arcadiam et Marinam augustas de fide.**
ACO 1.1.5, pp. 62–118.
Cf. CONCILIA OECUMENICA (ACO) (5000 001).

x47 **Libri v contra Nestorium.**
ACO 1.1.6, pp. 13–106.
Cf. CONCILIA OECUMENICA (ACO) (5000 001).

x48 **Ad Euoptium episcopum Ptolemaidis** (epistula 84).
ACO 1.1.6, pp. 110–111.
Cf. CONCILIA OECUMENICA (ACO) (5000 001).

x49 **Apologia xii anathematismorum contra Theodoretum.**
ACO 1.1.6, pp. 111–146.
Cf. CONCILIA OECUMENICA (ACO) (5000 001).

x50 **Ad Successum episcopum Diocaesareae** (epistula 45).
ACO 1.1.6, pp. 151–157.
Cf. CONCILIA OECUMENICA (ACO) (5000 001).

x51 **Ad Successum episcopum Diocaesareae** (epistula 46).
ACO 1.1.6, pp. 157–162.
Cf. CONCILIA OECUMENICA (ACO) (5000 001).

x52 **Contra eos qui Theotocon nolunt confiteri** [Dub.].
ACO 1.1.7, pp. 19–32.
Cf. CONCILIA OECUMENICA (ACO) (5000 001).

x53 **Apologia xii capitulorum contra orientales.**
ACO 1.1.7, pp. 33–65.

Cf. CONCILIA OECUMENICA (ACO) (5000 001).

x54 **Epistula ad Acacium Beroeensem.**
ACO 1.1.7, pp. 140–142.
Cf. CONCILIA OECUMENICA (ACO) (5000 001).

x55 **Epistula ad Joannem Antiochenum.**
ACO 1.1.7, p. 153.
Cf. CONCILIA OECUMENICA (ACO) (5000 001).

x56 **Epistula ad Joannem Antiochenum.**
ACO 1.1.7, pp. 153–154.
Cf. CONCILIA OECUMENICA (ACO) (5000 001).

x57 **Ad Theognostum et Charmosynum presbyteros et Leontium diaconum** (epistula 37).
ACO 1.1.7, p. 154.
Cf. CONCILIA OECUMENICA (ACO) (5000 001).

x58 **Epistula ad Maximianum Constantinopolitanum.**
ACO 1.1.7, pp. 162–163.
Cf. CONCILIA OECUMENICA (ACO) (5000 001).

x59 **Ad Eusebium presbyterum Antiochenum** (epistula 54).
ACO 1.1.7, pp. 164–165.
Cf. CONCILIA OECUMENICA (ACO) (5000 001).

x60 **Commonitorium ad Posidonium diaconum** (epistula 11a).
ACO 1.1.7, pp. 171–172.
Cf. CONCILIA OECUMENICA (ACO) (5000 001).

x61 **De concordia ecclesiarum** (homilia 16) (fragmentum).
ACO 1.1.7, p. 173.
Cf. CONCILIA OECUMENICA (ACO) (5000 001).

x62 **Scholia de incarnatione unigeniti** (fragmenta).
ACO 1.5.1, pp. 219–231.
Cf. CONCILIA OECUMENICA (ACO) (5000 002).
Cf. et 4090 026.

x63 **Ad Domnum episcopum Antiochiae** (epistula 77).
ACO 2.1.3, pp. 66–67.
Cf. CONCILIA OECUMENICA (ACO) (5000 003).

x64 **Ad monachos in Phua constitutos** (epistula 81).
ACO 3, pp. 201–202.
Cf. CONCILIA OECUMENICA (ACO) (5000 004).

x65 **Fragmentum in Psalmum 5.8** (in *Doctrina patrum*).
Diekamp, pp. 186–187 (fr. 21).
Cf. DOCTRINA PATRUM (7051 001).

x67 **De sancta trinitate dialogi vii** (fragmenta).
Diekamp, pp. 30 (fr. 5), 36 (fr. 7), 48 (fr. 3), 55 (fr. 4), 74 (fr. 6), 83 (fr. 8), 116 (fr. 8), 123 (fr. 10), 148 (lines 11–16), 193 (fr. 2).
Dup. partim 4090 023.
Cf. DOCTRINA PATRUM (7051 001).

x70 **Liber contra Synousiastas** (fragmenta Graeca).
Hespel, pp. 138–150, frr. 76–90.
Cf. FLORILEGIUM CYRILLIANUM (4147 001).

x72 **Contra Julianum imperatorem** (fragmenta e libris ii, viii, xii, xiii, xiv).
Hespel, pp. 185–187, frr. 176–180.
Cf. FLORILEGIUM CYRILLIANUM (4147 001).

x73 **Tractatus de inhumanatione.**
Hespel, p. 137, fr. 73.
Cf. FLORILEGIUM CYRILLIANUM (4147 001).

x75 **Sermo prosphoneticus ad Alexandrinos de fide** (homilia diversa 21) (fragmenta) (in *Doctrina patrum*).
Diekamp, pp. 17–18 (frr. 22–24), 21 (fr. 34), 66 (fr. 4).
Dup. partim 4090 017.
Cf. DOCTRINA PATRUM (7051 001).

x76 **Epistula ad Juvenalem et ceteros concilii legatos Constantinopolim missos** (epistula 32).
ACO 1.1.7, p. 137.
Cf. CONCILIA OECUMENICA (ACO) (5000 001).

x77 **Epistula ad Acacium Beroeensem** (epistula 33).
ACO 1.1.7, pp. 147–150.
Cf. CONCILIA OECUMENICA (ACO) (5000 001).

x78 **De incarnatione dei verbi** (homilia diversa 15).
Schwartz, pp. 13–15.
Cf. FLORILEGIUM ANTICHALCEDONIUM (4148 001).

x79 **Ad Rufum Thessalonicensem** (epistula 42).
Schwartz, p. 19.
Cf. FLORILEGIUM ANTICHALCEDONIUM (4148 001).

x80 **Ad Rufum Thessalonicensem** (epistula 43).
Schwartz, pp. 19–20.
Cf. FLORILEGIUM ANTICHALCEDONIUM (4148 001).

x81 **Ad Gennadium presbyterum et archimandritam** (epistula 56).
Schwartz, p. 17.
Cf. FLORILEGIUM ANTICHALCEDONIUM (4148 001).

x82 **Commonitorium ad Maximum diaconum Antiochenum** (epistula 57).
Schwartz, p. 21.
Cf. FLORILEGIUM ANTICHALCEDONIUM (4148 001).

x83 **Ad Maximum diaconum Antiochenum** (epistula 58).
Schwartz, pp. 20–21.
Cf. FLORILEGIUM ANTICHALCEDONIUM (4148 001).

x84 **Ad Joannem Antiochenum** (epistula 62).
Schwartz, p. 15.
Cf. FLORILEGIUM ANTICHALCEDONIUM (4148 001).

x85 **Ad Acacium Melitenum** (epistula 69).
Schwartz, pp. 15–16.
Cf. FLORILEGIUM ANTICHALCEDONIUM (4148 001).

x86 **Ad Lamponem presbyterum Alexandrinum** (epistula 70).
Schwartz, pp. 16–17.
Cf. FLORILEGIUM ANTICHALCEDONIUM (4148 001).

x87 **Ad Proclum Constantinopolitanum** (epistula 72).
Schwartz, pp. 17–19.
Cf. FLORILEGIUM ANTICHALCEDONIUM (4148 001).

x88 **Ad Atticum Constantinopolitanum** (epistula 76).
Schwartz, pp. 25–28.
Cf. FLORILEGIUM ANTICHALCEDONIUM (4148 001).

x89 **Ad Amphilochium episcopum Sidae** (epistula 82).
Schwartz, p. 20.
Cf. FLORILEGIUM ANTICHALCEDONIUM (4148 001).

x90 **Epistula ad monachos Constantinopolitanos** (fragmentum).
Schwartz, p. 34.
Cf. FLORILEGIUM ANTICHALCEDONIUM (4148 001).

x91 **De sancta trinitate dialogi vii** (fragmenta).
Schwartz, pp. 22–23.
Cf. FLORILEGIUM ANTICHALCEDONIUM (4148 001).

x92 **Commentarii in Matthaeum** (fragmenta e cod. Vat. gr. 1431).
Schwartz, pp. 42–45.
Cf. FLORILEGIUM ANTICHALCEDONIUM (4148 001).
Cf. et 4090 029.

x93 **Contra eunuchos** (homilia diversa 19).
de Boor, vol. 2, pp. 651–654.
Cf. GEORGIUS Monachus Chronogr. (3043 001).

4055 **Flavius CYRUS** Epic.
A.D. 5: Panopolitanus

001 **Epigrammata**, AG 1.99; 7.557; **9.**136, 623, 808–809; 15.9.
AG 9.813: Cf. ANONYMI EPIGRAMMATICI (AG) (0138 001).
Q: 270: Epigr.

002 **Homilia in nativitatem** (ap. Theophanem Confessorem), ed. T.C. Gregory, "The remarkable Christmas homily of Kyros Panopolites," *Greek, Roman and Byzantine Studies* 16 (1975) 318.
Q: Homilet.

0847 **CYRUS** Med.
ante A.D. 6: Edessenus

x01 **Fragmentum ap. Aëtium** (lib. 6).
CMG, vol. 8.2, p. 237.
Cf. AËTIUS Med. (0718 006).

4242 **CYRUS** Rhet.
    Incertum
  001 Περὶ διαφορᾶς στάσεως, ed. C. Walz, *Rhetores Graeci*, vol. 8. Stuttgart: Cotta, 1835 (repr. Osnabrück: Zeller, 1968): 387–399.
    Cod: Rhet.

1908 **DAIMACHUS** Hist.
    4 B.C.: Plataeeus
    Cf. et HELLENICA (0558).
  001 **Testimonia**, FGrH #65: 2A:15.
    NQ: 77: Test.
  002 **Fragmenta**, FGrH #65: 2A:15–17.
    Q: 492: Hist., Tact.

2482 **DAIMACHUS** Hist.
    vel Deimachus
    post 3 B.C.: Plataeeus
  001 **Testimonia**, FGrH #716: 3C:639.
    NQ: 100: Test.
  002 **Fragmenta**, FGrH #716: 3C:640–641.
    Q: 365: Hist.

2454 **DALION** Hist.
    4/3 B.C.?
  001 **Testimonia**, FGrH #666: 3C:277–278.
    NQ: 128: Test.
  002 **Fragmenta**, FGrH #666: 3C:278–279.
    Q: 184: Hist.

0158 **DAMAGETUS** Epigr.
    3 B.C.: Achaeus
  001 **Epigrammata**, AG **6**.277; **7**.9, 231, 355, 432, 438, 497, 540–541, 735; **16**.1, 95.
    Q: 417: Epigr.

DAMASCIUS Med.
    Cf. THEOPHILUS Protospatharius, DAMASCIUS et STEPHANUS Atheniensis Med. (0728).

4066 **DAMASCIUS** Phil.
    A.D. 5/6: Damascenus, Alexandrinus, Atheniensis
    Cf. et THEOPHILUS Protospatharius, DAMASCIUS et STEPHANUS Atheniensis Med. (0728).
  001 **Epigramma**, AG 7.553.
    Q: 16: Epigr.
  002 **Vita Isidori** (ap. *Sudam*, Hesychium, Photium et e cod. Vat. 1950), ed. C. Zintzen, *Damascii vitae Isidori reliquiae*. Hildesheim: Olms, 1967: 2–3, 5–97, 101–275, 279–299, 310–316.
    Dup. partim 4066 007.
    Q, Cod: 19,830: Biogr.
  003 **De principiis**, ed. C.É. Ruelle, *Damascii successoris dubitationes et solutiones*, vols. 1 & 2. Paris: Klincksieck, 1:1889; 2:1899 (repr. Brussels: Culture et Civilisation, 1964): 1:1–324; 2:1–4.
    Cod: 108,109: Phil.

  004 **In Parmenidem**, ed. Ruelle, *op. cit.*, vol. 2, 5–322.
    Cod: 112,749: Phil., Comm.
  005 **In Phaedonem** (versio 1), ed. L.G. Westerink, *The Greek commentaries on Plato's Phaedo*, vol. 2 [*Damascius*]. Amsterdam: North-Holland, 1977: 27–285.
    Cf. et 4066 008.
    Cod: 31,611: Phil., Comm.
  006 **In Philebum**, ed. L.G. Westerink, *Damascius. Lectures on the Philebus wrongly attributed to Olympiodorus*. Amsterdam: North-Holland, 1959: 3–121.
    Cod: 17,426: Phil., Comm.
  007 **Vita Isidori** (ap. Photium, *Bibl.* codd. 181, 242), ed. Zintzen, *op. cit.*, 4–18, 22–26, 38–46, 50–72, 76–112, 118–122, 130–134, 138–158, 162, 166–184, 190–198, 202–206, 210–220, 230, 234–238, 244, 248–254, 258–260, 268–292, 296, 300–309.
    Dup. partim 4066 002.
    Q: 10,957: Biogr.
  008 **In Phaedonem** (versio 2), ed. Westerink, *The Greek commentaries on Plato's Phaedo*, vol. 2, 289–371.
    Cf. et 4066 005.
    Cod: 10,951: Phil., Comm.
  x01 **Paradoxa**.
    Photius, *Bibliotheca* 130.
    Cf. PHOTIUS Theol., Scr. Eccl. et Lexicogr. (4040 001).
  x02 Περὶ ἀριθμοῦ καὶ τόπου καὶ χρόνου.
    Simplicius, *Physica* 183v45.
    Cf. SIMPLICIUS Phil. (4013 004).
  x03 **Commentarium in Aristotelis librum de caelo** (excerptum e cod. Vat. gr. 499) (olim sub auctore Damascio).
    Brandis, pp. 454a–455a.
    Cf. ANONYMI IN ARISTOTELIS LIBRUM DE CAELO (4195 001).

1868 **DAMASTES** Hist.
    5 B.C.: Sigeus
  001 **Testimonia**, FGrH #5: 1A:152–153.
    NQ: 279: Test.
  002 **Fragmenta**, FGrH #5: 1A:153–156, *8 addenda.
    fr. 4 bis: *P. Oxy*. 13.1611.
    Q, Pap: 836: Hist.

2627 **DAMIANUS** Scriptor De Opticis
    A.D. 4: fort. Larissaeus
  001 **Optica**, ed. R. Schöne, *Damianos Schrift über Optik*. Berlin: Reichsdruckerei, 1897: 2–22.
    Cod

2655 **<DAMIGERON Magus>**
    Incertum
  001 **De lapidibus**, ed. V. Rose, "Damigeron de lapidibus," *Hermes* 9 (1875) 481–490.
    Q

002 **De lapidibus** (e codd. V et A), ed. J. Mesk, "Ein unedierter Tractat περὶ λίθων," *Wiener Studien* (1898) 318–321.
Cod

1297 **DAMIPPUS** Phil.
3 B.C.
001 **Fragmenta**, ed. H. Thesleff, *The Pythagorean texts of the Hellenistic period.* Åbo: Åbo Akademi, 1965: 68–69.
Q: 520: Phil.

4067 **DAMOCHARIS** Gramm.
A.D. 6: Cous
001 **Epigrammata**, AG **6**.63; **7**.206; **9**.633; **16**.310.
Q: 174: Epigr.

0848 Servilius **DAMOCRATES** Poet. Med.
A.D. 1
x01 **Fragmenta ap. Galenum.**
K**12**.889–892; **13**.40–42, 220–227, 350–353, 455–457, 821–823, 915–923, 940–945, 988–990, 996–1005, 1047–1058; **14**.90–99, 115–135, 191–201.
Cf. GALENUS Med. (0057 076–078).

2493 **DAMOCRITUS** Hist.
1 B.C.–A.D. 1?
001 **Fragmentum**, FGrH #730: 3C:691.
Q: 33: Hist.

2273 **DAMON** Hist.
ante A.D. 3
001 **Fragmentum**, FGrH #389: 3B:266.
Q: 77: Hist.

2232 **DAMON** Mus.
5 B.C.: Atheniensis
001 **Testimonia**, ed. H. Diels and W. Kranz, *Die Fragmente der Vorsokratiker*, vol. 1, 6th edn. Berlin: Weidmann, 1951 (repr. Dublin: 1966): 381–382.
test. 1–8.
NQ: 367: Test.
002 **Fragmenta**, ed. Diels and Kranz, *op. cit.*, 382–384.
frr. 1–10.
Q: 523: Phil., Mus.

2244 **DAMON et PHINTIAS** Phil.
4 B.C.: Syracusanus
001 **Testimonium**, ed. H. Diels and W. Kranz, *Die Fragmente der Vorsokratiker*, vol. 1, 6th edn. Berlin: Weidmann, 1951 (repr. Dublin: 1966): 444.
NQ: 164: Test.

0849 Claudius **DAMONICUS** Med.
ante A.D. 1
x01 **Fragmenta ap. Galenum.**
K**12**.637; **13**.740.
Cf. GALENUS Med. (0057 076–077).

0438 **DAMOXENUS** Comic.
4/3 B.C.
001 **Fragmenta**, ed. T. Kock, *Comicorum Atticorum fragmenta*, vol. 3. Leipzig: Teubner, 1888: 348–351, 353.
frr. 1–3.
Q: 555: Comic.
002 **Fragmenta**, ed. A. Meineke, *Fragmenta comicorum Graecorum*, vol. 4. Berlin: Reimer, 1841 (repr. De Gruyter, 1970): 529–532, 536.
Q: 554: Comic.

0364 *DANAIS*
Incertum
001 **Danais**, ed. G. Kinkel, *Epicorum Graecorum fragmenta*, vol. 1. Leipzig: Teubner, 1877: 78.
fr. 1.
Q: [12]: Epic.

2615 **DAPHITAS** Gramm. vel Soph.
3 B.C.: Telmessensis
001 **Fragmentum**, ed. H. Lloyd-Jones and P. Parsons, *Supplementum Hellenisticum.* Berlin: De Gruyter, 1983: 173.
fr. 370.
Q: 16: Epigr.
x01 **Epigramma irrisorium.**
App. Anth. 5.20: Cf. ANTHOLOGIAE GRAECAE APPENDIX (7052 005).
Dup. 2615 001.

1894 **<DARES>** Hist.
8 B.C.?: Phrygius
001 **Testimonia**, FGrH #51: 1A:294.
NQ: 268: Test.

0851 **DARIUS** Med.
ante A.D. 1
x01 **Fragmenta ap. Galenum.**
K**13**.69, 832.
Cf. GALENUS Med. (0057 076–077).

4021 **DAVID** Phil.
A.D. 6: Thessalonicensis, Alexandrinus
Cf. et Pseudo-DAVID et Pseudo-ELIAS Phil. (4022).
001 **Prolegomena philosophiae**, ed. A. Busse, *Davidis prolegomena et in Porphyrii isagogen commentarium* [*Commentaria in Aristotelem Graeca* 18.2. Berlin: Reimer, 1904]: 1–79.
Cod: 29,971: Phil., Comm.
002 **In Porphyrii isagogen commentarium**, ed. Busse, *op. cit.*, 80–219.
Cod: 46,217: Phil., Comm.
x01 **In Aristotelis categorias commentaria.**
CAG 18.1, pp. 107–255.
Cf. ELIAS Phil. (4020 002).

4022 **Pseudo-DAVID et Pseudo-ELIAS** Phil.
A.D. 6/8: fort. Constantinopolitanus
Cf. et DAVID Phil. (4021).
Cf. et ELIAS Phil. (4020).

001 **In Porphyrii isagogen commentarium**, ed. L.G. Westerink, *Pseudo-Elias (Pseudo-David)*. *Lectures on Porphyry's isagoge*. Amsterdam: North-Holland, 1967: 1–136.
Cod: Phil., Comm.

0272 *DE ARBORIBUS AVIBUSQUE FABULAE*
ante A.D. 2/3
001 **Fragmenta** (*P. Heidelb.* 222), ed. E. Heitsch, *Die griechischen Dichterfragmente der römischen Kaiserzeit*, vol. 1, 2nd edn. Göttingen: Vandenhoeck & Ruprecht, 1963: 34–38.
frr. 1–5.
Pap: 321: Lyr.

2326 **DEI(L)OCHUS** Hist.
vel Deiochus
5–4 B.C.?: Cyzicenus, Proconnensis
001 **Testimonia**, FGrH #471: 3B:427.
NQ: 35: Test.
002 **Fragmenta**, FGrH #471: 3B:427–429.
Q: 634: Hist.
003 **Fragmentum**, ed. H.J. Mette, "Die 'Kleinen' griechischen Historiker heute," *Lustrum* 21 (1978) 30.
fr. 11.
Q: 29: Hist.

0877 **DELETIUS** Med.
ante A.D. 2
x01 **Fragmentum ap. Galenum**.
K13.300.
Cf. GALENUS Med. (0057 076).

1989 **Quintus DELLIUS** Hist.
1 B.C.
001 **Fragmenta**, FGrH #197: 2B:929.
Q: 127: Hist.

0535 **DEMADES** Orat. et Rhet.
4 B.C.: Atheniensis
001 **Fragmenta**, ed. V. de Falco, *Demade oratore. Testimonianze e frammenti*, 2nd edn. Naples: Libreria Scientifica Editrice, 1955: 19–54, 60–68, 83–87.
fr. 83: *P. Oxy.* 2.216.
Q, Cod, Pap: 6,539: Orat.
002 **Testimonium**, FGrH #227: 2B:955.
NQ: 43: Test.
003 **Fragmentum**, FGrH #227: 2B:955.
Q: 42: Hist.

1812 **DEMARATUS** Hist.
vel Demagetus
3–2 B.C.
001 **Fragmenta**, FGrH #42: 1A:264–265.
Q: 617: Hist., Myth.

2616 **DEMARETA** Poeta
ante A.D. 2
001 **Titulus**, ed. H. Lloyd-Jones and P. Parsons, *Supplementum Hellenisticum*. Berlin: De Gruyter, 1983: 174.
fr. 372.
NQ: 2: Poem.

2347 **DEMEAS** Hist.
4–3 B.C.?: Parius
001 **Fragmentum**, FGrH #502: 3B:479–481.
fr. 1: *IG* 12.5, no. 445.
Epigr: 566: Hist.

1298 *DEMETRII PHALEREI EPISTULA*
Incertum
Cf. et DEMETRIUS Phil. et Hist. (0624).
001 **Epistula**, ed. R. Hercher, *Epistolographi Graeci*. Paris: Didot, 1873 (repr. Amsterdam: Hakkert, 1965): 218.
Q: 179: Epist.

0439 **DEMETRIUS** Comic.
5/4 B.C.
001 **Fragmenta**, ed. T. Kock, *Comicorum Atticorum fragmenta*, vol. 1. Leipzig: Teubner, 1888: 795–796.
frr. 1–2, 4–5.
Q: 70: Comic.
002 **Fragmenta**, ed. A. Meineke, *Fragmenta comicorum Graecorum*, vol. 2.2. Berlin: Reimer, 1840 (repr. De Gruyter, 1970): 876–878.
Q: 71: Comic.
003 **Tituli**, ed. C. Austin, *Comicorum Graecorum fragmenta in papyris reperta*. Berlin: De Gruyter, 1973: 50.
fr. 77.
Pap: 5: Comic.

DEMETRIUS Epigr.
3 B.C.?: Halicarnassensis
AG 13.29.
Cf. NICAENETUS Epic. (0218 002).

0159 **DEMETRIUS** Epigr.
2 B.C.: Bithynius
001 **Epigramma**, AG 9.730.
AG 9.731: Cf. ANONYMI EPIGRAMMATICI (AG) (0138 001).
AG 9.732: Cf. Marcus ARGENTARIUS Epigr. (0132 001).
Q: 18: Epigr.

1756 **DEMETRIUS** Gramm.
3–2 B.C.: Scepsius
001 **Fragmenta**, ed. R. Gaede, *Demetrii Scepsii quae supersunt* [*Diss. Greifswald* (1880)]: 17–36, 38–52, 54–59.
frr. 1–75.
Q: 5,384: Gramm.

2208 **DEMETRIUS** Hist.
4 B.C.: fort. Argivus
001 **Testimonium**, FGrH #304: 3B:7.
NQ: 52: Test.

002 **Fragmentum**, FGrH #304: 3B:7.
Q: 27: Hist.

1957 **DEMETRIUS** Hist.
3 B.C.: Byzantius
001 **Testimonium**, FGrH #162: 2B:889.
NQ: 39: Test.

1299 **DEMETRIUS** Hist.
fiq Demetrius Judaeus Alexandrinus
3 B.C.?
Cf. et DEMETRIUS Judaeus Hist. (2485).
001 **Testimonium**, FGrH #643: 3C:188.
NQ: 29: Test.
002 **Fragmenta**, FGrH #643: 3C:189.
Q: 132: Hist.

2381 **DEMETRIUS** Hist.
3 B.C.?: Seriphius
001 **Fragmentum**, FGrH #549: 3B:535.
Q: 33: Hist.

1917 **DEMETRIUS** Hist.
3-2 B.C.: Callatianus
001 **Testimonia**, FGrH #85: 2A:202-203.
NQ: 130: Test.
002 **Fragmenta**, FGrH #85: 2A:203-204.
Q: 482: Hist., Geogr.

2522 **DEMETRIUS** Hist.
2 B.C.?
001 **Fragmentum**, FGrH #777: 3C:772.
Q: 82: Hist.

1901 **DEMETRIUS** Hist.
ante A.D. 2: Iliensis
001 **Fragmenta**, FGrH #59: 1A:298.
Q: 107: Hist., Myth.

1995 **DEMETRIUS** Hist.
A.D. 2: Sagalassensis
001 **Fragmentum**, FGrH #209: 2B:941.
Q: 15: Hist.

2511 **DEMETRIUS** Hist.
Incertum: Salaminius
001 **Fragmentum**, FGrH #756: 3C:736-737.
Q: 41: Hist.

2541 **DEMETRIUS** Hist.
Incertum: Odessius
001 **Testimonium**, FGrH #808: 3C:844.
NQ: 30: Test.

2572 **DEMETRIUS** Hist.
Incertum
001 **Fragmenta**, FGrH #852: 3C:936.
Q: 80: Hist.

0624 **DEMETRIUS** Phil. et Hist.
4-3 B.C.: Phalereus
Cf. et DEMETRII PHALEREI EPISTULA
(1298).

001 **Fragmenta**, ed. F. Wehrli, *Demetrios von Phaleron* [*Die Schule des Aristoteles*, vol. 4, 2nd edn. Basel: Schwabe, 1968]: 21-44.
Scripta: frr. 74-76.
Περὶ τύχης: frr. 79, 81.
Περὶ γήρως: frr. 82-83.
Περὶ εἰρήνης: fr. 89.
Σωκράτης: frr. 91-93, 95-97.
Περὶ ὀνείρων: fr. 99.
Apophthegmata: frr. 115-122.7.
Στρατηγικῶν: frr. 123-124.
Περὶ τῆς δεκαετίας. Περὶ τῆς πολιτείας. Ἀθηναίων καταδρομή: frr. 132-134, 136, 138a-138b.
Περὶ τῆς Ἀθήνησι νομοθεσίας. Περὶ τῶν Ἀθήνησι πολιτειῶν: frr. 139-141b, 143-147.
Ἀρχόντων ἀναγραφή: frr. 149-150.2, 152-154.
Historica incertae sedis: fr. 155.
Περὶ ῥητορικῆς: frr. 156-159, 161-166, 169-173.
Δημηγοριῶν συναγωγή. Πρεσβειῶν συναγωγή: frr. 183-184.
Περὶ Ἰλιάδος. Περὶ Ὀδυσσείας. Ὁμηρικός: frr. 190-193.
De Platone: fr. 195.
Apophthegmata (Dub. et Sp.): fr. 198.
Judaica (Dub. et Sp.): fr. 201.
Rhetorica (Dub. et Sp.): frr. 205-206.
Posthomerica (Dub. et Sp.): fr. 207.
Commentarium in Nicandri Theriaca (Dub. et Sp.): fr. 208.
Q, Pap: 4,763: Phil., Rhet., Gnom., Comm.
002 **Testimonia**, FGrH #228: 2B:956-960.
NQ: 1,613: Test.
003 **Fragmenta**, FGrH #228: **2B**:960-973; **3B**:744 addenda.
Q: 4,506: Hist., Rhet.
x01 **Septem sapientum apophthegmata**.
D-K vol. 1, pp. 63-66.
Cf. <SEPTEM SAPIENTES> (1667 002-003).
x02 **Formae epistolicae**.
Weichert, pp. 1-12.
Cf. DEMETRIUS Rhet. (1302 001-002).
x03 **De elocutione**.
Radermacher, pp. 3-62.
Cf. <DEMETRIUS> Rhet. (0613 001).

1301 **DEMETRIUS** Poet. Phil.
A.D. 1: Troezenius
002 **Fragmenta et titulus**, ed. H. Lloyd-Jones and P. Parsons, *Supplementum Hellenisticum*. Berlin: De Gruyter, 1983: 174-175.
frr. 374, 376.
Q: 22: Phil., Hexametr.

2617 **DEMETRIUS** Poeta
ante A.D. 3
001 **Fragmentum**, ed. H. Lloyd-Jones and P. Parsons, *Supplementum Hellenisticum*. Berlin: De Gruyter, 1983: 174.
fr. 373.
Q: 19: Hexametr.

1302 **DEMETRIUS** Rhet.
2/1 B.C.
001 **Formae epistolicae**, ed. V. Weichert, *Demetrii et Libanii qui feruntur τύποι ἐπιστολικοί et ἐπιστολιμαῖοι χαρακτῆρες*. Leipzig: Teubner, 1910: 1–12.
Cod: 1,897: Rhet.
002 **Formae epistolicae** (duo exempla spuria), ed. Weichert, *op. cit.*, 12.
Cod: 176: Rhet.

0613 **<DEMETRIUS>** Rhet.
1 B.C./A.D. 1?
001 **De elocutione**, ed. L. Radermacher, *Demetrii Phalerei qui dicitur de elocutione libellus*. Leipzig: Teubner, 1901 (repr. Stuttgart: 1967): 3–62.
Cod: 15,846: Rhet.

1849 **DEMETRIUS** Trag.
5 B.C.?
001 **Titulus** (+ dramatis personae), ed. B. Snell, *Tragicorum Graecorum fragmenta*, vol. 1. Göttingen: Vandenhoeck & Ruprecht, 1971: 189.
NQ: 10: Satyr.

DEMETRIUS I Poliorcetes Hist.
4 B.C.: Macedo
Cf. ADDITAMENTA (FGrH) (2433 021).

0958 **DEMETRIUS IXION** Gramm.
2 B.C.: Alexandrinus, Pergamenus
001 **Fragmenta**, ed. T. Staesche, *De Demetrio Ixione grammatico* [*Diss. Halle* (1883)]: 41–44, 46–47, 50–59.
Q: Gramm.

2485 **DEMETRIUS Judaeus** Hist.
3 B.C.: Alexandrinus
001 **Fragmenta**, FGrH #722: 3C:666–671.
Q: 1,632: Hist.

0440 **DEMETRIUS Junior** Comic.
4/3 B.C.
001 **Fragmentum**, ed. T. Kock, *Comicorum Atticorum fragmenta*, vol. 3. Leipzig: Teubner, 1888: 357–358.
fr. 1.
Q: 73: Comic.
002 **Fragmentum**, ed. A. Meineke, *Fragmenta comicorum Graecorum*, vol. 4. Berlin: Reimer, 1841 (repr. De Gruyter, 1970): 539.
Q: 52: Comic.

1300 **DEMETRIUS LACON** Phil.
2 B.C.
001 **Fragmenta** (*P. Herc.* 124, 188, 1006, 1013, 1014, 1055, 1061, 1113, 1258, 1429, 1642, 1647, 1696, 1786), ed. V. de Falco, *L'Epicureo Demetrio Lacone*. Naples: Cimmaruta, 1923: 25–60, 62–65, 69–82, 85–101, 103–107.
Pap: Phil.

002 Περὶ ποιημάτων (*P. Herc.* 188 + 1014), ed. C. Romeo, "Nuove letture nei libri 'sulla poesia' di Demetrio Lacone," *Cronache Ercolanesi* 8 (1978) 105–107, 111–123.
Pap: Phil.
003 **Fragmenta philosophica** (*P. Herc.* 1013), ed. C. Romeo, "Demetrio Lacone sulla grandezza del sole," *Cronache Ercolanesi* 9 (1979) 17–20.
Dup. partim 1300 001.
Pap: Phil.
004 **Fragmenta incerti operis** (*P. Herc.* 1012 + 1786), ed. E. Puglia, "Nuove letture nei P. Herc. 1012 e 1786 (Demetrii Laconis opera incerta)," *Cronache Ercolanesi* 10 (1980) 28–49, 51–52.
Pap: Phil.
005 Περὶ ποιημάτων (*P. Herc.* 1014), ed. C. Romeo, "Demetrio Lacone interprete di Alceo," *Cronache Ercolanesi* 12 (1982) 35, 36, 38, 40, 41.
Pap: Phil.
006 **Fragmenta incerti operis** (*P. Herc.* 1055), ed. E. Renna, "Nuove letture nel P. Herc. 1055 (libro incerto di Demetrio Lacone)," *Cronache Ercolanesi* 12 (1982) 46–49.
Dup. partim 1300 001.
Pap: Phil.

DEMETRIUS Scriptor Scholiorum
Incertum: Lampsacenus
Cf. SCHOLIA IN DIONYSIUM PERIEGETAM (5019 001).

0160 **DEMIURGUS** Epigr.
1 B.C.
001 **Epigramma**, AG 7.52.
Q: 12: Epigr.

1303 **DEMOCHARES** Orat. et Hist.
4–3 B.C.: Atheniensis
001 **Testimonia**, FGrH #75: 2A:133–134.
NQ: 394: Test.
002 **Fragmenta**, FGrH #75: 2A:134–136.
Q: 645: Hist.

0161 **DEMOCRITUS** Epigr.
ante A.D. 3?
001 **Epigramma**, AG 16.180.
Q: 35: Epigr.

1305 **DEMOCRITUS** Hist.
3 B.C.: Ephesius
001 **Testimonium**, FGrH #267: 3A:76.
NQ: 48: Test.
002 **Fragmenta**, FGrH #267: 3A:76.
Q: 154: Hist.

1304 **DEMOCRITUS** Phil.
5–4 B.C.: Abderita
Cf. et BOLUS Phil. (1306).
001 **Testimonia**, ed. H. Diels and W. Kranz, *Die Fragmente der Vorsokratiker*, vol. 2, 6th edn.

Berlin: Weidmann, 1952 (repr. Dublin: 1966): 81–129.

test. 1–170.

NQ: 19,869: Test.

002 **Fragmenta**, ed. Diels and Kranz, *op. cit.*, 130–224.

frr. 1–300, 302, 304–309.

fr. 300 = fragmenta Boli.

Q: 14,834: Phil., Gnom., Alchem.

x01 **Epigramma.**

AG 9.360: Cf. METRODORUS Epigr. (4077 001).

Pseudo-DEMOCRITUS Phil.

3 B.C.

Cf. BOLUS Phil. (1306).

2299 **DEMODAMAS** Hist.

4–3 B.C.: Halicarnassensis, Milesius

001 **Testimonia**, FGrH #428: 3B:324.

NQ: 121: Test.

002 **Fragmenta**, FGrH #428: 3B:324–325.

Q: 71: Hist.

0245 **DEMODOCUS** Eleg.

6 B.C.?: Lerius

001 **Fragmenta**, ed. M.L. West, *Iambi et elegi Graeci*, vol. 2. Oxford: Clarendon Press, 1972: 56–58.

frr. 1–6.

Q: 108: Eleg., Epigr., Iamb.

002 **Epigrammata**, AG 11.235–238.

Dup. 0245 001 (frr. 2–5).

Q: 89: Epigr.

2308 **DEMOGNETUS** Hist.

ante A.D. 2

001 **Fragmentum**, FGrH #445: 3B:376.

Q: 37: Hist.

1307 **DEMON** Hist.

4–3 B.C.: fort. Atheniensis

001 **Testimonium**, FGrH #327: 3B:87.

NQ: 22: Test.

002 **Fragmenta**, FGrH #327: 3B:87–96.

Q: 2,361: Hist., Paroem.

2969 **DEMONAX** Phil.

A.D. 2: Cyprius

001 **Fragmenta**, ed. F.W.A. Mullach, *Fragmenta philosophorum Graecorum*, vol. 2. Paris: Didot, 1867 (repr. Aalen: Scientia, 1968): 351–357.

frr. 1–67.

Q: 2,123: Phil.

0349 **DEMONAX** <Trag.>

Incertum

001 **Fragmenta**, ed. B. Snell, *Tragicorum Graecorum fragmenta*, vol. 1. Göttingen: Vandenhoeck & Ruprecht, 1971: 320.

frr. 1–3.

Q: 13: Trag.

0441 **DEMONICUS** Comic.

5/4 B.C.?

001 **Fragmentum**, ed. T. Kock, *Comicorum Atticorum fragmenta*, vol. 3. Leipzig: Teubner, 1888: 375.

fr. 1.

Q: 27: Comic.

002 **Fragmentum**, ed. A. Meineke, *Fragmenta comicorum Graecorum*, vol. 4. Berlin: Reimer, 1841 (repr. De Gruyter, 1970): 570.

Q: 28: Comic.

DEMOPHILUS Gnom.

Cf. SENTENTIAE PYTHAGOREORUM (1759 001).

1308 **DEMOSTHENES** Epic.

2 B.C.?: Bithynius

001 **Fragmenta**, ed. J.U. Powell, *Collectanea Alexandrina*. Oxford: Clarendon Press, 1925 (repr. 1970): 25–27.

frr. 4, 6, 7, 14.

Dup. partim 1308 002 (frr. 5, 6, 8, 14).

Q: 63: Epic., Hist.

002 **Fragmenta**, FGrH #699: 3C:552–554.

Dup. 1308 001 (frr. 4, 6, 7, 14).

Q: 641: Hist., Epic.

1819 **Pseudo-DEMOSTHENES** Epigr.

Incertum

001 **Epigramma**, ed. E. Diehl, *Anthologia lyrica Graeca*, fasc. 1, 3rd edn. Leipzig: Teubner, 1949: 135.

Q: 13: Epigr.

0014 **DEMOSTHENES** Orat.

4 B.C.: Atheniensis

Scholia: Cf. SCHOLIA IN DEMOSTHENEM (5017).

001 **Olynthiaca 1**, ed. S.H. Butcher, *Demosthenis orationes*, vol. 1. Oxford: Clarendon Press, 1903 (repr. 1966): [9–17].

Cod: 1,858: Orat.

002 **Olynthiaca 2**, ed. Butcher, *op. cit.*, vol. 1, [18–27].

Cod: 2,085: Orat.

003 **Olynthiaca 3**, ed. Butcher, *op. cit.*, vol. 1, [28–39].

Cod: 2,407: Orat.

004 **Philippica 1**, ed. Butcher, *op. cit.*, vol. 1, [40–55].

Cod: 3,338: Orat.

005 **De pace**, ed. Butcher, *op. cit.*, vol. 1, [57–63].

Cod: 1,488: Orat.

006 **Philippica 2**, ed. Butcher, *op. cit.*, vol. 1, [65–74].

Cod: 2,039: Orat.

007 **De Halonneso**, ed. Butcher, *op. cit.*, vol. 1, [76–88].

Cod: 2,494: Orat.

008 **De Chersoneso**, ed. Butcher, *op. cit.*, vol. 1, [90–109].
Cod: 4,291: Orat.

009 **Philippica 3**, ed. Butcher, *op. cit.*, vol. 1, [110–130].
Cod: 4,396: Orat.

010 **Philippica 4** [Sp.], ed. Butcher, *op. cit.*, vol. 1, [131–151].
Cod: 4,535: Orat.

011 **In epistulam Philippi** [Sp.], ed. Butcher, *op. cit.*, vol. 1, [152–158].
Cod: 1,324: Orat.

012 **[Philippi] epistula**, ed. Butcher, *op. cit.*, vol. 1, [158–165].
Cod: 1,456: Epist.

013 **Περὶ συντάξεως** [Sp.], ed. Butcher, *op. cit.*, vol. 1, [166–177].
Cod: 2,370: Orat.

014 **Περὶ τῶν συμμοριῶν**, ed. Butcher, *op. cit.*, vol. 1, [178–189].
Cod: 2,640: Orat.

015 **De Rhodiorum libertate**, ed. Butcher, *op. cit.*, vol. 1, [190–201].
Cod: 2,248: Orat.

016 **Pro Megalopolitanis**, ed. Butcher, *op. cit.*, vol. 1, [202–210].
Cod: 1,900: Orat.

017 **Περὶ τῶν πρὸς Ἀλέξανδρον συνθηκῶν** [Sp.], ed. Butcher, *op. cit.*, vol. 1, [211–220].
Cod: 1,831: Orat.

018 **De corona**, ed. Butcher, *op. cit.*, vol. 1, [225–332].
Cod: 22,893: Orat.

019 **De falsa legatione**, ed. Butcher, *op. cit.*, vol. 1, [341–451].
Cod: 23,576: Orat.

020 **Adversus Leptinem**, ed. Butcher, *op. cit.*, vol. 2.1 (1907; repr. 1966): [457–508].
Cod: 11,543: Orat.

021 **In Midiam**, ed. Butcher, *op. cit.*, vol. 2.1, [514–587].
Cod: 16,013: Orat.

022 **Adversus Androtionem**, ed. Butcher, *op. cit.*, vol. 2.1, [593–618].
Cod: 5,728: Orat.

023 **In Aristocratem**, ed. Butcher, *op. cit.*, vol. 2.1, [621–693].
Cod: 15,704: Orat.

024 **In Timocratem**, ed. Butcher, *op. cit.*, vol. 2.1, [700–767].
Cod: 14,896: Orat.

025 **In Aristogitonem 1**, ed. Butcher, *op. cit.*, vol. 2.1, [770–800].
Cod: 6,828: Orat.

026 **In Aristogitonem 2**, ed. Butcher, *op. cit.*, vol. 2.1, [800–808].
Cod: 1,718: Orat.

027 **In Aphobum 1**, ed. W. Rennie, *Demosthenis orationes*, vol. 2.2 (1921; repr. 1966): [813–835].
Cod: 4,687: Orat.

028 **In Aphobum 2**, ed. Rennie, *op. cit.*, vol. 2.2, [835–843].
Cod: 1,548: Orat.

029 **Contra Aphobum**, ed. Rennie, *op. cit.*, vol. 2.2, [844–862].
Cod: 4,006: Orat.

030 **Contra Onetorem 1**, ed. Rennie, *op. cit.*, vol. 2.2, [864–875].
Cod: 2,407: Orat.

031 **Contra Onetorem 2**, ed. Rennie, *op. cit.*, vol. 2.2, [876–880].
Cod: 966: Orat.

032 **Contra Zenothemin**, ed. Rennie, *op. cit.*, vol. 2.2, [882–891].
Cod: 1,956: Orat.

033 **Contra Apatourium** [Sp.], ed. Rennie, *op. cit.*, vol. 2.2, [892–904].
Cod: 2,596: Orat.

034 **Contra Phormionem**, ed. Rennie, *op. cit.*, vol. 2.2, [907–922].
Cod: 3,350: Orat.

035 **Contra Lacritum** [Sp.], ed. Rennie, *op. cit.*, vol. 2.2, [923–943].
Cod: 3,727: Orat.

036 **Pro Phormione**, ed. Rennie, *op. cit.*, vol. 2.2, [944–963].
Cod: 4,049: Orat.

037 **Contra Pantaenetum**, ed. Rennie, *op. cit.*, vol. 2.2, [966–984].
Cod: 3,860: Orat.

038 **Contra Nausimachum et Xenopeithea**, ed. Rennie, *op. cit.*, vol. 2.2, [984–993].
Cod: 1,900: Orat.

039 **Contra Boeotum 1**, ed. Rennie, *op. cit.*, vol. 2.2, [994–1007].
Cod: 2,803: Orat.

040 **Contra Boeotum 2** [Sp.], ed. Rennie, *op. cit.*, vol. 2.2, [1008–1026].
Cod: 3,987: Orat.

041 **Contra Spudiam**, ed. Rennie, *op. cit.*, vol. 3 (1931; repr. 1960): [1028–1037].
Cod: 2,017: Orat.

042 **Contra Phaenippum** [Sp.], ed. Rennie, *op. cit.*, vol. 3, [1038–1049].
Cod: 2,286: Orat.

043 **Contra Macartatum** [Sp.], ed. Rennie, *op. cit.*, vol. 3, [1050–1079].
Cod: 6,416: Orat.

044 **Contra Leocharem** [Sp.], ed. Rennie, *op. cit.*, vol. 3, [1081–1100].
Cod: 4,319: Orat.

045 **In Stephanum 1**, ed. Rennie, *op. cit.*, vol. 3, [1101–1128].
Cod: 5,850: Orat.

046 **In Stephanum 2** [Sp.], ed. Rennie, *op. cit.*, vol. 3, [1129–1137].
Cod: 1,900: Orat.

047 **In Evergum et Mnesibulum** [Sp.], ed. Rennie, *op. cit.*, vol. 3, [1139–1164].
Cod: 5,495: Orat.

048 **In Olympiodorum** [Sp.], ed. Rennie, *op. cit.*, vol. 3, [1167–1183].
Cod: 3,592: Orat.

049 **Contra Timotheum** [Sp.], ed. Rennie, *op. cit.*, vol. 3, [1184–1205].
Cod: 4,414: Orat.

050 **Contra Polyclem** [Sp.], ed. Rennie, *op. cit.*, vol. 3, [1206–1227].
Cod: 4,732: Orat.

051 **De corona trierarchiae**, ed. Rennie, *op. cit.*, vol. 3, [1228–1234].
Cod: 1,382: Orat.

052 **Contra Callippum** [Sp.], ed. Rennie, *op. cit.*, vol. 3, [1235–1245].
Cod: 2,168: Orat.

053 **Contra Nicostratum**, ed. Rennie, *op. cit.*, vol. 3, [1246–1255].
Cod: 2,063: Orat.

054 **In Cononem**, ed. Rennie, *op. cit.*, vol. 3, [1256–1271].
Cod: 3,259: Orat.

055 **Contra Calliclem**, ed. Rennie, *op. cit.*, vol. 3, [1272–1281].
Cod: 2,166: Orat.

056 **In Dionysodorum** [Sp.], ed. Rennie, *op. cit.*, vol. 3, [1282–1298].
Cod: 3,392: Orat.

057 **Contra Eubulidem**, ed. Rennie, *op. cit.*, vol. 3, [1299–1320].
Cod: 4,729: Orat.

058 **In Theocrinem** [Sp.], ed. Rennie, *op. cit.*, vol. 3, [1322–1344].
Cod: 4,795: Orat.

059 **In Neaeram** [Sp.], ed. Rennie, *op. cit.*, vol. 3, [1345–1388].
Cod: 9,416: Orat.

060 **Epitaphius**, ed. Rennie, *op. cit.*, vol. 3, [1388–1400].
Cod: 2,594: Orat.

061 **Eroticus** [Sp.], ed. Rennie, *op. cit.*, vol. 3, [1400–1418].
Cod: 3,735: Orat.

062 **Exordia**, ed. Rennie, *op. cit.*, vol. 3, [1418–1462].
Cod: 9,755: Orat.

063 **Epistulae**, ed. Rennie, *op. cit.*, vol. 3, [1462–1492].
Cod: 6,225: Epist.

064 **Fragmenta**, ed. J. Baiter and H. Sauppe, *Oratores Attici*. Zürich: Hoehr, 1850 (repr. Hildesheim: Olms, 1967): 251–257.
frr. 1–13.
Q: 2,527: Orat.

DEMOSTHENES Ophthalmicus Med.
Cf. DEMOSTHENES Philalethes Med. (0689).

0689 **DEMOSTHENES Philalethes** Med.
vel Demosthenes Ophthalmicus
A.D. 1

x01 **Fragmentum ap. Galenum.**
K12.843.
Cf. GALENUS Med. (0057 076).

x02 **Fragmenta ap. Oribasium.**
CMG, vol. 6.3, pp. 100, 104, 264.
Cf. ORIBASIUS Med. (0722 004).

x03 **Fragmenta ap. Aëtium** (lib. 7).
CMG, vol. 8.2, pp. 265, 283, 300, 306, 308, 322, 324, 325, 329, 373, 389.
Cf. AËTIUS Med. (0718 007).

2281 **DEMOTELES** Hist.
4–3 B.C.: Andrius

001 **Testimonium**, FGrH #400: 3B:293.
test. 1: *IG* 11.4, no. 544.
NQ: 49: Test.

2196 **[DERCYLLUS]** Hist.
Incertum

001 **Fragmenta**, FGrH #288: 3A:170–172.
Q: 499: Hist., Nat. Hist.

DERCYLUS Hist.
Cf. (H)AGIAS-DERCYLUS Hist. (1387).

0442 **DEXICRATES** Comic.
4/3 B.C.?

001 **Fragmentum**, ed. T. Kock, *Comicorum Atticorum fragmenta*, vol. 3. Leipzig: Teubner, 1888: 374.
fr. 1.
Q: 17: Comic.

002 **Fragmentum**, ed. A. Meineke, *Fragmenta comicorum Graecorum*, vol. 4. Berlin: Reimer, 1841 (repr. De Gruyter, 1970): 571.
Q: 17: Comic.

2141 **Publius Herennius DEXIPPUS** Hist.
A.D. 3: Atheniensis

001 **Testimonia**, FGrH #100: 2A:452–454.
test. 4: *IG* 3.716.
NQ: 483: Test.

002 **Fragmenta**, FGrH #100: 2A:454–480.
Q: 8,329: Hist.

2036 **DEXIPPUS** Phil.
A.D. 4

001 **In Aristotelis categorias commentarium**, ed. A. Busse, *Dexippi in Aristotelis categorias commentarium* [*Commentaria in Aristotelem Graeca* 4.2. Berlin: Reimer, 1888]: 1–71.
Cod: 22,898: Phil., Comm.

0371 **DIAGORAS** Lyr.
5 B.C.: Melius

001 **Fragmenta**, ed. D.L. Page, *Poetae melici Graeci*. Oxford: Clarendon Press, 1962 (repr. 1967 (1st edn. corr.)): 382.
fr. 1.
Dup. partim 0371 002.
Q: 24: Lyr.

002 **Fragmenta**, ed. M. Winiarczyk, *Diagorae Melii et Theodori Cyrenaei reliquiae*. Leipzig: Teubner, 1981: 29–30.
frr. 1–3: p. 29.
Imitationes: p. 30.
Dup. partim 0371 001.
Q: Lyr.

0854 **DIAGORAS** Med.
   3 B.C.: Cyprius
x01 **Fragmentum ap. Oribasium.**
   CMG, vol. 6.3, p. 106.
   Cf. ORIBASIUS Med. (0722 004).
x02 **Fragmentum ap. Aëtium** (lib. 7).
   CMG, vol. 8.2, p. 375.
   Cf. AËTIUS Med. (0718 007).

1309 *DIALEXEIS* (Δισσοὶ λόγοι)
   5/4 B.C.
001 **Fragmenta,** ed. H. Diels and W. Kranz, *Die
   Fragmente der Vorsokratiker,* vol. 2, 6th edn.
   Berlin: Weidmann, 1952 (repr. Dublin: 1966):
   405–416.
   frr. 1–9.
   Cod: 3,706: Phil.

0066 **DICAEARCHUS** Phil.
   4 B.C.: Messanius
001 **Fragmenta,** ed. F. Wehrli, *Dikaiarchos [Die
   Schule des Aristoteles,* vol. 1, 2nd edn. Basel:
   Schwabe, 1967]: 13–37.
   Περὶ ψυχῆς. Κορινθιακοὶ λόγοι. Λεσβιακοὶ
   λόγοι: frr. 5, 8a–b, 8g, 8i–k, 10a, 11–12e.
   Εἰς Τροφωνίου κατάβασις: frr. 13a–b, 19, 21–
   22.
   Περὶ τῆς ἐν Ἰλίῳ θυσίας: fr. 23.
   Biographica: frr. 26–27, 29–35b, 37–42, 44–46.
   Βίος Ἑλλάδος: frr. 49, 52–66.
   Πολιτεία Σπαρτιατῶν. Τριπολιτικός. Πελλη-
   ναίων, Κορινθίων, Ἀθηναίων πολιτεία: frr.
   70.1–72.
   Περὶ μουσικῶν ἀγώνων. Περὶ διονυσιακῶν
   ἀγώνων. Παναθηναικός. Ὀλυμπικός: frr. 73–
   89.
   Quaestiones Homericae: frr. 90–93.
   Περὶ Ἀλκαίου: frr. 94–99.
   Proverbia: frr. 100–103.1.
   Περίοδος γῆς. Πίνακες. Καταμετρήσεις τῶν ἐν
   Πελοποννήσῳ ὀρῶν: frr. 104, 106–107, 109–
   114.
   Dubia, spuria et fragmenta incertae sedis: frr.
   117–118.
   Q, Pap: 6,039: Phil., Biogr., Gramm., Hist.,
   Paroem.
x01 Περὶ τῶν ἐν τῇ Ἑλλάδι πόλεων.
   GGM, vol. 1, pp. 97–110.
   Cf. HERACLIDES Criticus Perieg. (1405 001).

0322 **DICAEOGENES** Trag.
   4 B.C.
001 **Fragmenta,** ed. B. Snell, *Tragicorum Graecorum fragmenta,* vol. 1. Göttingen: Vandenhoeck & Ruprecht, 1971: 191–192.
   frr. 1–2, 4–5.
   Q: 50: Trag.

1310 **DICTYS** Hist.
   A.D. 2/3: Cretensis
001 **Ephemeridos belli Troiani libri** (*P. Tebt.* 268),

   ed. W. Eisenhut, *Dictyis Cretensis ephemeridos
   belli Troiani libri.* Leipzig: Teubner, 1958:
   134–139.
   Pap: [634]
002 **Testimonia,** FGrH #49: 1A:273–275.
   NQ: 726: Test.
003 **Fragmenta,** FGrH #49: 1A:275–284.
   fr. 7a: *P. Tebt.* 268.
   Q, Pap: 3,173: Hist., Myth.

1311 *DIDACHE XII APOSTOLORUM*
   A.D. 2
001 Διδαχαὶ τῶν ἀποστολῶν, ed. J.P. Audet, *La
   Didachè. Instructions des Apôtres.* Paris: Le-
   coffre, 1958: 226–242.
   Cod: 2,323: Eccl.

2618 **DIDYMARCHUS** Poeta
   4 B.C.?
001 **Titulus,** ed. H. Lloyd-Jones and P. Parsons,
   Supplementum Hellenisticum. Berlin: De Gruyter, 1983: 175.
   fr. 378a.
   NQ: 5: Myth., Poem.

1312 **DIDYMUS** Gramm.
   1 B.C.: Alexandrinus
001 **Fragmentum,** FGrH #340: 3B:196–197.
   Q: 49: Hist.
002 **Fragmenta,** ed. M. Schmidt, *Didymi Chalcenteri grammatici Alexandrini fragmenta quae
   supersunt omnia.* Leipzig: Teubner, 1854 (repr.
   Amsterdam: Hakkert, 1964): 19–261, 299–405.
   Q: Gramm.
003 **In Demosthenem** (*P. Berol.* 9780), ed. L. Pearson and S. Stephens, *Didymi in Demosthenem
   commenta.* Stuttgart: Teubner, 1983: 1–54.
   Pap: 6,017: Gramm., Comm.
004 **De dubiis apud Platonem lectionibus** [Sp.], ed.
   E. Miller, "Opuscles divers," *Lexica Graeca
   minora* (ed. K. Latte & H. Erbse). Hildesheim:
   Olms, 1965: 245–252.
   Q: 1,888: Lexicogr.
x01 **Mensurae marmorum ac lignorum.**
   Hultsch, pp. 238–244.
   Cf. DIDYMUS Scriptor De Mensuris (0357
   001).

0855 **DIDYMUS** Med.
   A.D. 4/5: Alexandrinus
x01 **Fragmentum ap. Aëtium** (lib. 6).
   CMG, vol. 8.2, p. 155.
   Cf. AËTIUS Med. (0718 006).
x02 **Fragmentum ap. Aëtium** (lib. 9).
   Zervos, *Athena* 23, p. 389.
   Cf. AËTIUS Med. (0718 009).

2102 **DIDYMUS CAECUS** Scr. Eccl.
   A.D. 4: Alexandrinus
041 **In Genesim,** ed. P. Nautin and L. Doutreleau,
   Didyme l'Aveugle. Sur la Genèse, vols. 1–2

[*Sources chrétiennes* 233, 244. Paris: Cerf, 1:1976; 2:1978]: **1**:32–332; **2**:8–238.
Pap: 58,664: Exeget.

013 **Commentarii in Octateuchum et Reges** (in catenis), MPG 39: 1112–1116.
Q: 477: Exeget., Caten.

001 **Commentarii in Job** (1–4), ed. A. Henrichs, *Didymos der Blinde. Kommentar zu Hiob*, pt. 1 [*Papyrologische Texte und Abhandlungen* 1. Bonn: Habelt, 1968]: 24–308.
Pap: 19,583: Exeget.

002 **Commentarii in Job** (5.1–6.29), ed. A. Henrichs, *Didymos der Blinde. Kommentar zu Hiob*, pt. 2 [*Papyrologische Texte und Abhandlungen* 2. Bonn: Habelt, 1968]: 14–194.
Pap: 12,482: Exeget.

003 **Commentarii in Job** (7.20c–11), ed. U. Hagedorn, D. Hagedorn and L. Koenen, *Didymos der Blinde. Kommentar zu Hiob*, pt. 3 [*Papyrologische Texte und Abhandlungen* 3. Bonn: Habelt, 1968]: 2–220.
Pap: 16,425: Exeget.

004 **Commentarii in Job** (12.1–16.8a) (partim in catenis), ed. U. Hagedorn, D. Hagedorn and L. Koenen, *Didymos der Blinde. Kommentar zu Hiob*, pt. 4.1 [*Papyrologische Texte und Abhandlungen* 33.1. Bonn: Habelt, 1985]: 40–198.
Q, Pap: 16,559: Exeget., Caten.

014 **Commentarii in Job** (in catenis), MPG 39: 1120–1153.
Q: 7,230: Exeget., Caten.

016 **Commentarii in Psalmos 20–21**, ed. L. Doutreleau, A. Gesché and M. Gronewald, *Didymos der Blinde. Psalmenkommentar*, pt. 1 [*Papyrologische Texte und Abhandlungen* 7. Bonn: Habelt, 1969]: 2–228.
Pap: 24,836: Exeget.

017 **Commentarii in Psalmos 22–26.10**, ed. M. Gronewald, *Didymos der Blinde. Psalmenkommentar*, pt. 2 [*Papyrologische Texte und Abhandlungen* 4. Bonn: Habelt, 1968]: 2–246.
Pap: 25,434: Exeget.

018 **Commentarii in Psalmos 29–34**, ed. M. Gronewald, *Didymos der Blinde. Psalmenkommentar*, pt. 3 [*Papyrologische Texte und Abhandlungen* 8. Bonn: Habelt, 1969]: 2–414.
Pap: 45,353: Exeget.

019 **Commentarii in Psalmos 35–39**, ed. M. Gronewald, *Didymos der Blinde. Psalmenkommentar*, pt. 4 [*Papyrologische Texte und Abhandlungen* 6. Bonn: Habelt, 1969]: 2–314.
Pap: 32,875: Exeget.

049 **Commentarii in Psalmos 36.15–19**, ed. M. Gronewald, "Didymos der Blinde, Psalmenkommentar (Nachtrag der Seiten 248/49 des Tura-Papyrus)," *Zeitschrift für Papyrologie und Epigraphik* 46 (1982) 98–110.
Cf. et 2102 019.
Pap: 1,443: Exeget.

020 **Commentarii in Psalmos 40–44.4**, ed. M. Gronewald, *Didymos der Blinde. Psalmenkommentar*, pt. 5 [*Papyrologische Texte und Ab-*

handlungen 12. Bonn: Habelt, 1970]: 2–244.
Pap: 25,530: Exeget.

021 **Fragmenta in Psalmos** (e commentario altero), ed. E. Mühlenberg, *Psalmenkommentare aus der Katenenüberlieferung*, 2 vols. [*Patristische Texte und Studien* 15 & 16. Berlin: De Gruyter, 1:1975; 2:1977]: **1**:121–375; **2**:3–367.
Q: 159,008: Exeget.

022 **Fragmenta in Proverbia**, MPG 39: 1621–1645.
Q: 4,609: Exeget.

011 **Commentarii in Ecclesiasten** (1.1–8), ed. G. Binde and L. Liesenborghs, *Didymos der Blinde. Kommentar zum Ecclesiastes*, pt. 1 [*Papyrologische Texte und Abhandlungen* 25. Bonn: Habelt, 1979]: 2–240.
Pap: 16,841: Exeget.

047 **Commentarii in Ecclesiasten** (3–4.12), ed. M. Gronewald, *Didymos der Blinde. Kommentar zum Ecclesiastes*, pt. 2 [*Papyrologische Texte und Abhandlungen* 22. Bonn: Habelt, 1977]: 2–224.
Pap: 20,121: Exeget.

005 **Commentarii in Ecclesiasten** (5–6), ed. J. Kramer, *Didymos der Blinde. Kommentar zum Ecclesiastes*, pt. 3 [*Papyrologische Texte und Abhandlungen* 13. Bonn: Habelt, 1970]: 2–86.
Pap: 9,857: Exeget.

006 **Commentarii in Ecclesiasten** (7–8.8), ed. J. Kramer and B. Krebber, *Didymos der Blinde. Kommentar zum Ecclesiastes*, pt. 4 [*Papyrologische Texte und Abhandlungen* 16. Bonn: Habelt, 1972]: 2–154.
Pap: 15,424: Exeget.

048 **Commentarii in Ecclesiasten** (9.8–10.20), ed. M. Gronewald, *Didymos der Blinde. Kommentar zum Ecclesiastes*, pt. 5 [*Papyrologische Texte und Abhandlungen* 24. Bonn: Habelt, 1979]: 2–164.
Pap: 13,590: Exeget.

007 **Commentarii in Ecclesiasten** (11–12), ed. G. Binder and L. Liesenborghs, *Didymos der Blinde. Kommentar zum Ecclesiastes*, pt. 6 [*Papyrologische Texte und Abhandlungen* 9. Bonn: Habelt, 1969]: 2–244.
Pap: 16,065: Exeget.

023 **Fragmentum in Canticum canticorum** (in catenis), ed. J. Meurs, *Eusebii, Polychronii, Pselli in Canticum canticorum expositiones Graece*. Leiden: Meurs, 1617: 19.
Q: Exeget., Caten.

015 **Fragmenta in Jeremiam** (in catenis), ed. M. Ghisler, *In Ieremiam prophetam commentarii*, 2 vols. Lyon: Durand, 1623: **1**:39a; **2**:704, 754.
Q: Exeget., Caten.

010 **Commentarii in Zacchariam**, ed. L. Doutreleau, *Didyme l'Aveugle sur Zacharie*, 3 vols. [*Sources chrétiennes* 83, 84, 85. Paris: Cerf, 1962]: **83**:190–412; **84**:426–788; **85**:802–1086.
Cod, Pap: 91,483: Exeget.

025 **Fragmenta in Joannem** (in catenis), ed. J. Reuss, *Johannes-Kommentare aus der griechischen Kirche* [*Texte und Untersuchungen* 89.

Berlin: Akademie-Verlag, 1966]: 177–186.
Q: 2,420: Exeget., Caten.

026 **Fragmenta in epistulam ad Romanos** (in catenis), ed. K. Staab, *Pauluskommentar aus der griechischen Kirche aus Katenenhandschriften gesammelt.* Münster: Aschendorff, 1933: 1–6.
Q: 1,881: Exeget., Caten.

027 **Fragmenta in epistulam i ad Corinthios** (in catenis), ed. Staab, *op. cit.*, 6–14.
Q: 2,368: Exeget., Caten.

028 **Fragmenta in epistulam ii ad Corinthios** (in catenis), ed. Staab, *op. cit.*, 14–44.
Q: 9,842: Exeget., Caten.

046 **Fragmentum in epistulam ad Hebraeos** (in catenis), ed. Staab, *op. cit.*, 44–45.
Q: 125: Exeget., Caten.

030 **In epistulas catholicas brevis enarratio** (in catenis), ed. F. Zoepfl, *Didymi Alexandrini in epistulas canonicas brevis enarratio [Neutestamentliche Abhandlungen* 4.1. Münster: Aschendorff, 1914]: 1–4, 6–15, 17–25, 27–52, 57–63, 66–69, 73–91, 95–96.
Q: 6,448: Exeget., Caten.

008 **De trinitate** (lib. 1) [Sp.], ed. J. Hönscheid, *Didymus der Blinde. De trinitate, Buch 1 [Beiträge zur klassischen Philologie* 44. Meisenheim am Glan: Hain, 1975]: 14–238.
Cf. et 2102 009, 042, 043.
Cod: 23,675: Theol.

009 **De trinitate** (lib. 2.1–7) [Sp.], ed. I. Seiler, *Didymus der Blinde. De trinitate, Buch 2, Kapitel 1–7 [Beiträge zur klassischen Philologie* 52. Meisenheim am Glan: Hain, 1975]: 2–246.
Cf. et 2102 008, 042, 043.
Cod: 22,518: Theol.

042 **De trinitate** (lib. 2.8–27) [Sp.], MPG 39: 600–769.
Cf. et 2102 008, 009, 043.
Cod: 23,359: Theol.

043 **De trinitate** (lib. 3) [Sp.], MPG 39: 773–992.
Cf. et 2102 008, 009, 042.
Cod: 34,493: Theol.

012 **Contra Manichaeos**, MPG 39: 1085–1109.
Cod: 4,674: Theol.

032 **Ad philosophum** (ap. Joannem Damascenum, *Sacra parallela*), MPG 39: 1109.
Q: 14: Eccl.

033 **De incorporeo** (ap. Joannem Damascenum, *Sacra parallela*), MPG 39: 1109.
Q: 55: Eccl.

035 **Fragmenta** (ap. Maximum Confessorem, *Loci communes* [Sp.]), MPG 91: 725, 813, 821, 944, 948, 965, 968.
Q: 214: Phil., Eccl.

037 **Fragmenta** (ap. Antonium Melissam, *Loci communes*), MPG 136: 824, 892, 933, 952–953, 1084.
Q: 151: Eccl.

040 **Dialexis Montanistae et orthodoxi** [Sp.], ed. G. Ficker, "Widerlegung eines Montanisten," *Zeitschrift für Kirchengeschichte* 26 (1905) 449–458.
Cod: 2,380: Theol.

x01 **Συμβουλὴ ἠθική** (fragmentum ap. Socratem).
HE 4.23.
Cf. SOCRATES Scholasticus Hist. (2057 001).

x02 **De dogmatibus et contra Arianos** [Sp.] (ap. Basilium, *Adversus Eunomium* 4–5 [Sp.]).
MPG 29.672–768.
Cf. BASILIUS Theol. (2040 019).

x03 **Fragmentum in Osee** (ap. Joannem Damascenum, *Sacra parallela*).
MPG 95.1381.
Cf. JOANNES DAMASCENUS Theol. et Scr. Eccl. (2934 018).

x04 **Fragmentum in Lot et David** (ap. Joannem Damascenum, *Sacra parallela*).
MPG 96.141.
Cf. JOANNES DAMASCENUS Theol. et Scr. Eccl. (2934 018).

x05 **Fragmenta** (ap. Joannem Damascenum, *Sacra parallela*).
MPG **95**.1080, 1085, 1097, 1256, 1312, 1353, 1396, 1416, 1473, 1548, 1560; **96**.61, 73, 89, 101, 141, 220, 236, 248, 274, 320–321, 324, 325, 340, 344, 348, 360, 372–373, 397, 421, 436, 537.
Cf. JOANNES DAMASCENUS Theol. et Scr. Eccl. (2934 018–019).

x06 **Fragmenta in Isaiam** (ap. Joannem Damascenum, *Sacra parallela*).
MPG **95**.1093, 1169; **96**.525.
Cf. JOANNES DAMASCENUS Theol. et Scr. Eccl. (2934 018–019).

x07 **Fragmenta in Acta** (in catenis).
Cramer, vol. 3, pp. 21, 25, 34, 38, 40, 46, 48, 52, 65, 66, 69, 74, 79, 90, 94, 100, 112, 116, 119, 121, 128, 132, 139, 146, 147, 152, 153, 157, 166, 167, 168, 175, 187, 189, 191, 198, 215, 216, 230, 251, 269, 291, 295, 299, 304, 307, 309, 312, 317, 320, 331, 333, 335, 337, 341, 347, 367, 378, 394, 413.
Cf. CATENAE (Novum Testamentum) (4102 008).

x08 **Dialogus Didymi Caeci cum haeretico** (*P. Cairo Tura* 1090).
Kramer, pp. 206–210.
Cf. ECCLESIASTICA ADESPOTA (4156 001).

1809 **Claudius DIDYMUS Junior** Gramm.
A.D. 1

001 **Fragmentum** [Dub.], ed. M. Schmidt, *Didymi Chalcenteri grammatici Alexandrini fragmenta quae supersunt omnia.* Leipzig: Teubner, 1854 (repr. Amsterdam: Hakkert, 1964): 349.
Q: Gramm.

0357 **DIDYMUS** Scriptor De Mensuris
1 B.C.: Alexandrinus

001 **Mensurae marmorum ac lignorum**, ed. F. Hultsch, *Heronis Alexandrini geometricorum et stereometricorum reliquiae.* Berlin: Weidmann, 1864: 238–244.
Cod: 1,356: Metrolog.

0856 **DIEUCHES** Med.
3 B.C.
001 **Fragmentum**, ed. H. Lloyd-Jones and P. Parsons, *Supplementum Hellenisticum*. Berlin: De Gruyter, 1983: 176.
fr. 379.
Q: 9: Hexametr.
x01 **Fragmenta ap. Oribasium.**
CMG **6.1.1**, pp. 101, 102, 292; **6.3**, p. 167.
Cf. ORIBASIUS Med. (0722 001, 004).

1313 **DIEUCHIDAS** Hist.
4 B.C.: Megareus
001 **Testimonium**, FGrH #485: 3B:449.
NQ: 38: Test.
002 **Fragmenta**, FGrH #485: 3B:449–451.
Q: 708: Hist.

2324 **DINARCHUS** Hist.
ante 4 B.C.
001 **Testimonium**, FGrH #465: 3B:402.
NQ: 62: Test.

2280 **DINARCHUS** Hist.
4 B.C.?: Delius
001 **Testimonium**, FGrH #399: 3B:292.
NQ: 70: Test.
002 **Fragmenta**, FGrH #399: 3B:293.
Q: 127: Hist.

0029 **DINARCHUS** Orat.
4–3 B.C.: Corinthius, Atheniensis
004 **In Demosthenem**, ed. N.C. Conomis, *Dinarchi orationes cum fragmentis*. Leipzig: Teubner, 1975: 11–54.
Cod: 7,775: Orat.
005 **In Aristogitonem**, ed. Conomis, *op. cit.*, 54–64.
Cod: 1,831: Orat.
006 **In Philoclem**, ed. Conomis, *op. cit.*, 65–72.
Cod: 1,430: Orat.
007 **Fragmenta**, ed. Conomis, *op. cit.*, 73–145.
frr. 1–97.
Q: 8,491: Orat.
008 **Fragmenta incertae sedis**, ed. Conomis, *op. cit.*, 145–151.
frr. 3–42.
Q, Pap: 935: Orat.

1314 **DINIAS** Hist.
3 B.C.: Argivus
001 **Testimonium**, FGrH #306: 3B:10.
NQ: 50: Test.
002 **Fragmenta**, FGrH #306: 3B:10–13.
Q: 533: Hist.
003 **Fragmentum**, ed. H.J. Mette, "Die 'Kleinen' griechischen Historiker heute," *Lustrum* 21 (1978) 26.
fr. 3 bis.
Q: 77: Hist.

1315 **DINOLOCHUS** Comic.
5 B.C.
001 **Fragmentum**, ed. G. Kaibel, *Comicorum Grae-*

corum fragmenta, vol. 1.1 [*Poetarum Graecorum fragmenta*, vol. 6.1. Berlin: Weidmann, 1899]: 149–150.
fr. 4 + tituli.
Cod: 11: Comic.
002 **Tituli**, ed. C. Austin, *Comicorum Graecorum fragmenta in papyris reperta*. Berlin: De Gruyter, 1973: 50–51.
fr. 78.
Pap: 23: Comic.

1316 **DINON** Hist.
4 B.C.: Colophonius
001 **Testimonia**, FGrH #690: 3C:522.
NQ: 103: Test.
002 **Fragmenta**, FGrH #690: 3C:522–531.
fr. 29: *P. Oxy.* 15.1802.
Q, Pap: 2,960: Hist.

0285 **DINOSTRATUS** Math. et Phil.
4 B.C.
001 **Testimonium**, ed. F. Lasserre, *De Léodamas de Thasos à Philippe d'Oponte*. Naples: Bibliopolis, 1987: 127.
NQ: Test.
002 **Doctrina**, ed. Lasserre, *op. cit.*, 127–129.
NQ: Test.

DIO CASSIUS Hist.
Cf. CASSIUS DIO Hist. (0385).

0612 **DIO CHRYSOSTOMUS** Soph.
vel Dio Cocceianus
A.D. 1–2: Prusensis
Cf. et DIONIS EPISTULAE (1327).
Scholia: Cf. ARETHAS Philol. et Scr. Eccl. (2130 016).
001 **Orationes**, ed. J. von Arnim, *Dionis Prusaensis quem vocant Chrysostomum quae exstant omnia*, vols. 1–2, 2nd edn. Berlin: Weidmann, 1:1893; 2:1896 (repr. 1962): 1:1–338; 2:1–306.
De regno 1 (orat. 1): vol. 1, pp. 1–16.
De regno 2 (orat. 2): vol. 1, pp. 16–33.
De regno 3 (orat. 3): vol. 1, pp. 34–56.
De regno 4 (orat. 4): vol. 1, pp. 56–79.
Libycus mythos (orat. 5): vol. 1, pp. 79–83.
De tyrannide (orat. 6): vol. 1, pp. 83–95.
De virtute (orat. 8): vol. 1, pp. 95–102.
Isthmiaca (orat. 9): vol. 1, pp. 103–107.
De servis (orat. 10): vol. 1, pp. 107–115.
Trojana (orat. 11): vol. 1, pp. 115–154.
De dei cognitione (orat. 12): vol. 1, pp. 155–179.
De exilio (orat. 13): vol. 1, pp. 179–189.
Venator (orat. 7): vol. 1, pp. 189–219.
Rhodiaca (orat. 31): vol. 1, pp. 219–266.
Ad Alexandrinos (orat. 32): vol. 1, pp. 267–297.
Tarsica prior (orat. 33): vol. 1, pp. 297–316.
Tarsica altera (orat. 34): vol. 1, pp. 316–331.
Celaenis Phrygiae (orat. 35): vol. 1, pp. 331–338.

Borysthenitica (orat. 36): vol. 2, pp. 1–16.
Corinthiaca (orat. 37) [Sp.]: vol. 2, pp. 17–29.
Ad Nicomedienses (orat. 38): vol. 2, pp. 29–43.
Ad Nicaeenses (orat. 39): vol. 2, pp. 43–46.
De concordia cum Apamensibus (orat. 40): vol. 2, pp. 46–57.
Ad Apamenses (orat. 41): vol. 2, pp. 57–61.
Dialexis (orat. 42): vol. 2, pp. 61–63.
Politica (orat. 43): vol. 2, pp. 63–66.
Gratitudo (orat. 44): vol. 2, pp. 67–70.
Defensio (orat. 45): vol. 2, pp. 70–76.
De tumultu (orat. 46): vol. 2, pp. 76–80.
Contio (orat. 47): vol. 2, pp. 80–87.
In contione (orat. 48): vol. 2, pp. 87–93.
Recusatio magistratus (orat. 49): vol. 2, pp. 93–97.
De administratione (orat. 50): vol. 2, pp. 98–101.
Ad Diodorum (orat. 51): vol. 2, pp. 101–104.
De Philoctetae arcu (orat. 52): vol. 2, pp. 104–109.
De Homero (orat. 53): vol. 2, pp. 109–113.
De Socrate (orat. 54): vol. 2, pp. 113–114.
De Homero et Socrate (orat. 55): vol. 2, pp. 114–120.
De regno (orat. 56): vol. 2, pp. 121–125.
Nestor (orat. 57): vol. 2, pp. 125–129.
Achilles (orat. 58): vol. 2, pp. 129–131.
Philoctetes (orat. 59): vol. 2, pp. 131–134.
Nessus (orat. 60): vol. 2, pp. 134–137.
Chryseis (orat. 61): vol. 2, pp. 137–142.
De regno et tyrannide (orat. 62): vol. 2, pp. 142–144.
De fortuna 1 (orat. 63) [Sp.]: vol. 2, pp. 145–147.
De fortuna 2 (orat. 64) [Sp.]: vol. 2, pp. 147–155.
De fortuna 3 (orat. 65) [Sp.]: vol. 2, pp. 156–160.
De gloria 1 (orat. 66): vol. 2, pp. 160–169.
De gloria 2 (orat. 67): vol. 2, pp. 169–171.
De gloria 3 (orat. 68): vol. 2, pp. 171–174.
De virtute (orat. 69): vol. 2, pp. 174–177.
De philosophia (orat. 70): vol. 2, pp. 177–180.
De philosopho (orat. 71): vol. 2, pp. 181–184.
De habitu (orat. 72): vol. 2, pp. 184–189.
De fide (orat. 73): vol. 2, pp. 189–192.
De diffidentia (orat. 74): vol. 2, pp. 192–201.
De lege (orat. 75): vol. 2, pp. 202–204.
De consuetudine (orat. 76): vol. 2, pp. 205–206.
De invidia (orat. 77/78): vol. 2, pp. 206–219.
De divitiis (orat. 79): vol. 2, pp. 220–222.
De libertate (orat. 80): vol. 2, pp. 222–226.
De servitute et libertate 1 (orat. 14): vol. 2, pp. 227–232.
De servitute et libertate 2 (orat. 15): vol. 2, pp. 232–241.
De aegritudine (orat. 16): vol. 2, pp. 241–244.
De avaritia (orat. 17): vol. 2, pp. 244–250.
De dicendi exercitatione (orat. 18): vol. 2, pp. 250–257.

De audiendi affectione (orat. 19): vol. 2, pp. 257–258.
De secessu (orat. 20): vol. 2, pp. 259–266.
De pulchritudine (orat. 21): vol. 2, pp. 266–271.
De pace et bello (orat. 22): vol. 2, pp. 271–273.
De quod felix sit sapiens (orat. 23): vol. 2, pp. 273–276.
De felicitate (orat. 24): vol. 2, pp. 276–277.
De genio (orat. 25): vol. 2, pp. 278–281.
De consultatione (orat. 26): vol. 2, pp. 281–283.
De compotatione (orat. 27): vol. 2, pp. 283–285.
Melancomas 1 (orat. 29): vol. 2, pp. 286–291.
Melancomas 2 (orat. 28): vol. 2, pp. 292–294.
Charidemus (orat. 30): vol. 2, pp. 295–306.
Cod: 183,248: Orat., Rhet.

002 **Encomium comae**, ed. von Arnim, *op. cit.*, vol. 2, 307–308.
Cod: 411: Encom.

003 **Fragmenta**, ed. von Arnim, *op. cit.*, vol. 2, 309–310.
Q: 349: Orat., Rhet.

0443 **DIOCLES** Comic.
5 B.C.

001 **Fragmenta**, ed. T. Kock, *Comicorum Atticorum fragmenta*, vol. 1. Leipzig: Teubner, 1880: 766–769.
frr. 1–14, 16–18 + tituli.
Q: 99: Comic.

002 **Fragmenta**, ed. A. Meineke, *Fragmenta comicorum Graecorum*, vol. 2.2. Berlin: Reimer, 1840 (repr. De Gruyter, 1970): 838–841.
Q: 87: Comic.

003 **Fragmentum**, ed. J. Demiańczuk, *Supplementum comicum*. Krakau: Nakładem Akademii, 1912 (repr. Hildesheim: Olms, 1967): 39.
fr. 1.
Q: 2: Comic.

004 **Fragmenta**, ed. C. Austin, *Comicorum Graecorum fragmenta in papyris reperta*. Berlin: De Gruyter, 1973: 51.
frr. 79–80.
Pap: 6: Comic.

DIOCLES Gramm.
1 B.C.–A.D. 1
Cf. TYRANNION Junior Gramm. (1611).

2549 **DIOCLES** Hist.
3 B.C.: Peparethius
001 **Testimonia**, FGrH #820: 3C:894–895.
NQ: 84: Test.
002 **Titulus**, FGrH #820: 3C:895.
NQ: Hist.

2470 **DIOCLES** Hist.
3 B.C.?
001 **Fragmenta**, FGrH #693: 3C:532–533.
Q: 94: Hist.

2206 **[DIOCLES]** Hist.
Incertum: Rhodius
001 **Fragmentum**, FGrH #302: 3B:5.
Q: 52: Hist.

1317 **DIOCLES** Math.
3/1 B.C.?
001 **Fragmenta de speculis causticis**, ed. J.L. Heiberg, *Archimedis opera omnia*, vol. 3. Leipzig: Teubner, 1915 (repr. Stuttgart: 1972): 66–70, 160–176.
Q: Math.

0664 **DIOCLES** Med.
4 B.C.: Carystius
001 **Fragmentum**, *P. Ryl.* 1.39.
Pap
x01 **Fragmenta ap. Galenum**.
K**6**.455, 511–512, 544 in CMG, vol. **5.4.2**, pp. 202–203, 235, 255; K**8**.185–187; **9**.863; **11**.472–474; **12**.785, 880; **18**.1.7, 519.
Cf. GALENUS Med. (0057 037, 065, 075–076, 092, 095).
x02 **Fragmenta ap. Oribasium**.
CMG, vol. **6.1.1**, pp. 99, 121, 144, 268, 292; **6.2.1**, pp. 133, 276; **6.2.2**, pp. 141, 212; **6.3**, p. 166.
Cf. ORIBASIUS Med. (0722 001–004).
x03 **Fragmentum ap. Paulum**.
CMG, vol. 9.1, pp. 68–72.
Cf. PAULUS Med. (0715 001).
x04 **Fragmentum ap. Apollonium**.
CMG, vol. 11.1.1, p. 46.
Cf. APOLLONIUS Med. (0660 001).
x05 **Fragmentum ap. Pseudo-Dioscoridem**.
Sprengel, p. 47.
Cf. Pseudo-DIOSCORIDES Med. (1118 002).
x06 **Fragmentum ap. Erotianum**.
Nachmanson, p. 92.
Cf. EROTIANUS Gramm. et Med. (0716 001).
x07 **Fragmenta ap. Aëtium**.
Placita 5.14.3, 29.2.
Cf. AËTIUS Doxogr. (0528 001).
x08 **Fragmenta ap. Athenaeum**.
Deipnosophistae 2.53d, 61c, 68d; **3**.110b; 7.305b, 316c; 15.681b.
Cf. ATHENAEUS Soph. (0008 001).

0884 **DIOCLES** Med.
ante A.D. 2: Chalcedonius
x01 **Fragmentum ap. Galenum**.
K13.87.
Cf. GALENUS Med. (0057 076).

0162 **Julius DIOCLES** Rhet.
A.D. 1: Carystius
001 **Epigrammata**, AG **6**.186; 7.393; 9.109; 12.35.
Q: 163: Epigr.

4253 **DIOCLIDES** Phil.
4 B.C.: Atheniensis
001 **Testimonium**, ed. K. Döring, *Die Megariker*

[*Studien zur antiken Philosophie* 2. Amsterdam: Grüner, 1972]: 14, 46.
test. 148a (p. 46) = Stilpo (4262 001).
NQ: Test.

0444 **DIODORUS** Comic.
3 B.C.: Sinopensis
001 **Fragmenta**, ed. T. Kock, *Comicorum Atticorum fragmenta*, vol. 2. Leipzig: Teubner, 1884: 420–422.
frr. 1–3 + tituli.
Q: 310: Comic.
002 **Fragmenta**, ed. A. Meineke, *Fragmenta comicorum Graecorum*, vol. 3. Berlin: Reimer, 1840 (repr. De Gruyter, 1970): 543–546.
Q: 308: Comic.

2652 **DIODORUS** Eleg.
ante 1 B.C.: Elaita
001 **Titulus**, ed. H. Lloyd-Jones and P. Parsons, *Supplementum Hellenisticum*. Berlin: De Gruyter, 1983: 177.
fr. 381.
NQ: 5: Poem.

0163 **DIODORUS** Epigr.
fiq Diodorus Sardianus Rhet. vel Diodorus Tarsensis Gramm. vel Diodorus Zonas Sardianus Rhet.
1 B.C./A.D. 1
Cf. et DIODORUS Rhet. (0165).
Cf. et DIODORUS Gramm. (0166).
Cf. et DIODORUS ZONAS Rhet. (0164).
001 **Epigrammata**, AG **5**.122; 7.38, 40, 74, 370, 624, 632.
Q: 214: Epigr.

0166 **DIODORUS** Gramm.
1 B.C.: Tarsensis
Cf. et DIODORUS Epigr. (0163).
001 **Epigrammata**, AG **6**.348(?); 7.235, 700–701.
Q: 145: Epigr.

2315 **DIODORUS** Hist.
ante 3 B.C.?
001 **Fragmentum**, FGrH #452: 3B:381.
Q: 34: Hist.

0857 **DIODORUS** Med.
1 B.C.
x01 **Fragmenta ap. Galenum**.
K**12**.834; **13**.248, 361, 857.
Cf. GALENUS Med. (0057 076–077).

2265 **DIODORUS** Perieg.
4–3 B.C.
001 **Fragmenta**, FGrH #372: 3B:233–239.
Q: 1,577: Hist., Perieg.

2681 **DIODORUS** Phil.
4 B.C.: Aspendius
001 **Fragmentum**, ed. F.W.A. Mullach, *Fragmenta*

philosophorum Graecorum, vol. 2. Paris: Didot, 1867 (repr. Aalen: Scientia, 1968): 112.
Q: 14: Phil.

2383 **DIODORUS** Phil.
2 B.C.: Tyrius
001 **Fragmentum**, ed. F. Wehrli, *Hieronymos von Rhodos. Kritolaos und seine Schüler* [*Die Schule des Aristoteles*, vol. 10, 2nd edn. Basel: Schwabe, 1969]: 88.
fr. 4h.
Q: 44: Phil.

0165 **DIODORUS** Rhet.
fiq Diodorus Sardianus Junior
1 B.C.: Sardianus
Cf. et DIODORUS Epigr. (0163).
001 **Epigrammata**, AG **6**.243(?), 245(?); **9**.60, 219, 405, 776.
Q: 200: Epigr.
002 **Titulus**, ed. H. Lloyd-Jones and P. Parsons, *Supplementum Hellenisticum*. Berlin: De Gruyter, 1983: 178.
fr. 384.
NQ: 5: Lyr.

1318 **DIODORUS** Rhet.
Incertum
001 **Fragmentum de viris duobus**, ed. H. Hinck, *Polemonis declamationes quae exstant duae*. Leipzig: Teubner, 1873: 51–55.
Cod: 752: Rhet.

4134 **DIODORUS** Scr. Eccl.
A.D. 4: Tarsensis
005 **Fragmenta in epistulam ad Romanos** (in catenis), ed. K. Staab, *Pauluskommentar aus der griechischen Kirche aus Katenenhandschriften gesammelt*. Münster: Aschendorff, 1933: 83–112.
Q: 8,245: Exeget., Caten.

0073 **DIODORUS CRONUS** Phil.
3 B.C.: Iasensis, Atheniensis
001 **Testimonia**, ed. K. Döring, *Die Megariker* [*Studien zur antiken Philosophie* 2. Amsterdam: Grüner, 1972]: 28–44, 70.
test. 96–99, 101, 103–110, 112–117f, 119–131, 133–137, 141–143, 220.
test. 220 (p. 70) = Polyxenus (4277 001).
NQ: Test.

0060 **DIODORUS SICULUS** Hist.
1 B.C.: Siculus
001 **Bibliotheca historica** (lib. 1–20), ed. F. Vogel and K.T. Fischer (post I. Bekker & L. Dindorf), *Diodori bibliotheca historica*, 5 vols., 3rd edn. Leipzig: Teubner, 1:1888; 2:1890; 3:1893; 4–5:1906 (repr. Stuttgart: 1964): **1**:1–533; **2**:1–461; **3**:1–497; **4**:1–426; **5**:1–336.
Cod: 419,934: Hist.
003 **Bibliotheca historica** (lib. 21–40), ed. F.R. Wal-

ton, *Diodorus of Sicily*, vols. 11–12. Cambridge, Mass.: Harvard University Press, 11:1957; 12:1967 (repr. 11:1968): **11**:2–456; **12**:2–294.
Cod: 65,582: Hist.
002 **Fragmenta sedis incertae**, ed. Walton, *op. cit.*, vol. 12, 296–302.
frr. 1–14.
Q: 539: Hist.

0164 **DIODORUS ZONAS** Rhet.
1 B.C.: Sardianus
Cf. et DIODORUS Epigr. (0163).
001 **Epigrammata**, AG **6**.22, 98, 106; **7**.365, 404, 627(?); **9**.226, 312, 556; **11**.43.
AG 6.42: Cf. ANONYMI EPIGRAMMATICI (AG) (0138 001).
AG 6.256: Cf. ANTIPATER Epigr. (0114 001).
Q: 374: Epigr.

2128 **DIOGENES** Epigr.
A.D. 6: Amisenus
001 **Epigramma**, AG 7.613.
Q: 41: Epigr.

2348 **DIOGENES** Hist.
post 4 B.C.?: Sicyonius
001 **Testimonium**, FGrH #503: 3B:481.
NQ: 50: Test.

2469 **DIOGENES** Hist.
3 B.C.?
001 **Fragmentum**, FGrH #692: 3C:532.
Q: 29: Hist.

2328 **DIOGENES** Hist.
vel Diogenianus
A.D. 4–5?: Cyzicenus
001 **Testimonium**, FGrH #474: 3B:433.
NQ: 22: Test.
002 **Fragmenta**, FGrH #474: 3B:433–434.
Q: 93: Hist.

0859 **DIOGENES** Med.
1 B.C.–A.D. 1
x01 **Fragmenta ap. Galenum**.
K**12**.686; **13**.313.
Cf. GALENUS Med. (0057 076).
x02 **Fragmenta ap. Aëtium** (lib. 2–3).
CMG, vol. 8.1, pp. 166, 301.
Cf. AËTIUS Med. (0718 002–003).

1319 **DIOGENES** Phil.
5 B.C.: Apolloniates
001 **Testimonia**, ed. H. Diels and W. Kranz, *Die Fragmente der Vorsokratiker*, vol. 2, 6th edn. Berlin: Weidmann, 1952 (repr. Dublin: 1966): 51–58.
test. 1–33.
NQ: 2,888: Test.

002 **Fragmenta**, ed. Diels and Kranz, *op. cit.*, 59–66.
frr. 1–10.
Q: 1,364: Phil.

2314 **DIOGENES** Phil.
5 B.C.: Smyrnaeus
001 **Testimonium**, ed. H. Diels and W. Kranz, *Die Fragmente der Vorsokratiker*, vol. 2, 6th edn. Berlin: Weidmann, 1952 (repr. Dublin: 1966): 235.
test. 2.
NQ: 23: Test.

1320 **DIOGENES** Phil.
2 B.C.: Babylonius
001 **Testimonia et fragmenta**, ed. J. von Arnim, *Stoicorum veterum fragmenta*, vol. 3. Leipzig: Teubner, 1903 (repr. Stuttgart: 1968): 210–243.
Testimonia (frr. 1–16): pp. 210–212.
Logica (frr. 17–26): pp. 212–215.
Physica (frr. 27–37): pp. 215–218.
Ethica (frr. 38–53): pp. 218–221.
De musica (frr. 54–90): pp. 221–235.
De rhetorica (frr. 91–126): pp. 235–243.
Q, Pap: 11,291: Phil., Rhet., Mus.

1321 **DIOGENES** Phil.
A.D. 2: Oenoandensis
008 **Fragmenta**, ed. C.W. Chilton, *Diogenis Oenoandensis fragmenta*. Leipzig: Teubner, 1967: 1–93.
Epigr: 5,883: Phil.
001 **Fragmenta** (NF 1–4), ed. M.F. Smith, "Fragments of Diogenes of Oenoanda discovered and rediscovered," *American Journal of Archaeology* 74.1 (1970) 57, 59, 61–62.
Epigr: 277: Phil.
002 **Fragmenta** (NF 5–11, 14–16, HK 68), ed. M.F. Smith, "New fragments of Diogenes of Oenoanda," *American Journal of Archaeology* 75.4 (1971) 359–360, 366–367, 370, 372–374, 376, 382–383, 385–388.
Epigr: 1,028: Phil.
003 **Fragmenta** (NF 17–18), ed. M.F. Smith, "Two new fragments of Diogenes of Oenoanda," *Journal of Hellenic Studies* 92 (1972) 149–150, 154.
Epigr: 149: Phil.
004 **Fragmenta** (NF 19–31), ed. M.F. Smith, "Thirteen new fragments of Diogenes of Oenoanda," [*Österreichische Akademie der Wissenschaften*, Philosoph.-hist. Kl., Denkschriften, Bd. 117 (Vienna: Österreichische Akademie der Wissenschaften, 1974) 13, 17–18, 21–22, 26, 29, 33, 38–40, 42–44.
Epigr: 538: Phil.
005 **Fragmenta** (NF 12–13), ed. Smith, "Thirteen new fragments," 45–46.
Epigr: 108: Phil.
006 **Fragmenta** (NF 32–38), ed. M.F. Smith,

"Seven new fragments of Diogenes of Oenoanda," *Hermathena* 118 (1974) 113–114, 117, 120, 124, 126, 128.
Epigr: 137: Phil.
007 **Fragmenta** (NF 39–51), ed. M.F. Smith, "More new fragments of Diogenes of Oenoanda," *Cahiers de Philologie* 1 (1976) 286–288, 295–296, 298, 301–303, 306–311, 313.
Epigr: 693: Phil.
009 **Fragmenta** (NF 52–106), ed. M.F. Smith, "Fifty-five new fragments of Diogenes of Oenoanda," *Anatolian studies* 28 (1978) 46–90.
Epigr: Phil.
010 **Fragmenta** (NF 107–114), ed. M.F. Smith, "Eight new fragments of Diogenes of Oenoanda," *Anatolian studies* 29 (1979) 71–85.
Epigr: Phil.

0334 **DIOGENES** Phil. et Trag.
4 B.C.: Sinopensis
Cf. et DIOGENIS SINOPENSIS EPISTULAE (1325).
001 **Fragmenta**, ed. B. Snell, *Tragicorum Graecorum fragmenta*, vol. 1. Göttingen: Vandenhoeck & Ruprecht, 1971: 254–258.
frr. 1–7.
Q: 187: Trag.
x01 **Epigramma**.
AG 7.66: Cf. HONESTUS Epigr. (1440 001).

0320 **DIOGENES** Trag.
5 B.C.: Atheniensis
001 **Fragmentum**, ed. B. Snell, *Tragicorum Graecorum fragmenta*, vol. 1. Göttingen: Vandenhoeck & Ruprecht, 1971: 185.
fr. 1.
Q: 57: Trag.

0004 **DIOGENES LAERTIUS** Biogr.
A.D. 3: Laertius
001 **Vitae philosophorum**, ed. H.S. Long, *Diogenis Laertii vitae philosophorum*, 2 vols. Oxford: Clarendon Press, 1964 (repr. 1966): 1:1–246; 2:247–565.
Cod: 114,802: Biogr., Doxogr.
002 **Epigrammata**, AG 7.57, 85, 87–88, 91–92, 95–98, 101–102, 104–116, 118, 121–124, 126–127, 129–130, 133, 620, 706, 744.
Dup. partim 0004 001.
AG 7.89: Cf. CALLIMACHUS Philol. (0533 004).
Q: 1,120: Epigr.
x01 **Epigrammata** (*App. Anth.*).
Epigrammata sepulcralia: 2.380–381.
Epigrammata demonstrativa: 3.128–129.
Epigramma exhortatorium et supplicatorium: 4.46.
Epigrammata irrisoria: 5.34–42.
Problemata: 7.19–20.
App. Anth. 2.380–381: Cf. ANTHOLOGIAE GRAECAE APPENDIX (7052 002).

App. Anth. 3.128–129: Cf. ANTHOLOGIAE GRAECAE APPENDIX (7052 003).
App. Anth. 4.46: Cf. ANTHOLOGIAE GRAECAE APPENDIX (7052 004).
App. Anth. 5.34–42: Cf. ANTHOLOGIAE GRAECAE APPENDIX (7052 005).
App. Anth. 7.19–20: Cf. ANTHOLOGIAE GRAECAE APPENDIX (7052 007).

0097 <DIOGENIANUS> Paroemiogr.
A.D. 2: Heracleensis
001 **Paroemiae**, ed. E.L. von Leutsch and F.G. Schneidewin, *Corpus paroemiographorum Graecorum*, vol. 1. Göttingen: Vandenhoeck & Ruprecht, 1839 (repr. Hildesheim: Olms, 1965): 177–320.
Cod: 11,499: Paroem.
002 **Paroemiae** (litterarum ordine), ed. von Leutsch, *op. cit.*, vol. 2 (1851; repr. 1958): 1–52.
Cod: 5,070: Paroem.

1322 **DIOGENIANUS** Phil.
A.D. 2
001 **Fragmenta**, ed. A. Gercke, "Chrysippea," *Jahrbücher für classische Philologie*, suppl. 14 (1885) 748–755.
frr. 1–4.
Q: 2,553: Phil.

1325 *DIOGENIS SINOPENSIS EPISTULAE*
Incertum
Cf. et DIOGENES Phil. et Trag. (0334).
001 **Epistulae**, ed. R. Hercher, *Epistolographi Graeci*. Paris: Didot, 1873 (repr. Amsterdam: Hakkert, 1965): 235–258.
Q: 9,251: Epist.

1952 **DIOGNETUS** Hist.
post 4 B.C.: fort. Erythraeus
001 **Testimonia**, FGrH #120: 2B:626.
NQ: 44: Test.
002 **Fragmentum**, FGrH #120: 2B:626.
Q: 74: Hist.

DIOMEDES Gramm.
Incertum
Cf. COMMENTARIA IN DIONYSII THRACIS ARTEM GRAMMATICAM (4175 002, 004–005).

0860 **DIOMEDES** Med.
ante A.D. 2
x01 **Fragmenta ap. Galenum**.
K12.759, 771.
Cf. GALENUS Med. (0057 076).

0861 **DION** Med.
ante A.D. 1
x01 **Fragmentum ap. Oribasium**.
CMG, vol. 6.3, p. 103.
Cf. ORIBASIUS Med. (0722 004).

1327 *DIONIS EPISTULAE*
Incertum
Cf. et DIO CHRYSOSTOMUS Soph. (0612).
001 **Epistulae**, ed. R. Hercher, *Epistolographi Graeci*. Paris: Didot, 1873 (repr. Amsterdam: Hakkert, 1965): 259.
Cod: 275: Epist.

1323 **Aelius DIONYSIUS** Attic.
A.D. 2: Halicarnassensis
001 Ἀττικὰ ὀνόματα, ed. H. Erbse, *Untersuchungen zu den attizistischen Lexika [Abhandlungen der deutschen Akademie der Wissenschaften zu Berlin*, Philosoph.-hist. Kl. Berlin: Akademie-Verlag, 1950]: 95–151.
Q: 15,859: Lexicogr.

0445 **DIONYSIUS** Comic.
5/4 B.C.: Sinopensis
001 **Fragmenta**, ed. T. Kock, *Comicorum Atticorum fragmenta*, vol. 2. Leipzig: Teubner, 1884: 423–428.
frr. 1–11.
Q: 597: Comic.
002 **Fragmenta**, ed. A. Meineke, *Fragmenta comicorum Graecorum*, vol. 3. Berlin: Reimer, 1840 (repr. De Gruyter, 1970): 547–549, 551–555.
Q: 554: Comic.
003 **Fragmentum**, ed. Meineke, *FCG*, vol. 5.1 (1857; repr. 1970): ccxxi.
Q: 7: Comic.

0246 **DIONYSIUS** Eleg.
5 B.C.: Chalcus
001 **Fragmenta**, ed. M.L. West, *Iambi et elegi Graeci*, vol. 2. Oxford: Clarendon Press, 1972: 58–60.
frr. 1–6.
Q: 154: Eleg.

1326 **DIONYSIUS** Epic.
fiq Dionysius Perieg. vel Dionysius ὁ Κυκλογράφος Hist.
ante A.D. 3
Cf. et DIONYSIUS Perieg. (0084).
Cf. et DIONYSIUS ὁ Κυκλογράφος Hist. (1331).
001 **Fragmenta**, ed. E. Heitsch, *Die griechischen Dichterfragmente der römischen Kaiserzeit*, vol. 1, 2nd edn. Göttingen: Vandenhoeck & Ruprecht, 1963: 61–77.
frr. 1–28.
Q, Pap: 1,431: Epic.

2619 **DIONYSIUS** Epic.
Incertum: Corinthius
001 **Tituli**, ed. H. Lloyd-Jones and P. Parsons, *Supplementum Hellenisticum*. Berlin: De Gruyter, 1983: 178.
frr. 387–388.
NQ: 8: Poem.

0169 **DIONYSIUS** Epigr.
3 B.C.?: Cyzicenus
001 **Epigramma**, AG 7.78.
AG 7.462: Cf. DIONYSIUS Epigr. (0170 001).
Q: 40: Epigr.

0170 **DIONYSIUS** Epigr.
3 B.C.?: Rhodius
001 **Epigrammata**, AG 7.462(?), 716.
AG 7.51: Cf. ADAEUS Epigr. (0102 001).
AG 7.717: Cf. ANONYMI EPIGRAMMATICI
(AG) (0138 001).
Q: 50: Epigr.

0168 **DIONYSIUS** Epigr.
fiq Dionysius Sophista
A.D. 2?: Andrius
Cf. et DIONYSIUS Sophista <Epigr.> (0171).
001 **Epigramma**, AG 7.533.
Q: 20: Epigr.

0167 **DIONYSIUS** Epigr.
Incertum
001 **Epigrammata**, AG **6**.3; **12**.108.
AG 9.523: Cf. ANONYMI EPIGRAMMATICI
(AG) (0138 001).
Q: 53: Epigr.

0083 **DIONYSIUS** Geogr.
A.D. 2: Byzantius
Scholia: Cf. SCHOLIA IN DIONYSIUM BY-
ZANTIUM (5018).
002 **Titulus**, ed. H. Lloyd-Jones and P. Parsons,
Supplementum Hellenisticum. Berlin: De Gruy-
ter, 1983: 178.
fr. 386.
NQ: 3: Lyr.
003 **Per Bosporum navigatio**, ed. R. Güngerich,
*Dionysii Byzantii anaplus Bospori una cum
scholiis x saeculi*, 2nd edn. Berlin: Weidmann,
1958: 1–23, 31–35.
Cod: Perieg.

0069 **DIONYSIUS** Geogr.
A.D. 2?
001 **Descriptio Graeciae**, ed. K. Müller, *Geographi
Graeci minores*, vol. 1. Paris: Didot, 1855 (repr.
Hildesheim: Olms, 1965): 238–243.
Q: 940: Perieg., Iamb.

4178 **DIONYSIUS** Gramm.
2 B.C.: Alexandrinus
x01 **Fragmenta grammatica in Homeri opera** (in
scholiis).
Erbse, passim.
Cf. SCHOLIA IN HOMERUM (5026 001).

4186 **DIONYSIUS** Gramm.
ante 1 B.C.: Phaselinus
x01 **De Antimachi carminibus** (fragmentum ap.
vitam Nicandri).
Crugnola, p. 33.

Cf. SCHOLIA IN NICANDRUM (5031 001).
x02 **De poetis** (fragmentum ap. vitam Nicandri).
Crugnola, p. 33.
Cf. SCHOLIA IN NICANDRUM (5031 001).
x03 **De comparatione Arati et Homeri** (fragmentum ap. tertiam vitam Arati).
Martin, p. 17.
Cf. VITAE ARATI ET VARIA DE ARATO
(4161 004).
x04 **Fragmentum in illud:** Ὀρφεὺς Ὀδρύσης (fort.
auctore Dionysio Halicarnassensi Gramm. et
Mus.).
Cf. DIONYSIUS Gramm. et Mus. (4181 x02).
x05 **De poetis** *sive* **Commentarium de Pindaro**
(fragmentum in scholiis).
Drachmann, vol. 2, p. 31 (*Pyth.* 2).
Cf. SCHOLIA IN PINDARUM (5034 001).

4177 **DIONYSIUS** Gramm.
1 B.C.–A.D. 1
x01 Περὶ ὀνομασιῶν (fragmenta ap. Athenaeum).
Deipnosophistae **6**.255c; **11**.503c; **14**.641a.
Cf. ATHENAEUS Soph. (0008 001).
x02 Περὶ ὀνομασιῶν (fragmenta ap. Stephanum Byzantium).
Meineke, pp. 464, 482.
Cf. STEPHANUS Gramm. (4028 001).

4179 **DIONYSIUS** Gramm.
ante A.D. 3
x01 Περὶ ἀπόρων (fragmentum in scholiis ad Homerum).
Erbse, vol. 1, p. 251; FGrH 1A, p. 180, fr. 15.
Cf. SCHOLIA IN HOMERUM (5026 001).
Cf. DIONYSIUS ὁ Κυκλογράφος Hist. (1331
002).

4180 **DIONYSIUS** Gramm.
Incertum
x01 **Fragmenta grammatica in Euripidem** (in scho-
liis).
Schwartz, passim.
Cf. SCHOLIA IN EURIPIDEM (5023 001).

4181 **DIONYSIUS** Gramm. et Mus.
A.D. 2: Halicarnassensis
001 Περὶ ὁμοιοτήτων (fragmentum ap. Porphy-
rium), ed. R. Westphal, *Die Fragmente und die
Lehrsätze der griechischen Rhythmiker*. Leip-
zig: Teubner, 1861: 46.
Q: Mus.
x01 **Historia musica** (fragmentum ap. Stephanum
Byzantium).
Meineke, p. 646 (s.v. Ὑδρέα).
Cf. STEPHANUS Gramm. (4028 001).
x02 **Fragmentum in illud:** Ὀρφεὺς Ὀδρύσης (ap.
Sudam).
Adler, vol. 1.3, p. 565, no. 656.
Cf. SUDA (9010 001).

2466 **DIONYSIUS** Hist.
5 B.C.: Milesius

001 **Testimonia**, FGrH #687: 3C:410–411.
NQ: 61: Test.

002 **Fragmenta**, FGrH #687: 3C:411.
Q: 245: Hist.

2257 DIONYSIUS Hist.
5–4 B.C.

001 **Testimonium**, FGrH #357: 3B:217.
NQ: 13: Test.

1328 DIONYSIUS Hist.
4 B.C.?: Chalcidensis

001 **Fragmenta**, FHG 4: 393–396.
Q

1324 DIONYSIUS Hist.
4–3 B.C.?: Argivus

001 **Fragmentum**, FGrH #308: 3B:14.
Q: 167: Hist.

2538 DIONYSIUS Hist.
post 4 B.C.?: Olbianus

001 **Fragmentum**, FGrH #804: 3C:842.
Q: 59: Hist.

2483 DIONYSIUS Hist.
3 B.C.

001 **Testimonia**, FGrH #717: 3C:641.
NQ: 77: Test.

002 **Fragmentum**, FGrH #717: 3C:641–642.
Q: 91: Hist.

2446 DIONYSIUS Hist.
2 B.C./A.D. 1?

001 **Fragmentum**, FGrH #653: 3C:205.
Q: 30: Hist.

2354 DIONYSIUS Hist.
Incertum: Rhodius

001 **Testimonium**, FGrH #511: 3B:488.
NQ: 41: Test.

2390 [DIONYSIUS] Hist.
Incertum: Siculus

001 **Fragmentum**, FGrH #567: 3B:659.
Q: 61: Hist.

0793 DIONYSIUS Med.
3/1 B.C.: Aegaeus

x01 **Fragmenta**.
Photius, *Bibliotheca* 211.
Cf. PHOTIUS Theol., Scr. Eccl. et Lexicogr.
(4040 001).

0865 DIONYSIUS Med.
A.D. 2?: Samius

x01 **Fragmentum ap. Galenum**.
K13.745–746.
Cf. GALENUS Med. (0057 077).

0864 DIONYSIUS Med.
ante A.D. 4: fort. Hierapolitanus

x01 **Fragmentum ap. Oribasium**.
CMG, vol. 6.2.2, p. 281.
Cf. ORIBASIUS Med. (0722 003).

4182 DIONYSIUS Onir.
ante A.D. 2: Heliopolitanus

x01 **Fragmentum** (ap. Artemidorum Daldianum).
Pack, p. 190.
Cf. ARTEMIDORUS Onir. (0553 001).

0084 DIONYSIUS Perieg.
A.D. 2: fort. Alexandrinus
Cf. et DIONYSIUS Epic. (1326).
Vitae: Cf. VITAE DIONYSII PERIEGETAE
(4173).
Vitae et Scholia: Cf. SCHOLIA IN DIONY-
SIUM PERIEGETAM (5019).

001 **Orbis descriptio**, ed. K. Müller, *Geographi
Graeci minores*, vol. 2. Paris: Didot, 1861 (repr.
Hildesheim: Olms, 1965): 104–176.
Cod: 7,757: Perieg., Hexametr.

002 **Lithiaca vel lithica** (fragmenta), ed. Müller, *op.
cit.*, xxvi.
Q: 21: Nat. Hist.

003 **Ixeuticon** *sive De aucupio* (paraphrasis) (olim
sub auctore Eutecnio), ed. A. Garzya, *Dionysii
ixeuticon seu de aucupio libri tres in epitomen
metro solutam redacti*. Leipzig: Teubner, 1963:
1–49.
Cod: 8,319: Nat. Hist., Comm.

4254 DIONYSIUS Phil.
4 B.C.: Bithynius, Chalcedonius, Atheniensis

001 **Testimonia**, ed. K. Döring, *Die Megariker
[Studien zur antiken Philosophie* 2. Amsterdam: Grüner, 1972]: 10, 14.
test. 31, 45–46.
test. 31 (p. 10) = Euclides (4247 001).
test. 45–46 (p. 14) = Dionysius.
NQ: Test.

2683 DIONYSIUS Poeta
A.D. 2: Magnes

x01 **Epigramma sepulcrale**.
App. Anth. 2.339: Cf. ANTHOLOGIAE GRAE-
CAE APPENDIX (7052 002).

1329 DIONYSIUS Scr. Eccl.
A.D. 2: Corinthius

001 **Fragmenta**, ed. M.J. Routh, *Reliquiae sacrae*,
vol. 1, 2nd edn. Oxford: Oxford University
Press, 1846 (repr. Hildesheim: Olms, 1974):
179–183.
Epistula ad Romanos: pp. 179–181.
De reliquis septem epistulis: pp. 181–183.
Q: 646: Epist.

2952 DIONYSIUS Scr. Eccl.
A.D. 3: Alexandrinus

001 **Epistulae**, ed. C.L. Feltoe, *The letters and other
remains of Dionysius of Alexandria*. Cambridge:

Cambridge University Press, 1904: 5–21, 23–36, 38–40, 44–46, 49–64, 66–91, 94–105.

Ad Fabium Antiochenum: pp. 5–21.
Ad Germanum: pp. 23–36.
Ad Novatianum: pp. 38–39.
Ad Cornelium: p. 40.
Ad Stephanum Romanum: pp. 44–46.
Ad Xystum (Sixtum II) Romanum: pp. 49–52, 56–59.
Ad Philemonem presbyterum Romanum: pp. 52–55.
Ad Dionysium Romanum: pp. 55–56.
Ad Colonem (vel Cononem): pp. 60–62.
De paenitentia (fragmenta duo): pp. 62–64.
Ad Dometium et Didymum: pp. 66–69.
Ad Hermammonem: pp. 70–78.
Ad Alexandrinos: pp. 80–84.
Ad Hieracem: pp. 85–89.
Ex epistula secunda: p. 90.
Ex epistula quarta festali: p. 91.
Ad Basilidem: pp. 94–105.
Q: Epist.

002 **Fragmenta**, ed. Feltoe, *op. cit.*, 108–126, 131–164, 182–208, 210–229, 231–260.
De promissionibus: pp. 108–126.
De natura (adversus Epicureos): pp. 131–164.
Refutatio et apologia: pp. 182–198.
In Origenem [Dub.]: pp. 199–200.
In Job [Dub.]: pp. 201–208.
In Ecclesiasten [Dub.]: pp. 210–227.
In Canticum canticorum [Dub.]: pp. 228–229.
In Lucam [Sp.]: pp. 231–250.
In Acta apostolorum: p. 251.
In epistulam ad Romanos: p. 251.
In epistulam Jacobi [Dub.]: pp. 252–253.
In Apocalypsem [Dub.]: p. 253.
Ad Aphrodisium: pp. 254–256.
De gymnasio: p. 256.
De matrimonio: p. 257.
Fragmenta varia [Dub.]: pp. 257–260.
In Origenem: Dup. partim HIPPOLYTUS Scr. Eccl. (2115 004).
Q

003 **Ad Heuresium et Pasicriten** (fragmentum), ed. W.A. Bienert, "Neue Fragmente des Dionysius und des Petrus von Alexandrien aus Cod. Vatop. 236," Κληρονομία 5 (1973) 309.
Cod

004 **Commentarii in Ecclesiasten** (fragmenta duo), ed. Bienert, *op. cit.*, 310.
Cf. et 2952 002.
Cod

005 **Epistula ad Theodosium monachum**, MPG 78: 205–208.
Cod

006 **Epistula ad Ursenuphium lectorem**, MPG 78: 901–904.
Cod

007 **Epistula ad Paulum Samosatenum**, ed. E. Schwartz, "Eine fingierte Korrespondenz mit Paulus dem Samosatener," *Sitzungsberichte der bayerischen Akademie der Wissenschaften,*

Philosoph.-philol. und hist. Kl., Heft 3 (1927) 3–9.
Cod

x01 **Quaestiones et responsiones.**
Feltoe, pp. 259–260.
Cf. 2952 002.

2953 **DIONYSIUS** Scr. Eccl.
A.D. 3: Romanus
001 **Epistula ad Dionysium Alexandrinum**, ed. C.L. Feltoe, *The letters and other remains of Dionysius of Alexandria*. Cambridge: Cambridge University Press, 1904: 176–182.
Q: Epist.

4230 **DIONYSIUS** Soph.
A.D. 1–2: Milesius, Lesbius, Ephesius
x01 **Monodia de Chaeronea** (fragmentum ap. Philostratum, *Vitae sophistarum*).
Kayser, vol. 2, pp. 35–36.
Cf. Flavius PHILOSTRATUS Soph. (0638 003).

4184 **DIONYSIUS** Soph.
A.D. 5–6: Antiochenus
001 **Epistulae**, ed. R. Hercher, *Epistolographi Graeci*. Paris: Didot, 1873 (repr. Amsterdam: Hakkert, 1965): 260–274.
Cod: Epist.

0350 **<DIONYSIUS>** Trag. vel Comic.
Incertum: Scymnaeus
001 **Fragmentum**, ed. B. Snell, *Tragicorum Graecorum fragmenta*, vol. 1. Göttingen: Vandenhoeck & Ruprecht, 1971: 320.
fr. 1.
Q: 7: Trag.

0330 **DIONYSIUS I** <Trag.>
vel Dionysius Tyrannus Siceliae
4 B.C.: Syracusanus
001 **Fragmenta**, ed. B. Snell, *Tragicorum Graecorum fragmenta*, vol. 1. Göttingen: Vandenhoeck & Ruprecht, 1971: 242–246.
frr. 1–2, 3–12.
Q: 176: Trag., Satyr.
002 **Testimonium**, FGrH #557: 3B:568.
NQ: 12: Test.

0247 **DIONYSIUS II** <Eleg.>
vel Dionysius Tyrannus Siceliae
4 B.C.: Syracusanus
001 **Fragmenta**, ed. M.L. West, *Iambi et elegi Graeci*, vol. 2. Oxford: Clarendon Press, 1972: 60–61.
frr. 1–2.
Q: 14: Eleg.

2798 **Pseudo-DIONYSIUS AREOPAGITA** Theol. et Scr. Eccl.
A.D. 5–6: fort. Syrius
001 **De caelesti hierarchia**, ed. R. Roques, G. Heil

and M. de Gandillac, *Denys l'Aréopagite. La hiérarchie céleste* [*Sources chrétiennes* 58. Paris: Cerf, 1958 (repr. 1970)]: 70–225.
Cod: Theol.

002 **De ecclesiastica hierarchia**, MPG 3: 369–377, 392–404, 424–445, 472–485, 500–516, 529–537, 552–569.
Cod: Theol.

004 **De divinis nominibus**, MPG 3: 585–597, 636–652, 680–684, 693–736, 816–825, 856–857, 865–873, 889–897, 909–917, 936–940, 948–956, 969–972, 977–984.
Cod: Theol.

005 **De mystica theologia**, MPG 3: 997–1001, 1025, 1032–1033, 1040, 1045–1048.
Cod: Theol.

006 **Ad Gaium monachum** (epist. 1), MPG 3: 1065.
Cod: Epist., Theol.

007 **Ad Gaium monachum** (epist. 2), MPG 3: 1068–1069.
Cod: Epist., Theol.

008 **Ad Gaium monachum** (epist. 3), MPG 3: 1069.
Cod: Epist., Theol.

009 **Ad Gaium monachum** (epist. 4), MPG 3: 1072.
Cod: Epist., Theol.

010 **Ad Dorotheum ministrum** (epist. 5), MPG 3: 1073–1076.
Cod: Epist., Theol.

011 **Ad Sosipatrum sacerdotem** (epist. 6), MPG 3: 1077.
Cod: Epist., Theol.

012 **Ad Polycarpum antistitem** (epist. 7), MPG 3: 1077–1081.
Cod: Epist., Theol.

013 **Ad Demophilum monachum** (epist. 8), MPG 3: 1084–1100.
Cod: Epist., Theol.

014 **Ad Titum episcopum** (epist. 9), MPG 3: 1104–1113.
Cod: Epist., Theol.

015 **Ad Joannem theologum** (epist. 10), MPG 3: 1117–1120.
Cod: Epist., Theol.

0862 **DIONYSIUS CYRTUS** Med.
ante A.D. 1
x01 **Fragmentum ap. Galenum.**
K13.928.
Cf. GALENUS Med. (0057 077).

0863 **DIONYSIUS Empiricus** Med.
1 B.C.: fort. Milesius
x01 **Fragmenta ap. Galenum.**
K12.741–742, 760, 835.
Cf. GALENUS Med. (0057 076).

0081 **DIONYSIUS HALICARNASSENSIS** Rhet. et Hist.
1 B.C.: Halicarnassensis
Cf. et DIONYSIUS Sophista <Epigr.> (0171).

001 **Antiquitates Romanae**, ed. K. Jacoby, *Dionysii Halicarnasei antiquitatum Romanarum quae*

supersunt, 4 vols. Leipzig: Teubner, 1:1885; 2:1888; 3:1891; 4:1905 (repr. Stuttgart: 1967): 1:1–403; 2:1–408; 3:1–400; 4:1–336.
Cod: 295,922: Hist.

002 **De antiquis oratoribus**, ed. H. Usener and L. Radermacher, *Dionysii Halicarnasei quae exstant*, vol. 5. Leipzig: Teubner, 1899 (repr. Stuttgart: 1965): 3–7.
Cod: 915: Rhet.

003 **De Lysia**, ed. Usener and Radermacher, *op. cit.*, vol. 5, 8–53.
Cod: 7,951: Rhet.

004 **De Isocrate**, ed. Usener and Radermacher, *op. cit.*, vol. 5, 54–92.
Cod: 6,614: Rhet.

005 **De Isaeo**, ed. Usener and Radermacher, *op. cit.*, vol. 5, 93–124.
Cod: 5,434: Rhet.

006 **De Demosthenis dictione**, ed. Usener and Radermacher, *op. cit.*, vol. 5, 127–252.
Cod: 22,807: Rhet.

007 **Libri secundi de antiquis oratoribus reliquiae**, ed. Usener and Radermacher, *op. cit.*, vol. 5, 253–254.
Q: 244: Rhet.

008 **Ad Ammaeum**, ed. Usener and Radermacher, *op. cit.*, vol. 5, 257–279.
Cod: 3,598: Epist., Rhet.

009 **De Dinarcho**, ed. Usener and Radermacher, *op. cit.*, vol. 5, 297–321.
Cod: 4,413: Rhet.

010 **De Thucydide**, ed. Usener and Radermacher, *op. cit.*, vol. 5, 325–418.
Cod: 17,449: Rhet.

011 **De Thucydidis idiomatibus** (epistula ad Ammaeum), ed. Usener and Radermacher, *op. cit.*, vol. 5, 421–438.
Cod: 2,707: Epist., Rhet.

012 **De compositione verborum**, ed. Usener and Radermacher, *op. cit.*, vol. 6 (1929; repr. 1965): 3–143.
Cod: 21,576: Rhet.

013 **De compositione verborum** (epitome), ed. Usener and Radermacher, *op. cit.*, vol. 6, 145–194.
Cod: 9,989: Rhet.

014 **De imitatione** (fragmenta), ed. Usener and Radermacher, *op. cit.*, vol. 6, 197, 200, 202–216.
frr. 1–3, 6–6a, 9–10.
fr. 6 (De veterum censura): pp. 202.18–214.2.
Q: 2,162: Rhet.

015 **Epistula ad Pompeium Geminum**, ed. Usener and Radermacher, *op. cit.*, vol. 6, 221–248.
Cod: 4,535: Epist., Rhet.

016 **Ars rhetorica** [Sp.], ed. Usener and Radermacher, *op. cit.*, vol. 6, 255–292, 295–387.
Cod: 23,541: Rhet.

017 **Testimonium**, FGrH #251: 2B:1146.
NQ: 22: Test.

018 **Fragmenta**, FGrH #251: 2B:1146–1151.
Q: 1,782: Hist., Chronogr.

x01 **De veterum censura** (= Περὶ μιμήσεως).
Usener & Radermacher, vol. 6, pp. 202.18–
214.2.
Cf. 0081 014.

2620 **DIONYSIUS IAMBUS** Gramm. et Poeta
3 B.C.
001 **Fragmentum**, ed. H. Lloyd-Jones and P. Parsons, *Supplementum Hellenisticum*. Berlin: De Gruyter, 1983: 179.
fr. 389.
Q: 6: Hexametr.
x01 **Fragmentum de dialectis** (ap. Athenaeum).
Deipnosophistae 7.284b.
Cf. ATHENAEUS Soph. (0008 001).

4185 **DIONYSIUS LEPTUS** Gramm. et Rhet.
A.D. 2
x01 **Fragmentum ex commentario de Theodoride** (ap. Athenaeum).
Deipnosophistae 11.475f.
Cf. ATHENAEUS Soph. (0008 001).

2185 **DIONYSIUS** Μεταθέμενος Phil.
3 B.C.: Heracleota (Ponti)
001 **Fragmenta**, ed. J. von Arnim, *Stoicorum veterum fragmenta*, vol. 1. Leipzig: Teubner, 1905 (repr. Stuttgart: 1968): 93–96.
Q: 1,001: Phil.

1331 **DIONYSIUS** ὁ Κυκλογράφος Hist.
3/2 B.C.?: Samius
Cf. et DIONYSIUS Epic. (1326).
001 **Testimonia**, FGrH #15: 1A:178.
NQ: 54: Test.
002 **Fragmenta**, FGrH #15: 1A:178–180.
Q: 779: Hist., Myth.

1881 **DIONYSIUS SCYTOBRACHION** Gramm.
2 B.C.: Alexandrinus, fort. Mytilenensis vel Milesius
001 **Testimonia**, FGrH #32: 1A:228.
NQ: 196: Test.
002 **Fragmenta**, FGrH #32: 1A:229–257.
Q: 11,453: Hist., Myth.
003 **Fragmentum** (*P. Mich.* 1316), ed. H.J. Mette, "Die 'Kleinen' griechischen Historiker heute," *Lustrum* 21 (1978) 8.
fr. 14 bis.
Pap: 35: Hist.

0171 **DIONYSIUS Sophista** <Epigr.>
fiq Dionysius Halicarnassensis Rhet. et Hist.
A.D. 2?
Cf. et DIONYSIUS Epigr. (0168).
Cf. et DIONYSIUS HALICARNASSENSIS Rhet. et Hist. (0081).
001 **Epigrammata**, AG 5.81; 11.182.
AG 5.82–83: Cf. ANONYMI EPIGRAMMATICI (AG) (0138 001).
AG 10.38: Cf. TIMON Phil. (1735 002).
AG 12.60: Cf. MELEAGER Epigr. (1492 001).

AG 15.35: Cf. THEOPHANES CONFESSOR Chronogr. (4046 002).
Q: 33: Epigr.

0063 **DIONYSIUS THRAX** Gramm.
2 B.C.: Alexandrinus
Scholia: Cf. COMMENTARIA IN DIONYSII THRACIS ARTEM GRAMMATICAM (4175).
001 **Ars grammatica**, ed. G. Uhlig, *Grammatici Graeci*, vol. 1.1. Leipzig: Teubner, 1883 (repr. Hildesheim: Olms, 1965): 5–100.
Cf. et ANONYMI GRAMMATICI (0072 001).
Cod: 3,536: Gramm.
002 **Testimonium**, FGrH #512: 3B:488.
NQ: 40: Test.
003 **Fragmentum**, FGrH #512: 3B:488.
Q: 48: Hist.
004 **Fragmenta**, ed. K. Linke, *Die Fragmente des Grammatikers Dionysios Thrax* [*Sammlung griechischer und lateinischer Grammatiker* 3. Berlin: De Gruyter, 1977]: 13–33.
Q, Pap: 3,098: Gramm.

1909 **DIONYSODORUS** Hist.
4 B.C.?: Boeotus
001 **Testimonium**, FGrH #68: 2A:35.
NQ: 25: Test.
002 **Fragmentum**, FGrH #68: 2A:35.
Q: 52: Hist.

2574 **DIONYSOPHANES** Hist.
ante A.D. 3
001 **Fragmenta**, FGrH #856: 3C:943.
Q: 160: Hist.

0172 **DIOPHANES** Epigr.
1 B.C.: Myrinus
001 **Epigramma**, AG 5.309.
Q: 12: Epigr.

DIOPHANES Math.
vel Diophantus
A.D. 3?
Cf. DIOPHANTUS Math. (2039).

0395 **DIOPHANTUS** Comic.
Incertum
001 **Fragmentum**, ed. T. Kock, *Comicorum Atticorum fragmenta*, vol. 3. Leipzig: Teubner, 1888: 375.
fr. 1.
Q: 5: Comic.
002 **Fragmenta**, ed. A. Meineke, *Fragmenta comicorum Graecorum*, vol. 1. Berlin: Reimer, 1839 (repr. De Gruyter, 1970): 492.
Q: 9: Comic.

2712 **DIOPHANTUS** Epigr.
Incertum: Atheniensis
x01 **Epigramma exhortatorium et supplicatorium**.
App. Anth. 4.52: Cf. ANTHOLOGIAE GRAECAE APPENDIX (7052 004).

2539 **DIOPHANTUS** Hist.
      3 B.C.?
001   **Testimonium**, FGrH #805: 3C:842.
      NQ: 48: Test.
002   **Fragmenta**, FGrH #805: 3C:842-843.
      Q: 135: Hist.

2039 **DIOPHANTUS** Math.
      vel Diophanes
      A.D. 3?: Alexandrinus
      Scholia: Cf. SCHOLIA IN DIOPHANTUM
      (5021).
001   **Arithmeticorum libri sex**, ed. P. Tannery, *Dio-
      phanti Alexandrini opera omnia*, vol. 1. Leip-
      zig: Teubner, 1893 (repr. Stuttgart: 1974): 2-
      448.
      Cod: 46,559: Math.
002   **De polygonis numeris**, ed. Tannery, *op. cit.*,
      vol. 1, 450-480.
      Cod: 3,581: Math.
003   **Fragmentum** [Sp.] (e cod. Paris. suppl. gr. 387,
      fol. 181r), ed. Tannery, *op. cit.*, vol. 2 (1895;
      repr. 1974): 3.
      Cod: 94: Math.
004   **Fragmentum** [Sp.] (e cod. Paris. 453), ed.
      Tannery, *op. cit.*, vol. 2, 3-15.
      Cod: 2,625: Math.
005   **Fragmentum** [Sp.] (e cod. Paris. gr. 2448), ed.
      Tannery, *op. cit.*, vol. 2, 15-31.
      Cod: 3,287: Math.
x01   **Problema**.
      App. Anth. 7.3(?): Cf. ANTHOLOGIAE GRAE-
      CAE APPENDIX (7052 007).

0867 **DIOPHANTUS** Med.
      ante A.D. 1: Lycius
x01   **Fragmenta ap. Galenum**.
      K12.845; 13.281, 507, 805.
      Cf. GALENUS Med. (0057 076-078).

2621 **DIOPHILUS vel DIOPHILA** Poeta
      4-3 B.C.?
001   **Fragmentum**, ed. H. Lloyd-Jones and P. Par-
      sons, *Supplementum Hellenisticum*. Berlin: De
      Gruyter, 1983: 179-180.
      fr. 391: *P. Oxy.* 20.2258c, fr. 1.
      Pap: 56: Hexametr., Encom.

0173 **DIOSCORIDES** Epigr.
      3 B.C.: Alexandrinus
001   **Epigrammata**, AG **5**.52-56, 138, 193; **6**.126,
      220, 290; **7**.31, 37, 76, 162, 166-167, 178, 229,
      351, 407, 410-411, 430, 434, 450, 456, 484-
      485, 707-708; **9**.340, 568, 734; **11**.195, 363;
      12.14, 37, 42, 169-171.
      Dup. partim DIOSCURIDES Hist. (2409 002).
      AG 7.287: Cf. ANTIPATER Epigr. (0114 001).
      Q: 1,692: Epigr.

0656 **DIOSCORIDES PEDANIUS** Med.
      A.D. 1: Anazarbensis
      Cf. et Pseudo-DIOSCORIDES Med. (1118).

001   **De materia medica**, ed. M. Wellmann, *Pedanii
      Dioscuridis Anazarbei de materia medica libri
      quinque*, 3 vols. Berlin: Weidmann, 1:1907;
      2:1906; 3:1914 (repr. 1958): 1:1-255, 2:1-339,
      3:1-108.
      Cod: 97,500: Med.
002   **Euporista vel De simplicibus medicinis**, ed.
      Wellmann, *op. cit.*, vol. 3, 151-317.
      Cod: 32,395: Med.

1118 **Pseudo-DIOSCORIDES** Med.
      post A.D. 1
      Cf. et DIOSCORIDES PEDANIUS Med. (0656).
001   **De venenis eorumque praecautione et medica-
      tione** (= **Alexipharmaca**), ed. K. Sprengel, *Pe-
      danii Dioscoridis Anazarbei*, vol. 2 [*Medicorum
      Graecorum opera quae exstant* (ed. C.G. Kühn),
      vol. 26.2. Leipzig: Knobloch, 1830]: 1-41.
      Cod: 5,312: Med.
002   **De iis, quae virus ejaculantur, animalibus li-
      bellus, in quo et de rabioso cane** (= **Theriaca**),
      ed. Sprengel, *op. cit.*, 42-91.
      Cod: 6,493: Med.
003   **De lapidibus**, ed. C.É. Ruelle, *Les lapidaires de
      l'antiquité et du Moyen Age*, vol. 2.1. Paris:
      Leroux, 1898: 179-183.
      Cod: 1,095: Nat. Hist.

0870 **DIOSCORIDES Phacas** Med.
      1 B.C.: Alexandrinus
x01   **Fragmentum ap. Paulum**.
      CMG, vol. 9.1, p. 345.
      Cf. PAULUS Med. (0715 001).

2121 **DIOSCORUS** Epic.
      A.D. 6: Thebanus (Aegypti)
001   **Fragmenta**, ed. E. Heitsch, *Die griechischen
      Dichterfragmente der römischen Kaiserzeit*, vol.
      1, 2nd edn. Göttingen: Vandenhoeck & Rup-
      recht, 1963: 128-152.
      fr. 1, Encomium Justini II (*P. Cairo Cat.*
      2.67183): pp. 128-129.
      fr. 2, Encomium Joannis (*P. Cairo Cat.*
      1.67055v): pp. 129-130.
      fr. 3, Encomium Joannis (*P. Berol.* 10580 + *P.
      Cairo Cat.* 3.67317): pp. 130-133.
      fr. 4, Encomium Athanasii (*P. Cairo Cat.*
      1.67097v B C): pp. 133-134.
      fr. 5, Encomium Callinici (*P. Cairo Cat.*
      3.67315v): pp. 134-136.
      fr. 6, Encomium (*P. Cairo Cat.* 2.67177): pp.
      136-137.
      fr. 7, Encomium (*P. Cairo Cat.* 3.67316v): pp.
      137-138.
      fr. 8, Encomium (*P. Walters Art Gallery*, Balti-
      more, inv. 517): p. 138.
      fr. 9, Encomium (*P. Cairo Cat.* 1.67097 E): pp.
      138-139.
      fr. 10, Encomium (*P. Cairo Cat.* 2.67131v): pp.
      139-140.
      fr. 11, Encomium (*P. Cairo Cat.* 3.67279v): pp.
      140-141.

fr. 12, Encomium Romani domini (*P. Brit. Mus.* 1552 + *P. Rain.* 2070): pp. 141–142.

fr. 13, Encomium Constantini dioecetae (*P. Cairo Cat.* 1.67120v): pp. 142–143.

fr. 14, Encomium Dorothei comitis (*P. Cairo Cat.* 1.67120v): p. 143.

fr. 15, Encomium Constantini (*P. Cairo Cat.* 1.67120v): pp. 143–144.

fr. 16, Εἰς τὴν τύχην τῆς γενεθλίας (*P. Cairo Cat.* 1.67120v): p. 144.

fr. 17, Encomium Colluthi comitis (*P. Cairo Cat.* 1.67120v): pp. 144–145.

fr. 18, Encomium Joannis jurisconsulti (*P. Brit. Mus.* 1728 + 1745v): p. 145.

fr. 19, Encomium Hypatii excubitoris praefecti (*P. Cairo Cat.* 2.67185v A): pp. 145–146.

fr. 20, Encomium Pauli cancellarii (*P. Cairo Cat.* 2.67185v B): p. 146.

fr. 21, Epithalamium Callinici comitis (*P. Cairo Cat.* 2.67179 A): pp. 146–147.

fr. 22, Epithalamium (*P. Brit. Mus.* 1733 + *P. Cairo Cat.* 2.67181 et 67180): pp. 147–148.

fr. 23, Epithalamium acrostichum (*P. Cairo Cat.* 3.67318): pp. 148–149.

fr. 24, Epithalamium (*P. Brit. Mus.* 1728 + 1745v): pp. 149–150.

fr. 25, Epithalamium (*P. Brit. Mus.* 1745v): p. 150.

fr. 26, Achilles de Polyxena (*P. Cairo Cat.* 3.67316v): p. 151.

fr. 27, Apollo de Hyacintho et Daphne (*P. Cairo Cat.* 2.67188v): p. 151.

fr. 28, Symposiaca (*P. Cairo Cat.* 1.67097v F): pp. 151–152.

Pap: 3,728: Epic., Encom.

0868 **DIOSCORUS** Med.
ante A.D. 2
x01 **Fragmentum ap. Galenum.**
K13.204–205.
Cf. GALENUS Med. (0057 076).

2725 **DIOSCORUS I** Theol.
A.D. 5: Alexandrinus
x01 **Epistula** (inc. Ὁ μονογενὴς τοῦ θεοῦ υἱὸς λόγος) (ap. Eustathium, *Epistula de duabus naturis*).
MPG 86.1.933.
Cf. EUSTATHIUS Theol. (2810 001).
x02 **Epistula** (inc. Εἰ μὴ τὸ αἷμα) (ap. Eustathium, *Epistula de duabus naturis*).
MPG 86.1.933.
Cf. EUSTATHIUS Theol. (2810 001).

2409 **DIOSCURIDES** Hist.
vel Dioscorides
fiq Dioscurides Isocratis discipulus vel Dioscorides compositor constitutionis Laconicae vel Dioscurides Tarsensis Gramm.
4/1 B.C.?
001 **Testimonia,** FGrH #594: 3B:707.
test. 3: *Inscr. Cret. Cnossus* 12.
NQ: 90: Test.

002 **Fragmenta,** FGrH #594: 3B:707–713.
frr. 9–11 (auctore Dioscoride Alexandrino).
Dup. partim DIOSCORIDES Epigr. (0173 001).
Q: 2,025: Hist., Epigr.
003 **Fragmentum,** ed. H.J. Mette, "Die 'Kleinen' griechischen Historiker heute," *Lustrum* 21 (1978) 32.
fr. 3 bis.
Q: 36: Hist.

0174 **DIOTIMUS** Epic.
fiq Diotimus Epigr.
3 B.C.?: Adramyttenus
001 **Epigrammata,** AG **6.**267, 358; **7.**173, 227(?), 475(?), 733(?); **12.**36; **16.**158(?).
AG 7.261: Cf. DIOTIMUS Epigr. (0175 001).
Q: 297: Epigr.
002 **Fragmentum et titulus,** ed. H. Lloyd-Jones and P. Parsons, *Supplementum Hellenisticum.* Berlin: De Gruyter, 1983: 181–182.
frr. 393–394.
Dup. partim 0174 003 (fr. 2).
Q: 26: Epic.
003 **Fragmentum,** ed. G. Kinkel, *Epicorum Graecorum fragmenta,* vol. 1. Leipzig: Teubner, 1877: 213–214.
fr. 2.
Dup. partim 0174 002 (fr. 394).
Q: 21: Epic.

0175 **DIOTIMUS** Epigr.
4 B.C.: Atheniensis
001 **Epigrammata,** AG 7.261(?), 420.
Q: 74: Epigr.

DIOTIMUS Epigr.
fiq Diotimus Epic.
3 B.C.?
Cf. DIOTIMUS Epic. (0174).

0176 **DIOTIMUS** Epigr.
1 B.C.: Milesius
001 **Epigrammata,** AG **5.**106; **9.**391.
AG 16.158: Cf. DIOTIMUS Epic. (0174 001).
Q: 83: Epigr.

2340 **DIOTIMUS** Phil.
4 B.C.?: Tyrius
001 **Testimonia,** ed. H. Diels and W. Kranz, *Die Fragmente der Vorsokratiker,* vol. 2, 6th edn. Berlin: Weidmann, 1952 (repr. Dublin: 1966): 250.
test. 1–3.
NQ: 129: Test.

1332 **<DIOTOGENES>** Phil.
4 B.C./A.D. 2
001 **Fragmenta,** ed. H. Thesleff, *The Pythagorean texts of the Hellenistic period.* Åbo: Åbo Akademi, 1965: 71–77.
Q: 1,667: Phil.

0446 **DIOXIPPUS** Comic.
    4 B.C.?
001 **Fragmenta**, ed. T. Kock, *Comicorum Atticorum fragmenta*, vol. 3. Leipzig: Teubner, 1888: 358–360, 753.
    frr. 1–5 + titulus.
    Q: 72: Comic.
002 **Fragmenta**, ed. A. Meineke, *Fragmenta comicorum Graecorum*, vol. 4. Berlin: Reimer, 1841 (repr. De Gruyter, 1970): 541–543.
    Q: 75: Comic.

2316 **DIOXIPPUS** Hist.
    4 B.C.?: Corinthius
001 **Fragmentum**, FGrH #454: 3B:382–383.
    Q: 81: Hist.

0447 **DIPHILUS** Comic.
    4–3 B.C.: Sinopensis
001 **Fragmenta**, ed. T. Kock, *Comicorum Atticorum fragmenta*, vol. 2. Leipzig: Teubner, 1884: 541–580.
    frr. 1–8, 12–14, 16–24, 26–27, 29–36, 38, 40–46, 48–49, 51–69, 71–84, 86–123, 126–136 + tituli.
    Q: 2,297: Comic.
002 **Fragmenta**, ed. A. Meineke, *Fragmenta comicorum Graecorum*, vol. 4. Berlin: Reimer, 1841 (repr. De Gruyter, 1970): 375–381, 383–395, 397–428.
    Q: 2,213: Comic.
003 **Fragmenta**, ed. J. Demiańczuk, *Supplementum comicum*. Krakau: Nakładem Akademii, 1912 (repr. Hildesheim: Olms, 1967): 40.
    frr. 1–2.
    Q: 3: Comic.
004 **Fragmenta** (*P. Louvre* inv. no. 7733v), ed. F. Lasserre, "L'élégie de l'huître," *Quaderni urbinati di cultura classica* 19 (1975) 145–176.
    Pap

0248 **DIPHILUS** Epic. et Iamb.
    Incertum
001 **Fragmentum**, ed. M.L. West, *Iambi et elegi Graeci*, vol. 2. Oxford: Clarendon Press, 1972: 61.
    Q: 14: Iamb.

0177 **DIPHILUS** Epigr.
    4 B.C.: Atheniensis
001 **Epigramma**, AG 11.439.
    Q: 10: Epigr.

0872 **DIPHILUS** Med.
    3 B.C.: Siphnius
x01 **Fragmenta ap. Athenaeum.**
    Deipnosophistae 2.51a–b, 61d–e, 64b; 8.357a–358c.
    Cf. ATHENAEUS Soph. (0008 001).

4269 **DIPHILUS** Phil.
    3 B.C.: Bosporianus, Atheniensis

001 **Testimonium**, ed. K. Döring, *Die Megariker* [*Studien zur antiken Philosophie* 2. Amsterdam: Grüner, 1972]: 52, 61.
    test. 164a = Stilpo (4262 001).
    NQ: Test.

0279 ***DISCIPULORUM CANTIUNCULA***
    ante A.D. 4
001 **Fragmentum** (*P. Med.*), ed. E. Heitsch, *Die griechischen Dichterfragmente der römischen Kaiserzeit*, vol. 1, 2nd edn. Göttingen: Vandenhoeck & Ruprecht, 1963: 46–47.
    Pap: 43: Lyr.

1330 **DIUS** Hist.
    2 B.C.?
001 **Testimonium**, FGrH #785: 3C:797.
    NQ: 37: Test.
002 **Fragmentum**, FGrH #785: 3C:798.
    Q: 147: Hist.

1334 **DIUS** Phil.
    Incertum
001 **Fragmenta**, ed. H. Thesleff, *The Pythagorean texts of the Hellenistic period*. Åbo: Åbo Akademi, 1965: 70–71.
    Q: 286: Phil.

1911 **DIYLLUS** Hist.
    4–3 B.C.: Atheniensis
001 **Testimonia**, FGrH #73: 2A:130–131.
    NQ: 200: Test.
002 **Fragmenta**, FGrH #73: 2A:131–132.
    Q: 160: Hist.

7051 ***DOCTRINA PATRUM***
    A.D. 7–8
001 **Doctrina patrum** (fort. auctore Anastasio Sinaïta vel Anastasio Apocrisiario), ed. F. Diekamp, *Doctrina patrum de incarnatione verbi*. Münster: Aschendorff, 1907: 1–337.
    Cod: 65,265: Anthol., Gnom., Eccl., Exeget.

0873 **DOMITIUS NIGRINUS** Med.
    ante A.D. 2
x01 **Fragmentum ap. Galenum.**
    K13.1021.
    Cf. GALENUS Med. (0057 077).

2622 **DORIEUS** Poeta
    ante A.D. 2
001 **Epigramma**, ed. H. Lloyd-Jones and P. Parsons, *Supplementum Hellenisticum*. Berlin: De Gruyter, 1983: 182.
    fr. 396.
    Q: 56: Epigr.
x01 **Epigramma demonstrativum.**
    App. Anth. 3.95: Cf. ANTHOLOGIAE GRAECAE APPENDIX (7052 003).
    Dup. 2622 001.

1335 **DORION** Scr. Rerum Nat.
1 B.C.
x01 **Fragmenta ap. Athenaeum.**
Deipnosophistae 7.287c, 300f, 319d, 330a.
Cf. ATHENAEUS Soph. (0008 001).

1337 **DOROTHEUS** Astrol.
1 B.C.–A.D. 1 : Sidonius
001 **Fragmenta Graeca**, ed. D. Pingree, *Dorothei Sidonii carmen astrologicum.* Leipzig: Teubner, 1976: 323–330, 332–427.
Q, Cod: 27,536: Astrol.
002 **Fragmenta e Hephaestionis Ἀποτελεσματικῶν libris hausta**, ed. Pingree, *op. cit.*, 427–434.
Q: 1,412: Astrol.
003 **Fragmenta alia antiqua**, ed. Pingree, *op. cit.*, 435–437.
Q, Cod: 400: Astrol.

1336 **DOROTHEUS** Hist.
ante A.D. 1 : Atheniensis
001 **Testimonium**, FGrH #145: 2B:813.
NQ: 19: Test.
002 **Fragmenta**, FGrH #145: 2B:813–814.
Dup. partim [DOROTHEUS] Hist. (2197 001).
Q: 289: Hist., Nat. Hist.

2197 **[DOROTHEUS]** Hist.
Incertum: Chaldaeus
001 **Fragmenta**, FGrH #289: 3A:172–173.
Dup. partim DOROTHEUS Hist. (1336 002).
Q: 367: Hist., Nat. Hist.

0874 **DOROTHEUS** Med.
ante A.D. 1 : Heliopolitanus
x01 **Fragmenta ap. Galenum.**
K14.183, 187.
Cf. GALENUS Med. (0057 078).

1338 **DOSIADAS** Hist.
4–3 B.C.?: fort. Cydonius
001 **Testimonium**, FGrH #458: 3B:394.
NQ: 23: Test.
002 **Fragmenta**, FGrH #458: 3B:394–396.
Q: 524: Hist.

0208 **DOSIADAS** Lyr.
3/2 B.C.: Creticus
Scholia: Cf. SCHOLIA IN THEOCRITUM (5038 001).
001 **Βωμός**, ed. J.U. Powell, *Collectanea Alexandrina.* Oxford: Clarendon Press, 1925 (repr. 1970): 175.
Dup. partim 0208 002 (AG 15.26).
Q: 71: Epigr.
002 **Epigramma**, AG 15.26.
AG 15.26: Dup. 0208 001.
AG 15.27: Cf. SIMIAS Gramm. (0211 002).
Q: 72: Epigr.

1896 **[DOSITHEUS]** Hist.
Incertum

001 **Fragmenta**, FGrH #54 & #290: 1A:295–296; 3A:173–175.
Q: 672: Hist., Myth.

0875 **DOSITHEUS** Med.
ante A.D. 6
x01 **Fragmentum ap. Paulum.**
CMG, vol. 9.2, p. 308.
Cf. PAULUS Med. (0715 001).
x02 **Fragmentum ap. Aëtium** (lib. 8).
CMG, vol. 8.2, p. 530.
Cf. AËTIUS Med. (0718 008).

3027 **Joannes DOXAPATRES** Rhet.
A.D. 11 : Constantinopolitanus
001 **Prolegomena in Aphthonii progymnasmata**, ed. H. Rabe, *Prolegomenon sylloge* [*Rhetores Graeci* 14. Leipzig: Teubner, 1931]: 80–155.
Cod: Rhet., Comm.
002 **Prolegomena in Hermogenis librum περὶ στάσεων**, ed. Rabe, *op. cit.*, 304–318.
Cod: Rhet., Comm.
003 **Prolegomena in Hermogenis librum περὶ εὑρέσεως**, ed. Rabe, *op. cit.*, 360–374.
Cod: Rhet., Comm.
004 **Prolegomena in Hermogenis librum περὶ ἰδεῶν**, ed. Rabe, *op. cit.*, 420–426.
Cod: Rhet., Comm.
005 **Commentarium in Aphthonii progymnasmata**, ed. C. Walz, *Rhetores Graeci*, vol. 2. Stuttgart: Cotta, 1835 (repr. Osnabrück: Zeller, 1968): 145–564.
Cod: Rhet., Comm.
x01 **Prolegomena in Aphthonii progymnasmata** (olim sub auctore Joanne Doxapatre).
Rabe, *Prolegomenon sylloge*, pp. 158–170.
Cf. ANONYMI IN APHTHONIUM (5045 002).
x02 **Prolegomena in artem rhetoricam** (olim sub auctore Joanne Doxapatre).
Rabe, *Prolegomenon sylloge*, pp. 18–43.
Cf. RHETORICA ANONYMA (0598 005).
x03 **Excerpta de arte rhetorica** (olim sub auctore Joanne Doxapatre).
Walz, *Rhet. Graec.*, vol. 6, pp. 30–32.
Cf. RHETORICA ANONYMA (0598 003).

2249 **DRACO** Hist.
2 B.C.: Atheniensis
001 **Fragmentum**, FGrH #344: 3B:208.
Q: 38: Hist.

0448 **DROMO** Comic.
4 B.C.
001 **Fragmenta**, ed. T. Kock, *Comicorum Atticorum fragmenta*, vol. 2. Leipzig: Teubner, 1884: 419.
frr. 1–2.
Q: 47: Comic.
002 **Fragmenta**, ed. A. Meineke, *Fragmenta comicorum Graecorum*, vol. 3. Berlin: Reimer, 1840 (repr. De Gruyter, 1970): 541.
Q: 47: Comic.

0178 **DURIS** Epigr.
   4 B.C.: Eleaticus
 001 **Epigramma**, AG 9.424.
   Q: 52: Epigr.

1339 **DURIS** Hist.
   4–3 B.C.: Samius
 001 **Testimonia**, FGrH #76: 2A:136–138.
   NQ: 548: Test.
 002 **Fragmenta**, FGrH #76: 2A:138–158.
   fr. 25: *Inscr. Priene* 37.
   Q, Cod, Epigr: 5,561: Hist., Rhet.
 003 **Fragmenta**, ed. H.J. Mette, "Die 'Kleinen'
   griechischen Historiker heute," *Lustrum* 21
   (1978) 13–15.
   fr. 15 bis: *P. Oxy.* 24.2399.
   fr. 18b: *P. Oxy.* 32.2637.
   Pap: 481: Hist.
 004 **Fragmentum**, ed. D. Curiazi, "Hist. fragm.
   novum," *Museum criticum* 18 (1983) 209.
   Q: Hist.

1340 **<ECCELUS>** Phil.
   3/2 B.C.
 001 **Fragmentum**, ed. H. Thesleff, *The Pythagorean
   texts of the Hellenistic period*. Åbo: Åbo Akademi, 1965: 77–78.
   Q: 193: Phil.

4156 *ECCLESIASTICA ADESPOTA*
   Varia
 001 **Dialogus Didymi Caeci cum haeretico** (*P.
   Cairo Tura* 1090), ed. B. Kramer, "Protokoll
   eines Dialogs zwischen Didymos dem Blinden
   und einem Ketzer," *Zeitschrift für Papyrologie
   und Epigraphik* 32 (1978) 206–210.
   Pap: Dialog., Theol.
 002 **Homilia de Psalmis** (*P. Cairo Tura*) (fort. auctore quodam Alexandrino), ed. B. Kramer,
   "Eine Psalmenhomilie aus dem Tura-Fund,"
   Zeitschrift für Papyrologie und Epigraphik 16
   (1975) 180–204.
   Pap: Homilet.

2242 **ECHECRATES** Phil.
   5–4 B.C.
 001 **Testimonia**, ed. H. Diels and W. Kranz, *Die
   Fragmente der Vorsokratiker*, vol. 1, 6th edn.
   Berlin: Weidmann, 1951 (repr. Dublin: 1966):
   443.
   test. 1–4: auctores alii nominantur Diocles,
   Polymnastus, Phanto et Arion.
   NQ: 70: Test.

0249 **ECHEMBROTUS** Lyr. et Eleg.
   6 B.C.: Arcas
 001 **Fragmentum**, ed. M.L. West, *Iambi et elegi
   Graeci*, vol. 2. Oxford: Clarendon Press, 1972:
   62.
   Q: 18: Epigr.

2320 **ECHEMENES** Hist.
   ante A.D. 3: fort. Creticus
 001 **Fragmenta**, FGrH #459: 3B:396–397.
   Q: 83: Hist.

2289 **ECHEPHYLIDAS** Hist.
   4–3 B.C.?
 001 **Fragmenta**, FGrH #409: 3B:302.
   Q: 283: Hist.
 002 **Fragmenta**, ed. H.J. Mette, "Die 'Kleinen'
   griechischen Historiker heute," *Lustrum* 21
   (1978) 28.
   frr. 4a–b, 5a–b.
   Q: 144: Hist.

0449 **ECPHANTIDES** Comic.
   5 B.C.
 001 **Fragmenta**, ed. T. Kock, *Comicorum Atticorum fragmenta*, vol. 1. Leipzig: Teubner,
   1880: 9–10.
   frr. 1, 3, 5.
   Q: 17: Comic.
 002 **Fragmenta**, ed. A. Meineke, *Fragmenta comicorum Graecorum*, vol. 2.1. Berlin: Reimer,
   1839 (repr. De Gruyter, 1970): 12–13.
   Q: 17: Comic.
 003 **Titulus**, ed. C. Austin, *Comicorum Graecorum
   fragmenta in papyris reperta*. Berlin: De Gruyter, 1973: 52.
   NQ: 2: Comic.

1341 **<ECPHANTUS>** Phil.
   3 B.C.: Syracusanus vel Crotoniensis
 001 **Fragmenta** [Sp.], ed. H. Thesleff, *The Pythagorean texts of the Hellenistic period*. Åbo: Åbo
   Akademi, 1965: 79–84.
   Q: 1,480: Phil.
 002 **Testimonia**, ed. H. Diels and W. Kranz, *Die
   Fragmente der Vorsokratiker*, vol. 1, 6th edn.
   Berlin: Weidmann, 1951 (repr. Dublin: 1966):
   442.
   test. 1–5.
   NQ: 197: Test.

2156 **ELEAZAR** Hist.
   vel Khor ʿOhbut vel Chorobutus
   A.D. 4
 001 **Testimonium**, FGrH #224: 2B:951.
   NQ: 79: Test.

ELEAZARI EPISTULA
   Cf. PTOLEMAEI II PHILADELPHI ET ELEA-
   ZARI EPISTULAE (0050).

0231 *ELEGIACA ADESPOTA* (CA)
   Varia
 001 **Fragmenta**, ed. J.U. Powell, *Collectanea Alex-
   andrina*. Oxford: Clarendon Press, 1925 (repr.
   1970): 130–131.
   Aurea aetas (*P. Oxy.* 1.14) (fr. 1): p. 130.
   De Galatis (*P. Hamburgensis*) (fr. 2): p. 131.
   Pap: 186: Eleg.

0234 **ELEGIACA ADESPOTA** (IEG)
Varia
001 **Fragmenta**, ed. M.L. West, *Iambi et elegi Graeci*, vol. 2. Oxford: Clarendon Press, 1972: 1–15.
frr. 1–8, 10–12, 14–17, 19–62.
Q, Pap: 783: Eleg.

1897 **ELEUSIS** Hist.
3 B.C.
001 **Fragmentum**, FGrH #55: 1A:296.
Q: 105: Hist., Myth.

4020 **ELIAS** Phil.
A.D. 6: Alexandrinus
Cf. et Pseudo-DAVID et Pseudo-ELIAS Phil. (4022).
001 **In Porphyrii isagogen**, ed. A. Busse, *Eliae in Porphyrii isagogen et Aristotelis categorias commentaria* [*Commentaria in Aristotelem Graeca* 18.1. Berlin: Reimer, 1900]: 1–104.
Prolegomena philosophiae: pp. 1–34.
In Porphyrii isagogen: pp. 35–104.
Cod: 34,910: Phil., Comm.
002 **Eliae (olim Davidis) in Aristotelis categorias commentarium**, ed. Busse, *op. cit.*, 107–255.
Cod: 57,196: Phil., Comm.
003 **Commentarius in Aristotelis analytica priora**, ed. L.G. Westerink, "Introduction to Elias on the prior analytics," *Mnemosyne*, ser. 4, vol. 14 (1961) 134–139.
Cod: Phil., Comm.
x01 **Prolegomena philosophiae Platonicae** (olim sub auctore Olympiodoro, nunc fort. auctore Elia).
Westerink, pp. 3–55.
Cf. ANONYMUS DE PHILOSOPHIA PLATONICA (4227 001).

Pseudo-ELIAS Phil.
A.D. 6/8: fort. Constantinopolitanus
Cf. Pseudo-DAVID et Pseudo-ELIAS Phil. (4022).

1342 **EMPEDOCLES** Poet. Phil.
5 B.C.: Agrigentinus
002 **Epigramma**, AG 9.569.
AG 7.508: Cf. SIMONIDES Lyr. (0261 003).
Q: 56: Epigr.
003 **Testimonia**, ed. H. Diels and W. Kranz, *Die Fragmente der Vorsokratiker*, vol. 1, 6th edn. Berlin: Weidmann, 1951 (repr. Dublin: 1966): 276–307.
test. 1–98.
NQ: 13,382: Test.
004 **Fragmenta**, ed. Diels and Kranz, *op. cit.*, 308–374.
frr. 1–161.
fr. 112: Dup. partim 1342 002 (AG 9.569).
fr. 156: Dup. partim SIMONIDES Lyr. (0261 003) (AG 7.508).
Q: 12,288: Phil., Hexametr., Epigr.

x01 **Epigramma irrisorium**.
App. Anth. 5.4: Cf. ANTHOLOGIAE GRAECAE APPENDIX (7052 005).
Dup. partim 1342 004 (fr. 157).
x02 **Sphaera** [Sp.].
Maass, pp. 154–170.
Cf. VITAE ARATI ET VARIA DE ARATO (4161 014).

1984 **EMPYLUS** Hist.
1 B.C.: Rhodius
001 **Testimonia**, FGrH #191: 2B:926.
NQ: 69: Test.

0290 **ENCOMIUM DUCIS THEBAIDOS**
ante A.D. 5?
001 **Fragmentum** (*P. Berol.* 9799), ed. E. Heitsch, *Die griechischen Dichterfragmente der römischen Kaiserzeit*, vol. 2. Göttingen: Vandenhoeck & Ruprecht, 1964: 50–51.
Pap: 184: Hexametr., Encom.

2685 **ENNOEUS** Poeta
A.D. 3/4
x01 **Epigramma sepulcrale**.
App. Anth. 2.491(?): Cf. ANTHOLOGIAE GRAECAE APPENDIX (7052 002).

0356 **EPAPHRODITUS** Gramm.
A.D. 1: Chaeronensis, Romanus
001 **Fragmenta**, ed. E. Lünzner, *Epaphroditi grammatici quae supersunt* [*Diss. Bonn* (1866)]: 21–49.
Q: Gramm.

1343 **EPARCHIDES** Hist.
3 B.C.?: fort. Oeneius
001 **Fragmenta**, FGrH #437: 3B:369–370.
Q: 272: Hist.

2436 **EPHEMERIDES**
4 B.C.
001 **Ephemerides Alexandri** (fort. auctore Eumene Cardiano) (testimonia), FGrH #117: 2B:618.
NQ: 139: Test.
002 **Ephemerides Alexandri** (fort. auctore Eumene Cardiano) (fragmenta), FGrH #117: 2B:618–622.
Q: 1,080: Hist.

0450 **EPHIPPUS** Comic.
4 B.C.
001 **Fragmenta**, ed. T. Kock, *Comicorum Atticorum fragmenta*, vol. 2. Leipzig: Teubner, 1884: 250–264.
frr. 1–29.
Q: 780: Comic.
002 **Fragmenta**, ed. A. Meineke, *Fragmenta comicorum Graecorum*, vol. 3. Berlin: Reimer, 1840 (repr. De Gruyter, 1970): 322–323, 325–330, 332, 334–340.
Q: 747: Comic.

003 **Fragmentum**, ed. Meineke, *FCG*, vol. 5.1
(1857; repr. 1970): cxcvi.
Q: 13: Comic.

1936 **EPHIPPUS** Hist.
post 4 B.C.: Olynthius
001 **Testimonia**, FGrH #126: 2B:665.
NQ: 88: Test.
002 **Fragmenta**, FGrH #126: 2B:665–667.
Q: 551: Hist.

0536 **EPHORUS** Hist.
4 B.C.: Cumaeus
001 **Res publica Cretensium** (?) (fragmenta) (*P. Lit.
Lond.* 114 = Brit. Mus. inv. 187), ed. F.G.
Kenyon, "Deux papyrus grecs du British Museum," *Revue de Philologie* 21 (1897) 2.
Pap: Hist.
002 **Testimonia**, FGrH #70: 2A:37–43.
NQ: 2,109: Test.
003 **Fragmenta**, FGrH #70: 2A:43–109.
fr. 191: *P. Oxy.* 13.1610.
Q, Pap: 21,344: Hist., Rhet.
004 **Fragmenta**, ed. H.J. Mette, "Die 'Kleinen'
griechischen Historiker heute," *Lustrum* 21
(1978) 13.
frr. 120b1–120b2.
Q: 46: Hist.
x01 **Sicyonis historia** (*P. Oxy.* 11.1365).
FGrH #551, fr. 1b (= FGrH #105, fr. 2).
Cf. ADDITAMENTA (FGrH) (2433 024).
Cf. ANONYMI HISTORICI (FGrH) (1139 004).

1998 **EPHORUS Junior** Hist.
A.D. 3: Cumaeus
001 **Testimonium**, FGrH #212: 2B:943.
NQ: 21: Test.

1346 **EPHRAEM** Scr. Eccl.
A.D. 4?: Chersonensis
001 **De miraculo Clementis Romani**, MPG 2: 633–
646.
Cod

EPHRAEM GRAECUS Theol.
vel Ephraem Syrus
A.D. 4: Syrus
Cf. EPHRAEM SYRUS Theol. (4138).

4138 **EPHRAEM SYRUS** Theol.
vel Ephraem Graecus
A.D. 4: Syrus
001 **Sermo de virtutibus et vitiis**, ed. J.S. Assemani,
Sancti patris nostri Ephraem Syri opera omnia,
vol. 1. Rome, 1732: 1–18.
Q: 5,441: Homilet.

1344 *EPICA ADESPOTA* (CA)
Varia
001 **Epica adespota**, ed. J.U. Powell, *Collectanea*

Alexandrina. Oxford: Clarendon Press, 1925
(repr. 1970): 71–87.
Actaeonis epyllium (?) (fr. 1): pp. 71–72.
Epyllium Diomedis (fr. 2): pp. 72–75.
Telephi epyllium (?) (*P. Oxy.* 2.214) (fr. 3): pp.
76–77.
Epyllium incerti argumenti (*P. Oxy.* 15.1794)
(fr. 4): pp. 78–79.
Sine titulo (*P. Oxy.* 2.221, col. 9.1–9.3) (fr. 5):
p. 79.
Sine titulo (*P. Oxy.* 3.422) (fr. 6): p. 80.
Hymnus in Junonem (*P. Oxy.* 4.670) (fr. 7):
pp. 80–81.
Heraclea (?) (*P. Halensis* 1.182) (fr. 8): p. 81.
Hymnorum Ptolemaicorum fragmenta in Ar-
sinoen-Aphroditen (?) (*P. Chicaginiensis*) (fr.
9): pp. 82–87.
Q, Pap: 1,807: Epic.

1816 *EPICA ADESPOTA* (GDRK)
A.D. 1–7
001 **Lusus verborum**, ed. E. Heitsch, *Die griechischen Dichterfragmente der römischen Kaiserzeit*, vol. 1, 2nd edn. Göttingen: Vandenhoeck
& Ruprecht, 1963: 51.
Q: 8: Hexametr.
002 **Laudes Theonis gymnasiarchi** (*P. Oxy.*
7.1015), ed. Heitsch, *op. cit.*, 55.
Pap: 147: Hexametr., Encom.
003 **Fragmentum epicum** (*P. Brit. Mus.* 1181), ed.
Heitsch, *op. cit.*, 59–60.
Pap: 212: Epic.
004 **Exercitatio ethopoeiaca** (*P. Ryl.* 3.487), ed.
Heitsch, *op. cit.*, 78–79.
Pap: 143: Epic.
005 **Fragmentum epicum historicum** (*P. Argent.*
480 [= *P. Strassb.* inv. Gr. 480]), ed. Heitsch,
op. cit., 79–81.
Pap: 259: Epic., Encom., Hist.
006 **Mercurius mundi et Hermupolis magnae conditor** (*P. Argent.* 481 [= *P. Strassb.* inv. Gr.
481]), ed. Heitsch, *op. cit.*, 82–85.
Dup. ANONYMI HISTORICI (FGrH) (1139
029).
Pap: 399: Hexametr., Encom.
007 **Epithalamium** (*P. Ryl.* 1.17), ed. Heitsch, *op.
cit.*, 85.
Pap: 42: Hexametr.
008 **Exercitationes ethopoeiacae** (collectio C.
Graves), ed. Heitsch, *op. cit.*, 86–88.
Pap: 225: Epic.
009 **Encomium iambicum** (*P. Vindob.* gr. 29788b),
ed. Heitsch, *op. cit.*, 88–90.
Pap: 280: Iamb., Encom.
010 **Λόγος ἐπιβατήριος** (*P. Vindob.* gr. 29788a), ed.
Heitsch, *op. cit.*, 90–91.
Pap: 169: Hexametr.
011 **Laudatio professoris Smyrnaei in universitate
Beryti docentis** (*P. Berol.* 10559 A et B), ed.
Heitsch, *op. cit.*, 94–97.
Pap: 560: Iamb., Encom.

012 **Laudatio professoris in universitate Beryti docentis** (*P. Berol.* 10558), ed. Heitsch, *op. cit.*, 98–99.
Pap: 159: Iamb., Encom.

013 **Fragmentum epicum historicum** (*P. Berol.* 5003), ed. Heitsch, *op. cit.*, 99–103.
Pap: 498: Epic., Hist.

014 **Encomium** (*PSI* 149), ed. Heitsch, *op. cit.*, 103–104.
Pap: 84: Hexametr., Encom.

015 **Encomium Heraclii ducis** (*PSI* 253), ed. Heitsch, *op. cit.*, 104–108.
Pap: 452: Hexametr., Encom.

016 **Encomium ducis Romani** (*P. Flor.* 2.114), ed. Heitsch, *op. cit.*, 120–124.
Pap: 497: Hexametr., Encom.

017 **Polyxena et Achilles** (*P. Flor.* 390), ed. Heitsch, *op. cit.*, 124–125.
Pap: 91: Epic.

018 **Exercitatio ethopoeiaca** (Tab. lignea Caironensis), ed. Heitsch, *op. cit.*, 125.
Pap: 49: Hexametr.

019 **Carmen in Nilum crescentem** (*PSI* 845), ed. Heitsch, *op. cit.*, 126.
Pap: 93: Epic.

020 **In Thebas** (*P. Berol.* 5226v), ed. Heitsch, *op. cit.*, 127.
Pap: 18: Epic.

021 **Fragmentum** (sine titulo) (*P. Berol.* 5227r), ed. Heitsch, *op. cit.*, 127.
Pap: 9: Hexametr.

1345 *EPICA INCERTA* (CA)
Varia

001 **Fragmenta**, ed. J.U. Powell, *Collectanea Alexandrina*. Oxford: Clarendon Press, 1925 (repr. 1970): 89–90.
frr. 1–7.
Q: 28: Epic.

002 **Fragmentum**, ed. Powell, *op. cit.*, 251.
Pap: 31: Epic.

0521 **EPICHARMUS** Comic. et *PSEUDEPICHARMEA*
5 B.C.: Syracusanus

001 **Fragmenta Epicharmi**, ed. G. Kaibel, *Comicorum Graecorum fragmenta*, vol. 1.1 [*Poetarum Graecorum fragmenta*, vol. 6.1. Berlin: Weidmann, 1899]: 91–126, 128–132.
frr. 1, 5–7, 9–11, 19, 21, 23–25, 29–31, 33–35, 37–39, 42–51, 53–72, 76, 78–85, 87–91, 99–102, 107, 109–111, 113–118, 123–125, 127–128, 130–134, 136–137, 139–140, 146–155, 157–161, 164–166, 168–173, 179–180, 182, 185, 188–189, 207, 216–219, 221, 228–229, 232–233, 235, 238–239.
Dup. partim 0521 008.
Q: 1,971: Comic., Phil.

002 **Fragmenta Pseudepicharmea**, ed. Kaibel, *op. cit.*, 135–146.

frr. 239, 245–247, 249–250, 252–258, 261–290, 296–298.
Dup. partim 0521 008.
Q: 573: Comic., Gnom., Coq., Phil., Epigr.

003 **Fragmenta**, ed. J. Demiańczuk, *Supplementum comicum*. Krakau: Nakładem Akademii, 1912 (repr. Hildesheim: Olms, 1967): 123–125.
frr. 1–6.
fr. 2: *P. Hibeh* 1.1.
fr. 3: *P. Berol.* 9772.
Q, Pap: 282: Comic.

004 **Fragmenta Epicharmi**, ed. C. Austin, *Comicorum Graecorum fragmenta in papyris reperta*. Berlin: De Gruyter, 1973: 52–78.
frr. 81–85a.
Pap: 2,664: Comic.

005 **Fragmenta Pseudepicharmea**, ed. Austin, *op. cit.*, 79–83.
frr. 86–91.
Pap: 447: Comic.

006 **Fragmentum Epicharmi**, ed. Kaibel, *op. cit.*, vii.
fr. 100a.
Q: 12: Comic.

007 **Testimonia**, ed. H. Diels and W. Kranz, *Die Fragmente der Vorsokratiker*, vol. 1, 6th edn. Berlin: Weidmann, 1951 (repr. Dublin: 1966): 190–193.
test. 1–10.
NQ: 760: Test.

008 **Fragmenta**, ed. Diels and Kranz, *op. cit.*, 195–210.
frr. 1–65.
Fragmenta comica [Dub.] (frr. 1–7): pp. 195–199.
Sententiae Axiopisti [Sp.] (frr. 8–46): pp. 200–205.
Fragmenta ex Ennio [Sp.] (frr. 47–54): pp. 206–207 (verba Latina solum).
Fragmentum ex Axiopisti canone [Sp.] (fr. 55): p. 207 (verba Latina solum).
Constitutio Chrysogoni [Sp.] (frr. 56–57): p. 208.
Chiron [Sp.] (frr. 58–62): p. 209.
Coquinaria [Sp.] (fr. 63): p. 209.
Epigramma [Sp.] (fr. 64): p. 210.
Ad Antenorem [Sp.] (fr. 65): p. 210.
Dup. partim 0521 001–002.
Q: 2,514: Comic., Gnom., Coq., Phil., Epigr.

x01 **Epigramma exhortatorium et supplicatorium.**
App. Anth. 4.6(?): Cf. ANTHOLOGIAE GRAECAE APPENDIX (7052 004).

0451 **EPICRATES** Comic.
4 B.C.

001 **Fragmenta**, ed. T. Kock, *Comicorum Atticorum fragmenta*, vol. 2. Leipzig: Teubner, 1884: 282–288.
frr. 1–12 + tituli.
Q: 539: Comic.

002 **Fragmenta**, ed. A. Meineke, *Fragmenta comi-*

corum Graecorum, vol. 3. Berlin: Reimer, 1840 (repr. De Gruyter, 1970): 365–372.
Q: 492: Comic.

0557 **EPICTETUS** Phil.
A.D. 1–2: Hierapolitanus, Romanus
001 **Dissertationes ab Arriano digestae**, ed. H. Schenkl, *Epicteti dissertationes ab Arriano digestae*. Leipzig: Teubner, 1916 (repr. Stuttgart: 1965): 7–454.
Cod: 78,609: Phil.
002 **Enchiridion**, ed. Schenkl, *op. cit.*, 5*–38*.
Cod: 5,154: Phil.
003 **Dissertationum Epictetearum sive ab Arriano sive ab aliis digestarum fragmenta**, ed. Schenkl, *op. cit.*, 455–460, 462–475.
Q: 1,994: Phil.
004 **Gnomologium Epicteteum** (e Stobaei libris 1–2), ed. Schenkl, *op. cit.*, 476–477.
Q: 286: Gnom.
005 **Gnomologium Epicteteum** (e Stobaei libris 3–4), ed. Schenkl, *op. cit.*, 478–492.
Q: 1,921: Gnom.
006 **Arriani epistula ad Lucium Gellium**, ed. Schenkl, *op. cit.*, 5–6.
Dup. partim Flavius ARRIANUS Hist. et Phil. (0074 008).
Cod: 200: Epist.
x01 **Epigramma**.
AG 7.676.
Cf. ANONYMI EPIGRAMMATICI (AG) (0138 001).
x02 **Sententiae** (Moschionis).
Schenkl, pp. 493–494, frr. 1–25.
Cf. <MOSCHION> Gnom. (0575 001).
x03 **Hypothecae** (Moschionis).
Schenkl, pp. 495–496, frr. 1–18.
Cf. <MOSCHION> Gnom. (0575 002).

0537 **EPICURUS** Phil.
4–3 B.C.: Samius, Atheniensis
001 **Ratae sententiae**, ed. G. Arrighetti, *Epicuro. Opere*. Turin: Einaudi, 1960: 119–137.
Cod: 1,400: Phil.
002 **Gnomologium Vaticanum Epicureum**, ed. Arrighetti, *op. cit.*, 139–157.
Cod: 1,106: Gnom.
003 **Deperditorum librorum reliquiae**, ed. Arrighetti, *op. cit.*, 159–379.
Q, Pap: 14,653: Phil.
004 **Epistularum fragmenta**, ed. Arrighetti, *op. cit.*, 381–437.
Q, Pap: 3,829: Epist.
005 **Incertae sedis fragmenta**, ed. Arrighetti, *op. cit.*, 439–443.
Q, Pap: 169: Phil.
006 **Epistula ad Herodotum**, ed. P. von der Muehll, *Epicuri epistulae tres et ratae sententiae a Laertio Diogene servatae*. Leipzig: Teubner, 1922 (repr. Stuttgart: 1966): 3–27.
Cod: 4,610: Epist.

007 **Epistula ad Pythoclem**, ed. von der Muehll, *op. cit.*, 27–43.
Cod: 3,098: Epist.
008 **Epistula ad Menoeceum**, ed. von der Muehll, *op. cit.*, 44–50.
Cod: 1,354: Epist.
009 **Incerti operis fragmenta** (*P. Herc.* 1639), ed. W. Crönert, "Neues über Epikur und einige herkulanensische Rollen," *Rheinisches Museum* 56 (1901) 610–611.
Pap: Phil.

0880 **EPIDAURUS** Med.
ante A.D. 2
x01 **Fragmentum ap. Galenum**.
K13.985.
Cf. GALENUS Med. (0057 077).

0452 **EPIGENES** Comic.
4 B.C.
001 **Fragmenta**, ed. T. Kock, *Comicorum Atticorum fragmenta*, vol. 2. Leipzig: Teubner, 1884: 416–419.
frr. 1–8 + tituli.
Q: 120: Comic.
002 **Fragmenta**, ed. A. Meineke, *Fragmenta comicorum Graecorum*, vol. 3. Berlin: Reimer, 1840 (repr. De Gruyter, 1970): 537–540.
Q: 115: Comic.

1351 *EPIGONI*
fort. auctore Antimacho Teio
post 7 B.C.
Cf. et ANTIMACHUS Epic. (1141).
001 **Fragmentum**, ed. T.W. Allen, *Homeri opera*, vol. 5. Oxford: Clarendon Press, 1912 (repr. 1969): 115.
fr. 1.
Q: Epic.

0179 **EPIGONUS** Epigr.
1 B.C.?: Thessalonicensis
001 **Epigramma**, AG 9.261.
AG 9.260: Cf. SECUNDUS Epigr. (0274 001).
AG 9.406: Cf. ANTIGONUS Paradox. (0568 002).
Q: 27: Epigr.

0881 **EPIGONUS** Med.
A.D. 1
Cf. et EPIGONUS vel HERMON Med. (0922).
x01 **Fragmenta ap. Galenum**.
K13.492–493, 775.
Cf. GALENUS Med. (0057 077).

0922 **EPIGONUS vel HERMON** Med.
A.D. 1?
Cf. et EPIGONUS Med. (0881).
x01 **Fragmentum ap. Aëtium** (lib. 15).
Zervos, *Athena* 21, p. 39.
Cf. AËTIUS Med. (0718 015).

EPILOGUS MOSQUENSIS
Cf. MARTYRIUM POLYCARPI (1484 001).

0453 **EPILYCUS** Comic.
5/4 B.C.?
001 **Fragmenta**, ed. T. Kock, *Comicorum Atticorum fragmenta*, vol. 1. Leipzig: Teubner, 1880: 803–804.
frr. 1–3, 5–8.
Q: 37: Comic.
002 **Fragmenta**, ed. A. Meineke, *Fragmenta comicorum Graecorum*, vol. 2.2. Berlin: Reimer, 1840 (repr. De Gruyter, 1970): 887, 889.
Q: 26: Comic.
003 **Fragmentum**, ed. J. Demiańczuk, *Supplementum comicum*. Krakau: Nakładem Akademii, 1912 (repr. Hildesheim: Olms, 1967): 40.
fr. 1.
Q: 10: Comic.

1347 **EPIMENIDES** Phil.
6–5 B.C.: Creticus
001 **Testimonia**, FGrH #457: 3B:384–389.
NQ: 2,119: Test.
002 **Fragmenta**, FGrH #457: 3B:390–394.
Dup. partim 1347 004.
Q: 1,331: Hist., Phil., Theol.
003 **Testimonia**, ed. H. Diels and W. Kranz, *Die Fragmente der Vorsokratiker*, vol. 1, 6th edn. Berlin: Weidmann, 1951 (repr. Dublin: 1966): 27–31.
test. 1–8.
NQ: 1,527: Test.
004 **Fragmenta**, ed. Diels and Kranz, *op. cit.*, 31–37.
frr. 1–26.
Dup. partim 1347 002.
Q: 1,360: Hist., Phil., Theol.
005 **Fragmentum** (*P. Oxy.* 26.2442), ed. H.J. Mette, "Die 'Kleinen' griechischen Historiker heute," *Lustrum* 21 (1978) 29.
fr. 2 bis.
Pap: 40: Hist.

0454 **EPINICUS** Comic.
3/2 B.C.
001 **Fragmenta**, ed. T. Kock, *Comicorum Atticorum fragmenta*, vol. 3. Leipzig: Teubner, 1888: 330–331.
frr. 1–2.
Q: 142: Comic.
002 **Fragmenta**, ed. A. Meineke, *Fragmenta comicorum Graecorum*, vol. 4. Berlin: Reimer, 1841 (repr. De Gruyter, 1970): 505–506.
Q: 135: Comic.

1348 **EPIPHANES** Gnost.
A.D. 2
001 **De justitia** (fragmenta), ed. W. Völker, *Quellen zur Geschichte der christlichen Gnosis*. Tübingen: Mohr, 1932: 34–35.
Q

2021 **EPIPHANIUS** Scr. Eccl.
A.D. 4: Palaestinus, Constantiensis (Cypri)
001 **Ancoratus**, ed. K. Holl, *Epiphanius, Band 1: Ancoratus und Panarion* [*Die griechischen christlichen Schriftsteller* 25. Leipzig: Hinrichs, 1915]: 1–149.
Cod: 39,802: Theol.
002 **Panarion** (= **Adversus haereses**), ed. K. Holl, *Epiphanius, Bände 1–3: Ancoratus und Panarion* [*Die griechischen christlichen Schriftsteller* 25, 31, 37. Leipzig: Hinrichs, 1:1915; 2:1922; 3:1933]: 1:153–161, 169–233, 238–464; 2:5–210, 215–523; 3:2–229, 232–414, 416–526.
Epistula ab Acacio et Paulo: vol. 1, pp. 153–154.
Rescriptum ad Acacium et Paulum: vol. 1, pp. 155–161.
Haereses 1–33: vol. 1, pp. 169–233, 238–464.
Haereses 34–64: vol. 2, pp. 5–210, 215–523.
Haereses 65–80: vol. 3, pp. 2–229, 232–414, 416–496.
De fide: vol. 3, pp. 496–526.
Cod: 351,979: Theol., Epist.
003 **Anacephalaeosis** [Sp.], ed. Holl, *Epiphanius, Bände 1–3*, 1:162–168, 234–237; 2:1–4, 211–214; 3:1–2, 230–232, 415.
Cod: 4,529: Theol.
004 **De xii gemmis**, ed. C.É. Ruelle, *Les lapidaires de l'antiquité et du Moyen Age*, vol. 2.1. Paris: Leroux, 1898: 193–199.
Cod: 1,992: Med., Nat. Hist., Eccl., Exeget.
005 **De xii gemmis** (fragmenta ap. Anastasium Sinaïtam, *Quaestiones et responsiones*), MPG 89: 588–589.
Q: 603: Med., Nat. Hist., Eccl., Exeget.
006 **De xii gemmis** (fragmenta alia ap. Anastasium Sinaïtam, *Quaestiones et responsiones*), MPG 89: 596–597.
Q: 216: Med., Nat. Hist., Eccl., Exeget.
007 **Epistula ad Eusebium, Marcellum, Vivianum, Carpum et ad Aegyptios** (fragmentum), ed. K. Holl, *Gesammelte Aufsätze zur Kirchengeschichte*, vol. 2. Tübingen: Mohr, 1928 (repr. Darmstadt: Wissenschaftliche Buchgesellschaft, 1964): 204–207.
Cod: 828: Epist.
008 **Tractatus contra eos qui imagines faciunt** (fragmenta), ed. Holl, *Gesammelte Aufsätze*, 356–359.
Q: 398: Theol.
009 **Epistula ad Theodosium imperatorem** (fragmenta), ed. Holl, *Gesammelte Aufsätze*, 360–362.
Q: 464: Epist.
010 **Testamentum ad cives** (fragmenta), ed. Holl, *Gesammelte Aufsätze*, 363.
Q: 113: Theol.
011 **Epistula ad Joannem Hierosolymitanum** (fragmentum), ed. P. Maas, "Die ikonoklastischen Episode in dem Brief des Epiphanios an Johannes," *Byzantinische Zeitschrift* 30 (1929–1930) 281–283.
Q: 307: Epist., Theol.

012 **Homilia in festo palmarum** [Sp.], MPG 43: 428–437.
Cod: 2,107: Homilet.

013 **Homilia in divini corporis sepulturam** [Sp.], MPG 43: 440–464.
Cod: 5,344: Homilet.

014 **Homilia in Christi resurrectionem** (inc. Ὁ τῆς δικαιοσύνης) [Sp.], MPG 43: 465–477.
Cod: 2,680: Homilet.

015 **Homilia in assumptionem Christi** [Sp.], MPG 43: 477–485.
Cod: 1,537: Homilet.

016 **Homilia in laudes Mariae deiparae** [Sp.], MPG 43: 485–501.
Cod: 3,325: Homilet.

017 **Homilia in festo palmarum** (fragmentum) [Sp.], MPG 43: 501–505.
Cod: 793: Homilet.

018 **Tractatus de numerorum mysteriis** [Sp.], MPG 43: 507–517.
Cod: 1,739: Eccl.

019 **Fragmenta precationis et exorcismi** [Sp.], MPG 43: 537–538.
Cod: 57: Eccl.

020 **Enumeratio lxxii prophetarum et prophetissarum** [Sp.], ed. T. Schermann, *Prophetarum vitae fabulosae*. Leipzig: Teubner, 1907: 1–3.
Dup. VITAE PROPHETARUM (1750 001).
Cod: 285: Hagiogr.

021 **De prophetarum vita et obitu** (recensio prior) [Sp.], ed. Schermann, *op. cit.*, 4–25.
Dup. VITAE PROPHETARUM (1750 002).
Cod: 3,825: Hagiogr.

022 **De prophetarum vita et obitu** (recensio altera) [Sp.], ed. Schermann, *op. cit.*, 55–67.
Dup. VITAE PROPHETARUM (1750 004).
Cod: 2,593: Hagiogr.

023 **Index apostolorum** [Sp.], ed. Schermann, *op. cit.*, 107–117.
Dup. VITAE PROPHETARUM (1750 007).
Cod: 1,313: Hagiogr.

024 **Index discipulorum** [Sp.], ed. Schermann, *op. cit.*, 118–126.
Dup. VITAE PROPHETARUM (1750 008).
Cod: 1,265: Hagiogr.

025 **Nomina apostolorum** [Sp.], ed. T. Schermann, *Propheten und Apostellegenden* [*Texte und Untersuchungen* 31.3. Leipzig: Hinrichs, 1907]: 232.
Cod: 174: Eccl.

026 **Testimonia ex divinis et sacris scripturis** (= **De divina inhumanatione**) [Sp.], ed. R.V. Hotchkiss, *A Pseudo-Epiphanius testimony book*. Missoula, Montana: Scholars Press, 1974: 8–76.
Cod: 6,820: Eccl.

027 **Notitiae episcopatuum** [Sp.], ed. H. Gelzer, *Texte der Notitiae Episcopatuum* [*Abhandlungen der philosophisch-philologischen Classe der königlich bayerischen Akademie der Wissenschaften* 21.3. Munich: Franz, 1901]: 534–542.
Cod: 1,554: Eccl., Hist.

028 **Apophthegmata** (ap. *Apophthegmata patrum*) [Sp.], MPG 65: 161–168.
Q: 767: Gnom., Eccl.

029 **De fide** (fragmentum) [Sp.], ed. F. Diekamp, *Doctrina patrum de incarnatione verbi*. Münster: Aschendorff, 1907: 299.
Q: 64: Theol.

030 **De trinitate** (fragmentum) [Sp.], ed. Diekamp, *op. cit.*, 317.
Q: 36: Theol.

031 **Liturgia praesanctificatorum**, ed. D.N. Moraites, Ἡ λειτουργία τῶν προηγιασμένων. Thessalonica: University of Thessalonica, 1955: 53–77.
Cod

032 **Anaphora Graeca** (fragmenta) [Sp.], ed. G. Garitte, "Un opuscule grec traduit de l'arménien sur l'addition d'eau au vin eucharistique," *Muséon* 73 (1960) 298–299.
Cod: 285: Liturg.

033 **De mensuribus et ponderibus**, ed. E. Moutsoulas, "Τὸ 'Περὶ μέτρων καὶ σταθμῶν' ἔργον Ἐπιφανίου τοῦ Σαλαμῖνος," Θεολογία 44 (1973) 157–198.
Cod: 8,739: Metrolog.

035 **De mensuribus et ponderibus** (excerptum Graecum 1), ed. P. de Lagarde, *Symmicta* I. Göttingen: Dieterich, 1877: 211–223.
Cod

036 **De mensuribus et ponderibus** (excerptum Graecum 2), ed. de Lagarde, *op. cit.*, 223–225.
Cod: 633: Metrolog.

037 **De mensuribus et ponderibus** (excerptum Graecum 3), ed. J. Sakkelion, Πατμιακὴ βιβλιοθήκη. Athens: Papageorgios, 1890: 131–133.
Q: 829: Metrolog.

038 **De mensuribus et ponderibus** (excerptum Graecum 4), ed. F. Hultsch, *Metrologicorum scriptorum reliquiae*, vol. 1. Leipzig: Teubner, 1864: 259–276.
Q, Cod: 2,979: Metrolog.

039 **De mensuribus et ponderibus** (ap. Cosmam) (excerptum Graecum 6), ed. W. Wolska-Conus, *Cosmas Indicopleustès. Topographie chrétienne*, vol. 3 [*Sources chrétiennes* 197. Paris: Cerf, 1973]: 283–285.
Q: 197: Metrolog.

040 **De mensuribus et ponderibus** (ap. *Chronicon paschale*) (excerptum Graecum 7), MPG 92: 617, 644, 652.
Q: 176: Metrolog.

041 **De mensuribus et ponderibus** (ap. Joannem Damascenum) (excerptum Graecum 8), ed. B. Kotter, *Die Schriften des Johannes von Damaskos* [*Patristische Texte und Studien* 12. Berlin: De Gruyter, 1973]: 210–211.
Q: 286: Metrolog.

042 **Homilia in Christi resurrectionem** (inc. Νῦν τὸ πένθος) [Sp.], ed. P. Nautin, *Le dossier d'Hippolyte et de Méliton* [*Patristica* 1. Paris: Cerf, 1953]: 155–159.
Cod: 705: Homilet.

043 **Appendices ad indices apostolorum discipulorumque**, ed. Schermann, *Prophetarum vitae fabulosae*, 126–131.
Dup. VITAE PROPHETARUM (1750 009).
Cod: 616: Hagiogr.

x01 **Epistula ad Arabos.**
Haer. 78.2–25.
Cf. 2021 002.

x02 **Physiologus.**
Cf. PHYSIOLOGUS GRAECUS (2654 001–003).

1349 **EPISTULA A MARTYRIBUS LUGDUNENSIBUS**
A.D. 2

001 **Fragmentum epistulae a martyribus Lugdunensibus**, ed. M.J. Routh, *Reliquiae sacrae*, vol. 1, 2nd edn. Oxford: Oxford University Press, 1846 (repr. Hildesheim: Olms, 1974): 287.
Q: 76: Epist., Hagiogr.

1350 **EPISTULA AD DIOGNETUM**
A.D. 2

001 **Epistula ad Diognetum**, ed. H.-I. Marrou, *A Diognète*, 2nd edn. [*Sources chrétiennes* 33 bis. Paris: Cerf, 1965]: 52–84.
Dup. Pseudo-JUSTINUS MARTYR (0646 004).
Cod: 2,765: Epist., Apol.

1352 **EPISTULA ECCLESIARUM APUD LUGDUNUM ET VIENNAM**
A.D. 2

001 **Epistula ecclesiarum apud Lugdunum et Viennam**, ed. H. Musurillo, *The acts of the Christian martyrs*. Oxford: Clarendon Press, 1972: 62–84.
Cod: 3,822: Epist., Hagiogr.

0589 **EPISTULAE PRIVATAE**
3–1 B.C.

001 **Epistulae**, ed. S. Witkowsky, *Epistulae privatae Graecae quae in papyris aetatis Lagidarum servantur*, 2nd edn. Leipzig: Teubner, 1911: 4–137.
Pap: Epist.

1353 **EPITAPHIUM ABERCII**
A.D. 2

001 **Epitaphium**, ed. J. Quasten, *Monumenta eucharistica et liturgica vetustissima*, vol. 1.1 [*Florilegium patristicum tam veteris quam medii aevi auctores complectens*, vol. 7.1. Bonn: Hanstein, 1935]: 22, 24.
Epigr: 152: Epigr., Eccl.

2954 **EPITAPHIUM FLAVIAE**
A.D. 2

001 **Epitaphium Flaviae**, ed. E. Curtius and A. Kirchhoff, *Corpus inscriptionum Graecarum* 4. Berlin: Reimer, 1877 (repr. Hildesheim: Olms, 1977): 594 (no. 9595a).
Epigr

1570 **EPITAPHIUM PECTORII**
A.D. 2/3

001 **Epitaphium**, ed. J. Quasten, *Monumenta eucharistica et liturgica vetustissima*, vol. 1 [*Florilegium patristicum tam veteris quam medii aevi auctores complectens* 7.1. Bonn: Hanstein, 1935]: 24, 26.
Epigr: 65: Eccl., Eleg.

2139 **EPITAPHIUM SICILI**
Incertum

001 **Sicili epitaphium**, ed. K. Jan, *Musici scriptores Graeci*. Leipzig: Teubner, 1895 (repr. Hildesheim: Olms, 1962): 452.
Epigr: Mus.

0690 **ERASISTRATUS** Med.
3 B.C.: Ceus

x01 **Fragmenta ap. Galenum.**
K5.123, 125 in CMG, vol. **5.4.1.1**, pp. 80–82; K5.880 in *Script. Min.*, vol. 3, p. 86; K8.14, 311–313, 317–318, 321; 11.148–149, 155–156, 158, 160–161, 175–177, 196, 220–221, 225, 228, 230–231, 235–240, 246; **18.1.6–7**.
Cf. GALENUS Med. (0057 030, 033, 057, 068, 069, 092).

x02 **Fragmentum ap. Pseudo-Galenum.**
K1.184.
Cf. Pseudo-GALENUS Med. (0530 043).

x03 **Fragmenta ap. Oribasium.**
CMG, vol. 6.3, pp. 101, 167.
Cf. ORIBASIUS Med. (0722 004).

x04 **Fragmenta ap. Paulum.**
CMG, vol. 9.2, pp. 21, 346.
Cf. PAULUS Med. (0715 001).

x05 **Fragmentum ap. Aëtium** (lib. 7).
CMG, vol. 8.2, p. 265.
Cf. AËTIUS Med. (0718 007).

x06 **Fragmenta ap. Aëtium.**
Placita 5.29.1, 30.3.
Cf. AËTIUS Doxogr. (0528 001).

x07 **Fragmentum ap. Athenaeum.**
Deipnosophistae 7.324a.
Cf. ATHENAEUS Soph. (0008 001).

0226 **ERASTUS et CORISCUS** Phil.
4 B.C.: Scepsius

001 **Testimonia**, ed. F. Lasserre, *De Léodamas de Thasos à Philippe d'Oponte*. Naples: Bibliopolis, 1987: 105–109.
test. 1, 2b–9.
NQ: Test.

002 **Memoranda** (titulus), ed. Lasserre, *op. cit.*, 109.
fr. 1.
Pap: Phil.

2502 **ERATOSTHENES** Hist.
2 B.C.–A.D. 1: Cyrenaeus

001 **Testimonium**, FGrH #745: 3C:728.
NQ: 12: Test.

002 **Fragmenta**, FGrH #745: 3C:728.
Q: 89: Hist.

0222 ERATOSTHENES Philol. et ***ERATOS-
THENICA***
3–2 B.C.: Cyrenaeus

001 **Catasterismi**, ed. A. Olivieri, *Pseudo-Eratos-
thenis catasterismi* [*Mythographi Graeci* 3.1.
Leipzig: Teubner, 1897]: 1–52.
Cod: 7,906: Astron., Myth.

002 **Geographica**, ed. H. Berger, *Die geograph-
ischen Fragmente des Eratosthenes*. Leipzig:
Teubner, 1880 (repr. Amsterdam: Meridian,
1964): 1–382 (passim).
Q: Geogr.

003 **Mercurius**, ed. G. Bernhardy, *Eratosthenica*.
Berlin: Reimer, 1822 (repr. Osnabrück: Biblio
Verlag, 1968): 110–167 (passim).
Q: Epic.

004 **De mathematicis disciplinis**, ed. Bernhardy, *op.
cit.*, 168–174 (passim).
Q: Math., Mus.

005 **De cubi duplicatione**, ed. Bernhardy, *op. cit.*,
175–185 (passim).
Q: Math., Epigr.

006 **Opera philosophica**, ed. Bernhardy, *op. cit.*,
186–202 (passim).
Q: Phil.

007 **De antiqua comoedia**, ed. Bernhardy, *op. cit.*,
203–237 (passim).
Q: Gramm.

008 **De chronographiis**, ed. Bernhardy, *op. cit.*,
238–262 (passim).
Q: Hist., Chronogr.

009 **Fragmenta**, ed. J.U. Powell, *Collectanea Alexandrina*. Oxford: Clarendon Press, 1925 (repr.
1970): 59–68.
frr. 4, 6–12, 15–19, 22–27, 29–33, 35–37.
Q: 436: Epic., Epigr.

010 **Fragmentum Eratosthenicum**, ed. Powell, *op.
cit.*, 252.
Q: 6: Ignotum

011 **Testimonia**, FGrH #241: 2B:1010–1012.
test. 7: *P. Oxy.* 10.1241.
NQ: 621: Test.

012 **Fragmenta historica**, FGrH #241: 2B:1012–
1021.
fr. 8: *P. Oxy.* 3.409.
Q, Pap: 2,955: Hist., Chronogr.

013 **Fragmenta**, ed. H. Lloyd-Jones and P. Parsons,
Supplementum Hellenisticum. Berlin: De Gruyter, 1983: 183–186.
frr. 397–399.
fr. 397: *P. Oxy.* 42.3000.
Dup. partim 0222 009 (fr. 15).
Q, Pap: 125: Epic.

014 Περὶ Ὀλυμπιονικῶν (fragmentum) (fort. auctore Eratosthene), ed. C. Theodoridis, "Vier
neue Bruchstücke des Apollodoros von
Athen," *Rheinisches Museum*, N.F. 122 (1979)
16–17.
Q: Hist.

015 **De circa exornatione stellarum et etymologia
de quibus videntur**, ed. E. Maass, *Commentari-*

orum in Aratum reliquiae. Berlin: Weidmann,
1898 (repr. 1958): 134–136, 138.
Cod: 212: Astron.

x01 **Victores Olympici** (fort. auctore Phlegonte vel
Eratosthene).
FGrH #415.
Cf. ANONYMI HISTORICI (FGrH) (1139 026).

x02 **Fragmentum papyraceum** (*P. Oxy.* 30.2521)
(fort. auctore Eratosthene).
SH, p. 424, fr. 922.
Cf. ADESPOTA PAPYRACEA (SH) (2648 001).

4063 ERATOSTHENES Scholasticus Epigr.
A.D. 6

001 **Epigrammata**, AG 5.242, 277; **6.**77–78; **9.**444.
AG 5.243: Cf. MACEDONIUS II Epigr. (4064
001).
AG 5.244, 246: Cf. PAULUS Silentiarius Poet.
Christ. (4039 004).
AG 7.601: Cf. JULIANUS <Epigr.> (4050
001).
Q: 156: Epigr.

x01 **Epigrammata** (*App. Anth.*).
Epigramma dedicatorium: 1.119.
Epigramma demonstrativum: 3.68.
Epigramma exhortatorium et supplicatorium:
4.38.
App. Anth. 1.119: Cf. ANTHOLOGIAE GRAE-
CAE APPENDIX (7052 001).
App. Anth. 3.68: Cf. ANTHOLOGIAE GRAE-
CAE APPENDIX (7052 003).
App. Anth. 4.38: Cf. ANTHOLOGIAE GRAE-
CAE APPENDIX (7052 004).

EREN(N)IUS PHILO Hist. et Gramm.
Cf. (H)EREN(N)IUS PHILO Hist. et Gramm.
(1416).

2149 ERETES Hist.
vel Aretes vel Crates
3 B.C.?

001 **Fragmenta**, FGrH #242: 2B:1021.
Q: 133: Hist., Chronogr.

1354 ERGIAS Hist.
4 B.C.?: Rhodius

001 **Fragmenta**, FGrH #513: 3B:488–489.
Q: 321: Hist.

1355 ERINNA Lyr.
4 B.C.: Telia

001 **Fragmenta**, ed. E. Diehl, *Anthologia lyrica
Graeca*, vol. 1.4, 2nd edn. Leipzig: Teubner,
1936: 207–213.
frr. 1–5.
fr. 1b: *PSI* 1090.
frr. 3–5: Dup. 1355 002.
Dup. partim 1355 003 (frr. 401–402, [404]).
Q, Pap: 568: Hexametr., Epigr.

002 **Epigrammata**, AG **6.**352; **7.**710, 712.
Dup. partim 1355 001 (frr. 3–5).
Q: 139: Epigr.

003 **Fragmenta et titulus**, ed. H. Lloyd-Jones and
P. Parsons, *Supplementum Hellenisticum*. Berlin: De Gruyter, 1983: 186–189, 192–193.
frr. (+ titul.) 400–402, 404.
fr. 401: *PSI* 1090.
Dup. partim 1355 001 (frr. 1a–b, 2).
Q, Pap: 244: Hexametr.

0455 **ERIPHUS** Comic.
4 B.C.
001 **Fragmenta**, ed. T. Kock, *Comicorum Atticorum fragmenta*, vol. 2. Leipzig: Teubner,
1884: 428–430.
frr. 1–7.
Q: 203: Comic.
002 **Fragmenta**, ed. A. Meineke, *Fragmenta comicorum Graecorum*, vol. 3. Berlin: Reimer, 1840
(repr. De Gruyter, 1970): 556–559.
Q: 199: Comic.

0716 **EROTIANUS** Gramm. et Med.
A.D. 1
001 **Vocum Hippocraticarum collectio**, ed. E.
Nachmanson, *Erotiani vocum Hippocraticarum
collectio cum fragmentis*. Göteborg: Eranos,
1918: 3–96.
Cod: 12,167: Lexicogr., Med.
002 **Fragmenta**, ed. Nachmanson, *op. cit.*, 99–122.
Q: 2,489: Med., Comm.

5003 *EROTICA ADESPOTA*
Varia
001 **Sesonchosis** (*P. Oxy.* 15.1826), ed. F. Zimmermann, *Griechische Roman-Papyri und verwandte Texte*. Heidelberg: Bilabel, 1936: 36–
40.
Dup. partim ADDITAMENTA (FGrH) (2433
029) (fr. 194d).
Cf. et 5003 016, 017.
Pap: Narr. Fict.
002 **De Chione** (codex Thebanus deperditus), ed.
Zimmermann, *op. cit.*, 41–46.
Cod: Narr. Fict.
003 **Calligone** (*PSI* 981 = *P. Cairo* 47992), ed.
Zimmermann, *op. cit.*, 47–50.
Pap: Narr. Fict.
004 **Dionysius** (*PSI* 151), ed. Zimmermann, *op.
cit.*, 50–52.
Dup. partim ADDITAMENTA (FGrH) (2433
033) (fr. 28).
Pap: Narr. Fict.
006 **Metiochus et Parthenope** (?) (*P. Oxy.* 3.435 =
P. Yale inv. 45), ed. Zimmermann, *op. cit.*, 62.
Cf. et 5003 018.
Pap: Narr. Fict.
007 **Fragmenta** (*P. Berol.* inv. 10535), ed. Zimmer-
mann, *op. cit.*, 64–68.
Pap: Narr. Fict.
008 **Herpyllis** (*P. Dublin* inv. C3), ed. Zimmer-
mann, *op. cit.*, 68–78.
Pap: Narr. Fict.

009 **Antheia** (?) (*PSI* 726), ed. Zimmermann, *op.
cit.*, 79–84.
Pap: Narr. Fict.
010 **Olenius** (*PSI* 725), ed. Zimmermann, *op. cit.*,
90–92.
Pap: Narr. Fict.
013 **Tefnut** (*P. Lond.* 2.274 [= *P. Lit Lond.* 192 =
Brit. Mus. inv. 274]), ed. R. Reitzenstein, "Die
griechische Tefnut-Legende," *Sitzungsberichte
der Heidelberger Akademie der Wissenschaft*,
Phil.-hist. Kl. 1923.2. Heidelberg, 1923.
Pap: Narr. Fict.
014 **Tinouphis** (*P. Hauniensis* inv. 400), ed. M.
Haslam, "Narrative about Tinouphis in prosi-
metrum," *Papyri Greek and Egyptian edited by
various hands in honour of Eric Gardner Tur-
ner on the occasion of his seventieth birthday*.
London: Egypt Exploration Society, 1981: 41.
Pap: Narr. Fict.
015 **Iolaus** (*P. Oxy.* 42.3010), ed. P. Parsons, "A
Greek satyricon?," *Bulletin of the Institute of
Classical Studies* 18 (1971) 54.
Pap: Narr. Fict.
016 **Sesonchosis** (*P. Oxy.* 27.2466), ed. J. Rea, *The
Oxyrhynchus papyri*, pt. 27. London: Egypt
Exploration Society, 1962: 135–136.
Cf. et 5003 001, 017.
Pap: Narr. Fict.
017 **Sesonchosis** (*P. Oxy.* 47.3319), ed. S. West,
The Oxyrhynchus papyri, pt. 47 (1980): 15.
Cf. et 5003 001, 016.
Pap: Narr. Fict.
018 **Metiochus et Parthenope** (*P. Berol.* inv. 7927
+ 9588 + 21179), ed. H. Maehler, "Der Metio-
chos-Parthenope-Roman," *Zeitschrift für Pa-
pyrologie und Epigraphik* 23 (1976) 5–7.
Cf. et 5003 006.
Pap: Narr. Fict.
x01 **Ninus**.
Cf. NINUS (1804).
x02 **Ahiqar**.
Cf. HISTORIA ET SENTENTIAE DE AHIQAR
(3001 001–003).

2312 **ERXIAS** Hist.
ante 2 B.C.?
001 **Fragmentum**, FGrH #449: 3B:377.
Q: 46: Hist.

0180 **ERYCIUS** Epigr.
fiq Erycius Poeta
1 B.C.: Cyzicenus
Cf. et ERYCIUS Poeta (2653).
001 **Epigrammata**, AG **6**.96, 234, 255; **7**.36, 174,
230, 368, 377, 397; **9**.233, 237, 558, 824;
16.242.
Q: 571: Epigr.

2653 **ERYCIUS** Poeta
fiq Erycius Cyzicenus
1 B.C.?
Cf. et ERYCIUS Epigr. (0180).
001 **Fragmentum**, ed. H. Lloyd-Jones and P. Par-

sons, *Supplementum Hellenisticum*. Berlin: De Gruyter, 1983: 193.
fr. 407.
Q: 5: Hexametr.

1356 ***ESDRAS V/VI***
A.D. 2/3
001 **Fragmenta** (*P. Oxy.* 7.1010), ed. A.S. Hunt, *The Oxyrhynchus papyri*, pt. 7. London: Egypt Exploration Fund, 1910: 13–14.
Pap

0885 **Pseudo-ESDRAS**
ante A.D. 7
x01 **Fragmentum ap. Paulum.**
CMG, vol. 9.2, p. 303.
Cf. PAULUS Med. (0715 001).

0181 **ETRUSCUS** Epigr.
1 B.C.?
001 **Epigramma**, AG 7.381.
Q: 41: Epigr.

4099 ***ETYMOLOGICUM MAGNUM***
A.D. 12
001 **Etymologicum magnum**, ed. T. Gaisford, *Etymologicum magnum*. Oxford: Oxford University Press, 1848 (repr. Amsterdam: Hakkert, 1967): 1–826.
Cod: 359,646: Lexicogr.

2372 **EUAGON** Hist.
5 B.C.: Samius
001 **Testimonia**, FGrH #535: 3B:520.
NQ: 33: Test.
002 **Fragmenta**, FGrH #535: 3B:520–521.
Q: 170: Hist.

2425 **EUAGORAS** Hist.
A.D. 1/3?: Lindius
001 **Testimonium**, FGrH #619: 3C:153.
NQ: 36: Test.

2293 **EUALCES** Hist.
ante 3 B.C.: Ephesius
001 **Fragmentum**, FGrH #418: 3B:316.
Q: 19: Hist.

0456 **EUANGELUS** Comic.
post 4 B.C.
001 **Fragmentum**, ed. T. Kock, *Comicorum Atticorum fragmenta*, vol. 3. Leipzig: Teubner, 1888: 376.
fr. 1.
Q: 88: Comic.
002 **Fragmenta**, ed. A. Meineke, *Fragmenta comicorum Graecorum*, vol. 4. Berlin: Reimer, 1841 (repr. De Gruyter, 1970): 572.
Q: 90: Comic.

0886 **EUANGELUS** Med.
ante A.D. 1

x01 **Fragmentum ap. Galenum.**
K13.806.
Cf. GALENUS Med. (0057 077).

2623 **EUANTHES** Epic.
ante A.D. 2
001 **Titulus**, ed. H. Lloyd-Jones and P. Parsons, *Supplementum Hellenisticum*. Berlin: De Gruyter, 1983: 194.
fr. 409.
NQ: 4: Hymn.

1096 **EUARETUS** Trag.
4 B.C.
001 **Tituli**, ed. B. Snell, *Tragicorum Graecorum fragmenta*, vol. 1. Göttingen: Vandenhoeck & Ruprecht, 1971: 251.
frr. 1–2.
NQ: 16: Trag.

1800 **EUBOEUS** Parodius
5–4 B.C.: Parius
001 **Fragmenta**, ed. P. Brandt, *Parodorum epicorum Graecorum et Archestrati reliquiae* [*Corpusculum poesis epicae Graecae Ludibundae*, fasc. 1. Leipzig: Teubner, 1888]: 52.
frr. 1–2.
Dup. partim 1800 002 (frr. 411–412).
Q: 17: Parod.
002 **Fragmenta et titulus**, ed. H. Lloyd-Jones and P. Parsons, *Supplementum Hellenisticum*. Berlin: De Gruyter, 1983: 194.
frr. (+ titul.) 410–412.
frr. 411–412: Dup. 1800 001.
Q: 19: Parod.

0457 **EUBULIDES** Comic.
4 B.C.?
001 **Fragmentum**, ed. T. Kock, *Comicorum Atticorum fragmenta*, vol. 2. Leipzig: Teubner, 1884: 431.
fr. 1.
Q: 13: Comic.
002 **Fragmentum**, ed. A. Meineke, *Fragmenta comicorum Graecorum*, vol. 3. Berlin: Reimer, 1840 (repr. De Gruyter, 1970): 559.
Q: 13: Comic.

4257 **EUBULIDES** Phil.
4 B.C.: Milesius, Atheniensis
001 **Testimonia**, ed. K. Döring, *Die Megariker* [*Studien zur antiken Philosophie* 2. Amsterdam: Grüner, 1972]: 16–20.
test. 50–53b, 55–67.
NQ: Test.

0458 **EUBULUS** Comic.
4 B.C.
001 **Fragmenta**, ed. T. Kock, *Comicorum Atticorum fragmenta*, vol. 2. Leipzig: Teubner, 1884: 164–214.

frr. 1–4, 6–21, 23–32, 34–39, 41–57, 60–122, 124–131, 133–134, 136–151 + tituli.
Q: 2,745: Comic.

002 **Fragmenta**, ed. A. Meineke, *Fragmenta comicorum Graecorum*, vol. 3. Berlin: Reimer, 1840 (repr. De Gruyter, 1970): 203–205, 207–232, 234–255, 257–271.
Q: 2,584: Comic.

003 **Fragmenta**, ed. J. Demiańczuk, *Supplementum comicum*. Krakau: Nakładem Akademii, 1912 (repr. Hildesheim: Olms, 1967): 40–41.
frr. 1–2.
Q: 20: Comic.

004 **Titulus**, ed. C. Austin, *Comicorum Graecorum fragmenta in papyris reperta*. Berlin: De Gruyter, 1973: 83.
NQ: 2: Comic.

005 **Fragmentum**, ed. Kock, *CAF*, vol. 3 (1888): 738.
fr. 145b.
Q: 2: Comic.

006 **Fragmentum**, ed. Meineke, *FCG*, vol. 5.1 (1857; repr. 1970): clxxxvi.
Q: 2: Comic.

x01 **Aenigmata**.
App. Anth. 7.9–10: Cf. ANTHOLOGIAE GRAECAE APPENDIX (7052 007).
App. Anth. 7.10b addenda: Cf. ANTHOLOGIAE GRAECAE APPENDIX (7052 008).
Dup. partim 0458 002 (pp. 254–255).

0887 **EUBULUS** Med.
ante A.D. 1
x01 **Fragmenta ap. Galenum**.
K13.297, 911.
Cf. GALENUS Med. (0057 076–077).

0250 **EUCLIDES** Comic. vel Iamb.
ante 5 B.C.: fort. Atheniensis
001 **Fragmenta**, ed. M.L. West, *Iambi et elegi Graeci*, vol. 2. Oxford: Clarendon Press, 1972: 63.
frr. 1–2.
Q: 12: Iamb.

1799 **EUCLIDES** Geom.
3 B.C.: Alexandrinus
Scholia: Cf. SCHOLIA IN EUCLIDEM (5022).
001 **Elementa**, ed. E.S. Stamatis (post J.L. Heiberg), *Euclidis elementa*, vols. 1–4, 2nd edn. Leipzig: Teubner, 1:1969; 2:1970; 3:1972; 4:1973; **1**:1–179; **2**:1–227; **3**:1–210; **4**:1–186.
Lib. 1–4: vol. 1, pp. 1–179.
Lib. 5–9: vol. 2, pp. 1–227.
Lib. 10: vol. 3, pp. 1–210.
Lib. 11–13: vol. 4, pp. 1–186.
Lib. 14: Cf. HYPSICLES Math. et Astron. (0717 001).
Lib. 15: Cf. ANONYMUS Discipulus Isidori Milesii Mech. (4005 001).
Cod: 155,151: Math.

002 **Elementa** (demonstrationes alterae, lib. 1–3), ed. Stamatis (post Heiberg), *op. cit.*, vol. 1, 181–186.
Cod: 889: Math.

003 **Elementa** (demonstrationes alterae, lib. 5–9), ed. Stamatis (post Heiberg), *op. cit.*, vol. 2, 229–237, 239.
Cod: 1,693: Math.

004 **Elementa** (demonstrationes alterae, lib. 10), ed. Stamatis (post Heiberg), *op. cit.*, vol. 3, 211–234.
Cod: 4,179: Math.

005 **Elementa** (demonstrationes alterae, lib. 11–13), ed. Stamatis (post Heiberg), *op. cit.*, vol. 4, 187–206.
Cod: 4,153: Math.

006 **Elementa** (recensio altera, lib. 11.36–12.17), ed. Stamatis (post Heiberg), *op. cit.*, vol. 4, 207–238.
Cod: 10,336: Math.

007 **Data**, ed. H. Menge, *Euclidis opera omnia*, vol. 6. Leipzig: Teubner, 1896: 2–186.
Cod: 19,734: Math.

008 **Data** (demonstrationes alterae), ed. Menge, *Euclidis opera omnia*, vol. 6, 190–230.
Cod: 4,346: Math.

009 **Optica**, ed. J.L. Heiberg, *Euclidis opera omnia*, vol. 7. Leipzig: Teubner, 1895: 2–120.
Cod: 11,383: Math.

010 **Opticorum recensio Theonis**, ed. Heiberg, *Euclidis opera omnia*, vol. 7, 144–246.
Cod: 10,384: Math.

011 **Catoptrica** (recensio Theonis?), ed. Heiberg, *Euclidis opera omnia*, vol. 7, 286–342.
Cod: 5,409: Math.

012 **Phaenomena**, ed. Menge, *Euclidis opera omnia*, vol. 8. Leipzig: Teubner, 1916: 2–104.
Cod: 8,333: Astron.

013 **Phaenomena** (recensio b), ed. Menge, *Euclidis opera omnia*, vol. 8, 44–82, 86–102, 106–112.
Cod: 5,282: Astron.

014 **Phaenomena** (demonstrationes alterae recensionis b), ed. Menge, *Euclidis opera omnia*, vol. 8, 114–132.
Cod: 2,409: Astron.

015 **Sectio canonis** [Sp.], ed. Menge, *Euclidis opera omnia*, vol. 8, 158–180.
Cod: 2,487: Mus.

016 **Fragmenta**, ed. Heiberg, *Euclidis opera omnia*, vol. 8, 227, 236–284.
Q, Cod: 10,956: Math.

017 **Epigramma**, ed. Heiberg, *Euclidis opera omnia*, vol. 8, 286.
Q: 49: Epigr.

x01 **Problema**.
App. Anth. 7.2: Cf. ANTHOLOGIAE GRAECAE APPENDIX (7052 007).
Dup. 1799 017.

x03 **Introductio harmonica**.
Menge, pp. 186–222.
Cf. CLEONIDES Mus. (0361 001).

4247 **EUCLIDES** Phil.
5–4 B.C.: Megarensis, Atheniensis
001 **Testimonia**, ed. K. Döring, *Die Megariker*
[Studien zur antiken Philosophie 2. Amsterdam: Grüner, 1972]: 3–14.
test. 2–13, 15–19, 21–25, 27, 29–37, 39–44e.
NQ: Test.

2356 **EUCRATES** Hist.
ante A.D. 3
001 **Fragmenta**, FGrH #514: 3B:490.
Q: 24: Hist.

2343 **EUDEMUS** Hist.
5 B.C.?: Naxius vel Parius
001 **Testimonia**, FGrH #497: 3B:469.
NQ: 109: Test.

2365 **EUDEMUS** Hist.
4 B.C.?
001 **Titulus**, FGrH #524: 3B:503.
NQ: Hist.

0735 **EUDEMUS** Med.
3 B.C.: Alexandrinus
001 **Fragmenta**, *P. Ryl.* 1.21.
Pap

1357 **EUDEMUS** Phil.
4 B.C.: Rhodius
001 **Fragmenta**, ed. F. Wehrli, *Eudemos von Rho-*
dos [*Die Schule des Aristoteles*, vol. 8, 2nd edn.
Basel: Schwabe, 1969]: 11–72.
Κατηγορίαι (?): frr. 7–8.
Ἀναλυτικά: frr. 9–16, 18–20, 22, 24.
Περὶ λέξεως: frr. 25–29.
Περὶ γωνίας: fr. 30.
Φυσικά: frr. 31–123b.
Τὰ μετὰ τὰ φυσικά (?): fr. 124.
Historia animalium (?): frr. 126–132.
Γεωμετρικὴ ἱστορία: frr. 133–141.
Ἀριθμητικὴ ἱστορία: fr. 142.
Ἀστρολογικὴ ἱστορία: frr. 143–149.
Historia theologiae (?): fr. 150.
Q: 20,895: Phil., Nat. Hist., Math.

0888 **EUDEMUS** Poet. Med.
A.D. 1
001 **Fragmentum**, ed. H. Lloyd-Jones and P. Par-
sons, *Supplementum Hellenisticum*. Berlin: De
Gruyter, 1983: 195.
fr. 412a: Dup. partim 0888 x01.
Q: 106: Eleg., Med.
x01 **Fragmenta ap. Galenum.**
K14.185, 201.
Dup. partim 0888 001 (fr. 412a).
Cf. GALENUS Med. (0057 078).

1376 **EUDEMUS** Rhet.
A.D. 2?: fort. Argivus
001 Περὶ λέξεων ῥητορικῶν (excerpta), ed. B.

Niese, "Excerpta ex Eudemi codice Parisino n.
2635," *Philologus*, suppl. 15 (1922) 145–160.
Cod: 2,310: Lexicogr.

0903 **EUDEMUS Senior** Med.
ante A.D. 2
x01 **Fragmentum ap. Galenum.**
K13.291.
Cf. GALENUS Med. (0057 076).

1847 **EUDORUS** Hist.
1 B.C.: Alexandrinus
x01 **Testimonium.**
FGrH #650.
Cf. ARISTON Phil. (2447 001).

2989 **EUDORUS** Phil.
1 B.C.: Alexandrinus
001 **De simulacris in speculis** (*P. Oxy.* 13.1609)
(fort. auctore Eudoro Alexandrino), ed. B.P.
Grenfell, *The Oxyrhynchus papyri*, pt. 13.
London: Egypt Exploration Fund, 1919: 95–
97.
Pap: Phil.
x01 **Commentarius in Platonis Theaetetum.**
Diels & Schubart, pp. 3–51.
Cf. ANONYMI COMMENTARIUS IN PLATO-
NIS THEAETETUM (1128 001).

1358 **EUDOXUS** Astron.
4 B.C.: Cnidius
001 **Fragmenta**, ed. F. Lasserre, *Die Fragmente des*
Eudoxos von Knidos. Berlin: De Gruyter, 1966:
39–127.
frr. 2–11, 13–20, 22–30, 32–43, 45, 47–48, 50–
54, 56–57, 59, 62–130, 132–133, 137, 139,
141–143, 147a–173b, 174b, 176–192a, 193a–
313, 315–326, 328–339, 341, 344a–363, 365–
368, 370–374.
Q, Pap: 18,414: Astron., Geogr., Math., Iamb.
002 **Fragmenta** [Sp.], ed. F. Boll, *Codices German-*
ici [*Catalogus codicum astrologorum Graecorum*
7. Brussels: Lamertin, 1908]: 183–187.
Cod: [1,922]
003 **Ars astronomica** [Sp.] (*P. Par.* 1), ed. F. Blass,
Eudoxi ars astronomica qualis in charta Aegyp-
tiaca superest [*Programm. Kiel* (1887)]: 12–25.
Pap: 3,267: Astron.

0399 **EUDOXUS** Comic.
4–3 B.C.?
001 **Fragmenta**, ed. A. Kock, *Comicorum Atticorum*
fragmenta, vol. 3. Leipzig: Teubner, 1888: 332.
frr. 1–2.
Q: 6: Comic.
002 **Tituli**, ed. A. Meineke, *Fragmenta comicorum*
Graecorum, vol. 4. Berlin: Reimer, 1841 (repr.
De Gruyter, 1970): 508.
NQ: 3: Comic.

1915 **EUDOXUS** Hist.
3 B.C.: Rhodius

001 **Testimonia**, FGrH #79: 2A:159.
NQ: 107: Test.

002 **Fragmenta**, FGrH #79: 2A:159–160.
Q: 234: Hist.

2399 **EUDROMUS** Phil.
2 B.C.

001 **Fragmenta**, ed. J. von Arnim, *Stoicorum veterum fragmenta*, vol. 3. Leipzig: Teubner, 1903 (repr. Stuttgart: 1968): 268.
Q: 78: Phil.

0251 **EUENUS** Eleg.
5–4 B.C.: Parius

001 **Fragmenta**, ed. M.L. West, *Iambi et elegi Graeci*, vol. 2. Oxford: Clarendon Press, 1972: 64–67.
frr. 1–9a.
Q: 158: Eleg., Hexametr., Iamb.

x01 **Epigrammata exhortatoria et supplicatoria.**
App. Anth. 4.13–15: Cf. ANTHOLOGIAE GRAECAE APPENDIX (7052 004).
Dup. partim 0251 001 (frr. 1, 3, 5).

0183 **EUENUS** Epigr.
1 B.C.?: Atheniensis

001 **Epigramma**, AG 9.602.
Q: 51: Epigr.

0182 **EUENUS** Gramm.
1 B.C.?: Ascalonius

001 **Epigrammata**, AG **9**.62, 75, 122, 251, 717–718; **11**.49; **12**.172; **16**.165–166.
Q: 256: Epigr.

0184 **EUGENES** Epigr.
post 3 B.C.

001 **Epigramma**, AG 16.308.
Q: 43: Epigr.

0891 **EUGENIUS** Med.
A.D. 1–2

x01 **Fragmentum ap. Galenum.**
K13.114.
Cf. GALENUS Med. (0057 076).

0892 **EUGERASIA** Med.
ante A.D. 2

x01 **Fragmentum ap. Galenum.**
K13.244.
Cf. GALENUS Med. (0057 076).

1905 **EUHEMERUS** Scriptor De Sacra Historia
4–3 B.C.: Messenius

001 **Testimonia**, FGrH #63: 1A:300–302.
NQ: 646: Test.

002 **Fragmenta**, FGrH #63: 1A:302–313, *20 addenda.
Q: 3,918: Hist., Myth.

2824 **EULOGIUS** Theol.
A.D. 6–7: Alexandrinus

001 **Fragmentum in Psalmum 31.1–2**, MPG 86.2: 2964.
Cod: Exeget.

002 **Fragmenta tria in Lucam**, MPG 86.2: 2961–2964.
Cod: Exeget.

003 **Fragmentum in Joannem 21.16**, MPG 86.2: 2961.
Cod: Exeget.

004 **De trinitate et de incarnatione** (fragmentum), ed. O. Bardenhewer, "Ungedruckte Excerpte aus einer Schrift des Patriarchen Eulogios von Alexandrien über Trinität und Inkarnation," *Theologische Quartalschrift* 78 (1896) 353–401.
Cod: Theol.

x01 **Dubitationes orthodoxi** (fragmenta in *Doctrina patrum*).
Diekamp, pp. 152–155.
Cf. DOCTRINA PATRUM (7051 001).

x02 **Defensiones** (fragmenta in *Doctrina patrum*).
Diekamp, pp. 209–210, 211–213.
Cf. DOCTRINA PATRUM (7051 001).

1972 **EUMACHUS** Hist.
3–2 B.C.: Neapolitanus

001 **Fragmenta**, FGrH #178: 2B:906.
Q: 70: Hist.

1361 **EUMEDES** Comic.
post 4 B.C.?

001 **Titulus**, ed. T. Kock, *Comicorum Atticorum fragmenta*, vol. 3. Leipzig: Teubner, 1888: 377.
NQ: 2: Comic.

0298 **EUMELUS** Epic.
8 B.C.?: Corinthius
Cf. et TITANOMACHIA (1737).

001 **Fragmentum**, ed. D.L. Page, *Poetae melici Graeci*. Oxford: Clarendon Press, 1962 (repr. 1967 (1st edn. corr.)): 361.
fr. 1.
Q: 16: Lyr., Hymn.

002 **Fragmenta**, ed. G. Kinkel, *Epicorum Graecorum fragmenta*, vol. 1. Leipzig: Teubner, 1877: 188, 191, 193, 195.
frr. 2, 9, 11, 13, 16.
Dup. partim 0298 001, 004 (fr. 2).
Q: 130: Epic., Lyr., Hymn.

003 **Testimonia**, FGrH #451: 3B:378.
NQ: 56: Test.

004 **Corinthiaca** (fragmenta), FGrH #451: 3B:378–381.
Dup. partim 0298 002 (fr. 2).
Q: 935: Hist., Epic.

1913 **EUMELUS** Hist.
3 B.C.?

001 **Fragmenta**, FGrH #77: 2A:158.
Q: 113: Hist., Rhet.

EUMENES Hist.
4 B.C.: Cardianus
Cf. EPHEMERIDES (2436 001–002).

0890 **EUMERUS** Med.
ante A.D. 2
x01 **Fragmenta ap. Galenum.**
K12.774, 777, 778, 788.
Cf. GALENUS Med. (0057 076).

2723 **EUMETIS** Epigr.
ante A.D. 2
x01 **Aenigma.**
App. Anth. 7.6(?): Cf. ANTHOLOGIAE GRAE-
CAE APPENDIX (7052 007).

2050 **EUNAPIUS** Hist. et Soph.
A.D. 4–5: Sardianus
Scholia: Cf. ARETHAS Philol. et Scr. Eccl.
(2130 x01).
001 **Vitae sophistarum,** ed. J. Giangrande, *Eunapii
vitae sophistarum.* Rome: Polygraphica, 1956:
1–101.
Cod: 22,059: Biogr.
002 **Fragmenta historica,** ed. L. Dindorf, *Historici
Graeci minores,* vol. 1. Leipzig: Teubner, 1870:
205–274.
Q: 16,162: Hist.

0459 **EUNICUS** Comic.
5 B.C.
001 **Fragmentum,** ed. T. Kock, *Comicorum Atticorum fragmenta,* vol. 1. Leipzig: Teubner,
1880: 781.
fr. 1 + titulus.
Q: 9: Comic.
002 **Fragmentum,** ed. A. Meineke, *Fragmenta
comicorum Graecorum,* vol. 2.2. Berlin: Reimer, 1840 (repr. De Gruyter, 1970): 856.
Q: 8: Comic.

EUNOMIANUS Epigr.
AG 9.193.
Cf. PHILOSTORGIUS Scr. Eccl. (2058 006).

0893 **EUNOMUS** Med.
A.D. 1
x01 **Fragmentum ap. Galenum.**
K13.851.
Cf. GALENUS Med. (0057 077).

0185 **EUODUS** Epigr.
A.D. 2/3
001 **Epigrammata,** AG 16.116, 155.
Q: 22: Epigr.

0396 **EUPHANES** Comic.
4 B.C.
001 **Fragmentum,** ed. T. Kock, *Comicorum Atticorum fragmenta,* vol. 2. Leipzig: Teubner,
1884: 296–297.
fr. 1.
Q: 12: Comic.

1912 **EUPHANTUS** Phil.
4–3 B.C.: Olynthius, Atheniensis

001 **Testimonia,** FGrH #74: 2A:132.
test. 3: *P. Herc.* 1112.
Dup. partim 1912 003.
NQ: 135: Test.
002 **Fragmenta,** FGrH #74: 2A:132–133.
Dup. partim 1912 003.
Q: 294: Hist.
003 **Testimonia,** ed. K. Döring, *Die Megariker
[Studien zur antiken Philosophie* 2. Amster-
dam: Grüner, 1972]: 20–21.
test. 68–72.
Dup. partim 1912 001–002.
NQ: Test.

0221 **EUPHORION** Epic.
3 B.C.: Chalcidensis
001 **Fragmenta,** ed. J.U. Powell, *Collectanea Alexandrina.* Oxford: Clarendon Press, 1925 (repr.
1970): 29–34, 36–47, 49–56, 58.
frr. 2–5, 8–14, 16–17, 21, 23–25, 30, 33–35,
38, 40–44, 46–48, 50–54, 57–61, 63–66, 73–
75, 77–96, 98, 103–104, 107–108, 110–114,
118–125, 127–141, 145, 149–154, 157–162,
175–176 + tituli.
frr. 48, 63, 86, 130: Dup. partim 0221 002 (frr.
418, 426, 428, 429).
frr. 140–141: Dup. 0221 004.
Q: 1,116: Epic., Epigr.
002 **Fragmenta,** ed. H. Lloyd-Jones and P. Parsons,
Supplementum Hellenisticum. Berlin: De Gruyter, 1983: 196–199, 205–207, 210–218, 221–
233.
frr. 413–454.
frr. 413–416: *PSI* 1390.
frr. 418–421: *P. Oxy.* 19.2219.
frr. 422–427: *P. Oxy.* 19.2220.
fr. 428: *P. Oxy.* 30.2525.
fr. 429: *P. Berol.* 13873.
frr. 430–431: *P. Oxy.* 17.2085.
fr. 432: *P. Oxy.* 30.2528.
frr. 433–452: *P. Oxy.* 30.2526.
fr. 453: *P. Berol.* 9780.
fr. 454: *P. Oxy.* 30.2527.
Dup. partim 0221 001 (frr. 48, 63, 86, 130).
Q, Pap: 2,018: Epic.
003 **Fragmenta prosaica,** ed. B.A. van Groningen,
Euphorion. Amsterdam: Hakkert, 1977: 226–
248.
Dup. partim 0221 001–002.
Q: [1,096]
004 **Epigrammata,** AG 6.279; 7.651.
Dup. partim 0221 001 (frr. 140–141).
Q: 63: Epigr.

0894 **EUPHRANOR** Med.
A.D. 1
x01 **Fragmentum ap. Galenum.**
K13.525.
Cf. GALENUS Med. (0057 077).

0460 **EUPHRO** Comic.
3 B.C.
001 **Fragmenta,** ed. T. Kock, *Comicorum Atti-*

corum fragmenta, vol. 3. Leipzig: Teubner, 1888: 317–324.
frr. 1–12.
Q: 576: Comic.

002 **Fragmenta**, ed. A. Meineke, *Fragmenta comicorum Graecorum*, vol. 4. Berlin: Reimer, 1841 (repr. De Gruyter, 1970): 486–487, 489–495.
Q: 582: Comic.

0210 **EUPHRONIUS** Lyr.
3 B.C.: Chersonesites
001 **Priapeia**, ed. J.U. Powell, *Collectanea Alexandrina.* Oxford: Clarendon Press, 1925 (repr. 1970): 176.
Q: 28: Lyr.

2129 **EUPITHIUS** Epigr.
A.D. 3: Atheniensis
001 **Epigramma**, AG 9.206.
Q: 27: Epigr.

2486 **EUPOLEMUS Judaeus** Hist.
2 B.C.: Palaestinus
001 **Testimonia**, FGrH #723: 3C:671–672.
NQ: 166: Test.
002 **Fragmenta**, FGrH #723: 3C:672–678.
frr. 1–4, *5.
Q: 1,914: Hist., Epist.

2487 **Pseudo-EUPOLEMUS Judaeus** Hist.
vel Anonymus Samaritanus
2 B.C.?
001 **Fragmenta**, FGrH #724: 3C:678–679.
Q: 523: Hist.

0461 **EUPOLIS** Comic.
5 B.C.
001 **Fragmenta**, ed. T. Kock, *Comicorum Atticorum fragmenta*, vol. 1. Leipzig: Teubner, 1880: 258–270, 272–355, 357–369.
frr. 1–16, 18–32, 34–38, 42–52, 58, 60–79, 86, 88–121, 128–134, 138–141, 143–144, 146–163, 168–177, 179–188, 190–192, 198–236, 242–248, 250–259, 261–272, 275–293, 295–362, 372, 374–453, 455–459.
Q: 2,936: Comic.
002 **Fragmenta**, ed. A. Meineke, *Fragmenta comicorum Graecorum*, vol. 2.1. Berlin: Reimer, 1839 (repr. De Gruyter, 1970): 426, 428–433, 435, 437–438, 440–444, 447–453, 455–458, 460–461, 463–475, 477, 479–482, 484–486, 488–495, 497–502, 505–521, 523–526, 528–543, 546–568, 577.
p. 447, fr. 1: lines 3–4 supplied from vol. 5.1, p. lxx.
p. 520: fr. 35 supplied from vol. 5.1, p. lxxxii.
Q: 2,840: Comic.
003 **Fragmenta**, ed. J. Demiańczuk, *Supplementum comicum.* Krakau: Nakładem Akademii, 1912 (repr. Hildesheim: Olms, 1967): 41–53.
frr. 1–27.
fr. 7–12: *P. Cairo* inv. 43227.
Q, Pap: 668: Comic.

004 **Fragmenta**, ed. C. Austin, *Comicorum Graecorum fragmenta in papyris reperta.* Berlin: De Gruyter, 1973: 83–119.
frr. 92–100.
Pap: 2,804: Comic.
005 **Fragmenta**, ed. Meineke, *FCG*, vol. 5.1 (1857; repr. 1970): lxviii, lxxviii–lxxix, xc–xci.
Q: 45: Comic.
006 **Fragmentum**, ed. A. Guida, "Frammenti inediti di Eupoli, Teleclide, Teognide, Giuliano e Imerio da un nuovo codice del Lexicon Vindobonense," *Prometheus* 5 (1979) 201.
Q

0006 **EURIPIDES** Trag.
5 B.C.: Atheniensis
Cf. et EURIPIDIS EPISTULAE (1367).
Vita et scholia: Cf. SCHOLIA IN EURIPIDEM (5023).
001 **Cyclops**, ed. G. Murray, *Euripidis fabulae*, vol. 1. Oxford: Clarendon Press, 1902 (repr. 1966).
Cod: 4,470: Satyr.
002 **Alcestis**, ed. Murray, *op. cit.*, vol. 1.
Cod: 7,090: Trag.
003 **Medea**, ed. Murray, *op. cit.*, vol. 1.
Cod: 8,395: Trag.
004 **Heraclidae**, ed. Murray, *op. cit.*, vol. 1.
Cod: 6,644: Trag.
005 **Hippolytus**, ed. Murray, *op. cit.*, vol. 1.
Cod: 8,648: Trag.
006 **Andromacha**, ed. Murray, *op. cit.*, vol. 1.
Cod: 7,764: Trag.
007 **Hecuba**, ed. Murray, *op. cit.*, vol. 1.
Cod: 7,677: Trag.
008 **Supplices**, ed. Murray, *op. cit.*, vol. 2, 3rd edn. (1913; repr. 1966).
Cod: 7,549: Trag.
009 **Hercules**, ed. Murray, *op. cit.*, vol. 2.
Cod: 8,469: Trag.
010 **Ion**, ed. Murray, *op. cit.*, vol. 2.
Cod: 10,101: Trag.
011 **Troiades**, ed. Murray, *op. cit.*, vol. 2.
Cod: 7,634: Trag.
012 **Electra**, ed. Murray, *op. cit.*, vol. 2.
Cod: 8,264: Trag.
013 **Iphigenia Taurica**, ed. Murray, *op. cit.*, vol. 2.
Cod: 9,029: Trag.
014 **Helena**, ed. Murray, *op. cit.*, vol. 3 (1902; repr. 1966).
Cod: 10,582: Trag.
015 **Phoenissae**, ed. Murray, *op. cit.*, vol. 3.
Cod: 10,478: Trag.
016 **Orestes**, ed. Murray, *op. cit.*, vol. 3.
Cf. et CANTICUM EURIPIDIS (2138 001).
Cod: 10,754: Trag.
017 **Bacchae**, ed. Murray, *op. cit.*, vol. 3.
Cod: 8,208: Trag.
018 **Iphigenia Aulidensis**, ed. Murray, *op. cit.*, vol. 3.
Cod: 10,048: Trag.
019 **Rhesus**, ed. Murray, *op. cit.*, vol. 3.
Cod: 5,800: Trag.
020 **Fragmenta**, ed. A. Nauck, *Tragicorum Grae-*

corum fragmenta. Leipzig: Teubner, 1889
(repr. Hildesheim: Olms, 1964): 363–378,
380–410, 412–419, 421–427, 429–468, 470–
496, 498–513, 515–516, 518–578, 580–599,
601–609, 611–612, 616–623, 625–667, 670–
716.

frr. 1–38, 40–63, 65–177, 179–181, 183–224,
226–369, 371–426, 428–478, 480–484, 486–
487, 489–495, 497–513, 515–567, 569–588,
590–740, 742–779, 781–819, 821–837, 839–
850, 852–859, 861–880, 882–890, 892–924,
926–941, 943–953, 955–1003, 1005–1015,
1017–1020, 1023–1092, 1095–1115, 1117,
1123–1127, 1129–1132 + tituli.

Q, Cod, Pap: 18,087: Trag., Satyr.

021 **Fragmenta papyracea**, ed. C. Austin, *Nova
fragmenta Euripidea in papyris reperta.* Berlin:
De Gruyter, 1968: 12–21, 23–40, 42–48, 50–
58, 60–65, 67–87.

frr. 1–156 + tituli.

Q, Pap: 4,950: Trag.

022 **Epinicium in Alcibiadem** (fragmenta), ed. D.L.
Page, *Poetae melici Graeci.* Oxford: Clarendon
Press, 1962 (repr. 1967 (1st edn. corr.)): 391.

frr. 1–2.

Q: 39: Lyr., Encom.

023 **Fragmenta Phaethontis**, ed. J. Diggle, *Euripides. Phaethon.* Cambridge: Cambridge University Press, 1970: 55–69.

Cf. et 0006 032.

Q, Cod, Pap: 1,328: Trag.

024 **Fragmenta Antiopes**, ed. J. Kambitsis, *L'Anti-
ope d'Euripide.* Athens: Hourzamanis, 1972: 1–
19, 130, 134.

frr. 1–48, 910N, 911N.

Q, Pap: 1,507: Trag.

025 **Fragmenta Alexandri**, ed. B. Snell, *Euripides
Alexandros und andere Strassburger Papyri mit
Fragmenten griechischer Dichter [Hermes Ein-
zelschriften* 5 (1937)]: 5–21.

frr. 2–7, 9*, 11*, 13–14*, 16, 18, 23, 25*, 26–
29, 30*–31*, 32–41, 43–44, 45*, 46–58, 60,
62–68.

Pap: 1,366: Trag.

026 **Fragmenta Hypsipyles**, ed. G.W. Bond, *Euripides. Hypsipyle.* Oxford: Clarendon Press,
1963: 23–52, 157.

p. 23: fr. 752N.

pp. 23–24: fr. 61+82.

p. 24: frr. 70+96, 764N.

p. 25: frr. I.i, 2.

pp. 25–27: fr. I.ii.

pp. 27–28: fr. I.iii.

pp. 28–30: fr. I.iv.

p. 30: fr. 4.

pp. 30–32: fr. I.v.

p. 32: frr. 753N, 6, 7.

p. 33: fr. 8/9.

pp. 33–34: fr. 10.

p. 34: frr. 12+14, 11.

pp. 34–35: fr. 754N.

p. 35: fr. 32.

pp. 35–36: fr. 20/21.

p. 36: fr. 34/35.

pp. 36–37: fr. 18.

p. 37: frr. 19, 31+38, 33.

p. 38: frr. 36, 23, 24, 758N, 760N.

p. 39: frr. 27, 28.

pp. 39–44: frr. 22 et 60.

p. 44: fr. 63.

pp. 44–45: fr. 57.

pp. 45–46: fr. 58.

p. 46: frr. 59, 81.

pp. 46–48: fr. 64.

p. 48: fr. ap. Lydum.

p. 49: frr. 62, 76, 66.

p. 50: frr. 72, 73, 74.

p. 51: frr. 755N, 756N, 761N, 762N, 763N,
765N, 766N, 767N.

p. 52: frr. 769N, fragmenta dubia (a= 856N;
b= *P. Petrie* 2.49d).

p. 157: addendum (= *P. Hamb.* 118b).

Pap: 3,016: Trag.

027 **Fragmenta Phrixei** (*P. Oxy.* 34.2685), ed. J.
Rea, *The Oxyrhynchus papyri*, pt. 34. London:
Egypt Exploration Society, 1968: 10–13.

Pap: 137: Trag.

028 **Fragmenta fabulae incertae**, ed. Snell, *Hermes
Einzelschriften* 5, 79–82.

Pap: 633: Trag.

029 **Fragmenta**, ed. D.L. Page, *Select papyri*, vol. 3
[*Literary papyri*]. London: Heinemann, 1941
(repr. 1970): 54–70, 74–76, 82–108, 112–118,
122–134, 154–158.

frr. 8–18, 26–28 + tituli.

Pap: 4,858: Trag.

030 **Fragmenta Oenei**, ed. J. von Arnim, *Supplementum Euripideum.* Bonn: Marcus & Weber,
1913: 38, 39–40.

Pap: 77: Trag.

031 **Epigrammata**, AG 10.107, 107b.

Q: 28: Epigr.

032 **Fragmenta Phaethontis incertae sedis**, ed.
Diggle, *op. cit.*, 70–71.

frr. 3, 5, 6.

Cf. et 0006 023.

Q: 17: Trag.

033 **Fragmenta**, ed. B. Snell, *Tragicorum Graecorum fragmenta. Supplementum.* Hildesheim:
Olms, 1964: 3–20.

frr. 11a–c, 13a, *42a, **42b, *42c, 73a, 78a,
87a, **114a, **124.4, **125a(?), 155a, **164a,
179, 182a, 184.1, 185.4–5, *264a, 265a, 282a,
308.1, *312a, 330a, **330b, *360a, 369a–b,
379a, 386a, 397a, **426a, 447a, 472a, 477a,
539a, 554a, 556, 617a, 645a, 646a, 660a, 665a,
674a, 681a, *683a, 705a, 708a, 741a, 751a,
**790a, 799a, 813a, 838a, 845a, 860, 882a,
*889a, 898a, 908a, *908b, 913, 920a, 921.3,
925a–b, 926a, 929a, *941a, 942a, 944a, 954a,
955a–i, 989a, 1007a–f, 1007g(?), 1009a, 1024,
1043a, 1087, 1097a, 1098a, 1100a, 1110a,
1128a–b.

Q, Pap: 808: Trag., Satyr.

x01 **Epigrammata** (*App. Anth.*).
Epigrammata sepulcralia: 2.22–25.
Epigrammata demonstrativa: 3.27–28.
App. Anth. 2.22–25: Cf. ANTHOLOGIAE
GRAECAE APPENDIX (7052 002).
App. Anth. 3.27–28: Cf. ANTHOLOGIAE
GRAECAE APPENDIX (7052 003).

1840 **EURIPIDES II** Trag.
5 B.C.
001 **Tituli**, ed. B. Snell, *Tragicorum Graecorum
fragmenta*, vol. 1. Göttingen: Vandenhoeck &
Ruprecht, 1971: 94.
NQ: 3: Trag.

1367 *EURIPIDIS EPISTULAE*
A.D. 2?
Cf. et EURIPIDES Trag. (0006).
001 **Epistulae**, ed. R. Hercher, *Epistolographi
Graeci*. Paris: Didot, 1873 (repr. Amsterdam:
Hakkert, 1965): 275–279.
Cod: 1,881: Epist.

1360 **<EURYPHAMUS>** Phil.
vel Euryphemos
3 B.C.: Metapontinus
001 **Fragmentum**, ed. H. Thesleff, *The Pythagorean
texts of the Hellenistic period*. Åbo: Åbo Akademi, 1965: 85–87.
Q: 728: Phil.

0895 **EURYPHON** Med.
5 B.C.: Cnidius
x01 **Fragmenta ap. Galenum**.
K17.1.886, 888 in CMG, vol. **5.10.2.2**, pp. 54,
55.
Cf. GALENUS Med. (0057 091).
x02 **Fragmentum ap. Anonymum Londinensem**.
Iatrica 4.31–40.
Cf. ANONYMUS LONDINENSIS Med. (0643
001).

1363 **EURYTUS** Lyr.
Incertum: Lacedaemonius
001 **Fragmentum**, ed. T. Bergk, *Poetae lyrici
Graeci*, vol. 3. Leipzig: Teubner, 1882: 639.
Q: [2]: Lyr.

1362 **<EURYTUS>** Phil.
vel Eurysus
3 B.C.: fort. Crotoniensis
001 **Fragmentum**, ed. H. Thesleff, *The Pythagorean
texts of the Hellenistic period*. Åbo: Åbo Akademi, 1965: 88.
Q: 167: Phil.
002 **Testimonia**, ed. H. Diels and W. Kranz, *Die
Fragmente der Vorsokratiker*, vol. 1, 6th edn.
Berlin: Weidmann, 1951 (repr. Dublin: 1966):
419–420.
test. 1–3.
NQ: 321: Test.

0896 **EUSCHEMUS** Med.
ante A.D. 2
x01 **Fragmentum ap. Galenum**.
K13.287.
Cf. GALENUS Med. (0057 076).

2146 **EUSEBIUS** Hist.
A.D. 3
001 **Testimonium**, FGrH #101: 2A:480.
NQ: 19: Test.
002 **Fragmenta**, FGrH #101: 2A:480–482.
Q: 576: Hist., Tact.

2640 **EUSEBIUS** Phil.
A.D. 4: Myndius
001 **Fragmenta**, ed. F.W.A. Mullach, *Fragmenta
philosophorum Graecorum*, vol. 3. Paris: Didot,
1881 (repr. Aalen: Scientia, 1968): 7–18.
frr. 1–63.
Q: 3,225: Phil.

4124 **EUSEBIUS** Scr. Eccl.
A.D. 4: Emesenus
001 **De arbitrio, voluntate Pauli et domini passione**
(fragmenta ap. Theodoretum, *Eranistes*), ed.
É.M. Buytaert, *L'héritage littéraire d'Eusèbe
d'Émèse* [*Bibliothèque du Muséon* 24. Louvain:
Bureaux du Muséon, 1949]: 9*–15*.
Q: Homilet.
003 **Homilia de paenitentia** (olim sub auctore Basilio), ed. Buytaert, *op. cit.*, 16*–29*.
Dup. BASILIUS Theol. (2040 060).
Cod: Homilet.
004 **Fragmenta in Octateuchum** (in catenis), ed. R.
Devreesse, *Les anciens commentateurs grecs de
l'Octateuque et des Rois* [*Studi e Testi* 201. Vatican City: Biblioteca Apostolica Vaticana,
1959]: 57–102.
Q: Exeget., Caten.
005 **Fragmenta in Reges** (in catenis), ed. Devreesse, *op. cit.*, 102–103.
Q: Exeget., Caten.
006 **Fragmenta in Octateuchum** (in catenis), ed.
Buytaert, *op. cit.*, 153*–154*.
frr. 1–3.
Q: Exeget., Caten.
007 **Fragmenta in epistulam ad Romanos** (in catenis), ed. K. Staab, *Pauluskommentar aus der
griechischen Kirche aus Katenenhandschriften
gesammelt*. Münster: Aschendorff, 1933: 46.
Q: 199: Exeget., Caten.
008 **Fragmenta in epistulam ad Galatas** (in catenis), ed. Staab, *op. cit.*, 46–52.
Q: 1,531: Exeget., Caten.
009 **Fragmentum in epistulam i ad Corinthios** (in
catenis) [Dub.], ed. Staab, *op. cit.*, 52.
Q: 68: Exeget., Caten.
012 **Fragmenta in Octateuchum** (in catenis) [Dub.],
ed. Buytaert, *op. cit.*, 157*–158*.
frr. 1–5.
Q: Exeget., Caten.

013 **Fragmentum in Isaiam** (in catenis) [Dub.], ed. Buytaert, *op. cit.*, 158*.
fr. 6.
Q: Exeget., Caten.

2720 **Pseudo-EUSEBIUS** Scr. Eccl.
A.D. 5/7: Alexandrinus
Vita: Cf. JOANNES Notarius Biogr. (3167 001).

001 **De jejunio** (sermo 1), MPG 86.1: 313–324.
Cod: Homilet.

002 **De caritate** (sermo 2), MPG 86.1: 324–328.
Cod: Homilet.

003 **De incarnatione domini** (sermo 3), MPG 86.1: 328–332.
Cod: Homilet.

004 **Quod qui infirmatur deo gratias agere debeat et in Job** (sermo 4), MPG 86.1: 332–341.
Cod: Homilet.

005 **De eo qui gratiam communicare possit non habenti et de presbyteris** (sermo 5) (e cod. Vat. gr. 1633), MPG 86.1: 341–349.
Dup. partim 2720 034.
Cod: Homilet.

006 **De iis qui laqueis impliciti pereunt** (sermo 6), MPG 86.1: 349–353.
Dup. partim 2720 037.
Cod: Homilet.

007 **De neomeniis et de sabbatis et de non observandis avium vocibus** (sermo 7), MPG 86.1: 353–357.
Cod: Homilet.

008 **De commemoratione sanctorum** (sermo 8), MPG 86.1: 357–361.
Cod: Homilet.

009 **De epulatione** (sermo 9), MPG 86.1: 364–365.
Cod: Homilet.

010 **De Christi nativitate** (sermo 10), MPG 86.1: 365–372.
Cod: Homilet.

011 **De baptismo** (sermo 11), MPG 86.1: 372–380.
Cod: Homilet.

012 **In illud:** *Tu es qui venturus es, an alium exspectamus?* (sermo 12), MPG 86.1: 380–384.
Cod: Homilet., Exeget.

013 **De adventu Joannis in infernum et de ibi inclusis** (sermo 13) (e cod. Vindob. theol. gr. 307), MPG 86.1: 509–525.
Dup. partim 2720 014.
Cod: Homilet.

014 **De adventu Joannis in infernum et de ibi inclusis** (sermo 13) (e cod. Vat. gr. 1633), MPG 86.1: 509–526.
Dup. partim 2720 013.
Cod: Homilet.

015 **De proditione Judae** (sermo 14) (e cod. Vindob. theol. gr. 307), MPG 86.1: 525–536.
Dup. partim 2720 016–017, 035.
Cod: Homilet.

016 **De proditione Judae** (sermo 14) (e cod. Vat. gr. 1633), MPG 86.2: 525–536.

Dup. partim 2720 015, 017, 035.
Cod: Homilet.

017 **De proditione Judae** (sermo 14) (e cod. Hierosol. Sab. 30), ed. Hippolytus Monachus, "Δύο λόγοι ἐπ᾽ ὀνόματι τοῦ ἁγ. Ἰωάννου τοῦ Χρυσοστόμου," Νέα Σιών 20 (1925) 752–755.
Dup. partim 2720 015–016, 035.
Cod: Homilet.

018 **In diabolum et Orcum** (sermo 15) (e cod. Vat. gr. 1633), MPG 86.1: 383–406.
Dup. partim 2720 019–020.
Cod: Homilet.

019 **In diabolum et Orcum** (sermo 15) (recensio altera) (e cod. Vindob. theol. gr. 307), MPG 86.1: 383–406.
Dup. partim 2720 018, 020.
Cod: Homilet.

020 **In diabolum et Orcum** (sermo 15) (recensio tertia) (e cod. Vindob. theol. gr. 284), MPG 86.1: 383–406.
Dup. partim 2720 018–019.
Cod: Homilet.

021 **De die dominica** (sermo 16), MPG 86.1: 413–421.
Dup. partim 2720 022–023.
Cod: Homilet.

022 **De die dominica** (sermo 16) (e codd. Paris. gr. 929 + 947) (olim sub auctore Joanne Chrysostomo), ed. F. Nau, "Sur diverses homélies pseudépigraphiques, sur les oeuvres attribuées à Eusèbe d'Alexandrie et sur un nouveau manuscrit de la chaîne *contra severianos*," *Revue de l'Orient chrétien* 13 (1908) 414–415.
Dup. partim 2720 021, 023.
Cod: Homilet.

023 **De die dominica** (sermo 16) (e cod. Paris. gr. 769), ed. Nau, *op. cit.*, 415–418.
Dup. partim 2720 021–022.
Cod: Homilet.

026 **De Christi passione** (sermo 17), MPG 62: 721–724.
Dup. partim 2720 036.
Cod: Homilet.

027 **De domini resurrectione** (sermo 18), MPG 61: 733–738.
Cod: Homilet.

028 **De domini ascensione** (sermo 19), MPG 64: 45–48.
Dup. partim 2720 038.
Cod: Homilet.

029 **In secundum adventum domini nostri** (sermo 20), MPG 61: 775–778.
Cod: Homilet.

030 **De eleemosyna et in divitem atque Lazarum** (sermo 21), MPG 86.1: 424–452.
Cod: Homilet.

031 **De astronomis** (sermo 22), MPG 86.1: 452–461.
Cod: Homilet.

032 **Fragmenta e sermonibus i–viii, xvi–xviii, xxii,** ed. K. Holl, *Fragmente vornicänischer Kirchenväter aus den Sacra Parallela herausgegeben*

[*Texte und Untersuchungen*, N.F. 5.2. Leipzig: Hinrichs, 1899]: 214–233.
frr. 474–501.
Dup. partim 2720 001–008, 021–023, 026–027, 031.
Cod: Homilet.

034 **De eo qui gratiam communicare possit non habenti et de presbyteris** (sermo 5) (e cod. Vindob. theol. gr. 10), MPG 61: 783–786.
Dup. partim 2720 005.
Cod: Homilet.

035 **De proditione Judae** (sermo 14) (e cod. Hierosol. Sab. 259), ed. J. Zellinger, *Studien zu Severian von Gabala* [*Münsterische Beiträge zur Theologie* 8. Münster: Aschendorff, 1926]: 142–145.
Dup. partim 2720 015–017.
Cod: Homilet.

036 **De Christi passione** (sermo 17) (*P. Lit. Lond.* 245), ed. M. Gronewald, "Kein durchtriebener Räuber (P. Lit. Lond. 245 = Ps. Eusebius, Sermo 17)," *Zeitschrift für Papyrologie und Epigraphik* 34 (1979) 24–25.
Dup. partim 2720 026.
Pap: Homilet.

037 **De iis qui laqueis impliciti pereunt** (sermo 6) (fragmenta recensionis ap. Niconem Nigri Montis) (e codd. Coislin. 37, mss. gr. 879 + 880), ed. Nau, *op. cit.*, 411–412.
Dup. partim 2720 006.
Q: Homilet.

038 **De domini ascensione** (sermo 19) (e cod. Athon. Causocalyb. 6) (sub auctore Cyrillo Alexandrino), ed. C. Papadopoulos, "Λόγος εἰς τὴν ἀνάληψιν τοῦ κυρίου ἀνέκδοτος ἐπ' ὀνόματι Κυρίλλου 'Αλεξανδρείας" in Εἰς μνήμην Σπυρίδωνος Λάμπρου. Athens: Hestia, 1935: 39–41.
Dup. partim 2720 028.
Cod: Homilet.

2018 **EUSEBIUS** Scr. Eccl. et Theol.
A.D. 4: Caesariensis
Scholia: Cf. SCHOLIA IN EUSEBIUM (5049).

001 **Praeparatio evangelica**, ed. K. Mras, *Eusebius Werke, Band 8: Die Praeparatio evangelica* [*Die griechischen christlichen Schriftsteller* 43.1 & 43.2. Berlin: Akademie-Verlag, 43.1:1954; 43.2:1956]: **43.1**:3–613; **43.2**:3–426.
Cod: 241,486: Apol.

002 **Historia ecclesiastica**, ed. G. Bardy, *Eusèbe de Césarée. Histoire ecclésiastique*, 3 vols. [*Sources chrétiennes* 31, 41, 55. Paris: Cerf, 1:1952; 2:1955; 3:1958 (repr. 3:1967)]: **1**:3–215; **2**:4–231; **3**:3–120.
Cod: 102,980: Hist., Eccl.

003 **De martyribus Palaestinae** (recensio brevior), ed. Bardy, *op. cit.*, vol. 3, 121–174.
Cod: 8,099: Hagiogr.

004 **De martyribus Palaestinae** (recensio prolixior), ed. Bardy, *op. cit.*, vol. 3, 128–138, 140–142, 153–167.
Cod: 4,485: Hagiogr.

005 **Demonstratio evangelica**, ed. I.A. Heikel, *Eusebius Werke, Band 6: Die Demonstratio evangelica* [*Die griechischen christlichen Schriftsteller* 23. Leipzig: Hinrichs, 1913]: 1–492.
Cod: 161,238: Apol.

006 **Demonstratio evangelica** (fragmenta libri xv), ed. Heikel, *GCS* 23, 493–496.
Cod: 935: Apol.

007 **Contra Marcellum**, ed. E. Klostermann and G.C. Hansen, *Eusebius Werke, Band 4: Gegen Marcell. Über die kirchliche Theologie. Die Fragmente Marcells* [*Die griechischen christlichen Schriftsteller* 14, 2nd edn. Berlin: Akademie-Verlag, 1972]: 1–58.
Cod: 18,255: Theol.

008 **Epistula ad Flacillum**, ed. Klostermann and Hansen, *op. cit.*, 60.
Cod: 186: Epist.

009 **De ecclesiastica theologia**, ed. Klostermann and Hansen, *op. cit.*, 61–182.
Cod: 42,089: Theol.

010 **De theophania** (fragmenta), ed. H. Gressmann, *Eusebius Werke, Band 3.2: Die Theophanie* [*Die griechischen christlichen Schriftsteller* 11.2. Leipzig: Hinrichs, 1904]: 3*–35*.
Cod: 8,802: Apol.

011 **Onomasticon**, ed. E. Klostermann, *Eusebius Werke, Band 3.1: Das Onomastikon* [*Die griechischen christlichen Schriftsteller* 11.1. Leipzig: Hinrichs, 1904]: 2–176.
Cod: 18,382: Lexicogr., Geogr.

012 **In cantica canticorum interpretatio**, ed. J.B. Pitra, *Analecta sacra spicilegio Solesmensi parata*, vol. 3. Venice: St. Lazarus Monastery, 1883: 530–537.
Cod: 1,650: Exeget.

013 **Epistula ad Carpianum ad canones evangeliorum praemissa**, ed. E. Nestle, *Novum Testamentum Graece*, 25th edn. London: United Bible Societies, 1963 (repr. 1971): 32*–33*.
Cod: 383: Epist.

014 **Epistula ad Caesarienses**, ed. H.G. Opitz, *Athanasius Werke*, vol. 2.1. Berlin: De Gruyter, 1935: 28–31.
Q: 1,219: Epist.

015 **Epistula ad Alexandrum Alexandrinum**, ed. Opitz, *op. cit.*, vol. 3.1 (1934): 14–15.
Q: 253: Epist.

016 **Epistula ad Euphrationem**, ed. Opitz, *op. cit.*, vol. 3.1, 4–6.
Q: 300: Epist.

017 **Contra Hieroclem**, ed. C.L. Kayser, *Flavii Philostrati opera*, vol. 1. Leipzig: Teubner, 1870 (repr. Hildesheim: Olms, 1964): 369–413.
Cod: 10,823: Apol.

018 **De mensuris et ponderibus** (fragmenta), ed. F. Hultsch, *Metrologicorum scriptorum reliquiae*, vol. 1. Leipzig: Teubner, 1864 (repr. Stuttgart: 1971): 276–278.
Cod: 378: Metrolog.

019 **Commentarius in Isaiam**, ed. J. Ziegler, *Eusebius Werke, Band 9: Der Jesajakommentar* [*Die griechischen christlichen Schriftsteller*. Berlin: Akademie-Verlag, 1975]: 3–411.
Cod: 161,118: Exeget.

020 **Vita Constantini**, ed. F. Winkelmann, *Eusebius Werke, Band 1.1: Über das Leben des Kaisers Konstantin* [*Die griechischen christlichen Schriftsteller*. Berlin: Akademie-Verlag, 1975]: 3–151.
Cod: 39,170: Biogr., Encom.

021 **Constantini imperatoris oratio ad coetum sanctorum**, ed. I.A. Heikel, *Eusebius Werke, Band 1: Über das Leben Constantins. Constantins Rede an die heilige Versammlung. Tricennatsrede an Constantin* [*Die griechischen christlichen Schriftsteller* 7. Leipzig: Hinrichs, 1902]: 151–192.
= Vita Constantini lib. 4 (appendix) vel lib. 5.
Cod: 12,021: Apol., Exeget., Hexametr.

022 **De laudibus Constantini**, ed. Heikel, *GCS* 7, 195–259.
Cod: 20,162: Apol., Encom.

023 **Generalis elementaria introductio** (= **Eclogae propheticae**), ed. T. Gaisford, *Eusebii Pamphili episcopi Caesariensis eclogae propheticae*. Oxford: Oxford University Press, 1842: 1–236.
Cod: 53,621: Apol.

024 **Generalis elementaria introductio** (fragmenta), ed. K. Holl, *Fragmente vornicänischer Kirchenväter aus den Sacra Parallela* [*Texte und Untersuchungen* 20. Leipzig: Hinrichs, 1899]: 121, 213–214.
Q: 263: Apol.

025 **Antiquorum martyriorum collectio** (fragmenta), MPG 20: 1520–1533.
Cod: 3,045: Hagiogr.

026 **Passio sanctorum decem martyrum Aegyptiorum** (fragmenta), MPG 20: 1533–1536.
Cod: 441: Hagiogr.

027 **Epistula ad Constantiam Augustam**, MPG 20: 1545–1549.
Q: 829: Epist.

028 **Quaestiones evangelicae ad Stephanum**, MPG 22: 880–936.
Cod: 11,826: Exeget.

029 **Quaestiones evangelicae ad Marinum**, MPG 22: 937–957.
Cod: 3,924: Exeget.

030 **Supplementa ad quaestiones ad Stephanum**, MPG 22: 957–976.
Q: 3,594: Exeget.

031 **Supplementa ad quaestiones ad Marinum**, MPG 22: 984–1005.
Q: 5,215: Exeget.

032 **Supplementa minora ad quaestiones ad Marinum**, MPG 22: 1008–1016.
Q: 1,458: Exeget.

033 **De vitis prophetarum** (fragmenta), MPG 22: 1261–1272.
Cod: 1,720: Hagiogr.

034 **Commentaria in Psalmos**: MPG 23:66–1396; 24:9–76.
Cod: 311,746: Exeget.

035 **Fragmenta in proverbia**, MPG 24: 76–78.
Q: 94: Exeget.

036 **Fragmenta in Danielem**, MPG 24: 525–528.
Q: 554: Exeget.

037 **Fragmenta in Lucam**, MPG 24: 529–605.
Q: 16,330: Exeget.

038 **Fragmenta in Hebraeos**, MPG 24: 605.
Q: 81: Exeget.

039 **De solemnitate paschali**, MPG 24: 693–706.
Q: 2,545: Theol.

040 **Chronicon**, ed. A. Schöne, *Eusebi chronicorum canonum quae supersunt*, 2 vols. Berlin: Weidmann, 1:1875; 2:1866 (repr. 1967): 1:2–286; 2:4–190.
Cod: Chronogr.

2717 **EUSTATHIUS** Epigr.
A.D. 11: Iconiensis

x01 **Epigramma exhortatorium et supplicatorium**.
App. Anth. 4.116: Cf. ANTHOLOGIAE GRAECAE APPENDIX (7052 004).

2637 **EUSTATHIUS** Hist.
A.D. 5–6: Epiphaniensis

001 **Fragmenta**, ed. L. Dindorf, *Historici Graeci minores*, vol. 1. Leipzig: Teubner, 1870: 354–363.
Q

4083 **EUSTATHIUS** Philol. et Scr. Eccl.
A.D. 12: Thessalonicensis

001 **Commentarii ad Homeri Iliadem**, ed. M. van der Valk, *Eustathii archiepiscopi Thessalonicensis commentarii ad Homeri Iliadem pertinentes*, vols. 1–4. Leiden: Brill, 1:1971; 2:1976; 3:1979; 4:1987: 1:1–802; 2:1–838; 3:1–944; 4:1–991.
vol. 1 = Lib. A–Δ.
vol. 2 = Lib. E–I.
vol. 3 = Lib. K–Π.
vol. 4 = Lib. P–Ω.
Cod: 820,814: Comm.

002 **Commentarii ad Homeri Iliadem** (lib. Σ–Ω), ed. G. Stallbaum, *Eustathii archiepiscopi Thessalonicensis commentarii ad Homeri Iliadem*, vol. 4. Leipzig: Weigel, 1830 (repr. Hildesheim: Olms, 1970): 47–386.
Text to be replaced by van der Valk edition (cf. 4083 001).
Cod: 246,524: Comm.

003 **Commentarii ad Homeri Odysseam**, ed. G. Stallbaum, *Eustathii archiepiscopi Thessalonicensis commentarii ad Homeri Odysseam*, 2 vols. in 1. Leipzig: Weigel, 1:1825; 2:1826 (repr. Hildesheim: Olms, 1970): 1:1–443; 2:1–334.
Cod: 566,007: Comm.

005 **Prooemium commentarii in Pindari opera**, ed.

A.B. Drachmann, *Scholia vetera in Pindari carmina*, vol. 3. Leipzig: Teubner, 1927 (repr. Amsterdam: Hakkert, 1966): 285-306.
Cod: Comm.

006 **Commentarium in Dionysii periegetae orbis descriptionem**, ed. K. Müller, *Geographi Graeci minores*, vol. 2. Paris: Didot, 1861 (repr. Hildesheim: Olms, 1965): 201-407.
Cod: Comm.

x01 **Scholia in Aristophanis nubes.**
Cf. SCHOLIA IN ARISTOPHANEM (5014 005).

2810 **EUSTATHIUS** Theol.
A.D. 6: Constantinopolitanus
001 **Epistula de duabus naturis**, MPG 86.1: 901-942.
Q: Epist., Theol.

2499 **EUSTOCHIUS** Soph.
A.D. 4: Cappadox
001 **Testimonium**, FGrH #738: 3C:713-714.
NQ: 18: Test.
002 **Fragmentum**, FGrH #738: 3C:714.
Q: 56: Hist.

4031 **EUSTRATIUS** Phil.
A.D. 11-12: Nicaeensis
001 **In Aristotelis analyticorum posteriorum librum secundum commentarium**, ed. M. Hayduck, *Eustratii in analyticorum posteriorum librum secundum commentarium* [*Commentaria in Aristotelem Graeca* 21.1. Berlin: Reimer, 1907]: 1-270.
Cod: 108,899: Phil., Comm.
002 **In Aristotelis ethica Nicomachea i commentaria**, ed. G. Heylbut, *Eustratii et Michaelis et anonyma in ethica Nicomachea commentaria* [*Commentaria in Aristotelem Graeca* 20. Berlin: Reimer, 1892]: 1-121.
Cod: 46,390: Phil., Comm.
003 **In Aristotelis ethica Nicomachea vi commentaria**, ed. Heylbut, *op. cit.*, 256-406.
Cod: 61,730: Phil., Comm.

0752 **EUTECNIUS** Soph.
vel Eutechnius
A.D. 3/10
001 **Paraphrasis in Nicandri theriaca**, ed. I. Gualandri, *Eutecnii paraphrasis in Nicandri theriaca*. Milan: Istituto Editoriale Cisalpino, 1968: 21-70.
Cod: 12,857: Med., Nat. Hist., Comm.
002 **Paraphrasis in Nicandri alexipharmaca**, ed. M. Geymonat, *Eutecnii paraphrasis in Nicandri alexipharmaca*. Milan: Istituto Editoriale Cisalpino, 1976: 25-58.
Cod: Med., Nat. Hist., Comm.
003 **Paraphrasis in Oppiani cynegetica** (fort. auctore Eutecnio), ed. O. Tüselmann, *Die Paraphrase des Euteknios zu Oppians Kynegetika* [*Abhandlungen der königlichen Gesellschaft der*

Wissenschaften zu Göttingen, Philol.-hist. Kl., N.F. 4.1. Berlin: Weidmann, 1900]: 8-43.
Cod: Comm., Nat. Hist.

005 **Paraphrasis in Oppiani halieutica** (fort. auctore Eutecnio), ed. M. Papathomopoulos, Ἀνωνύμου παράφρασις εἰς τὰ Ὀππιανοῦ Ἁλιευτικά. Joannina: University of Joannina Press, 1976: 1-29.
Cod: Nat. Hist., Comm.

x01 **Paraphrasis in Oppiani ixeutica** (olim sub auctore Eutecnio).
Garzya, pp. 1-49.
Cf. DIONYSIUS Perieg. (0084 003).

0462 **EUTHYCLES** Comic.
5/4 B.C.?
001 **Fragmenta**, ed. T. Kock, *Comicorum Atticorum fragmenta*, vol. 1. Leipzig: Teubner, 1880: 805.
frr. 1-4.
Q: 23: Comic.
002 **Fragmenta**, ed. A. Meineke, *Fragmenta comicorum Graecorum*, vol. 2.2. Berlin: Reimer, 1840 (repr. De Gruyter, 1970): 890.
Q: 19: Comic.

0897 **EUTHYDEMUS** Med.
2 B.C.: Atheniensis
001 **Fragmentum**, ed. H. Lloyd-Jones and P. Parsons, *Supplementum Hellenisticum*. Berlin: De Gruyter, 1983: 233-234.
fr. 455.
Q: 92: Hexametr., Coq.
x01 **Fragmentum ap. Athenaeum.**
Deipnosophistae 7.315f.
Cf. ATHENAEUS Soph. (0008 001).

2170 **EUTHYMENES** Hist.
2 B.C.?
001 **Fragmentum**, FGrH #243: 2B:1021-1022.
Q: 43: Hist., Chronogr.

4072 **EUTOCIUS** Math.
A.D. 5-6: Ascalonius
001 **Commentarii in libros de sphaera et cylindro**, ed. J.L. Heiberg and E. Stamatis, *Archimedis opera omnia cum commentariis Eutocii*, vol. 3. Leipzig: Teubner, 1915 (repr. Stuttgart: 1972): 2-224.
Cod: Math., Comm.
002 **Commentarius in dimensionem circuli**, ed. Heiberg and Stamatis, *op. cit.*, 228-260.
Cod: Math., Comm.
003 **Commentarius in libros de planorum aequilibriis**, ed. Heiberg and Stamatis, *op. cit.*, 264-318.
Cod: Math., Comm.
004 **Commentaria in conica**, ed. J.L. Heiberg, *Apollonii Pergaei quae Graece exstant*, vol. 2. Leipzig: Teubner, 1893 (repr. Stuttgart: 1974): 168-360.
Cod: Math., Comm.

4068 **EUTOLMIUS** Epigr.
A.D. 4
001 **Epigrammata**, AG **6**.86; **7**.608, 611; **9**.587.
Q: 81: Epigr.

0898 **EUTONIUS** Med.
ante A.D. 4
x01 **Fragmentum ap. Oribasium.**
CMG, vol. 6.3, p. 93.
Cf. ORIBASIUS Med. (0722 004).

2236 **EUTROPIUS** Hist.
A.D. 4
001 **Breviarium ab urbe condita** (Paeanii translatio), ed. S.P. Lambros, "Παιανίου μετάφρασις
εἰς τὴν τοῦ Εὐτροπίου Ῥωμαϊκὴν ἱστορίαν,"
Νέος Ἑλληνομνήμων 9 (1912) 9–113.
Cod: 25,695: Hist.

2158 **EUTYCHIANUS** Hist.
A.D. 4: Cappadox
001 **Fragmentum**, FGrH #226: 2B:954.
Q: 206: Hist.

0899 **EUTYCHIANUS** Med.
ante A.D. 4
x01 **Fragmentum ap. Oribasium.**
CMG, vol. 6.2.2, p. 272.
Cf. ORIBASIUS Med. (0722 005).

4110 **EVAGRIUS** Scr. Eccl.
A.D. 4: Ponticus
001 **Practicus**, ed. A. Guillaumont and C. Guillau-
mont, *Évagre le Pontique. Traité pratique ou le
moine*, vol. 2 [*Sources chrétiennes* 171. Paris:
Cerf, 1971]: 482–712.
Q
010 **Sententiae ad monachos**, ed. H. Gressmann,
*Nonnenspiegel und Mönchsspiegel des Euagrios
Pontikos* [*Texte und Untersuchungen* 39.4.
Leipzig: Hinrichs, 1913]: 152–165.
Q
011 **Ad virginem**, ed. Gressmann, *op. cit.*, 146–151.
Q

2733 **EVAGRIUS** Scholasticus Scr. Eccl.
A.D. 6: Epiphaniensis (Syriae), Antiochenus
001 **Historia ecclesiastica**, ed. J. Bidez and L. Parmentier, *The ecclesiastical history of Evagrius
with the scholia*. London: Methuen, 1898 (repr.
New York: AMS Press, 1979): 5–241.
Cod: 55,947: Hist., Eccl.

1364 *EVANGELIUM AEGYPTIUM*
A.D. 2
001 **Evangelium Aegyptium**, ed. E. Klostermann,
Apocrypha II. Evangelien, 2nd edn. [*Kleine
Texte* 8. Bonn: Marcus & Weber, 1910]: 12–13.
Cod: 211: Evangel., Apocryph.
x01 **Fragmenta.**
P. Oxy. 2.210; 4.655.

Cf. FRAGMENTA EVANGELIORUM INCER-
TORUM (1378 005, 007).

*EVANGELIUM APOCRYPHUM SECUN-
DUM MATTHIAM*
Cf. MATTHIAE TRADITIONES (1560).

1366 *EVANGELIUM BARTHOLOMAEI*
A.D. 3
001 **Evangelium Bartholomaei**, ed. N. Bonwetsch,
"Die apokryphen Fragen des Bartholomäus,"
*Nachrichten von der Gesellschaft der Wissen-
schaften zu Göttingen*, Philol.-hist. Kl (1897)
9–29.
Cod: 4,156: Evangel., Apocryph.
002 **Fragmenta evangelii Bartholomaei**, ed. A. Wil-
mart and E. Tisserant, "Fragments grecs et
latins de l'Évangile de Barthélemy," *Revue
Biblique* 10 (1913) 185–190, 321–333.
Cod: 2,462: Evangel., Apocryph.

1368 *EVANGELIUM EBIONITUM*
A.D. 2/3
Cf. et EVANGELIUM SECUNDUM HE-
BRAEOS (1374).
001 **Evangelium Ebionitum**, ed. E. Klostermann,
Apocrypha II. Evangelien, 2nd edn. [*Kleine
Texte* 8. Bonn: Marcus & Weber, 1910]: 9–12.
Q: 539: Evangel., Apocryph.

1372 *EVANGELIUM EVAE*
ante A.D. 4
001 **Evangelium Evae**, ed. E. Klostermann, *Apocrypha II. Evangelien*, 2nd edn. [*Kleine Texte* 8.
Bonn: Marcus & Weber, 1910]: 15.
Q: 143: Evangel., Apocryph.

1369 *EVANGELIUM MARIAE*
ante A.D. 3?
001 **Evangelium Mariae**, ed. E. Preuschen, *Antilegomena*, 2nd edn. Giessen: Töpelmann, 1905:
82–83.
Q: 175: Evangel., Apocryph.
002 **Fragmentum**, *P. Ryl.* 3.463.
Pap: Evangel., Apocryph.

1370 *EVANGELIUM NAASSENUM*
A.D. 1/2?
001 **Sermo Naassenorum** (fragmenta), ed. W.
Völker, *Quellen zur Geschichte der christlichen
Gnosis*. Tübingen: Mohr, 1932: 11–25.
Q: Evangel., Apocryph.

1371 *EVANGELIUM PETRI*
A.D. 2
001 **Evangelium Petri**, ed. M.G. Mara, *Évangile de
Pierre* [*Sources chrétiennes* 201. Paris: Cerf,
1973]: 40–66.
Cod: Evangel., Apocryph.

1373 *EVANGELIUM PHILIPPI*
A.D. 2/3?

001 **Evangelium Philippi**, ed. E. Klostermann, *Apocrypha II. Evangelien*, 2nd edn. [*Kleine Texte* 8. Bonn: Marcus & Weber, 1910]: 15.
Q: 104: Evangel., Apocryph.

1374 *EVANGELIUM SECUNDUM HEBRAEOS*
A.D. 1/2
Cf. et EVANGELIUM EBIONITUM (1368).
001 **Evangelium secundum Hebraeos**, ed. E. Klostermann, *Apocrypha II. Evangelien*, 2nd edn. [*Kleine Texte* 8. Bonn: Marcus & Weber, 1910]: 5-9.
frr. 5-6, 9-10, 15-16, 22, 27.
Q: 313: Evangel., Apocryph.

1375 *EVANGELIUM THOMAE*
A.D. 2?
001 **Evangelium Thomae**, ed. E. Klostermann, *Apocrypha II. Evangelien*, 2nd edn. [*Kleine Texte* 8. Bonn: Marcus & Weber, 1910]: 13.
Q: 101: Evangel., Apocryph.
x01 **Evangelium Thomae** (fragmenta).
P. Oxy. 1.1; 4.654, 655.
Cf. FRAGMENTA EVANGELIORUM INCERTORUM (1378 004, 006-007).

0343 **EZECHIEL** Trag.
2 B.C.: fort. Alexandrinus
001 Ἐξαγωγή, ed. B. Snell, *Tragicorum Graecorum fragmenta*, vol. 1. Göttingen: Vandenhoeck & Ruprecht, 1971: 288-301.
Q: 1,661: Trag.

1968 **FABIUS CERYLLIANUS** Hist.
A.D. 3-4?
001 **Fragmentum**, FGrH #217: 2B:947.
Q: 72: Hist.

2542 **Quintus FABIUS PICTOR** Hist.
3 B.C.: Romanus
001 **Testimonia**, FGrH #809: 3C:845-848.
NQ: 1,352: Test.
002 **Fragmenta**, FGrH #809: 3C:849-876.
Q: 10,706: Hist.

1377 **FAVORINUS** Phil. et Rhet.
A.D. 2: Arelatensis
001 **Fragmenta**, ed. E. Mensching, *Favorin von Arelate*, vol. 1 [*Texte und Kommentare. Eine altertumswissenschaftliche Reihe*, vol. 3. Berlin: De Gruyter, 1963]: 65-67, 69, 71, 73-75, 77, 80-81, 84, 88-89, 91-92, 94, 97-101, 103, 110, 114-116, 118-122, 124-127, 130-131, 133, 138-142, 144-147, 150-154.
frr. 1-21: Memorabilia.
frr. 22-51a: Omnigena historia.
frr. 51-66: Memorabilia vel Omnigena historia.
fr. 67: Epitome (Omnigena historia?).
Dup. partim 1377 003.
Q: 2,492: Polyhist.
002 **De fuga** (*P. Vat. Gr.* 11), ed. M. Norsa and G.

Vitelli, *Il papiro Vaticano greco 11* [*Studi e Testi* 53. Vatican City: Biblioteca Apostolica Vaticana, 1931]: 17-32.
Dup. partim 1377 003.
Pap: 8,582: Phil.
003 **Fragmenta**, ed. A. Barigazzi, *Favorino di Arelate. Opere*. Florence: Monnier, 1966: 152-161, 163-166, 171, 174, 179-186, 190-191, 193-194, 196-207, 216-219, 221-239, 241, 375-409, 525-526, 528-551.
fr. 7: Περὶ τῆς δημώδους σωφροσύνης.
fr. 8: Περὶ εὐχῆς.
frr. 9-17: Περὶ γήρως.
frr. 18-21: Περὶ Σωκράτους καὶ τῆς κατ᾿ αὐτὸν ἐρωτικῆς τέχνης.
fr. 25: Περὶ ἰδεῶν.
fr. 27: Πυρρωνείων τρόπων ιʹ.
fr. 28: Plutarchus sive de Academiae ratione.
fr. 29: Περὶ τῆς καταληπτικῆς φαντασίας.
fr. 30: Ad Epictetum.
fr. 31: Alcibiades.
frr. 32-51: Memorabilia.
frr. 53-93: Omnigena historia.
fr. 96: De fuga (*P. Vat. Gr.* 11).
frr. 97-141: Fragmenta incertae sedis.
Dup. partim 1377 001-002.
Q, Pap: 15,896: Phil., Polyhist.
x01 **De fortuna**.
von Arnim, vol. 2, pp. 147-155 (orat. 64).
Cf. DIO CHRYSOSTOMUS Soph. (0612 001).
x02 **Corinthiaca**.
von Arnim, vol. 2, pp. 17-29 (orat. 37).
Cf. DIO CHRYSOSTOMUS Soph. (0612 001).

0901 **FLAVIANUS** Med.
ante A.D. 2: Cretensis
x01 **Fragmentum ap. Galenum**.
K13.72.
Cf. GALENUS Med. (0057 076).

0902 **FLAVIUS** Med.
ante A.D. 2
x01 **Fragmentum ap. Galenum**.
K13.294.
Cf. GALENUS Med. (0057 076).

4148 *FLORILEGIUM ANTICHALCEDONIUM*
A.D. 5
001 **Florilegium** (cod. Vat. gr. 1431), ed. E. Schwartz, *Codex Vaticanus gr. 1431, eine antichalkedonische Sammlung aus der Zeit Kaiser Zenos* [*Abhandlungen der bayerischen Akademie der Wissenschaften*, Philosoph.-philol. und hist. Kl., Bd. 32, Abh. 6. Munich: Oldenbourg, 1927]: 13-62.
Cod: Anthol., Exeget.

4147 *FLORILEGIUM CYRILLIANUM*
post A.D. 6
001 **Florilegium Cyrillianum**, ed. R. Hespel, *Le florilège cyrillien réfuté par Sévère d'Antioche*

[*Bibliothèque du Muséon* 37. Louvain: Université de Louvain, 1955]: 103–208.
frr. 1–230.
Cod: 25,491: Anthol., Exeget.

2646 *FRAGMENTA ADESPOTA* (SH)
Varia
001 **Frustula adespota ex auctoribus**, ed. H. Lloyd-Jones and P. Parsons, *Supplementum Hellenisticum*. Berlin: De Gruyter, 1983: 517–561, 863.
frr. 1000–1185, 1134a.
Q: 844: Hexametr., Eleg., Iamb.

1817 *FRAGMENTA ANONYMA* (PsVTGr)
Varia
001 **Fragmenta**, ed. A.-M. Denis, *Fragmenta pseudepigraphorum quae supersunt Graeca* [*Pseudepigrapha veteris testamenti Graece* 3. Leiden: Brill, 1970]: 229–238.
Q, Pap: 1,784: Pseudepigr.

1378 *FRAGMENTA EVANGELIORUM INCERTORUM*
ante A.D. 3
Cf. et AGRAPHA (1776).
001 **Fragmenta**, *P. Cairo* 10735.
Pap: Evangel., Apocryph.
002 **Fragmenta**, *P. Egerton* 2.
Pap: Evangel., Apocryph.
003 **Fragmentum** (*P. Rain.*), ed. G. Bickell, "Das nichtkanonische Evangelienfragment," *Mittheilungen aus der Sammlung der Papyrus Erzherzog Rainer* 1 (Vienna, 1887): 54.
Pap: Evangel., Apocryph.
004 **Logia Jesu** (fragmenta) (*P. Oxy.* 1.1), ed. B.P. Grenfell and A.S. Hunt, *The Oxyrhynchus papyri*, pt. 1. London: Egypt Exploration Fund, 1898: 3.
Cf. et 1378 006.
Cf. et AGRAPHA (1776 001).
Pap: Evangel., Apocryph.
005 **Fragmenta** (*P. Oxy.* 2.210), ed. Grenfell and Hunt, *op. cit.*, pt. 2 (1899): 10.
Pap: Evangel., Apocryph.
006 **Logia Jesu** (fragmenta) (*P. Oxy.* 4.654), ed. Grenfell and Hunt, *op. cit.*, pt. 4 (1904): 3–6, 8–9.
Cf. et 1378 004.
Cf. et AGRAPHA (1776 001).
Pap: Evangel., Apocryph.
007 **Fragmentum evangelii apocryphi** (*P. Oxy.* 4.655), ed. Grenfell and Hunt, *op. cit.*, pt. 4, 24.
Pap: Evangel., Apocryph.
008 **Fragmentum evangelii apocryphi** (*P. Oxy.* 5.840), ed. Grenfell and Hunt, *op. cit.*, pt. 5 (1908): 6–7.
Pap: Evangel., Apocryph.
009 **Fragmentum evangelii apocryphi** (*P. Oxy.* 10.1224), ed. Grenfell and Hunt, *op. cit.*, pt. 10 (1914): 6–9.
Pap: Evangel., Apocryph.

1379 *FRAGMENTUM ALCHEMICUM*
ante A.D. 2
001 **Fragmentum** (*P. Oxy.* 3.467), ed. B.P. Grenfell and A.S. Hunt, *The Oxyrhynchus papyri*, pt. 3. London: Egypt Exploration Fund, 1903: 138–139.
Pap: Alchem.

2287 *FRAGMENTUM STOICUM*
Incertum
001 **Fragmentum**, ed. J. von Arnim, *Stoicorum veterum fragmenta*, vol. 1. Leipzig: Teubner, 1905 (repr. Stuttgart: 1968): 142.
Q: 29: Phil.

1381 *FRAGMENTUM SYNODICAE EPISTULAE CONCILII CAESARIENSIS*
A.D. 2
001 **Fragmentum epistulae**, ed. M.J. Routh, *Reliquiae sacrae*, vol. 2, 2nd edn. Oxford: Oxford University Press, 1846 (repr. Hildesheim: Olms, 1974): 3.
Q: 77: Epist.

1382 *FRAGMENTUM TELIAMBICUM*
ante A.D. 3
001 **Fragmentum teliambicum** (*P. Oxy.* 1.15), ed. D. Young (post E. Diehl), *Theognis*. Leipzig: Teubner, 1971: 122.
Dup. partim SCOLIA ALPHABETICA (0273 002).
Pap: 78: Hexametr., Lyr.

0186 **Marcus Cornelius FRONTO** Rhet.
A.D. 2: Numidianus
001 **Ad Marcum Caesarem et invicem** (lib. 1), ed. M.P.J. van den Hout, *M. Cornelii Frontonis epistulae*. Leiden: Brill, 1954 (repr. New York: Arno, 1975): 16–17, 20–23.
Herodi Attico (epist. 8): pp. 16–17.
Matri Caesaris (epist. 10): pp. 20–23.
Cod: 886: Epist.
002 **Ad Marcum Caesarem et invicem** (lib. 2), ed. van den Hout, *op. cit.*, 32–33.
Matri Caesaris (epist. 12).
Cod: 305: Epist.
003 **Ad amicos** (lib. 1), ed. van den Hout, *op. cit.*, 165.
Apollonidae (epist. 2).
Cod: 71: Epist.
004 **Additamentum epistularum variarum acephalum**, ed. van den Hout, *op. cit.*, 228–239.
Appiano (epist. 5): pp. 228–233.
Epistula acephala (epist. 8): pp. 234–239.
Cod: 2,308: Epist.
005 **Epigrammata**, AG 12.174, 233.
Q: 56: Epigr.
x01 **Epigramma demonstrativum**.
App. Anth. 3.125: Cf. ANTHOLOGIAE GRAECAE APPENDIX (7052 003).

4069 **GABRIELIUS** Epigr.
A.D. 6: Constantinopolitanus

001 **Epigramma**, AG 16.208.
Q: 14: Epigr.

0188 **GAETULICUS I** Epigr.
A.D. 1
001 **Epigrammata**, AG **5.**17; **6.**154, 190, 331; **7.**71,
244, 245(?), 275, 354.
Q: 332: Epigr.

0187 **GAETULICUS II** Epigr.
A.D. 1
001 **Epigramma**, AG 11.409.
Q: 37: Epigr.

0822 **GAIUS** Med.
ante A.D. 1: Neapolitanus
Cf. et ANONYMUS NEAPOLITANUS Med.
(1119).
Cf. et GAIUS Med. (0904).
x01 **Fragmentum ap. Galenum.**
K13.830.
Cf. GALENUS Med. (0057 077).

0904 **GAIUS** Med.
fiq Gaius Neapolitanus
ante A.D. 2
Cf. et GAIUS Med. (0822).
x01 **Fragmentum ap. Galenum.**
K12.771.
Cf. GALENUS Med. (0057 076).

0572 **GAIUS** Scr. Eccl.
vel Caius
A.D. 3: Romanus
001 **Fragmenta**, ed. M.J. Routh, *Reliquiae sacrae*,
vol. 2, 2nd edn. Oxford: Oxford University
Press, 1846 (repr. Hildesheim: Olms, 1974):
127–134.
Fragmenta ex dialogo vel disputatione cum
Proclo sive Proculo Montanista: pp. 127–128.
Fragmenta ex parvo labyrintho Caii vel anon-
ymi scriptoris: pp. 129–134.
Q: 1,064: Eccl., Dialog.

3039 **Joannes GALENUS** Gramm.
A.D. 12: Constantinopolitanus
001 **Allegoriae in Hesiodi theogoniam**, ed. H.
Flach, *Glossen und Scholien zur hesiodischen
Theogonie.* Leipzig: Teubner, 1876 (repr. Osna-
brück: Biblio Verlag, 1970): 295–365.
Cod: 20,301: Schol.
002 **Allegoriae in Homeri Iliadem 4.1–4**, ed. Flach,
op. cit., 420–424.
Cod: 1,282: Schol.
x01 **Scholia in Hesiodi opera et dies.**
Gaisford, pp. 23–447 passim.
Cf. SCHOLIA IN HESIODUM (5025 002).

0057 **GALENUS** Med.
vel Claudius Galenus
A.D. 2: Pergamenus
006 **De constitutione artis medicae ad Patrophi-
lum**, ed. C.G. Kühn, *Claudii Galeni opera*

omnia, vol. 1. Leipzig: Knobloch, 1821 (repr.
Hildesheim: Olms, 1964): 224–304.
Cod: 12,396: Med.
007 **Ars medica**, ed. Kühn, *op. cit.*, vol. 1, 305–412.
Cod: 16,776: Med.
011 **De anatomicis administrationibus libri ix**, ed.
Kühn, *op. cit.*, vol. 2 (1821; repr. 1964): 215–
731.
Cod: 81,247: Med.
012 **De ossibus ad tirones**, ed. Kühn, *op. cit.*, vol.
2, 732–778.
Cod: 7,165: Med.
013 **De venarum arteriarumque dissectione**, ed.
Kühn, *op. cit.*, vol. 2, 779–830.
Cod: 7,824: Med.
014 **De nervorum dissectione**, ed. Kühn, *op. cit.*,
vol. 2, 831–856.
Cod: 3,736: Med.
018 **De motu musculorum libri ii**, ed. Kühn, *op.
cit.*, vol. 4 (1822; repr. 1964): 367–464.
Cod: 15,264: Med.
114 **De causis respirationis**, ed. Kühn, *op. cit.*, vol.
4, 465–469.
Cod: 706: Med.
021 **De semine libri ii**, ed. Kühn, *op. cit.*, vol. 4,
512–651.
Cod: 21,557: Med.
022 **De foetuum formatione libellus**, ed. Kühn, *op.
cit.*, vol. 4, 652–702.
Cod: 8,011: Med.
084 **De substantia facultatum naturalium fragmentum (= De propriis placitis fragmentum)**, ed.
Kühn, *op. cit.*, vol. 4, 757–766.
Cf. et 0057 026.
Cod: 1,424: Med., Phil.
031 **De usu pulsuum**, ed. Kühn, *op. cit.*, vol. 5
(1823; repr. 1965): 149–180.
Cod: 4,655: Med.
040 **De dignotione ex insomniis**, ed. Kühn, *op. cit.*,
vol. 6 (1823; repr. 1965): 832–835.
Cod: 527: Med.
041 **De morborum differentiis**, ed. Kühn, *op. cit.*,
vol. 6, 836–880.
Cod: 6,905: Med.
042 **De causis morborum liber**, ed. Kühn, *op. cit.*,
vol. 7 (1824; repr. 1965): 1–41.
Cod: 6,336: Med.
043 **De symptomatum differentiis liber**, ed. Kühn,
op. cit., vol. 7, 42–84.
Cod: 6,857: Med.
044 **De symptomatum causis libri iii**, ed. Kühn, *op.
cit.*, vol. 7, 85–272.
Cod: 30,535: Med.
045 **De differentiis febrium libri ii**, ed. Kühn, *op.
cit.*, vol. 7, 273–405.
Cod: 21,703: Med.
048 **De typis liber**, ed. Kühn, *op. cit.*, vol. 7, 463–
474.
Cod: 1,651: Med.
049 **Adversos eos qui de typis scripserunt vel de
circuitibus**, ed. Kühn, *op. cit.*, vol. 7, 475–512.
Cod: 5,801: Med.

050 **De plenitudine liber,** ed. Kühn, *op. cit.*, vol. 7, 513–583.
Cod: 11,502: Med.

051 **De tremore, palpitatione, convulsione et rigore liber,** ed. Kühn, *op. cit.*, vol. 7, 584–642.
Cod: 9,451: Med.

053 **De marcore liber,** ed. Kühn, *op. cit.*, vol. 7, 666–704.
Cod: 6,018: Med.

055 **De inaequali intemperie liber,** ed. Kühn, *op. cit.*, vol. 7, 733–752.
Cod: 3,278: Med.

056 **De difficultate respirationis libri iii,** ed. Kühn, *op. cit.*, vol. 7, 753–960.
Cod: 33,093: Med.

057 **De locis affectis libri vi,** ed. Kühn, *op. cit.*, vol. 8 (1824; repr. 1965): 1–452.
Cod: 72,559: Med.

058 **De pulsibus libellus ad tirones,** ed. Kühn, *op. cit.*, vol. 8, 453–492.
Cod: 6,221: Med.

059 **De differentia pulsuum libri iv,** ed. Kühn, *op. cit.*, vol. 8, 493–765.
Cod: 44,391: Med.

060 **De dignoscendis pulsibus libri iv,** ed. Kühn, *op. cit.*, vol. 8, 766–961.
Cod: 32,375: Med.

061 **De causis pulsuum libri iv,** ed. Kühn, *op. cit.*, vol. 9 (1825; repr. 1965): 1–204.
Cod: 33,321: Med.

062 **De praesagitione ex pulsibus libri iv,** ed. Kühn, *op. cit.*, vol. 9, 205–430.
Cod: 37,699: Med.

063 **Synopsis librorum suorum de pulsibus,** ed. Kühn, *op. cit.*, vol. 9, 431–533.
Cod: 16,348: Med.

065 **De diebus decretoriis libri iii,** ed. Kühn, *op. cit.*, vol. 9, 769–941.
Cod: 28,286: Med.

066 **De methodo medendi libri xiv,** ed. Kühn, *op. cit.*, vol. 10 (1825; repr. 1965): 1–1021.
Cod: 163,139: Med.

067 **Ad Glauconem de medendi methodo libri ii,** ed. Kühn, *op. cit.*, vol. 11 (1826; repr. 1965): 1–146.
Cod: 23,690: Med.

068 **De venae sectione adversus Erasistratum,** ed. Kühn, *op. cit.*, vol. 11, 147–186.
Cod: 6,173: Med.

069 **De venae sectione adversus Erasistrateos Romae degentes,** ed. Kühn, *op. cit.*, vol. 11, 187–249.
Cod: 9,371: Med.

070 **De curandi ratione per venae sectionem,** ed. Kühn, *op. cit.*, vol. 11, 250–316.
Cod: 10,398: Med.

071 **De hirundinibus, revulsione, cucurbitula, incisione et scarificatione,** ed. Kühn, *op. cit.*, vol. 11, 317–322.
Cod: 726: Med.

075 **De simplicium medicamentorum temperamentis ac facultatibus libri xi,** ed. Kühn, *op. cit.*, vols. 11 & 12 (1826; repr. 1965): 11:379–892; 12:1–377.
Cod: 139,244: Med.

076 **De compositione medicamentorum secundum locos libri x,** ed. Kühn, *op. cit.*, vols. 12 & 13 (1827; repr. 1965): 12:378–1007; 13:1–361.
Cod: 150,524: Med.

077 **De compositione medicamentorum per genera libri vii,** ed. Kühn, *op. cit.*, vol. 13, 362–1058.
Cod: 109,210: Med.

078 **De antidotis libri ii,** ed. Kühn, *op. cit.*, vol. 14 (1827; repr. 1965): 1–209.
Cod: 28,945: Med.

079 **De theriaca ad Pisonem,** ed. Kühn, *op. cit.*, vol. 14, 210–294.
Cod: 13,556: Med.

083 **De praenotione ad Posthumum (Epigenem),** ed. Kühn, *op. cit.*, vol. 14, 599–673.
Cod: 11,530: Med.

092 **In Hippocratis aphorismos commentarii vii,** ed. Kühn, *op. cit.*, vols. 17.2 & 18.1 (1829; repr. 1965): 17.2:345–887; 18.1:1–195.
Cod: 102,970: Med., Comm.

095 **In Hippocratis librum de articulis et Galeni in eum commentarii iv,** ed. Kühn, *op. cit.*, vol. 18.1, 300–345, 423–767.
Cod: 55,499: Med., Comm.

096 **De humero iis modis prolapso quos Hippocrates non vidit,** ed. Kühn, *op. cit.*, vol. 18.1, 346–422.
Cod: 10,593: Med.

100 **In Hippocratis librum de fracturis commentarii iii,** ed. Kühn, *op. cit.*, vol. 18.2 (1830; repr. 1965): 318–628.
Cod: 44,698: Med., Comm.

101 **In Hippocratis librum de officina medici commentarii iii,** ed. Kühn, *op. cit.*, vol. 18.2, 629–925.
Cod: 43,376: Med., Comm.

102 **De musculorum dissectione ad tirones,** ed. Kühn, *op. cit.*, vol. 18.2, 926–1026.
Cod: 15,368: Med.

106 **Linguarum seu dictionum exoletarum Hippocratis explicatio,** ed. Kühn, *op. cit.*, vol. 19 (1830; repr. 1965): 62–157.
Cod: 9,956: Med., Lexicogr.

002 **De optima doctrina,** ed. J. Marquardt, *Claudii Galeni Pergameni scripta minora*, vol. 1. Leipzig: Teubner, 1884 (repr. Amsterdam: Hakkert, 1967): 82–92.
Cod: 1,916: Med.

103 **De consuetudinibus,** ed. J. Marquardt, I. Müller and G. Helmreich, *Claudii Galeni Pergameni scripta minora*, vol. 2. Leipzig: Teubner, 1891 (repr. Amsterdam: Hakkert, 1967): 9–31.
Cod: 4,181: Med.

027 **Quod animi mores corporis temperamenta sequantur,** ed. Marquardt, Müller, and Helmreich, *op. cit.*, vol. 2, 32–79.
Cod: 8,840: Med.

105 **De ordine librorum suorum ad Eugenianum**, ed. Marquardt, Müller, and Helmreich, *op. cit.*, vol. 2, 80–90.
Cod: 2,051: Med., Phil.

104 **De libris propriis liber**, ed. Marquardt, Müller, and Helmreich, *op. cit.*, vol. 2, 91–124.
Cod: 6,514: Med., Phil.

004 **De sectis ad eos qui introducuntur**, ed. Marquardt, Müller and Helmreich, *op. cit.*, vol. 3 (1893; repr. 1967): 1–32.
Cod: 6,494: Med.

033 **Thrasybulus sive utrum medicinae sit an gymnasticae hygieine**, ed. Marquardt, Müller, and Helmreich, *op. cit.*, vol. 3, 33–100.
Cod: 14,352: Med., Phil.

010 **De naturalibus facultatibus**, ed. Marquardt, Müller, and Helmreich, *op. cit.*, vol. 3, 101–257.
Cod: 33,104: Med., Phil.

017 **De usu partium**, ed. G. Helmreich, *Galeni de usu partium libri xvii*. Leipzig: Teubner, 1:1907; 2:1909 (repr. Amsterdam: Hakkert, 1968): 1:1–496; 2:1–451.
Cod: 202,076: Med.

009 **De temperamentis libri iii**, ed. G. Helmreich, *Galeni de temperamentis libri iii*. Leipzig: Teubner, 1904 (repr. Stuttgart: 1969): 1–115.
Cod: 28,600: Med.

054 **De tumoribus praeter naturam**, ed. J. Reedy, *Galen. De tumoribus praeter naturam* [*Diss. University of Michigan* (1968)]: 1–28.
Cod: 4,309: Med.

064 **De crisibus libri iii**, ed. B. Alexanderson, *Galenos*. Περὶ κρίσεων [*Studia Graeca et Latina Gothoburgensia* 23. Göteborg: Elanders, 1967]: 69–212.
Cod: 34,406: Med.

016 **De uteri dissectione**, ed. D. Nickel, *Galeni de uteri dissectione* [*Corpus medicorum Graecorum*, vol. 5.2.1. Berlin: Akademie-Verlag, 1971]: 34–58.
Cod: 3,295: Med.

028 **De propriorum animi cuiuslibet affectuum dignotione et curatione**, ed. W. de Boer, *Galeni de propriorum animi cuiuslibet affectuum dignotione et curatione* [*Corpus medicorum Graecorum*, vol. 5.4.1.1. Leipzig: Teubner, 1937]: 3–37.
Cod: 8,605: Med.

029 **De animi cuiuslibet peccatorum dignotione et curatione (= De animi cuiuslibet peccatorum dignotione et medela)**, ed. W. de Boer, *Galeni de animi cuiuslibet peccatorum dignotione et curatione* [*Corpus medicorum Graecorum*, vol. 5.4.1.1. Leipzig: Teubner, 1937]: 41–68.
Cod: 6,707: Med.

030 **De atra bile**, ed. W. de Boer, *Galeni de atra bile libellus* [*Corpus medicorum Graecorum*, vol. 5.4.1.1. Leipzig: Teubner, 1937]: 71–93.
Cod: 6,484: Med.

032 **De placitis Hippocratis et Platonis**, ed. P. De Lacy, *Galen. On the doctrines of Hippocrates and Plato* [*Corpus medicorum Graecorum*, vol. 5.4.1.2, pts. 1–2. Berlin: Akademie-Verlag, 1978]: 1:65–358; 2:360–608.
N.B.: Text in the TLG data bank is based upon the editor's 1975 typescript.
Cod: 98,571: Med., Phil., Comm.

036 **De sanitate tuenda libri vi**, ed. K. Koch, *Galeni de sanitate tuenda libri vi* [*Corpus medicorum Graecorum*, vol. 5.4.2. Leipzig: Teubner, 1923]: 3–198.
Cod: 69,757: Med.

037 **De alimentorum facultatibus libri iii**, ed. G. Helmreich, *Galeni de alimentorum facultatibus libri iii* [*Corpus medicorum Graecorum*, vol. 5.4.2. Leipzig: Teubner, 1923]: 201–386.
Cod: 46,318: Med.

038 **De rebus boni malique suci**, ed. G. Helmreich, *Galeni de rebus boni malique suci libellus* [*Corpus medicorum Graecorum*, vol. 5.4.2. Leipzig: Teubner, 1923]: 389–429.
Cod: 10,678: Med.

019 **De victu attenuante**, ed. K. Kalbfleisch, *Galeni de victu attenuante* [*Corpus medicorum Graecorum*, vol. 5.4.2. Leipzig: Teubner, 1923]: 433–451.
Cod: 6,663: Med.

039 **De ptisana**, ed. O. Hartlich, *Galeni qui fertur de ptisana libellus* [*Corpus medicorum Graecorum*, vol. 5.4.2. Leipzig: Teubner, 1923]: 455–463.
Cod: 2,300: Med.

085 **In Hippocratis de natura hominis librum commentarii iii**, ed. J. Mewaldt, *Galeni in Hippocratis de natura hominis commentaria tria* [*Corpus medicorum Graecorum*, vol. 5.9.1. Leipzig: Teubner, 1914]: 3–88.
Cod: 25,350: Med.

086 **In Hippocratis vel Polybi opus de salubri victus ratione privatorum commentarius (= Galeni in Hippocratis de natura hominis commentarius tertius)**, ed. Mewaldt, *CMG* 5.9.1, 89–113.
Cod: 6,764: Med.

087 **In Hippocratis de victu acutorum commentaria iv**, ed. G. Helmreich, *Galeni in Hippocratis de victu acutorum commentaria iv* [*Corpus medicorum Graecorum*, vol. 5.9.1. Leipzig: Teubner, 1914]: 117–366.
Cod: 69,473: Med.

088 **In Hippocratis prorrheticum i commentaria iii**, ed. H. Diels, *Galeni in Hippocratis prorrheticum i commentaria iii* [*Corpus medicorum Graecorum*, vol. 5.9.2. Leipzig: Teubner, 1915]: 3–178.
Cod: 47,475: Med.

052 **De comate secundum Hippocratem liber**, ed. J. Mewaldt, *Galeni de comate secundum Hippocratem liber* [*Corpus medicorum Graecorum*, vol. 5.9.2. Leipzig: Teubner, 1915]: 181–187.
Cod: 1,820: Med.

099 **In Hippocratis prognosticum commentaria iii**,

ed. J. Heeg, *Galeni in Hippocratis prognosticum commentaria iii* [*Corpus medicorum Graecorum*, vol. 5.9.2. Leipzig: Teubner, 1915]: 197–378.
Cod: 43,712: Med.

089 **In Hippocratis librum primum epidemiarum commentarii iii**, ed. E. Wenkebach, *Galeni in Hippocratis epidemiarum librum i commentaria iii* [*Corpus medicorum Graecorum*, vol. 5.10.1. Leipzig: Teubner, 1934]: 6–151.
Cod: 40,571: Med.

090 **In Hippocratis librum iii epidemiarum commentarii iii**, ed. E. Wenkebach, *Galeni in Hippocratis epidemiarum librum iii commentaria iii* [*Corpus medicorum Graecorum*, vol. 5.10.2.1. Leipzig: Teubner, 1936]: 1–187.
Cod: 42,913: Med.

091 **In Hippocratis librum vi epidemiarum commentarii vi**, ed. E. Wenkebach, *Galeni in Hippocratis sextum librum epidemiarum commentaria i–vi* [*Corpus medicorum Graecorum*, vol. 5.10.2.2. Leipzig: Teubner, 1940]: 3–351.
Cod: 79,741: Med.

115 **Quomodo morborum simulantes sint deprehendendi**, ed. K. Deichgräber and F. Kudlien, *Galens Kommentare zu den Epidemien des Hippokrates* [*Corpus medicorum Graecorum*, vol. 5.10.2.4. Berlin: Akademie-Verlag, 1960]: 113–116.
Cod: 871: Med.

093 **Adversus Lycum libellus**, ed. E. Wenkebach, *Galeni adversus Lycum et adversus Iulianum libelli* [*Corpus medicorum Graecorum*, vol. 5.10.3. Berlin: Akademie-Verlag, 1951]: 3–29.
Cod: 7,717: Med.

094 **Adversus ea quae a Juliano in Hippocratis aphorismos enuntiata sunt libellus**, ed. Wenkebach, *CMG* 5.10.3, 33–70.
Cod: 7,971: Med.

035 **De venereis** (ap. Oribasium), ed. J. Raeder, *Oribasii collectionum medicarum reliquiae* [*Corpus medicorum Graecorum*, vol. 6.1.1. Leipzig: Teubner, 1928]: 187–189.
Q: 416: Med.

073 **Quos quibus catharticis medicamentis et quando purgare oporteat** (ap. Oribasium), ed. Raeder, *CMG* 6.1.1, 221–227.
Q: 2,043: Med.

121 **De melancholia** (ap. Aëtium), ed. A. Olivieri, *Aëtii Amideni libri medicinales v–viii* [*Corpus medicorum Graecorum*, vol. 8.2. Berlin: Akademie-Verlag, 1950]: 143–146.
Q: 1,077: Med.

005 **In Platonis Timaeum commentarii fragmenta**, ed. H.O. Schröder, *Galeni in Platonis Timaeum commentarii fragmenta* [*Corpus medicorum Graecorum, supplementum*, vol. 1. Leipzig: Teubner, 1934]: 9–26.
Cod: 5,359: Phil., Comm.

015 **De instrumento odoratus**, ed. J. Kollesch, *Galeni de instrumento odoratus* [*Corpus medicorum Graecorum, supplementum*, vol. 5. Berlin: Akademie-Verlag, 1964]: 30–64.
Cod: 4,585: Med.

001 **Adhortatio ad artes addiscendas**, ed. E. Wenkebach, "Galens Protreptikosfragment," *Quellen und Studien zur Geschichte der Naturwissenschaften und Medizin* 4.3 (1935) 90–120.
Cod: 5,224: Med.

003 **Quod optimus medicus sit quoque philosophus**, ed. E. Wenkebach, "Der hippokratische Arzt als das Ideal Galens," *Quellen und Studien zur Geschichte der Naturwissenschaften und Medizin* 3.4 (1933) 170–175.
Cod: 1,438: Med., Phil.

008 **De elementis ex Hippocrate libri ii**, ed. G. Helmreich, *Galeni de elementis ex Hippocrate libri ii*. Erlangen: Deichert, 1878: 1–69.
Cod: 13,951: Med., Comm.

020 **De utilitate respirationis liber**, ed. R. Noll, *Galeni περὶ χρείας ἀναπνοῆς libellus* [*Diss. Marburg* (1915)]: 1–33.
Cod: 6,350: Med.

023 **An in arteriis natura sanguis contineatur**, ed. F. Albrecht, *Galeni an in arteriis natura sanguis contineatur* [*Diss. Marburg* (1911)]: 1–21.
Cod: 4,884: Med.

024 **De optima corporis nostri constitutione**, ed. G. Helmreich, *Galenus de optima corporis constitutione. Idem de bono habitu* [*Programm Gymnasium Hof, 1900–1901* (1901)]: 7–16.
Cod: 1,820: Med.

025 **De bono habitu liber**, ed. Helmreich, *Programm Hof*, 16–20.
Cod: 837: Med.

026 **De propriis placitis fragmenta inedita**, ed. G. Helmreich, "Galeni περὶ τῶν ἑαυτῷ δοκούντων fragmenta inedita," *Philologus* 52 (1894) 432–434.
Cf. et 0057 084.
Cod: 1,049: Med., Phil.

034 **De parvae pilae exercitio**, ed. E. Wenkebach, "Galenos von Pergamon: Allgemeine Ertüchtigung durch Ballspiel. Eine sporthygienische Schrift aus dem zweiten Jahrhundert n. Chr.," *Sudhoffs Archiv für Geschichte der Medizin und der Naturwissenschaften* 31 (1938) 258–272.
Cod: 1,791: Med.

046 **De morborum temporibus liber**, ed. I. Wille, *Die Schrift Galens Περὶ τῶν ἐν ταῖς νόσοις καιρῶν und ihre Überlieferung*, pt. 2 [*Diss. Kiel* (1960)]: 1–70.
Cod: 5,673: Med.

047 **De totius morbi temporibus liber**, ed. Wille, *op. cit.*, 70–114.
Cod: 3,777: Med.

072 **De purgantium medicamentorum facultate**, ed. J. Ehlert, *Galeni de purgantium medicamentorum facultate* [*Diss. Göttingen* (1959)]: 1–21.
Cod: 3,132: Med.

074 **Pro puero epileptico consilium**, ed. W. Keil, *Galeni puero epileptico consilium* [*Diss. Göttingen* (1959)]: 1–23.
Cod: 3,327: Med.

080 **De septimestri partu**, ed. H. Schöne, "Galenos' Schrift über die Siebenmonatskinder,"

Quellen und Studien zur Geschichte der Naturwissenschaften und Medizin 3.4 (1933) 127–130.
Cod: 1,351: Med.

081 **Institutio logica**, ed. K. Kalbfleisch, *Galeni institutio logica*. Leipzig: Teubner, 1896: 3–49.
Cod: 8,730: Phil.

082 **De sophismatis seu captionibus penes dictionem**, ed. K. Gabler, *Galeni libellus de captionibus quae per dictionem fiunt* [*Diss. Rostock* (1903)]: 1–16.
Cod: 2,585: Rhet.

107 **De experientia medica**, ed. R. Walzer, *Galen on medical experience*. London: Oxford University Press, 1944: 93–96, 113–114.
Cod: 1,021: Med.

111 **Quod qualitates incorporeae sint**, ed. J. Westenberger, *Galeni qui fertur de qualitatibus incorporeis libellus* [*Diss. Marburg* (1906)]: 1–19.
Cod: 3,371: Med.

0530 **Pseudo-GALENUS** Med.
post A.D. 2

043 **De optima secta ad Thrasybulum liber**, ed. C.G. Kühn, *Claudii Galeni opera omnia*, vol. 1. Leipzig: Knobloch, 1821 (repr. Hildesheim: Olms, 1964): 106–223.
Cod: 18,213: Med.

032 **De theriaca ad Pamphilianum**, ed. Kühn, *op. cit.*, vol. 14 (1827; repr. 1965): 295–310.
Cod: 2,240: Med.

029 **De remediis parabilibus libri iii**, ed. Kühn, *op. cit.*, vol. 14, 311–581.
Cod: 36,890: Med.

012 **Introductio seu medicus**, ed. Kühn, *op. cit.*, vol. 14, 674–797.
Cod: 19,693: Med., Phil.

005 **De fasciis liber**, ed. Kühn, *op. cit.*, vol. 18.1 (1829; repr. 1965): 768–827.
Cod: 8,609: Med.

041 **Definitiones medicae**, ed. Kühn, *op. cit.*, vol. 19 (1830; repr. 1965): 346–462.
Cod: 15,715: Med., Phil.

009 **De humoribus liber**, ed. Kühn, *op. cit.*, vol. 19, 485–496.
Cod: 1,746: Med.

023 **Praesagitio omnino vera expertaque**, ed. Kühn, *op. cit.*, vol. 19, 512–518.
Cod: 913: Med.

036 **De venae sectione**, ed. Kühn, *op. cit.*, vol. 19, 519–528.
Cod: 1,315: Med.

024 **Prognostica de decubitu ex mathematica scientia**, ed. Kühn, *op. cit.*, vol. 19, 529–573.
Cod: 6,880: Med., Astrol.

033 **De urinis**, ed. Kühn, *op. cit.*, vol. 19, 574–601.
Cod: 3,983: Med.

034 **De urinis compendium**, ed. Kühn, *op. cit.*, vol. 19, 602–608.
Cod: 976: Med.

035 **De urinis ex Hippocrate, Galeno et aliis quibusdam**, ed. Kühn, *op. cit.*, vol. 19, 609–628.
Cod: 3,096: Med.

026 **De pulsibus ad Antonium disciplinae studiosum ac philosophum**, ed. Kühn, *op. cit.*, vol. 19, 629–642.
Cod: 2,120: Med.

045 **De affectuum renibus insidentium dignotione et curatione liber adscriptitius**, ed. Kühn, *op. cit.*, vol. 19, 643–698.
Cod: 8,517: Med.

031 **De succedaneis liber**, ed. Kühn, *op. cit.*, vol. 19, 721–747.
Cod: 2,218: Med.

037 **De victus ratione in morbis acutis ex Hippocratis sententia liber**, ed. J. Westenberger, *Galeni de diaeta Hippocratis in morbis acutis* [*Corpus medicorum Graecorum*, vol. 5.9.1. Leipzig: Teubner, 1914]: 369–392.
Cod: 5,711: Med.

020 **De partibus philosophiae**, ed. R. Kotrc, Γαλήνου τοῦ ἰατροῦ περὶ εἴδων φιλοσοφίας [*Corpus medicorum Graecorum* (in press)]: 6–14.
N.B.: Text in the TLG data bank is based upon the editor's 1975 typescript.
Cod: 2,244: Phil.

001 **De causa affectionum**, ed. G. Helmreich, *Handschriftliche Studien zu Galen* [*Programm Gymnasium Ansbach* (1911)]: 5–19.
Cod: 3,407: Med.

002 **An animal sit quod est in utero**, ed. H. Wagner, *Galeni qui fertur libellus* Εἰ ζῷον τὸ κατὰ γαστρός [*Diss. Marburg* (1914)]: 1–18.
Cod: 3,827: Med.

003 Λέξεις βοτανῶν, ed. A. Delatte, *Anecdota Atheniensia et alia*, vol. 2. Paris: Droz, 1939: 358–393.
Cod: 1,452: Lexicogr.

006 **Ad Gaurum quomodo animetur fetus**, ed. K. Kalbfleisch, "Die neuplatonische, fälschlich dem Galen zugeschriebene Schrift Πρὸς Γαῦρον περὶ τοῦ πῶς ἐμψυχοῦνται τὰ ἔμβρυα, *Abhandlungen der königlichen Akademie der Wissenschaften zu Berlin*, Philol.-hist. Kl. (Berlin: Reimer, 1895): 33–62.
Cod: 9,936: Med.

022 **De ponderibus et mensuris**, ed. F. Hultsch, *Metrologicorum scriptorum reliquiae*, vol. 1. Leipzig, Stuttgart: Teubner (repr. 1971): 218–244.
Cod: 3,942: Metrolog.

042 **De historia philosophica**, ed. H. Diels, *Doxographi Graeci*. Berlin: Reimer, 1879 (repr. De Gruyter, 1965): 597–648.
Cod: 11,549: Phil., Doxogr.

046 **De signis ex urinis** (fort. auctore Magno Emeseno). ed. P. Moraux, "Anecdota Graeca minora vi: Pseudo-Galen, de signis ex urinis," *Zeitschrift für Papyrologie und Epigraphik* 60 (1985) 68–74.
Cod: 1,813: Med.

2452 **GALITAS** (?) Hist.
3 B.C.?

001 **Testimonium**, FGrH #818: 3C:894.
NQ: 40: Test.

0189 **Gaius Cornelius GALLUS** <Epigr.>
      1 B.C.
001   **Epigramma**, AG 16.89.
      Q: 38: Epigr.

0905 **Aelius GALLUS** Med.
      1 B.C.
      Cf. et GALLUS Med. (0797).
      Cf. et Marcus GALLUS Med. (0804).
x01   **Fragmenta ap. Galenum**.
      K12.625–626, 738; **14**.114, 158–159, 161–162,
      170–171.
      Cf. GALENUS Med. (0057 076, 078).

0797 **GALLUS** Med.
      fiq Aelius Gallus
      1 B.C.?
      Cf. et Aelius GALLUS Med. (0905).
x01   **Fragmenta ap. Galenum**.
      K12.784; **13**.77, 138, 202–203, 310, 472–473,
      556, 838.
      Cf. GALENUS Med. (0057 076–077).

0804 **Marcus GALLUS** Med.
      fiq Aelius Gallus
      1 B.C.?
      Cf. et Aelius GALLUS Med. (0905).
x01   **Fragmentum ap. Galenum**.
      K13.179–180.
      Cf. GALENUS Med. (0057 076).

2137 **GAUDENTIUS** Phil. et Mus.
      A.D. 2/6
001   **Harmonica introductio**, ed. K. Jan, *Musici
      scriptores Graeci*. Leipzig: Teubner, 1895 (repr.
      Hildesheim: Olms, 1962): 327–355.
      Cod: Mus.

0190 **GAURADAS** Epigr.
      Incertum
001   **Epigramma**, AG 16.152.
      Q: 50: Epigr.

2663 **GEMELLUS** Epigr.
      A.D. 2
x01   **Epigramma dedicatorium**.
      App. Anth. 1.182: Cf. ANTHOLOGIAE GRAE-
      CAE APPENDIX (7052 001).

0906 **GEMELLUS** Med.
      ante A.D. 2
x01   **Fragmentum ap. Galenum**.
      K13.299.
      Cf. GALENUS Med. (0057 076).

1383 **GEMINUS** Astron.
      1 B.C.
001   **Elementa astronomiae**, ed. G. Aujac, *Géminos.
      Introduction aux phénomènes*. Paris: Les Belles
      Lettres, 1975: 1–98.
      Cod: 20,938: Astron.
002   **Calendarium** [Sp.?], ed. Aujac, *op. cit.*, 98–108.
      Cod: 1,723: Astron.

003   **De Posidonii meteorologicis** (epitome ap. Sim-
      plicium), ed. Aujac, *op. cit.*, 111–113.
      Q
004   Περὶ τῆς τῶν μαθημάτων τάξεως (**vel** θεωρίας),
      ed. Aujac, *op. cit.*, 114–117.
      Q
005   **Fragmenta optica** [Dub.], ed. R. Schöne, *Da-
      mianos Schrift über Optik*. Berlin: Reichs-
      druckerei, 1897: 22–30.
      Q

      GEMINUS Epigr.
      Cf. TULLIUS GEMINUS Epigr. (1742).

      GENETHLIUS Rhet. et Soph.
      A.D. 3: Petraeus
      Cf. MENANDER Rhet. (2586 001).

0907 **GENNADIUS** Med.
      ante A.D. 2
x01   **Fragmentum ap. Galenum**.
      K12.760.
      Cf. GALENUS Med. (0057 076).

2762 **GENNADIUS I** Scr. Eccl.
      A.D. 5: Constantinopolitanus
004   **Fragmenta in epistulam ad Romanos** (in ca-
      tenis), ed. K. Staab, *Pauluskommentar aus der
      griechischen Kirche aus Katenenhandschriften
      gesammelt*. Münster: Aschendorff, 1933: 352–
      418.
      Q: 20,174: Exeget., Caten.
005   **Fragmenta in epistulam i ad Corinthios** (in ca-
      tenis), ed. Staab, *op. cit.*, 418–419.
      Q: 259: Exeget., Caten.
006   **Fragmentum in epistulam ii ad Corinthios** (in
      catenis), ed. Staab, *op. cit.*, 419.
      Q: 26: Exeget., Caten.
007   **Fragmenta in epistulam ad Galatas** (in ca-
      tenis), ed. Staab, *op. cit.*, 419–420.
      Q: 340: Exeget., Caten.
008   **Fragmentum in epistulam ii ad Thessalonicen-
      ses** (in catenis), ed. Staab, *op. cit.*, 420.
      Q: 30: Exeget., Caten.
009   **Fragmenta in epistulam ad Hebraeos** (in ca-
      tenis), ed. Staab, *op. cit.*, 420–422.
      Q: 375: Exeget., Caten.

2030 *GEOGRAPHICA ADESPOTA* (GGM)
      Incertum
001   **Fragmenta**, ed. K. Müller, *Geographi Graeci
      minores*, vol. 2. Paris: Didot, 1861 (repr.
      Hildesheim: Olms, 1965): 509–511.
      Cod: 209: Geogr.

4087 **Joannes GEOMETRES** Rhet. et Poeta
      vel Cyriotes vel Joannes Cyriotis
      A.D. 10: Constantinopolitanus
x01   **Epigrammata demonstrativa**.
      App. Anth. 3.241, 284: Cf. ANTHOLOGIAE
      GRAECAE APPENDIX (7052 003).

4080 **GEOPONICA**
A.D. 10
001 **Geoponica**, ed. H. Beckh, *Geoponica*. Leipzig: Teubner, 1895: 1–529.
Cod: 83,504: Nat. Hist.

2690 **GEORGIUS** <Epigr.>
A.D. 12: Corcyraeus
x01 **Epigramma sepulcrale.**
App. Anth. 2.747: Cf. ANTHOLOGIAE GRAE-CAE APPENDIX (7052 002).

GEORGIUS Gramm.
Incertum
Cf. COMMENTARIA IN DIONYSII THRACIS ARTEM GRAMMATICAM (4175 004).

4241 **GEORGIUS Diaereta** Soph.
Incertum
x01 **Prolegomena in Hermogenis librum** περὶ εὑρέσεως (olim sub auctore Georgio Diaereta). Rabe, pp. 351–360.
Cf. JOANNES Rhet. (4157 001).
x02 **Commentarium in Hermogenis librum** περὶ εὑρέσεως (olim sub auctore Georgio Diaereta, nunc fort. auctore Joanne Sardiano). Walz, vol. 6, pp. 512–543.
Cf. JOANNES Rhet. (4157 002).

3043 **GEORGIUS Monachus** Chronogr.
vel Georgius Hamartolus vel Georgius Pecca-tor
A.D. 9: Alexandrinus
Cf. et GEORGIUS MONACHUS CONTINUA-TUS (3051).
001 **Chronicon** (lib. 1–4), ed. C. de Boor, *Georgii monachi chronicon*, 2 vols. Leipzig: Teubner, 1904 (repr. Stuttgart: 1978 (1st edn. corr. P. Wirth)): 1:1–382; 2:383–804.
Dup. partim 3043 002.
Cod: 156,324: Hist., Chronogr.
002 **Chronicon breve** (lib. 1–6) (redactio recentior), MPG 110: 41–1260.
Dup. partim 3043 001.
Lib. 5 = *Georgius Monachus Continuatus* (re-dactio A).
Cod: 212,143: Hist., Chronogr.
x01 **Chronicon breve** (lib. 7–8) (redactio recentior). MPG 110.1261–1285.
Cf. SYMEON METAPHRASTES Biogr. et Hist. (3115 001).

3051 **GEORGIUS MONACHUS CONTINUATUS**
A.D. 10
Cf. et GEORGIUS Monachus Chronogr. (3043).
001 **Chronicon** (continuatio) (redactio A), ed. I. Bekker, *Theophanes Continuatus, Ioannes Ca-meniata, Symeon Magister, Georgius Monachus* [*Corpus scriptorum historiae Byzantinae.* Bonn: Weber, 1838]: 763–924.
= Vitae recentiorum imperatorum.
Cod: Hist., Chronogr.

002 **Chronicon** (continuatio) (redactio B), ed. V.M. Istrin, *Chronika Georgia Hamartola ii.* St. Pe-tersburg, 1922: 1–65.
= Vitae recentiorum imperatorum.
Cod: Hist., Chronogr.
x01 **Chronicon** (lib. 5) (redactio A).
MPG 110.1035–1193.
Cf. GEORGIUS Monachus Chronogr. (3043 002).

4240 **GEORGIUS MONUS** Soph.
A.D. 5: Alexandrinus
002 **De syllogismis** (excerptum e cod. Paris. gr. 2919, fol. 107v–111v), ed. L. Schilling, "Quaestiones rhetoricae selectae," *Jahrbücher für classische Philologie*, suppl. 28 (1903) 671–676.
E commentario inedito in Hermogenis librum περὶ στάσεων.
Cod: Rhet., Comm.
003 **Commentarium in Hermogenis librum** περὶ στάσεων (excerpta e cod. Paris. gr. 2919), ed. Schilling, *op. cit.*, 667–668, 677–681, 684–690, 695–703, 707–712, 714–716, 719–722, 724–763, 765–766.
Cod: Rhet., Comm.

2971 **GEORGIUS PECCATOR** Poeta
A.D. 4–5?
001 **Hymnus** (olim sub auctore Synesio), ed. A. Dell'Era, *Sinesio di Cirene. Inni.* Rome: Tum-minelli, 1968: 169.
Cod: 48: Hymn.

2701 **GEORGIUS PISIDES** Poeta
A.D. 7: Pisides, Constantinopolitanus
x01 **Epigrammata.**
AG 1.120, 121: Cf. ANONYMI EPIGRAMMAT-ICI (AG) (0138 001).
x02 **Epigramma demonstrativum.**
App. Anth. 3.254: Cf. ANTHOLOGIAE GRAE-CAE APPENDIX (7052 003).

3045 **GEORGIUS SYNCELLUS** Chronogr.
A.D. 8–9: Constantinopolitanus
001 **Ecloga chronographica**, ed. A.A. Mosshammer, *Georgius Syncellus. Ecloga chronographica.* Leipzig: Teubner, 1984: 1–478.
Cod: Chronogr.

0191 **GERMANICUS CAESAR** <Epigr.>
1 B.C.–A.D. 1
001 **Epigrammata**, AG 9.17–18, 387(?).
AG 7.73: Cf. TULLIUS GEMINUS Epigr. (1742 001).
AG 9.387: Cf. et HADRIANUS Imperator (0195 001).
Q: 124: Epigr.

4070 **GERMANUS** Epigr.
A.D. 4
001 **Epigramma**, AG 14.148.
Q: 48: Epigr.

4159 GERMANUS Gramm.
Incertum
x01 **Scholia in Pindarum.**
Abel, pp. 40–480 passim.
Cf. SCHOLIA IN PINDARUM (5034 004).

0908 GLAUCIAS Med.
2 B.C.: Tarentinus
x01 **Fragmentum ap. Galenum.**
K13.835.
Cf. GALENUS Med. (0057 077).
x02 **Fragmentum ap. Oribasium.**
CMG, vol. 6.2.1, p. 283.
Cf. ORIBASIUS Med. (0722 001).

2191 GLAUCIPPUS Hist.
Incertum
001 **Fragmentum,** FGrH #363: 3B:224.
Q: 76: Hist.

0192 GLAUCUS Epigr.
Incertum: Atheniensis
001 **Epigrammata,** AG **9.**774–775; **16.**111.
Q: 82: Epigr.

0193 GLAUCUS Epigr.
Incertum: Nicopolitanus
001 **Epigrammata,** AG **7.**285; **9.**341; **12.**44.
Q: 105: Epigr.

2460 GLAUCUS Hist.
2 B.C./A.D. 3
001 **Fragmenta,** FGrH #674: 3C:338–339.
Q: 206: Hist.

1385 GLAUCUS Hist.
ante A.D. 3
001 **Fragmentum,** FGrH #806: 3C:843.
fr. 1: *P. Oxy.* 15.1802.
Pap: 75: Hist.

2991 *GLOSSARIA BILINGUIA*
Varia
001 **Glossarium Graecolatinum** (*P. Berol.* 21246),
ed. J. Kramer, *Glossaria bilinguia in papyris et
membranis reperta* [*Papyrologische Texte und
Abhandlungen* 30. Bonn: Habelt, 1983]: 20–24.
Pap: Lexicogr.
002 **Glossarium alphabeticum Graecolatinum (s–v)**
(*P. Reinach* 2069 [= *P. Sorbonne* inv. 2069]),
ed. Kramer, *op. cit.,* 30–35.
Pap: Lexicogr.
003 **Glossarium alphabeticum Graecolatinum (l–m)**
(*P. Reinach* inv. 2140), ed. Kramer, *op. cit.,* 42.
Pap: Lexicogr.
004 **Glossarium Graecolatinum** (fragmenta Helm-
stadiensia et folium Wallraffianum), ed. Kramer, *op. cit.,* 47–53.
Pap: Lexicogr.
005 **Glossarium piscium Graecolatinum** (*P. Laur.*
inv. III/418), ed. Kramer, *op. cit.,* 61.
Pap: Lexicogr.

006 **Glossarium holerum et piscium Graecolatinum
i** (*P. Oxy.* 33.2660), ed. Kramer, *op. cit.,* 63–64.
Pap: Lexicogr.
007 **Glossarium holerum et piscium Graecolatinum
ii** (*P. Oxy.* 33.2660a), ed. Kramer, *op. cit.,* 67.
Pap: Lexicogr.
008 **Glossarium signorum zodiacorum et nominum
ventorum Graecolatinum** (*P. Oxy.* 46.3315),
ed. Kramer, *op. cit.,* 69.
Pap: Lexicogr.
009 **Glossarium nominum animalium Graecolatinum** (*P. Lund* 5), ed. Kramer, *op. cit.,* 71.
Pap: Lexicogr.
010 **Glossarium rerum pertinentium ad homines
Graecolatinum** (*PSI* sine numero), ed. Kramer,
op. cit., 73–75.
Pap: Lexicogr.
011 **Glossarium nominum mensium Graecolatinum**
(*P. Fayûm* 135v), ed. Kramer, *op. cit.,* 77.
Pap: Lexicogr.
012 **Glossarium nominum deorum Graecolatinum**
(*P. Mich.* inv. 2458), ed. Kramer, *op. cit.,* 79–
80.
Pap: Lexicogr.
013 **Glossarium nominum vulgarium Graecolati-
num** (*P. Lond.* 2.481 [= *P. Lit. Lond.* 187 =
Brit. Mus. inv. 481]), ed. Kramer, *op. cit.,* 83–
84.
Pap: Lexicogr.
014 **Glossarium rerum pertinentium ad hospitium
Graecolatinum** (*P. Louvre Eg.* inv. 2329 [= *P.
Louvre* inv. 4 bis]), ed. Kramer, *op. cit.,* 90–91.
Pap: Lexicogr.
015 **Glossarium Graeco-Latino-Copticum** (*P. Berol.*
inv. 10582), ed. Kramer, *op. cit.,* 99–103.
Pap: Lexicogr.
016 **Typi epistulares e lingua Latina in Graecam**
(*P. Bonon.* 5 [= *P. Bonon.* inv. 1]), ed. Kramer,
op. cit., 111–117.
Pap: Lexicogr., Epist.

0194 GLYCON Epigr.
Incertum
001 **Epigramma,** AG 10.124.
AG 10.124b–126: Cf. ANONYMI EPIGRAM-
MATICI (AG) (0138 001).
Q: 17: Epigr.

0911 GLYTUS Med.
ante A.D. 1?
x01 **Fragmentum ap. Galenum.**
K13.1036–1037.
Cf. GALENUS Med. (0057 077).

2945 *GNOMOLOGIUM VATICANUM*
A.D. 14
001 **Gnomologium Vaticanum,** ed. L. Sternbach,
*Gnomologium Vaticanum e codice Vaticano
Graeco 743* [*Texte und Kommentare* 2 (repr.
Berlin: De Gruyter, 1963)]: 4–204.
Cod

2255 **GORGIAS** Hist.
A.D. 1–2?: Atheniensis
001 **Testimonium**, FGrH #351: 3B:214.
NQ: 66: Test.
002 **Fragmenta**, FGrH #351: 3B:214.
Q: 60: Hist., Gramm.

0593 **GORGIAS** Rhet. et Soph.
5–4 B.C.: Leontinus
001 **Testimonium**, FGrH #407: 3B:301.
NQ: 46: Test.
002 **Testimonia**, ed. H. Diels and W. Kranz, *Die Fragmente der Vorsokratiker*, vol. 2, 6th edn. Berlin: Weidmann, 1952 (repr. Dublin: 1966): 271–279.
test. 1–35.
NQ: 2,998: Test.
003 **Fragmenta**, ed. Diels and Kranz, *op. cit.*, 279–306.
frr. 1–8, 10–27, 29–31.
frr. 1–5: Περὶ τοῦ μὴ ὄντος ἢ περὶ φύσεως.
frr. 5a–6: Epitaphius.
frr. 7–8a: Olympicus.
fr. 10: Encomium in Eleos.
fr. 11: Encomium in Helenam.
fr. 11a: Apologia pro Palamede.
frr. 12–14: Τέχνη.
frr. 15–27: Fragmenta incertae sedis.
frr. 29–31: Fragmenta incerta.
Q, Cod: 7,074: Phil., Rhet., Encom.

2357 **GORGON** Hist.
2 B.C.?: fort. Rhodius
001 **Fragmenta**, FGrH #515: 3B:490–491.
Q: 78: Hist.

2369 **GORGOSTHENES** Hist.
5 B.C.: Rhodius
001 **Testimonium**, FGrH #529: 3B:505.
NQ: 18: Test.

1872 **GORGUS** Epigr.
ante 2 B.C.: Colophonius
001 **Testimonium**, FGrH #17: 1A:182.
test. l: *Inscr. Athen. Mitt.* 11.428.
NQ: 40: Test.

0964 **Chrysantus GRATIANUS** Med.
ante A.D. 2
x01 **Fragmentum ap. Galenum.**
K12.631–632.
Cf. GALENUS Med. (0057 076).

9006 **GREGORIUS** Paroemiogr.
A.D. 13: Cyprius
001 **Paroemiae**, ed. E.L. von Leutsch and F.G. Schneidewin, *Corpus paroemiographorum Graecorum*, vol. 1. Göttingen: Vandenhoeck & Ruprecht, 1839 (repr. Hildesheim: Olms, 1965): 349–378.
Cod: 2,814: Paroem.

002 **Paroemiae** (e cod. Leidense), ed. von Leutsch, *op. cit.*, vol. 2 (1851; repr. 1958): 53–92.
Cod: 3,521: Paroem.
003 **Paroemiae** (e cod. Mosquense), ed. von Leutsch, *op. cit.*, vol. 2, 93–130.
Cod: 4,341: Paroem.
004 **Paroemiae** (e cod. Vat.), ed. von Leutsch, *op. cit.*, vol. 2, 131–134.
Cod: 702: Paroem.

2022 **GREGORIUS NAZIANZENUS** Theol.
vel Gregorius Theologus
A.D. 4: Nazianzenus, Constantinopolitanus
001 **Epistulae**, ed. P. Gallay, *Saint Grégoire de Nazianze. Lettres*, 2 vols. Paris: Les Belles Lettres, 1:1964; 2:1967: **1**:1–118; **2**:1–148.
Epist. 1–100: vol. 1.
Epist. 103–201, 203–249: vol. 2.
Cod: 42,908: Epist.
002 **Epistulae theologicae**, ed. P. Gallay, *Grégoire de Nazianze. Lettres théologiques* [*Sources chrétiennes* 208. Paris: Cerf, 1974]: 36–94.
Epist. 101: pp. 36–68.
Epist. 102: pp. 70–84.
Epist. 202: pp. 86–94.
Cod: 4,507: Epist., Theol.
003 **Christus patiens** [Dub.] (fort. auctore Constantino Manasse), ed. A. Tuilier, *Grégoire de Nazianze. La passion du Christ* [*Sources chrétiennes* 149. Paris: Cerf, 1969]: 124–338.
Cod: 16,043: Trag.
004 **De vita sua**, ed. C. Jungck, *Gregor von Nazianz. De vita sua*. Heidelberg: Winter, 1974: 54–148.
Cod: 11,888: Biogr., Iamb.
005 **Funebris in laudem Caesarii fratris oratio** (orat. 7), ed. F. Boulenger, *Grégoire de Nazianze. Discours funèbres en l'honneur de son frère Césaire et de Basile de Césarée*. Paris: Picard, 1908: 2–56.
Cod: 5,549: Orat., Encom.
006 **Funebris oratio in laudem Basilii Magni Caesareae in Cappadocia episcopi** (orat. 43), ed. Boulenger, *op. cit.*, 58–230.
Cod: 17,970: Orat., Encom.
007 **Adversus Eunomianos** (orat. 27), ed. J. Barbel, *Gregor von Nazianz. Die fünf theologischen Reden*. Düsseldorf: Patmos-Verlag, 1963: 38–60.
Cod: 2,105: Theol., Orat.
008 **De theologia** (orat. 28), ed. Barbel, *op. cit.*, 62–126.
Cod: 7,443: Theol., Orat.
009 **De filio** (orat. 29), ed. Barbel, *op. cit.*, 128–168.
Cod: 4,901: Theol., Orat.
010 **De filio** (orat. 30), ed. Barbel, *op. cit.*, 170–216.
Cod: 4,947: Theol., Orat.
011 **De spiritu sancto** (orat. 31), ed. Barbel, *op. cit.*, 218–276.
Cod: 6,288: Theol., Orat.
012 **Comparatio vitarum** (= carmen morale 8), ed.

H.M. Werhahn, *Gregorii Nazianzeni* σύγκρισις βίων [*Klassisch-philologische Studien* 15. Wiesbaden: Harrassowitz, 1953]: 22–29.
Cod: 1,599: Iamb.

013 **De testamentis et adventu Christi** (= carmen dogmaticum 9, additamentum inter vv. 18 et 19), ed. B. Wyss, *Phyllobolia für Peter von der Mühll*. Basel: Schwabe, 1946: 161–163.
Dup. partim 2022 059 (carm. 9).
Cod: 424: Hexametr.

014 **Alphabeticum paraeneticum 1** (e cod. Patm. 33), ed. J. Sakkelion, Πατμιακὴ βιβλιοθήκη. Athens: Papageorgiu, 1890: 18–19.
Cod: 145: Iamb., Gnom.

015 **In sanctum pascha et in tarditatem** (orat. 1), MPG 35: 396–401.
Cod: 845: Orat.

016 **Apologetica** (orat. 2), MPG 35: 408–513.
Cod: 14,922: Orat., Apol.

017 **Ad eos qui ipsum acciverant nec occurrerant** (orat. 3), MPG 35: 517–525.
Cod: 1,042: Orat.

018 **Contra Julianum imperatorem 1** (orat. 4), MPG 35: 532–664.
Cod: 18,851: Orat., Invectiv.

019 **Contra Julianum imperatorem 2** (orat. 5), MPG 35: 664–720.
Cod: 7,878: Orat., Invectiv.

020 **De pace 1** (orat. 6), MPG 35: 721–752.
Cod: 4,821: Orat.

021 **In laudem sororis Gorgoniae** (orat. 8), MPG 35: 789–817.
Cod: 4,475: Orat., Encom.

022 **Apologeticus ad patrem** (orat. 9), MPG 35: 820–825.
Cod: 1,206: Orat., Apol.

023 **In seipsum ad patrem et Basilium magnum** (orat. 10), MPG 35: 828–832.
Cod: 801: Orat., Apol.

024 **Ad Gregorium Nyssenum** (orat. 11), MPG 35: 832–841.
Cod: 1,616: Orat., Apol.

025 **Ad patrem** (orat. 12), MPG 35: 844–849.
Cod: 1,229: Orat.

026 **In consecratione Eulalii Doarensium episcopi** (orat. 13), MPG 35: 852–856.
Cod: 646: Orat.

027 **De pauperum amore** (orat. 14), MPG 35: 857–909.
Cod: 8,551: Orat.

028 **In Machabaeorum laudem** (orat. 15), MPG 35: 912–933.
Cod: 3,246: Orat., Encom., Hagiogr.

029 **In patrem tacentem** (orat. 16), MPG 35: 933–964.
Cod: 4,712: Orat.

030 **Ad cives Nazianzenos** (orat. 17), MPG 35: 964–981.
Cod: 2,648: Orat.

031 **Funebris oratio in patrem** (orat. 18), MPG 35: 985–1044.
Cod: 9,574: Orat., Encom.

032 **Ad Julianum tributorum exaequatorem** (orat. 19), MPG 35: 1044–1064.
Cod: 3,292: Orat.

033 **De dogmate et constitutione episcoporum** (orat. 20), MPG 35: 1065–1080.
Cod: 2,471: Orat., Theol.

034 **In laudem Athanasii** (orat. 21), MPG 35: 1081–1128.
Cod: 7,310: Orat., Encom., Hagiogr.

035 **De pace 2** (orat. 22), MPG 35: 1132–1152.
Cod: 3,543: Orat.

036 **De pace 3** (orat. 23), MPG 35: 1152–1168.
Cod: 2,704: Orat.

037 **In laudem Cypriani** (orat. 24), MPG 35: 1169–1193.
Cod: 3,776: Orat., Encom., Hagiogr.

038 **In laudem Heronis philosophi** (orat. 25), MPG 35: 1197–1225.
Cod: 4,411: Orat., Encom.

039 **In seipsum, cum rure rediisset, post ea quae a Maximo perpetrata fuerant** (orat. 26), MPG 35: 1228–1252.
Cod: 4,095: Orat.

040 **De moderatione in disputando** (orat. 32), MPG 36: 173–212.
Cod: 6,621: Orat., Theol.

041 **Contra Arianos et de seipso** (orat. 33), MPG 36: 213–237.
Cod: 3,431: Orat., Theol.

042 **In Aegyptiorum adventum** (orat. 34), MPG 36: 241–256.
Cod: 2,403: Orat.

043 **De martyribus et adversus Arianos** (orat. 35) [Sp.], MPG 36: 257–261.
Cod: 1,064: Orat.

044 **De seipso et ad eos qui ipsum cathedram Constantinopolitanam affectare dicebant** (orat. 36), MPG 36: 265–279.
Cod: 2,629: Orat., Apol.

045 **In dictum evangelii: Cum consummasset Jesus hos sermones** (orat. 37), MPG 36: 281–308.
Cod: 4,366: Orat., Exeget.

046 **In theophania** (orat. 38), MPG 36: 312–333.
Cod: 3,550: Orat.

047 **In sancta lumina** (orat. 39), MPG 36: 336–360.
Cod: 4,012: Orat.

048 **In sanctum baptisma** (orat. 40), MPG 36: 360–425.
Cod: 10,900: Orat.

049 **In pentecosten** (orat. 41), MPG 36: 428–452.
Cod: 3,776: Orat.

050 **Supremum vale** (orat. 42), MPG 36: 457–492.
Cod: 5,797: Orat.

051 **In novam Dominicam** (orat. 44), MPG 36: 608–621.
Cod: 2,224: Orat.

052 **In sanctum pascha** (orat. 45), MPG 36: 624–664.
Cod: 6,819: Orat.

053 **Significatio in Ezechielem** [Sp.], MPG 36: 665–669.
Cod: 533: Exeget.

054 **Fragmentum ex oratione contra astronomos** [Sp.], MPG 36: 675–678.
Cod: 917: Orat.

055 **Liturgia sancti Gregorii** [Sp.], MPG 36: 700–733.
Cod: 5,875: Liturg.

056 Ἀλάτιον σκευασθὲν ὑπὸ τῆς ἐνεργείας τοιᾶσδε, ed. J.L. Ideler, *Physici et medici Graeci minores*, vol. 1. Berlin: Reimer, 1841 (repr. Amsterdam: Hakkert, 1963): 297–298.
Cod: 91: Med.

057 **Epigrammata**, AG 1.51, 92(?); 8.1–254.
Dup. partim 2022 063.
Q: 6,776: Epigr.

058 **Testamentum**, ed. J.B. Pitra, *Iuris ecclesiastici Graecorum historia et monumenta*, vol. 2. Rome: Congregatio de Propaganda Fide, 1868: 155–159.
Cod

059 **Carmina dogmatica**, MPG 37: 397–522.
De patre (carm. 1): coll. 397–401.
De filio (carm. 2): coll. 401–408.
De spiritu sancto (carm. 3): coll. 408–415.
De mundo (carm. 4): coll. 415–425.
De providentia (carm. 5): coll. 424–429.
De eodem argumento (carm. 6): coll. 430–438.
De substantiis mente praeditis (carm. 7): coll. 438–446.
De anima (carm. 8): coll. 446–456.
De testamentis et adventu Christi (carm. 9): coll. 456–464.
De incarnatione adversus Apollinarium (carm. 10): coll. 464–470.
De Christi incarnatione (carm. 11): coll. 470–471.
De veris scripturae libris (carm. 12): coll. 472–474.
Patriarchae filii Jacob (carm. 13): col. 475.
Plagae Aegypti (carm. 14): coll. 475–476.
Moysis decalogus (carm. 15): coll. 476–477.
Eliae et Elisaei miracula (carm. 16): coll. 477–479.
Epigramma in templum Eliae quod Χηρεῖον appellabatur (carm. 17): coll. 479–480.
De Christi genealogia (carm. 18): coll. 480–487.
Discipuli Christi duodecim (carm. 19): col. 488.
Miracula Christi secundum Matthaeum (carm. 20): coll. 488–491.
Miracula Christi secundum Marcum (carm. 21): coll. 491–492.
Miracula Christi secundum Lucam (carm. 22): coll. 492–494.
Miracula Christi secundum Joannem (carm. 23): col. 494.
Parabolae Christi et aenigmata secundum Matthaeum (carm. 24): coll. 495–496.
Parabolae Christi secundum Marcum (carm. 25): coll. 496–497.
Parabolae Christi secundum Lucam (carm. 26): coll. 497–498.
Parabolae Christi secundum omnes evangelistas (carm. 27): coll. 498–506.
Tempestas a Christo sedata (carm. 28): coll. 506–507.
Hymnus ad deum (carm. 29) [Sp.]: coll. 507–508.
Hymnus alius ad deum (carm. 30): coll. 508–510.
Hymnus alius (carm. 31) [Dub.]: coll. 510–511.
Hymnus vespertinus (carm. 32) [Dub.]: coll. 511–514.
Actio gratiarum (carm. 33) [Dub.]: col. 514.
Alia gratiarum actio (carm. 34) [Dub.]: coll. 515–517.
Precatio ante scripturae lectionem (carm. 35) [Dub.]: coll. 517–518.
Precatio ante iter suscipiendum (carm. 36): coll. 518–520.
Alia de prospero itinere precatio (carm. 37) [Dub.]: coll. 520–521.
Alia precatio (carm. 38) [Dub.]: coll. 521–522.
Carm. 9: Dup. 2022 013.
Carm. 28: Dup. partim 2022 057 (AG 1.92).
Cod: 11,038: Hexametr., Eleg., Epigr., Hymn., Lyr., Iamb., Poem.

060 **Carmina moralia**, MPG 37: 521–968.
In laudem virginitatis (carm. 1): coll. 521–578.
Praecepta ad virgines (carm. 2): coll. 578–632.
Exhortatio ad virgines (carm. 3) [Dub.]: coll. 632–640.
Ad virginem (carm. 4): coll. 640–642.
Ad monachos in monasterio degentes (carm. 5): coll. 642–643.
De pudicitia (carm. 6): coll. 643–648.
De castitate (carm. 7): coll. 648–649.
Comparatio vitarum (carm. 8): coll. 649–667.
De virtute (carm. 9): coll. 667–680.
De virtute (carm. 10): coll. 680–752.
Dialogus cum mundo (carm. 11): coll. 752–753.
De naturae humanae fragilitate (carm. 12): coll. 753–754.
De eodem argumento (carm. 13): coll. 754–755.
De humana natura (carm. 14): coll. 755–765.
De exterioris hominis vilitate (carm. 15): coll. 766–778.
De vitae itineribus (carm. 16): coll. 778–781.
Variorum vitae generum beatitudines (carm. 17): coll. 781–786.
De vita humana (carm. 18) [Sp.]: coll. 786–787.
De eodem argumento (carm. 19) [Sp.]: coll. 787–788.
De desiderio (carm. 20) [Sp.]: col. 788.
De morte carorum (carm. 21) [Sp.]: col. 789.
De falsis amicis (carm. 22): col. 789.
De eodem argumento (carm. 23) [Sp.]: col. 790.
Dialogus adversus eos qui frequenter jurant (carm. 24): coll. 790–813.
Adversus iram (carm. 25): coll. 813–851.

In nobilem male moratum (carm. 26): coll. 851–854.

De eodem argumento (carm. 27): coll. 854–856.

Adversus opum amantes (carm. 28): coll. 856–884.

Adversus mulieres se nimis ornantes (carm. 29): coll. 884–908.

Versus iambici acrostichi (carm. 30): coll. 908–910.

Distichae sententiae (carm. 31): coll. 910–915.

Aliae generis eiusdem sententiae (carm. 32) [Sp.]: coll. 916–927.

Tetrastichae sententiae (carm. 33): coll. 927–945.

Definitiones minus exactae (carm. 34): coll. 945–964.

De philosophica paupertate (carm. 35): col. 965.

De eodem argumento (carm. 36): coll. 965–966.

De patientia (carm. 37): col. 966.

De eodem argumento (carm. 38): col. 967.

De fortuna et providentia (carm. 39) [Sp.]: coll. 967–968.

De rerum humanarum vanitate (carm. 40) [Sp.]: col. 968.

Carm. 8: Dup. 2022 012.

Carm. 28: Dup. partim 2022 057 (AG 1.92).

Cod: 38,594: Hexametr., Eleg., Lyr., Iamb., Gnom., Poem.

061 **Carmina de se ipso**, MPG 37: 969–1029, 1166–1452.

Carm. 1–10: coll. 969–1029.

Carm. 12–99: coll. 1166–1452.

Carm. 90–91, 93–98: Dup. partim 2022 057 (AG 8.77–82, 84).

Carm. 99 est dubium.

Carm. 11 (De vita sua): Cf. 2022 004.

Cod: 29,518: Hexametr., Eleg., Epigr., Iamb., Biogr.

062 **Carmina quae spectant ad alios**, MPG 37: 1451–1577.

Ad Hellenium pro monachis exhortatorium (carm. 1): coll. 1451–1477.

Ad Julianum (carm. 2): coll. 1477–1480.

Ad Vitalianum (carm. 3): coll. 1480–1505.

Nicobuli filii ad patrem (carm. 4): coll. 1505–1521.

Nicobuli patris ad filium (carm. 5): coll. 1521–1542.

Ad Olympiadem (carm. 6): coll. 1542–1550.

Ad Nemesium (carm. 7): coll. 1551–1577.

Carm. 8 (Ad Seleucum): Cf. AMPHILOCHIUS Scr. Eccl. (2112 002).

Cod: 11,350: Eleg., Hexametr.

063 **Epitaphia**, MPG 38: 11–82.

Epitaph. 1–3, 6–78, 80–128 etiam exstant in *Anthologia Graeca* (lib. 8): Dup. partim 2022 057.

Epitaph. 129 spurium est.

Cod: Epigr.

064 **Epigrammata**, MPG 38: 81–130.

Epigr. 26–29, 47–94 etiam exstant in *Anthologia Graeca* (lib. 8): Dup. partim 2022 057.

Epigr. 30 spurium est.

Cod: Epigr.

065 **Alphabeticum A** [Sp.], ed. C. Müller, "Handschriftliches zu Ignatius Diaconus," *Byzantinische Zeitschrift* 3 (1894) 521.

Cod

066 Ὁ προτρεπτικὸς εἰς ὑπομονὴν ἢ πρὸς τοὺς νεωστὶ βεβαπτισμένους, ed. A. Guida, "Un nuovo testo di Gregorio Nazianzeno," *Prometheus* 2 (1976) 222–226.

Dup. partim CLEMENS ALEXANDRINUS Theol. (0555 008) (fr. 44).

Dup. partim Pseudo-MACARIUS Scr. Eccl. (2109 001) (sermo 62).

Dup. partim MAXIMUS CONFESSOR Theol. et Poeta (2892 081).

Cod: Homilet.

x01 **Epigramma demonstrativum**.

App. Anth. 3.161: Cf. ANTHOLOGIAE GRAECAE APPENDIX (7052 003).

x02 **Metaphrasis in Ecclesiasten** [Sp.].

MPG 10.998–1017.

Cf. GREGORIUS THAUMATURGUS Scr. Eccl. (2063 006).

x03 **Alphabeticum paraeneticum 2** (e cod. Vind. philos. gr. 165 N).

FCG 4.356–357.

Cf. MENANDER Comic. (0541 047).

2017 **GREGORIUS NYSSENUS** Theol.

A.D. 4: Nyssenus

030 **Contra Eunomium**, ed. W. Jaeger, *Gregorii Nysseni opera*, vols. 1.1 & 2.2. Leiden: Brill, 1960: **1.1**:3–409; **2.2**:3–311.

Cod: 172,463: Theol., Apol.

031 **Refutatio confessionis Eunomii**, ed. Jaeger, *Gregorii Nysseni opera*, vol. 2.2 (1960): 312–410.

Cod: 23,674: Apol., Theol.

001 **Ad Eustathium de sancta trinitate**, ed. F. Mueller, *Gregorii Nysseni opera*, vol. 3.1 (1958): 3–16.

Cod: 2,792: Theol.

002 **Ad Graecos ex communibus notionibus**, ed. Mueller, *op. cit.*, vol. 3.1, 19–33.

Cod: 3,111: Theol.

003 **Ad Ablabium quod non sint tres dei**, ed. Mueller, *op. cit.*, vol. 3.1, 37–57.

Cod: 4,092: Theol.

004 **Ad Simplicium de fide**, ed. Mueller, *op. cit.*, vol. 3.1, 61–67.

Cod: 1,604: Theol.

005 **Adversus Arium et Sabellium de patre et filio**, ed. Mueller, *op. cit.*, vol. 3.1, 71–85.

Cod: 4,019: Theol.

006 **Adversus Macedonianos de spiritu sancto**, ed. Mueller, *op. cit.*, vol. 3.1, 89–115.

Cod: 7,710: Theol.

007 **Ad Theophilum adversus Apollinaristas**, ed. Mueller, *op. cit.*, vol. 3.1, 119–128.
Cod : 1,732 : Theol.

008 **Antirrheticus adversus Apollinarium**, ed. Mueller, *op. cit.*, vol. 3.1, 131–233.
Cod : 27,511 : Theol.

081 **In illud: *Tunc et ipse filius***, ed. J.K. Downing, *Gregorii Nysseni opera*, vol. 3.2 (1986): 1–28.
Cod : 5,315 : Exeget.

082 **Contra fatum**, ed. J. McDonough, *Gregorii Nysseni opera*, vol. 3.2, 31–63.
Cod : 6,704 : Theol., Phil.

083 **De infantibus praemature abreptis**, ed. H. Hörner, *Gregorii Nysseni opera*, vol. 3.2, 67–97.
Cod : 6,642 : Theol., Phil.

084 **De pythonissa ad Theodosium episcopum**, ed. Hörner, *Gregorii Nysseni opera*, vol. 3.2, 101–108. 101–108.
Cod : 1,510 : Epist., Exeget.

027 **In inscriptiones Psalmorum**, ed. J. McDonough, *Gregorii Nysseni opera*, vol. 5 (1962): 24–175.
Cod : 36,066 : Exeget.

028 **In sextum Psalmum**, ed. McDonough, *Gregorii Nysseni opera*, vol. 5, 187–193.
Cod : 1,593 : Exeget.

029 **In Ecclesiasten** (homiliae 8), ed. P. Alexander, *Gregorii Nysseni opera*, vol. 5, 277–442.
Cod : 31,078 : Homilet., Exeget.

032 **In Canticum canticorum** (homiliae 15), ed. H. Langerbeck, *Gregorii Nysseni opera*, vol. 6 (1960): 3–469.
Cod : 79,915 : Homilet., Exeget.

024 **De instituto Christiano**, ed. Jaeger, *Gregorii Nysseni opera*, vol. 8.1 (1963): 40–89.
Cod : 9,149 : Phil., Theol.

025 **De professione Christiana ad Harmonium**, ed. Jaeger, *Gregorii Nysseni opera*, vol. 8.1, 129–142.
Cod : 2,564 : Theol., Phil.

026 **De perfectione Christiana ad Olympium monachum**, ed. Jaeger, *Gregorii Nysseni opera*, vol. 8.1, 173–214.
Cod : 7,842 : Theol., Phil.

033 **Epistulae**, ed. G. Pasquali, *Gregorii Nysseni opera*, vol. 8.2, 2nd edn. (1959): 3–95.
Ad Flavianum episcopum (epist. 1): pp. 3–12.
De iis qui adeunt Hierosolyma (epist. 2): pp. 13–19.
Ad Eustathiam et Ambrosiam (epist. 3): pp. 19–27.
Ad Eusebium (epist. 4): pp. 27–30.
Ad Sebastenos (epist. 5): pp. 31–34 (*item* pp. 92–95).
Ad Ablabium episcopum (epist. 6): pp. 34–36.
Ad Hierium praefectum (epist. 7): pp. 36–37.
Ad Antiochianum (epist. 8): pp. 37–38.
Ad Stagirium sophistam (epist. 9): pp. 38–39.
Ad Otreium episcopum (epist. 10): pp. 39–40.
Ad Eupatrium scholasticum (epist. 11): pp. 41–42.

Ad Eupatrium scholasticum (epist. 12): pp. 42–44.
Ad Libanium sophistam (epist. 13): pp. 44–46.
Ad Libanium sophistam (epist. 14): pp. 46–48.
Ad Joannem et Maximianum (epist. 15): pp. 48–49.
Ad Strategium presbyterum (epist. 16): pp. 49–50.
Ad presbyteros in Nicomedia (epist. 17): pp. 51–58.
Ad Otreium episcopum (epist. 18): pp. 58–61.
Ad Joannem (epist. 19): pp. 62–68.
Ad Adelphium scholasticum (epist. 20): pp. 68–72.
Ad Ablabium episcopum (epist. 21): pp. 73–74.
Ad episcopos (epist. 22): p. 74.
Sine titulo (epist. 23): p. 74.
Ad Heraclianum haereticum (epist. 24): pp. 75–79.
Ad Amphilochium Iconiensem (epist. 25): pp. 79–83.
Epistula Stagirii sophistae ad Gregorium (epist. 26) [Sp.?]: pp. 83–84.
Ad Stagirium sophistam (epist. 27) [Sp.]: pp. 84–85.
Sine titulo (epist. 28) [Sp.]: pp. 85–86.
Ad Petrum Sebastenum (epist. 29): pp. 87–89.
Epistula Petri Sebasteni ad Gregorium (epist. 30): pp. 89–91.
Cod : 19,280 : Epist.

009 **De mortuis non esse dolendum**, ed. G. Heil, *Gregorii Nysseni opera*, vol. 9.1 (1967): 28–68.
Cod : 9,338 : Homilet., Phil.

010 **De beneficentia** (*vulgo* **De pauperibus amandis i**), ed. A. van Heck, *Gregorii Nysseni opera*, vol. 9.1, 93–108.
Cod : 3,176 : Homilet.

011 **In illud: *Quatenus uni ex his fecistis mihi fecistis*** (*vulgo* **De pauperibus amandis ii**), ed. van Heck, *op. cit.*, vol. 9.1, 111–127.
Cod : 3,777 : Homilet., Exeget.

012 **Contra usurarios**, ed. E. Gebhardt, *Gregorii Nysseni opera*, vol. 9.1, 195–207.
Cod : 2,915 : Homilet.

013 **Contra fornicarios**, ed. Gebhardt, *op. cit.*, vol. 9.1, 211–217.
Cod : 1,296 : Homilet.

014 **In diem luminum** (*vulgo* **In baptismum Christi oratio**), ed. Gebhardt, *op. cit.*, vol. 9.1, 221–242.
Cod : 4,566 : Homilet.

015 **In sanctum pascha** (*vulgo* **In Christi resurrectionem oratio iii**), ed. Gebhardt, *op. cit.*, vol. 9.1, 245–270.
Cod : 5,694 : Homilet.

016 **De tridui inter mortem et resurrectionem domini nostri Jesu Christi spatio** (*vulgo* **In Christi resurrectionem oratio i**), ed. Gebhardt, *op. cit.*, vol. 9.1, 273–306.
Cod : 6,253 : Homilet.

017 **In sanctum et salutare pascha** (*vulgo* **In Christi resurrectionem oratio iv**), ed. Gebhardt, *op. cit.*, vol. 9.1, 309–311.
Cod: 642: Homilet.

018 **In luciferam sanctam domini resurrectionem** (*vulgo* **In Christi resurrectionem oratio v**) [Sp.], ed. Gebhardt, *op. cit.*, vol. 9.1, 315–319.
Cod: 1,071: Homilet.

019 **In ascensionem Christi**, ed. Gebhardt, *op. cit.*, vol. 9.1, 323–327.
Cod: 990: Homilet.

020 **De deitate adversus Evagrium** (*vulgo* **In suam ordinationem**), ed. Gebhardt, *op. cit.*, vol. 9.1, 331–341.
Cod: 2,087: Homilet.

021 **Oratio funebris in Meletium episcopum**, ed. A. Spira, *Gregorii Nysseni opera*, vol. 9.1, 441–457.
Cod: 2,475: Homilet., Encom.

022 **Oratio consolatoria in Pulcheriam**, ed. Spira, *op. cit.*, vol. 9.1, 461–472.
Cod: 2,840: Homilet., Encom.

023 **Oratio funebris in Flacillam imperatricem**, ed. Spira, *op. cit.*, vol. 9.1, 475–490.
Cod: 3,014: Homilet., Encom.

034 **De creatione hominis sermo primus** [Sp.], ed. H. Hörner, *Gregorii Nysseni opera*, suppl. (1972): 2–40.
Cod: 4,622: Homilet.

035 **De creatione hominis sermo alter** [Sp.], ed. Hörner, *Gregorii Nysseni opera*, suppl., 41–72.
Cod: 4,211: Homilet.

036 **De paradiso** [Sp.], ed. Hörner, *Gregorii Nysseni opera*, suppl., 2a–39a, 40.
Cod: 1,675: Homilet.

037 **De creatione hominis sermo primus** (recensio C) [Sp.], ed. Hörner, *Gregorii Nysseni opera*, suppl., 2a–39a, 40.
Cod: 5,775: Homilet.

038 **De creatione hominis sermo alter** (recensio C) [Sp.], ed. Hörner, *Gregorii Nysseni opera*, suppl., 41a–72a.
Cod: 4,683: Homilet.

039 **De paradiso** (recensio ΛF) [Sp.], ed. Hörner, *Gregorii Nysseni opera*, suppl., 75a–84a.
Cod: 1,927: Homilet.

040 **Encomium in sanctum Stephanum protomartyrem i**, ed. O. Lendle, *Gregorius Nyssenus. Encomium in sanctum Stephanum protomartyrem*. Leiden: Brill, 1968: 4–44.
Cod: 3,925: Encom., Hagiogr.

041 **Vita sanctae Macrinae**, ed. P. Maraval, *Grégoire de Nysse. Vie de sainte Macrine* [*Sources chrétiennes* 178. Paris: Cerf, 1971]: 136–266.
Cod: 9,131: Hagiogr., Epist.

042 **De vita Mosis**, ed. J. Daniélou, *Grégoire de Nysse. La vie de Moïse*, 3rd edn. [*Sources chrétiennes* 1 ter. Paris: Cerf, 1968]: 44–326.
Cod: 30,573: Hagiogr., Exeget., Phil., Theol.

043 **De virginitate**, ed. M. Aubineau, *Grégoire de*

Nysse. Traité de la virginité [*Sources chrétiennes* 119. Paris: Cerf, 1966]: 246–560.
Cod: 20,454: Theol., Phil.

044 **De virginitate** (recensio altera), ed. Aubineau, *op. cit.*, 258–260, 508, 514–516, 546–548.
Cod: 634: Phil., Theol.

046 **Oratio catechetica magna**, ed. J. Srawley, *The catechetical oration of Gregory of Nyssa*. Cambridge: Cambridge University Press, 1903 (repr. 1956): 1–164.
Cod: 20,996: Apol., Theol.

047 **De oratione dominica orationes v**, ed. F. Oehler, *Gregor's Bischof's von Nyssa Abhandlung von der Erschaffung des Menschen und fünf Reden auf das Gebet*. Leipzig: Engelmann, 1859: 202–314.
Cod: 16,472: Homilet., Exeget.

048 **In Basilium fratrem**, ed. J. Stein, *Encomium of Saint Gregory Bishop of Nyssa on his brother Saint Basil*. Washington, D.C.: The Catholic University of America, 1928: 2–60.
Cod: 6,327: Encom., Hagiogr.

049 **Oratio in diem natalem Christi**, ed. F. Mann, *Die Weihnachtspredigt Gregors von Nyssa Überlieferungsgeschichte und Text* [*Diss. Münster (1975)*]: 263–292.
Cod: 4,931: Homilet.

051 **In annuntiationem** [Sp.], ed. D. Montagna, "La lode alla theotokos nei testi greci dei secoli iv–vii," *Marianum* 24 (1962) 536–539.
Cod: 1,764: Encom., Hagiogr.

052 **Inventio imaginis in Camulianis** [Sp.], ed. E. Dobschütz, *Christusbilder. Untersuchungen zur christlichen Legende* [*Texte und Untersuchungen* 18. Leipzig: Hinrichs, 1899]: 12**–18**.
Cod: 865: Hagiogr.

053 **Orationes viii de beatitudinibus**, MPG 44: 1193–1301.
Cod: 23,092: Homilet., Exeget.

055 **Ad imaginem dei et ad similitudinem** [Sp.], MPG 44: 1328–1345.
Cod: 4,139: Theol., Exeget.

056 **Dialogus de anima et resurrectione**, MPG 46: 12–160.
Cod: 24,400: Theol., Phil., Dialog.

058 **Testimonia adversus Judaeos** [Sp.], MPG 46: 193–233.
Cod: 6,764: Theol.

059 **Adversus eos qui castigationes aegre ferunt**, MPG 46: 308–316.
Cod: 1,980: Homilet.

060 **De iis qui baptismum differunt**, MPG 46: 416–432.
Cod: 3,111: Homilet.

061 **Decem syllogismi contra Manichaeos** [Sp.], MPG 46: 541.
Cod: 234: Phil., Theol.

062 **De deitate filii et spiritus sancti**, MPG 46: 553–576.
Cod: 4,752: Homilet., Theol.

063 **De spiritu sancto** *sive* **In pentecosten,** MPG
46: 696–701.
Cod: 1,285: Homilet.

064 **Encomium in sanctum Stephanum protomar-**
tyrem ii, MPG 46: 721–736.
Cod: 2,468: Encom., Hagiogr.

065 **De sancto Theodoro,** MPG 46: 736–748.
Cod: 2,522: Encom., Hagiogr.

066 **Encomium in xl martyres i,** MPG 46: 749–772.
Cod: 4,813: Encom., Hagiogr.

067 **Encomium in xl martyres ii,** MPG 46: 773–
788.
Cod: 3,004: Encom., Hagiogr.

068 **In sanctum Ephraim,** MPG 46: 820–849.
Cod: 6,413: Encom., Hagiogr.

069 **De vita Gregorii Thaumaturgi,** MPG 46: 893–
957.
Cod: 13,944: Encom., Hagiogr.

070 **Epistula xxvi ad Evagrium monachum** [Sp.],
MPG 46: 1101–1108.
Cod: 1,132: Epist.

071 **Sermo in illud:** *Hic est filius meus dilectus*
(ap. Joannem Damascenum, *Sacra parallela*)
(fragmenta), MPG 46: 1109–1112.
Q: 217: Homilet., Exeget.

072 **Sermo in Mariam et Joseph** (ap. Joannem
Damascenum, *Sacra parallela*) (fragmentum),
MPG 46: 1112.
Q: 108: Homilet.

073 **De occursu domini** [Sp.], MPG 46: 1152–1181.
Cod: 6,101: Homilet., Hagiogr.

074 **Tractatus ad Xenodorum** (fragmentum), ed. F.
Diekamp, *Analecta patristica* [*Orientalia Chris-
tiana analecta* 117. Rome: Pont. Institutum
Orientalium Studiorum, 1938 (repr. 1962)]:
14–15.
Cod: 112: Phil.

075 **Sermo in sanctum Romanum** (ap. Joannem
Damascenum, *Sacra parallela*) (fragmentum),
MPG 96: 476–477.
Q: 65: Homilet., Hagiogr., Encom.

076 **Epistula canonica ad Letoium,** MPG 45: 221–
236.
Cod: 3,133: Epist., Eccl.

077 **Liber de cognitione dei** (= Θεογνωσία) (fragmenta ap. Euthymium Zigabenum, *Panoplia
dogmatica*) [Sp.], MPG 130: 28–29, 257–276,
312–317.
Q: 5,079: Theol.

078 **Apologia in hexaemeron,** MPG 44: 61–124.
Cod: 14,827: Apol., Exeget., Theol.

079 **De opificio hominis,** MPG 44: 124–256.
Cod: 28,105: Theol., Exeget.

080 **Epistula ad Philippum monachum** (ap. Joannem Damascenum, *Contra Jacobitas*) (fragmentum), MPG 46: 1112.
Q: 54: Epist.

x01 **Ad Petrum fratrem de differentia essentiae**
hypostaseos.
Basilius, *Epist.* 38.
Cf. BASILIUS Theol. (2040 004).

x02 **De anima** [Sp.].
Nemesius, *De natura hominis*, cap. 2–3.
Cf. NEMESIUS Theol. (0743 001).

4092 **GREGORIUS PARDUS** Gramm. et Rhet.
vel Georgius Pardus vel Georgius Prodromus
vel Gregorius Corinthius vel Gregorius Smyrnaeus
A.D. 11–12: Corinthius

002 **Commentarium in Hermogenis librum** περὶ
μεθόδου δεινότητος, ed. C. Walz, *Rhetores
Graeci*, vol. 7. Stuttgart: Cotta, 1834 (repr.
Osnabrück: Zeller, 1968): 1090–1352.
Cod: Rhet., Comm.

2063 **GREGORIUS THAUMATURGUS** Scr. Eccl.
A.D. 3: Neocaesariensis

001 **In Originem oratio panegyrica,** ed. H. Crouzel,
*Grégoire le Thaumaturge. Remerciement à Ori-
gène suivi de la lettre d'Origène à Grégoire*
[*Sources chrétiennes* 148. Paris: Cerf, 1969]:
94–182.
Cod: 9,302: Orat., Encom.

005 **Epistula canonica,** FONTI II: 19–30.
Cod: 1,223: Epist.

006 **Metaphrasis in Ecclesiasten Salamonis,** MPG
10: 988–1017.
Cod: 5,249: Exeget.

008 **Ad Tatianum de anima per capita disputatio**
[Sp.], MPG 10: 1137–1145.
Dup. partim MAXIMUS CONFESSOR Theol.
et Poeta (2892 043).
Cod: 1,609: Theol.

009 **In annuntiationem sanctae virginis Mariae**
(homiliae 1–2) [Sp.], MPG 10: 1145–1169.
Cod: 5,216: Homilet.

010 **Sermo in omnes sanctos** [Sp.], MPG 10: 1197–
1204.
Cod: 674: Homilet.

013 **Fragmentum in evangelium Matthaei 6.22–23**
(in catenis), MPG 10: 1189.
Q: 185: Exeget., Caten.

016 **Fragmentum in Job** (in catenis), ed. J.B. Pitra,
Analecta sacra spicilegio Solesmensi parata, vol.
3. Venice: St. Lazarus Monastery, 1883: 589–
591.
Cod: 461: Exeget., Caten.

017 **Exorcismus,** ed. A. Strittmatter, "Ein griechisches Exorzismusbüchlein. Ms. car. C 143b
der Zentralbibliothek in Zürich," *Orientalia
Christiana* 26.2 (Rome, 1932): 129–137.
Cod

018 **Precatio,** ed. Strittmatter, *op. cit.,* 141–143.
Cod

020 **De deitate et tribus personis,** ed. C.P. Caspari,
"Nogle nye kirkehistoriske Anecdota II. Et
Gregorius Thaumaturgus tillagt Fragment,"
*Theologisk Tidsskrift for den evangelisk-luther-
ske Kirche i Norge*, ser. 2, vol. 8 (1882) 53–59.
Q

021 **Sententiae** (ap. Antonium Melissam), ed. V.

Ryssel, *Gregorius Thaumaturgus. Sein Leben und seine Schriften.* Leipzig: Fernau, 1880: 52–53.
frr. 1–6.
Q: 119: Gnom.

022 Εἰς τὸ οὐδὲν εἴδωλον ἐν κόσμῳ (fragmentum), ed. K. Holl, *Fragmente vornicänischer Kirchenväter aus den Sacra parallela herausgegeben* [*Texte und Untersuchungen* 20. Leipzig: Hinrichs, 1899]: 159.
fr. 405.
Q: 32: Theol.

025 **Fragmenta in Jeremiam** (in catenis), ed. Pitra, *op. cit.*, 591–595.
Q: 1,150: Exeget., Caten.

026 **Fragmentum in Matthaeum** (in catenis, typus C), ed. B. Corderius, *Symbolarum in Matthaeum tomus alter, quo continetur catena patrum Graecorum triginta collectore Niceta episcopo Serrarum.* Toulouse, 1647.
Q: Exeget., Caten.

028 **De fide capitula duodecim**, ed. L. Casson and E.L. Hettich, *Excavations at Nessana, vol. 2: literary papyri.* Princeton: Princeton University Press, 1950: 155–158.
Cf. et 2063 x02.
Pap: 553: Theol.

x01 **Fragmentum** (in *Doctrina patrum*).
Diekamp, p. 251 (vv. 7–8).
Cf. DOCTRINA PATRUM (7051 001).

x02 **De fide capitula duodecim** (= **Liber de dei verbi incarnatione**).
ACO 1.1.6, pp. 146–151.
Cf. CONCILIA OECUMENICA (ACO) (5000 001).
Cf. et 2063 028.

x03 **Confessio fidei.**
ACO 3, p. 3.
Cf. CONCILIA OECUMENICA (ACO) (5000 004).

2118 *GRYLLUS*
ante A.D. 3
001 **Fragmentum** (*P. Oxy.* 22.2331), ed. E. Heitsch, *Die griechischen Dichterfragmente der römischen Kaiserzeit*, vol. 2. Göttingen: Vandenhoeck & Ruprecht, 1964: 48–49.
Pap: 81: Lyr.

1758 **HABRON** Gramm.
A.D. 1: Phrygius, Rhodius
001 **Fragmenta**, ed. R. Berndt, "Die Fragmente des Grammatikers Habron," *Philologische Wochenschrift* 35 (1915) coll. 1452–1455, 1483.
frr. 1–21.
Q: Gramm.

2259 **HABRON** Hist.
2 B.C.?: Atheniensis
001 **Testimonium**, FGrH #359: 3B:218.
NQ: 19: Test.

HADRIANUS Rhet.
A.D. 2: Tyrius
Cf. ADRIANUS Rhet. et Soph. (0666).

0195 **HADRIANUS Imperator**
A.D. 1–2: Romanus
001 **Epigrammata**, AG 6.332; 7.674; 9.137, 387(?), 402.
AG 9.17, 387: Cf. (et) GERMANICUS CAESAR <Epigr.> (0191 001).
AG 9.137: Cf. et ANONYMI EPIGRAMMATICI (AG) (0138 001).
Q: 163: Epigr.

x01 **Epigramma dedicatorium.**
App. Anth. 1.242: Cf. ANTHOLOGIAE GRAECAE APPENDIX (7052 001).

2358 **HAGELOCHUS** Hist.
post 3 B.C.
001 **Titulus**, FGrH #516: 3B:491.
NQ: Hist.

2359 **HAGESTRATUS** Hist.
post 3 B.C.
001 **Titulus**, FGrH #517: 3B:491.
NQ: Hist.

1387 **(H)AGIAS-DERCYLUS** Hist.
4 B.C.
001 **Testimonia**, FGrH #305: 3B:7.
NQ: 31: Test.
002 **Fragmenta**, FGrH #305: 3B:7–10, 757 addenda.
Q: 759: Hist.

0909 **HALIEUS** Med.
ante A.D. 1
x01 **Fragmenta ap. Galenum.**
K13.645, 785–786, 802, 1025–1026, 1032.
Cf. GALENUS Med. (0057 077).

1974 **HANNIBAL Rex Carthaginiensium** Hist.
3–2 B.C.: Carthaginiensis
001 **Testimonium**, FGrH #181: 2B:909.
NQ: 37: Test.

HANNO Rex Carthaginiensium <Geogr.>
Cf. PERIPLUS HANNONIS (0064).

1388 **HARMODIUS** Hist.
3 B.C.?: Lepreates
001 **Fragmenta**, FGrH #319: 3B:32–33.
Q: 376: Hist.

0720 **HARMODIUS** Trag.
1 B.C.: Tarsensis
001 **Titulus**, ed. B. Snell, *Tragicorum Graecorum fragmenta*, vol. 1. Göttingen: Vandenhoeck & Ruprecht, 1971: 309.
NQ: 2: Satyr.

0912 **HARPALUS** Med.
ante A.D. 1
x01 **Fragmenta ap. Galenum.**
K**13**.928–929; **14**.167.
Cf. GALENUS Med. (0057 077–078).

0914 **HARPOCRAS** Med.
A.D. 1–2: Alexandrinus
x01 **Fragmenta ap. Galenum.**
K**12**.631, 943; **13**.729, 838, 840–841, 978.
Cf. GALENUS Med. (0057 076–077).

1389 **HARPOCRATION** Gramm.
A.D. 1/2?: Alexandrinus
001 **Lexicon in decem oratores Atticos,** ed. W.
Dindorf, *Harpocrationis lexicon in decem ora-
tores Atticos,* vol. 1. Oxford: Oxford University
Press, 1853 (repr. Groningen: Bouma, 1969):
1–310.
Cod: 40,215: Lexicogr.

0913 **HARPOCRATION** Med.
ante A.D. 1?
x01 **Fragmentum ap. Galenum.**
K**12**.629.
Cf. GALENUS Med. (0057 076).

0691 *HARPOCRATIONIS EPISTULA*
fort. auctore Harpocratione Alexandrino
A.D. 4?
Cf. et CYRANIDES (1482).
001 **Epistula,** ed. C. Graux, "Lettre inédite d'Harpocration à un empereur," *Revue philologique* 2
(1878) 70–77.
Cod: 1,054: Epist., Med., Astrol.

0196 **HECATAEUS** Epigr.
3 B.C.: Thasius
001 **Epigramma,** AG 7.167.
Q: 42: Epigr.

0538 **HECATAEUS** Hist.
6–5 B.C.: Milesius
001 **Testimonia,** FGrH #1: 1A:1–7, *1 addenda.
NQ: 2,451: Test.
002 **Fragmenta,** FGrH #1: 1A:7–47, *1–*4 addenda.
Q: 11,822: Hist., Myth., Perieg.
003 **Fragmenta,** ed. H.J. Mette, "Die 'Kleinen'
griechischen Historiker heute," *Lustrum* 21
(1978) 6.
fr. 145 bis a–b.
Q: 89: Hist.

1390 **HECATAEUS** Hist.
4–3 B.C.: Abderita
001 **Testimonia,** FGrH #264: 3A:11–12.
NQ: 603: Test.
002 **Fragmenta,** FGrH #264: 3A:12–64.
Q: 24,721: Hist., Myth.
003 **Testimonia,** ed. H. Diels and W. Kranz, *Die*

Fragmente der Vorsokratiker, vol. 2, 6th edn.
Berlin: Weidmann, 1952 (repr. Dublin: 1966):
240–241.
test. 1–6.
NQ: 214: Test.
004 **Fragmenta,** ed. Diels and Kranz, *op. cit.,* 241–
245.
frr. 1–16.
Q: 1,794: Phil., Hist.

0197 **HEDYLE** Epigr.
4–3 B.C.
001 **Fragmentum,** ed. H. Lloyd-Jones and P. Parsons, *Supplementum Hellenisticum.* Berlin: De
Gruyter, 1983: 234.
fr. 456.
Q: 34: Epigr.

0198 **HEDYLUS** Epigr.
3 B.C.: Atheniensis vel Samius
001 **Epigrammata,** AG 5.161, 199; **6**.292; **11**.123,
414.
Q: 156: Epigr.
002 **Fragmentum et titulus,** ed. H. Lloyd-Jones and
P. Parsons, *Supplementum Hellenisticum.* Ber-
lin: De Gruyter, 1983: 235.
frr. 458–459.
Q: 48: Eleg., Epigr.
x01 **Epigrammata** (*App. Anth.*).
Epigramma dedicatorium: 1.115.
Epigramma sepulcrale: 2.134.
Epigramma demonstrativum: 3.67.
Epigrammata exhortatoria et supplicatoria:
4.25–26.
Epigrammata irrisoria: 5.16–18.
App. Anth. 1.115: Cf. ANTHOLOGIAE GRAE-
CAE APPENDIX (7052 001).
App. Anth. 2.134: Cf. ANTHOLOGIAE GRAE-
CAE APPENDIX (7052 002).
App. Anth. 3.67: Cf. ANTHOLOGIAE GRAE-
CAE APPENDIX (7052 003).
App. Anth. 4.25–26: Cf. ANTHOLOGIAE
GRAECAE APPENDIX (7052 004).
App. Anth. 5.16–18: Cf. ANTHOLOGIAE
GRAECAE APPENDIX (7052 005).

1391 **HEGEMON** Epic.
fiq Hegemon Epigr.
3 B.C.?: Alexandrinus (Troadis)
001 **Epigramma,** AG 7.436.
Q: 25: Epigr.
002 **Titulus,** ed. H. Lloyd-Jones and P. Parsons,
Supplementum Hellenisticum. Berlin: De Gruyter, 1983: 236.
fr. 462.
NQ: 2: Hist., Epic.
003 **Testimonium,** FGrH #110: 2B:523.
NQ: 24: Test.
004 **Fragmentum,** FGrH #110: 2B:523–524.
Q: 106: Hist., Epic.

1925 HEGEMON Epigr.
fiq Hegemon Epic.
3 B.C.
Cf. et HEGEMON Epic. (1391).
x01 **Epigramma.**
AG 7.436.
Cf. HEGEMON Epic. (1391 001).

0463 HEGEMON Parodius
5 B.C.: Thasius
001 **Fragmentum,** ed. T. Kock, *Comicorum Atticorum fragmenta,* vol. 1. Leipzig: Teubner, 1880: 700.
fr. 1.
Q: 14: Comic.
002 **Fragmentum,** ed. A. Meineke, *Fragmenta comicorum Graecorum,* vol. 2.2. Berlin: Reimer, 1840 (repr. De Gruyter, 1970): 743.
Q: 14: Comic.
003 **Fragmentum,** ed. P. Brandt, *Parodorum epicorum Graecorum et Archestrati reliquiae [Corpusculum poesis epicae Graecae Ludibundae,* fasc. 1. Leipzig: Teubner, 1888]: 42–44.
Q: 151: Parod.

1392 HEGESANDER Hist.
3 B.C.: Delphicus
001 **Fragmenta,** FHG 4: 412–422.
Q: Hist.

1393 HEGESIANAX Epic. et Astron.
2 B.C.: Alexandrinus (Troadis)
001 **Fragmenta,** ed. J.U. Powell, *Collectanea Alexandrina.* Oxford: Clarendon Press, 1925 (repr. 1970): 8–9.
frr. 1–2.
Dup. 1393 004 (frr. 465–467).
Q: 36: Epic., Astron.
002 **Testimonia,** FGrH #45: 1A:268–270, *19 addenda.
NQ: 638: Test.
003 **Fragmenta,** FGrH #45: 1A:270–272.
Q: 739: Hist., Myth.
004 **Fragmenta et titulus,** ed. H. Lloyd-Jones and P. Parsons, *Supplementum Hellenisticum.* Berlin: De Gruyter, 1983: 237–238.
frr. (+ titul.) 465–467.
Dup. 1393 001 (frr. 1–2).
Q: 39: Epic., Astron.

HEGESIAS Epic.
Cf. CYPRIA (1296).

1394 HEGESIAS Hist. et Orat.
3 B.C.: Magnes
001 **Testimonia,** FGrH #142: 2B:804–806.
NQ: 1,028: Test.
002 **Fragmenta,** FGrH #142: 2B:806–811.
Q, Cod: 1,523: Hist., Encom.

1395 HEGESINUS Epic.
ante A.D. 2

001 **Fragmentum** [Dub.], ed. G. Kinkel, *Epicorum Graecorum fragmenta,* vol. 1. Leipzig: Teubner, 1877: 208.
Dup. partim 1395 003.
Q: 28: Epic.
002 **Testimonia,** FGrH #331: 3B:165.
NQ: 88: Test.
003 **Fragmentum** [Dub.], FGrH #331: 3B:165.
Dup. partim 1395 001.
Q: 69: Hist., Epic.

0464 HEGESIPPUS Comic.
3 B.C.
001 **Fragmenta,** ed. T. Kock, *Comicorum Atticorum fragmenta,* vol. 3. Leipzig: Teubner, 1888: 312–314.
frr. 1–3.
Q: 238: Comic.
002 **Fragmenta,** ed. A. Meineke, *Fragmenta comicorum Graecorum,* vol. 4. Berlin: Reimer, 1841 (repr. De Gruyter, 1970): 479–481.
Q: 234: Comic.

1396 HEGESIPPUS Epigr.
3 B.C.
001 **Epigrammata,** AG **6.**124, 178, 266; **7.**276, 320, 446, 545; **13.**12.
Q: 234: Epigr.

1397 HEGESIPPUS Hist.
4 B.C.?: Mecybernaeus
001 **Testimonia,** FGrH #391: 3B:273.
NQ: 53: Test.
002 **Fragmenta,** FGrH #391: 3B:273–275.
Q: 740: Hist.

1398 HEGESIPPUS Scr. Eccl.
A.D. 2: Palaestinus
001 **Fragmenta** (ex incerto libro), ed. M.J. Routh, *Reliquiae sacrae,* vol. 1, 2nd edn. Oxford: Oxford University Press, 1846 (repr. Hildesheim: Olms, 1974): 207–219.
Q: 1,766: Hagiogr., Exeget.

1831 HEGETOR Med.
2 B.C.
x01 **Fragmentum ap. Apollonium.**
CMG, vol. 11.1.1, pp. 78–80.
Cf. APOLLONIUS Med. (0660 001).

2420 HEGIAS Hist.
post 4 B.C.?: Troezenius
001 **Fragmentum,** FGrH #606: 3B:739.
Q: 75: Hist.

2256 HELICON Math., Astron. et Phil.
4 B.C.: Cyzicenus
001 **Testimonia,** ed. F. Lasserre, *De Léodamas de Thasos à Philippe d'Oponte.* Naples: Bibliopolis, 1987: 141–143.
test. 1–4.
NQ: Test.

HELIODORUS Gramm.
A.D. 6/9?
Cf. COMMENTARIA IN DIONYSII THRACIS
ARTEM GRAMMATICAM (4175 003, 005–006).

0692 **HELIODORUS** Med.
A.D. 1
Cf. et ANTYLLUS et HELIODORUS Med. (0852).
x01 **Fragmenta ap. Oribasium.**
CMG, vol. **6.2.1**, pp. 120–125, 164–165, 166, 168, 176, 216–227, 232–234, 236, 239–240, 258–260, 273–275, 279–281; **6.2.2**, pp. 4–12, 13–43, 57, 60–69.
Cf. ORIBASIUS Med. (0722 001).
x02 **Fragmentum ap. Paulum.**
CMG, vol. 9.1, p. 371.
Cf. PAULUS Med. (0715 001).

1400 **HELIODORUS** Perieg.
2 B.C.?: Atheniensis
001 **Testimonia**, FGrH #373: 3B:239.
NQ: 62: Test.
002 **Fragmenta**, FGrH #373: 3B:239–241.
Q: 340: Hist., Perieg.

HELIODORUS Phil.
Incertum: Prusensis
Cf. ANONYMI IN ARISTOTELIS ETHICA
NICOMACHEA (4033 003).

0658 **HELIODORUS** Scr. Erot.
A.D. 3?
001 **Aethiopica**, ed. R.M. Rattenbury, T.W. Lumb and J. Maillon, *Héliodore. Les Éthiopiques (Théagène et Chariclée)*, 3 vols., 2nd edn. Paris: Les Belles Lettres, 1960: **1**:2–124; **2**:2–164; **3**:2–126.
Cod: 80,126: Narr. Fict.
002 **Epigrammata**, AG 9.485, 490.
Q: 84: Epigr.

0750 **HELIODORUS** Trag.
ante 1 B.C.: Atheniensis
001 Ἰταλικὰ θαύματα, ed. A. Meineke, *Commentationum miscellanearum fasciculus primus.* Halle: Bäntsch, 1822: 36–37.
Dup. partim 0750 002 (fr. 472).
Q: 105: Hexametr., Med.
002 **Fragmenta**, ed. H. Lloyd-Jones and P. Parsons, *Supplementum Hellenisticum.* Berlin: De Gruyter, 1983: 240–242.
frr. 471–474.
fr. 472 (Ἰταλικὰ θαύματα): Dup. 0750 001.
Q: 183: Hexametr., Med.

1401 **HELLADIUS** Epigr.
A.D. 1–2
001 **Epigramma**, AG 11.423.
Q: 13: Epigr.

2438 **HELLADIUS** Hist.
A.D. 4: Antinoupolitanus
001 **Testimonium**, FGrH #635: 3C:183.
NQ: 98: Test.

4245 **HELLANICUS** Gramm.
3–2 B.C.: Alexandrinus
001 **Fragmenta grammatica**, ed. F. Montanari, *I frammenti dei grammatici Agathokles, Hellanikos, Ptolemaios Epithetes* [*Sammlung griechischer und lateinischer Grammatiker* 7. Berlin: De Gruyter, 1988]: 57–61.
Q: Gramm.

0539 **HELLANICUS** Hist.
5 B.C.: Lesbius
001 **Testimonia**, FGrH #4, #323a, #687a: **1A**:104–107; **3B**:40–41: **3C**:412.
NQ: 1,551: Test.
002 **Fragmenta**, FGrH #4, #323a, #601a, #608a, #645a, #687a: **1A**:107–152, *6–*8 addenda; **3B**:41–50, 732–733; **3C**:1–2, 190, 412–414.
fr. 124b (*PSI* 1173): vol. 1A, p. *6 addenda.
fr. 189 (*P. Oxy.* 10.1241): vol. 1A, p. 150.
fr. 201 bis (*P. Giessen* 307v): vol. 1A, p. *7 addenda.
Q, Pap: 18,331: Hist., Myth.
003 **Fragmentum** (*P. Oxy.* 26.2442), ed. H.J. Mette, "Die 'Kleinen' griechischen Historiker heute," *Lustrum* 21 (1978) 7.
fr. 133 bis.
Pap: 78: Hist.

0558 *HELLENICA*
fort. auctore Cratippo vel Daimacho
4 B.C.?
Cf. et CRATIPPUS Hist. (1907).
Cf. et DAIMACHUS Hist. (2482).
001 **Fragmenta Florentina** (*PSI* 1304), ed. V. Bartoletti, *Hellenica Oxyrhynchia.* Leipzig: Teubner, 1959: 1–5.
Pap: 747: Hist.
002 **Fragmenta Londinensia** (*P. Oxy.* 5.842), ed. Bartoletti, *op. cit.*, 6–37.
Pap: 5,348: Hist.
003 **Fragmenta Londinensia incertae sedis** (*P. Oxy.* 5.842), ed. Bartoletti, *op. cit.*, 37–41.
Pap: 611: Hist.
004 **Fragmenta** (*P. Oxy.* 5.842), FGrH #66: 2A:17–35.
Pap: 5,218: Hist.
005 **Fragmentum** (*P. Cairo* inv. 26/6/27/1–35), ed. H.J. Mette, "Die 'Kleinen' griechischen Historiker heute," *Lustrum* 21 (1978) 11–12.
Pap: 445: Hist.

0465 **HENIOCHUS** Comic.
4 B.C.: Atheniensis
001 **Fragmenta**, ed. T. Kock, *Comicorum Atticorum fragmenta*, vol. 2. Leipzig: Teubner, 1884: 431–434.
frr. 1–5 + tituli.
Q: 245: Comic.

002 **Fragmenta**, ed. A. Meineke, *Fragmenta comi-corum Graecorum*, vol. 3. Berlin: Reimer, 1840 (repr. De Gruyter, 1970): 560–563.
Q: 240: Comic.

2043 **HEPHAESTION** Astrol.
A.D. 4: Thebanus
001 **Apotelesmatica**, ed. D. Pingree, *Hephaestionis Thebani apotelesmaticorum libri tres*, vol. 1. Leipzig: Teubner, 1973: 1–333.
Q, Cod: 74,652: Astrol.
002 **Apotelesmatica** (epitomae quattuor), ed. Pingree, *op. cit.*, vol. 2 (1974): 1–350.
Cod: 87,301: Astrol.
003 **Excerptum** (e cod. Paris. gr. 2506), ed. Pingree, *op. cit.*, vol. 2, VI–VII.
Cod: 407: Astrol.
004 **Excerptum** (e cod. Marcian. gr. 334), ed. Pingree, *op. cit.*, vol. 2, X–XI.
Cod: 473: Astrol.
005 **Excerptum** (e cod. Vat. gr. 1056), ed. Pingree, *op. cit.*, vol. 2, XXI–XXII.
Cod: 222: Astrol.

1402 **HEPHAESTION** Gramm.
A.D. 2
001 **Enchiridion de metris**, ed. M. Consbruch, *Hephaestionis enchiridion cum commentariis veteribus*. Leipzig: Teubner, 1906 (repr. Stuttgart: 1971): 1–58.
Cod: 7,847: Gramm.
002 **Introductio metrica**, ed. Consbruch, *op. cit.*, 58–62.
Cod: 650: Gramm.
003 **De poematis**, ed. Consbruch, *op. cit.*, 62–73.
Cod: 1,645: Gramm.
004 **De signis**, ed. Consbruch, *op. cit.*, 73–76.
Cod: 580: Gramm.
005 **Fragmenta Hephaestionea**, ed. Consbruch, *op. cit.*, 76–78.
frr. 1–5.
Cod: 323: Gramm.

0883 **HERACLAS** Med.
A.D. 1–2
x01 **Fragmentum ap. Oribasium**.
CMG, vol. 6.2.1, pp. 262–268.
Cf. ORIBASIUS Med. (0722 001).

1403 **HERACLEON** Gnost.
A.D. 2
001 **Fragmenta**, ed. W. Völker, *Quellen zur Geschichte der christlichen Gnosis*. Tübingen: Mohr, 1932: 63–86.
Q

0567 **HERACLEON** Gramm.
A.D. 1: Ephesius
001 **Fragmenta**, ed. R. Berndt, *Die Fragmente des Homererklärers Herakleon* [*Programm Gymnasium Insterburg* (1914)]: 18–24.
Q: Gramm.

0466 **HERACLIDES** Comic.
4 B.C.
Cf. et <HERACLITUS> Comic. (1784).
001 **Fragmentum**, ed. T. Kock, *Comicorum Atticorum fragmenta*, vol. 2. Leipzig: Teubner, 1884: 435.
fr. 1.
Q: 29: Comic.
002 **Fragmentum**, ed. A. Meineke, *Fragmenta comicorum Graecorum*, vol. 3. Berlin: Reimer, 1840 (repr. De Gruyter, 1970): 565.
Q: 27: Comic.

1410 **HERACLIDES** Epigr.
1 B.C.–A.D. 1: Sinopensis
001 **Epigrammata**, AG 7.281, 392.
AG 7.465: Cf. HERACLITUS Epigr. (1415 001).
Q: 63: Epigr.

1408 **HERACLIDES** Gramm.
A.D. 1–2: Milesius
001 **Fragmenta**, ed. L. Cohn, *De Heraclide Milesio grammatico*. Berlin: Calvary, 1884: 37–64, 66–79, 81–91, 93–107.
Περὶ καθολικῆς προσῳδίας (frr. 1–15): pp. 37–44.
Περὶ δυσκλίτων ῥημάτων (frr. 16–55): pp. 45–64, 66–79, 81–91, 93–102.
Fragmenta sedis incertae (frr. 56–60): pp. 103–106.
Fragmenta dubia (frr. 61–62): pp. 106–107.
Q: 12,544: Gramm.
002 Περὶ δυσκλίτων ῥημάτων (fragmentum) (*P. Rain.* 3.33A = *P. Vindob.* gr. 29815A), ed. A. Wouters, *The grammatical papyri from Graeco-Roman Egypt. Contributions to the study of the 'ars grammatica' in antiquity*. Brussels: Paleis der Academiën, 1979: 243–246.
Pap: 415: Gramm.

1406 **HERACLIDES** Hist.
4 B.C.: Cumaeus
001 **Testimonium**, FGrH #689: 3C:517.
NQ: 40: Test.
002 **Fragmenta**, FGrH #689: 3C:517–522.
Q: 1,259: Hist.

1979 **HERACLIDES** Hist.
1 B.C.?: Magnes
001 **Testimonium**, FGrH #187: 2B:918.
NQ: 10: Test.

0694 **HERACLIDES** Med.
1 B.C.: Tarentinus
Cf. et HERACLIDES Med. (1033).
x01 **Fragmenta ap. Galenum**.
K12.402–403, 435, 454–455, 583–584, 639–640, 691–693, 730, 741, 785, 835, 847–848, 867, 957; **13**.33, 328, 507–508, 717–728, 811–812, 826, 854, 857; **14**.186–187.
Cf. GALENUS Med. (0057 076–078).
x02 **Fragmentum ap. Aëtium** (lib. 6).

CMG, vol. 8.2, p. 230.
Cf. AËTIUS Med. (0718 006).

x03 **Fragmenta ap. Athenaeum.**
Deipnosophistae **2.**64a, 64e; **3.**120b.
Cf. ATHENAEUS Soph. (0008 001).

x04 **Fragmenta ap. Hippiatrica.**
Oder & Hoppe, vol. 2, pp. 194, 199.
Cf. HIPPIATRICA (0738 006).

0916 **HERACLIDES** Med.
1 B.C.–A.D. 1: Erythraeus
Cf. et HERACLIDES Med. (1033).

x01 **Fragmentum ap. Paulum.**
CMG, vol. 9.2, p. 371.
Cf. PAULUS Med. (0715 001).

1033 **HERACLIDES** Med.
fiq Heraclides Tarentinus vel Heraclides Erythraeus
1 B.C./A.D. 1?
Cf. et HERACLIDES Med. (0694).
Cf. et HERACLIDES Med. (0916).

x01 **Fragmentum ap. Alexandrum Trallianum.**
Puschmann, vol. 2, p. 527.
Cf. ALEXANDER Med. (0744 003).

0915 **HERACLIDES** Med.
ante A.D. 1: Ephesius

x01 **Fragmentum ap. Oribasium.**
CMG, vol. 6.2.2, p. 278.
Cf. ORIBASIUS Med. (0722 003).

1954 **HERACLIDES** Phil.
2 B.C.: Tarsensis

001 **Fragmentum**, ed. J. von Arnim, *Stoicorum veterum fragmenta*, vol. 3. Leipzig: Teubner, 1903 (repr. Stuttgart: 1968): 258.
Q: 21: Phil.

1844 **HERA[CLIDES]** Trag.
5 B.C.

001 **Titulus**, ed. B. Snell, *Tragicorum Graecorum fragmenta*, vol. 1. Göttingen: Vandenhoeck & Ruprecht, 1971: 155.
NQ: 7: Trag.

1405 **HERACLIDES Criticus** Perieg.
3–2 B.C.

001 **Descriptio Graeciae** (sub auctore Dicaearcho vel Athenaeo), ed. K. Müller, *Geographi Graeci minores*, vol. 1. Paris: Didot, 1855 (repr. Hildesheim: Olms, 1965): 97–110.
Cod: 2,862: Perieg.

1407 **HERACLIDES LEMBUS** Hist.
2 B.C.: Alexandrinus

001 **Excerpta politiarum**, ed. M.R. Dilts, *Heraclidis Lembi excerpta politiarum* [*Greek, Roman and Byzantine monographs* 5. Durham: Duke University Press, 1971]: 14–40.
Dup. partim ARISTOTELES Phil. et CORPUS ARISTOTELICUM (0086 051).
Cod: 2,935: Phil., Hist.

002 **Fragmenta**, FHG 3: 167–171.
Q

003 **Hermippi** περὶ νομοθετῶν (epitome) (*P. Oxy.* 11.1367), ed. B.P. Grenfell and A.S. Hunt, *The Oxyrhynchus papyri*, pt. 11. London: Egypt Exploration Fund, 1915: 116–117.
Pap

1409 **HERACLIDES PONTICUS** Phil.
4 B.C.: Heracleensis

001 **Fragmenta**, ed. F. Wehrli, *Herakleides Pontikos* [*Die Schule des Aristoteles*, vol. 7, 2nd edn. Basel: Schwabe, 1969]: 13–54.
Scripta: frr. 22–23, 25.
Περὶ τοῦ ῥητορεύειν ἢ Πρωταγόρας: fr. 33.
Ἡρακλείτου ἐξηγήσεις: fr. 39.
Περὶ τῶν Πυθαγορείων: frr. 40–41.
Περὶ εὐδαιμονίας: fr. 44.
Περὶ βίων: fr. 45.
Περὶ δικαιοσύνης: frr. 48–51a, 51c.
Περὶ σωφροσύνης: fr. 52.
Περὶ ἡδονῆς: frr. 55–61.
Ἐρωτικός: frr. 64–65.
Ζωροάστρης: frr. 68–70.
Περὶ τῶν ἐν Ἅιδου: fr. 72.
Ἄβαρις: frr. 73–75.
Περὶ τῆς ἄπνου ἢ περὶ νόσων: frr. 76–80, 82–87, 89.
Περὶ ψυχῆς. Κατ᾽ ἰδίαν περὶ ψυχῆς: frr. 90–93, 95–98a, 98d–100, 102.
Περὶ τῶν ἐν οὐρανῷ: frr. 104–108, 110, 112–117.
Περὶ φύσεως. Περὶ εἰδώλων. Λύσεις: frr. 118–123.
Περὶ νήσων: frr. 124–125, 127.
Geographica et ethnographica: frr. 128a–129.
Περὶ χρησμῶν. Περὶ χρηστηρίων: frr. 130, 131b–131c, 135–140.
Περὶ ἀρχῆς: frr. 144–145.
Περὶ νόμων: frr. 146–150.
Περὶ εὑρημάτων: fr. 152.
Κτίσεις ἱερῶν: frr. 153–155.
Historica: fr. 156.
Συναγωγὴ τῶν ἐν μουσικῇ (διαλαμψάντων): frr. 157–163.
Homerica: fr. 167.
Περὶ Ὁμήρου: frr. 169–170.
Λύσεων Ὁμηρικῶν: frr. 171–175.
Περὶ τῆς Ὁμήρου καὶ Ἡσιόδου ἡλικίας: frr. 176–177.
De scriptis tragicis: fr. 181.
Q, Pap: 10,562: Phil., Hist., Geogr., Comm.

0283 **HERACLIDES PONTICUS Junior** Gramm.
A.D. 1: Ponticus
Cf. et HERACLIDES LEMBUS Hist. (1407).

001 **Fragmenta**, ed. E. Heitsch, *Die griechischen Dichterfragmente der römischen Kaiserzeit*, vol. 2. Göttingen: Vandenhoeck & Ruprecht, 1964: 41.
frr. 1–2.
Dup. partim 0283 002 (frr. 480–481).
Q: 16: Lyr.

002 **Fragmenta et titulus,** ed. H. Lloyd-Jones and P. Parsons, *Supplementum Hellenisticum.* Berlin: De Gruyter, 1983: 242–244.
frr. (+ titul.) 475, 480–481.
Dup. partim 0283 001 (frr. 1–2).
Q: 13: Lyr.

1411 *HERACLITI EPHESII EPISTULAE*
Incertum
Cf. et HERACLITUS Phil. (0626).
Cf. et Pseudo-HERACLITI EPISTULAE (1412).
001 **Epistulae,** ed. R. Hercher, *Epistolographi Graeci.* Paris: Didot, 1873 (repr. Amsterdam: Hakkert, 1965): 280–283, 285–288.
Cod: 1,994: Epist.

1412 *Pseudo-HERACLITI EPISTULAE*
Incertum
Cf. et HERACLITUS Phil. (0626).
Cf. et HERACLITI EPHESII EPISTULAE (1411).
001 **Epistulae,** ed. A.-M. Denis, *Fragmenta pseudepigraphorum quae supersunt Graeca* [*Pseudepigrapha veteris testamenti Graece* 3. Leiden: Brill, 1970]: 157–160.
Cod: 1,194: Epist.

1784 <HERACLITUS> Comic.
fiq Heraclides
4 B.C.
Cf. et HERACLIDES Comic. (0466).
001 **Titulus,** ed. T. Kock, *Comicorum Atticorum fragmenta,* vol. 2. Leipzig: Teubner, 1884: 435.
NQ: 2: Comic.
002 **Titulus,** ed. A. Meineke, *Fragmenta comicorum Graecorum,* vol. 1. Berlin: Reimer, 1839 (repr. De Gruyter, 1970): 422.
NQ: 2: Comic.

HERACLITUS Epigr.
fiq Heraclitus Ephesius Phil.
6–5 B.C.?
AG 9.359, 524.
Cf. POSIDIPPUS Epigr. (1632 001).
Cf. PLATO Comic. (0497 005).
Cf. ANONYMI EPIGRAMMATICI (AG) (0138 001).

1415 **HERACLITUS** Epigr.
3 B.C.: Halicarnassensis
001 **Epigramma,** AG 7.465.
Q: 50: Epigr.

1962 **HERACLITUS** Hist.
3 B.C.: Lesbius
001 **Testimonia,** FGrH #167: 2B:893.
NQ: 35: Test.

1413 **HERACLITUS** Paradox.
post 4 B.C.?
001 **De incredibilibus,** ed. N. Festa, *Palaephati*

περὶ ἀπίστων [*Mythographi Graeci* 3.2. Leipzig: Teubner, 1902]: 73–87.
Cod: 1,823: Paradox.

0626 **HERACLITUS** Phil.
6–5 B.C.: Ephesius
Cf. et HERACLITI EPHESII EPISTULAE (1411).
Cf. et Pseudo-HERACLITI EPISTULAE (1412).
001 **Testimonia,** ed. H. Diels and W. Kranz, *Die Fragmente der Vorsokratiker,* vol. 1, 6th edn. Berlin: Weidmann, 1951 (repr. Dublin: 1966): 139–149.
test. 1–23.
NQ: 3,764: Test.
002 **Fragmenta,** ed. Diels and Kranz, *op. cit.,* 150–182.
frr. 1–139.
Q: 3,600: Phil.

1414 **HERACLITUS** Phil.
A.D. 1?
001 **Allegoriae** (= **Quaestiones Homericae**), ed. F. Buffière, *Héraclite. Allégories d'Homère.* Paris: Les Belles Lettres, 1962: 1–88.
Cod: 14,825: Comm., Myth.

2671 **HERACLIUS** Epigr.
Incertum
x01 **Epigramma dedicatorium.**
App. Anth. 1.195: Cf. ANTHOLOGIAE GRAECAE APPENDIX (7052 001).

0917 **HERAS** Med.
1 B.C./A.D. 1: Cappadox
Cf. et BAPHULLUS vel HERAS Med. (0820).
x01 **Fragmenta ap. Galenum.**
K12.398–400, 439, 593, 610–614, 819, 929, 941–942; **13**.297–298, 338, 422–423, 431–432, 511–513, 544–549, 557–560, 747, 765–768, 774–775, 815–816, 914–915, 986, 1045–1046; **14**.201.
Cf. GALENUS Med. (0057 076–078).
x02 **Fragmentum ap. Paulum.**
CMG, vol. 9.2, p. 318.
Cf. PAULUS Med. (0715 001).
x03 **Fragmentum ap. Aëtium** (lib. 12).
Kostomiris, p. 106.
Cf. AËTIUS Med. (0718 012).
x04 **Fragmenta ap. Aëtium** (lib. 15).
Zervos, *Athena* 21, pp. 53, 67, 136.
Cf. AËTIUS Med. (0718 015).

2336 **HEREAS** Hist.
vel Heragoras
4–3 B.C.?: Megareus
001 **Fragmenta,** FGrH #486: 3B:451–452.
Q: 401: Hist.

1416 **(H)EREN(N)IUS PHILO** Hist. et Gramm.
A.D. 1–2: Byblius
Cf. et <AMMONIUS> Gramm. (0708).
Cf. et PHILO <Epigr.> (1593).

001 **De diversis verborum significationibus** (e cod.
Paris. suppl. gr. 1238), ed. V. Palmieri, *Herennius Philo. De diversis verborum significationibus.* Naples: n.p., 1983: 125–239.
Cod

002 **Supplementum glossarum,** ed. K. Nickau, *Ammonii qui dicitur liber de adfinium vocabulorum differentia.* Leipzig: Teubner, 1966: 156–159.
Cod: 663: Lexicogr.

003 **De propria dictione** (epitome) (e cod. Venet. Marciano gr. 512), ed. Palmieri, *op. cit.,* 247–252.
Cod

004 **De aetatum cognitione** (epitome) (e cod. Ambrosiano C 222 et cod. Berol. Phill. 1527), ed. Palmieri, *op. cit.,* 243.
Cod

005 **Testimonia,** FGrH #790: 3C:802–803.
NQ: 216: Test.

006 **Fragmenta,** FGrH #790: 3C:803–824.
frr. 1–7: Φοινικικὴ ἱστορία.
frr. 9–11: Περὶ Ἰουδαίων.
frr. 12–13: Παράδοξος ἱστορία.
fr. 14: Περὶ χρηστομαθίας.
frr. 15–51: Περὶ πόλεων καὶ οὓς ἑκάστη αὐτῶν ἐνδόξους ἤνεγκε.
frr. 52–53: Περὶ κτήσεως καὶ ἐκλογῆς βιβλίων (περὶ ἰατρῶν).
frr. 55–57: Fragmenta varia.
Q: 6,010: Hist., Paradox.

2169 HERILLUS Phil.
3 B.C.: Carthaginiensis
001 **Fragmenta,** ed. J. von Arnim, *Stoicorum veterum fragmenta,* vol. 1. Leipzig: Teubner, 1905 (repr. Stuttgart: 1968): 91–93.
Q: 600: Phil.

2426 HERMAEUS Hist.
A.D. 1?
001 **Fragmenta,** FGrH #620: 3C:153–154.
Q: 194: Hist.

1417 HERMAGORAS Rhet.
1 B.C.–A.D. 1
001 **Fragmenta,** ed. D. Matthes, *Hermagorae Temnitae testimonia et fragmenta.* Leipzig: Teubner, 1962: 56–59.
Q

1380 HERMAGORAS Minor Rhet.
A.D. 1/2
001 **Fragmenta,** ed. D. Matthes, *Hermagorae Temnitae testimonia et fragmenta.* Leipzig: Teubner, 1962: 59–65.
Q

1418 HERMAPION Hist.
A.D. 1?
001 **Fragmenta,** FGrH #658: 3C:206–208.
Q: 673: Hist.

1439 HERMARCHUS Phil.
3 B.C.: Mytilenensis
001 **Fragmenta,** ed. K. Krohn, *Der Epikureer Hermarchos* [*Diss.* Berlin (1921)].
Q, Pap

0974 HERMAS Med.
ante A.D. 2
x01 **Fragmentum ap. Philumenum.**
CMG, vol. 10.1.1, p. 13.
Cf. PHILUMENUS Med. (0671 001).

1419 HERMAS Scr. Eccl.
A.D. 2
001 **Pastor,** ed. M. Whittaker, *Die apostolischen Väter I. Der Hirt des Hermas* [*Die griechischen christlichen Schriftsteller* 48, 2nd edn. Berlin: Akademie-Verlag, 1967]: 1–98.
Cod: 27,917: Apocalyp.

002 **Fragmenta** (ap. Antiochum), ed. Whittaker, *op. cit.,* 101, 103.
Q: 255: Apocalyp.

003 **Fragmenta** (*P. Oxy.* 3.404), ed. Whittaker, *op. cit.,* 109, 111.
Pap: 113: Apocalyp.

004 **Fragmentum in F** (cod. Paris. gr. 1143), ed. Whittaker, *op. cit.,* 118.
Cod: 145: Apocalyp.

2437 HERMATELES Hist.
A.D. 2?
001 **Testimonium,** FGrH #657: 3C:205–206.
NQ: 22: Test.

[HERMES TRISMEGISTUS]
Cf. CORPUS HERMETICUM (1286).

0213 HERMESIANAX Eleg.
4–3 B.C.: Colophonius
001 **Fragmenta,** ed. J.U. Powell, *Collectanea Alexandrina.* Oxford: Clarendon Press, 1925 (repr. 1970): 96, 98–100.
frr. 1, 7.
Q: 577: Eleg.

002 **Testimonia,** FGrH #691: 3C:531–532.
NQ: 147: Test.

003 **Fragmenta,** FGrH #691: 3C:532.
Q: 109: Hist.

2532 [HERMESIANAX] Hist.
Incertum: Cyprius
001 **Fragmenta,** FGrH #797: 3C:835–836.
Q: 227: Hist.

2384 HERMIAS Hist.
4 B.C.?: Methymnaeus
001 **Testimonium,** FGrH #558: 3B:568.
NQ: 28: Test.

002 **Fragmentum,** FGrH #558: 3B:568.
Q: 19: Hist.

2440 HERMIAS Hist.
A.D. 4/5: Hermupolitanus

001 **Testimonium**, FGrH #638: 3C:185.
NQ: 55: Test.

1420 **HERMIAS** Iamb.
3 B.C.?: Curiensis
Cf. et HERMIAS Poeta (2624).
001 **Fragmentum**, ed. J.U. Powell, *Collectanea Alexandrina*. Oxford: Clarendon Press, 1925 (repr. 1970): 237.
Q: 27: Iamb.

0919 **HERMIAS** Med.
ante A.D. 2
x01 **Fragmentum ap. Galenum.**
K12.754.
Cf. GALENUS Med. (0057 076).

0531 **HERMIAS** Phil.
A.D. 2/6
001 **Irrisio gentilium philosophorum**, ed. H. Diels, *Doxographi Graeci*. Berlin: Reimer, 1879 (repr. De Gruyter, 1965): 651–656.
Cod: 1,867: Doxogr.

2317 **HERMIAS** Phil.
A.D. 5: Alexandrinus
001 **In Platonis Phaedrum scholia**, ed. P. Couvreur, *Hermeias von Alexandrien. In Platonis Phaedrum scholia*. Paris: Bouillon, 1901 (repr. Hildesheim: Olms, 1971): 1–266.
Cod: Schol.

2624 **HERMIAS** Poeta
fiq Hermias Curiensis
3 B.C.?
Cf. et HERMIAS Iamb. (1420).
001 **Fragmentum**, ed. H. Lloyd-Jones and P. Parsons, *Supplementum Hellenisticum*. Berlin: De Gruyter, 1983: 244.
fr. 484.
Q: 7: Poem.

1796 **HERMINUS** Phil.
A.D. 2
001 **Fragmenta**, ed. H. Schmidt, *De Hermino peripatetico* [*Diss. Marburg* (1907)].
Q

0252 **HERMIPPUS** Comic.
5 B.C.: Atheniensis
001 **Fragmenta**, ed. T. Kock, *Comicorum Atticorum fragmenta*, vol. 1. Leipzig: Teubner, 1880: 224–243, 245–253.
frr. 1–6, 8, 10–32, 34–63, 66–68, 70–71, 75–97.
Q: 941: Comic.
002 **Fragmenta**, ed. A. Meineke, *Fragmenta comicorum Graecorum*, vol. 2.1. Berlin: Reimer, 1839 (repr. De Gruyter, 1970): 379–395, 397–408, 410–417.
Q: 890: Comic.
003 **Fragmenta**, ed. J. Demiańczuk, *Supplementum*

comicum. Krakau: Nakładem Akademii, 1912 (repr. Hildesheim: Olms, 1967): 53.
frr. 1–3.
Q: 10: Comic.
004 **Fragmenta**, ed. M.L. West, *Iambi et elegi Graeci*, vol. 2. Oxford: Clarendon Press, 1972: 67–69.
frr. 2–6 + titulus.
Q: 53: Iamb.
005 **Fragmentum** (*P. Oxy.* 13.1611), ed. C. Austin, *Comicorum Graecorum fragmenta in papyris reperta*. Berlin: De Gruyter, 1973: 120.
fr. 101 + titulus.
Pap: 11: Comic.

1421 **HERMIPPUS** Gramm. et Hist.
fiq Hermippus Astronomus
3 B.C.: Smyrnaeus
001 **Fragmenta**, ed. F. Wehrli, *Hermippos der Kallimacheer* [*Die Schule des Aristoteles*, suppl. 1. Basel: Schwabe, 1974]: 11–41.
De magis: fr. 3.
Βίοι: frr. 5–17, 19–71, 73–79, 81–94.
Φαινόμενα. Καταστηρισμοί(?): frr. 95–98, 101–102.
Fragmenta incertae sedis: frr. 103–104.
Q, Pap: 6,897: Biogr., Astrol., Nat. Hist.
002 **Fragmentum astrologicum**, ed. W. Kroll, *Codices Romani* [*Catalogus codicum astrologorum Graecorum* 5.2. Brussels: Lamertin, 1906]: 71.
Cod
003 **Titulus**, ed. H. Lloyd-Jones and P. Parsons, *Supplementum Hellenisticum*. Berlin: De Gruyter, 1983: 245.
fr. 485.
NQ: 3: Astrol.

0207 **HERMOCLES** Lyr.
4–3 B.C.: Cyzicenus
001 **Ithyphalli**, ed. J.U. Powell, *Collectanea Alexandrina*. Oxford: Clarendon Press, 1925 (repr. 1970): 173–174.
Q: 178: Lyr.

1422 **HERMOCREON** Epigr.
Incertum
001 **Epigrammata**, AG **9**.327; **16**.11.
Q: 48: Epigr.

1423 **HERMODORUS** Epigr.
Incertum
001 **Epigramma**, AG 16.170.
AG 9.77: Cf. ANTIPATER Epigr. (0114 001).
Q: 28: Epigr.

0095 **HERMODORUS** Phil.
4 B.C.: Syracusanus
001 **Testimonia et fragmenta**, ed. M.I. Parente, *Senocrate-Ermodoro. Frammenti*. Naples: Bibliopolis, 1982: 157–160.
frr. 1–9.
Q, Pap: Phil.

002 **De Platone** (fort. auctore Hermodoro Syracusano), ed. F. Lasserre, *De Léodamas de Thasos à Philippe d'Oponte*. Naples: Bibliopolis, 1987: 217–223.
Dup. partim PHILODEMUS Phil. (1595 602).
Pap: Phil., Biogr.

1424 **HERMOGENES** Hist.
post 4 B.C.?
001 **Fragmenta**, FGrH #795: 3C:833–834.
Q: 288: Hist.

2143 **HERMOGENES** Hist.
3–2 B.C.: fort. Prienaeus
001 **Testimonia**, FGrH #481: 3B:445.
NQ: 61: Test.

0921 **HERMOGENES** Med.
A.D. 2: Smyrnaeus
001 **Testimonium**, FGrH #579: 3B:690.
test. 1: *Inscr. Smyrna* (*CIG* 331).
NQ: 66: Test.
x01 **Fragmentum ap. Oribasium.**
CMG, vol. 6.2.2, p. 287.
Cf. ORIBASIUS Med. (0722 003).

0592 **HERMOGENES** Rhet.
A.D. 2–3: Tarsensis
Scholia: Cf. SCHOLIA IN HERMOGENEM (5043).
001 **Progymnasmata** [Dub.], ed. H. Rabe, *Hermogenis opera*. Leipzig: Teubner, 1913 (repr. Stuttgart: 1969): 1–27.
Cod: 4,088: Rhet.
002 Περὶ στάσεων, ed. Rabe, *op. cit.*, 28–92.
Cod: 10,906: Rhet.
003 Περὶ εὑρέσεως [Sp.], ed. Rabe, *op. cit.*, 93–212.
Cod: 21,237: Rhet.
004 Περὶ ἰδεῶν λόγου, ed. Rabe, *op. cit.*, 213–413.
Cod: 41,547: Rhet.
005 Περὶ μεθόδου δεινότητος [Sp.], ed. Rabe, *op. cit.*, 414–456.
Cod: 6,753: Rhet.
006 **Testimonia**, FGrH #851: 3C:936.
NQ: 56: Test.
007 **Titulus**, FGrH #851: 3C:936.
NQ: Hist.

0240 **HERMOLOCHUS** Lyr.
4 B.C.?
001 **Fragmentum**, ed. D.L. Page, *Poetae melici Graeci*. Oxford: Clarendon Press, 1962 (repr. 1967 (1st edn. corr.)): 447.
fr. 1.
Q: 37: Lyr.

HERMON Med.
Cf. EPIGONUS vel HERMON Med. (0922).

1425 **HERMONAX** Epic.
vel Hermon
4 B.C./A.D. 2: Delius

001 **Fragmenta**, ed. J.U. Powell, *Collectanea Alexandrina*. Oxford: Clarendon Press, 1925 (repr. 1970): 251–252.
frr. 1–2.
Q: 63: Epic.

0923 **HERMOPHILUS** Med.
ante A.D. 2
x01 **Fragmentum ap. Galenum.**
K12.781.
Cf. GALENUS Med. (0057 076).
x02 **Fragmentum ap. Aëtium** (lib. 7).
CMG, vol. 8.2, p. 388.
Cf. AËTIUS Med. (0718 007).

2468 **HERMOTIMUS** Math.
4 B.C.: Colophonius
001 **Testimonium**, ed. F. Lasserre, *De Léodamas de Thasos à Philippe d'Oponte*. Naples: Bibliopolis, 1987: 147.
NQ: Test.
002 **Doctrina**, ed. Lasserre, *op. cit.*, 147–148.
frr. 1–5.
NQ: Test.

0650 **HERODAS** Mimogr.
vel Herondas
3 B.C.
001 **Mimiambi**, ed. I.C. Cunningham, *Herodas. Mimiambi*. Oxford: Clarendon Press, 1971: 27–56.
Q, Pap: 5,009: Mim.

2166 **HERODES I Rex Judaeorum** Hist.
1 B.C.: Palaestinus
001 **Fragmentum**, FGrH #236: 2B:988–990.
Q: 548: Hist.

1426 **HERODES ATTICUS** Soph.
A.D. 2: Atheniensis, Romanus
001 Περὶ πολιτείας [Dub.], ed. U. Albini, [*Erode Attico*]. Περὶ πολιτείας. Florence: Le Monnier, 1968: 29–35.
Cod: 1,909: Orat.

0015 **HERODIANUS** Hist.
A.D. 2–3: Syrus
001 **Ab excessu divi Marci**, ed. K. Stavenhagen, *Herodiani ab excessu divi Marci libri octo*. Leipzig: Teubner, 1922 (repr. Stuttgart: 1967): 1–223.
Cod: 48,889: Hist.

0087 **Aelius HERODIANUS et Pseudo-HERODIANUS** Gramm. et Rhet.
A.D. 2: Alexandrinus, Romanus
001 **De prosodia catholica**, ed. A. Lentz, *Grammatici Graeci*, vol. 3.1. Leipzig: Teubner, 1867 (repr. Hildesheim: Olms, 1965): 3–547.
Cod: 143,838: Gramm.

002 **De enclisi** (epitome ap. Arcadium), ed. Lentz, *op. cit.*, vol. 3.1, 551–564.
Q: 2,934: Gramm.

003 Περὶ κυρίων καὶ ἐπιθέτων καὶ προσηγορικῶν μονόβιβλον, ed. Lentz, *op. cit.*, vol. 3.2 (1870; repr. 1965): 1–6.
Q: 1,962: Gramm.

004 Περὶ διχρόνων, ed. Lentz, *op. cit.*, vol. 3.2, 7–20.
Cod: 4,040: Gramm.

005 Περὶ πνευμάτων, ed. Lentz, *op. cit.*, vol. 3.2, 20.
Q: 74: Gramm.

006 Περὶ Ἀττικῆς προσῳδίας, ed. Lentz, *op. cit.*, vol. 3.2, 20–21.
Q: 154: Gramm.

007 Περὶ Ἰλιακῆς προσῳδίας, ed. Lentz, *op. cit.*, vol. 3.2, 22–128.
Cod: 40,308: Gramm.

008 Περὶ Ὀδυσσειακῆς προσῳδίας, ed. Lentz, *op. cit.*, vol. 3.2, 129–165.
Cod: 9,710: Gramm.

009 Περὶ παθῶν, ed. Lentz, *op. cit.*, vol. 3.2, 166–389.
Περὶ παθῶν: pp. 166–388.
Ἐκ τῶν Ἡρωδιανοῦ ὑπομνημάτων τῶν περὶ παθῶν Διδύμου: p. 389.
Cf. et 0087 034.
Q: 41,556: Gramm.

010 Περὶ συντάξεως τῶν στοιχείων, ed. Lentz, *op. cit.*, vol. 3.2, 390–406.
Q: 6,139: Gramm.

011 Περὶ ὀρθογραφίας, ed. Lentz, *op. cit.*, vol. 3.2, 407–611.
Q: 54,459: Gramm.

012 Περὶ ὀνομάτων, ed. Lentz, *op. cit.*, vol. 3.2, 612–633.
Q: 8,125: Gramm.

013 Περὶ κλίσεως ὀνομάτων, ed. Lentz, *op. cit.*, vol. 3.2, 634–777.
Q: 55,098: Gramm.

014 Εἰς τὸ περὶ γενῶν Ἀπολλωνίου ὑπόμνημα, ed. Lentz, *op. cit.*, vol. 3.2, 777.
Q: 57: Gramm.

015 Μονόβιβλον περὶ τοῦ ὕδωρ, ed. Lentz, *op. cit.*, vol. 3.2, 777.
Q: 86: Gramm.

016 Περὶ τοῦ ζώς, ed. Lentz, *op. cit.*, vol. 3.2, 778.
Q: 102: Gramm.

017 Περὶ συζυγιῶν, ed. Lentz, *op. cit.*, vol. 3.2, 779.
Q: 78: Gramm.

018 Μονόβιβλον περὶ τοῦ μὴ πάντα τὰ ῥήματα κλίνεσθαι εἰς πάντας τοὺς χρόνους, ed. Lentz, *op. cit.*, vol. 3.2, 779–784.
Q: 1,586: Gramm.

019 Περὶ μετοχῶν, ed. Lentz, *op. cit.*, vol. 3.2, 784–785.
Q: 164: Gramm.

020 Μονόβιβλον περὶ τοῦ ἦν, ed. Lentz, *op. cit.*, vol. 3.2, 785–786.
Q: 114: Gramm.

021 Περὶ ῥημάτων, ed. Lentz, *op. cit.*, vol. 3.2, 787–824.
Q: 15,993: Gramm.

022 Περὶ τῶν εἰς μῖ, ed. Lentz, *op. cit.*, vol. 3.2, 825–844.
Q: 9,760: Gramm.

023 Περὶ ἀντωνυμιῶν, ed. Lentz, *op. cit.*, vol. 3.2, 845–846.
Q: 480: Gramm.

024 Περὶ ἐπιρρημάτων, ed. Lentz, *op. cit.*, vol. 3.2, 846.
Q: 66: Gramm.

025 Περὶ σχημάτων, ed. Lentz, *op. cit.*, vol. 3.2, 847–849.
Q: 711: Gramm.

026 Περὶ παρωνύμων, ed. Lentz, *op. cit.*, vol. 3.2, 849–897.
Q: 15,428: Gramm.

027 Περὶ ῥηματικῶν ὀνομάτων, ed. Lentz, *op. cit.*, vol. 3.2, 897–903.
Q: 2,256: Gramm.

028 Περὶ μονοσυλλάβων, ed. Lentz, *op. cit.*, vol. 3.2, 903–904.
Q: 251: Gramm.

029 Περὶ γάμου καὶ συμβιώσεως, ed. Lentz, *op. cit.*, vol. 3.2, 904.
Q: 70: Gramm.

030 Συμπόσιον, ed. Lentz, *op. cit.*, vol. 3.2, 904–906.
Q: 616: Gramm.

031 Προτάσεις, ed. Lentz, *op. cit.*, vol. 3.2, 907.
Q: 124: Gramm.

032 Εἰς τὴν Ἀπολλωνίου εἰσαγωγήν, ed. Lentz, *op. cit.*, vol. 3.2, 907.
Q: 55: Gramm.

033 Περὶ μονήρους λέξεως, ed. Lentz, *op. cit.*, vol. 3.2, 908–952.
Cod: 11,290: Gramm.

Περὶ παθῶν (supplementum), ed. Lentz, *op. cit.*, vol. 3.2, 167–170, 172, 174–181, 183–190, 192–196, 200–202, 205, 208–211, 214–218, 222–223, 226, 228–230, 232–237, 240–243, 245–247, 249–250, 253–259, 262–272, 274–279, 281–282, 286, 288–293, 298–299, 301–302, 304, 307–313, 315–320, 324–325, 327, 330–338, 340–350, 352–362, 364–366, 369–371, 373–374, 378, 382–383, 386–388.
Cf. et 0087 009.
Q: 15,556: Gramm.

035 **De figuris**, ed. L. Spengel, *Rhetores Graeci*, vol. 3. Leipzig: Teubner, 1856 (repr. Frankfurt am Main: Minerva, 1966): 83–104.
Cod: 4,078: Rhet.

036 **Partitiones**, ed. J.F. Boissonade, *Herodiani partitiones*. London, 1819 (repr. Amsterdam: Hakkert, 1963): 1–282.
Cod: 33,224: Gramm.

037 **Philetaerus**, ed. A. Dain, *Le "Philétaeros" attribué à Hérodien*. Paris: Les Belles Lettres, 1954: 41–72.
Cod: 5,207: Gramm.

038 Περὶ τῶν ζητουμένων κατὰ πάσης κλίσεως ὀνόματος (e cod. Paris. suppl. gr. 1238), ed. Dain, *op. cit.*, 73–74.
Cf. et 0087 047.
Cod: 312: Gramm.

039 **Fragmenta**, ed. Dain, *op. cit.*, 75–82.
Cod: 1,714: Gramm.

040 **De versibus**, ed. W. Studemund, "Der Pseudo-Herodianische Tractat über die εἴδη des Hexameters," *Jahrbücher für classische Philologie* 95 (1867) 618–619.
Cod: 253: Gramm.

041 **Schematismi Homerici**, ed. P. Egenolff, "Zu Herodianos technikos," *Jahrbücher für classische Philologie* 149 (1894) 338–345.
Cod: 2,543: Lexicogr.

042 Περὶ ἀριθμῶν (ap. Stephanum), *TGL* 8.345 (appendix).
Q: 393: Gramm.

043 Περὶ αὐθυποτάκτων καὶ ἀνυποτάκτων, ed. I. Bekker, *Anecdota Graeca*, vol. 3. Berlin: Reimer, 1821 (repr. Graz: Akademische Druck- und Verlagsanstalt, 1965): 1086–1088.
Cod: 803: Gramm.

044 Περὶ σολοικισμοῦ καὶ βαρβαρισμοῦ, ed. A. Nauck, *Lexicon Vindobonense*. St. Petersburg: Eggers, 1867 (repr. Hildesheim: Olms, 1965): 294–312.
Cod: 2,678: Rhet.

045 Περὶ παραγωγῶν γενικῶν ἀπὸ διαλέκτων, ed. J.A. Cramer, *Anecdota Graeca e codd. manuscriptis bibliothecarum Oxoniensium*, vol. 3. Oxford: Oxford University Press, 1836 (repr. Amsterdam: Hakkert, 1963): 228–236.
Cod: 2,616: Gramm.

046 Ζητούμενα τῶν μερῶν τοῦ λόγου, ed. J. Pierson and G.A. Koch, *Moeridis Atticistae lexicon Atticum*. Leipzig: Lauffer, 1830 (repr. Hildesheim: Olms, 1969): 412–437.
Cod: 1,586: Gramm.

047 Περὶ τῶν ζητουμένων κατὰ πάσης κλίσεως ὀνόματος (e cod. Barocciano 76), ed. Cramer, *op. cit.*, 246–255.
Cf. et 0087 038.
Cod: 2,527: Gramm.

048 Περὶ κλίσεως ῥημάτων, ed. Cramer, *op. cit.*, 256–262.
Cod: 1,541: Gramm.

049 Περὶ λέξεως τῶν στίχων, ed. F. de Furia, *Appendix ad Draconem Stratonicensem*. Leipzig: Weigel, 1814: 88.
Cod: 232: Gramm., Rhet.

050 Παρεκβολαὶ τοῦ μεγάλου ῥήματος, ed. J. La Roche, Παρεκβολαὶ τοῦ μεγάλου ῥήματος ἐκ τῶν Ἡρωδιανοῦ [*Programm Akad. Gymn. Vienna* (1863)]: 4–37.
Cod: 14,934: Gramm.

052 Ἀπορίαι καὶ λύσεις, ed. A. Manuzio, *Thesaurus. Cornucopiae et horti Adonidis*. Venice: Aldus, 1496.
Cod

x01 **De impropriis**.
Cf. <AMMONIUS> Gramm. (0708 002).

2625 **HERODICUS** Gramm.
2 B.C.: Babylonius

001 **Fragmenta**, ed. H. Lloyd-Jones and P. Parsons, *Supplementum Hellenisticum*. Berlin: De Gruyter, 1983: 247–248.
frr. 494–495.
Q: 135: Hexametr., Epigr.

x01 **Epigramma irrisorium**.
App. Anth. 5.25: Cf. ANTHOLOGIAE GRAECAE APPENDIX (7052 005).
Dup. partim 2625 001 (fr. 494).

1427 **HERODORUS** Hist.
5–4 B.C.: Heracleota

001 **Testimonia**, FGrH #31: 1A:215.
NQ: 54: Test.

002 **Fragmenta**, FGrH #31: 1A:215–228, *12–*13 addenda.
Q: 3,933: Hist., Myth., Geogr.

0016 **HERODOTUS** Hist.
5 B.C.: Halicarnassensis, Thurius

001 **Historiae**, ed. Ph.-E. Legrand, *Hérodote. Histoires*, 9 vols. Paris: Les Belles Lettres, 1:1932 (repr. 1970); 2:1930 (repr. 1963); 3:1939 (repr. 1967); 4, 3rd edn.:1960; 5:1946 (repr. 1968); 6:1948 (repr. 1963); 7:1951 (repr. 1963); 8:1953 (repr. 1964); 9:1954 (repr. 1968): 1:13–204; 2:65–194; 3:37–185; 4:47–201; 5:18–147; 6:7–128; 7:24–235; 8:9–161; 9:9–109.
Cod: 189,489: Hist.

Pseudo-HERODOTUS
Cf. VITAE HOMERI (1805 001).

0926 **HERODOTUS** Med.
A.D. 1–2
Cf. et CRITO et HERODOTUS Med. (0882).
Cf. et HERODOTUS et PHILUMENUS Med. (0910).

001 Περὶ βοηθημάτων (*P. Tebt.* 2.272), ed. M.-H. Marganne, "Un fragment de médecin Hérodote: P. Tebt. II 272" in *Proceedings of the sixteenth international congress of papyrology (1980)* [*American studies in papyrology* 23. Chico, California: Scholars Press, 1981]: 75–76.
Pap: Med.

x01 **Fragmentum ap. Galenum**.
K13.801.
Cf. GALENUS Med. (0057 077).

x02 **Fragmenta ap. Oribasium**.
CMG, vol. **6.1.1**, pp. 144–146, 147–151, 175–177, 182, 209, 217, 253, 254, 261; **6.1.2**, pp. 46, 53–55, 59–61, 75–78; **6.2.2**, p. 284; **6.3**, pp. 204–206.
Cf. ORIBASIUS Med. (0722 001, 003, 004).

x03 **Fragmentum ap. Aëtium** (lib. 4).
CMG, vol. 8.1, p. 389.
Cf. AËTIUS Med. (0718 004).

x04 **Fragmenta ap. Aëtium** (lib. 5).
CMG, vol. 8.2, pp. 98, 107–111.
Cf. AËTIUS Med. (0718 005).

x05　**Fragmenta ap. Aëtium** (lib. 9).
Zervos, *Athena* 23, pp. 276–279, 299, 366–368.
Cf. AËTIUS Med. (0718 009).

x06　**Fragmentum ap. Aëtium** (lib. 15).
Zervos, *Athena* 21, p. 61.
Cf. AËTIUS Med. (0718 015).

x07　Διάγνωσις περὶ τῶν ὀξέων καὶ χρονίων νοσ-
ημάτων [Dub.].
Fuchs, *RhM* 58, pp. 69–114.
Cf. ANONYMI MEDICI (0721 026).

0910　**HERODOTUS et PHILUMENUS** Med.
A.D. 2?
Cf. et HERODOTUS Med. (0926).
Cf. et PHILUMENUS Med. (0671).

x01　**Fragmentum ap. Aëtium** (lib. 5).
CMG, vol. 8.2, p. 97.
Cf. AËTIUS Med. (0718 005).

0559　**HERON** Mech.
A.D. 1?: Alexandrinus

001　**Pneumatica**, ed. W. Schmidt, *Heronis Alexandrini opera quae supersunt omnia*, vol. 1. Leipzig: Teubner, 1899: 2–332.
Cod: 22,951: Mech.

002　**De automatis**, ed. Schmidt, *op. cit.*, vol. 1,
338–452.
Cod: 9,375: Mech.

003　**Fragmenta de horoscopiis**, ed. Schmidt, *op.
cit.*, vol. 1, 456, 506.
Q: 303: Metrolog.

004　**Mechanicorum fragmenta**, ed. L. Nix and W.
Schmidt, *Heronis Alexandrini opera*, vol. 2.1
(1900): 256–298.
Q: 3,278: Mech.

005　**Catoptrica**, ed. Nix and Schmidt, *op. cit.*, vol.
2.1, 368–372.
Q: 501: Mech.

006　**Metrica**, ed. H. Schöne, *Heronis Alexandrini
opera*, vol. 3 (1903): 2–184.
Cod: 21,173: Metrolog., Math.

007　**Dioptra**, ed. Schöne, *op. cit.*, vol. 3, 188–314.
Cod: 13,353: Metrolog., Mech.

008　**Definitiones**, ed. J.L. Heiberg, *Heronis Alexandrini opera*, vol. 4 (1903): 2–168.
Cod: 15,039: Math.

009　**Geometrica**, ed. Heiberg, *op. cit.*, vol. 4, 172–
448.
Cod: 34,086: Math.

010　**Stereometrica**, ed. Heiberg, *Heronis Alexandrini opera*, vol. 5 (1914): 2–162.
Cod: 18,189: Metrolog., Math.

011　**De mensuris**, ed. Heiberg, *op. cit.*, vol. 5, 164–
218.
Cod: 5,159: Metrolog.

012　**Belopoeica**, ed. H. Diels and E. Schramm,
Herons Belopoiika [*Abhandlungen der königlich
preussischen Akademie der Wissenschaften*,
Philosoph.-hist. Kl. 2. Berlin: Reimer, 1918]:
5–55.
Cod: 5,667: Mech.

013　Χειροβαλλίστρας κατασκευὴ καὶ συμμετρία,
ed. V. Prou, *La chirobaliste d'Héron d'Alex-
andrie* [*Notices et extraits des manuscrits de la
Bibliothèque Nationale* 26.2. Paris: Imprimerie
Nationale, 1877]: 116–149.
Cod: 1,168: Mech.

014　**Fragmenta Heroniana**, ed. F. Hultsch, *Metrologicorum scriptorum reliquiae*, vol. 1. Leipzig:
Teubner, 1864 (repr. Stuttgart: 1971): 180–
197, 202–205.
Cod: 2,807: Metrolog.

015　**Geodaesia** [Sp.], ed. Heiberg, *Heronis Alexandrini opera*, vol. 5, LXX–XCIII.
Cod: 4,993: Metrolog.

016　**Liber geeponicus** [Sp.], ed. F. Hultsch, *Heronis
Alexandrini geometricorum et stereometricorum
reliquiae*. Berlin: Weidmann, 1864: 208–234.
Cod: 6,747: Metrolog.

0927　**HERON** Med.
ante A.D. 1

x01　**Fragmentum ap. Galenum**.
K12.745.
Cf. GALENUS Med. (0057 076).

2419　**HEROPHANES** Hist.
post 1 B.C.: Troezenius

001　**Fragmentum**, FGrH #605: 3B:739.
Q: 93: Hist.

0928　**HEROPHILUS** Med.
4–3 B.C.: Chalcedonius
Cf. et TROPHILUS <Paradox.> (0588).

x01　**Fragmenta ap. Galenum**.
K2.570–571, 895, in CMG, vol. 2.1, p. 42;
K4.596–597; 8.592, 956, 959; 12.843; 13.308.
Cf. GALENUS Med. (0057 011, 016, 021, 059,
060, 076).

x02　**Fragmentum ap. Oribasium**.
CMG, vol. 6.2.1, p. 36.
Cf. ORIBASIUS Med. (0722 001).

x03　**Fragmentum ap. Anonymum Londinensem**.
Iatrica 21.22.
Cf. ANONYMUS LONDINENSIS Med. (0643
001).

x04　**Fragmentum ap. Soranum**.
CMG, vol. 4, pp. 130–131.
Cf. SORANUS Med. (0565 001).

2311　**HEROPYTHUS** Hist.
5–4 B.C.: fort. Colophonius

001　**Fragmenta**, FGrH #448: 3B:377.
Q: 108: Hist.

2516　**HESIANAX** Hist.
Incertum

001　**Fragmentum**, FGrH #763: 3C:745.
Q: 58: Hist.

0020　**HESIODUS** Epic.
8/7 B.C.?: Ascraeus
Cf. et AEGIMIUS (0668).

Vita: Cf. VITAE HESIODI PARTICULA (1749).
Scholia: Cf. SCHOLIA IN HESIODUM (5025).

001 **Theogonia**, ed. M.L. West, *Hesiod. Theogony*.
Oxford: Clarendon Press, 1966: 111–149.
Cod: 6,969: Epic.

002 **Opera et dies**, ed. F. Solmsen, *Hesiodi opera*.
Oxford: Clarendon Press, 1970: 49–85.
Cod: 5,900: Epic.

003 **Scutum**, ed. Solmsen, *op. cit.*, 88–107.
Cod: 3,336: Epic.

004 **Fragmenta**, ed. R. Merkelbach and M.L. West,
Fragmenta Hesiodea. Oxford: Clarendon Press,
1967: 3–78, 80–117, 119–127, 129–137, 139–
141, 144, 147, 149–156, 158, 160–169, 171–
172, 176–178, 181–186, 188–190.
frr. 1, 5, 7–14, 16–17a, 21–23a, 25–27, 29–31,
33–37, 40–41, 43a, 44–49, 51, 54a, 55–62, 64–
67, 69–70, 73, 75–77, 79–86, 88–124, 128–
129, 132–137, 141, 143–146, 150–151, 154,
156, 158–159, 161, 165, 167, 169–181, 185–
188, 190, 193, 195–201, 203–206, 209, 211,
212b, 215, 217, 221, 227–229, 231, 233–236,
239–240, 242–245, 248–249, 251–253, 257,
259b, 264, 266a, 266c, 268–276, 278, 280–281,
283, 286, 288–291, 293–294, 296, 298, 301–
310, 313–324, 328–333, 335–339, 343, 357,
361–363, 372–373, 380–381, 384, 386, 388,
392–393, 403, 405–406, 412.
Q, Pap: 11,229: Epic.

005 **Testimonia**, ed. H. Diels and W. Kranz, *Die
Fragmente der Vorsokratiker*, vol. 1, 6th edn.
Berlin: Weidmann, 1951 (repr. Dublin: 1966):
38.
test. 1–3.
NQ: 76: Test.

006 **Fragmenta astronomica**, ed. Diels and Kranz,
op. cit., 38–40.
frr. 1–8.
Q: 593: Astron., Phil., Hexametr.

007 **Fragmenta**, ed. R. Merkelbach and M.L. West,
Hesiodi opera (ed. F. Solmsen), 2nd edn. Ox-
ford: Clarendon Press, 1983: 227–232.
Q, Pap: 727: Epic.

008 **Fragmentum** (ap. Maximum Tyrium), ed. R.
Renehan, "A new Hesiodic fragment," *Classi-
cal Philology* 81 (1986) 221.
Dup. partim 0020 004 (fr. 1, v. 16).
Q

x01 **Problema**.
App. Anth. 7.1: Cf. ANTHOLOGIAE GRAE-
CAE APPENDIX (7052 007).
Dup. partim 0020 004 (fr. 278).

1428 **HESTIAEUS** Hist.
ante A.D. 1

001 **Fragmenta**, FGrH #786: 3C:799.
Q: 103: Hist.

0225 **HESTIAEUS** Phil.
4 B.C.: Perinthius

001 **Testimonia**, ed. F. Lasserre, *De Léodamas de*

Thasos à Philippe d'Oponte. Naples: Bibliopolis, 1987: 99.
test. 1, 2b.
NQ: Test.

002 **Fragmenta**, ed. Lasserre, *op. cit.*, 99–102.
frr. 1–5c.
Q: Phil.

4085 **HESYCHIUS** Lexicogr.
A.D. 5: Alexandrinus

001 **Epistula ad Eulogium**, ed. K. Latte, *Hesychii
Alexandrini lexicon*, vol. 1. Copenhagen:
Munksgaard, 1953: 1–2.
Cod: 578: Epist.

002 **Lexicon (A–O)**, ed. Latte, *op. cit.*, vols. 1 & 2
(1966): **1**:3–492; **2**:1–806.
Cod: 235,260: Lexicogr.

003 **Lexicon (Π–Ω)**, ed. M. Schmidt, *Hesychii Alexandrini lexicon*, vols. 3–4. Halle, 3:1861;
4:1862 (repr. Amsterdam: Hakkert, 1965):
3:251–439; **4**:1–336.
Cod: 67,413: Lexicogr.

2274 **HESYCHIUS Illustrius** Hist.
A.D. 6: Milesius

001 **Fragmentum**, FGrH #390: 3B:266–272.
Dup. partim 2274 006.
Cod: 1,977: Hist.

002 **Onomatologi**, ed. J. Flach, *Hesychii Milesii
onomatologi quae supersunt*. Leipzig: Teubner,
1882: 1–240.
Cod: Lexicogr.

003 **De viris illustribus**, ed. J. Flach, *Hesychii Mi-
lesii qui fertur de viris illustribus liber*. Leipzig:
Teubner, 1880: 1–55.
Cod: Biogr.

004 **Homilia in natalem Christi**, ed. L. Dindorf,
Chronicon paschale, vol. 2 [*Corpus scriptorum
historiae Byzantinae*. Bonn: Weber, 1832]: 116.
Cod: Homilet.

005 **Πάτρια Κωνσταντινουπόλεως**, ed. T. Preger,
Scriptores originum Constantinopolitanarum,
vol. 1. Leipzig: Teubner, 1901 (repr. New
York: Arno, 1975): 1–18.
Cod: [2,130]: Hist.

006 **Fragmenta**, FHG 4: 145–177.
Dup. partim 2274 001.
Q, Cod: Hist.

007 **Vita Aristotelis (vita Menagiana)** [Sp.], ed. I.
Düring, *Aristotle in the ancient biographical
tradition*. Göteborg: Elanders, 1957: 82–89.
Cod: Biogr.

0929 **HICESIUS** Med.
1 B.C.

x01 **Fragmentum ap. Galenum**.
K13.788.
Cf. GALENUS Med. (0057 077).

x02 **Fragmentum ap. Paulum**.
CMG, vol. 9.2, p. 359.
Cf. PAULUS Med. (0715 001).

x03 **Fragmentum ap. Aëtium** (lib. 15).
Zervos, *Athena* 21, p. 58.
Cf. AËTIUS Med. (0718 015).

x04 **Fragmentum ap. Athenaeum.**
Deipnosophistae 15.681c, 689c.
Cf. ATHENAEUS Soph. (0008 001).

2240 **HICETAS** Phil.
5 B.C.: Syracusanus

001 **Testimonia**, ed. H. Diels and W. Kranz, *Die Fragmente der Vorsokratiker*, vol. 1, 6th edn. Berlin: Weidmann, 1951 (repr. Dublin: 1966): 441–442.
test. 1–2.
NQ: 79: Test.

0930 **HIERAX** Med.
ante A.D. 2: Thebanus
Cf. et ANONYMUS THEBANUS Med. (1086).

x01 **Fragmenta ap. Galenum.**
K12.775–776; 13.829.
Cf. GALENUS Med. (0057 076–077).

2370 **HIEROBOLUS** Hist.
4 B.C.: Rhodius

001 **Testimonium**, FGrH #530: 3B:505.
NQ: 18: Test.

2408 **HIEROCLES** Hist.
A.D. 3?

001 **Fragmenta**, FHG 4: 430.
Q

1429 **HIEROCLES** Phil.
A.D. 2

001 Ἠθικὴ Στοιχείωσις, ed. J. von Arnim, *Hierokles. Ethische Elementarlehre (Papyrus 9780)* [*Berliner Klassikertexte* 4. Berlin: Weidmann, 1906]: 7–47.
Pap: 3,946: Phil.

002 **Fragmenta ethica** (ap. Stobaeum), ed. von Arnim, *op. cit.*, 48–63.
Q: 5,404: Phil.

003 **Fragmenta** (ap. *Sudam*), ed. von Arnim, *op. cit.*, 64.
Q: 108: Phil.

2571 **HIEROCLES** Phil.
A.D. 5
Scholia: Cf. ARETHAS Philol. et Scr. Eccl. (2130 036).

001 **In aureum carmen**, ed. F.G. Köhler, *Hieroclis in aureum Pythagoreorum carmen commentarius*. Stuttgart: Teubner, 1974: 5–122.
Cod: 26,580: Comm.

x01 **De providentia et fato.**
Photius, *Bibliotheca* 214, 251.
Cf. PHOTIUS Theol., Scr. Eccl. et Lexicogr. (4040 001).

2404 **HIEROCLES et PHILAGRIUS** Scriptores Facetiarum
A.D. 4?

001 **Facetiae**, ed. A. Thierfelder, *Philogelos der Lachfreund von Hierokles und Philagrios*. Munich: Heimeran, 1968: 28–126.
Cod

2360 **HIERON** Hist.
Incertum

001 **Titulus**, FGrH #518: 3B:491.
NQ: Hist.

1953 **HIERONYMUS** Hist.
3 B.C.: Cardianus

001 **Testimonia**, FGrH #154: 2B:829–830.
NQ: 553: Test.

002 **Fragmenta**, FGrH #154: 2B:830–835.
Q: 1,825: Hist.

x01 **Epistula cuidam Macedoniae regi.**
FGrH #153, fr. 1.
Cf. ANONYMI HISTORICI (FGrH) (1139 007).

2526 **HIERONYMUS** Hist.
ante A.D. 1: Aegyptius

001 **Fragmenta**, FGrH #787: 3C:799–800.
Q: 117: Hist.

1430 **HIERONYMUS** Phil.
3 B.C.: Rhodius

001 **Fragmenta**, ed. F. Wehrli, *Hieronymos von Rhodos. Kritolaos und seine Schüler* [*Die Schule des Aristoteles*, vol. 10, 2nd edn. Basel: Schwabe, 1969]: 13–23.
Ethica et teleologia: frr. 11–13, 15a–16, 18.
Educatio: frr. 19–20.
De ira: frr. 22–23.
Περὶ ἐποχῆς: fr. 24.
Περὶ μέθης: frr. 25–28.
Περὶ ποιητῶν: frr. 29–33.
Σποράδην ὑπομνήματα. Ἱστορικὰ ὑπομνήματα: frr. 34–49.
Rhetorica: frr. 52a–52b.
Theoria de perceptione: fr. 53.
Q, Pap: 2,730: Rhet.

0745 **HIEROPHILUS** Soph. et Phil.
A.D. 4/6?

001 **De nutriendi methodo**, ed. J.L. Ideler, *Physici et medici Graeci minores*, vol. 1. Berlin: Reimer, 1841 (repr. Amsterdam: Hakkert, 1963): 409–417.
Cod: 2,326: Med.

002 Πῶς ὀφείλει διαιτᾶσθαι ἄνθρωπος ἐφ' ἑκάστῳ μηνί, ed. A. Delatte, *Anecdota Atheniensia et alia*, vol. 2. Paris: Droz, 1939: 546–566.
Cod: 2,150: Med.

2051 **HIMERIUS** Soph.
A.D. 4: Prusensis, Atheniensis

001 **Declamationes et orationes**, ed. A. Colonna, *Himerii declamationes et orationes cum deperditarum fragmentis*. Rome: Polygraphica, 1951: 13–248.
Declamatio Hyperidis pro Demosthene (orat. 1): pp. 13–16.

Quia semper exercitationibus vacandum sit
(orat. 74): pp. 247–248.
Declamatio Corinthi habita (orat. 75) (titulus
solum): p. 248.
Cod: 42,880: Orat.

002 **Fragmenta ex incertis orationibus**, ed. Colonna, *op. cit.*, 249–253.
Q: 374: Orat.

003 **Fragmenta** (*P. Oslo* inv. 1478), ed. S. Eitrem
and L. Amundsen, "Fragments from the
speeches of Himerios, P. Oslo inv. no. 1478,"
Classica et mediaevalia 17 (1956) 29–30.
frr. e–f.
Pap: 107: Orat.

004 **Fragmenta**, ed. A. Guida, "Frammenti inediti
di Eupoli, Teleclide, Teognide, Giuliano e
Imerio da un nuovo codice del Lexicon Vindobonense," *Prometheus* 5 (1979) 210, 212, 213.
Q

2501 **HIPPAGORAS** Hist.
3 B.C.?

001 **Fragmentum**, FGrH #743: 3C:722.
Q: 40: Hist.

1431 **HIPPARCHUS** Astron. et Geogr.
2 B.C.: Nicaeensis

001 **Fragmenta** [Sp.?], ed. S. Weinstock, *Codices
Britannici* [*Catalogus codicum astrologorum
Graecorum* 9.1. Brussels: Academia, 1951]:
189–190.
Cod

002 **Fragmenta geographica**, ed. D.R. Dicks, *The
geographical fragments of Hipparchus*. London:
Athlone Press, 1960: 56–102.
Q: 5,424: Geogr.

003 **In Arati et Eudoxi phaenomena commentariorum libri iii**, ed. C. Manitius, *Hipparchi in
Arati et Eudoxi phaenomena commentariorum
libri iii*. Leipzig: Teubner, 1894: 2–280.
Cod: 28,852: Comm.

0468 **HIPPARCHUS** Comic.
3 B.C.?

001 **Fragmenta**, ed. T. Kock, *Comicorum Atticorum fragmenta*, vol. 3. Leipzig: Teubner,
1888: 272–274.
frr. 1–3, 5.
Q: 91: Comic.

002 **Fragmenta**, ed. A. Meineke, *Fragmenta comicorum Graecorum*, vol. 4. Berlin: Reimer, 1841
(repr. De Gruyter, 1970): 431–432.
Q: 89: Comic.

1433 **HIPPARCHUS** <Epigr.>
6 B.C.: Atheniensis

001 **Fragmenta**, ed. E. Diehl, *Anthologia lyrica
Graeca*, fasc. 1, 3rd edn. Leipzig: Teubner,
1949: 75.
frr. 1–2.
Q, Epigr: 13: Epigr.

2626 **HIPPARCHUS** Parodius
ante A.D. 2

001 **Fragmenta**, ed. H. Lloyd-Jones and P. Parsons,
Supplementum Hellenisticum. Berlin: De Gruyter, 1983: 249.
frr. 496–497.
Q: 28: Parod.

1432 <**HIPPARCHUS**> Phil.
3 B.C.

001 **Fragmentum**, ed. H. Thesleff, *The Pythagorean
texts of the Hellenistic period*. Åbo: Åbo Akademi, 1965: 89–91.
Q: 616: Phil.

2406 **HIPPASUS** Hist.
ante 1 B.C.: Lacon

001 **Testimonium**, FGrH #589: 3B:703.
NQ: 40: Test.

002 **Fragmentum**, FGrH #589: 3B:704.
Q: 68: Hist.

2260 **HIPPASUS** Phil.
6 B.C.: Metapontinus

001 **Testimonia**, ed. H. Diels and W. Kranz, *Die
Fragmente der Vorsokratiker*, vol. 1, 6th edn.
Berlin: Weidmann, 1951 (repr. Dublin: 1966):
107–110.
test. 1–15.
NQ: 1,403: Test.

002 **Tituli**, ed. H. Thesleff, *The Pythagorean texts
of the Hellenistic period*. Åbo: Åbo Akademi,
1965: 93.
NQ: 7: Phil.

1435 **HIPPIAS** Hist.
post 4 B.C.?: Erythraeus

001 **Fragmentum**, FGrH #421: 3B:317–318.
Q: 399: Hist.

1434 **HIPPIAS** Soph.
5 B.C.: Eleus

001 **Testimonia**, FGrH #6: 1A:156.
NQ: 146: Test.

002 **Fragmenta**, FGrH #6: 1A:156–158.
Q: 507: Hist., Geogr.

003 **Testimonia**, ed. H. Diels and W. Kranz, *Die
Fragmente der Vorsokratiker*, vol. 2, 6th edn.
Berlin: Weidmann, 1952 (repr. Dublin: 1966):
326–330.
test. 1–16.
NQ: 1,500: Test.

004 **Fragmenta**, ed. Diels and Kranz, *op. cit.*, 330–
333.
frr. 1–4, 6, 8–21.
Q: 818: Phil., Geogr.

x01 **Epigramma sepulcrale**.
App. Anth. 2.26(?): Cf. ANTHOLOGIAE
GRAECAE APPENDIX (7052 002).

0738 *HIPPIATRICA*
A.D. 9

001 **Hippiatrica Berolinensia**, ed. E. Oder and K. Hoppe, *Corpus hippiatricorum Graecorum*, vol. 1. Leipzig: Teubner, 1924 (repr. Stuttgart: 1971): 1–439.
Cod: 84,239: Med.

002 **Appendices ad hippiatrica Berolinensia**, ed. Oder and Hoppe, *op. cit.*, vol. 1, 440–450.
Cod: 2,382: Med.

003 **Hippiatrica Parisina**, ed. Oder and Hoppe, *op. cit.*, vol. 2 (1927; repr. 1971): 29–114.
Cod: 16,855: Med.

004 **Fragmenta Anatolii**, ed. Oder and Hoppe, *op. cit.*, vol. 2, 115–121.
Cod: 1,039: Med.

005 **Fragmenta Timothei Gazaei**, ed. Oder and Hoppe, *op. cit.*, vol. 2, 121–124.
Cod: 512: Med.

006 **Hippiatrica Cantabrigiensia**, ed. Oder and Hoppe, *op. cit.*, vol. 2, 125–252.
Cod: 26,259: Med.

007 **Additamenta Londinensia ad hippiatrica Cantabrigiensia**, ed. Oder and Hoppe, *op. cit.*, vol. 2, 253–271.
Cod: 4,214: Med.

008 **Excerpta Lugdunensia**, ed. Oder and Hoppe, *op. cit.*, vol. 2, 272–313.
Cod: 11,612: Med.

009 **Fragmenta Anatolii de equis**, ed. Oder and Hoppe, *op. cit.*, vol. 2, 325–330.
Cod: 1,485: Med.

010 **Fragmenta Anatolii de bubus**, ed. Oder and Hoppe, *op. cit.*, vol. 2, 330–336.
Cod: 1,907: Med.

2992 **HIPPOBOTUS** Phil. et Hist.
3 B.C.

001 **Fragmenta**, ed. M. Gigante, "Frammenti di Ippoboto. Contributo alla storia della storiografia filosofica," *Omaggio a Piero Treves*. Padua: Antenore, 1983: 179–193.
Q: Phil., Hist.

2235 **HIPPOCRATES** Math.
5 B.C.: Chius

001 **Testimonia**, ed. H. Diels and W. Kranz, *Die Fragmente der Vorsokratiker*, vol. 1, 6th edn. Berlin: Weidmann, 1951 (repr. Dublin: 1966): 395–397.
test. 1–6: alter auctor nominatur Aeschylus.
NQ: 808: Test.

0627 **HIPPOCRATES** Med. et *CORPUS HIPPO-CRATICUM*
5–4 B.C.: Cous

001 **De prisca medicina**, ed. É. Littré, *Oeuvres complètes d'Hippocrate*, vol. 1. Paris: Baillière, 1839 (repr. Amsterdam: Hakkert, 1973): 570–636.
Cod: 5,705: Med.

002 **De aëre aquis et locis**, ed. Littré, *op. cit.*, vol. 2 (1840; repr. 1961): 12–92.
Cod: 7,685: Med.

003 **Prognosticon**, ed. Littré, *op. cit.*, vol. 2, 110–190.
Cod: 5,363: Med.

004 **De diaeta in morbis acutis**, ed. Littré, *op. cit.*, vol. 2, 224–376.
Cod: 6,381: Med.

005 **De diaeta acutorum [Sp.]**, ed. Littré, *op. cit.*, vol. 2, 394–528.
Cod: 5,569: Med.

006 **De morbis popularibus** (= Epidemiae), ed. Littré, vols. 2; 3 (1841; repr. 1961); 5 (1846; repr. 1962): **2**:598–716; **3**:24–148; **5**:72–138, 144–196, 204–258, 266–356, 364–468.
Lib. 1: vol. 2, pp. 598–716.
Lib. 2: vol. 5, pp. 72–138.
Lib. 3: vol. 3, pp. 24–148.
Lib. 4: vol. 5, pp. 144–196.
Lib. 5: vol. 5, pp. 204–258.
Lib. 6: vol. 5, pp. 266–356.
Lib. 7: vol. 5, pp. 364–468.
Cod: 43,404: Med.

007 **De capitis vulneribus**, ed. Littré, *op. cit.*, vol. 3, 182–260.
Cod: 5,130: Med.

008 **De officina medici**, ed. Littré, *op. cit.*, vol. 3, 272–336.
Cod: 2,221: Med.

009 **De fracturis**, ed. Littré, *op. cit.*, vol. 3, 412–562.
Cod: 11,593: Med.

010 **De articulis**, ed. Littré, *op, cit.*, vol. 4 (1844; repr. 1962): 78–326.
Cod: 21,905: Med.

011 **Vectiarius**, ed. Littré, *op. cit.*, vol. 4, 340–394.
Cod: 5,091: Med.

012 **Aphorismi**, ed. Littré, *op. cit.*, vol. 4, 458–608.
Cod: 7,374: Med.

013 **Jusjurandum**, ed. Littré, *op. cit.*, vol. 4, 628–632.
Cf. et 0627 057.
Cod: 262: Med.

014 **Lex**, ed. Littré, *op. cit.*, vol. 4, 638–642.
Cod: 335: Med.

015 **De humoribus**, ed. Littré, *op. cit.*, vol. 5, 476–502.
Cod: 2,330: Med.

016 **Prorrheticon**, ed. Littré, *op. cit.*, vols. 5 & 9 (1861; repr. 1962): **5**:510–572; **9**:6–74.
Cod: 10,563: Med.

017 **Coa praesagia**, ed. Littré, *op. cit.*, vol. 5, 588–732.
Cod: 13,170: Med.

018 **De arte**, ed. Littré, *op. cit.*, vol. 6 (1849; repr. 1962): 2–26.
Cod: 2,801: Med.

019 **De natura hominis**, ed. Littré, *op. cit.*, vol. 6, 32–68.
Cod: 4,017: Med.

020 **De diaeta salubri**, ed. Littré, *op. cit.*, vol. 6, 72–86.
Cod: 1,509: Med.

021 **De flatibus**, ed. Littré, *op. cit.*, vol. 6, 90–114.
Cod: 2,923: Med.

022 **De humidorum usu**, ed. Littré, *op. cit.*, vol. 6, 118–136.
Cod: 1,532: Med.

023 **De morbis i–iii**, ed. Littré, *op. cit.*, vols. 6 & 7 (1851; repr. 1962): 6:140–204; 7:8–114, 118–160.
Cf. et 0627 024.
Cod: 26,143: Med.

024 **De semine, de natura pueri, de morbis iv**, ed. Littré, *op. cit.*, vol. 7, 470–614.
Cf. et 0627 023.
Cod: 19,474: Med.

025 **De affectionibus**, ed. Littré, *op. cit.*, vol. 6, 208–270.
Cod: 7,640: Med.

026 **De locis in homine**, ed. Littré, *op. cit.*, vol. 6, 276–348.
Cod: 8,723: Med.

027 **De morbo sacro**, ed. Littré, *op. cit.*, vol. 6, 352–396.
Cod: 4,876: Med.

028 **De ulceribus**, ed. Littré, *op. cit.*, vol. 6, 400–432.
Cod: 3,434: Med.

029 **De haemorrhoidibus**, ed. Littré, *op. cit.*, vol. 6, 436–444.
Cod: 928: Med.

030 **De fistulis**, ed. Littré, *op. cit.*, vol. 6, 448–460.
Cod: 1,603: Med.

031 **De diaeta i–iv**, ed. Littré, *op. cit.*, vol. 6, 466–662.
Cod: 20,472: Med.

032 **De affectionibus interioribus**, ed. Littré, *op. cit.*, vol. 7, 166–302.
Cod: 16,553: Med.

033 **De natura muliebri**, ed. Littré, *op. cit.*, vol. 7, 312–430.
Cod: 12,199: Med.

034 **De septimestri partu**, ed. Littré, *op. cit.*, vol. 7, 436–452.
Cod: 1,722: Med.

035 **De octimestri partu**, ed. Littré, *op. cit.*, vol. 7, 452–460.
Cod: 804: Med.

036 **De mulierum affectibus i–iii**, ed. Littré, *op. cit.*, vol. 8 (1853; repr. 1962): 10–462.
Lib. 1: pp. 10–232.
Lib. 2: pp. 234–406.
Lib. 3 (= De sterilibus): pp. 408–462.
Cod: 50,007: Med.

037 **De virginum morbis**, ed. Littré, *op. cit.*, vol. 8, 466–470.
Cod: 472: Med.

038 **De superfetatione**, ed. Littré, *op. cit.*, vol. 8, 476–508.
Cod: 3,485: Med.

039 **De exsectione foetus**, ed. Littré, *op. cit.*, vol. 8, 512–518.
Cod: 495: Med.

040 **De anatome**, ed. Littré, *op. cit.*, vol. 8, 538–540.
Cod: 260: Med.

041 **De dentitione**, ed. Littré, *op. cit.*, vol. 8, 544–548.
Cod: 403: Med.

042 **De glandulis**, ed. Littré, *op. cit.*, vol. 8, 556–574.
Cod: 1,810: Med.

043 **De carnibus**, ed. Littré, *op. cit.*, vol. 8, 584–614.
Cod: 3,467: Med.

045 **De corde**, ed. Littré, *op. cit.*, vol. 9, 80–92.
Cod: 1,062: Med.

046 **De alimento**, ed. Littré, *op. cit.*, vol. 9, 98–120.
Cod: 1,339: Med.

047 **De visu**, ed. Littré, *op. cit.*, vol. 9, 152–160.
Cod: 806: Med.

048 **De ossium natura**, ed. Littré, *op. cit.*, vol. 9, 168–196.
Cod: 3,411: Med.

049 **De medico**, ed. Littré, *op. cit.*, vol. 9, 204–220.
Cod: 1,552: Med.

050 **De decente habitu**, ed. Littré, *op. cit.*, vol. 9, 226–244.
Cod: 1,558: Med.

051 **Praeceptiones**, ed. Littré, *op. cit.*, vol. 9, 250–272.
Cod: 1,384: Med.

052 **De judicationibus**, ed. Littré, *op. cit.*, vol. 9, 276–294.
Cod: 2,025: Med.

053 **De diebus judicatoriis**, ed. Littré, *op. cit.*, vol. 9, 298–306.
Cod: 1,316: Med.

055 **Epistulae**, ed. Littré, *op. cit.*, vol. 9, 312–428.
Cod: 12,141: Epist.

044 **De septimanis** (= **De hebdomadibus**), ed. W.H. Roscher, *Die hippokratische Schrift von der Siebenzahl* [*Studien zur Geschichte und Kultur des Altertums* 6. Paderborn: Schöningh, 1913 (repr. New York: Johnson Reprint, 1967)]: 1–10, 20–23, 29–31, 36–37, 42–43, 45, 48–50, 68–69, 72–73, 74–79.
Cod: 2,162: Med.

054 **De purgantibus** (= **De remediis**), ed. H. Schöne, "Hippokrates. Περὶ φαρμάκων," *Rheinisches Museum* 73 (1924) 440–443.
Cod: 504: Med.

056 **De septimestri partu** [Sp.], ed. H. Grensemann, *Hippokrates. Über Achtmonatskinder. Über das Siebenmonatskind* [*Corpus medicorum Graecorum*, vol. 1.2.1. Berlin: Akademie-Verlag, 1968]: 122–124.
Cod: 414: Med.

057 **Jusjurandum metricum**, ed. J.L. Heiberg, *Hippocratis opera* [*Corpus medicorum Graecorum*, vol. 1.1. Leipzig: Teubner, 1927]: 5–6.
Dup. partim JUSJURANDUM MEDICUM (0740 001).
Cf. et 0627 013.
Cod: 74: Med., Hexametr.

0751 **Pseudo-HIPPOCRATES** Med.
post 5 B.C.

001 **Epistula ad Ptolemaeum regem**, ed. J.F. Boissonade, *Anecdota Graeca*, vol. 3. Paris: Imprimerie Nationale, 1831 (repr. Hildesheim:
Olms, 1962): 422–428.
Cod: 801: Epist.

002 **Epistula ad Ptolemaeum regem de hominis
fabrica**, ed. F.Z. Ermerins, *Anecdota medica
Graeca*. Leiden: Luchtmans, 1840 (repr. Amsterdam: Hakkert, 1963): 279–297.
Cod: 1,503: Epist., Med.

003 Περὶ διαφόρων καὶ παντοίων τροφῶν, ed. A.
Delatte, *Anecdota Atheniensia et alia*, vol. 2.
Paris: Droz, 1939: 479–482.
Cod: 657: Med.

004 Περὶ διαφορᾶς τροφῶν πρὸς Πτολεμαῖον, ed.
Delatte, *op. cit.*, 483–499.
Cod: 2,753: Med.

005 Ἑρμηνεία περὶ ἐνεργῶν λίθων, ed. C.É. Ruelle,
Les lapidaires de l'antiquité et du Moyen Age,
vol. 2.1. Paris: Leroux, 1898: 185–190.
Cod: 1,645: Nat. Hist., Lexicogr.

007 **Qualem oportet esse discipulum** *sive* **Testa-
mentum**, ed. K. Deichgräber, *Medicus gratiosus
[Abhandlungen der geistes- und sozialwissen-
schaftlichen Klasse* Jahrgang 1970, Nr. 3.
Mainz: Akademie der Wissenschaften und der
Literatur, 1970]: 97.
Cod: Med.

2698 **HIPPODAMAS** Epigr.
Incertum: Salaminius

x01 **Epigramma demonstrativum.**
App. Anth. 3.17: Cf. ANTHOLOGIAE GRAE-
CAE APPENDIX (7052 003).

1436 **<HIPPODAMUS>** Phil.
3 B.C.: Milesius

001 **Fragmenta** [Sp.], ed. H. Thesleff, *The Pythago-
rean texts of the Hellenistic period*. Åbo: Åbo
Akademi, 1965: 94–102.
Q: 2,677: Phil.

002 **Testimonia**, ed. H. Diels and W. Kranz, *Die
Fragmente der Vorsokratiker*, vol. 1, 6th edn.
Berlin: Weidmann, 1951 (repr. Dublin: 1966):
389–391.
test. 1–5: auctor alter nominatur Phaleas.
NQ: 672: Test.

2115 **HIPPOLYTUS** Scr. Eccl.
A.D. 3: Romanus

060 **Refutatio omnium haeresium (= Philosophumena)**, ed. M. Marcovich, *Hippolytus. Refutatio omnium haeresium [Patristische Texte und
Studien 25.* Berlin: De Gruyter, 1986]: 53–417.
Cod: 74,005: Phil., Theol., Hist.

002 **Contra haeresin Noeti**, ed. R. Butterworth,
Hippolytus of Rome. Contra Noetum. London:
Heythrop College (University of London),
1977: 43–93.
Cod: 4,564: Homilet.

003 **De antichristo**, ed. H. Achelis, *Hippolyt's
kleinere exegetische und homiletische Schriften
[Die griechischen christlichen Schriftsteller* 1.2.
Leipzig: Hinrichs, 1897]: 1–47.
Cod: 10,616: Exeget.

004 **Fragmenta in Genesim**, ed. Achelis, *op. cit.*,
51–53, 55–71.
frr. 1–6, 8–52.
Cf. et 2115 005, 038.
Cod: 2,433: Exeget.

005 **Fragmenta in Genesim** [Sp.], ed. Achelis, *op.
cit.*, 72–81.
frr. 53–81.
Cf. et 2115 004, 033.
Q, Cod: 1,059: Exeget.

006 **De benedictione Balaam** (fragmentum ex
Leontio), ed. Achelis, *op. cit.*, 82.
Cf. et 2115 046.
Cod: 75: Exeget., Homilet.

007 **In canticum Mosis**, ed. Achelis, *op. cit.*, 83–84.
frr. 1–3.
Q: 239: Exeget.

008 **Ex interpretatione Ruth**, ed. Achelis, *op. cit.*,
120.
Cod: 242: Exeget.

009 **In Helcanam et Annam**, ed. Achelis, *op. cit.*,
121–122.
frr. 1–4.
Q: 266: Exeget.

010 **Fragmentum de engastrimytho** [Sp.], ed. Achelis, *op. cit.*, 123.
Cod: 228: Exeget., Homilet.

011 **Fragmenta in Psalmos**, ed. Achelis, *op. cit.*,
130, 146–147, 153.
frr. 1, 18–20, 37.
Cf. et 2115 012, 052.
Q: 436: Exeget.

012 **Fragmenta in Psalmos** [Sp.], ed. Achelis, *op.
cit.*, 131–145, 147–153.
frr. 2–17, 21–36, 38.
Cf. et 2115 011, 052.
Q, Cod: 4,308: Exeget.

013 **Fragmenta in Proverbia**, ed. Achelis, *op. cit.*,
157–167, 176–178.
frr. 1–29, 54.
Cf. et 2115 044, 045, 053.
Q, Cod: 2,499: Exeget.

014 **Fragmenta in Proverbia** [Dub.], ed. Achelis,
op. cit., 168.
frr. 30–31.
Q: 26: Exeget.

015 **Fragmenta in Proverbia** [Sp.], ed. Achelis, *op.
cit.*, 169–175.
frr. 32–53.
Q: 813: Exeget.

016 **In Ecclesiasten** (fragmentum e cod. Vat. 1694),
ed. Achelis, *op. cit.*, 179.
Cod: 67: Exeget.

017 **Fragmentum in Ecclesiasten** [Sp.], ed. Achelis,
op. cit., 179.
Q: 21: Exeget.

018 **In principium Isaiae**, ed. Achelis, *op. cit.*, 180.
Q: 123: Exeget.

019 **Fragmentum in Ezechielem**, MPG 10: 632–633.
Q: 138: Exeget.

020 **Fragmentum in Matthaeum 6.11** [Sp.], ed. Achelis, *op. cit.*, 208.
Q: 59: Exeget.

021 **Fragmentum de distributione talantorum** (Matth. 25.24), ed. H. Achelis, *op. cit.*, 209.
Q: 99: Exeget.

022 **De duobus latronibus** (Joh. 19.33–34), ed. Achelis, *op. cit.*, 211.
Q: 142: Exeget.

023 **In evangelium Joannis et de resurrectione Lazari** [Dub.], ed. Achelis, *op. cit.*, 215–220, 224–227.
Q: 1,328: Exeget.

024 **De resurrectione ad Mammaeam imperatricem** (fragmenta ap. Theodoretum, *Eranistes*), ed. Achelis, *op. cit.*, 253.
frr. 7–8.
Cf. et 2115 025, 048.
Q: 112: Epist., Theol.

025 **Fragmentum de resurrectione et incorruptione** (ap. Anastasium Sinaïtam, *Viae dux*), ed. Achelis, *op. cit.*, 254.
Cf. et 2115 024, 048.
Q: 96: Theol.

026 **De theophania** [Dub.], ed. Achelis, *op. cit.*, 257–263.
Q: 2,012: Exeget., Homilet.

027 **Demonstratio temporum paschatis** (in catenis), ed. Achelis, *op. cit.*, 267–271.
frr. 1–3, 5, 7.
Q: 371: Homilet., Exeget., Caten.

028 **Narratio de virgine Corinthiaca** [Dub.], ed. Achelis, *op. cit.*, 275–277.
Cod: 341: Exeget., Homilet.

029 **De consummatione mundi** [Sp.], ed. Achelis, *op. cit.*, 289–309.
Cod: 8,216: Exeget.

030 **Commentarium in Danielem**, ed. M. Lefèvre, *Hippolyte. Commentaire sur Daniel* [*Sources chrétiennes* 14. Paris: Cerf, 1947]: 70–386.
Cf. et 2115 032, 035.
Q, Cod: 34,647: Exeget.

031 **In Canticum canticorum**, ed. G.N. Bonwetsch and H. Achelis, *Hippolytus Werke*, vol. 1 [*Die griechischen christlichen Schriftsteller* 1.1. Leipzig: Hinrichs, 1897]: 343.
Cf. et 2115 049.
Q: 132: Exeget.

032 **Commentarium in Danielem 1.18**, ed. M. Richard, "Les difficultés d'une édition du commentaire de S. Hippolyte sur Daniel," *Revue d'histoire des textes* 2 (1972) 5–7.
Cf. et 2115 030, 035.
Cod: 484: Exeget.

033 **De benedictionibus Isaaci et Jacobi**, ed. M. Brière, L. Mariès and B.-C. Mercier, *Hippolyte de Rome. Sur les bénédictions d'Isaac, de Jacob et de Moïse* [*Patrologia Orientalis* 27 (1954)]: 2–114.

Cf. et 2115 005.
Cod: 8,356: Exeget., Homilet.

034 **De benedictione Mosis** (fragmenta), ed. Brière, Mariès, and Mercier, *op. cit.*, ix.
Q: 107: Exeget., Homilet.

035 **Fragmentum in Danielem 1.18.3**, ed. M. Richard, "Le chapitre sur l'église du commentaire sur Daniel de Saint-Hippolyte," *Revue d'histoire des textes* 3 (1973) 16.
Cf. et 2115 030, 032.
Cod: 40: Exeget.

036 **Chronicon**, ed. R. Helm (post A. Bauer), *Hippolytus Werke*, vol. 4, 2nd edn. [*Die griechischen christlichen Schriftsteller* 46. Berlin: Akademie-Verlag, 1955]: 6–69, 128–134.
Q, Cod: 10,632: Hist., Chronogr.

037 **Chronicon** (fragmentum) (*P. Oxy.* 6.870), ed. B.P. Grenfell and A.S. Hunt, *The Oxyrhynchus papyri*, pt. 6. London: Egypt Exploration Fund, 1908: 176.
Pap: 107: Hist., Chronogr.

038 **Fragmentum in Genesim 4.23** (e cod. Ath. bibl. nat. 2492), ed. M. Richard, "Un fragment inédit de S. Hippolyte sur Genèse 4.23," *Serta Turyniana: Studies in Greek literature and palaeography in honor of Alexander Turyn.* Urbana: University of Illinois Press, 1974: 396–397.
Cf. et 2115 004.
Cod: 235: Exeget.

039 **Demonstratio adversus Judaeos** [Sp.], ed. E. Schwartz, "Zwei Predigten Hippolyts," *Sitzungsberichte der bayerischen Akademie der Wissenschaften*, Philosoph.-hist. Kl., Heft 3. Munich, 1936: 19–23.
Cod: 1,333: Homilet.

042 **De universo**, ed. K. Holl, *Fragmente vornicänischer Kirchenväter aus den Sacra Parallela* [*Texte und Untersuchungen* 20. Leipzig: Hinrichs, 1899]: 137–143.
Cf. et 2115 043, 058, x05.
Q: 1,176: Theol., Phil.

043 **De universo** (fragmenta), ed. W.J. Malley, "Four unedited fragments of the 'De universo' of the Pseudo-Josephus found in the Chronicon of George Hamartolus (Coislin 305)," *Journal of Theological Studies*, n.s. 16 (1965) 15–16.
Cf. et 2115 042, 058, x05.
Q: 328: Theol., Phil.

044 **Fragmenta in Proverbia** (e cod. Coislin. 193), ed. M. Richard, "Les fragments du commentaire de S. Hippolyte sur les proverbes de Salomon," *Muséon* 79 (1966) 75–94.
frr. 1–48, 52–79.
Cf. et 2115 013.
Cod: 2,527: Exeget.

045 **Fragmenta in Proverbia** (e Pseudo-Anastasio Sinaïta), ed. Richard, *Muséon* 79, 82–94.
frr. 37–61, 65, 67–72, 74–76.
Cf. et 2115 013.
Q: 824: Exeget.

046 **De benedictione Balaam** (fragmenta ap. Irenaeum), ed. W.W. Harvey, *Sancti Irenaei episcopi Lugdunensis libri quinque adversus haereses*, vol. 2. Cambridge: Cambridge University Press, 1857: 486, 489–491, 509.
frr. 15, 20–27.
Cf. et 2115 006.
Q: 388: Exeget., Homilet.

047 **Fragmentum e traditione apostolica** [Sp.], ed. M. Richard, "Quelques nouveaux fragments des pères anténicéens et nicéens," *Symbolae Osloenses* 38 (1963) 79.
Cod: 33: Eccl.

048 **De resurrectione ad Mammaeam imperatricem** (cod. Achrid. Mus. nat. 86), ed. Richard, *Symbolae Osloenses* 38, 79–80.
Cf. et 2115 024, 025.
Cod: 68: Epist., Theol.

049 **In Canticum canticorum** (paraphrasis), ed. M. Richard, "Une paraphrase grecque résumée du commentaire d'Hippolyte sur le cantique des cantiques," *Muséon* 77 (1964) 140–154.
Cf. et 2115 031.
Cod: 3,331: Exeget.

050 **Fragmenta varia** [Dub.], ed. Harvey, *op. cit.*, 497–498.
frr. 33–34.
Dup. partim IRENAEUS Scr. Eccl. (1447 005) (frr. 33–34).
Q: 90: Exeget.

051 **Fragmentum in Helcanam et Annam**, ed. P. Nautin, *Le dossier d'Hippolyte et de Méliton* [*Patristica* 1. Paris: Cerf, 1953]: 34.
Q: 46: Exeget.

052 **Fragmenta in Psalmos**, ed. Nautin, *op. cit.*, 167–183.
Cf. et 2115 011, 012.
Q: 1,999: Exeget.

053 **Fragmenta in Proverbia**, ed. M. Richard, "Les fragments du commentaire de S. Hippolyte sur les proverbes de Salomon," *Muséon* 78 (1965) 263–271, 273–277, 279–288.
frr. 1–14, 16–20, 26, 29–31.
frr. 30–31 dubia sunt.
Dup. partim 2115 013.
Q: 1,840: Exeget.

055 **Traditio apostolica**, ed. B. Botte, *Hippolyte de Rome. La tradition apostolique d'après les anciennes versions*, 2nd edn. [*Sources chrétiennes* 11 bis. Paris: Cerf, 1968]: 42–46, 66, 96, 112.
Oratio consecrationis episcopi: pp. 42–46.
De lectore: p. 66.
De jejunio: p. 96.
De fructibus quos oportet offerre episcopo: p. 112.
Q: 369: Eccl.

056 **Contra Beronem et Heliconem** [Sp.], ed. F. Diekamp, *Doctrina patrum de incarnatione verbi*. Münster: Aschendorff, 1907: 321–326.
Q: 1,602: Theol.

057 **Canon paschalis**, ed. M. Guarducci, *Epigrafia*

greca iv. *Epigrafi sacre pagane e cristiane*. Rome: Istituto Poligrafico, 1978: 542–543.
Epigr: 80: Eccl.

058 **De universo** (fragmentum ap. Joannem Philoponum, *De opificio mundi*), ed. P.A. de Lagarde, *Hippolyti Romani quae feruntur omnia graece*. Leipzig: Teubner, 1858 (repr. Osnabrück: Zeller, 1966): 124.
fr. 17.
Cf. et 2115 042, 043, x05.
Q: 68: Theol., Phil.

059 **Syntagma** (fragmentum ap. *Chronicon paschale*), MPG 10: 868–869.
Q: 261: Eccl., Epist.

x01 **Contra Artemonem** *sive* **Parvus labyrinthus** [Dub.].
Eusebius, HE 5.28.
Cf. EUSEBIUS Scr. Eccl. et Theol. (2018 002).

x02 **De xii apostolis** [Sp.].
Schermann, pp. 164–167.
Cf. VITAE PROPHETARUM (1750 012).

x03 **De lxx apostolis** [Sp.].
Schermann, pp. 167–170.
Cf. VITAE PROPHETARUM (1750 012).

x04 **Adversus Graecos**.
Cf. De universo (2115 042, 043, 058, x05).

x05 **De universo** (fragmenta).
Photius, *Bibliotheca* 48.
Cf. PHOTIUS Theol., Scr. Eccl. et Lexicogr. (4040 001).
Cf. et 2115 042, 043, 058.

1437 **HIPPON** Phil.
vel Hipponax
5 B.C.: Rheginus

001 **Testimonia**, ed. H. Diels and W. Kranz, *Die Fragmente der Vorsokratiker*, vol. 1, 6th edn. Berlin: Weidmann, 1951 (repr. Dublin: 1966): 385–387.
test. 1–19.
NQ: 1,150: Test.

002 **Fragmenta**, ed. Diels and Kranz, *op. cit.*, 387–389.
frr. 1–4.
Q: 361: Phil.

x01 **Epigramma sepulcrale** [Sp.].
App. Anth. 2.340: Cf. ANTHOLOGIAE GRAECAE APPENDIX (7052 002).
Dup. 1437 002 (fr. 2).

0233 **HIPPONAX** Iamb.
6 B.C.: Ephesius

001 **Fragmenta**, ed. M.L. West, *Iambi et elegi Graeci*, vol. 1. Oxford: Clarendon Press, 1971: 110–152, 154, 156–160, 162–171.
frr. 1–10, 12–17, 19–30, 32, 34–44, 47–54, 56–125, 127–129a, 132, 135–135b, 144–145, 147, 148b, 151a, 154–155b, 158, 161, 165b, 166–167, 172, 175–177, 182.
Q, Pap: 2,256: Iamb., Hexametr.

2391 **HIPPOSTRATUS** Hist.
3 B.C.?
001 **Testimonia**, FGrH #568: 3B:659.
NQ: 78: Test.
002 **Fragmenta**, FGrH #568: 3B:660–661.
Q: 416: Hist.

0351 **[HIPPOTHOON]** Trag.
vel Hippothous
Incertum
001 **Fragmenta**, ed. B. Snell, *Tragicorum Graecorum fragmenta*, vol. 1. Göttingen: Vandenhoeck & Ruprecht, 1971: 321–322.
frr. 1–6.
Q: 69: Trag.

1438 **HIPPYS** Hist.
5 B.C.?: Rheginus
001 **Testimonium**, FGrH #554: 3B:540–541.
NQ: 40: Test.
002 **Fragmenta**, FGrH #554: 3B:541–543.
Q: 587: Hist.

1386 **HISTORIA ALEXANDRI MAGNI**
post 4 B.C.
Cf. et ANONYMI HISTORICI in FGrH (1139
007).
001 **Recensio** *a*, ed. W. Kroll, *Historia Alexandri
Magni*, vol. 1. Berlin: Weidmann, 1926: 1–146.
Cod: 31,522: Narr. Fict.
002 **Recensio** *β*, ed. L. Bergson, *Der griechische
Alexanderroman. Rezension β*. Stockholm:
Almqvist & Wiksell, 1965: 1–192.
Cod: 27,729: Narr. Fict.
010 **Recensio** *β* (e cod. Leidensi Vulc. 93), ed.
Bergson, *op. cit.*, 193–204.
Cod: 2,718: Narr. Fict.
011 **Recensio** *β* (e cod. Paris. gr. 1685 et cod. Mes-
sinensi 62), ed. Bergson, *op. cit.*, 205–207.
Cod: 587: Narr. Fict.
003 **Recensio** *γ* (lib. 1), ed. U. von Lauenstein, *Der
griechische Alexanderroman. Rezension γ. Buch
I* [*Beiträge zur klassischen Philologie* 4. Meisenheim am Glan: Hain, 1962]: 2–150.
Cod: 16,408: Narr. Fict.
004 **Recensio** *γ* (lib. 2), ed. H. Engelmann, *Der
griechische Alexanderroman. Rezension γ. Buch
II* [*Beiträge zur klassischen Philologie* 12. Meisenheim am Glan: Hain, 1963]: 152–328.
Cod: 18,492: Narr. Fict.
005 **Recensio** *γ* (lib. 3), ed. F. Parthe, *Der griechische Alexanderroman. Rezension γ. Buch III*
[*Beiträge zur klassischen Philologie* 33. Meisenheim am Glan: Hain, 1969]: 330–462.
Cod: 11,555: Narr. Fict.
020 **Recensio** *δ* (e cod. Vat. gr. 1700, 88v–89r), ed.
G. Ballaira, "Frammenti inediti della perduta
recensione δ del romanzo di Alessandro in un
codice Vaticano," *Bollettino del comitato per la
preparazione della edizione nazionale dei classici
greci e latini* 13 (1965) 29.
Cod: 260: Narr. Fict.

006 **Recensio** *ε*, ed. J. Trumpf, *Anonymi Byzantini
vita Alexandri regis Macedonum*. Stuttgart:
Teubner, 1974: 1–178.
Cod: 24,971: Narr. Fict.
007 **Recensio** *λ* (lib. 3), ed. H. van Thiel, *Die
Rezension λ des Pseudo-Kallisthenes*. Bonn: Habelt, 1959: 37–65.
Cod: 6,366: Narr. Fict.
008 **Recensio** *λ* (Pseudo-Methodius, redactio 1),
ed. van Thiel, *op. cit.*, 72, 74.
Cod: 435: Narr. Fict.
009 **Recensio** *λ* (Pseudo-Methodius, redactio 2),
ed. van Thiel, *op. cit.*, 73, 75.
Cod: 359: Narr. Fict.
013 **Recensio** *E* (cod. Eton College 163), ed. A.
Lolos and V.L. Konstantinopulos, *Ps.-Kallis-
thenes: Zwei mittelgriechische Prosa-Fassungen
des Alexanderromans*, 2 vols. [*Beiträge zur
klassischen Philologie* 141 & 150. Meisenheim
am Glan: Hain, 1983]: 1:87–309; 2:11–207.
vol. 1: ed. Lolos.
vol. 2: ed. Konstantinopulos.
Cod: 46,536: Narr. Fict.
012 **Recensio** *F* (cod. Flor. Laurentianus Ashburn
1444), ed. Lolos and Konstantinopulos, *op. cit.*,
vol. 1, 86–308; 2, 10–206.
Dup. partim 1386 014.
Cod: 48,332: Narr. Fict.
015 **Recensio** *K* (cod. 236 Kutlumussiu-Kloster des
Athos), ed. K. Mitsakis, "Διήγησις περὶ τοῦ
Ἀλεξάνδρου καὶ τῶν μεγάλων πολέμων," *By-
zantinisch-neugriechische Jahrbücher* 20 (1970)
263–290.
Cod: 12,099: Narr. Fict.
014 **Recensio** *V* (cod. Vind. theol. gr. 244), ed. K.
Mitsakis, *Der byzantinische Alexanderroman
nach dem Codex Vind. Theol. gr. 244* [*Miscellanea Byzantina Monacensia* 7. Munich: Institut für Byzantinistik und neugriechische Philologie der Universität, 1967]: 21–87.
Dup. partim 1386 012.
Cod: 19,701: Narr. Fict.
016 **Recensio** *φ*, ed. G. Veloudis, Ἡ φυλλάδα τοῦ
μεγαλέξαντρου. Διήγησις Ἀλεξάνδρου τοῦ
Μακεδόνος [Νέα Ἑλληνικὴ Βιβλιοθήκη 39.
Athens: Hermes, 1977]: 5–117.
Cod: 38,461: Narr. Fict.
018 **Recensio Byzantina poetica** (cod. Marcianus
408), ed. S. Reichmann, *Das byzantinische
Alexandergedicht nach dem codex Marcianus
408 herausgegeben* [*Beiträge zur klassischen
Philologie* 13. Meisenheim am Glan: Hain,
1963].
Cod: 40,784: Narr. Fict., Iamb.
019 **Recensio poetica** (recensio R), ed. D. Holton,
Διήγησις τοῦ Ἀλεξάνδρου. *The tale of Alex-
ander. The rhymed version* [Βυζαντινὴ καὶ
Νεοελληνικὴ βιβλιοθήκη. Thessalonica: n.p.,
1974]: 103–185.
Cod: 22,882: Narr. Fict., Iamb.

3001 HISTORIA ET SENTENTIAE DE AHIQAR
2/1 B.C.

001 **Historia et sententiae de Ahiqar** (e vita G Aesopi, recensio 3), ed. B.E. Perry, *Fragmenta pseudepigraphorum quae supersunt Graeca* (ed. A.-M. Denis) [*Pseudepigrapha veteris testamenti Graece* 3. Leiden: Brill, 1970]: 133–147.
Q: Narr. Fict.

002 **Historia et sententiae de Ahiqar** (e vita W Aesopi, recensio 2), ed. Perry, *op. cit.*, 133–147.
Q: Narr. Fict.

003 **Historia et sententiae de Ahiqar** (e vita Aesopi sub auctore Maximo Planude, recensio 1), ed. F.C. Conybeare, J.R. Harris and A. Smith Lewis, *The story of Ahikar from the Syriac, Arabic, Armenian, Ethiopic, Greek and Slavonic versions.* London: Clay, 1898: 119–124.
Q: Narr. Fict.

2744 HISTORIA MONACHORUM IN AEGYPTO
fort. auctore monacho Hierosolymitano
A.D. 5

001 **Historia monachorum in Aegypto,** ed. A.J. Festugière, *Historia monachorum in Aegypto.* Brussels: Société des Bollandistes, 1971: 4–138.
Cod: 20,865: Hagiogr.

4065 Manuel HOLOBOLUS Rhet.
vel Maximus Holobolus
A.D. 13

001 **Scholia in Besantini βωμόν,** ed. C. Wendel, "Die Technopägnien-Scholien des Rhetors Holobolos," *Byzantinische Zeitschrift* 19 (1910) 336–337.
Cod: Schol.

002 **Commentarium in Theocriti syringem,** ed. F. Dübner, *Scholia in Theocritum.* Paris: Didot, 1849: 111–113.
Cod: Comm.

x01 **Epigrammata** (*App. Anth.*).
Epigramma demonstrativum: 3.214.
Epigramma exhortatorium et supplicatorium: 4.89.
App. Anth. 3.214: Cf. ANTHOLOGIAE GRAE-CAE APPENDIX (7052 003).
App. Anth. 4.89: Cf. ANTHOLOGIAE GRAE-CAE APPENDIX (7052 004).

0012 HOMERUS Epic.
8 B.C.
Cf. et VERSUS HEROICI (1802).
Vitae: Cf. VITAE HOMERI (1805).
Scholia: Cf. SCHOLIA IN HOMERUM (5026).

001 **Ilias,** ed. T.W. Allen, *Homeri Ilias,* vols. 2–3. Oxford: Clarendon Press, 1931: 2:1–356; 3:1–370.
Cod: 115,477: Epic.

002 **Odyssea,** ed. P. von der Muehll, *Homeri Odyssea.* Basel: Helbing & Lichtenhahn, 1962: 1–456.
Cod: 87,765: Epic.

003 **Epigrammata,** AG 7.153; **14.**147.
AG 10.32: Cf. PALLADAS Epigr. (2123 001).
Q: 59: Epigr.

x01 **Epigramma dedicatorium.**
App. Anth. 1.2(?): Cf. ANTHOLOGIAE GRAE-CAE APPENDIX (7052 001).

0253 [HOMERUS] <Epic.>
7/6 B.C.: fort. Colophonius

001 **Margites** (fragmenta), ed. M.L. West, *Iambi et elegi Graeci,* vol. 2. Oxford: Clarendon Press, 1972: 72–73, 75–76.
frr. 1–3, 4b, 7.
Q, Pap: 138: Hexametr., Iamb.

1440 HONESTUS Epigr.
A.D. 1: Byzantius vel Corinthius

001 **Epigrammata,** AG 5.20; 7.66, 274; **9.**216, 225, 230, 250, 292; **11.**32, 45.
Q: 312: Epigr.

x01 **Epigrammata dedicatoria.**
App. Anth. 1.134–137: Cf. ANTHOLOGIAE GRAECAE APPENDIX (7052 001).

2052 HORAPOLLO Gramm.
A.D. 4/5?: Nilous

001 **Hieroglyphica** (translatio Philippi), ed. F. Sbordone, *Hori Apollinis hieroglyphica.* Naples: Loffredo, 1940: 1–216.
Cod: 8,844: Comm.

002 **Testimonia,** FGrH #630: 3C:180.
NQ: 180: Test.

HYBRIAS Lyr.
PMG, p. 478.
Cf. CARMINA CONVIVIALIA (PMG) (0296 001).

0932 HYBRISTUS Med.
ante 3 B.C.: Oxyrhynchites

x01 **Fragmentum ap. Galenum.**
K14.188.
Cf. GALENUS Med. (0057 078).

0933 HYGIENUS Med.
A.D. 1/2

x01 **Fragmenta ap. Galenum.**
K12.488, 788; **13.**353, 512, 747.
Cf. GALENUS Med. (0057 076–077).

0742 HYMNI ANONYMI
Varia

001 **Naassenorum carmina,** ed. E. Heitsch, *Die griechischen Dichterfragmente der römischen Kaiserzeit,* vol. 1, 2nd edn. Göttingen: Vandenhoeck & Ruprecht, 1963: 155–157.
fr. 1, sine titulo: pp. 155–156.
fr. 2, In Attinem: pp. 156–157.
fr. 3, In Attinem: p. 157.
Q: 225: Hymn.

002 **Christianorum carmina,** ed. Heitsch, *op. cit.,* vol. 1, 157–164.

fr. 1, In Christum salvatorem: pp. 157-159.

fr. 2, In trinitatem (*P. Oxy.* 15.1786): p. 160.

fr. 3, In Christum (*P. Berol. Mus.* 8299): p. 161.

fr. 4, De moribus Christianorum (*P. Amh.* 1, 23-28): pp. 161-164.

Q, Pap: 521: Hymn.

003 **Carminis de mundi creatione exordium**, ed. Heitsch, *op. cit.*, vol. 1, 164-165.
Pap: 55: Hymn.

004 **Hymnus in Jovem**, ed. Heitsch, *op. cit.*, vol. 1, 165.
Q: 30: Hymn.

005 **Hymnus in Isim** (*PSI* 844), ed. Heitsch, *op. cit.*, vol. 1, 165-166.
Pap: 97: Hymn.

006 **Hymnus in Sarapidem** (*P. Schubart* 12), ed. Heitsch, *op. cit.*, vol. 1, 166.
Pap: 58: Hymn.

007 **Aretalogia Sarapidis** (*P. Berol.* 10525), ed. Heitsch, *op. cit.*, vol. 1, 167-168.
Pap: 153: Hymn.

008 **Hymnus in Apollinem**, ed. Heitsch, *op. cit.*, vol. 1, 168.
Q: 47: Hymn.

009 **Paean in Apollinem** (*P. Berol.* 6870v), ed. Heitsch, *op. cit.*, vol. 1, 169-170.
Pap: 51: Hymn.

010 **Hymnus in Asclepium**, ed. Heitsch, *op. cit.*, vol. 1, 171.
Q: 66: Hymn.

011 **Hymnus in Hecatam**, ed. Heitsch, *op. cit.*, vol. 1, 171.
Q: 50: Hymn.

012 **Hymnus in Fortunam** (*P. Berol. Mus.* 9734v), ed. Heitsch, *op. cit.*, vol. 1, 172.
Dup. partim LYRICA ADESPOTA (CA) (0230 001) (fr. 34).
Pap: 63: Hymn.

013 **Hymnus in Dionysum** (*P. Ross. Georg.* 1.11), ed. Heitsch, *op. cit.*, vol. 1, 173-175.
Pap: 427: Hymn.

014 **Carmen mystarum** (*P. Argent.* 1313), ed. Heitsch, *op. cit.*, vol. 1, 175-176.
Pap: 74: Hymn.

015 **Descensus ad inferos** (*P. Brit. Mus.* 1192), ed. Heitsch, *op. cit.*, vol. 1, 177-179.
Pap: 258: Poem.

016 **Hymni e papyris magicis collecti**, ed. Heitsch, *op. cit.*, vol. 1, 180-199.

fr. 1, In Pantocratorem (*P. Gr. Lugd. Bat.* 1.384, col. 7-8): p. 180.

fr. 2, In Pana (-Pantocratorem) (*P. Louvre* 2391, col. 17): p. 180.

fr. 3, In Solem (*P. Paris. Bibl. Nat.* suppl. gr. 574, fol. 11v): p. 181.

fr. 4, In Solem (*P. Paris. Bibl. Nat.* suppl. gr. 574 + *P. Brit.* Mus. gr. 122 + *P. Berol.* 5025 A et B): pp. 181-183.

fr. 5, In Solem (*P. Louvre* 2391, col. 8 et 9): pp. 183-184.

fr. 6, In Typhona (*P. Paris. Bibl. Nat.* suppl. gr. 574, fol. 4r): p. 185.

fr. 7, In Typhona (*P. Paris. Bibl. Nat.* suppl. gr. 574, fol. 4v-5r): p. 186.

fr. 8, In Mercurium (*P. Argent.* gr. 1179v): pp. 186-187.

fr. 9, In Lunam (*P. Paris. Bibl. Nat.* suppl. gr. 574, fol. 25v-26v): pp. 187-191.

fr. 10, In Lunam (*P. Paris Bibl. Nat.* suppl. gr. 574, fol. 30v-31v): pp. 191-193.

fr. 11, In Lunam (*P. Paris. Bibl. Nat.* suppl. gr. 574, fol. 28r-29v): pp. 193-195.

fr. 12, In Dianam (-Lunam) (*P. Paris. Bibl. Nat.* suppl. gr. 574, fol. 28): pp. 195-196.

fr. 13, In Hecatam (*P. Paris. Bibl. Nat.* suppl. gr. 574, fol. 30): pp. 197-198.

fr. 14, In Venerem (*P. Paris. Bibl. Nat.* suppl. gr. 574, fol. 32r): pp. 198-199.

Cod, Pap: 2,863: Hymn., Magica

017 **Hymnus in omnes deos**, ed. Heitsch, *op. cit.*, vol. 2 (1964): 43.
fr. S3.
Q: 66: Hymn.

018 **Hymnus in Apollinem**, ed. Heitsch, *op. cit.*, vol. 2, 44.
fr. S5.
Q: 31: Hymn.

019 **Hymnus in Isim**, ed. F.H. von Gärtringen, *Inscriptiones insularum Maris Aegaei praeter Delum* [*Inscriptiones Graecae*, vol. 12.5. Berlin: Reimer, 1909]: 214-217.
no. 739.
Epigr: Hymn.

020 **Φῶς ἱλαρόν**, ed. W. Christ and M. Paranikas, *Anthologia Graeca carminum Christianorum.* Leipzig: Teubner, 1871 (repr. Hildesheim: Olms, 1963): 40.
Cod: Hymn.

0013 ***HYMNI HOMERICI***
8-6 B.C.
Cf. et VERSUS HEROICI (1802).

001 **Fragmenta hymni in Bacchum**, ed. T.W. Allen, W.R. Halliday and E.E. Sikes, *The Homeric hymns*, 2nd edn. Oxford: Clarendon Press, 1936: 1-2.
Q, Cod: 149: Hymn.

002 **In Cererem**, ed. Allen, Halliday, and Sikes, *op. cit.*, 2-20.
Cod: 3,401: Hymn.

003 **In Apollinem**, ed. Allen, Halliday, and Sikes, *op. cit.*, 20-42.
Cod: 3,842: Hymn.

004 **In Mercurium**, ed. Allen, Halliday, and Sikes, *op. cit.*, 42-64.
Cod: 4,030: Hymn.

005 **In Venerem**, ed. Allen, Halliday, and Sikes, *op. cit.*, 64-75.
Cod: 2,067: Hymn.

006 **In Venerem**, ed. Allen, Halliday, and Sikes, *op. cit.*, 75.
Cod: 135: Hymn.

007 **In Bacchum**, ed. Allen, Halliday, and Sikes, *op. cit.*, 76-78.
Cod: 429: Hymn.

008 **In Martem**, ed. Allen, Halliday, and Sikes, *op. cit.*, 78.
Cod: 104: Hymn.

009 **In Dianam**, ed. Allen, Halliday, and Sikes, *op. cit.*, 79.
Cod: 60: Hymn.

010 **In Venerem**, ed. Allen, Halliday, and Sikes, *op. cit.*, 79.
Cod: 42: Hymn.

011 **In Minervam**, ed. Allen, Halliday, and Sikes, *op. cit.*, 79.
Cod: 38: Hymn.

012 **In Junonem**, ed. Allen, Halliday, and Sikes, *op. cit.*, 80.
Cod: 30: Hymn.

013 **In Cererem**, ed. Allen, Halliday, and Sikes, *op. cit.*, 80.
Cod: 22: Hymn.

014 **In matrem deorum**, ed. Allen, Halliday, and Sikes, *op. cit.*, 80.
Cod: 50: Hymn.

015 **In Herculem**, ed. Allen, Halliday, and Sikes, *op. cit.*, 81.
Cod: 64: Hymn.

016 **In Aesculapium**, ed. Allen, Halliday, and Sikes, *op. cit.*, 81.
Cod: 35: Hymn.

017 **In Dioscuros**, ed. Allen, Halliday, and Sikes, *op. cit.*, 81–82.
Cod: 30: Hymn.

018 **In Mercurium**, ed. Allen, Halliday, and Sikes, *op. cit.*, 82.
Cod: 77: Hymn.

019 **In Pana**, ed. Allen, Halliday, and Sikes, *op. cit.*, 82–84.
Cod: 342: Hymn.

020 **In Volcanum**, ed. Allen, Halliday, and Sikes, *op. cit.*, 84.
Cod: 54: Hymn.

021 **In Apollinem**, ed. Allen, Halliday, and Sikes, *op. cit.*, 85.
Cod: 40: Hymn.

022 **In Neptunum**, ed. Allen, Halliday, and Sikes, *op. cit.*, 85.
Cod: 45: Hymn.

023 **In Jovem**, ed. Allen, Halliday, and Sikes, *op. cit.*, 85.
Cod: 25: Hymn.

024 **In Vestam**, ed. Allen, Halliday, and Sikes, *op. cit.*, 85–86.
Cod: 36: Hymn.

025 **In Musas et Apollinem**, ed. Allen, Halliday, and Sikes, *op. cit.*, 86.
Cod: 55: Hymn.

026 **In Bacchum**, ed. Allen, Halliday, and Sikes, *op. cit.*, 86.
Cod: 93: Hymn.

027 **In Dianam**, ed. Allen, Halliday, and Sikes, *op. cit.*, 87.
Cod: 133: Hymn.

028 **In Minervam**, ed. Allen, Halliday, and Sikes, *op. cit.*, 87–88.
Cod: 114: Hymn.

029 **In Vestam**, ed. Allen, Halliday, and Sikes, *op. cit.*, 88–89.
Cod: 100: Hymn.

030 **In Tellurem matrem omnium**, ed. Allen, Halliday, and Sikes, *op. cit.*, 89.
Cod: 137: Hymn.

031 **In Solem**, ed. Allen, Halliday, and Sikes, *op. cit.*, 89–90.
Cod: 128: Hymn.

032 **In Lunam**, ed. Allen, Halliday, and Sikes, *op. cit.*, 90–91.
Cod: 126: Hymn.

033 **In Dioscuros**, ed. Allen, Halliday, and Sikes, *op. cit.*, 91–92.
Cod: 119: Hymn.

034 **Eἰς ξένους**, ed. Allen, Halliday, and Sikes, *op. cit.*, 92.
Cod: 31: Hymn.

0030 **HYPERIDES** Orat.
4 B.C.: Atheniensis

001 **In Demosthenem**, ed. C. Jensen, *Hyperidis orationes sex.* Leipzig: Teubner, 1917 (repr. Stuttgart: 1963): 2–24.
Pap: 2,695: Orat.

002 **Pro Lycophrone**, ed. Jensen, *op. cit.*, 25–37.
Pap: 1,725: Orat.

003 **Pro Euxenippo**, ed. Jensen, *op. cit.*, 38–56.
Pap: 3,121: Orat.

004 **In Philippidem**, ed. Jensen, *op. cit.*, 57–68.
Pap: 1,210: Orat.

005 **In Athenogenem**, ed. Jensen, *op. cit.*, 69–89.
Pap: 2,585: Orat.

006 **Epitaphius**, ed. Jensen, *op. cit.*, 90–114.
Pap: 2,346: Orat.

007 **Fragmenta**, ed. Jensen, *op. cit.*, 115–154.
frr. 1–43, 45–179, 181–212, 219–276.
Q: 6,681: Orat.

2277 **HYPERMENES** Hist.
ante A.D. 2

001 **Fragmentum**, FGrH #394: 3B:284.
Q: 47: Hist.

2396 **HYPEROCHUS** Hist.
post 3 B.C.: Cumaeus

001 **Fragmenta**, FGrH #576: 3B:678–679.
Q: 191: Hist.

002 **Titulus**, ed. H. Lloyd-Jones and P. Parsons, *Supplementum Hellenisticum.* Berlin: De Gruyter, 1983: 249.
titul. 498.
NQ: 2: Hist., Poem.

5005 ***HYPOTHESES*** (in papyris)
Varia

001 **Heros Menandri** (hypothesis) (*P. Cair.* 43227), ed. F.H. Sandbach, *Menandri reliquiae selectae.* Oxford: Clarendon Press, 1972: 133.
Dup. partim MENANDER Comic. (0541 037) (fr. 140).
Pap: Hypoth., Comic.

002 **Hiereia, Imbrioi et Thrasyleon Menandri**
(hypotheses) (*P. Oxy.* 10.1235), ed. B.P. Grenfell and A.S. Hunt, *The Oxyrhynchus papyri*,
pt. 10. London: Egypt Exploration Fund,
1914: 83–86.
Pap: Hypoth., Comic.

003 **Dyscolus Menandri** (hypothesis) (*P. Bodmer* 4),
ed. V. Martin, *Papyrus Bodmer IV. Ménandre,
le dyscolos*. Geneva: Bibliotheca Bodmeriana,
1958: 16–17.
Diplomatic text: p. 16.
Reading text: p. 17.
Dup. 5005 004, 055.
Pap: Hypoth., Comic.

004 **Dyscolus Menandri** (hypothesis) (*P. Bodmer* 4),
ed. Sandbach, *op. cit.*, 45.
Dup. 5005 003, 055.
Pap: Hypoth., Comic.

005 **Dis exapaton Menandri** (hypothesis) (*P. IFAO*
inv. 337), ed. B. Boyaval, "Hypothesis de Ménandre," *Zeitschrift für Papyrologie und Epigraphik* 6 (1970) 6.
Dup. partim MENANDER Comic. (0541 037)
(fr. 119).
Cf. et 5005 006.
Pap: Hypoth., Comic.

006 **Dis exapaton Menandri** (hypothesis) (*P. IFAO*
inv. 337, variae lectiones), ed. L. Koenen, "Zu
der Menander-Hypothesis P. IFAO inv. nr.
337," *Zeitschrift für Papyrologie und Epigraphik* 8 (1971) 136.
Dup. partim MENANDER Comic. (0541 037)
(fr. 203).
Cf. et 5005 005.
Pap: Hypoth., Comic.

007 **Ἑαυτὸν τιμωρούμενος Menandri** (hypothesis)
(*P. Oxy.* 31.2534), ed. J.W.B. Barns, *The Oxyrhynchus papyri*, pt. 31. London: Egypt Exploration Society, 1966: 13.
Dup. partim MENANDER Comic. (0541 037)
(fr. 111).
Pap: Hypoth., Comic.

008 **Comoedia** (?) (hypothesis) (*P. Schubart* 26), ed.
W. Schubart, *Griechische literarische Papyri*.
Berlin: Akademie-Verlag, 1950: 55.
Dup. partim COMICA ADESPOTA (CGFPR)
(0662 006) (fr. 340).
Pap: Hypoth., Comic.

009 **Euripidis hypotheses**, ed. C. Austin, *Nova
fragmenta Euripidea in papyris reperta*. Berlin:
De Gruyter, 1968: 12, 59, 67, 88–103.
fr. 1, Aeolus (*P. Oxy.* 27.2457): pp. 88–89.
fr. 4, Archelaus (*P. Oxy.* 27.2455, fr. 9): p. 12.
fr. 6, Busiris (?) (*P. Oxy.* 27.2455, fr. 19): p. 90.
fr. 9, Melanippe Sapiens (*P. Oxy.* 27.2455, frr.
1–2): p. 90.
fr. 10, Medea (*P. IFAO, PSP* 248 + *P. Oxy.*
27.2455, fr. 1): pp. 90–92.
fr. 11, Oedipus (*P. Oxy.* 27.2455, fr. 4): p. 59.
fr. 14, Rhadamanthys (*PSI* 12.1286): p. 92.
fr. 17, Sisyphus (?) (*P. Oxy.* 27.2455, fr. 7): p.
93.

fr. 18, Sciron (*P. Oxy.* 27.2455, frr. 6 + 5): p.
94.
fr. 18a, Sciron (?) (*P. Amherst* 2.17): p. 95.
fr. 19, Scyrii (*PSI* 12.1286): pp. 95–96.
fr. 20, Syleus (*P. Oxy.* 27.2455, fr. 18): p. 96.
fr. 21, Tennes (*P. Oxy.* 27.2455, fr. 14): p. 97.
fr. 22, Telephus (?) (*P. Oxy.* 27.2455, fr. 12): p.
67.
fr. 23, Temenidae (?) (*P. Oxy.* 27.2455, fr. 11):
pp. 97–98.
fr. 24, Temenus (*P. Oxy.* 27.2455, frr. 8 + 10):
p. 98.
fr. 27, Phaethon (*P. Oxy.* 27.2455, fr. 14): p.
99.
fr. 28, Philoctetes (*P. Oxy.* 27.2455, fr. 17): p.
100.
fr. 30, Phoenix (*P. Oxy.* 27.2455, fr. 14): p.
101.
fr. 31, Phrixus i (*P. Oxy.* 27.2455, frr. 14 +
16): pp. 101–102.
fr. 32, Phrixus ii (*P. Oxy.* 27.2455, fr. 17): pp.
102–103.
fr. 33, Chrysippus (*P. Oxy.* 27.2455, fr. 17): p.
103.
fr. 34, Fabula incerta (*P. Oxy.* 27.2455, fr. 21):
p. 103.
Pap: Hypoth., Trag., Satyr.

010 **Temenus vel Temenidae** (?) **Euripidis** (hypo-
thesis) (*P. Mich.* inv. 1319), ed. E. Turner,
"Archelaos," *Papyrologica Lugduno-Batava* 17.
Leiden: Brill, 1968: 133.
titulus in papyro = Διηγήματα.
Dup. 5005 011–012.
Cf. et 5005 009 (frr. 23–24), 011–014.
Pap: Hypoth., Trag.

011 **Temenus vel Temenidae** (?) **Euripidis** (hypothesis) (*P. Mich.* inv. 1319), ed. A. Harder, "A
new identification in P. Oxy. 2455?," *Zeitschrift für Papyrologie und Epigraphik* 35
(1979) 8.
Dup. 5005 010, 012.
Cf. et 5005 009 (frr. 23–24), 010, 012–014.
Pap: Hypoth., Trag.

012 **Temenus vel Temenidae** (?) **Euripidis** (hypo-
thesis) (*P. Mich.* inv. 1319), ed. J. Rusten,
"The return of the Heracleidae," *Zeitschrift für
Papyrologie und Epigraphik* 40 (1980) 39.
Dup. 5005 010–011.
Cf. et 5005 009 (frr. 23–24), 010–011, 013–
014.
Pap: Hypoth., Trag.

013 **Temenus vel Temenidae** (?) **Euripidis** (hypo-
thesis) (*P. Mich.* inv. 1319), ed. W. Luppe,
"Der Temenos-Papyrus, P. Mich. inv. nr.
1319," *Philologus* 122 (1978) 7–8.
Cf. et 5005 009 (frr. 23–24), 010–012, 014.
Pap: Hypoth., Trag.

014 **Temenus vel Temenidae** (?) **Euripidis** (hypothesis) (*P. Mich.* inv. 1319 + *P. Oxy.* 27.2455),
ed. W. Luppe, "Zu einigen kleinen Bruch-

stücken der Euripides-Hypotheseis P. Oxy. 2455," *Zeitschrift für Papyrologie und Epigraphik* 49 (1982) 16–17.
Cf. et 5005 009 (frr. 23–24), 010–013.
Pap: Hypoth., Trag.

015 **Syleus (?) Euripidis** (hypothesis) (*P. Strassb. gr.* 2676, fr. Aa), ed. J. Schwartz, "Wartetext 7," *Zeitschrift für Papyrologie und Epigraphik* 4 (1969) 43.
Cf. et 5005 016.
Pap: Hypoth., Satyr.

016 **Syleus (?) Euripidis** (hypothesis) (*P. Strassb. gr.* 2676, fr. Aa), ed. H. Mette, "Hypothesis von Euripides Syleus?," *Zeitschrift für Papyrologie und Epigraphik* 4 (1969) 173.
Cf. et 5005 015.
Pap: Hypoth., Satyr.

018 **Auge Euripidis** (hypothesis) (*P. Colon.* 1.1), ed. B. Kramer, *Kölner Papyri* 1 [*Sonderreihe papyrologica Coloniensia* 7. Opladen: Westdeutscher Verlag, 1976]: 12.
Cf. et 5005 019.
Pap: Hypoth., Trag.

019 **Auge Euripidis** (hypothesis) (*P. Colon.* 1.1), ed. L. Koenen, "Eine Hypothesis zur Auge des Euripides und Tegeatische Plynterien (P. Colon. inv. nr. 264)," *Zeitschrift für Papyrologie und Epigraphik* 4 (1969) 8, 11.
Diplomatic text: p. 8.
Reading text: p. 11.
= editio princeps.
Cf. et 5005 018.
Pap: Hypoth., Trag.

020 **Peliades Euripidis** (hypothesis) (*P. Amst.* 1.7), ed. R.P. Salomons, P. Sijpestein and K. Worp, "Diegese zu Euripides Peliaden (?)," *Die Amsterdamer Papyri* 1. Zutphen: Terra Publishing Company, 1980: 16–17.
Cf. et 5005 021.
Pap: Hypoth., Trag.

021 **Peliades (?) Euripidis** (hypothesis) (*P. Amst.* 1.7), ed. P.J. Sijpestein, "The rejuvenation cure of Pelias," *Zeitschrift für Papyrologie und Epigraphik* 9 (1972) 109–110.
= editio princeps.
Cf. et 5005 020.
Pap: Hypoth., Trag.

022 **Alexander et Andromache Euripidis** (hypotheses) (*P. Oxy.* 52.3650), ed. R.A. Coles, *The Oxyrhynchus papyri*, pt. 52. London: Egypt Exploration Society, 1984: 14–15.
Cf. et 5005 023.
Pap: Hypoth., Trag.

023 **Alexander et Andromache Euripidis** (hypothesis) (*P. Oxy.* 52.3650), ed. H.M. Cockle, *A new Oxyrhynchus papyrus: the hypothesis of Euripides' Alexandros* [*Bulletin of the Institute of Classical Studies*, suppl. 32 (1974)]: 8, 12, 67.
Diplomatic text (hypothesis Alexandri): p. 8.
Reading text (hypothesis Alexandri): p. 12.

Reading text (hypothesis Andromaches): p. 67.
= editio princeps.
Cf. et 5005 022.
Pap: Hypoth., Trag.

024 **Bellerophon et Busiris Euripidis** (hypotheses) (*P. Oxy.* 52.3651), ed. H.M. Cockle, *The Oxyrhynchus papyri*, pt. 52, 19–20.
Pap: Hypoth., Trag., Satyr.

025 **Hypsipyle et Phrixus i Euripidis** (hypotheses) (*P. Oxy.* 52.3652), ed. Cockle, *The Oxyrhynchus papyri*, pt. 52, 24.
Pap: Hypoth., Trag.

026 **Tragoedia Aeschyli** (hypothesis?) (*P. Oxy.* 20.2255, fr. 42), ed. E. Lobel, *The Oxyrhynchus papyri*, pt. 20. London: Egypt Exploration Society, 1952: 28.
Dup. partim AESCHYLUS Trag. (0085 008) (fr. 527).
Cf. et 5005 027.
Pap: Hypoth., Trag.

027 **Tragoedia Aeschyli** (hypothesis?) (*P. Oxy.* 20.2255, fr. 42), ed. S. Radt, *Tragicorum Graecorum fragmenta*, vol. 3. Göttingen: Vandenhoeck & Ruprecht, 1985: 497.
fr. 451x.
Dup. partim AESCHYLUS Trag. (0085 008) (fr. 527).
Cf. et 5005 026.
Pap: Hypoth., Trag.

028 **Laius Aeschyli** (hypothesis) (*P. Oxy.* 20.2256, fr. 1), ed. Lobel, *The Oxyrhynchus papyri*, pt. 20, 29.
Dup. partim AESCHYLUS Trag. (0085 008) (fr. 169).
Cf. et 5005 029.
Pap: Hypoth., Trag.

029 **Laius Aeschyli** (hypothesis) (*P. Oxy.* 20.2256, fr. 1), ed. Radt, *TrGF* 3, 231.
ante fr. 121.
Dup. partim AESCHYLUS Trag. (0085 008) (fr. 169).
Cf. et 5005 028.
Pap: Hypoth., Trag.

030 **Laius Aeschyli** (hypothesis) (*P. Oxy.* 20.2256, fr. 2), ed. Lobel, *The Oxyrhynchus papyri*, pt. 20, 30.
Dup. partim AESCHYLUS Trag. (0085 008) (fr. 169).
Cf. et 5005 031.
Pap: Hypoth., Trag.

031 **Laius Aeschyli** (hypothesis) (*P. Oxy.* 20.2256, fr. 2), ed. Radt, *TrGF* 3, 51.
test. 58b.
Dup. partim AESCHYLUS Trag. (0085 008) (fr. 169).
Cf. et 5005 030.
Pap: Hypoth., Trag.

032 **Danaides Aeschyli** (hypothesis) (*P. Oxy.* 20.2256, fr. 3), ed. Lobel, *The Oxyrhynchus papyri*, pt. 20, 30.

Dup. partim AESCHYLUS Trag. (0085 008) (fr. 122).
Cf. et 5005 033.
Pap: Hypoth., Trag.

033 **Danaides Aeschyli** (hypothesis) (*P. Oxy.* 20.2256, fr. 3), ed. Radt, *TrGF* 3, 55.
test. 70.
Dup. partim AESCHYLUS Trag. (0085 008) (fr. 122).
Cf. et 5005 032.
Pap: Hypoth., Trag.

034 **Danaides (?) Aeschyli** (hypothesis) (*P. Oxy.* 20.2256, fr. 4), ed. Lobel, *The Oxyrhynchus papyri*, pt. 20, 31.
Dup. partim AESCHYLUS Trag. (0085 008) (fr. 169).
Cf. et 5005 035.
Pap: Hypoth., Trag.

035 **Danaides (?) Aeschyli** (hypothesis) (*P. Oxy.* 20.2256, fr. 4), ed. Radt, *TrGF* 3, 496.
fr. 451v.
Dup. partim AESCHYLUS Trag. (0085 008) (fr. 169).
Cf. et 5005 034.
Pap: Hypoth., Trag.

036 **Philoctetes (?) Aeschyli** (hypothesis) (*P. Oxy.* 20.2256, fr. 5), ed. Lobel, *The Oxyrhynchus papyri*, pt. 20, 32.
Dup. partim AESCHYLUS Trag. (0085 008) (fr. 392).
Cf. et 5005 037.
Pap: Hypoth., Trag.

037 **Philoctetes (?) Aeschyli** (hypothesis) (*P. Oxy.* 20.2256, fr. 5), ed. Radt, *TrGF* 3, 496–497.
fr. 451w.
Dup. partim AESCHYLUS Trag. (0085 008) (fr. 392).
Cf. et 5005 036.
Pap: Hypoth., Trag.

038 **Aitnaiai Aeschyli** (hypothesis) (*P. Oxy.* 20.2257, fr. 1), ed. Lobel, *The Oxyrhynchus papyri*, pt. 20, 66–67.
Dup. partim AESCHYLUS Trag. (0085 008) (fr. 26).
Cf. et 5005 039.
Pap: Hypoth., Trag.

039 **Aitnaiai Aeschyli** (hypothesis) (*P. Oxy.* 20.2257, fr. 1), ed. Radt, *TrGF* 3, 494.
fr. 451t.
Dup. partim AESCHYLUS Trag. (0085 008) (fr. 26).
Cf. et 5005 038.
Pap: Hypoth., Trag.

040 **Nauplius et Niobe Sophoclis** (hypotheses) (*P. Oxy.* 52.3653, frr. 1–2), ed. Cockle, *The Oxyrhynchus papyri*, pt. 52, 30–33.
Diplomatic text (hypothesis Nauplii): p. 30.
Reading text (hypothesis Nauplii): p. 31.
Diplomatic text (hypothesis Niobes): p. 32.
Reading text (hypothesis Niobes): p. 33.
Cf. et 5005 042.
Pap: Hypoth., Trag.

042 **Niobe Sophoclis** (hypothesis) (*P. Oxy.* 52.3653, fr. 2), ed. Radt, *TrGF* 3, 575–576.
n. ad vol. 4, p. 363 + fr. 441aa.
Cf. et 5005 040.
Pap: Hypoth., Trag.

043 **Rhadamanthys Critiae** (hypothesis) (*PSI* 12.1286), ed. Radt, *TrGF* 1 (1971): 179.
fr. 15.
Cf. et 5005 009 (fr. 14).
Pap: Hypoth., Trag.

044 **Tennes Critiae** (hypothesis) (*P. Oxy.* 27.2455, fr. 1), ed. Radt, *TrGF* 1, 182–183.
fr. 20.
Cf. et 5005 009 (fr. 21).
Pap: Hypoth., Trag.

045 **Tereus tragici ignoti** (hypothesis) (*P. Oxy.* 42.3013), ed. P. Parsons, *The Oxyrhynchus papyri*, pt. 42. London: Egypt Exploration Society, 1974: 48–49.
Diplomatic text: p. 48.
Reading text: p. 49.
Pap: Hypoth., Trag.

047 **Tragoedia (?)** (hypothesis?) (*P. Harris* 21), ed. J.E. Powell, *The Rendel Harris papyri of Woodbrooke College, Birmingham*. Cambridge: Cambridge University Press, 1936: 15.
Pap: Hypoth., Myth.

049 **Theseus (?)** (hypothesis?) (*MPER*, n.s. 3.45), ed. H. Oellacher, *Griechische literarische Papyri* 2 [*Mitteilungen aus der Papyrussammlung der Nationalbibliothek in Wien*, n.s. 3. Vienna: Rohrer, 1939]: 72.
Pap: Hypoth., Myth.

050 **Dionysalexandrus i Cratini** (hypothesis) (*P. Oxy.* 4.663), ed. B.P. Grenfell and A.S. Hunt, *The Oxyrhynchus papyri*, pt. 4. London: Egypt Exploration Fund, 1904: 71–72.
Dup. partim CRATINUS Comic. (0434 004) (fr. 70).
Pap: Hypoth., Comic.

051 **Dionysalexandrus i Cratini** (hypothesis) (*P. Oxy.* 4.663), ed. R. Kassel and C. Austin, *Poetae comici Graeci* 4. Berlin: De Gruyter, 1983: 140.
Dup. partim CRATINUS Comic. (0434 004) (fr. 70).
Pap: Hypoth., Comic.

052 **Dionysalexandrus i Cratini** (hypothesis) (*P. Oxy.* 35.2739), ed. E. Lobel, *The Oxyrhynchus papyri*, pt. 35. London: Egypt Exploration Society, 1968: 48.
Dup. partim CRATINUS Comic. (0434 004) (fr. 69).
Pap: Hypoth., Comic.

053 **Danaides** (hypothesis?) (*P. Hibeh* 2.221), ed. E.G. Turner, *The Hibeh papyri* 2. London: Egypt Exploration Society, 1951: 141.
Pap: Hypoth., Trag.

054 **Hypothesis (?)** (*P. Giss.* inv. 302 [= *P. Giss. univ.* 41]), ed. H. Eberhart, *Mitteilungen aus der Papyrussammlung der Giessener Universi-*

tätsbibliothek 4. Giessen: Universitätsdruckerei
Giessen, 1935: 27–28 (no. 41).
Pap: Hypoth., Comic.

055 **Dyscolus Menandri** (hypothesis) (*P. Bodmer* 4),
ed. E. Handley, *Menander of Athens. Dyscolus.*
Cambridge, Mass.: Harvard University Press,
1965: 77.
Dup. 5005 003–004.
Pap: Hypoth., Comic.

0717 **HYPSICLES** Math. et Astron.
2 B.C.: Alexandrinus
Scholia: Cf. SCHOLIA IN EUCLIDEM (5022).

001 **Hypsiclis liber sive elementorum liber xiv qui
fertur**, ed. E.S. Stamatis (post J.L. Heiberg),
Euclidis elementa, vol. 5.1, 2nd edn. Leipzig:
Teubner, 1977: 1–22.
Cf. et EUCLIDES Geom. (1799 001).
Cod: 3,840: Math.

002 **Anaphoricus**, ed. V. de Falco and M. Krause,
"Hypsikles. Die Aufgangszeiten der Gestirne,"
*Abhandlungen der Akademie der Wissenschaften
in Göttingen*, Philol.-hist. Kl., ser. 3, no. 62
(Göttingen: Vandenhoeck & Ruprecht, 1966):
34–40.
Cod: 1,864: Astron.

1983 **HYPSICRATES** Hist.
1 B.C.–A.D. 1: Amisenus
001 **Testimonium**, FGrH #190: 2B:923.
NQ: 18: Test.

002 **Fragmenta**, FGrH #190: **2B**:923–926; **3B**:743
addenda.
fr. 12: *P. Oxy.* 18.2192.
Q, Pap: 1,021: Hist., Gramm.

9026 *IAMBICA ADESPOTA*
Varia
001 **Fragmentum**, ed. E.L. von Leutsch, *Corpus
paroemiographorum Graecorum*, vol. 2. Göttingen: Vandenhoeck & Ruprecht, 1851 (repr.
Hildesheim: Olms, 1958): 232.
Cod: Iamb.

1821 *IAMBICA ADESPOTA* (ALG)
Varia
001 **Fragmenta iambica adespota**, ed. E. Diehl,
Anthologia lyrica Graeca, fasc. 3, 3rd edn.
Leipzig: Teubner, 1952: 73–79.
frr. 1–16b, 18–33.
Q: 268: Iamb.

002 **Anonymorum iambica**, ed. Diehl, *op. cit.*, 68–
72.
frr. 1–2.
Pap: 184: Iamb.

0235 *IAMBICA ADESPOTA* (IEG)
Varia
001 **Fragmenta**, ed. M.L. West, *Iambi et elegi
Graeci*, vol. 2. Oxford: Clarendon Press, 1972:
16–28.
frr. 1–42, 49–61.
Q, Pap: 451: Iamb.

2140 **IAMBLICHUS** Alchem.
post A.D. 3
001 **Fragmenta**, ed. M. Berthelot, *Collection des
anciens alchimistes grecs.* Paris: Steinheil, 1887
(repr. London: Holland Press, 1963): 285–289.
Cod

2023 **IAMBLICHUS** Phil.
A.D. 3–4: Chalcidensis
Scholia: Cf. SCHOLIA IN IAMBLICHUM
PHILOSOPHUM (5027).

001 **De vita Pythagorica**, ed. U. Klein (post L.
Deubner), *Iamblichi de vita Pythagorica liber.*
Leipzig: Teubner, 1937 (repr. Stuttgart: 1975):
1–147.
Cod: 30,873: Biogr., Phil.

002 **Protrepticus**, ed. H. Pistelli, *Iamblichi protrepticus ad fidem codicis Florentini.* Leipzig: Teubner, 1888 (repr. Stuttgart: 1967): 3–126.
Cod: 26,867: Phil.

003 **De communi mathematica scientia**, ed. U.
Klein (post N. Festa), *Iamblichi de communi
mathematica scientia liber.* Leipzig: Teubner,
1891 (repr. Stuttgart: 1975): 3–99.
Cod: 20,536: Math., Phil.

004 **In Nicomachi arithmeticam introductionem**,
ed. U. Klein (post H. Pistelli), *Iamblichi in
Nicomachi arithmeticam introductionem liber.*
Leipzig: Teubner, 1894 (repr. Stuttgart: 1975):
3–125.
Cod: 27,506: Math., Phil., Comm.

005 **Theologoumena arithmeticae**, ed. V. de Falco,
[Iamblichi] theologoumena arithmeticae. Leip-
zig: Teubner, 1922: 1–87.
Cod: 17,193: Math.

006 **De mysteriis**, ed. E. des Places, *Jamblique. Les
mystères d'Égypte.* Paris: Les Belles Lettres,
1966: 38–215.
Cod: 42,940: Phil., Theol.

007 **Fragmenta exegetica**, ed. B.D. Larsen, *Jamblique de Chalcis. Exégète et philosophe. Appendice: testimonia et fragmenta exegetica.* Aarhus:
Universitetsforlaget, 1972: 9–130.
Q

008 **In Platonis dialogos commentariorum fragmenta**, ed. J.M. Dillon, *Iamblichi Chalcidensis
in Platonis dialogos commentariorum fragmenta.*
Leiden: Brill, 1973: 72–224.
Q

009 **Sententiae**, ed. D.J. O'Meara, "New fragments
of Iamblichus' collection of Pythagorean doctrines," *American Journal of Philology* 102
(1981) 26–40.
Q

1441 **IAMBLICHUS** Scr. Erot.
A.D. 2
001 **Babyloniaca**, ed. E. Habrich, *Iamblichi Baby-
loniacorum reliquiae.* Leipzig: Teubner, 1960:
5–79.
Fragmenta (frr. 1–89): pp. 5–69.

Fragmenta incertae sedis (frr. 90–100): pp. 70–72.

Fragmenta dubia (frr. 101–126): pp. 73–79.
Q, Cod: 4,024: Narr. Fict.

0293 **IBYCUS** Lyr.
6 B.C.: Rheginus
001 **Fragmenta**, ed. D.L. Page, *Poetae melici Graeci*. Oxford: Clarendon Press, 1962 (repr. 1967 (1st edn. corr.)): 144–150, 152–162, 164–167.
frr. 1–2, 4–7, 12, 17, 21–22, 25, 29–40, 48–49, 51–53, 56–57.
Q, Pap: 717: Lyr.
002 **Fragmenta**, ed. D.L. Page, *Supplementum lyricis Graecis*. Oxford: Clarendon Press, 1974: 44–73.
fr. S151: *P. Oxy.* 15.1790 + 17.2081.
frr. S152–S162: *P. Oxy.* 15.1790.
frr. S163–S165: *P. Oxy.* 17.2081.
frr. S166–S219: *P. Oxy.* 35.2735.
frr. S220–S257: *P. Oxy.* 32.2637.
fr. S258: ex Herodiano, *De prosodia catholica*.
Dup. partim 0293 001.
Q, Pap: 2,679: Lyr.

2226 **ICCUS** Phil.
6 B.C.: Tarentinus
001 **Testimonia**, ed. H. Diels and W. Kranz, *Die Fragmente der Vorsokratiker*, vol. 1, 6th edn. Berlin: Weidmann, 1951 (repr. Dublin: 1966): 216–217.
test. 1–3.
NQ: 230: Test.

4255 **ICHTHYAS** Phil.
4 B.C.: Atheniensis
001 **Testimonium**, ed. K. Döring, *Die Megariker* [*Studien zur antiken Philosophie* 2. Amsterdam: Grüner, 1972]: 11, 15, 46.
test. 32a–b, 33, 47–48, 147.
test. 32a–b, 33 = Euclides (4247 001).
test. 47–48 = Ichthyas.
test. 147 = Stilpo (4262 001).
NQ: Test.

0935 **ICODOTUS** Med.
ante A.D. 2
x01 **Fragmentum ap. Galenum**.
K13.311–312.
Cf. GALENUS Med. (0057 076).

2628 **IDAEUS** Epic.
Incertum: Rhodius
001 **Titulus**, ed. H. Lloyd-Jones and P. Parsons, *Supplementum Hellenisticum*. Berlin: De Gruyter, 1983: 250.
fr. 502.
NQ: 2: Epic.

2304 **IDAEUS** Phil.
5 B.C.: Himeraeus

001 **Testimonium**, ed. H. Diels and W. Kranz, *Die Fragmente der Vorsokratiker*, vol. 2, 6th edn. Berlin: Weidmann, 1952 (repr. Dublin: 1966): 51.
NQ: 402: Test.

0936 **IDIUS** Med.
ante A.D. 2
x01 **Fragmentum ap. Galenum**.
K13.297.
Cf. GALENUS Med. (0057 076).

1442 **IDOMENEUS** Hist.
4–3 B.C.: Lampsacenus
001 **Testimonia**, FGrH #338: 3B:189.
NQ: 291: Test.
002 **Fragmenta**, FGrH #338: 3B:190–195.
Dup. partim 1442 003.
Q: 1,610: Hist., Hexametr.
003 **Fragmenta**, ed. A. Angeli, "I frammenti di Idomeno di Lampsaco," *Cronache Ercolanesi* 11 (1981) 64–72.
frr. 16, 18, 30–31, 35: *P. Herc.* 1418.
frr. 20, 29, 32–34: *P. Herc.* 176.
fr. 21: *P. Herc.* 1471.
Dup. partim 1442 002.
Q, Pap

2380 **IDOMENEUS** Hist.
Incertum
001 **Testimonium**, FGrH #547: 3B:532.
NQ: 10: Test.

9012 **IGNATIUS** Biogr. et Poeta
vel Ignatius Diaconus Hagiae Sophiae vel Ignatius Melodus
A.D. 8–9: Nicaeensis, Constantinopolitanus
001 **Epigrammata**, AG 15.29–31, 39.
Q: 124: Epigr.
002 **Vita Nicephori**, ed. C. de Boor, *Nicephori archiepiscopi Constantinopolitani opuscula historica*. Leipzig: Teubner, 1880 (repr. New York: Arno, 1975): 139–217.
Cod: Biogr.

9011 **IGNATIUS** Epigr.
A.D. 9
001 **Epigramma**, AG 1.109.
Q: 25: Epigr.

1443 **IGNATIUS** Scr. Eccl.
A.D. 1–2: Antiochenus
001 **Epistulae vii genuinae** (recensio media), ed. P.T. Camelot, *Ignace d'Antioche. Polycarpe de Smyrne. Lettres. Martyre de Polycarpe*, 4th edn. [*Sources chrétiennes* 10. Paris: Cerf, 1969]: 56–154.
Ad Ephesios (epist. 1): pp. 56–78.
Ad Magnesios (epist. 2): pp. 80–92.
Ad Trallianos (epist. 3): pp. 94–104.
Ad Romanos (epist. 4): pp. 106–118.
Ad Philadelphios (epist. 5): pp. 120–130.

Ad Smyrnaeos (epist. 6): pp. 132–144.
Ad Polycarpum (epist. 7): pp. 146–154.
Cod: 8,105: Epist.

002 **Epistulae interpolatae et epistulae suppositi-
ciae** (recensio longior) [Sp.], ed. F.X. Funk and
F. Diekamp, *Patres apostolici*, vol. 2, 3rd edn.
Tübingen: Laupp, 1913: 83–268.
Epistula Mariae ad Ignatium (epist. 13): pp.
83–87.
Ad Mariam Cassobolitam (epist. 1): pp. 88–92.
Ad Trallianos (epist. 2): pp. 94–112.
Ad Magnesios (epist. 3): pp. 112–132.
Ad Tarsenses (epist. 4): pp. 132–144.
Ad Philippenses (epist. 5): pp. 144–159.
Ad Philadelphios (epist. 6): pp. 159–190.
Ad Smyrnaeos (epist. 7): pp. 190–204.
Ad Polycarpum (epist. 8): pp. 204–211.
Ad Antiochenos (epist. 9): pp. 212–222.
Ad Heronem diaconum ecclesiae Antiochenae
(epist. 10): pp. 224–234.
Ad Ephesios (epist. 11): pp. 234–258.
Ad Romanos (epist. 12): pp. 258–268.
Cod: 20,125: Epist.

003 **Fragmenta** (e cod. Florent. Laur. 6.4) [Sp.], ed.
J.H. Crehan, *A new fragment of Ignatius' Ad
Polycarpum* in *Studia Patristica* 1 [*Texte und
Untersuchungen* 63. Berlin: Akademie-Verlag,
1957]: 24.
Cod

x01 **Fragmenta** (ap. Joannem Damascenum, *Sacra
parallela*) [Sp.].
MPG **95**.1208c, 1548c–d, 1564d; **96**.81a, 264d,
429a, 429b.
Cf. JOANNES DAMASCENUS Theol. et Scr.
Eccl. (2934 018).

1444 ***ILIAS PARVA***
fort. auctore Cinaethone Lacedaemonio vel
Lesche Mytilenensi
7/6 B.C.?

001 **Fragmenta**, ed. T.W. Allen, *Homeri opera*, vol.
5. Oxford: Clarendon Press, 1912 (repr. 1969):
129–133, 135.
frr. 1–2, 4–6, 10–12, 19.
Q: Epic.

1445 ***ILIU PERSIS***
fort. auctore Arctino Milesio vel Lesche Mytilenensi
7/6 B.C.?

001 **Fragmenta**, ed. T.W. Allen, *Homeri opera*, vol.
5. Oxford: Clarendon Press, 1912 (repr. 1969):
138–140.
frr. 1, 3, 5–6.
Q: Epic.

2731 **IOMEDES** Epigr.
A.D. 2/3

x01 **Epigramma sepulcrale.**
App. Anth. 2.665: Cf. ANTHOLOGIAE GRAE-
CAE APPENDIX (7052 002).

1446 **ION** Eleg.
5 B.C.: Samius

001 **Fragmentum**, ed. E. Diehl, *Anthologia lyrica
Graeca*, fasc. 1, 3rd edn. Leipzig: Teubner,
1949: 87.
Epigr: 27: Epigr.

002 **Epigramma**, AG 7.43.
AG 7.44: Cf. ANONYMI EPIGRAMMATICI
(AG) (0138 001).
Q: 26: Epigr.

0308 **ION** Poeta et Phil.
5 B.C.: Chius

001 **Fragmenta**, ed. B. Snell, *Tragicorum Graecorum fragmenta*, vol. 1. Göttingen: Vandenhoeck & Ruprecht, 1971: 96–114.
frr. 1–29, 31–43, 43b–43c, 44–68.
Q: 551: Trag., Satyr.

002 **Fragmenta**, ed. M.L. West, *Iambi et elegi
Graeci*, vol. 2. Oxford: Clarendon Press, 1972:
78–80.
frr. 26–30, 32.
Q: 223: Eleg.

003 **Fragmenta**, ed. D.L. Page, *Poetae melici
Graeci*. Oxford: Clarendon Press, 1962 (repr.
1967 (1st edn. corr.)): 384–386.
frr. 5–7.
Q: 47: Lyr., Trag.

004 **Fragmentum**, ed. D.L. Page, *Supplementum
lyricis Graecis*. Oxford: Clarendon Press, 1974:
105.
fr. S316: *P. Oxy.* 35.2737.
Dup. ALCMAN Lyr. (0291 002) (fr. S2).
Dup. TERPANDER Lyr. (0299 002) (fr. S6).
Pap: 4: Lyr.

005 **Tituli**, ed. Page, *PMG*, 383–384.
frr. 1, 3–4.
NQ: 9: Lyr., Hymn., Encom.

006 **Testimonia**, FGrH #392: 3B:276–278.
NQ: 528: Test.

007 **Fragmenta**, FGrH #392: 3B:278–283.
Q: 1,871: Hist.

008 **Testimonia**, ed. H. Diels and W. Kranz, *Die
Fragmente der Vorsokratiker*, vol. 1, 6th edn.
Berlin: Weidmann, 1951 (repr. Dublin: 1966):
377–378.
test. 1–7.
NQ: 490: Test.

009 **Fragmenta**, ed. Diels and Kranz, *op. cit.*, 379–
381.
frr. 1–5.
Q: 358: Phil., Eleg., Epigr.

0311 **IOPHON** Trag.
5 B.C.

001 **Fragmenta**, ed. B. Snell, *Tragicorum Graecorum fragmenta*, vol. 1. Göttingen: Vandenhoeck & Ruprecht, 1971: 134–135.
frr. 1–2c.
Q: 41: Trag., Satyr.

4071 **IRENAEUS** Epigr.
    A.D. 6
  001 **Epigrammata**, AG 5.249, 251, 253.
    Q: 103: Epigr.

1447 **IRENAEUS** Theol.
    A.D. 2: Lugdunensis
  001 **Adversus haereses** (libri 1–2), ed. W.W. Har-
    vey, *Sancti Irenaei episcopi Lugdunensis libri*
    quinque adversus haereses, vol. 1. Cambridge:
    Cambridge University Press, 1857: 1–188,
    192–198, 204–207, 209–212, 214–216, 220–
    230, 232–233, 241–242, 331, 345, 347, 351–
    352, 360, 362, 370, 374–375, 380.
    Q: 22,657: Theol.
  002 **Adversus haereses** (liber 3), ed. A. Rousseau
    and L. Doutreleau, *Irénée de Lyon. Contre les*
    hérésies, livre 3, vol. 2 [*Sources chrétiennes* 211.
    Paris: Cerf, 1974]: 22–24, 28, 32–44, 50, 84–
    86, 106–108, 128, 160–170, 176–178, 182–
    184, 190–192, 196–198, 206–208, 214–216,
    246–248, 320, 336–338, 348–350, 364–374,
    378, 398–406, 414, 428–430, 434–436.
    Q: 3,064: Theol.
  004 **Adversus haereses 3.9** (*P. Oxy.* 3.405), ed.
    Rousseau and Doutreleau, *SC* 211, 104, 107–
    108.
    Pap: 139: Theol.
  007 **Adversus haereses** (liber 4), ed. A. Rousseau,
    B. Hemmerdinger, L. Doutreleau and C. Mer-
    cier, *Irénée de Lyon. Contre les hérésies, livre 4*,
    vol. 2 [*Sources chrétiennes* 100. Paris: Cerf,
    1965]: 418–420, 432–434, 440, 446, 472, 610–
    612, 628, 634, 640–642, 672, 712–714, 726,
    788, 790, 810, 816–818, 830, 910–912, 920–
    930, 940–956, 968–970, 974, 978–982.
    Q: 2,436: Theol.
  008 **Adversus haereses** (liber 5), ed. A. Rousseau,
    L. Doutreleau and C. Mercier, *Irénée de Lyon.*
    Contre les hérésies, livre 5, vol. 2 [*Sources chré-*
    tiennes 153. Paris: Cerf, 1969]: 14–16, 20–24,
    32–48, 50, 52, 54, 62, 64, 66, 68, 70, 74, 98,
    114, 116, 118, 120, 140, 142, 144, 146, 148,
    150, 166–168, 172–174, 216–222, 232–234,
    300–304, 334–336, 342–380, 384, 394, 416,
    452–458.
    Q: 4,581: Theol.
  003 **Adversus haereses 5.3–13** (*P. Jena*), ed. Rous-
    seau, Doutreleau and Mercier, *SC* 153, 49, 51,
    53, 55, 56, 60, 63, 65, 67, 69, 71, 76, 78–96,
    99–100, 103–115, 117, 119–126, 141, 143,
    145, 147, 149, 152–164.
    Pap: 2,274: Theol.
  005 **Fragmenta deperditorum operum**, ed. Harvey,
    op. cit., vol. 2 (1857): 470–511.
    frr. 1–47.
    frr. 33–34: Dup. HIPPOLYTUS Scr. Eccl.
    (2115 050).
    Q, Cod: 3,763: Exeget.
  006 **Fragmentum**, ed. A. de Santos Otero, "Dos
    capitulos ineditos del original griego de Ireneo
    de Lyon (*Adversus haereses II:50–51*) en el

codice Vatopedi 236," *Emerita* 41 (1973) 486–
488.
Cod

0017 **ISAEUS** Orat.
    5–4 B.C.: Atheniensis, fort. Chalcidicus
  001 **De Cleonymo**, ed. P. Roussel, *Isée. Discours*,
    2nd edn. Paris: Les Belles Lettres, 1960: 20–
    32.
    Cod: 2,698: Orat.
  002 **De Menecle**, ed. Roussel, *op. cit.*, 36–48.
    Cod: 2,737: Orat.
  003 **De Pyrrho**, ed. Roussel, *op. cit.*, 52–71.
    Cod: 4,535: Orat.
  004 **De Nicostrato**, ed. Roussel, *op. cit.*, 74–81.
    Cod: 1,818: Orat.
  005 **De Dicaeogene**, ed. Roussel, *op. cit.*, 88–102.
    Cod: 3,059: Orat.
  006 **De Philoctemone**, ed. Roussel, *op. cit.*, 108–
    124.
    Cod: 3,727: Orat.
  007 **De Apollodoro**, ed. Roussel, *op. cit.*, 129–140.
    Cod: 2,715: Orat.
  008 **De Cirone**, ed. Roussel, *op. cit.*, 144–158.
    Cod: 3,110: Orat.
  009 **De Astyphilo**, ed. Roussel, *op. cit.*, 162–173.
    Cod: 2,334: Orat.
  010 **De Aristarcho**, ed. Roussel, *op. cit.*, 179–186.
    Cod: 1,808: Orat.
  011 **De Hagnia**, ed. Roussel, *op. cit.*, 190–205.
    Cod: 3,580: Orat.
  012 **Pro Euphileto**, ed. Roussel, *op. cit.*, 211–215.
    Cod: 853: Orat.
  013 **Fragmenta**, ed. Roussel, *op. cit.*, 220–230.
    Q: 975: Orat.

1449 **ISIDORUS** Epigr.
    1 B.C.?: Aegeates
  001 **Epigrammata**, AG 7.156, 280, 293, 532; **9**.94.
    Q: 182: Epigr.

4052 **ISIDORUS** Epigr.
    A.D. 6: Bolbythiotus
  001 **Epigrammata**, AG **6**.58; **9**.11.
    Q: 70: Epigr.

0070 **ISIDORUS** Geogr.
    1 B.C.–A.D. 1: Characenus
  001 **Testimonia**, FGrH #781: 3C:777–778.
    NQ: 198: Test.
  002 **Fragmenta**, FGrH #781: 3C:778–785.
    Q, Cod: 1,860: Hist., Perieg.

1448 **ISIDORUS** Gnost.
    A.D. 2
  001 **Fragmenta**, ed. W. Völker, *Quellen zur Ge-*
    schichte der christlichen Gnosis. Tübingen:
    Mohr, 1932: 41–43.
    Q

0938 **ISIDORUS** Med.
    ante A.D. 2: Antiochenus

x01 **Fragmenta ap. Galenum**.
K13.250, 295–296, 341, 833, 834–835, 885, 908.
Cf. GALENUS Med. (0057 076–077).

0939 **ISIDORUS** Med.
ante A.D. 2: Memphiticus
x01 **Fragmentum ap. Aëtium** (lib. 7).
CMG, vol. 8.2, p. 387.
Cf. AËTIUS Med. (0718 007).

0359 **ISIDORUS** Scriptor Hymnorum
ante 1 B.C.: Aegyptius
001 **Hymni in Isim**, ed. V.F. Vanderlip, *The four Greek hymns of Isidorus and the cult of Isis* [*American studies in papyrology* 12. Toronto: Hakkert, 1972]: 17–18, 34–35, 49–50, 63–64.
Epigr: 948: Hymn.

0352 **ISIDORUS** Trag.
Incertum
001 **Fragmenta**, ed. B. Snell, *Tragicorum Graecorum fragmenta*, vol. 1. Göttingen: Vandenhoeck & Ruprecht, 1971: 323.
frr. 1–2.
Q: 30: Trag.

1083 **ISIGONUS** Paradox.
3 B.C./A.D. 1: Nicaeensis
001 **Fragmenta**, ed. A. Giannini, *Paradoxographorum Graecorum reliquiae*. Milan: Istituto Editoriale Italiano, 1965: 147–148.
Q

0010 **ISOCRATES** Orat.
5–4 B.C.: Atheniensis
Vita et scholia: Cf. SCHOLIA IN ISOCRATEM (5028).
001 **In Euthynum** (orat. 21), ed. G. Mathieu and É. Brémond, *Isocrate. Discours*, vol. 1. Paris: Les Belles Lettres, 1929 (repr. 1963): 7–11.
Cod: 1,138: Orat.
002 **In Callimachum** (orat. 18), ed. Mathieu and Brémond, *op. cit.*, vol. 1, 19–34.
Cod: 3,698: Orat.
003 **In Lochitem** (orat. 20), ed. Mathieu and Brémond, *op. cit.*, vol. 1, 39–44.
Cod: 1,151: Orat.
004 **De bigis** (orat. 16), ed. Mathieu and Brémond, *op. cit.*, vol. 1, 51–64.
Cod: 3,017: Orat.
005 **Trapeziticus** (orat. 17), ed. Mathieu and Brémond, *op. cit.*, vol. 1, 71–87.
Cod: 3,476: Orat.
006 **Aegineticus** (orat. 19), ed. Mathieu and Brémond, *op. cit.*, vol. 1, 93–106.
Cod: 3,036: Orat.
007 **Ad Demonicum** (orat. 1), ed. Mathieu and Brémond, *op. cit.*, vol. 1, 122–135.
Cod: 3,000: Orat.
008 **In sophistas** (orat. 13), ed. Mathieu and Brémond, *op. cit.*, vol. 1, 144–150.
Cod: 1,382: Orat., Rhet.

009 **Helenae encomium** (orat. 10), ed. Mathieu and Brémond, *op. cit.*, vol. 1, 163–179.
Cod: 3,893: Orat., Rhet., Encom.
010 **Busiris** (orat. 11), ed. Mathieu and Brémond, *op. cit.*, vol. 1, 188–200.
Cod: 2,833: Orat., Rhet., Encom.
011 **Panegyricus** (orat. 4), ed. Mathieu and Brémond, *op. cit.*, vol. 2 (1938; repr. 1967 (1st edn. rev. et corr.)): 15–64.
Cod: 11,249: Orat.
012 **Plataicus** (orat. 14), ed. Mathieu and Brémond, *op. cit.*, vol. 2, 74–88.
Cod: 3,353: Orat.
013 **Ad Nicoclem** (orat. 2), ed. Mathieu and Brémond, *op. cit.*, vol. 2, 97–111.
Cod: 3,119: Orat.
014 **Nicocles** (orat. 3), ed. Mathieu and Brémond, *op. cit.*, vol. 2, 120–137.
Cod: 3,908: Orat.
015 **Evagoras** (orat. 9), ed. Mathieu and Brémond, *op. cit.*, vol. 2, 146–168.
Cod: 4,820: Orat.
016 **Archidamus** (orat. 6), ed. Mathieu and Brémond, *op. cit.*, vol. 2, 175–205.
Cod: 6,412: Orat.
017 **De pace** (orat. 8), ed. Mathieu, *op. cit.*, vol. 3 (1942; repr. 1966): 12–51.
Cod: 8,278: Orat.
018 **Areopagiticus** (orat. 7), ed. Mathieu, *op. cit.*, vol. 3, 63–84.
Cod: 4,743: Orat.
019 **Antidosis** (orat. 15), ed. Mathieu, *op. cit.*, vol. 3, 103–181.
Cod: 18,731: Orat.
020 **Philippus** (orat. 5), ed. Mathieu and Brémond, *op. cit.*, vol. 4 (1962): 19–60.
Cod: 9,031: Orat.
021 **Panathenaicus** (orat. 12), ed. Mathieu and Brémond, *op. cit.*, vol. 4, 87–159.
Cod: 16,409: Orat.
022 **Ad Dionysium** (epist. 1), ed. Mathieu and Brémond, *op. cit.*, vol. 4, 185–187.
Cod: 633: Epist.
023 **Ad filios Jasonis** (epist. 6), ed. Mathieu and Brémond, *op. cit.*, vol. 4, 188–192.
Cod: 920: Epist.
024 **Ad Archidamum** (epist. 9), ed. Mathieu and Brémond, *op. cit.*, vol. 4, 193–198.
Cod: 1,179: Epist.
025 **Ad reges Mytilenaeos** (epist. 8), ed. Mathieu and Brémond, *op. cit.*, vol. 4, 199–202.
Cod: 683: Epist.
026 **Ad Timotheum** (epist. 7), ed. Mathieu and Brémond, *op. cit.*, vol. 4, 203–206.
Cod: 805: Epist.
027 **Ad Philippum** (epist. 2), ed. Mathieu and Brémond, *op. cit.*, vol. 4, 207–213.
Cod: 1,321: Epist.
028 **Ad Alexandrum** (epist. 5), ed. Mathieu and Brémond, *op. cit.*, vol. 4, 214–215.
Cod: 296: Epist.

029 **Ad Antipatrum** (epist. 4), ed. Mathieu and Brémond, *op. cit.*, vol. 4, 216–220.
Cod: 860: Epist.

030 **Ad Philippum** (epist. 3), ed. Mathieu and Brémond, *op. cit.*, vol. 4, 221–223.
Cod: 432: Epist.

031 **Fragmenta**, ed. Mathieu and Brémond, *op. cit.*, vol. 4, 229–232, 234–239.
frr. 1–2, 4–6, 8–41.
Q: 1,408: Rhet.

1450 **ISTER** Hist.
vel Istrus
3 B.C.: Cyrenaeus

001 **Testimonia**, FGrH #334: 3B:168.
NQ: 135: Test.

002 **Fragmenta**, FGrH #334: 3B:169–186.
Q, Cod: 4,663: Hist.

003 **Fragmentum** (*P. Oxy.* 26.2442), ed. H.J. Mette, "Die 'Kleinen' griechischen Historiker heute," *Lustrum* 21 (1978) 27.
fr. 41 bis.
Pap: 47: Hist.

0201 **ISYLLUS** Lyr.
3 B.C.: Epidaurius

001 **Fragmenta** (*IG* 4.950), ed. J.U. Powell, *Collectanea Alexandrina*. Oxford: Clarendon Press, 1925 (repr. 1970): 132–135.
Epigr: 561: Lyr., Hymn.

0934 **JACOBUS Psychrestus** Med.
A.D. 5: Alexandrinus

x01 **Fragmentum ap. Aëtium** (lib. 12).
Kostomiris, p. 92.
Cf. AËTIUS Med. (0718 012).

x02 **Fragmentum ap. Alexandrum Trallianum**.
Puschmann, vol. 2, pp. 161–163, 565, 571.
Cf. ALEXANDER Med. (0744 003).

2183 **JASON** Hist.
ante 2 B.C.?: Nyssenus
Cf. et JASON Hist. (2309).

001 **Fragmentum**, FGrH #632: 3C:182.
Q: 32: Hist.

2309 **JASON** Hist.
fiq Jason Nyssenus
ante 2 B.C.?
Cf. et JASON Hist. (2183).

001 **Titulus**, FGrH #446: 3B:376.
NQ: Hist.

1975 **JASON** Hist.
2 B.C.: Cyrenaeus

001 **Testimonium**, FGrH #182: 2B:910.
NQ: 214: Test.

2575 **JASON** Hist.
Incertum: Byzantius

001 **Fragmentum**, FGrH #12c: 1A:*10 addenda.
Q: 33: Hist., Nat. Hist.

1921 **JASON** Hist. et Gramm.
A.D. 2: Argivus

001 **Testimonium**, FGrH #94: 2A:445–446.
NQ: 46: Test.

2576 **JOANNES** Gramm.
fiq Joannes Philoponus Phil.
A.D. 6: Alexandrinus
Cf. et JOANNES PHILOPONUS Phil. (4015).

001 **Compendia** περὶ Αἰολίδος, ed. O. Hoffmann, *Die griechischen Dialekte*, vol. 2. Göttingen: Vandenhoeck & Ruprecht, 1893: 206–208, 213–222.
Cod

x01 **Tonica praecepta**.
Dindorf, pp. 3–42.
Cf. JOANNES PHILOPONUS Phil. (4015 016).

2578 **JOANNES** Gramm. et Poeta
A.D. 6: Gazaeus

001 Ἔκφρασις τοῦ κοσμικοῦ πίνακος, ed. P. Friedländer, *Johannes von Gaza und Paulus Silentiarius. Kunstbeschreibungen justinianischer Zeit*. Leipzig: Teubner, 1912: 135–164.
Cod: [4,194]

002 **Anacreontea**, ed. T. Bergk, *Poetae lyrici Graeci*, vol. 3, 4th edn. Leipzig: Teubner, 1882: 342–348.
Cod

0727 **JOANNES** Med.
A.D. 7: Alexandrinus

001 **Commentarii in Hippocratis librum de natura pueri**, ed. F.R. Dietz, *Scholia in Hippocratem et Galenum*, vol. 2. Königsberg: Borntraeger, 1834 (repr. Amsterdam: Hakkert, 1966): 205–235.
Cod: 8,621: Med., Comm.

4157 **JOANNES** Rhet.
ante A.D. 10: Sardianus

001 **Prolegomena in Hermogenis librum** περὶ εὑρέσεως (olim sub auctore Georgio Diaereta), ed. H. Rabe, *Prolegomenon sylloge* [*Rhetores Graeci* 14. Leipzig: Teubner, 1931]: 351–360.
Cod: Rhet., Comm.

002 **Commentarium in Hermogenis librum** περὶ εὑρέσεως (olim sub auctore Georgio Diaereta, nunc fort. auctore Joanne Sardiano), ed. C. Walz, *Rhetores Graeci*, vol. 6. Stuttgart: Cotta, 1834 (repr. Osnabrück: Zeller, 1968): 512–543.
Cod: Rhet., Comm.

004 **Commentarium in Aphthonii progymnasmata**, ed. H. Rabe, *Ioannis Sardiani commentarium in Aphthonii progymnasmata* [*Rhetores Graeci* 15. Leipzig: Teubner, 1928]: 1–268.
Cod: Rhet., Comm.

4235 **JOANNES** Rhet.
A.D. 11: Siculus

001 **Prolegomena in Hermogenis librum** περὶ ἰδεῶν, ed. H. Rabe, *Prolegomenon sylloge*

[*Rhetores Graeci* 14. Leipzig: Teubner, 1931]:
393-420.
Cod: Rhet., Comm.

002 **Commentarium in Hermogenis librum** περὶ
ἰδεῶν, ed. C. Walz, *Rhetores Graeci*, vol. 6.
Stuttgart: Cotta, 1834 (repr. Osnabrück: Zeller,
1968): 80-504.
Cod: Rhet., Comm.

3173 **JOANNES** Scr. Eccl.
A.D. 8: Hierosolymitanus

001 **Adversus iconoclastas** (olim sub auctore
Joanne Damasceno), MPG 96: 1348-1361.
Cod: 3,034: Theol.

002 **De sacris imaginibus contra Constantinum
Cabalinum** (olim sub auctore Joanne Damasceno), MPG 95: 309-344.
Cod: 6,936: Theol.

2498 **JOANNES I** Hist.
2 B.C.: Hyrcanus

001 **Testimonium,** FGrH #736: 3C:700.
NQ: 49: Test.

4201 **JOANNES CHORTASMENUS** Gramm.
vel Ignatius
A.D. 14-15: Constantinopolitanus, Selymbrius

001 **In Aristotelis sophisticos elenchos** (excerpta e
codd. Bolon., B.U. gr. 3637; Lond., B.L. Harl.
5697; Flor. Laur. 71-76; Vat. gr. 1766), ed. S.
Ebbesen, *Commentators and commentaries on
Aristotle's sophistici elenchi. A study of post-
Aristotelian ancient and medieval writings on
fallacies*, vol. 2 [*Corpus Latinum commentariorum in Aristotelem Graecorum. De Wulf-
mansion Centre* 7. Leiden: Brill, 1981]: 315-
320.
E capitulo in sophisticos elenchos: pp. 315-
319.
Scholion marginale iuxta paraphrasim sophisticorum elenchorum: p. 320.
Cod: Comm.

2062 **JOANNES CHRYSOSTOMUS** Scr. Eccl.
A.D. 4-5: Antiochenus, Constantinopolitanus

001 **Ad Theodorum lapsum** (lib. 2) (= **Epistula ad
Theodorum monachum**), ed. J. Dumortier,
Jean Chrysostome. A Théodore [*Sources chrétiennes* 117. Paris: Cerf, 1966]: 46-78.
Cod: 3,099: Epist., Eccl.

002 **Ad Theodorum lapsum** (lib. 1), ed. Dumortier,
SC 117, 80-218.
Cod: 14,551: Eccl.

003 **Adversus oppugnatores vitae monasticae** (lib.
1-3), MPG 47: 319-386.
Cod: 32,255: Eccl.

004 **Ad Demetrium de compunctione** (lib. 1), MPG
47: 393-410.
Cod: 7,963: Eccl.

005 **Ad Stelechium de compunctione** (lib. 2), MPG
47: 411-422.
Cod: 5,741: Eccl.

006 **Ad Stagirium a daemone vexatum** (lib. 1-3),
MPG 47: 423-494.
Cod: 33,064: Eccl.

007 **Contra eos qui subintroductas habent virgines,**
ed. J. Dumortier, *Saint Jean Chrysostome. Les
cohabitations suspectes*. Paris: Les Belles
Lettres, 1955: 44-94.
Cod: 9,277: Epist., Eccl.

008 **Quod regulares feminae viris cohabitare non
debeant,** ed. Dumortier, *Les cohabitations suspectes*, 95-137.
Cod: 8,648: Epist., Eccl.

009 **De virginitate,** ed. H. Musurillo and B. Grillet,
Jean Chrysostome. La virginité [*Sources chrétiennes* 125. Paris: Cerf, 1966]: 92-394.
Cod: 31,995: Eccl.

010 **Ad viduam juniorem,** ed. G.H. Ettlinger and
B. Grillet, *Jean Chrysostome. A une jeune
veuve. Sur le mariage unique* [*Sources chrétiennes* 138. Paris: Cerf, 1968]: 112-159.
Cod: 4,727: Eccl.

011 **De non iterando conjugio,** ed. Ettlinger and
Grillet, *op. cit.*, 160-201.
Cod: 4,295: Eccl.

085 **De sacerdotio** (lib. 1-6), ed. A.-M. Malingrey,
Jean Chrysostome. Sur le sacerdoce [*Sources
chrétiennes* 272. Paris: Cerf, 1980]: 60-362.
De sacerdotio (lib. 7): Cf. 2062 119.
Cod: 32,119: Eccl.

496 **Sermo cum presbyter fuit ordinatus,** ed.
Malingrey, *SC* 272, 388-418.
Cod: 2,752: Homilet.

012 **De incomprehensibili dei natura** (= **Contra
Anomoeos**, homiliae 1-5), ed. A.-M. Malingrey, *Jean Chrysostome. Sur l'incompréhensibilité de Dieu* [*Sources chrétiennes* 28 bis. Paris:
Cerf, 1970]: 92-322.
Cod: 21,310: Homilet.

014 **De beato Philogonio** (= **Contra Anomoeos**, homilia 6), MPG 48: 747-756.
Cod: 3,536: Homilet., Encom., Hagiogr.

015 **De consubstantiali** (= **Contra Anomoeos**, homilia 7), MPG 48: 755-768.
Cod: 5,657: Homilet.

016 **De petitione matris filiorum Zebedaei** (= **Contra Anomoeos**, homilia 8), MPG 48: 767-778.
Cod: 4,197: Homilet.

017 **In quatriduanum Lazarum** (= **Contra Anomoeos**, homilia 9) [Sp.], MPG 48: 779-784.
Cod: 1,987: Homilet.

018 **De Christi precibus** (= **Contra Anomoeos**, homilia 10), MPG 48: 783-796.
Cod: 4,948: Homilet.

019 **Contra Anomoeos** (homilia 11), MPG 48: 795-
802.
Cod: 2,922: Homilet.

020 **De Christi divinitate** (= **Contra Anomoeos**, homilia 12), MPG 48: 801-812.
Cod: 4,258: Homilet.

372 **Contra Judaeos et gentiles quod Christus sit**

deus, ed. N.G. McKendrick, *Quod Christus sit Deus* [*Diss. Fordham* (1966)].
Cod: Apol.

021 **Adversus Judaeos** (orationes 1-8), MPG 48: 843-942.
Cod: 46,300: Homilet.

022 **In Kalendas**, MPG 48: 953-962.
Cod: 4,220: Homilet.

023 **De Lazaro** (homiliae 1-7), MPG 48: 963-1054.
Cod: 40,378: Homilet.

024 **Ad populum Antiochenum** (homiliae 1-21), MPG 49: 15-222.
Cod: 98,986: Homilet.

025 **Ad illuminandos catecheses 1-2** (series prima et secunda), MPG 49: 223-240.
Cod: 8,610: Homilet.

026 **De diabolo tentatore** (homiliae 1-3), MPG 49: 241-276.
Cod: 13,481: Homilet.

027 **De paenitentia** (homiliae 1-9), MPG 49: 277-350.
Homiliae 7-9 sunt spuriae.
Cod: 32,239: Homilet.

028 **In diem natalem**, MPG 49: 351-362.
Cod: 5,003: Homilet.

029 **De baptismo Christi**, MPG 49: 363-372.
Cod: 3,764: Homilet.

030 **De proditione Judae** (homiliae 1-2), MPG 49: 373-392.
Cod: 9,139: Homilet.

031 **De coemeterio et de cruce**, MPG 49: 393-398.
Cod: 2,356: Homilet.

032 **De cruce et latrone** (homilia 1), MPG 49: 399-408.
Cod: 3,765: Homilet.

033 **De cruce et latrone** (homilia 2), MPG 49: 407-418.
Cod: 4,831: Homilet.

034 **De resurrectione mortuorum**, MPG 50: 417ter-432.
Cod: 6,590: Homilet.

035 **Adversus ebriosos et de resurrectione domini nostri Jesu Christi**, MPG 50: 433-442.
Cod: 3,684: Homilet.

036 **In ascensionem domini nostri Jesu Christi**, MPG 50: 441-452.
Cod: 4,141: Homilet.

037 **De sancta pentecoste** (homiliae 1-2), MPG 50: 453-470.
Cod: 7,511: Homilet.

486 **De laudibus sancti Pauli apostoli** (homiliae 1-7), ed. A. Piédagnel, *Jean Chrysostome. Panégyriques de S. Paul* [*Sources chrétiennes* 300. Paris: Cerf, 1982]: 112-320.
Cod: 16,161: Homilet., Encom., Hagiogr.

039 **De sancto Meletio Antiocheno**, MPG 50: 515-520.
Cod: 2,227: Homilet., Encom., Hagiogr.

040 **In sanctum Lucianum martyrem**, MPG 50: 519-526.
Cod: 2,147: Homilet., Encom., Hagiogr.

041 **De sancto hieromartyre Babyla**, MPG 50: 527-534.
Cod: 2,173: Homilet., Encom., Hagiogr.

373 **De Babyla contra Julianum et gentiles**, ed. M. Schatkin, *Critical edition of, and introduction to, St. John Chrysostom's "De sancto Babyla, contra Iulianum et gentiles"* [*Diss. Fordham* (1967)]: 1-106.
Cod: 18,204: Apol.

042 **In Juventinum et Maximum martyres**, MPG 50: 571-578.
Cod: 2,281: Homilet., Encom., Hagiogr.

043 **De sancta Pelagia virgine et martyre**, MPG 50: 579-584.
Cod: 2,572: Homilet., Encom., Hagiogr.

044 **In sanctum Ignatium martyrem**, MPG 50: 587-596.
Cod: 4,129: Homilet., Encom., Hagiogr.

045 **In sanctum Eustathium Antiochenum**, MPG 50: 597-606.
Cod: 3,247: Homilet., Encom., Hagiogr.

046 **In sanctum Romanum** (homilia 1), MPG 50: 605-612.
Cod: 2,752: Homilet., Encom., Hagiogr.

047 **De Maccabeis** (homiliae 1-3), MPG 50: 617-628.
Cod: 4,556: Homilet., Encom., Hagiogr.

048 **De sanctis Bernice et Prosdoce**, MPG 50: 629-640.
Cod: 5,354: Homilet., Encom., Hagiogr.

049 **In quatriduanum Lazarum**, MPG 50: 641-644.
Cod: 1,327: Homilet.

050 **De sanctis martyribus**, MPG 50: 645-654.
Cod: 3,223: Homilet., Encom., Hagiogr.

051 **Non esse ad gratiam concionandum**, MPG 50: 653-662.
Cod: 3,996: Homilet.

052 **Homilia in martyres**, MPG 50: 661-666.
Cod: 1,228: Homilet., Encom., Hagiogr.

053 **In sanctum Julianum martyrem**, MPG 50: 665-676.
Cod: 4,063: Homilet., Encom., Hagiogr.

054 **In sanctum Barlaam martyrem**, MPG 50: 675-682.
Cod: 2,888: Homilet., Encom., Hagiogr.

055 **De sancta Droside martyre**, MPG 50: 683-694.
Cod: 4,427: Homilet., Encom., Hagiogr.

056 **In martyres Aegyptios**, MPG 50: 693-698.
Cod: 1,781: Homilet., Encom., Hagiogr.

057 **De sancto hieromartyre Phoca**, MPG 50: 699-706.
Cod: 3,017: Homilet., Encom., Hagiogr.

058 **De sanctis martyribus**, MPG 50: 705-712.
Cod: 2,470: Homilet., Encom., Hagiogr.

059 **De terrae motu**, MPG 50: 713-716.
Cod: 1,468: Homilet.

060 **De fato et providentia** (orationes 1-6), MPG 50: 749-774.
Cod: 11,488: Homilet.

061 **De decem millium talentorum debitore**, MPG 51: 17*-30.
Cod: 5,940: Homilet., Exeget.

062 **In illud:** *Pater, si possibile est, transeat*, MPG 51: 31–40.
Cod: 4,256: Homilet., Exeget.

063 **In paralyticum demissum per tectum**, MPG 51: 47–64.
Cod: 6,763: Homilet., Exeget.

064 **In principium Actorum** (homiliae 1–4), MPG 51: 65–112.
Cod: 20,353: Homilet., Exeget.

065 **De mutatione nominum** (homiliae 1–4), MPG 51: 113–156.
Cod: 19,015: Homilet., Exeget.

066 **De gloria in tribulationibus**, MPG 51: 155–164.
Cod: 3,929: Homilet., Exeget.

067 **In illud:** *Diligentibus deum omnia cooperantur in bonum*, MPG 51: 165–172.
Cod: 2,800: Homilet., Exeget.

068 **In illud:** *Si esurierit inimicus*, MPG 51: 171–186.
Cod: 6,435: Homilet., Exeget.

069 **In illud:** *Salutate Priscillam et Aquilam* (sermones 1–2), MPG 51: 187–208.
Cod: 9,098: Homilet., Exeget.

070 **In illud:** *Propter fornicationes autem unusquisque suam uxorem habeat*, MPG 51: 207–218.
Cod: 4,379: Homilet., Exeget.

071 **De libello repudii**, MPG 51: 217–226.
Cod: 3,475: Homilet., Exeget.

072 **Quales ducendae sint uxores (= Encomium ad Maximum)**, MPG 51: 225–242.
Cod: 7,877: Homilet., Encom.

073 **In dictum Pauli:** *Nolo vos ignorare*, MPG 51: 241–252.
Cod: 5,071: Homilet., Exeget.

074 **In dictum Pauli:** *Oportet haereses esse*, MPG 51: 251–260.
Cod: 3,684: Homilet., Exeget.

075 **De eleemosyna**, MPG 51: 261–272.
Cod: 4,926: Homilet.

076 **In illud:** *Habentes eundem spiritum* (homiliae 1–3), MPG 51: 271–302.
Cod: 13,391: Homilet., Exeget.

077 **In illud:** *Utinam sustineretis modicum*, MPG 51: 301–310.
Cod: 3,931: Homilet., Exeget.

078 **De profectu evangelii**, MPG 51: 311–320.
Cod: 4,507: Homilet., Exeget.

079 **In illud:** *Vidua eligatur*, MPG 51: 321–338.
Cod: 7,157: Homilet., Exeget.

080 **In Heliam et viduam**, MPG 51: 337–348.
Cod: 4,126: Homilet., Exeget.

081 **De futurae vitae deliciis**, MPG 51: 347–354.
Cod: 2,522: Homilet.

082 **Peccata fratrum non evulganda**, MPG 51: 353–364.
Cod: 4,605: Homilet.

083 **Non esse desperandum**, MPG 51: 363–372.
Cod: 3,058: Homilet.

084 **In illud:** *In faciem ei restiti*, MPG 51: 371–388.
Cod: 7,500: Homilet., Exeget.

089 **In Eutropium**, MPG 52: 391–396.
Cod: 2,165: Homilet.

090 **Cum Saturninus et Aurelianus acti essent in exsilium**, MPG 52: 413–420.
Cod: 2,136: Homilet.

374 **De regressu**, ed. A. Wenger, "L'homélie de saint Jean Chrysostome 'à son retour d'Asie'," *Revue des études byzantines* 19 (1961) 114–122.
Cod: 1,503: Homilet.

091 **Sermo antequam iret in exsilium**, MPG 52: 427*–432.
Cod: 1,934: Homilet.

092 **Sermo cum iret in exsilium**, MPG 52: 435*–438.
Cod: 868: Homilet.

375 **Post reditum a priore exsilio** (sermo 1), ed. B. de Montfaucon, *Sancti patris nostri Ioannis Chrysostomi opera omnia*, vol. 3. Paris: Guerin, 1721: 424.
Cod: Homilet.

093 **Post reditum a priore exsilio** (sermo 2), MPG 52: 443–448.
Cod: 2,013: Homilet.

086 **Quod nemo laeditur nisi a se ipso**, ed. A.-M. Malingrey, *Lettre d'exil à Olympias et à tous les fidèles* [Sources chrétiennes 103. Paris: Cerf, 1964]: 56–144.
Cod: 8,570: Epist., Eccl.

087 **Ad eos qui scandalizati sunt**, ed. A.-M. Malingrey, *Jean Chrysostome. Sur la providence de Dieu* [Sources chrétiennes 79. Paris: Cerf, 1961]: 52–276.
Cod: 21,081: Eccl.

094 **Ad Innocentium papam** (epist. 1), MPG 52: 529–536.
Cod: 1,987: Epist.

095 **Ad Innocentium papam** (epist. 2), MPG 52: 535–536.
Cod: 569: Epist.

096 **Epistula ad episcopos, presbyteros et diaconos**, MPG 52: 541*–542*.
Cod: 679: Epist.

097 **Epistulae 18–242**, MPG 52: 623–748.
Epistulae 125, 233, 237–241 sunt spuriae.
Epistulae 1–17: Cf. Epistulae ad Olympiadem (2062 088).
Epistula 125: Cf. et Epistula ad Cyriacum (2062 376).
Epistula 233: Cf. et Epistula ad Antiochum (2062 344).
Cod: 47,804: Epist.

088 **Epistulae ad Olympiadem** (epist. 1–17), ed. A.-M. Malingrey, *Jean Chrysostome. Lettres à Olympias*, 2nd edn. [Sources chrétiennes 13 bis. Paris: Cerf, 1968]: 106–388.
Cod: 29,965: Epist., Eccl.

344 **Epistula ad Antiochum** (epist. 233) [Sp.], ed. P.G. Nicolopoulos, Αἱ εἰς τὸν Ἰωάννην τὸν

Χρυσόστομον ἐσφαλμένως ἀποδιδόμεναι ἐπιστολαί. Athens: Tsiveriotes, 1973: 497.
Dup. partim 2062 097 (MPG 52.739).
Cod: 150: Epist.

376 **Epistula ad Cyriacum** (epist. 125 + recensiones), ed. Nicolopoulos, *op. cit.*, 381–391, 395–411, 413–419, 423–449.
Dup. partim 2062 097 (MPG 52.681–685).
Cod: 13,184: Epist.

098 **Laus Diodori episcopi**, MPG 52: 761–766.
Cod: 1,068: Homilet., Encom.

099 **In sanctum pascha**, MPG 52: 765–772.
Cod: 2,809: Homilet.

112 **In Genesim** (homiliae 1–67), MPG **53**:21–385; **54**:385–580.
Cod: 282,363: Homilet., Exeget.

113 **In Genesim** (sermones 1–9), MPG 54: 581–630.
Cod: 22,678: Homilet., Exeget.

114 **De Anna** (sermones 1–5), MPG 54: 631–676.
Cod: 20,347: Homilet., Exeget.

115 **De Davide et Saule** (homiliae 1–3), MPG 54: 675–708.
Cod: 14,852: Homilet., Exeget.

143 **Expositiones in Psalmos**, MPG 55: 39–498.
Cod: 207,105: Exeget.

144 **In illud:** *Ne timueritis cum dives factus fuerit homo* (homiliae 1–2), MPG 55: 499–518.
Cod: 8,519: Homilet., Exeget.

145 **In Psalmum 145**, MPG 55: 519–528.
Cod: 4,115: Homilet., Exeget.

497 **In Isaiam**, ed. J. Dumortier, *Jean Chrysostome. Commentaire sur Isaïe* [Sources chrétiennes 304. Paris: Cerf, 1983]: 36–356.
Cod: 37,747: Exeget.

498 **In illud:** *Vidi dominum* (homiliae 1–6), ed. J. Dumortier, *Jean Chrysostome. Homélies sur Ozias* [Sources chrétiennes 277. Paris: Cerf, 1981]: 42–228.
Cod: 19,137: Homilet., Exeget.

148 **In illud Isaiae:** *Ego dominus deus feci lumen*, MPG 56: 141–152.
Cod: 5,038: Homilet., Exeget.

149 **In illud:** *Domine, non est in homine*, MPG 56: 153–162.
Cod: 3,968: Homilet., Exeget.

150 **De prophetiarum obscuritate** (homiliae 1–2), MPG 56: 163–192.
Cod: 12,721: Homilet.

180 **In illud:** *Filius ex se nihil facit*, MPG 56: 247–256.
Cod: 4,527: Homilet., Exeget.

175 **Contra ludos et theatra**, MPG 56: 263–270.
Cod: 2,387: Homilet.

151 **In illud:** *Hoc scitote quod in novissimis diebus*, MPG 56: 271–280.
Cod: 3,856: Homilet., Exeget.

152 **In Matthaeum** (homiliae 1–90), MPG **57**:13–472; **58**:471–794.
Cod: 328,440: Homilet., Exeget.

153 **In Joannem** (homiliae 1–88), MPG 59: 23–482.
Cod: 227,691: Homilet., Exeget.

154 **In Acta apostolorum** (homiliae 1–55), MPG 60: 13–384.
Cod: 179,725: Homilet., Exeget.

155 **In epistulam ad Romanos** (homiliae 1–32), MPG 60: 391–682.
Cod: 143,874: Homilet., Exeget., Hypoth.

156 **In epistulam i ad Corinthios** (homiliae 1–44), MPG 61: 9–382.
Cod: 179,224: Homilet., Exeget., Hypoth.

157 **In epistulam ii ad Corinthios** (homiliae 1–30), MPG 61: 381–610.
Cod: 97,925: Homilet., Exeget.

158 **In epistulam ad Galatas commentarius**, MPG 61: 611–682.
Cod: 31,373: Exeget.

159 **In epistulam ad Ephesios** (homiliae 1–24), MPG 62: 9–176.
Cod: 77,349: Homilet., Exeget., Hypoth.

160 **In epistulam ad Philippenses** (homiliae 1–15), MPG 62: 177–298.
Cod: 52,139: Homilet., Exeget., Hypoth.

161 **In epistulam ad Colossenses** (homiliae 1–12), MPG 62: 299–392.
Cod: 42,302: Homilet., Exeget.

162 **In epistulam i ad Thessalonicenses** (homiliae 1–11), MPG 62: 391–468.
Cod: 35,398: Homilet., Exeget.

163 **In epistulam ii ad Thessalonicenses** (homiliae 1–5), MPG 62: 467–500.
Cod: 14,999: Homilet., Exeget., Hypoth.

164 **In epistulam i ad Timotheum** (homiliae 1–18), MPG 62: 501–600.
Cod: 46,694: Homilet., Exeget., Hypoth.

165 **In epistulam ii ad Timotheum** (homiliae 1–10), MPG 62: 599–662.
Cod: 30,211: Homilet., Exeget.

166 **In epistulam ad Titum** (homiliae 1–6), MPG 62: 663–700.
Cod: 16,862: Homilet., Exeget.

167 **In epistulam ad Philemonem** (homiliae 1–3), MPG 62: 701–720.
Cod: 7,835: Homilet., Exeget., Hypoth.

168 **In epistulam ad Hebraeos** (homiliae 1–34), MPG 63: 9–236.
Cod: 104,920: Homilet., Exeget., Hypoth.

169 **Homilia dicta postquam reliquiae martyrum**, MPG 63: 467–472.
Cod: 2,007: Homilet.

170 **Homilia dicta praesente imperatore**, MPG 63: 473–478.
Cod: 2,372: Homilet.

171 **Quod frequenter conveniendum sit**, MPG 63: 461–468.
Cod: 3,346: Homilet.

172 **Adversus eos qui non adfuerant**, MPG 63: 477–486.
Cod: 3,550: Homilet.

173 **De studio praesentium**, MPG 63: 485–492.
Cod: 2,868: Homilet.

174 **Adversus catharos**, MPG 63: 491–494.
Cod: 976: Homilet.

176 **Homilia dicta in templo sanctae Anastasiae,** MPG 63: 493–500.
Cod: 3,391: Homilet.

177 **Homilia habita postquam presbyter Gothus concionatus fuerat,** MPG 63: 499–510.
Cod: 4,789: Homilet.

178 **In illud:** *Pater meus usque modo operatur,* MPG 63: 511–516.
Cod: 2,731: Homilet., Exeget.

179 **In illud:** *Messis quidem multa,* MPG 63: 515–524.
Cod: 3,618: Homilet., Exeget.

181 **De Eleazaro et septem pueris,** MPG 63: 523–530.
Cod: 3,209: Homilet.

182 **In poenitentiam Ninivitarum** [Sp.], MPG 64: 424–433.
Cod: 2,156: Homilet.

183 **Commentarius in Job** (prooemium tantum), MPG 64: 504–506.
Cod: 451: Exeget.

184 **Fragmenta in Job** (in catenis), MPG 64: 505–656.
Q: 29,081: Exeget., Caten.

185 **Fragmenta in Proverbia** (in catenis), MPG 64: 660–740.
Q: 16,237: Exeget., Caten.

186 **Fragmenta in Jeremiam** (in catenis), MPG 64: 740–1037.
Q: 56,086: Exeget., Caten.

187 **Fragmenta in epistulas catholicas,** MPG 64: 1040–1061.
Q: 4,068: Exeget.

378 **De inani gloria et de educandis liberis,** ed. A.-M. Malingrey, *Jean Chrysostome. Sur la vaine gloire et l'éducation des enfants* [Sources chrétiennes 188. Paris: Cerf, 1972]: 64–196.
Cod: 9,283: Eccl.

379 **In illud:** *Apparuit gratia dei omnibus hominibus,* ed. A. Wenger, "Une homélie inédite de Jean Chrysostome sur l'épiphanie," *Revue des études byzantines* 29 (1971) 123–135.
Cod: 2,357: Homilet., Exeget.

380 **Catechesis de juramento** (series prima), ed. A. Papadopoulos-Kerameus, *Varia Graeca sacra.* St. Petersburg: Kirschbaum, 1909 (repr. Leipzig: Zentralantiquariat der DDR, 1975): 154–166.
Cod: 3,309: Homilet.

381 **Catechesis ultima ad baptizandos** (series prima), ed. Papadopoulos-Kerameus, *op. cit.,* 166–175.
Cod: 2,873: Homilet.

382 **Catecheses ad illuminandos 1–8** (series tertia), ed. A. Wenger, *Jean Chrysostome. Huit catéchèses baptismales,* 2nd edn. [Sources chrétiennes 50 bis. Paris: Cerf, 1970]: 108–260.
Homilia 3 = Ad neophytos.
Cod: 26,080: Homilet.

383 **Fragmenta ex homiliis diversis,** ed. S. Haidacher, "Chrysostomos-Fragmente im Maxi-

mos-Florilegium und in den Sacra Parallela," *Byzantinische Zeitschrift* 16 (1907) 173–186.
Ex homilia ὅτι χρὴ γενναίως φέρειν τὴν πενίαν (frr. 6–8): pp. 173–175.
Ex homilia εἰς τὴν χήραν τὴν τὰ δύο λεπτὰ προσενέγκασαν ἐν τῷ γαζοφυλακίῳ (fr. 9): p. 175.
Ex homilia in sanctum Stephanum (fr. 10): p. 176.
Ex homilia in sanctum Romanum martyrem (fr. 11): p. 176.
Ex homilia de Constantino imperatore (fr. 12): p. 176.
Ἐκ τοῦ εἰς τὰς Βασιλείας γ' λόγου (fr. 13): pp. 176–177.
Εἰς τὴν β' Βασιλειῶν (fr. 14): p. 177.
Ἐκ τῆς εἰς τὸν Βασίλειον ὁμιλίας (fr. 15): p. 177.
In martyrem Julianum (fr. 16): p. 177.
In Lazarum (fr. 17): p. 178.
Ἐκ τῆς πη' ἐπιστολῆς (fr. 18): p. 178.
Fragmenta varia sine lemmate (frr. 19–56): pp. 178–186.
Q: Homilet., Exeget., Hagiogr., Encom., Epist.

384 **Fragmenta ex homiliis diversis,** ed. G. Bardy, "Les citations de saint Jean Chrysostome dans le florilège du cod. Vatican. graec. 1142," *Revue de l'Orient chrétien* 23 (1922–1923) 430–431.
Εἰς τὸ μυστικὸν δεῖπνον: pp. 430–431.
Εἰς τὸ πάθος τοῦ κυρίου: p. 431.
Q: 185: Homilet.

386 **Fragmentum in Matth. 3.16** (ap. Nilum Ancyranum, epist. 293), MPG 79: 345.
Q: Homilet.

387 **Fragmentum incertum** (ap. Nilum Ancyranum, epist. 294), MPG 79: 345–348.
Q

385 **Fragmenta incerta in eclogis,** ed. S. Haidacher, "Studien über Chrysostomus-Eklogen," *Österreichische Akademie der Wissenschfaten,* Philosoph.-hist. Kl., Sitzungsberichte, Bd. 144, Abh. 4. Vienna: Österreichische Akademie der Wissenschaften, 1902: 23–28.
Q: Homilet.

388 **In parabolam de ficu** (ap. Anastasium Sinaïtam, *Quaestiones et responsiones*), MPG 89: 365–368.
Q: Homilet.

389 **De jejunio** (ap. Anastasium Sinaïtam, *Quaestiones et responsiones*), MPG 89: 340.
Q: Homilet.

390 **In Petrum, Jacobum et Joannem** (ap. Eustratium Constantinopolitanum, *De statu animarum post mortem*), ed. L. Allacci, *De utriusque ecclesiae occidentalis perpetua...consensione.* Rome: Maronita, 1655.
Q: Homilet.

116 **Comparatio regis et monachi** [Dub.], MPG 47: 387–392.
Cod: 2,245: Eccl., Phil.

117 Ascetam facetiis uti non debere [Sp.], MPG 48: 1055–1060.
Cod: 2,622: Homilet.

118 De jejunio et eleemosyna [Sp.], MPG 48: 1059–1062.
Cod: 1,737: Homilet.

119 De sacerdotio (lib. 7) [Sp.], MPG 48: 1067–1070.
De sacerdotio (lib. 1–6): Cf. 2062 085.
Cod: 1,671: Eccl.

120 Christi discipulum benignum esse debere [Sp.], MPG 48: 1069–1072.
Cod: 1,333: Homilet.

121 De fugienda simulata specie [Sp.], MPG 48: 1073–1076.
Cod: 1,161: Homilet.

122 Contra Judaeos, gentiles et haereticos et in illud: *Vocatus est Jesus ad nuptias* [Sp.], MPG 48: 1075–1080.
Cod: 2,978: Homilet., Exeget.

123 De sancta trinitate [Sp.], MPG 48: 1087–1096.
Cod: 5,332: Homilet.

402 In sanctam Pelagiam [Sp.], ed. P. Franchi de' Cavalieri, *Note agiografiche* 8 [*Studi e Testi* 65. Vatican City: Biblioteca Apostolica Vaticana, 1935]: 301–303.
Cod: 682: Homilet., Encom., Hagiogr.

124 In Romanum martyrem (homilia 2) [Sp.], MPG 50: 611–618.
Cod: 1,996: Homilet., Encom., Hagiogr.

125 In proditionem Judae [Sp.], MPG 50: 715–720.
Cod: 1,151: Homilet.

126 In Bassum martyrem [Dub.], MPG 50: 719–726.
Cod: 2,156: Homilet., Encom., Hagiogr.

127 In sanctos Petrum et Heliam [Sp.], MPG 50: 725–736.
Cod: 4,856: Homilet.

128 De beato Abraham [Sp.], MPG 50: 737–746.
Cod: 3,753: Homilet., Encom.

129 De sancta Thecla martyre [Sp.], MPG 50: 745–748.
Cf. et 2062 488.
Cod: 963: Homilet., Encom.

488 De sancta Thecla martyre (e cod. Athon. Panteleimon 58) [Sp.], ed. M. Aubineau, "Le panégyrique de Thècle attribué à Jean Chrysostome: la fin retrouvée d'un texte mutilé," *Analecta Bollandiana* 93 (1975) 351–352.
Cf. et 2062 129.
Cod: 187: Homilet., Encom.

130 De precatione (orat. 1–2) [Sp.], MPG 50: 775–786.
Cod: 4,869: Homilet.

131 In oraculum Zachariae redditum [Sp.], MPG 50: 785–788.
Cod: 1,137: Homilet.

132 In laudem conceptionis sancti Joannis Baptistae [Sp.], MPG 50: 787–792.
Cod: 2,226: Homilet., Encom.

133 In annuntiationem beatae virginis [Sp.], MPG 50: 791–796.
Cod: 1,440: Homilet.

134 In illud: *Exiit edictum* [Sp.], MPG 50: 795–800.
Cod: 2,842: Homilet., Exeget.

135 In sanctum Joannem praecursorem [Sp.], MPG 50: 801–806.
Cod: 2,396: Homilet., Encom., Hagiogr.

136 In sanctam theophaniam seu baptismum Christi [Sp.], MPG 50: 805–808.
Cod: 1,403: Homilet.

137 De occursu domini, de deipara et Symeone [Sp.], MPG 50: 807–812.
Cod: 2,203: Homilet., Exeget.

138 In sancta et magna parasceve [Sp.], MPG 50: 811–816.
Cod: 2,242: Homilet.

139 In venerabilem crucem sermo [Sp.], MPG 50: 815–820.
Cod: 2,323: Homilet.

140 In triduanam resurrectionem domini [Sp.], MPG 50: 821–824.
Cod: 1,793: Homilet.

141 De angusta porta et in orationem dominicam [Sp.], MPG 51: 41–48.
Cod: 3,178: Homilet., Exeget.

142 Homilia de capto Eutropio [Dub.], MPG 52: 395–414.
Cod: 8,286: Homilet.

101 De Chananaea [Dub.], MPG 52: 449–460.
Cod: 4,959: Homilet.

499 Epistula ad Caesarium [Sp.], ed. Nicolopoulos, *op. cit.*, 513–518.
Cod: 742: Epist., Eccl.

100 In ascensionem (sermo 1) [Sp.], MPG 52: 791–794.
Cod: 772: Homilet.

103 In ascensionem (sermo 2) [Sp.], MPG 52: 793–796.
Cod: 1,640: Homilet.

104 In ascensionem (sermo 3) [Sp.], MPG 52: 797–800.
Cod: 1,102: Homilet.

105 In ascensionem (sermo 4) [Sp.], MPG 52: 799–802.
Cod: 1,680: Homilet.

106 In ascensionem (sermo 5) [Sp.], MPG 52: 801–802.
Cod: 491: Homilet.

107 In pentecosten (sermo 1) [Sp.], MPG 52: 803–808.
Cod: 2,314: Homilet.

108 In pentecosten (sermo 2) [Sp.], MPG 52: 807–809.
Cod: 1,226: Homilet.

110 De adoratione pretiosae crucis [Sp.], MPG 52: 835–840.
Cod: 2,800: Homilet.

111 De confessione pretiosae crucis [Sp.], MPG 52: 841–844.
Cod: 1,903: Homilet.

196 **In Psalmum 50** [Sp.], MPG 55: 527–532.
Q: 1,498: Homilet., Exeget.

197 **Prooemia in Psalmos** (fragmenta) [Sp.], MPG 55: 531–538.
Prooemium in Psalmos: pp. 531–534.
Argumentum Psalmorum: pp. 533–538.
Q: 3,005: Homilet., Exeget., Hypoth.

198 **In illud:** *Verumtamen frustra conturbatur* [Sp.], MPG 55: 559–564.
Cod: 2,064: Homilet., Exeget.

199 **In Psalmum 50** (homilia 1) [Sp.], MPG 55: 565–575.
Cf. et 2062 500.
Cod: 5,840: Homilet., Exeget.

500 **In Psalmum 50** (homilia 1) [Sp.] (*P. Berol.* 6788 A), ed. K. Treu, "Ein Berliner Chrysostomos-Papyrus (P. 6788 A)," *Studia patristica* 12 (1975) 74–75.
Cf. et 2062 199.
Pap: 68: Homilet., Exeget.

200 **In Psalmum 50** (homilia 2) [Sp.], MPG 55: 575–588.
Cod: 7,707: Homilet., Exeget.

201 **In Psalmum 75** [Sp.], MPG 55: 593–598.
Cod: 2,384: Homilet., Exeget.

202 **De turture seu de ecclesia sermo** [Sp.], MPG 55: 599–602.
Cod: 2,198: Homilet.

203 **In Psalmum 92** [Sp.], MPG 55: 611–616.
Cod: 2,109: Homilet., Exeget.

204 **In Psalmum 94** [Sp.], MPG 55: 615–620.
Cod: 1,991: Homilet., Exeget.

205 **In Psalmum 100** [Sp.], MPG 55: 629–636.
Cod: 3,778: Homilet., Exeget.

206 **In Psalmos 101–107** [Sp.], MPG 55: 635–674.
Q: 24,382: Homilet., Exeget.

207 **In Psalmum 118** (homiliae 1–3) [Sp.], MPG 55: 675–708.
Cod: 20,763: Homilet., Exeget.

208 **In Psalmum 139** [Sp.], MPG 55: 707–710.
Cod: 1,703: Homilet., Exeget.

209 **Interpretatio in Danielem prophetam** [Sp.], MPG 56: 193–246.
Cod: 21,458: Exeget.

210 **De Melchisedech** [Sp.], MPG 56: 257–262.
Cod: 1,923: Homilet.

211 **De perfecta caritate** [Sp.], MPG 56: 279–290.
Cod: 4,938: Homilet.

212 **De continentia** [Sp.], ed. S. Haidacher, "Drei unedierte Chrysostomus-Texte einer Baseler Handschrift," *Zeitschrift für katholische Theologie* 30 (1906) 575–581.
Cod: 1,534: Homilet.

213 **Synopsis scripturae sacrae** [Sp.], MPG 56: 313–386.
Cod: 32,599: Exeget.

214 **In natalem Christi diem** [Dub.], MPG 56: 385–394.
Cod: 3,077: Homilet.

215 **In Genesim** (sermo 1) [Sp.], MPG 56: 519–522.
Cod: 1,791: Homilet., Exeget.

216 **In Genesim** (sermo 3) [Sp.], MPG 56: 525–538.
Cod: 7,713: Homilet., Exeget.

217 **Contra theatra** [Sp.], MPG 56: 541–554.
Cod: 6,778: Homilet.

218 **In Job** (sermones 1–4) [Sp.], MPG 56: 563–582.
Cod: 12,350: Homilet.

219 **In Eliam prophetam** [Sp.], MPG 56: 583–586.
Cod: 1,942: Homilet.

220 **De Joseph et de castitate** [Sp.], MPG 56: 587–590.
Cod: 2,009: Homilet.

221 **De Susanna** [Sp.], MPG 56: 589–594.
Cod: 2,202: Homilet.

222 **De tribus pueris** [Sp.], MPG 56: 593–600.
Cod: 3,019: Homilet.

224 **In decollationem sancti Joannis** [Sp.], MPG 59: 485–490.
Cod: 2,264: Homilet., Hagiogr.

225 **In praecursorem domini** [Sp.], MPG 59: 489–492.
Cod: 904: Homilet., Hagiogr.

226 **In Petrum et Paulum** [Sp.], MPG 59: 491–496.
Cod: 1,695: Homilet., Encom., Hagiogr.

227 **In duodecim apostolos** [Sp.], MPG 59: 495–498.
Dup. partim VITAE PROPHETARUM (1750 022).
Cod: 1,024: Homilet., Encom., Hagiogr.

228 **In sanctum Thomam apostolum** [Sp.], MPG 59: 497–500.
Cod: 1,246: Homilet., Encom., Hagiogr.

229 **In sanctum Stephanum protomartyrem** [Sp.], MPG 59: 501–508.
Cod: 3,811: Homilet., Encom., Hagiogr.

230 **In illud:** *Sufficit tibi gratia mea* [Sp.], MPG 59: 507–516.
Cod: 5,098: Homilet., Exeget.

231 **In parabolam de filio prodigo** [Sp.], MPG 59: 515–522.
Cod: 3,436: Homilet., Exeget.

232 **In saltationem Herodiadis** [Sp.], MPG 59: 521–526.
Cod: 1,774: Homilet., Exeget., Hagiogr.

233 **In illud:** *Collegerunt Judaei* [Sp.], MPG 59: 525–528.
Cod: 1,169: Homilet., Exeget.

234 **In decem virgines** [Sp.], MPG 59: 527–532.
Cod: 2,001: Homilet., Exeget.

235 **In Samaritanam** [Sp.], MPG 59: 535–542.
Cod: 4,481: Homilet., Exeget.

236 **De caeco nato** [Sp.], MPG 59: 543–554.
Cod: 6,483: Homilet., Exeget.

237 **De pseudoprophetis** [Sp.], MPG 59: 553–568.
Cod: 8,653: Homilet.

238 **De circo** [Sp.], MPG 59: 567–570.
Cod: 1,272: Homilet.

239 **In illud:** *Attendite ne eleemosynam vestram faciatis coram hominibus* [Sp.], MPG 59: 571–574.
Cod: 1,853: Homilet., Exeget.

240 **In principium indictionis, in martyres** [Sp.], MPG 59: 575–578.
Cod: 1,639: Homilet.
241 **In illud:** *Simile est regnum caelorum patri familias* [Sp.], MPG 59: 577–586.
Cod: 4,162: Homilet., Exeget.
242 **In parabolam de ficu** [Sp.], MPG 59: 585–590.
Cod: 2,425: Homilet., Exeget.
243 **De pharisaeo** [Sp.], MPG 59: 589–592.
Cod: 1,148: Homilet.
244 **De Lazaro et divite** [Sp.], MPG 59: 591–596.
Cod: 1,681: Homilet., Exeget.
245 **In publicanum et pharisaeum** [Sp.], MPG 59: 595–600.
Cod: 1,807: Homilet.
246 **De caeco et Zacchaeo** [Sp.], MPG 59: 599–610.
Cod: 5,478: Homilet.
247 **In Joannem theologum** [Sp.], MPG 59: 609–614.
Cod: 2,667: Homilet., Encom.
248 **De negatione Petri** [Sp.], MPG 59: 613–620.
Cod: 2,853: Homilet., Exeget.
249 **In secundum domini adventum** [Sp.], MPG 59: 619–628.
Cod: 3,858: Homilet., Exeget.
250 **Interpretatio orationis** *Pater noster* [Sp.], MPG 59: 627–628.
Cod: 523: Homilet., Exeget.
251 **In principium indictionis** [Sp.], MPG 59: 673–674.
Cod: 719: Homilet.
252 **In venerandum crucem** [Sp.], MPG 59: 675–678.
Cod: 2,017: Homilet.
253 **In exaltationem venerandae crucis** [Sp.], MPG 59: 679–682.
Cod: 1,821: Homilet.
254 **In sanctum Stephanum** [Sp.], MPG 59: 699–702.
Cod: 893: Homilet., Encom., Hagiogr.
255 **In mediam hebdomadam jejuniorum** [Sp.], MPG 59: 701–704.
Cod: 742: Homilet.
256 **In ramos palmarum** [Sp.], MPG 59: 703–708.
Cod: 2,638: Homilet.
257 **Contra haereticos et in sanctam deiparam** [Sp.], MPG 59: 709–714.
Cod: 2,401: Homilet.
258 **In latronem** [Sp.], MPG 59: 719–722.
Cod: 1,308: Homilet.
259 **Sermo catecheticus in pascha** [Sp.], MPG 59: 721–724.
Cod: 335: Homilet.
260 **In sanctum pascha** (sermo 1) [Sp.] (fort. auctore Apollinare Laodicense), ed. P. Nautin, *Homélies pascales*, vol. 2 [*Sources chrétiennes* 36. Paris: Cerf, 1953]: 55–75.
Cod: 1,759: Homilet.
261 **In sanctum pascha** (sermo 2) [Sp.] (fort. auctore Apollinare Laodicense), ed. Nautin, *SC* 36, 77–101.
Cod: 2,114: Homilet.

262 **In sanctum pascha** (sermo 3) [Sp.] (fort. auctore Apollinare Laodicense), ed. Nautin, *SC* 36, 103–117.
Cod: 1,168: Homilet.
263 **In sanctum pascha** (sermo 4) [Sp.], MPG 59: 731–732.
Cod: 721: Homilet.
264 **In sanctum pascha** (sermo 5) [Sp.], MPG 59: 731–736.
Cod: 2,108: Homilet.
265 **In sanctum pascha** (sermo 6) [Sp.], ed. P. Nautin, *Homélies pascales*, vol. 1 [*Sources chrétiennes* 27. Paris: Cerf, 1950]: 117–191.
Cod: 6,158: Homilet.
266 **In sanctum pascha** (sermo 7) [Sp.], ed. F. Floëri and P. Nautin, *Homélies pascales*, vol. 3 [*Sources chrétiennes* 48. Paris: Cerf, 1957]: 111–173.
Cod: 5,536: Homilet.
267 **In synaxim archangelorum** [Sp.], MPG 59: 755–756.
Cod: 848: Homilet., Encom.
268 **De paenitentia** [Sp.], MPG 59: 757–766.
Cod: 5,435: Homilet.
269 **De paenitentia** (sermo 1) [Sp.], MPG 60: 681–700.
Cod: 10,713: Homilet.
270 **De paenitentia** (sermo 2) [Sp.], MPG 60: 699–706.
Cod: 3,801: Homilet.
271 **De paenitentia** (sermo 3) [Sp.], MPG 60: 705–708.
Cod: 1,391: Homilet.
272 **De eleemosyna** [Sp.], MPG 60: 707–712.
Cod: 2,475: Homilet.
273 **De jejunio** (sermones 1–7) [Sp.], MPG 60: 711–724.
Cod: 7,043: Homilet.
274 **De patientia** (sermo 1) [Sp.], MPG 60: 723–730.
Cod: 3,953: Homilet.
275 **De patientia** (sermo 2) [Sp.], MPG 60: 729–736.
Cod: 3,295: Homilet.
276 **De salute animae** [Sp.], MPG 60: 735–738.
Cod: 1,832: Homilet.
277 **In catechumenos** [Sp.], MPG 60: 739–742.
Cod: 1,545: Homilet.
278 **De corruptoribus virginum** [Sp.], MPG 60: 741–744.
Cod: 1,738: Homilet.
279 **Contra haereticos** [Sp.], MPG 60: 745–748.
Cod: 1,292: Homilet.
280 **De eleemosyna** [Sp.], MPG 60: 747–752.
Cod: 2,775: Homilet.
281 **Epistula ad monachos** [Sp.], ed. Nicolopoulos, *op. cit.*, 481–493.
Cod: 2,692: Epist., Eccl.
282 **In annuntiationem sanctissimae deiparae** [Sp.], MPG 60: 755–760.
Cod: 1,863: Homilet., Hagiogr.

283 **De remissione peccatorum** [Sp.], MPG 60: 759-764.
Cod: 2,590: Homilet., Exeget.

284 **De non judicando proximo** [Sp.], MPG 60: 763-766.
Cod: 1,537: Homilet., Exeget.

285 **De paenitentia** [Sp.], MPG 60: 765-768.
Cod: 1,174: Homilet.

286 **De spe** [Sp.], MPG 60: 771-774.
Cod: 1,208: Homilet.

287 **De caritate** [Sp.], MPG 60: 773-776.
Cod: 877: Homilet.

288 **Caritatem secundum deum rem esse deo dignam** [Sp.], MPG 61: 681-684.
Cod: 1,202: Homilet.

289 **In proditionem Judae** [Sp.], MPG 61: 687-690.
Cod: 809: Homilet.

290 **In illud:** *Memor fui dei* [Sp.], MPG 61: 689-698.
Cod: 5,397: Homilet., Exeget.

291 **In Rachelem et infantes** [Sp.], MPG 61: 697-700.
Cod: 1,047: Homilet.

292 **In Herodem et infantes** [Sp.], MPG 61: 699-702.
Cod: 1,290: Homilet.

293 **In Martham, Mariam et Lazarum** [Sp.], MPG 61: 701-706.
Cod: 3,056: Homilet., Hagiogr.

294 **In illud:** *Exeuntes pharisaei* [Sp.], MPG 61: 705-710.
Cod: 2,094: Homilet., Exeget.

295 **In meretricem et in pharisaeum** [Sp.], MPG 61: 709-712.
Cod: 683: Homilet.

296 **In assumptionem domini nostri Jesu Christi** [Sp.], MPG 61: 711-712.
Cod: 876: Homilet.

297 **In ramos palmarum** [Sp.], MPG 61: 715-720.
Cod: 2,371: Homilet.

298 **In laudem sancti Joannis theologi** (homilia 1) [Sp.], MPG 61: 719-720.
Cod: 715: Homilet., Encom., Hagiogr.

299 **In laudem sancti Joannis theologi** (homilia 2) [Sp.], MPG 61: 719-722.
Cod: 677: Homilet., Encom., Hagiogr.

300 **In transfigurationem** [Sp.], MPG 61: 721-724.
Cod: 956: Homilet.

301 **De siccitate** [Sp.], MPG 61: 723-726.
Cod: 1,270: Homilet.

302 **In Jordanem fluvium** [Sp.], MPG 61: 725-728.
Cod: 1,395: Homilet.

303 **In pharisaeum et meretricem** [Sp.], MPG 61: 727-734.
Cod: 4,326: Homilet.

304 **In Christi natalem diem** [Sp.], MPG 61: 737-738.
Cod: 1,123: Homilet., Hagiogr.

305 **In illud:** *Ascendit dominus in templo* [Sp.], MPG 61: 739-742.
Cod: 1,739: Homilet., Exeget.

306 **In mediam pentecosten** [Sp.], MPG 61: 741-744.
Cod: 912: Homilet.

307 **In Samaritanam, in die mediae pentecostes** [Sp.], MPG 61: 743-746.
Cod: 1,083: Homilet.

308 **In illud:** *Pater si possibile est* [Sp.], MPG 61: 751-756.
Cod: 2,633: Homilet., Exeget.

309 **In illud:** *Homo quidam descendebat* [Sp.], MPG 61: 755-758.
Cod: 1,096: Homilet., Exeget.

310 **In natale sancti Joannis prophetae** [Sp.], MPG 61: 757-762.
Cod: 3,076: Homilet.

311 **In natale domini nostri Jesu Christi** [Sp.], MPG 61: 763-768.
Cod: 1,991: Homilet., Encom.

312 **In Zacchaeum publicanum** [Sp.], MPG 61: 767-768.
Cod: 1,030: Homilet., Exeget.

313 **In centurionem** [Sp.], MPG 61: 769-772.
Cod: 2,206: Homilet.

314 **In illud:** *Exiit qui seminat* [Sp.], MPG 61: 771-776.
Cod: 1,958: Homilet., Exeget.

315 **In drachmam et in illud:** *Homo quidam habebat duos filios* [Sp.], MPG 61: 781-784.
Cod: 1,481: Homilet., Exeget.

316 **De jejunio** [Sp.], MPG 61: 787-790.
Cod: 1,297: Homilet.

317 **In filium viduae** [Sp.], MPG 61: 789-794.
Cod: 1,920: Homilet., Exeget.

318 **In publicanum et pharisaeum** [Sp.], MPG 62: 723-728.
Cod: 2,117: Homilet., Exeget.

319 **In ingressum sanctorum jejuniorum** [Sp.], MPG 62: 727-728.
Cod: 475: Homilet.

320 **De jejunio, dominica quinta jejuniorum** [Sp.], MPG 62: 731-732.
Cod: 840: Homilet.

321 **De jejunio** [Sp.], MPG 62: 731-738.
Cod: 3,698: Homilet.

322 **De oratione** [Sp.], MPG 62: 737-740.
Cod: 1,060: Homilet.

323 **In illud:** *Ignem veni mittere in terram* [Sp.], MPG 62: 739-742.
Cod: 1,666: Homilet., Exeget.

324 **Admonitiones spirituales** [Sp.], MPG 62: 741-744.
Cod: 1,446: Homilet.

325 **In principium jejuniorum** [Sp.], MPG 62: 745-748.
Cod: 1,446: Homilet.

326 **In adorationem venerandae crucis** [Sp.], MPG 62: 747-754.
Cod: 3,983: Homilet.

327 **In resurrectionem domini** [Sp.], MPG 62: 753-756.
Cod: 804: Homilet.

328 **In parabolam Samaritani** [Sp.], MPG 62: 755–758.
Cod: 1,705: Homilet., Exeget.

329 **De jejunio** [Sp.], MPG 62: 757–760.
Cod: 722: Homilet.

330 **De jejunio, de Davide** [Sp.], MPG 62: 759–764.
Cod: 2,996: Homilet.

331 **In annuntiationem deiparae** [Sp.], MPG 62: 763–770.
Cod: 3,081: Homilet.

332 **De eleemosyna** [Sp.], MPG 62: 769–770.
Cod: 1,136: Homilet.

333 **De caritate** [Sp.], MPG 62: 769–772.
Cod: 1,098: Homilet.

334 **In Lazarum** (homilia 1) [Sp.], MPG 62: 771–776.
Cod: 2,158: Homilet.

335 **In Lazarum** (homilia 2) [Sp.], MPG 62: 775–778.
Cod: 1,288: Homilet.

336 **In Lazarum** (homilia 3) [Sp.], MPG 62: 777–780.
Cod: 636: Homilet.

337 **De mansuetudine sermo** [Sp.], MPG 63: 549–556.
Cod: 2,362: Homilet.

338 **Eclogae i–xlviii ex diversis homiliis** [Sp.], MPG 63: 567–902.
Cod: 160,345: Homilet., Encom.

339 **Liturgia** (forma brevior e cod. Barber. gr. 336), ed. F.E. Brightman, *Liturgies eastern and western*, vol. 1. Oxford: Clarendon Press, 1896: 309–344.
Cod: Liturg.

340 **Liturgia** (forma brevior e cod. Vat. gr.), ed. N. Krasnoselčev, *Svjedjenija o njekotoryh liturgičeskich rukopisjah Vatikanskoj Biblioteki.* Kazan, 1885: 283–295.
Cod: Liturg.

341 **Liturgia** (forma brevior e cod. Leningr. gr. 226), ed. M.I. Orlov, *Liturgija svjatogo Vasilija Velikago.* St. Petersburg, 1909: 384–404.
Cod: Liturg.

342 **Liturgia** (forma brevior Constantinopolitana e cod. Sevastianov 474), ed. Krasnoselčev, *op. cit.*, 237–280.
Cod: Liturg.

343 **Liturgia** (forma integra hodierna), ed. Brightman, *op. cit.*, 353–399.
Cod: Liturg.

487 **Liturgia** (forma integra hodierna) [Sp.], ed. P. De Meester, *La divine liturgie de s. Jean Chrysostome.* Rome, 1907.
Cod: Liturg.

345 **Oratio ante lectionem** [Sp.], MPG 63: 923–924.
Cod: 83: Liturg.

346 **Oratio secunda** [Sp.], MPG 63: 923–928.
Cod: 1,905: Eccl.

347 **In novam dominicam et in apostolum Thomam** [Sp.], MPG 63: 927–930.
Cod: 2,112: Homilet., Exeget.

348 **In sanctum Stephanum** (homilia 1) [Sp.], MPG 63: 929–932.
Cod: 1,141: Homilet., Hagiogr.

349 **In sanctum Stephanum** (homilia 2) [Sp.], MPG 63: 931–934.
Cod: 386: Homilet., Hagiogr.

350 **In sanctum Stephanum** (homilia 3) [Sp.], MPG 63: 933–934.
Cod: 456: Homilet., Hagiogr.

351 **De patientia et de consummatione huius saeculi** [Sp.], MPG 63: 937–942.
Cod: 2,391: Homilet.

352 **De paenitentia et in lectionem de Davide et de uxore Uriae** [Sp.], MPG 64: 11–16.
Cod: 2,077: Homilet., Exeget.

353 **De iis qui in jejunio continenter vivunt** [Sp.], MPG 64: 15–16.
Cod: 828: Homilet.

354 **Sermo exhortatorius de temperantia** [Sp.], MPG 64: 17–18.
Cod: 618: Homilet.

355 **Quod grave sit dei clementiam contemnere** [Sp.], MPG 64: 17–18.
Cod: 172: Homilet.

356 **In sanguinis fluxu laborantem** [Sp.], MPG 64: 17–20.
Cod: 1,309: Homilet.

357 **Quod mari similis sit haec vita** [Sp.], MPG 64: 19–22.
Cod: 1,197: Homilet.

358 **In illud:** *Simile est regnum caelorum grano sinapis* [Sp.], MPG 64: 21–26.
Cod: 1,515: Homilet., Exeget.

359 **In illud:** *Si qua in Christo nova creatura* [Sp.], MPG 64: 25–34.
Cod: 5,831: Homilet., Exeget.

360 **In evangelii dictum et de virginitate** [Sp.], MPG 64: 37–44.
Cod: 3,363: Homilet.

361 **De cognitione dei et in sancta theophania** [Sp.], MPG 64: 43–46.
Cod: 1,009: Homilet.

362 **In lacum Genesareth et in sanctum Petrum apostolum** [Sp.], MPG 64: 47–52.
Cod: 2,488: Homilet., Hagiogr.

363 **De eleemosyna** [Sp.], MPG 64: 433–444.
Cod: 1,952: Homilet.

364 **Ad eos qui magni aestimant opes** [Sp.], MPG 64: 453–461.
Cod: 1,461: Homilet.

365 **De precatione** [Sp.], MPG 64: 461–465.
Cod: 1,084: Homilet.

366 **De virtute animi** [Sp.], MPG 64: 473–480.
Cod: 1,352: Homilet.

367 **Ad Eudoxiam** (epist. 1–7) [Sp.], ed. Nicolopoulos, *op. cit.*, 286, 287, 289–290, 295–297, 503–504, 507.
Q, Cod: 1,621: Epist.

368 **Precatio in obsessos** [Sp.], MPG 64: 1061.
Cod: 146: Liturg.

369 **Precatio** [Sp.], MPG 64: 1061–1064.
Cod: 102: Liturg.

370 **Precatio** [Sp.], MPG 64: 1064.
Cod: 114: Liturg.

371 **Precatio** [Sp.], MPG 64: 1064–1068.
Cod: 870: Liturg.

403 **De oratione Annae et quod utilis est pauper-tas,** *Savile* 5: 78–83.
Cod: Homilet.

404 **In publicanum et pharisaeum,** *Savile* 5: 261–264.
Cod: Homilet.

405 **Quod stantem non superbire et lapsum non desperare oportet,** *Savile* 5: 351–355.
Cod: Homilet.

406 **In illud:** *Voluntarie enim peccantibus, Savile* 5: 807–814.
Cod: Homilet.

407 **In vivificam sepulturam et triduanam resurrec-tionem Christi,** *Savile* 5: 912–916.
Cod: Homilet.

408 **De jejunio, et quod optimum sacrificium est beneficia dei agnoscere,** *Savile* 6: 886–889.
Cod: Homilet.

409 **De jejunio sanctae quadragesimae, et quod ignauorum nulla erit excusatio,** *Savile* 6: 889–893.
Cod: Homilet.

410 **Quod animae curam curae corporis praeferre debemus,** *Savile* 6: 893–896.
Cod: Homilet.

411 **De non vituperandis sacerdotibus,** *Savile* 6: 896–902.
Cod: Homilet.

412 **In transfigurationem domini** [Sp.], ed. C. Da-tema and P. Allen, *Leontii presbyteri Constanti-nopolitani homiliae [Corpus Christianorum. Series Graeca* 17. Turnhout: Brepols, 1987]: 433–448.
Cod: Homilet., Exeget.

413 **In natale domini et in sanctam Mariam geni-tricem** [Sp.], ed. F.J. Leroy, "Une nouvelle homélie acrostiche sur la nativité," *Muséon* 77 (1964) 163–173.
Cod: 1,764: Homilet.

414 **Visio Danielis** [Sp.], ed. A. Vassiliev, *Anecdota Graeco-Byzantina,* vol. 1. Moscow: Imperial University Press, 1893: 33–38.
Cod: 1,697: Homilet.

415 **De cruce et latrone** [Sp.], ed. A. Wenger, "Le sermon lxxx de la collection augustinienne de Mai restitué à Sévérien de Gabala," *Augustinus Magister. Congrès international augustinien* 1. Paris: Études Augustiniennes, 1954: 177–182.
Cod: 1,623: Homilet.

416 **In recens baptizatos et in sanctum pascha** [Sp.], ed. F. Combefis, *Sancti Ioannis Chryso-stomi de educandis liberis liber aureus.* Paris: Bertier, 1656: 169–177.
Cod

417 **In infirmos** [Sp.], ed. Vassiliev, *op. cit.,* 323–327.
Cod: 1,359: Homilet.

418 **In omnes sanctos** [Sp.], ed. K.I. Dyobouniotes,

"'Ο ὑπ' ἀριθμ. 108 κῶδιξ τῆς Ἰ. Συνόδου τῆς Ἐκκλησίας τῆς Ἑλλάδος," Ἐκκλησιαστικὸς Φάρος 9 (1912) 303–305.
Cod: 847: Encom., Hagiogr.

419 **In magnam feriam v** [Sp.], ed. R. Trautmann and R. Klostermann, "Noch ein griechischer Text zum Codex Suprasliensis," *Zeitschrift für slavische Philologie* 13 (1936) 338–341.
Cod: 633: Homilet.

420 **De meretrice** [Sp.], ed. R. Abicht, "Quellen-nachweise zum Codex Suprasliensis," *Archiv für slavische Philologie* 16 (1894) 149–153.
Cod: 1,244: Homilet.

421 **Epistula ad abbatem** [Sp.], ed. Nicolopoulos, *op. cit.,* 455–478.
Cod: 3,428: Epist.

422 **In sancta lumina** [Sp.], ed. Combefis, *op. cit.,* 118–168.
Cod: Homilet.

423 **In nativitatem Joannis Baptistae** [Sp.], ed. F. Halkin, *Inédits byzantins d'Ochrida, Candie et Moscou [Subsidia hagiographica* 38. Brussels: Société des Bollandistes, 1963]: 87–94.
Cod: 1,405: Homilet., Hagiogr.

424 **In Christi ascensionem** [Sp.], ed. C. Baur, "Drei unedierte Festpredigten aus der Zeit der nestorianischen Streitigkeiten," *Traditio* 9 (1953) 122–124.
Cod: 572: Homilet.

425 **In illud:** *Dominus regnavit* **et in illud:** *Dies diei dicit verbum* [Sp.], ed. F. Nau, "Le texte grec de trois homélies de Nestorius, et une homélie inédite sur le Psaume 96," *Revue de l'Orient chrétien* 15 (1910) 120–124.
Cod: 1,192: Homilet., Exeget.

426 **In assumptionem domini** [Sp.], ed. Baur, *op. cit.,* 116–119.
Cod: 918: Liturg.

427 **In resurrectionem domini** [Sp.], ed. M. Aubi-neau, *Homélies pascales [Sources chrétiennes* 187. Paris: Cerf, 1972]: 318–324.
Cod: 485: Homilet.

428 **Deprecatio** [Sp.], ed. M. Richard, "Témoins grecs des fragments xiii et xv de Méliton de Sardes," *Muséon* 85 (1972) 318–321.
Cod: 812: Liturg.

429 **Epitimia lxxiii** [Sp.], ed. J.B. Pitra, *Spicilegium Solesmense,* vol. 4. Paris: Didot, 1858 (repr. Graz: Akademische Druck- und Verlagsanstalt, 1963): 461–464.
Cod: 1,356: Jurisprud., Eccl.

430 **In illud:** *Nolite thesaurizare vobis thesauros in terra* [Sp.], ed. Hippolytus Monachus, "Δύο λόγοι ἐπ' ὀνόματι τοῦ ἁγ. Ἰωάννου τοῦ Χρυσοστόμου," Νέα Σιών 20 (1925) 629–633.
Cod: 1,443: Homilet., Exeget.

431 **De utilitate tentationum,** ed. B. de Montfau-con, *Sancti patris nostri Johannis Chrysostomi opera omnia,* vol. 13. Venice, 1741: appendix.
Cod: Homilet.

432 **In catenas sancti Petri** [Sp.], ed. E. Batareikh, "Discours inédit sur les chaînes de S. Pierre

attribué à S. Jean Chrysostome," Χρυσοστο-μικά 3. Rome: Pustet, 1908: 978–1005.
Cod: 6,972: Homilet., Exeget.

433 **Stichoi** [Sp.], ed. J.B. Pitra, *Iuris ecclesiastici Graecorum historia et monumenta*, vol. 2. Rome: Congregatio de Propaganda Fide, 1868: 170.
Cod: 83: Poem.

434 **In passionem salvatoris nostri Jesu Christi** [Sp.], ed. Hippolytus Monachus, "Ἐπ᾽ ὀνόματι Ἰωάννου τοῦ Χρυσοστόμου φερόμενοι λόγοι," Νέα Σιών 18 (1923) 691–692.
Cod: 403: Homilet.

435 **In ramos palmarum** [Sp.], ed. Hippolytus Monachus, Νέα Σιών 18, 309–313.
Cod: 1,296: Homilet.

436 **In synaxim incorporalium** [Sp.], ed. Halkin, *op cit.*, 133–146.
Cod: 2,193: Homilet., Hagiogr.

437 **Encomium in sanctum Joannem evangelistam** [Sp.], ed. Hippolytus Monachus, "Ἰωάννου τοῦ Χρυσοστόμου ἐγκώμιον εἰς Ἰωάννην τὸν εὐαγγελιστήν," Νέα Σιών 17 (1922) 665–667, 725–728.
Cod: 1,718: Homilet., Encom., Hagiogr.

438 **In sanctum pascha** [Sp.], ed. Baur, *op. cit.*, 108–110.
Cod: 1,080: Homilet.

440 **In nativitatem** [Sp.], ed. Datema and Allen, *Leontii presbyteri Constantinopolitani homiliae*, 381–387.
Cod: Homilet.

441 **Sermones animae utiles**, ed. M.N. Speranskij, "Perevodnije sborniki izrečenij v slavjano-russkoj pis'mennosti," *Čtenija v imper. Obščestvě istorii i drevnostej rossijskich pri Moskovskom Universitetě*, fasc. 2 (1905) 204–218.
Cod: Homilet.

442 **Oratio de hypapante** [Sp.], ed. E. Bickersteth, "Edition and translation of a hypapante homily ascribed to John Chrysostom," *Orientalia Christiana periodica* 32 (1966) 56–76.
Cod: 3,090: Homilet.

443 **In illud: *Credidi propter quod locutus sum*** [Sp.], ed. S. Haidacher, "Drei unedierte Chrysostomus-Texte einer Baseler Handschrift," *Zeitschrift für katholische Theologie* 31 (1907) 351–358.
Cod: 1,966: Exeget., Homilet.

444 **In Christi natalem** [Sp.], ed. S.G. Mercati, "Antica omelia metrica εἰς τὴν Χριστοῦ γένναν," *Biblica* 1 (1920) 84–90.
Cod: 533: Homilet., Poem.

445 **Encomium in sanctos martyres** [Sp.], ed. M. Aubineau, "Une homélie grecque inédite 'sur tous les martyrs' attribuée à Jean Chrysostome," *Forma futuri. Studi in onore del Cardinale Michele Pellegrino*. Turin: Erasmo, 1975: 622–623.
Cod: 312: Homilet., Encom., Hagiogr.

446 **Encomium in sanctum Polycarpum**, ed. A. Hilgenfeld, "Des Chrysostomus Lobrede auf Polykarp," *Zeitschrift für wissenschaftliche Theologie* 45 (1902) 570–572.
Cod: 568: Encom., Hagiogr.

447 **In illud: *Quando ipsi subiciet omnia*** [Sp.], ed. Haidacher, *ZKT* 31, 150–167.
Cod: 4,279: Homilet., Exeget.

448 **De descensu ad inferos et de latrone** [Sp.], ed. H. Brunellus, *Sanctorum patrum orationes et epistolae selectae*, vol. 1. Rome, 1585: 145–155.
Cod: Homilet.

489 **De nativitate Joannis Baptistae** [Sp.], ed. C. Datema, "An unedited homily of Ps. Chrysostom on the birth of John the Baptist," *Byzantion* 52 (1982) 76–80.
Cod: 1,193: Homilet., Hagiogr.

449 **De nativitate Christi** [Sp.], ed. M. Capaldo, "La source principale du sermon sur la nativité attribué à Jean l'exarque," *Polata Knigopisnaja* 9 (1984) 3–29.
Cod: Homilet.

490 **Oratio de exaltatione crucis** [Sp.] (fort. auctore Severiano Gabalense), ed. B.S. Pseftogkas, "Ἡ ψευδοχρυσοστόμεια ὁμιλία στὸν τίμιο καὶ ζωοποιὸ σταυρό (BHG3 415m καὶ 415n) εἶναι τοῦ Σεβεριανοῦ Γαβάλων," Γρηγόριος ὁ Παλαμᾶς 62 (1979) 299–318.
Cod: Homilet.

452 **Oratio de epiphania** [Sp.], ed. A. Wenger, "Une homélie inédite (de Sévérien de Gabala?) sur l'épiphanie," *Analecta Bollandiana* 95 (1977) 81–90.
Cod: 1,386: Homilet.

504 **In pentecosten (et) in illos qui rosis sepulcra ornant** [Sp.], ed. Datema and Allen, *Leontii presbyteri Constantinopolitani homiliae*, 397–406.
Cod: Homilet.

455 **Sermones prophylactici** (sermo 2) [Sp.], ed. G. Astruc-Morize, *Pseudochrysostomi sermo prophylacticus ii* [*Corpus Christianorum. Series Graeca*. Turnhout: Brepols, 1976]: 25–39.
Cod: Homilet.

459 **In sanctum Thomam et in oeconomiam domini nostri** [Sp.], ed. C. Datema and P. Allen, "BHG 1841s: An unedited homily of Ps. Chrysostom on Thomas," *Byzantion* 56 (1986), 32–52.
Cod: Homilet., Hagiogr.

463 **De nativitate** [Sp.], ed. S.J. Voicu, "Une homélie pseudo-chrysostomienne pour la Noël," *Byzantion* 43 (1973) 486–494.
Cod: 806: Homilet.

464 **In illud: *Genimina viperarum*** [Sp.], ed. J. Kecskeméti, *Sévérien de Gabala. Homélie inédite sur le saint-esprit* [*Diss. Paris* (1978)].
Cod: Homilet., Exeget.

465 **Oratio in patres Nicaenos** (excerptum), ed. V. Grecu, "Izvorul principal bizantin... Omiliile patriarhului Ioan xiv Caleca," *Studii şi cercetari* 35. Bucharest, 1939: 138–140.
Cod: Homilet., Encom.

491 **In sanctum pascha** [Sp.], ed. C. Datema and P. Allen, "Text and tradition of two Easter homilies of Ps. Chrysostom," *Jahrbuch der österreichischen Byzantinistik* 30 (1981) 98–102.
Cod: 1,059: Homilet.

492 **In resurrectionem domini** [Sp.], ed. C. Datema and P. Allen, "Leontius, presbyter of Constantinople – a compiler?," *Jahrbuch der österreichischen Byzantinistik* 29 (1980) 12–18.
Cod: 1,430: Homilet.

473 **In nativitatem Christi** (fragmenta duo) [Sp.], ed. M. Jugie, "La mort et l'assomption de la sainte Vierge dans la tradition des cinq premiers siècles," *Échos d'Orient* 25 (1926) 134, adn. 1.2.
Cod: 76: Homilet.

484 **In sanctum Paulum apostolum** (excerptum), ed. L. Petit, X. Sidéridès and M. Jugie, *Oeuvres complètes de Gennade Scholarios*, vol. 3. Paris, 1930: 427–430.
Cod: 1,178: Homilet.

503 **Catechesis baptismalis** [Sp.] (e cod. Ambros. F 41 sup. gr. 338), ed. J. Paramelle, "Une catéchèse baptismale inconnue du début du Ve siècle," *Mémorial André-Jean Festugière. Antiquité païenne et chrétienne*. Geneva: Cramer, 1984: 173–177.
Cod: Homilet.

502 **De nativitate Joannis Baptistae** [Sp.], ed. C. Datema, "Another unedited homily of Ps. Chrysostom on the birth of John the Baptist," *Byzantion* 53 (1983) 480–490.
Cod: 1,327: Homilet.

494 **In operarios undecimae horae** [Sp.], ed. S.J. Voicu, "*In operarios undecimae horae*: una omelia pseudocrisostomica arianeggiante," *Augustinianum* 18 (1978) 353–356.
Cod: 1,567: Homilet., Theol.

495 **In Ecclesiasten** [Sp.], ed. S. Leanza, *Procopii Gazaei catena in Ecclesiasten necnon Pseudochrysostomi commentarius in eundem Ecclesiasten* [Corpus Christianorum. Series Graeca 4. Turnhout: Brepols, 1978]: 67–97.
Cod: 6,830: Exeget.

493 **In resurrectionem domini B** [Sp.], ed. Datema and Allen, *JÖByz* 30, 94–97.
Cod: 1,216: Homilet.

x01 **Ad neophytos.**
Cf. 2062 382.

x02 **Epistula ad Epiphanium** (ap. Socratem).
HE 6.14.
Cf. SOCRATES Scholasticus Hist. (2057 001).

x03 **Apocalypsis apocrypha sancti Joannis altera** [Sp.].
Nau, pp. 215–221.
Cf. APOCALYPSIS JOANNIS (1158 002).

x04 **Epistula ad Theophilum Alexandrinum** (ap. Palladium).
Coleman-Norton, p. 41.
Cf. PALLADIUS Scr. Eccl. (2111 004).

x05 **Epistula ad Theophilum Alexandrinum** (ap. Palladium).
Coleman-Norton, p. 42.
Cf. PALLADIUS Scr. Eccl. (2111 004).

x06 **Epistula ad Theophili partium episcopos** (ap. Palladium).
Coleman-Norton, p. 49.
Cf. PALLADIUS Scr. Eccl. (2111 004).

x07 **Epistula ad Theophili partium episcopos** (ap. Palladium).
Coleman-Norton, p. 63.
Cf. PALLADIUS Scr. Eccl. (2111 004).

x08 **Epistula ad imperatorem** (ap. Palladium).
Coleman-Norton, p. 55.
Cf. PALLADIUS Scr. Eccl. (2111 004).

x09 **Ex enarratione in epistulam ad Hebraeos** (ap. Joannem Damascenum, *De imaginibus*, orat. 1.53, 2.49, 3.51).
Kotter, vol. 3, p. 155.
Cf. JOANNES DAMASCENUS Theol. et Scr. Eccl. (2934 005).

x10 **Ex narratione in parabolam seminis** (ap. Joannem Damascenum, *De imaginibus*, orat. 2.61).
Kotter, vol. 3, p. 163.
Cf. JOANNES DAMASCENUS Theol. et Scr. Eccl. (2934 005).

x11 **Fragmentum incertum** (ap. Joannem Damascenum, *De imaginibus*, orat. 3.95).
Kotter, vol. 3, p. 186.
Cf. JOANNES DAMASCENUS Theol. et Scr. Eccl. (2934 005).

x12 **In sanctum Flavianum Antiochenum** (ap. Joannem Damascenum, *De imaginibus*, orat. 3.102–104).
Kotter, vol. 3, p. 188.
Cf. JOANNES DAMASCENUS Theol. et Scr. Eccl. (2934 005).

x13 **Contra Julianum** (ap. Joannem Damascenum, *De imaginibus*, orat. 3.121).
Kotter, vol. 3, p. 193.
Cf. JOANNES DAMASCENUS Theol. et Scr. Eccl. (2934 005).

x14 **In pentecosten** (sermo 3) [Sp.].
MPG 52.809–812.
Cf. BASILIUS Scr. Eccl. (2800 012).

x15 **Daemones non gubernare mundum** (ap. Georgium, *Chronicon*).
de Boor, vol. 1, pp. 108–112.
Cf. GEORGIUS Monachus Chronogr. (3043 001)

2934 **JOANNES DAMASCENUS** Theol. et Scr. Eccl.
vel Joannes Arela vel Joannes Monachus Sancti Sabae
A.D. 7–8: Damascenus

001 **Institutio elementaris**, ed. B. Kotter, *Die Schriften des Johannes von Damaskos*, vol. 1 [Patristische Texte und Studien 7. Berlin: De Gruyter, 1969]: 20–26.
Cod: 2,312: Phil., Theol.

002 **Dialectica** *sive* **Capita philosophica** (recensio fusior), ed. Kotter, *op. cit.*, vol. 1, 47–95, 101–142.
= pars operis *Fons scientiae.*
Cf. et Dialectica (recensio brevior) (2934 067).
Cf. et Dialectica (recensio brevior, ἕτερον κεφάλαιον) (2934 068).
Cod: 21,912: Phil., Theol.

003 **Fragmentum philosophica** (e cod. Oxon. Bodl. Auct. T.1.6), ed. Kotter, *op.cit.*, vol. 1, 151–173.
Cod: 8,252: Phil.

004 **Expositio fidei**, ed. Kotter, *op. cit.*, vol. 2 [*PTS* 12 (1973)]: 3–239.
= pars operis *Fons scientiae.*
Cod: 61,353: Theol.

005 **Orationes de imaginibus tres**, ed. Kotter, *op. cit.*, vol. 3 [*PTS* 17 (1975)]: 65–200.
Cod: 31,133: Theol.

006 **De haeresibus**, ed. Kotter, *op. cit.*, vol. 4 [*PTS* 22 (1981)]: 19–67.
= pars operis *Fons scientiae.*
Cod: 10,758: Theol.

007 **Contra Jacobitas**, ed. Kotter, *op. cit.*, vol. 4, 109–153.
Cod: 13,434: Theol., Exeget.

008 **De duabus in Christo voluntatibus**, ed. Kotter, *op. cit.*, vol. 4, 173–231.
Cod: 14,124: Theol.

009 **De fide contra Nestorianos**, ed. Kotter, *op. cit.*, vol. 4, 238–253.
Cod: 4,950: Theol.

010 **Contra Nestorianos**, ed. Kotter, *op. cit.*, vol. 4, 263–288.
Cod: 7,513: Theol.

011 **Epistula de hymno trisagio**, ed. Kotter, *op. cit.*, vol. 4, 304–332.
Cod: 7,455: Epist.

012 **Contra Manichaeos**, ed. Kotter, *op. cit.*, vol. 4, 351–398.
Cod: 15,776: Theol., Dialog.

013 **De natura composita** *sive* **Contra acephalos**, ed. Kotter, *op. cit.*, vol. 4, 409–417.
Cod: 2,415: Theol.

014 **Disputatio Christiani et Saraceni** [Dub.], ed. Kotter, *op. cit.*, vol. 4, 427–438.
Cod: 2,406: Phil., Theol., Dialog.

015 **Canon paschalis**, ed. F. Rühl, *Chronologie des Mittelalters und der Neuzeit.* Berlin: Reuther & Reichard, 1897: 168–169.
Cod

016 **Sacra parallela** (recensio libri primi) (fragmenta e cod. Paris. B.N. Coislin. 276), ed. J.B. Pitra, *Analecta sacra spicilegio Solesmensi parata*, vol. 2. Paris: Tusculum, 1884 (repr. Farnborough: Gregg Press, 1966): 304–310.
Cod: Theol.

017 **Sacra parallela** (recensio libri secundi) (cod. Vat. gr. 1553), MPG 86: 2017–2100.
Cod: Theol.

018 **Sacra parallela** (recensiones secundum alphabeti litteras dispositae, quae tres libros conflant)
(fragmenta e cod. Vat. gr. 1236), MPG 95 & 96: **95**.1040–1588; **96**.9–441.
Cod: 176,720: Theol.

019 **Sacra parallela** (recensiones secundum alphabeti litteras dispositae, quae tres libros conflant) (fragmenta e cod. Berol. B.N. gr. 46 [= parallela Rupefucaldina]), MPG 96: 441–544.
Cod: 19,726: Theol.

020 **De recta sententia liber**, MPG 94: 1421–1432.
Cod: Theol.

021 **De sacris jejuniis**, MPG 95: 64–77.
Cod: 2,281: Eccl.

022 **Homilia in nativitatem Mariae** (e codd. Paris. gr. 1171 + Vat. gr. 455), ed. P. Voulet, *S. Jean Damascène. Homélies sur la nativité et la dormition* [*Sources chrétiennes* 80. Paris: Cerf, 1961]: 46–78.
Cf. et 2934 026.
Cod: Homilet.

023 **Homilia i in dormitionem Mariae** (e codd. Paris. suppl. gr. 241 + Vat. gr. 1671), ed. Voulet, *op. cit.*, 80–120.
Cf. et 2934 027.
Cod: Homilet.

024 **Homilia ii in dormitionem Mariae** (e codd. Paris. gr. 1470 + suppl. gr. 241), ed. Voulet, *op. cit.*, 122–176.
Cf. et 2934 028.
Cod: Homilet.

025 **Homilia iii in dormitionem Mariae** (e codd. Paris. gr. 1470 + suppl. gr. 241), ed. Voulet, *op. cit.*, 178–196.
Cf. et 2934 029.
Cod: Homilet.

026 **Homilia in nativitatem Mariae** (e codd. Paris. gr. 1171, Vat. gr. 455, Paris. suppl. gr. 1012, Athon. Protat. 57, Athon. Xeropot. 39), ed. A. Gievtic, Ἁγίου Ἰωάννου Δαμασκηνοῦ. Ἡ θεοτόκος. Τεσσέρεις θεομητορικὲς ὁμιλίες [Ἐπὶ τὰς πηγάς. Ἐκλεκτὰ πατερικὰ κείμενα 2. Athens: Εὐαγὲς Ἵδρυμα ""Ὅσιος Ἰωάννης ὁ Ῥῶσσος," 1970]: 64–98.
Cf. et 2934 022.
Cod: Homilet.

027 **Homilia i in dormitionem Mariae** (e codd. Vindob. hist. gr. 45; Athen. Mus. Benakis 141; Vat. gr. 1671, 455; Paris. gr. 1173, 1453; Paris. suppl. gr. 241), ed. Gievtic, *op. cit.*, 100–143.
Cf. et 2934 023.
Cod: Homilet.

028 **Homilia ii in dormitionem Mariae** (e codd. Vat. gr. 455, 1671; Paris. gr. 1171, 1173, 1453, 1470; Paris. suppl. gr. 241; Vindob. hist. gr. 45; Athen. Mus. Benakis 141), ed. Gievtic, *op. cit.*, 144–203.
Cf. et 2934 024.
Cod: Homilet.

029 **Homilia iii in dormitionem Mariae** (e codd. Vindob. hist. gr. 45; Athen. Mus. Benakis 141; Paris. gr. 1470; Paris. suppl. gr. 241), ed. Gievtic, *op. cit.*, 204–223.
Cf. et 2934 025.
Cod: Homilet.

030 **Sermo in hypapanten domini**, ed. N. Camarda, *Epigrafi ed opusculi ellenici inediti*. Palermo: Lima, 1873: 98–134.
Cod: Homilet.

031 **Sermo in nativitatem domini** (auctore Joanne Damasceno vel Joanne Euboeense), ed. S. Eustratiades, "Λόγος εἰς τὴν γέννησιν τοῦ κυρίου καὶ θεοῦ καὶ σωτῆρος ἡμῶν Ἰησοῦ Χριστοῦ," Νέος ποιμήν 3 (1921) 23–42.
Cod: Homilet.

032 **Concertationes cum Saracenis ex ore Joannis Damasceni** [Dub.], MPG 94: 1596b–1597c.
Cod: Theol., Dialog.

033 **De draconibus** (fragmentum) [Dub.], MPG 94: 1600–1601.
Cod

034 **De strygibus** (fragmentum) [Dub.], MPG 94: 1604.
Cod

035 **De sancta trinitate** (fragmentum) [Dub.], MPG 95: 9–17.
Cod: 1,217: Theol.

036 **De octo spiritibus nequitiae** (fragmentum) [Sp.], MPG 95: 80–84.
Cod: 811: Phil., Theol.

037 **De virtutibus et vitiis** (fragmenta) [Sp.], MPG 95: 85–97.
Cod: 2,318: Phil., Theol.

038 **Contra Severianos** (fragmentum) [Dub.], MPG 95: 225–228.
Cod: 479: Theol.

039 **Qua ratione homo imago dei** (fragmentum) [Dub.], MPG 95: 228.
Cod: 134: Theol.

040 **De theologia** (fragmentum) [Dub.], MPG 95: 228–229.
Cod: 235: Theol.

041 **De animato** (fragmentum) [Dub.], MPG 95: 229.
Cod: 192: Phil.

042 **De partibus animae** (fragmentum) [Dub.], MPG 95: 229–232.
Cod: 223: Phil.

043 **De unione** (fragmentum) [Dub.], MPG 95: 232–233.
Cod: 207: Phil., Theol.

044 **Ex thesauro orthodoxiae Nicetae Choniatae** (fragmentum) [Dub.], MPG 95: 233.
Q: 130: Theol.

045 **Fragmenta in Lucam** (in catenis) [Dub.], MPG 95: 233–236.
Q: 179: Exeget., Caten.

046 **De mensibus Macedonicis** (fragmenta) [Dub.], MPG 95: 236–237.
Cod: 453: Hist.

047 **Quid est homo?** (fragmentum) [Dub.], MPG 95: 244–245.
Cod: 461: Phil., Epist.

048 **Oratio de his qui in fide dormierunt** [Sp.], MPG 95: 248–277.
Cod: 5,344: Theol., Poem.

050 **Epistula ad Theophilum imperatorem de sanc**tis et venerandis imaginibus [Sp.], MPG 95: 345–385.
Cod: 7,723: Epist., Theol.

051 **De azymis** (fragmenta duo) [Sp.], MPG 95: 388–396.
Cod: 2,095: Theol.

052 **De immaculato corpore** [Sp.], MPG 95: 405–412.
Cod: 1,229: Theol.

053 **Commentarii in epistulas Pauli** [Sp.], MPG 95: 441–1033.
In epistulam ad Romanos: coll. 441–569.
In epistulam i ad Corinthios: coll. 569–705.
In epistulam ii ad Corinthios: coll. 705–776.
In epistulam ad Galatas: coll. 776–821.
In epistulam ad Ephesios: coll. 821–856.
In epistulam ad Philippenses: coll. 856–884.
In epistulam ad Colossenses: coll. 884–904.
In epistulam i ad Thessalonicenses: coll. 905–917.
In epistulam ii ad Thessalonicenses: coll. 917–929.
In epistulam ad Hebraeos: coll. 929–997.
In epistulam i ad Timotheum: coll. 997–1016.
In epistulam ii ad Timotheum: coll. 1016–1025.
In epistulam ad Titum: coll. 1025–1029.
In epistulam ad Philemonem: coll. 1029–1033.
Cod: 107,275: Exeget.

054 **Homilia in transfigurationem domini**, MPG 96: 545–576.
Cod: 6,037: Homilet.

055 **Homilia in ficum arefactam**, MPG 96: 576–588.
Cod: 2,545: Homilet.

056 **Homilia in sabbatum sanctum**, MPG 96: 601–644.
Cod: 7,499: Homilet.

057 **Sermo in annuntiationem Mariae** [Sp.], MPG 96: 648–661.
Cod: 2,636: Homilet.

059 **Encomium in sanctum Joannem Chrysostomum**, MPG 96: 761–781.
Cod: 3,869: Encom., Hagiogr.

060 **Laudatio sanctae Barbarae**, MPG 96: 781–813.
Cod: 6,694: Encom., Hagiogr.

061 **Deprecationes i–iii** [Dub.], MPG 96: 816–817.
Cod: 566: Liturg.

062 **Passio sancti Artemii** [Dub.], MPG 96: 1252–1320.
Cod: 13,815: Hagiogr.

064 **Fragmenta in Matthaeum** (e catena Nicetae) [Dub.], MPG 96: 1408–1413.
Q: 1,302: Exeget., Caten.

066 **Vita Barlaam et Joasaph** [Sp.], ed. G.R. Woodward and H. Mattingly, *[St. John Damascene]. Barlaam and Joasaph*. Cambridge, Mass.: Harvard University Press, 1914 (repr. 1983): 2–610.
Cod: 66,645: Narr. Fict., Hagiogr.

067 **Dialectica** *sive* **Capita philosophica** (recensio brevior), ed. Kotter, *op. cit.*, vol. 1, 47–50, 57–59, 74–81, 87–88, 95–101, 111.

Cf. et Dialectica (recensio fusior) (2934 002).
Cf. et Dialectica (recensio brevior, ἕτερον
κεφάλαιον) (2934 068).
Cod: 16,729: Phil., Theol.

068 **Dialectica** *sive* **Capita philosophica** (recensio
brevior, ἕτερον κεφάλαιον), ed. Kotter, *op. cit.*,
vol. 1, 142–146.
Cf. et Dialectica (recensio fusior) (2934 002).
Cf. et Dialectica (recensio brevior) (2934 067).
Cod: 1,299: Phil., Theol.

069 **Libellus orthodoxiae** [Sp.], ed. M. Gordillo,
"Damascenica. I. Vita Marciana. II. Libellus
orthodoxiae," *Orientalia Christiana* 8.2 [n. 29]
(Rome, 1926): 86–92.
Cod: Theol.

070 **De generatione hominis** [Sp.], ed. K. Krumbacher, "Studien zu den Legenden des hei-
ligen Theodosios," *Sitzungsberichte der bayerischen Akademie der Wissenschaften*,
Philosoph.-philol. und hist. Kl (1892) 345–
347.
Cod: Phil., Theol.

071 Διδασκαλικαὶ ἑρμηνεῖαι [Sp.], ed. P. Tannery,
"Fragments de Jean Damascène," *Revue des
études grecques* 6 (1893) 86–91, 273–274, 276–
277.
Cod

072 **Carmina**, MPG 96: 818–856.
Cod: Eleg., Iamb., Poem.

073 **Carmina** (tria stichera anastasima et tria idio-
mela), ed. W. Christ and M. Paranikas, *Anthologia Graeca carminum Christianorum.* Leipzig: Teubner, 1871 (repr. Hildesheim: Olms,
1963): 117–121.
Cod: Poem.

074 **Carmina** (canones), ed. Christ and Paranikas,
op. cit., 205–236.
Cod: Iamb., Poem.

075 **Homilia de Maria deipara**, ed. J.E. Bickersteth,
"Unedited Greek homilies (acephalous, anonymous or attributed to John Chrysostom) for
festivals of the virgin Mary," *Orientalia Christiana periodica* 46 (1980) 474–480.
Cod: Homilet.

x02 **De sacris imaginibus contra Constantinum
Cabalinum** [Sp.].
MPG 95.309–344.
Cf. JOANNES Scr. Eccl. (3173 002).

x03 **Adversus iconoclastas** [Sp.].
MPG 96.1348–1361.
Cf. JOANNES Scr. Eccl. (3173 001).

x04 **Homilia in nativitatem Mariae** [Sp.].
MPG 96.680–697.
Cf. THEODORUS STUDITES Scr. Eccl. et
Theol. (2714 001).

x05 **Epistula de confessione** [Sp.].
Holl, pp. 110–127.
Cf. SYMEON Neotheologus Theol. et Poeta
(3116 001).

x06 **Philosophia Christiana dividitur in tres partes**
(nonnumquam sub auctore Joanne Dama-
sceno).
Epifanovič, p. 61.

Cf. MAXIMUS CONFESSOR Theol. et Poeta
(2892 064).

4143 **JOANNES Diaconus** Rhet.
Incertum: Constantinopolitanus

001 **Commentarius in Hermogenis librum** περὶ
μεθόδου δεινότητος (excerpta e cod. Vat. gr.
2228), ed. H. Rabe, "Aus Rhetoren-Hand-
schriften," *Rheinisches Museum* 63 (1908) 133–
150.
Cod: Rhet., Comm.

3062 **JOANNES Italus** Phil. et Rhet.
vel Joannes Cluniacensis
A.D. 11: Italus, Constantinopolitanus

001 **Commentarium in Aristotelis librum de interpretatione** (fragmenta), ed. C.A. Brandis, *Aristotelis opera*, vol. 4, 2nd edn. Berlin: Reimer,
1836 (repr. De Gruyter, 1961): 94b–95b, 121a
(nota).
Q: Phil., Comm.

2871 **JOANNES MALALAS** Chronogr.
fiq Joannes Scholasticus
A.D. 5–6: Antiochenus

001 **Chronographia**, ed. L. Dindorf, *Ioannis Mala-
lae chronographia* [*Corpus scriptorum historiae
Byzantinae.* Bonn: Weber, 1831]: 23–496.
Cod: 91,268: Chronogr.

002 **Chronologica** (fort. auctore anonymo excerptorum chronologicorum), ed. Dindorf, *op. cit.*,
3–22.
Cod: 3,485: Chronogr.

003 **Chronographia** (eclogae e cod. Paris. gr. 1336),
ed. J.A. Cramer, *Anecdota Graeca e codd.
manuscriptis bibliothecae regiae Parisiensis*, vol.
2. Oxford: Oxford University Press, 1839 (repr.
Hildesheim: Olms, 1967): 231–242.
Cod: 3,613: Hist., Chronogr.

3167 **JOANNES Notarius** Biogr.
A.D. 5/7: fort. Alexandrinus

001 **Vita Eusebii Alexandrini**, MPG 86.1: 297–309.
Cod: Biogr.

4015 **JOANNES PHILOPONUS** Phil.
vel Joannes Grammaticus
A.D. 6: Alexandrinus

001 **In Aristotelis categorias commentarium**, ed. A.
Busse, *Philoponi (olim Ammonii) in Aristotelis
categorias commentarium* [*Commentaria in
Aristotelem Graeca* 13.1. Berlin: Reimer, 1898]:
1–205.
Cod: 67,258: Phil., Comm.

002 **In Aristotelis analytica priora commentaria**,
ed. M. Wallies, *Ioannis Philoponi in Aristotelis
analytica priora commentaria* [*Commentaria in
Aristotelem Graeca* 13.2. Berlin: Reimer, 1905]:
1–485.
Cod: 165,959: Phil., Comm.

003 **In Aristotelis analytica posteriora commentaria**
(prooemium e codd. BRL), ed. M. Wallies,
Ioannis Philoponi in Aristotelis analytica poste-

riora commentaria cum Anonymo in librum ii
[Commentaria in Aristotelem Graeca 13.3. Berlin: Reimer, 1909]: xxvii–xxx.
Cod: 1,600: Phil., Comm.

004 **In Aristotelis analytica posteriora commentaria**, ed. Wallies, *CAG* 13.3, 1–440.
Cod: 147,906: Phil., Comm.

005 **In Aristotelis meteorologicorum librum primum commentarium**, ed. M. Hayduck, *Ioannis Philoponi in Aristotelis meteorologicorum librum primum commentarium [Commentaria in Aristotelem Graeca* 14.1. Berlin: Reimer, 1901]: 1–131.
Cod: 53,855: Phil., Nat. Hist., Comm.

006 **In Aristotelis libros de generatione et corruptione commentaria**, ed. H. Vitelli, *Ioannis Philoponi in* Aristotelis libros de generatione et corruptione *commentaria [Commentaria in Aristotelem Graeca* 14.2. Berlin: Reimer, 1897]: 1–314.
Cod: 108,122: Phil., Nat. Hist., Comm.

007 **In libros de generatione animalium commentaria**, ed. M. Hayduck, *Ioannis Philoponi (Michaelis Ephesii) in libros de generatione animalium commentaria [Commentaria in Aristotelem Graeca* 14.3. Berlin: Reimer, 1903]: 1–249.
Cod: 96,011: Phil., Nat. Hist., Comm.

008 **In Aristotelis libros de anima commentaria**, ed. M. Hayduck, *Ioannis Philoponi in Aristotelis de anima libros commentaria [Commentaria in Aristotelem Graeca* 15. Berlin: Reimer, 1897]: 1–607.
Liber iii spurius est; fort. auctore Stephano Phil. (9019).
Cod: 240,876: Phil., Comm.

009 **In Aristotelis physicorum libros commentaria**, ed. H. Vitelli, *Ioannis Philoponi in Aristotelis physicorum libros octo commentaria*, 2 vols. *[Commentaria in Aristotelem Graeca* 16 & 17. Berlin: Reimer, 16:1887; 17:1888]: **16:**1–495; 17:496–908.
Cod: 308,938: Phil., Nat. Hist., Comm.

010 **De aeternitate mundi**, ed. H. Rabe, *Ioannes Philoponus. De aeternitate mundi contra Proclum.* Leipzig: Teubner, 1899 (repr. Hildesheim: Olms, 1963): 1–646.
Cod: 146,246: Phil.

011 **De opificio mundi**, ed. W. Reichardt, *Joannis Philoponi de opificio mundi libri vii.* Leipzig: Teubner, 1897: 1–308.
Cod: 64,598: Phil.

012 **De vocabulis quae diversum significatum exhibent secundum differentiam accentus**, ed. L.W. Daly, *Iohannis Philoponi de vocabulis quae diversum significatum exhibent secundum differentiam accentus.* Philadelphia: American Philosophical Society, 1983: 3–53, 55–139, 141–195, 197–238.
Recensio A: pp. 3–53.
Recensio B: pp. 55–94.
Recensio C: pp. 95–139.
Recensio D: pp. 141–195.
Recensio E: pp. 197–238.

Cod: Lexicogr.

013 **Compendium** περὶ διαλέκτων, ed. O. Hoffmann, *Die griechischen Dialekte*, vol. 2. Göttingen: Vandenhoeck & Ruprecht, 1893: 204.
Cod

014 **In Nicomachi arithmeticam introductionem** (lib. 1), ed. R. Hoche, Ἰωάννου Γραμματικοῦ Ἀλεξανδρέως. Εἰς τὸ πρῶτον τῆς Νικομάχου ἀριθμητικῆς εἰσαγωγῆς. Leipzig: Teubner, 1864.
Cod

015 **In Nicomachi arithmeticam introductionem** (lib. 2), ed. R. Hoche, Ἰωάννου Γραμματικοῦ Ἀλεξανδρέως. Εἰς τὸ δεύτερον τῆς Νικομάχου ἀριθμητικῆς εἰσαγωγῆς. Berlin: Calvary, 1867: 1–37.
Cod

016 **Tonica praecepta**, ed. W. Dindorf, Ἰωάννου Ἀλεξανδρέως τονικὰ παραγγέλματα. Αἰλίου Ἡρωδιανοῦ περὶ σχημάτων. Leipzig: Reimer, 1825: 3–42.
Cod

017 **De usu astrolabii eiusque constructione**, ed. H. Hase, "Joannis Alexandrini, cognomine Philoponi, de usu astrolabii ejusque constructione libellus," *Rheinisches Museum* 6 (1839) 129–156.
Cod: 8,048: Mech.

x01 **In Aristotelis categorias** (fragmenta e cod. Paris. 2051) (olim sub auctore Joanne Philopono).
Brandis, pp. 46a, 51b.
Cf. ANONYMI IN ARISTOTELIS CATEGORIAS (4027 003).

x02 **In Porphyrii isagogen** (fragmenta e cod. Bodl. [Barocc.] 145) (olim sub auctore Joanne Philopono).
Brandis, pp. 10a–12b.
Cf. ANONYMUS BYZANTINUS IN PORPHYRII ISAGOGEN (4168 001).

x03 **In Aristotelis librum de caelo** (fragmentum e codd. Marc. gr. 257 + 263) (olim sub auctore Joanne Philopono).
Brandis, pp. 467b–468a.
Cf. ANONYMI IN ARISTOTELIS LIBRUM DE CAELO (4195 002).

x04 **In Aristotelis categorias** (fragmenta e cod. Marc. 217) (olim sub auctore Ammonio, nunc fort. auctore Joanne Philopono).
Busse, p. 140 (in apparatu ad vv. 6 et 8).
Cf. ANONYMI IN ARISTOTELIS CATEGORIAS (4027 004).

3155 **JOANNES Protospatharius** Gramm.
A.D. 13–14: Constantinopolitanus

001 Ἐξήγησις φυσικὴ τῶν ἡμερῶν Ἡσιόδου, ed. T. Gaisford, *Poetae minores Graeci*, vol. 2 [*Scholia ad Hesiodum*]. Leipzig: Kühn, 1823: 448–459.
Cod: 3,773: Schol.

3063 **JOANNES SCYLITZES** Hist.
vel Joannes Cyropalata vel Joannes Thracesius
A.D. 11–12: Constantinopolitanus

Cf. et SCYLITZES CONTINUATUS (3064).

001 **Synopsis historiarum**, ed. J. Thurn, *Ioannis Scylitzae synopsis historiarum* [*Corpus fontium historiae Byzantinae 5. Series Berolinensis*. Berlin: De Gruyter, 1973]: 3–500.
Cod: Hist., Chronogr.

003 Ὑπόμνησις, ed. J. Zepos and P. Zepos (post C.E. Zachariä von Lingenthal), *Jus Graeco-romanum*, vol. 1 [*Novellae et aureae bullae imperatorum post Justinianum*]. Athens: Fexis, 1931 (repr. Aalen: Scientia, 1962): 319–321.
Cod: Jurisprud.

0526 **Flavius JOSEPHUS** Hist.
A.D. 1: Palaestinus, Romanus

001 **Antiquitates Judaicae**, ed. B. Niese, *Flavii Iosephi opera*, vols. 1–4. Berlin: Weidmann, 1:1887; 2:1885; 3:1892; 4:1890 (repr. 1955): 1:3–362; 2:3–392; 3:3–409; 4:3–320.
Cod: 322,394: Hist.

002 **Josephi vita**, ed. Niese, *op. cit.*, vol. 4, 321–389.
Cod: 16,293: Biogr., Apol.

003 **Contra Apionem** (= De Judaeorum vetustate), ed. Niese, *op. cit.*, vol. 5 (1889; repr. 1955): 3–99.
Cod: 23,540: Apol.

004 **De bello Judaico libri vii**, ed. Niese, *op. cit.*, vol. 6 (1895; repr. 1955): 3–628.
Cod: 129,064: Hist.

x01 **Machabaeorum iv** [Sp.].
Rahlfs, vol. 1, pp. 1157–1184.
Cf. SEPTUAGINTA (0527 026).

1451 *JOSEPHUS ET ASENETH*
A.D. 2

001 **Confessio et precatio Aseneth**, ed. M. Philonenko, *Joseph et Aséneth*. Leiden: Brill, 1968: 128–220.
Cod: 8,641: Hagiogr., Narr. Fict., Pseudepigr.

3151 **JOSEPHUS RHACENDYTA** Phil.
vel Josephus Pinarus
A.D. 13–14: Ithacensis, Thessalonicensis, Constantinopolitanus

002 **Synopsis artis rhetoricae**, ed. C. Walz, *Rhetores Graeci*, vol. 3. Stuttgart: Cotta, 1834 (repr. Osnabrück: Zeller, 1968): 467–569.
Cap. 13 (pp. 547–558): Dup. partim MENANDER Rhet. (2586 002).
Cod: Rhet., Comm., Iamb.

1452 **JUBA II Rex Mauretaniae** <Hist.>
1 B.C.–A.D. 1: Mauretanicus

001 **Testimonia**, FGrH #275: 3A:127–130.
NQ: 1,153: Test.

002 **Fragmenta**, FGrH #275: 3A:130–155.
Q: 7,527: Hist., Nat. Hist.

x01 **Epigramma irrisorium**.
App. Anth. 5.29: Cf. ANTHOLOGIAE GRAECAE APPENDIX (7052 005).
Dup. 1452 002 (fr. 104).

2180 **JUDAS** Hist.
A.D. 3

001 **Testimonium**, FGrH #261: 2B:1229.
NQ: 61: Test.

4050 **JULIANUS** <Epigr.>
fiq Julianus Meteorus Scholasticus
A.D. 6: Aegyptius
Cf. et JULIANUS <Epigr.> (4054).

001 **Epigrammata**, AG 5.298; **6**.12, 18–20, 25–26, 28–29, 67–68; **7**.32–33, 58–59, 69–70, 561–562, 565, 576–577, 580–582, 584–587, 590–592, 594–595, 597–601, 603, 605; **9**.398, 445–447, 652, 654, 661, 738–739, 763, 771, 793–798; **16**.87–88, 107–108, 113, 130, 139, 157, 173, 181, 203, 325, 388.
AG 6.186: Cf. Julius DIOCLES Rhet. (0162 001).
AG 9.9, 9b: Cf. Julius POLYAENUS Epigr. (1620 001).
AG 16.218: Cf. Joannes BARBUCALLUS Gramm. (4051 001).
Q: 2,122: Epigr.

x01 **Epigramma demonstrativum**.
App. Anth. 3.179: Cf. ANTHOLOGIAE GRAECAE APPENDIX (7052 003).

4053 **JULIANUS** <Epigr.>
A.D. 6

001 **Epigrammata**, AG 11.367–369.
Q: 47: Epigr.

4054 **JULIANUS** <Epigr.>
fiq Julianus Praefectus Aegypti
Incertum
Cf. et JULIANUS <Epigr.> (4050).

001 **Epigramma**, AG 9.481.
Q: 32: Epigr.

0940 **JULIANUS** Med.
A.D. 2: Alexandrinus

x01 **Fragmenta ap. Galenum**.
K**13**.557; **18**.1.248, 255–257, 296 in CMG, vol. 5.10.3, pp. 34, 40–42, 68, 69.
Cf. GALENUS Med. (0057 077, 094).

x02 **Fragmentum ap. Paulum**.
CMG, vol. 9.2, pp. 280–281.
Cf. PAULUS Med. (0715 001).

2003 **Flavius Claudius JULIANUS Imperator** Phil.
vel Julianus Apostata
A.D. 4: Constantinopolitanus

001 Ἐγκώμιον εἰς τὸν αὐτοκράτορα Κωνστάντιον, ed. J. Bidez, *L'empereur Julien. Oeuvres complètes*, vol. 1.1. Paris: Les Belles Lettres, 1932: 10–68.
Cod: 11,824: Encom.

002 Εὐσεβίας τῆς βασιλίδος ἐγκώμιον, ed. Bidez, *op. cit.*, vol. 1.1, 73–105.
Cod: 6,970: Encom.

003 Περὶ τῶν τοῦ αὐτοκράτορος πράξεων ἢ περὶ βασιλείας, ed. Bidez, *op. cit.*, vol. 1.1, 116–180.
Cod: 13,313: Phil.

004 Ἐπὶ τῇ ἐξόδῳ τοῦ ἀγαθωτάτου Σαλουστίου παραμυθητικὸς εἰς ἑαυτόν, ed. Bidez, *op. cit.*, vol. 1.1, 189–206.
Cod: 3,083: Phil.

005 Ἀθηναίων τῇ βουλῇ καὶ τῷ δήμῳ, ed. Bidez, *op. cit.*, vol. 1.1, 213–235.
Cod: 4,766: Epist.

006 Θεμιστίῳ φιλοσόφῳ, ed. G. Rochefort, *L'empereur Julien. Oeuvres complètes*, vol. 2.1 (1963): 12–30.
Cod: 3,382: Epist.

007 Πρὸς Ἡράκλειον κυνικὸν περὶ τοῦ πῶς κυνιστέον καὶ εἰ πρέπει τῷ κυνὶ μύθους πλάττειν, ed. Rochefort, *op. cit.*, vol. 2.1, 43–90.
Cod: 9,016: Orat.

008 Εἰς τὴν μητέρα τῶν θεῶν, ed. Rochefort, *op. cit.*, vol. 2.1, 103–131.
Cod: 5,867: Orat., Phil., Theol.

009 Εἰς τοὺς ἀπαιδεύτους κύνας, ed. Rochefort, *op. cit.*, vol. 2.1, 144–173.
Cod: 5,777: Orat.

010 Συμπόσιον ἢ Κρόνια sive **Caesares**, ed. C. Lacombrade, *L'empereur Julien. Oeuvres complètes*, vol. 2.2 (1964): 32–71.
Cod: 6,889: Satura

011 Εἰς τὸν βασιλέα Ἥλιον πρὸς Σαλούστιον, ed. Lacombrade, *op. cit.*, vol. 2.2, 100–138.
Cod: 7,621: Orat.

012 **Misopogon** (sc. Ἀντιοχικὸς ἢ Μισοπώγων), ed. Lacombrade, *op. cit.*, vol. 2.2, 156–199.
Cod: 8,493: Satura

013 **Epistulae**, ed. Bidez, *L'empereur Julien. Oeuvres complètes*, vol. 1.2, 2nd edn. (1960): 12–23, 26, 51–77, 84–91, 133–200, 205–207.
Cod: 20,165: Epist.

014 **Poematia et fragmenta**, ed. Bidez, *op. cit.*, vol. 1.2, 214–217.
frr. 161, 165–170, 176–178.
Dup. partim 2003 018.
Q: 352: Epigr., Orat., Phil.

015 **Epistulae dubiae**, ed. Bidez, *op. cit.*, vol. 1.2, 222–231.
Cod: 1,626: Epist.

016 **Epistulae spuriae**, ed. Bidez, *op. cit.*, vol. 1.2, 246–249.
Cod: 392: Epist.

017 **Contra Galilaeos**, ed. C.J. Neumann, *Juliani imperatoris librorum contra Christianos quae supersunt*. Leipzig: Teubner, 1880: 163–233.
Q

018 **Epigrammata**, AG **9**.365, 368; **16**.115(?).
AG 7.747: Cf. LIBANIUS Rhet. et Soph. (2200 011).
AG 11.108, 109: Cf. ANONYMI EPIGRAMMATICI (AG) (0138 001).
Q: 125: Epigr.

019 **Testimonia**, FGrH #238: 2B:990–991.
NQ: 200: Test.

020 **Fragmentum**, ed. A. Guida, "Frammenti inediti di Eupoli, Teleclide, Teognide, Giuliano e Imerio da un nuovo codice del Lexicon Vindobonense," *Prometheus* 5 (1979) 208.
Q: 28: Orat.

x01 **Aenigmata**.
App. Anth. 7.22–23: Cf. ANTHOLOGIAE GRAECAE APPENDIX (7052 007).
Dup. partim 2003 014 (fr. 169).

0737 **JULIANUS** Scriptor Legis De Medicis
fiq Julianus Imperator
A.D. 4?

001 **Lex de medicis**, ed. J.L. Ideler, *Physici et medici Graeci minores*, vol. 2. Berlin: Reimer, 1842 (repr. Amsterdam: Hakkert, 1963): 464.
Cod: 69: Med.

JULIANUS Theurgus Phil.
A.D. 2
Cf. ORACULA CHALDAICA (1550 001).

1757 **JULIUS** Epic.
ante A.D. 5

001 **Fragmenta**, ed. E. Heitsch, *Die griechischen Dichterfragmente der römischen Kaiserzeit*, vol. 1, 2nd edn. Göttingen: Vandenhoeck & Ruprecht, 1963: 77.
frr. 1–2.
Q: 35: Epic.

2956 **Sextus JULIUS AFRICANUS** Hist.
A.D. 2–3: Hierosolymitanus, Alexandrinus

001 **Chronographiae** (fragmenta), ed. M.J. Routh, *Reliquiae sacrae*, vol. 2. Oxford: Oxford University Press, 1846 (repr. Hildesheim: Olms, 1974): 238–308.
Q

002 **Cesti** (fragmenta), ed. J.R. Vieillefond, *Les "Cestes" de Julius Africanus*. Florence: Sansoni, 1970: 103–323.
Q, Cod, Pap

003 **Epistula ad Origenem**, ed. W. Reichardt, *Die Briefe des Sextus Julius Africanus an Aristides und Origenes* [*Texte und Untersuchungen* 34.3. Leipzig: Hinrichs, 1909]: 78–80.
Cod

004 **Epistula ad Aristidem**, ed. Reichardt, *op. cit.*, 53–62.
Q, Cod

1453 **JUNCUS** Phil.
A.D. 2?

x01 **Fragmenta ap. Stobaeum**.
Anth. IV.50a.27; 50b.85; 50c.95; 53.35.
Cf. Joannes STOBAEUS (2037 001).

0943 **JUNIAS** Med.
ante A.D. 2?

x01 **Fragmentum ap. Oribasium**.
CMG, vol. 6.2.2, p. 299.
Cf. ORIBASIUS Med. (0722 003).

2673 **JUNIOR** Poeta
Incertum

x01 **Epigramma dedicatorium**.
App. Anth. 1.199: Cf. ANTHOLOGIAE GRAECAE APPENDIX (7052 001).

0740 *JUSJURANDUM MEDICUM*
Incertum
001 **Jusjurandum medicum**, ed. U.C. Bussemaker,
Poetae bucolici et didactici. Paris: Didot, 1862:
90.
Dup. partim HIPPOCRATES Med. et CORPUS
HIPPOCRATICUM (0627 057).
Cod: 77: Med., Hexametr.

2734 **Flavius JUSTINIANUS Imperator** Theol.
vel Petrus Sabbatius
A.D. 5-6: Constantinopolitanus
001 **Contra monophysitas**, ed. M. Amelotti, R.
Albertella and M. Migliardi (post E. Schwartz),
Drei dogmatische Schriften Justinians, 2nd edn.
[*Legum Iustiniani imperatoris vocabularium.
Subsidia 2.* Milan: Giuffrè, 1973]: 6-78.
Cod: Theol.
004 **Epistula contra tria capitula**, ed. Amelotti,
Albertella, and Migliardi, *op. cit.*, 82-126.
Cod: Epist., Theol.
005 **Edictum rectae fidei**, ed. Amelotti, Albertella,
and Migliardi, *op. cit.*, 130-168.
Cod: Theol.
008 **Decretum ad abbatem montis Sinai**, ed. M.
Amelotti and L.M. Zingale, *Scritti teologici ed
ecclesiastici di Giustiniano.* Milan: Giuffrè,
1977: 200-201.
Cod: Eccl.
010 **De confirmatione digestorum**, ed. T. Mommsen, *Digesta Iustiniani Augusti*, vol. 1. Berlin:
Weidmann, 1870 (repr. 1962): xxxiii*-li*.
= pars operis *Corpus juris civilis.*
Cod: Jurisprud.
011 **Digesta**, ed. T. Mommsen and P. Krüger, *Digesta Iustiniani Augusti*, vols. 1 & 2 (1870;
repr. 1963): 1:passim; 2:passim.
= pars operis *Corpus juris civilis.*
Cod: Jurisprud.
012 **Codex Justinianus**, ed. P. Krüger, *Corpus iuris
civilis*, vol. 2. Berlin: Weidmann, 1877 (repr.
1970): passim.
= pars operis *Corpus juris civilis.*
Cod: Jurisprud.
013 **Novellae**, ed. R. Schöll and W. Kroll, *Corpus
iuris civilis*, vol. 3 (1895; repr. 1968): 1-795.
= pars operis *Corpus juris civilis.*
Cod: 213,249: Jurisprud.
014 **Appendix constitutionum dispersarum**, ed.
Schöll and Kroll, *op. cit.*, vol. 3, 797-798.
= pars operis *Corpus juris civilis.*
Cod: 410: Jurisprud.
026 **Constitutiones** (fragmenta papyracea), ed. M.
Amelotti and G.I. Luzzatto, *Le costituzioni
giustinianee nei papiri e nelle epigrafi* [*Legum
Iustiniani imperatoris vocabularium. Subsidia
1.* Milan: Giuffrè, 1972]: 18-19, 22-23, 26-27,
30, 33, 34, 37, 39, 42-44, 50-51, 54, 58, 60,
61, 62, 64, 69.
Pap: Jurisprud.
027 **Constitutiones** (fragmenta epigraphica), ed.
Amelotti and Luzzatto, *op. cit.*, 87-89, 90, 92,

93, 94-95, 96, 97-98, 101, 103, 106-107, 109,
111-112.
Epigr: Jurisprud.
015 **Contra Nestorianos** (ap. *Chronicon paschale*),
ed. Amelotti and Zingale, *op. cit.*, 32-34.
Q: Theol.
016 **Contra Nestorianos et Acephalos** (ap. acta concilii oecumenici vi), ed. Amelotti and Zingale,
op. cit., 38.
Q: Theol.
017 **Troparium**, ed. Amelotti and Zingale, *op. cit.*,
44.
Cod: Hymn.
018 **Constitutio contra Anthimum, Severum, Petrum et Zooram**, ed. Amelotti and Zingale, *op.
cit.*, 46-54.
Dup. partim CONCILIA OECUMENICA (ACO)
(5000 004) (vol. 3, pp. 119-123).
Q: Theol.
019 **Epistula dogmatica ad Zoilum**, ed. Amelotti
and Zingale, *op. cit.*, 58-60.
Q: Epist., Theol.
020 **Edictum contra Origenem**, ed. Amelotti and
Zingale, *op. cit.*, 68-118.
Q: Theol.
021 **Epistula ad synodum de Origene**, ed. Amelotti
and Zingale, *op. cit.*, 122-124.
Q: Epist., Theol.
022 **Epistula ad synodum de Theodoro Mopsues-
teno et reliquis**, ed. Amelotti and Zingale, *op.
cit.*, 150-156.
Q: Epist., Theol.
023 **Edictum de aphthartodocetismo** (fragmentum),
ed. Amelotti and Zingale, *op. cit.*, 194.
Q: Theol.
024 **Edictum de asylo**, ed. Amelotti and Zingale,
op. cit., 204.
Cod: Eccl.
025 **Edictum de asylo**, ed. Amelotti and Zingale,
op. cit., 208.
Cod: Eccl.

1454 **JUSTINUS** Gnost.
A.D. 2
001 **Fragmenta**, ed. W. Völker, *Quellen zur Ge-
schichte der christlichen Gnosis.* Tübingen:
Mohr, 1932: 27-33.
Q

0645 **JUSTINUS MARTYR** Apol.
A.D. 2: Samaritanus, Romanus
001 **Apologia**, ed. E.J. Goodspeed, *Die ältesten
Apologeten.* Göttingen: Vandenhoeck & Ruprecht, 1915: 26-77.
Cod: 15,239: Apol.
002 **Apologia secunda**, ed. Goodspeed, *op. cit.*, 78-
89.
Cod: 3,504: Apol.
003 **Dialogus cum Tryphone**, ed. Goodspeed, *op.
cit.*, 90-265.
Cod: 53,732: Apol., Dialog.
004 **Fragmenta operum deperditorum**, ed. J.C.T.

Otto, *Corpus apologetarum Christianorum sae-culi secundi*, vol. 3, 3rd edn. Jena: Mauke, 1879 (repr. Wiesbaden: Sändig, 1971): 250–264.
frr. 1–20.
Q: 715: Apol.

0646 Pseudo-JUSTINUS MARTYR
A.D. 3/5
Cf. et ACTA JUSTINI ET SEPTEM SODA-LIUM (0384).

001 **Oratio ad gentiles**, ed. J.C.T. Otto, *Corpus apologetarum Christianorum saeculi secundi*, vol. 3, 3rd edn. Jena: Mauke, 1879 (repr. Wiesbaden: Sändig, 1971): 2–18.
Cod: 1,090: Orat., Apol.

002 **Cohortatio ad gentiles**, ed. Otto, *op. cit.*, vol. 3, 18–126.
Cod: 11,276: Apol.

003 **De monarchia**, ed. Otto, *op. cit.*, vol. 3, 126–158.
Cod: 1,955: Apol.

004 **Epistula ad Diognetum**, ed. Otto, *op. cit.*, vol. 3, 158–210.
Dup. EPISTULA AD DIOGNETUM (1350 001).
Cod: 2,728: Epist., Apol.

005 **De resurrectione**, ed. Otto, *op. cit.*, vol. 3, 210–248.
Cod: 3,519: Apol.

006 **Expositio rectae fidei**, ed. Otto, *op. cit.*, vol. 4, 3rd edn. (1880; repr. 1969): 2–66.
Cod: 5,981: Theol.

007 **Epistula ad Zenam et Serenum**, ed. Otto, *op. cit.*, vol. 4, 66–98.
Cod: 3,597: Epist.

008 **Confutatio dogmatum quorundam Aristotelicorum**, ed. Otto, *op. cit.*, vol. 4, 100–222.
Cod: 16,818: Apol.

009 **Quaestiones et responsiones ad orthodoxos**, ed. Otto, *op. cit.*, vol. 5, 3rd edn. (1881; repr. 1969): 2–246.
Cod: 29,353: Apol.

010 **Quaestiones Christianorum ad gentiles**, ed. Otto, *op. cit.*, vol. 5, 246–326.
Cod: 12,757: Apol.

011 **Quaestiones gentilium ad Christianos**, ed. Otto, *op. cit.*, vol. 5, 326–366.
Cod: 5,415: Apol.

012 **Fragmenta**, ed. Otto, *op. cit.*, vol. 5, 368–374.
frr. 1–7.
Q, Cod: 560: Apol.

0944 JUSTUS Med.
A.D. 2
x01 **Fragmenta ap. Oribasium**.
CMG, vol. 6.1.1, pp. 298, 300.
Cf. ORIBASIUS Med. (0722 001).

x02 **Fragmentum ap. Paulum**.
CMG, vol. 9.2, p. 287.
Cf. PAULUS Med. (0715 001).

x03 **Fragmentum ap. Aëtium** (lib. 3).

CMG, vol. 8.1, p. 306.
Cf. AËTIUS Med. (0718 003).

2497 JUSTUS Judaeus Hist.
A.D. 1: Tiberiensis
001 **Testimonia**, FGrH #734: 3C:695–699.
NQ: 1,466: Test.
002 **Fragmenta**, FGrH #734: 3C:699.
Q: 196: Hist.

1455 *KERYGMA PETRI*
A.D. 2
001 **Kerygma Petri**, ed. E. Klostermann, *Apocrypha I. Reste des Petrusevangeliums, der Petrusapokalypse und des Kerygma Petri*, 2nd edn. [*Kleine Texte* 3. Bonn: Marcus & Weber, 1908]: 13–16.
Q: Apocryph.

2937 LACHARES Soph.
A.D. 5: Atheniensis
001 **De metris rhetoricis** (e cod. Paris. 1983), ed. W. Studemund, *Pseudo-Castoris excerpta rhetorica*. Breslau: Breslau University Press, 1888: 13–26.
Cod: Rhet.

002 **Rhetorica** (fragmentum e cod. Paris. suppl. gr. 670), ed. H. Graeven, "Ein Fragment des Lachares," *Hermes* 30 (1895) 291–298.
Cod: Rhet.

004 **De orationibus Demosthenis**, ed. F. Blass, *Die attische Beredsamkeit*, vol. 3.1. Leipzig: Teubner, 1893 (repr. Hildesheim: Olms, 1962): 590–642.
Cod: Rhet.

1456 LACO Epigr.
Incertum
001 **Epigramma**, AG 6.203.
Q: 64: Epigr.

2525 LAETUS Hist.
vel Mochus
ante 2 B.C.?
001 **Testimonium**, FGrH #784: 3C:795.
NQ: 43: Test.
002 **Fragmenta**, FGrH #784: 3C:795–797.
Q: 736: Hist.

1930 LAMACHUS Hist.
4 B.C.: fort. Smyrnaeus
001 **Testimonium**, FGrH #116: 2B:617.
NQ: 84: Test.

0945 LAMPON Med.
ante A.D. 1: Pelusiota
x01 **Fragmenta ap. Galenum**.
K12.682; 13.133–134.
Cf. GALENUS Med. (0057 076).

0370 LAMPROCLES Lyr.
5 B.C.: Atheniensis

001 **Fragmenta**, ed. D.L. Page, *Poetae melici Graeci*. Oxford: Clarendon Press, 1962 (repr. 1967 (1st edn. corr.)): 379–380.
frr. 1–2.
Q: 23: Lyr., Hymn.

0918 **LAMYNTHIUS** Lyr.
5 B.C.: Milesius
001 **Titulus**, ed. D.L. Page, *Poetae melici Graeci*. Oxford: Clarendon Press, 1962 (repr. 1967 (1st edn. corr.)): 442.
fr. 1.
NQ: 2: Lyr.

0946 **LAODICUS** <Med.>
ante A.D. 1
x01 **Fragmentum ap. Galenum**.
K12.626.
Cf. GALENUS Med. (0057 076).

0469 **LAON** Comic.
3 B.C.?
001 **Fragmenta**, ed. T. Kock, *Comicorum Atticorum fragmenta*, vol. 3. Leipzig: Teubner, 1888: 382.
frr. 1–2.
Q: 31: Comic.
002 **Fragmenta**, ed. A. Meineke, *Fragmenta comicorum Graecorum*, vol. 4. Berlin: Reimer, 1841 (repr. De Gruyter, 1970): 574.
Q: 32: Comic.

2321 **LAOSTHENIDAS** Hist.
1 B.C.?: fort. Creticus
001 **Titulus**, FGrH #462: 3B:400.
NQ: Hist.

0366 **LASUS** Lyr.
6 B.C.: Hermioneus
001 **Fragmentum**, ed. D.L. Page, *Poetae melici Graeci*. Oxford: Clarendon Press, 1962 (repr. 1967 (1st edn. corr.)): 365.
fr. 1.
Q: 20: Lyr., Hymn.
002 **Tituli**, ed. Page, *op. cit.*, 365.
frr. 2–3.
NQ: 3: Lyr.

2159 **LEANDR(I)US** Hist.
vel Leandrus
ante 3 B.C.: Milesius
001 **Fragmenta**, FGrH #492: 3B:461–464.
frr. 10–19.
Q: 646: Hist.

1941 **LEO** Hist.
fiq Leo discipulus Aristotelis
4 B.C.?: Byzantius
001 **Testimonia**, FGrH #132: 2B:676.
NQ: 195: Test.
002 **Fragmenta**, FGrH #132: 2B:677.
Q: 255: Hist.

1978 **LEO** Hist.
4/3 B.C.: Pellaeus
001 **Testimonium**, FGrH #659: 3C:208–209.
NQ: 201: Test.
002 **Fragmenta**, FGrH #659: 3C:209–211.
Q: 697: Hist., Epist.

2375 **LEO** Hist.
2 B.C.: Samius
001 **Testimonium**, FGrH #540: 3B:523.
test. 1: *Inscr. Samos* (Heraion inv. 197).
NQ: 75: Test.

2186 **LEO** Hist.
2 B.C./A.D. 2: Alabandeus
001 **Testimonium**, FGrH #278: 3A:157–158.
NQ: 23: Test.
002 **Fragmenta**, FGrH #279: 3A:158.
Q: 113: Hist.

0078 **LEO** Math. et Phil.
5–4 B.C.?: Atheniensis
001 **Testimonium**, ed. F. Lasserre, *De Léodamas de Thasos à Philippe d'Oponte*. Naples: Bibliopolis, 1987: 81.
NQ: Test.
002 **Fragmenta**, ed. Lasserre, *op. cit.*, 81–82.
frr. 1–2c.
fragmentum 2 dubium est.
Q: Phil., Math.
003 **Doctrina**, ed. Lasserre, *op. cit.*, 82–85.
frr. 1–8.
NQ: Test.

0723 **LEO** Phil.
A.D. 9: Constantinopolitanus
001 **De natura hominum synopsis**, ed. R. Renehan, *Leo the physican. Epitome on the nature of man* [*Corpus medicorum Graecorum*, vol. 10.4. Berlin: Akademie-Verlag, 1969]: 16–61.
Cod: 7,038: Med., Phil.
002 **Conspectus medicinae**, ed. F.Z. Ermerins, *Anecdota medica Graeca*. Leiden: Luchtmans, 1840 (repr. Amsterdam: Hakkert, 1963): 80–86, 89–217.
Cod: 10,463: Med.

2944 **LEO VI SAPIENS Imperator** Phil., Scr. Eccl. et Poeta
vel Leo Philosophus
A.D. 9–10: Constantinopolitanus
001 **Strategemata** (e cod. Flor.), ed. E. Woelfflin and J. Melber, *Polyaeni strategematon libri viii*. Leipzig: Teubner, 1887 (repr. Stuttgart: 1970): 507–540.
Cod: Tact.
x01 **Epigramma**.
AG 9.581.
Cf. ANONYMI EPIGRAMMATICI (AG) (0138 001).
x02 **Epigramma** (oraculum).

App. Anth. 6.225: Cf. ANTHOLOGIAE GRAE-
CAE APPENDIX (7052 006).

x03 **Cantica matutina.**
MPG 107.300–307.
Cf. CONSTANTINUS VII PORPHYROGENI-
TUS Imperator (3023 016).

x04 **Strategicon** (sub auctore Pseudo-Mauricio).
Mihäescu, pp. 28–380.
Cf. Pseudo-MAURICIUS Tact. (3075 001).

2710 **LEO BARDALAS** Epigr.
A.D. 13–14

x01 **Epigrammata** (*App. Anth.*).
Epigramma demonstrativum: 3.418.
Epigrammata exhortatoria et supplicatoria:
4.117–120.
App. Anth. 3.418: Cf. ANTHOLOGIAE GRAE-
CAE APPENDIX (7052 003).
App. Anth. 4.117–120: Cf. ANTHOLOGIAE
GRAECAE APPENDIX (7052 004).

4187 **LEO MAGENTINUS** Phil.
A.D. 13: Mytilenensis

001 **Commentarium in Aristotelis librum de interpretatione** (fragmenta e cod. Paris. gr. 1917),
ed. C.A. Brandis, *Aristotelis opera*, vol. 4. Berlin: Reimer, 1836 (repr. De Gruyter, 1961):
95b, 100b–101a nota, 102a–b nota, 104a–b
nota, 113b nota, 122a nota, 127a nota, 129a
nota, 135b nota.
Cod: Phil., Comm.

002 **Commentarium in Aristotelis librum de inter-
pretatione** [Sp.], ed. A. Manuzio, *Ammonii
Hermei commentaria in librum Peri Hermenias.
Margentini* [sic] *archiepiscopi Mitylenensis in
eundem enarratio.* Venice: Aldus, 1503.
Cod: Phil., Comm.

003 **Commentarium in Aristotelis analytica priora,**
ed. J.F. Trincavelli, *Ioannis Grammatici Philoponi commentaria in priora analytica Aristotelis. Magentini commentaria in eadem. Libellus
de syllogismis.* Venice: Zanetti, 1536.
Cod: Phil., Comm.

006 **Commentarium in Aristotelis sophisticos elenchos** (excerpta e cod. Vat. gr. 244), ed. A.
Bülow-Jacobsen and S. Ebbesen, "Vaticanus
Urbinas Graecus 35. An edition of the scholia
on Aristotle's sophistici elenchi," *Cahiers de
l'Institut du moyen-âge grec et latin* 43 (1982)
114–116.
Cod: Phil., Comm.

007 **Commentarium in Aristotelis sophisticos elenchos** (excerpta e cod. Vat. gr. 244), ed. S.
Ebbesen, "*Hoc aliquid–quale quid* and the
signification of appellatives," Φιλοσοφία 5–6
(1975–1976) 383–388.
Cod: Phil., Comm.

010 **Commentarium in Aristotelis sophisticos elen-
chos** (excerpta e cod. Vat. gr. 244), ed. S.
Ebbesen, *Commentators and commentaries on
Aristotle's sophistici elenchi. A study of post-
Aristotelian ancient and medieval writings on*

fallacies, vol. 1 [*Corpus Latinum commentariorum in Aristotelem Graecorum. De Wulf-
mansion Centre* 7. Leiden: Brill, 1981]: 305–
311, 316.
Cod: Phil., Comm.

008 **Commentarium in Aristotelis sophisticos elenchos** (excerpta praecipue e cod. Vat. gr. 244),
ed. Ebbesen, *op. cit.,* vol. 2 (1981): 280–306.
Cod: Phil., Comm.

009 **Commentarium in Aristotelis categorias** (excerptum e cod. Vat. gr. 244), ed. Ebbesen, *op.
cit.,* vol. 2, 278–279.
Cod: Phil., Comm.

9016 **LEO Philosophus** Gramm.
A.D. 9–10

001 **Epigrammata,** AG **9**.200–203, 214, 361, 578–
579; **15**.12.
AG 16.387c: Cf. ANONYMI EPIGRAMMATICI
(AG) (0138 001).
Q: 404: Epigr.

x01 **Epigrammata** (*App. Anth.*).
Epigramma demonstrativum: 3.255.
Epigramma exhortatorium et supplicatorium:
4.77.
Epigramma irrisorium: 5.58.
App. Anth. 3.255: Cf. ANTHOLOGIAE GRAE-
CAE APPENDIX (7052 003).
App. Anth. 4.77: Cf. ANTHOLOGIAE GRAE-
CAE APPENDIX (7052 004).
App. Anth. 5.58: Cf. ANTHOLOGIAE GRAE-
CAE APPENDIX (7052 005).

0100 **LEODAMAS** Phil. et Math.
5–4 B.C.: Thasius

001 **Testimonia,** ed. F. Lasserre, *De Léodamas de
Thasos à Philippe d'Oponte.* Naples: Bibliopolis, 1987: 43–44.
test. 1–3.
NQ: Test.

002 **Doctrina,** ed. Lasserre, *op. cit.,* 45–46.
frr. 1–3.
NQ: Test.

1458 **LEONIDAS** Epigr.
4–3 B.C.: Tarentinus

001 **Epigrammata,** AG **5**.188, 206; **6**.4, 13, 35, 44,
110, 120, 129–131, 154, 188, 200, 202, 204–
205, 211, 221, 226, 262–263, 281, 286, 288–
289, 293, 296, 298, 300, 302, 305, 309, 334,
355; **7**.13, 19, 35, 67, 163, 173, 190, 198, 264,
266, 273, 283, 295, 316, 408, 422, 440, 448,
452, 455, 463, 466, 472–472b, 478, 480, 503–
504, 506, 648, 652, 654–665, 715, 719, 726,
731, 736, 740; **9**.24–25, 99, 107, 179, 316, 318,
320, 322, 326, 329, 335, 337, 563, 719, 744;
10.1; **16**.171, 182, 190, 206, 230, 236, 261,
306–307.
AG 6.189: Cf. MOERO Epic. (0220 002).
AG 7.187: Cf. PHILIPPUS Epigr. (1589 001).
AG 9.435: Cf. THEOCRITUS Bucol. (0005
005).

AG 16.213: Cf. STRATON Epigr. (1697 001).
AG 16.213: Cf. et MELEAGER Epigr. (1492 001).
Q: 4,282: Epigr.
x01 **Epigramma exhortatorium et supplicatorium.**
App. Anth. 4.39: Cf. ANTHOLOGIAE GRAE-
CAE APPENDIX (7052 004).

1457 **Julius LEONIDAS** Math. et Astrol.
A.D. 1: Alexandrinus
001 **Epigrammata,** AG **6.**321–322, 324–329; **7.**547–
550, 668, 675; **9.**12, 42, 78–80, 106, 123, 344–
356; **11.**9, 70, 187, 199–200, 213; **12.**20.
AG 6.323: Cf. NICODEMUS Epigr. (1536 001).
AG 7.676: Cf. ANONYMI EPIGRAMMATICI
(AG) (0138 001).
Q: 1,042: Epigr.

0948 **LEONIDAS** Med.
vel Leonides
A.D. 1: Alexandrinus
x01 **Fragmentum ap. Paulum.**
CMG, vol. 9.2, p. 122.
Cf. PAULUS Med. (0715 001).
x02 **Fragmenta ap. Aëtium** (lib. 6–7).
CMG, vol. 8.2, pp. 123, 320.
Cf. AËTIUS Med. (0718 006–007).
x03 **Fragmenta ap. Aëtium** (lib. 15).
Zervos, *Athena* 21, pp. 17, 24, 34.
Cf. AËTIUS Med. (0718 015).
x04 **Fragmenta ap. Aëtium** (lib. 16).
Zervos, *Gynaekologie des Aëtios,* pp. 58, 60, 61,
68.
Cf. AËTIUS Med. (0718 016).

2554 **LEONIDES** Hist.
Incertum
001 **Fragmentum,** FGrH #827: 3C:899–900.
Q: 43: Hist.

LEONTEUS Trag.
A.D. 1: Argivus
AG 9.20.
Cf. ANONYMI EPIGRAMMATICI (AG) (0138
001).

4167 **LEONTIUS** Mech.
A.D. 7
001 **De sphaerae Arateae constructione,** ed. E.
Maass, *Commentariorum in Aratum reliquiae.*
Berlin: Weidmann, 1898 (repr. 1958): 561–
567.
Cod: 2,238: Mech., Astron.
x01 **De zodiaco** (olim sub auctore Leontio).
Martin, pp. 529–532.
Cf. VITAE ARATI ET VARIA DE ARATO
(4161 008).

2819 **LEONTIUS** Theol.
A.D. 6: Hierosolymitanus
001 **Contra monophysitas,** MPG 86.2: 1769–1901.
Cod: Theol.

002 **Contra Nestorianos,** MPG 86: 1400–1768.
Cod: Theol.

4062 **LEONTIUS Minotaurus** Epigr.
A.D. 6
001 **Epigrammata,** AG **5.**295; **7.**149–150, 571, 573,
575, 579; **9.**614, 624, 630, 650, 681; **16.**32, 33,
37, 245, 272, 283–288, 357.
AG 9.20: Cf. ANONYMI EPIGRAMMATICI
(AG) (0138 001).
Q: 672: Epigr.

0949 **LEPIDIANUS** Med.
ante A.D. 4
x01 **Fragmentum ap. Oribasium.**
CMG, vol. 6.2.2, p. 246.
Cf. ORIBASIUS Med. (0722 003).

1459 **LEPIDUS** Hist.
Incertum
001 **Fragmenta,** FGrH #838: 3C:905.
Q: 200: Hist.

1460 **LESBONAX** Gramm.
ante A.D. 2
001 **De figuris,** ed. D.L. Blank, *Lesbonax.* Περὶ
σχημάτων [*Sammlung griechischer und lateinischer Grammatiker* 7. Berlin: De Gruyter,
1988]: 177–208.
Cod: Gramm.

0649 **LESBONAX** Rhet.
A.D. 2
001 Πολιτικός, ed. F. Kiehr, *Lesbonactis sophistae
quae supersunt* [*Diss. Strassburg* (1906)]: 25–
27.
Cod: 339: Rhet.
002 Προτρεπτικὸς **A,** ed. Kiehr, *op. cit.,* 27–32.
Cod: 1,327: Rhet.
003 Προτρεπτικὸς **B,** ed. Kiehr, *op. cit.,* 32–37.
Cod: 865: Rhet.

LESCHES
7 B.C.?: Mytilenensis
Cf. ILIAS PARVA (1444).
Cf. ILIU PERSIS (1445).

1967 **LESCHIDES** Hist.
3/2 B.C.
001 **Testimonium,** FGrH #172: 2B:895.
Dup. partim 1967 002.
NQ: 27: Test.
002 **Titulus,** ed. H. Lloyd-Jones and P. Parsons,
Supplementum Hellenisticum. Berlin: De Gruyter, 1983: 250.
fr. 503.
Dup. partim 1967 001.
NQ: 2: Epic.

1461 **LEUCIPPUS** Phil.
5 B.C.: Eleaticus vel Abderita vel Milesius
001 **Testimonia,** ed. H. Diels and W. Kranz, *Die*

Fragmente der Vorsokratiker, vol. 2, 6th edn. Berlin: Weidmann, 1952 (repr. Dublin: 1966): 70–79.
test. 1–37.
NQ: 3,849: Test.

002 **Fragmenta**, ed. Diels and Kranz, *op. cit.*, 80–81.
frr. 1–2.
fr. 1a: *P. Herc.* 1788.
Q, Pap: 111: Phil.

0470 **LEUCO** Comic.
5–4 B.C.

001 **Fragmentum**, ed. T. Kock, *Comicorum Atticorum fragmenta*, vol. 1. Leipzig: Teubner, 1880: 703–704.
fr. 1 + tituli.
Q: 15: Comic.

002 **Fragmentum**, ed. A. Meineke, *Fragmenta comicorum Graecorum*, vol. 2.2. Berlin: Reimer, 1840 (repr. De Gruyter, 1970): 749.
Q: 10: Comic.

003 **Fragmentum**, ed. C. Austin, *Comicorum Graecorum fragmenta in papyris reperta*. Berlin: De Gruyter, 1973: 120–121.
fr. 102.
Pap: 16: Comic.

2200 **LIBANIUS** Rhet. et Soph.
A.D. 4: Antiochenus, Constantinopolitanus, Nicomediensis

004 **Orationes 1–64**, ed. R. Foerster, *Libanii opera*, vols. 1–4. Leipzig: Teubner, 1.1–1.2:1903; 2:1904; 3:1906; 4:1908 (repr. Hildesheim: Olms, 1963): **1.1**:79–320; **1.2**:354–535; **2**:9–572; **3**:4–487; **4**:6–498.
Cod: 260,529: Orat.

005 **Declamationes 1–51**, ed. Foerster, *op. cit.*, vols. 5 (1909; repr. 1963); 6 (1911; repr. 1963); 7 (1913; repr. 1963): **5**:13–564; **6**:7–658; **7**:7–736.
Cod: 220,315: Rhet.

012 **Declamatio 3** (Legatio Menelai, Theorema), ed. Foerster, *op. cit.*, vol. 5, 210–211.
Cod: 102: Rhet.

006 **Progymnasmata**, ed. Foerster, *op. cit.*, vol. 8 (1915; repr. 1963): 24–571.
Cod: 69,308: Rhet.

007 **Argumenta orationum Demosthenicarum**, ed. Foerster, *op. cit.*, vol. 8, 600–681.
Cod: 12,379: Hypoth.

008 **Characteres epistolici** [Sp.], ed. Foerster, *op. cit.*, vol. 9 (1927; repr. 1963): 27–47.
Cod: 2,450: Rhet.

001 **Epistulae 1–1544**, ed. Foerster, *op. cit.*, vols. 10 (1921; repr. 1963) & 11 (1922; repr. 1963): **10**:1–758; **11**:1–562.
Cod: 226,218: Epist.

002 **Epistulae pseudepigraphae**, ed. Foerster, *op. cit.*, vol. 11, 563–571.
Cod: 1,234: Epist.

003 **Epistularum Basilii et Libanii quod fertur**

commercium, ed. Foerster, *op. cit.*, vol. 11, 572–597.
Cod: 3,269: Epist.

009 **Fragmenta de declamationibus**, ed. Foerster, *op. cit.*, vol. 11, 637–648.
frr. 48–50.
Cod: 1,311: Rhet.

013 **Fragmenta**, ed. Foerster, *op. cit.*, vol. 11, 653–662, 664–668.
frr. 54–56, 57a–b, 58–82, 84–85, 88–93.
Q, Cod: 789: Rhet.

010 **Fragmentum**, *P. Rain.* 3.60.
Pap

011 **Epigramma**, AG 7.747.
Q: 15: Epigr.

1774 *LIBER ELCHESAI*
A.D. 2

001 **Liber Elchesai**, ed. A. Hilgenfeld, *Novum Testamentum extra canonem receptum*, fasc. 3, 2nd edn. Leipzig: Weigel, 1881: 229–240.
Q: Apocryph.

1462 *LIBER ELDAD ET MODAD*
ante A.D. 2

001 **Fragmentum**, ed. A.-M. Denis, *Fragmenta pseudepigraphorum quae supersunt Graeca* [*Pseudepigrapha veteris testamenti Graece* 3. Leiden: Brill, 1970]: 68.
Q: 20: Pseudepigr.

1463 *LIBER ENOCH*
vel *I Enoch*
2/1 B.C.

001 **Apocalypsis Enochi**, ed. M. Black, *Apocalypsis Henochi Graece* [*Pseudepigrapha veteris testamenti Graece* 3. Leiden: Brill, 1970]: 19–44.
Cod: 8,603: Apocalyp., Pseudepigr.

002 **Apocalypsis Enochi** (recensio ap. Syncellum), ed. Black, *op. cit.*, 21–26, 29–30, 32–33, 37.
Q: 2,227: Apocalyp., Pseudepigr.

1859 *LIBER JANNES ET MAMBRES*
vel *Liber Jamnes et Mambres*
Incertum

001 **Fragmentum**, ed. A.-M. Denis, *Fragmenta pseudepigraphorum quae supersunt Graeca* [*Pseudepigrapha veteris testamenti Graece* 3. Leiden: Brill, 1970]: 69.
Q: 19: Pseudepigr.

1464 *LIBER JUBILAEORUM*
2/1 B.C.

001 **Fragmenta**, ed. A.-M. Denis, *Fragmenta pseudepigraphorum quae supersunt Graeca* [*Pseudepigrapha veteris testamenti Graece* 3. Leiden: Brill, 1970]: 70–101.
Q, Cod: 3,162: Pseudepigr.

0374 **LICYMNIUS** Lyr.
5 B.C.: Chius

001 **Fragmenta**, ed. D.L. Page, *Poetae melici*

Graeci. Oxford: Clarendon Press, 1962 (repr.
1967 (1st edn. corr.)): 396–397.
frr. 2–4.
Q: 31: Lyr., Hymn.
002 **Titulus**, ed. Page, *op. cit.*, 396.
fr. 1.
NQ: 2: Lyr., Hymn.

0203 **LIMENIUS** Lyr.
2 B.C.: Atheniensis
001 **Paean Delphicus ii et prosodium in Apollinem**, ed. J.U. Powell, *Collectanea Alexandrina.*
Oxford: Clarendon Press, 1925 (repr. 1970):
149–150.
Epigr: 287: Lyr., Hymn.

0950 **LINGON** Med.
ante A.D. 2
x01 **Fragmentum ap. Galenum**.
K13.286.
Cf. GALENUS Med. (0057 076).

1465 **[LINUS]** Epic.
Incertum
001 **Testimonia**, ed. M.L. West, *The Orphic poems.*
Oxford: Clarendon Press, 1983: 62–65.
test. 1–4, 6–9, 12.
NQ: Test.
002 **Fragmenta**, ed. West, *op. cit.*, 65–67.
frr. 1–7, 9–11.
Q

2630 **LOBO** Poeta
3 B.C.?: Argivus
001 **Fragmenta et titulus**, ed. H. Lloyd-Jones and
P. Parsons, *Supplementum Hellenisticum.* Berlin: De Gruyter, 1983: 251–257.
frr. 504–526.
Q: 398: Epigr., Poem.
002 **Epigrammata in poetas ante Alexandrinorum
aetatem condita**, ed. W. Crönert, "De Lobone
Argivo," *Charites Friedrich Leo zum sechzigs-
ten Geburtstag dargebracht.* Berlin: Weidmann,
1911: 142–145.
Q: 377: Epigr.

0951 **LOGADIUS** Soph.
ante A.D. 6
x01 **Fragmentum ap. Paulum**.
CMG, vol. 9.2, p. 287.
Cf. PAULUS Med. (0715 001).
x02 **Fragmentum ap. Aëtium** (lib. 3).
CMG, vol. 8.1, p. 302.
Cf. AËTIUS Med. (0718 003).

LOGIA JESU
Cf. AGRAPHA (1776).

1466 **LOLLIANUS** Scr. Erot.
fiq Publius Hordeonius Lollianus Ephesius
A.D. 2

001 **Φοινικικά** (fragmenta), ed. A. Henrichs, *Die
Phoinikika des Lollianos* [*Papyrologische Texte
und Abhandlungen* 14. Bonn: Habelt, 1972]:
82–103.
Pap: 1,457: Narr. Fict.

1467 **LOLLIANUS** Soph.
A.D. 2: Ephesius
001 **Fragmenta**, ed. O. Schissel, "Lollianos aus
Ephesos," *Philologus* 82 (1927) 185–188.
Q

0143 **LOLLIUS BASSUS** Epigr.
A.D. 1: Smyrnaeus
001 **Epigrammata**, AG 5.125; 7.243, 372, 386, 391;
9.30, 53, 236, 279, 289; 10.102; 11.72.
AG 9.283: Cf. CRINAGORAS Epigr. (0154
001).
Q: 416: Epigr.

2178 **Cassius LONGINUS** Phil. et Rhet.
A.D. 3: Atheniensis, Palmyrenus
001 **Ars rhetorica**, ed. L. Spengel, *Rhetores Graeci*,
vol. 1. Leipzig: Teubner, 1853 (repr. Frankfurt
am Main: Minerva, 1966): 299–320.
Cod: 5,688: Rhet.
002 **Excerpta**, ed. Spengel, *op. cit.*, 325–328.
Cod: 683: Rhet.
004 **Fragmenta**, ed. M. Consbruch, *Hephaestionis
enchiridion cum commentariis veteribus.* Leipzig: Teubner, 1906 (repr. Stuttgart: 1971): 81–
89.
Τὰ προλεγόμενα εἰς τὸ τοῦ Ἡφαιστίωνος ἐγ-
χειρίδιον: pp. 81–87.
Περὶ βραχείας συλλαβῆς: pp. 87–89.
Cod: Gramm.
005 **Fragmenta**, ed. J. Toup, *Dionysii Longini quae
supersunt graece et latine.* Oxford: Clarendon
Press, 1778: 107–108, 120–131.
Q, Cod: Phil., Rhet.

0560 **[LONGINUS]** Rhet.
A.D. 1?
001 **De sublimitate**, ed. D.A. Russell, *'Longinus'.
On the sublime.* Oxford: Clarendon Press,
1964: 1–56.
Cod: 12,948: Rhet.

0561 **LONGUS** Scr. Erot.
A.D. 2?: fort. Lesbius
001 **Daphnis et Chloe**, ed. G. Dalmeyda, *Longus.
Pastorales (Daphnis et Chloé).* Paris: Les Belles
Lettres, 1934 (repr. 1971): 2–106.
Cod: 20,929: Narr. Fict.

0734 **<LUCAS Apostolus>** Med.
post A.D. 1
001 **Σκευασία ἁλατίου**, ed. J.L. Ideler, *Physici et
medici Graeci minores*, vol. 1. Berlin: Reimer,
1841 (repr. Amsterdam: Hakkert, 1963): 297.
Cod: 128: Med.

0062 **LUCIANUS** Soph.
A.D. 2: Samosatenus
Scholia: Cf. SCHOLIA IN LUCIANUM (5029).

001 **Phalaris**, ed. A.M. Harmon, *Lucian*, vol. 1.
Cambridge, Mass.: Harvard University Press,
1913 (repr. 1961): 2-30.
Cod: 2,951: Rhet.

002 **Hippias**, ed. Harmon, *op. cit.*, vol. 1, 34-44.
Cod: 999: Rhet.

003 **Bacchus**, ed. Harmon, *op. cit.*, vol. 1, 48-58.
Cod: 1,048: Rhet.

004 **Hercules**, ed. Harmon, *op. cit.*, vol. 1, 62-70.
Cod: 780: Rhet.

005 **Electrum**, ed. Harmon, *op. cit.*, vol. 1, 74-78.
Cod: 625: Rhet.

006 **Muscae encomium**, ed. Harmon, *op. cit.*, vol.
1, 82-94.
Cod: 1,206: Rhet., Encom.

007 **Nigrinus**, ed. M.D. Macleod, *Luciani opera*,
vol. 1. Oxford: Clarendon Press, 1972: 31-45.
Cod: 4,114: Phil., Epist.

008 **Demonax**, ed. Harmon, *op. cit.*, vol. 1, 142-
172.
Cod: 3,179: Biogr.

009 **De domo**, ed. Harmon, *op. cit.*, vol. 1, 176-
206.
Cod: 3,203: Rhet.

010 **Patriae encomium**, ed. Harmon, *op. cit.*, vol. 1,
210-218.
Cod: 984: Rhet., Encom.

011 **Macrobii**, ed. Harmon, *op. cit.*, vol. 1, 222-244.
Cod: 2,199: Paradox.

012 **Verae historiae**, ed. Macleod, *Luciani opera*,
vol. 1, 82-125.
Cod: 11,310: Satura, Narr. Fict.

013 **Calumniae non temere credendum**, ed. Harmon, *op. cit.*, vol. 1, 360-392.
Cod: 3,235: Rhet.

014 **Lis consonantium (= Judicium vocalium)**, ed.
Harmon, *op. cit.*, vol. 1, 396-408.
Cod: 1,188: Gramm., Satura

015 **Symposium**, ed. Macleod, *Luciani opera*, vol.
1, 144-163.
Cod: 4,777: Satura, Dialog.

016 **Cataplus**, ed. Harmon, *op. cit.*, vol. 2 (1915;
repr. 1960): 2-56.
Cod: 4,131: Satura, Dialog.

017 **Juppiter confutatus**, ed. Harmon, *op. cit.*, vol.
2, 60-86.
Cod: 2,377: Satura, Dialog.

018 **Juppiter tragoedus**, ed. Harmon, *op. cit.*, vol. 2,
90-168.
Cod: 6,865: Satura, Dialog.

019 **Gallus**, ed. Harmon, *op. cit.*, vol. 2, 172-238.
Cod: 5,842: Satura, Dialog.

020 **Prometheus**, ed. Harmon, *op. cit.*, vol. 2, 242-
264.
Cod: 2,419: Satura, Dialog.

021 **Icaromenippus**, ed. Harmon, *op. cit.*, vol. 2,
268-322.
Cod: 5,372: Satura, Dialog.

022 **Timon**, ed. Macleod, *Luciani opera*, vol. 1,
310-336.
Cod: 6,070: Satura, Dialog.

023 **Charon sive contemplantes**, ed. Harmon, *op.
cit.*, vol. 2, 396-446.
Cod: 4,340: Satura, Dialog.

024 **Vitarum auctio**, ed. Harmon, *op. cit.*, vol. 2,
450-510.
Cod: 3,747: Satura, Dialog.

025 **Revivescentes sive piscator**, ed. Harmon, *op.
cit.*, vol. 3 (1921; repr. 1969): 2-80.
Cod: 6,621: Satura, Dialog.

026 **Bis accusatus sive tribunalia**, ed. Harmon, *op.
cit.*, vol. 3, 84-150.
Cod: 5,861: Satura, Dialog.

027 **De sacrificiis**, ed. Harmon, *op. cit.*, vol. 3, 154-
170.
Cod: 1,830: Rhet.

028 **Adversus indoctum et libros multos ementem**,
ed. Harmon, *op. cit.*, vol. 3, 174-210.
Cod: 3,916: Satura, Invectiv.

029 **Somnium sive vita Luciani**, ed. Harmon, *op.
cit.*, vol. 3, 214-232.
Cod: 1,837: Rhet.

030 **De parasito sive artem esse parasiticam**, ed.
Harmon, *op. cit.*, vol. 3, 236-316.
Cod: 6,685: Satura, Dialog.

031 **Philopseudes sive incredulus**, ed. Harmon, *op.
cit.*, vol. 3, 320-380.
Cod: 6,401: Satura, Dialog.

032 **Dearum judicium**, ed. Harmon, *op. cit.*, vol. 3,
384-408.
Cod: 2,090: Satura, Dialog.

033 **De mercede conductis potentium familiaribus**,
ed. Harmon, *op. cit.*, vol. 3, 412-480.
Cod: 7,251: Satura

034 **Anacharsis**, ed. Harmon, *op. cit.*, vol. 4 (1925;
repr. 1961): 2-68.
Cod: 6,527: Rhet., Dialog.

035 **Menippus sive necyomantia**, ed. Harmon, *op.
cit.*, vol. 4, 72-108.
Cod: 3,379: Satura, Dialog.

036 **De luctu**, ed. Harmon, *op. cit.*, vol. 4, 112-130.
Cod: 1,802: Rhet.

037 **Rhetorum praeceptor**, ed. Harmon, *op. cit.*,
vol. 4, 134-170.
Cod: 3,572: Satura

038 **Alexander**, ed. Harmon, *op. cit.*, vol. 4, 174-
252.
Cod: 7,021: Satura, Invectiv.

039 **Imagines**, ed. Harmon, *op. cit.*, vol. 4, 256-
294.
Cod: 3,329: Rhet., Dialog.

040 **Pro imaginibus**, ed. Harmon, *op. cit.*, vol. 4,
298-334.
Cod: 3,585: Rhet., Dialog.

041 **De Syria dea**, ed. Harmon, *op. cit.*, vol. 4, 338-
410.
Cod: 6,367: Satura

042 **De morte Peregrini**, ed. Harmon, *op. cit.*, vol.
5 (1936; repr. 1972): 2-50.
Cod: 4,285: Satura, Invectiv.

043 **Fugitivi**, ed. Harmon, *op. cit.*, vol. 5, 54–98.
Cod: 3,278: Satura, Dialog.

044 **Toxaris vel amicitia**, ed. Harmon, *op. cit.*, vol. 5, 102–206.
Cod: 9,918: Narr. Fict., Dialog.

045 **De saltatione**, ed. Harmon, *op. cit.*, vol. 5, 210–288.
Cod: 7,126: Encom., Dialog.

046 **Lexiphanes**, ed. Harmon, *op. cit.*, vol. 5, 292–326.
Cod: 2,929: Satura, Dialog.

047 **Eunuchus**, ed. Harmon, *op. cit.*, vol. 5, 330–344.
Cod: 1,341: Satura, Dialog.

048 **De astrologia**, ed. Harmon, *op. cit.*, vol. 5, 348–368.
Cod: 2,001: Satura

049 **Pseudologista**, ed. Harmon, *op. cit.*, vol. 5, 372–414.
Cod: 4,004: Satura, Invectiv.

050 **Deorum concilium**, ed. Harmon, *op. cit.*, vol. 5, 418–440.
Cod: 1,902: Satura, Dialog.

051 **Tyrannicida**, ed. Harmon, *op. cit.*, vol. 5, 444–472.
Cod: 2,916: Rhet.

052 **Abdicatus**, ed. Harmon, *op. cit.*, vol. 5, 476–524.
Cod: 4,884: Rhet.

053 **Quomodo historia conscribenda sit**, ed. K. Kilburn, *Lucian*, vol. 6. Cambridge, Mass.: Harvard University Press, 1959 (repr. 1968): 2–72.
Cod: 7,639: Satura, Hist.

054 **Dipsades**, ed. Kilburn, *op. cit.*, vol. 6, 76–84.
Cod: 945: Rhet.

055 **Saturnalia**, ed. Kilburn, *op. cit.*, vol. 6, 88–138.
Cod: 5,286: Satura, Dialog.

056 **Herodotus**, ed. Kilburn, *op. cit.*, vol. 6, 142–150.
Cod: 937: Rhet.

057 **Zeuxis**, ed. Kilburn, *op. cit.*, vol. 6, 154–168.
Cod: 1,611: Rhet.

058 **Pro lapsu inter salutandum**, ed. Kilburn, *op. cit.*, vol. 6, 172–188.
Cod: 1,631: Rhet.

059 **Apologia**, ed. Kilburn, *op. cit.*, vol. 6, 192–212.
Cod: 2,101: Rhet.

060 **Harmonides**, ed. Kilburn, *op. cit.*, vol. 6, 216–224.
Cod: 995: Rhet.

061 **Hesiodus**, ed. Kilburn, *op. cit.*, vol. 6, 228–236.
Cod: 942: Rhet., Dialog.

062 **Scytha**, ed. Kilburn, *op. cit.*, vol. 6, 240–256.
Cod: 1,862: Rhet.

063 **Hermotimus**, ed. Kilburn, *op. cit.*, vol. 6, 260–414.
Cod: 14,455: Satura, Dialog.

064 **Prometheus es in verbis**, ed. Kilburn, *op. cit.*, vol. 6, 418–426.
Cod: 1,033: Rhet.

065 **Navigium**, ed. Kilburn, *op. cit.*, vol. 6, 430–486.
Cod: 5,504: Satura, Dialog.

066 **Dialogi mortuorum**, ed. Macleod, *Lucian*, vol. 7. Cambridge, Mass.: Harvard University Press, 1961: 2–174.
Cod: 11,885: Satura, Dialog.

067 **Dialogi marini**, ed. Macleod, *Lucian*, vol. 7, 178–236.
Cod: 4,197: Satura, Dialog.

068 **Dialogi deorum**, ed. Macleod, *Lucian*, vol. 7, 240–352.
Cod: 8,021: Satura, Dialog.

069 **Dialogi meretricii**, ed. Macleod, *Lucian*, vol. 7, 356–466.
Cod: 8,303: Satura, Dialog.

070 **Soloecista**, ed. Macleod, *Lucian*, vol. 8. Cambridge, Mass.: Harvard University Press, 1967: 4–44.
Cod: 1,875: Rhet., Satura, Dialog.

071 **Podagra**, ed. Macleod, *Lucian*, vol. 8, 324–354.
Cod: 1,813: Satura

x01 **Epigrammata**.
Cf. Pseudo-LUCIANUS Soph. (0061 009–010).

x02 **Oracula ficta**.
App. Anth. 6.296–307: Cf. ANTHOLOGIAE GRAECAE APPENDIX (7052 006).
Dup. partim 0062 038, 042.

0061 **Pseudo-LUCIANUS Soph.**
post A.D. 2

001 **Asinus**, ed. M.D. Macleod, *Lucian*, vol. 8. Cambridge, Mass.: Harvard University Press, 1967: 52–144.
Cod: 9,802: Narr. Fict.

002 **Amores**, ed. Macleod, *op. cit.*, 150–234.
Cod: 7,747: Satura, Dialog.

003 **Demosthenis encomium**, ed. Macleod, *op. cit.*, 238–300.
Cod: 5,224: Rhet., Dialog., Encom.

004 **Halcyon**, ed. Macleod, *op. cit.*, 306–316.
Cod: 948: Satura, Dialog.

005 **Ocypus**, ed. Macleod, *op. cit.*, 358–376.
Cod: 1,131: Satura

006 **Cynicus**, ed. Macleod, *op. cit.*, 380–410.
Cod: 2,487: Satura, Dialog.

007 **Philopatris**, ed. Macleod, *op. cit.*, 416–464.
Cod: 3,402: Satura, Dialog.

008 **Charidemus**, ed. Macleod, *op. cit.*, 468–502.
Cod: 3,500: Satura, Dialog., Encom.

009 **Epigramma**, ed. Macleod, *op. cit.*, 526.
Q: 33: Epigr.

010 **Epigrammata**, AG **6**.17; **7**.308; **9**.120, 367; **10**.26–29, 31, 35–37, 41–42, 122; **11**.274, 294, 396–397, 400–405, 410, 427–436; **16**.154, 163–164, 238.
AG 6.20: Cf. JULIANUS <Epigr.> (4050 001).
AG 6.164; 11.10, 68, 239, 278, 408: Cf. LUCILLIUS Epigr. (1468 001).
AG 7.339; 9.74; 10.30; 11.420: Cf. ANONYMI EPIGRAMMATICI (AG) (0138 001).
AG 10.58: Cf. PALLADAS Epigr. (2123 001).

AG 11.17: Cf. NICARCHUS II Epigr. (1532 001).

AG 11.129: Cf. CEREALIUS Epigr. (0151 001).
Q: 1,141: Epigr.

x01 **Nero.**
Cf. Flavius PHILOSTRATUS Soph. (0638 005).

x02 **Epistulae.**
Cf. ANACHARSIDIS EPISTULAE (0037 001).
Cf. PHALARIDIS EPISTULAE (0053 001).

x03 **Epigramma demonstrativum.**
App. Anth. 3.132: Cf. ANTHOLOGIAE GRAE-
CAE APPENDIX (7052 003).
Dup. 0061 009.

2957 **LUCIANUS** Theol. et Int. Vet. Test.
A.D. 4: Antiochenus

002 **In Job 2.9–10** (fragmentum), ed. D. Hagedorn,
Der Hiobkommentar des Arianers Julian [*Pa-
tristische Texte und Studien* 14. Berlin: De
Gruyter, 1973]: 30–33.
Q: Exeget.

x01 **Epistula ad Antiochenos** (fragmentum ap.
Chronicon paschale).
Dindorf, p. 516.
Cf. CHRONICON PASCHALE (2371 001).

1468 **LUCILLIUS** Epigr.
A.D. 1

001 **Epigrammata,** AG **5.**68; **6.**164, 166; **9.**55, 572;
11.10–11, 68–69, 75–81, 83–85, 87–95, 99–
101, 103–107, 111–116, 131–143, 148, 153–
155, 159–161, 163–165, 171–172, 174–179,
183–185, 189–192, 194, 196–197, 205–208,
210–212, 214–217, 233–234, 239–240, 245–
247, 249, 253–254, 256–259, 264–266, 276–
279, 295, 308–315, 388–393, 408.
AG 9.573: Cf. AMMIANUS Epigr. (0109 001).
AG 9.574; 11.282, 316, 394: Cf. ANONYMI
EPIGRAMMATICI (AG) (0138 001).
AG 10.122; 11.294, 433: Cf. Pseudo-
LUCIANUS Soph. (0061 010).
AG 11.173: Cf. PHILIPPUS Epigr. (1589 001).
AG 11.195: Cf. DIOSCORIDES Epigr. (0173
001).
AG 11.281, 293: Cf. PALLADAS Epigr. (2123
001).
Q: 3,903: Epigr.

0952 **LUCIUS** Med.
A.D. 1: fort. Tarsensis

x01 **Fragmenta ap. Galenum.**
K12.488, 787, 828; **13.**287, 292–293, 295, 746,
829, 850, 852, 853–854, 857, 934, 969.
Cf. GALENUS Med. (0057 076–077).

x02 **Fragmentum ap. Aëtium** (lib. 12).
Kostomiris, p. 80.
Cf. AËTIUS Med. (0718 012).

x03 **Fragmenta ap. Aëtium** (lib. 15).
Zervos, *Athena* 21, pp. 30, 92.
Cf. AËTIUS Med. (0718 015).

2686 **LUCULLUS** Epigr.
A.D. 3/4

x01 **Epigramma sepulcrale.**
App. Anth. 2.496: Cf. ANTHOLOGIAE GRAE-
CAE APPENDIX (7052 002).

1977 **Lucius Licinius LUCULLUS** Hist.
1 B.C.

001 **Testimonia,** FGrH #185: 2B:917.
NQ: 180: Test.

2439 **LUPERCUS** Gramm.
A.D. 3: Berytensis

001 **Testimonium,** FGrH #636: 3C:183–184.
NQ: 57: Test.

1469 **LYCEAS** Hist.
4 B.C.?: Naucratites

001 **Fragmenta,** FGrH #613: 3C:120–121.
Q: 389: Hist.

2212 **LYCEAS** Hist.
ante A.D. 2: fort. Argivus

001 **Fragmenta,** FGrH #312: 3B:21–22.
Q: 279: Hist.

002 **Titulus,** ed. H. Lloyd-Jones and P. Parsons,
Supplementum Hellenisticum. Berlin: De Gruyter, 1983: 257.
titul. 527.
NQ: 3: Epic.

0953 **LYCOMEDES** Med.
ante A.D. 1

x01 **Fragmentum ap. Galenum.**
K13.92.
Cf. GALENUS Med. (0057 076).

2246 **LYCON** Phil.
vel Lycus
4 B.C.: Tarentinus vel Iasensis

001 **Testimonia,** ed. H. Diels and W. Kranz, *Die
Fragmente der Vorsokratiker,* vol. 1, 6th edn.
Berlin: Weidmann, 1951 (repr. Dublin: 1966):
445–446.
test. 1–5.
NQ: 171: Test.

1138 **LYCON** Phil.
3 B.C.: Alexandrinus (Troadis)

001 **Fragmenta,** ed. F. Wehrli, *Lykon und Ariston
von Keos* [*Die Schule des Aristoteles,* vol. 6, 2nd
edn. Basel: Schwabe, 1968]: 11–15.
Testamentum: fr. 15.
Fragmenta incertae sedis: frr. 18, 20–25, 27–
28.
Fragmentum dubium: fr. 29.
Q: 958: Phil.

2444 **LYCOPHRON** Soph.
4 B.C.

001 **Testimonia,** ed. H. Diels and W. Kranz, *Die*

Fragmente der Vorsokratiker, vol. 2, 6th edn. Berlin: Weidmann, 1952 (repr. Dublin: 1966): 307–308.
test. 1–6.
NQ: 386: Test.

0341 **LYCOPHRON** Trag.
4–3 B.C.: Chalcidicus, Alexandrinus
Vita et Scholia: Cf. SCHOLIA IN LYCO-PHRONEM (5030).
001 **Fragmenta**, ed. B. Snell, *Tragicorum Graecorum fragmenta*, vol. 1. Göttingen: Vandenhoeck & Ruprecht, 1971: 275–278.
frr. 2–5 + tituli (frr. 1–1k, 4a–4c, 6–9).
Q: 141: Trag., Satyr.
002 **Alexandra**, ed. L. Mascialino, *Lycophronis Alexandra*. Leipzig: Teubner, 1964: 1–65.
Cod: 7,527: Trag.

0381 **LYCOPHRONIDES** Lyr.
4 B.C.
001 **Fragmenta**, ed. D.L. Page, *Poetae melici Graeci*. Oxford: Clarendon Press, 1962 (repr. 1967 (1st edn. corr.)): 446.
frr. 1–2.
Q: 49: Lyr.

0034 **LYCURGUS** Orat.
4 B.C.: Atheniensis
001 **Oratio in Leocratem**, ed. N.C. Conomis (post C. Scheibe & F. Blass), *Lycurgi oratio in Leocratem*. Leipzig: Teubner, 1970: 33–90.
Cod: 11,217: Orat.
002 **Fragmenta**, ed. Conomis, *op. cit.*, 91–92, 95–118, 120.
Ἀπολογισμὸς ὧν πεπολίτευται (fr. 1): pp. 91–92.
Κατ᾿ Ἀριστογείτονος (fr. 2): pp. 95–96.
Κατ᾿ Αὐτολύκου (fr. 3): p. 97.
Πρὸς Δημάδην ὑπὲρ τῶν εὐθυνῶν (fr. 4): p. 98.
Περὶ τῆς διοικήσεως (fr. 5): pp. 98–100.
Περὶ τῆς ἱερείας (fr. 6): pp. 100–105.
Περὶ τῆς ἱερωσύνης sive Κροκωνιδῶν διαδικασία πρὸς Κοιρωνίδας (fr. 7): pp. 105–107.
Κατὰ Ἰσχυρίου (fr. 8): p. 107.
Κατὰ Κηφισοδότου ὑπὲρ τῶν Δημάδου τιμῶν (fr. 9): pp. 107–108.
Κατὰ Λυκόφρονος εἰσαγγελία Α΄Β΄ (frr. 10–11): pp. 109–112.
Κατὰ Λυσικλέους (fr. 12): p. 113.
Πρὸς τὰς μαντείας sive Περὶ τῶν μαντειῶν (fr. 13): pp. 113–114.
Κατὰ Μενεσαίχμου εἰσαγγελία sive Δηλιακός (fr. 14): pp. 114–118.
Fragmenta sedis incertae (fr. 15): pp. 118, 120.
Q, Pap: 3,581: Orat.

1470 **LYCUS** Hist.
4–3 B.C.: Rheginus
001 **Testimonia**, FGrH #570: 3B:664.
NQ: 145: Test.

002 **Fragmenta**, FGrH #570: 3B:664–668.
Q: 1,198: Hist.
003 **Fragmenta**, ed. H.J. Mette, "Die 'Kleinen' griechischen Historiker heute," *Lustrum* 21 (1978) 31–32.
fr. 1 bis a–b.
Q: 88: Hist.

2267 **LYCUS** Hist.
post 4 B.C.
001 **Fragmenta**, FGrH #380: 3B:249–250.
Q: 225: Hist.

0955 **LYCUS** Med.
2–1 B.C.: Neapolitanus
Cf. et ANONYMUS NEAPOLITANUS Med. (1119).
x01 **Fragmenta ap. Oribasium**.
CMG, vol. **6.1.1**, pp. 278, 293; **6.1.2**, p. 28; **6.2.1**, p. 46; **6.3**, pp. 22, 119.
Cf. ORIBASIUS Med. (0722 001, 004).
x02 **Fragmentum ap. Paulum**.
CMG, vol. 9.2, p. 17.
Cf. PAULUS Med. (0715 001).
x03 **Fragmentum ap. Aëtium** (lib. 3).
CMG, vol. 8.1, p. 349.
Cf. AËTIUS Med. (0718 003).

0954 **LYCUS** Med.
A.D. 2: Macedonius
x01 **Fragmenta ap. Galenum**.
K18.1.198, 216 in CMG, vol. 5.10.3, pp. 4, 13.
Cf. GALENUS Med. (0057 093).

2580 **Joannes Laurentius LYDUS** Hist.
A.D. 6: Philadelphius, Constantinopolitanus
001 **De magistratibus populi Romani**, ed. A.C. Bandy, *Ioannes Lydus. On powers or the magistracies of the Roman state*. Philadelphia: American Philosophical Society, 1983: 2–256.
Cod: 30,840: Hist.
002 **De mensibus**, ed. R. Wünsch, *Ioannis Lydi liber de mensibus*. Leipzig: Teubner, 1898 (repr. Stuttgart: 1967): 1–184.
Cod: 32,714: Hist.
003 **De ostentis**, ed. C. Wachsmuth, *Ioannis Laurentii Lydi liber de ostentis et calendaria Graeca omnia*. Leipzig: Teubner, 1897: 3–160.
Cod: 22,720: Hist.

0471 **LYNCEUS** Comic.
4/3 B.C.: Samius
001 **Fragmentum**, ed. T. Kock, *Comicorum Atticorum fragmenta*, vol. 3. Leipzig: Teubner, 1888: 274–275.
fr. 1.
Q: 158: Comic.
002 **Fragmentum**, ed. A. Meineke, *Fragmenta comicorum Graecorum*, vol. 4. Berlin: Reimer, 1841 (repr. De Gruyter, 1970): 433.
Q: 157: Comic.

0230 **LYRICA ADESPOTA** (CA)
Varia

001 **Fragmenta lyrica**, ed. J.U. Powell, *Collectanea Alexandrina*. Oxford: Clarendon Press, 1925 (repr. 1970): 177–200.
Παρακλαυσίθυρον (fr. 1): pp. 177–179.
Mimi fragmenta (fr. 2): pp. 180–181.
Κωμαστής (fr. 3): pp. 181–182.
Παῖς ἀλέκτορα ἀπολέσας (fr. 4): pp. 182–183.
Marisaeum melos (fr. 5): p. 184.
Helenae querimonia (fr. 6): p. 185.
Saltus montanus (fr. 7): p. 185.
Aphorismi erotici (fr. 8): p. 186.
Fragmentum Pseudo-Alcmanis (fr. 9): p. 186.
Laudes Homeri (fr. 10): pp. 187–188.
Cassandrae oracula (fr. 11): pp. 188–189.
Choliambi anonymi (frr. 12–15): p. 190.
Scolia (sine titulo) (frr. 16–17, 21): pp. 190–192.
Musae (scolion) (fr. 18): p. 191.
Εὐφωρατίς (scolion) (fr. 19): p. 191.
Mnemosyne (scolion) (fr. 20): pp. 191–192.
Fragmenta dithyramborum (frr. 22–25): pp. 192–193.
Partheneion (fr. 26): p. 193.
Fragmenta Phalaecea (frr. 27–30): pp. 193–194.
Ἐπῳδοί (fr. 31): p. 194.
Nautarum cantilena (fr. 32): p. 195.
Ῥοδίοις ἀνέμοις (fr. 33): pp. 195–196.
Hymnus in Fortunam (fr. 34): p. 196.
Εἰς τὴν φύσιν Πυθαγόρου (fr. 35): p. 197.
Εἰς τὴν Ἶσιν (fr. 36): p. 198.
Aulodiae (fr. 37): pp. 199–200.
Monodia (fr. 38): p. 200.
fr. 31: Dup. partim CALLIMACHUS Philol. (0533 001) (Pfeiffer, fr. 197).
fr. 32: Dup. partim NAUTARUM CANTIUN-CULAE (0269 001) (Heitsch, 1:32–33).
fr. 33: Dup. partim NAUTARUM CANTI-UNCULAE (0269 002) (Heitsch, 1:33).
fr. 34: Dup. partim HYMNI ANONYMI (0742 012) (Heitsch, 1:172).
frr. 35–36: Dup. partim AEGIMIUS (0668 001) (Heitsch, 1:26–28, frr. 4–5).
fr. 37: Dup. ANONYMI AULODIA (1836 001).
fr. 37: Dup. partim SCOLIA ALPHABETICA (0273 001) (Heitsch, 1:38–40).
fr. 38: Dup. MONODIA (0277 001) (Heitsch, 1:45).
Q, Cod, Pap: 2,089: Hexametr., Lyr., Encom., Hymn., Mim.

0297 **LYRICA ADESPOTA** (PMG)
Varia

001 **Fragmenta**, ed. D.L. Page, *Poetae melici Graeci*. Oxford: Clarendon Press, 1962 (repr. 1967 (1st edn. corr.)): 484–546, 548–551.
frr. 1–9, 11–53, 55–63, 66–127.
Q, Pap, Epigr: 2,852: Lyr.

1471 **LYRICA ADESPOTA** (SLG)
Varia

001 **Fragmenta**, ed. D.L. Page, *Supplementum lyricis Graecis*. Oxford: Clarendon Press, 1974: 106–151.
fr. S317: ex Euphronii cratere.
fr. S318: ex Himerio, *Orat.* 46.
frr. S319–S386: *P. Oxy.* 32.2623.
frr. S387–S442: *P. Oxy.* 32.2624.
frr. S443–S444: *P. Oxy.* 32.2620.
frr. S445–S448: *P. Oxy.* 32.2626.
fr. S449: *P. Oxy.* 32.2627.
frr. S450–S451: *P. Oxy.* 32.2628.
fr. S452: *P. Oxy.* 32.2629.
fr. S453: *P. Oxy.* 32.2630.
fr. S454: *P. Oxy.* 32.2631.
frr. S455–S456: *P. Oxy.* 32.2632.
fr. S457: *P. Oxy.* 32.2633.
fr. S458: *P. Oxy.* 39.2879.
fr. S459: *P. Oxy.* 39.2880.
frr. S460–S472: *P. Oxy.* 32.2625.
fr. S473: *P. Oxy.* 32.2635.
fr. S474: *P. Oxy.* 29.2506.
fr. S475: *P. Mich.* 3499.
fr. S477: *P. Mich.* 3498.
Q, Pap, Epigr: 2,786: Lyr.

2402 **LYSANDER** Hist.
vel Cleon Halicarnassensis
5/4 B.C.

001 **Testimonia**, FGrH #583: 3B:694–695.
NQ: 578: Test.

2298 **LYSANIAS** Hist.
ante A.D. 2: Mallotes

001 **Fragmentum**, FGrH #426: 3B:322.
Q: 141: Hist.

0956 **LYSIAS** Med.
ante A.D. 1

x01 **Fragmentum ap. Galenum.**
K13.49.
Cf. GALENUS Med. (0057 076).

0540 **LYSIAS** Orat.
5–4 B.C.: Atheniensis

001 **De caede Eratosthenis**, ed. U. Albini, *Lisia. I discorsi*. Florence: Sansoni, 1955: 6–16.
Cod: 2,525: Orat.

002 **Epitaphius** [Sp.], ed. Albini, *op. cit.*, 320–337.
Cod: 4,251: Orat.

003 **Contra Simonem**, ed. Albini, *op. cit.*, 20–29.
Cod: 2,280: Orat.

004 Περὶ τραύματος ἐκ προνοίας ὑπὲρ οὗ καὶ πρὸς ὃν ‹ἄδηλον›, ed. Albini, *op. cit.*, 34–38.
Cod: 1,010: Orat.

005 **Pro Callia**, ed. Albini, *op. cit.*, 42–43.
Cod: 292: Orat.

006 **In Andocidem** [Sp.], ed. Albini, *op. cit.*, 342–353.
Cod: 2,744: Orat.

007 **Areopagiticus**, ed. Albini, *op. cit.*, 48–56.
Cod: 2,119: Orat.

008 **Κατηγορία πρὸς τοὺς συνουσιαστὰς κακολογιῶν** [Sp.], ed. Albini, *op. cit.*, 358–362.
Cod: 1,078: Orat.

009 **Pro milite** [Sp.], ed. Albini, *op. cit.*, 366–370.
Cod: 926: Orat.

010 **In Theomnestum 1**, ed. Albini, *op. cit.*, 60–66.
Cod: 1,544: Orat.

011 **In Theomnestum 2** [Sp.], ed. Albini, *op. cit.*, 372–374.
Cod: 574: Orat.

012 **In Eratosthenem**, ed. Albini, *op. cit.*, 70–90.
Cod: 5,052: Orat.

013 **In Agoratum**, ed. Albini, *op. cit.*, 94–116.
Cod: 5,074: Orat.

014 **In Alcibiadem 1**, ed. Albini, *op. cit.*, 120–130.
Cod: 2,501: Orat.

015 **In Alcibiadem 2**, ed. Albini, *op. cit.*, 132–134.
Cod: 632: Orat.

016 **Pro Mantitheo**, ed. Albini, *op. cit.*, 138–143.
Cod: 1,193: Orat.

017 **Πρὸς τὸ δημόσιον περὶ τῶν Ἐράτωνος χρημάτων**, ed. Albini, *op. cit.*, 148–151.
Cod: 621: Orat.

018 **Περὶ τῆς δημεύσεως <τῶν> τοῦ Νικίου ἀδελφοῦ ἐπίλογος**, ed. Albini, *op. cit.*, 156–161.
Cod: 1,410: Orat.

019 **Ὑπὲρ τῶν Ἀριστοφάνους χρημάτων, πρὸς τὸ δημόσιον**, ed. Albini, *op. cit.*, 166–180.
Cod: 3,260: Orat.

020 **Pro Polystrato** [Sp.], ed. Albini, *op. cit.*, 378–386.
Cod: 1,994: Orat.

021 **Ἀπολογία δωροδοκίας ἀπαράσημος**, ed. Albini, *op. cit.*, 184–189.
Cod: 1,354: Orat.

022 **Κατὰ τῶν σιτοπωλῶν**, ed. Albini, *op. cit.*, 194–199.
Cod: 1,175: Orat.

023 **In Pancleonem**, ed. Albini, *op. cit.*, 204–207.
Cod: 804: Orat.

024 **<Ὑπὲρ τοῦ ἀδυνάτου>**, ed. Albini, *op. cit.*, 212–218.
Cod: 1,485: Orat.

025 **[Δήμου καταλύσεως] ἀπολογία**, ed. Albini, *op. cit.*, 222–230.
Cod: 2,117: Orat.

026 **<Περὶ τῆς Εὐάνδρου δοκιμασίας>**, ed. Albini, *op. cit.*, 234–240.
Cod: 1,441: Orat.

027 **In Epicratem**, ed. Albini, *op. cit.*, 244–247.
Cod: 794: Orat.

028 **In Ergoclem**, ed. Albini, *op. cit.*, 252–256.
Cod: 959: Orat.

029 **In Philocratem**, ed. Albini, *op. cit.*, 260–263.
Cod: 704: Orat.

030 **In Nicomachum**, ed. Albini, *op. cit.*, 268–276.
Cod: 1,971: Orat.

031 **In Philonem**, ed. Albini, *op. cit.*, 280–288.
Cod: 1,894: Orat.

032 **In Diogitonem**, ed. Albini, *op. cit.*, 292–300.
Cod: 1,784: Orat.

033 **Olympiacus**, ed. Albini, *op. cit.*, 304–306.
Cod: 457: Orat.

034 **Περὶ τοῦ μὴ καταλῦσαι τὴν πάτριον πολιτείαν Ἀθήνησι**, ed. Albini, *op. cit.*, 310–313.
Cod: 584: Orat.

035 **Fragmenta**, ed. Albini, *op. cit.*, 394–407.
Πρὸς Ἱπποθέρσην, ὑπὲρ θεραπαίνης: pp. 394–397.
Πρὸς Θεόμνηστον: pp. 397–398.
Κατὰ Θεοζοτίδου: pp. 399–400.
Πρὸς Αἰσχίνης τὸν Σωκρατικὸν χρέως: pp. 400–401.
Πρὸς Ἀρχεβιάδην: p. 402.
Κατὰ Τείσιδος: pp. 402–404.
Πρὸς τοὺς Ἱπποκράτους παῖδας: pp. 404–405.
Ὑπὲρ Φερενίκου περὶ τοῦ Ἀνδροκλείδου κλήρου: pp.405–406.
Πρὸς Κινησίαν ὑπὲρ Φανίου παρανόμων: pp. 406–407.
Q, Pap: 2,516: Orat.

036 **Fragmenta**, ed. T. Thalheim, *Lysiae orationes* (editio maior), 2nd edn. Leipzig: Teubner, 1913: 328–366, 368–370.
frr. 1–102b, 109b: pp. 328–366, 368.
frr. 110–115 (epistulae): pp. 369–370.
fr. 116 (vocabula singula): p. 370.
Q, Pap: 5,940: Orat., Epist.

037 **Fragmentum**, *P. Rain.* 1.13.
Pap

2262 **LYSIMACHIDES** Hist.
1 B.C.–A.D. 1?

001 **Fragmenta**, FGrH #366: 3B:226–228.
Q: 560: Hist.

0574 **LYSIMACHUS** Hist.
4–3 B.C.: Alexandrinus

001 **Fragmenta**, FGrH #382: 3B:251–258.
fr. 21: *P. Oxy.* 15.1790.
Q, Pap: 2,021: Hist., Paradox.

002 **Fragmenta**, ed. H.J. Mette, "Die 'Kleinen' griechischen Historiker heute," *Lustrum* 21 (1978) 27–28.
frr. 12b, 23 (olim 21).
fr. 23: *P. Oxy.* 15.1790.
Q, Pap: 138: Hist.

1965 **LYSIMACHUS** Hist.
3–2 B.C.

001 **Testimonium**, FGrH #170: 2B:895.
NQ: 47: Test.

2427 **LYSIMACHUS** Hist.
1 B.C.–A.D. 1?

001 **Testimonia**, FGrH #621: 3C:154–155.
NQ: 101: Test.

002 **Fragmenta**, FGrH #621: 3C:155–156.
Q: 473: Hist.

0472 **LYSIPPUS** Comic.
5 B.C.

001 **Fragmenta**, ed. T. Kock, *Comicorum Atticorum fragmenta*, vol. 1. Leipzig: Teubner, 1880: 700–703.
frr. 1–5, 7–10 + tituli.
Q: 98: Comic.

002 **Fragmenta**, ed. A. Meineke, *Fragmenta comicorum Graecorum*, vol. 2.2. Berlin: Reimer, 1840 (repr. De Gruyter, 1970): 744–746, 748.
Q: 151: Comic.

003 **Titulus**, ed. C. Austin, *Comicorum Graecorum fragmenta in papyris reperta*. Berlin: De Gruyter, 1973: 121.
NQ: 2: Comic.

0633 **<LYSIS>** Phil.
4/2 B.C.: Tarentinus

001 **Epistula ad Hipparchum**, ed. H. Thesleff, *The Pythagorean texts of the Hellenistic period*. Åbo: Åbo Akademi, 1965: 111–114.
Q: 545: Phil., Epist.

002 **Testimonia**, ed. H. Diels and W. Kranz, *Die Fragmente der Vorsokratiker*, vol. 1, 6th edn. Berlin: Weidmann, 1951 (repr. Dublin: 1966): 420–421.
test. 1–5: auctores alii nominantur Archippus et Opsimus.
NQ: 200: Test.

1472 **LYSISTRATUS** Epigr.
5 B.C.: Atheniensis

001 **Epigramma**, AG 9.509.
Q: 6: Epigr.

2318 **MACARIUS** Hist.
3 B.C.?: Cous

001 **Fragmenta**, FGrH #456: 3B:384.
fr. 1b: Dup. partim PHYLARCHUS Hist. (1609 002–003).
Q: 83: Hist., Hexametr.

MACARIUS Paroemiogr.
A.D. 14: Philadelphius
Cf. Macarius CHRYSOCEPHALUS Paroemiogr. (9008).

MACARIUS Scr. Eccl.
A.D. 4: Aegyptius
Cf. Pseudo-MACARIUS Scr. Eccl. (2109).

2109 **Pseudo-MACARIUS** Scr. Eccl.
vel Symeon vel Macarius-Symeon
A.D. 4: Mesopotamius

001 **Sermones 64** (collectio B), ed. H. Berthold, *Makarios/Symeon Reden und Briefe*, 2 vols. [*Die griechischen christlichen Schriftsteller*. Berlin: Akademie-Verlag, 1973]: 1:3–265; 2:3–219.
Cod: 142,336: Homilet.

002 **Homiliae spirituales 50** (collectio H), ed. H. Dörries, E. Klostermann and M. Kroeger, *Die 50 geistlichen Homilien des Makarios* [*Patristische Texte und Studien* 4. Berlin: De Gruyter, 1964]: 1–322.
Cod: 77,443: Homilet.

003 **Sermones 1–22, 24–27**, ed. E. Klostermann and H. Berthold, *Neue Homilien des Makarius/Symeon* [*Texte und Untersuchungen* 72. Berlin: Akademie-Verlag, 1961]: 1–113, 128–158.
Cod: 34,616: Homilet.

004 **Homiliae 7** (collectio HA), ed. G.L. Marriott, *Macarii anecdota* [*Harvard Theological Studies* 5. Cambridge, Mass.: Harvard University Press, 1918 (repr. New York: Kraus, 1969)]: 19–48.
Cod: 9,200: Homilet.

005 **Epistula magna**, ed. W. Jaeger, *Two rediscovered works of ancient Christian literature: Gregory of Nyssa and Macarius*. Leiden: Brill, 1954: 233–301.
Cod: 13,588: Epist.

006 **Sermo 23** (recensio excerpta), ed. Klostermann and Berthold, *op. cit.*, 114, 116, 118, 120, 122, 124, 126.
Cod: 597: Homilet.

007 **Sermo 23** (recensio completa), ed. Klostermann and Berthold, *op. cit.*, 115, 117, 119, 121, 123, 125, 127.
Cod: 1,957: Homilet.

008 **Sermo 28** (recensio expletior), ed. Klostermann and Berthold, *op. cit.*, 160, 162, 164, 166–170.
Cod: 1,735: Homilet.

009 **Sermo 28** (recensio brevior), ed. Klostermann and Berthold, *op. cit.*, 161, 163, 165.
Cod: 886: Homilet.

010 **Preces**, MPG 34: 445–448.
Cod: 366: Liturg.

011 **Apophthegmata**, MPG 34: 236–261.
Cod: 4,871: Gnom., Eccl.

012 **Opusculum 1** (= **De custodia cordis**), MPG 34: 821–841.
Cod: 4,110: Eccl.

013 **Sermo 17** (excerpta), ed. Klostermann and Berthold, *op. cit.*, 91–94.
Cod: 147: Homilet.

0202 **MACE(DONIUS)** Lyr.
Incertum

001 **Paean in Apollinem et Aesculapium** (*IG* 3.1.171b), ed. J.U. Powell, *Collectanea Alexandrina*. Oxford: Clarendon Press, 1925 (repr. 1970): 138–139.
Epigr: 147: Lyr., Hymn.

x01 **Epigramma exhortatorium et supplicatorium**.
App. Anth. 4.53(?): Cf. ANTHOLOGIAE GRAECAE APPENDIX (7052 004).
Dup. 0202 001.

1473 **MACEDONIUS I** Epigr.
1 B.C.?: Thessalonicensis

001 **Epigrammata**, AG 9.275; 11.27, 39.
Q: 85: Epigr.

4064 MACEDONIUS II Epigr.
A.D. 6: Thessalonicensis

001 **Epigrammata**, AG **5**.223–225, 227, 229, 231,
233, 235, 238, 240, 243, 245, 247, 271; **6**.30,
40, 56, 69–70, 73, 83, 175–176; **7**.566; **9**.625,
645, 648–649; **10**.67, 70–71; **11**.58–59, 61, 63,
366, 370, 374–375, 380; **16**.51.
Q: 1,643: Epigr.

0957 MACHAERION Med.
ante A.D. 2

x01 **Fragmentum ap. Galenum.**
K13.797.
Cf. GALENUS Med. (0057 077).

x02 **Fragmentum ap. Paulum.**
CMG, vol. 9.2, p. 364.
Cf. PAULUS Med. (0715 001).

x03 **Fragmentum ap. Aëtium** (lib. 15).
Zervos, *Athena* 21, p. 41.
Cf. AËTIUS Med. (0718 015).

MACHAON Med.
Cf. ASCLEPIUS et MACHAON Med. (0879).

0473 MACHON Comic.
3 B.C.: Corinthius, Sicyonius, Alexandrinus

001 **Fragmenta**, ed. A.S.F. Gow, *Machon. The fragments.* Cambridge: Cambridge University
Press, 1965: 35–56.
frr. 1–21.
Q: 2,986: Comic.

002 **Fragmenta**, ed. T. Kock, *Comicorum Atticorum fragmenta*, vol. 3. Leipzig: Teubner,
1888: 324–325.
frr. 1–2.
Q: 96: Comic.

003 **Fragmenta**, ed. A. Meineke, *Fragmenta comicorum Graecorum*, vol. 4. Berlin: Reimer, 1841
(repr. De Gruyter, 1970): 496–497.
Q: 96: Comic.

2339 MAEANDRIUS Hist.
ante 3 B.C.: Milesius

001 **Fragmenta**, FGrH #491: 3B:459–461.
frr. 1–9.
fr. 1a–c: *Inscr. Priene* 37.
Q, Epigr: 960: Hist.

1474 Quintus MAECIUS Epigr.
1 B.C.

001 **Epigrammata**, AG **5**.114, 117, 130, 133; **6**.33,
89, 230(?), 233; **9**.249, 403, 411; **16**.198.
AG 7.635: Cf. ANTIPHILUS Epigr. (0118 001).
Q: 467: Epigr.

5002 *MAGICA*
Varia

001 **Papyri magicae**, ed. K. Preisendanz and A.
Henrichs, *Papyri Graecae magicae. Die griechischen Zauberpapyri*, vols. 1–2, 2nd edn. Stuttgart: Teubner, 1:1973; 2:1974: 1:1–62, 66–200;
2:1–208.

P1 (*P. Berol.* 5025): vol. 1, pp. 1–18.
P2 (*P. Berol.* 5026): vol. 1, pp. 18–30.
P3 (*P. Louvre* 2391): vol. 1, pp. 30–62.
P4 (*P. Bibl. Nat. suppl. gr.* 574): vol. 1, pp. 66–
180.
P5 (*P. Brit. Mus.* XLVI): vol. 1, pp. 180–198.
P5a (*P. Holmiensis*): vol. 1, p. 198.
P6 (*P. Brit. Mus.* XLVII): vol. 1, pp. 198–200.
P7–P11c (*P. Brit. Mus.* CXXI–CXXV,
CXLVII–CXLVIII): vol. 2, pp. 1–56.
P12–P13 (*P. Mus. van Oudheden, Leiden* J384
& J395): vol. 2, pp. 57–131.
P14 (*P. Brit. Mus.* 10070 + *P. Leiden* J383):
vol. 2, pp. 132–133.
P15 (*P. Alex.* inv. 491): vol. 2, pp. 133–134.
P16 (*P. Louvre* 3378): vol. 2, pp. 135–137.
P17a–c (*P. Strassb.* 1167, 1179, 574): vol. 2,
pp. 138–140.
P18a–P22b (*P. Berol.* 955, 956, 9909, 11737,
7504, 9566, 9873, 13895): vol. 2, pp. 140–150.
P23–P24b (*P. Oxy.* 3.412, 6.886, 887, 959):
vol. 2, pp. 150–152.
P25c (amuletum Cairense): vol. 2, p. 153.
P26–P29 (*P. Oxy.* 12.1477, 1478; 16.2061,
2062, 2063; 11.1383): vol. 2, pp. 153–155.
P30a–f (*P. Fayûm* 137; *P. Rain.* 26; *P. Berol.*
7318/19, 13302, 13300, 13304): vol. 2, p. 156.
P31a–c (*P. Fayûm* 138; *P. Oxy.* 8.1148, 1149):
vol. 2, p. 157.
P32 (*P. Harawa* 312): vol. 2, pp. 157–158.
P32a (*P. Harawa* in Ashmol. Mus.): vol. 2, p.
158.
P33 (*P. Tebtunis* 275): vol. 2, p. 159.
P34 (*P. Fayûm* 5): vol. 2, pp. 159–160.
P35 (*PSI* 29): vol. 2, pp. 160–162.
P36–P39 (*P. Oslo* 1, 2, 3, 4): vol. 2, pp. 163–
177.
P40 (*P. gr. Nat. Bibl.* Vienna 1): vol. 2, p. 178.
P41–P47 (*P. Rain.* 13, 16b, 12, 16, 14, 15, 2):
vol. 2, pp. 179–181.
P50 (*Perg. R.* 527 in exhibitione, catalog. 125):
vol. 2, p. 182.
P51–P52 (*P. Univ. Bibl. Leipzig* 9.418,
46.429): vol. 2, pp. 182–184.
P57 (*P. Mich.*, cryptogram.): vol. 2, pp. 184–
186.
P58 (*P. Giessen* 266 [= *P. Iand.* 87]): vol. 2, p.
186.
P59 (*P. Cairo* 10563): vol. 2, p. 187.
P60 (*P. Brux.* 10563): vol. 2, p. 188.
P61 (*P. Brit. Mus.* 10588): vol. 2, pp. 189–192.
P62 (*P. Leiden* 21): vol. 2, pp. 192–196.
P63–P65 (*P. Vienna* 323, 29273, 29272): vol.
2, p. 197.
P66–P68 (*P. Cairo* 60139, 60140, 60636): vol.
2, pp. 198–201.
P69–P71 (*P. Mich.* 1463, 7, 193): vol. 2, pp.
201–203.
P72 (*P. Oslo* 75): vol. 2, p. 204.
P73–P74 (*P. Oxy.* 9.1213, 6.923): vol. 2, p.
205.

P75 (*P. Berol.* 13307): vol. 2, p. 205.
P76 (*P. Brit. Mus.* 1267d): vol. 2, p. 205.
P77 (*P. Harris* 55): vol. 2, p. 206.
P78 (*P. Heidelb.* 2170): vol. 2, p. 207.
P79–P80 (*P. Prag.* 1.18, 21): vol. 2, pp. 207–208.
P81 (*P. Oxy.* 12.1566): vol. 2, p. 208.
Pap: 70,696: Magica
002 **Papyri magicae** (fragmenta Christiana), ed. Preisendanz and Henrichs, *op. cit.*, vol. 2, 209–232.
P1–P2 (*P. Oxy.* 6.925, 7.1060): pp. 209–210.
P2a (*P. gr. Vienna* 19889): p.210.
P3 (*P. Oslo* 5): pp. 210–211.
P4–5b (*P. Oxy.* 8.1077, 6.924, 8.1151): pp. 211–213.
P5c (*P. Cairo* 10696): pp. 213–214.
P5d (*P. Brit. Mus.* 1176): p. 214.
P6a–c (*P. Oxy.* 8.1152; 7.1058, 1059): pp. 214–215.
P6d (*P. gr. Vienna* 19909): p. 215.
P7–8b (*P. Oxy.* 11.1384, 16.1926, 8.1150): pp. 215–216.
P9 (*P. Berol.* 954): p. 217.
P10–P12 (*P. Rain.* 1, 3, 5): pp. 218–220.
P13–P13a (*P. Cairo* 10263, 67188): pp. 220–222.
P14 (*P. Heidelb.* 1359): p. 223.
Pap: 3,545: Magica
003 **Papyri magicae** (ostraca), ed. Preisendanz and Henrichs, *op. cit.*, vol. 2, 233–235.
Pap: 408: Magica
004 **Papyri magicae** (tabulae), ed. Preisendanz and Henrichs, *op. cit.*, vol. 2, 236.
Pap: 194: Magica

0474 **MAGNES** Comic.
5 B.C.
001 **Fragmenta**, ed. T. Kock, *Comicorum Atticorum fragmenta*, vol. 1. Leipzig: Teubner, 1880: 7–9.
frr. 1–7 + tituli.
Q: 55: Comic.
002 **Fragmenta**, ed. A. Meineke, *Fragmenta comicorum Graecorum*, vol. 2.1. Berlin: Reimer, 1839 (repr. De Gruyter, 1970): 9–11.
Q: 46: Comic.
003 **Fragmentum**, ed. J. Demiańczuk, *Supplementum comicum*. Krakau: Nakładem Akademii, 1912 (repr. Hildesheim: Olms, 1967): 54.
fr. 1.
Q: 2: Comic.

2157 **MAGNUS** Hist.
A.D. 4: Carrhaeus
001 **Testimonia**, FGrH #225: 2B:951–952.
NQ: 148: Test.
002 **Fragmenta**, FGrH #225: 2B:952–954.
Q: 710: Hist.

0961 **MAGNUS** Med.
A.D. 1: Philadelphius

x01 **Fragmenta ap. Galenum**.
K13.80, 829, 831.
Cf. GALENUS Med. (0057 076–077).

0962 **MAGNUS** Med.
ante A.D. 2: Tarsensis
x01 **Fragmentum ap. Galenum**.
K13.313.
Cf. GALENUS Med. (0057 076).

0965 **MAGNUS** Med.
A.D. 2: Ephesius
x01 **Fragmentum ap. Galenum**.
K8.640–641.
Cf. GALENUS Med. (0057 059).
x02 **Fragmentum ap. Oribasium**.
CMG, vol. 6.2.2, p. 217.
Cf. ORIBASIUS Med. (0722 003).

0959 **MAGNUS** Med.
A.D. 4
001 **Epigramma**, AG 16.270.
Q: 25: Epigr.

0960 **MAGNUS Archiatrus** Med.
A.D. 2
x01 **Fragmentum ap. Galenum**.
K14.262.
Cf. GALENUS Med. (0057 079).

0963 **MAGNUS ὁ κλινικός** Med.
ante A.D. 2
x01 **Fragmentum ap. Galenum**.
K12.829.
Cf. GALENUS Med. (0057 076).

1807 **MAGO** <Med.>
3/2 B.C.: Carthaginiensis
x01 **Fragmentum ap. Hippiatrica**.
Oder & Hoppe, vol. 1, pp. 141–142.
Cf. HIPPIATRICA (0738 001).

0920 **[MAIA]** Med.
Incertum
x01 **Fragmentum ap. Galenum**.
K13.840.
Cf. GALENUS Med. (0057 077).

1475 **MAIISTAS** Epic.
3 B.C.
001 **Aretalogia** (*IG* 11.4.1299), ed. J.U. Powell, *Collectanea Alexandrina*. Oxford: Clarendon Press, 1925 (repr. 1970): 69–71.
Epigr: 456: Epic.

2382 **MALACUS** Hist.
ante A.D. 3
001 **Fragmentum**, FGrH #552: 3B:539.
Q: 70: Hist.

2582 **MALCHUS** Hist.
A.D. 5–6: Philadelphius, Constantinopolitanus

001 **Fragmenta**, FHG 4: 111–132.
Q: Hist.

1476 **MAMERCUS** Eleg.
4 B.C.
001 **Epigramma**, ed. E. Diehl, *Anthologia lyrica Graeca*, fasc. 1, 3rd edn. Leipzig: Teubner, 1949: 112.
Q: 12: Epigr.
x01 **Epigramma dedicatorium**.
App. Anth. 1.84: Cf. ANTHOLOGIAE GRAE-CAE APPENDIX (7052 001).
Dup. 1476 001.

3074 **Constantinus MANASSES** Poeta et Hist.
A.D. 12: Constantinopolitanus
001 **Compendium chronicum**, ed. I. Bekker, *Constantini Manassis breviarium historiae metricum* [*Corpus scriptorum historiae Byzantinae*. Bonn: Weber, 1837]: 1–286.
Cod: Hist., Chronogr., Poem.
002 **Vita Oppiani**, ed. A. Colonna, "De Oppiani vita antiquissima," *Bollettino del comitato per la preparazione dell'edizione nazionale dei classici greci e latini* 12 (1964) 38–39.
Cod: Biogr.
003 **Carmen astronomicum** (olim sub auctore Theodoro Prodromo), ed. E. Miller, "Poëmes astronomiques de Théodore Prodrome et de Jean Camatère," *Notices et extraits des manuscrits de la Bibliothèque Nationale* 23.2 (1872) 8–39.
Cod: Astron., Poem.
x01 **Christus patiens** (fort. auctore Constantino Manasse).
Tuilier, pp. 124–338.
Cf. GREGORIUS NAZIANZENUS Theol. (2022 003).

2583 **MANETHO** Astrol.
A.D. 4?
001 Ἀποτελεσματικά, ed. A. Koechly, *Poetae bucolici et didactici*. Paris: Didot, 1862: 41–101.
Cod

1477 **MANETHO** Hist.
3 B.C.: Aegyptius
001 **Testimonia**, FGrH #609: 3C:5–10.
NQ: 1,358: Test.
002 **Fragmenta**, FGrH #609: 3C:11–13, 16–55, 80–112.
frr. 1–24 = Manetho.
frr. 25–28 = Pseudo-Manetho.
fr. 11: *P. Baden* 59.
Q, Pap: 11,945: Hist., Chronogr., Epist.

1478 **Pseudo-MANETHO** Hist.
Incertum
001 **Fragmenta**, FGrH #610: 3C:112–118.
Cf. et MANETHO Hist. (1477 002).
Q: 1,628: Hist., Chronogr.

0966 **MANETHO** Med.
3 B.C.?
x01 **Fragmentum ap. Paulum**.
CMG, vol. 9.2, p. 324.
Cf. PAULUS Med. (0715 001).

MANI-CODEX
A.D. 4
Cf. ANONYMUS MANICHAEUS Biogr. (4282).

0967 **MANTIAS** Med.
2 B.C.
x01 **Fragmenta ap. Galenum**.
K13.162, 751.
Cf. GALENUS Med. (0057 076–077).

0200 *MANTISSA PROVERBIORUM*
Incertum
001 **Mantissa proverbiorum**, ed. E.L. von Leutsch, *Corpus paroemiographorum Graecorum*, vol. 2. Göttingen: Vandenhoeck & Ruprecht, 1851 (repr. Hildesheim: Olms, 1958): 745–779.
Cod: 4,302: Paroem.

2716 **MANUEL** Epigr.
A.D. 9
x01 **Epigramma exhortatorium et supplicatorium**.
App. Anth. 4.115: Cf. ANTHOLOGIAE GRAE-CAE APPENDIX (7052 004).

2585 **MARCELLINUS** Biogr.
fiq Marcellinus Gramm. et Rhet.
A.D. 4?
001 **Vita Thucydidis**, ed. H.S. Jones, *Thucydidis historiae*, vol. 1. Oxford: Clarendon Press, 1942 (repr. 1970 (1st edn. rev.)): xi–xx.
Cod: Biogr.

4234 **MARCELLINUS** Gramm. et Rhet.
fiq Marcellinus Biogr.
A.D. 5?
Cf. et SYRIANI, SOPATRI ET MARCELLINI SCHOLIA AD HERMOGENIS STATUS (2047).
x01 **Introductio in prolegomena Hermogenis artis rhetoricae** (fort. auctore Marcellino Gramm. et Rhet.).
Walz, vol. 4, pp. 1–38.
Cf. ANONYMI IN HERMOGENEM (5024 001).

0667 **MARCELLINUS I** Med.
A.D. 2
001 **De pulsibus**, ed. H. Schöne, "Marcellinos' Pulslehre. Ein griechisches Anekdoton," *Festschrift zur 49. Versammlung deutscher Philologen und Schulmänner*. Basel: Birkhäuser, 1907: 455–471.
Cod: 5,088: Med.

0968 **MARCELLINUS II** Med.
ante A.D. 1

x01 **Fragmentum ap. Galenum.**
K13.90.
Cf. GALENUS Med. (0057 076).

x02 **Fragmentum ap. Alexandrum Trallianum.**
Puschmann, vol. 2, p. 357.
Cf. ALEXANDER Med. (0744 003).

2676 **MARCELLUS** Epigr.
A.D. 2?

x01 **Epigrammata dedicatoria.**
App. Anth. 1.263–264: Cf. ANTHOLOGIAE
GRAECAE APPENDIX (7052 001).

2458 **MARCELLUS** Hist.
Incertum

001 **Fragmenta,** FGrH #671: 3C:283–284.
Q: 298: Hist.

0281 **MARCELLUS** Poet. Med.
A.D. 2: Sidetes

001 **De piscibus fragmentum,** ed. E. Heitsch, *Die
griechischen Dichterfragmente der römischen
Kaiserzeit,* vol. 2. Göttingen: Vandenhoeck &
Ruprecht, 1964: 17–22.
Cod: 633: Hexametr., Med., Nat. Hist.

x01 **Fragmentum ap. Paulum.**
CMG, vol. 9.1, p. 331.
Cf. PAULUS Med. (0715 001).

x02 **Fragmentum ap. Aëtium** (lib. 6).
CMG, vol. 8.2, p. 151.
Cf. AËTIUS Med. (0718 006).

2041 **MARCELLUS** Theol.
A.D. 4: Ancyranus

001 **Fragmenta,** ed. E. Klostermann and G.C. Hansen, *Eusebius Werke,* vol. 4, 2nd edn. [*Die
griechischen christlichen Schriftsteller* 14. Berlin: Akademie-Verlag, 1972]: 185–215.
Fragmenta e libro contra Asterium (frr. 1–128):
pp. 185–214.
Epistula ad Julium papam (fr. 129): pp. 214–
215.
Q: 11,193: Theol., Epist.

002 **De sancta ecclesia** [Sp.] (olim auctore Anthimo
vel Marcello), ed. G. Mercati, *Anthimi Nicomediensis episcopi et martyris de sancta ecclesia
in Note di letteratura biblica e cristiana antica
[Studi e Testi* 5. Rome: Biblioteca Apostolica
Vaticana, 1905]: 87–98.
Q

004 **Expositio fidei,** ed. H. Nordberg, *Athanasiana
I* [*Commentationes humanarum litterarum*
30.2. Helsinki: Centraltryckeriet, 1962]: 49–56.
Cod: 1,107: Theol.

005 **De incarnatione et contra Arianos,** MPG 26:
984–1028.
Cod: 7,510: Theol.

x01 **Sermo major de fide.**
Athanasius, *Sermo major de fide* [Sp.].
Cf. ATHANASIUS Theol. (2035 023).

x02 **Contra theopaschitas.**
Athanasius, *Epist. ad Liberium* [Sp.].
Cf. ATHANASIUS Theol. (2035 033).

1479 ***MARCI AURELII EPISTULA***
post A.D. 2
Cf. et MARCUS AURELIUS ANTONINUS Imperator Phil. (0562).

001 **Epistula ad senatum, qua testatur Christianos
victoriae causam fuisse,** ed. J.C.T. Otto, *Corpus apologetarum Christianorum saeculi secundi,* vol. 1, 3rd edn. Jena: Mauke, 1876
(repr. Wiesbaden: Sändig, 1969): 246–252.
Cod: 448: Epist.

4003 **MARCIANUS** Geogr.
A.D. 3/5: Heracleensis

001 **Periplus maris exteri,** ed. K. Müller, *Geographi
Graeci minores,* vol. 1. Paris: Didot, 1855 (repr.
Hildesheim: Olms, 1965): 515–562.
Cod: 12,066: Perieg.

002 **Menippi periplus maris interni** (epitome Marciani), ed. Müller, *op. cit.,* 563–572.
Cod: 2,439: Perieg.

003 **Artemidori geographia** (epitome Marciani), ed.
Müller, *op. cit.,* 574–576.
Q: 510: Geogr.

0969 **MARCIANUS** Med.
ante A.D. 4: Africanus

x01 **Fragmentum ap. Oribasium.**
CMG, vol. 6.2.2, p. 243.
Cf. ORIBASIUS Med. (0722 003).

x02 **Fragmentum ap. Aëtium** (lib. 7).
CMG, vol. 8.2, p. 387.
Cf. AËTIUS Med. (0718 007).

x03 **Fragmentum ap. Aëtium** (lib. 8).
CMG, vol. 8.2, p. 485.
Cf. AËTIUS Med. (0718 008).

x04 **Fragmentum ap. Aëtium** (lib. 9).
Zervos, *Athena* 23, pp. 331, 389.
Cf. AËTIUS Med. (0718 009).

x05 **Fragmentum ap. Aëtium** (lib. 11).
Daremberg-Ruelle, p. 571.
Cf. AËTIUS Med. (0718 011).

x06 **Fragmentum ap. Aëtium** (lib. 12).
Kostomiris, p. 28.
Cf. AËTIUS Med. (0718 012).

1035 **MARCINUS** Med.
ante A.D. 6: Thrax

x01 **Fragmentum ap. Alexandrum Trallianum.**
Puschmann, vol. 1, p. 565.
Cf. ALEXANDER Med. (0744 003).

2958 **MARCION** Theol.
A.D. 2: Sinopensis

001 **Antitheses,** ed. A. von Harnack, *Marcion: Das
Evangelium vom fremden Gott,* 2nd edn. [*Texte
und Untersuchungen* 45. Leipzig: Hinrichs,
1924]: 256*–313*.
Q

002 **Evangelium**, ed. von Harnack, *op. cit.*, 183*–
240*.
Q

003 **Apostolicum**, ed. von Harnack, *op. cit.*, 67*–
127*.
Q

1823 **MARCUS** Gnost.
A.D. 2
001 **Fragmenta**, ed. W. Völker, *Quellen zur Ge-
schichte der christlichen Gnosis.* Tübingen:
Mohr, 1932: 136–141.
Q

0970 **MARCUS** Med.
ante A.D. 2
x01 **Fragmentum ap. Galenum**.
K12.750.
Cf. GALENUS Med. (0057 076).

0562 **MARCUS AURELIUS ANTONINUS Imperator** Phil.
A.D. 2: Romanus
Cf. et MARCI AURELII EPISTULA (1479).
001 **Τὰ εἰς ἑαυτόν**, ed. A.S.L. Farquharson, *The
meditations of the emperor Marcus Aurelius*,
vol. 1. Oxford: Clarendon Press, 1944 (repr.
1968): 4–250.
Cod: 29,724: Phil.

0972 **MARCUS TELENTIUS** Med.
ante A.D. 2
x01 **Fragmentum ap. Galenum**.
K13.973.
Cf. GALENUS Med. (0057 077).

MARGITES
Cf. [HOMERUS] <Epic.> (0253).

1480 **MARIA JUDAEA** Alchem.
3/2 B.C.
001 **Fragmenta**, ed. M. Berthelot, *Collection des
anciens alchimistes grecs.* Paris: Steinheil, 1887
(repr. London: Holland Press, 1963): 93, 102,
103, 146, 149, 152, 157, 169, 173, 182, 192,
193, 195, 196–197, 198, 200, 201, 236–237,
351, 356, 357, 382, 404.
Q: Alchem.

4073 **MARIANUS** Epigr.
A.D. 5–6
001 **Epigrammata**, AG **9**.626–627, 657, 668–669;
16.201.
Q: 343: Epigr.

4074 **MARINUS** Epigr.
fiq Marinus Phil.
Incertum
Cf. et MARINUS Phil. (4075).
001 **Epigrammata**, AG 1.23, 28.
Q: 54: Epigr.

0973 **MARINUS** Med.
A.D. 2: fort. Alexandrinus
x01 **Fragmentum ap. Galenum**.
K13.25.
Cf. GALENUS Med. (0057 076).

4075 **MARINUS** Phil.
A.D. 5: Neapolitanus (Samariae)
001 **Epigrammata**, AG 9.196–197.
Q: 53: Epigr.
002 **Commentarium in Euclidis data**, ed. H.
Menge, *Euclidis opera omnia*, vol. 6. Leipzig:
Teubner, 1896: 234–256.
Cod: Comm.
003 **Vita Procli**, ed. R. Masullo, *Marino di Neapoli.
Vita di Proclo.* Naples: d'Auria, 1985.
Cod: Biogr.

2432 *MARMOR PARIUM*
3 B.C.
001 **Marmor Parium** (*IG* 12.5, 444), FGrH #239:
2B:992–1005.
Epigr: 2,489: Hist., Chronogr.

1481 **MARSYAS Pellaeus et MARSYAS Philippeus**
Hist.
post 4 B.C.: Pellaeus, Philippeus
001 **Testimonia**, FGrH #135–136: 2B:736–737.
NQ: 135: Test.
002 **Fragmenta Marsyae Pellaei**, FGrH #135–136:
2B:737.
Q: 90: Hist.
003 **Fragmenta Marsyae Philippei**, FGrH #135–
136: 2B:737–739.
Q: 257: Hist.
004 **Fragmenta Marsyae Pellaei vel Marsyae Philippei**, FGrH #135–136: 2B:739–741.
Q: 740: Hist.

2011 *MARTYRIUM AGAPAE, IRENAE, CHIO-
NAE ET SODALIUM*
post A.D. 4
001 **Martyrium Agapae, Irenae, Chionae et sodalium**, ed. H. Musurillo, *The acts of the Christian martyrs.* Oxford: Clarendon Press, 1972:
280–292.
Cod: 1,813: Hagiogr.

0390 *MARTYRIUM CARPI, PAPYLI ET AGA-
THONICAE*
A.D. 2
001 **Martyrium sanctorum Carpi, Papyli et Aga-
thonicae**, ed. H. Musurillo, *The acts of the
Christian martyrs.* Oxford: Clarendon Press,
1972: 22–28.
Cod: 1,003: Hagiogr.

2008 *MARTYRIUM CONONIS*
post A.D. 4
001 **Martyrium Cononis**, ed. H. Musurillo, *The acts*

of the Christian martyrs. Oxford: Clarendon Press, 1972: 186–192.
Cod: 982: Hagiogr.

2010 **MARTYRIUM DASII**
post A.D. 4
001 **Martyrium Dasii**, ed. H. Musurillo, *The acts of the Christian martyrs.* Oxford: Clarendon Press, 1972: 272–278.
Cod: 1,102: Hagiogr.

1483 **MARTYRIUM ET ASCENSIO ISAIAE**
A.D. 2
001 **Fragmenta**, ed. A.-M. Denis, *Fragmenta pseudepigraphorum quae supersunt Graeca* [*Pseudepigrapha veteris testamenti Graece* 3. Leiden: Brill, 1970]: 105–114.
Q, Cod, Pap: 1,439: Pseudepigr., Hagiogr.

2657 **MARTYRIUM IGNATII**
post A.D. 2
001 **Martyrium Ignatii Antiocheni** (martyrium Antiochenum), ed. F.X. Funk and F. Diekamp, *Patres apostolici*, vol. 2, 3rd edn. Tübingen: Laupp, 1913: 324–338.
Cod: Hagiogr.
002 **Martyrium Ignatii Antiocheni** (martyrium Romanum), ed. Funk and Diekamp, *op. cit.*, 340–362.
Cod: Hagiogr.

2009 **MARTYRIUM MARINI**
post A.D. 3
001 **Martyrium Marini**, ed. H. Musurillo, *The acts of the Christian martyrs.* Oxford: Clarendon Press, 1972: 240–242.
Q: 265: Hagiogr.

MARTYRIUM PAULI
Cf. ACTA PAULI (0388 002).

MARTYRIUM PERPETUAE ET FELICITATIS
post A.D. 3
Cf. PASSIO PERPETUAE ET FELICITATIS (2016).

MARTYRIUM PETRI
Cf. ACTA PETRI (0389 001).

2005 **MARTYRIUM PIONII**
A.D. 4?
001 **Martyrium Pionii presbyteri et sodalium**, ed. H. Musurillo, *The acts of the Christian martyrs.* Oxford: Clarendon Press, 1972: 136–166.
Cod: 4,480: Hagiogr.

1484 **MARTYRIUM POLYCARPI**
fort. auctore Marcione
post A.D. 2
001 **Epistula ecclesiae Smyrnensis de martyrio sancti Polycarpi**, ed. H. Musurillo, *The acts of the Christian martyrs.* Oxford: Clarendon Press, 1972: 2–20.
Appendix 1 (cap. 22): p. 18.
Appendix 2 (Epilogus Mosquensis): pp. 18–20.
Cod: 2,718: Epist., Hagiogr.

2007 **MARTYRIUM POTAMIAENAE ET BASILIDIS**
post A.D. 3
001 **Martyrium Potamiaenae et Basilidis**, ed. H. Musurillo, *The acts of the Christian martyrs.* Oxford: Clarendon Press, 1972: 132–134.
Q: 402: Hagiogr.

1485 **MARTYRIUM PTOLEMAEI ET LUCII**
A.D. 2
001 **Martyrium Ptolemaei et Lucii**, ed. H. Musurillo, *The acts of the Christian martyrs.* Oxford: Clarendon Press, 1972: 38–40.
Cod: 515: Hagiogr.

1888 **MATRIS** Hist.
3 B.C.?: Thebanus
001 **Testimonia**, FGrH #39: 1A:260.
NQ: 138: Test.
002 **Fragmenta**, FGrH #39: 1A:260.
Q: 76: Hist., Myth., Encom.

1486 **MATRON** Parodius
4 B.C.: Pitanaeus
001 **Convivium Atticum**, ed. P. Brandt, *Parodorum epicorum Graecorum et Archestrati reliquiae* [*Corpusculum poesis epicae Graecae Ludibundae*, fasc. 1. Leipzig: Teubner, 1888]: 60–71.
Dup. partim 1486 003 (fr. 534).
Q: 894: Parod.
002 **Fragmenta**, ed. Brandt, *op. cit.*, 91–93.
frr. 1–6.
Dup. partim 1486 003 (frr. 535–540).
Q: 136: Parod.
003 **Fragmenta**, ed. H. Lloyd-Jones and P. Parsons, *Supplementum Hellenisticum.* Berlin: De Gruyter, 1983: 259–262, 266–268.
frr. 534–540.
Dup. 1486 001–002.
Q: 1,002: Parod.

1560 **MATTHIAE TRADITIONES**
fiq *Evangelium apocryphum secundum Matthiam*
ante A.D. 2
001 **Matthiae traditiones**, ed. E. Preuschen, *Antilegomena*, 2nd edn. Giessen: Töpelmann, 1905: 13–15.
Q: 511: Evangel., Apocryph.

3075 **Pseudo-MAURICIUS** Tact.
vel Urbicius
A.D. 6–10: Constantinopolitanus
001 **Strategicon** (sub nomine Mauricii Imperatoris vel Urbicii), ed. H. Mihăescu, *Mauricius. Arta*

militară [*Scriptores Byzantini* 6. Bucharest: Academie Republicii Socialiste România, 1970]: 28–380.
Pinax: pp. 28–40.
Introductio: pp. 42–46.
Strategicon (lib. 1–12): pp. 48–380.
Cod: Tact.

Flavius MAURICIUS Imperator
A.D. 6–7: Constantinopolitanus
Cf. Pseudo-MAURICIUS Tact. (3075).

2709 **Joannes MAUROPUS** Rhet. et Poeta
A.D. 11: Euchaitenus (Paphlagoniae), Constantinopolitanus
x01 **Epigramma demonstrativum.**
App. Anth. 3.411: Cf. ANTHOLOGIAE GRAECAE APPENDIX (7052 003).

1040 **MAXIMIANUS** Med.
ante A.D. 6
x01 **Fragmentum ap. Alexandrum Trallianum.**
Puschmann, vol. 2, p. 57.
Cf. ALEXANDER Med. (0744 003).

1487 **MAXIMUS** Astrol.
A.D. 2/4?
001 Περὶ καταρχῶν, ed. A. Ludwich, *Maximi et Ammonis carminum de actionum auspiciis reliquiae.* Leipzig: Teubner, 1877: 3–48.
Cod: 4,108: Astrol., Hexametr.
002 Περὶ καταρχῶν (epitome), ed. Ludwich, *op. cit.*, 79–96.
Cod: 2,305: Astrol.

2675 **MAXIMUS** Epigr.
post A.D. 2: fort. Apamensis
x01 **Epigramma dedicatorium.**
App. Anth. 1.248(?): Cf. ANTHOLOGIAE GRAECAE APPENDIX (7052 001).

2025 **MAXIMUS** Rhet.
A.D. 4?: Byzantius vel Epirota
001 Περὶ τῶν ἀλύτων ἀντιθέσεων (fort. auctore Maximo Byzantio), ed. C. Walz, *Rhetores Graeci*, vol. 5. Stuttgart: Cotta, 1833 (repr. Osnabrück: Zeller, 1968): 577–590.
Cod: 3,025: Rhet.

0563 **MAXIMUS** Soph.
A.D. 2: Tyrius
001 **Philosophumena,** ed. H. Hobein, *Maximi Tyrii philosophumena.* Leipzig: Teubner, 1910: 1–484.
Cod: 68,363: Rhet.

1488 **MAXIMUS** Theol.
A.D. 2
001 **Fragmentum ex libro de materia,** ed. M.J. Routh, *Reliquiae sacrae*, vol. 2, 2nd edn. Ox-

ford: Oxford University Press, 1846 (repr. Hildesheim: Olms, 1974): 87–107.
Q: 3,273: Theol.

2892 **MAXIMUS CONFESSOR** Theol. et Poeta
vel Maximus Homologetes
A.D. 6–7: Chrysopolitanus, Constantinopolitanus
001 **Quaestiones ad Thalassium,** ed. C. Laga and C. Steel, *Maximi confessoris quaestiones ad Thalassium i: quaestiones i–lv* [*Corpus Christianorum. Series Graeca* 7. Turnhout: Brepols, 1980]: 3–539.
Pinax: pp. 3–7.
Quaestiones: pp. 9–539.
Cod: Theol., Exeget.
002 **Quaestiones et dubia,** ed. J.H. Declerck, *Maximi confessoris quaestiones et dubia* [*Corpus Christianorum. Series Graeca* 10. Turnhout: Brepols, 1982]: 3–170.
Cod: Theol., Exeget.
005 **Expositio in Psalmum lix,** MPG 90: 856–872.
Cod: Exeget.
006 **Orationis dominicae expositio,** MPG 90: 872–909.
Cod: Exeget.
007 **Liber asceticus,** MPG 90: 912–956.
Cod: Theol., Dialog.
008 **Capita de caritate,** ed. A. Ceresa-Gastaldo, *Massimo confessore. Capitoli sulla carità.* Rome: Editrice Studium, 1963: 48–238.
Prologus ad Elpidium: p. 48.
Centuriae quattuor: pp. 50–238.
Cod: Eccl.
009 **Capita theologica et oecumenica** *sive* **Capita gnostica,** MPG 90: 1084–1173.
Cod: Theol.
010 **Capita xv,** MPG 90: 1177–1185.
Cod: Theol.
011 **Diversa capita ad theologiam et oeconomiam spectantia deque virtute et vitio** [Sp.] (fort. ab Antonio Melissa confecta), MPG 90: 1185–1392.
Cod: Theol.
012 **Quaestiones ad Theopemptum,** ed. M. Gitlbauer, "Die Überreste griechischer Tachygraphie im Codex Vaticanus graecus 1809," *Denkschriften der kaiserlichen Akademie der Wissenschaften*, Philosoph.-hist. Kl. 28. Vienna: Gerold, 1878: 85–89.
fr. 11.
Cod: Exeget.
013 **Ad Marinum presbyterum,** MPG 91: 9–37.
Cod: Theol.
014 **Ad Marinum presbyterum ex tractatu de operationibus et voluntatibus** (cap. 50), MPG 91: 40–45.
Cod: Theol.
015 **Ex tractatu de operationibus et voluntatibus** (cap. 51), MPG 91: 45–56.
Cod: Theol.

016 **Ad Georgium presbyterum ac hegumenum,** MPG 91: 56–61.
Cod: Theol.

017 **Ad eos qui dicunt dicendam unam Christi operationem,** MPG 91: 64–65.
Cod: Theol.

018 **In illud:** *Pater si fieri potest transeat a me calix,* MPG 91: 65–69.
Cod: Theol., Exeget.

019 **Tomus dogmaticus ad Marinum diaconum,** MPG 91: 69–89.
Cod: Theol.

020 **Exemplum epistulae ad episcopum Nicandrum,** MPG 91: 89–112.
Cod: Theol., Epist.

021 **Ad catholicos per Siciliam constitutos,** MPG 91: 112–132.
Cod: Theol.

022 **Ad Marinum Cypri presbyterum,** MPG 91: 133–137.
Cod: Theol., Epist.

023 **Ex epistula Romae scripta,** MPG 91: 137–140.
Cod: Theol., Epist.

025 **De duabus Christi naturis,** MPG 91: 145–149.
Cf. et 2892 065.
Cod: Theol.

026 **Variae definitiones,** MPG 91: 149–153.
Cf. et 2892 070.
Cod: Theol.

027 **Spiritalis tomus ac dogmaticus,** MPG 91: 153–184.
Cod: Theol.

028 **De duabus unius Christi nostri voluntatibus,** MPG 91: 184–212.
Cod: Theol.

029 **Distinctionum quibus res dirimuntur definitiones,** MPG 91: 212–213.
Cod: Theol.

030 **Unionum definitiones,** MPG 91: 213–216.
Cod: Theol.

031 **Theodori Byzantini diaconi quaestiones cum Maximi solutionibus,** MPG 91: 216–228.
Cod: Theol.

032 **Tomus dogmaticus ad Marinum presbyterum,** MPG 91: 228–245.
Cod: Theol.

033 **De qualitate, proprietate et differentia seu distinctione ad Theodorum presbyterum in Mazario,** MPG 91: 245–257.
Cod: Theol.

034 **Fragmenta duo,** MPG 91: 257–260.
Cod: Theol.

035 **De substantia seu essentia et natura, deque hypostasi et persona capita x,** MPG 91: 260–264.
Cf. et 2892 071.
Cod: Theol.

037 **De substantia seu essentia et natura et hypostasi,** MPG 91: 265–268.
Cod: Theol.

038 **Fieri non posse ut dicatur una in Christo voluntas,** MPG 91: 268–269.
Cod: Theol.

039 **Capita x de duplici voluntate domini,** MPG 91: 269–273.
Cod: Theol.

040 **Ex quaestionibus a Theodoro monacho illi propositis,** MPG 91: 276–280.
Cf. et 2892 069.
Cod: Theol.

041 **Diversae definitiones,** MPG 91: 280–285.
Cod: Theol.

042 **Disputatio cum Pyrrho,** MPG 91: 288–353.
Cod: Theol., Dialog.

043 **Opusculum de anima** [Sp.], MPG 91: 353–361.
Dup. partim GREGORIUS THAUMATURGUS Scr. Eccl. (2063 008).
Cf. et 2892 086.
Cod: Theol.

044 **Epistulae xlv,** MPG 91: 364–649.
Epist. 1: Dup. partim ATHANASIUS Theol. (2035 076).
Epist. 8: cf. et 2892 078, 107.
Epist. 11: cf. et 2892 108.
Epist. 15: cf. et 2892 072, 080.
Cod: Theol., Epist.

045 **Epistula secunda ad Thomam,** ed. P. Canart, "La deuxième lettre à Thomas de s. Maxime le confesseur," *Byzantion* 34 (1964) 429–445.
Cod: Theol., Epist.

046 **Epistula ad Anastasium monachum discipulum,** MPG 90: 132–133.
Cod: Theol., Epist.

050 **Mystagogia,** MPG 91: 657–717.
Cod: Liturg.

051 **Ambiguorum liber,** MPG 91: 1032–1417.
Cod: Theol., Exeget.

053 **Computus ecclesiasticus,** MPG 19: 1217–1280.
Cod: Eccl.

054 **Quaestiones et dubia** (e cod. Dresd. gr. 187a), ed. S.L. Epifanovič, *Materialy k izučeniju žizni i tvorenij prep. Maksima Ispovědnika (Matériaux pour servir à l'étude de la vie et des oeuvres de S. Maxime le confesseur).* Kiev, 1917: 26–27.
Cod: Exeget.

055 **De cibo angelorum et Christi post resurrectionem** (e cod. Dresd. gr. 187a), ed. Epifanovič, *op. cit.,* 27–28.
Cod: Exeget.

056 **De triginta argenteis Judae** (e cod. Vindob. theol. gr. 165), ed. Epifanovič, *op. cit.,* 28.
Cod: Exeget.

057 **De gradibus ecclesiasticis Jesu Christi** (e cod. Vindob. theol. gr. 165), ed. Epifanovič, *op. cit.,* 28.
Cod: Exeget.

058 **De divina inhumanatione** (e cod. Vindob. 157), ed. Epifanovič, *op. cit.,* 28–29.
Cod: Exeget.

059 **In apostoli verbum:** *semetipsum exinanivit,*

formam servi accipiens (e cod. Mosq. synod. gr. 444 [324]), ed. Epifanovič, *op. cit.*, 29-33.
Cod: Exeget.

060 **Capita gnostica** (e cod. Mosq. synod. 425 [439]), ed. Epifanovič, *op. cit.*, 33-56.
Cod: Exeget.

062 **Capita practica xiii-xx** (e cod. Mosq. synod. 425 [439]), ed. Epifanovič, *op. cit.*, 59-60.
Cod: Exeget.

063 **De veritate et pietate** (e cod. Hierosol. S. Sabae 408), ed. Epifanovič, *op. cit.*, 60-61.
Cod: Theol.

064 **Philosophia Christiana dividitur in tres partes** (e cod. Hierosol. S. Sabae 283) (nonnumquam sub auctore Joanne Damasceno), ed. Epifanovič, *op. cit.*, 61.
Cod: Theol.

065 **Caput contra Arianos** (e cod. Vindob. gr. 248 [307]), ed. Epifanovič, *op. cit.*, 61-62.
Textus = additamentum ad opusculum *De duabus Christi naturis.*
Cf. et 2892 025.
Cod: Theol.

066 **Capita de proprietatibus duarum Christi naturarum** (cap. 58, 59, 92 e cod. Mosq. 247 [509]), ed. Epifanovič, *op. cit.*, 62-63.
Cod: Theol.

067 **Capita xiii de voluntatibus** (e cod. Vat. gr. 507), ed. Epifanovič, *op. cit.*, 64-65.
Cod: Theol.

068 **Capita x de voluntatibus et energiis** (e cod. Mosq. synod. gr. 425 [439]), ed. Epifanovič, *op. cit.*, 66-67.
Cod: Theol.

069 **E quaestionibus a Theodoro monacho illi propositis** (e cod. Paris gr. 854), ed. Epifanovič, *op. cit.*, 67-68.
Textus = additamentum ad opusculum *Ex quaestionibus a Theodoro monacho illi propositis.*
Cf. et 2892 040.
Cod: Theol.

070 **Definitiones** (e codd. Mosq. synod. gr. 425 [439] + Paris gr. 854), ed. Epifanovič, *op. cit.*, 68-70.
Textus = additamenta ad opusculum *Variae definitiones.*
Cf. et 2892 026.
Cod: Theol.

071 **Capita de substantia et hypostasi** (e cod. Paris. gr. 854), ed. Epifanovič, *op. cit.*, 70-71.
Textus = additamenta ad opusculum *De substantia seu essentia et natura, deque hypostasi et persona.*
Cf. et 2892 035.
Cod: Theol.

072 **Ex epistula dogmatica ad Cosmam diaconum Alexandrinum** (e cod. Paris. gr. 854), ed. Epifanovič, *op. cit.*, 71-72.
Textus = additamentum ad epistulam 15.
Cf. et 2892 044.
Cod: Theol., Epist.

073 **Definitiones de voluntate** (e cod. Paris. gr. 854), ed. Epifanovič, *op. cit.*, 72-75.
Cod: Theol.

074 **Definitiones variae de energia** (e cod. Paris. gr. 854), ed. Epifanovič, *op. cit.*, 76-77.
Cod: Theol.

075 **Theorema** (e cod. Paris. gr. 887), ed. Epifanovič, *op. cit.*, 78-80.
Cod: Theol.

076 **Compendiosa fidei expositio** (e cod. Paris. gr. 214a), ed. Epifanovič, *op. cit.*, 80-82.
Cod: Theol.

077 **De adventu domini** (e cod. Paris. gr. 922), ed. Epifanovič, *op. cit.*, 82-83.
Cod: Theol.

078 **Ad Sophronium monachum** (e cod. Vat. gr. 507), ed. Epifanovič, *op. cit.*, 84.
Textus = fragmentum epistulae 8.
Cf. et 2892 044, 107.
Cod: Theol., Epist.

079 **Ad Stephanum presbyterum et hegumenum** (e cod. Laurent., Plut. 57 cod. 7), ed. Epifanovič, *op. cit.*, 84.
Cod: Theol.

080 **Appendix ad epistulam xv ad Cosmam** (e cod. Mosq. synod. 425), ed. Epifanovič, *op. cit.*, 85.
Textus = additamentum ad epistulam 15.
Cf. et 2892 044.
Cod: Theol., Epist.

081 **Ad neophytos de patientia** (e cod. Vat. gr. 507), ed. Epifanovič, *op. cit.*, 85-91.
Dup. partim CLEMENS ALEXANDRINUS Theol. (0555 008) (fr. 44).
Dup. partim GREGORIUS NAZIANZENUS Theol. (2022 066).
Dup. partim Pseudo-MACARIUS Scr. Eccl. (2109 001) (sermo 62).
Cod: Homilet.

082 **De miseria et brevitate vitae humanae versus** (e cod. Vindob. gr. 164 [153]), ed. Epifanovič, *op. cit.*, 91.
Lineae 1-2: Dup. PALLADAS Epigr. (2123 001) (AG 10.58).
Cod: Epigr.

084 **In isagogen Porphyrii et in categorias Aristotelis** (e cod. Vat. gr. 507), ed. M. Roueché, "Byzantine philosophical texts of the seventh century," *Jahrbuch der Österreichischen Byzantinistik* 23 (1974) 70-71.
Cod: Phil., Comm.

085 **Scholia in categorias Aristotelis** (e cod. Hierosol. patr. gr. 106), ed. Epifanovič, *op. cit.*, 93-99.
Cod: Schol.

086 **Ad Anianum de anima** (e cod. Paris. gr. 1019a), ed. Epifanovič, *op. cit.*, 99-100.
Textus = additamentum ad *Opusculum de anima.*
Cf. et 2892 043.
Cod: Theol.

087 **Scholia in corpus Areopagiticum** (fragmenta

sub auctoribus Maximo et Joanne Scholastico),
MPG 4: 16–432, 528–576.
Cf. et 2892 088.
Cod: Schol., Eccl.

088 **Scholia in corpus Areopagiticum** (e codd.
Mosq. synod. gr. 109 [35] + Mosq. synod. gr.
110 [35] + Paris gr. 441 + Paris gr. 444) (sub
auctoribus Maximo et Joanne Scholastico), ed.
Epifanovič, *op. cit.*, 101–208.
Cf. et 2892 087.
Cod: Schol., Eccl.

089 **Epistula ad ignotum** (fragmentum), ed. Gitlbauer, *op. cit.*, 84.
fr. 8.
Cod: Epist.

090 **Fragmentum**, ed. Gitlbauer, *op. cit.*, 84–85.
fr. 9.
Cod: Theol.

091 **Capita ascetica iv**, ed. Gitlbauer, *op. cit.*, 89–
90.
fr. 12.
Cod: Eccl.

092 **Capita ascetica vii**, ed. Gitlbauer, *op. cit.*, 94–
95.
fr. 18.
Cod: Eccl.

093 **Scholia in Psalmos** (in catenis, typus VIII: catena Nicetae), MPG 69: 700–715 passim.
Q: Exeget., Caten.

094 **Scholia in Odas** (in catenis: catena multiplex),
ed. B. Corderius, *Expositio patrum Graecorum
in Psalmos*, vol. 3. Antwerp, 1646: passim.
Q: Exeget., Caten.

097 **Scholia in Ecclesiasten** (in catenis: catena
trium patrum), ed. S. Lucà, *Anonymus in Ecclesiasten commentarius qui dicitur catena
trium patrum* [*Corpus Christianorum. Series
Graeca* 11. Turnhout: Brepols, 1983]: 3–87
passim.
Q: Exeget., Caten.

098 **Scholia in Matthaeum** (in catenis, typus C:
catena Nicetae), ed. B. Corderius, *Symbolarum
in Matthaeum tomus alter, quo continetur catena patrum Graecorum triginta collectore Niceta episcopo Serrarum*. Toulouse, 1647: passim.
Q: Exeget., Caten.

099 **Scholia in Lucam** (in catenis, typus F: catena
Nicetae), ed. A. Mai, *Scriptorum veterum nova
collectio*, vol. 9. Rome: Biblioteca Apostolica
Vaticana, 1837: 626–724 passim.
Q: Exeget., Caten.

101 **Fragmentum de fine mundi**, ed. F. Boll, *Codices Germanici* [*Catalogus codicum astrologorum
Graecorum* 7. Brussels: Lamertin, 1908]: 100–
101.
Q: Theol., Phil.

102 **Capita varia** [Sp.], MPG 90: 1401–1461.
Cod: Exeget.

103 **Loci communes** [Sp.], MPG 91: 721–1017.
Cod: Comm., Exeget.

104 **Hymni** [Sp.], MPG 91: 1417–1424.
Cod: Hymn.

105 **Ad regem Achridae** (fragmentum ex opere lxiii
dubiorum) [Sp.], MPG 90: 1461.
Cod: Theol.

107 **Epistula 8** (fragmentum), ed. R. Devreesse,
"La fin inédite d'une lettre de saint Maxime:
un baptême forcé de Juifs et de Samaritains à
Carthage en 632," *Revue des sciences religieuses*
17 (1937) 34–35.
Cf. et 2892 044, 078.
Cod: Epist., Theol.

108 **Epistula 11** (fragmentum), ed. Gitlbauer, *op.
cit.*, 90.
fr. 13.
Cf. et 2892 044.
Cod: Theol., Epist.

x01 **Fragmenta** (in *Doctrina patrum*).
Diekamp, pp. 137–138, 210–211, 296–297,
300.
Cf. DOCTRINA PATRUM (7051 001).

x02 **Scholia in Acta** (in catenis: catena Andreae).
Cramer, vol. 3, pp. 1–424 passim.
Cf. CATENAE (Novum Testamentum) (4102
008).

x04 **Scholia in epistulas catholicas** (in catenis: catena Andreae).
Cramer, vol. 8, passim.
Cf. CATENAE (Novum Testamentum) (4102
040–046).

x05 **Capita vii de duabus naturis domini** (sub auc-
tore Eulogio Alexandrino).
Diekamp, pp. 152–155.
Cf. EULOGIUS Theol. (2824 x01).

x06 **Scholia in Canticum canticorum** [Dub.] (in ca-
tenis, typus B1: catena trium patrum).
MPG 87.2.1756–1780 passim.
Cf. PROCOPIUS Rhet. et Scr. Eccl. (2598 015).

x07 **Scholia in epistulam ad Romanos** (in catenis,
typus Monacensis).
Cramer, vol. 4, pp. 163–529 passim.
Cf. CATENAE (Novum Testamentum) (4102
011).

x08 **Scholia in epistulam ad Hebraeos** (in catenis:
catena Nicetae).
Cramer, vol. 7, pp. 279–598 passim.
Cf. CATENAE (Novum Testamentum) (4102
039).

1939 **MEDIUS** Hist.
post 4 B.C.?: Larissaeus
001 **Testimonia**, FGrH #129: 2B:670–671.
NQ: 289: Test.
002 **Fragmentum**, FGrH #129: 2B:671–672.
Q: 445: Hist.

1489 **MEGASTHENES** Hist.
4–3 B.C.
001 **Testimonia**, FGrH #715: 3C:603–604.
NQ: 370: Test.
002 **Fragmenta**, FGrH #715: 3C:604–639.
Q: 12,194: Hist.

0976 **MEGES** Med.
A.D. 1: Sidonius

x01 **Fragmentum ap. Galenum.**
K12.845.
Cf. GALENUS Med. (0057 076).

x02 **Fragmentum ap. Oribasium.**
CMG, vol. 6.2.1, pp. 142–144.
Cf. ORIBASIUS Med. (0722 001).

1490 **<MEGILLUS>** Phil.
3/2 B.C.: Lacon

001 **Fragmentum**, ed. H. Thesleff, *The Pythagorean texts of the Hellenistic period*. Åbo: Åbo Akademi, 1965: 115.
Q: 67: Phil.

MELAMPUS Gramm.
Incertum
Cf. COMMENTARIA IN DIONYSII THRACIS ARTEM GRAMMATICAM (4175 002, 004).

1365 **MELAMPUS** Scriptor De Divinatione
3 B.C.

001 Περὶ ἐλαιῶν τοῦ σώματος, ed. J.G.F. Franz, *Scriptores physiognomoniae veteres*. Altenburg: Richter, 1780: 501–508.
Cod

002 Περὶ παλμῶν ἀρχομένου ἀπὸ κεφαλῆς ἕως ποδῶν (e cod. Berol. 1577), ed. H. Diels, "Anonyme Version des Phillippsianus," *Abhandlungen der königlich preussischen Akademie der Wissenschaften*, Philosoph.-hist. Kl., Abh. 4. Berlin: Reimer, 1908: 7–9.
Cf. et 1365 006.
Cod

003 Περὶ παλμῶν μαντικὴ πρὸς Πτολεμαῖον βασιλέα (versio A), ed. H. Diels, "Die griechischen Zuckungsbücher (Melampus περὶ παλμῶν)," *Abhandlungen der königlich preussischen Akademie der Wissenschaften*, Philosoph.-hist. Kl., Abh. 4. Berlin: Reimer, 1907: 21–32.
Cod

004 Περὶ παλμῶν τί σημαίνουσιν ἐν ἑκάστῳ μέρει (versio P), ed. Diels, *APAW* (1907), 35–38.
Cod

005 **Lunarium**, ed. D. Bassi, F. Cumont, A. Martini and A. Olivieri, *Codices Italici* [*Catalogus codicum astrologorum Graecorum* 4. Brussels: Lamertin, 1903]: 110–113.
Cod

006 Περὶ παλμῶν ἀρχομένου ἀπὸ κεφαλῆς ἕως ποδῶν (P. Flor. 3.391), ed. Diels, *APAW* (1908), 12–15.
Cf. et 1365 002.
Pap

0373 **MELANIPPIDES** Lyr.
5 B.C.: Melius

001 **Fragmenta**, ed. D.L. Page, *Poetae melici Graeci*. Oxford: Clarendon Press, 1962 (repr. 1967 (1st edn. corr.)): 392–395.
frr. 1–7.
Q: 113: Lyr., Hymn.

1491 **MELANTHIUS** Hist.
4 B.C.?: fort. Atheniensis

001 **Fragmenta**, FGrH #326: 3B:86–87.
Q: 311: Hist.

0344 **MELANTHIUS** Trag.
2 B.C.: Rhodius

001 **Fragmentum**, ed. B. Snell, *Tragicorum Graecorum fragmenta*, vol. 1. Göttingen: Vandenhoeck & Ruprecht, 1971: 303.
fr. 1.
Q: 12: Trag.

0254 **MELANTHIUS** Trag. et Eleg.
5 B.C.: Atheniensis

001 **Fragmentum**, ed. M.L. West, *Iambi et elegi Graeci*, vol. 2. Oxford: Clarendon Press, 1972: 81.
fr. 1.
Q: 12: Eleg.

002 **Titulus**, ed. B. Snell, *Tragicorum Graecorum fragmenta*, vol. 1. Göttingen: Vandenhoeck & Ruprecht, 1971: 138.
NQ: 2: Trag.

1492 **MELEAGER** Epigr.
2–1 B.C.: Gadarensis

001 **Epigrammata**, AG 4.1; 5.8, 24, 57, 96, 136–137, 139–141, 143–144, 147–149, 151–152, 154–157, 160, 163, 165–166, 171–180, 182, 184, 187, 190–192, 195, 196–198, 204, 208, 212, 214–215; 6.162–163; 7.13, 79, 182, 195–196, 207, 352, 417–419, 421, 428, 461, 468, 470, 476, 535; 9.16, 331, 363; 11.223; 12.23, 33, 41, 47–49, 52–54, 56–57, 59–60, 63, 65, 68, 70, 72, 74, 76, 78, 80–86, 92, 94–95, 101, 106, 109–110, 113–114, 117, 119, 122, 125–128, 132–133, 137, 141, 144, 147, 154, 157–159, 164–165, 167, 256–257; 16.134, 213.
AG 5.2, 82, 99, 168, 195b; 12.79: Cf. ANONYMI EPIGRAMMATICI (0138 001).
AG 5.189: Cf. ASCLEPIADES Epigr. (0137 001).
AG 7.31: Cf. DIOSCORIDES Epigr. (0173 001).
AG 12.234–235; 16.213: Cf. (et) STRATON Epigr. (1697 001).
Q: 5,928: Epigr.

0730 **MELETIUS** Med.
A.D. 7/9

001 **De natura hominis**, ed. J.A. Cramer, *Anecdota Graeca e codd. manuscriptis bibliothecarum Oxoniensium*, vol. 3. Oxford: Oxford University Press, 1836 (repr. Amsterdam: Hakkert, 1963): 5–157.
Cod: 41,338: Med.

002 **Hypothesis ad opus De natura hominis** (e cod. Barocciano 131), ed. Cramer, *op. cit.*, 1–4.
Cod: 928: Med.

0977 **MELETUS** Med.
ante A.D. 1
x01 **Fragmentum ap. Galenum.**
K12.946.
Cf. GALENUS Med. (0057 076).

1848 **MELETUS Junior** Trag.
5-4 B.C.: Atheniensis
001 **Titulus**, ed. B. Snell, *Tragicorum Graecorum fragmenta*, vol. 1. Göttingen: Vandenhoeck & Ruprecht, 1971: 188.
NQ: 1: Trag.

1493 **MELINNO** Lyr.
2 B.C.?: Lesbia
001 Εἰς Ῥώμην, ed. H. Lloyd-Jones and P. Parsons, *Supplementum Hellenisticum*. Berlin: De Gruyter, 1983: 268-269.
fr. 541.
Q: 90: Lyr.

0051 **<MELISSA>** Phil.
3 B.C.?
001 **Fragmentum epistulae ad Clearetam**, ed. H. Thesleff, *The Pythagorean texts of the Hellenistic period*. Åbo: Åbo Akademi, 1965: 115-116.
Q: 221: Phil., Epist.

2282 **MELISSEUS** Hist.
ante 4 B.C.?
001 **Fragmenta**, FGrH #402: 3B:297.
Q: 162: Hist.

1494 **MELISSUS** Phil.
5 B.C.: Samius
001 **Testimonia**, ed. H. Diels and W. Kranz, *Die Fragmente der Vorsokratiker*, vol. 1, 6th edn. Berlin: Weidmann, 1951 (repr. Dublin: 1966): 258-267.
test. 1-14.
NQ: 3,687: Test.
002 **Fragmenta**, ed. Diels and Kranz, *op. cit.*, 268-276.
frr. 1-12.
Q: 1,105: Phil.

4280 **Theodorus MELITENIOTES** Gramm.
A.D. 14: Constantinopolitanus
x01 **Scholia in Homeri Iliadem** (e cod. Genevensi gr. 44).
Nicole, vol. 2, pp. 3-214.
Cf. SCHOLIA IN HOMERUM (5026 004).

2955 **MELITIUS et MELITIANI** Theol.
A.D. 4: Lycopolitanus (Melitius)
001 **Epistulae Melitianorum**, ed. H.I. Bell, *Jews and Christians in Egypt. The Jewish troubles in Alexandria and the Athanasian controversy*. Oxford: Oxford University Press, 1924: 38-99.
Pap
x01 **Breviarium a Melitio datum Alexandro episcopo.**

Opitz, pp. 149-151.
Cf. ATHANASIUS Theol. (2035 005).

1495 **MELITO** Apol.
A.D. 2: Sardianus
001 **De pascha** (*P. Beatty* 8 + *P. Bodmer* 13 + *P. Oxy.* 13.1600), ed. O. Perler, *Méliton de Sardes. Sur la Pâque et fragments* [*Sources chrétiennes* 123. Paris: Cerf, 1966]: 60-126.
Pap: 4,499: Homilet., Apol.
002 **Fragmentum** (*P. Bodmer* 12), ed. Perler, *op. cit.*, 128.
Pap: 30: Hymn.
003 **Fragmenta**, ed. Perler, *op. cit.*, 218-224, 226, 228-236.
frr. 1-4, 6-7, 8b-12.
Q: 1,553: Apol., Exeget., Homilet.
x01 **Deprecatio.**
Richard, *Muséon* 85, pp. 318-321.
Cf. JOANNES CHRYSOSTOMUS Scr. Eccl. (2062 428).

2250 **MELITO** Hist.
A.D. 2?: fort. Atheniensis
001 **Fragmentum**, FGrH #345: 3B:208.
Q: 29: Hist.

0978 **MELITO** Med.
A.D. 1
x01 **Fragmentum ap. Galenum.**
K13.843.
Cf. GALENUS Med. (0057 077).

0825 **MELITO** Trag.
A.D. 1
001 **Titulus**, ed. B. Snell, *Tragicorum Graecorum fragmenta*, vol. 1. Göttingen: Vandenhoeck & Ruprecht, 1971: 314.
NQ: 1: Trag.

1496 **MEMNON** Hist.
1 B.C.-A.D. 1?: fort. Heracleota
001 **Testimonium**, FGrH #434: 3B:336-337.
NQ: 141: Test.
002 **Fragmenta**, FGrH #434: 3B:337-368.
Cod: 11,314: Hist.

4258 **MEMNON** <Phil.>
4/3 B.C.?: fort. Atheniensis
001 **Testimonium**, ed. K. Döring, *Die Megariker* [*Studien zur antiken Philosophie* 2. Amsterdam: Grüner, 1972]: 20, 21.
test. 69 = Euphantus (1912 003).
NQ: Test.

1497 **MENAECHMUS** Hist.
4 B.C.: Sicyonius
001 **Testimonia**, FGrH #131: 2B:673.
NQ: 112: Test.
002 **Fragmenta**, FGrH #131: 2B:673-676.
Q: 706: Hist.
x01 **Sicyonis historia** (*P. Oxy.* 11.1365).

FGrH #551, fr. 1b (= FGrH #105, fr. 2).
Cf. ADDITAMENTA (FGrH) (2433 024).
Cf. ANONYMI HISTORICI (FGrH) (1139 004).

0270 **MENAECHMUS** Math. et Phil.
4 B.C.
001 **Testimonia**, ed. F. Lasserre, *De Léodamas de Thasos à Philippe d'Oponte*. Naples: Bibliopolis, 1987: 117.
test. 1–3.
NQ: Test.
002 **Fragmentum et titulus**, ed. Lasserre, *op. cit.*, 118.
frr. 1–2.
fr. 1 = De Platonis politiis (titulus).
Q: Phil.
003 **Doctrina**, ed. Lasserre, *op. cit.*, 118–124.
frr. 1–7.
NQ: Test.

0541 **MENANDER** Comic.
4–3 B.C.: Atheniensis
Cf. et MENANDRI ET PHILISTIONIS SENTENTIAE (1791).
001 **Aspis**, ed. F.H. Sandbach, *Menandri reliquiae selectae*. Oxford: Clarendon Press, 1972: 3–25.
Pap: 3,267: Comic.
002 **Aspidis fragmenta aliunde nota**, ed. Sandbach, *op. cit.*, 25–26.
frr. 1–2.
Q: 37: Comic.
003 **Georgus**, ed. Sandbach, *op. cit.*, 29–33.
Pap: 688: Comic.
004 **Georgi fragmenta aliunde nota**, ed. Sandbach, *op. cit.*, 34–35.
frr. 1–7.
Q, Pap: 131: Comic.
005 **Dis exapaton**, ed. Sandbach, *op. cit.*, 39–41.
Pap: 402: Comic.
006 **Dis exapatontis fragmenta aliunde nota**, ed. Sandbach, *op. cit.*, 41–42.
frr. 1–5.
Q, Pap: 34: Comic.
007 **Dyscolus**, ed. Sandbach, *op. cit.*, 47–91.
Pap: 6,694: Comic.
008 **Epitrepontum fragmenta**, ed. Sandbach, *op. cit.*, 97–98, 120–121, 130.
frr. 1–10.
Q: 105: Comic.
009 **Epitrepontes**, ed. Sandbach, *op. cit.*, 98–130.
Pap: 4,493: Comic.
010 **Heros**, ed. Sandbach, *op. cit.*, 135–139.
Pap: 532: Comic.
011 **Herois fragmenta aliunde nota**, ed. Sandbach, *op. cit.*, 139–141.
frr. 1–8, 10.
Q: 82: Comic.
012 **Theophorumene**, ed. Sandbach, *op. cit.*, 145.
Pap: 118: Comic.
013 **Theophorumenae fragmentum dubium**, ed. Sandbach, *op. cit.*, 146.
Pap: 104: Comic.

014 **Theophorumenae fragmenta aliunde nota**, ed. Sandbach, *op. cit.*, 147–148.
frr. 1–5.
Q: 153: Comic.
015 **Carchedonius**, ed. Sandbach, *op. cit.*, 153–154.
Pap: 154: Comic.
016 **Carchedonii fragmenta aliunde nota**, ed. Sandbach, *op. cit.*, 154–155.
frr. 1–7.
Q: 46: Comic.
017 **Citharista**, ed. Sandbach, *op. cit.*, 159–161.
Pap: 400: Comic.
018 **Citharistae fragmenta aliunde nota**, ed. Sandbach, *op. cit.*, 162–164.
frr. 1–12.
Q, Pap: 161: Comic.
019 **Colax**, ed. Sandbach, *op. cit.*, 167–171.
Pap: 627: Comic.
020 **Colacis fragmenta aliunde nota**, ed. Sandbach, *op. cit.*, 172–173.
frr. 2–7.
Q: 103: Comic.
021 **Coneazomenae**, ed. Sandbach, *op. cit.*, 177–178.
Pap: 126: Comic.
022 **Coneazomenarum fragmentum aliunde notum**, ed. Sandbach, *op. cit.*, 178.
fr. 1.
Q: 15: Comic.
023 **Misumenus**, ed. Sandbach, *op. cit.*, 181, 183–194.
Pap: 1,600: Comic.
024 **Misumeni fragmenta**, ed. Sandbach, *op. cit.*, 182–183, 194–195.
frr. 2–11.
Q: 78: Comic.
025 **Periciromene**, ed. Sandbach, *op. cit.*, 199–221.
Pap: 3,152: Comic.
026 **Periciromenae fragmenta aliunde nota**, ed. Sandbach, *op. cit.*, 221.
frr. 1–2.
Q: 13: Comic.
027 **Perinthia**, ed. Sandbach, *op. cit.*, 225–226.
Pap: 152: Comic.
028 **Perinthiae fragmenta aliunde nota**, ed. Sandbach, *op. cit.*, 226–228.
frr. 1–10.
Q: 93: Comic.
029 **Samia**, ed. Sandbach, *op. cit.*, 231–265.
Pap: 5,424: Comic.
030 **Samiae fragmentum aliunde notum**, ed. Sandbach, *op. cit.*, 265.
Q: 10: Comic.
031 **Sicyonius**, ed. Sandbach, *op. cit.*, 269–284.
Pap: 2,215: Comic.
032 **Sicyonii fragmenta aliunde nota**, ed. Sandbach, *op. cit.*, 284–286.
frr. 1–6, 10–11.
Q, Pap: 104: Comic.
033 **Phasma**, ed. Sandbach, *op. cit.*, 289–293.
Pap: 637: Comic.

034 **Fabula incerta**, ed. Sandbach, *op. cit.*, 297–299.
Pap: 342: Comic.

035 **Fragmentum dubium** (*P. Oxy.* 31.2533), ed.
Sandbach, *op. cit.*, 300.
Pap: 69: Comic.

036 **Fragmenta longiora apud alios auctores servata**, ed. Sandbach, *op. cit.*, 303–324.
frr. 59–60, 97, 208–210, 215, 250–251, 264,
276, 286–287, 303–304, 333–336, 397, 416a–
b, 417, 451, 538, 568, 581, 592, 612, 614, 620,
656, 714, 718, 722, 740, 745, 754, 794, 795.
Dup. partim 0541 045.
Q, Pap: 2,238: Comic.

037 **Fragmenta**, ed. C. Austin, *Comicorum Graecorum fragmenta in papyris reperta.* Berlin: De
Gruyter, 1973: 121–196.
frr. 103–104, 106–107, 110–111, 113, 119,
121–122, 124, 128–129, 131–135, 138, 140,
142–143, 145–148, 151, 157–159, 163, 165,
167–168, 171, 173, 180–181, 183, 186–187,
190, 193, 195, 202–204 + tituli.
Pap: 4,142: Comic.

038 **Misumeni nova fragmenta**, ed. E.G. Turner,
"New fragments of the *Misoumenos* of Menander," *Bulletin of the Institute of Classical
Studies*, suppl. 17 (1965) 25–73.
Dup. 0541 023 (partim); 0541 024 (partim);
0541 037 (CGFPR, pp. 149–164, fr. 153).
Pap: 1,257: Comic.

039 **Fragmenta**, ed. T. Kock, *Comicorum Atticorum fragmenta*, vol. 3. Leipzig: Teubner,
1888: 3–152, 155–164, 166–241, 246–271.
frr. 1, 3–6, 8–33, 36, 39, 41–42, 48, 50–55, 59–
100, 102–107, 109–120, 123–132, 134–151,
153–162, 164–171, 173–181, 183–185, 187–
189, 191–258, 260–275, 278–314, 316–333,
335–389, 391–411, 413, 415–443, 445–458,
460–463, 465–494, 497–544, 546–720, 722–
734, 736–749, 751–864, 866–895, 897–907,
912–930, 962–963, 965–986, 988–1116, 1121,
1127 + tituli.
Q: 12,000: Comic.

040 **Fragmenta**, ed. A. Meineke, *Fragmenta comicorum Graecorum*, vol. 4. Berlin: Reimer, 1841
(repr. De Gruyter, 1970): 69–79, 81–189, 191–
215, 217–296, 298–300, 302, 305, 307, 321–
332, 876.
Q: 10,779: Comic.

041 **Fragmenta**, ed. J. Demiańczuk, *Supplementum
comicum.* Krakau: Nakładem Akademii, 1912
(repr. Hildesheim: Olms, 1967): 54–62.
frr. 1–18, 20–24.
Q: 246: Comic.

042 **Sententiae e codicibus Byzantinis**, ed. S. Jaekel, *Menandri sententiae.* Leipzig: Teubner,
1964: 33–83.
Cod: 5,299: Gnom., Iamb.

044 **Epigrammata**, AG 7.72; 11.438.
AG 11.286: Cf. PALLADAS Epigr. (2123 001).
Q: 24: Epigr.

045 **Fragmenta**, ed. A. Körte and A. Thierfelder,

Menandri quae supersunt, vol. 2, 2nd edn.
Leipzig: Teubner, 1959: 14–251, 267–271,
295, 298.
frr. 1–3, 5–8, 10–28, 30, 33–40, 42–43, 45–50,
53–73, 76–90, 93–94, 97–98a, 100–101, 104–
106, 109–125, 127–139, 141–159, 161–164,
166, 171–181, 185–190, 192–216, 218–224,
226–231, 235, 238–244, 248–259, 263–267,
269–272, 274–282, 284, 286–292, 294–298,
300–309, 311–331, 333–354, 358–368, 371–
376, 380–390, 392, 394–398, 401–405, 407–
412, 416–428, 431–443, 446–456, 459, 462–
703, 705–722, 724–807, 809, 932–937, 939–
941, 944–950, addenda 317a, 669a, 715a.
Dup. partim 0541 036.
Q: 9,889: Comic.

046 **Epigramma**, ed. Meineke, *FCG*, vol. 4, 335.
Q: 19: Epigr.

047 **Sententiae**, ed. Meineke, *FCG*, vol. 4, 340–
362.
Q: 4,515: Gnom.

048 **Sententiae e papyris**, ed. Jaekel, *op. cit.*, 3–25.
frr. 1–20.
Pap: 1,577: Gnom.

049 **Fragmenta**, ed. Meineke, *FCG*, vol. 5.1 (1857;
repr. 1970): ccxliv, ccxlviii, ccli, ccliii, cclxiii,
cclxxix, cclxxxiv, ccxcii–ccxciii, 109–110.
Q: 152: Comic.

050 **Misumeni fragmenta** (*P. Oxy.* 48.3368–3371),
ed. E. Turner, *The Oxyrhynchus papyri*, pt. 48.
London: Egypt Exploration Society, 1981: 9,
10–12, 21.
Pap

051 **Epitrepontum fragmenta** (*P. Oxy.* 50.3532),
ed. Turner, *The Oxyrhynchus papyri*, pt. 50
(1983): 39.
Pap

052 **Epitrepontum fragmenta** (*P. Oxy.* 50.3533),
ed. Turner, *The Oxyrhnchus papyri*, pt. 50, 43,
45, 47.
Pap

053 **Colacis fragmenta** (*P. Oxy.* 50.3534), ed. E.W.
Handley, *The Oxyrhynchus papyri*, pt. 50, 50.
Pap

1498 **MENANDER** Hist.
ante 2 B.C.: Ephesius

001 **Testimonia**, FGrH #783: 3C:788–789.
NQ: 221: Test.

002 **Fragmenta**, FGrH #783: 3C:789–795.
Q: 1,146: Hist.

2586 **MENANDER** Rhet.
A.D. 3/4: Laodicensis

001 Διαίρεσις τῶν ἐπιδεικτικῶν (olim sub auctore
Genethlio), ed. D.A. Russell and N.G. Wilson,
Menander rhetor. Oxford: Clarendon Press,
1981: 2–74.
Cod: 9,130: Rhet.

002 Περὶ ἐπιδεικτικῶν, ed. Russell and Wilson, *op.
cit.*, 76–224.

Cap. 1 (pp. 76–94): Dup. partim JOSEPHUS
RHACENDYTA Phil. (3151 002).
Cod: 20,201: Rhet.

4076 **MENANDER Protector** Hist.
A.D. 6: Constantinopolitanus
001 **Epigramma**, AG 1.101.
Q: 47: Epigr.
003 **De legationibus Romanorum ad gentes** (fragmenta ap. Constantinum Porphyrogenitum, *De
legationibus*), ed. C. de Boor, *Excerpta historica
iussu imp. Constantini Porphyrogeniti confecta,
vol. 1: excerpta de legationibus*, pt. 1. Berlin:
Weidmann, 1903: 170–221.
Q: 15,779: Hist.
004 **De legationibus gentium ad Romanos** (fragmenta ap. Constantinum Porphyrogenitum, *De
legationibus*), ed. de Boor, *op. cit.*, pt. 2, 442–
477.
Q: 11,625: Hist.
005 **De sententiis** (ap. Constantinum Porphyrogenitum, *De sententiis*), ed. U.P. Boissevain,
*Excerpta historica iussu imp. Constantini Por-
phyrogeniti confecta, vol. 4: excerpta de sententiis*. Berlin: Weidmann, 1906: 18–26.
Cod: 1,921: Hist.
006 **Fragmentum** (e cod. Paris. gr. 1140A) [Dub.],
ed. F. Halkin, "Un nouvel extrait de l'historien
byzantin Menandre?" in *Zetesis (Festschrift E.
de Strycker)*. Antwerp: De Nederlandsche
Boekhandel, 1973: 664–665.
Cod: 344: Hist.

1791 *MENANDRI ET PHILISTIONIS SENTEN-
TIAE*
Incertum
Cf. et MENANDER Comic. (0541 042, 045).
001 **Comparatio Menandri et Philistionis**, ed. S.
Jaekel, *Menandri sententiae*. Leipzig: Teubner,
1964: 87–120.
Q: 4,287: Gnom.
002 **Sententiae Menandri et Philistionis**, ed. A.
Meineke, *Fragmenta comicorum Graecorum*,
vol. 4. Berlin: Reimer, 1841 (repr. De Gruyter,
1970): 335–338.
Q: 359: Gnom.

1499 **MENECLES** Hist.
2 B.C.: Barcaeus
001 **Fragmenta**, FGrH #270: 3A:83–84.
Q: 568: Hist.

2325 **MENECLES** Hist.
2 B.C.: Teius
001 **Testimonium**, FGrH #466: 3B:402–403.
test. 1: *Inscr. Cret.* 1.280.
NQ: 98: Test.

MENECLES Perieg.
Cf. CALLICRATES-MENECLES Perieg.
(1236).

2684 **MENECLES** Phil.
post 3 B.C.
x01 **Epigramma sepulcrale**.
App. Anth. 2.383: Cf. ANTHOLOGIAE GRAE-
CAE APPENDIX (7052 002).

0523 **MENECRATES** Comic.
post 5 B.C.
001 **Titulus**, ed. T. Kock, *Comicorum Atticorum
fragmenta*, vol. 3. Leipzig: Teubner, 1888: 383.
NQ: 5: Comic.
002 **Titulus**, ed. A. Meineke, *Fragmenta comicorum
Graecorum*, vol. 1. Berlin: Reimer, 1839 (repr.
De Gruyter, 1970): 493.
NQ: 9: Comic.
003 **Fragmentum**, ed. J. Demiańczuk, *Supplementum comicum*. Krakau: Nakładem Akademii,
1912 (repr. Hildesheim: Olms, 1967): 63.
fr. 1.
Q: 8: Comic.

1501 **MENECRATES** Epigr.
4–3 B.C.: Samius
001 **Epigrammata**, AG 9.54–55.
Q: 35: Epigr.

1502 **MENECRATES** Epigr.
1 B.C.: Smyrnaeus
001 **Epigramma**, AG 9.390.
Q: 42: Epigr.

1503 **MENECRATES** Hist.
4 B.C.: Xanthius
001 **Fragmenta**, FGrH #769: 3C:761–762.
Q: 504: Hist.

2475 **MENECRATES** Hist.
post 4 B.C.?
001 **Fragmenta**, FGrH #701: 3C:555.
Q: 246: Hist.

0639 **MENECRATES** Med.
4 B.C.: Syracusanus
001 **Epistula** [Sp.], ed. R. Hercher, *Epistolographi
Graeci*. Paris: Didot, 1873 (repr. Amsterdam:
Hakkert, 1965): 399.
Q: 58: Epist.

0980 **Tiberius Claudius MENECRATES** Med.
A.D. 1
x01 **Fragmenta ap. Galenum**.
K12.846, 946.
Cf. GALENUS Med. (0057 076).

1500 **MENECRATES** Poet. Phil.
4 B.C.: Ephesius
001 **Fragmentum et titulus**, ed. H. Lloyd-Jones and
P. Parsons, *Supplementum Hellenisticum*. Berlin: De Gruyter, 1983: 269–270.
frr. (+ titul.) 543–544.
Q: 13: Hexametr.

0982 **MENECRITUS** Med.
ante A.D. 4
x01 **Fragmentum ap. Oribasium.**
CMG, vol. 6.2.1, p. 286.
Cf. ORIBASIUS Med. (0722 001).

0224 **MENEDEMUS** Phil.
4 B.C.: Pyrrhaeus
001 **Testimonia**, ed. F. Lasserre, *De Léodamas de Thasos à Philippe d'Oponte.* Naples: Bibliopolis, 1987: 93–95.
test. 1, 3c–8.
NQ: Test.
002 **Philocrates** (fragmentum), ed. Lasserre, *op. cit.*, 95–96.
fr. 1.
Q: Phil.

1504 **MENELAUS** Epic.
post 1 B.C.?: Aegaeus
001 **Testimonia**, FGrH #384: 3B:261–262.
NQ: 81: Test.
002 **Fragmenta**, FGrH #384: 3B:262.
Dup. partim 1504 003.
Q: 131: Hist., Epic.
003 **Fragmenta et titulus**, ed. H. Lloyd-Jones and P. Parsons, *Supplementum Hellenisticum.* Berlin: De Gruyter, 1983: 271–272.
frr. (+ titul.) 551–555.
Dup. partim 1504 002.
Q: 14: Epic.

0983 **MENELAUS** Med.
ante A.D. 2
x01 **Fragmentum ap. Galenum.**
K14.173.
Cf. GALENUS Med. (0057 078).

0984 **MENEMACHUS** Med.
A.D. 1: Aphrodisiensis
x01 **Fragmenta ap. Oribasium.**
CMG, vol. **6.1.1**, p. 220; **6.1.2**, p. 58.
Cf. ORIBASIUS Med. (0722 001).

1505 **MENESTHENES** Hist.
ante A.D. 3
001 **Fragmentum**, FHG 4: 451–452.
Q

0985 **MENESTHEUS** Med.
ante A.D. 2
x01 **Fragmentum ap. Galenum.**
K13.830.
Cf. GALENUS Med. (0057 077).

2228 **MENESTOR** Phil.
5 B.C.: Sybarita
001 **Testimonia**, ed. H. Diels and W. Kranz, *Die Fragmente der Vorsokratiker*, vol. 1, 6th edn.

Berlin: Weidmann, 1951 (repr. Dublin: 1966): 375–376.
test. 1–7.
NQ: 497: Test.

1787 **[MENIPPUS]** Comic.
Incertum
001 **Tituli**, ed. T. Kock, *Comicorum Atticorum fragmenta*, vol. 3. Leipzig: Teubner, 1888: 383.
NQ: 3: Comic.
002 **Tituli**, ed. A. Meineke, *Fragmenta comicorum Graecorum*, vol. 1. Berlin: Reimer, 1839 (repr. De Gruyter, 1970): 494.
NQ: 12: Comic.

0079 **MENIPPUS** Geogr.
1 B.C.: Pergamenus
002 **Fragmenta**, ed. K. Müller, *Geographi Graeci minores*, vol. 1. Paris: Didot, 1855 (repr. Hildesheim: Olms, 1965): 572–573.
Q: 216: Geogr.
x01 **Menippi periplus Maris Interni** (epitome Marciani).
GGM, vol. 1, pp. 563–572.
Cf. MARCIANUS Geogr. (4003 002).

2517 **MENIPPUS** Hist.
ante 1 B.C.
001 **Titulus**, FGrH #766: 3C:758.
NQ: Hist.

0986 **MENIPPUS** Med.
ante A.D. 1
x01 **Fragmentum ap. Galenum.**
K14.172.
Cf. GALENUS Med. (0057 078).

0052 **MENIPPUS** Phil.
3 B.C.: Gadarensis
001 **Epistula** [Sp.], ed. R. Hercher, *Epistolographi Graeci.* Paris: Didot, 1873 (repr. Amsterdam: Hakkert, 1965): 400.
Q: 62: Epist.

MENO Med.
Cf. ANONYMUS LONDINENSIS Med. (0643 001).

1506 **MENODOTUS** Hist.
3 B.C.?: Samius
001 **Fragmenta**, FGrH #541: 3B:524–526.
Q: 1,053: Hist.

1916 **MENODOTUS** Hist.
2 B.C.: Perinthius
Cf. et MENODOTUS Hist. (1506).
001 **Testimonium**, FGrH #82: 2A:189.
NQ: 26: Test.

0989 **MENOETIUS** Med.
ante A.D. 2

x01 **Fragmenta ap. Galenum.**
K13.509, 511–512.
Cf. GALENUS Med. (0057 077).

2631 **MENOPHILUS** Poeta
Incertum: Damascenus
001 **Fragmentum**, ed. H. Lloyd-Jones and P. Parsons, *Supplementum Hellenisticum*. Berlin: De Gruyter, 1983: 272–273.
fr. 558.
Q: 107: Hexametr.

2202 **[MENYLLUS]** Hist.
Incertum
001 **Fragmenta**, FGrH #295: 3A:178–179.
Q: 116: Hist.

1021 *MEROPIS*
6 B.C.
001 **Fragmenta** (*P. Colon.* inv. 5604), ed. L. Koenen and R. Merkelbach, *Collectanea papyrologica. Texts published in honor of H.C. Youtie*, vol. 1 (ed. A.E. Hanson) [*Papyrologische Texte und Abhandlungen* 19. Bonn: Habelt, 1976]: 9, 11, 13, 15.
Pap

0268 **MESOMEDES** Lyr.
A.D. 2: Creticus
001 **Fragmenta**, ed. E. Heitsch, *Die griechischen Dichterfragmente der römischen Kaiserzeit*, vol. 1, 2nd edn. Göttingen: Vandenhoeck & Ruprecht, 1963: 25–32.
frr. 1–13.
frr. 4–5: Dup. partim LYRICA ADESPOTA (CA) (0230 001) (fr. 35–36).
Q, Cod: 879: Hymn.
002 **Epigrammata**, AG 14.63; 16.323.
Q: 103: Epigr.

0475 **METAGENES** Comic.
5 B.C.
001 **Fragmenta**, ed. T. Kock, *Comicorum Atticorum fragmenta*, vol. 1. Leipzig: Teubner, 1880: 704–710.
frr. 1–10, 12–16, 19.
Q: 222: Comic.
002 **Fragmenta**, ed. A. Meineke, *Fragmenta comicorum Graecorum*, vol. 2.2. Berlin: Reimer, 1840 (repr. De Gruyter, 1970): 751–756, 758–759.
p. 758: fr. 3 supplied from vol. 5.1, p. 115.
Q: 223: Comic.

2959 **METHODIUS** Scr. Eccl.
A.D. 3–4: Olympius
001 **Symposium** *sive* **Convivium decem virginum**, ed. H. Musurillo and V.-H. Debidour, *Méthode d'Olympe. Le banquet* [*Sources chrétiennes* 95. Paris: Cerf, 1963]: 42–332.
Cod
002 **De libero arbitrio**, ed. G.N. Bonwetsch, *Metho-*

dius [*Die griechischen christlichen Schriftsteller* 27. Leipzig: Hinrichs, 1917]: 145–206.
Cod
003 **De resurrectione**, ed. Bonwetsch, *op. cit.*, 226, 242–352, 361–363, 368–371, 373–382, 384–386, 388, 391–400, 403, 405, 410–416, 420.
Cod
004 **De lepra ad Sistelium**, ed. Bonwetsch, *op. cit.*, 455–464, 466–467, 469.
Cod
005 **De creatis** (fragmenta ap. Photium, *Bibl.* cod. 235), ed. Bonwetsch, *op. cit.*, 493–500.
Q
006 **Adversus Porphyrium** (fragmenta), ed. Bonwetsch, *op. cit.*, 503–507.
Q
007 **Fragmenta in Job** (in catenis), ed. Bonwetsch, *op. cit.*, 511–519.
Q: Exeget., Caten.
008 **De martyribus** (fragmenta), ed. Bonwetsch, *op. cit.*, 520.
Q
009 **Fragmentum de resurrectione** (e cod. Vat. gr. 2022) [Sp.], ed. Bonwetsch, *op. cit.*, 423–424.
Cod
010 **Fragmenta incerta** [Sp.], ed. Bonwetsch, *op. cit.*, 520–521.
Q
011 **In Genesim** (in catenis), ed. R. Devreesse, *Les anciens commentateurs de l'Octateuque et des Rois* [*Studi e Testi* 201. Vatican City: Biblioteca Apostolica Vaticana, 1959]: 54.
Q: Exeget., Caten.
012 **Sermo de Simeone et Anna** [Sp.], MPG 18: 348–381.
Cod
013 **Sermo in ramos palmarum** [Sp.], MPG 18: 384–397.
Cod
014 **Apocalypsis** (recensio 1) [Sp.], ed. A. Lolos, *Die Apokalypse des Ps.-Methodios* [*Beiträge zur klassischen Philologie* 83. Meisenheim am Glan: Hain, 1976]: 46–140.
Cod
015 **Apocalypsis** (recensio 2) [Sp.], ed. Lolos, *BKP* 83, 47–141.
Cod
016 **Apocalypsis** (recensio 3) [Sp.], ed. A. Lolos, *Die dritte und vierte Redaktion des Ps.-Methodios* [*Beiträge zur klassischen Philologie* 94. Meisenheim am Glan: Hain, 1978]: 22, 25–38, 40–75.
Cod
017 **Apocalypsis** (recensio 4) [Sp.], ed. Lolos, *BKP* 94, 23, 39–69, 76–78.
Cod

2708 **METHODIUS I** Scr. Eccl.
vel Methodius Confessor
A.D. 9: Constantinopolitanus
001 **Encomium et vita Theophanis** (e cod. Mosq. synod. 159 Vlad.), ed. D. Spyridonov, "Βίος τοῦ ὁσίου πατρὸς ἡμῶν καὶ ὁμολογητοῦ Θεο-

φάνους. Ποίημα Μεθοδίου πατριάρχου Κωνσταντινουπόλεως," Ἐκκλησιαστικὸς Φάρος 12
(1913) 95–96, 113–165.
Cod: Biogr., Encom.

x01 **Epigramma demonstrativum.**
App. Anth. 3.310: Cf. ANTHOLOGIAE GRAE-
CAE APPENDIX (7052 003).

1507 **<METOPUS>** Phil.
3 B.C.: Metapontinus

001 **Fragmenta,** ed. H. Thesleff, *The Pythagorean
texts of the Hellenistic period.* Åbo: Åbo Akademi, 1965: 116–121.
Q: 1,441: Phil.

4077 **METRODORUS** Epigr.
fiq Metrodorus Byzantius Gramm.
A.D. 4?

001 **Epigrammata,** AG 9.360, 712.
Q: 93: Epigr.

x01 **Epigrammatum arithmeticorum collectio.**
AG **14**.116–146.
Cf. ANONYMI EPIGRAMMATICI (AG) (0138
001).

1976 **METRODORUS** Hist.
1 B.C.: Scepsius

001 **Testimonia,** FGrH #184: 2B:912–914.
NQ: 761: Test.

002 **Fragmenta,** FGrH #184: 2B:914–917.
Q: 856: Hist.

1508 **METRODORUS** Phil.
4 B.C.: Chius

001 **Fragmenta,** FGrH #43: 1A:266, *15 addenda.
Q: 298: Hist., Myth.

002 **Testimonia,** ed. H. Diels and W. Kranz, *Die
Fragmente der Vorsokratiker,* vol. 2, 6th edn.
Berlin: Weidmann, 1952 (repr. Dublin: 1966):
231–233.
test. 1–25.
NQ: 1,034: Test.

003 **Fragmenta,** ed. Diels and Kranz, *op. cit.,* 233–
234.
frr. 1–6.
Q: 279: Phil., Myth.

1773 **METRODORUS** Phil.
4–3 B.C.: Lampsacenus

001 **Fragmenta,** ed. A. Körte, "Metrodori Epicurei
fragmenta," *Jahrbücher für classische Philologie,* suppl. 17. Leipzig: Teubner, 1890: 537–
552, 554–565.
Q

1811 **METRODORUS Major** Phil.
6 B.C.: Lampsacenus

001 **Testimonia,** ed. H. Diels and W. Kranz, *Die
Fragmente der Vorsokratiker,* vol. 2, 6th edn.
Berlin: Weidmann, 1952 (repr. Dublin: 1966):
49–50.
test. 1–6.
NQ: 345: Test.

4270 **METRODORUS Theorematicus** Phil.
4 B.C.: Atheniensis

001 **Testimonium,** ed. K. Döring, *Die Megariker
[Studien zur antiken Philosophie* 2. Amsterdam: Grüner, 1972]: 52, 61.
test. 164a = Stilpo (4262 001).
NQ: Test.

2531 **METROPHANES** Hist.
A.D. 3/4?

001 **Testimonium,** FGrH #796: 3C:834.
NQ: 29: Test.

002 **Fragmentum,** FGrH #796: 3C:835.
Q: 47: Hist.

9017 **MICHAEL** Epigr.
A.D. 10

001 **Epigramma,** AG 1.122.
Q: 24: Epigr.

2704 **MICHAEL** Epigr.
Incertum

x01 **Epigrammata demonstrativa.**
App. Anth. 3.275–276: Cf. ANTHOLOGIAE
GRAECAE APPENDIX (7052 003).

4034 **MICHAEL** Phil.
A.D. 11–12: Ephesius

001 **In ethica Nicomachea ix–x commentaria,** ed.
G. Heylbut, *Eustratii et Michaelis et anonyma
in ethica Nicomachea commentaria [Commen-
taria in Aristotelem Graeca* 20. Berlin: Reimer,
1892]: 461–620.
Cod: 65,713: Phil., Comm.

002 **In parva naturalia commentaria,** ed. P. Wendland, *Michaelis Ephesii in parva naturalia commentaria [Commentaria in Aristotelem Graeca*
22.1. Berlin: Reimer, 1903]: 1–149.
Cod: 51,594: Phil., Nat. Hist., Comm.

003 **In libros de partibus animalium commentaria,**
ed. M. Hayduck, *Michaelis Ephesii in libros de
partibus animalium, de animalium motione, de
animalium incessu commentaria [Commentaria
in Aristotelem Graeca* 22.2. Berlin: Reimer,
1904]: 1–99.
Cod: 41,075: Phil., Nat. Hist., Comm.

004 **In libros de animalium motione commentarium,** ed. Hayduck, *CAG* 22.2, 103–131.
Cod: 10,030: Phil., Nat. Hist., Comm.

005 **In librum de animalium incessu commentarium,** ed. Hayduck, *CAG* 22.2, 135–170.
Cod: 13,851: Phil., Nat. Hist., Comm.

006 **In librum quintum ethicorum Nicomacheorum
commentarium,** ed. M. Hayduck, *Michaelis
Ephesii in librum quintum ethicorum Nicomacheorum commentarium [Commentaria in
Aristotelem Graeca* 22.3. Berlin: Reimer, 1901]:
1–72.
Cod: 29,038: Phil., Comm.

007 **Commentarium in Aristotelis librum de interpretatione** (fragmenta) (e cod. Paris. 1917), ed.
C.A. Brandis, *Aristotelis opera,* vol. 4. Berlin:

Reimer, 1836 (repr. De Gruyter, 1961): 100a
nota, 102b nota, 103b nota, 105a nota, 107b
nota, 112a nota, 132a nota, 133a nota.
Cod: Phil., Comm.

008 **In Aristotelis sophisticos elenchos commentarius** (= Pseudo-Alexander 1) (olim sub auctore
Alexandro Aphrodisiensi), ed. M. Wallies, *Alexandri quod fertur in Aristotelis sophisticos
elenchos commentarium* [*Commentaria in Aristotelem Graeca* 2.3. Berlin: Reimer, 1898]: 1–
198.
Cf. et 4034 011.
Cod: 73,265: Phil., Comm.

011 **Scholion in Aristotelis sophisticos elenchos** (e
cod. Vat. gr. 269 et 244 in marginibus) (=
Pseudo-Alexander 1), ed. S. Ebbesen, *Commentators and commentaries on Aristotle's sophistici elenchi. A study of post-Aristotelian
ancient and medieval writings on fallacies*, vol.
1 [*Corpus Latinum commentariorum in Aristotelem Graecorum. De Wulf-mansion Centre* 7.
Leiden: Brill, 1981]: 277.
Cf. et 4034 008.
Cod: Schol.

009 **In Aristotelis sophisticos elenchos commentarius** (selecta) (= Pseudo-Alexander 2 + commentarium 5), ed. Ebbesen, *op. cit.*, vol. 2
(1981): 153–199.
Cod: Phil., Comm.

**MICHAEL ANDREOPULUS Translator Syn-
tipae**
A.D. 11
Cf. SYNTIPAS (3118 001).

3079 **MICHAEL ATTALIATES** Hist.
A.D. 11–12: Constantinopolitanus
001 **Historia**, ed. I. Bekker, *Michaelis Attaliotae his-
toria* [*Corpus scriptorum historiae Byzantinae.*
Bonn: Weber, 1853]: 3–322.
Cod: Hist.

002 Πόνημα νομικὸν ἤτοι σύνοψις πραγματική, ed.
J. Zepos and P. Zepos, *Jus Graecoromanum*,
vol. 7 [*Prochiron auctum*]. Athens: Fexis, 1931
(repr. Aalen: Scientia, 1962): 411–497.
Cod: Jurisprud., Epigr.

005 **Diataxis**, ed. P. Gautier, "La diataxis de Michel Attaliate," *Revue des études byzantines* 39
(1981) 17–130.
Cod: Eccl.

4078 **MICHAELIUS** Gramm.
A.D. 6
001 **Epigramma**, AG 16.316.
Q: 39: Epigr.

1509 **<MILON>** <Phil.>
Incertum: Crotoniensis
001 **Fragmentum**, ed. H. Thesleff, *The Pythagorean
texts of the Hellenistic period.* Åbo: Åbo Akademi, 1965: 122–123.
Q: 65: Phil.

1510 ***MIMI ANONYMI***
ante A.D. 3
001 **Fragmentum** (*P. Oxy.* 3.413), ed. D.L. Page,
Select papyri, vol. 3 [*Literary papyri*]. London:
Heinemann, 1941 (repr. 1970): 338–348.
Pap: [1,340]: Mim.

002 **Fragmentum** (*P. Oxy.* 3.413), ed. Page, *op. cit.*,
352–360.
Pap: Mim.

003 **Fragmentum** (*P. Lit. Lond.* 97), ed. Page, *op.
cit.*, 362–366.
Pap: Mim.

004 **Fragmentum** (*P. Lit. Lond.* 52), ed. Page, *op.
cit.*, 368–370.
Pap: Mim.

0255 **MIMNERMUS** Eleg.
7 B.C.: Colophonius, Smyrnaeus
001 **Fragmenta**, ed. M.L. West, *Iambi et elegi
Graeci*, vol. 2. Oxford: Clarendon Press, 1972:
83–90.
frr. 1–9, 11–12, 13a–17, 22, 24–26.
Q: 610: Eleg., Iamb.

002 **Epigramma**, AG 9.50.
AG 9.50: Dup. partim 0255 001 (fr. 7).
AG 7.405: Cf. PHILIPPUS Epigr. (1589 001).
Q: 15: Epigr.

003 **Fragmenta**, FGrH #578: 3B:688–690.
Q: 498: Hist., Eleg.

1511 **MIMNERMUS** Trag.
ante 4 B.C.?
001 **Fragmenta**, ed. A. Nauck, *Tragicorum Graecorum fragmenta.* Leipzig: Teubner, 1889
(repr. Hildesheim: Olms, 1964): 829–830.
frr. 1–2.
Q: 30: Trag.

0991 **MINUCIANUS** Med.
1 B.C.–A.D. 1
x01 **Fragmentum ap. Galenum.**
K13.930.
Cf. GALENUS Med. (0057 077).

2890 **MINUCIANUS** Rhet.
A.D. 2: Atheniensis
001 **Fragmenta**, ed. S. Glöckner, *Quaestiones rhetoricae. Historiae artis rhetoricae qualis fuerit
aevo imperatorio capita selecta* [*Breslauer philologische Abhandlungen* 8.2. Breslau: Marcus,
1901]: 22–50.
Q: Rhet.

002 **Fragmentum**, ed. O. Schissel, "Ein Minukian-
zitat in der Redelehre des Rufus," *Philologische
Wochenschrift* 47 (1927) 829–830.
Q: Rhet.

2903 **MINUCIANUS Junior** Rhet.
A.D. 3: Atheniensis
001 Περὶ ἐπιχειρημάτων, ed. C. Hammer (post L.

Spengel), *Rhetores Graeci*, vol. 1.2. Leipzig:
Teubner, 1894: 340–351.
Cod: Rhet.

1512 MINYAS
ante 5 B.C.
001 **Fragmentum**, ed. G. Kinkel, *Epicorum Graecorum fragmenta*, vol. 1. Leipzig: Teubner,
1877: 215.
fr. 1.
Q: 16: Epic.

0992 MITHRIDATES VI Eupator <Med.>
2–1 B.C.
x01 **Fragmenta ap. Galenum.**
K13.23, 52–53, 54–56, 329–330; **14**.148, 152–
155, 164.
Cf. GALENUS Med. (0057 076, 078).
x02 **Fragmentum ap. Paulum.**
CMG, vol. 9.2, p. 297.
Cf. PAULUS Med. (0715 001).

0039 MITHRIDATIS EPISTULA
1 B.C.?
Cf. et BRUTI EPISTULAE (1803).
001 **Epistula**, ed. R. Hercher, *Epistolographi Graeci*.
Paris: Didot, 1873 (repr. Amsterdam: Hakkert,
1965): 177–178.
Cod: 353: Epist.

1513 MNASALCES Epigr.
3 B.C.: Sicyonius
001 **Epigrammata**, AG **6**.9, 110, 125, 128, 264, 268;
7.54, 171, 192, 194, 212, 242, 488, 491; **9**.70,
324, 333; **12**.138.
AG 7.490: Cf. ANYTE Epigr. (0121 001).
Q: 486: Epigr.
x01 **Epigrammata** (*App. Anth.*).
Epigramma demonstrativum: 3.71.
Epigramma irrisorium: 5.14.
App. Anth. 3.71: Cf. ANTHOLOGIAE GRAE-
CAE APPENDIX (7052 003).
App. Anth. 5.14: Cf. ANTHOLOGIAE GRAE-
CAE APPENDIX (7052 005).

0993 MNASEAS Med.
vel Mnasaeus
A.D. 1
x01 **Fragmentum ap. Galenum.**
K13.445.
Cf. GALENUS Med. (0057 077).
x02 **Fragmenta ap. Oribasium.**
CMG, vol. **6.2.2**, p. 271; **6.3**, pp. 83, 87, 492.
Cf. ORIBASIUS Med. (0722 003–005).
x03 **Fragmentum ap. Paulum.**
CMG, vol. 9.2, p. 353.
Cf. PAULUS Med. (0715 001).
x04 **Fragmentum ap. Aëtium** (lib. 15).
Zervos, *Athena* 21, p. 83.
Cf. AËTIUS Med. (0718 015).

x05 **Fragmentum ap. Alexandrum Trallianum.**
Puschmann, vol. 2, pp. 107–109.
Cf. ALEXANDER Med. (0744 003).

1514 MNASEAS Perieg.
3 B.C.: Patrensis
001 **Fragmenta**, FHG 3: 149–158.
Q
002 **Fragmenta**, ed. H.J. Mette, "Die 'Kleinen'
griechischen Historiker heute," *Lustrum* 21
(1978) 39–40.
frr. 25 bis a–b, 34 bis, 51.
fr. 51: *P. Oxy.* 13.1611.
Q, Pap: 410: Hist.

0476 MNESIMACHUS Comic.
4 B.C.
001 **Fragmenta**, ed. T. Kock, *Comicorum Atticorum fragmenta*, vol. 2. Leipzig: Teubner,
1884: 436–438, 441–442.
frr. 1–4, 7–11.
Q: 448: Comic.
002 **Fragmenta**, ed. A. Meineke, *Fragmenta comicorum Graecorum*, vol. 3. Berlin: Reimer, 1840
(repr. De Gruyter, 1970): 567–570, 576–579.
Q: 451: Comic.

2565 MNESIMACHUS Hist.
4/3 B.C.?: Phaselinus
001 **Fragmenta**, FGrH #841: 3C:927–928.
Q: 243: Hist.

1959 MNESIPTOLEMUS Hist.
3–2 B.C.: Cumaeus
001 **Testimonia**, FGrH #164: 2B:890.
NQ: 201: Test.

0701 MNESITHEUS Med.
4 B.C.: Atheniensis
Cf. et MNESITHEUS Med. (0805).
x01 **Fragmenta ap. Galenum.**
K6.512–513, 645–646 in CMG, vol. 5.4.2, pp.
235–236, 321–322.
Cf. GALENUS Med. (0057 037).
x02 **Fragmenta ap. Oribasium.**
CMG, vol. **6.1.1**, pp. 62–64, 261, 288–290;
6.2.2, p. 135.
Cf. ORIBASIUS Med. (0722 001–002).
x03 **Fragmenta ap. Athenaeum.**
Deipnosophistae 1.32d; **2**.54b–c, 59b; **3**.80c,
80e, 92b–c, 106d; **8**.357a–358c; **11**.483f–484b.
Cf. ATHENAEUS Soph. (0008 001).

0805 MNESITHEUS Med.
fiq Mnesitheus Atheniensis vel Mnesitheus
Cyzicenus
4/3 B.C.?
Cf. et MNESITHEUS Med. (0701).
Cf. et MNESITHEUS Med. (0702).
x01 **Fragmentum ap. Oribasium.**
CMG, vol. 6.2.2, p. 84.
Cf. ORIBASIUS Med. (0722 002).

0702 **MNESITHEUS** Med.
3 B.C.?: Cyzicenus
Cf. et MNESITHEUS Med. (0805).
x01 **Fragmentum ap. Oribasium.**
CMG, vol. 6.1.1, p. 100.
Cf. ORIBASIUS Med. (0722 001).

1890 **MODERATUS** Phil.
A.D. 1: Gaditanus
001 **Fragmenta**, ed. F.W.A. Mullach, *Fragmenta philosophorum Graecorum*, vol. 2. Paris: Didot, 1867 (repr. Aalen: Scientia, 1968): 48–49.
frr. 1–3.
Q: 368: Phil.
x01 **Fragmenta ap. Porphyrium.**
VP 48.
Cf. PORPHYRIUS Phil. (2034 002).
x02 **Fragmenta ap. Simplicium.**
CAG 9, pp. 230–231.
Cf. SIMPLICIUS Phil. (4013 004).

1515 **MOERIS** Attic.
A.D. 2
001 **Lexicon Atticum**, ed. I. Bekker, *Harpocration et Moeris*. Berlin: Reimer, 1833: 187–214.
Cod: Lexicogr.

0220 **MOERO** Epic.
4–3 B.C.: Byzantia
001 **Fragmenta**, ed. J.U. Powell, *Collectanea Alexandrina*. Oxford: Clarendon Press, 1925 (repr. 1970): 21–23.
frr. 1–3 + tituli.
Q: 129: Epic., Epigr.
002 **Epigrammata**, AG 6.119, 189.
Dup. 0220 001 (frr. 2–3).
Q: 53: Epigr.

1516 **MOLPIS** Hist.
2–1 B.C.: Lacon
001 **Testimonium**, FGrH #590: 3B:704.
NQ: 42: Test.
002 **Fragmenta**, FGrH #590: 3B:704–705.
Q: 188: Hist.

2968 **MONIMUS** Phil.
4 B.C.: Syracusanus
001 **Fragmenta**, ed. F.W.A. Mullach, *Fragmenta philosophorum Graecorum*, vol. 2. Paris: Didot, 1867 (repr. Aalen: Scientia, 1968): 345.
frr. 1–2.
Q: 29: Phil.

0277 *MONODIA*
ante A.D. 2
001 **Mirmillonis amatrix** (*P. Ryl.* 1.15), ed. E. Heitsch, *Die griechischen Dichterfragmente der römischen Kaiserzeit*, vol. 1, 2nd edn. Göttingen: Vandenhoeck & Ruprecht, 1963: 45.
Dup. partim LYRICA ADESPOTA (CA) (0230 001) (fr. 38).
Pap: 93: Lyr.

1044 **MONOIMUS** Gnost.
A.D. 2: Arabius
x01 **Fragmenta.**
Hippolytus, *Refut.* 8.12.1–8.15.2.
Cf. HIPPOLYTUS Scr. Eccl. (2115 001).

1771 **MONTANUS et MONTANISTAE** Theol.
A.D. 2: Phrygius (Montanus)
001 **Oracula**, ed. P. de Labriolle, *La crise montaniste*. Paris: Leroux, 1913: 37–38, 43, 45–46, 60–61, 68–69, 71, 73, 86–87, 95–97.
Q: 754: Orac.
x01 **Fragmenta ap. Epiphanium.**
Haer. 48.10–11.
Cf. EPIPHANIUS Scr. Eccl. (2021 002).
x02 **Fragmenta ap. Didymum** (*Trin.* 3.41).
MPG 39.984.
Cf. DIDYMUS CAECUS Scr. Eccl. (2102 043).
x03 **Fragmenta** (in *Doctrina patrum*).
Diekamp, p. 306 (fr. 14).
Cf. DOCTRINA PATRUM (7051 001).

0314 **MORSIMUS** Trag.
5 B.C.: Atheniensis
001 **Fragmentum**, ed. B. Snell, *Tragicorum Graecorum fragmenta*, vol. 1. Göttingen: Vandenhoeck & Ruprecht, 1971: 148.
fr. 1.
Q: 8: Trag.

0575 **<MOSCHION>** Gnom.
Incertum
001 **Sententiae**, ed. H. Schenkl, *Epicteti dissertationes ab Arriano digestae*. Leipzig: Teubner, 1916 (repr. Stuttgart: 1965): 493–494.
frr. 1–25.
Q: [583]
002 **Hypothecae**, ed. Schenkl, *op. cit.*, 495–496.
frr. 1–18.
Q

1517 **MOSCHION** Hist. et Paradox.
3 B.C.?
001 **Fragmenta**, FGrH #575: 3B:675–678.
Q: 1,402: Hist., Paradox.

0339 **MOSCHION** Trag.
3 B.C.
001 **Fragmenta**, ed. B. Snell, *Tragicorum Graecorum fragmenta*, vol. 1. Göttingen: Vandenhoeck & Ruprecht, 1971: 264–268.
frr. 1–10, 12.
Q: 416: Trag.

0994 **MOSCHION** ὁ διορθωτής Med.
1 B.C.
Cf. et APHRODAS et MOSCHION Med. (0866).
x01 **Fragmenta ap. Galenum.**
K13.528, 537–539, 646–649, 853.
Cf. GALENUS Med. (0057 077).

x02 **Fragmentum ap. Aëtium** (lib. 15).
Zervos, *Athena* 21, p. 63.
Cf. AËTIUS Med. (0718 015).

x03 **Fragmentum ap. Alexandrum Trallianum.**
Puschmann, vol. 1, p. 571.
Cf. ALEXANDER Med. (0744 003).

x04 **Fragmentum ap. Hippiatrica.**
Oder & Hoppe, vol. 2, p. 194.
Cf. HIPPIATRICA (0738 006).

9025 **Manuel MOSCHOPULUS** Gramm.
A.D. 13–14: Constantinopolitanus

001 **Scholia in Iliadem**, ed. L. Bachmann, *Scholia in Homeri Iliadem*, pt. 1. Rostock: Adler, 1835: 1–52.
Cod: Schol.

002 **Scholia in Batrachomyomachiam** (e cod. Ottoboniano gr. 150), ed. A. Ludwich, *Moschopuli in Batrachomyomachiam commentarii*, pt. 1 [*Programm Königsberg* (1890)].
Cod: Schol.

003 **Scholia in Batrachomyomachiam** (e cod. Ambrosiano H 22), ed. Ludwich, *op. cit.*, pt. 2 (1892): 5–24.
Cod: Schol.

x01 **Scholia in Pindarum.**
Abel, pp. 44–480 passim.
Cf. SCHOLIA IN PINDARUM (5034 004).

x02 **Scholia in Hesiodi opera et dies.**
Gaisford, pp. 23–447 passim.
Cf. SCHOLIA IN HESIODUM (5025 002).

x03 **Scholia in Aristophanis plutum** (fort. auctore Moschopulo).
Dübner, pp. 333, 345, 349.
Cf. SCHOLIA IN ARISTOPHANEM (5014 014) (vv. 172, 355, 455).

x04 **Scholia in Sophoclis Oedipum tyrannum.**
Longo, pp. 3–92.
Cf. SCHOLIA IN SOPHOCLEM (5037 005).

0035 **MOSCHUS** Bucol.
2 B.C.: Syracusanus

001 **Eros drapeta**, ed. A.S.F. Gow, *Bucolici Graeci.* Oxford: Clarendon Press, 1952 (repr. 1969): 132–133.
Cod: 253: Bucol.

002 **Europa**, ed. Gow, *op. cit.*, 133–139.
Cod: 1,146: Bucol.

003 **Epitaphius Bionis** [Sp.], ed. Gow, *op. cit.*, 140–145.
Cod: 926: Bucol.

004 **Megara** [Sp.], ed. Gow, *op. cit.*, 146–150.
Cod: 898: Bucol.

005 **Fragmenta**, ed. Gow, *op. cit.*, 151–152.
Q: 268: Bucol., Epigr.

006 **Epigrammata**, AG **9**.440; **16**.200.
Dup. 0035 001 (pp. 132–133) et 0035 005 (p. 152, fr. 4).
Q: 284: Epigr.

4231 **Demetrius MOSCHUS** Philol.
A.D. 15–16: fort. Lacedaemonius

001 **Hypothesis in Orphicum librum de lapidibus**, ed. R. Halleux and J. Schamp, *Les lapidaires grecs*. Paris: Les Belles Lettres, 1985: 80–81.
Cod

2856 **Joannes MOSCHUS** Scr. Eccl.
vel Joannes Eucrates
A.D. 6–7: Aegyptius, Antiochenus, Constantinopolitanus

001 **Pratum spirituale**, MPG 87.3: 2852–3112.
Cod: Hagiogr.

002 **Pratum spirituale** (cap. 120–122, 131–132), ed. P. Pattenden, "The text of the pratum spirituale," *Journal of Theological Studies*, n.s. 26 (1975) 49–54.
Cod: Hagiogr.

003 **Prologus in pratum spirituale** [Sp.], ed. H. Usener, *Sonderbare Heilige I. Der heilige Tychon*. Leipzig: Teubner, 1907: 91–93.
Cod: Hagiogr.

2181 **MOSES** Alchem.
A.D. 2?

001 **Fragmenta**, ed. M. Berthelot, *Collection des anciens alchimistes grecs*. Paris: Steinheil, 1887 (repr. London: Holland Press, 1963): 38–39, 300–315.
Cod

2414 **MOSMES** (?) Hist.
post 4 B.C.?

001 **Fragmentum**, FGrH #614: 3C:122.
Q: 48: Hist.

1519 **MUNDUS MUNATIUS** Epigr.
A.D. 1?

001 **Epigramma**, AG 9.103.
Q: 53: Epigr.

0808 **MUSA** Med.
fiq Antonius Musa vel Petronius
A.D. 1?
Cf. et ANTONIUS MUSA Med. (0669).
Cf. et PETRONIUS Med. (1026).

x01 **Fragmenta ap. Galenum.**
K12.956; 13.832.
Cf. GALENUS Med. (0057 076–077).

x02 **Fragmenta ap. Oribasium.**
CMG, vol. **6.2.2**, p. 192; **6.3**, pp. 93, 494.
Cf. ORIBASIUS Med. (0722 003–005).

x03 **Fragmentum ap. Paulum.**
CMG, vol. 9.2, p. 317.
Cf. PAULUS Med. (0715 001).

0576 **MUSAEUS** Epic.
2 B.C.?: Ephesius

001 **Testimonium**, FGrH #455: 3B:383.
NQ: 22: Test.

002 **Fragmentum**, FGrH #455: 3B:383.
Q: 86: Hist.

003 **Tituli**, ed. H. Lloyd-Jones and P. Parsons,

Supplementum Hellenisticum. Berlin: De Gruyter, 1983: 274.
frr. 560–561.
NQ: 7: Epic.

2691 **[MUSAEUS]** Phil.
Incertum: Eleusinius
001 **Testimonia**, ed. H. Diels and W. Kranz, *Die Fragmente der Vorsokratiker*, vol. 1, 6th edn. Berlin: Weidmann, 1951 (repr. Dublin: 1966): 20–22.
test. 1–11.
NQ: 600: Test.
002 **Fragmenta**, ed. Diels and Kranz, *op. cit.*, 22–27.
frr. 1–22.
Q: 1,240: Phil., Theol.

4082 **MUSAEUS Grammaticus** Epic.
A.D. 5/6
001 **Hero et Leander**, ed. H. Färber, *Hero und Leander*. Munich: Heimeran, 1961: 6–26.
Cod: 2,185: Epic.

1520 **MUSICIUS** Epigr.
ante A.D. 3
001 **Epigramma**, AG 9.39.
Q: 28: Epigr.

0628 **Gaius MUSONIUS RUFUS** Phil.
A.D. 1: Volsiniensis
001 **Dissertationum a Lucio digestarum reliquiae**, ed. C.E. Lutz, *Musonius Rufus "The Roman Socrates."* New Haven: Yale University Press, 1947: 32–128.
frr. 1–21.
fr. 15: *P. Harris* 1 (inv. 3).
Q, Pap: 15,647: Phil.
002 **Fragmenta minora**, ed. Lutz, *op. cit.*, 131–141, 144.
frr. 22–48, 50–51, 53.
Q: 1,165: Phil., Gnom.
003 **Epistulae spuriae**, ed. O. Hense, *C. Musonii Rufi reliquiae*. Leipzig: Teubner, 1905: 137–143.
Cod: 1,363: Epist.
004 **Fragmentum**, ed. G.D. Kilpatrick, "A fragment of Musonius," *Classical Review* 63 (1949) 94.
Q: 23: Phil.

0509 **<MYIA>** Phil.
3/2 B.C.
001 **Epistula ad Phyllidem**, ed. H. Thesleff, *The Pythagorean texts of the Hellenistic period.* Åbo: Åbo Akademi, 1965: 123–124.
Q: 301: Phil., Epist.

1522 **MYRINUS** Epigr.
1 B.C.?
001 **Epigrammata**, AG **6**.108, 254; 7.703; 11.67.
Q: 137: Epigr.

4271 **MYRMEX** Phil.
4 B.C.: Atheniensis
001 **Testimonia**, ed. K. Döring, *Die Megariker* [*Studien zur antiken Philosophie* 2. Amsterdam: Grüner, 1972]: 52, 61.
test. 164a–b = Stilpo (4262 001).
NQ: Test.

1523 **MYRON** Hist.
3 B.C.?: Prienaeus
001 **Testimonium**, FGrH #106: 2B:509.
NQ: 149: Test.
002 **Fragmenta**, FGrH #106: 2B:509–515.
Q, Epigr: 2,063: Hist.

2331 **MYRSILUS** Hist.
3 B.C.: Methymnaeus
001 **Testimonia**, FGrH #477: 3B:437.
NQ: 50: Test.
002 **Fragmenta**, FGrH #477: 3B:437–442.
Q: 1,608: Hist., Paradox.

0477 **MYRTILUS** Comic.
5 B.C.
001 **Fragmenta**, ed. T. Kock, *Comicorum Atticorum fragmenta*, vol. 1. Leipzig: Teubner, 1880: 253–254.
frr. 3–4 + tituli.
Q: 19: Comic.
002 **Fragmenta**, ed. A. Meineke, *Fragmenta comicorum Graecorum*, vol. 2.1. Berlin: Reimer, 1839 (repr. De Gruyter, 1970): 418–419.
Q: 18: Comic.
003 **Fragmentum**, ed. Kock, *CAF*, vol. 3 (1888): 717.
fr. 3b.
Q: 7: Comic.

MYSON Phil.
7–6 B.C.: Lacon
Cf. <SEPTEM SAPIENTES> (1667 006).

1524 **NAUMACHIUS** Epic.
A.D. 2
001 **Fragmentum**, ed. E. Heitsch, *Die griechischen Dichterfragmente der römischen Kaiserzeit*, vol. 1, 2nd edn. Göttingen: Vandenhoeck & Ruprecht, 1963: 92–94.
Q: 525: Epic.

0478 **NAUSICRATES** Comic.
4 B.C.
001 **Fragmenta**, ed. T. Kock, *Comicorum Atticorum fragmenta*, vol. 2. Leipzig: Teubner, 1884: 295–296.
frr. 1–3.
Q: 132: Comic.
002 **Fragmenta**, ed. A. Meineke, *Fragmenta comicorum Graecorum*, vol. 4. Berlin: Reimer, 1841 (repr. De Gruyter, 1970): 575, 578.
Q: 87: Comic.

003 **Fragmentum**, ed. J. Demiańczuk, *Supplementum comicum*. Krakau: Nakładem Akademii, 1912 (repr. Hildesheim: Olms, 1967): 64.
fr. 1.
Q: 2: Comic.

2334 **NAUSIPHANES** Phil.
4–3 B.C.: Teius
001 **Testimonia**, ed. H. Diels and W. Kranz, *Die Fragmente der Vorsokratiker*, vol. 2, 6th edn. Berlin: Weidmann, 1952 (repr. Dublin: 1966): 246–247.
test. 1–9.
NQ: 504: Test.
002 **Fragmenta**, ed. Diels and Kranz, *op. cit.*, 248–250.
frr. 1–4.
Q: 889: Phil.

0269 ***NAUTARUM CANTIUNCULAE***
ante A.D. 2/3
001 **Fragmentum** (*P. Oxy.* 3.425), ed. E. Heitsch, *Die griechischen Dichterfragmente der römischen Kaiserzeit*, vol. 1, 2nd edn. Göttingen: Vandenhoeck & Ruprecht, 1963: 33.
Dup. partim LYRICA ADESPOTA (CA) (0230 001) (fr. 32).
Pap: 20: Lyr.
002 **Ad Rhodios ventos** (*P. Oxy.* 11.1383), ed. Heitsch, *op. cit.*, 33.
Dup. partim LYRICA ADESPOTA (CA) (0230 001) (fr. 33).
Pap: 41: Lyr.

4155 ***NAUTICUS LAPIDARIUS***
Incertum
001 **Nauticus lapidarius liber**, ed. R. Halleux and J. Schamp, *Les lapidaires grecs*. Paris: Les Belles Lettres, 1985: 188–189.
Cod: Nat. Hist.

1525 **NEANTHES** Hist.
3 B.C.: Cyzicenus
001 **Testimonia**, FGrH #84: 2A:191.
NQ: 84: Test.
002 **Fragmenta**, FGrH #84: 2A:192–202.
fr. 34: *P. Herc.* 327, fr. 4.
Q, Pap: 3,426: Hist.

1966 **NEANTHES Junior** Hist.
3–2 B.C.: Cyzicenus
001 **Fragmentum**, FGrH #171: 2B:895.
Q: 33: Hist.

1942 **NEARCHUS** Hist.
4–3 B.C.?: Cretensis
001 **Testimonia**, FGrH #133: 2B:677–680.
test. 2: *Inscr. Delphi.*
NQ: 998: Test.
002 **Fragmenta**, FGrH #133: 2B:681–722.
Q: 15,337: Hist., Perieg.

0995 **[NECHEPSO et PETOSIRIS]** Astrol.
ante 2 B.C.: Aegyptius
001 **Fragmenta**, ed. E. Riess, "Nechepsonis et Petosiridis fragmenta magica," *Philologus*, suppl. 6 (1891–1893) 332–387.
Q, Cod
002 **Testimonium**, FGrH #663: 3C:214.
NQ: 26: Test.
x01 **Fragmentum ap. Aëtium** (lib. 2).
CMG, vol. 8.1, p. 164.
Cf. AËTIUS Med. (0718 002).
x02 **Fragmentum ap. Aëtium** (lib. 15).
Zervos, *Athena* 21, p. 42.
Cf. AËTIUS Med. (0718 015).

0996 **NEILAMMON** Med.
ante A.D. 7
x01 **Fragmentum ap. Paulum**.
CMG, vol. 9.2, p. 338.
Cf. PAULUS Med. (0715 001).

4079 **NEILUS** Epigr.
A.D. 5
001 **Epigrammata**, AG 1.33; **16**.247.
Q: 49: Epigr.

0743 **NEMESIUS** Theol.
A.D. 4: Emesenus
001 **De natura hominis**, ed. B. Einarson, *Nemesius of Emesa* (typescript) [*Corpus medicorum Graecorum* (in press)]: 35–368.
Cod: 37,934: Med., Phil.

0025 **NEOCLIDES** Math. et Phil.
5–4 B.C.: Atheniensis
001 **Testimonium**, ed. F. Lasserre, *De Léodamas de Thasos à Philippe d'Oponte*. Naples: Bibliopolis, 1987: 77.
NQ: Test.

0307 **NEOPHRON** Trag.
5 B.C.
001 **Fragmenta**, ed. B. Snell, *Tragicorum Graecorum fragmenta*, vol. 1. Göttingen: Vandenhoeck & Ruprecht, 1971: 92–94.
frr. 1–3.
Q: 146: Trag.

1526 **NEOPTOLEMUS** Gramm.
3 B.C.: Parianus
001 **Fragmenta**, ed. J.U. Powell, *Collectanea Alexandrina*. Oxford: Clarendon Press, 1925 (repr. 1970): 27–28.
frr. 1–2, 3, 6.
Dup. partim 1526 003 (frr. 2, 4, 5).
Q: 39: Epic.
002 **Testimonium**, FGrH #702: 3C:555.
NQ: 18: Test.
003 **Fragmenta**, FGrH #702: 3C:556.
Dup. partim 1526 001 (frr. 2, 3, 6).
Q: 202: Hist., Epic., Epigr.

004 **Fragmenta**, ed. H.J. Mette, "Neoptolemos von Parion," *Rheinisches Museum* 123 (1980) 1–13.
Q

1527 **NEPUALIUS** Phil.
vel Neptunalius vel Neptunianus
A.D. 2?
001 Περὶ τῶν κατὰ ἀντιπάθειαν καὶ συμπάθειαν, ed. W. Gemoll, *Nepualii fragmentum περὶ τῶν κατὰ ἀντιπάθειαν καὶ συμπάθειαν et Democriti περὶ συμπαθειῶν καὶ ἀντιπαθειῶν [Städtisches Realprogymnasium zu Striegau* (1884)]: 1–3.
Cod

0998 **NERO Imperator**
A.D. 1: Romanus
x01 **Fragmentum ap. Paulum.**
CMG, vol. 9.2, p. 359.
Cf. PAULUS Med. (0715 001).

2456 **NESSAS** Phil.
5 B.C.: Chius
001 **Testimonia**, ed. H. Diels and W. Kranz, *Die Fragmente der Vorsokratiker*, vol. 2, 6th edn. Berlin: Weidmann, 1952 (repr. Dublin: 1966): 230.
test. 1–2.
NQ: 66: Test.
002 **Fragmenta**, ed. Diels and Kranz, *op. cit.*, 230.
frr. 1–2.
Q: 47: Phil.

1528 **NESTOR** Epic.
A.D. 2–3: Larandensis
001 **Epigrammata**, AG 9.128–129, 364, 537.
AG 9.536: Cf. ANONYMI EPIGRAMMATICI (AG) (0138 001).
Q: 108: Epigr.
x01 **Epigramma dedicatorium.**
App. Anth. 1.299?: Cf. ANTHOLOGIAE GRAECAE APPENDIX (7052 001).

0218 **NICAENETUS** Epic.
3 B.C.: Abderita
001 **Fragmenta**, ed. J.U. Powell, *Collectanea Alexandrina.* Oxford: Clarendon Press, 1925 (repr. 1970): 1–4.
frr. 1–7.
Q: 239: Epic., Epigr.
002 **Epigrammata**, AG 6.225; 7.502; 13.29; 16.191.
Dup. partim 0218 001 (frr. 3–5, 7).
Q: 125: Epigr.
x01 **Epigramma exhortatorium et dedicatorium.**
App. Anth. 4.40: Cf. ANTHOLOGIAE GRAECAE APPENDIX (7052 004).
Dup. partim 0218 001 (fr. 6).

0022 **NICANDER** Epic.
fiq Nicander Colophonius Hist.
3/2 B.C.: Colophonius
Vita et Scholia: Cf. SCHOLIA IN NICANDRUM (5031).
Cf. et NICANDER Hist. (1933).

001 **Theriaca**, ed. A.S.F. Gow and A.F. Scholfield, *Nicander. The poems and poetical fragments.* Cambridge: Cambridge University Press, 1953: 28–92.
Cod, Pap: 6,380: Epic., Med., Nat. Hist.
002 **Alexipharmaca**, ed. Gow and Scholfield, *op. cit.*, 94–136.
Cod: 4,149: Epic., Med., Nat. Hist.
003 **Fragmenta**, ed. Gow and Scholfield, *op. cit.*, 138–166.
Oetaica (frr. 16, 18): p. 138.
Thebaica (fr. 19): p. 138.
Sicelia (frr. 21–22): pp. 138–140.
Europia (frr. 26–27): p. 140.
Ophiaca (frr. 31–32): p. 142.
Heteroeumena (frr. 43, 50, 59, 62): pp. 142–144.
Georgica (frr. 68–76, 78–87, 90–91): pp. 144–160.
Cynegetica (?) (frr. 98, 100): p. 162.
Hymnus in Attalum (?) (fr. 104): p. 162.
Epigrammata (frr. 105–107): pp. 162–164.
Incertae sedis fragmenta (frr. 108–112): pp. 164–166.
Q: 1,332: Epic., Med., Nat. Hist., Hymn., Epigr.
004 **Fragmenta prosaica**, ed. O. Schneider, *Nicandrea.* Leipzig: Teubner, 1856.
Q
005 **Fragmenta**, ed. H. Lloyd-Jones and P. Parsons, *Supplementum Hellenisticum.* Berlin: De Gruyter, 1983: 274, 277–278.
frr. 562–563a.
fr. 562: *P. Oxy.* 37.2812.
fr. 563 (commentarius in *Theriaca*): *P. Oxy.* 19.2221.
fr. 563a (commentarius in *Theriaca*): *P. Mil. Vogl.* 2.45.
Pap: 163: Hexametr., Comm.
006 **Epigrammata**, AG 7.435, 526; 9.503b.
Dup. partim 0022 001 (p. 76, v. 741), 003 (pp. 162–164).
AG 11.7: Cf. NICARCHUS II Epigr. (1532 001).
Q: 80: Epigr.
x01 **Fragmenta.**
FGrH #271–272.
Cf. NICANDER Hist. (1933 001–002).

1529 **NICANDER** Gramm.
3/1 B.C.: Thyatirius
001 **Testimonium**, FGrH #343: 3B:205.
NQ: 19: Test.
002 **Fragmenta**, FGrH #343: 3B:205–207.
Q: 785: Hist.

1933 **NICANDER** Hist.
fiq Nicander Epic.
3/2 B.C.: Colophonius
Cf. et NICANDER Epic. (0022).
001 **Testimonia**, FGrH #271–272: 3A:85–86.
NQ: 788: Test.

002 **Fragmenta,** FGrH #271-272: **3A**:87-95; **3B**:753 addenda.
Q: 3,027: Hist., Hexametr.

2474 **NICANDER** Hist.
2 B.C.?: Chalcedonius
001 **Fragmenta,** FGrH #700: 3C:554-555.
Q: 87: Hist.

1530 **NICANOR** Gramm.
A.D. 2: Alexandrinus
001 **Testimonium,** FGrH #628: 3C:178.
NQ: 65: Test.
002 **Fragmenta,** FGrH #628: 3C:178-179.
Q: 165: Hist.
003 Περὶ Ἰλιακῆς στιγμῆς, ed. L. Friedländer, *Nicanoris περὶ Ἰλιακῆς στιγμῆς reliquiae emendatiores,* 2nd edn. Berlin: Borntraeger, 1857 (repr. Hakkert, 1967): 141-278.
Q
004 Περὶ Ὀδυσσειακῆς στιγμῆς, ed. O. Carnuth, *Nicanoris περὶ Ὀδυσσειακῆς στιγμῆς reliquiae emendatiores.* Berlin: Borntraeger, 1875 (repr. Hakkert, 1967): 21-68.
Q

1948 **NICANOR** Hist.
ante 2 B.C.
001 **Fragmenta,** FGrH #146: 2B:814-815.
Q: 153: Hist.

2494 **NICARCHUS** Hist.
A.D. 1?
001 **Fragmentum,** FGrH #731: 3C:691-692.
Q: 88: Hist.

1531 **NICARCHUS I** Epigr.
4-3 B.C.
001 **Epigrammata,** AG **6**.31, 285; **7**.159, 166; **9**.330.
Q: 245: Epigr.

1532 **NICARCHUS II** Epigr.
A.D. 1
001 **Epigrammata,** AG **5**.38-40; **9**.576; **11**.1, 7, 17-18, 71, 73-74, 82, 96, 102, 110, 124, 162, 169-170, 186, 241-243, 251-252, 328-332, 395, 398, 406-407, 415.
AG 5.67: Cf. CAPITO Epigr. (0149 001).
AG 5.98: Cf. ARCHIAS Epigr. (0126 001).
AG 11.72: Cf. LOLLIUS BASSUS Epigr. (0143 001).
AG 11.118-122: Cf. CALLICTER Epigr. (0148 001).
AG 11.244: Cf. ANONYMI EPIGRAMMATICI (AG) (0138 001).
Q: 1,355: Epigr.

2361 **NICASYLUS** Hist.
Incertum
001 **Titulus,** FGrH #519: 3B:492.
NQ: Hist.

3152 **NICEPHORUS** Biogr.
A.D. 10: Constantinopolitanus
Cf. et THEODORUS Protosecretarius Biogr. (3154).
001 **Vita Theophanis Confessoris,** ed. C. de Boor, *Theophanis chronographia,* vol. 2. Leipzig: Teubner, 1885 (repr. Hildesheim: Olms, 1963): 13-27.
Cod: Biogr.

3086 **NICEPHORUS I** Theol., Scr. Eccl. et Hist.
vel Nicephorus Confessor vel Nicephorus Homologetes vel Nicephorus Patriarcha I
A.D. 8-9: Constantinopolitanus
001 **Breviarium historicum de rebus gestis post imperium Mauricii** (e cod. Vat. gr. 977), ed. C. de Boor, *Nicephori archiepiscopi Constantinopolitani opuscula historica.* Leipzig: Teubner, 1880 (repr. New York: Arno, 1975): 3-77.
Cod: Hist., Chronogr.
002 **Chronographia brevis** [Dub.], ed. de Boor, *op. cit.,* 81-135.
Cod: Hist., Chronogr.

3088 **NICEPHORUS BRYENNIUS** Hist.
vel Nicephorus Botaniata
A.D. 11-12: Constantinopolitanus
002 **Historiae,** ed. P. Gautier, *Nicéphore Bryennios. Histoire [Corpus fontium historiae Byzantinae 9. Series Bruxellensis.* Brussels: Byzantion, 1975]: 55-311.
Anonymi praefatio ad Bryennii historias: pp. 55-71.
Bryennii prooemium ad historias: pp. 71-73.
Historiae (lib. i-iv): pp. 75-311.
Cod: Hist.

4145 **NICEPHORUS GREGORAS** Polyhist.
A.D. 13-14: Heracleensis, Constantinopolitanus
001 **Byzantina historia,** ed. L. Schopen and I. Bekker, *Nicephori Gregorae historiae Byzantinae,* 3 vols. [Corpus scriptorum historiae Byzantinae.* Bonn: Weber, 1:1829; 2:1830; 3:1855]: 1:3-568; 2:571-1146; 3:3-567.
Cod: Hist.
x01 **Epigramma sepulcrale.**
App. Anth. 2.774: Cf. ANTHOLOGIAE GRAECAE APPENDIX (7052 002).

2633 **NICERATUS** Epic.
5 B.C.: Heracleota
001 **Titulus,** ed. H. Lloyd-Jones and P. Parsons, *Supplementum Hellenisticum.* Berlin: De Gruyter, 1983: 278.
fr. 564.
NQ: 2: Epic.

NICERATUS Epigr.
AG 13.29.
Cf. NICAENETUS Epic. (0218 002).

0999 **NICERATUS** Med.
1 B.C.–A.D. 1
x01 **Fragmenta ap. Galenum.**
K13.87, 96, 98, 110, 180, 232, 233–234.
Cf. GALENUS Med. (0057 076).

2705 **NICETAS DAVID** Gramm., Phil. et Scr.
Eccl.
vel Nicetas Philosophus vel Nicetas Rhetor
fiq Nicetas Paphlagonius
A.D. 9–10: Paphlagonius, Constantinopolitanus
x01 **Epigramma demonstrativum.**
App. Anth. 3.285: Cf. ANTHOLOGIAE GRAE-
CAE APPENDIX (7052 003).

0046 *NICIAE EPISTULA*
Incertum
001 **Epistula**, ed. R. Hercher, *Epistolographi Graeci.*
Paris: Didot, 1873 (repr. Amsterdam: Hakkert,
1965): 405–406.
Q: 768: Epist.

1533 **NICIAS** Epigr.
3 B.C.: Milesius
001 **Epigrammata**, AG **6.**122, 127, 270; **7.**200;
9.315, 564; **16.**188.
AG 11.398: Cf. NICARCHUS II Epigr. (1532
001).
Q: 181: Epigr.
002 **Fragmentum**, ed. H. Lloyd-Jones and P. Parsons, *Supplementum Hellenisticum.* Berlin: De
Gruyter, 1983: 279.
fr. 566.
Q: 16: Hexametr.

1837 **NICIAS** Gramm.
1 B.C.?: fort. Cous
001 **Fragmenta**, ed. R. Berndt, "Die Fragmente des
Grammatikers Nicias," *Philologische Wochenschrift* 30 (1910) coll. 508–510.
Q

2217 **NICIAS** Hist.
ante A.D. 3
001 **Fragmentum**, FGrH #318: 3B:31.
Q: 78: Hist.

1902 **<NICIAS>** Hist.
Incertum: Mallotes
001 **Fragmenta**, FGrH #60: 1A:298.
Q: 184: Hist., Myth., Nat. Hist.

0479 **NICO** Comic.
post 5 B.C.
001 **Fragmentum**, ed. T. Kock, *Comicorum Atticorum fragmenta*, vol. 3. Leipzig: Teubner,
1888: 389.
fr. 1.
Q: 19: Comic.

002 **Fragmentum**, ed. A. Meineke, *Fragmenta
comicorum Graecorum*, vol. 4. Berlin: Reimer,
1841 (repr. De Gruyter, 1970): 578.
Q: 20: Comic.

1937 **NICOBULE** Hist.
4 B.C.
001 **Testimonia**, FGrH #127: 2B:667.
NQ: 32: Test.
002 **Fragmenta**, FGrH #127: 2B:667.
Q: 91: Hist.

0480 **NICOCHARES** Comic.
4 B.C.
001 **Fragmenta**, ed. T. Kock, *Comicorum Atticorum fragmenta*, vol. 1. Leipzig: Teubner,
1880: 770–774.
frr. 1–3, 5, 7–9, 11–12, 14–21 + tituli.
Q: 116: Comic.
002 **Fragmenta**, ed. A. Meineke, *Fragmenta comicorum Graecorum*, vol. 2.2. Berlin: Reimer,
1840 (repr. De Gruyter, 1970): 842–846.
Q: 88: Comic.
003 **Fragmenta**, ed. J. Demiańczuk, *Supplementum
comicum.* Krakau: Nakładem Akademii, 1912
(repr. Hildesheim: Olms, 1967): 64–66.
frr. 1–5, 7.
Q: 30: Comic.

2279 **NICOCHARES** Hist.
ante 4 B.C.
001 **Testimonium**, FGrH #398: 3B:292.
NQ: 37: Test.

1534 **NICOCLES** Hist.
ante 1 B.C.: Lacon
001 **Fragmenta**, FGrH #587: 3B:701–702.
Q: 289: Hist.

1535 **NICOCRATES** Hist.
ante 2 B.C.
001 **Fragmenta**, FGrH #376: 3B:242–244.
fr. 1: *P. Mich.* 4913.
Q, Pap: 681: Hist.

1536 **NICODEMUS** Epigr.
Incertum: Heracleensis
001 **Epigrammata**, AG **6.**314–320, 323; **9.**53.
Q: 131: Epigr.

0481 **NICOLAUS** Comic.
4 B.C.?
001 **Fragmenta**, ed. T. Kock, *Comicorum Atticorum fragmenta*, vol. 3. Leipzig: Teubner,
1888: 383–384, 386.
frr. 1–2.
Q: 277: Comic.
002 **Fragmentum**, ed. A. Meineke, *Fragmenta
comicorum Graecorum*, vol. 4. Berlin: Reimer,
1841 (repr. De Gruyter, 1970): 579–580.
Q: 275: Comic.

2713 **NICOLAUS** Epigr.
A.D. 14?
x01 **Epigrammata exhortatoria et supplicatoria.**
App. Anth. 4.106–107: Cf. ANTHOLOGIAE
GRAECAE APPENDIX (7052 004).

0577 **NICOLAUS** Hist.
1 B.C.: Damascenus
001 **Testimonia**, FGrH #90: 2A:324–328.
NQ: 1,119: Test.
002 **Fragmenta**, FGrH #90: 2A:328–430.
Q: 35,523: Hist., Biogr., Encom.

1001 **NICOLAUS** Med.
ante A.D. 2
x01 **Fragmentum ap. Galenum.**
K13.831.
Cf. GALENUS Med. (0057 077).
x02 **Fragmentum ap. Paulum.**
CMG, vol. 9.2, p. 358.
Cf. PAULUS Med. (0715 001).

2904 **NICOLAUS** Rhet. et Soph.
A.D. 5: Myrensis (Lyciae), Atheniensis, Constantinopolitanus
001 **Progymnasmata**, ed. J. Felten, *Nicolai pro-*
gymnasmata [*Rhetores Graeci* 11. Leipzig:
Teubner, 1913]: 1–79.
pp. 59–63: Dup. partim 2904 002–003.
Q, Cod: Rhet.
002 **Progymnasmata** (caput περὶ συγκρίσεως e cod.
Brit. Mus. addit. 11889), ed. Felten, *op. cit.*, v–
vi.
Dup. partim 2904 001, 003.
Cod: Rhet.
003 **Progymnasmata** (capita περὶ συγκρίσεως, περὶ
ἠθοποιίας, περὶ ἐκφράσεως, περὶ θέσεως, περὶ
νόμου εἰσφορᾶς e cod. Ambros. 523), ed. Felten, *op. cit.*, 60–79.
Dup. partim 2904 001–002.
Cod: Rhet.

4144 **NICOLAUS CALLICLES** Med. et Poeta
fiq Nicolaus magister medicorum
A.D. 11–12: Constantinopolitanus
x01 **Epigrammata sepulcralia.**
App. Anth. 2.771–773: Cf. ANTHOLOGIAE
GRAECAE APPENDIX (7052 002).

0482 **NICOMACHUS** Comic.
3 B.C.
001 **Fragmenta**, ed. T. Kock, *Comicorum Atti-*
corum fragmenta, vol. 3. Leipzig: Teubner,
1888: 386–389.
frr. 1–4.
Q: 335: Comic.
002 **Fragmenta**, ed. A. Meineke, *Fragmenta comi-*
corum Graecorum, vol. 4. Berlin: Reimer, 1841
(repr. De Gruyter, 1970): 583–584, 587–588.
Q: 311: Comic.

1537 **NICOMACHUS** Epigr.
ante 2 B.C.
001 **Epigramma**, AG 7.299.
Q: 29: Epigr.

1538 **NICOMACHUS** Hist.
ante A.D. 2
001 **Fragmentum**, FGrH #662: 3C:213–214.
Q: 46: Hist.

1961 **NICOMACHUS** Hist.
A.D. 3–4?
001 **Fragmentum**, FGrH #215: 2B:946.
Q: 258: Hist.

0358 **NICOMACHUS** Math.
A.D. 2: Gerasenus
001 **Introductio arithmetica**, ed. R. Hoche, *Nico-*
machi Geraseni Pythagorei introductionis arith-
meticae libri ii. Leipzig: Teubner, 1866: 1–70,
73–147.
Cod: 24,279: Math.
002 **Harmonicum enchiridion**, ed. K. Jan, *Musici*
scriptores Graeci. Leipzig: Teubner, 1895 (repr.
Hildesheim: Olms, 1962): 236–265.
Cod: 5,229: Mus.
003 **Theologoumena arithmeticae**, ed. V. de Falco,
[Iamblichi] theologoumena arithmeticae. Leipzig: Teubner, 1922: 17–30, 42, 56–71.
Q: 5,785: Math.
004 **Excerpta**, ed. Jan, *op. cit.*, 266–282.
Cod: 2,443: Mus.

NICOMACHUS Med.
Cf. ALCIMION vel NICOMACHUS Med.
(0823).

1843 **NICOMACHUS** Trag.
5 B.C.: Atheniensis
001 **Tituli**, ed. B. Snell, *Tragicorum Graecorum*
fragmenta, vol. 1. Göttingen: Vandenhoeck &
Ruprecht, 1971: 155.
NQ: 3: Trag., Satyr.

0342 **NICOMACHUS** Trag.
3 B.C.: Alexandrinus (Troadis)
001 **Fragmenta**, ed. B. Snell, *Tragicorum Grae-*
corum fragmenta, vol. 1. Göttingen: Vandenhoeck & Ruprecht, 1971: 285–287.
frr. 1–16.
Q: 42: Trag.

NICOMEDES Epigr.
AG 9.53.
Cf. NICODEMUS Epigr. (1536 001).
Cf. LOLLIUS BASSUS Epigr. (0143 001).

2520 **NICOMEDES** Hist.
4 B.C.?: Acanthius
001 **Fragmenta**, FGrH #772: 3C:766–767.
Q: 197: Hist.

2674 **NICOMEDES** Med.
vel Nicodemus
A.D. 2

x01 **Epigramma dedicatorium.**
App. Anth. 1.247(?): Cf. ANTHOLOGIAE
GRAECAE APPENDIX (7052 001).

NICOMEDES Rex Bithyniae <Med.>
Cf. CODAMUS vel NICOMEDES Rex Bithyniae <Med.> (0838).

0483 **NICOPHON** Comic.
5–4 B.C.: Atheniensis

001 **Fragmenta,** ed. T. Kock, *Comicorum Atticorum fragmenta*, vol. 1. Leipzig: Teubner,
1880: 775–780.
frr. 1–29.
Q: 183: Comic.

002 **Fragmenta,** ed. A. Meineke, *Fragmenta comicorum Graecorum*, vol. 2.2. Berlin: Reimer,
1840 (repr. De Gruyter, 1970): 848–854.
Q: 155: Comic.

0484 **NICOSTRATUS** Comic.
4 B.C.

001 **Fragmenta,** ed. T. Kock, *Comicorum Atticorum fragmenta*, vol. 2. Leipzig: Teubner,
1884: 219–230, 581.
frr. 1–13, 15–22, 24–36, 38–40, 42 + titulus.
Q: 562: Comic.

002 **Fragmenta,** ed. A. Meineke, *Fragmenta comicorum Graecorum*, vol. 3. Berlin: Reimer, 1840
(repr. De Gruyter, 1970): 278–290.
Q: 527: Comic.

003 **Fragmentum,** ed. J. Demiańczuk, *Supplementum comicum*. Krakau: Nakładem Akademii,
1912 (repr. Hildesheim: Olms, 1967): 66.
fr. 1.
Q: 9: Comic.

004 **Titulus,** ed. Kock, *CAF*, vol. 3 (1888): 739.
NQ: 2: Comic.

005 **Fragmenta,** ed. Meineke, *FCG*, vol. 5.1 (1857;
repr. 1970): 84.
Q: 6: Comic.

2523 **NICOSTRATUS** Hist.
ante 2 B.C.

001 **Fragmentum,** FGrH #778: 3C:772.
Q: 98: Hist.

2144 **NICOSTRATUS** Hist.
A.D. 3: Trapezius

001 **Testimonium,** FGrH #98: 2A:452.
NQ: 43: Test.

1005 **NICOSTRATUS** Med.
ante A.D. 2

x01 **Fragmenta ap. Galenum.**
K13.139, 279, 299, 308, 985; 14.208.
Cf. GALENUS Med. (0057 076–078).

1539 **NICOSTRATUS** Soph.
A.D. 2: Macedo

x01 **Fragmenta ap. Stobaeum.**
Anth. IV.22.102; 23.62–65.
Cf. Joannes STOBAEUS (2037 001).

0997 **NILEUS** Med.
vel Neileus vel Neilus
3 B.C.

x01 **Fragmenta ap. Galenum.**
K12.765–766; 13.182.
Cf. GALENUS Med. (0057 076).

x02 **Fragmenta ap. Oribasium.**
CMG, vol. 6.2.2, pp. 203, 245; 6.3, p. 100.
Cf. ORIBASIUS Med. (0722 003–004).

x03 **Fragmenta ap. Paulum.**
CMG, vol. 9.2, pp. 342, 371.
Cf. PAULUS Med. (0715 001).

x04 **Fragmentum ap. Aëtium** (lib. 7).
CMG, vol. 8.2, p. 375.
Cf. AËTIUS Med. (0718 007).

x05 **Fragmentum ap. Aëtium** (lib. 9).
Zervos, *Athena* 23, p. 308.
Cf. AËTIUS Med. (0718 009).

1804 *NINUS*
1 B.C.?

001 **Fragmenta A-B** (*P. Berol.* 6926), ed. F. Zimmermann, *Griechische Roman-Papyri und verwandte Texte*. Heidelberg: Bilabel, 1936: 14–35.
Pap: 1,455: Narr. Fict.

002 **Fragmentum C** (*PSI* 1305), ed. M. Norsa, *PSI* 13 (1949): 82–86.
Pap: Narr. Fict.

2045 **NONNUS** Epic.
A.D. 5/6: Panopolitanus

001 **Dionysiaca,** ed. R. Keydell, *Nonni Panopolitani Dionysiaca*, 2 vols. Berlin: Weidmann, 1959:
1:1–500; 2:1–509.
Cod: 129,061: Epic.

002 **Paraphrasis sancti evangelii Joannei,** ed. A. Scheindler, *Paraphrasis s. evangelii Ioannei*.
Leipzig: Teubner, 1881: 3–228.
Cod: 23,202: Evangel., Hexametr., Exeget.

003 **Epigramma,** AG 10.120.
Q: 14: Epigr.

1006 **NONNUS** Med.
ante A.D. 6

x01 **Fragmentum ap. Aëtium** (lib. 7).
CMG, vol. 8.2, p. 382.
Cf. AËTIUS Med. (0718 007).

1540 **NOSSIS** Epigr.
4 B.C.: Locra

001 **Epigrammata,** AG 5.170; 6.132, 265, 273(?),
275, 353–354; 7.414, 718; 9.332, 604–605.
Q: 336: Epigr.

1541 *NOSTOI*
post 7 B.C.
Cf. et ATRIDARUM REDITUS (1212).

001 **Fragmenta,** ed. T.W. Allen, *Homeri opera*, vol.

5. Oxford: Clarendon Press, 1912 (repr. 1969): 140–142.
frr. 2, 6, 8, 11.
Q: Epic.

0031 *NOVUM TESTAMENTUM*
A.D. 1

001 **Evangelium secundum Matthaeum**, ed. K. Aland, M. Black, C.M. Martini, B.M. Metzger and A. Wikgren, *The Greek New Testament*, 2nd edn. Stuttgart: Württemberg Bible Society, 1968: 1–117.
Cod: 19,521: Relig., Evangel.

002 **Evangelium secundum Marcum**, ed. Aland, Black, Martini, Metzger, and Wikgren, *op. cit.*, 118–198.
Cod: 12,076: Relig., Evangel.

003 **Evangelium secundum Lucam**, ed. Aland, Black, Martini, Metzger, and Wikgren, *op. cit.*, 199–319.
Cod: 20,728: Relig., Evangel.

004 **Evangelium secundum Joannem**, ed. Aland, Black, Martini, Metzger, and Wikgren, *op. cit.*, 320–415.
Cod: 16,576: Relig., Evangel.

005 **Acta apostolorum**, ed. Aland, Black, Martini, Metzger, and Wikgren, *op. cit.*, 416–528.
Cod: 19,551: Relig., Acta

006 **Epistula Pauli ad Romanos**, ed. Aland, Black, Martini, Metzger, and Wikgren, *op. cit.*, 529–577.
Cod: 7,573: Relig., Epist.

007 **Epistula Pauli ad Corinthios i**, ed. Aland, Black, Martini, Metzger, and Wikgren, *op. cit.*, 578–620.
Cod: 7,266: Relig., Epist.

008 **Epistula Pauli ad Corinthios ii**, ed. Aland, Black, Martini, Metzger, and Wikgren, *op. cit.*, 621–647.
Cod: 4,761: Relig., Epist.

009 **Epistula Pauli ad Galatas**, ed. Aland, Black, Martini, Metzger, and Wikgren, *op. cit.*, 648–663.
Cod: 2,379: Relig., Epist.

010 **Epistula Pauli ad Ephesios**, ed. Aland, Black, Martini, Metzger, and Wikgren, *op. cit.*, 664–680.
Cod: 2,605: Relig., Epist.

011 **Epistula Pauli ad Philippenses**, ed. Aland, Black, Martini, Metzger, and Wikgren, *op. cit.*, 681–691.
Cod: 1,731: Relig., Epist.

012 **Epistula Pauli ad Colossenses**, ed. Aland, Black, Martini, Metzger, and Wikgren, *op. cit.*, 692–703.
Cod: 1,684: Relig., Epist.

013 **Epistula Pauli ad Thessalonicenses i**, ed. Aland, Black, Martini, Metzger, and Wikgren, *op. cit.*, 704–713.
Cod: 1,574: Relig., Epist.

014 **Epistula Pauli ad Thessalonicenses ii**, ed. Aland, Black, Martini, Metzger, and Wikgren, *op. cit.*, 714–719.

Cod: 879: Relig., Epist.

015 **Epistula Pauli ad Timotheum i**, ed. Aland, Black, Martini, Metzger, and Wikgren, *op. cit.*, 720–730.
Cod: 1,717: Relig., Epist.

016 **Epistula Pauli ad Timotheum ii**, ed. Aland, Black, Martini, Metzger, and Wikgren, *op. cit.*, 731–738.
Cod: 1,337: Relig., Epist.

017 **Epistula Pauli ad Titum**, ed. Aland, Black, Martini, Metzger, and Wikgren, *op. cit.*, 739–743.
Cod: 720: Relig., Epist.

018 **Epistula Pauli ad Philemonem**, ed. Aland, Black, Martini, Metzger, and Wikgren, *op. cit.*, 744–746.
Cod: 365: Relig., Epist.

019 **Epistula Pauli ad Hebraeos**, ed. Aland, Black, Martini, Metzger, and Wikgren, *op. cit.*, 747–778.
Cod: 5,286: Relig., Epist.

020 **Epistula Jacobi**, ed. Aland, Black, Martini, Metzger, and Wikgren, *op. cit.*, 779–790.
Cod: 1,857: Relig., Epist.

021 **Epistula Petri i**, ed. Aland, Black, Martini, Metzger, and Wikgren, *op. cit.*, 791–804.
Cod: 1,790: Relig., Epist.

022 **Epistula Petri ii**, ed. Aland, Black, Martini, Metzger, and Wikgren, *op. cit.*, 805–812.
Cod: 1,180: Relig., Epist.

023 **Epistula Joannis i**, ed. Aland, Black, Martini, Metzger, and Wikgren, *op. cit.*, 813–826.
Cod: 2,250: Relig., Epist.

024 **Epistula Joannis ii**, ed. Aland, Black, Martini, Metzger, and Wikgren, *op. cit.*, 827–829.
Cod: 264: Relig., Epist.

025 **Epistula Joannis iii**, ed. Aland, Black, Martini, Metzger, and Wikgren, *op. cit.*, 830–831.
Cod: 235: Relig., Epist.

026 **Epistula Juda**, ed. Aland, Black, Martini, Metzger, and Wikgren, *op. cit.*, 832–835.
Cod: 489: Relig., Epist.

027 **Apocalypsis Joannis**, ed. Aland, Black, Martini, Metzger, and Wikgren, *op. cit.*, 836–895.
Cod: 10,224: Relig., Apocalyp.

1543 **NUMENIUS** Epigr.
ante A.D. 2: Tarsensis

001 **Epigramma**, AG 12.28.
AG 12.60: Cf. MELEAGER Epigr. (1492 001).
AG 12.237: Cf. STRATON Epigr. (1697 001).
Q: 18: Epigr.

0704 **NUMENIUS** Med.
fiq Numenius Heracleota
3 B.C.?
Cf. et NUMENIUS Poet. Didac. (0703).

x01 **Fragmentum ap. Philumenum.**
CMG, vol. 10.1.1, p. 22.
Cf. PHILUMENUS Med. (0671 001).

1542 **NUMENIUS** Phil.
A.D. 2: Apamensis

001 **Fragmenta**, ed. É. des Places, *Numénius. Fragments*. Paris: Les Belles Lettres, 1974: 42–94, 99–102.
Περὶ τἀγαθοῦ (frr. 1–22): pp. 1–61.
Περὶ τῶν παρὰ Πλάτωνι ἀπορρήτων (fr. 23): pp. 61–62.
Περὶ τῆς τῶν Ἀκαδημαϊκῶν πρὸς Πλάτωνα διαστάσεως (frr. 24–28): pp. 62–80.
Περὶ ἀφθαρσίας ψυχῆς (fr. 29): p. 80.
Incertorum operum fragmenta (frr. 30–33, 35–51, 53–54, 56–59): pp. 80–94, 99–101.
Fragmentum dubium (fr. 60): pp. 101–102.
Q: 10,512: Phil.

0703 **NUMENIUS** Poet. Didac.
fiq Numenius Med.
3 B.C.: Heracleota
Cf. et NUMENIUS Med. (0704 001).
001 **Fragmenta et tituli**, ed. H. Lloyd-Jones and P. Parsons, *Supplementum Hellenisticum*. Berlin: De Gruyter, 1983: 279–285.
frr. (+ titul.) 568–592.
Dup. partim 0703 x01.
Q: 321: Hexametr.
x01 **Fragmenta ap. Athenaeum**.
Deipnosophistae 7.282a; 286f; 287c; 295b; 304d, e, f; 305c; 306c–d; 308e; 309c, f; 313d, e; 315b; 319b; 320d, e; 321b; 322b, f; 326a, f; 327a, b, f; 328a, d; **9**.371b.
Dup. partim 0703 001 (frr. 569–588).
Cf. ATHENAEUS Soph. (0008 001).

1544 **NYMPHIS** Hist.
4–3 B.C.: Heracleota
001 **Testimonia**, FGrH #432: 3B:328–329.
NQ: 178: Test.
002 **Fragmenta**, FGrH #432: 3B:329–334, 758 addenda.
Q: 1,648: Hist.

0578 **NYMPHODORUS** Hist.
4 B.C.: Syracusanus
001 **Testimonia**, FGrH #572: 3B:668–669.
NQ: 104: Test.
002 **Fragmenta**, FGrH #572: 3B:669–674.
Q: 1,524: Hist., Perieg.

1007 **NYMPHODOTUS** Med.
ante A.D. 2
x01 **Fragmentum ap. Galenum**.
K13.926.
Cf. GALENUS Med. (0057 077).
x02 **Fragmentum ap. Oribasium**.
CMG, vol. 6.2.2, p. 217.
Cf. ORIBASIUS Med. (0722 003).
x03 **Fragmentum ap. Paulum**.
CMG, vol. 9.2, p. 322.
Cf. PAULUS Med. (0715 001).

1545 **OCELLUS** Phil.
vel Occelus
5 B.C.: Lucanus

001 **De universi natura** [Sp.], ed. R. Harder, *Ocellus Lucanus* [*Neue philologische Untersuchungen*, vol. 1. Berlin: Weidmann, 1926]: 11–25.
Cod: 4,071: Phil.
002 **Fragmenta** [Sp.], ed. Harder, *op. cit.*, 26–27.
frr. 1–3.
Q: 308: Phil.
003 **Testimonia**, ed. H. Diels and W. Kranz, *Die Fragmente der Vorsokratiker*, vol. 1, 6th edn. Berlin: Weidmann, 1951 (repr. Dublin: 1966): 440–441.
test. 1–8.
NQ: 348: Test.

1243 **ODAE SALOMONIS**
A.D. 1–2
001 **Oda Salomonis** (11.1–24) (*P. Bodmer* 11), ed. M. Testuz, *Papyrus Bodmer X–XII*. Geneva: Bibliotheca Bodmeriana, 1959: 60–68.
Pap

1546 **OECHALIAE HALOSIS**
fort. auctore Creophylo Samio vel Chio
Incertum
001 **Fragmentum**, ed. T.W. Allen, *Homeri opera*, vol. 5. Oxford: Clarendon Press, 1912 (repr. 1969): 146.
fr. 1.
Q: Epic.

2866 **OECUMENIUS** Rhet. et Phil.
A.D. 6
001 **Commentarius in Apocalypsin**, ed. H.C. Hoskier, *The complete commentary of Oecumenius on the Apocalypse*. Ann Arbor: University of Michigan Press, 1928: 29–260.
Cod: 55,840: Exeget.
002 **Fragmenta in epistulam ad Romanos** (in catenis), ed. K. Staab, *Pauluskommentar aus der griechischen Kirche aus Katenenhandschriften gesammelt*. Münster: Aschendorff, 1933: 423–432.
Q: 1,856: Exeget., Caten.
003 **Fragmenta in epistulam i ad Corinthios** (in catenis), ed. Staab, *op. cit.*, 432–443.
Q: 3,021: Exeget., Caten.
004 **Fragmenta in epistulam ii ad Corinthios** (in catenis), ed. Staab, *op. cit.*, 444–446.
Q: 433: Exeget., Caten.
005 **Fragmenta in epistulam ad Galatas** (in catenis), ed. Staab, *op. cit.*, 446–448.
Q: 464: Exeget., Caten.
006 **Fragmenta in epistulam ad Ephesios** (in catenis), ed. Staab, *op. cit.*, 448–452.
Q: 920: Exeget., Caten.
007 **Fragmenta in epistulam ad Philippenses** (in catenis), ed. Staab, *op. cit.*, 452–453.
Q: 330: Exeget., Caten.
008 **Fragmenta in epistulam ad Colossenses** (in catenis), ed. Staab, *op. cit.*, 453–455.
Q: 553: Exeget., Caten.

009 **Fragmenta in epistulam i ad Thessalonicenses** (in catenis), ed. Staab, *op. cit.*, 456–457.
Q: 337: Exeget., Caten.

010 **Fragmenta in epistulam ii ad Thessalonicenses** (in catenis), ed. Staab, *op. cit.*, 457–458.
Q: 212: Exeget., Caten.

011 **Fragmenta in epistulam i ad Timotheum** (in catenis), ed. Staab, *op. cit.*, 458–460.
Q: 499: Exeget., Caten.

012 **Fragmenta in epistulam ii ad Timotheum** (in catenis), ed. Staab, *op. cit.*, 460–461.
Q: 193: Exeget., Caten.

013 **Fragmenta in epistulam ad Titum** (in catenis), ed. Staab, *op. cit.*, 461.
Q: 126: Exeget., Caten.

014 **Fragmentum in epistulam ad Philemonem** (in catenis), ed. Staab, *op. cit.*, 462.
Q: 16: Exeget., Caten.

015 **Fragmenta in epistulam ad Hebraeos** (in catenis), ed. Staab, *op. cit.*, 462–469.
Q: 1,741: Exeget., Caten.

4154 **Pseudo-OECUMENIUS** Scr. Eccl.
post A.D. 7

001 **Prooemium commentarii in Apocalypsin** (e cod. Coislin. 224), ed. J.A. Cramer, *Catenae Graecorum patrum in Novum Testamentum*, vol. 8. Oxford: Oxford University Press, 1840 (repr. Hildesheim: Olms, 1967): 173–175.
Cod: Exeget., Caten.

002 **Commentarius in Apocalypsin** (e cod. Coislin. 224), ed. Cramer, *op. cit.*, 497–582.
Cod: Exeget., Caten.

1547 ***OEDIPODEA***
fort. auctore Cinaethone Lacedaemonio
post 7 B.C.

001 **Fragmenta**, ed. T.W. Allen, *Homeri opera*, vol. 5. Oxford: Clarendon Press, 1912 (repr. 1969): 112.
frr. 1–2.
Q: Epic.

0971 **OENIADES** Lyr.
4 B.C.: Thebanus

001 **Titulus**, ed. D.L. Page, *Poetae melici Graeci*. Oxford: Clarendon Press, 1962 (repr. 1967 (1st edn. corr.)): 443.
NQ: 2: Lyr.

1548 **OENOMAUS** Phil.
A.D. 2: Gadarensis

001 **Fragmenta**, ed. F.W.A. Mullach, *Fragmenta philosophorum Graecorum*, vol. 2. Paris: Didot, 1867 (repr. Aalen: Scientia, 1968): 361–385.
frr. 1–14.
Q: 8,581: Phil.

002 **Epigramma**, AG 9.749.
Q: 15: Epigr.

2234 **OENOPIDES** Phil.
5 B.C.: Chius

001 **Testimonia**, ed. H. Diels and W. Kranz, *Die Fragmente der Vorsokratiker*, vol. 1, 6th edn. Berlin: Weidmann, 1951 (repr. Dublin: 1966): 393–395.
test. 1–14.
NQ: 819: Test.

2373 **OLYMPICHUS** Hist.
ante 2 B.C.: Samius

001 **Fragmentum**, FGrH #537: 3B:522.
Q, Epigr: 22: Hist.

1008 **OLYMPICUS** Med.
A.D. 2: Milesius

x01 **Fragmentum ap. Galenum.**
K10.67–68.
Cf. GALENUS Med. (0057 066).

2589 **OLYMPIODORUS** Alchem.
fiq Olympiodorus Phil.
A.D. 6?
Cf. et OLYMPIODORUS Phil. (4019).

001 Εἰς τὸ κατ᾽ ἐνέργειαν Ζοσίμου ὅσα ἀπὸ Ἑρμοῦ καὶ τῶν φιλοσόφων ἦσαν εἰρημένα (= **De arte sacra**), ed. M. Berthelot, *Collection des anciens alchimistes grecs*. Paris: Steinheil, 1887 (repr. London: Holland Press, 1963): 69–104.
Cod

002 **Fragmenta**, ed. Berthelot, *op. cit.*, 104–106.
Cod

2590 **OLYMPIODORUS** Hist.
A.D. 5: Thebanus (Aegypti)

001 **Fragmenta**, ed. L. Dindorf, *Historici Graeci minores*, vol. 1. Leipzig: Teubner, 1870: 450–471.
Q

002 **Blemyomachia** (*P. Berol.* 5003), ed. H. Livrea, *Anonymi fortasse Olympiodori Thebani Blemyomachia (P. Berol. 5003)*. Meisenheim am Glan: Hain, 1978: 36–53.
Pap

4019 **OLYMPIODORUS** Phil.
fiq Olympiodorus Alchem.
A.D. 6: Alexandrinus
Cf. et OLYMPIODORUS Alchem. (2589).

001 **Prolegomena**, ed. A. Busse, *Olympiodori prolegomena et in categorias commentarium* [*Commentaria in Aristotelem Graeca* 12.1. Berlin: Reimer, 1902]: 1–25.
Cod: 10,066: Phil., Comm.

002 **In Aristotelis categorias commentarium**, ed. Busse, *op. cit.*, 26–148.
Cod: 50,220: Phil., Comm.

003 **In Aristotelis meteora commentaria**, ed. G. Stüve, *Olympiodori in Aristotelis meteora commentaria* [*Commentaria in Aristotelem Graeca* 12.2. Berlin: Reimer, 1900]: 1–338.
Cod: 113,456: Phil., Nat. Hist., Comm.

004 **In Platonis Alcibiadem commentarii**, ed. L.G. Westerink, *Olympiodorus. Commentary on the*

first Alcibiades of Plato. Amsterdam: Hakkert, 1956 (repr. 1982): 1–144.
Cod: 50,719: Phil., Comm.

005 **In Platonis Gorgiam commentaria**, ed. L.G. Westerink, *Olympiodori in Platonis Gorgiam commentaria.* Leipzig: Teubner, 1970: 1–268.
Cod: 64,789: Phil., Comm.

006 **In Platonis Phaedonem commentaria**, ed. L.G. Westerink, *The Greek commentaries on Plato's Phaedo*, vol. 1 [*Olympiodorus*]. Amsterdam: North-Holland, 1976: 39–181.
Cod: 19,110: Phil., Comm.

008 **Scholia in Aristotelis librum de interpretatione** (e cod. Vat. Urbin. gr. 35), ed. L. Tarán, *Anonymous commentary on Aristotle's de interpretatione* [*Beiträge zur klassischen Philologie* 95. Meisenheim am Glan: Hain, 1978]: xxvi–xli.
Cod: 2,588: Comm., Phil.

x01 **In Philebum.**
Westerink, pp. 3–121.
Cf. DAMASCIUS Phil. (4066 006).

x02 **Epigramma demonstrativum.**
App. Anth. 3.177: Cf. ANTHOLOGIAE GRAECAE APPENDIX (7052 003).

x03 **Ethicorum Nicomacheorum paraphrasis** (olim sub auctore Olympiodoro).
Heylbut, pp. 1–233.
Cf. ANONYMI IN ARISTOTELIS ETHICA NICOMACHEA (4033 003).

x04 **Prolegomena philosophiae Platonicae** (olim sub auctore Olympiodoro, nunc fort. auctore Elia).
Westerink, pp. 3–55.
Cf. ANONYMUS DE PHILOSOPHIA PLATONICA (4227 001).

1022 **OLYMPIUS** Med.
A.D. 1?

x01 **Fragmentum ap. Aëtium** (lib. 11).
Daremberg-Ruelle, p. 579.
Cf. AËTIUS Med. (0718 011).

1990 **OLYMPUS** Hist.
1 B.C.

001 **Fragmentum**, FGrH #198: 2B:929–930.
Q: 90: Hist.

0648 **ONASANDER** Tact.
vel Onosander
A.D. 1

001 **Strategicus**, ed. W.A. Oldfather, A.S. Pease and J.B. Titchener, *Aeneas Tacticus, Asclepiodotus, Onasander.* Cambridge, Mass.: Harvard University Press, 1923 (repr. 1962): 368–526.
Cod: 12,629: Tact.

1999 **ONASIMUS** Hist.
A.D. 3–4?: Cyprius vel Lacedaemonius

001 **Testimonium**, FGrH #216: 2B:946.
NQ: 33: Test.

002 **Fragmenta**, FGrH #216: 2B:947.
Q: 309: Hist.

1889 **ONASUS** Hist.
2 B.C./A.D. 1

001 **Fragmenta**, FGrH #41: 1A:263.
Q: 96: Hist., Myth.

1549 **<ONATAS>** Phil.
vel Onatus
fiq Onetor Atheniensis
3 B.C.: Crotoniensis

001 **Fragmenta**, ed. H. Thesleff, *The Pythagorean texts of the Hellenistic period.* Åbo: Åbo Akademi, 1965: 139–140.
Q: 486: Phil.

1943 **ONESICRITUS** Hist.
4–3 B.C.: Astypaleius

001 **Testimonia**, FGrH #134: 2B:723–725.
NQ: 740: Test.

002 **Fragmenta**, FGrH #134: 2B:725–736.
Q: 3,989: Hist., Narr. Fict.

2362 **ONOMASTUS** Hist.
Incertum

001 **Titulus**, FGrH #520: 3B:492.
NQ: Hist.

0485 **OPHELIO** Comic.
4 B.C.

001 **Fragmenta**, ed. T. Kock, *Comicorum Atticorum fragmenta*, vol. 2. Leipzig: Teubner, 1884: 293–294.
frr. 1–3, 5 + tituli.
Q: 36: Comic.

002 **Fragmenta**, ed. A. Meineke, *Fragmenta comicorum Graecorum*, vol. 3. Berlin: Reimer, 1840 (repr. De Gruyter, 1970): 380–381.
Q: 31: Comic.

0023 **OPPIANUS** Epic.
A.D. 2: Anazarbensis
Vitae: Cf. VITAE OPPIANI (4172).
Scholia: Cf. SCHOLIA IN OPPIANUM (5032 002).

001 **Halieutica**, ed. A.W. Mair, *Oppian, Colluthus, Tryphiodorus.* Cambridge, Mass.: Harvard University Press, 1928 (repr. 1963): 200–514.
Cod: 22,910: Epic., Nat. Hist.

0024 **OPPIANUS** Epic.
A.D. 2–3: Apamensis
Vitae: Cf. VITAE OPPIANI (4172).
Scholia: Cf. SCHOLIA IN OPPIANUM (5032 001).

001 **Cynegetica**, ed. A.W. Mair, *Oppian, Colluthus, Tryphiodorus.* Cambridge, Mass.: Harvard University Press, 1928 (repr. 1963): 2–198.
Cod: 13,586: Epic., Nat. Hist.

5001 ***ORACULA***
Varia
Cf. et ORACULA CHALDAICA (1550).
Cf. et ORACULA SIBYLLINA (1551).
Cf. et ORACULA TIBURTINA (2960).

x01 **Oracula.**
Ammon: 178–179.
Amphilytus Acarnan: 207.
Apollo anonymus: 144, 155.
Apollo Chalcedonius: 143.
Apollo Clarius: 134–139.
Apollo Colophonius: 140.
Apollo incertus: 156–173.
Apollo Ismenius: 132–133.
Apollo Milesius: 123–131.
Apollo Pythius: 1–122; 24b, 107 addenda.
Apollo Sarpedonius: 141–142.
Asclepius: 180–181.
Bacis: 205–206.
Diopithes: 220.
Euclus: 221.
Hecate: 193–204.
Hermes: 182.
Musaeus: 222.
Oracula ficta: 277, 291–323.
Oracula varia: 226–263, 265–276.
Pan: 191–192.
Peliades: 223.
Phaennis: 224.
Serapis: 183–189.
Sibylla: 208–219.
Trophonius: 190.
Vergilius: 264.
Zeus Belus: 174.
Zeus Dodonaeus: 175–177.
App. Anth. 6.1–323: Cf. ANTHOLOGIAE
GRAECAE APPENDIX (7052 006).
App. Anth. 6.24b, 107 addenda: Cf. ANTHO-
LOGIAE GRAECAE APPENDIX (7052 008).

x02 **Oraculum Herophilae Sibyllae.**
App. Anth. 3.123: Cf. ANTHOLOGIAE GRAE-
CAE APPENDIX (7052 003).

x03 **Oraculum Leonis Imperatoris.**
Cf. LEO VI SAPIENS Imperator Phil., Scr.
Eccl. et Poeta (2944 x02).

1550 *ORACULA CHALDAICA*
A.D. 2
001 **Oracula** (fragmenta) (olim sub auctore Juliano
Theurgo), ed. É. des Places, *Oracles chal-
daïques*. Paris: Les Belles Lettres, 1971: 66–
121.
Oracula Chaldaica (frr. 1–186 bis): pp. 66–110.
Vocabula Chaldaica varia (frr. 187–210): pp.
111–115.
Fragmenta dubia (frr. 211–226): pp. 116–121.
Q: 2,791: Orac.

1551 *ORACULA SIBYLLINA*
2 B.C.–A.D. 4
001 **Oracula**, ed. J. Geffcken, *Die Oracula Sibyllina*
[*Die griechischen christlichen Schriftsteller* 8.
Leipzig: Hinrichs, 1902]: 1–226.
Cod: 29,475: Orac.
002 **Fragmenta**, ed. Geffcken, *op. cit.*, 227–233.
Q: 663: Orac.
003 **Fragmentum**, *P. Flor.* 3.389.
Pap: Orac.

x01 **Aenigmata.**
App. Anth. 7.25–26: Cf. ANTHOLOGIAE
GRAECAE APPENDIX (7052 007).
Dup. partim 1551 001 (1.141–146, 326–331).

2960 *ORACULA TIBURTINA*
A.D. 4
001 **Prophetia**, ed. P.J. Alexander, *The oracle of
Baalbek. The Tiburtine Sibyl in Greek dress*
[*Dumbarton Oaks Studies* 10. Washington,
D.C.: Dumbarton Oaks, 1967]: 9–22.
Cod: Orac.

1552 *ORATIO JOSEPHI*
ante A.D. 3
001 **Fragmenta**, ed. A.-M. Denis, *Fragmenta pseudepigraphorum quae supersunt Graeca* [*Pseudepigrapha veteris testamenti Graece* 3. Leiden:
Brill, 1970]: 61–62.
Q: 258: Pseudepigr.

1858 *ORATIO MANASSIS*
1 B.C./A.D. 4?
001 **Oratio**, ed. A.-M. Denis, *Fragmenta pseudepigraphorum quae supersunt Graeca* [*Pseudepigrapha veteris testamenti Graece* 3. Leiden:
Brill, 1970]: 115–117.
Q: 497: Pseudepigr.

1010 **ORESTINUS** Med.
1 B.C.?
x01 **Fragmentum ap. Galenum.**
K12.402.
Cf. GALENUS Med. (0057 076).

0722 **ORIBASIUS** Med.
A.D. 4: Pergamenus
001 **Collectiones medicae** (lib. 1–16, 24–25, 43–
50), ed. J. Raeder, *Oribasii collectionum medicarum reliquiae*, vols. 1–4 [*Corpus medicorum
Graecorum*, vols. 6.1.1–6.2.2. Leipzig: Teubner,   6.1.1:1928;   6.1.2:1929;   6.2.1:1931;
6.2.2:1933]: **6.1.1:**4–27, 30–65, 67–91, 93–109,
111–153,   155–192,   194–245,   247–300;
6.1.2:4–237,   239–297,   298;   **6.2.1:**4–291;
6.2.2:4–69.
Lib. 1–14: vols. 6.1.1–6.1.2.
Lib. 15–16: vol. 6.1.2.
Lib. 24–25, 43–48: vol. 6.2.1.
Lib. 49–50: vol. 6.2.2.
Cod: 300,268: Med.
002 **Collectiones medicae** (libri incerti), ed. Raeder,
CMG 6.2.2, 75–180.
Cod: 38,850: Med.
003 **Eclogae medicamentorum**, ed. Raeder, *CMG*
6.2.2, 185–307.
Cod: 44,010: Med.
004 **Synopsis ad Eustathium filium**, ed. J. Raeder,
*Oribasii synopsis ad Eustathium et libri ad Eu-
napium* [*Corpus medicorum Graecorum*, vol.
6.3. Leipzig: Teubner, 1926 (repr. Amsterdam:
Hakkert, 1964)]: 3–313.
Synopsis operis: p. 3.

Pinaces et synopsis ad Eustathium: pp. 4–313.
Cod: 78,038: Med.

005 **Libri ad Eunapium** (lib. 1–4), ed. Raeder, *CMG* 6.3, 317–318, 320–347, 349–393, 396–433, 436–498.
Cod: 57,605: Med.

010 **Testimonia**, FGrH #221: 2B:950.
NQ: 63: Test.

2042 **ORIGENES** Theol.
A.D. 2–3: Alexandrinus, Caesariensis

047 **Commentarii in Genesim** (fragmenta), MPG 12: 45–92.
Q: 7,070: Exeget.

048 **Selecta in Genesim**, MPG 12: 92–145.
Q: 10,034: Exeget.

022 **Homiliae in Genesim** (in catenis), ed. W.A. Baehrens, *Origenes Werke*, vol. 6 [*Die griechischen christlichen Schriftsteller* 29. Leipzig: Teubner, 1920]: 23–30.
Q: 1,079: Homilet., Exeget., Caten.

066 **Adnotationes in Genesim**, MPG 17: 12–16.
Q: 679: Exeget.

049 **Fragmenta ex commentariis in Exodum** (= **In illud:** *Induravit dominus cor Pharaonis*), MPG 12: 264–281.
Q: 3,474: Exeget.

050 **Selecta in Exodum**, MPG 12: 281–297.
Q: 3,293: Exeget.

067 **Adnotationes in Exodum**, MPG 17: 16–17.
Q: 267: Exeget.

023 **Homiliae in Exodum**, ed. Baehrens, *GCS* 29, 217–218, 221–230.
Q: 944: Homilet., Exeget.

051 **Selecta in Leviticum**, MPG 12: 397–404.
Q: 1,542: Exeget.

068 **Adnotationes in Leviticum**, MPG 17: 17–22.
Q: 671: Exeget.

024 **Homiliae in Leviticum**, ed. Baehrens, *GCS* 29, 332–334, 395, 402–407, 409–416.
Q: 1,517: Homilet., Exeget.

052 **Selecta in Numeros**, MPG 12: 576–584.
Q: 1,752: Exeget.

069 **Adnotationes in Numeros**, MPG 17: 21–24.
Q: 242: Exeget.

053 **Selecta in Deuteronomium**, MPG 12: 805–817.
Q: 2,501: Exeget.

070 **Adnotationes in Deuteronomium**, MPG 17: 24–36.
Q: 2,319: Exeget.

025 **In Jesu Nave homiliae xxvi** (in catenis), ed. W.A. Baehrens, *Origenes Werke*, vol. 7 [*Die griechischen christlichen Schriftsteller* 30. Leipzig: Teubner, 1921]: 290–291, 293, 298–302, 305, 308, 310, 312, 394–398, 406–445, 448–456, 460–463.
Cf. et 2042 080.
Q: 4,452: Homilet., Caten.

080 **Homiliae in librum Jesu Nave** (addendum), ed. Baehrens, *GCS* 30, 621.
Cf. et 2042 025.
Q: Homilet.

054 **Selecta in Jesum Nave**, MPG 12: 820–824.
Q: 967: Exeget.

071 **Adnotationes in Jesum filium Nave**, MPG 17: 36–37.
Q: 193: Exeget.

055 **Selecta in Judices**, MPG 12: 949.
Q: 278: Exeget.

072 **Adnotationes in Judices**, MPG 17: 37–40.
Q: 211: Exeget.

056 **In Ruth** (fragmentum), MPG 12: 989.
Q: 54: Exeget.

013 **De engastrimytho** (= Homilia in i Reg. [i Sam.] 28.3–25), ed. E. Klostermann, *Origenes Werke*, vol. 3 [*Die griechischen christlichen Schriftsteller* 6. Leipzig: Hinrichs, 1901]: 283–294.
Cod: 3,671: Homilet., Exeget.

014 **Fragmenta in librum primum Regnorum** (in catenis), ed. Klostermann, *GCS* 6, 295–303.
Q: 1,968: Exeget., Caten.

015 **Fragmentum in librum primum Regnorum** (in catenis), ed. Klostermann, *GCS* 6, 304.
Q: 86: Exeget., Caten.

057 **Selecta in Job** (e codd. Paris.), MPG 12: 1032–1049.
Q: 3,583: Exeget.

073 **Enarrationes in Job** (e codd. Marc. gr. 21, 538), MPG 17: 57–105.
Q: 8,876: Exeget.

086 **Homiliae in Job** (fragmenta e codd. Vat.), ed. J.B. Pitra, *Analecta sacra spicilegio Solesmensi parata*, vol. 2. Paris: Tusculum, 1884 (repr. Farnborough: Gregg Press, 1966): 361–391.
Q: Homilet., Exeget.

058 **Selecta in Psalmos** [Dub.], MPG 12: 1053–1320, 1368–1369, 1388–1389, 1409–1685.
Q, Cod: 107,208: Exeget.

074 **Excerpta in Psalmos** [Dub.], MPG 17: 105–149.
Q: 9,126: Exeget.

044 **Fragmenta in Psalmos 1–150** [Dub.], ed. Pitra, *Analecta sacra spicilegio Solesmensi parata*, vols. 2 & 3 (Venice: St. Lazarus Monastery, 1883): 2:444–483; 3:1–236, 242–245, 248–364.
Cod: 86,530: Exeget.

059 **Fragmenta ex commentariis in Proverbia**, MPG 13: 17–33.
Q: 3,452: Exeget.

075 **Expositio in Proverbia**, MPG 17: 161–252.
Q: 18,525: Exeget.

026 **Libri x in Canticum canticorum** (fragmenta), ed. W.A. Baehrens, *Origenes Werke*, vol. 8 [*Die griechischen christlichen Schriftsteller* 33. Leipzig: Teubner, 1925]: 90–92, 96, 98, 101, 108–109, 111, 126, 128–132, 141–146, 154–155, 161–162, 165–166, 168–169, 174–175, 178–184, 191–194, 199–202, 220–221, 224, 226, 230–233, 235–237, 240–241.
Dup. partim 2042 076.
Cf. et 2042 081.
Q: 2,806: Exeget.

076 **Scholia in Canticum canticorum**, MPG 17: 253–288.
Dup. partim 2042 026.
Q: 7,197: Exeget.

081 **Libri x in Canticum canticorum** (addenda), ed. Baehrens, *GCS* 33, liii–liv.
Cf. et 2042 026.
Q: Exeget.

060 **In Canticum canticorum** (libri duo quos scripsit in adulescentia), MPG 13: 36.
Q: 172: Exeget.

009 **In Jeremiam** (homiliae 1–11), ed. P. Nautin, *Origène. Homélies sur Jérémie*, vol. 1 [*Sources chrétiennes* 232. Paris: Cerf, 1976]: 196–430.
Cod: 24,992: Homilet., Exeget.

021 **In Jeremiam** (homiliae 12–20), ed. Klostermann, *GCS* 6, 85–194.
Cf. et 2042 084.
Cod: 33,153: Homilet., Exeget.

084 **Fragmenta in Jeremiam** (e *Philocalia*), ed. Klostermann, *GCS* 6, 195–198.
Cf. et 2042 021.
Q: 757: Homilet., Exeget.

010 **Fragmenta in Jeremiam** (in catenis), ed. Klostermann, *GCS* 6, 199–232.
Q: 8,308: Exeget., Caten.

011 **Fragmenta in Lamentationes** (in catenis), ed. Klostermann, *GCS* 6, 235–278.
Q: 10,580: Exeget., Caten.

012 **Fragmentum in Lamentationes** (in catenis), ed. Klostermann, *GCS* 6, 279.
Q: 172: Exeget., Caten.

061 **Fragmenta ex commentariis in Ezechielem**, MPG 13: 664–665.
Q: 468: Exeget.

027 **Homiliae in Ezechielem**, ed. Baehrens, *GCS* 33, 319–320, 323, 327–329, 336–337, 340, 354–355, 378, 390, 396, 426–427, 434–435, 450–452.
Cf. et 2042 082.
Cod: 1,384: Homilet., Exeget.

082 **Homiliae in Ezechielem** (addendum), ed. Baehrens, *GCS* 33, lv.
Cf. et 2042 027.
Q: Homilet.

062 **Selecta in Ezechielem**, MPG 13: 768–825.
Q: 11,987: Exeget.

063 **Fragmentum ex commentariis in Osee**, MPG 13: 825–828.
Q: 575: Exeget.

029 **Commentarium in evangelium Matthaei** (lib. 10–11), ed. R. Girod, *Origène. Commentaire sur l'évangile selon Matthieu*, vol. 1 [*Sources chrétiennes* 162. Paris: Cerf, 1970]: 140–386.
Cod: 22,406: Exeget.

030 **Commentarium in evangelium Matthaei** (lib. 12–17), ed. E. Klostermann, *Origenes Werke*, vol. 10.1–10.2 [*Die griechischen christlichen Schriftsteller* 40.1–40.2. Leipzig: Teubner, 10.1:1935; 10.2:1937]: **10.1**:69–304; **10.2**:305–703.
Cod: 95,260: Exeget.

028 **Commentariorum series in evangelium Matthaei** (Mt. 22.34–27.63), ed. E. Klostermann, *Origenes Werke*, vol. 11 [*Die griechischen christlichen Schriftsteller* 38.2. Leipzig: Teubner, 1933]: 4, 21–22, 42–43, 54, 83–84, 86, 93–101, 103, 108, 110, 112–114, 118–128, 130–138, 140, 144–151, 156–157, 159–163, 166, 171, 178, 180, 189, 191–192, 206, 219–220, 222, 227, 229–230, 233, 236–242, 244–248, 250–255, 257–266, 270–278, 283–284, 287, 293–295.
Q: 4,732: Exeget.

031 **Fragmenta ex commentariis in evangelium Matthaei**, ed. E. Klostermann and E. Benz, *Origenes Werke*, vol. 12 [*Die griechischen christlichen Schriftsteller* 41.1. Leipzig: Teubner, 1941]: 3–5.
Cf. et 2042 085.
Q: 495: Exeget.

085 **Fragmenta ex commentariis in evangelium Matthaei** (in catenis), ed. Klostermann and Benz, *GCS* 41.1, 13–235.
Cf. et 2042 031.
Q: Exeget., Caten.

032 **Fragmenta in evangelium Matthaei**, ed. E. Klostermann and E. Benz, *Zur Überlieferung der Matthäuserklärung des Origenes* [*Texte und Untersuchungen* 47.2. Leipzig: Hinrichs, 1931]: 4–8.
Q: 517: Exeget.

077 **Scholia in Matthaeum**, MPG 17: 289–309.
Cod: 4,429: Exeget.

016 **Homiliae in Lucam**, ed. M. Rauer, *Origenes Werke*, vol. 9, 2nd edn. [*Die griechischen christlichen Schriftsteller* 49 (35). Berlin: Akademie-Verlag, 1959]: 3–51, 54–90, 92–96, 99–109, 111, 114–123, 125–130, 132–139, 141–145, 154–155, 157–158, 160–166, 168–174, 177–179, 181, 183, 186–203, 205–206, 209–212, 214–222.
Cod: 12,366: Homilet., Exeget.

017 **Fragmenta in Lucam** (in catenis), ed. Rauer, *GCS* 49 (35), 227–336.
Q: 20,706: Homilet., Exeget., Caten.

078 **Scholia in Lucam**, MPG 17: 312–369.
Cod: 12,047: Exeget.

005 **Commentarii in evangelium Joannis** (lib. 1, 2, 4, 5, 6, 10, 13), ed. C. Blanc, *Origène. Commentaire sur saint Jean*, 3 vols. [*Sources chrétiennes* 120, 157, 222. Paris: Cerf, 1:1966; 2:1970; 3:1975]: 1:56–390; 2:128–580; 3:34–282.
Lib. 19, 20, 28, 32: Cf. 2042 079.
Cod: 96,316: Exeget.

079 **Commentarii in evangelium Joannis** (lib. 19, 20, 28, 32), ed. E. Preuschen, *Origenes Werke*, vol. 4 [*Die griechischen christlichen Schriftsteller* 10. Leipzig: Hinrichs, 1903]: 298–480.
Lib. 1, 2, 4, 5, 6, 10, 13: Cf. 2042 005.
Cod: 61,431: Exeget.

006 **Fragmenta in evangelium Joannis** (in catenis), ed. Preuschen, *GCS* 10, 483–574.
Q: 22,566: Exeget., Caten.

064 **Fragmentum ex homiliis in Acta apostolorum**, MPG 14: 829–832.
Q: 196: Homilet., Exeget.

039 **Commentarii in Romanos** (cod. Athon. Laura 184 B64), ed. O. Bauernfeind, *Der Römerbrieftext des Origenes nach dem codex von der Goltz* [*Texte und Untersuchungen* 44.3. Leipzig: Hinrichs, 1923]: 91–119.
Cod: 5,761: Exeget.

036 **Commentarii in epistulam ad Romanos** (I.1–XII.21) (in catenis), ed. A. Ramsbotham, "Documents: The commentary of Origen on the epistle to the Romans," *Journal of Theological Studies* 13 & 14 (1912) 13:210–224, 357–368; 14:10–22.
Q: 13,938: Exeget., Caten.

037 **Commentarii in epistulam ad Romanos** (e cod. Vindob. gr. 166), ed. K. Staab, "Neue Fragmente aus dem Kommentar des Origenes zum Römerbrief," *Biblische Zeitschrift* 18 (1928) 74–82.
Q: 1,692: Exeget.

038 **Commentarii in Romanos** (III.5–V.7) (*P. Cair.* 88748 + cod. Vat. gr. 762), ed. J. Scherer, *Le commentaire d'Origène sur Rom. III.5–V.7*. Cairo: L'Institut Français d'Archéologie Orientale, 1957: 124–232.
Q, Cod, Pap: 11,868: Exeget.

034 **Fragmenta ex commentariis in epistulam i ad Corinthios** (in catenis), ed. C. Jenkins, "Documents: Origen on I Corinthians," *Journal of Theological Studies* 9 & 10 (1908) 9:232–247, 353–372, 500–514; 10:29–51.
Q: 26,284: Exeget., Caten.

035 **Fragmenta ex commentariis in epistulam ad Ephesios** (in catenis), ed. J.A.F. Gregg, "Documents: The commentary of Origen upon the epistle to the Ephesians," *Journal of Theological Studies* 3 (1902) 234–244, 398–420, 554–576.
Q: 18,328: Exeget., Caten.

065 **Ex homiliis in epistulam ad Hebraeos**, MPG 14: 1308–1309.
Q: 185: Homilet., Exeget.

042 **Scholia in Apocalypsem** (scholia 1, 3–39), ed. C. Diobouniotis and A. von Harnack, *Der Scholien-Kommentar des Origenes zur Apokalypse Johannis* [*Texte und Untersuchungen* 38.3. Leipzig: Hinrichs, 1911]: 21–44.
Dup. partim 2042 043.
Cod: 5,262: Exeget.

043 **Scholia in Apocalypsem** (scholia 28–38), ed. C.H. Turner, "Document: Origen, scholia in Apocalypsin," *Journal of Theological Studies* 25 (1923) 1–15.
Dup. partim 2042 042.
Cod: 1,888: Exeget.

007 **Exhortatio ad martyrium**, ed. P. Koetschau, *Origenes Werke*, vol. 1 [*Die griechischen christlichen Schriftsteller* 2. Leipzig: Hinrichs, 1899]: 3–47.
Cod: 12,657: Eccl.

001 **Contra Celsum**, ed. M. Borret, *Origène. Contre Celse*, 4 vols. [*Sources chrétiennes* 132, 136, 147, 150. Paris: Cerf, 1:1967; 2:1968; 3–4:1969]: 1:64–476; 2:14–434; 3:14–382; 4:14–352.
Cod: 166,590: Apol.

008 **De oratione**, ed. P. Koetschau, *Origenes Werke*, vol. 2 [*Die griechischen christlichen Schriftsteller* 3. Leipzig: Hinrichs, 1899]: 297–403.
Cod: 28,725: Theol.

046 **De resurrectione libri ii** (fragmenta), MPG 11: 96.
Q: 263: Theol.

087 **De pascha**, ed. O. Guéraud and P. Nautin, *Sur la Pâque. Traité inédit publié d'après un papyrus de Toura* [*Christianisme antique* 2. Paris: Beauchesne, 1979].
Pap: Exeget.

018 **Dialogus cum Heraclide**, ed. J. Scherer, *Entretien d'Origène avec Héraclide* [*Sources chrétiennes* 67. Paris: Cerf, 1960]: 52–110.
Cod: 5,607: Theol., Dialog.

002 **De principiis**, ed. H. Görgemanns and H. Karpp, *Origenes vier Bücher von den Prinzipien*. Darmstadt: Wissenschaftliche Buchgesellschaft, 1976: 462–560, 668–764.
Q, Cod: 13,821: Theol.

003 **Fragmenta de principiis**, ed. Görgemanns and Karpp, *op. cit.*, 82, 94, 96, 136, 146, 154, 162, 164, 168, 192, 220, 226, 240, 244, 262, 284–286, 310, 364, 388, 392, 400, 648, 730, 772–774, 782, 784–786, 794, 796, 808, 810, 812.
Q: 2,521: Theol.

004 **Fragmenta alia de principiis**, ed. Görgemanns and Karpp, *op. cit.*, 228, 392, 394.
Q: 169: Theol.

033 **Epistula ad Gregorium Thaumaturgum**, ed. P. Koetschau, *Des Gregorios Thaumaturgos Dankrede an Origenes*. Freiburg: Mohr, 1894: 40–44.
Q: 858: Epist.

040 **Epistula ad ignotum** (Fabianum Romanum), ed. P. Nautin, *Lettres et écrivains chrétiens des 2e et 3e siècles* [*Patristica* 2. Paris: Cerf, 1961]: 250–251.
Q: 123: Epist.

045 **Epistula ad Africanum**, MPG 11: 48–85.
Cod: 5,404: Epist.

041 **Epistula quibusdam qui ei obtrectabant** (ad Alexandrum Hierosolymitanum), ed. Nautin, *Patristica* 2, 126.
Q: 118: Epist.

083 **Hexapla**, ed. F. Field, *Origenis hexaplorum quae supersunt*, 2 vols. Oxford: Oxford University Press, 1875 (repr. Hildesheim: Olms, 1964): 1:7–806; 2:4–1034.
Cod

019 **Philocalia** *sive* **Ecloga de operibus Origenis a Basilio et Gregorio Nazianzeno facta** (cap. 1–27), ed. J.A. Robinson, *The philocalia of*

Origen. Cambridge: Cambridge University Press, 1893: 1–256.
Dup. partim 2042 020.
Cod: 65,752: Exeget.

020 **Philocalia** *sive* **Ecloga de operibus Origenis a Basilio et Gregorio Nazianzeno facta** (cap. 23, 25–27), ed. É. Junod, *Origène. Philocalie 21–27: sur le libre arbitre [Sources chrétiennes 226.* Paris: Cerf, 1976]: 130–314.
Dup. partim 2042 019.
Cod: 14,424: Exeget.

0924 **ORIGENIA** Med.
ante A.D. 1

x01 **Fragmenta ap. Galenum.**
K13.58, 85, 143.
Cf. GALENUS Med. (0057 076).

2591 **ORION** Gramm.
A.D. 5: Thebanus (Aegypti), Alexandrinus, Constantinopolitanus, Caesariensis (fort. Cappadociae)

001 **Etymologicum**, ed. F.G. Sturz, *Orionis Thebani etymologicon.* Leipzig: Weigel, 1820 (repr. Hildesheim: Olms, 1973): 1–172.
Cod: Lexicogr.

002 **Etymologicum** (excerpta e cod. regio 2610), ed. G.H.K. Koës, *Orionis Thebani etymologicon* (ed. F.G. Sturz). Leipzig: Weigel, 1820 (repr. Hildesheim: Olms, 1973): 173–184.
Cod: Lexicogr.

003 **Etymologicum** (excerpta e cod. regio Paris. 2630), ed. Koës, *op. cit.*, 185–192.
Cod: Lexicogr.

004 **Anthologion**, ed. F.G. Schneidewin, *Coniectanea critica.* Göttingen: Dieterich, 1839: 41–58.
Cod: Anthol., Gnom., Poem.

005 **Fragmenta** (e cod. Darmstadino 2773), ed. F.G. Sturz, *Etymologicum Graecae linguae Gudianum.* Leipzig: Weigel, 1818: 611–617.
Cod: Lexicogr.

006 **Excerpta ex etymologico** (e cod. Vat. gr. 1456), ed. A.M. Micciarelli Collesi, "Nuovi 'excerpta' dall' 'etimologico' di Orione," *Byzantion* 40 (1970) 521–542.
Cod: Lexicogr.

1011 **ORION** Med.
ante A.D. 1

x01 **Fragmentum ap. Galenum.**
K13.1038.
Cf. GALENUS Med. (0057 077).

0579 ***ORPHICA***
Varia

001 **Hymni**, ed. W. Quandt, *Orphei hymni*, 3rd edn. Berlin: Weidmann, 1962 (repr. 1973): 1–57.
Cod: 6,844: Hymn., Hexametr.

002 **Argonautica**, ed. G. Dottin, *Les argonautiques*

d'Orphée. Paris: Les Belles Lettres, 1930: 3–54.
Cod: 9,013: Epic.

003 **Lithica**, ed. E. Abel, *Orphei lithica.* Berlin: Calvary, 1881: 15–38.
Cod: 5,025: Nat. Hist., Hexametr.

004 **Lithica kerygmata**, ed. Abel, *op. cit.*, 138–153.
Cod: 2,767: Nat. Hist.

005 **Fragmenta**, ed. O. Kern, *Orphicorum fragmenta.* Berlin: Weidmann, 1922 (repr. 1972): 80–344 (passim).
Q, Pap, Epigr

007 **Fragmentum astrologicum**, ed. M.A. Sangin, *Codices Rossici [Catalogus codicum astrologorum Graecorum* 12. Brussels: Lamertin, 1936]: 158–161.
Cod

008 **Fragmenta**, ed. A. Giannini, *Paradoxographorum Graecorum reliquiae.* Milan: Istituto Editoriale Italiano, 1965: 384–385.
Q

009 **Testimonia**, ed. H. Diels and W. Kranz, *Die Fragmente der Vorsokratiker*, vol. 1, 6th edn. Berlin: Weidmann, 1951 (repr. Dublin: 1966): 1–6.
test. 1–16.
NQ: 1,251: Test.

010 **Fragmenta**, ed. Diels and Kranz, *op. cit.*, 6–20.
frr. 1–23.
fr. 15a: *P. Berol.* 44.
fr. 19: *IG* 14.641.
fr. 23: *P. Gurob* 1.
Q, Pap, Epigr: 2,929: Phil., Theol.

011 **Lithica**, ed. R. Halleux and J. Schamp, *Les lapidaires grecs.* Paris: Les Belles Lettres, 1985: 82–123.
Text to replace Abel edition (0579 003).
Cod: Nat. Hist., Hexametr.

012 **Lithica kerygmata**, ed. Halleux and Schamp, *op. cit.*, 146–177.
Orphei lithica kerygmata (cap. 1–25): pp. 146–165.
Socratis et Dionysii lithica (cap. 26–53): pp. 166–177.
Text to replace Abel edition (0579 004).
Cod: Nat. Hist.

013 **Fragmenta** (*P. Derveni*) [editor not given], "Der orphische Papyrus von Derveni," *Zeitschrift für Papyrologie und Epigraphik* 47 (1982) 1*–12*.
Pap: Theol.

x01 **Epigrammata** (*App. Anth.*).
Epigramma dedicatorium: 1.1(?).
Epigramma exhortatorium et supplicatorium: 4.47(?).
App. Anth. 1.1(?): Cf. ANTHOLOGIAE GRAECAE APPENDIX (7052 001).
App. Anth. 4.47(?): Cf. ANTHOLOGIAE GRAECAE APPENDIX (7052 004).

x02 **Hieros logos.**
PsVTGr 3.164–167.

Cf. PSEUDO-AUCTORES HELLENISTAE (PsVTGr) (1639 001).

2480 ORTHAGORAS Hist.
1 B.C.?
001 **Fragmenta**, FGrH #713: 3C:601–603.
Q: 462: Hist.

2995 ORUS Gramm.
A.D. 5: Alexandrinus, Constantinopolitanus
001 **Vocum Atticarum collectio** (fragmenta ap. Zonarae lexicon), ed. K. Alpers, *Das attizistische Lexikon des Oros* [*Sammlung griechischer und lateinischer Grammatiker* 4. Berlin: De Gruyter, 1981]: 149–193.
Q: Lexicogr.
002 **Vocum Atticarum collectio** (fragmenta ap. alios auctores et Ori scripta alia), ed. Alpers, *op. cit.*, 194–260.
Q: Lexicogr.

1016 <OSTANES Magus>
5 B.C.
001 **Fragmenta**, ed. J. Bidez and F. Cumont, *Les mages hellénisés*, vol. 2. Paris: Les Belles Lettres, 1938: 302, 318, 322, 329–330, 331, 334–335.
Q

1012 OTHO Med.
ante 1 B.C.: Siculus
x01 **Fragmentum ap. Galenum.**
K12.403.
Cf. GALENUS Med. (0057 076).

1013 PACCIUS ANTIOCHUS Med.
fiq Antiochus Romanus
A.D. 1
Cf. et ANTIOCHUS Med. (0778).
x01 **Fragmenta ap. Galenum.**
K**12**.751, 760, 772, 782; **13**.284, 984.
Cf. GALENUS Med. (0057 076–077).

1203 *PAEANES* (CA)
4–2 B.C.
001 **Paean Erythraeus in Aesculapium**, ed. J.U. Powell, *Collectanea Alexandrina*. Oxford: Clarendon Press, 1925 (repr. 1970): 136.
Epigr: 88: Lyr., Hymn.
002 **Paean Erythraeus ad urbem Dium repertus**, ed. Powell, *op. cit.*, 137.
Epigr: 95: Lyr., Hymn.
003 **Fragmentum Erythraeum paeanis in Apollinem**, ed. Powell, *op. cit.*, 140.
Epigr: 75: Lyr., Hymn.
004 **Fragmentum Erythraeum paeanis in Seleucum**, ed. Powell, *op. cit.*, 140.
Epigr: 14: Lyr., Hymn.
005 **Paean Delphicus i in Apollinem**, ed. Powell, *op. cit.*, 141–142.
Epigr: 181: Lyr., Hymn.

006 **Fragmentum paeanis in Titum Flamininum**, ed. Powell, *op. cit.*, 173.
Q: 27: Lyr., Hymn.

PAEANIUS Translator Eutropii Breviarii
A.D. 4
Cf. EUTROPIUS Hist. (2236 001).

2665 Mettius PAEON Epigr.
Incertum: Sidetes
x01 **Epigrammata dedicatoria.**
App. Anth. 1.187–188: Cf. ANTHOLOGIAE GRAECAE APPENDIX (7052 001).

2512 PAEON Hist.
3 B.C.?: Amathusiacus
001 **Fragmenta**, FGrH #757: 3C:737.
Q: 200: Hist.

4272 PAEONIUS Phil.
4 B.C.: Atheniensis
001 **Testimonium**, ed. K. Döring, *Die Megariker* [*Studien zur antiken Philosophie* 2. Amsterdam: Grüner, 1972]: 52, 61.
test. 164a = Stilpo (4262 001).
NQ: Test.

2450 PALAEPHATUS Gramm.
Incertum: Aegyptius
001 **Testimonium**, FGrH #660: 3C:211–212.
NQ: 41: Test.
002 **Fragmentum**, FGrH #660: 3C:212.
Q: 162: Hist.

1553 <PALAEPHATUS> Myth.
4 B.C.?: fort. Atheniensis vel Aegyptius
001 **De incredibilibus**, ed. N. Festa, *Palaephati περὶ ἀπίστων* [*Mythographi Graeci* 3.2. Leipzig: Teubner, 1902]: 1–72.
Cod: 7,819: Myth.
002 **Testimonia**, FGrH #44: 1A:266–267, *16–*17 addenda.
NQ: 434: Test.
003 **Fragmenta**, FGrH #44: 1A:267–268, *17–*19 addenda.
fr. 3 bis: *P. Oxy.* 13.1611.
Q: 571: Hist., Myth.

2123 PALLADAS Epigr.
A.D. 4–5: Alexandrinus
001 **Epigrammata**, AG 5.71–72, 257; **6**.60–61, 85; 7.607, 610, 681–688; **9**.5–6, 119, 165–176, 180–183, 377–379, 393–395, 397, 400–401, 441, 484, 486–487, 489, 502–503, 508, 528, 773; **10**.32, 34, 44–63, 65, 72–73, 75, 77–99; 11.54–55, 62, 204, 255, 263, 280–281, 283–293, 299–307, 317, 323, 340–341, 349, 351, 353, 355, 357, 371, 373, 377–378, 381, 383–387; **15**.20; **16**.20, 194, 207, 282, 317.
AG 7.339; 9.134–135, 399, 501; 11.273, 343: Cf. ANONYMI EPIGRAMMATICI (AG) (0138 001).

AG 9.9b: Cf. Julius POLYAENUS Epigr. (1620 001).

AG 9.57: Cf. PAMPHILUS Epigr. (1554 001).

AG 9.118: Cf. BESANTINUS Poeta (0144 001).

AG 9.120; 11.294, 430: Cf. Pseudo-LUCIANUS Soph. (0061 010).

AG 9.503b: Cf. NICANDER Epic. (0022 006).

AG 10.121: Cf. RARUS Epigr. (1653 001).

AG 11.295, 310: Cf. LUCILLIUS Epigr. (1468 001).

Q: 4,582: Epigr.

x01 **Epigramma demonstrativum** (auctore Pallada vel Agathia).
App. Anth. 3.145(?): Cf. ANTHOLOGIAE GRAECAE APPENDIX (7052 003).
Cf. et AGATHIAS Scholasticus Hist. et Epigr. (4024 x01).

2564 **PALLADIUS** Hist.
A.D. 4: Methonaeus
001 **Testimonia**, FGrH #837: 3C:904.
NQ: 60: Test.
002 **Titulus**, FGrH #837: 3C:904.
NQ: Hist.

0726 **PALLADIUS** Med.
A.D. 6: Alexandrinus
001 **Commentarii in Hippocratis librum sextum de morbis popularibus**, ed. F.R. Dietz, Scholia in Hippocratem et Galenum, vol. 2. Königsberg: Borntraeger, 1834 (repr. Amsterdam: Hakkert, 1966): 1–39, 73–88, 92–204.
Cod: 46,389: Med., Comm.
002 **Synopsis de febribus**, ed. J.L. Ideler, Physici et medici Graeci minores, vol. 1. Berlin: Reimer, 1841 (repr. Amsterdam: Hakkert, 1963): 107–120.
Cf. et THEOPHILUS Protospatharius et STEPHANUS Atheniensis Med. (0746 001).
Cod: 3,742: Med.
003 Περὶ βρώσεως καὶ πόσεως, ed. Dietz, op. cit., vii–viii.
Cod: 242: Med.
004 **Scholia in Hippocratis de fracturis**, ed. D. Irmer, Palladius. Kommentar zu Hippokrates 'De fracturis' und seine Parallelversion unter dem Namen des Stephanus von Alexandria [Hamburger philologische Studien 45. Hamburg: Buske, 1977]: 16–88.
Cod: 8,120: Med., Comm.
005 **Commentarium in Galeni de sectis** (excerptum e cod. Laur. plut. 74, 11), ed. H. Rabe, Prolegomenon sylloge [Rhetores Graeci 14. Leipzig: Teubner, 1931]: 16–17.
Cod: Rhet., Comm.

2111 **PALLADIUS** Scr. Eccl.
A.D. 4–5: Helenopolitanus
001 **Historia Lausiaca** (recensio G), ed. G.J.M. Bartelink, Palladio. La storia Lausiaca. Verona: Fondazione Lorenzo Valla, 1974: 4–292.
Cod: 29,734: Hist., Hagiogr.
002 **Prooemium ad historiam Lausiacam** [Sp.], ed.

C. Butler, The Lausiac history of Palladius, vol. 2. Cambridge: Cambridge University Press, 1904 (repr. Hildesheim: Olms, 1967): 3–5.
Cod: 593: Hist., Eccl.
003 **Epistula ad Lausum**, ed. Butler, op. cit., 6–7.
Cod: 302: Epist.
004 **Dialogus de vita Joannis Chrysostomi**, ed. P.R. Coleman-Norton, Palladii dialogus de vita S. Joanni Chrysostomi. Cambridge: Cambridge University Press, 1928: 3–147.
Cod: 35,922: Hagiogr., Dialog.
005 **De gentibus Indiae et Bragmanibus** [Sp.], ed. W. Berghoff, Palladius. De gentibus Indiae et Bragmanibus. Meisenheim am Glan: Hain, 1967: 2–55.
Cod: 6,923: Narr. Fict.

1828 **PAMPHILA** Hist.
A.D. 1: Epidauria
001 **Fragmenta**, FHG 3: 520–522.
Q

1554 **PAMPHILUS** Epigr.
fiq Pamphilus Alexandrinus Gramm.
2 B.C.
001 **Epigrammata**, AG 7.201; 9.57.
Q: 44: Epigr.

PAMPHILUS Gramm.
2 B.C.: Alexandrinus
Cf. PAMPHILUS Epigr. (1554).

1014 **PAMPHILUS** Med.
ante A.D. 2: Romanus
x01 **Fragmentum ap. Galenum**.
K13.68.
Cf. GALENUS Med. (0057 076).

1015 **PAMPHILUS** <Med.>
ante A.D. 6
x01 **Fragmentum ap. Aëtium** (lib. 16).
Zervos, Gynaekologie des Aëtios, p. 171.
Cf. AËTIUS Med. (0718 016).

2495 **PAMPHILUS** Phil.
4 B.C.
001 **Testimonia**, ed. F. Lasserre, De Léodamas de Thasos à Philippe d'Oponte. Naples: Bibliopolis, 1987: 155–156.
test. 2–4b.
NQ: Test.

2634 **PAMPHILUS** Poeta
ante 4 B.C.: Siculus
001 **Fragmentum**, ed. H. Lloyd-Jones and P. Parsons, Supplementum Hellenisticum. Berlin: De Gruyter, 1983: 286.
fr. 597.
Q: 16: Iamb.

2961 **PAMPHILUS** Scr. Eccl.
A.D. 3–4: Caesariensis
001 **Fragmentum in Psalmum 71** (in catenis) [Sp.],

ed. J.B. Pitra, *Analecta sacra spicilegio Soles-mense parata*, vol. 3. Venice: St. Lazarus Monastery, 1883: 469–470.
Q: Exeget., Caten.

1399 PAMPHILUS Trag.
4 B.C.: Atheniensis
001 **Titulus**, ed. B. Snell, *Tragicorum Graecorum fragmenta*, vol. 1. Göttingen: Vandenhoeck & Ruprecht, 1971: 189.
NQ: 1: Trag.

2597 PAMPHOS Poeta
post 4 B.C.
x01 **Fragmentum** (ap. Philostratum, *Heroicus*).
Kayser, vol. 2, p. 162.
Cf. Flavius PHILOSTRATUS Soph. (0638 004).

4038 PAMPREPIUS Epic.
A.D. 5: Panopolitanus
001 **Fragmenta** (*P. Vindob.* 29788 A-C), ed. E. Heitsch, *Die griechischen Dichterfragmente der römischen Kaiserzeit*, vol. 1, 2nd edn. Göttingen: Vandenhoeck & Ruprecht, 1963: 109–120.
frr. 1–4.
Pap: 1,609: Epic., Encom.
002 **Testimonium**, FGrH #749: 3C:732.
NQ: 17: Test.
003 **Titulus**, FGrH #749: 3C:732.
NQ: Hist.

1359 PANAETIUS Phil.
2 B.C.: Rhodius
001 **Fragmenta**, ed. M. van Straaten, *Panaetii Rhodii fragmenta*, 3rd edn. Leiden: Brill, 1962: 19–20, 24, 28–31, 33, 42–44, 48–52.
Q

0256 PANARCES Scriptor Aenigmatum
5 B.C.
001 **Fragmenta**, ed. M.L. West, *Iambi et elegi Graeci*, vol. 2. Oxford: Clarendon Press, 1972: 91.
Q: 58: Iamb.

1555 PANCRATES Epic.
A.D. 2: Aegyptius
001 **Fragmenta**, ed. E. Heitsch, *Die griechischen Dichterfragmente der römischen Kaiserzeit*, vol. 1, 2nd edn. Göttingen: Vandenhoeck & Ruprecht, 1963: 52–54.
frr. 1–4.
fr. 1: *P. Brit. Mus.* 1109b.
fr. 2: *P. Oxy.* 8.1085.
fr. 4 = fragmentum dubium.
fr. 4: Dup. 1555 003 (fr. 1).
fr. 4: Dup. partim PANCRATES Epigr. (1556 001) (fr. 602).
Q, Pap: 320: Hexametr., Epigr.
002 **Testimonium**, FGrH #625: 3C:160.
NQ: 127: Test.

003 **Fragmentum**, FGrH #625: 3C:160.
fr. 1: Dup. partim 1555 001 (fr. 4).
fr. 1: Dup. partim PANCRATES Epigr. (1556 001) (fr. 602).
Q: 26: Hist., Epigr.

1556 PANCRATES Epigr.
3/2 B.C.: Arcadius
001 **Fragmenta**, ed. H. Lloyd-Jones and P. Parsons, *Supplementum Hellenisticum*. Berlin: De Gruyter, 1983: 286–287.
frr. 598–600, 602.
fr. 602: Dup. partim PANCRATES Epic. (1555 001) (fr. 4).
fr. 602: Dup. partim PANCRATES Epic. (1555 003) (fr. 1).
Q: 57: Hexametr., Epigr.
002 **Epigrammata**, AG 6.117, 356; 7.653.
Q: 78: Epigr.

2120 PANTELEIUS Epic.
ante A.D. 5
001 **Fragmentum**, ed. E. Heitsch, *Die griechischen Dichterfragmente der römischen Kaiserzeit*, vol. 1, 2nd edn. Göttingen: Vandenhoeck & Ruprecht, 1963: 81–82.
Q: 61: Epic.

4261 PANTHOIDES Phil.
3 B.C.: Atheniensis
001 **Testimonia**, ed. K. Döring, *Die Megariker* [*Studien zur antiken Philosophie* 2. Amsterdam: Grüner, 1972]: 19, 39, 45.
test. 63, 131, 145–146.
test. 63, 131 (pp. 19, 39) = Diodorus Cronus (0073 001).
test. 145–146 (p. 45) = Panthoides.
NQ: Test.

1557 PANYASSIS Epic.
5 B.C.: Halicarnassensis
001 **Fragmenta**, ed. V.J. Matthews, *Panyassis of Halikarnassos*. Leiden: Brill, 1974: 43, 48, 50, 74–76, 88, 91, 100, 131, 135, 138, 142.
frr. 1–2, 4, 5, 12–16, 18, 28–30, 32.
Q: 453: Epic.
002 **Testimonium**, FGrH #440: 3B:371.
NQ: 33: Test.

1558 PAPIAS Scr. Eccl.
A.D. 2: Hierapolitanus
001 **Fragmenta**, ed. K. Bihlmeyer and W. Schneemelcher (post F.X. Funk), *Die apostolischen Väter*, 3rd edn. Tübingen: Mohr, 1970: 134–139.
Q: 1,676: Exeget.

2032 PAPPUS Math.
A.D. 4: Alexandrinus
001 **Synagoge**, ed. F. Hultsch, *Pappi Alexandrini collectionis quae supersunt*, 3 vols. Berlin:

Weidmann, 1:1876; 2:1877; 3:1878: **1**:2–470;
2:474–1020; **3**:1022–1134.
Lib. 2–5: vol. 1.
Lib. 6–7: vol. 2.
Lib. 8: vol. 3.
Cod: 140,874: Math.

002 **Commentaria in Ptolemaei syntaxin mathema-
ticam 5–6**, ed. A. Rome, *Commentaires de
Pappus et de Théon d'Alexandrie sur l'Alma-
geste*, vol. 1 [*Studi e Testi* 54. Rome: Biblioteca
Apostolica Vaticana, 1931]: 1–314.
Cod: 62,548: Math., Comm.

x01 **Introductio harmonica**.
Menge, pp. 186–222.
Cf. CLEONIDES Mus. (0361 001).

ΠΑΡΑΔΟΣΕΙΣ ΤΟΥ ΜΑΤΘΙΟΥ
Cf. MATTHIAE TRADITIONES (1560).

0580 *PARADOXOGRAPHUS FLORENTINUS*
vel *Anonymus Florentinus*
A.D. 2?

001 **Mirabilia de aquis**, ed. A. Giannini, *Paradoxo-
graphorum Graecorum reliquiae*. Milan: Istituto
Editoriale Italiano, 1965: 316–328.
Cod: 1,234: Paradox.

0581 *PARADOXOGRAPHUS PALATINUS*
vel *Anonymus Palatinus*
A.D. 3?

001 **Admiranda**, ed. A. Giannini, *Paradoxographorum Graecorum reliquiae*. Milan: Istituto Editoriale Italiano, 1965: 354–360.
Cod: 621: Paradox.

0582 *PARADOXOGRAPHUS VATICANUS*
vel *Anonymus Vaticanus*
A.D. 2?

001 **Admiranda**, ed. A. Giannini, *Paradoxographorum Graecorum reliquiae*. Milan: Istituto Editoriale Italiano, 1965: 332–350.
Cod: 1,617: Paradox.

1772 *PARALEIPOMENA JEREMIOU*
A.D. 2?

001 **Paraleipomena Jeremiou**, ed. R.A. Kraft and
A.-E. Purintun, *Texts and translations 1.
Pseudepigrapha series 1*. Missoula, Montana:
Society of Biblical Literature, 1972: 12–48.
Cod: 4,195: Pseudepigr.

1785 **PARAMONUS** Comic.
Incertum

001 **Tituli**, ed. T. Kock, *Comicorum Atticorum
fragmenta*, vol. 3. Leipzig: Teubner, 1888: 355.
NQ: 3: Comic.

4174 *PARAPHRASES IN DIONYSIUM PERIE-
GETAM*
Incertum

001 **In Dionysii periegetae orbis descriptionem**,
ed. K. Müller, *Geographi Graeci minores*, vol.

2. Paris: Didot, 1861 (repr. Hildesheim: Olms,
1965): 409–425.
Dup. partim 4174 002.
Cod: Comm., Geogr.

002 **In Dionysii periegetae orbis descriptionem**,
ed. A. Ludwich, *Aristarchs Homerische Textkritik nach den Fragmenten des Didymos*, vol.
2. Leipzig: Teubner, 1885 (repr. Hildesheim:
Olms, 1971): 556–574.
Dup. partim 4174 001.
Cod: Comm., Geogr.

4279 *PARAPHRASES IN HOMERI OPERA*
Varia

001 **Paraphrasis in Iliadem**, ed. I. Bekker, *Scholia
in Homeri Iliadem*, vol. 2. Berlin: Reimer,
1825: 651–811.
Cod: Comm.

1561 **PARDALAS** Epigr.
Incertum: Sardianus

x01 **Epigramma dedicatorium**.
App. Anth. 1.190: Cf. ANTHOLOGIAE GRAE-
CAE APPENDIX (7052 001).

PARMENIDES Epigr.
AG 9.113.
Cf. PARMENION Epigr. (1563 001).

1562 **PARMENIDES** Poet. Phil.
5 B.C.: Eleaticus

001 **Testimonia**, ed. H. Diels and W. Kranz, *Die
Fragmente der Vorsokratiker*, vol. 1, 6th edn.
Berlin: Weidmann, 1951 (repr. Dublin: 1966):
217–227.
test. 1–54.
NQ: 4,493: Test.

002 **Fragmenta**, ed. Diels and Kranz, *op. cit.*, 227–
246.
frr. 1–25.
Q: 3,198: Phil., Hexametr.

1563 **PARMENION** Epigr.
1 B.C.: Macedo

001 **Epigrammata**, AG **5**.33–34; **7**.183–184, 239;
9.27, 43, 69, 113–114, 304, 342; **11**.4, 65;
16.216, 222.
AG 7.240: Cf. ADAEUS Epigr. (0102 001).
AG 11.5: Cf. CALLICTER Epigr. (0148 001).
Q: 366: Epigr.

1564 **PARMENISCUS** Gramm.
2–1 B.C.

001 **Fragmenta**, ed. M. Breithaupt, *De Parmenisco
grammatico*. Leipzig: Teubner, 1915: 2–54.
Q

2225 **PARM(EN)ISCUS** Phil.
6 B.C.: Metapontinus

001 **Testimonia**, ed. H. Diels and W. Kranz, *Die
Fragmente der Vorsokratiker*, vol. 1, 6th edn.

Berlin: Weidmann, 1951 (repr. Dublin: 1966): 112–113.
test. 1–3.
NQ: 171: Test.

1565 **[PARMENO]** Epigr.
3 B.C.
001 **Epigramma**, AG 13.18.
Q: 35: Epigr.

1566 **PARMENO** Iamb.
3 B.C.: Byzantius
001 **Fragmenta**, ed. J.U. Powell, *Collectanea Alexandrina*. Oxford: Clarendon Press, 1925 (repr. 1970): 237.
frr. 1–3.
fr. 1: Dup. 1566 x01.
fr. 3: Dup. 1566 002.
Q: 36: Iamb., Epigr.
002 **Fragmentum**, ed. H. Lloyd-Jones and P. Parsons, *Supplementum Hellenisticum*. Berlin: De Gruyter, 1983: 288.
fr. 604a.
Dup. partim 1566 001 (fr. 3).
Q: 29: Iamb.
x01 **Epigramma demonstrativum**.
App. Anth. 3.124: Cf. ANTHOLOGIAE GRAECAE APPENDIX (7052 003).
Dup. partim 1566 001 (fr. 1).

1801 *PARODICA ANONYMA*
Varia
001 **Incertorum fragmenta**, ed. P. Brandt, *Parodorum epicorum Graecorum et Archestrati reliquiae* [*Corpusculum poesis epicae Graecae Ludibundae*, fasc. 1. Leipzig: Teubner, 1888]: 96–99, 101–104, 107, 109–110.
frr. 1–9.
Q: 376: Parod.
002 **Fragmenta dubia**, ed. Brandt, *op. cit.*, 112–113.
frr. 1–3.
Q: 25: Parod.
003 **Galeomyomachia** (*P. Mich.* inv. 6946), ed. H.S. Schibli, "Fragments of a weasel and mouse war," *Zeitschrift für Papyrologie und Epigraphik* 53 (1983) 13, 15, 17.
Pap: Parod.

2227 **PARON** Phil.
6 B.C.
001 **Testimonium**, ed. H. Diels and W. Kranz, *Die Fragmente der Vorsokratiker*, vol. 1, 6th edn. Berlin: Weidmann, 1951 (repr. Dublin: 1966): 217.
NQ: 78: Test.

1567 **PARRHASIUS** Epigr.
5/4 B.C.: Ephesius
001 **Epigrammata**, ed. E. Diehl, *Anthologia lyrica Graeca*, fasc. 1, 3rd edn. Leipzig: Teubner, 1949: 110–111.
frr. 1–3.
Q: 65: Epigr.

x01 **Epigrammata demonstrativa**.
App. Anth. 3.20–22: Cf. ANTHOLOGIAE GRAECAE APPENDIX (7052 003).
Dup. 1567 001.

1568 **PARTHAX** Hist.
ante A.D. 2
001 **Fragmenta**, FGrH #825: 3C:898.
Q: 95: Hist.

0655 **PARTHENIUS** Myth.
1 B.C.: Nicaeensis vel Myrleanus
001 **Narrationes amatoriae**, ed. E. Martini, *Parthenii Nicaeni quae supersunt* [*Mythographi Graeci* 2.1, suppl. Leipzig: Teubner, 1902]: 41–92.
Cod: 7,148: Myth., Narr. Fict.
002 **Poesis reliquiae**, ed. Martini, *op. cit.*, 11–37.
Elegiarum reliquiae (frr. 1–10): pp. 11–17.
Carmina forma incerta (frr. 11–21): pp. 18–22, 24, 26.
Incertae sedis fragmenta (frr. 22–46): pp. 26–37.
Dup. partim 0655 003.
Q: 221: Eleg., Poem.
003 **Fragmenta et tituli**, ed. H. Lloyd-Jones and P. Parsons, *Supplementum Hellenisticum*. Berlin: De Gruyter, 1983: 291–300, 302–304, 306–315.
frr. (+ titul.) 606–612b, 614–636, 639–664, 666.
frr. 609–612b, 614: *P. Gen.* 97.
fr. 626: *P. Lit. Lond.* 64.
Dup. partim 0655 002.
Q, Pap: 575: Eleg., Poem.

4263 **PASICLES** Phil.
4 B.C.: Thebanus, Atheniensis
001 **Testimonia**, ed. K. Döring, *Die Megariker* [*Studien zur antiken Philosophie* 2. Amsterdam: Grüner, 1972]: 46.
test. 148a–148b = Stilpo (4262 001).
NQ: Test.

1017 **PASIO** Med.
ante A.D. 1
x01 **Fragmentum ap. Oribasium**.
CMG, vol. 6.3, p. 95.
Cf. ORIBASIUS Med. (0722 004).
x02 **Fragmentum ap. Paulum**.
CMG, vol. 9.2, p. 318.
Cf. PAULUS Med. (0715 001).
x03 **Fragmentum ap. Aëtium** (lib. 15).
Zervos, *Athena* 21, p. 89.
Cf. AËTIUS Med. (0718 015).

2016 *PASSIO PERPETUAE ET FELICITATIS*
post A.D. 3
001 **Passio Perpetuae et Felicitatis**, ed. J.A. Robinson, *The passion of S. Perpetua* [*Texts and Studies* 1.2. Cambridge: Cambridge University

Press, 1891 (repr. Nendeln, Liechtenstein: Kraus, 1967)]: 61-95.
Cod: 4,063: Hagiogr.

PASSIO SPERATI ET SOCIORUM
A.D. 2
Cf. ACTA SCILLITANORUM MARTYRUM (0391).

PASTOR HERMAE
Cf. HERMAS Scr. Eccl. (1419 001).

2479 **PATROCLES** Hist.
4/3 B.C.
001 **Testimonia**, FGrH #712: 3C:597-598.
NQ: 427: Test.
002 **Fragmenta**, FGrH #712: 3C:598-601.
Q: 1,284: Hist.

0324 **PATROCLES** Trag.
4 B.C.: Thurius
001 **Fragmenta**, ed. B. Snell, *Tragicorum Graecorum fragmenta*, vol. 1. Göttingen: Vandenhoeck & Ruprecht, 1971: 197.
frr. 1-2.
Q: 47: Trag.

1018 **PATROCLUS** Med.
1 B.C.?
x01 **Fragmentum ap. Galenum.**
K13.1019.
Cf. GALENUS Med. (0057 077).

PAULI ET CORINTHIORUM EPISTULAE
(*P. Bodmer 10*)
Cf. ACTA PAULI (0388 003).

1020 **PAULINUS** Med.
ante A.D. 1
x01 **Fragmentum ap. Galenum.**
K13.211-213.
Cf. GALENUS Med. (0057 076).

2053 **PAULUS** Astrol.
A.D. 4: Alexandrinus
001 **Elementa apotelesmatica**, ed. E. Boer, *Pauli Alexandrini elementa apotelesmatica*. Leipzig: Teubner, 1958: 1-100.
Cod: 16,092: Astrol.
002 **Anacephalaeosis**, ed. Boer, *op. cit.*, xxi-xxiv.
Cod: 1,011: Astrol.

1019 **PAULUS** Med.
A.D. 4?
x01 **Fragmentum ap. Oribasium.**
CMG, vol. 6.2.2, p. 287.
Cf. ORIBASIUS Med. (0722 004).

0715 **PAULUS** Med.
A.D. 7: Aegineta
001 **Epitomae medicae libri septem**, ed. J.L. Heiberg, *Paulus Aegineta*, 2 vols. [*Corpus medi-*

corum Graecorum, vols. 9.1 & 9.2. Leipzig: Teubner, 9.1:1921; 9.2:1924]: **9.1**:3-388; **9.2**:5-411.
Cod: 206,400: Med.

4039 **PAULUS Silentiarius** Poet. Christ.
A.D. 6
001 **Descriptio Sanctae Sophiae**, ed. P. Friedländer, *Johannes von Gaza und Paulus Silentiarius*. Leipzig: Teubner, 1912: 227-256.
Cod
002 **Descriptio ambonis**, ed. Friedländer, *op. cit.*, 257-265.
Cod
004 **Epigrammata**, AG 5.217, 219, 221, 226, 228, 230, 232, 234, 236, 239, 241, 244, 246, 248, 250, 252, 254-256, 258-260, 262, 264, 266, 268, 270, 272, 274-275, 279, 281, 283, 286, 288, 290-291, 293, 300-301; **6**.54, 57, 64-66, 71, 75, 81-82, 84, 168; **7**.4, 307, 560, 563, 588, 604, 606, 609; **9**.396, 443, 620, 651, 658, 663-664, 764-765, 770, 782; **10**.15, 74, 76; **11**.60; **16**.57, 77, 118, 277-278.
AG 7.600: Cf. JULIANUS <Epigr.> (4050 001).
AG 9.444: Cf. ERATOSTHENES Scholasticus Epigr. (4063 001).
AG 9.766-769: Cf. AGATHIAS Scholasticus Hist. et Epigr. (4024 002).
Q: 3,434: Epigr.
x01 **In thermas Pythicas** [Sp.].
App. Anth. 4.75: Cf. ANTHOLOGIAE GRAECAE APPENDIX (7052 004).

0047 *PAUSANIAE I ET XERXIS EPISTULAE*
Incertum
001 **Epistulae**, ed. R. Hercher, *Epistolographi Graeci*. Paris: Didot, 1873 (repr. Amsterdam: Hakkert, 1965): 407.
Q: 150: Epist.

1569 **PAUSANIAS** Attic.
A.D. 2
001 Ἀττικῶν ὀνομάτων συναγωγή, ed. H. Erbse, *Untersuchungen zu den attizistischen Lexika* [*Abhandlungen der deutschen Akademie der Wissenschaften zu Berlin*, Philosoph.-hist. Kl. Berlin: Akademie-Verlag, 1950]: 152-221.
Q: 21,684: Lexicogr.

PAUSANIAS Geogr.
2 B.C.?: Damascenus
Cf. Pseudo-SCYMNUS (0068).

2407 **PAUSANIAS** Hist.
post 1 B.C.?: Lacon
001 **Testimonium**, FGrH #592: 3B:707.
NQ: 18: Test.

2573 **PAUSANIAS** Hist.
A.D. 4: Antiochenus vel Damascenus
001 **Testimonium**, FGrH #854: 3C:938.
NQ: 81: Test.

002 **Fragmenta**, FGrH #854: 3C:938–942.
Q: 1,944: Hist., Chronogr.

0525 **PAUSANIAS** Perieg.
A.D. 2: fort. Lydius
Scholia: Cf. SCHOLIA IN PAUSANIAM (5033).
001 **Graeciae descriptio**, ed. F. Spiro, *Pausaniae Graeciae descriptio*, 3 vols. Leipzig: Teubner, 1903 (repr. Stuttgart: 1:1967): **1**:1–420; **2**:1–389; **3**:1–217.
Cod: 224,602: Geogr., Perieg.

2401 **PAUSANIAS II Rex Lacedaemonis** Hist.
4 B.C.: Lacedaemonius
001 **Testimonia**, FGrH #582: 3B:693–694.
NQ: 261: Test.

2266 **PAXAMUS** Hist. et Scr. Rerum Nat.
1 B.C.
001 **Testimonium**, FGrH #377: 3B:245.
NQ: 24: Test.
x01 **Fragmenta** (ap. *Geoponica*).
Beckh, pp. 36–37, 79, 112, 151–152, 195, 208, 248–249, 274, 288, 298, 303, 320, 361–364, 380, 384, 387–388, 390–391, 395–396, 421–422, 447, 450, 476, 499, 516–517.
Cf. GEOPONICA (4080 001).

2592 **Joannes PEDIASIMUS** Gramm.
vel Joannes Diaconus Galenus vel Joannes Didascalus vel Galenus Aquanimus vel Galenus Tranquillus
A.D. 13–14: Bulgarius
001 **Tractatus de duodecim Herculis laboribus**, ed. R. Wagner, *Apollodori bibliotheca. Pediasimi libellus de duodecim Herculis laboribus* [*Mythographi Graeci* 1. Leipzig: Teubner, 1894]: 249–259.
Cod: Myth.
003 **Scholia in Hesiodi scutum** (scholia paraphrastica Pediasimi et exegesis Joannis Tzetzae), ed. T. Gaisford, *Poetae minores Graeci*, vol. 2 [*Scholia ad Hesiodum*]. Leipzig: Kühn, 1823: 609–654.
Cod: 13,343: Schol.
004 **Scholia in Aristotelis analytica priora**, ed. V. de Falco, *Ioannis Pediasimi in Aristotelis analytica scholia selecta*. Naples: Sangiovanni, 1926: 3–86.
Cod: Schol.
005 **Scholia in Aristotelis analytica posteriora**, ed. de Falco, *op. cit.*, 89–120.
Cod: Schol.
006 **Scholia in Theocriti syringem**, ed. F. Dübner, *Scholia in Theocritum*. Paris: Didot, 1849: 110–111.
Cod: Schol.
007 **Scholia in Aristotelis analytica priora et posteriora**, ed. V. de Falco, "Altri scolii di Giovanni Pediasimo agli analitici," *Byzantinische Zeitschrift* 28 (1928) 251–269.
Cod: Schol.

0275 ***PEIRAZOMENE***
ante A.D. 3
001 **Fragmentum** (*P. Brit. Mus.* 2208), ed. E. Heitsch, *Die griechischen Dichterfragmente der römischen Kaiserzeit*, vol. 1, 2nd edn. Göttingen: Vandenhoeck & Ruprecht, 1963: 41–42.
Pap: 142: Lyr.

2019 **PELAGIUS** Alchem.
A.D. 3?
001 **Fragmenta**, ed. M. Berthelot, *Collection des anciens alchimistes grecs*. Paris: Steinheil, 1887 (repr. London: Holland Press, 1963): 89, 199, 253–261.
Cod

1571 **<PEMPELUS>** Phil.
3/2 B.C.
001 **Fragmenta**, ed. H. Thesleff, *The Pythagorean texts of the Hellenistic period*. Åbo: Åbo Akademi, 1965: 141–142.
Q: 227: Phil.

0629 **PERIANDER** <Phil.>
7–6 B.C.: Corinthius
Cf. et <SEPTEM SAPIENTES> (1667).
001 **Epistulae** [Sp.], ed. R. Hercher, *Epistolographi Graeci*. Paris: Didot, 1873 (repr. Amsterdam: Hakkert, 1965): 408.
Q: 113: Epist.

1572 **<PERICTIONE>** Phil.
4/2 B.C.
001 **Fragmenta**, ed. H. Thesleff, *The Pythagorean texts of the Hellenistic period*. Åbo: Åbo Akademi, 1965: 142–146.
Q: 1,176: Phil.

1023 **PERIGENES** Med.
1 B.C.?
x01 **Fragmenta ap. Galenum.**
K13.33–34, 69–70, 73.
Cf. GALENUS Med. (0057 076).

0064 ***PERIPLUS HANNONIS***
4 B.C.
001 **Periplus Hannonis**, ed. K. Müller, *Geographi Graeci minores*, vol. 1. Paris: Didot, 1855 (repr. Hildesheim: Olms, 1965): 1–14.
Cod: 681: Perieg.

0071 ***PERIPLUS MARIS ERYTHRAEI***
fort. auctore Arriano
post A.D. 2
001 **Anonymi (Arriani, ut fertur) periplus maris Erythraei**, ed. K. Müller, *Geographi Graeci minores*, vol. 1. Paris: Didot, 1855 (repr. Hildesheim: Olms, 1965): 257–305.
Cod: 6,561: Perieg.

0077 **PERIPLUS MARIS MAGNI**
vel *Stadiasmus*
post A.D. 3
001 **Stadiasmus sive periplus Maris Magni**, ed. K. Müller, *Geographi Graeci minores*, vol. 1. Paris: Didot, 1855 (repr. Hildesheim: Olms, 1965): 427-514.
Cod: 5,980: Perieg.

PERIPLUS MARIS RUBRI
Cf. PERIPLUS MARIS ERYTHRAEI (0071).

0075 **PERIPLUS PONTI EUXINI**
fort. auctore Arriano
post A.D. 6
001 **Anonymi (Arriani, ut fertur) periplus ponti Euxini**, ed. K. Müller, *Geographi Graeci minores*, vol. 1. Paris: Didot, 1855 (repr. Hildesheim: Olms, 1965): 402-423.
Cod: 5,783: Perieg.

1573 **PERITAS** Epigr.
Incertum
001 **Epigramma**, AG 16.236.
Q: 28: Epigr.

2403 **PERSAEUS** Hist.
4-3 B.C.: Citieus
001 **Testimonia**, FGrH #584: 3B:696-697.
NQ: 330: Test.
002 **Fragmenta**, FGrH #584: 3B:697-700.
Q: 926: Hist.

1574 **PERSAEUS** Phil.
4-3 B.C.: Citiensis
001 **Fragmenta**, ed. J. von Arnim, *Stoicorum veterum fragmenta*, vol. 1. Leipzig: Teubner, 1905 (repr. Stuttgart: 1968): 96-102.
Q: 2,008: Phil.

1575 **PERSES** Epigr.
4 B.C.: Thebanus
001 **Epigrammata**, AG 6.112, 272, 274; 7.445, 487, 501, 539, 730; 9.334.
Q: 257: Epigr.

2722 **PERSEUS** Epigr.
Incertum
x01 **Problema**.
App. Anth. 7.4(?): Cf. ANTHOLOGIAE GRAECAE APPENDIX (7052 007).

2635 **PERSINUS** Poeta
4 B.C.: Ephesius vel Milesius
001 **Titulus**, ed. H. Lloyd-Jones and P. Parsons, *Supplementum Hellenisticum*. Berlin: De Gruyter, 1983: 316.
fr. 666c.
NQ: 3: Poem.

2323 **PETELLIDAS** Hist.
ante 1 B.C.: Creticus

001 **Fragmentum**, FGrH #464: 3B:401-402.
Q: 114: Hist.

1024 **PETINUS** Med.
ante A.D. 1
x01 **Fragmentum ap. Galenum**.
K13.57.
Cf. GALENUS Med. (0057 076).

[PETOSIRIS]
Cf. [NECHEPSO et PETOSIRIS] Astrol. (0995).

2247 **PETRON** Phil.
6 B.C.
001 **Testimonium**, ed. H. Diels and W. Kranz, *Die Fragmente der Vorsokratiker*, vol. 1, 6th edn. Berlin: Weidmann, 1951 (repr. Dublin: 1966): 106.
NQ: 129: Test.

1025 **PETRONAS** Med.
5 B.C.: Aegineta
x01 **Fragmentum ap. Galenum**.
K15.436 in CMG, vol. 5.9.1, p. 126.
Cf. GALENUS Med. (0057 087).

1026 **PETRONIUS** Med.
fiq Musa
A.D. 1
Cf. et MUSA Med. (0808).
x01 **Fragmentum ap. Galenum**.
K13.831.
Cf. GALENUS Med. (0057 077).

2678 **<PETRONIUS APOLLODORUS>** Epigr.
A.D. 4
x01 **Epigramma dedicatorium**.
App. Anth. 1.340: Cf. ANTHOLOGIAE GRAECAE APPENDIX (7052 001).

1027 **PETRUS** Med.
ante A.D. 6
x01 **Fragmentum ap. Aëtium** (lib. 7).
CMG, vol. 8.2, p. 386.
Cf. AËTIUS Med. (0718 007).

2962 **PETRUS** Scr. Eccl.
A.D. 3-4: Alexandrinus
001 **De deitate** (fragmentum), ed. M. Richard, "Le florilège du cod. Vatopédi 236 sur le corruptible et l'incorruptible," *Muséon* 86 (1973) 268-269.
Q
002 **De adventu domini** (fragmentum), MPG 18: 521.
Q
003 **De anima** (fragmenta), ed. W.A. Bienert, "Neue Fragmente des Dionysius und des Petrus von Alexandrien aus Cod. Vatop. 236," Κληρονομία 5 (1973) 311-312.
Cod

004 **Epistula canonica** (e Περὶ μετανοίας) (canones 1–14), FONTI II: 578–596.
Cod

005 **De paschate ad Tricentium** (fragmenta), MPG 18: 512–517.
Q

006 **De paschate ad Tricentium** (canon 15 epistulae canonicae) (fragmentum), FONTI II: 597.
Cod

007 **Epistula ad clericos suos** (fragmentum), ed. M. Richard, "Quelques nouveaux fragments des pères anténicéens et nicéens," *Symbolae Osloenses* 38 (1963) 80.
Q

008 **Epistula festalis** (fragmenta), ed. Richard, *Muséon* 86, 267–268.
Q

011 **Didascalia** (fragmentum) [Sp.], ed. J.M. Heer, "Ein neues Fragment der Didaskalie des Märtyrerbischofs Petros von Alexandrien," *Oriens Christianus* 2 (1902) 344–351.
Q

012 **Didascalia** (fragmenta) [Sp.], ed. K. Holl, *Fragmente vornicänischer Kirchenväter aus den Sacra Parallela* [*Texte und Untersuchungen* 20. Leipzig: Hinrichs, 1899]: 234.
Q

013 **Didascalia** (fragmentum ap. Eliam Cretensem) [Sp.], MPG 36: 895.
Q

x01 **De deitate** (fragmenta).
ACO **1.1.2**, p. 39; **1.1.7**, pp. 36, 89, 90.
Cf. CONCILIA OECUMENICA (ACO) (5000 001).

x02 **De anima** (fragmentum).
ACO 3, p. 197.
Cf. CONCILIA OECUMENICA (ACO) (5000 004).

2997 **PETRUS** Scr. Eccl.
A.D. 4: Sebastenus

x01 **Epistula ad Gregorium fratrem.**
Pasquali, *Epist.* 30, pp. 89–91.
Cf. GREGORIUS NYSSENUS Theol. (2017 033).

2732 **PETRUS MONGUS** Scr. Eccl.
A.D. 5: Alexandrinus

x01 **Epistula ad Acacium** (ap. Evagrium, *Historia ecclesiastica*).
Bidez & Parmentier, pp. 115–116.
Cf. EVAGRIUS Scholasticus Scr. Eccl. (2733 001).

2593 **PETRUS PATRICIUS** Hist.
A.D. 6: Thessalonicensis, Constantinopolitanus

001 **De scientia politica** (fragmenta), ed. A. Mai, *Scriptorum veterum nova collectio*, vol. 2. Rome: Biblioteca Apostolica Vaticana, 1827: 590–609.
Cod: Hist.

x01 **Fragmenta historiae** (ap. Constantinum Porphyrogenitum, *De legationibus*).
de Boor, vol. 1.2, pp. 390–396.
Cf. CONSTANTINUS VII PORPHYROGENITUS Imperator (3023 001).

x02 **Fragmenta historiae** (ap. Constantinum Porphyrogenitum, *De sententiis*.
Boissevain, pp. 241–271.
Cf. CONSTANTINUS VII PORPHYROGENITUS Imperator (3023 004).

x03 Περὶ τῆς πολιτικῆς καταστάσεως (fragmenta ap. Constantinum Porphyrogenitum, *De ceremoniis*).
Reiske, vol. 1, pp. 386–389 (lib. 1, cap. 84–85).
Cf. CONSTANTINUS VII PORPHYROGENITUS Imperator (3023 010).

PHACELLUS (?) Epigr.
AG 7.650.
Cf. PHALAECUS Epigr. (1581 001).

1576 **PHAEDIMUS** <Epic.>
Incertum

001 **Fragmentum**, ed. G. Kinkel, *Epicorum Graecorum fragmenta*, vol. 1. Leipzig: Teubner, 1877: 214.
Q: 6: Epic.

1577 **PHAEDIMUS** Epigr.
3 B.C.: Macedo vel Paphlagonius

001 **Epigrammata**, AG **6.**271; **7.**739; **13.**2, 22.
Q: 140: Epigr.

002 **Fragmentum**, ed. H. Lloyd-Jones and P. Parsons, *Supplementum Hellenisticum*. Berlin: De Gruyter, 1983: 316.
fr. 669.
Q: 9: Hexametr.

PHAEDRI EPISTULA
Epist. Graec., p. 627.
Cf. SOCRATICORUM EPISTULAE (0637 001).

1578 **PHAENIAS** Phil.
vel Phanias
4 B.C.: Eresius

001 **Fragmenta**, ed. F. Wehrli, *Phainias von Eresos. Chamaileon. Praxiphanes* [*Die Schule des Aristoteles*, vol. 9, 2nd edn. Basel: Schwabe, 1969]: 10–21.
Logica: fr. 8.
Πρὸς Διόδωρον: fr. 9.
Πρὸς τοὺς σοφιστάς: fr. 10.
Περὶ τῶν ἐν Σικελίᾳ τυράννων: frr. 11–13.
Τυράννων ἀναίρεσις ἐκ τιμωρίας: frr. 14–16.
Πρυτάνεις Ἐρεσίων: frr. 17a–19.
Historica: frr. 20–29.
Περὶ τῶν Σωκρατικῶν: frr. 30–31.
Περὶ ποιητῶν: frr. 32–33.
Mirabilia: frr. 34–35.
Περὶ φυτῶν (= φυτικά): frr. 37–48, 50.
Fragmentum dubium: fr. 51.
Q: 3,609: Phil., Hist., Paradox., Nat. Hist.

1579 **PHAËNNUS** Epigr.
3 B.C.
  001 **Epigrammata**, AG 7.197, 437.
Q: 49: Epigr.

2366 **PHAENNUS** Hist.
Incertum
  001 **Titulus**, FGrH #525: 3B:503.
NQ: Hist.

1580 **PHAESTUS** Epic.
post 4 B.C.
  001 **Fragmentum**, ed. J.U. Powell, *Collectanea Al-
exandrina*. Oxford: Clarendon Press, 1925
(repr. 1970): 28.
Dup. partim 1580 002.
Dup. 1580 003 (fr. 670).
Q: 7: Epic.
  002 **Fragmenta**, FGrH #593: 3B:707.
Dup. partim 1580 001.
Dup. partim 1580 003 (fr. 670).
Q: 54: Hist., Epic.
  003 **Fragmentum**, ed. H. Lloyd-Jones and P. Par-
sons, *Supplementum Hellenisticum*. Berlin: De
Gruyter, 1983: 316.
fr. 670.
Dup. 1580 001.
Dup. partim 1580 002.
Q: 8: Epic.

1581 **PHALAECUS** Epigr.
4 B.C.: Phoceus
  001 **Epigrammata**, AG **6**.165; **7**.650; **13**.5–6, 27.
Q: 225: Epigr.
  x01 **Epigramma dedicatorium** (*App. Anth.*).
App. Anth. 1.117: Cf. ANTHOLOGIAE GRAE-
CAE APPENDIX (7052 001).

0053 *PHALARIDIS EPISTULAE*
A.D. 2?
  001 **Epistulae**, ed. R. Hercher, *Epistolographi
Graeci*. Paris: Didot, 1873 (repr. Amsterdam:
Hakkert, 1965): 409–459.
Cod: 18,336: Epist.

2667 **PHALERNUS** Poeta et Soph.
A.D. 2–3
  x01 **Epigramma dedicatorium.**
App. Anth. 1.191: Cf. ANTHOLOGIAE GRAE-
CAE APPENDIX (7052 001).

1582 **PHANIAS** Gramm.
3 B.C.
  001 **Epigrammata**, AG **6**.294–295, 297, 299, 304,
307; **7**.537; **12**.31.
Q: 357: Epigr.

0975 **PHANIUS** Med.
ante A.D. 1
  x01 **Fragmentum ap. Galenum.**
K13.840.
Cf. GALENUS Med. (0057 077).

0214 **PHANOCLES** Eleg.
3 B.C.?
  001 **Fragmenta**, ed. J.U. Powell, *Collectanea Alexandrina*. Oxford: Clarendon Press, 1925 (repr.
1970): 106–108.
frr. 1–3.
Q: 201: Eleg.
  x01 **Fragmentum papyraceum** (*P. Sorbonne* inv.
2254) (fort. auctore Phanocle).
SH, pp. 478–479, fr. 970.
Cf. ADESPOTA PAPYRACEA (SH) (2648 002).

1583 **PHANODEMUS** Hist.
4 B.C.: Atheniensis
  001 **Testimonia**, FGrH #325: 3B:77–78, 757 addenda.
test. 2: *IG²* 2.223.
test. 3a: *IG* 7.4252.
test. 3b: *IG* 7.4253.
test. 4: *IG* 7.4254.
test. 5: *Inscr. Delphi.*
test. 8: *P. Oxy.* 17.2082.
NQ: 597: Test.
  002 **Fragmenta**, FGrH #325: 3B:79–85.
Q, Cod: 2,091: Hist.

2278 **PHANODICUS** Hist.
2 B.C.?
  001 **Fragmenta**, FGrH #397: 3B:291–292.
Q: 341: Hist.

2471 **PHARNUCHUS** Hist.
1 B.C.–A.D. 1?: Nisibenus
  001 **Testimonium**, FGrH #694: 3C:533.
NQ: 33: Test.

0979 **Apius PHASCUS** Med.
ante A.D. 2
  x01 **Fragmentum ap. Galenum.**
K12.841–842.
Cf. GALENUS Med. (0057 076).

0486 **PHERECRATES** Comic.
5 B.C.
  001 **Fragmenta**, ed. T. Kock, *Comicorum Atticorum fragmenta*, vol. 1. Leipzig: Teubner,
1880: 145–175, 177–188, 190–209.
frr. 1–13, 15–17, 19–56, 58–65, 67–73, 75–91,
93–98, 100–109, 113–132, 134–138, 141–191,
195–249 + tituli.
Q: 2,483: Comic.
  002 **Fragmenta**, ed. A. Meineke, *Fragmenta comicorum Graecorum*, vol. 2.1. Berlin: Reimer,
1839 (repr. De Gruyter, 1970): 252–272, 274–
300, 305, 309–316, 318–327, 335–355, 357–
360.
p. 338, fr. 7: line 7 supplied from vol. 5.1, p.
lvii.
Q: 2,340: Comic.
  003 **Fragmenta**, ed. J. Demiańczuk, *Supplementum*

comicum. Krakau: Nakładem Akademii, 1912 (repr. Hildesheim: Olms, 1967): 66–71.
frr. 1–22.
Q: 94: Comic.

004 **Fragmentum,** ed. C. Austin, *Comicorum Graecorum fragmenta in papyris reperta.* Berlin: De Gruyter, 1973: 196.
fr. 205.
Pap: 12: Comic.

005 **Fragmentum,** ed. Kock, *CAF,* vol. 3 (1888): 716.
fr. 155b.
Q: 16: Comic.

006 **Fragmenta,** ed. Meineke, *FCG,* vol. 5.1 (1857; repr. 1970): li.
Q: 6: Comic.

1584 **PHERECYDES** Hist.
5 B.C.: Atheniensis
Cf. et ANTIOCHUS-PHERECYDES Hist. (2221).
001 **Testimonia,** FGrH #3: 1A:58–59.
Dup. partim ANTIOCHUS-PHERECYDES Hist. (2221 001).
NQ: 206: Test.
002 **Fragmenta,** FGrH #3: 1A:59–104, *5 addenda.
Dup. partim ANTIOCHUS-PHERECYDES Hist. (2221 002).
Q: 15,426: Hist., Myth.

2329 **PHERECYDES** Hist.
4 B.C./A.D. 2: Lerius
001 **Testimonium,** FGrH #475: 3B:434.
NQ: 22: Test.
002 **Fragmenta,** FGrH #475: 3B:434–435.
Q: 322: Hist.

0630 **PHERECYDES** Phil. et Myth.
6 B.C.: Syrius
Cf. et PHERECYDIS EPISTULA (1585).
001 **Testimonia,** ed. H. Diels and W. Kranz, *Die Fragmente der Vorsokratiker,* vol. 1, 6th edn. Berlin: Weidmann, 1951 (repr. Dublin: 1966): 43–46.
test. 1–12.
NQ: 1,384: Test.
002 **Fragmenta,** ed. Diels and Kranz, *op. cit.,* 47–51.
frr. 1–14.
Q, Pap: 966: Phil., Theol.

1585 *PHERECYDIS EPISTULA*
Incertum
Cf. et PHERECYDES Phil. et Myth. (0630).
001 **Epistula,** ed. R. Hercher, *Epistolographi Graeci.* Paris: Didot, 1873 (repr. Amsterdam: Hakkert, 1965): 460.
Q: 127: Epist.

2636 **PHERENICUS** Epic.
2 B.C./A.D. 2?: Heracleota
001 **Fragmentum,** ed. H. Lloyd-Jones and P. Par-

sons, *Supplementum Hellenisticum.* Berlin: De Gruyter, 1983: 317.
fr. 671.
Q: 31: Epic.

1880 **PHIDALIUS** Hist.
Incertum: Corinthius
001 **Fragmenta,** FGrH #30: 1A:214.
NQ: 368: Hist., Myth.

1586 **PHILAENIS** Scriptor De Aphrodisiis
3 B.C.?: Samia
001 **Fragmenta** (*P. Oxy.* 39.2891), ed. E. Lobel, *The Oxyrhynchus papyri,* pt. 39. London: Egypt Exploration Society, 1972: 53–54.
Pap

1079 **PHILAGRIUS** Med.
A.D. 4–5: Epirotes
x01 **Fragmentum ap. Oribasium.**
CMG, vol. **6.1.1,** pp. 133–138; **6.3,** pp. 109, 111, 312.
Cf. ORIBASIUS Med. (0722 001, 004).
x02 **Fragmentum ap. Paulum.**
CMG, vol. 9.2, pp. 285, 333, 366.
Cf. PAULUS Med. (0715 001).
x03 **Fragmentum ap. Aëtium** (lib. 3).
CMG, vol. 8.1, p. 299.
Cf. AËTIUS Med. (0718 003).
x04 **Fragmentum ap. Aëtium** (lib. 5).
CMG, vol. 8.2, p. 112.
Cf. AËTIUS Med. (0718 005).
x05 **Fragmentum ap. Aëtium** (lib. 7).
CMG, vol. 8.2, pp. 374, 376, 381.
Cf. AËTIUS Med. (0718 007).
x06 **Fragmentum ap. Aëtium** (lib. 8).
CMG, vol. 8.2, pp. 475, 516.
Cf. AËTIUS Med. (0718 008).
x07 **Fragmentum ap. Aëtium** (lib. 9).
Zervos, *Athena* 23, p. 305.
Cf. AËTIUS Med. (0718 009).
x08 **Fragmentum ap. Aëtium** (lib. 11).
Daremberg-Ruelle, pp. 95, 123, 573–574.
Cf. AËTIUS Med. (0718 011).
x09 **Fragmentum ap. Aëtium** (lib. 12).
Kostomiris, pp. 46, 50, 52, 85, 88, 89, 111.
Cf. AËTIUS Med. (0718 012).
x10 **Fragmentum ap. Aëtium** (lib. 15).
Zervos, *Athena* 21, p. 29.
Cf. AËTIUS Med. (0718 015).
x11 **Fragmentum ap. Aëtium** (lib. 16).
Zervos, *Gynaekologie des Aëtios,* pp. 103–105.
Cf. AËTIUS Med. (0718 016).

PHILAGRIUS Scriptor Facetiarum
A.D. 4?
Cf. HIEROCLES et PHILAGRIUS Scriptores Facetiarum (2404).

2966 **PHILEAS** Scr. Eccl.
A.D. 3–4: Thmuitanus
001 **Apologia** (fragmenta), ed. V. Martin, *Papyrus*

Bodmer XX. Apologie de Philéas évêque de Thmouis. Geneva: Bibliotheca Bodmeriana, 1964.
Pap

002 **Epistula ad Thmuitanos** (ap. Eusebium), ed. H. Musurillo, *The acts of the Christian martyrs.* Oxford: Clarendon Press, 1972: 320–324.
Q: 677: Epist., Hagiogr.

0487 **PHILEMON** Comic.
4–3 B.C.: Syracusanus
001 **Fragmenta**, ed. T. Kock, *Comicorum Atticorum fragmenta*, vol. 2. Leipzig: Teubner, 1884: 478–539.
frr. 2–18, 20–39, 41–44, 46–77, 79–86, 88–211, 213, 219–220, 222–240, 243–247 + tituli.
fr. 89: *P. Cairo* inv. 56226.
fr. 233: Tabula lignea Cairensis.
Q, Pap: 4,361: Comic.
002 **Fragmenta**, ed. A. Meineke, *Fragmenta comicorum Graecorum*, vol. 4. Berlin: Reimer, 1839 (repr. De Gruyter, 1970): 3–64, 67.
Q: 4,192: Comic.
003 **Fragmenta**, ed. J. Demiańczuk, *Supplementum comicum.* Krakau: Nakładem Akademii, 1912 (repr. Hildesheim: Olms, 1967): 71–72.
frr. 1–3.
fr. 3: *P. Oxy.* 9.39 (col. 7, v. 32).
Q, Pap: 56: Comic.
004 **Fragmenta**, ed. C. Austin, *Comicorum Graecorum fragmenta in papyris reperta.* Berlin: De Gruyter, 1973: 197–200.
frr. 206, 212–214.
Pap: 136: Comic.
006 **Titulus**, ed. Kock, *CAF*, vol. 3 (1888): 749.
NQ: 2: Comic.
007 **Fragmentum**, ed. Kock, *CAF*, vol. 3, 750.
fr. 224b.
Q: 2: Comic.
008 **Epigramma**, AG 9.450.
AG 10.82: Cf. PALLADAS Epigr. (2123 001).
Q: 17: Epigr.
009 **Fragmenta**, ed. Meineke, *FCG*, vol. 5.1 (1857; repr. 1970): ccxxxiv, ccxxxviii–ccxxxix.
p. ccxxxiv: Dup. partim 0487 002 (vol. 4, p. 47, fr. 39).
p. ccxxxix: Dup. partim 0541 040 (vol. 4, p. 242, fr. 28).
Q: 77: Comic.
x01 **Sententia ap. Menandrum** (tabula lignea Cairensis).
Menandri sententiae, fr. 15.
Cf. MENANDER Comic. (0541 048).

0488 **PHILEMON Junior** Comic.
3 B.C.
001 **Fragmenta**, ed. T. Kock, *Comicorum Atticorum fragmenta*, vol. 2. Leipzig: Teubner, 1884: 540.
frr. 1–3 + titulus.
Q: 106: Comic.

002 **Fragmenta**, ed. A. Meineke, *Fragmenta comicorum Graecorum*, vol. 4. Berlin: Reimer, 1841 (repr. De Gruyter, 1970): 68.
Q: 91: Comic.

1384 **PHILEMON III** Comic.
3 B.C.?
001 **Titulus**, ed. T. Kock, *Comicorum Atticorum fragmenta*, vol. 2. Leipzig: Teubner, 1884: 540.
NQ: [1]: Comic.

2718 **Manuel PHILES** Poeta
A.D. 13–14: Ephesius, Constantinopolitanus
x01 **Epigrammata** (*App. Anth.*).
Epigramma exhortatorium et supplicatorium: 4.141.
Epigramma irrisorium: 5.79.
App. Anth. 4.141: Cf. ANTHOLOGIAE GRAECAE APPENDIX (7052 004).
App. Anth. 5.79: Cf. ANTHOLOGIAE GRAECAE APPENDIX (7052 005).

0489 **PHILETAERUS** Comic.
4 B.C.
001 **Fragmenta**, ed. T. Kock, *Comicorum Atticorum fragmenta*, vol. 2. Leipzig: Teubner, 1884: 230–235.
frr. 1, 3–18, 20 + tituli.
Q: 324: Comic.
002 **Fragmenta**, ed. A. Meineke, *Fragmenta comicorum Graecorum*, vol. 3. Berlin: Reimer, 1840 (repr. De Gruyter, 1970): 292–299.
Q: 307: Comic.
003 **Fragmentum**, ed. J. Demiańczuk, *Supplementum comicum.* Krakau: Nakładem Akademii, 1912 (repr. Hildesheim: Olms, 1967): 72.
fr. 1.
Q: 2: Comic.

0212 **PHILETAS** Eleg. et Gramm.
vel Philitas
4–3 B.C.: Cous
001 **Fragmenta**, ed. J.U. Powell, *Collectanea Alexandrina.* Oxford: Clarendon Press, 1925 (repr. 1970): 90–95.
frr. 1–4, 6–14, 16–26.
Dup. partim 0212 002, x01.
Q: 300: Eleg., Epigr., Hexametr.
002 **Fragmenta poetica**, ed. W. Kuchenmüller, *Philetae Coi reliquiae* [*Diss. Berlin* (1928)]: 38–41, 49–50, 52, 58, 61, 64, 66, 68, 72, 74, 76–78, 80–87.
frr. 1–8, 10–28.
Dup. partim 0212 001, 004.
Q: 311: Eleg., Epigr.
003 **Fragmenta grammatica**, ed. Kuchenmüller, *op. cit.*, 91–96, 98–100, 102–111.
frr. 29–59.
Q: 871: Gramm.
004 **Fragmenta**, ed. H. Lloyd-Jones and P. Parsons,

Supplementum Hellenisticum. Berlin: De Gruyter, 1983: 318–320.
frr. 673–674, 675a–675d.
fr. 673: *P. Oxy.* 20.2258a.
fr. 674: *P. Oxy.* 20.2260.
Dup. partim 0212 002 (frr. 16, 24–26).
Q, Pap: 42: Eleg., Poem.

x01 **Epigramma exhortatorium et supplicatorium.**
App. Anth. 4.36: Cf. ANTHOLOGIAE GRAECAE APPENDIX (7052 004).
Dup. partim 0212 001 (fr. 12).

1587 **PHILIADES** Eleg.
5 B.C.: Megareus
001 **Fragmentum,** ed. E. Diehl, *Anthologia lyrica Graeca,* fasc. 1, 3rd edn. Leipzig: Teubner, 1949: 87.
Q: 13: Epigr.

x01 **Epigramma demonstrativum.**
App. Anth. 3.19: Cf. ANTHOLOGIAE GRAECAE APPENDIX (7052 003).
Dup. 1587 001.

1588 **PHILICUS** Lyr.
3 B.C.: Corcyraeus
001 **Fragmenta,** ed. H. Lloyd-Jones and P. Parsons, *Supplementum Hellenisticum.* Berlin: De Gruyter, 1983: 321–324.
frr. 676–680.
frr. 678–680: *PSI* 1282.
Q, Pap: 414: Hymn.

2692 **PHILINNA** Poeta
ante 1 B.C.: Thessala
x01 **Incantamenta hexametrica** (*P. Amh.* 11) (fort. auctore Philinna).
SH, p. 399, fr. 900.
Cf. ADESPOTA PAPYRACEA (SH) (2648 001).

1969 **PHILINUS** Hist.
3 B.C.: Agrigentinus
001 **Testimonia,** FGrH #174: 2B:897.
NQ: 109: Test.
002 **Fragmenta,** FGrH #174: 2B:897–900.
Q: 883: Hist.

1030 **PHILINUS** Med.
3 B.C.: Cous
x01 **Fragmenta ap. Galenum.**
K13.113, 842.
Cf. GALENUS Med. (0057 076–077).
x02 **Fragmentum ap. Philumenum.**
CMG, vol. 10.1.1, p. 10.
Cf. PHILUMENUS Med. (0671 001).

0490 **PHILIPPIDES** Comic.
4 B.C.
001 **Fragmenta,** ed. T. Kock, *Comicorum Atticorum fragmenta,* vol. 3. Leipzig: Teubner, 1888: 301–312.
frr. 1–29, 31–40 + titulus.
Q: 463: Comic.
002 **Fragmenta,** ed. A. Meineke, *Fragmenta comi-*

corum Graecorum, vol. 4. Berlin: Reimer, 1841 (repr. De Gruyter, 1970): 467–477, 478.
478: fr. 18 supplied from vol. 5.1, p. cccxv.
Q: 439: Comic.

1781 **PHILIPPUS** Comic.
4 B.C.
001 **Fragmentum,** ed. T. Kock, *Comicorum Atticorum fragmenta,* vol. 2. Leipzig: Teubner, 1884: 215.
fr. 1.
Q: 4: Comic.
002 **Fragmentum,** ed. A. Meineke, *Fragmenta comicorum Graecorum,* vol. 1. Berlin: Reimer, 1839 (repr. De Gruyter, 1970): 342.
Q: 2: Comic.

1589 **PHILIPPUS** Epigr.
A.D. 1: Thessalonicensis
001 **Epigrammata,** AG **4.**2; **6.**5, 36, 38, 62, 90, 92, 94, 99, 101–104, 107, 203, 231, 236, 240, 247, 251, 259; **7.**186–187, 234, 362, 382–383, 385, 394, 405, 554, 692; **9.**11, 22, 56, 83, 85, 88–89, 232, 240, 247, 253–255, 262, 264–265, 267, 274, 285, 290, 293, 299, 307, 311, 416, 438, 543, 561, 575, 708–709, 742, 777–778; **11.**33, 36, 173, 321, 347; **13.**1; **16.**25, 52, 81, 93, 104, 137, 141, 177, 193, 215, 240.
AG 6.114: Cf. SIMIAS Gramm. (0211 002).
AG 7.237: Cf. ALPHEUS Epigr. (0108 001).
AG 9.266, 269: Cf. ANTIPATER Epigr. (0114 001).
AG 9.562: Cf. CRINAGORAS Epigr. (0154 001).
AG 9.563: Cf. LEONIDAS Epigr. (1458 001).
Q: 3,413: Epigr.

1590 **PHILIPPUS** Hist.
3 B.C.?: Theangelius
001 **Fragmenta,** FGrH #741: 3C:718.
Q: 261: Hist.

2142 **PHILIPPUS** Hist.
A.D. 2: Pergamenus
001 **Testimonium,** FGrH #95: 2A:446.
test. 1: *IG* 4.1153.
NQ: 24: Test.
002 **Fragmentum,** FGrH #95: 2A:446.
fr. 1: *IG* 4.1153.
Epigr: 66: Hist.

2188 **PHILIPPUS** Hist.
A.D. 4?: Amphipolitanus
001 **Testimonia,** FGrH #280: 3A:159.
NQ: 51: Test.
002 **Fragmentum,** FGrH #280: 3A:159.
Q: 20: Hist.

4176 **PHILIPPUS** Math., Astron. et Phil.
4 B.C.: Opuntius
001 **Testimonia,** ed. F. Lasserre, *De Léodamas de*

Thasos à Philippe d'Oponte. Naples: Bibliopolis, 1987: 159–161.
test. 1–3, 4b–6.
NQ: Test.

002 **Fragmenta et tituli**, ed. Lasserre, *op. cit.*, 161–183.
frr. 1–14c, 15a–36, 38–47, 50–76a, 77.
Q, Pap: Math., Astron., Phil.

003 **Doctrina**, ed. Lasserre, *op. cit.*, 183–188.
frr. 1–5, 7–10b.
NQ: Test.

x01 **Epinomis.**
Burnet, vol. 5 (St. II.973a–992e).
Cf. PLATO Phil. (0059 035).

0990 **PHILIPPUS** <Med.>
fiq Philippus Xerus Rheginus
ante A.D. 2: Macedo

x01 **Fragmentum ap. Galenum.**
K14.149–150.
Cf. GALENUS Med. (0057 078).

1031 **PHILIPPUS** Med.
A.D. 2

x01 **Fragmenta ap. Galenum.**
K13.88, 105, 304.
Cf. GALENUS Med. (0057 076).

x02 **Fragmentum ap. Paulum.**
CMG, vol. 9.2, p. 317.
Cf. PAULUS Med. (0715 001).

4265 **PHILIPPUS** Phil.
4 B.C.: Megarensis, Atheniensis

001 **Fragmentum**, ed. K. Döring, *Die Megariker* [*Studien zur antiken Philosophie* 2. Amsterdam: Grüner, 1972]: 52, 61.
fr. 164a (p. 52) = Stilpo (4262 001).
Q: Phil.

0048 **PHILIPPUS II Rex Macedonum** <Epist.>
5–4 B.C.: Macedonius

001 **Epistulae**, ed. R. Hercher, *Epistolographi Graeci*. Paris: Didot, 1873 (repr. Amsterdam: Hakkert, 1965): 461–467.
Q: 2,414: Epist.

x01 **Epigramma irrisorium.**
App. Anth. 5.10: Cf. ANTHOLOGIAE GRAECAE APPENDIX (7052 005).

PHILIPPUS Translator Hieroglyphicorum
post A.D. 5?
Cf. HORAPOLLO Gramm. (2052 001).

0491 **PHILISCUS** Comic.
fiq Philiscus Corcyraeus Epigr.
4 B.C.?
Cf. et PHILISCUS Epigr. (2131).

001 **Fragmenta**, ed. T. Kock, *Comicorum Atticorum fragmenta*, vol. 2. Leipzig: Teubner, 1884: 443–444.
frr. 1–5 + tituli.
Q: 60: Comic.

002 **Fragmenta**, ed. A. Meineke, *Fragmenta comi-*

corum Graecorum, vol. 3. Berlin: Reimer, 1840 (repr. De Gruyter, 1970): 579–580.
Q: 44: Comic.

003 **Fragmentum**, ed. C. Austin, *Comicorum Graecorum fragmenta in papyris reperta*. Berlin: De Gruyter, 1973: 200.
fr. 215.
Pap: 112: Comic.

2131 **PHILISCUS** Epigr.
fiq Philiscus Comic.
3 B.C.: Corcyraeus
Cf. et PHILISCUS Comic. (0491).

001 **Epigramma**, AG 11.441.
Q: 8: Epigr.

0257 **PHILISCUS** Rhet.
5–4 B.C.: Milesius

001 **Fragmentum**, ed. M.L. West, *Iambi et elegi Graeci*, vol. 2. Oxford: Clarendon Press, 1972: 93.
Q: 67: Eleg.

002 **Fragmentum**, FGrH #337 bis: 3B:757 addenda.
Q: 37: Hist.

x01 **Epigramma sepulcrale.**
App. Anth. 2.124: Cf. ANTHOLOGIAE GRAECAE APPENDIX (7052 002).
Dup. 0257 001.

0335 **PHILISCUS** Trag.
4 B.C.: Aegineta

001 **Fragmentum**, ed. B. Snell, *Tragicorum Graecorum fragmenta*, vol. 1. Göttingen: Vandenhoeck & Ruprecht, 1971: 259.
fr. 1.
Q: 13: Trag.

1870 **PHILISTIDES** Hist.
5 B.C.?: Mallotes

001 **Testimonia**, FGrH #11: 1A:165, *9 addenda.
NQ: 63: Test.

002 **Fragmenta**, FGrH #11: 1A:165–166.
Q: 267: Hist., Myth.

1591 **PHILISTUS** Hist.
5–4 B.C.: Syracusanus

001 **Testimonia**, FGrH #556: 3B:551–558.
NQ: 2,724: Test.

002 **Fragmenta**, FGrH #556: 3B:558–567.
fr. 77: *P. Oxy.* 1.222.
Q, Pap: 2,249: Hist.

2422 **PHILISTUS** Hist.
post 4 B.C.?: Naucratites

001 **Testimonia**, FGrH #615: 3C:122.
NQ: 88: Test.

1592 **PHILITAS** Epigr.
ante 1 B.C.: Samius

001 **Epigrammata**, AG **6**.210; 7.481.
Q: 64: Epigr.

2594 **PHILLIS** Hist.
4 B.C.: Delius
001 **Fragmenta,** FHG 4: 476.
Q

1593 **PHILO** <Epigr.>
fiq (H)eren(n)ius Philo
A.D. 1?
Cf. et (H)EREN(N)IUS PHILO Hist. et Gramm.
(1416).
001 **Epigramma,** AG 11.419.
Q: 16: Epigr.

2457 **PHILO** Hist.
3 B.C.
001 **Testimonium,** FGrH #670: 3C:283.
NQ: 57: Test.
002 **Fragmenta,** FGrH #670: 3C:283.
Q: 123: Hist.

1599 **PHILO** Mech.
3–2 B.C.: Byzantius
001 **Belopoeica,** ed. H. Diels and E. Schramm,
Philons Belopoiika [*Abhandlungen der preuss-
ischen Akademie der Wissenschaften,*
Philosoph.-hist. Kl., no. 16. Berlin: Reimer,
1919]: 7–68.
= Mathematica syntaxis, liber 4.
Cod: 10,999: Mech.
002 **Parasceuastica et poliorcetica,** ed. H. Diels and
E. Schramm, *Exzerpte aus Philons Mechanik B.
VII und VIII* [*Abhandlungen der preussischen
Akademie der Wissenschaften,* Philosoph.-hist.
Kl., no. 12. Berlin: Reimer, 1920]: 17–84.
Parasceuastica = Mathematica syntaxis, liber 7.
Poliorcetica = Mathematica syntaxis, liber 8.
Cod: 9,695: Mech.

0706 **PHILO** Med.
A.D. 1/2: Tarsensis
001 **Fragmentum,** ed. H. Lloyd-Jones and P. Par-
sons, *Supplementum Hellenisticum.* Berlin: De
Gruyter, 1983: 332–333.
fr. 690.
Dup. 0706 x01.
Q: 171: Med., Eleg.
x01 **Fragmentum ap. Galenum.**
K13.267–269.
Dup. 0706 001.
Cf. GALENUS Med. (0057 076).
x02 **Fragmenta ap. Oribasium.**
CMG **6.3,** pp. 112, 496.
Cf. ORIBASIUS Med. (0722 004–005).
x03 **Fragmentum ap. Paulum.**
CMG **9.2,** p. 300.
Cf. PAULUS Med. (0715 001).
x04 **Fragmentum ap. Aëtium** (lib. 9).
Zervos, *Athena* 23, p. 349.
Cf. AËTIUS Med. (0718 009).

2595 **PHILO** Paradox.
A.D. 4/6: Byzantius

001 **De septem orbis spectaculis,** ed. R. Hercher,
*Aeliani de natura animalium, varia historia,
epistolae et fragmenta. Porphyrii philosophi de
abstinentia et de antro nympharum. Philonis
Byzantii de septem orbis spectaculis.* Paris: Didot, 1858: 101–105.
Cod

4260 **PHILO** Phil.
3–2 B.C.: Atheniensis
001 **Testimonia,** ed. K. Döring, *Die Megariker*
[*Studien zur antiken Philosophie* 2. Amsterdam: Grüner, 1972]: 29, 31, 41–42, 43–44, 45.
test. 101, 104, 110, 135–137, 141–142 (pp. 29,
31, 41–42, 43–44, 45) = Diodorus Cronus
(0073 001).
test. 144(?) (p. 45) = Philo.
NQ: Test.

2013 **PHILO** Phil.
2–1 B.C.: Larissaeus
002 **Testimonia et fragmenta,** ed. H.J. Mette, "Philon von Larisa und Antiochos von Askalon,"
Lustrum 28–29 (1986–1987) 12–15.
Q: Phil.

2638 **PHILO** Poeta
5 B.C.?: Metapontinus vel Nicomediensis
001 **Fragmentum,** ed. H. Lloyd-Jones and P. Parsons, *Supplementum Hellenisticum.* Berlin: De
Gruyter, 1983: 332.
fr. 689a.
Q: 6: Poem.

0018 **PHILO JUDAEUS** Phil.
1 B.C.–A.D. 1: Alexandrinus
001 **De opificio mundi,** ed. L. Cohn, *Philonis Alexandrini opera quae supersunt,* vol. 1. Berlin:
Reimer, 1896 (repr. De Gruyter, 1962): 1–60.
Cod: 13,672: Phil., Theol., Exeget.
002 **Legum allegoriarum libri i–iii,** ed. Cohn, *op.
cit.,* vol. 1, 61–169.
Cod: 33,082: Exeget.
003 **De cherubim,** ed. Cohn, *op. cit.,* vol. 1, 170–
201.
Cod: 7,831: Phil., Exeget.
004 **De sacrificiis Abelis et Caini,** ed. Cohn, *op.
cit.,* vol. 1, 202–257.
Cod: 9,828: Exeget.
005 **Quod deterius potiori insidiari soleat,** ed.
Cohn, *op. cit.,* vol. 1, 258–298.
Cod: 11,566: Exeget.
006 **De posteritate Caini,** ed. P. Wendland, *op. cit.,*
vol. 2 (1897; repr. 1962): 1–41.
Cod: 11,367: Phil., Theol., Exeget.
007 **De gigantibus,** ed. Wendland, *op. cit.,* vol. 2,
42–55.
Cod: 3,338: Phil., Exeget.
008 **Quod deus sit immutabilis,** ed. Wendland, *op.
cit.,* vol. 2, 56–94.
Cod: 9,213: Phil., Theol., Exeget.

009 **De agricultura**, ed. Wendland, *op. cit.*, vol. 2, 95–132.
Cod: 9,200: Phil., Theol., Exeget.

010 **De plantatione**, ed. Wendland, *op. cit.*, vol. 2, 133–169.
Cod: 9,172: Phil., Theol., Exeget.

011 **De ebrietate**, ed. Wendland, *op. cit.*, vol. 2, 170–214.
Cf. et 0018 036.
Cod: 11,964: Phil., Exeget.

012 **De sobrietate**, ed. Wendland, *op. cit.*, vol. 2, 215–228.
Cod: 3,719: Phil., Exeget.

013 **De confusione linguarum**, ed. Wendland, *op. cit.*, vol. 2, 229–267.
Cod: 10,751: Phil., Exeget.

014 **De migratione Abrahami**, ed. Wendland, *op. cit.*, vol. 2, 268–314.
Cod: 13,146: Exeget.

015 **Quis rerum divinarum heres sit**, ed. Wendland, *op. cit.*, vol. 3 (1898; repr. 1962): 1–71.
Cod: 16,515: Phil., Theol., Exeget.

016 **De congressu eruditionis gratia**, ed. Wendland, *op. cit.*, vol. 3, 72–109.
Cod: 9,258: Phil., Exeget.

017 **De fuga et inventione**, ed. Wendland, *op. cit.*, vol. 3, 110–155.
Cod: 11,419: Exeget.

018 **De mutatione nominum**, ed. Wendland, *op. cit.*, vol. 3, 156–203.
Cod: 13,718: Exeget.

019 **De somniis** (lib. i–ii), ed. Wendland, *op. cit.*, vol. 3, 204–306.
Cf. et 0018 039.
Cod: 27,040: Onir., Exeget.

020 **De Abrahamo**, ed. Cohn, *op. cit.*, vol. 4 (1902; repr. 1962): 1–60.
Cod: 13,617: Phil., Exeget.

021 **De Josepho**, ed. Cohn, *op. cit.*, vol. 4, 61–118.
Cod: 13,088: Phil., Exeget.

022 **De vita Mosis** (lib. i–ii), ed. Cohn, *op. cit.*, vol. 4, 119–268.
Cod: 32,002: Biogr., Phil., Exeget.

023 **De decalogo**, ed. Cohn, *op. cit.*, vol. 4, 269–307.
Cod: 8,619: Phil., Exeget.

024 **De specialibus legibus** (lib. i–iv), ed. Cohn, *op. cit.*, vol. 5 (1906; repr. 1962): 1–265.
Cod: 58,218: Phil., Theol., Exeget.

025 **De virtutibus**, ed. Cohn, *op. cit.*, vol. 5, 266–335.
Cod: 12,421: Phil.

026 **De praemiis et poenis + De exsecrationibus**, ed. Cohn, *op. cit.*, vol. 5, 336–376.
Cod: 9,303: Phil.

027 **Quod omnis probus liber sit**, ed. Cohn and S. Reiter, *op. cit.*, vol. 6 (1915; repr. 1962): 1–45.
Cod: 7,769: Phil.

028 **De vita contemplativa**, ed. Cohn and Reiter, *op. cit.*, vol. 6, 46–71.
Cod: 4,701: Phil.

029 **De aeternitate mundi**, ed. Cohn and Reiter, *op. cit.*, vol. 6, 72–119.
Cod: 9,401: Phil.

030 **In Flaccum**, ed. Cohn and Reiter, *op. cit.*, vol. 6, 120–154.
Cod: 9,103: Phil., Apol.

031 **Legatio ad Gaium**, ed. Cohn and Reiter, *op. cit.*, vol. 6, 155–223.
Cf. et 0018 039.
Cod: 17,824: Phil., Apol.

032 **Hypothetica** *sive* **Apologia pro Judaeis**, ed. Cohn and Reiter, *Philonis Alexandrini opera quae supersunt* (editio minor), vol. 6. Berlin: Reimer, 1915: 191–200.
Q: 2,610: Apol.

033 **De providentia**, ed. F.H. Colson, *Philo*, vol. 9. Cambridge, Mass.: Harvard University Press, 1941 (repr. 1967): 454–506.
Q: 4,341: Theol.

034 **Quaestiones in Genesim** (fragmenta), ed. F. Petit, *Quaestiones in Genesim et in Exodum. Fragmenta Graeca* [*Les oeuvres de Philon d'Alexandrie* 33. Paris: Cerf, 1978]: 41–81, 83–153, 155–160, 162–183, 185–213, 216–228.
Q: 9,574: Exeget.

035 **Quaestiones in Exodum** (fragmenta), ed. Petit, *op. cit.*, 233–278, 281–306.
Q: 3,612: Exeget.

036 **De ebrietate ii**, ed. P. Wendland, *Neu entdeckte Fragmente Philos nebst einer Untersuchung über die ursprüngliche Gestalt der Schrift de sacrificiis Abelis et Caini*. Berlin: Reimer, 1891: 22–25.
Cf. et 0018 011.
Q: 599: Phil.

038 Περὶ ἀριθμῶν *sive* Ἀριθμητικά (fragmenta), ed. K. Staehle, *Die Zahlenmystik bei Philon von Alexandreia*. Leipzig: Teubner, 1931: 19–51, 53–59, 62–70, 75.
Q: 10,198: Phil., Math., Metrolog.

039 **Fragmenta**, ed. H. Lewy, "Neue Philontexte in der Überarbeitung des Ambrosius. Mit einem Anhang: Neu gefundene griechische Philonfragmente," *Sitzungsberichte der preussischen Akademie der Wissenschaften zu Berlin*, Philosoph.-hist. Kl., 1932. Berlin: De Gruyter, 1932: 80–84.
Legatio ad Gaium (frr. 17–18): pp. 80–81.
De somniis (fr. 19): p. 81.
Fragmenta incertae sedis (frr. 20–32): pp. 81–84.
Q: 481: Apol., Onir., Phil.

040 **Fragmenta**, ed. J.R. Harris, *Fragments of Philo Judaeus*. Cambridge: Cambridge University Press, 1886: 6–11, 75–85, 87–110.
Q: Phil., Exeget.

041 **De deo** (*P. Berol.* inv. 17027), ed. K. Stahlschmidt, "Eine unbekannte Schrift Philons von Alexandrien (oder eines ihm nahestehenden Verfassers)," *Aegyptus* 22 (1942) 162–165.
Pap: 255: Theol.

042 **Fragmenta incerti operis** (*P. Oxy.* 18.2158),
ed. C.H. Roberts, *The Oxyrhynchus papyri*, pt.
18. London: Egypt Exploration Society, 1941:
3.
Pap: 83: Ignotum

047 **De mundo** [Sp.], ed. J. Mangey, *Philo Judaeus.
Opera omnia*, vol. 2. London: Bowyer, 1742:
601–624.
Cod: Phil.

1594 **PHILO Judaeus Senior** Epic.
fiq Philo Senior Hist.
2 B.C.

002 **Fragmenta**, ed. H. Lloyd-Jones and P. Parsons,
Supplementum Hellenisticum. Berlin: De Gruy-
ter, 1983: 328–330.
frr. 681–686.
Dup. partim 1594 004.
Q: 147: Epic.

003 **Testimonia**, FGrH #729: 3C:689–690.
NQ: 79: Test.

004 **Fragmenta**, FGrH #729: 3C:690–691.
Dup. partim 1594 002.
Q: 274: Hist., Epic.

PHILO Senior Hist.
2 B.C.
Cf. PHILO Judaeus Senior Epic. (1594).

0583 **PHILOCHORUS** Hist.
4–3 B.C.: Atheniensis

001 **Testimonia**, FGrH #328: 3B:97–98.
NQ: 372: Test.

002 **Fragmenta**, FGrH #328: 3B:98–160.
fr. 98: *P. Oxy.* 10.1241.
fr. 229: *P. Oxy.* 6.853.
Q, Pap: 17,343: Hist., Epist.

003 **Fragmentum** (*P. Oslo* 1662), ed. H.J. Mette,
"Die 'Kleinen' griechischen Historiker heute,"
Lustrum 21 (1978) 26.
fr. 34c.
Pap: 73: Hist.

1794 **PHILOCLES** Comic.
Incertum

001 **Titulus**, ed. T. Kock, *Comicorum Atticorum
fragmenta*, vol. 3. Leipzig: Teubner, 1888: 366.
NQ: 2: Comic.

1034 **PHILOCLES** Med.
ante A.D. 1

x01 **Fragmentum ap. Galenum.**
K13.1034–1035.
Cf. GALENUS Med. (0057 077).

0312 **PHILOCLES** Trag.
5 B.C.

001 **Fragmenta**, ed. B. Snell, *Tragicorum Graecorum fragmenta*, vol. 1. Göttingen: Vandenhoeck & Ruprecht, 1971: 141–142.
frr. 1, 3–5.
Q: 35: Trag.

2415 **PHILOCRATES** Hist.
4 B.C.?

001 **Fragmenta**, FGrH #601: 3B:733.
Q: 61: Hist.

0205 **PHILODAMUS** Lyr.
4 B.C.: Scarpheus

001 **Paean in Dionysum**, ed. J.U. Powell, *Collectanea Alexandrina.* Oxford: Clarendon Press,
1925 (repr. 1970): 165–169.
Epigr: 513: Lyr., Hymn.

002 **Paean in Dionysum** (fragmenta incerti ordinis),
ed. Powell, *op. cit.*, 169–170.
Epigr: 16: Lyr., Hymn.

1595 **PHILODEMUS** Phil.
1 B.C.: Gadarensis

001 Κατὰ τῆς ἀποδείξεως ἐκ τῶν Ζήνωνος σχολῶν
(*P. Herc.* 1389, subscriptio), ed. D. Comparetti,
"Relazione sui papiri Ercolanesi," *Atti della R.
Accademia dei Lincei*, ser. 3, vol. 5. Rome: Sal-
viucci, 1880: 178.
Pap: 6: Phil.

010 Περὶ αἱρέσεων καὶ φυγῶν (*P. Herc.* 1251), ed.
W. Schmid, *Ethica Epicurea. Pap. Herc. 1251*
[*Studia Herculanensia* 1. Leipzig: Harrassowitz,
1939]: 9–53.
Pap: 2,054: Phil.

020 Περὶ αἰσθήσεως (?) (*P. Herc.* 19/698), ed. W.
Scott, *Fragmenta Herculanensia.* Oxford: Cla-
rendon Press, 1885: 257–299.
Pap: 2,818: Phil.

030 Περὶ βίων καὶ ἠθῶν (*P. Herc.* 168, col. 1), ed.
E. Bignone, "Epicurea," *Atti della Accademia
delle Scienze di Torino* 47 (1912) 671–673.
Pap: 144: Phil.

031 Περὶ βίων καὶ ἠθῶν (*P. Herc.* 168, col. 2), ed.
E. Bignone, "Philodemea," *Rivista di filologia e
di istruzione classica* 47 (1919) 416–418.
Pap: 87: Phil.

040 Περὶ γάμου (?) (*P. Herc.* 312), ed. W. Crönert,
Kolotes und Menedemos. Leipzig: Avenarius,
1906 (repr. Amsterdam: Hakkert, 1965): 126.
Pap: Phil.

053 Περὶ Ἐπικούρου (*P. Herc.* 1232, frr. 3; 5; 6,
coll. 1–3; 7, col. 3; 8, coll. 1–2; 9, coll. 1–2;
subscriptio), ed. A. Vogliano, *Epicuri et Epicureorum scripta in Herculanensibus papyris servata.* Berlin: Weidmann, 1928: 65–73.
Pap: 1,637: Phil.

055 Περὶ Ἐπικούρου (lib. ii) (*P. Herc.* 1289, fr. 1;
fr. 6, coll. 2–6; subscriptio), ed. Vogliano, *op.
cit.*, 59–61.
Pap: 308: Phil.

060 Περὶ ἐπιχαιρεκακίας (?) (*P. Herc.* 1678), ed. D.
Bassi, "Papiro Ercolanese inedito 1678 (Φιλο-
δήμου περὶ ἐπιχαιρεκακίας)," *Rivista Indo-
Greco-Italica* 4 (1920) 65 (n. 1), 66 (+ nn. 13–
14), 67.
Pap: 311: Phil.

070 Περὶ ἔρωτος (?) (*P. Herc.* 1167, 1384, fragmenta), ed. F. Sbordone, "Nuovi frammenti

dei papiri Ercolanesi," *Parola del passato* 103 (1965) 311–312.
Pap: 78: Phil.

080 Περὶ εὐσεβείας (*P. Herc.* 229, 242, 243, 247, 248, 433, 1077, 1088, 1098, 1428, 1609, 1610, 1648), ed. T. Gomperz, *Philodem. Über Frömmigkeit* [*Herkulanische Studien* 2. Leipzig: Teubner, 1866]: 5–151.
Pap: Phil.

081 Περὶ εὐσεβείας (*P. Herc.* 242, 243, 247, 248, 433, 1088, 1428, 1602, 1609, 1610, 1648), ed. A. Schober, *Philodemi περὶ εὐσεβείας libelli partem priorem restituit* [*Diss. Königsberg* (unpublished) (1923)]: 1–103.
Pap: Phil.

082 Περὶ εὐσεβείας (*P. Herc.* 242; 243; 247; 248; 433; 1428, fr. 3; 1609), ed. A. Henrichs, "Philodems de pietate als mythographische Quelle," *Cronache Ercolanesi* 5 (1975) 8–13, 18–19, 21–22, 35.
Pap: Phil.

088 Περὶ εὐσεβείας (*P. Herc.* 243, fr. 2.1-27b), ed. A. Henrichs, "Die Kekropidensage im P. Herc. 243: von Kallimachos zu Ovid," *Cronache Ercolanesi* 13 (1983) 37.
Pap: Phil.

089 Περὶ εὐσεβείας (*P. Herc.* 243, fr. 6.1-19), ed. A. Henrichs, "Ein neues Likymniosfragment bei Philodem," *Zeitschrift für Papyrologie und Epigraphik* 57 (1984) 53–57.
Pap: Phil.

091 Περὶ εὐσεβείας (*P. Herc.* 243, frr. 3.1-28, 4.3-12; 247, fr. 6a.1-22; 433, fr. 2a.1-21; 1088, fr. 2b.3-10; 1428, frr. 11.1-7, 23.1-9, 23a.1-11; 1610, fr. 3.3-19), ed. A. Henrichs, "Toward a new edition of Philodemus' treatise 'On piety'," *Greek, Roman and Byzantine studies* 13 (1972) 72–73, 77, 78 (n. 32), 80, 84, 86–87, 92, 94.
Pap: Phil.

095 Περὶ εὐσεβείας (*P. Herc.* 1088, fr. 2a.1-30; 2b.1-7), ed. W. Luppe, "Atlas-Zitate im 1. Buch von Philodems 'de pietate'," *Cronache Ercolanesi* 13 (1983) 45–48, 50–52.
Pap: Phil.

096 Περὶ εὐσεβείας (*P. Herc.* 1098, fr. 9.13-14), ed. D. Sedley, "The structure of Epicurus' 'On nature'," *Cronache Ercolanesi* 4 (1974) 91.
Pap: Phil.

098 Περὶ εὐσεβείας (*P. Herc.* 1428, coll. 1-15), ed. A. Henrichs, "Die Kritik der stoischen Theologie im P. Herc. 1428," *Cronache Ercolanesi* 4 (1974) 12–26.
Pap: Phil.

099 Περὶ εὐσεβείας (*P. Herc.* 1428, frr. 16 et 19), ed. A. Henrichs, "Two doxographical notes: Democritus and Prodicus on religion," *Harvard studies in classical philology* 79 (1975) 96, 107.
Pap: Phil.

100 Περὶ εὐσεβείας (*P. Herc.* 1428, fr. 16), ed. M.

Marcovich, "Democritus on gods: P. Herc. 1428, fr. 16," *Zeitschrift für Papyrologie und Epigraphik* 19 (1975) 244.
Pap: Phil.

101 Περὶ εὐσεβείας (*P. Herc.* 1428, fr. 16), ed. M. Gigante and G. Indelli, "Democrito nei papiri ercolanesi di Filodemo" in *Democrito e l'atomismo antico* (ed. F. Romano), *Siculorum Gymnasium*, n.s. 33.1, 1980: 451 (n. 3).
Pap: Phil.

102 Περὶ εὐσεβείας (*P. Herc.* 1602, fr. 7.7, 13-19), ed. A. Henrichs, "Ein Meropiszitat in Philodems de pietate," *Cronache Ercolanesi* 7 (1977) 124.
Pap: Phil.

113 Περὶ θανάτου (*P. Herc.* 807, col. 18), ed. A. Ievolo, "Testimonianze biografiche e motivi dossografici di Teofrasto nei papiri ercolanesi," *Cronache Ercolanesi* 3 (1973) 96.
Pap: Phil.

115 Περὶ θανάτου (*P. Herc.* 1050), ed. S. Mekler, "Φιλόδημος περὶ θανάτου δ. Philodemos über den Tod, viertes Buch. Nach der Oxforder und Neapolitaner Abschrift," *Sitzungsberichte der kaiserlichen Akademie der Wissenchaften*, Philosoph.-hist. Kl., Bd. 109. Vienna: Gerold, 1885: 308–353.
Pap: 13,185: Phil.

116 Περὶ θανάτου (*P. Herc.* 1050), ed. T. Kuiper, *Philodemus over den Dood.* Amsterdam: Paris, 1925: 139–165.
Pap: 4,989: Phil.

117 Περὶ θανάτου (*P. Herc.* 1050, col. 3a.3-13), ed. M. Gigante, "Filodemo de morte iv.3," *Rendiconti dell'Accademia di Archeologia, Lettere e Belle Arti di Napoli* 28 (1953) 129.
Dup. partim 1595 118.
Pap: 57: Phil.

118 Περὶ θανάτου (*P. Herc.* 1050, coll. 1.1-24, 2.1-23, 3.26-39, 3a.1-13), ed. Gigante, *RAAN* 28, 119–122, 124–125.
Pap: 282: Phil.

119 Περὶ θανάτου (*P. Herc.* 1050, coll. 4-9), ed. M. Gigante, "Philodemi de morte IV coll. 4-9," *Parola del passato* 13 (1958) 51–58.
Pap: 781: Phil.

132 Περὶ θεῶν (lib. i) (*P. Herc.* 26 + subscriptio), ed. H. Diels, *Philodemos über die Götter, erstes Buch* [*Abhandlungen der königlich preussischen Akademie der Wissenschaften*, Philosoph.-hist. Kl., 1915, no. 7. Berlin: Reimer, 1916 (repr. Leipzig: Zentralantiquariat der DDR, 1970)]: 9–42, 44–45.
Pap: 4,285: Phil.

135 Περὶ θεῶν (lib. iii) (*P. Herc.* 89, subscriptio et fragmenta), ed. Crönert, *Kolotes und Menedemos*, (n. 512).
= De victu deorum.
Pap: Phil.

138 Περὶ θεῶν (lib. iii) (*P. Herc.* 152/157), ed. H.

Diels, *Philodemos über die Götter, drittes Buch* [*Abhandlungen der königlich preussischen Akademie der Wissenschaften*, Philosoph.-hist. Kl., 1916, no. 4. Berlin: Reimer, 1917 (repr. Leipzig: Zentralantiquariat der DDR, 1970)]: 13–69.
= De victu deorum.
Pap: 5,458: Phil.

139 Περὶ θεῶν (lib. iii) (*P. Herc.* 152/157, fragmenta), ed. R. Philippson, "Nachträgliches zur epikureischen Götterlehre," *Hermes* 53 (1918) 381, 384–387.
= De victu deorum.
Pap: 487: Phil.

141 Περὶ θεῶν (lib. iii) (*P. Herc.* 152/157, fr. 75), ed. G. Arrighetti, "Filodemo. Gli dèi iii fr. 75 (Antifane, gli stoici e i πράγματα)," *Cronache Ercolanesi* 13 (1983) 29.
= De victu deorum.
Pap: Phil.

143 Περὶ θεῶν (?) (*P. Herc.* 1638, frr. 1–3), ed. D. Bassi, "Frammenti inediti di opere di Filodemo (περὶ μουσικῆς–περὶ θεῶν?–περὶ ῥητορικῆς) in papiri Ercolanesi," *Rivista di filologia e di istruzione classica* 38 (1910) 327.
Pap: Phil.

150 Περὶ κακιῶν (*P. Herc.* 253, fr. 12.1–8), ed. A. Körte, "Augusteer bei Philodem," *Rheinisches Museum* 45 (1890) 172.
olim Περὶ φιλαργυρίας.
Pap: Phil.

151 Περὶ κακιῶν (*P. Herc.* 253, col. 12.4–5), ed. Crönert, *Kolotes und Menedemos*, 127 (n. 534).
olim Περὶ φιλαργυρίας.
Pap: Phil.

164 Περὶ κολακείας (*P. Herc.* 222, fragmenta), ed. T. Gargiulo, "P. Herc. 222: Filodemo sull'adulazione," *Cronache Ercolanesi* 11 (1981) 106–109.
= De vitiis vii.
Pap: Phil.

168 Περὶ κολακείας (*P. Herc.* 223, frr. 1–8), ed. M. Gigante and G. Indelli, "Bione e l'epicureismo," *Cronache Ercolanesi* 8 (1978) 127–131.
= De vitiis vii.
Pap: Phil.

172 Περὶ κολακείας (*P. Herc.* 1082), ed. L. Spengel, "Die herculanensischen Rollen," *Philologus*, suppl. 2 (1863) 526–527.
= De vitiis vii.
Pap: Phil.

173 Περὶ κολακείας (*P. Herc.* 1082, col. 11.1–7), ed. Crönert, *Kolotes und Menedemos*, 127 (n. 534).
= De vitiis vii.
Pap: Phil.

175 Περὶ κολακείας (*P. Herc.* 1089, coll. 1–9), ed. E.A. Méndez, "P. Herc. 1089: Filodemo 'sobre la adulación'," *Cronache Ercolanesi* 13 (1983) 125–126.
= De vitiis vii.
Pap: Phil.

179 Περὶ κολακείας (*P. Herc.* 1457, fragmenta), ed. Crönert, *Kolotes und Menedemos*, 91 (n. 447), 130 (n. 542), 178 (n. 34), 182 (n. 91, line 38 + n. 447).
= De vitiis vii.
Pap: Phil.

181 Περὶ κολακείας (*P. Herc.* 1457, frr. 11.1–9; 12.4–8; 16.8–9, 13; 3.31–37), ed. U.E. Paoli, "Papiro Ercolanese 1457," *Rivista di filologia e di istruzione classica* 43 (1915) 312, 314–315.
= De vitiis vii.
Pap: Phil.

182 Περὶ κολακείας (*P. Herc.* 1457, col. 5, fr. 6–col. 7, v. 20), ed. E. Kondo, "I caratteri di Teofrasto nei papiri ercolanesi," *Cronache Ercolanesi* 1 (1971) 74–75.
= De vitiis vii.
Pap: Phil.

185 Περὶ κολακείας (*P. Herc.* 1457, fragmenta), ed. E. Kondo, "Per l'interpretazione del pensiero filodemeo sulla adulazione nel P. Herc. 1457," *Cronache Ercolanesi* 4 (1974) 45, 46 (nn. 26–27), 47 (nn. 30, 33, 42–44), 48 (+ nn. 46, 49–51), 49 (+ nn. 61, 63), 50 (+ n. 65), 51, 52 (+ n. 83), 53 (+ n. 89), 54–55.
= De vitiis vii.
Pap: Phil.

190 Περὶ κολακείας (*P. Herc.* 1675, subscriptio et fragmenta), ed. V. de Falco, "Appunti sul περὶ κολακείας di Filodemo, Pap. erc. 1675," *Rivista Indo-Greco-Italica* 10 (1926) 15–26.
= De vitiis vii.
Pap: Phil.

199 Περὶ μαθήσεως (?) (*P. Herc.* 862), ed. Scott, *Fragmenta Herculanensia*, 313–325.
Pap: 859: Phil.

200 Περὶ μανίας (*P. Herc.* 57), ed. D. Bassi, "Notizie di papiri Ercolanesi inediti," *Rivista di filologia e di istruzione classica* 45 (1917) 457–458, 460–465.
Pap: 499: Phil.

221 Περὶ μουσικῆς (*P. Herc.* 225, 411, 424, 1094, 1497, 1572, 1575, 1576, 1578, 1583), ed. D.A. van Krevelen, *Philodemus. De muziek met vertaling en commentaar.* Hilversum: Schipper, 1939: 2–228.
Dup. partim 1595 222, 230.
Pap: 13,553: Phil., Mus.

222 Περὶ μουσικῆς (lib. i) (*P. Herc.* 225, 411, 424, 1094, 1572, 1583), ed. G.M. Rispoli, "Il primo libro del περὶ μουσικῆς di Filodemo," *Ricerche sui papiri Ercolanesi* 1. Naples: Giannini, 1969: 39–241.
Dup. partim 1595 221.
Pap: 3,441: Phil., Mus.

230 Περὶ μουσικῆς (lib. iv) (*P. Herc.* 1497 + subscriptio), ed. A.J. Neubecker, *Über die Musik iv. Buch.* Naples: Bibliopolis, 1986: 35–90.
Dup. partim 1595 221.
Pap: Phil., Mus.

241 Περὶ οἰκονομίας (*P. Herc.* 1424), ed. C. Jensen, *Philodemi περὶ οἰκονομίας qui dicitur libellus.* Leipzig: Teubner, 1906: 1–76.
= De vitiis ix.
Pap: 5,910: Phil.

251 Περὶ ὁμιλίας (*P. Herc.* 873), ed. F. Amoroso, "Filodemo sulla conversazione," *Cronache Ercolanesi* 5 (1975) 65–68.
Pap: Phil.

261 Περὶ ὀργῆς (*P. Herc.* 182), ed. K. Wilke, *Philodemi de ira liber.* Leipzig: Teubner, 1914: 1–100.
Pap: 7,422: Phil.

264 Περὶ ὀργῆς (*P. Herc.* 182, fragmenta), ed. R. Philippson, "Philodems Buch über den Zorn. Ein Beitrag zu seiner Wiederherstellung und Auslegung," *Rheinisches Museum* 71 (1916) 427–459.
Pap: 2,132: Phil.

271 Περὶ παρρησίας (*P. Herc.* 1471), ed. A. Olivieri, *Philodemi περὶ παρρησίας libellus.* Leipzig: Teubner, 1914: 1–68.
Pap: 5,927: Phil.

274 Περὶ παρρησίας (*P. Herc.* 1471, fragmenta), ed. M. Gigante, "Philodème: sur la liberté de parole," *Actes du 8ᵉ Congrès de l'Association G. Budé.* Paris: Les Belles Lettres, 1969: 196–217.
Pap: Phil.

275 Περὶ παρρησίας (*P. Herc.* 1471, col. 12), ed. M. Gigante, "Testimonianze di Filodemo su Maison," *Cronache Ercolanesi* 1 (1971) 67.
Pap: Phil.

281 Περὶ πλούτου (*P. Herc.* 163), ed. A. Tepedino Guerra, "Il primo libro 'sulla ricchezza' di Filodemo," *Cronache Ercolanesi* 8 (1978) 61–74.
Pap: Phil.

290 Περὶ ποιημάτων (lib. i–iii) (*P. Herc.* 460 + 1073, 994, 1074 + 1081 + 1676), ed. F. Sbordone, "Eufonia e synthesis nella poetica di Filodemo," *Museum philologum Londiniense* 2 (1977) 257–258.
Pap: Phil.

294 Περὶ ποιημάτων (lib. i) (*P. Herc.* 994), ed. F. Sbordone, Φιλοδήμου περὶ ποιημάτων tractatus tres [*Ricerche sui papiri Ercolanesi* 2. Naples: Giannini, 1976]: 2–113.
Pap: 4,938: Phil.

296 Περὶ ποιημάτων (lib. i) (*P. Herc.* 994), ed. M.L. Nardelli, "P. Herc. 994, col. X," *Cronache Ercolanesi* 12 (1982) 135–136.
Pap: Phil.

301 Περὶ ποιημάτων (lib. ii) (*P. Herc.* 460, 1073), ed. Sbordone, Φιλοδήμου περὶ ποιημάτων tractatus tres, 117–187.
Pap: 3,742: Phil.

304 Περὶ ποιημάτων (lib. ii) (?) (*P. Herc.* 407, 466, fragmenta), ed. R. Schächter, "De Homero in Philodemi περὶ ποιημάτων libro ii laudato," *Eos* 31 (1928) 445.
Pap: 56: Phil.

310 Περὶ ποιημάτων (lib. ii) (?) (*P. Herc.* 466, frag-

mentum), ed. F. Sbordone, "Il papiro Ercolanese 444," *Rendiconti dell'Accademia di Archeologia, Lettere e Belle Arti di Napoli* 35 (1960) 109.
Pap: 47: Phil.

316 Περὶ ποιημάτων (lib. iii) (*P. Herc.* 1074, 1081, 1676), ed. Sbordone, Φιλοδήμου περὶ ποιημάτων tractatus tres, 191–267.
Pap: 3,481: Phil.

317 Περὶ ποιημάτων (lib. iii) (*P. Herc.* 1074.23 + 1081.25, 1091.16 + 1074.22), ed. H.J. Mette, "Zu Philodem, περὶ ποιημάτων," *Zeitschrift für Papyrologie und Epigraphik* 34 (1979) 59–61.
Pap: 236: Phil.

319 Περὶ ποιημάτων (lib. iii) (*P. Herc.* 1081, fragmenta), ed. C. Jensen, *Philodemos über die Gedichte, fünftes Buch.* Berlin: Weidmann, 1923 (repr. 1973): 143, 147.
Pap: 66: Phil.

326 Περὶ ποιημάτων (lib. iv) (*P. Herc.* 207), ed. F. Sbordone, "Il quarto libro del περὶ ποιημάτων di Filodemo," *Ricerche sui papiri Ercolanesi* 1. Naples: Giannini, 1969: 299–337.
Pap: 1,085: Phil.

328 Περὶ ποιημάτων (lib. iv) (?) (*P. Herc.* 1581, fragmenta), ed. M.L. Nardelli, "La catarsi poetica nel P. Herc. 1581," *Cronache Ercolanesi* 8 (1978) 99–101.
Pap: Phil.

330 Περὶ ποιημάτων (lib. v) (*P. Herc.* 228, frr. 4, 6), ed. Jensen, *Philodemos über die Gedichte, fünftes Buch,* 154–155.
Pap: 132: Phil.

332 Περὶ ποιημάτων (lib. v) (*P. Herc.* 228, fr. 2, col. 2; fr. 3, col. 1), ed. C. Coppola, "Frammenti inediti del P. Herc. 228," *Cronache Ercolanesi* 13 (1983) 103.
Pap: Phil.

336 Περὶ ποιημάτων (lib. v) (*P. Herc.* 1425, 1538), ed. Jensen, *Philodemos über die Gedichte, fünftes Buch,* 3–79.
Pap: 5,076: Phil.

338 Περὶ ποιημάτων (lib. v) (*P. Herc.* 1425, 1538, fragmenta), ed. C. Jensen, "Herakleides vom Pontus bei Philodem und Horaz," *Sitzungsberichte der königlich preussischen Akademie der Wissenschaften zu Berlin.* Berlin: Reimer, 1936: 292–320.
Dup. partim 1595 336.
Pap: Phil.

344 Περὶ ποιημάτων (loci incerti) (*P. Herc.* 403, fragmenta), ed. F. Sbordone, "Ancora un papiro ercolanese della *Poetica* di Filodemo: n. 403," *Studi filologici e storici in onore di Vittorio de Falco.* Naples: Libreria Scientifica, 1971: 344–348, 350–351.
Pap: 358: Phil.

346 Περὶ ποιημάτων (loci incerti) (*P. Herc.* 444, fragmenta), ed. Sbordone, *RAAN* 35, 101–107.
Pap: 1,003: Phil.

348 Περὶ ποιημάτων (?) (*P. Herc.* 1275, subscriptio), ed. D. Comparetti, "Relazione sui papiri

Ercolanesi," *Atti della R. Accademia dei Lincei*, ser. 3, vol. 5. Rome: Salviucci, 1880: 178. Pap: 6: Phil.

350 Περὶ ποιημάτων (?) (*P. Herc.* 1677, fragmenta), ed. T. Gomperz, "Philodem und die ästhetischen Schriften der herculanischen Bibliothek," *Sitzungsberichte der philosophisch-historischen Classe der kaiserlichen Akademie der Wissenschaften* 123. Vienna: Tempsky, 1891: 69. Pap: Phil.

362 Περὶ προνοίας (*P. Herc.* 1670), ed. D. Bassi, "Notizie di papiri Ercolanesi inediti," *Rivista di filologia e di istruzione classica* 44 (1916) 51–62. Pap: 605: Phil.

366 Περὶ προνοίας (*P. Herc.* 1670, fragmenta), ed. M. Ferrario, "Filodemo sulla provvidenza (*P. Herc.* 1670)," *Cronache Ercolanesi* 2 (1972) 75, 76 (+ n. 48), 77 (+ n. 59), 78 (+ nn. 67–68, 71–72), 79–82, 84–92, 94. Pap: Phil.

370 Περὶ ῥητορικῆς (*P. Herc.* 220, 221, 224, 240, 245, 250, 380, 398, 408, 409, 425, 426, 455, 467, 468, 473, 1004, 1007, 1015/832, 1078/1080, 1079, 1086, 1095, 1114, 1117, 1423, 1426, 1427, 1506, 1573, 1580, 1612, 1633, 1669, 1672, 1674), ed. S. Sudhaus, *Philodemi volumina rhetorica*, vols. 1–2. Leipzig: Teubner, 1:1892; 2:1896 (repr. Amsterdam: Hakkert, 1964): 1:1–385; 2:1–303. Pap: 70,642: Phil., Rhet.

372 Περὶ ῥητορικῆς (*P. Herc.* 224, fr. 12.1–13), ed. Crönert, *Kolotes und Menedemos*, 67. Pap: Phil., Rhet.

374 Περὶ ῥητορικῆς (*P. Herc.* 232, fragmenta), ed. Bassi, *RFIC* 38, 340. Pap: 100: Phil., Rhet.

375 Περὶ ῥητορικῆς (*P. Herc.* 234, frr. 1–4), ed. Bassi, *RFIC* 38, 341. Pap: 47: Phil., Rhet.

376 Περὶ ῥητορικῆς (*P. Herc.* 410, coll. 1–4), ed. Bassi, *RFIC* 38, 341–342. Pap: 126: Phil., Rhet.

380 Περὶ ῥητορικῆς (*P. Herc.* 449, frr. 1–4), ed. Bassi, *RFIC* 38, 342–343. Pap: 15: Phil., Rhet.

382 Περὶ ῥητορικῆς (*P. Herc.* 453, frr. 1–4), ed. Bassi, *RFIC* 38, 343–345. Pap: 180: Phil., Rhet.

384 Περὶ ῥητορικῆς (*P. Herc.* 463), ed. F. Longo Auricchio, "Frammenti inediti di un libro della retorica di Filodemo (P. Herc. 463)," *Cronache Ercolanesi* 12 (1982) 69–74. Pap: Phil., Rhet.

386 Περὶ ῥητορικῆς (*P. Herc.* 470, frr. 1–5), ed. Bassi, *RFIC* 38, 345–346. Pap: 109: Phil., Rhet.

388 Περὶ ῥητορικῆς (*P. Herc.* 1001, subscriptio), ed. Bassi, *RFIC* 44, 482–483. Pap: 5: Phil., Rhet.

392 Περὶ ῥητορικῆς (*P. Herc.* 1004, fragmenta), ed. M.G. Cappelluzzo, "Per una nuova edizione di un libro della retorica filodemea," *Cronache Ercolanesi* 6 (1976) 70–76. Pap: Phil., Rhet.

400 Περὶ ῥητορικῆς (*P. Herc.* 1118, frr. 1–3), ed. Bassi, *RFIC* 38, 346–347. Pap: 54: Phil., Rhet.

402 Περὶ ῥητορικῆς (*P. Herc.* 1119, frr. 1, 3–5, 8–12), ed. Bassi, *RFIC* 38, 347. Pap: 37: Phil., Rhet.

410 Περὶ ῥητορικῆς (?) (*P. Herc.* 1574, frr. 1–6), ed. Bassi, *RFIC* 38, 348–351. Pap: 234: Phil., Rhet.

412 Περὶ ῥητορικῆς (*P. Herc.* 1605, frr. 1–4), ed. Bassi, *RFIC* 38, 351. Pap: 21: Phil., Rhet.

414 Περὶ ῥητορικῆς (*P. Herc.* 1606, frr. 1–4), ed. Bassi, *RFIC* 38, 352. Pap: 70: Phil., Rhet.

416 Περὶ ῥητορικῆς (?) (*P. Herc.* 1636, fragmenta), ed. Bassi, *RFIC* 44, 481–482. 481–482. Pap: 67: Phil., Rhet.

418 Περὶ ῥητορικῆς (*P. Herc.* 1641, frr. 1–3), ed. Bassi, *RFIC* 38, 352. Pap: 14: Phil., Rhet.

424 Περὶ ῥητορικῆς (lib. i–ii) (*P. Herc.* 408, 409, 425, 1079, 1086, 1117, 1573, 1580, 1672, 1674), ed. F. Longo Auricchio, Φιλοδήμου περὶ ῥητορικῆς *libri primi et secundi* [*Ricerche sui papiri Ercolanesi* 3. Naples: Giannini, 1977]: 3–279. Dup. partim 1595 388. Pap: 13,445: Phil., Rhet.

426 Περὶ ῥητορικῆς (lib. i) (*P. Herc.* 1790, frr. c + d², g¹ + h², r² + q¹, s² + t¹, u² + v¹), ed. F. Sbordone, "Recenti tentativi di svolgimento dei papiri ercolanesi," *Cronache Ercolanesi* 1 (1971) 33–35. Pap: Phil., Rhet.

430 Περὶ ῥητορικῆς (lib. ii) (*P. Herc.* 1674, coll. 44.19–49, 48.23–49.27), ed. F. Longo Auricchio, "I filosofi megarici nella 'retorica' di Filodemo," *Cronache Ercolanesi* 5 (1975) 77–78. Pap: Phil., Rhet.

432 Περὶ ῥητορικῆς (lib. iv) (*P. Herc.* 1673, col. 13.13–23), ed. Ievolo, *CronErc* 3, 95. Pap: Phil., Rhet.

437 Περὶ ῥητορικῆς (lib. iv, pars ii) (*P. Herc.* 1007, fragmenta), ed. Gigante, *CronErc* 1, 65–66. Pap: Phil., Rhet.

442 Περὶ ῥητορικῆς (lib. v) (*P. Herc.* 1669, frr. 1–39b), ed. M. Ferrario, "Frammenti del v libro della 'retorica' di Filodemo," *Cronache Ercolanesi* 10 (1980) 65–79. Pap: Phil., Rhet.

472 Περὶ σημειώσεων (*P. Herc.* 1065), ed. P.H. De Lacy, E.A. De Lacy, M. Gigante, F. Longo Auricchio and A. Tepedino Guerra, *Philodemus: On methods of inference*, rev. edn. [*La*

scuola di Epicuro 1. Naples: Bibliopolis, 1978]:
29–87.
Pap: 8,639: Phil.

480 Περὶ τῆς Σωκράτους αἱρέσεως (?) (P. Herc. 495
(?), 558 (?), fragmenta), ed. W. Crönert, "Her-
culanensische Bruchstücke einer Geschichte
des Sokrates und seiner Schule," Rheinisches
Museum 57 (1902) 286–290, 292–298.
Pap: Phil.

482 Περὶ τῆς Σωκράτους αἱρέσεως (?) (P. Herc. 495
(?), fragmentum), ed. Bassi, RFIC 44, 484.
Pap: Phil.

492 Περὶ τοῦ καθ᾽ Ὅμηρον ἀγαθοῦ βασιλέως (P.
Herc. 1507), ed. T. Dorandi, Filodemo. Il buon
re secondo Omero [La scuola di Epicuro, vol. 3.
Naples: Bibliopolis, 1982]: 75–120.
Pap: Phil.

500 Περὶ τῶν Ζήνωνος σχολῶν (P. Herc. 300, fr.
9n + P. Herc. 1003, subscriptio et fragmenta),
ed. W. Crönert, "Die λογικὰ ζητήματα des
Chrysippos," Hermes 36 (1901) 572–576.
Pap: Phil.

512 Περὶ τῶν Στωικῶν (P. Herc. 155, 339), ed. T.
Dorandi, "Filodemo. Gli stoici (P. Herc. 155 e
339)," Cronache Ercolanesi 12 (1982) 99–103.
olim Περὶ τῶν φιλοσόφων.
Pap: Phil.

520 Περὶ ὕβρεως (?) (P. Herc. 1017, fragmentum),
ed. D. Bassi, "Φιλοδήμου περὶ ὕβρεως?," Rivista Indo-Greco-Italica 5 (1921) 16.
Pap: Phil.

532 Περὶ ὑπερηφανίας (P. Herc. 1008, fr. 1 + coll.
1–24), ed. C. Jensen, Philodemi περὶ κακιῶν
liber decimus. Leipzig: Teubner, 1911: 3–43.
= De vitiis x.
Dup. partim 1595 534.
Pap: Phil.

534 Περὶ ὑπερηφανίας (P. Herc. 1008, fr. 1 + coll.
1–10), ed. C. Jensen, Ein neuer Brief Epikurs
[Abhandlungen der Gesellschaft der Wissen-
schaften zu Göttingen, Philol.-hist. Kl., ser. 3,
no. 5. Berlin: Weidmann, 1933]: 13–33.
= De vitiis x.
Dup. partim 1595 532.
Pap: Phil.

536 Περὶ ὑπερηφανίας (P. Herc. 1008, subscriptio),
ed. M. Capasso, "Il presunto papiro di Fania,"
Cronache Ercolanesi 8 (1978) 157.
= De vitiis x.
Pap: Phil.

551 Περὶ φιλαργυρίας (?) (P. Herc. 465, fr. 12.15–
21), ed. W. Crönert, "Neues über Epikur und
einige herkulanensische Rollen," Rheinisches
Museum 56 (1901) 625.
Pap: Phil.

553 Περὶ φιλαργυρίας (?) (P. Herc. 1645, fragmen-
tum), ed. W. Crönert, "Fälschungen in den
Abschriften der herkulanensischen Rollen,"
Rheinisches Museum 53 (1898) 594.
Pap: Phil.

560 Περὶ φιλοδοξίας (?) (P. Herc. 1025, fragmen-

tum), ed. Crönert, Kolotes und Menedemos, 91
(n. 447).
Pap: Phil.

572 Περὶ χάριτος (P. Herc. 1414), ed. A. Tepedino
Guerra, "Filodemo sulla gratitudine," Cron-
ache Ercolanesi 7 (1977) 100–102.
Pap: Phil.

582 Πραγματεῖαι (P. Herc. 310 (?), 1418), ed. C.
Diano, Lettere di Epicuro e dei suoi. Florence:
Sansoni, 1946: 7–20, 27 (+ n. 1), 29–30 (+
app. crit.), 32, 40.
Pap: Phil.

588 Πραγματεῖαι (P. Herc. 1418), ed. L. Spina, "Il
trattato di Filodemo su Epicuro e altri (P.
Herc. 1418)," Cronache Ercolanesi 7 (1977) 49–
68.
Pap: Phil.

595 Πρὸς τοὺς [σοφιστάς] (P. Herc. 1005, fragmenta), ed. F. Sbordone, Philodemi adversus
[sophistas]. Naples: Loffredo, 1947: 3–115.
Pap: 5,113: Phil.

602 Σύνταξις τῶν φιλοσόφων (P. Herc. 164, 1021),
ed. S. Mekler, Academicorum philosophorum
index Herculanensis, 2nd edn. Berlin: Weidmann, 1958: 3–113.
= Index academicorum.
Pap: Phil.

606 Σύνταξις τῶν φιλοσόφων (P. Herc. 327, frr. 1–
6b), ed. Crönert, Kolotes und Menedemos, 128.
= De Eleaticis.
Pap: Phil.

610 Σύνταξις τῶν φιλοσόφων (P. Herc. 1018), ed.
A. Traversa, Index stoicorum Herculanensis.
Genoa: University of Genoa Press, 1952: 1–
110, 117.
= Index stoicorum.
Pap: Phil.

616 Σύνταξις τῶν φιλοσόφων (P. Herc. 1021, coll.
1*.1–2.5, 2.36–43, 3.1–14, 3.34–5.19, 10.16–
24), ed. K. Gaiser, "La biografia di Platone in
Filodemo: nuovi dati dal P. Herc. 1021,"
Cronache Ercolanesi 13 (1983) 55–60.
= Index academicorum.
Pap: Phil.

618 Σύνταξις τῶν φιλοσόφων (P. Herc. 1508, coll.
3–5, fragmenta), ed. Crönert, Kolotes und Menedemos, 131.
= De Pythagoreis.
Pap: Phil.

632 Incerti operis de Epicuro fragmenta (P. Herc.
671, 861, fragmenta), ed. Crönert, Hermes 36,
577–578.
Pap: Phil.

636 Incerti operis de Epicuro fragmentum (P.
Herc. 986, frr. 2.4–8, 12.8–10, 14.6, 21.1–8,
24.6–10), ed. Crönert, RhM 56, 618–619.
Pap: Phil.

638 Incerti operis de Epicuro fragmenta (P. Herc.
998, frr. 11.2–8, 12.4–8, 16.4–7), ed. Crönert,
RhM 56, 619–620.
Pap: Phil.

640 **Incerti operis de Epicuro fragmentum** (*P. Herc.* 1036), ed. Crönert, *RhM* 56, 625.
Pap: Phil.

642 **Incerti operis de Epicuro fragmentum** (*P. Herc.* 1084, fr. 1.1–16), ed. Crönert, *RhM* 56, 616–617.
Pap: Phil.

644 **Incerti operis de Epicuro fragmentum** (*P. Herc.* 1188), ed. Crönert, *RhM* 56, 625 (+ n. 3).
Pap: Phil.

646 **Incerti operis de Epicuro fragmentum** (*P. Herc.* 1188), ed. Crönert, *Kolotes und Menedemos*, 184 (n. 133).
Pap: Phil.

648 **Incerti operis de Epicuro fragmenta** (*P. Herc.* 1735, frr. 2 + 1, 10 + 3), ed. F. Sbordone, "Recenti tentativi di svolgimento dei papiri ercolanesi," *Cronache Ercolanesi* 1 (1971) 31–32.
Pap: Phil.

660 **Incerti operis fragmenta** (*P. Herc.* 118, fragmenta), ed. Crönert, *RhM* 56, 615.
Pap: Phil.

662 **Incerti operis fragmenta** (*P. Herc.* 300 (?), fr. 6), ed. H. Usener, *Epicurea*. Leipzig: Teubner, 1887 (repr. Stuttgart: 1966): 346.
fr. 161a.
Pap: Phil.

664 **Incerti operis fragmenta** (*P. Herc.* 415, fragmenta), ed. D. Bassi, "Papiri ercolanesi inediti," *Classici e Neolatini* 3 (1908) 18–19.
Pap: Phil.

666 **Incerti operis fragmenta** (*P. Herc.* 421, fragmenta), ed. Bassi, *Classici e Neolatini* 3, 10.
Pap: Phil.

668 **Incerti operis fragmenta** (*P. Herc.* 461, frr. 1+2, 3+4, 6+5, 8+9), ed. F. Sbordone, "Recenti tentativi di svolgimento dei papiri ercolanesi," *Cronache Ercolanesi* 1 (1971) 38–39.
Pap: Phil.

672 **Incerti operis fragmentum** (*P. Herc.* 1504), ed. Sbordone, *CronErc* 1, 30.
Pap: Phil.

674 **Incerti operis fragmenta** (*P. Herc.* 1692, frr. 1–5), ed. Bassi, *RFIC* 38, 335–340.
Pap: 366: Phil.

678 **Incerti operis fragmentum** (*P. Herc.* 1784, fragmentum), ed. F. Sbordone, "Nuovi frammenti dei papiri Ercolanesi," *Parola del passato* 103 (1965) 313.
Pap: 16: Phil.

730 **Epigrammata**, AG 5.4, 13, 25, 46, 107, 112, 115, 120–121, 123–124, 126, 131–132, 306, 308(?); **6**.246(?), 349; **7**.222; **9**.412, 570; **10**.21, 103; **11**.30, 34–35, 41, 44, 318; **12**.173; **16**.234.
AG 5.8, 24: Cf. MELEAGER Epigr. (1492 001).
AG 5.80: Cf. PLATO Phil. (0059 039).
AG 5.113; 6.246(?): Cf. (et) Marcus ARGENTARIUS Rhet. et Epigr. (0132 001).

AG 5.114: Cf. Quintus MAECIUS Epigr. (1474 001).
AG 5.308(?): Cf. et ANTIPHILUS Epigr. (0118 001).
Q: 1,361: Epigr.

x01 **Vita Philonidis** (*P. Herc.* 1044).
Crönert, pp. 942–959.
Cf. ANONYMUS EPICUREUS Phil. (1779 003).

1596 **PHILOLAUS** Phil.
5 B.C.: Crotoniensis

001 **Testimonia**, ed. H. Diels and W. Kranz, *Die Fragmente der Vorsokratiker*, vol. 1, 6th edn. Berlin: Weidmann, 1951 (repr. Dublin: 1966): 398–406.
test. 1–29.
NQ: 3,279: Test.

002 **Fragmenta**, ed. Diels and Kranz, *op. cit.*, 406–419.
frr. 1–23.
Q: 2,302: Phil.

003 **Fragmenta** [Sp.], ed. H. Thesleff, *The Pythagorean texts of the Hellenistic period*. Åbo: Åbo Akademi, 1965: 149–151.
Q: 261: Phil.

x01 **Epigramma**.
AG 7.126.
Cf. DIOGENES LAERTIUS Biogr. (0004 002).

1598 **PHILOMNESTUS** Hist.
ante A.D. 3

001 **Fragmenta**, FGrH #527: 3B:504.
Q: 156: Hist.

0492 **PHILONIDES** Comic.
5 B.C.

001 **Fragmenta**, ed. T. Kock, *Comicorum Atticorum fragmenta*, vol. 1. Leipzig: Teubner, 1880: 254–257.
frr. 1–18 + tituli.
Q: 105: Comic.

002 **Fragmenta**, ed. A. Meineke, *Fragmenta comicorum Graecorum*, vol. 2.1. Berlin: Reimer, 1839 (repr. De Gruyter, 1970): 421–424.
Q: 51: Comic.

003 **Fragmenta**, ed. J. Demiańczuk, *Supplementum comicum*. Krakau: Nakładem Akademii, 1912 (repr. Hildesheim: Olms, 1967): 73.
frr. 1–2.
Q: 24: Comic.

1934 **PHILONIDES** Hist.
post 4 B.C.: Cretensis

001 **Testimonia**, FGrH #121: 2B:627.
test. 1a: *Inscr. Olympia* 5.276.
NQ: 69: Test.

002 **Fragmentum**, FGrH #121: 2B:627.
Q: 55: Hist.

1036 **PHILONIDES** Med.
A.D. 1: Dyrrachinus, Siculus

x01 **Fragmentum ap. Galenum.**
K13.978.
Cf. GALENUS Med. (0057 077).

x02 **Fragmentum ap. Athenaeum.**
Deipnosophistae 15.675a–e.
Cf. ATHENAEUS Soph. (0008 001).

PHILONIDES Epicureus Phil.
P. Herc. 1044.
Cf. ANONYMUS EPICUREUS Phil. (1779 003)

0493 **PHILOSTEPHANUS** Comic.
Incertum

001 **Fragmentum,** ed. T. Kock, *Comicorum Atticorum fragmenta,* vol. 3. Leipzig: Teubner, 1888: 393.
fr. 1.
Q: 28: Comic.

002 **Fragmentum,** ed. A. Meineke, *Fragmenta comicorum Graecorum,* vol. 4. Berlin: Reimer, 1841 (repr. De Gruyter, 1970): 589.
Q: 28: Comic.

0584 **PHILOSTEPHANUS** Hist.
3 B.C.: Cyrenaeus

001 **De mirabilibus fluviis,** ed. A. Giannini, *Paradoxographorum Graecorum reliquiae.* Milan: Istituto Editoriale Italiano, 1965: 21–23.
frr. 1–8.
Dup. partim 0584 002–003, x01.
Q: Paradox., Epigr.

002 **Fragmenta,** FHG 3: 28–34.
frr. 1–37.
Dup. partim 0584 001, 003, x01.
Q: Hist., Epigr.

003 **Fragmenta,** ed. H. Lloyd-Jones and P. Parsons, *Supplementum Hellenisticum.* Berlin: De Gruyter, 1983: 335.
frr. 691, 693.
Dup. partim 0584 001–002, x01.
Q: 31: Epigr.

x01 **Epigramma.**
App. Anth. 3.66b addenda: Cf. ANTHOLOGIAE GRAECAE APPENDIX (7052 008).
Dup. partim 0584 001–003.

2058 **PHILOSTORGIUS** Scr. Eccl.
A.D. 4–5: Cappadox

001 **Historia ecclesiastica** (fragmenta ap. Photium), ed. F. Winkelmann (post J. Bidez), *Philostorgius. Kirchengeschichte,* 3rd edn. [*Die griechischen christlichen Schriftsteller.* Berlin: Akademie-Verlag, 1981]: 4–150.
Q: Hist., Eccl.

002 **Historia ecclesiastica** (fragmenta e vita Constantini) (cod. Angelic. 22), ed. Winkelmann, *op. cit.,* 8–10, 12–17, 20–24, 26.
Q: Hist., Eccl.

003 **Historia ecclesiastica** (fragmenta e passione Artemii), ed. Winkelmann, *op. cit.,* 7–150 passim.
Q: Hist., Eccl.

006 **Epigramma,** AG 9.193.
AG 9.194: Cf. ANONYMI EPIGRAMMATICI (AG) (0138 001).
Q: 10: Epigr.

2527 **PHILOSTRATUS** Hist.
1 B.C.?

001 **Fragmentum,** FGrH #789: 3C:801–802.
Q: 127: Hist.

2145 **PHILOSTRATUS** Hist.
A.D. 3: Atheniensis

001 **Testimonium,** FGrH #99: 2A:452.
NQ: 21: Test.

002 **Fragmentum,** FGrH #99: 2A:452.
Q: 84: Hist.

0638 **Flavius PHILOSTRATUS** Soph.
A.D. 2–3: Lemnius

001 **Vita Apollonii,** ed. C.L. Kayser, *Flavii Philostrati opera,* vol. 1. Leipzig: Teubner, 1870 (repr. Hildesheim: Olms, 1964): 1–344.
Cod: 87,068: Narr. Fict., Biogr.

002 **Apollonii epistulae,** ed. Kayser, *op. cit.,* vol. 1, 345–368.
Cod: 5,523: Epist.

003 **Vitae sophistarum,** ed. Kayser, *op. cit.,* vol. 2 (1871; repr. 1964): 1–127.
Cod: 29,905: Biogr.

004 **Heroicus,** ed. Kayser, *op. cit.,* vol. 2, 128–219.
Cod: 22,617: Myth., Dialog.

005 **Nero,** ed. Kayser, *op. cit.,* vol. 2, 220–224.
Cod: 1,046: Hist., Dialog.

006 **Epistulae et dialexeis,** ed. Kayser, *op. cit.,* vol. 2, 225–260.
Cod: 7,784: Epist., Rhet.

007 **De gymnastica,** ed. Kayser, *op. cit.,* vol. 2, 261–293.
Cod: 7,925: Hist., Physiognom.

009 **Epigramma,** AG 16.110.
Q: 48: Epigr.

0652 **PHILOSTRATUS Junior** Soph.
A.D. 3: Lemnius

001 **Imagines,** ed. C.L. Kayser, *Flavii Philostrati opera,* vol. 2. Leipzig: Teubner, 1871 (repr. Hildesheim: Olms, 1964): 390–420.
Cod: 7,438: Rhet.

1600 **PHILOSTRATUS Major** Soph.
A.D. 2–3: Lemnius

001 **Imagines,** ed. O. Benndorf and K. Schenkl, *Philostrati maioris imagines.* Leipzig: Teubner, 1893: 3–129.
Cod: 23,750: Rhet.

1037 **PHILOTAS** Med.
A.D. 2?

x01 **Fragmenta ap. Galenum.**
K**12.**752, 838; **13.**745.
Cf. GALENUS Med. (0057 076–077).

3111 PHILOTHEUS Scriptor Cletorologii
A.D. 9–10: Constantinopolitanus
x01 **Cletorologion.**
Reiske, vol. 2, pp. 702–791.
Cf. CONSTANTINUS VII PORPHYROGENITUS Imperator (3023 010).

1601 PHILOXENUS Epigr.
3 B.C.
001 **Epigramma**, AG 9.319.
Q: 25: Epigr.

1602 PHILOXENUS Gramm.
1 B.C.: Alexandrinus
001 **Fragmenta**, ed. C. Theodoridis, *Die Fragmente des Grammatikers Philoxenos* [*Sammlung griechischer und lateinischer Grammatiker 2.* Berlin: De Gruyter, 1976]: 93–387.
Q

0379 PHILOXENUS Lyr.
5–4 B.C.: Cytherius
001 **Fragmenta**, ed. D.L. Page, *Poetae melici Graeci.* Oxford: Clarendon Press, 1962 (repr. 1967 (1st edn. corr.)): 423, 426–428, 430–432.
frr. 2, 6–11, 15–20.
Q: 98: Lyr.
002 **Tituli**, ed. Page, *op. cit.*, 423, 428–429.
frr. 1, 12–14.
NQ: 9: Lyr.

0380 PHILOXENUS Lyr.
5–4 B.C.: fort. Leucadius
001 **Fragmenta**, ed. D.L. Page, *Poetae melici Graeci.* Oxford: Clarendon Press, 1962 (repr. 1967 (1st edn. corr.)): 433–441.
frr. a–e.
Q: 629: Lyr., Hymn.
002 **Fragmentum** [Sp.], ed. J.U. Powell, *Collectanea Alexandrina.* Oxford: Clarendon Press, 1925 (repr. 1970): 251.
fr. 9.
Q: 14: Poem.

1039 Claudius PHILOXENUS Med.
2–1 B.C.: Alexandrinus
x01 **Fragmenta ap. Galenum.**
K12.683–684, 731, 735, 736, 743; **13.**539–540, 645, 742–743, 819–820.
Cf. GALENUS Med. (0057 076–077).
x02 **Fragmentum ap. Paulum.**
CMG, vol. 9.2, p. 303.
Cf. PAULUS Med. (0715 001).

2344 PHILTEAS Hist.
ante 4 B.C.?
001 **Testimonium**, FGrH #498: 3B:469.
NQ: 36: Test.
002 **Fragmenta**, FGrH #498: 3B:469–470.
Q: 134: Hist.

0671 PHILUMENUS Med.
A.D. 2: Alexandrinus
Cf. et HERODOTUS et PHILUMENUS Med. (0910).
001 **De venenatis animalibus eorumque remediis**, ed. M. Wellmann, *Philumeni de venenatis animalibus eorumque remediis* [*Corpus medicorum Graecorum*, vol. 10.1.1. Leipzig: Teubner, 1908]: 4–40.
Cod: 9,626: Med.

0494 PHILYLLIUS Comic.
5–4 B.C.
001 **Fragmenta**, ed. T. Kock, *Comicorum Atticorum fragmenta*, vol. 1. Leipzig: Teubner, 1880: 781–789.
frr. 1–8, 10–15, 17–23, 25–33 + tituli.
Q: 238: Comic.
002 **Fragmenta**, ed. A. Meineke, *Fragmenta comicorum Graecorum*, vol. 2.2. Berlin: Reimer, 1840 (repr. De Gruyter, 1970): 857–865.
Q: 207: Comic.
003 **Fragmenta**, ed. J. Demiańczuk, *Supplementum comicum.* Krakau: Nakładem Akademii, 1912 (repr. Hildesheim: Olms, 1967): 73–74.
frr. 1–2.
Q: 4: Comic.
004 **Titulus**, ed. C. Austin, *Comicorum Graecorum fragmenta in papyris reperta.* Berlin: De Gruyter, 1973: 201.
NQ: 2: Comic.

1603 <PHINTYS> Phil.
3 B.C.
001 **Fragmenta**, ed. H. Thesleff, *The Pythagorean texts of the Hellenistic period.* Åbo: Åbo Akademi, 1965: 151–154.
Q: 741: Phil.

0585 Publius Aelius PHLEGON Paradox.
A.D. 2: Trallianus
001 **De mirabilibus**, ed. A. Giannini, *Paradoxographorum Graecorum reliquiae.* Milan: Istituto Editoriale Italiano, 1965: 170–218.
Dup. partim 0585 003.
Cod: 5,254: Paradox.
002 **Testimonia**, FGrH #257: 2B:1159–1160.
NQ: 314: Test.
003 **Fragmenta**, FGrH #257: **2B:**1160–1194; **3B:**744–745 addenda.
Dup. partim 0585 001.
Cf. et 0585 x02.
Q, Cod: 10,370: Hist., Chronogr., Paradox.
x01 **Fragmentum ap. Paradoxographum Florentinum 35** [Dub.].
PGR, p. 324.
Cf. PARADOXOGRAPHUS FLORENTINUS (0580 001).
x02 **Chronicon Olympicum** (fort. auctore Phlegonte).
FGrH #257a.

Cf. ANONYMI HISTORICI (FGrH) (1139 019).

x03 **Victores Olympici** (fort. auctore Phlegonte vel Eratosthene).
FGrH #415.
Cf. ANONYMI HISTORICI (FGrH) (1139 026).

2124 **PHOCAS Diaconus** Epigr.
Incertum
001 **Epigramma**, AG 9.772.
Q: 13: Epigr.

2272 **PHOCUS** Phil.
Incertum: Samius
001 **Titulus**, ed. H. Diels and W. Kranz, *Die Fragmente der Vorsokratiker*, vol. 1, 6th edn. Berlin: Weidmann, 1951 (repr. Dublin: 1966): 41.
NQ: Test.

PHOCYLIDEA
Cf. Pseudo-PHOCYLIDES Gnom. (1605).

1604 **PHOCYLIDES** Eleg. et Gnom.
6 B.C.: Milesius
001 **Sententiae**, ed. E. Diehl, *Anthologia lyrica Graeca*, fasc. 1, 3rd edn. Leipzig: Teubner, 1949: 57–60.
frr. 1–[17].
fr. [17]: Dup. 1604 002.
Q: 270: Eleg., Gnom., Hexametr.
002 **Epigramma**, AG 10.117.
Dup. partim 1604 001 (fr. [17]).
Q: 30: Epigr.

1605 **Pseudo-PHOCYLIDES** Gnom.
A.D. 1/2
001 **Sententiae**, ed. D. Young (post E. Diehl), *Theognis*. Leipzig: Teubner, 1971: 95–112.
Cod: 1,606: Gnom., Hexametr.

2596 **PHOEBAMMON** Soph.
A.D. 5/6?: Antinoupolitanus
001 **De figuris** (fort. auctore Phoebammone alio), ed. L. Spengel, *Rhetores Graeci*, vol. 3. Leipzig: Teubner, 1856 (repr. Frankfurt am Main: Minerva, 1966): 43–56.
Cod: Rhet.
002 **Prolegomena in Hermogenis librum** περὶ ἰδεῶν (fort. auctore Phoebammone alio), ed. H. Rabe, *Prolegomenon sylloge*. Leipzig: Teubner, 1935: 375–388.
Dup. partim SYRIANUS Phil. (4017 003).
Cod: Rhet., Comm.
x01 **Commentarium in Thucydidem** (fragmentum) (fort. auctore Phoebammone alio).
Hude, p. 46.
Cf. SCHOLIA IN THUCYDIDEM (5039 001).
x02 **Commentarium in Hermogenis librum** περὶ στάσεων (fragmenta ap. Christophorum) (fort. auctore Phoebammone alio).
Rabe, *RhM* 50:244, 246–248; 54:633.

Cf. CHRISTOPHORUS Rhet. (4007 001).

x03 **Commentarium in Hermogenis librum** περὶ μεθόδου δεινότητος vel in librum περὶ στάσεων (fragmentum ap. Joannem Diaconum) (fort. auctore Phoebammone alio).
Rabe, p. 143.
Cf. JOANNES Diaconus Rhet. (4143 001).

0495 **PHOENICIDES** Comic.
3 B.C.
001 **Fragmenta**, ed. T. Kock, *Comicorum Atticorum fragmenta*, vol. 3. Leipzig: Teubner, 1888: 333–334.
frr. 1–4 + titulus.
Q: 200: Comic.
002 **Fragmenta**, ed. A. Meineke, *Fragmenta comicorum Graecorum*, vol. 4. Berlin: Reimer, 1841 (repr. De Gruyter, 1970): 509–511.
Q: 200: Comic.
003 **Titulus**, ed. C. Austin, *Comicorum Graecorum fragmenta in papyris reperta*. Berlin: De Gruyter, 1973: 201.
NQ: 2: Comic.

1606 **PHOENIX** Iamb.
3 B.C.: Colophonius
001 **Fragmenta**, ed. J.U. Powell, *Collectanea Alexandrina*. Oxford: Clarendon Press, 1925 (repr. 1970): 231–236.
frr. 1–6.
fr. 6: *P. Heidelb.* inv. 310.
Q, Pap: 473: Iamb.
002 **Fragmenta** (*P. Strassb.* [W.G. 304–307]), ed. A.D. Knox, *Herodes, Cercidas, and the Greek choliambic poets*. Cambridge, Mass.: Harvard University Press, 1929 (repr. 1967): 256–262.
frr. 4–6, 8.
Pap

1788 **PHORMIS** Comic.
vel Phormus
Incertum
001 **Fragmentum**, ed. T. Kock, *Comicorum Atticorum fragmenta*, vol. 3. Leipzig: Teubner, 1888: 393.
fr. 1.
Q: 3: Comic.
002 **Titulus**, ed. G. Kaibel, *Comicorum Graecorum fragmenta*, vol. 1.1 [*Poetarum Graecorum fragmenta*, vol. 6.1. Berlin: Weidmann, 1899]: 148.
NQ: 2: Comic.

1607 *PHORONIS*
7 B.C.?
001 **Fragmenta**, ed. G. Kinkel, *Epicorum Graecorum fragmenta*, vol. 1. Leipzig: Teubner, 1877: 210–211.
frr. 1–2, 4–5.
Q: 78: Epic.

4040 **PHOTIUS** Theol., Scr. Eccl. et Lexicogr.
A.D. 9: Constantinopolitanus
Scholia: Cf. ARETHAS Philol. et Scr. Eccl.
(2130 018–019).

001 **Bibliotheca**, ed. R. Henry, *Photius. Bibliothèque*, 8 vols. Paris: Les Belles Lettres, 1:1959; 2:1960; 3:1962; 4:1965; 5:1967; 6:1971; 7:1974; 8:1977: 1:1–191; 2:8–203; 3:8–227; 4:8–174; 5:8–201; 6:8–194; 7:8–228; 8:8–214.
Cod: 360,682: Theol., Hist., Orat., Phil., Med., Narr. Fict., Lexicogr.

002 **Quaestiones ad Amphilochium**, MPG 101: 45–1172.
Cod

003 **Contra Manichaeos**, MPG 102: 16–264.
Cod

004 **De spiritus sancti mystagogia**, MPG 102: 280–400.
Cod

005 **Homilia 1: In sanctae Mariae nativitatem**, MPG 102: 548–561.
Cod

006 **Homilia 3: In dedicatione novae basilicae**, MPG 102: 564–573.
Cod

007 **Homilia 4: Sancti Athanasii encomium**, MPG 102: 576.
Cod

008 **Carmina**, MPG 102: 576–584.
Cod

009 **Epistulae**, ed. B. Laourdas and L.G. Westerink, *Photii patriarchae Constantinopolitani epistulae et Amphilochia*, vols. 1–6.1. Leipzig: Teubner, 1:1983; 2:1984; 3:1985; 4:1986; 5:1986; 6.1:1987: 1:2–197; 2:1–253; 3:4–166; 4:1–190; 5:1–263; 6.1:1–138.
Cod: Epist.

010 **Syntagma canonum**, MPG 104: 441–976.
Cod

011 **Epigramma**, AG 9.203.
Q: 65: Epigr.

012 **Interrogationes decem**, MPG 104: 1220–1232.
Cod

013 **Nomocanon**, MPG 104: 980–1217.
Cod

028 **Commentarii in Matthaeum** (in catenis), ed. J. Reuss, *Matthäus-Kommentare aus der griechischen Kirche* [*Texte und Untersuchungen* 61. Berlin: Akademie-Verlag, 1957]: 270–337.
Q: 18,327: Exeget., Caten.

027 **Commentarii in Joannem** (in catenis), ed. J. Reuss, *Johannes-Kommentare aus der griechischen Kirche* [*Texte und Untersuchungen* 89. Berlin: Akademie-Verlag, 1966]: 359–412.
Q: 15,403: Exeget., Caten.

014 **Fragmenta in epistulam ad Romanos** (in catenis), ed. K. Staab, *Pauluskommentar aus der griechischen Kirche aus Katenenhandschriften gesammelt*. Münster: Aschendorff, 1933: 470–544.
Q: 25,607: Exeget., Caten.

015 **Fragmenta in epistulam I ad Corinthios** (in catenis), ed. Staab, *op. cit.*, 544–583.
Q: 12,896: Exeget., Caten.

016 **Fragmenta in epistulam ii ad Corinthios** (in catenis), ed. Staab, *op. cit.*, 583–604.
Q: 7,048: Exeget., Caten.

017 **Fragmenta in epistulam ad Galatas** (in catenis), ed. Staab, *op. cit.*, 604–610.
Q: 1,826: Exeget., Caten.

018 **Fragmenta in epistulam ad Ephesios** (in catenis), ed. Staab, *op. cit.*, 611–621.
Q: 3,489: Exeget., Caten.

019 **Fragmenta in epistulam ad Philippenses** (in catenis), ed. Staab, *op. cit.*, 621–630.
Q: 2,931: Exeget., Caten.

020 **Fragmenta in epistulam ad Colossenses** (in catenis), ed. Staab, *op. cit.*, 631–633.
Q: 577: Exeget., Caten.

021 **Fragmenta in epistulam I ad Thessalonicenses** (in catenis), ed. Staab, *op. cit.*, 633–636.
Q: 900: Exeget., Caten.

022 **Fragmenta in epistulam ii ad Thessalonicenses** (in catenis), ed. Staab, *op. cit.*, 636.
Q: 138: Exeget., Caten.

023 **Fragmenta in epistulam i ad Timotheum** (in catenis), ed. Staab, *op. cit.*, 636–637.
Q: 145: Exeget., Caten.

024 **Fragmentum in epistulam ii ad Timotheum** (in catenis), ed. Staab, *op. cit.*, 637.
Q: 22: Exeget., Caten.

025 **Fragmentum in epistulam ad Philemonem** (in catenis), ed. Staab, *op. cit.*, 637.
Q: 15: Exeget., Caten.

026 **Fragmenta in epistulam ad Hebraeos** (in catenis), ed. Staab, *op. cit.*, 637–652.
Q: 4,627: Exeget., Caten.

029 **Lexicon**, ed. C. Theodoridis, *Photii patriarchae lexicon*, vol. 1 (A–Δ). Berlin: De Gruyter, 1982: 3–440.
Epistula dedicatoria: pp. 3–4.
Lexicon (A–Δ): pp. 7–440.
Cod: Lexicogr., Epist.

4274 **PHRASIDEMUS** Phil.
4 B.C.: Atheniensis

001 **Testimonium**, ed. K. Döring, *Die Megariker* [*Studien zur antiken Philosophie* 2. Amsterdam: Grüner, 1972]: 52, 61.
test. 165 = Stilpo (4262 001).
NQ: Test.

1608 **PHRYNICHUS** Attic.
A.D. 2: Arabius

001 **Praeparatio sophistica** (epitome), ed. J. de Borries, *Phrynichi sophistae praeparatio sophistica*. Leipzig: Teubner, 1911: 1–129.
Cod: 16,134: Lexicogr.

002 **Eclogae**, ed. E. Fischer, *Die Ekloge des Phrynichos* [*Sammlung griechischer und lateinischer Grammatiker* 1. Berlin: De Gruyter, 1974]: 60–109.
Cod: 9,000: Lexicogr.

003 **Eclogae** (familia q), ed. Fischer, *op. cit.*, 109–124.
Cod: 3,701: Lexicogr.

004 **Eclogae** (familia T), ed. Fischer, *op. cit.*, 124–130.
Cod: 1,449: Lexicogr.

005 **Praeparatio sophistica** (fragmenta), ed. de Borries, *op. cit.*, 130–180.
frr. 1–370.
Q, Cod: 7,914: Lexicogr.

0496 **PHRYNICHUS** Comic.
5 B.C.: Atheniensis

001 **Fragmenta**, ed. T. Kock, *Comicorum Atticorum fragmenta*, vol. 1. Leipzig: Teubner, 1880: 369–391.
frr. 1–3, 5–10, 13–15, 18–25, 27–29, 31–40, 43, 45–46, 48, 50–70, 73–95.
Q: 550: Comic.

002 **Fragmenta**, ed. A. Meineke, *Fragmenta comicorum Graecorum*, vol. 2.1. Berlin: Reimer, 1839 (repr. De Gruyter, 1970): 580–584, 586–590, 592–606.
Q: 502: Comic.

003 **Fragmenta**, ed. J. Demiańczuk, *Supplementum comicum*. Krakau: Nakładem Akademii, 1912 (repr. Hildesheim: Olms, 1967): 74–76.
frr. 1–8.
Q: 36: Comic.

004 **Tituli**, ed. C. Austin, *Comicorum Graecorum fragmenta in papyris reperta*. Berlin: De Gruyter, 1973: 201.
NQ: 3: Comic.

005 **Fragmentum**, ed. Meineke, *FCG*, vol. 5.1 (1857; repr. 1970): xcvi.
Q: 9: Comic.

0303 **PHRYNICHUS** Trag.
6 B.C.: Atheniensis

001 **Fragmenta**, ed. B. Snell, *Tragicorum Graecorum fragmenta*, vol. 1. Göttingen: Vandenhoeck & Ruprecht, 1971: 72–79.
frr. 1–2, 3a, 4–14, 16–17, 20–24.
Q: 208: Trag., Comic.

x01 **Epigramma demonstrativum.**
App. Anth. 3.18: Cf. ANTHOLOGIAE GRAECAE APPENDIX (7052 003).

0876 **PHRYNICHUS II** Trag.
Incertum: Atheniensis

001 **Tituli**, ed. B. Snell, *Tragicorum Graecorum fragmenta*, vol. 1. Göttingen: Vandenhoeck & Ruprecht, 1971: 323.
NQ: 2: Trag.

1609 **PHYLARCHUS** Hist.
3 B.C.: Atheniensis

001 **Testimonia**, FGrH #81: 2A:161–162.
NQ: 404: Test.

002 **Fragmenta**, FGrH #81: 2A:162–189.
fr. 84: Dup. 1609 003 (fr. 694a).

fr. 84: Dup. partim MACARIUS Hist. (2318 001) (fr. 1b).
Q: 8,287: Hist., Hexametr.

003 **Fragmentum**, ed. H. Lloyd-Jones and P. Parsons, *Supplementum Hellenisticum*. Berlin: De Gruyter, 1983: 336.
fr. 694a.
Dup. partim 1609 002 (fr. 84).
Dup. partim MACARIUS Hist. (2318 001) (fr. 1b).
Q: 18: Hexametr.

1038 **PHYLOTIMUS** Med.
3 B.C.: Cous

x01 **Fragmenta ap. Galenum.**
K6.720, 726–727 in CMG, vol. 5.4.2, pp. 368, 372.
Cf. GALENUS Med. (0057 037).

x02 **Fragmenta ap. Oribasium.**
CMG, vol. 6.1.1, pp. 64, 107, 151.
Cf. ORIBASIUS Med. (0722 001).

x03 **Fragmenta ap. Athenaeum.**
Deipnosophistae 2.53f; **3.**79a.
Cf. ATHENAEUS Soph. (0008 001).

2654 ***PHYSIOLOGUS GRAECUS***
A.D. 2/4?

001 **Physiologus**, ed. F. Sbordone, *Physiologus*. Rome: Dante Alighieri-Albrighi, Segati, 1936 (repr. Hildesheim: Olms, 1976): 1–325.
Cod

002 **Physiologus**, ed. D. Offermanns, *Der Physiologus nach den Handschriften G und M*. Meisenheim am Glan: Hain, 1966.
Cod

003 **Physiologus**, ed. D. Kaimakis, *Der Physiologus nach der ersten Redaktion*. Meisenheim am Glan: Hain, 1974: 6a–141a, 143b, 148b.
Cod

2963 **PIERIUS** Scr. Eccl.
A.D. 3–4: Alexandrinus

001 **Fragmentum** (ap. Philippum Sidensem), ed. C. de Boor, *Neue Fragmente des Papias, Hegesippus und Pierius in bisher unbekannten Excerpten aus der Kirchengeschichte des Philippus Sidetes* [*Texte und Untersuchungen* 5.2. Leipzig: Hinrichs, 1888]: 170–171.
Q

0258 **PIGRES** Eleg.
6–5 B.C.

001 **Fragmentum**, ed. M.L. West, *Iambi et elegi Graeci*, vol. 2. Oxford: Clarendon Press, 1972: 93.
Q: 14: Eleg.

0033 **PINDARUS** Lyr.
6–5 B.C.: Boeotus
Vitae: Cf. VITAE PINDARI ET VARIA DE PINDARO (4170).
Scholia: Cf. SCHOLIA IN PINDARUM (5034).

001 **Olympia**, ed. H. Maehler (post B. Snell), *Pindari carmina cum fragmentis*, pt. 1, 5th edn. Leipzig: Teubner, 1971: 2–6, 8–15, 17–34, 36–40, 42–56, 58.
Cod: 6,102: Lyr., Encom.

002 **Pythia**, ed. Maehler (post Snell), *op. cit.*, pt. 1, 59–64, 66–91, 93–121.
Cod: 7,719: Lyr., Encom.

003 **Nemea**, ed. Maehler (post Snell), *op. cit.*, pt. 1, 122–139, 141–143, 145–162.
Cod: 5,119: Lyr., Encom.

004 **Isthmia**, ed. Maehler (post Snell), *op. cit.*, pt. 1, 163–181, 183–184, 186–190.
Cod: 3,066: Lyr., Encom.

005 **Fragmenta**, ed. Maehler (post Snell), *op. cit.*, pt. 2, 4th edn. (1975): 1–161, 215–216.
Isthmia, frr. 1–2, 4–8, 10–14, 15 (= 6a(d)), 16–27, 28 (= 6a(c)): pp. 1–7.
Hymni, frr. 29–30, 32–40, 42–47, 49, 50–51, (= 33a), 51a–51b, 51d, 51f: pp. 8–15.
Paeanes, frr. 52a–52w, 57, 59–61, 66–67, 70: pp. 16–71.
Dithyrambi, frr. 70a–70d, 71–72, 74, 74a, 75–78, 80, 81 (= post 70b), 82, 83 (= 75), 84–85, 86, 86a, pp. 72–84 70b), 82, 83 (= 75), 84–85, 86, 86a, 87 (= 33c), 88 (= 33D): pp. 72–84.
Prosodia, frr. 89a–89b, 92–94: pp. 85–86.
Parthenia, frr. 94a–97, 99, 104b, 104c–104d (= 94a–94b): pp. 87–94.
Hyporchemata, frr. 105–106, 107a–107b, 108–113, 116–117 (= 94c): pp. 95–99.
Encomia, frr. 118–128: pp. 100–104.
Threni, frr. 128a–131b, 133–138, 139 (= 128c): pp. 105–112.
Fragmenta incertorum librorum, frr. 140a–141, 142 (= 108b), 143–144, 145 (= 35a), 146, 147 (= 33b), 148, 150–153, 155–166, 167 (= 128f), 168b, 169a–169b, 170–173, 177, 178 (= 35c), 179–185, 187–196, 198a–198b, 199, 201–207, 209–215c, 216 (= 35b), 217, 219–234, 236–246b, 247 (= 85a), 248, 249b (= post 70b), 250a, 252 (= prae 165), 255–256, 258 (= 243), 259–260, 273, 277–278 (= 223), 282, 287–288, 292, 294–297, 299–300, 302–307, 309–311, 313–314, 317–321, 325–327, 329–332: pp. 113–151.
Fragmenta dubia, frr. 333–335, 337–342, 346–359: pp. 152–161.
Fragmenta addenda et corrigenda, frr. 52w(k), 94e, 124e, 169b: pp. 215–216.
Q, Pap: 9,106: Lyr., Encom., Hymn.

x01 **Epigramma sepulcrale**.
App. Anth. 2.10: Cf. ANTHOLOGIAE GRAECAE APPENDIX (7052 002).

1610 **PINYTUS** Epigr.
A.D. 1: Bithynius

001 **Epigramma**, AG 7.16.
Q: 16: Epigr.

0288 **PISANDER** Epic.
7/6 B.C.: Camirensis

002 **Fragmenta**, ed. G. Kinkel, *Epicorum Graecorum fragmenta*, vol. 1. Leipzig: Teubner, 1877: 251–252.
frr. 7–11.
Dup. partim PISANDER Epic. (0522 001).
Q: 30: Epic.

003 **Epigramma**, AG 7.304.
Q: 30: Epigr.

0522 **PISANDER** Epic.
A.D. 3?: Larandensis

001 **Fragmenta**, ed. E. Heitsch, *Die griechischen Dichterfragmente der römischen Kaiserzeit*, vol. 2. Göttingen: Vandenhoeck & Ruprecht, 1964: 46–47.
frr. 7, 16–20.
Dup. partim PISANDER Epic. (0288 002).
Q: 31: Hexametr.

0393 **PISANDER** Myth.
2 B.C.

001 **Testimonia**, FGrH #16: 1A:*10 addenda.
NQ: 244: Test.

002 **Fragmenta**, FGrH #16: 1A:181–182, *11 addenda.
Q: 749: Hist., Myth.

0049 *PISISTRATI EPISTULA*
Incertum

001 **Epistula**, ed. R. Hercher, *Epistolographi Graeci*. Paris: Didot, 1873 (repr. Amsterdam: Hakkert, 1965): 490.
Q: 213: Epist.

2395 **PISISTRATUS** Hist.
Incertum: Liparaeus

001 **Fragmentum**, FGrH #574: 3B:674.
Q: 21: Hist.

1612 **PISO** Epigr.
A.D. 1–2

001 **Epigramma**, AG 11.424.
Q: 13: Epigr.

1613 *PITTACI EPISTULA*
Incertum
Cf. et PITTACUS <Lyr.>. (0631).

001 **Epistula**, ed. R. Hercher, *Epistolographi Graeci*. Paris: Didot, 1873 (repr. Amsterdam: Hakkert, 1965): 491.
Q: 54: Epist.

0631 **PITTACUS** <Lyr.>
7–6 B.C.: Mytilenensis
Cf. et <SEPTEM SAPIENTES> (1667).

001 **Fragmentum**, ed. T. Bergk, *Poetae lyrici Graeci*, vol. 3, 4th edn. Leipzig: Teubner, 1882: 198.
Q: 23: Lyr.

002 **Epigramma**, AG 11.440.
Q: 8: Epigr.

2677 **PIUS** Gramm.
A.D. 2-3
001 **Fragmenta**, ed. E. Hiller, "Der Grammatiker
Pius und die ἀπολογίαι πρὸς τὰς ἀθετήσεις
᾽Αριστάρχου," *Philologus* 28 (1869) 86-115
(passim).
Q

4146 **Maximus PLANUDES** Polyhist.
A.D. 13-14: Nicomediensis
001 **Commentarium in arithmetica Diophanti**, ed.
P. Tannery, *Diophanti Alexandrini opera omnia*, vol. 2. Leipzig: Teubner, 1895 (repr. Stuttgart: 1974): 125-255.
Cod: Math., Comm.
002 **Prolegomena in artem rhetoricam**, ed. H.
Rabe, *Prolegomenon sylloge* [*Rhetores Graeci* 14.
Leipzig: Teubner, 1931]: 64-73.
Cod: Rhet., Comm.
003 **Prolegomena in Hermogenis librum** περὶ στάσεων, ed. C. Walz, Rhetores Graeci, vol. 5.
Stuttgart: Cotta, 1833 (repr. Osnabrück: Zeller,
1968): 222-230.
Cod: Rhet., Comm.
004 **Πῶς ἐπιγνωσόμεθα τὰς στάσεις**, ed. Walz, *op.
cit.*, 231.
Cod: Rhet., Comm.
005 **Commentarium in Hermogenis librum** περὶ
στάσεων, ed. Walz, *op. cit.*, 232-363.
Cod: Rhet., Comm.
006 **Prolegomena in Hermogenis librum** περὶ εὑρέσεως, ed. Walz, *op. cit.*, 363-369.
Cod: Rhet., Comm.
007 **Commentarium in Hermogenis librum** περὶ
εὑρέσεως, ed. Walz, *op. cit.*, 370-436.
Cod: Rhet., Comm.
008 **Prolegomena in Hermogenis librum** περὶ
ἰδεῶν, ed. Walz, *op. cit.*, 437-439.
Dup. partim ANONYMI IN HERMOGENEM
(5024 013).
Cod: Rhet., Comm.
009 **Commentarium in Hermogenis librum** περὶ
ἰδεῶν, ed. Walz, *op. cit.*, 439-561.
Cod: Rhet., Comm.
010 **Commentarium in Hermogenis librum** περὶ
μεθόδου δεινότητος, ed. Walz, *op. cit.*, 562-576.
Cod: Rhet., Comm.
x01 **Epigrammata** (*App. Anth.*).
Epigramma sepulcrale: 2.775.
Epigramma demonstrativum: 3.422.
Epigrammata irrisoria: 5.80-82.
App. Anth. 2.775: Cf. ANTHOLOGIAE GRAE-
CAE APPENDIX (7052 002).
App. Anth. 3.422: Cf. ANTHOLOGIAE GRAE-
CAE APPENDIX (7052 003).
App. Anth. 5.80-82: Cf. ANTHOLOGIAE
GRAECAE APPENDIX (7052 005).
x02 **Vita Aesopi**.
Eberhard, pp. 226-305.
Cf. VITAE AESOPI (1765 003).
x03 **Scholia in Sophoclem**.
Longo, pp. 95-164.
Cf. SCHOLIA IN SOPHOCLEM (5037 005).

0497 **PLATO** Comic.
5-4 B.C.: Atheniensis
001 **Fragmenta**, ed. T. Kock, *Comicorum Atticorum fragmenta*, vol. 1. Leipzig: Teubner,
1880: 601-627, 629-659, 661-667.
frr. 1-59, 62-69, 71-74, 76-79, 82-98, 104-
124, 126-131, 134-138, 142-164, 166-169,
171-178, 180-202, 205-209, 211, 221-259,
263, 265, 267.
Q: 2,013: Comic.
002 **Fragmenta**, ed. A. Meineke, *Fragmenta comicorum Graecorum*, vol. 2.2. Berlin: Reimer,
1840 (repr. De Gruyter, 1970): 615-622, 624-
641, 643-650, 652-657, 659-662, 664-677,
679-687, 693.
p. 693: fr. 45 supplied from vol. 5.1, p. cix.
Q: 1,824: Comic.
003 **Fragmenta**, ed. J. Demiańczuk, *Supplementum
comicum*. Krakau: Nakładem Akademii, 1912
(repr. Hildesheim: Olms, 1967): 76-82.
frr. 1-28.
fr. 28: *P. Berol.* inv. 9772.
Q, Pap: 102: Comic.
004 **Fragmenta**, ed. C. Austin, *Comicorum Graecorum fragmenta in papyris reperta*. Berlin: De
Gruyter, 1973: 202-203.
frr. 216-217.
Pap: 32: Comic.
005 **Epigramma**, AG 9.359.
Q: 82: Epigr.
006 **Fragmentum**, ed. Kock, *CAF*, vol. 3 (1888):
729.
fr. 207b.
Q: 4: Comic.
007 **Fragmenta**, ed. Meineke, *FCG*, vol. 5.1 (1857;
repr. 1970): xcvi, xcix, cix.
Q: 47: Comic.

1042 **PLATO** Med.
ante A.D. 1
x01 **Fragmentum ap. Galenum**.
K13.60.
Cf. GALENUS Med. (0057 076).

0059 **PLATO** Phil.
5-4 B.C.: Atheniensis
Cf. et SOCRATICORUM EPISTULAE (0637).
Scholia: Cf. SCHOLIA IN PLATONEM (5035).
001 **Euthyphro**, ed. J. Burnet, *Platonis opera*, vol. 1.
Oxford: Clarendon Press, 1900 (repr. 1967): St
I.2a-16a.
Cod: 5,464: Phil., Dialog.
002 **Apologia Socratis**, ed. Burnet, *op. cit.*, vol. 1, St
I.17a-42a.
Cod: 8,854: Phil.
003 **Crito**, ed. Burnet, *op. cit.*, vol. 1, St I.43a-54e.
Cod: 4,329: Phil., Dialog.
004 **Phaedo**, ed. Burnet, *op. cit.*, vol. 1, St I.57a-
118a.
Cod: 22,633: Phil., Dialog.
005 **Cratylus**, ed. Burnet, *op. cit.*, vol. 1, St I.383a-
440e.
Cod: 19,201: Phil., Dialog.

006 **Theaetetus**, ed. Burnet, *op. cit.*, vol. 1, St
I.142a–210d.
Cod: 23,803: Phil., Dialog.

007 **Sophista**, ed. Burnet, *op. cit.*, vol. 1, St I.216a–
268d.
Cod: 17,414: Phil., Dialog.

008 **Politicus**, ed. Burnet, *op. cit.*, vol. 1, St II.257a–
311c.
Cod: 18,592: Phil., Dialog.

009 **Parmenides**, ed. Burnet, *op. cit.*, vol. 2 (1901;
repr. 1967): St III.126a–166c.
Cod: 16,434: Phil., Dialog.

010 **Philebus**, ed. Burnet, *op. cit.*, vol. 2, St II.11a–
67b.
Cod: 19,054: Phil., Dialog.

011 **Symposium**, ed. Burnet, *op. cit.*, vol. 2, St
III.172a–223d.
Cod: 17,530: Phil., Dialog.

012 **Phaedrus**, ed. Burnet, *op. cit.*, vol. 2, St
III.227a–279c.
Cod: 17,221: Phil., Dialog.

013 **Alcibiades i** [Sp.], ed. Burnet, *op. cit.*, vol. 2, St
II.103a–135c.
Cod: 11,317: Phil., Dialog.

014 **Alcibiades ii** [Sp.], ed. Burnet, *op. cit.*, vol. 2, St
II.138a–151c.
Cod: 4,422: Phil., Dialog.

015 **Hipparchus** [Sp.], ed. Burnet, *op. cit.*, vol. 2, St
II.225a–232c.
Cod: 2,426: Phil., Dialog.

016 **Amatores** [Sp.], ed. Burnet, *op. cit.*, vol. 2, St
I.132a–139a.
Cod: 2,424: Phil., Dialog.

017 **Theages** [Sp.], ed. Burnet, *op. cit.*, vol. 3 (1903;
repr. 1968): St I.121a–131a.
Cod: 3,650: Phil., Dialog.

018 **Charmides**, ed. Burnet, *op. cit.*, vol. 3, St
II.153a–176d.
Cod: 8,410: Phil., Dialog.

019 **Laches**, ed. Burnet, *op. cit.*, vol. 3, St II.178a–
201c.
Cod: 8,021: Phil., Dialog.

020 **Lysis**, ed. Burnet, *op. cit.*, vol. 3, St II.203a–
223b.
Cod: 7,319: Phil., Dialog.

021 **Euthydemus**, ed. Burnet, *op. cit.*, vol. 3, St
I.271a–307c.
Cod: 13,030: Phil., Dialog.

022 **Protagoras**, ed. Burnet, *op. cit.*, vol. 3, St
I.309a–362a.
Cod: 18,077: Phil., Dialog.

023 **Gorgias**, ed. Burnet, *op. cit.*, vol. 3, St I.447a–
527e.
Cod: 27,824: Phil., Dialog.

024 **Meno**, ed. Burnet, *op. cit.*, vol. 3, St II.70a–
100c.
Cod: 10,396: Phil., Dialog.

025 **Hippias major** [Dub.], ed. Burnet, *op. cit.*, vol.
3, St III.281a–304e.
Cod: 8,911: Phil., Dialog.

026 **Hippias minor**, ed. Burnet, *op. cit.*, vol. 3, St
I.363a–376c.
Cod: 4,505: Phil., Dialog.

027 **Ion**, ed. Burnet, *op. cit.*, vol. 3, St I.530a–542b.
Cod: 4,091: Phil., Dialog.

028 **Menexenus**, ed. Burnet, *op. cit.*, vol. 3, St
II.234a–249e.
Cod: 4,908: Phil., Dialog.

029 **Clitophon** [Dub.], ed. Burnet, *op. cit.*, vol. 4
(1902; repr. 1968): St III.406a–410e.
Cod: 1,575: Phil., Dialog.

030 **Respublica**, ed. Burnet, *op. cit.*, vol. 4, St
II.327a–621d.
Cod: 89,358: Phil., Dialog.

031 **Timaeus**, ed. Burnet, *op. cit.*, vol. 4, St III.17a–
92c.
Cod: 24,104: Phil., Dialog.

032 **Critias**, ed. Burnet, *op. cit.*, vol. 4, St III.106a–
121c.
Cod: 5,040: Phil., Dialog.

033 **Minos** [Sp.], ed. Burnet, *op. cit.*, vol. 5 (1907;
repr. 1967): St II.313a–321d.
Cod: 3,078: Phil., Dialog.

034 **Leges**, ed. Burnet, *op. cit.*, vol. 5, St II.624a–
969d.
Cod: 106,298: Phil., Dialog.

035 **Epinomis** [Dub.] (fort. auctore Philippo Opun-
tio), ed. Burnet, *op. cit.*, vol. 5, St II.973a–
992e.
Cod: 6,389: Phil., Dialog.

036 **Epistulae** [Dub.], ed. Burnet, *op. cit.*, vol. 5, St
III.309a–363e.
Cod: 17,213: Epist.

037 **Definitiones** [Sp.], ed. Burnet, *op. cit.*, vol. 5, St
III.411a–416a.
Cod: 1,738: Phil.

038 **Spuria**, ed. Burnet, *op. cit.*, vol. 5, St III.364a–
406a.
De justo: 372a–375d.
De virtute: 376a–379d.
Demodocus: 380a–386b.
Sisyphus: 387b–391d.
Eryxias: 392a–406a.
Axiochus: 364a–372a.
Cod: 14,839: Phil., Dialog.

039 **Epigrammata**, AG **5**.78–80; **6**.1, 43; **7**.99–100,
256, 259, 265, 268–269, 669–670; **9**.3, 44, 51,
506, 747, 823; **16**.13, 160–161, 210, 248.
Dup. 0059 041.
AG 7.35: Cf. LEONIDAS Epigr. (1458 001).
AG 7.217: Cf. ASCLEPIADES Epigr. (0137
001).
AG 9.39: Cf. MUSICIUS Epigr. (1520 001).
AG 9.45: Cf. STATYLLIUS FLACCUS Epigr.
(1694 001).
AG 9.759, 826; 16.12, 162: Cf. ANONYMI EPI-
GRAMMATICI (AG) (0138 001).
AG 9.827: Cf. AMMONIUS Epigr. (0289 002).
AG 16.11: Cf. HERMOCREON Epigr. (1422
001).
Q: 639: Epigr.

040 **Fragmenta tragica**, ed. B. Snell, *Tragicorum*

Graecorum fragmenta, vol. 1. Göttingen: Vandenhoeck & Ruprecht, 1971: 186.
frr. 1–3.
Q: 10: Trag.

041 **Epigrammata**, ed. E. Diehl, *Anthologia lyrica Graeca*, fasc. 1, 3rd edn. Leipzig: Teubner, 1949: 102–110.
frr. 1–33.
Dup. 0059 039.
Q: 766: Epigr.

x01 **Epigramma demonstrativum.**
App. Anth. 3.33: Cf. ANTHOLOGIAE GRAECAE APPENDIX (7052 003).
Dup. partim 0059 041 (fr. 14).

1614 **PLATO Junior** Epigr.
Incertum

001 **Epigrammata**, AG 9.13, 748, 751.
AG 9.13b: Cf. ANTIPHILUS Epigr. (0118 001).
AG 16.210: Cf. PLATO Phil. (0059 039).
Q: 48: Epigr.

1615 **PLATONIUS** Gramm.
Incertum

001 **Fragmenta de comoedia Graeca**, ed. G. Kaibel, *Comicorum Graecorum fragmenta*, vol. 1.1 [*Poetarum Graecorum fragmenta*, vol. 6.1. Berlin: Weidmann, 1899]: 3–6.
Περὶ διαφορᾶς κωμῳδιῶν: pp. 3–5.
Περὶ διαφορᾶς χαρακτήρων: p. 6.
Cod: 893: Gramm.

1043 **PLATYSEMUS** Med.
ante A.D. 4

x01 **Fragmentum ap. Oribasium.**
CMG, vol. 6.2.2, p. 263.
Cf. ORIBASIUS Med. (0722 003).

1895 **PLESIMACHUS** Hist.
Incertum

001 **Fragmentum**, FGrH #52: 1A:295.
Q: 66: Hist., Myth.

2000 **PLOTINUS** Phil.
A.D. 3: Lycopolitanus, Alexandrinus, Romanus

001 **Enneades**, ed. P. Henry and H.-R. Schwyzer, *Plotini opera*, 3 vols. Leiden: Brill, 1:1951; 2:1959; 3:1973: **1**:48–142, 145–253, 255–417; **2**:3–258, 260–427; **3**:2–328.
Cod: 216,398: Phil.

0007 **PLUTARCHUS** Biogr. et Phil.
A.D. 1–2: Chaeronensis

001 **Theseus**, ed. K. Ziegler, *Plutarchi vitae parallelae*, vol. 1.1, 4th edn. Leipzig: Teubner, 1969: 1–35.
Cod: 7,972: Biogr.

002 **Romulus**, ed. Ziegler, *Vitae*, vol. 1.1, 35–76.
Cod: 9,727: Biogr.

003 **Comparatio Thesei et Romuli**, ed. Ziegler, *Vitae*, vol. 1.1, 76–81.
Cod: 1,206: Biogr.

007 **Solon**, ed. Ziegler, *Vitae*, vol. 1.1, 82–123.
Cod: 9,051: Biogr.

008 **Publicola**, ed. Ziegler, *Vitae*, vol. 1.1, 124–152.
Cod: 6,168: Biogr.

009 **Comparatio Solonis et Publicolae**, ed. Ziegler, *Vitae*, vol. 1.1, 152–156.
Cod: 999: Biogr.

010 **Themistocles**, ed. Ziegler, *Vitae*, vol. 1.1, 157–197.
Cod: 8,453: Biogr.

011 **Camillus**, ed. Ziegler, *Vitae*, vol. 1.1, 197–248.
Cod: 11,602: Biogr.

024 **Aristides**, ed. Ziegler, *Vitae*, vol. 1.1, 249–287.
Cod: 8,606: Biogr.

025 **Cato Maior**, ed. Ziegler, *Vitae*, vol. 1.1, 287–324.
Cod: 8,493: Biogr.

026 **Comparatio Aristidis et Catonis**, ed. Ziegler, *Vitae*, vol. 1.1, 324–331.
Cod: 1,536: Biogr.

035 **Cimon**, ed. Ziegler, *Vitae*, vol. 1.1, 332–359.
Cod: 6,271: Biogr.

036 **Lucullus**, ed. Ziegler, *Vitae*, vol. 1.1, 359–419.
Cod: 14,069: Biogr.

037 **Comparatio Cimonis et Luculli**, ed. Ziegler, *Vitae*, vol. 1.1, 419–423.
Cod: 1,037: Biogr.

012 **Pericles**, ed. Ziegler, *Vitae*, vol. 1.2, 3rd edn. (1964): 1–47.
Cod: 10,584: Biogr.

013 **Fabius Maximus**, ed. Ziegler, *Vitae*, vol. 1.2, 47–81.
Cod: 8,046: Biogr.

014 **Comparatio Periclis et Fabii Maximi**, ed. Ziegler, *Vitae*, vol. 1.2, 81–84.
Cod: 756: Biogr.

038 **Nicias**, ed. Ziegler, *Vitae*, vol. 1.2, 85–125.
Cod: 9,517: Biogr.

039 **Crassus**, ed. Ziegler, *Vitae*, vol. 1.2, 126–177.
Cod: 10,692: Biogr.

040 **Comparatio Niciae et Crassi**, ed. Ziegler, *Vitae*, vol. 1.2, 177–182.
Cod: 1,270: Biogr.

016 **Marcius Coriolanus**, ed. Ziegler, *Vitae*, vol. 1.2, 183–226.
Cod: 9,765: Biogr.

015 **Alcibiades**, ed. Ziegler, *Vitae*, vol. 1.2, 226–274.
Cod: 10,624: Biogr.

017 **Comparatio Alcibiadis et Marcii Coriolani**, ed. Ziegler, *Vitae*, vol. 1.2, 274–279.
Cod: 1,129: Biogr.

054 **Demosthenes**, ed. Ziegler, *Vitae*, vol. 1.2, 280–312.
Cod: 7,370: Biogr.

055 **Cicero**, ed. Ziegler, *Vitae*, vol. 1.2, 312–368.
Cod: 12,578: Biogr.

056 **Comparatio Demosthenis et Ciceronis**, ed. Ziegler, *Vitae*, vol. 1.2, 368-373.
Cod: 1,039: Biogr.

049 **Phocion**, ed. Ziegler, *Vitae*, vol. 2.1, 2nd edn. (1964): 1-31.
Cod: 8,422: Biogr.

050 **Cato Minor**, ed. Ziegler, *Vitae*, vol. 2.1, 32-92.
Cod: 17,099: Biogr.

060 **Dion**, ed. Ziegler, *Vitae*, vol. 2.1, 93-135.
Cod: 12,217: Biogr.

061 **Brutus**, ed. Ziegler, *Vitae*, vol. 2.1, 135-179.
Cod: 12,354: Biogr.

062 **Comparatio Dionis et Bruti**, ed. Ziegler, *Vitae*, vol. 2.1, 179-183.
Cod: 963: Biogr.

019 **Aemilius Paullus**, ed. Ziegler, *Vitae*, vol. 2.1, 184-222.
Cod: 10,177: Biogr.

018 **Timoleon**, ed. Ziegler, *Vitae*, vol. 2.1, 222-255.
Cod: 9,148: Biogr.

020 **Comparatio Aemilii Paulli et Timoleontis**, ed. Ziegler, *Vitae*, vol. 2.1, 255-256.
Cod: 495: Biogr.

042 **Sertorius**, ed. Ziegler, *Vitae*, vol. 2.1, 257-281.
Cod: 6,878: Biogr.

041 **Eumenes**, ed. Ziegler, *Vitae*, vol. 2.1, 281-301.
Cod: 5,684: Biogr.

043 **Comparatio Eumenis et Sertorii**, ed. Ziegler, *Vitae*, vol. 2.1, 301-302.
Cod: 412: Biogr.

027 **Philopoemen**, ed. Ziegler, *Vitae*, vol. 2.2, 2nd edn. (1968): 1-27.
Cod: 5,997: Biogr.

028 **Titus Flamininus**, ed. Ziegler, *Vitae*, vol. 2.2, 28-56.
Cod: 6,140: Biogr.

029 **Comparatio Philopoemenis et Titi Flaminini**, ed. Ziegler, *Vitae*, vol. 2.2, 56-59.
Cod: 576: Biogr.

021 **Pelopidas**, ed. Ziegler, *Vitae*, vol. 2.2, 60-105.
Cod: 9,850: Biogr.

022 **Marcellus**, ed. Ziegler, *Vitae*, vol. 2.2, 105-147.
Cod: 8,830: Biogr.

023 **Comparatio Pelopidae et Marcelli**, ed. Ziegler, *Vitae*, vol. 2.2, 148-151.
Cod: 848: Biogr.

047 **Alexander**, ed. Ziegler, *Vitae*, vol. 2.2, 152-253.
Cod: 20,808: Biogr.

048 **Caesar**, ed. Ziegler, *Vitae*, vol. 2.2, 253-337.
Cod: 16,522: Biogr.

057 **Demetrius**, ed. Ziegler, *Vitae*, vol. 3.1, 2nd edn. (1971): 1-60.
Cod: 12,745: Biogr.

058 **Antonius**, ed. Ziegler, *Vitae*, vol. 3.1, 60-148.
Cod: 19,144: Biogr.

059 **Comparatio Demetrii et Antonii**, ed. Ziegler, *Vitae*, vol. 3.1, 149-152.
Cod: 924: Biogr.

030 **Pyrrhus**, ed. Ziegler, *Vitae*, vol. 3.1, 153-203.
Cod: 11,321: Biogr.

031 **Marius**, ed. Ziegler, *Vitae*, vol. 3.1, 203-263.
Cod: 13,323: Biogr.

063 **Aratus**, ed. Ziegler, *Vitae*, vol. 3.1, 264-317.
Cod: 12,262: Biogr.

064 **Artaxerxes**, ed. Ziegler, *Vitae*, vol. 3.1, 318-351.
Cod: 7,653: Biogr.

051 **Agis et Cleomenes**, ed. Ziegler, *Vitae*, vol. 3.1, 352-415.
Cod: 13,975: Biogr.

052 **Tiberius et Gaius Gracchus**, ed. Ziegler, *Vitae*, vol. 3.1, 416-458.
Cod: 9,550: Biogr.

053 **Comparatio Agidis et Cleomenis cum Tiberio et Gaio Graccho**, ed. Ziegler, *Vitae*, vol. 3.1, 458-463.
Cod: 1,005: Biogr.

004 **Lycurgus**, ed. B. Perrin, *Plutarch's lives*, vol. 1. Cambridge, Mass.: Harvard University Press, 1914 (repr. 1967): 204-302.
Cod: 9,749: Biogr.

005 **Numa**, ed. Perrin, *Plutarch's lives*, vol. 1, 306-382.
Cod: 7,773: Biogr.

006 **Comparatio Lycurgi et Numae**, ed. Perrin, *Plutarch's lives*, vol. 1, 382-400.
Cod: 1,642: Biogr.

032 **Lysander**, ed. Perrin, *Plutarch's lives*, vol. 4 (1916; repr. 1968): 234-320.
Cod: 8,425: Biogr.

033 **Sulla**, ed. Perrin, *Plutarch's lives*, vol. 4, 324-444.
Cod: 11,958: Biogr.

034 **Comparatio Lysandri et Sullae**, ed. Perrin, *Plutarch's lives*, vol. 4, 444-456.
Cod: 1,270: Biogr.

044 **Agesilaus**, ed. Perrin, *Plutarch's lives*, vol. 5 (1917; repr. 1968): 2-112.
Cod: 11,137: Biogr.

045 **Pompeius**, ed. Perrin, *Plutarch's lives*, vol. 5, 116-324.
Cod: 20,853: Biogr.

046 **Comparatio Agesilai et Pompeii**, ed. Perrin, *Plutarch's lives*, vol. 5, 326-336.
Cod: 1,125: Biogr.

065 **Galba**, ed. Perrin, *Plutarch's lives*, vol. 11 (1926; repr. 1962): 206-272.
Cod: 6,395: Biogr.

066 **Otho**, ed. Perrin, *Plutarch's lives*, vol. 11, 276-318.
Cod: 4,295: Biogr.

081 **Regum et imperatorum apophthegmata** [Sp.?] (172b-208a), ed. W. Nachstädt, *Plutarchi moralia*, vol. 2.1. Leipzig: Teubner, 1935 (repr. 1971): 1-109.
Cod: 16,811: Phil., Gnom.

082 **Apophthegmata Laconica** [Sp.?] (208b-242d), ed. Nachstädt, *Plutarchi moralia*, vol. 2.1, 110-165, 167-224.

Apophthegmata Laconica (208b–236e): pp.
110–165, 167–203.

Instituta Laconica (236f–240b): pp. 204–215.

Lacaenarum apophthegmata (240c–242d): pp.
216–224.

Cod: 17,043: Phil., Gnom.

083 **Mulierum virtutes** (242e–263c), ed. Nachstädt,
Plutarchi moralia, vol. 2.1, 225–272.

Cod: 9,861: Phil., Hist.

084 **Aetia Romana et Graeca** (263d–304f), ed. J.B.
Titchener, *Plutarchi moralia*, vol. 2.1, 273–
366.

= Quaestiones Romanae et Graecae.

Cod: 20,354: Polyhist.

085 **Parallela minora** [Sp.] (305a–316b), ed. Nachstädt, *Plutarchi moralia*, vol. 2.2 (1935; repr.
1971): 1–42.

Cod: 5,175: Hist., Myth.

086 **De fortuna Romanorum** (316c–326c), ed.
Nachstädt, *Plutarchi moralia*, vol. 2.2, 43–74.

Cod: 4,981: Rhet.

087 **De Alexandri magni fortuna aut virtute** (326d–
345b), ed. Nachstädt, *Plutarchi moralia*, vol.
2.2, 75–120.

Cod: 8,721: Rhet.

088 **De gloria Atheniensium** (345c–351b), ed.
Nachstädt, *Plutarchi moralia*, vol. 2.2, 121–
136.

Cod: 2,842: Rhet.

089 **De Iside et Osiride** (351c–384c), ed. W. Sieveking, *Plutarchi moralia*, vol. 2.3 (1935; repr.
1971): 1–80.

Cod: 16,666: Phil., Theol.

090 **De E apud Delphos** (384d–394c), ed. Sieveking, *Plutarchi moralia*, vol. 3 (1929; repr.
1972): 1–24.

Cod: 5,116: Phil., Theol., Dialog.

091 **De Pythiae oraculis** (394d–409d), ed. Sieveking, *Plutarchi moralia*, vol. 3, 25–59.

Cod: 7,521: Phil., Theol., Dialog.

092 **De defectu oraculorum** (409e–438d), ed.
Sieveking, *Plutarchi moralia*, vol. 3, 59–122.

Cod: 14,196: Phil., Theol., Dialog.

093 **An virtus doceri possit** (439a–440c), ed. M.
Pohlenz, *Plutarchi moralia*, vol. 3, 123–127.

Cod: 1,091: Phil., Rhet.

094 **De virtute morali** (440d–452d), ed. Pohlenz,
Plutarchi moralia, vol. 3, 127–156.

Cod: 6,116: Phil.

095 **De cohibenda ira** (452f–464d), ed. Pohlenz,
Plutarchi moralia, vol. 3, 157–186.

Cod: 5,792: Phil., Dialog.

096 **De tranquillitate animi** (464e–477f), ed. Pohlenz, *Plutarchi moralia*, vol. 3, 187–220.

Cod: 6,469: Phil.

097 **De fraterno amore** (478a–492d), ed. Pohlenz,
Plutarchi moralia, vol. 3, 221–254.

Cod: 6,970: Phil.

098 **De amore prolis** (493a–497e), ed. Pohlenz,
Plutarchi moralia, vol. 3, 255–267.

Cod: 2,348: Phil., Rhet.

099 **An vitiositas ad infelicitatem sufficiat** (498a–

500a), ed. Pohlenz, *Plutarchi moralia*, vol. 3,
268–273.

Cod: 923: Phil.

100 **Animine an corporis affectiones sint peiores**
(500b–502a), ed. Pohlenz, *Plutarchi moralia*,
vol. 3, 273–279.

Cod: 910: Phil.

101 **De garrulitate** (502b–515a), ed. Pohlenz, *Plutarchi moralia*, vol. 3, 279–311.

Cod: 6,250: Phil.

102 **De curiositate** (515b–523b), ed. Pohlenz, *Plutarchi moralia*, vol. 3, 311–332.

Cod: 3,975: Phil.

103 **De cupiditate divitiarum** (523c–528b), ed.
Pohlenz, *Plutarchi moralia*, vol. 3, 332–346.

Cod: 2,361: Phil.

104 **De vitioso pudore** (528c–536d), ed. Pohlenz,
Plutarchi moralia, vol. 3, 346–365.

Cod: 3,861: Phil.

105 **De invidia et odio** (536e–538e), ed. Pohlenz,
Plutarchi moralia, vol. 3, 365–371.

Cod: 1,056: Phil.

106 **De laude ipsius** (539a–547f), ed. Pohlenz, *Plutarchi moralia*, vol. 3, 371–393.

Cod: 4,281: Phil., Rhet.

107 **De sera numinis vindicta** (548a–568a), ed.
Pohlenz, *Plutarchi moralia*, vol. 3, 394–444.

Cod: 9,781: Phil., Theol., Dialog.

108 **De fato** [Sp.] (568b–574f), ed. Sieveking, *Plutarchi moralia*, vol. 3, 445–460.

Cod: 3,572: Phil., Rhet.

109 **De genio Socratis** (575a–598f), ed. Sieveking,
Plutarchi moralia, vol. 3, 460–511.

Cod: 12,039: Phil., Theol., Dialog.

110 **De exilio** (599a–607f), ed. Sieveking, *Plutarchi
moralia*, vol. 3, 512–532.

Cod: 4,375: Phil.

111 **Consolatio ad uxorem** (608a–612b), ed. Sieveking, *Plutarchi moralia*, vol. 3, 533–542.

Cod: 2,047: Phil., Epist.

112 **Quaestiones convivales** (612c–748d), ed. C.
Hubert, *Plutarchi moralia*, vol. 4 (1938; repr.
1971): 1–335.

Cod: 66,199: Polyhist., Phil., Dialog.

113 **Amatorius** (748e–771e), ed. Hubert, *Plutarchi
moralia*, vol. 4, 336–396.

Cod: 11,677: Phil., Dialog.

114 **Amatoriae narrationes** [Sp.] (771e–775e), ed.
Hubert, *Plutarchi moralia*, vol. 4, 396–405.

Cod: 1,877: Narr. Fict.

121 **Vitae decem oratorum** [Sp.] (832b–852e), ed. J.
Mau, *Plutarchi moralia*, vol. 5.2.1 (1971): 1–
49.

Cod: 9,754: Biogr.

125 **Aetia physica** (911c–919e), ed. Hubert, *Plutarchi moralia*, vol. 5.3, 2nd edn. (1960): 1–26.

= Quaestiones naturales.

Cod: 4,437: Nat. Hist.

126 **De facie in orbe lunae** (920b–945e), ed. Pohlenz, *Plutarchi moralia*, vol. 5.3, 31–89.

Cod: 13,440: Phil., Astron., Dialog.

127 **De primo frigido** (945f–955c), ed. Hubert, *Plutarchi moralia*, vol. 5.3, 90–114.
Cod: 5,278: Phil., Nat. Hist.

128 **Aquane an ignis sit utilior** [Sp.] (955d–958e), ed. Hubert, *Plutarchi moralia*, vol. 6.1 (1954; repr. 1959): 1–10.
Cod: 1,718: Rhet.

129 **De sollertia animalium** (959a–985c), ed. Hubert, *Plutarchi moralia*, vol. 6.1, 11–75.
Cod: 13,178: Phil., Nat. Hist., Dialog.

130 **Bruta animalia ratione uti** (985d–992e), ed. Hubert, *Plutarchi moralia*, vol. 6.1, 76–93.
Cod: 3,610: Phil., Nat. Hist., Dialog.

131 **De esu carnium i** (993a–996c), ed. Hubert, *Plutarchi moralia*, vol. 6.1, 94–104.
Cod: 1,690: Phil., Rhet.

132 **De esu carnium ii** (996d–999b), ed. Hubert, *Plutarchi moralia*, vol. 6.1, 105–112.
Cod: 1,330: Phil., Rhet.

133 **Platonicae quaestiones** (999c–1011e), ed. Hubert, *Plutarchi moralia*, vol. 6.1, 113–142.
Cod: 6,581: Phil.

134 **De animae procreatione in Timaeo** (1012b–1030c), ed. Hubert, *Plutarchi moralia*, vol. 6.1, 143–188.
Cod: 9,925: Phil.

135 **Epitome libri de animae procreatione in Timaeo** (1030d–1032f), ed. Hubert, *Plutarchi moralia*, vol. 6.1, 189–194.
Cod: 1,248: Phil.

136 **De Stoicorum repugnantiis** (1033a–1057b), ed. R. Westman (post M. Pohlenz), *Plutarchi moralia*, vol. 6.2, 2nd edn. (1959): 2–58.
Cod: 12,602: Phil.

137 **Stoicos absurdiora poetis dicere** (1057c–1058e), ed. Westman (post Pohlenz), *Plutarchi moralia*, vol. 6.2, 59–61.
Cod: 540: Phil.

138 **De communibus notitiis adversus Stoicos** (1058e–1086b), ed. Westman (post Pohlenz), *Plutarchi moralia*, vol. 6.2, 62–122.
Cod: 14,372: Phil., Dialog.

139 **Non posse suaviter vivi secundum Epicurum** (1086c–1107c), ed. Westman (post Pohlenz), *Plutarchi moralia*, vol. 6.2, 173–215.
Cod: 10,278: Phil., Dialog.

140 **Adversus Colotem** (1107d–1127e), ed. Westman (post Pohlenz), *Plutarchi moralia*, vol. 6.2, 173–215.
Cod: 10,441: Phil.

141 **De latenter vivendo** (1128a–1130e), ed. Westman (post Pohlenz), *Plutarchi moralia*, vol. 6.2, 216–223.
Cod: 1,325: Phil.

143 **De libidine et aegritudine**, ed. Ziegler and Pohlenz, *Plutarchi moralia*, vol. 6.3, 3rd edn. (1966): 51–59.
Cod: 1,727: Phil.

144 **Parsne an facultas animi sit vita passiva**, ed. Ziegler and Pohlenz, *Plutarchi moralia*, vol. 6.3, 60–64.
Cod: 1,139: Phil.

145 **Fragmenta**, ed. F.H. Sandbach, *Plutarchi moralia*, vol. 7 (1967): 13–138.
Q, Cod: 23,639: Biogr., Epist., Myth., Nat. Hist., Phil., Rhet., Theol.

067 **De liberis educandis** [Sp.] (1a–14c), ed. F.C. Babbitt, *Plutarch's moralia*, vol. 1. Cambridge, Mass.: Harvard University Press, 1927 (repr. 1969): 4–68.
Cod: 6,339: Phil., Rhet.

068 **Quomodo adolescens poetas audire debeat** (14d–37b), ed. Babbitt, *Plutarch's moralia*, vol. 1, 74–196.
Cod: 10,493: Phil., Rhet.

069 **De recta ratione audiendi** (37b–48d), ed. Babbitt, *Plutarch's moralia*, vol. 1, 204–258.
Cod: 5,299: Phil., Rhet.

070 **Quomodo adulator ab amico internoscatur** (48e–74e), ed. Babbitt, *Plutarch's moralia*, vol. 1, 264–394.
Cod: 12,265: Phil.

071 **Quomodo quis suos in virtute sentiat profectus** (75a–86a), ed. Babbitt, *Plutarch's moralia*, vol. 1, 400–456.
Cod: 5,270: Phil.

072 **De capienda ex inimicis utilitate** (86b–92f), ed. Babbitt, *Plutarch's moralia*, vol. 2 (1928; repr. 1962): 4–40.
Cod: 3,145: Phil.

073 **De amicorum multitudine** (93a–97b), ed. Babbitt, *Plutarch's moralia*, vol. 2, 46–68.
Cod: 1,905: Phil.

074 **De fortuna** (97c–100a), ed. Babbitt, *Plutarch's moralia*, vol. 2, 74–88.
Cod: 1,314: Phil., Rhet.

075 **De virtute et vitio** (100b–101e), ed. Babbitt, *Plutarch's moralia*, vol. 2, 94–100.
Cod: 695: Phil.

076 **Consolatio ad Apollonium** [Sp.] (101f–122a), ed. Babbitt, *Plutarch's moralia*, vol. 2, 108–210.
Cod: 9,580: Epist., Phil.

077 **De tuenda sanitate praecepta** (122b–137e), ed. Babbitt, *Plutarch's moralia*, vol. 2, 216–292.
Cod: 7,141: Phil., Med., Dialog.

078 **Conjugalia praecepta** (138a–146a), ed. Babbitt, *Plutarch's moralia*, vol. 2, 298–342.
Cod: 3,853: Phil.

079 **Septem sapientium convivium** (146b–164d), ed. Babbitt, *Plutarch's moralia*, vol. 2, 348–448.
Cod: 8,983: Phil., Dialog.

080 **De superstitione** (164e–171f), ed. Babbitt, *Plutarch's moralia*, vol. 2, 454–494.
Cod: 3,469: Phil., Theol.

115 **Maxime cum principibus philosopho esse disserendum** (776a–779c), ed. H.N. Fowler, *Plutarch's moralia*, vol. 10 (1936; repr. 1969): 28–46.
Cod: 1,596: Phil.

116 **Ad principem ineruditum** (779d–782f), ed. Fowler, *Plutarch's moralia*, vol. 10, 52–70.
Cod: 1,649: Phil.

117 **An seni respublica gerenda sit** (783b–797f),

ed. Fowler, *Plutarch's moralia*, vol. 10, 76–
152.
Cod: 6,968: Phil.

118 **Praecepta gerendae reipublicae** (798a–825f),
ed. Fowler, *Plutarch's moralia*, vol. 10, 158–
298.
Cod: 12,890: Phil.

119 **De unius in republica dominatione, populari
statu, et paucorum imperio** (826a–827c), ed.
Fowler, *Plutarch's moralia*, vol. 10, 304–310.
Cod: 582: Phil.

120 **De vitando aere alieno** (827d–832a), ed. Fowler, *Plutarch's moralia*, vol. 10, 316–338.
Cod: 2,087: Phil.

122 **Comparationis Aristophanis et Menandri compendium** (853a–854d), ed. Fowler, *Plutarch's
moralia*, vol. 10, 462–472.
Cod: 763: Rhet.

123 **De Herodoti malignitate** (854e–874c), ed. L.
Pearson, *Plutarch's moralia*, vol. 11 (1965;
repr. 1970): 8–128.
Cod: 9,433: Rhet.

146 Παροιμίαι αἷς ᾿Αλεξανδρεῖς ἐχρῶντο, ed. E.L.
von Leutsch and F.G. Schneidewin, *Corpus
paroemiographorum Graecorum*, vol. 1. Göttingen: Vandenhoeck & Ruprecht, 1839 (repr.
Hildesheim: Olms, 1965): 321–342.
Q, Cod: 2,807: Paroem.

147 ᾿Εκλογὴ περὶ τῶν ἀδυνάτων, ed. von Leutsch
and Schneidewin, *op. cit.*, 343–348.
Q, Cod: 172: Paroem.

148 **Fragmenta**, FGrH #388: 3B:264–265.
Q: 507: Hist., Myth.

149 **De proverbiis Alexandrinorum** [Sp.], ed. O.
Crusius, *Plutarchi de proverbiis Alexandri-
norum libellus ineditus*. Tübingen: Fues &
Kostenbader, 1887: 1–24.
Cod: Paroem.

0094 **Pseudo-PLUTARCHUS**
post A.D. 2

001 **De fluviis**, ed. K. Müller, *Geographi Graeci
minores*, vol. 2. Paris: Didot, 1861 (repr. Hildesheim: Olms, 1965): 637–665.
Cod: 6,879: Geogr.

002 **De musica** (1131b–1147a), ed. K. Ziegler, *Plu-
tarchi moralia*, vol. 6.3, 3rd edn. Leipzig:
Teubner, 1966: 1–37.
Cod: 8,504: Mus., Dialog.

003 **Placita philosophorum** (874d–911c), ed. J.
Mau, *Plutarchi moralia*, vol. 5.2.1. Leipzig:
Teubner, 1971: 50–153.
Cod: 17,825: Doxogr.

004 **Titulus**, ed. A. Giannini, *Paradoxographorum
Graecorum reliquiae*. Milan: Istituto Editoriale
Italiano, 1965: 396.
NQ: [10]: Paradox.

x01 **Stromata**.
Plutarchi moralia, vol. 7, pp. 110–114.
Cf. PLUTARCHUS Biogr. et Phil. (0007 145)
(fr. 179).

x02 **Apophthegmata Romana**.
Ofenloch, pp. 206–210.

Cf. Pseudo-CAECILIUS Rhet. (1234 001).

x03 **Vita Homeri**.
Allen, vol. 5, pp. 239–245.
Cf. VITAE HOMERI (1805 002).

0987 **PODANITES** Med.
ante A.D. 2

x01 **Fragmentum ap. Galenum**.
K13.115.
Cf. GALENUS Med. (0057 076).

0625 **POLEMAEUS** Trag.
1 B.C.: Ephesius

001 **Tituli**, ed. B. Snell, *Tragicorum Graecorum
fragmenta*, vol. 1. Göttingen: Vandenhoeck &
Ruprecht, 1971: 309.
frr. 1–2.
NQ: 3: Trag., Satyr.

0586 **POLEMON** Perieg.
3–2 B.C.: Iliensis

001 **Fragmenta**, FHG 3: 108–148.
Q

002 **Testimonium et fragmenta**, ed. H.J. Mette,
"Die 'Kleinen' griechischen Historiker heute,"
Lustrum 21 (1978) 40–41.
frr. 4 bis, 37 bis, 65 bis, 75 bis.
testimonium: *IG* 8.281.
fr. 4 bis: *P. Oxy.* 13.1611.
fr. 65 bis: *P. Oxy.* 18.2176.
Q, Pap, Epigr: 263: Hist.

1617 **Marcus Antonius POLEMON** Soph.
A.D. 1–2

001 **Declamationes**, ed. H. Hinck, *Polemonis decla-
mationes quae exstant duae*. Leipzig: Teubner,
1873: 3–39.
In Cynaegirum: pp. 3–17.
In Callimachum: pp. 17–39.
Cod: 6,268: Rhet.

002 **Fragmentum physiognomonicum**, ed. J.A. Cramer, *Anecdota Graeca e codd. manuscriptis bibliothecarum Oxoniensium*, vol. 4. Oxford: Oxford University Press, 1836 (repr. Amsterdam:
Hakkert, 1963): 255.
Q: 30: Physiognom.

2233 **Pseudo-POLEMON**
A.D. 2

001 **Physiognomonica**, ed. R. Foerster, *Scriptores
physiognomonici Graeci et Latini*, vol. 1. Leipzig: Teubner, 1893: 427–431.
Cod

002 **Epitome Adamantiana**, ed. Foerster, *op. cit.*,
298–347, 351–397, 401–426.
Cod

1616 **POLEMON I** <Epigr.>
vel Polemon II
1 B.C./A.D. 1

001 **Epigrammata**, AG 5.68; 9.746; 11.38.
Q: 88: Epigr.

x01 **Epigrammata** (*App. Anth.*).

Epigramma demonstrativum: 3.106.
Epigramma irrisorium: 5.30.
App. Anth. 3.106: Cf. ANTHOLOGIAE GRAE-
CAE APPENDIX (7052 003).
App. Anth. 5.30: Cf. ANTHOLOGIAE GRAE-
CAE APPENDIX (7052 005).

0498 **POLIOCHUS** Comic.
5/3 B.C.
001 **Fragmenta**, ed. T. Kock, *Comicorum Atticorum fragmenta*, vol. 3. Leipzig: Teubner,
1888: 390.
frr. 1–2.
Q: 58: Comic.
002 **Fragmenta**, ed. A. Meineke, *Fragmenta comicorum Graecorum*, vol. 4. Berlin: Reimer, 1841
(repr. De Gruyter, 1970): 589–590.
Q: 59: Comic.

2477 **POLLES** Hist.
Incertum: Aegaeus
001 **Testimonia**, FGrH #705: 3C:565.
NQ: 87: Test.

1045 **POLLES** Med.
fiq Polles Aegaeus Phil.
ante A.D. 4
x01 **Fragmentum ap. Oribasium.**
CMG, vol. 6.2.1, p. 177 scholia.
Cf. ORIBASIUS Med. (0722 001).
x02 **Fragmenta ap. Oribasium.**
CMG, vol. 6.3, pp. 65, 67–68.
Cf. ORIBASIUS Med. (0722 004).
x03 **Fragmenta ap. Aëtium** (lib. 15).
Zervos, *Athena* 21, pp. 73, 74, 75, 77, 78, 79,
82.
Cf. AËTIUS Med. (0718 015).

1618 **POLLIANUS** Epigr.
A.D. 2
001 **Epigrammata**, AG 11.127–128, 130, 167;
16.150.
Q: 179: Epigr.

1985 **Asinius POLLIO** Hist.
1 B.C.–A.D. 1: Trallianus
001 **Testimonium**, FGrH #193: 2B:928.
NQ: 60: Test.

0542 **Julius POLLUX** Gramm.
A.D. 2
001 **Onomasticon**, ed. E. Bethe, *Pollucis onomas-
ticon*, 2 vols. [*Lexicographi Graeci* 9.1–9.2.
Leipzig: Teubner, 9.1:1900; 9.2:1931 (repr.
Stuttgart: 1967)]: **9.1**:1–305; **9.2**:1–248.
Cod: 127,434: Lexicogr., Rhet., Epist.

1869 **POLUS** Rhet. et Hist.
5 B.C.: Agragantinus
001 **Testimonium**, FGrH #7: 1A:158.
NQ: 38: Test.

1619 **POLUS LUCANUS** Phil.
Incertum
x01 **Fragmentum ap. Stobaeum.**
Anth. III.9.51.
Cf. Joannes STOBAEUS (2037 001).

1620 **Julius POLYAENUS** Epigr.
fiq Gaius Julius Polyaenus Soph. et Hist.
1 B.C.
Cf. et Gaius Julius POLYAENUS Soph. et Hist.
(1988).
001 **Epigrammata**, AG 9.7–9b.
Q: 101: Epigr.

1621 **POLYAENUS** Epigr.
A.D. 2: Sardianus
001 **Epigramma**, AG 9.1.
Q: 38: Epigr.

0616 **POLYAENUS** Rhet.
A.D. 2: Macedo
001 **Strategemata**, ed. E. Woelfflin and J. Melber,
Polyaeni strategematon libri viii. Leipzig:
Teubner, 1887 (repr. Stuttgart: 1970): 2–301,
305–425.
Cod: 63,853: Tact.
002 **Excerpta Polyaeni**, ed. Woelfflin and Melber,
op. cit., 429–504.
Cod: 16,439: Tact.
003 **Testimonia**, FGrH #639: 3C:185.
NQ: 20: Test.
004 **Fragmenta**, FGrH #639: 3C:185–186.
Q: 202: Hist.

1988 **Gaius Julius POLYAENUS** Soph. et Hist.
fiq Julius Polyaenus Epigr.
1 B.C.: Sardianus
Cf. et Julius POLYAENUS Epigr. (1620).
001 **Testimonium**, FGrH #196: 2B:929.
NQ: 24: Test.

1886 **POLYARCHUS** Hist.
vel Polyanthus
ante A.D. 2: Cyrenaeus
001 **Fragmenta**, FGrH #37: 1A:259.
Q: 48: Hist., Myth.

0543 **POLYBIUS** Hist.
3–2 B.C.: Megalopolitanus
001 **Historiae**, ed. T. Buettner-Wobst, *Polybii historiae*, vols. 1–4. Leipzig: Teubner, 1:1905;
2:1889; 3:1893; 4:1904 (repr. Stuttgart: 1:1962;
2–3:1965; 4:1967): 1:1–361; 2:1–380; 3:1–430;
4:1–512.
Q, Cod: 327,805: Hist.
002 **Fragmenta ex incertis libris**, ed. Buettner-
Wobst, *op. cit.*, vol. 4, 513–545.
frr. 1–237.
Q: 4,236: Hist.
003 **Testimonium**, FGrH #173: 2B:896.
NQ: 221: Test.

2177 **Tiberius Claudius POLYBIUS** Hist.
      1 B.C.–A.D. 1
001   **Fragmentum,** FGrH #254: 2B:1153.
      Q: 71: Hist., Chronogr.

0605 **POLYBIUS** Rhet.
      Incertum: Sardianus
001   **Fragmenta de figuris,** ed. L. Spengel, *Rhetores Graeci,* vol. 3. Leipzig: Teubner, 1856 (repr. Frankfurt am Main: Minerva, 1966): 105–109.
      Cod: 745: Rhet.
002   **De barbarismo et soloecismo,** ed. A. Nauck, *Lexicon Vindobonense.* St. Petersburg: Eggers, 1867 (repr. Hildesheim: Olms, 1965): 283–289.
      Cod: 946: Rhet.

1622 **POLYCARPUS** Scr. Eccl.
      A.D. 1–2: Smyrnaeus
001   **Epistula ad Philippenses,** ed. K. Bihlmeyer and W. Schneemelcher (post F.X. Funk), *Die apostolischen Väter,* 3rd edn. Tübingen: Mohr, 1970: 114–120.
      Cod: 1,184: Epist.

1624 **POLYCHARMUS** Hist.
      post 4 B.C.?: Naucratites
      Cf. et POLYCHARMUS Hist. (1623).
001   **Fragmentum,** FGrH #640: 3C:187.
      Q: 216: Hist.

1623 **POLYCHARMUS** Hist.
      fiq Polycharmus Naucratites
      2 B.C.?
      Cf. et POLYCHARMUS Hist. (1624).
001   **Fragmenta,** FGrH #770: 3C:762–765.
      Q: 1,088: Hist.

1938 **POLYCLITUS** Hist.
      post 4 B.C.: Larissaeus
001   **Testimonia,** FGrH #128: 2B:668.
      NQ: 47: Test.
002   **Fragmenta,** FGrH #128: 2B:668–670.
      Q: 900: Hist.

1625 **POLYCLITUS** Phil.
      5 B.C.: Argivus
001   **Testimonia,** ed. H. Diels and W. Kranz, *Die Fragmente der Vorsokratiker,* vol. 1, 6th edn. Berlin: Weidmann, 1951 (repr. Dublin: 1966): 391.
      test. 1–3.
      NQ: 344: Test.
002   **Fragmenta,** ed. Diels and Kranz, *op. cit.,* 392–393.
      frr. 1–2.
      Q: 262: Phil.

2410 **POLYCRATES** Hist.
      4 B.C.: Atheniensis
001   **Testimonium,** FGrH #597: 3B:730.
      NQ: 69: Test.

1627 **POLYCRATES** Hist.
      ante 1 B.C.: Lacon
001   **Fragmentum,** FGrH #588: 3B:702–703.
      Q: 244: Hist.

1626 **POLYCRATES** Scr. Eccl.
      A.D. 2: Ephesinus
001   **Fragmentum synodicae epistulae,** ed. M.J. Routh, *Reliquiae sacrae,* vol. 2, 2nd edn. Oxford: Oxford University Press, 1846 (repr. Hildesheim: Olms, 1974): 13–16.
      Q: 352: Epist.

2385 **POLYCRITUS** Hist.
      4 B.C.?: Mendaeus
001   **Testimonia,** FGrH #559: 3B:568.
      NQ: 103: Test.
002   **Fragmenta,** FGrH #559: 3B:568–570.
      Q: 385: Hist.
003   **Titulus,** ed. H. Lloyd-Jones and P. Parsons, *Supplementum Hellenisticum.* Berlin: De Gruyter, 1983: 337.
      fr. 696.
      NQ: 2: Epic., Hist.

1041 **POLYDEUCES** Med.
      ante A.D. 6
x01   **Fragmentum ap. Alexandrum Trallianum.** Puschmann, vol. 2, p. 15.
      Cf. ALEXANDER Med. (0744 003).

2327 **POLYGNOSTUS** Hist.
      Incertum
001   **Titulus,** FGrH #473: 3B:433.
      NQ: Hist.

1048 **POLYIDUS** Med.
      ante A.D. 1
x01   **Fragmenta ap. Galenum.** K13.826, 834.
      Cf. GALENUS Med. (0057 077).
x02   **Fragmenta ap. Oribasium.** CMG, vol. **6.2.2,** p. 216; **6.3,** p. 494.
      Cf. ORIBASIUS Med. (0722 003, 005).
x03   **Fragmentum ap. Paulum.** CMG, vol. 9.2, p. 318.
      Cf. PAULUS Med. (0715 001).

0331 **<POLYIDUS>** Trag.
      4 B.C.: Selymbrianus
001   **Fragmentum,** ed. B. Snell, *Tragicorum Graecorum fragmenta,* vol. 1. Göttingen: Vandenhoeck & Ruprecht, 1971: 249.
      fr. 2.
      Q: 24: Trag.

1839 **POLYPHRASMON** Trag.
      5 B.C.
001   **Tituli,** ed. B. Snell, *Tragicorum Graecorum fragmenta,* vol. 1. Göttingen: Vandenhoeck & Ruprecht, 1971: 85.
      NQ: 2: Trag., Satyr.

1628 POLYSTRATUS Epigr.
2 B.C.: Aegyptius
001 **Epigrammata**, AG **7**.297; **12**.91.
Q: 80: Epigr.

1629 POLYSTRATUS Phil.
3–2 B.C.
001 Περὶ ἀλόγου καταφρονήσεως (*P. Herc.*
336/1150), ed. K. Wilke, *Polystrati Epicurei
περὶ ἀλόγου καταφρονήσεως libellus.* Leipzig:
Teubner, 1905: 3–33.
Pap: 2,687: Phil.
002 **Fragmenta** (*P. Herc.* 346), ed. A. Vogliano,
*Epicuri et Epicureorum scripta in Herculanen-
sibus papyris servata.* Berlin: Weidmann, 1928:
77–89.
Pap: 2,496: Phil.

4277 POLYXENUS Soph.
4 B.C.: Atheniensis, Syracusanus
001 **Testimonia**, ed. K. Döring, *Die Megariker
[Studien zur antiken Philosophie* 2. Amsterdam: Grüner, 1972]: 67–70.
test. 211–220.
NQ: Test.

0499 POLYZELUS Comic.
5–4 B.C.
001 **Fragmenta**, ed. T. Kock, *Comicorum Atticorum fragmenta*, vol. 1. Leipzig: Teubner,
1880: 789–793.
frr. 2–4, 6–12 + tituli.
Q: 110: Comic.
002 **Fragmenta**, ed. A. Meineke, *Fragmenta comicorum Graecorum*, vol. 2.2. Berlin: Reimer,
1840 (repr. De Gruyter, 1970): 867, 869–872.
Q: 90: Comic.
003 **Fragmentum**, ed. J. Demiańczuk, *Supplementum comicum.* Krakau: Nakładem Akademii,
1912 (repr. Hildesheim: Olms, 1967): 82.
fr. 1.
Q: 3: Comic.

1630 POLYZELUS Hist.
3 B.C.?: Rhodius
001 **Fragmenta**, FGrH #521: 3B:492–494.
Q: 362: Hist.

POMPEIUS <Epigr.>
AG 9.647.
Cf. ANONYMI EPIGRAMMATICI (AG) (0138
001).

0346 POMPEIUS MACER <Trag.>
1 B.C.–A.D. 1
001 **Fragmentum**, ed. B. Snell, *Tragicorum Graecorum fragmenta*, vol. 1. Göttingen: Vandenhoeck & Ruprecht, 1971: 313.
fr. 1.
Q: 41: Trag.

1631 POMPEIUS MACER Junior Epigr.
1 B.C.–A.D. 1
001 **Epigrammata**, AG **7**.219; **9**.28.
Q: 79: Epigr.

1051 POMPEIUS SABINUS Med.
A.D. 2
Cf. et SABINUS Med. (1066).
x01 **Fragmentum ap. Galenum**.
K13.1027.
Cf. GALENUS Med. (0057 077).

PORPHYRIUS Gramm.
Incertum
Cf. COMMENTARIA IN DIONYSII THRACIS
ARTEM GRAMMATICAM (4175 004).

2034 PORPHYRIUS Phil.
vel Malchus
A.D. 3: Tyrius, Romanus
Scholia: Cf. SCHOLIA IN PORPHYRIUM
(5036).
001 **Vita Plotini**, ed. P. Henry and H.-R. Schwyzer,
Plotini opera, vol. 1. Leiden: Brill, 1951: 1–41.
Cod: 8,123: Biogr.
002 **Vita Pythagorae**, ed. A. Nauck, *Porphyrii
philosophi Platonici opuscula selecta*, 2nd edn.
Leipzig: Teubner, 1886 (repr. Hildesheim:
Olms, 1963): 17–52.
Cod: 6,077: Biogr., Phil.
003 **De abstinentia**, ed. Nauck, *op. cit.*, 85–269.
Cod: 36,196: Phil.
004 **De antro nympharum**, ed. Seminar Classics
609, *Porphyry. The cave of the nymphs in the
Odyssey [Arethusa Monographs* 1. Buffalo: De-
partment of Classics, State University of New
York, 1969]: 2–34.
Cod: 4,993: Comm.
005 **Ad Marcellam**, ed. W. Pötscher, *Porphyrios.*
Πρὸς Μαρκέλλαν. Leiden: Brill, 1969: 6–38.
Cod: 4,676: Phil., Epist.
006 **Isagoge sive quinque voces**, ed. A. Busse, *Porphyrii isagoge et in Aristotelis categorias commentarium [Commentaria in Aristotelem
Graeca* 4.1. Berlin: Reimer, 1887]: 1–22.
Cod: 5,907: Phil., Comm.
007 **In Aristotelis categorias expositio per interro-
gationem et responsionem**, ed. Busse, *op. cit.*,
55–142.
Cod: 31,264: Phil., Comm.
008 **Sententiae ad intelligibilia ducentes**, ed. E.
Lamberz, *Porphyrii sententiae ad intelligibilia
ducentes.* Leipzig: Teubner, 1975: 1–59.
Cod: 7,813: Phil., Gnom.
009 **In Platonis Timaeum commentaria** (fragmenta), ed. A.R. Sodano, *Porphyrii in Platonis
Timaeum commentariorum fragmenta.* Naples:
n.p., 1964: 1–48, 60–69.
Cod: 10,834: Exeget., Comm.
010 **Chronica**, FHG 3: 689–702, 706–707, 711–
717, 719–725.
Q: 5,886: Hist., Chronogr.

011 **De philosophia ex oraculis**, ed. G. Wolff, *Porphyrii de philosophia ex oraculis haurienda.* Berlin: Springer, 1856 (repr. Hildesheim: Olms, 1962): 109–185.
Cod: 3,921: Phil., Orac.

012 Περὶ ἀγαλμάτων, ed. J. Bidez, *Vie de Porphyre le philosophe néo-platonicien.* Leipzig: Teubner, 1913 (repr. Hildesheim: Olms, 1964): *1–*23.
Cod: 3,106: Phil.

013 **Epistula ad Anebonem**, ed. A.R. Sodano, *Porfirio. Lettera ad Anebo.* Naples: L'Arte Tipografica, 1958: 1–31.
Cod: 3,924: Epist., Phil.

014 **Quaestionum Homericarum ad Iliadem pertinentium reliquiae**, ed. H. Schrader, *Porphyrii quaestionum Homericarum ad Iliadem pertinentium reliquiae*, fasc. 1 & 2. Leipzig: Teubner, 1:1880; 2:1882: 1:1–180; 2:183–278.
Cod: 69,704: Comm.

015 **Zetemata codicis Vaticani**, ed. Schrader, *Porphyrii quaestionum Homericarum ad Iliadem pertinentium reliquiae*, fasc. 2, 281–335.
Cod: 12,704: Comm.

016 **Quaestionum Homericarum ad Odysseam pertinentium reliquiae**, ed. H. Schrader, *Porphyrii quaestionum Homericarum ad Odysseam pertinentium reliquiae.* Leipzig: Teubner, 1890: 1–134.
Cod: 26,018: Comm.

017 **Quaestionum Homericarum liber i** (recensio V), ed. A.R. Sodano, *Porphyrii quaestionum Homericarum liber i.* Naples: Giannini, 1970: 1–134.
Cod: 12,995: Comm.

018 **Quaestionum Homericarum liber i** (recensio X), ed. Sodano, *Porphyrii quaestionum Homericarum liber i*, 3–37, 39–134.
Cod: 12,508: Comm.

019 **Quaestionum Homericarum liber i** (recensio T), ed. Sodano, *Porphyrii quaestionum Homericarum liber i*, 86–89, 95–97.
Cod: 158: Comm.

020 **Quaestionum Homericarum liber i** (recensio B), ed. Sodano, *Porphyrii quaestionum Homericarum liber i*, 86–89, 95–97.
Cod: 124: Comm.

021 Εἰς τὰ ἁρμονικὰ Πτολεμαίου ὑπόμνημα, ed. I. Düring, *Porphyrios. Kommentar zur Harmonielehre des Ptolemaios.* Göteborg: Elanders, 1932: 3–174.
Cod: 58,903: Comm., Mus.

022 **Commentarium in Platonis Timaeum** (fragmentum incertum), ed. Sodano, *Porphyrii in Platonis Timaeum commentariorum fragmenta*, 116–118.
Cod: 290: Comm., Phil.

023 **Contra Christianos** (fragmenta), ed. A. von Harnack, *Porphyrius. Gegen die Christen [Abhandlungen der königlich preussischen Akademie der Wissenschaften*, Philosoph.-hist. Kl. 1.

Berlin: Reimer, 1916]: 45, 47–51, 54–67, 75–85, 87–94, 96–103.
Dup. partim 2034 025.
Q: 10,420: Phil.

024 **Testimonia**, FGrH #260: 2B:1197–1198.
NQ: 140: Test.

025 **Fragmenta**, FGrH #260: 2B:1208–1213, 1220–1229.
Dup. partim 2034 023, 027.
Q: 5,343: Hist., Phil.

026 **Symmikta zetemata** (fragmenta), ed. H. Dörrie, *Porphyrios. Symmikta Zetemata [Zetemata 20.* Munich: Beck, 1959]: passim.
Q

027 **Historia philosophiae** (fragmenta), ed. Nauck, *op. cit.*, 4–16.
Dup. partim 2034 025.
Q: 1,928: Hist., Phil.

028 **Introductio in tetrabiblum Ptolemaei**, ed. A. Boer and S. Weinstock, *Codices Romani [Catalogus codicum astrologorum Graecorum 5.4.* Brussels: Academia, 1940]: 190–228.
Cod

029 **In Platonis Parmenidem commentaria** (fragmenta), ed. P. Hadot, *Porphyre et Victorinus*, vol. 2. Paris: Études Augustiniennes, 1968: 64–112.
Cod: 3,498: Phil., Comm.

x01 **Ad Gaurum quomodo animetur fetus.** Kalbfleisch, pp. 33–62.
Cf. Pseudo-GALENUS Med. (0530 006).

0500 **POSIDIPPUS** Comic.
3 B.C.

001 **Fragmenta**, ed. T. Kock, *Comicorum Atticorum fragmenta*, vol. 3. Leipzig: Teubner, 1888: 335–348.
frr. 1–7, 9–34, 36–44.
Q: 641: Comic.

002 **Fragmenta**, ed. A. Meineke, *Fragmenta comicorum Graecorum*, vol. 4. Berlin: Reimer, 1841 (repr. De Gruyter, 1970): 513–521, 523–527.
Q: 599: Comic.

003 **Fragmentum**, ed. C. Austin, *Comicorum Graecorum fragmenta in papyris reperta.* Berlin: De Gruyter, 1973: 203–204.
fr. 218 + titulus.
Pap: 56: Comic.

POSIDIPPUS Eleg.
3 B.C.: Thebanus
Cf. POSIDIPPUS Epigr. (1632 004).

1632 **POSIDIPPUS** Epigr.
fiq Posidippus Hist.
3 B.C.: Pellaeus
Cf. et POSIDIPPUS Hist. (2310).

001 **Epigrammata**, AG 5.134, 183, 186, 194, 202, 209, 211, 213; 7.170, 267; 9.359; 12.45, 77, 98, 120, 131, 168; 16.68, 119, 275.
AG 5.215: Cf. MELEAGER Epigr. (1492 001).

AG 12.17: Cf. ANONYMI EPIGRAMMATICI
(AG) (0138 001).
Q: 777: Epigr.

002 **Epigrammata** (*P. Didot* 28–34), ed. D.L. Page,
Select papyri, vol. 3 [*Literary papyri*]. Cambridge, Mass.: Harvard University Press, 1941
(repr. 1970): 444–448.
fr. 104.
Pap: Epigr.

004 **Fragmenta et tituli**, ed. H. Lloyd-Jones and P.
Parsons, *Supplementum Hellenisticum*. Berlin:
De Gruyter, 1983: 338, 340–341, 343.
frr. 698–700, 705–706.
fr. 705: *P. Berol.* 17 (= *Tabula cerata Berol.*
14283).
Q, Pap: 197: Eleg., Epigr.

x01 **Epigrammata** (*App. Anth.*).
Epigramma dedicatorium: 1.116.
Epigrammata demonstrativa: 3.77–81.
Epigramma irrisorium: 5.15.
App. Anth. 1.116: Cf. ANTHOLOGIAE GRAE-
CAE APPENDIX (7052 001).
App. Anth. 3.77–81: Cf. ANTHOLOGIAE
GRAECAE APPENDIX (7052 003).
App. Anth. 5.15: Cf. ANTHOLOGIAE GRAE-
CAE APPENDIX (7052 005).

x02 **Fragmentum elegiacum** (*P. Lit. Lond.* 60)
(fort. auctore Posidippo).
SH, pp. 463–464, fr. 961.
Cf. ADESPOTA PAPYRACEA (SH) (2648 002).

x03 **Epigrammata** [Dub.] (*P. Cairo* inv. 65445).
SH, pp. 491, 493, frr. 978–979.
Cf. ADESPOTA PAPYRACEA (SH) (2648 003).

2310 **POSIDIPPUS** Hist.
fiq Posidippus Pellaeus
4–3 B.C.?
Cf. et POSIDIPPUS Epigr. (1632).
001 **Fragmenta**, FGrH #447: 3B:376.
Q: 146: Hist.

2639 **POSIDONIUS** Epic.
ante A.D. 2: Corinthius
001 **Titulus**, ed. H. Lloyd-Jones and P. Parsons,
Supplementum Hellenisticum. Berlin: De Gruyter, 1983: 344.
fr. 709.
NQ: 2: Epic.

1964 **POSIDONIUS** Hist.
2 B.C.
001 **Fragmenta**, FGrH #169: 2B:893–894.
Q: 227: Hist.

2187 **POSIDONIUS** Hist.
A.D. 2?: Olbiopolitanus
001 **Testimonia**, FGrH #279: 3A:158.
NQ: 90: Test.

1866 **POSIDONIUS** Med.
A.D. 4–5?
x01 **Fragmenta** ap. Aëtium (lib. 6).

CMG, vol. 8.2, pp. 125, 133, 147, 150, 152,
158, 159.
Cf. AËTIUS Med. (0718 006).

1052 **POSIDONIUS** Phil.
2–1 B.C.: Apamensis, Rhodius
001 **Fragmenta**, ed. W. Theiler, *Posidonios. Die
Fragmente*, vol. 1. Berlin: De Gruyter, 1982:
16–72, 75–238, 242–244, 255–269, 279–280,
285, 290–297, 307, 310–346, 348–350, 354–
357, 375–386.
Dup. partim 1052 003.
Q: 106,815: Phil., Hist., Geogr., Nat. Hist.,
Math., Tact.

002 **Testimonia**, FGrH #87: 2A:222–224.
NQ: 903: Test.

003 **Fragmenta**, FGrH #87: 2A:225–317.
Dup. partim 1052 001.
Q: 36,366: Hist., Geogr., Nat. Hist.

2333 **POSSIS** Hist.
3–2 B.C.?: Magnes
001 **Fragmenta**, FGrH #480: 3B:444.
Q: 95: Hist.
002 **Titulus**, ed. H. Lloyd-Jones and P. Parsons,
Supplementum Hellenisticum. Berlin: De Gruyter, 1983: 344.
fr. 710.
NQ: 3: Hist., Epic.

2544 **Aelius POSTUMIUS ALBINUS** Hist.
2 B.C.: Romanus
001 **Testimonia**, FGrH #812: 3C:881–882.
NQ: 452: Test.
002 **Fragmenta**, FGrH #812: 3C:882–883.
Q: 393: Hist.

1949 **POTAMON** Hist.
1 B.C.–A.D. 1: Mytilenensis
001 **Testimonia**, FGrH #147: 2B:815.
NQ: 183: Test.
002 **Fragmentum**, FGrH #147: 2B:816.
Q: 29: Hist.

0663 **PRAECEPTA SALUBRIA**
fort. auctore Asclepiade Bithynio
1 B.C.?
001 **Praecepta salubria**, ed. U.C. Bussemaker,
Poetae bucolici et didactici. Paris: Didot, 1862:
132–134.
Cod: 614: Med.

0278 **PRAELUSIO MIMI**
A.D. 2
001 **Fragmentum** (*P. Giessen* 1.1), ed. E. Heitsch,
*Die griechischen Dichterfragmente der röm-
ischen Kaiserzeit*, vol. 1, 2nd edn. Göttingen:
Vandenhoeck & Ruprecht, 1963: 46.
Pap: 66: Lyr., Mim.

1053 **PRASION** Med.
ante A.D. 2

x01 **Fragmentum ap. Galenum.**
K13.854.
Cf. GALENUS Med. (0057 077).

1833 **PRATINAS** Trag.
6–5 B.C.: Phliasius
001 **Fragmenta**, ed. B. Snell, *Tragicorum Grae-*
corum fragmenta, vol. 1. Göttingen: Vandenhoeck & Ruprecht, 1971: 81–83.
frr. 1–6.
Dup. 1833 002.
Q: 145: Trag., Lyr., Satyr.
002 **Fragmenta**, ed. D.L. Page, *Poetae melici*
Graeci. Oxford: Clarendon Press, 1962 (repr.
1967 (1st edn. corr.)): 367–369.
frr. 1–5.
Dup. 1833 001.
Q: 135: Trag., Satyr.

2151 **PRAXAGORAS** Hist.
A.D. 4: Atheniensis
001 **Testimonium**, FGrH #219: 2B:948–949.
NQ: 546: Test.

0672 **PRAXAGORAS** Med.
4 B.C.: Cous
x01 **Fragmenta ap. Galenum.**
K2.906 in CMG, vol. 5.2.1, p. 54; K17.2.838;
18.1.7.
Cf. GALENUS Med. (0057 016, 092).

0372 **PRAXILLA** Lyr.
5 B.C.: Sicyonia
001 **Fragmenta**, ed. D.L. Page, *Poetae melici*
Graeci. Oxford: Clarendon Press, 1962 (repr.
1967 (1st edn. corr.)): 387–388, 390.
frr. 1–4, 8.
Q: 67: Lyr., Hymn.

2335 **PRAXION** Hist.
4 B.C.?: fort. Megareus
001 **Fragmentum**, FGrH #484: 3B:448–449.
Q: 36: Hist.

0089 **PRAXIPHANES** Phil.
4–3 B.C.: Mytilenensis, Rhodius
001 **Fragmenta**, ed. F. Wehrli, *Phainias von Eresos.*
Chamaileon. Praxiphanes [*Die Schule des Aris-*
toteles, vol. 9, 2nd edn. Basel: Schwabe, 1969]:
93–100.
Περὶ φιλίας (?): fr. 7.
Grammatica: frr. 8–10, 19.
Περὶ ποιητῶν (?). Περὶ ποιημάτων: frr. 11–16.
Περὶ ἱστορίας: fr. 18.
Commentarium in Homerum: frr. 20–21.
Commentarium in Hesiodum (?): fr. 22a–22b.
Commentarium in Sophoclem (?): fr. 23.
Q, Pap: 1,346: Phil., Gramm.

1633 **PRAXITELES** <Epigr.>
4 B.C.: Cous
001 **Epigramma**, ed. E. Diehl, *Anthologia lyrica*

Graeca, fasc. 1, 3rd edn. Leipzig: Teubner,
1949: 135.
Dup. partim SIMONIDES Lyr. (0261 003) (AG
16.204).
Q: 23: Epigr.

1054 **PRIMION** Med.
ante A.D. 1
x01 **Fragmentum ap. Galenum.**
K13.695.
Cf. GALENUS Med. (0057 077).

1055 **PRISCIANUS** Med.
ante A.D. 4
x01 **Fragmentum ap. Oribasium.**
CMG, vol. 6.2.1, p. 218.
Cf. ORIBASIUS Med. (0722 003).

4014 **PRISCIANUS** Phil.
A.D. 6: Lydus
001 **Metaphrasis in Theophrastum**, ed. I. Bywater,
Prisciani Lydi quae extant [*Commentaria in*
Aristotelem Graeca, suppl. 1.2. Berlin: Reimer,
1886]: 1–37.
Cod: 13,867: Phil., Comm.
x01 **In Aristotelis libros de anima commentaria**
(fort. auctore Prisciano Lydo).
Hayduck, pp. 1–329.
Cf. SIMPLICIUS Phil. (4013 005).

2641 **PRISCUS** Epic.
fiq Clutorius Priscus
1 B.C.–A.D. 1?
001 **Titulus**, ed. H. Lloyd-Jones and P. Parsons,
Supplementum Hellenisticum. Berlin: De Gruyter, 1983: 344.
fr. 710a.
NQ: 2: Epic.

1056 **PROCLUS** Med.
1 B.C.
x01 **Fragmentum ap. Oribasium.**
CMG, vol. 6.3, p. 95.
Cf. ORIBASIUS Med. (0722 004).
x02 **Fragmentum ap. Paulum.**
CMG, vol. 9.2, p. 313.
Cf. PAULUS Med. (0715 001).

4036 **PROCLUS** Phil.
A.D. 5: Atheniensis
001 **In Platonis rem publicam commentarii**, ed. W.
Kroll, *Procli Diadochi in Platonis rem publicam*
commentarii, 2 vols. Leipzig: Teubner, 1:1899;
2:1901 (repr. Amsterdam: Hakkert, 1965): 1:1–
296; 2:1–368.
Cod: 167,711: Phil., Comm.
002 **Hypotyposis astronomicarum positionum**, ed.
C. Manitius, *Procli Diadochi hypotyposis astro-*
nomicarum positionum. Leipzig: Teubner,
1909 (repr. Stuttgart: 1974): 2–238.
Cod: 24,977: Astron.

003 **Epigramma**, AG 7.341.
Dup. partim 4036 017.
Q: 27: Epigr.

004 **Theologia Platonica** (lib. 1–5), ed. D. Saffrey
and L.G. Westerink, *Proclus. Théologie platoni-
cienne*, vols. 1–5. Paris: Les Belles Lettres,
1:1968; 2:1974; 3:1978; 4:1981; 5:1987: **1**:1–
125; **2**:1–73; **3**:1–102; **4**:1–113; **5**.1–148.
Dup. partim 4036 020.
Cod: 124,159: Phil.

005 **Institutio theologica**, ed. E.R. Dodds, *Proclus.
The elements of theology*, 2nd edn. Oxford: Cla-
rendon Press, 1963 (repr. 1977): 2–184.
Cod: 28,278: Phil.

006 **Institutio physica**, ed. A. Ritzenfeld, *Procli
Diadochi Lycii institutio physica*. Leipzig:
Teubner, 1912: 2–58.
Cod: 7,688: Phil.

007 **In Platonis Alcibiadem i**, ed. L.G. Westerink,
*Proclus Diadochus. Commentary on the first
Alcibiades of Plato*. Amsterdam: North-
Holland, 1954: 1–158.
Cod: 68,762: Phil., Comm.

008 **In Platonis Parmenidem**, ed. V. Cousin, *Procli
philosophi Platonici opera inedita*, pt. 3. Paris:
Durand, 1864 (repr. Hildesheim: Olms, 1961):
617–1244.
Cod: 177,636: Phil., Comm.

009 **In Platonis Cratylum commentaria**, ed. G. Pasquali, *Procli Diadochi in Platonis Cratylum
commentaria*. Leipzig: Teubner, 1908: 1–113.
Cod: 28,788: Phil., Comm.

010 **In Platonis Timaeum commentaria**, ed. E.
Diehl, *Procli Diadochi in Platonis Timaeum
commentaria*, 3 vols. Leipzig: Teubner, 1:1903;
2:1904; 3:1906 (repr. Amsterdam: Hakkert,
1965): **1**:1–458; **2**:1–317; **3**:1–358.
Cod: 325,501: Phil., Comm.

011 **In primum Euclidis elementorum librum commentarii**, ed. G. Friedlein, *Procli Diadochi in
primum Euclidis elementorum librum commentarii*. Leipzig: Teubner, 1873: 3–436.
Cod: 84,453: Math., Comm.

012 **De decem dubitationibus circa providentiam**,
ed. H. Boese, *Procli Diadochi tria opuscula*.
Berlin: De Gruyter, 1960: 5–108.
Cod: 13,405: Phil.

013 **De providentia et fato et eo quod in nobis ad
Theodorum mechanicum**, ed. Boese, *op. cit.*,
117–137, 141–155, 159–163, 169–171.
Cod: 5,479: Phil.

014 **De malorum subsistentia**, ed. Boese, *op. cit.*,
173–191, 211–265.
Cod: 9,437: Phil.

015 **Hymni 1–7**, ed. E. Vogt, *Procli hymni*. Wiesbaden: Harrassowitz, 1957: 27–33.
Cod: 1,151: Hymn.

016 **Hymnorum fragmenta**, ed. Vogt, *op. cit.*, 33.
frr. 1–2.
Q: 15: Hymn.

017 **Epigrammata**, ed. Vogt, *op. cit.*, 34.
Epigr. 1: Dup. 4036 003.
Q, Cod: 70: Epigr.

018 **De sacrificio et magia**, ed. J. Bidez, *Catalogue
des manuscrits alchimiques grecs*, vol. 6. Brussels: Lamertin, 1928: 148–151.
Cod: 1,048: Phil.

020 **Excerpta e Platonica Procli theologia**, ed.
Cousin, *op. cit.*, 1243–1258.
Dup. partim 4036 004.
Cod: 3,599: Phil.

021 **Eclogae de philosophia Chaldaica**, ed. É. des
Places, *Oracles chaldaïques*. Paris: Les Belles
Lettres, 1971: 206–212.
Cod: 1,502: Phil., Comm.

022 **Paraphrasis Ptolemaei tetrabiblou** [Dub.], ed.
L. Allacci, *Procli diadochi paraphrasis in Ptole-
maei libros iv de siderum effectionibus*. Leiden:
Elzevir, 1635.
Cod: Comm., Astrol.

023 **Chrestomathia** [Dub.], ed. A. Severyns, *Re-
cherches sur la Chrestomathie de Proclus*, vol. 4.
Paris: Les Belles Lettres, 1963: 67–74, 77–85,
87–97.
Vita Homeri: pp. 67–74.
Cyclicorum enarrationes: pp. 77–85, 87–97.
Dup. partim VITAE HOMERI (1805 003).
Cod

024 **Σφαῖρα**, ed. J. Bainbridge, *Procli sphaera.
Ptolemaei de hypothesibus planetarum liber sin-
gularis*. London, 1620.
Cod

x01 **Prolegomena et scholia in Hesiodi opera et
dies**.
Pertusi, pp. 1–259 passim; Gaisford, pp. 3–9,
23–447 passim.
Cf. SCHOLIA IN HESIODUM (5025 001–002).

x02 **Characteres epistolici**.
Foerster, vol. 9, pp. 27–47.
Cf. LIBANIUS Rhet. et Soph. (2200 008).

x03 **Epigramma demonstrativum**.
App. Anth. 3.166: Cf. ANTHOLOGIAE GRAE-
CAE APPENDIX (7052 003).

4029 **PROCOPIUS** Hist.
A.D. 6: Caesariensis

001 **De bellis**, ed. G. Wirth (post J. Haury), *Procopii Caesariensis opera omnia*, vols. 1–2. Leipzig: Teubner, 1:1962; 2:1963: **1**:1, 4–145, 148–
305, 307–417, 419–552; **2**:1, 4–147, 150–294,
197–484, 487–678.
Lib. 1–2 = De bello Persico, lib. 1–2.
Lib. 3–4 = De bello Vandalico, lib. 1–2.
Lib. 5–8 = De bello Gothico, lib. 1–4.
Cod: 231,931: Hist.

002 **Historia arcana** (= **Anecdota**), ed. Wirth (post
Haury), *op. cit.*, vol. 3 (1963): 1, 4–186.
Cod: 33,481: Hist.

003 **De aedificiis** (lib. 1–6), ed. Wirth (post Haury),
op. cit., vol. 4 (1964): 1, 5–186.
Cod: 37,272: Hist.

2598 **PROCOPIUS** Rhet. et Scr. Eccl.
A.D. 5–6: Gazaeus

001 **Catena in Octateuchum**, MPG 87.1: 21–1220.
Cod: Caten.

002 **Catena in Canticum canticorum**, MPG 87.2: 1545–1753.
Cod: Caten.

003 **Catena in Ecclesiasten** (e cod. Marc. 22), ed. S. Leanza, *Procopii Gazaei catena in Ecclesiasten necnon Pseudochrysostomi commentarius in eundem Ecclesiasten* [*Corpus Christianorum. Series Graeca* 4. Turnhout: Brepols, 1978]: 5–39.
Cod: Caten.

004 **Catena in Isaiam**, MPG 87.2: 1817–2717.
Cod: Caten.

005 **Epistulae 1–166**, ed. A. Garzya and R.J. Loenertz, *Procopii Gazaei epistolae et declamationes* [*Studia patristica et Byzantina* 9. Ettal: Buch-Kunstverlag, 1963]: 3–80.
Cod: Epist.

006 **Epistula** (e cod. Barocciano gr. 131), ed. L.G. Westerink, "Ein unbekannter Brief des Prokopios von Gaza," *Byzantinische Zeitschrift* 60 (1967) 2.
Cod: Epist.

008 **Declamationes**, ed. Garzya and Loenertz, *op. cit.*, 83–98.
Cod: Rhet.

009 **Descriptio imaginis**, ed. P. Friedländer, *Spätantiker Gemäldezyklus in Gaza* [*Studi e testi* 89. Vatican City: Biblioteca Apostolica Vaticana, 1939]: 5–19.
Cod: Rhet.

010 **Horologium**, ed. H. Diels, "Über die von Prokop beschriebene Kunstuhr von Gaza," *Abhandlungen der königlich preussischen Akademie der Wissenschaften*, Philosoph.-hist. Kl. 26.7 (Berlin: Reimer, 1917): 27–39.
Cod: Rhet.

011 **Panegyricus in Anastasium imperatorem**, ed. C. Kempen, *Procopii Gazaei in imperatorem Anastasium panegyricus*. Bonn: Georg, 1918: 1–17.
Cod: Encom.

012 **Refutatio Procli** (fragmentum e cod. Vat. gr. 1096), ed. A. Mai, *Classici auctores e Vaticanis codicibus editi*, vol. 4. Rome: Biblioteca Apostolica Vaticana, 1831: 274–275.
Cod: Phil., Theol.

013 **Στίχων Ὁμηρικῶν μεταφράσεις**, ed. A. Brinkmann, "Die Homermetaphrasen des Prokopios von Gaza," *Rheinisches Museum* 63 (1908) 618–623.
Cod: Rhet.

014 **Commentarii in proverbia** [Sp.], MPG 87.1: 1221–1544.
Cod: Exeget.

015 **Fragmenta in Canticum** [Sp.], MPG 87.2: 1756–1780.
Cod: Exeget., Caten.

018 **Orationes deperditae** (fragmenta), ed. I. Bekker, *Anecdota Graeca*, vol. 1. Berlin: Nauck, 1814 (repr. Graz: Akademische Druck-

und Verlagsanstalt, 1965): 125, 133, 135, 139, 153, 169.
Cod: Rhet.

019 **Epistula** (e cod. Escur. gr. 234), ed. E.V. Maltese, "Un'epistola inedita di Procopio di Gaza," *La parola del passato* 39 (1984) 53–54.
Cod: Epist.

x01 **Descriptio basilicae sanctae Sophiae** [Sp.].
Wirth, vol. 4, pp. 8–17.
Cf. PROCOPIUS Hist. (4029 003).

1634 **PRODICUS** Soph.
5–4 B.C.: Ceus

001 **Testimonia**, ed. H. Diels and W. Kranz, *Die Fragmente der Vorsokratiker*, vol. 2, 6th edn. Berlin: Weidmann, 1952 (repr. Dublin: 1966): 308–312.
test. 1–20.
NQ: 1,488: Test.

002 **Fragmenta**, ed. Diels and Kranz, *op. cit.*, 312–319.
frr. 1–11.
Q: 1,903: Phil., Rhet.

2721 **Theodorus PRODROMUS** Polyhist. et Poeta
vel Theodorus Ptochoprodromus vel Theodorus Protoprodromus
A.D. 11–12: Constantinopolitanus

001 **Epithalamium fortunatissimis imperatoris filiis**, ed. P. Gautier, *Nicéphore Bryennios. Histoire* [*Corpus fontium historiae Byzantinae* 9. Series Bruxellensis. Brussels: Byzantion, 1975]: 341–355.
Cod: Encom.

002 **Epitaphius in Theodoram nurum Bryennii**, ed. Gautier, *op. cit.*, 355–367.
Cod: Iamb.

x01 **Epigramma irrisorium**.
App. Anth. 5.78: Cf. ANTHOLOGIAE GRAECAE APPENDIX (7052 005).

x02 **Carmen astronomicum** (olim sub auctore Theodoro Prodromo).
Miller, pp. 8–39.
Cf. Constantinus MANASSES Poeta et Hist. (3074 003).

x03 **In Aristotelis analytica posteriora ii** (fragmenta).
Brandis, *Aristotelis opera*, vol. 4, p. 241a.
Cf. ANONYMI IN ARISTOTELIS ANALYTICA POSTERIORA (4191 002).

x04 **Περὶ γραμματικῆς** (fort. auctore Theodoro Prodromo).
Göttling, pp. 1–197.
Cf. THEODOSIUS Gramm. (2020 003).

x05 **Περὶ τόνου** (fort. auctore Theodoro Prodromo).
Göttling, pp. 198–201.
Cf. THEODOSIUS Gramm. (2020 004).

1057 **PROËCHIUS** Med.
fiq Proëchius Arsinoeticus Episcopus
A.D. 5

x01 **Fragmentum ap. Paulum.**

CMG, vol. 9.2, p. 339.
Cf. PAULUS Med. (0715 001).

2300 **PROMATHIDAS** Hist.
4–3 B.C.: fort. Heracleota
001 **Testimonia**, FGrH #430: 3B:325.
NQ: 31: Test.
002 **Fragmenta**, FGrH #430: 3B:325–327.
frr. 1–6: Promathidas.
frr. 7–8: Promathidas Junior.
Q: 740: Hist.
003 **Titulus**, ed. H. Lloyd-Jones and P. Parsons,
Supplementum Hellenisticum. Berlin: De Gruyter, 1983: 345.
fr. 711 (auctore Promathida vel Promathida
Juniore).
NQ: 2: Iamb.

PROMATHIDAS Junior Hist.
1 B.C.
Cf. PROMATHIDAS Hist. (2300 002–003).

2548 **PROMATHION** Hist.
3 B.C.?
001 **Fragmentum**, FGrH #817: 3C:893–894.
Q: 215: Hist.

0397 **PRONOMUS** Lyr.
5 B.C.: Thebanus
001 **Titulus**, ed. D.L. Page, *Poetae melici Graeci*.
Oxford: Clarendon Press, 1962 (repr. 1967 (1st
edn. corr.)): 396.
NQ: 4: Lyr., Hymn.

2729 **PRORUS** Phil.
5 B.C.: Cyrenaeus
001 **Titulus**, ed. H. Thesleff, *The Pythagorean texts
of the Hellenistic period*. Åbo: Åbo Akademi,
1965: 154.
Cf. et <CLINIAS> Phil. (1277 002).
NQ: 4: Phil.

1790 **PROTAGORAS** Astrol.
fiq Protagoras Cyzicenus
3 B.C.: Nicaeensis
001 **Fragmenta**, ed. D. Bassi, F. Cumont, A. Martini and A. Olivieri, *Codices Italici [Catalogus
codicum astrologorum Graecorum* 4. Brussels:
Lamertin, 1903]: 150–151.
Cod

1635 **PROTAGORAS** Soph.
5 B.C.: Abderita
001 **Testimonia**, ed. H. Diels and W. Kranz, *Die
Fragmente der Vorsokratiker*, vol. 2, 6th edn.
Berlin: Weidmann, 1952 (repr. Dublin: 1966):
253–262.
test. 1–30.
NQ: 3,814: Test.
002 **Fragmenta**, ed. Diels and Kranz, *op. cit.*, 262–
268.
frr. 1–10.
Q: 1,039: Phil.

003 **Fragmentum**, ed. J. Mejer, "The alleged new
fragment of Protagoras," *Hermes* 100.2 (1972)
175.
Q: 20: Phil.

1636 **PROTAGORIDES** Hist.
2 B.C.?: Cyzicenus
001 **Testimonia**, FGrH #853: 3C:937.
NQ: 56: Test.
002 **Fragmenta**, FGrH #853: 3C:937.
Q: 208: Hist.

1058 **PROTEUS** Med.
ante A.D. 2
x01 **Fragmentum ap. Galenum.**
K12.787.
Cf. GALENUS Med. (0057 076).
x02 **Fragmentum ap. Paulum.**
CMG, vol. 9.2, p. 343.
Cf. PAULUS Med. (0715 001).

1637 ***PROTEVANGELIUM JACOBI***
A.D. 2
001 **Protevangelium Jacobi**, ed. É. Strycker, *La
forme la plus ancienne du protévangile de
Jacques*. Brussels: Société des Bollandistes,
1961: 64–190.
Textus omnibus testibus communis (cap. 1.1–
37.14, 42.7–49.17): pp. 64–146, 172–190.
Textus Z (= *P. Bodmer* 5) + textus omnibus
testibus communis (cap. 37.14–16, 38.1–42.7):
pp. 146, 152–172.
Textus ceterorum testium + textus omnibus
testibus communis (cap. 37a.1–42a.23): pp.
148–172.
Cod, Pap: 5,138: Evangel., Apocryph.

1638 **PROXENUS** Hist.
3 B.C.: Epirota
001 **Fragmenta**, FGrH #703: 3C:556–560.
Q: 990: Hist.

2297 **PROXENUS** Hist.
3 B.C.?: Chalcidensis
001 **Fragmenta**, FGrH #425: 3B:322.
Q: 64: Hist.

1059 **PROXENUS** Med.
ante A.D. 1
x01 **Fragmentum ap. Galenum.**
K13.61.
Cf. GALENUS Med. (0057 076).

PSALMUS NAASSENUS
Heitsch, vol. 1, pp. 155–156.
Cf. HYMNI ANONYMI (0742 001).

1914 **PSAON** Hist.
3 B.C.: Plataeeus
001 **Testimonia**, FGrH #78: 2A:158–159.
NQ: 143: Test.

PSELLUS Epigr.
fiq Michael Psellus
AG 14.5, 35, 58.
Cf. ANONYMI EPIGRAMMATICI (AG) (0138 001).

2702 **Michael PSELLUS** Polyhist.
vel Constantinus Psellus vel Constantius Psellus vel Michael Psellus Minor
A.D. 11: Constantinopolitanus
001 **Chronographia**, ed. É. Renauld, *Michel Psellos. Chronographie ou histoire d'un siècle de Byzance (976–1077)*, 2 vols. Paris: Les Belles Lettres, 1:1926; 2:1928 (repr. 1967): 1:1–154; 2:1–185.
Cod: 78,393: Hist.
x01 **Epigrammata** (*App. Anth.*).
Epigramma demonstrativum: 3.267.
Problemata: 7.34–45.
App. Anth. 3.267: Cf. ANTHOLOGIAE GRAECAE APPENDIX (7052 003).
App. Anth. 7.34–45: Cf. ANTHOLOGIAE GRAECAE APPENDIX (7052 007).

PSEUDEPICHARMEA
Cf. EPICHARMUS Comic. et PSEUDEPICHARMEA (0521).

1639 **PSEUDO-AUCTORES HELLENISTAE** (in PsVTGr)
Varia
001 **Fragmenta**, ed. A.-M. Denis, *Fragmenta pseudepigraphorum quae supersunt Graeca [Pseudepigrapha veteris testamenti Graece* 3. Leiden: Brill, 1970]: 161–173.
Aeschylus: pp. 161–162.
Sophocles: pp. 162–163, 167–168, 173.
Euripides: pp. 163, 171.
Orpheus: pp. 163–167.
Pythagoras: p. 167.
Diphilus: pp. 168–169, 171.
Menander: pp. 169–170.
Hesiodus: p. 173.
(Hesiodus), Homerus, Callimachus/Linus: pp. 171–172.
Q: 2,081: Trag., Comic., Phil., Epic., Hexametr.

PSEUDO-CALLISTHENES
A.D. 3?
Cf. HISTORIA ALEXANDRI MAGNI (1386).

PTOCHOPRODROMICA
A.D. 11–12
Cf. Theodorus PRODROMUS Polyhist. et Poeta (2721).

Theodorus PTOCHOPRODROMUS Polyhist.
A.D. 11–12
Cf. Theodorus PRODROMUS Polyhist. et Poeta (2721).

0050 **PTOLEMAEI II PHILADELPHI ET ELEAZARI EPISTULAE**
Incertum
001 **Epistulae**, ed. R. Hercher, *Epistolographi Graeci*. Paris: Didot, 1873 (repr. Amsterdam: Hakkert, 1965): 599–600.
Q: 443: Epist.

1640 **PTOLEMAEUS** Epigr.
ante 1 B.C.
001 **Epigramma**, AG 7.314.
Q: 17: Epigr.

1641 **PTOLEMAEUS** Gnost.
A.D. 2
001 **Epistula ad Floram**, ed. G. Quispel, *Ptolémée. Lettre à Flora*, 2nd edn. [*Sources chrétiennes* 24 bis. Paris: Cerf, 1966]: 50–72.
Q: 2,124: Epist.

1643 **PTOLEMAEUS** Gramm.
2 B.C./A.D. 2: Ascalonita
001 **Περὶ προσῳδίας Ὁμηρικῆς** (fragmenta), ed. M. Baege, *De Ptolemaeo Ascalonita [Diss. Halle* (1883)]: 173–198.
Q
002 **Fragmenta**, ed. Baege, *op. cit.*, 198–200.
Περὶ μέτρων: p. 198.
Περὶ τῆς Κρατητείου αἱρέσεως: p. 198.
Fragmenta incertae sedis: pp. 199–200.
Q
003 **Περὶ διαφορᾶς λέξεων**, ed. H. Heylbut, "Ptolemaeus περὶ διαφορᾶς λέξεων," *Hermes* 22 (1887) 388–410.
Cod

1646 **PTOLEMAEUS** Hist.
3–2 B.C.: Megalopolitanus
001 **Testimonia**, FGrH #161: 2B:887.
NQ: 142: Test.
002 **Fragmenta**, FGrH #161: 2B:888.
Q: 166: Hist.

1991 **PTOLEMAEUS** Hist.
1 B.C.–A.D. 1
001 **Fragmentum**, FGrH #199: 2B:930.
Q: 59: Hist.

1647 **PTOLEMAEUS** Hist.
ante A.D. 1: Mendesicus
001 **Testimonia**, FGrH #611: 3C:118.
NQ: 152: Test.
002 **Fragmenta**, FGrH #611: 3C:119.
Q: 208: Hist., Chronogr.

0363 **Claudius PTOLEMAEUS** Math.
A.D. 2: Alexandrinus
001 **Syntaxis mathematica**, ed. J.L. Heiberg, *Claudii Ptolemaei opera quae exstant omnia*, vols. 1.1–1.2. Leipzig: Teubner, 1.1:1898; 1.2:1903: 1.1:3–546; 1.2:1–608.
Cod: 229,217: Math.

002 **Phaseis**, ed. Heiberg, *op. cit.*, vol. 2 (1907): 3–67.
Cod: 9,913: Astron.

003 **Hypotheses**, ed. Heiberg, *op. cit.*, vol. 2, 70–106.
Cod: 4,497: Astron.

004 **Inscriptio Canobi**, ed. Heiberg, *op. cit.*, vol. 2, 149–155.
Cod: 1,217: Astron.

005 Προχείρων κανόνων διάταξις καὶ ψηφοφορία, ed. Heiberg, *op. cit.*, vol. 2, 159–185.
Cod: 5,257: Astron.

006 **De analemmate**, ed. Heiberg, *op. cit.*, vol. 2, 194–216.
Cod: 2,375: Astron.

007 **Apotelesmatica** (= **Tetrabiblos**), ed. F. Boll and E. Boer, *Claudii Ptolemaei opera quae exstant omnia*, vol. 3.1. Leipzig: Teubner, 1940 (repr. 1957): 1–213.
Cod: 40,328: Astrol.

008 **De judicandi facultate et animi principatu**, ed. F. Lammert, *Claudii Ptolemaei opera quae exstant omnia*, vol. 3.2, 2nd edn. Leipzig: Teubner, 1961: 3–25.
Cod: 4,153: Phil.

009 **Geographia** (lib. 1–3), ed. K. Müller, *Claudii Ptolemaei geographia*, vol. 1.1. Paris: Didot, 1883: 1–570.
Cf. et 0363 014.
Cod: 36,012: Geogr.

010 **Harmonica**, ed. I. Düring, *Die Harmonielehre des Klaudios Ptolemaios* [*Göteborgs Högskolas Årsskrift* 36. Göteborg: Elanders, 1930]: 2–111.
Cod: 29,782: Mus.

011 **Musica**, ed. K. Jan, *Musici scriptores Graeci*. Leipzig: Teubner, 1895 (repr. Hildesheim: Olms, 1962): 411–420.
Cod: 1,156: Mus.

012 **Fragmenta**, ed. Heiberg, *op. cit.*, vol. 2, 263–270.
frr. 1–8.
Q: 1,555: Math., Mech.

013 **Epigramma**, AG 9.577.
Q: 25: Epigr.

014 **Geographia** (lib. 4–8), ed. C.F.A. Nobbe, *Claudii Ptolemaei geographia*, vols. 1–2. Leipzig: Teubner, 1:1843; 2:1845 (repr. Hildesheim: Olms, 1966): 1:222–284; 2:1–264.
Cf. et 0363 009.
Cod: 54,611: Geogr.

x01 **Epigramma demonstrativum**.
App. Anth. 3.120: Cf. ANTHOLOGIAE GRAECAE APPENDIX (7052 003).

1642 **Pseudo-PTOLEMAEUS**
post A.D. 2

001 **Fructus sive centiloquium**, ed. E. Boer, *Claudii Ptolemaei opera quae exstant omnia*, vol. 3.2, 2nd edn. Leipzig: Teubner, 1961: 37–61.
Cod: 2,806: Astrol.

1060 **PTOLEMAEUS** Med.
2–1 B.C.: Cyrenaeus

x01 **Fragmenta ap. Galenum**.
K12.584, 789; **13**.101, 849.
Cf. GALENUS Med. (0057 076–077).

1644 **PTOLEMAEUS** Phil. et Gramm.
A.D. 1–2: Chennus

001 Καινὴ ἱστορία (fragmenta), ed. A. Chatzis, *Der Philosoph und Grammatiker Ptolemaios Chennos*. Paderborn: Schöningh, 1914 (repr. New York: Johnson Reprint, 1967): 10–45.
Q

002 **Fragmenta**, ed. Chatzis, *op. cit.*, 46–51.
Fragmentum incertae sedis (fr. 1): p. 46.
Fragmenta probabili modo ad Καινὴν ἱστορίαν referenda (frr. 2–7): pp. 46–50.
Fragmenta dubia (frr. 8–11): pp. 50–51.
Q

003 **Reliquarum scriptionum fragmenta**, ed. Chatzis, *op. cit.*, 53–56.
frr. 1–7.
Q

004 **Titulus**, ed. A. Giannini, *Paradoxographorum Graecorum reliquiae*. Milan: Istituto Editoriale Italiano, 1965: 396.
NQ: Paradox.

1944 **PTOLEMAEUS I SOTER** Hist.
4–3 B.C.

001 **Testimonia**, FGrH #138: 2B:752–753.
NQ: 132: Test.

002 **Fragmenta**, FGrH #138: 2B:753–769.
Q: 7,012: Hist.

2693 **PTOLEMAEUS III EUERGETES I** <Epigr.>
3 B.C.

001 **Epigramma**, ed. H. Lloyd-Jones and P. Parsons, *Supplementum Hellenisticum*. Berlin: De Gruyter, 1983: 345.
fr. 712.
Q: 29: Epigr.

x01 **Epigramma demonstrativum**.
App. Anth. 3.39: Cf. ANTHOLOGIAE GRAECAE APPENDIX (7052 003).
Dup. 2693 001.

0604 **PTOLEMAEUS IV PHILOPATOR** Trag.
3 B.C.

001 **Titulus**, ed. B. Snell, *Tragicorum Graecorum fragmenta*, vol. 1. Göttingen: Vandenhoeck & Ruprecht, 1971: 283.
NQ: 1: Trag.

1645 **PTOLEMAEUS VIII EUERGETES II** <Hist.>
2 B.C.

001 **Testimonia**, FGrH #234: 2B:983.
NQ: 39: Test.

002 **Fragmenta**, FGrH #234: 2B:983–987.
Q: 1,058: Hist.

4246 **PTOLEMAEUS** ὁ Ἐπιθέτης Gramm.
2 B.C.: Alexandrinus
001 **Fragmenta grammatica**, ed. F. Montanari, *I frammenti dei grammatici Agathokles, Hellanikos, Ptolemaios Epithetes* [*Sammlung griechischer und lateinischer Grammatiker* 7. Berlin: De Gruyter, 1988]: 89–93.
Q, Pap: Gramm.

1814 **PTOLEMAIS** Phil.
post 4 B.C.: Cyrenensis
001 **Fragmenta de musica**, ed. H. Thesleff, *The Pythagorean texts of the Hellenistic period.* Åbo: Åbo Akademi, 1965: 242–243.
Q: 459: Phil., Mus.

1061 **PUBLIUS** Med.
1 B.C.
x01 **Fragmenta ap. Galenum**.
K13.281, 533, 842, 852.
Cf. GALENUS Med. (0057 076–077).

1062 **PYRAMUS** Med.
ante A.D. 2
x01 **Fragmentum ap. Galenum**.
K12.777.
Cf. GALENUS Med. (0057 076).

2349 **[PYRANDER]** Hist.
vel Pyrandrus
Incertum
001 **Fragmentum**, FGrH #504: 3B:481.
Q: 32: Hist.

1648 **PYRGION** Hist.
ante A.D. 3
001 **Fragmentum**, FGrH #467: 3B:403.
Q: 106: Hist.

2563 **PYRRHO** Hist.
ante A.D. 2: Liparaeus
001 **Fragmentum**, FGrH #836: 3C:903.
Q: 128: Hist.

2160 **PYRRHUS** Hist.
3 B.C.: fort. Epirotes
001 **Fragmenta**, FGrH #229: 2B:973.
Q: 212: Hist.

1649 **PYTHAENETUS** Hist.
3–2 B.C.?
001 **Fragmenta**, FGrH #299: 3B:2–3.
Q: 304: Hist.

0632 **<PYTHAGORAS>** Phil.
6–5 B.C.
001 **Carmen aureum**, ed. D. Young (post E. Diehl), *Theognis.* Leipzig: Teubner, 1971: 86–94.
Cod: 553: Phil., Theol., Hexametr.
002 **Fragmenta**, ed. H. Thesleff, *The Pythagorean texts of the Hellenistic period.* Åbo: Åbo Aka-

demi, 1965: 157–159, 162–165, 168–174, 185–186.
Epigramma, p. 174: Dup. 0632 005.
Q: 1,793: Phil., Epist., Hexametr., Epigr.
004 **Fragmenta astrologica**, ed. J. Heeg, *Codices Romani* [*Catalogus codicum astrologorum Graecorum* 5.3. Brussels: Lamertin, 1910]: 114.
Cf. et 0632 007.
Cod
005 **Epigramma**, AG 7.746.
Dup. partim 0632 002 (p. 174).
Q: 8: Epigr.
006 **Testimonia**, ed. H. Diels and W. Kranz, *Die Fragmente der Vorsokratiker*, vol. 1, 6th edn. Berlin: Weidmann, 1951 (repr. Dublin: 1966): 96–105.
test. 1–21.
NQ: 3,866: Test.
007 **Fragmenta astrologica**, ed. K.O. Zuretti, *Codices Hispanienses* [*Catalogus codicum astrologorum Graecorum* 11.2. Brussels: Lamertin, 1934]: 124–125, 135–138, 139–144.
Cf. et 0632 004.
Cod
x01 **Fragmentum**.
PsVTGr 3.167.
Dup. partim 0632 002 (p. 174).
Cf.   PSEUDO-AUCTORES   HELLENISTAE (PsVTGr) (1639 001).

2239 **PYTHAGORISTAE** (D-K) Phil.
Varia
001 **Testimonia et fragmenta**, ed. H. Diels and W. Kranz, *Die Fragmente der Vorsokratiker*, vol. 1, 6th edn. Berlin: Weidmann, 1951 (repr. Dublin: 1966): 446–480.
Pythagoristae ex Iamblicho: pp. 446–448.
Anonymus Pythagoreus: pp. 448–462.
Ἀκούσματα καὶ σύμβολα: pp. 462–466.
Ἐκ τῶν Ἀριστοξένου Πυθαγορικῶν ἀποφάσεων καὶ Πυθαγορικοῦ βίου: pp. 467–478.
Fragmenta Pythagorica e comoedia media: pp. 478–480.
Q: 14,392: Phil., Comic.

2682 **PYTHEAS** Epigr.
ante A.D. 3: Arcadius
x01 **Epigramma sepulcrale**.
App. Anth. 2.156: Cf. ANTHOLOGIAE GRAECAE APPENDIX (7052 002).

1650 **PYTHEAS** Perieg.
4 B.C.: Massiliensis
001 **Fragmenta**, ed. H.J. Mette, *Pytheas von Massalia.* Berlin: De Gruyter, 1952: 17–29, 34–35.
frr. 1–9b, 14–15.
Q: 3,710: Geogr., Perieg.

1651 **PYTHERMUS** Hist.
3–2 B.C.: Ephesius
001 **Fragmenta**, FGrH #80: 2A:160–161.
Q: 177: Hist.

PYTHERMUS Lyr.
6 B.C.: Teius
PMG, p. 479, fr. 27.
Cf. CARMINA CONVIVIALIA (PMG) (0296 001).

2179 **PYTHEUS-SATYRUS** Hist.
4 B.C.
001 **Testimonium**, FGrH #429: 3B:325.
NQ: 23: Test.
002 **Fragmenta**, FGrH #429: 3B:325.
Q: 78: Hist.

1834 **PYTHION** Med.
ante A.D. 1
x01 **Fragmentum ap. Galenum.**
K13.536.
Cf. GALENUS Med. (0057 077).

1063 **PYTHIUS** Med.
ante A.D. 1
x01 **Fragmentum ap. Galenum.**
K12.879–880.
Cf. GALENUS Med. (0057 076).

2560 **PYTHOCLES** Hist.
Incertum: Samius
001 **Fragmenta**, FGrH #833: 3C:902.
Q: 191: Hist.

0337 **PYTHON** Trag.
4 B.C.
001 **Fragmentum**, ed. B. Snell, *Tragicorum Graecorum fragmenta*, vol. 1. Göttingen: Vandenhoeck & Ruprecht, 1971: 260.
fr. 1.
Q: 119: Satyr.

1652 **QUADRATUS** Apol.
A.D. 2: Atheniensis
x01 **Fragmentum ap. Eusebium.**
HE 4.3.1–2.
Cf. EUSEBIUS Scr. Eccl. et Theol. (2018 002).

1064 **QUADRATUS** Med.
ante A.D. 1
x01 **Fragmentum ap. Galenum.**
K13.1034.
Cf. GALENUS Med. (0057 077).

2046 **QUINTUS** Epic.
A.D. 4: Smyrnaeus
001 **Posthomerica**, ed. F. Vian, *Quintus de Smyrne. La suite d'Homère*, 3 vols. Paris: Les Belles Lettres, 1:1963; 2:1966; 3:1969: 1:12–44, 56–81, 96–126, 136–159; 2:18–44, 67–92, 105–134, 144–163, 180–202; 3.16–36, 48–68, 88–111, 128–151, 176–203.
Cod: 62,202: Epic.
x01 **Epigramma.**
AG 16.92: Cf. ANONYMI EPIGRAMMATICI (AG) (0138 001).

1065 **QUINTUS** Med.
A.D. 2
x01 **Fragmentum ap. Oribasium.**
CMG, vol. 6.3, p. 115.
Cf. ORIBASIUS Med. (0722 004).

1653 **RARUS** Epigr.
Incertum
001 **Epigramma**, AG 10.121.
Q: 41: Epigr.

1068 *RES GESTAE DIVI AUGUSTI*
A.D. 1
001 **Res gestae** (monumentum Ancyranum), ed. H. Volkmann, *Das Monumentum Ancyranum*, 3rd edn. [*Kleine Texte* 29–30. Berlin: De Gruyter, 1969].
Epigr: Hist.

0598 *RHETORICA ANONYMA*
Varia
001 Περὶ μεγαλοπρεπείας (*P. Oxy.* 3.410), ed. L. Radermacher, *Artium scriptores* [Österreichische Akademie der Wissenschaften, Philosoph.-hist. Kl., Sitzungsberichte, Bd. 227, Abh. 3. Vienna: Rohrer, 1951]: 231–232.
Pap: 324: Rhet.
002 Περὶ τρόπων, ed. L. Spengel, *Rhetores Graeci*, vol. 3. Leipzig: Teubner, 1856 (repr. Frankfurt am Main: Minerva, 1966): 227–229.
Cod: 421: Rhet.
003 **Excerpta de arte rhetorica** (olim sub auctore Joanne Doxapatre), ed. C. Walz, *Rhetores Graeci*, vol. 6. Stuttgart: Cotta, 1834 (repr. Osnabrück: Zeller, 1968): 30–32.
Ὅρος τοῦ ἁπλῶς προγυμνάσματος (excerptum e codd. Med. plut. 55.5 + Taur. 230): p. 30.
Ἡ διαίρεσις τῶν ιδ´ στάσεων (excerptum e codd. Med. plut. 55.5 + Taur. 230 + Paris. gr. 817): pp. 31–32.
Cod: Rhet.
004 **Prolegomena in artem rhetoricam**, ed. H. Rabe, *Prolegomenon sylloge* [*Rhetores Graeci* 14. Leipzig: Teubner, 1931]: 14–16.
Cod: Rhet.
005 **Prolegomena in artem rhetoricam** (olim sub auctore Joanne Doxapatre), ed. Rabe, *op. cit.*, 18–43.
Poema Maximi Planudis: p. 43.
Cod: Rhet., Hexametr.
006 **Prolegomena de arte rhetorica**, ed. Rabe, *op. cit.*, 59–64.
Excerptum e cod. Paris. 2977 (pp. 59–60): Dup. partim ANONYMI IN APHTHONIUM (5045 004).
Excerptum e cod. Paris. 1983 (pp. 60–64): Dup. partim ANONYMI IN APHTHONIUM (5045 003).
Cod: Rhet.
007 **Prolegomena in artem rhetoricam**, ed. Walz, *op. cit.*, vol. 6, 33–41.
Cod: Rhet.

008 **Prolegomena de inventione**, ed. Walz, *op. cit.*, vol. 7 (1834; repr. 1968): 52–54.
Cod: Rhet.

009 Σημειῶδες εἰς τὰς εὑρέσεις, ed. Walz, *op. cit.*, vol. 7, 74–76.
Cod: Rhet.

010 **In librum** περὶ ἰδεῶν, ed. Walz, *op. cit.*, vol. 7, 77–89.
Cod: Rhet., Comm.

011 **Progymnasmata**, ed. Walz, *op. cit.*, vol. 1 (1832; repr. 1968): 597–648.
Cod: Rhet.

013 Περὶ τῶν τεσσάρων μερῶν τοῦ τελείου λόγου (e cod. Paris. gr. 2918), ed. Walz, *op. cit.*, vol. 3 (1834; repr. 1968): 570–587.
Cod: Rhet.

014 Περὶ τῶν ὀκτὼ μερῶν τοῦ ῥητορικοῦ λόγου (e cod. Paris. 2918), ed. Walz, *op. cit.*, vol. 3, 588–609.
Cod: Rhet.

015 **Epitome artis rhetoricae** (e cod. Ven. 444), ed. Walz, *op. cit.*, vol. 3, 610–612.
Cod: Rhet.

016 **Epitome artis rhetoricae**, ed. Walz, *op. cit.*, vol. 3, 617–669.
Cod: Rhet., Poem.

017 **Expositio artis rhetoricae**, ed. Walz, *op. cit.*, vol. 3, 725–748.
Cod: Rhet.

018 **Problemata rhetorica in status**, ed. Walz, *op. cit.*, vol. 8 (1835; repr. 1968): 402–413.
Cod: Rhet.

019 Περὶ τῶν τοῦ λόγου σχημάτων, ed. Spengel, *op. cit.*, vol. 3, 110–160.
Cod: Rhet.

020 **De synecdoche**, ed. Walz, *op. cit.*, vol. 8, 691–693.
Cod: Rhet.

021 **De figuris**, ed. Spengel, *op. cit.*, vol. 3, 171–173.
Cod: Rhet.

022 Περὶ τῶν σχημάτων τοῦ λόγου, ed. Spengel, *op. cit.*, vol. 3, 174–188.
Cod: Rhet.

023 Περὶ ποιητικῶν τρόπων, ed. Spengel, *op. cit.*, vol. 3, 207–214.
Cod: Rhet.

0219 **RHIANUS** Epic.
3 B.C.: Benaeus

001 **Fragmenta**, ed. J.U. Powell. Oxford: Clarendon Press, 1925 (repr. 1970): 9–21.
frr. 1, 10, 13, 16, 19–20, 25, 30–32, 34, 36, 38–39, 41, 47, 50–51, 54–58, 60, 66–76 + tituli.
Dup. partim 0219 002–003, 005, x04.
Q: 776: Epic., Epigr.

002 **Epigrammata**, AG **6**.34, 173, 278; **7**.315; **12**.38, 58, 93, 121, 142(?), 146.
Dup. partim 0219 001 (frr. 66–76).
Q: 393: Epigr.

003 **Fragmentum et titulus**, ed. H. Lloyd-Jones and

P. Parsons, *Supplementum Hellenisticum*. Berlin: De Gruyter, 1983: 347.
frr. 715–716.
Dup. partim 0219 001.
Q: 4: Epic.

004 **Testimonia**, FGrH #265: 3A:64.
NQ: 136: Test.

005 **Fragmenta**, FGrH #265: 3A:65–73.
Dup. partim 0219 001.
Q: 2,356: Hist., Epic.

006 **Fragmenta**, ed. H.J. Mette, "Die 'Kleinen' griechischen Historiker heute," *Lustrum* 21 (1978) 24–25.
frr. 41 bis a–b, 41 ter a–b, 41 quater, 47 bis.
fr. 41 ter a–b: *P. Oxy.* 39.2883.
fr. 41 quater: *P. Oxy.* 30.2522.
fr. 47 bis: *P. Oxy.* 27.2463.
Q, Pap: 363: Hist.

x01 **Fragmentum hexametricum** (*P. Oxy.* 30.2522).
SH, pp. 425–426, fr. 923.
Cf. ADESPOTA PAPYRACEA (SH) (2648 001).

x02 **Fragmentum hexametricum** (*P. Oxy.* 39.2883).
SH, p. 447, fr. 946.
Cf. ADESPOTA PAPYRACEA (SH) (2648 001).

x03 **Fragmenta hexametrica** [Dub.] (*P. Oxy.* 37.2819).
SH, pp. 442–445, frr. 941–945.
Cf. ADESPOTA PAPYRACEA (SH) (2648 001).

x04 **Epigramma irrisorium**.
App. Anth. 5.21: Cf. ANTHOLOGIAE GRAECAE APPENDIX (7052 005).
Dup. 0219 001 (fr. 75).

1654 **RHINTHON** Comic.
vel Rhinton
3 B.C.: Syracusanus

001 **Fragmenta**, ed. G. Kaibel, *Comicorum Graecorum fragmenta*, vol. 1.1 [*Poetarum Graecorum fragmenta*, vol. 6.1. Berlin: Weidmann, 1899]: 185–187.
frr. 3, 7, 8, 10, 12 + tituli.
Q: 63: Comic.

002 **Titulus**, ed. C. Austin, *Comicorum Graecorum fragmenta in papyris reperta*. Berlin: De Gruyter, 1973: 204.
NQ: 2: Comic.

1655 **RHODO** Scr. Eccl.
A.D. 2

x01 **Fragmentum ap. Eusebium**.
HE 5.13.2–7.
Cf. EUSEBIUS Scr. Eccl. et Theol. (2018 002).

1067 **RIPALUS** Med.
ante A.D. 2

x01 **Fragmentum ap. Galenum**.
K13.64.
Cf. GALENUS Med. (0057 076).

2881 **ROMANUS MELODUS** Hymnogr.
A.D. 6: Emesenus, Berytensis, Constantinopolitanus

001 **Cantica**, ed. J. Grosdidier de Matons, *Romanos le Mélode. Hymnes*, vols. 1–5 [*Sources chrétiennes* 99, 110, 114, 128, 283. Paris: Cerf, 1:1964; 2:1965; 3:1965; 4:1967; 5:1981]: **1**:70–92, 102–126, 138–164, 172–192, 202–244, 258–292, 306–340, 360–402, 410–426; **2**.20–40, 48–76, 86–110, 118–128, 138–160, 172–196, 204–224, 234–258, 268–292, 300–320, 328–352, 360–378; **3**.20–42, 54–76, 86–100, 110–130, 138–142, 154–178, 198–224, 234–260, 268–270, 278–300, 322–364; **4**.28–52, 68–96, 110–140, 158–186, 202–230, 242–260, 282–310, 324–352, 378–420, 430–450, 458–482, 500–540, 550–562, 576–600; **5**.28–60, 86–122, 136–170, 180–206, 232–266, 296–326, 342–370, 410–452, 470–498, 512–524, 536–540.
Hymn. 1–8 + hymnus de Ninive: vol. 1.
Hymn. 9–20: vol. 2.
Hymn. 21–31: vol. 3.
Hymn. 32–45: vol. 4.
Hymn. 46–56: vol. 5.
Cod: 84,238: Hymn.

002 **Cantica genuina**, ed. P. Maas and C.A. Trypanis, *Sancti Romani Melodi cantica: cantica genuina*. Oxford: Clarendon Press, 1963: 276–280, 294–311, 447–453, 487–510.
Hymn. 35, 38–39, 52, 57–59.
Cod: 8,626: Hymn.

003 **Cantica dubia**, ed. P. Maas and C.A. Trypanis, *Sancti Romani Melodi cantica: cantica dubia*. Berlin: De Gruyter, 1970: 1–185.
Hymn. 60–89.
Cod: 33,387: Hymn.

005 Ἀκάθιστος ὕμνος [Dub.], ed. C.A. Trypanis, *Fourteen early Byzantine cantica* [*Wiener byzantinistische Studien* 5. Vienna: Böhlaus, 1968]: 29–39.
Cod: 1,583: Hymn.

1656 **RUFINUS** Epigr.
A.D. 2: fort. Samius

001 **Epigrammata**, AG 5.9, 12, 14–15, 18–19, 21–22, 27–28, 35–37, 41–44, 47–48, 60–62, 66, 69–71, 73–77, 87–88, 92–94, 97, 103.
AG 5.23: Cf. CALLIMACHUS Philol. (0533 001).
AG 5.50, 90, 95: Cf. ANONYMI EPIGRAMMATICI (AG) (0138 001).
AG 5.89: Cf. Marcus ARGENTARIUS Rhet. et Epigr. (0132 001).
Q: 1,372: Epigr.

4041 **RUF(IN)US** Epigr.
Incertum

001 **Epigramma**, AG 5.284.
Q: 14: Epigr.

2688 **RUFUS** Epigr.
A.D. 3?

x01 **Epigramma sepulcrale.**

App. Anth. 2.625: Cf. ANTHOLOGIAE GRAECAE APPENDIX (7052 002).

2553 **RUFUS** Hist.
A.D. 2–3?

001 **Testimonia**, FGrH #826: 3C:898–899.
NQ: 353: Test.

002 **Fragmentum**, FGrH #826: 3C:899.
Q: 35: Hist.

0564 **RUFUS** Med.
A.D. 1–2: Ephesius

001 **De renum et vesicae morbis**, ed. C. Daremberg and C.É. Ruelle, *Oeuvres de Rufus d'Éphèse*. Paris: Imprimerie Nationale, 1879 (repr. Amsterdam: Hakkert, 1963): 1–63.
Cod: 7,110: Med.

002 **De satyriasmo et gonorrhoea**, ed. Daremberg and Ruelle, *op. cit.*, 64–84.
Cod: 2,399: Med.

003 **De corporis humani appellationibus**, ed. Daremberg and Ruelle, *op. cit.*, 133–167.
Cod: 4,995: Med.

004 **De partibus corporis humani**, ed. Daremberg and Ruelle, *op. cit.*, 168–185.
Cod: 2,334: Med.

005 **De ossibus**, ed. Daremberg and Ruelle, *op. cit.*, 186–194.
Cod: 1,089: Med.

006 **Quaestiones medicinales**, ed. H. Gärtner, *Rufus von Ephesos. Die Fragen des Arztes an den Kranken* [*Corpus medicorum Graecorum, supplementum*, vol. 4. Berlin: Akademie-Verlag, 1962]: 24–46.
Cod: 3,487: Med.

007 **Synopsis de pulsibus**, ed. Daremberg and Ruelle, 219–232.
Cod: 1,860: Med.

x01 **Fragmenta ap. Galenum.**
K12.425; 13.92.
Cf. GALENUS Med. (0057 076).

x02 **Fragmenta ap. Oribasium.**
CMG **6.1.1**, pp. 20, 59, 61, 97, 117, 126, 127, 128, 189, 227, 267, 270, 290, 291, 297; **6.2.1**, pp. 102, 131, 133, 150, 165, 166, 167, 168, 184, 191; **6.2.2**, pp. 43, 106, 109, 117, 136; **6.3**, pp. 8, 14, 16, 17, 19, 92, 108, 119, 120, 148, 162, 199, 236, 237, 266, 328, 496.
Cf. ORIBASIUS Med. (0722 001, 002, 004, 005).

x03 **Fragmenta ap. Paulum.**
CMG **9.1**, pp. 62, 65, 108, 184; **9.2**, p. 287.
Cf. PAULUS Med. (0715 001).

x04 **Fragmenta ap. Aëtium** (lib. 1–3).
CMG 8.1, pp. 121, 180, 183, 265–268, 305, 307, 337.
Cf. AËTIUS Med. (0718 001–003).

x05 **Fragmenta ap. Aëtium** (lib. 5, 6, 8).
CMG 8.2, pp. 82, 146, 151, 410.
Cf. AËTIUS Med. (0718 005, 006, 008).

x06 **Fragmenta ap. Aëtium** (lib. 11).
Daremberg-Ruelle, pp. 87–88, 98–104, 109–112, 113–117, 126.
Cf. AËTIUS Med. (0718 011).

x07 **Fragmenta ap. Aëtium** (lib. 12).
Kostomiris, pp. 47, 48.
Cf. AËTIUS Med. (0718 012).

x08 **Fragmenta ap. Aëtium** (lib. 16).
Zervos, *Gynaekologie des Aëtios*, p. 160.
Cf. AËTIUS Med. (0718 016).

0606 **RUFUS** Soph.
A.D. 2: Perinthius

001 **Ars rhetorica**, ed. L. Spengel, *Rhetores Graeci*, vol. 1. Leipzig: Teubner, 1853 (repr. Frankfurt am Main: Minerva, 1966): 463–470.
Text to be replaced by Hammer edition: cf. 0606 002.
Cod: 1,549: Rhet.

002 **Ars rhetorica**, ed. C. Hammer (post L. Spengel), *Rhetores Graeci*, vol. 1.2. Leipzig: Teubner, 1894: 399–407.
Cod: [1,549]: Rhet.

2546 **Publius RUTILIUS RUFUS** Hist.
2–1 B.C.

001 **Testimonia**, FGrH #815: 3C:887–889.
NQ: 734: Test.

002 **Fragmenta**, FGrH #815: 3C:889–892.
Q: 1,012: Hist.

1066 **SABINUS** Med.
fiq Pompeius Sabinus
A.D. 1–2
Cf. et POMPEIUS SABINUS Med. (1051).

x01 **Fragmentum ap. Galenum.**
K15.25 in CMG, vol. 5.9.1, p. 15.
Cf. GALENUS Med. (0057 085).

x02 **Fragmentum ap. Oribasium.**
CMG, vol. 6.1.2, p. 15.
Cf. ORIBASIUS Med. (0722 001).

3006 **SALLUSTIUS** Gramm. et Soph.
fiq Sallustius Cynicus
A.D. 5

x01 **Hypothesis in Sophoclis Oedipum Coloneum.**
de Marco, pp. 3–4.
Cf. SCHOLIA IN SOPHOCLEM (5037 006).

2049 **SALLUSTIUS** Phil.
A.D. 4

001 **De deis et mundo**, ed. G. Rochefort, *Saloustios. Des dieux et du monde*. Paris: Les Belles Lettres, 1960: 2–25.
Cod: 5,459: Phil.

1825 ***SALOMONIS EPISTULAE***
ante 2 B.C.

x01 **Epistulae.**
FGrH #723, fr. 2.
Cf. EUPOLEMUS Judaeus Hist. (2486 002).

1657 ***SAMIORUM ANNALES***
fort. auctore Aethlio Samio
5–4 B.C.?
Cf. et AETHLIUS Hist. (0686).

001 **Fragmenta**, FGrH #544: 3B:527.
Q: 89: Hist.

1658 **SAMUS** Epigr.
vel Samius
3 B.C.: Macedonius

001 **Epigramma**, AG 6.116.
AG 7.647: Cf. SIMONIDES Lyr. (0261 001).
Q: 35: Epigr.

x01 **Epigramma demonstrativum.**
App. Anth. 3.72: Cf. ANTHOLOGIAE GRAECAE APPENDIX (7052 003).

0501 **SANNYRION** Comic.
5 B.C.

001 **Fragmenta**, ed. T. Kock, *Comicorum Atticorum fragmenta*, vol. 1. Leipzig: Teubner, 1880: 793–795.
frr. 1–4, 6–8, 10–11.
Q: 71: Comic.

002 **Fragmenta**, ed. A. Meineke, *Fragmenta comicorum Graecorum*, vol. 2.2. Berlin: Reimer, 1840 (repr. De Gruyter, 1970): 873–875.
Q: 69: Comic.

003 **Fragmenta**, ed. J. Demiańczuk, *Supplementum comicum*. Krakau: Nakładem Akademii, 1912 (repr. Hildesheim: Olms, 1967): 83.
frr. 1–3.
Q: 5: Comic.

004 **Titulus**, ed. C. Austin, *Comicorum Graecorum fragmenta in papyris reperta*. Berlin: De Gruyter, 1973: 204.
NQ: 2: Comic.

005 **Titulus**, ed. Kock, *CAF*, vol. 3 (1888): 731.
NQ: [1]: Comic.

0009 **SAPPHO** Lyr.
7–6 B.C.: Lesbia
Cf. et SAPPHO et ALCAEUS Lyr. (1815).
Cf. et SAPPHUS vel ALCAEI FRAGMENTA (0387).

001 **Fragmenta**, ed. E. Lobel and D.L. Page, *Poetarum Lesbiorum fragmenta*. Oxford: Clarendon Press, 1955 (repr. 1968 (1st edn. corr.)): 2, 5–68, 70–103, 108–110.
frr. 1–88, 90–192, 210–211, 213.
Q, Pap, Epigr: 5,741: Lyr.

004 **Fragmentis addenda**, ed. Lobel and Page, *op. cit.*, 338–339.
frr. 214, 29(25)+24a.
Pap: 111: Lyr.

002 **Epigrammata**, AG 6.269(?); 7.489, 505.
Q: 71: Epigr.

003 **Fragmenta**, ed. D.L. Page, *Supplementum lyricis Graecis*. Oxford: Clarendon Press, 1974: 74–76, 150.

frr. S259–S261: *P. Oxy.* 32.2637.
fr. S261a: *P. Colon.* 5860.
fr. S476: *P. Colon.* inv. 8.
Pap: 236: Lyr.

1815 SAPPHO et ALCAEUS Lyr.
7–6 B.C.
Cf. et ALCAEUS Lyr. (0383).
Cf. et SAPPHO Lyr. (0009).
Cf. et SAPPHUS vel ALCAEI FRAGMENTA
(0387).
001 **Fragmenta**, ed. D.L. Page, *Supplementum lyricis Graecis.* Oxford: Clarendon Press, 1974: 87–97.
frr. S273–S285: *P. Oxy.* 29.2506.
fr. S286: *P. Mich.* inv. 3498.
Pap: 830: Lyr.

0387 *SAPPHUS vel ALCAEI FRAGMENTA*
7–6 B.C.
Cf. et ALCAEUS Lyr. (0383).
Cf. et SAPPHO Lyr. (0009).
Cf. et SAPPHO et ALCAEUS Lyr. (1815).
001 **Fragmenta**, ed. E. Lobel and D.L. Page, *Poetarum Lesbiorum fragmenta.* Oxford: Clarendon Press, 1955 (repr. 1968 (1st edn. corr.)): 292–297.
frr. 1–8, 10–14, 16–27.
Q, Pap: 177: Lyr.
002 **Fragmenta**, ed. D.L. Page, *Supplementum lyricis Graecis.* Oxford: Clarendon Press, 1974: 98–102.
frr. S287–S312: *P. Oxy.* 39.2878.
Pap: 394: Lyr.

1659 SATRIUS Epigr.
fiq Satyrus
1 B.C.
Cf. et SATYRUS Epigr. (1660).
001 **Epigramma**, AG 6.11.
Q: 35: Epigr.

0608 SATYRUS Biogr.
3/2 B.C.: Oxyrhynchites
001 **Vita Euripidis** (*P. Oxy.* 9.1176), ed. G. Arrighetti, *Satiro. Vita di Euripide.* Pisa: Libreria Goliardica Editrice, 1964: 37–81.
Pap: 3,118: Biogr.
002 **Fragmenta**, FHG 3: 159–164.
Q

1660 SATYRUS Epigr.
1 B.C.
Cf. et SATRIUS Epigr. (1659).
001 **Epigrammata**, AG **10**.6, 11, 13; **16**.153, 195.
Q: 148: Epigr.

1661 SATYRUS Hist.
3 B.C.: Alexandrinus
001 **Fragmentum** (*P. Oxy.* 27.2465), ed. H.J.

Mette, "Die 'Kleinen' griechischen Historiker heute," *Lustrum* 21 (1978) 33–35.
fr. 1b.
Pap: 804: Hist.
002 **Fragmentum**, FGrH #631: 3C:180–182.
Q: 263: Hist.

1069 SATYRUS Med.
A.D. 2
x01 **Fragmentum ap. Galenum**.
K16.524 in CMG, vol. 5.9.2, p. 20.
Cf. GALENUS Med. (0057 088).

1873 SATYRUS "Zeta" Hist.
2 B.C.
001 **Fragmenta**, FGrH #20: 1A:184–185.
Q: 561: Hist., Myth.

1518 Quintus Mucius SCAEVOLA Epigr.
1 B.C.
001 **Epigramma**, AG 9.217.
Q: 41: Epigr.

2330 SCAMON Hist.
4 B.C.: Mytilenensis
001 **Testimonia**, FGrH #476: 3B:435–436.
NQ: 90: Test.
002 **Fragmenta**, FGrH #476: 3B:436–437.
Q: 263: Hist.

5008 *SCHOLIA IN AELIUM ARISTIDEM*
Varia
Cf. et ARETHAS Philol. et Scr. Eccl. (2130 016).
001 **Scholia in Aelium Aristidem** (scholia vetera), ed. W. Dindorf, *Aristides*, vol. 3. Leipzig: Reimer, 1829 (repr. Hildesheim: Olms, 1964): 1–734.
Παναθηναϊκός: pp. 1–343.
Ῥώμης ἐγκώμιον: p. 343.
Ἱεροὶ λόγοι βʹ: pp. 343–344.
Ἱεροὶ λόγοι γʹ: p. 344.
Ἱεροὶ λόγοι δʹ: p. 344.
Ἱεροὶ λόγοι εʹ: p. 344.
Λευκτρικὸς αʹ: pp. 345–353.
Λευκτρικὸς βʹ et hypothesis: pp. 353–355.
Λευκτρικὸς γʹ: p. 355.
Λευκτρικὸς δʹ: p. 356.
Συμμαχικὸς αʹ: p. 356.
Ῥοδιακός: p. 356.
Περὶ ῥητορικῆς: pp. 356–432.
Ὑπερ τῶν τεττάρων: pp. 433–733.
  Hypotheses duo: pp. 433–439.
    Ὑπὲρ Περικλέους: pp. 439–515.
  Κίμων et hypothesis: pp. 515–531.
  Μιλτιάδης et hypothesis: pp. 531–573.
  Θεμιστοκλῆς et hypothesis: pp. 574–733.
Πρὸς Καπίτωνα: pp. 733–734.
Αἰγύπτιος: p. 734.
Cod: Schol., Epigr., Hypoth.

5009 **SCHOLIA IN AESCHINEM**
Varia
001 **Scholia in Aeschinem** (scholia vetera), ed. F.
Schultz, *Aeschinis orationes.* Leipzig: Teubner,
1865 (repr. New York: Arno, 1973): 253–355.
In Timarchum: pp. 253–283.
De falsa legatione: pp. 284–314.
In Ctesiphontem: pp. 315–355.
Cod: 31,936: Schol.

5010 **SCHOLIA IN AESCHYLUM**
Varia
001 **Scholia in Aeschylum** (scholia vetera), ed. O.L.
Smith, *Scholia Graeca in Aeschylum quae ex-
stant omnia,* vols. 1 & 2.2. Leipzig: Teubner,
1:1976; 2.2:1982: **1**:1–83; **2.2**:1–423.
Argumentum et scholia vetera in Agamemno-
nem: vol. 1, pp. 1–14.
Scholia vetera in Choephoros: vol. 1, pp. 15–
41.
Hypothesis et scholia vetera in Eumenides: vol.
1, pp. 42–65.
Scholia vetera in Supplices: vol. 1, pp. 66–83.
Hypotheses in Septem contra Thebas: vol. 2.2,
pp. 1–8.
Versus de Oedipode et eius filiis: vol. 2.2, pp.
8–9.
Scholium de Amphione et Zetho: vol. 2.2, p. 9.
Scholia in Septem contra Thebas: vol. 2.2, pp.
10–423.
Scholia in Eumenides: Dup. partim 5010 023.
Cod: 108,029: Schol., Hypoth.
002 **Scholia prototricliniana in Aeschylum** (scholia
recentiora), ed. Smith, *op. cit.,* vol. 1, 84–94.
In Agamemnonem: pp. 84–89.
In Eumenides: pp. 90–94.
In Eumenides: Dup. partim 5010 023.
Cod: 2,240: Schol.
003 **Scholia in Aeschylum** (scholia recentiora De-
metrii Triclinii), ed. Smith, *op. cit.,* vol. 1, 95–
218.
Hypothesis et scholia in Agamemnonem: pp.
95–206.
Hypothesis et scholia in Eumenides: pp. 207–
218.
Cod: 21,585: Schol., Hypoth.
004 **Scholia in Persas** (scholia vetera), ed. W. Dindorf, *Aeschyli tragoediae superstites et deperditarum fragmenta,* vol. 3 [*Scholia Graeca ex codicibus aucta et emendata*]. Oxford: Oxford
University Press, 1851 (repr. Hildesheim:
Olms, 1962): 70–92.
Hypothesis: pp. 70–71.
Scholia: pp. 71–92.
Dup. partim 5010 006, 010, 011.
Cod: Schol., Hypoth.
005 **Scholia in Prometheum vinctum** (scholia vetera), ed. C.J. Herington, *The older scholia on
the Prometheus bound.* Leiden: Brill, 1972: 59–
242.
Vitae Aeschyli (secundum commentarium A +
supplementa): pp. 59–64.

Argumenta ad Prometheum: pp. 65–66.
Scholia: pp. 67–239.
Epigrammata de Prometheo: pp. 240–241.
Epigramma de Aetna monte: pp. 241–242.
Epigrammata: Dup. partim ANTHOLOGIAE
GRAECAE APPENDIX (7052 003–004).
Cod: 32,577: Schol., Biogr., Hypoth.
006 **Scholia in Persas** (scholia vetera et recentiora
Thomae Magistri et Demetrii Triclinii), ed. L.
Massa Positano, *Demetrii Triclinii in Aeschyli
Persas scholia,* 2nd edn. Naples: Libreria Scien-
tifica Editrice, 1963: 23–128.
Hypothesis Thomae Magistri: pp. 23–28.
Scholia: pp. 28–72.
Glossae: pp. 73–128.
Dup. partim 5010 004, 009.
Cod: Schol., Hypoth.
007 **Scholia in Prometheum vinctum** (scholia re-
centiora Thomae Magistri et Demetrii Tricli-
nii) (e cod. Neapol. II.F.31), ed. H.W. Smyth,
"The commentary on Aeschylus' Prometheus
in the codex Neapolitanus," *Harvard studies in
classical philology* 32 (1921) 3–82.
Argumentum: p. 3.
Scholia: pp. 3–82.
Cod: Schol., Hypoth.
008 **Scholia in Septem contra Thebas** (scholia re-
centiora Demetrii Triclinii), ed. W. Dindorf,
"Über die mediceische Handschrift des
Aeschylus und deren Verhältniss zu den
übrigen Handschriften," *Philologus* 21 (1864)
193–223.
Cod: Schol.
009 **Scholia in Aeschylum** (scholia recentiora), ed.
Dindorf, *Aeschyli tragoediae superstites et deper-
ditarum fragmenta,* vol. 3, 166–512.
Hypothesis ad Prometheum: p. 166.
Scholia in Prometheum: pp. 166–296.
Hypothesis ad Septem contra Thebas: pp. 297–
299.
Scholia in Septem contra Thebas: pp. 299–414.
Hypotheses ad Persas: pp. 415–421.
Scholia in Persas: pp. 421–503.
Scholia in Agamemnonem: pp. 504–510.
Scholia in Eumenides: pp. 511–512.
Scholia in Persas: Dup. partim 5010 006, 021.
Cod: Schol., Hypoth.
010 **Scholia et glossae in Persas** (scholia vetera et
recentiora Thomae Magistri et Demetrii Tri-
clinii) (e cod. Laur. 31.8), ed. Massa Positano,
op. cit., 155–161.
Dup. partim 5010 004.
Cod: Schol.
011 **Scholia in Persas** (scholia vetera) (e cod. Me-
diceo 32.9), ed. O. Dähnhardt, *Scholia in
Aeschyli Persas.* Leipzig: Teubner, 1894: 7, 9,
11–217, 221–275.
Dup. partim 5010 004.
Cod: Schol.
012 **Scholia in Persas** (scholia recentiora), ed. J.
Vitelli and N. Wecklein, *Aeschyli fabulae cum
lectionibus et scholiis codicis Medicei et in Aga-*

memnonem codicis Florentini, vol. 2 [*Persae*].
Berlin: Calvary, 1885: 6, 10, 11, 15, 23, 40, 43,
45, 48.
Scholia ad vv. 64, 127, 138, 229, 372, 379,
730, 776, 820, 893.
Cod: Schol.

014 **Scholia in Septem contra Thebas** (scholia recentiora), ed. Vitelli and Wecklein, *Aeschyli
fabulae cum lectionibus et scholiis codicis Medicei et in Agamemnonem codicis Florentini*,
vol. 3 [*Septem adversus Thebas*] (1885): 3–5, 9,
17, 28, 34, 36–38, 47, 52, 55, 67, 73.
Scholia 2 (glossa), 4, 20, 25, 26, 43, (98), 197,
351, 437, 444, 448, 450, 476, 483, 498, 665,
731, 763, 960, 1046.
Cod: Schol.

017 **Scholia in Eumenides** (scholion recentius), ed.
Vitelli and Wecklein, *Aeschyli fabulae cum lectionibus et scholiis codicis Medicei et in Agamemnonem codicis Florentini*, vol. 7 [*Eumenides*] (1885): 22.
Scholion 341.
Cod: Schol.

018 **Scholia et glossae in Prometheum vinctum**
(scholia recentiora), ed. Vitelli and Wecklein,
*Aeschyli fabulae cum lectionibus et scholiis codi-
cis Medicei et in Agamemnonem codicis Florentini*, vol. 1 [*Prometheus*] (1885): 4–5, 7, 11, 14,
18, 32, 41, 45, 51, 53, 56, 57.
Scholia et glossae 27, 35, 42, 77, 154, 207,
291, 573, 738, 841, 948, 993, 1048, 1079,
1089.
Cod: Schol.

019 **Scholia de metris Aeschyli** (scholia recentiora
Demetrii Triclinii), ed. Dindorf, *Aeschyli tra-
goediae superstites et deperditarum fragmenta*,
vol. 3, 513–531.
Scholia in Septem contra Thebas: pp. 513–517.
Scholia in Persas: pp. 518–521.
Scholia in Agamemnonem: pp. 522–528.
Scholia in Eumenides: pp. 529–531.
Cod: Schol.

020 **Argumentum in margine et glossae interline-
ariae ad Persas** (glossae recentiores) (e codd.
Vindob. 197; Palatino 18; Guelferbytano 88;
Lipsiensi rep. I.4.43; Cantabrigiensi 1), ed.
Dähnhardt, *op. cit.*, 1894, 7, 9, 11–217, 221–
275.
Cod: Schol., Hypoth.

021 **Scholia in Persas** (scholia recentiora), ed.
Dähnhardt, *op. cit.*, 2–274.
Argumentum: pp. 2–8.
Scholia: pp. 10–274.
Dup. partim 5010 009.
Cod: Schol., Hypoth.

022 **Catalogus in fabulas** (e cod. Mediceo 32.9), ed.
Dindorf, *Aeschyli tragoediae superstites et deper-
ditarum fragmenta*, vol. 3, 9–10.
Cod: Schol.

023 **Scholia in Eumenides** (scholia vetera et recentiora Demetrii Triclinii) (e cod. Neapol.
II.F.31), ed. A. Turyn, *The manuscript tra-*

dition of the tragedies of Aeschylus. New York:
Polish Institute of Arts and Sciences, 1943
(repr. Hildesheim: Olms, 1967): 125–137.
Dup. partim 5010 001, 002.
Cod: Schol.

5044 **SCHOLIA IN ALCMANEM**
Varia

001 **Scholia in Alcmanem** (scholia vetera), ed. C.
Calame, *Alcman.* Rome: Ateneo, 1983: 25–26,
40–49, 54–55, 58, 65–72, 78, 100–105, 107–
110, 177, 179–180, 185, 187, 192–195, 201–
203.
P. Oxy. 24.2387: p. 78.
P. Oxy. 24.2389: pp. 25–26, 44–49, 54, 65–71,
177.
P. Oxy. 24.2390: pp. 100–105, 109–110, 201–
203.
P. Oxy. 24.2391: pp. 192–193.
P. Oxy. 24.2392: p. 58.
P. Oxy. 24.2393: pp. 72, 201.
P. Oxy. 24.2394: pp. 185, 187.
P. Oxy. 29.2506: pp. 54–55, 107–108, 194.
P. Oxy. 35.2737: pp. 25, 179–180.
P. Oxy. 37.2812: p. 195.
P. Paris. 71 [*P. Louv.* inv. 3320]: pp. 40–44.
Pap: Schol.

5011 **SCHOLIA IN ANTHOLOGIAM GRAECAM**
Varia
Cf. et Joannes TZETZES Gramm. et Poeta
(9022 007).

001 **Scholia ad epigrammata arithmetica in Anthologia Graeca** (scholia recentiora), ed. P. Tannery, *Diophanti Alexandrini opera omnia*, vol.
2. Leipzig: Teubner, 1895 (repr. Stuttgart:
1974): 43–72.
Cod: Schol.

5012 **SCHOLIA IN APOLLONIUM RHODIUM**
Varia

001 **Scholia in Apollonii Rhodii Argonautica**
(scholia vetera), ed. K. Wendel, *Scholia in
Apollonium Rhodium vetera.* Berlin: Weid-
mann, 1935 (repr. 1974): 1–329.
Apollonii genus: pp. 1–2.
Apollonii vita: p. 2.
Argumentum: pp. 2–4.
Catalogus Argonautarum: pp. 4–6.
Scholia: pp. 7–329.
Cod: 66,207: Schol., Biogr., Hypoth.

5013 **SCHOLIA IN ARATUM**
Varia

001 **Scholia in Aratum** (scholia vetera), ed. J. Martin, *Scholia in Aratum vetera.* Stuttgart: Teubner, 1974: 37–45, 49–207, 209–527.
Cod: 65,126: Schol.

002 **Scholia in Aratum** (scholia vetera) (*P. Berol.*
5865), ed. Martin, *op. cit.*, 560–562.
Cod: 111: Schol.

003 **Scholia in Aratum** (scholia vetera), ed. Martin, *op. cit.*, 563–564.
Scholia in cod. Laurentiano xxxi 32: pp. 563–564.
Scholia in cod. Marciano 465: p. 564.
Cod: 234: Schol.

004 **Scholia in Aratum** (scholia vetera) (e codd. Palat. gr. 40 (P) + Paris gr. 2860), ed. Martin, *op. cit.*, 565–568.
Cod: 773: Schol.

005 **Scholia in Aratum** (scholia vetera) (e cod. Perusino A 35), ed. Martin, *op. cit.*, 571–572.
Cod: 138: Schol.

006 **Scholia in Aratum** (scholia vetera) (e cod. Paris gr. 2728), ed. E. Maass, *Commentariorum in Aratum reliquiae*. Berlin: Weidmann, 1898 (repr. 1958): 177.
Cod: 71: Schol.

5047 *SCHOLIA IN ARISTIDEM QUINTILIANUM*
Varia

001 **Scholia in Aristidis Quintiliani librum de musica** (scholia recentiora), ed. R.P. Winnington-Ingram, *Aristidis Quintiliani de musica libri tres*. Leipzig: Teubner, 1963: 4, 6, 7, 11, 12, 97, 98, 103 in apparatu.
Cod: Schol.

5014 *SCHOLIA IN ARISTOPHANEM*
Varia

001 **Scholia in Acharnenses** (scholia vetera et recentiora Triclinii), ed. N.G. Wilson, *Prolegomena de comoedia. Scholia in Acharnenses, Equites, Nubes [Scholia in Aristophanem 1.1B*. Groningen: Bouma, 1975]: 1–150.
Argumenta: pp. 1–2.
Scholia: pp. 3–150.
Argumentum 2 (epigramma est): Dup. ARISTOPHANES Gramm. (0644 007) (fr. 5).
Cf. et 5014 022.
Cod, Pap: 31,738: Schol., Hypoth.

002 **Scholia in equites** (scholia vetera et recentiora Triclinii), ed. D.M. Jones and N.G. Wilson, *Prolegomena de comoedia. Scholia in Acharnenses, Equites, Nubes [Scholia in Aristophanem 1.2*. Groningen: Wolters-Noordhoff, 1969]: 1–277.
Argumenta: pp. 1–3.
Epigramma Aristophanis grammatici: pp. 3–4.
Dramatis personae: p. 4.
Scholia et glossae: pp. 5–277.
Argumentum 7 (epigramma est): Dup. ARISTOPHANES Gramm. (0644 007) (fr. 6).
Cod, Pap: 54,703: Schol., Hypoth., Epigr.

003 **Scholia in nubes** (scholia vetera), ed. D. Holwerda, *Prolegomena de comoedia. Scholia in Acharnenses, Equites, Nubes [Scholia in Aristophanem 1.3.1*. Groningen: Bouma, 1977]: 1–250.
Argumenta: pp. 1–5.
Dramatis personae: p. 6.

Scholia et glossae: pp. 7–250.
Subscriptiones: p. 250.
Cod: 41,167: Schol., Hypoth.

004 **Scholia in nubes** (scholia scholiorumque partes editionis Aldinae propria), ed. W.J.W. Koster, *Prolegomena de comoedia. Scholia in Acharnenses, Equites, Nubes [Scholia in Aristophanem 1.3.1*. Groningen: Bouma, 1977]: 256–282.
Cod: 5,900: Schol.

005 **Scholia in nubes** (scholia recentiora Eustathii, Thomae Magistri et Triclinii), ed. Koster, *Prolegomena de comoedia. Scholia in Acharnenses, Equites, Nubes [Scholia in Aristophanem 1.3.2*. Groningen: Bouma, 1974]: 3–198.
Scholia Eustathiana: pp. 3–7.
Argumenta: pp. 8–12.
Dramatis personae: p. 14.
Scholia Thomana et Tricliniana: pp. 14–198.
Subscriptiones: p. 198.
Cod: 32,148: Schol., Hypoth.

006 **Scholia in nubes** (scholia anonyma recentiora), ed. Koster, *Prolegomena de comoedia. Scholia in Acharnenses, Equites, Nubes [Scholia in Aristophanem 1.3.2*. Groningen: Bouma, 1974]: 199–465.
Scholia anonyma: pp. 199–465.
Subscriptiones: p. 465.
Cod: 66,228: Schol., Hypoth.

007 **Scholia in vespas** (scholia vetera, recentiora Tricliniana et Aldina), ed. Koster, *Scholia in Vespas, Pacem, Aves et Lysistratam [Scholia in Aristophanem 2.1*. Groningen: Bouma, 1978]: 3–238.
Argumenta: pp. 3–6.
Dramatis personae: p. 7.
Scholia et glossae: pp. 8–238.
Subscriptiones: p. 238.
Argumentum 1 (epigramma est): Dup. ARISTOPHANES Gramm. (0644 007) (fr. 7).
Cod: 41,173: Schol., Hypoth., Epigr.

008 **Scholia in pacem** (scholia vetera et recentiora Triclinii), ed. Holwerda, *Scholia in Vespas, Pacem, Aves et Lysistratam [Scholia in Aristophanem 2.2*. Groningen: Bouma, 1982]: 1–182.
Argumenta: pp. 1–4.
Dramatis personae: p. 5.
Scholia et glossae: pp. 6–182.
Subscriptio: p. 182.
Argumentum 4 (epigramma est): Dup. ARISTOPHANES Gramm. (0644 007) (fr. 8).
Cod: 39,944: Schol., Hypoth., Epigr.

009 **Scholia in aves** (scholia vetera), ed. F. Dübner, *Scholia Graeca in Aristophanem*. Paris: Didot, 1877 (repr. Hildesheim: Olms, 1969): 209–247.
Argumenta: pp. 209–210.
Scholia: pp. 210–247.
Argumentum 4 (epigramma est): Dup. ARISTOPHANES Gramm. (0644 007) (fr. 9).
Cod: 28,413: Schol., Hypoth., Epigr.

010 **Scholia in Lysistratam** (scholia vetera), ed. Dübner, *op. cit.*, 248–263.

Argumenta: p. 248.
Scholia: pp. 248–263.
Argumentum 2 (epigramma est): Dup. AN-
THOLOGIAE GRAECAE APPENDIX (7052
003) (epigr. 83).
Cod: 9,397: Schol., Hypoth., Epigr.

011 **Scholia in Thesmophoriazusas** (scholia vetera),
ed. Dübner, *op. cit.*, 264–272.
Cod: 4,937: Schol.

012 **Scholia in ranas** (scholia vetera), ed. Dübner,
op. cit., 273–314.
Argumenta: pp. 273–274.
Scholia: pp. 274–314.
Argumentum 2 (epigramma est): Dup. AN-
THOLOGIAE GRAECAE APPENDIX (7052
003) (epigr. 84).
Argumentum 3: sub auctore Thoma Magistro.
Cod: 30,877: Schol., Hypoth., Epigr.

013 **Scholia in ecclesiazusas** (scholia vetera), ed.
Dübner, *op. cit.*, 315–322.
Argumenta: p. 315.
Scholia: pp. 315–322.
Argumentum 2 (epigramma est): Dup. ARIS-
TOPHANES Gramm. (0644 007) (fr. 10).
Cod: 4,017: Schol., Hypoth., Epigr.

014 **Scholia in plutum** (scholia vetera et fort. recen-
tiora sub auctore Moschopulo), ed. Dübner, *op.
cit.*, 323–387.
Argumenta: pp. 323–324.
Scholia: pp. 324–387.
Scholia ad versas 172, 355, 455 fort. sub auc-
tore Moschopulo.
Argumentum 6 (epigramma est): Dup. ARIS-
TOPHANES Gramm. (0644 007) (fr. 11).
Cod: 50,090: Schol., Hypoth., Epigr.

015 **Commentarium in plutum** (recensio 1) (scholia
recentiora Tzetzae), ed. L. Massa Positano, *Jo.
Tzetzae commentarii in Aristophanem* [*Scholia
in Aristophanem* 4.1. Groningen: Bouma,
1960]: 1, 3–30, 32–35, 37–39, 41, 46–63, 65–
71, 73–94, 96–113, 115–119, 121–143, 145–
166, 168, 170–175, 177–181, 184–196, 198,
200–202, 204–206, 208–233.
Argumentum: p. 1.
Dramatis personae: p. 3.
Scholia: pp. 3–233.
Cf. et 5014 021.
Cod: 14,028: Schol., Hypoth.

016 **Glossae in plutum** (scholia recentiora Tzetzae),
ed. Massa Positano, *Jo. Tzetzae commentarii in
Aristophanem* [*Scholia in Aristophanem* 4.1],
234–269.
Cod: 6,112: Schol.

017 **Commentarium in nubes** (scholia recentiora
Tzetzae), ed. Holwerda, *Jo. Tzetzae commenta-
rii in Aristophanem* [*Scholia in Aristophanem*
4.2. Groningen: Bouma, 1960]: 367–689.
Argumenta: pp. 367–373.
Dramatis personae: p. 374.
Scholia et glossae: pp. 374–689.
Cod: 43,293: Schol., Hypoth.

018 **Commentarium in ranas** (scholia recentiora

Tzetzae), ed. Koster, *Jo. Tzetzae commentarii
in Aristophanem* [*Scholia in Aristophanem* 4.3.
Groningen: Bouma, 1962]: 691–918, 920–929,
931, 939–947, 950–951, 955–957, 961–978,
980, 983–985, 987–1000, 1002–1012, 1014–
1015, 1018–1041, 1043–1051, 1053–1066,
1068–1069, 1071–1074, 1080–1081, 1083–
1086, 1088–1104, 1106–1107, 1109–1118,
1120.
Argumenta: pp. 691–702.
Dramatis personae: pp. 703–704.
Scholia et glossae: pp. 704–1120.
Cf. et 5014 023.
Cod: 25,353: Schol., Hypoth.

019 **Argumentum in equites** (argumentum Tzetzi-
anum), ed. Koster, *Jo. Tzetzae commentarii in
Aristophanem* [*Scholia in Aristophanem* 4.3],
1121–1122.
Argumentum: p. 1121.
Dramatis personae: p. 1122.
Cod: 305: Schol., Hypoth.

020 **Commentarium in aves** (scholia vetera et re-
centiora Tzetzae), ed. Koster, *Jo. Tzetzae com-
mentarii in Aristophanem* [*Scholia in Aristo-
phanem* 4.3], 1123–1129, 1131–1164.
Argumenta: pp. 1123–1124, 1125–1128.
Dramatis personae: pp. 1124–1125.
Scholia et glossae ad argumentum iii: p. 1129.
Scholia et glossae ad Aves: pp. 1131–1164.
Cod: 6,465: Schol., Hypoth.

021 **Commentarium in plutum** (recensio 2) (scholia
recentiora Tzetzae), ed. Massa Positano, *Jo.
Tzetzae commentarii in Aristophanem* [*Scholia
in Aristophanem* 4.1], 1–221, 223–233.
Argumentum: pp. 1–2.
Dramatis personae: p. 3.
Scholia: pp. 3–233.
Cf. et 5014 015.
Cod: 27,783: Schol., Hypoth.

022 **Scholia in Acharnenses** (scholia vetera) (*P.
Oxy.* 6.856), ed. B.P. Grenfell and A.S. Hunt,
*Prolegomena de comoedia. Scholia in Achar-
nenses, Equites, Nubes* (ed. N. G. Wilson)
[*Scholia in Aristophanem* 1.1B. Groningen:
Bouma, 1975]: vii–ix.
Cf. et 5014 001.
Pap: 512: Schol.

023 **Commentarium in ranas** (scholia recentiora
Tzetzae) (cod. Ambrosianus gr. C 222 inf.), ed.
Koster, *Jo. Tzetzae commentarii in Aristophanem* [*Scholia in Aristophanem* 4.3], 703–704,
708, 714, 723–724, 726, 775, 778–779, 787,
790, 802–803, 805, 811, 820, 825–826, 829–
830, 837, 839–841, 846–847, 850, 854, 860–
861, 863–865, 868, 871, 874–875, 886, 896,
904–906, 911, 913–987, 991–1018, 1020–
1041, 1047–1097, 1099–1120.
Dramatis personae: pp. 703–704.
Scholia et glossae: pp. 708–1120.
Cf. et 5014 018.
Cod: 12,267: Schol.

5015 *SCHOLIA IN ARISTOTELEM*

Varia

Cf. et ANONYMI IN ARISTOTELIS ANALY-
TICA POSTERIORA (4191).

Cf. et ANONYMI IN ARISTOTELIS ANALY-
TICA PRIORA (4190).

Cf. et ANONYMI IN ARISTOTELIS ARTEM
RHETORICAM (4026).

Cf. et ANONYMI IN ARISTOTELIS CATEGO-
RIAS (4027).

Cf. et ANONYMI IN ARISTOTELIS ETHICA
NICOMACHEA (4033).

Cf. et ANONYMI IN ARISTOTELIS LIBRUM
DE CAELO (4195).

Cf. et ANONYMI IN ARISTOTELIS LIBRUM
DE INTERPRETATIONE (4165).

Cf. et ANONYMI IN ARISTOTELIS META-
PHYSICA (4196).

Cf. et ANONYMI IN ARISTOTELIS PHYSICA
(4194).

Cf. et ANONYMI IN ARISTOTELIS SOPHIS-
TICOS ELENCHOS (4193).

Cf. et ANONYMI IN ARISTOTELIS TOPICA
(4192).

Cf. et LEO MAGENTINUS Phil. (4187).

Cf. et MAXIMUS CONFESSOR Theol. et Poeta
(2892 084–085).

Cf. et Joannes PEDIASIMUS Gramm. (2592
004–005, 007).

001 **Scholia in Aristotelis sophisticos elenchos**
(scholia recentiora) (e cod. Vat. Urb. gr. 35),
ed. A. Bülow-Jacobsen and S. Ebbesen, "Vaticanus Urbinas Graecus 35. An edition of the
scholia on Aristotle's sophistici elenchi,"
Cahiers de l'Institut du moyen-âge grec et latin
43 (1982) 55–113.
Cod: Schol.

002 **Scholia in Aristotelis sophisticos elenchos**
(scholia recentiora), ed. S. Ebbesen, *Commen-*
tators and commentaries on Aristotle's sophistici
elenchi. A study of post-Aristotelian ancient and
medieval writings on fallacies, vol. 2 [*Corpus*
Latinum commentariorum in Aristotelem Grae-
corum. De Wulf-mansion Centre 7. Leiden:
Brill, 1981]: 321–330.
Cod: Schol.

003 **Scholia in Aristotelis ethica Nicomachea**
(scholia vetera et recentiora) (e cod. Paris. gr.
1854), ed. J.A. Cramer, *Anecdota Graeca e*
codd. manuscriptis bibliothecae regiae Parisien-
sis, vol. 1. Oxford: Oxford University Press,
1839 (repr. Hildesheim: Olms, 1967): 180–
244.
Cod: Schol.

5016 *SCHOLIA IN CALLIMACHUM*

Varia

001 **Scholia in Callimachum** (scholia vetera), ed. R.
Pfeiffer, *Callimachus*, vols. 1–2. Oxford: Clarendon Press, 1:1949; 2:1953: 1:3, 7, 11, 13,
17, 19, 30–34, 45–51, 53–54, 64, 114, 116,
118, 120, 122, 161, 163–168, 170, 175, 177,

179, 181, 218–221, 226, 311–315; 2:100–106,
114–116, 121, 123–124.
Argumentum Hecalae: vol. 1, p. 226.
Pap: Schol., Hypoth.

002 **Scholia in Callimachi hymnos** (scholia vetera),
ed. Pfeiffer, *op. cit.*, vol. 2, 41–79.
Cod, Pap: Schol.

003 **Diegeseis in Callimachum** (scholia vetera), ed.
Pfeiffer, *op. cit.*, vols. 1 & 2, 1:71, 85–87, 91–
92, 95, 97–99, 101–103, 105–111, 123, 163,
172, 174, 177, 185, 189, 193, 195–196, 198–
200, 205, 216, 217–218, 223, 227; 2:41, 46,
107–108, 110–112.
Pap: Schol.

5048 *SCHOLIA IN CLEMENTEM ALEXANDRI-NUM*

Varia

001 **Scholia in protrepticum et paedagogum**
(scholia recentiora partim sub auctore Aretha),
ed. O. Stählin and U. Treu, *Clemens Alexan-*
drinus, vol. 1, 3rd edn. [*Die griechischen christ-*
lichen Schriftsteller 12. Berlin: Akademie-
Verlag, 1972]: 295–340.
Cod: Schol., Eccl.

5017 *SCHOLIA IN DEMOSTHENEM*

Varia

001 **Scholia in Demosthenem** (scholia vetera) (fort.
auctore Ulpiano), ed. M.R. Dilts, *Scholia De-*
mosthenica, 2 vols. Leipzig: Teubner, 1:1983;
2:1986: 1:14–235; 2:1–384.
Scholia in orationes: vol. 1, pp. 14–119, 121–
235; vol. 2, pp. 1–384.
Hypothesis in Pacem: vol. 1, pp. 120–121.
Scholion in Philippi epistulam: vol. 1, p. 162.
Cod: 184,241: Schol., Hypoth.

5018 *SCHOLIA IN DIONYSIUM BYZANTIUM*

Varia

001 **Scholia in Dionysii Byzantii per Bosporum**
navigationem (scholia recentiora), ed. R. Güngerich, *Dionysii Byzantii anaplus Bospori una*
cum scholiis x saeculi, 2nd edn. Berlin: Weidmann, 1958: 36–40.
Epigramma (p. 40): Dup. partim ANONYMI
EPIGRAMMATICI (AG) (0138 001) (AG
7.169).
Cod: Schol.

5019 *SCHOLIA IN DIONYSIUM PERIEGETAM*

Varia

001 **Scholia in Dionysii periegetae orbis descrip-**
tionem (scholia vetera) (olim sub auctore De-
metrio Lampsaceno), ed. K. Müller, *Geographi*
Graeci minores, vol. 2. Paris: Didot, 1861 (repr.
Hildesheim: Olms, 1965): 427–457.
Vita Dionysii: pp. 427–428.
Scholia: pp. 428–457.
Appendix ad scholia: p. 457.
Dup. partim 5019 002.
Cod: Schol., Biogr.

002 **Scholia in Dionysii periegetae orbis descriptionem** (scholia vetera), ed. A. Ludwich, *Aristarchs Homerische Textkritik nach den Fragmenten des Didymos*, vol. 2. Leipzig: Teubner, 1885 (repr. Hildesheim: Olms, 1971): 575–587.
Vita Dionysii: pp. 575–576.
Scholia: pp. 576–587.
Dup. partim 5019 001.
Cod: Schol.

5020 *SCHOLIA IN DIONYSIUM THRACEM*
Varia

x01 **Scholia in Dionysii Thracis artem grammaticam** (scholia vetera et recentiora).
Hilgard, vol. 1.3, pp. 1–586.
Cf. COMMENTARIA IN DIONYSII THRACIS ARTEM GRAMMATICAM (4175 001–007).

5021 *SCHOLIA IN DIOPHANTUM*
Varia
Cf. et Maximus PLANUDES Polyhist. (4146 001).

001 **Scholia in Diophanti arithmetica** (scholia recentiora e codd. Matr. Bibl. Nat. 4678; Vat. gr. 191 et 304), ed. A. Allard, "Les scolies aux arithmétiques de Diophante d'Alexandrie dans le Matritensis Bibl. Nat. 4678 et les Vaticani gr. 191 et 304," *Byzantion* 53 (1983) 682–710.
Cod: Schol.

002 **Scholia in Diophanti arithmetica** (scholia vetera), ed. P. Tannery, *Diophanti Alexandrini opera omnia*, vol. 2. Leipzig: Teubner, 1895 (repr. Stuttgart: 1974): 256–260.
Cod: Schol.

5022 *SCHOLIA IN EUCLIDEM*
Varia
Cf. et PROCLUS Phil. (4036 011).

001 **Scholia in Euclidis elementa** (scholia vetera et recentiora), ed. E.S. Stamatis (post J.L. Heiberg), *Euclidis opera omnia*, vols. 5.1–5.2, 2nd edn. Leipzig: Teubner, 1977: **5.1**:39–243; **5.2**:1–350.
Scholia in libros 1–5: vol. 5.1, pp. 39–243.
Scholia in libros 6–13: vol. 5.2, pp. 1–309.
Appendix scholiorum 1 (in libros 14–15): vol. 5.2, pp. 311–324.
Appendix scholiorum 2 (in libros 14–15): vol. 5.2, pp. 325–336.
Appendix scholiorum 3 (in libros 14–15): vol. 5.2, pp. 337–350.
Cod: Schol.

002 **Scholia in Euclidis data** (scholia vetera), ed. H. Menge, *Euclidis opera omnia*, vol. 6. Leipzig: Teubner, 1896: 261–319, 323–336.
Scholia: pp. 261–319.
Appendix scholiorum: pp. 323–336.
Cf. et 5022 007.
Cod: Schol.

003 **Scholia in Euclidis optica** (scholia vetera), ed. J.L. Heiberg, *Euclidis opera omnia*, vol. 7. Leipzig: Teubner, 1895: 125–141.
Cod: Schol.

004 **Scholia in opticorum recensionem Theonis** (scholia vetera), ed. Heiberg, *op. cit.*, vol. 7, 251–284.
Cod: Schol.

005 **Scholia in Euclidis catoptrica** (scholia vetera), ed. Heiberg, *op. cit.*, vol. 7, 347–362.
Cf. et 5022 007.
Cod: Schol.

006 **Scholia in Euclidis phaenomena** (scholia vetera), ed. Menge, *op. cit.*, vol. 8 (1916): 134–156.
Cod: Schol.

007 **Scholia in Euclidis data et catoptrica** (scholia vetera), ed. Menge, *op. cit.*, vol. 8, 290–292.
Scholia e cod. Vat. gr. 1038 sub fine datorum: pp. 290–291.
Scholion ad catoptrica prop. 1 e cod. Vat. gr. 204: pp. 291–292.
Cf. et 5022 002, 005.
Cod: Schol.

5023 *SCHOLIA IN EURIPIDEM*
Varia

001 **Scholia in Euripidem** (scholia vetera), ed. E. Schwartz, *Scholia in Euripidem*, 2 vols. Berlin: Reimer, 1:1887; 2:1891 (repr. De Gruyter, 1966): **1**:1–6, 9–415; **2**: 1–343, 345–376.
Vita Euripidis: vol. 1, pp. 1–6.
Argumentum Hecubae: vol. 1, p. 9.
Scholia in Hecubam: vol. 1, pp. 10–91.
Argumentum Orestis: vol. 1, pp. 92–93.
Scholia in Orestem: vol. 1, pp. 94–241.
Argumentum Phoenissarum: vol. 1, pp. 242–244.
Scholia in Phoenissas: vol. 1, pp. 245–415.
Argumentum Hippolyti: vol. 2, pp. 1–2.
Scholia in Hippolytum: vol. 2, pp. 3–136.
Argumentum Medeae: vol. 2, pp. 137–139.
Scholia in Medeam: vol. 2, pp. 140–213.
Argumentum Alcestis: vol. 2, pp. 214–215.
Scholia in Alcestem: vol. 2, pp. 216–244.
Argumentum Andromachae: vol. 2, pp. 245–246.
Scholia in Andromacham: vol. 2, pp. 247–322.
Argumentum Rhesi: vol. 2, pp. 323–325.
Scholia in Rhesum: vol. 2, pp. 326–343, 345.
Argumentum Troiadum: vol. 2, p. 346.
Scholia in Troiades: vol. 2, pp. 347–376.
Cf. et 5023 004, 005, 006.
Cod: 163,202: Schol., Biogr., Hypoth.

003 **Scholia in Euripidem** (cod. Hierosolymitanus patriarchalis 36), ed. S.G. Daitz, *The scholia in the Jerusalem palimpsest of Euripides*. Heidelberg: Winter, 1979: 15–105.
Hecuba: pp. 15–24.
Phoenissae: pp. 25–37.
Orestes: pp. 38–69.
Andromacha: pp. 69–84.

Hippolytus: pp. 85–89.

Medea: pp. 89–105.

Cod: 10,117: Schol.

004 **Glossae codicis Vaticani 909 in Euripidis Rhesum** (scholia vetera), ed. Schwartz, *op. cit.*, vol. 2, 326–327, 330–334, 336–339, 342–343. Cf. et 5023 001, 005.

Cod: 869: Schol.

005 **Glossae codicis C in Euripidis Rhesum** (scholia vetera), ed. Schwartz, *op. cit.*, vol. 2, 326–328, 331, 333, 337–338, 342–343. Cf. et 5023 001, 004.

Cod: 184: Schol.

006 **Glossae in Euripidis Troiades** (scholia vetera), ed. Schwartz, *op. cit.*, vol. 2, 348–376. Cf. et 5023 001.

Cod: 1,128: Schol.

007 **Scholia in Euripidem** (scholia metrica recentiora Demetrii Triclinii), ed. H. Wagenvoort, "Demetrii Triclinii scholia metrica e codice Angelico aucta et emendata," *Mnemosyne*, n.s. 41 (1913) 314–332.

Scholia in Hecubam: pp. 314–317.

Argumentum Orestis: pp. 317–318.

Scholia in Orestem: pp. 318–323.

Scholia in Phoenissas: pp. 323–328.

Scholia alia: pp. 329–332.

Cod: Schol., Hypoth.

5049 *SCHOLIA IN EUSEBIUM*

Varia

001 **Scholia in praeparationem evangelicam** (scholia recentiora partim sub auctore Aretha), ed. K. Mras, *Eusebius Werke, Band 8: Die Praeparatio evangelica [Die griechischen christlichen Schriftsteller* 43.1 & 43.2. Berlin: Akademie-Verlag, 43.1:1954; 43.2:1956]: passim (in apparatu).

Cod: Schol., Eccl.

5043 *SCHOLIA IN HERMOGENEM*

Varia

Cf. et ANONYMI IN HERMOGENEM (5024).

Cf. et SYRIANI, SOPATRI ET MARCELLINI SCHOLIA AD HERMOGENIS STATUS (2047).

Cf. et CHRISTOPHORUS Rhet. (4007 001).

Cf. et Joannes DOXAPATRES Rhet. (3027 002–004).

Cf. et GREGORIUS PARDUS Gramm. et Rhet. (4092 002).

Cf. et JOANNES Rhet. (4157 001–002).

Cf. et JOANNES Rhet. (4235 001–002).

Cf. et JOANNES Diaconus Rhet. (4143 001).

Cf. et MARCELLINUS Gramm. et Rhet. (4234 x01).

Cf. et PHOEBAMMON Soph. (2596 002, x02–x03).

Cf. et Maximus PLANUDES Polyhist. (4146 003, 005–010).

Cf. et SOPATER Rhet. (2031 002).

Cf. et SYRIANUS Phil. (4017 002–004).

Cf. et TROILUS Soph. (2127 001).

001 **Scholion in Hermogenem** (scholion recentius) (excerptum e cod. Venet. 444), ed. C. Walz, *Rhetores Graeci*, vol. 4. Stuttgart: Cotta, 1833 (repr. Osnabrück: Zeller, 1968): 31 (in apparatu).

Cod: Schol.

007 **Scholia in Hermogenis librum** περὶ στάσεων (scholia recentiora in margine e codd. Paris. 2921, 2923 + Venet. class. XI, cod. 2), ed. Walz, *op. cit.*, vol. 4, 47–709 passim (in apparatu).

Cod: Schol.

002 **Scholia in Hermogenis librum** περὶ μεθόδου δεινότητος (scholia minora recentiora e cod. Paris. gr. 2977), ed. Walz, *op. cit.*, vol. 5 (1833; repr. 1968): 562–575.

Cod: Schol.

004 **Scholion in Hermogenis librum** περὶ στάσεων (scholion recentius in margine inferiore e cod. Monacensi 8), ed. Walz, *op. cit.*, vol. 5, 253 (in apparatu).

Cod: Schol.

005 **Scholia in Hermogenis librum** περὶ εὑρέσεως (scholia minora recentiora e codd. Paris. gr. 2977 + Farnesino II.E.5), ed. Walz, *op. cit.*, vol. 5, 372, 373, 374, 389, 397, 399, 400, 402, 412, 424, 430 (in apparatu).

Cod: Schol.

006 **Scholia in Hermogenis librum** περὶ ἰδεῶν (scholia minora recentiora e codd. Paris. gr. 2916 + Monacensi 8), ed. Walz, *op. cit.*, vol. 5, 443–548 passim (in apparatu).

Cod: Schol.

003 **Scholia in Hermogenis librum** περὶ στάσεων (scholia minora recentiora e codd. Paris. gr. 1983, 2916, 2977 + Farnesino II.E.5), ed. Walz, *op. cit*, vol. 7 (1834; repr. 1968): 105–684 passim (in apparatu).

Cod: Schol.

008 **Scholia in Hermogenis librum** περὶ εὑρέσεως (scholia minora recentiora e codd. Paris. 1983, 2916, 2977 + Farnesino II.E.5), ed. Walz, *op. cit.*, vol. 7, 701–859 passim (in apparatu).

Cod: Schol.

009 **Scholia in Hermogenis librum** περὶ ἰδεῶν (scholia minora recentiora e codd. Paris. 1983, 2916, 2977 + Farnesino II.E.5), ed. Walz, *op. cit.*, vol. 7, 861–1087 passim (in apparatu).

Cod: Schol.

010 **Scholia in Hermogenis librum** περὶ μεθόδου δεινότητος (scholia recentiora e cod. Mediceo plut. XVI), ed. Walz, *op. cit.*, vol. 7, 1091–1332 passim (in apparatu).

Cod: Schol.

5025 *SCHOLIA IN HESIODUM*

Varia

Cf. et Joannes GALENUS Gramm. (3039 001).

Cf. et JOANNES Protospatharius Gramm. (3155 001).

Cf. et Joannes PEDIASIMUS Gramm. (2592 003).

Cf. et Joannes TZETZES Gramm. et Poeta (9022 x01).

001 **Scholia in opera et dies** (scholia vetera), ed. A. Pertusi, *Scholia vetera in Hesiodi opera et dies.* Milan: Societa Editrice Vita e Pensiero, 1955: 1-259.
Prolegomena: pp. 1-5.
Scholia: pp. 6-259.
Dup. partim 5025 002 (verba ex Proclo).
Cod: 49,780: Schol.

002 **Scholia in opera et dies** (scholia vetera partim Procli et recentiora partim Moschopuli, Tzetzae et Joannis Galeni), ed. T. Gaisford, *Poetae minores Graeci*, vol. 2 [*Scholia ad Hesiodum*]. Leipzig: Kühn, 1823: 3-447.
Prolegomena Procli: pp. 3-9.
Interpretatio Joannis Tzetzae: pp. 10-22.
Scholia: pp. 23-447.
Prolegomena Procli et scholia: Dup. partim 5025 001 (verba ex Proclo).
Cod: 105,575: Schol.

003 **Scholia in theogoniam** (scholia vetera), ed. L. di Gregorio, *Scholia vetera in Hesiodi theogoniam.* Milan: Societa Editrice Vita e Pensiero, 1975: 1-123.
Cod: 18,911: Schol.

004 **Glossae in theogoniam**, ed. H. Flach, *Glossen und Scholien zur hesiodischen Theogonie.* Leipzig: Teubner, 1876 (repr. Osnabrück: Biblio Verlag, 1970): 183-204.
Cod: 4,240: Schol.

5026   *SCHOLIA IN HOMERUM*
Varia

Cf. et Joannes GALENUS Gramm. (3039 002).
Cf. et Manuel MOSCHOPULUS Gramm. (9025 001).
Cf. et PARAPHRASES IN HOMERI OPERA (4279).

001 **Scholia in Iliadem** (scholia vetera), ed. H. Erbse, *Scholia Graeca in Homeri Iliadem (scholia vetera)*, vols. 1-5, 7. Berlin: De Gruyter, 1:1969; 2:1971; 3:1974; 4:1975; 5:1977; 7:1988: 1:3-538; 2:1-545; 3:1-557, 559-680; 4.1-649; 5.1-643; 7.285-286, 301-302.
Cod, Pap: 560,935: Schol.

003 **Scholia in Iliadem** (scholia vetera et recentiora e cod. Genevensi gr. 44), ed. J. Nicole, *Les scolies genevoises de l'Iliade*, vol. 1. Geneva: Georg, 1891 (repr. Hildesheim: Olms, 1966): 3-222.
Dup. partim 5026 001.
Cod: Schol.

004 **Scholia in Iliadem** (scholia recentiora Theodori Meliteniotis) (e cod. Genevensi gr. 44), ed. Nicole, *op. cit.*, vol. 2 (1891; repr. 1966): 3-214.
Cod: Schol.

005 **Scholia minora in Iliadem** (glossae et scholia vetera), ed. V. de Marco, *Scholia minora in Homeri Iliadem*, pt. 1 [Λέξεις Ὁμηρικαί]. Vatican City: n.p., 1946.
Cod: Schol.

007 **Scholia in Odysseam** (scholia vetera), ed. W. Dindorf, *Scholia Graeca in Homeri Odysseam*, 2 vols. Oxford: Oxford University Press, 1855 (repr. Amsterdam: Hakkert, 1962): 1:7-402; 2:403-732.
Dup. partim 5026 008.
Cod: 170,839: Schol., Hypoth.

008 **Scholia in Odysseam 1.1-309** (scholia vetera), ed. A. Ludwich, *Scholia in Homeri Odysseae A 1-309 auctiora et emendatiora.* Königsberg: Hartung, 1888-1890 (repr. Hildesheim: Olms, 1966): 4-27, 31-36, 47-70, 73-93, 98-120.
Argumentum: pp. 4-5.
Scholia: pp. 5-27, 31-36, 47-70, 73-93, 98-120.
Dup. partim 5026 007.
Cod: Schol.

009 **Inscriptiones et hypothesis in Odysseam**, ed. Dindorf, *op. cit.*, vol. 1, 1-6.
Inscriptiones: pp. 1-3.
Hypothesis: pp. 3-6.
Cod: 1,258: Schol., Hypoth.

011 **Scholia in Iliadem** (scholia vetera) (= D scholia), ed. J. Lascaris, *Scholia in Homeri Iliadem quae vocantur Didymi.* Rome, 1517 (repr. Oxford: Oxford University Press, 1675): 1-718.
Hypothesis: ante p. 1.
Scholia: pp. 1-718.
Cod: Schol., Hypoth.

012 **Scholia in Odysseam** (scholia vetera) (= D scholia), ed. F. Asolani, *Didymi antiquissimi auctoris interpretatio in Odysseam.* Venice: Aldus, 1528: 3-128.
Hypothesis: p. 3.
Scholia: pp. 3-128.
Cod: Schol., Hypoth.

5027   *SCHOLIA IN IAMBLICHUM PHILOSOPHUM*
Varia

001 **Scholia in librum Iamblichi in Nicomachi arithmeticam introductionem** (scholia vetera et recentiora), ed. U. Klein (post H. Pistelli), *Iamblichi in Nicomachi arithmeticam introductionem liber.* Leipzig: Teubner, 1894 (repr. Stuttgart: 1975): 126-132.
Cod: Schol.

5028   *SCHOLIA IN ISOCRATEM*
Varia

001 **Scholia in Isocratem** (scholia vetera), ed. W. Dindorf, *Scholia Graeca in Aeschinem et Isocratem.* Oxford: Oxford University Press, 1852: 101-124.
Vita: pp. 101-106.

Hypotheses: pp. 107–118.
Scholia: pp. 118–124.
Cod: 5,607: Schol., Hypoth., Biogr.

5029 SCHOLIA IN LUCIANUM
Varia

001 **Scholia in Lucianum** (scholia vetera et recentiora Arethae), ed. H. Rabe, *Scholia in Lucianum.* Leipzig: Teubner, 1906 (repr. Stuttgart: 1971): 1–285.
Epigramma Pseudo-Luciani: p. 1.
Phalaris: pp. 1–8.
Hippias: pp. 8–9.
Bacchus: p. 9.
Hercules: pp. 9–10.
Electrum: p. 10.
Muscae encomium: pp. 10–11.
Nigrinus: pp. 11–13.
Demonax: pp. 13–15.
De domo: pp. 15–17.
Patriae encomium: p. 17.
Macrobii: pp. 17–18.
Verae historiae: pp. 18–25.
Calumniae non temere credendum: pp. 25–28.
Lis consonantium (= Judicium vocalium): pp. 28–29.
Symposium: pp. 29–35.
Soloecista: pp. 36–40.
Cataplus: pp. 41–53.
Juppiter confutatus: pp. 53–57.
Juppiter tragoedus: pp. 57–85.
Gallus: pp. 85–95.
Prometheus: pp. 95–98.
Icaromenippus: pp. 98–109.
Timon: pp. 109–119.
Charon sive contemplantes: pp. 119–122.
Vitarum auctio: pp. 122–131.
Revivescentes sive piscator: pp. 131–137.
Bis accusatus sive tribunalia: pp. 137–148.
De sacrificiis: pp. 148–150.
Adversus indoctum et libros multos ementem: pp. 151–154.
Somnium sive vita Luciani: pp. 154–155.
De parasito sive artem esse parasiticam: pp. 155–161.
Philopseudes sive incredulus: pp. 161–164.
Dearum judicium: pp. 164–165.
De mercede conductis potentium familiaribus: pp. 165–168.
Anacharsis: pp. 168–171.
Menippus sive necyomantia: pp. 171–173.
Asinus Pseudo-Luciani: p. 173.
De luctu: pp. 173–174.
Rhetorum praeceptor: pp. 174–180.
Alexander: pp. 180–185.
Imagines: pp. 185–186.
De Syria dea: pp. 186–187.
De saltatione: pp. 188–190.
Lexiphanes: pp. 190–202.
Eunuchus: pp. 202–203.
De astrologia: p. 203.
Amores Pseudo-Luciani: pp. 203–206.

Pro imaginibus: pp. 206–208.
Pseudologista: pp. 208–211.
Deorum concilium: pp. 211–213.
Tyrannicida: p. 213.
Abdicatus: pp. 213–215.
De morte Peregrini: pp. 215–222.
Fugitivi: pp. 222–223.
Toxaris vel amicitia: pp. 223–224.
Demosthenis encomium Pseudo-Luciani: pp. 224–226.
Quomodo historia conscribenda sit: pp. 226–231.
Dipsades: pp. 231–232.
Saturnalia: pp. 232–233.
Herodotus: pp. 233–234.
Zeuxis: p. 234.
Pro lapsu inter salutandum: pp. 234–235.
Apologia: pp. 234–238.
Harmonides: p. 239.
Hesiodus: pp. 239–240.
Scytha: p. 240.
Podagra: p. 241.
Hermotimus: pp. 241–247.
Prometheus es in verbis: pp. 247–248.
Halycon Pseudo-Luciani: p. 248.
Navigium: pp. 248–250.
Dialogi mortuorum: pp. 250–264.
Dialogi marini: pp. 264–268.
Dialogi deorum: pp. 268–274.
Dialogi meretricii: pp. 275–285.
Halycon Pseudo-Luciani (p. 248): Dup. partim 5029 002.
Scholia in Jovem Tragoedum, pp. 71–74, 78–82: Dup. partim ARETHAS Philol. et Scr. Eccl. (2130 033) (pp. 333–339).
Cod: 58,123: Schol.

002 **Scholia in Pseudo-Luciani Halcyonem** (scholia vetera), ed. W.C. Greene, *Scholia Platonica.* Haverford, Pennsylvania: American Philological Association, 1938: 405–407.
Dup. partim 5029 001 (Rabe, p. 248).
Cod: 300: Schol.

5030 SCHOLIA IN LYCOPHRONEM
Varia

001 **Scholia in Lycophronem** (scholia vetera et recentiora partim Isaac et Joannis Tzetzae), ed. E. Scheer, *Lycophronis Alexandra*, vol. 2. Berlin: Weidmann, 1958: 1–398.
Introductio in Lycophronem (olim sub auctore Isaac Tzetza, nunc auctore Joanne Tzetza): pp. 1–4.
Genus: pp. 4–7.
Hypothesis: p. 7.
Scholia: pp. 8–398.
Cod: Schol., Biogr., Hypoth.

5031 SCHOLIA IN NICANDRUM
Varia

001 **Scholia et glossae in Nicandri theriaca** (scholia vetera et recentiora), ed. A. Crugnola, *Scholia*

in Nicandri theriaka. Milan: Istituto Editoriale Cisalpino, 1971: 34–321.
Vita Nicandri: pp. 33–34.
Scholia: pp. 34–321.
Dup. partim 5031 003.
Cod, Pap: Schol.

002 **Scholia et glossae in Nicandri alexipharmaca** (scholia vetera et recentiora), ed. M. Geymonat, *Scholia in Nicandri alexipharmaca.* Milan: Istituto Editoriale Cisalpino, 1974: 29–212.
Dup. partim 5031 003.
Cod: Schol.

003 **Scholia in Nicandri theriaca et alexipharmaca** (scholia vetera et recentiora), ed. U.C. Bussemaker, *Scholia et paraphrases in Nicandrum et Oppianum* in *Scholia in Theocritum* (ed. F. Dübner). Paris: Didot, 1849: 173–219.
Dup. partim 5031 001, 002.
Cod: Schol.

5032 ***SCHOLIA IN OPPIANUM***
Varia

001 **Scholia et glossae in cynegetica** (scholia vetera et recentiora), ed. U.C. Bussemaker, *Scholia et paraphrases in Nicandrum et Oppianum* in *Scholia in Theocritum* (ed. F. Dübner). Paris: Didot, 1849: 243–259.
Cod: Schol.

002 **Scholia et glossae in halieutica** (scholia vetera et recentiora), ed. Bussemaker, *op. cit.,* 260–364.
Tzetzae epigrammata: pp. 260, 276.
Cod: Schol., Epigr.

5033 ***SCHOLIA IN PAUSANIAM***
Varia

001 **Scholia in Pausaniae periegesin** (scholia vetera sub auctore Agathia), ed. F. Spiro, "Pausanias-Scholien," *Hermes* 29 (1894) 145–149.
Cod: Schol.

5034 ***SCHOLIA IN PINDARUM***
Varia

001 **Scholia in Pindarum** (scholia vetera), ed. A.B. Drachmann, *Scholia vetera in Pindari carmina,* 3 vols. Leipzig: Teubner, 1:1903; 2:1910; 3:1927 (repr. Amsterdam: Hakkert, 1:1969; 2:1967; 3:1966): 1:12–395; 2:1–270; 3:1–278.
Scholia in Olympia i–xiv: vol. 1, pp. 12–395.
Hypothesis Pythiorum: vol. 2, pp. 1–5.
Scholia in Pythia i–xii: vol. 2, pp. 5–270.
Hypothesis Nemeorum: vol. 3, pp. 1–5.
Scholia in Nemea i–xi: vol. 3, pp. 5–191.
Hypothesis Isthmiorum: vol. 3, pp. 192–195.
Scholia in Isthmia i–viii: vol. 3, pp. 195–278.
Dup. partim 5034 003, 004, 007.
Cod: 184,604: Schol., Hypoth.

002 **Capitula ad praefationem scholiorum ad Pindari carmina,** ed. Drachmann, *op. cit.,* vol. 3, 306–311.
Cod: 1,252: Schol.

003 **Scholia in Pythia v–vii** (scholia vetera et recentiora Thomae Magistri et Triclinii) (e cod. Flor.), ed. T. Mommsen, *Scholia Thomano-Tricliniana in Pindari Pythia v–xii ex cod. Florentino edita* [*Programm Gymnasium Frankfurt.* Frankfurt am Main: Mahlau & Waldschmidt, 1867]: 4–36.
Dup. partim 5034 001, 005.
Cod: 10,039: Schol.

004 **Scholia et glossae in Olympia et Pythia** (scholia recentiora Triclinii, Thomae Magistri, Moschopuli, Germani) (collecta a Triclinio), ed. E. Abel, *Scholia recentia in Pindari epinicia,* vol. 1. Berlin: Calvary, 1891: 40–480.
Demetrii Triclinii scholia metrica: pp. 40–43.
Scholia in Olympia i–xiv: pp. 44–428.
Scholia in Pythia i–ii: pp. 429–480.
Scholia in Pythia: Dup. partim 5034 005.
Cod: 75,188: Schol.

005 **Scholia in Pindarum** (scholia vetera et recentiora partim Thomae Magistri et Alexandri Phortii) (e cod. Patm.), ed. D. Semitelos, Πινδάρου σχόλια Πατμιακά. Athens: Hermes, 1875: 1–133.
Scholia in Olympia i–xiv: pp. 1–22.
Scholia in Pythia i–xii: pp. 23–122.
Scholia in Nemea i–xi: pp. 122–130.
Scholia in Isthmia i–ii, iv–vi, viii: pp. 130–133.
Scholia in Pythia: Dup. partim 5034 001, 003, 004.
Cod: 29,063: Schol.

006 **Scholia in paeanes** (scholia vetera) (*P. Oxy.* 5.841), ed. E. Diehl, *Supplementum lyricum. Neue Bruchstücke.* Bonn: Marcus & Weber, 1917: 52–71.
Pap: Schol.

007 **Scholia in Nemea et Isthmia** (scholia vetera et recentiora partim Thomae Magistri et Triclinii), ed. T. Mommsen, *Scholia recentiora Thomano-Tricliniana in Pindari Nemea et Isthmia.* Leipzig: Teubner, 1865: 1–32.
Scholia in Nemea i–xi: pp. 1–28.
Scholia in Isthmia iii–vi: pp. 28–32.
Dup. partim 5034 001.
Cod: 6,798: Schol.

008 **Scholia in Pythia 5.92 et 5.106** (scholia recentiora e cod. Pal. C), ed. A. Boeckh, *Pindari opera quae supersunt,* vol. 2.2. Leipzig: Weigel, 1821: 382–384.
Cod: Schol.

5035 ***SCHOLIA IN PLATONEM***
Cf. et HERMIAS Phil. (2317 001).
Varia

001 **Scholia in Platonem** (scholia vetera), ed. W.C. Greene, *Scholia Platonica.* Haverford, Pennsylvania: American Philological Association, 1938: 1–405, 407–413.
Euthyphro: pp. 1–4.
Apologia: pp. 4–7.
Crito: p. 7.
Phaedo: pp. 8–15.

Cratylus: pp. 16–18.
Theaetetus: pp. 18–40.
Sophista: pp. 40–44.
Politicus: pp. 44–47.
Parmenides: pp. 47–50.
Philebus: pp. 50–55.
Symposium: pp. 55–67.
Phaedrus: pp. 67–88.
Alcibiades i: pp. 89–107.
Alcibiades ii: pp. 107–108.
Hipparchus: pp. 108–110.
Amatores: pp. 110–111.
Theages: pp. 111–112.
Charmides: pp. 112–116.
Laches: pp. 116–118.
Lysis: pp. 118–121.
Euthydemus: pp. 121–125.
Protagoras: pp. 125–128.
Gorgias: pp. 128–170.
Meno: pp. 170–174.
Hippias Major: pp. 174–178.
Hippias Minor: pp. 178–180.
Ion: pp. 180–182.
Menexenus: pp. 182–186.
Clitophon: pp. 186–187.
Respublica: pp. 187–276.
Timaeus: pp. 277–289.
Critias: pp. 290–293.
Minos: pp. 293–295.
Leges: pp. 296–380.
Epinomis: pp. 380–384.
Epistulae: pp. 384–400.
Definitiones: pp. 400–402.
De justo: p. 402.
De virtute: pp. 402–403.
Demodocus: pp. 403–404.
Sisyphus: pp. 404–405.
Eryxias: pp. 407–408.
Axiochus: pp. 409–413.
Dup. partim 5035 003.
Cod: 63,572: Schol.

002 **Scholia in Platonem** (scholia recentiora Arethae), ed. Greene, *op. cit.*, 417–480.
Euthyphro: pp. 417–419.
Apologia: pp. 419–423.
Crito: pp. 423–424.
Phaedo: pp. 424–426.
Cratylus: pp. 426–427.
Theaetetus: pp. 427–445.
Sophista: pp. 445–446.
Politicus: p. 446.
Parmenides: p. 447.
Philebus: p. 447.
Symposium: pp. 447–448.
Phaedrus: p. 449.
Alcibiades i: pp. 449–453.
Hipparchus: p. 453.
Amatores: p. 454.
Theages: p. 454.
Charmides: p. 454.
Laches: p. 455.
Lysis: pp. 456–458.

Euthydemus: p. 458.
Protagoras: p. 458.
Gorgias: pp. 459–479.
Meno: p. 480.
Dup. partim 5035 003.
Cod: 10,639: Schol.

003 **Scholia in Platonem** (scholia vetera et recentiora), ed. K.F. Hermann, *Platonis dialogi secundum Thrasylli tetralogias dispositi*, vol. 6. Leipzig: Teubner, 1902: 223–396.
Euthyphro: pp. 223–226.
Apologia: pp. 226–229.
Crito: pp. 229–230.
Phaedo: pp. 230–235.
Cratylus: pp. 235–237.
Theaetetus: pp. 237–249.
Sophista: pp. 249–251.
Politicus: pp. 251–252.
Parmenides: pp. 252–253.
Philebus: pp. 254–255.
Symposium: pp. 255–262.
Phaedrus: pp. 262–276.
Alcibiades i: pp. 276–284.
Alcibiades ii: pp. 284–285.
Hipparchus: pp. 285–286.
Amatores: pp. 286–287.
Theages: pp. 287–288.
Charmides: pp. 288–291.
Laches: pp. 291–292.
Lysis: pp. 292–294.
Euthydemus: pp. 295–296.
Protagoras: pp. 296–297.
Gorgias: pp. 297–324.
Meno: pp. 324–325.
Hippias Major: pp. 325–327.
Hippias Minor: pp. 327–328.
Ion: p. 328.
Menexenus: pp. 328–330.
Clitophon: pp. 330–331.
Respublica: pp. 331–363.
Timaeus: pp. 363–369.
Critias: pp. 369–370.
Minos: pp. 370–372.
Leges: pp. 372–390.
Epinomis: p. 390.
Epistulae: pp. 390–392.
De justo: p. 392.
Sisyphus: pp. 392–393.
Halcyon: pp. 393–394.
Eryxias: p. 394.
Axiochus: pp. 394–396.
Dup. partim 5035 001–002.
Halycon (pp. 393–394): Dup. partim SCHOLIA IN LUCIANUM (5029 002).
Cod: Schol.

004 **Scholia in Platonis Parmenidem** (scholia vetera), ed. V. Cousin, *Procli philosophi Platonici opera inedita*, pt. 3. Paris: Durand, 1864 (repr. Hildesheim: Olms, 1961): 1257–1314.
Cod: [15,162]: Schol.

5036 SCHOLIA IN PORPHYRIUM
Varia
Cf. et MAXIMUS CONFESSOR Theol. et Poeta
(2892 084).
001 **Scholia in Porphyrii librum de abstinentia,** ed.
J. Bouffartigue and M. Patillon, *Porphyre. De
l'abstinence,* vol. 2. Paris: Les Belles Lettres,
1979: 193–195.
Cod: Schol.

5037 SCHOLIA IN SOPHOCLEM
Varia
001 **Scholia in Sophoclis Ajacem** (scholia vetera),
ed. G.A. Christodoulos, Τὰ ἀρχαῖα σχόλια εἰς
Αἴαντα τοῦ Σοφοκλέους. Athens: University of
Athens Press, 1977: 9–10, 13–260.
Hypothesis: pp. 9–10.
Scholia et glossae: pp. 13–260.
Cod: 24,028: Schol., Hypoth.
002 **Scholia et glossae in Sophoclis Ajacem** (glossae
et scholia recentiora), ed. Christodoulos, *op.
cit.,* 263–353.
Cod: 17,937: Schol.
003 **Hypotheses et excerpta interpretationum alle-
goricarum in Sophoclis Ajacem,** ed. Christo-
doulos, *op. cit.,* 354–355.
Argumentum codicis N: p. 354.
Argumentum codicis G: p. 354.
Excerpta interpretationum allegoricarum codi-
cis V: pp. 354–355.
Cod: 668: Schol., Hypoth.
004 **Scholia in Sophoclem** (scholia vetera), ed. P.N.
Papageorgius, *Scholia in Sophoclis tragoedias
vetera.* Leipzig: Teubner, 1888: 1–468.
Ajax: pp. 1–96.
Electra: pp. 97–160.
Oedipus tyrannus: pp. 161–212.
Antigone: pp. 213–277.
Trachiniae: pp. 278–349.
Philoctetes: pp. 350–394.
Oedipus Coloneus: pp. 395–468.
Ajax: Dup. partim 5037 001.
Oedipus Coloneus: Dup. partim 5037 006.
Cod: Schol.
005 **Scholia in Sophoclis Oedipum tyrannum**
(scholia recentiora), ed. O. Longo, *Scholia By-
zantina in Sophoclis Oedipum tyrannum.* Pa-
dua: Antenore, 1971: 3–92, 95–164, 167–265,
269–297.
Scholia Moschopuli: pp. 3–92.
Scholia Planudea: pp. 95–164.
Scholia Thomae Magistri: pp. 167–265.
Scholia Triclinii de metris: pp. 269–284.
Scholia Triclinii: pp. 285–290.
Figurae Triclinii: pp. 291–293.
Variae lectiones codicum Triclinianorum: pp.
294–297.
Cod: 45,140: Schol.
006 **Scholia in Sophoclis Oedipum Coloneum**
(scholia vetera), ed. V. de Marco, *Scholia in
Sophoclis Oedipum Coloneum.* Rome: Bret-
schneider, 1952: 1–68.

Hypotheses 1–3: pp. 1–3.
Hypothesis Sallustii Pythagorei: pp. 3–4.
Scholia: pp. 5–68.
Epigramma: p. 68.
Dup. partim 5037 004.
Cod: 13,446: Schol., Hypoth., Epigr.

5041 SCHOLIA IN TATIANUM
A.D. 9–10
x01 **Scholia in orationem ad Graecos** (scholia re-
centiora sub auctore Aretha).
Schwartz, pp. 44–47.
Cf. ARETHAS Philol. et Scr. Eccl. (2130 015).

5038 SCHOLIA IN THEOCRITUM
Varia
Cf. et Joannes PEDIASIMUS Gramm. (2592
006).
Cf. et Manuel HOLOBOLUS Rhet. (4065 002).
001 **Scholia in Theocritum** (scholia vetera), ed. K.
Wendel, *Scholia in Theocritum vetera.* Leipzig:
Teubner, 1914 (repr. Stuttgart: 1967): 1–352.
Vita et prolegomena: pp. 1–7.
Anecdoton Estense: pp. 7–13.
Argumenta et scholia: pp. 23–335.
Scholia in Theocriti, Simiae, Dosiadae, et Be-
santini technopaegnia: pp. 336–352.
Cod: 54,762: Schol., Biogr., Hypoth.

5046 SCHOLIA IN THEONEM RHETOREM
Varia
001 **Scholia in progymnasmata** (scholia recentiora),
ed. C. Walz, *Rhetores Graeci,* vol. 1. Stuttgart:
Cotta, 1832 (repr. Osnabrück: Zeller, 1968):
257–262.
Cod: Schol., Rhet.

5039 SCHOLIA IN THUCYDIDEM
Varia
001 **Scholia in Thucydidem** (scholia vetera et recentiora), ed. K. Hude, *Scholia in Thucydidem
ad optimos codices collata.* Leipzig: Teubner,
1927 (repr. New York: Arno, 1973): 1–434.
Cod, Pap: 104,371: Schol., Epigr.

5040 SCHOLIA IN XENOPHONTEM
Varia
001 **Scholia in anabasin Cyri** (scholia vetera), ed.
L. Dindorf, *Xenophontis expeditio Cyri,* 2nd
edn. Oxford: Oxford University Press, 1855:
381–396.
Cod: Schol.

2514 Publius Cornelius SCIPIO Hist.
3–2 B.C.: Romanus
001 **Testimonia,** FGrH #811: 3C:880–881.
NQ: 60: Test.

2163 Publius Cornelius SCIPIO Major Hist.
3–2 B.C.: Romanus

001 **Fragmentum**, FGrH #232: 2B:979–980.
Q: 1,011: Hist., Epist.

2164 **Publius Cornelius SCIPIO NASICA CORCU-
LUM** Hist.
2 B.C.: Romanus
001 **Fragmenta**, FGrH #233: 2B:981–982.
Q: 691: Hist.

1662 **SCIRAS** Comic.
3 B.C.
001 **Fragmentum**, ed. G. Kaibel, *Comicorum Graecorum fragmenta*, vol. 1.1 [*Poetarum Graecorum fragmenta*, vol. 6.1. Berlin: Weidmann,
1899]: 190.
fr. 1.
Q: 12: Comic.

0353 **<SCLERIAS>** Trag.
Incertum
001 **Fragmenta**, ed. B. Snell, *Tragicorum Graecorum fragmenta*, vol. 1. Göttingen: Vandenhoeck & Ruprecht, 1971: 323–324.
frr. 1–2, 4.
Q: 42: Trag.

0273 *SCOLIA ALPHABETICA*
ante A.D. 3
001 **Fragmenta** (*P. Oxy.* 15.1795), ed. E. Heitsch,
*Die griechischen Dichterfragmente der röm-
ischen Kaiserzeit*, vol. 1, 2nd edn. Göttingen:
Vandenhoeck & Ruprecht, 1963: 38–40.
Dup. ANONYMI AULODIA (1836 001).
Dup. partim LYRICA ADESPOTA (CA) (0230
001) (fr. 37).
Pap: 291: Hexametr., Lyr.
002 **Fragmenta** (*P. Oxy.* 1.15), ed. Heitsch, *op. cit.*,
40–41.
Dup. FRAGMENTUM TELIAMBICUM (1382
001).
Pap: 99: Hexametr., Lyr.

SCOLIA ANONYMA
PMG, pp. 472–482, frr. 1–25, 28–31, 33.
CA, pp. 190–192, frr. 16–17, 21.
Cf. CARMINA CONVIVIALIA (PMG) (0296
001).
Cf. LYRICA ADESPOTA (CA) (0230 001).

2238 **SCOPAS** (?) Hist.
ante 2 B.C.
001 **Testimonium**, FGrH #413: 3B:305.
NQ: 23: Test.
002 **Fragmentum**, FGrH #413: 3B:306.
Q: 59: Hist.

0065 **SCYLAX** Perieg.
5/4 B.C.: Caryandensis
001 **Periplus Scylacis**, ed. K. Müller, *Geographi
Graeci minores*, vol. 1. Paris: Didot, 1855 (repr.
Hildesheim: Olms, 1965): 15–96.
Cod: 9,047: Perieg.

002 **Testimonia**, FGrH #709: 3C:587–589.
NQ: 712: Test.

003 **Fragmenta**, FGrH #709: 3C:589–592.
Q: 902: Hist., Perieg.

3064 *SCYLITZES CONTINUATUS*
A.D. 11
Cf. et JOANNES SCYLITZES Hist. (3063).
002 **Continuatio Scylitzae**, ed. E.T. Tsolakes, Ἡ
συνέχεια τῆς χρονογραφίας τοῦ Ἰωάννου Σκυ-
λίτση [Ἑταιρεία Μακεδονικῶν Σπουδῶν. Ἴδ-
ρυμα Μελετῶν Χερσονήσου τοῦ Αἵμου 105.
Thessalonica: n.p., 1968]: 103–186.
Cod: Hist., Chronogr.

0068 **Pseudo-SCYMNUS** Geogr.
vel Pausanias Damascenus
1 B.C.
001 **Ad Nicomedem regem, vv. 1–980** (*sub titulo
Orbis descriptio*), ed. K. Müller, *Geographi
Graeci minores*, vol. 1. Paris: Didot, 1855 (repr.
Hildesheim: Olms, 1965): 196–237.
Cod: 5,805: Perieg., Iamb.
002 **Ad Nicomedem regem, vv. 722–1026**, ed. A.
Diller, *The tradition of the minor Greek geogra-
phers*. Lancaster, Pennsylvania: American
Philological Association, 1952: 165–176.
Dup. partim 0068 001.
Cod: 1,688: Perieg., Iamb.

0259 **SCYTHINUS** Poet. Phil.
4 B.C.: Teius
001 **Fragmenta**, ed. M.L. West, *Iambi et elegi
Graeci*, vol. 2. Oxford: Clarendon Press, 1972:
96.
frr. 1–2.
Q: 55: Iamb.
002 **Testimonia**, FGrH #13: 1A:176.
NQ: 44: Test.
004 **Fragmentum**, FGrH #13: 1A:176–177.
Q: 160: Hist., Myth.
003 **Epigrammata**, AG 12.22, 232.
Q: 98: Epigr.

0274 **SECUNDUS** Epigr.
A.D. 1: Tarentinus
001 **Epigrammata**, AG 9.36, 260, 301; 16.214.
Q: 164: Epigr.

SECUNDUS Phil.
A.D. 2: Atheniensis
Cf. VITA ET SENTENTIAE SECUNDI (1521).

1810 **SELEUCUS** Gramm.
A.D. 1: Alexandrinus
001 **Fragmenta**, ed. R. Reitzenstein, *Geschichte der
griechischen Etymologika*. Leipzig: Teubner,
1897 (repr. Amsterdam: Hakkert, 1964): 157–
165.
Q: [2,151]
002 Περὶ Ἑλληνισμοῦ (fragmentum), ed. H. Fun-

aioli, *Grammaticae Romanae fragmenta*, vol. 1. Leipzig: Teubner, 1907: 450–451.
Q

003 **Testimonia**, FGrH #341: 3B:197.
NQ: 84: Test.

004 **Fragmenta**, FGrH #341 & #634: **3B**:197–198; **3C**:183.
Q: 442: Hist.

005 **Fragmenta**, ed. M. Müller, *De Seleuco Homerico* [*Diss. Göttingen* (1891)]: 34–53.
Q

2524 **SELEUCUS** Gramm.
A.D. 3–4: Emesenus

001 **Testimonium**, FGrH #780: 3C:777.
NQ: 27: Test.

0209 **SELEUCUS** Lyr.
2 B.C.

001 'Ιλαρὰ ᾄσματα, ed. J.U. Powell, *Collectanea Alexandrina*. Oxford: Clarendon Press, 1925 (repr. 1970): 176.
Q: 18: Lyr.

2464 **SEMERONIUS** Hist.
Incertum: Babylonius

001 **Fragmentum**, FGrH #686: 3C:410.
Q: 71: Hist.

0260 **SEMONIDES** Eleg. et Iamb.
7 B.C.: Samius, Amorginus

001 **Fragmenta**, ed. M.L. West, *Iambi et elegi Graeci*, vol. 2. Oxford: Clarendon Press, 1972: 97–109, 111–112.
frr. 1–28, 30–31a, 41–42.
Q: 1,063: Iamb.

002 **Testimonia**, FGrH #534: 3B:520.
NQ: 90: Test.

1663 **SEMUS** Gramm.
3–2 B.C.?: Delius

001 **Testimonium**, FGrH #396: 3B:285.
NQ: 33: Test.

002 **Fragmenta**, FGrH #396: 3B:285–291.
Q: 1,400: Hist.

2431 **Lucius Annaeus SENECA** Phil.
1 B.C.–A.D. 1: Cordubensis

001 **Fragmenta**, FGrH #644: 3C:189–190.
Q: 221: Hist.

SENECA Iatrosophista <Epigr.>
AG 1.90.
Cf. SOPHRONIUS Soph., Scr. Eccl. et Epigr. (4042 016).

1664 **SENIORES ALEXANDRINI** Scr. Eccl.
A.D. 2

001 **Fragmenta**, ed. J.B. Pitra, *Analecta sacra spicilegio Solesmensi parata*, vol. 2. Paris: Tusculum, 1884 (repr. Farnborough: Gregg Press, 1966): 335–345.
Cod: 1,741: Exeget.

1665 **SENIORES APUD IRENAEUM** Scr. Eccl.
A.D. 2–3

001 **Reliquiae plurium anonymorum**, ed. M.J. Routh, *Reliquiae sacrae*, vol. 1, 2nd edn. Oxford: Oxford University Press, 1846 (repr. Hildesheim: Olms, 1974): 47–48, 56–59.
Q: 472: Nat. Hist., Eccl.

1759 *SENTENTIAE PYTHAGOREORUM*
A.D. 2–3?

001 **Sententiae Pythagoreorum** (fort. auctore vel collectore Demophilo), ed. A. Elter, *Gnomica homoeomata*, pt. 5 [*Programm zur Feier des Geburtstages seiner Majestät des Kaisers und Königs am 27. Januar 1904*. Bonn: Georg, 1905]: coll. 1–36.
Q, Cod: 3,373: Gnom.

002 **Sententiae Pythagoreorum**, ed. H. Chadwick, *The sentences of Sextus*. Cambridge: Cambridge University Press, 1959: 84–94.
Cod: 1,920: Gnom.

1666 *SENTENTIAE SEXTI*
A.D. 2/3

001 **Sententiae Sexti**, ed. H. Chadwick, *The sentences of Sextus*. Cambridge: Cambridge University Press, 1959: 12–72.
Cod: 4,867: Gnom.

1667 <**SEPTEM SAPIENTES**> Phil.
7–6 B.C.
Cf. et BIAS <Phil.> (1223).
Cf. et CHILON <Phil.> (1261).
Cf. et CLEOBULUS Lyr. et Epigr. (1274).
Cf. et PERIANDER <Phil.> (0629).
Cf. et PITTACUS <Lyr.> (0631).
Cf. et SOLON Nomographus et Poeta (0263).
Cf. et THALES Phil. (1705).

001 **Testimonia**, ed. H. Diels and W. Kranz, *Die Fragmente der Vorsokratiker*, vol. 1, 6th edn. Berlin: Weidmann, 1951 (repr. Dublin: 1966): 61–62.
test. 1–3.
NQ: 561: Test.

002 **Apophthegmata** (ex collectione Demetrii Phalerei) (ap. Stobaeum), ed. Diels and Kranz, *op. cit.*, 63–66.
Q: 889: Phil., Gnom.

004 **Sententiae**, ed. F.W.A. Mullach, *Fragmenta philosophorum Graecorum*, vol. 1. Paris: Didot, 1860 (repr. Aalen: Scientia, 1968): 215–216.
Cod: 565: Gnom.

005 **Praecepta** (sub auctore Sosiade) (ap. Stobaeum), ed. Mullach, *op. cit.*, 217–218.
Q: 413: Gnom.

006 **Apophthegmata** (ap. auctores diversos), ed. Mullach, *op. cit.*, 219–235.
Septem sapientum apophthegmata: Divisiones 1–7, pp. 219–231.
Eorundem vii sapientum de re familiari effata: Divisio 8, p. 231.
Eorundem dicta de republica: Divisio 9, pp. 231–232.

Anacharsis Gnuri filii apophthegmata: Divisio
10, pp. 232–234.

Mysonis apophthegmata: Divisio 11, p. 234.

Incerti epigramma in vii sapientes: Divisio 12,
p. 235.

Antipatri in eosdem epigramma: Divisio 13, p.
235.

Q: 4,206: Gnom., Epigr.

0527 *SEPTUAGINTA*
Varia

001 **Genesis**, ed. A. Rahlfs, *Septuaginta*, vol. 1, 9th
edn. Stuttgart: Württembergische Bibelanstalt,
1935 (repr. 1971): 1–86.
Cod: 34,304: Relig., Hist.

002 **Exodus**, ed. Rahlfs, *op. cit.*, vol. 1, 86–158.
Cod: 26,553: Relig., Hist.

003 **Leviticus**, ed. Rahlfs, *op. cit.*, vol. 1, 158–209.
Cod: 20,336: Relig., Hist.

004 **Numeri**, ed. Rahlfs, *op. cit.*, vol. 1, 210–283.
Cod: 26,811: Relig., Hist.

005 **Deuteronomium**, ed. Rahlfs, *op. cit.*, vol. 1,
284–354.
Cod: 24,297: Relig., Hist.

006 **Josue** (Cod. Vaticanus + Cod. Alexandrinus),
ed. Rahlfs, *op. cit.*, vol. 1, 354–405.
Cod. Vat. + Cod. Alex.: 354–381, 384–388,
392–405.
Cod. Vat. solum: 382–384, 388–392.
Cod: 15,847: Relig., Hist.

007 **Josue** (Cod. Alexandrinus), ed. Rahlfs, *op. cit.*,
vol. 1, 382–384, 388–392.
Cod: 1,195: Relig., Hist.

008 **Judices** (Cod. Alexandrinus), ed. Rahlfs, *op.
cit.*, vol. 1, 405–495.
Cod: 16,883: Relig., Hist.

009 **Judices** (Cod. Vaticanus), ed. Rahlfs, *op. cit.*,
vol. 1, 405–495.
Cod: 16,519: Relig., Hist.

010 **Ruth**, ed. Rahlfs, *op. cit.*, vol. 1, 495–501.
Cod: 2,200: Relig., Narr. Fict.

011 **Regnorum i** (Samuelis i in textu Masoretico),
ed. Rahlfs, *op. cit.*, vol. 1, 502–564.
Cod: 21,243: Relig., Hist.

012 **Regnorum ii** (Samuelis ii in textu Masoretico),
ed. Rahlfs, *op. cit.*, vol. 1, 565–622.
Cod: 18,914: Relig., Hist.

013 **Regnorum iii** (Regum i in textu Masoretico),
ed. Rahlfs, *op. cit.*, vol. 1, 623–693.
Cod: 22,061: Relig., Hist.

014 **Regnorum iv** (Regum ii in textu Masoretico),
ed. Rahlfs, *op. cit.*, vol. 1, 693–752.
Cod: 19,990: Relig., Hist.

015 **Paralipomenon i** *sive* **Chronicon i**, ed. Rahlfs,
op. cit., vol. 1, 752–811.
Cod: 17,451: Relig., Hist.

016 **Paralipomenon ii** *sive* **Chronicon ii**, ed. Rahlfs,
op. cit., vol. 1, 811–873.
Cod: 22,679: Relig., Hist.

017 **Esdras i** (liber apocryphus), ed. Rahlfs, *op. cit.*,
vol. 1, 873–903.
Cod: 9,624: Relig., Hist., Apocryph.

018 **Esdras ii** (Ezra et Nehemias in textu Masoretico), ed. Rahlfs, *op. cit.*, vol. 1, 903–950.
Cod: 14,219: Relig., Hist.

019 **Esther**, ed. Rahlfs, *op. cit.*, vol. 1, 951–973.
Cod: 6,237: Relig., Narr. Fict.

020 **Judith**, ed. Rahlfs, *op. cit.*, vol. 1, 973–1002.
Cod: 9,736: Relig., Narr. Fict., Apocryph.

021 **Tobias** (Cod. Vaticanus + Cod. Alexandrinus),
ed. Rahlfs, *op. cit.*, vol. 1, 1002–1039.
Cod: 5,856: Relig., Narr. Fict., Apocryph.

022 **Tobias** (Cod. Sinaiticus), ed. Rahlfs, *op. cit.*,
vol. 1, 1002–1039.
Cod: 7,636: Relig., Narr. Fict., Apocryph.

023 **Machabaeorum i**, ed. Rahlfs, *op. cit.*, vol. 1,
1039–1099.
Cod: 19,535: Relig., Hist., Apocryph.

024 **Machabaeorum ii**, ed. Rahlfs, *op. cit.*, vol. 1,
1099–1139.
Cod: 12,762: Relig., Hist., Apocryph.

025 **Machabaeorum iii**, ed. Rahlfs, *op. cit.*, vol. 1,
1139–1156.
Cod: 5,484: Relig., Narr. Fict., Apocryph.

026 **Machabaeorum iv**, ed. Rahlfs, *op. cit.*, vol. 1,
1157–1184.
Cod: 8,489: Relig., Hagiogr., Apocryph.

027 **Psalmi**, ed. Rahlfs, *op. cit.*, vol. 2, 9th edn.
(1935; repr. 1971): 1–164.
Cod: 35,353: Relig., Hymn., Poem.

028 **Odae**, ed. Rahlfs, *op. cit.*, vol. 2, 164–183.
Oda 12, Oratio Manassis: apocrypha est.
Cod: 4,234: Relig., Hymn., Poem.

029 **Proverbia**, ed. Rahlfs, *op. cit.*, vol. 2, 183–238.
Cod: 11,265: Relig., Paroem.

030 **Ecclesiastes**, ed. Rahlfs, *op. cit.*, vol. 2, 238–
260.
Cod: 4,573: Relig., Poem.

031 **Canticum**, ed. Rahlfs, *op. cit.*, vol. 2, 260–270.
Cod: 2,037: Relig., Poem.

032 **Job**, ed. Rahlfs, *op. cit.*, vol. 2, 271–345.
Cod: 13,664: Relig., Narr. Fict., Poem.

033 **Sapientia Salomonis**, ed. Rahlfs, *op. cit.*, vol. 2,
345–376.
Cod: 6,985: Relig., Pseudepigr.

034 **Ecclesiasticus** *sive* **Siracides** (Sapientia Jesu
filii Sirach), ed. Rahlfs, *op. cit.*, vol. 2, 377–
471.
Cod: 18,760: Relig., Apocryph.

035 **Psalmi Salomonis**, ed. Rahlfs, *op. cit.*, vol. 2,
471–489.
Cod: 4,969: Relig., Poem., Pseudepigr.

036 **Osee**, ed. Rahlfs, *op. cit.*, vol. 2, 490–501.
Cod: 4,205: Relig., Prophet.

037 **Amos**, ed. Rahlfs, *op. cit.*, vol. 2, 502–511.
Cod: 3,409: Relig., Prophet.

038 **Michaeas**, ed. Rahlfs, *op. cit.*, vol. 2, 512–519.
Cod: 2,515: Relig., Prophet.

039 **Joel**, ed. Rahlfs, *op. cit.*, vol. 2, 519–524.
Cod: 1,693: Relig., Prophet.

040 **Abdias**, ed. Rahlfs, *op. cit.*, vol. 2, 524–526.
Cod: 505: Relig., Prophet.

041 **Jonas**, ed. Rahlfs, *op. cit.*, vol. 2, 526–529.
Cod: 1,136: Relig., Narr. Fict., Prophet.

042 **Nahum**, ed. Rahlfs, *op. cit.*, vol. 2, 530–533.
Cod: 1,006: Relig., Prophet.

043 **Habacuc**, ed. Rahlfs, *op. cit.*, vol. 2, 533–537.
Cod: 1,162: Relig., Prophet.

044 **Sophonias**, ed. Rahlfs, *op. cit.*, vol. 2, 538–542.
Cod: 1,289: Relig., Prophet.

045 **Aggaeus**, ed. Rahlfs, *op. cit.*, vol. 2, 542–545.
Cod: 1,005: Relig., Prophet.

046 **Zacharias**, ed. Rahlfs, *op. cit.*, vol. 2, 545–561.
Cod: 5,243: Relig., Prophet.

047 **Malachias**, ed. Rahlfs, *op. cit.*, vol. 2, 561–565.
Cod: 1,490: Relig., Prophet.

048 **Isaias**, ed. Rahlfs, *op. cit.*, vol. 2, 566–656.
Cod: 28,804: Relig., Prophet.

049 **Jeremias**, ed. Rahlfs, *op. cit.*, vol. 2, 656–748.
Cod: 30,810: Relig., Prophet.

050 **Baruch**, ed. Rahlfs, *op. cit.*, vol. 2, 748–756.
Cod: 2,803: Relig., Hymn., Poem., Prophet., Apocryph.

051 **Threni** *seu* **Lamentationes**, ed. Rahlfs, *op. cit.*, vol. 2, 756–766.
Cod: 2,422: Relig., Poem.

052 **Epistula Jeremiae**, ed. Rahlfs, *op. cit.*, vol. 2, 766–770.
Cod: 1,370: Relig., Epist., Apocryph.

053 **Ezechiel**, ed. Rahlfs, *op. cit.*, vol. 2, 770–863.
Cod: 31,395: Relig., Prophet.

054 **Susanna** (translatio Graeca), ed. Rahlfs, *op. cit.*, vol. 2, 864–870.
Cod: 853: Relig., Narr. Fict., Apocryph.

055 **Susanna** (Theodotionis versio), ed. Rahlfs, *op. cit.*, vol. 2, 864–870.
Cod: 1,230: Relig., Narr. Fict., Apocryph.

056 **Daniel** (translatio Graeca), ed. Rahlfs, *op. cit.*, vol. 2, 870–936.
Cod: 11,398: Relig., Narr. Fict., Apocalyp.

057 **Daniel** (Theodotionis versio), ed. Rahlfs, *op. cit.*, vol. 2, 870–936.
Cod: 11,096: Relig., Narr. Fict., Apocalyp.

058 **Bel et Draco** (translatio Graeca), ed. Rahlfs, *op. cit.*, vol. 2, 936–941.
Cod: 960: Relig., Narr. Fict., Apocryph.

059 **Bel et Draco** (Theodotionis versio), ed. Rahlfs, *op. cit.*, vol. 2, 936–941.
Cod: 939: Relig., Narr. Fict., Apocryph.

1669 **SERAPION** Astrol.
fiq Serapion Alexandrinus
1 B.C.?: Antiochenus

001 **Fragmenta**, ed. A. Olivieri, *Codices Florentini* [*Catalogus codicum astrologorum Graecorum* 1. Brussels: Lamertin, 1898]: 99–102.
Cod

002 **Fragmenta**, ed. F. Cumont and F. Boll, *Codices Romani* [*Catalogus codicum astrologorum Graecorum* 5.1. Brussels: Lamertin, 1904]: 179–180.
Cod

003 **Fragmenta**, ed. J. Heeg, *Codices Romani* [*Catalogus codicum astrologorum Graecorum* 5.3. Brussels: Lamertin, 1910]: 96–97, 125.
Cod

004 **Fragmenta**, ed. P. Boudreaux, *Codices Parisini* [*Catalogus codicum astrologorum Graecorum* 8.4. Brussels: Lamertin, 1921]: 225–232.
Cod

1668 **SERAPION** Epigr.
ante A.D. 1: Alexandrinus

001 **Epigramma**, AG 7.400.
Q: 27: Epigr.

1070 **SERAPION** Med.
3 B.C.: Alexandrinus

x01 **Fragmenta ap. Galenum.**
K13.509–510, 833.
Cf. GALENUS Med. (0057 077).

x02 **Fragmentum ap. Oribasium.**
CMG, vol. 6.2.2, p. 285.
Cf. ORIBASIUS Med. (0722 003).

x03 **Fragmentum ap. Paulum.**
CMG, vol. 9.2, p. 360.
Cf. PAULUS Med. (0715 001).

x04 **Fragmentum ap. Aëtium** (lib. 15).
Zervos, *Athena* 21, p. 88.
Cf. AËTIUS Med. (0718 015).

1670 **SERAPION** Scr. Eccl.
A.D. 2–3: Antiochenus

001 **Fragmenta**, ed. M.J. Routh, *Reliquiae sacrae*, vol. 1, 2nd edn. Oxford: Oxford University Press, 1846 (repr. Hildesheim: Olms, 1974): 451–453.
Fragmentum ex epistula ad Caricum et Pontium: pp. 451–452.
Fragmentum ex libro de evangelio, quod sub nomine Petri ferebatur: pp. 452–453.
Q: 339: Epist., Theol.

0347 **SERAPION** Trag.
A.D. 1

001 **Fragmentum**, ed. B. Snell, *Tragicorum Graecorum fragmenta*, vol. 1. Göttingen: Vandenhoeck & Ruprecht, 1971: 315.
fr. 1.
Q: 14: Trag.

2055 **SERENUS** Geom.
A.D. 4: Antinoensis

001 **De sectione cylindri**, ed. J.L. Heiberg, *Sereni Antinoensis opuscula*. Leipzig: Teubner, 1896: 2–116.
Cod: 12,938: Math.

002 **De sectione coni**, ed. Heiberg, *op. cit.*, 120–302.
Cod: 20,007: Math.

1671 **SERENUS** Gnom.
fiq Aelius Serenus Gramm.
A.D. 2?: fort. Atheniensis

x01 **Fragmenta ap. Stobaeum.**
Anth. III.5.36–38; 6.17–19; 7.62; 11.23;

13.48–49, 58; 29.96; 39.27; **IV**.2.26; 6.20;
19.48; 22f.134; 24a.11.
Cf. Joannes STOBAEUS (2037 001).

1072 **SERGIUS** Med.
ante A.D. 2: Babylonius
x01 **Fragmenta ap. Galenum.**
K12.746, 751.
Cf. GALENUS Med. (0057 076).

1073 **Clemens SERTORIUS** Med.
ante A.D. 2
x01 **Fragmentum ap. Galenum.**
K13.1037.
Cf. GALENUS Med. (0057 077).

1672 **SERVIUS** Hist.
Incertum
001 **Fragmentum,** FGrH #47: 1A:272.
Q: 75: Hist., Myth.

1820 **SEUTHES** Astrol.
ante A.D. 2
001 **Fragmenta,** ed. W. Kroll, *Codices Romani [Ca-*
talogus codicum astrologorum Graecorum, vol.
5.2. Brussels: Lamertin, 1906]: 114.
Q

4139 **SEVERIANUS** Scr. Eccl.
A.D. 4: Gabalensis
039 **Fragmenta in epistulam ad Romanos** (in catenis), ed. K. Staab, *Pauluskommentar aus der*
griechischen Kirche aus Katenenhandschriften
gesammelt. Münster: Aschendorff, 1933: 213–
225.
Q: 3,054: Exeget., Caten.
040 **Fragmenta in epistulam i ad Corinthios** (in catenis), ed. Staab, *op. cit.,* 225–277.
Q: 14,909: Exeget., Caten.
041 **Fragmenta in epistulam ii ad Corinthios** (in catenis), ed. Staab, *op. cit.,* 278–298.
Q: 5,165: Exeget., Caten.
042 **Fragmenta in epistulam ad Galatas** (in catenis), ed. Staab, *op. cit.,* 298–304.
Q: 1,581: Exeget., Caten.
043 **Fragmenta in epistulam ad Ephesios** (in catenis), ed. Staab, *op. cit.,* 304–313.
Q: 2,248: Exeget., Caten.
044 **Fragmenta in epistulam ad Philippenses** (in
catenis), ed. Staab, *op. cit.,* 313–314.
Q: 412: Exeget., Caten.
045 **Fragmenta in epistulam ad Colossenses** (in catenis), ed. Staab, *op. cit.,* 314–328.
Q: 3,811: Exeget., Caten.
046 **Fragmenta in epistulam i ad Thessalonicenses**
(in catenis), ed. Staab, *op. cit.,* 328–331.
Q: 796: Exeget., Caten.
047 **Fragmenta in epistulam ii ad Thessalonicenses**
(in catenis), ed. Staab, *op. cit.,* 332–336.
Q: 1,197: Exeget., Caten.

048 **Fragmenta in epistulam i ad Timotheum** (in
catenis), ed. Staab, *op. cit.,* 336–341.
Q: 1,736: Exeget., Caten.
049 **Fragmenta in epistulam ii ad Timotheum** (in
catenis), ed. Staab, *op. cit.,* 342–344.
Q: 624: Exeget., Caten.
050 **Fragmenta in epistulam ad Titum** (in catenis),
ed. Staab, *op. cit.,* 344–345.
Q: 173: Exeget., Caten.
051 **Fragmentum in epistulam ad Philemonem** (in
catenis), ed. Staab, *op. cit.,* 345.
Q: 34: Exeget., Caten.
052 **Fragmenta in epistulam ad Hebraeos** (in catenis), ed. Staab, *op. cit.,* 345–351.
Q: 1,665: Exeget., Caten.

1074 **SEVERUS** Med.
fiq Severus Iatrosophista
A.D. 1
Cf. et SEVERUS Iatrosophista Med. (0748).
x01 **Fragmentum ap. Galenum.**
K12.734.
Cf. GALENUS Med. (0057 076).
x02 **Fragmentum ap. Paulum.**
CMG, vol. 9.2, p. 337.
Cf. PAULUS Med. (0715 001).
x03 **Fragmenta ap. Aëtium** (lib. 7).
CMG, vol. 8.2, pp. 279, 296, 331, 337, 341,
396.
Cf. AËTIUS Med. (0718 007).
x04 **Fragmentum ap. Alexandrum Trallianum.**
Puschmann, vol. 2, p. 44.
Cf. ALEXANDER Med. (0744 003).

2970 **SEVERUS** Phil.
A.D. 2
001 Περὶ ψυχῆς (fragmentum), ed. F.W.A. Mullach, *Fragmenta philosophorum Graecorum,*
vol. 3. Paris: Didot, 1881 (repr. Aalen: Scientia, 1968): 204–205.
Q: 399: Phil.

4239 **SEVERUS** Soph.
A.D. 4: Alexandrinus, Antiochenus, Constan-
tinopolitanus
001 **Narrationes et ethopoeia,** ed. C. Walz, *Rhetores*
Graeci, vol. 1. Stuttgart: Cotta, 1832 (repr.
Osnabrück: Zeller, 1968): 537–548.
Cod: Rhet.

0748 **SEVERUS Iatrosophista** Med.
A.D. 1?
Cf. et SEVERUS Med. (1074).
001 **De instrumentis infusoriis seu clysteribus ad**
Timotheum, ed. F.R. Dietz, *Severi iatrosophis-*
tae de clysteribus liber [Diss. med. Königsberg
(1836)]: 1–43.
Cod: 9,605: Med.

SEXTUS Phil.
Cf. SENTENTIAE SEXTI (1666).

0544 **SEXTUS EMPIRICUS** Phil.
A.D. 2–3
001 **Pyrrhoniae hypotyposes**, ed. H. Mutschmann, *Sexti Empirici opera*, vol. 1. Leipzig: Teubner, 1912: 3–131, 133–209.
Cod: 53,497: Phil.
002 **Adversus mathematicos**, ed. Mutschmann and J. Mau, *Sexti Empirici opera*, vols. 2 (1914) & 3, 2nd edn. (1961): 2:3–429; 3:1–177.
Lib. 1 (Adversus mathematicos et grammaticos): vol. 3, pp. 1–82.
Lib. 2 (Adversus rhetores): vol. 3, pp. 83–106.
Lib. 3 (Adversus geometras): vol. 3, pp. 107–132.
Lib. 4 (Adversus arithmeticos): vol. 3, pp. 133–140.
Lib. 5 (Adversus astrologos): vol. 3, pp. 141–162.
Lib. 6 (Adversus musicos): vol. 3, pp. 163–177.
Lib. 7 (Adversus dogmaticos 1) (= Adversus logicos 1): vol. 2, pp. 3–103.
Lib. 8 (Adversus dogmaticos 2) (= Adversus logicos 2): vol. 2, pp. 104–212.
Lib. 9 (Adversus dogmaticos 3) (= Adversus physicos 1): vol. 2, pp. 213–302.
Lib. 10 (Adversus dogmaticos 4) (= Adversus physicos 2): vol. 2, pp. 303–374.
Lib. 11 (Adversus dogmaticos 5) (= Adversus ethicos): vol. 2, pp. 375–429.
Cod: 155,837: Phil.

SEXTUS JULIUS AFRICANUS Hist.
Cf. Sextus JULIUS AFRICANUS Hist. (2956).

SIBYLLA TIBURTINA
A.D. 4: Tiburtina
Cf. ORACULA TIBURTINA (2960).

1970 **SILENUS** Hist.
3 B.C.: fort. Calactinus
001 **Testimonia**, FGrH #175: 2B:900.
NQ: 111: Test.
002 **Fragmenta**, FGrH #175: 2B:900–903.
Q: 751: Hist.

1877 **SILENUS** Hist.
3/2 B.C.?: Chius
001 **Fragmenta**, FGrH #27: 1A:211–212.
Q: 177: Hist., Myth.

0603 **SILENUS** Trag.
2 B.C.
001 **Titulus**, ed. B. Snell, *Tragicorum Graecorum fragmenta*, vol. 1. Göttingen: Vandenhoeck & Ruprecht, 1971: 309.
NQ: 1: Trag.

0211 **SIMIAS** Gramm.
vel Simmias
4–3 B.C.: Rhodius
Scholia: Cf. SCHOLIA IN THEOCRITUM (5038).

001 **Fragmenta**, ed. J.U. Powell, *Collectanea Alexandrina*. Oxford: Clarendon Press, 1925 (repr. 1970): 109, 111–119.
frr. 1, 3–4, 6–26.
Dup. partim 0211 002.
Q: 671: Hexametr., Epigr.
002 **Epigrammata**, AG **6**.113–114; **7**.21–22, 60, 193, 203, 647; **15**.22, 24, 27.
Dup. partim 0211 001 (frr. 18–22, 24–26).
AG 6.116: Cf. SAMUS Epigr. (1658 001).
AG 7.20: Cf. SIMONIDES Lyr. (0261 003).
Q: 561: Epigr.
x01 **Fragmentum hexametricum** (*P. Mich.* 3.139) (fort. auctore Simia Rhodio).
SH, p. 411, fr. 906.
Cf. ADESPOTA PAPYRACEA (SH) (2648 001).

1673 **SIMMIAS** Epigr.
5–4 B.C.: Thebanus
001 **Epigrammata**, AG 7.21–22, 60.
Q: 105: Epigr.

0988 **SIMMIAS** Med.
ante A.D. 2: Medus
x01 **Fragmentum ap. Galenum**.
K14.180.
Cf. GALENUS Med. (0057 078).

4266 **SIMMIAS** Phil.
4 B.C.: Syracusanus, Atheniensis
001 **Testimonia**, ed. K. Döring, *Die Megariker* [*Studien zur antiken Philosophie* 2. Amsterdam: Grüner, 1972]: 50, 52, 61.
test. 153 (p. 50), 164a (p. 52) = Stilpo (4262 001).
NQ: Test.

2600 **SIMON** Scriptor De Re Equestri
5 B.C.: Atheniensis
001 **De forma et delectu equorum**, ed. K. Widdra, Ξενοφῶντος περὶ ἱππικῆς. Leipzig: Teubner, 1964: 41–44.
Cod: 552: Nat. Hist.
002 **Fragmenta**, ed. F. Ruehl, *Xenophontis scripta minora*, vol. 2. Leipzig: Teubner, 1912: 196–197.
frr. 1–6.
Q: 180: Nat. Hist.

1674 **<SIMON MAGUS>** Gnost.
A.D. 1
001 **Apophasis megale** (fragmenta), ed. W. Völker, *Quellen zur Geschichte der christlichen Gnosis*. Tübingen: Mohr, 1932: 1–11.
Q

1906 **SIMONIDES** Epic.
Incertum: Carystius vel Eretrius
001 **Testimonium**, FGrH #55c: 1A:*20 addenda.
NQ: 19: Test.
002 **Tituli**, ed. H. Lloyd-Jones and P. Parsons,

Supplementum Hellenisticum. Berlin: De Gruyter, 1983: 348.
frr. 720–722.
NQ: 8: Epic., Iamb.

1958 **SIMONIDES** Hist.
3–2 B.C.: Magnes
001 **Testimonium**, FGrH #163: 2B:889.
NQ: 34: Test.

0261 **SIMONIDES** Lyr.
6–5 B.C.: Ceus
001 **Fragmenta**, ed. M.L. West, *Iambi et elegi Graeci*, vol. 2. Oxford: Clarendon Press, 1972: 112–117.
frr. 2–17 + titulus.
Q: 269: Eleg., Epigr.
002 **Fragmenta**, ed. D.L. Page, *Poetae melici Graeci*. Oxford: Clarendon Press, 1962 (repr. 1967 (1st edn. corr.)): 238–241, 244–274, 276–318.
frr. 1–4, 6–7, 9–12, 14–22, 26, 28, 33, 36–41, 45–46, 48, 50, 54–55, 59, 62, 66–67, 70, 72, 74, 76, 78–82, 85, 87–90, 92–98, 100, 103, 107, 109–111, 113, 115, 117–121, 125–126, 128, 131, 133–134 + tituli.
Q, Pap: 3,962: Lyr., Encom.
003 **Epigrammata**, AG 5.159; **6**.2, 50, 52, 197, 212–217; **7**.20, 24–25, 77, 177, 248–251, 253–254b, 258, 270, 296, 300–302, 344, 348–349, 431, 442–443, 496, 507, 508–516, 647, 650b, 677; **9**.700, 757–758; **10**.105; **13**.11, 14, 19–20, 26, 28, 30; **16**.2–3, 23–24, 26, 60, 82, 204, 232.
AG 7.508: Dup. partim EMPEDOCLES Poet. Phil. (1342 004) (fr. 156).
AG 16.204: Dup. PRAXITELES <Epigr.> (1633 001).
AG 5.161: Cf. HEDYLUS Epigr. (0198 001).
AG 6.144: Cf. ANACREON Lyr. (0237 004).
AG 7.22: Cf. SIMIAS Gramm. (0211 002).
AG 7.187: Cf. PHILIPPUS Epigr. (1589 001).
AG 7.257, 347, 507b: Cf. ANONYMI EPIGRAMMATICI (AG) (0138 001).
AG 7.344b: Cf. CALLIMACHUS Philol. (0533 001).
AG 7.345: Cf. AESCHRION Lyr. (0679 001).
AG 9.147: Cf. ANTAGORAS Epic. (0215 002).
Q: 1,688: Epigr.
004 **Testimonium**, FGrH #8: 1A:158.
NQ: 29: Test.
005 **Fragmenta**, FGrH #8: 1A:159, *8–*9 addenda.
Q, Pap: 208: Hist., Myth.
x01 **Epigrammata** (*App. Anth.*).
Epigrammata dedicatoria: 1.23, 24(?), 25.
Epigrammata sepulcralia: 2.4–6.
Epigrammata demonstrativa: 3.6–14.
Epigrammata exhortatoria et supplicatoria: 4.2–6.
Epigrammata irrisoria: 5.3.
App. Anth. 1.23, 24(?), 25: Cf. ANTHOLO-

GIAE GRAECAE APPENDIX (7052 001).
App. Anth. 2.4–6: Cf. ANTHOLOGIAE GRAECAE APPENDIX (7052 002).
App. Anth. 3.6–14: Cf. ANTHOLOGIAE GRAECAE APPENDIX (7052 003).
App. Anth. 4.2–6: Cf. ANTHOLOGIAE GRAECAE APPENDIX (7052 004).
App. Anth. 5.3: Cf. ANTHOLOGIAE GRAECAE APPENDIX (7052 005).

SIMONIS EPISTULA
Epist. Graec., p. 618.
Cf. SOCRATICORUM EPISTULAE (0637 001).

4013 **SIMPLICIUS** Phil.
A.D. 6: Atheniensis
001 **In Aristotelis quattuor libros de caelo commentaria**, ed. J.L. Heiberg, *Simplicii in Aristotelis de caelo commentaria* [*Commentaria in Aristotelem Graeca* 7. Berlin: Reimer, 1894]: 1–361, 365–731.
Cod: 268,079: Phil., Nat. Hist., Comm.
002 **De caelo i** (interpretatio Graeca ex Kc), ed. Heiberg, *op. cit.*, 361–364.
Cod: 491: Phil., Nat. Hist., Comm.
003 **In Aristotelis categorias commentarium**, ed. K. Kalbfleisch, *Simplicii in Aristotelis categorias commentarium* [*Commentaria in Aristotelem Graeca* 8. Berlin: Reimer, 1907]: 1–438.
Cod: 171,042: Phil., Comm.
004 **In Aristotelis physicorum libros commentaria**, ed. H. Diels, *Simplicii in Aristotelis physicorum libros octo commentaria*, 2 vols. [*Commentaria in Aristotelem Graeca* 9 & 10. Berlin: Reimer, 9:1882; 10:1895]: **9**:1–800; **10**:801–1366.
Cod: 537,087: Phil., Nat. Hist., Math., Comm.
005 **In Aristotelis libros de anima commentaria** [Sp.?] (fort. auctore Prisciano Lydo), ed. M. Hayduck, *Simplicii in libros Aristotelis de anima commentaria* [*Commentaria in Aristotelem Graeca* 11. Berlin: Reimer, 1882]: 1–329.
Cod: 139,474: Phil., Comm.
006 **Commentarius in Epicteti enchiridion**, ed. F. Dübner, *Theophrasti characteres*. Paris: Didot, 1842: 1–138.
Cod: 61,219: Phil., Comm.

2245 **SIMUS** Phil.
4 B.C.
001 **Testimonia**, ed. H. Diels and W. Kranz, *Die Fragmente der Vorsokratiker*, vol. 1, 6th edn. Berlin: Weidmann, 1951 (repr. Dublin: 1966): 444–445.
test. 1–3: auctores alii nominantur Myonides et Euphranor.
NQ: 116: Test.

0398 **SIMYLUS** Comic.
4/3 B.C.
001 **Fragmentum**, ed. T. Kock, *Comicorum Atti-*

corum fragmenta, vol. 2. Leipzig: Teubner, 1884: 444.
fr. 1 + titulus.
Q: 4: Comic.

002 **Fragmentum**, ed. A. Meineke, *Fragmenta comicorum Graecorum*, vol. 1. Berlin: Reimer, 1839 (repr. De Gruyter, 1970): 424.
Q: 2: Comic.

1675 **SIMYLUS** Eleg.
fiq Simylus Iamb.
3 B.C.?
Cf. et SIMYLUS Iamb. (1676).

002 **Fragmenta**, ed. H. Lloyd-Jones and P. Parsons, *Supplementum Hellenisticum*. Berlin: De Gruyter, 1983: 349–350.
frr. 724–725.
Q: 61: Eleg.

1676 **SIMYLUS** Iamb.
fiq Simylus Eleg.
4 B.C./A.D. 2
Cf. et SIMYLUS Eleg. (1675).

001 **Fragmenta**, ed. A. Meineke, *Fragmenta comicorum Graecorum*, vol. 1. Berlin: Reimer, 1839 (repr. De Gruyter, 1970): xiii–xv.
Dup. 1676 002.
Q: 190: Comic., Iamb.

002 **Fragmenta**, ed. H. Lloyd-Jones and P. Parsons, *Supplementum Hellenisticum*. Berlin: De Gruyter, 1983: 350–351.
frr. 726–728.
Dup. 1676 001.
Q: 159: Iamb.

1893 **SISYPHUS** Hist.
3 B.C.: Cous
001 **Testimonium**, FGrH #50: 1A:284.
NQ: 38: Test.
002 **Fragmenta**, FGrH #50: 1A:284–294.
Q: 3,498: Hist., Myth.

2644 **SMINTHES** Astron.
4 B.C.?
001 **Titulus**, ed. H. Lloyd-Jones and P. Parsons, *Supplementum Hellenisticum*. Berlin: De Gruyter, 1983: 351.
fr. 729.
NQ: 2: Astron., Poem.

1677 **SOCRATES** Epigr.
Incertum
001 **Epigramma**, AG 14.1.
Q: 56: Epigr.

1678 **SOCRATES** Hist.
ante 1 B.C.: Argivus
001 **Testimonium**, FGrH #310: 3B:15.
NQ: 28: Test.
002 **Fragmenta**, FGrH #310: 3B:15–20.
Q: 1,499: Hist., Nat. Hist.

1679 **SOCRATES** Hist.
1 B.C.: Rhodius
001 **Fragmenta**, FGrH #192: 2B:927–928.
Q: 290: Hist.

1000 **SOCRATES** Med.
A.D. 1?
x01 **Fragmentum ap. Pseudo-Galenum.**
K14.501.
Cf. Pseudo-GALENUS Med. (0530 029).

0262 **SOCRATES** Phil.
5–4 B.C.: Atheniensis
Cf. et SOCRATIS EPISTULAE (0636).
001 **Fragmenta**, ed. M.L. West, *Iambi et elegi Graeci*, vol. 2. Oxford: Clarendon Press, 1972: 118–119.
frr. 1–3.
Q: 31: Eleg., Hexametr.

x01 **Epigramma exhortatorium et supplicatorium.**
App. Anth. 4.16(?): Cf. ANTHOLOGIAE GRAECAE APPENDIX (7052 004).
Dup. partim 0262 001 (fr. 1).

0021 **SOCRATES Junior** Phil. et Math.
4 B.C.: Atheniensis
001 **Testimonia**, ed. F. Lasserre, *De Léodamas de Thasos à Philippe d'Oponte*. Naples: Bibliopolis, 1987: 69–71.
test. 1–5a, 5c–8.
NQ: Test.
002 **Doctrina**, ed. Lasserre, *op. cit.*, 71–73.
frr. 1–2.
fragmentum 2 dubium est.
NQ: Test.

2057 **SOCRATES Scholasticus** Hist.
A.D. 4–5: Constantinopolitanus
001 **Historia ecclesiastica**, ed. W. Bright, *Socrates' ecclesiastical history*, 2nd edn. Oxford: Clarendon Press, 1893: 1–330.
Cod: 104,077: Hist., Eccl.

0637 *SOCRATICORUM EPISTULAE*
Incertum
Cf. et SOCRATIS EPISTULAE (0636).
001 **Epistulae**, ed. R. Hercher, *Epistolographi Graeci*. Paris: Didot, 1873 (repr. Amsterdam: Hakkert, 1965): 616–629, 634–635.
Cod: 6,218: Epist.

1003 **SOCRATION** Med.
ante A.D. 2
x01 **Fragmentum ap. Galenum.**
K12.835–836.
Cf. GALENUS Med. (0057 076).

0636 *SOCRATIS EPISTULAE*
Incertum
Cf. et SOCRATES Phil. (0262).
Cf. et SOCRATICORUM EPISTULAE (0637).
001 **Epistulae**, ed. R. Hercher, *Epistolographi*

Graeci. Paris: Didot, 1873 (repr. Amsterdam: Hakkert, 1965): 609–616.
Cod: 3,098: Epist.

1680 **<SODAMUS>** Eleg.
Incertum: Tegeates
001 **Fragmentum,** ed. E. Diehl, *Anthologia lyrica Graeca,* fasc. 1, 3rd edn. Leipzig: Teubner, 1949: 127.
Q: 14: Epigr.

1786 **SOGENES** Comic.
Incertum
001 **Titulus,** ed. T. Kock, *Comicorum Atticorum fragmenta,* vol. 3. Leipzig: Teubner, 1888: 355.
NQ: 2: Comic.

1075 **SOLON** Med.
ante A.D. 1: Smyrnaeus
x01 **Fragmentum ap. Galenum.**
K12.630.
Cf. GALENUS Med. (0057 076).

0263 **SOLON** Nomographus et Poeta
7–6 B.C.: Atheniensis
Cf. et <SEPTEM SAPIENTES> (1667).
Cf. et SOLONIS EPISTULAE (1681).
Cf. et SOLONIS LEGES (1808).
001 **Fragmenta,** ed. M.L. West, *Iambi et elegi Graeci,* vol. 2. Oxford: Clarendon Press, 1972: 120–144.
frr. 1–4a, 4c, 5–7, 9–21, 22a, 23–28, 31–34, 36–40, 43.
Q: 1,845: Eleg., Hexametr., Iamb.
x01 **Epigrammata** (*App. Anth.*).
Epigramma demonstrativum: 3.5.
Epigramma exhortatorium et supplicatorium: 4.1.
Dup. partim 0263 001 (fr. 27).
App. Anth. 3.5: Cf. ANTHOLOGIAE GRAECAE APPENDIX (7052 003).
App. Anth. 4.1: Cf. ANTHOLOGIAE GRAECAE APPENDIX (7052 004).

1681 *SOLONIS EPISTULAE*
Incertum
Cf. et SOLON Nomographus et Poeta (0263).
001 **Epistulae,** ed. R. Hercher, *Epistolographi Graeci.* Paris: Didot, 1873 (repr. Amsterdam: Hakkert, 1965): 636–637.
Q: 461: Epist.

1808 *SOLONIS LEGES*
6 B.C.
Cf. et SOLON Nomographus et Poeta (0263).
001 **Fragmenta,** ed. E. Ruschenbusch, Σόλωνος νόμοι [*Historia Einzelschriften* 9 (1966)]: 70–126.
Q, Pap, Epigr

1682 **SOPATER** Comic.
4–3 B.C.: Paphius

001 **Fragmenta,** ed. G. Kaibel, *Comicorum Graecorum fragmenta,* vol. 1.1 [*Poetarum Graecorum fragmenta,* vol. 6.1. Berlin: Weidmann, 1899]: 192–197.
frr. 1–21, 23–25.
Q: 314: Comic.

2031 **SOPATER** Rhet.
A.D. 4: Atheniensis
Cf. et SYRIANI, SOPATRI ET MARCELLINI SCHOLIA AD HERMOGENIS STATUS (2047).
001 Διαίρεσις ζητημάτων, ed. C. Walz, *Rhetores Graeci,* vol. 8. Stuttgart: Cotta, 1835 (repr. Osnabrück: Zeller, 1968): 2–385.
Cod: 92,266: Rhet.
002 **Scholia ad Hermogenis status seu artem rhetoricam,** ed. Walz, *op. cit.,* vol. 5 (1833; repr. 1968): 1–211.
Dup. partim SYRIANI, SOPATRI ET MARCELLINI SCHOLIA AD HERMOGENIS STATUS (2047 001).
Cod: 55,814: Rhet., Comm.
003 **Prolegomena in Aristidem,** ed. W. Dindorf, *Aristides,* vol. 3. Leipzig: Reimer, 1829 (repr. Hildesheim: Olms, 1964): 737–757.
Dup. partim 2031 004.
Cod: 5,343: Rhet.
004 **Prolegomena in Aristidem,** ed. F.W. Lenz, *The Aristeides prolegomena* [*Mnemosyne,* suppl. 5. Leiden: Brill, 1959]: 111–119, 121–125, 127–151, 153–155, 157–166, 169–172.
Dup. partim 2031 003.
Cod: Rhet.
005 **Progymnasmatum fragmenta,** ed. H. Rabe, *Aphthonii progymnasmata.* Leipzig: Teubner, 1926: 59–69.
Cod: Rhet.
006 **Paraphrases,** ed. S. Glöckner, "Aus Sopatros μεταποιήσεις," *Rheinisches Museum* 65 (1910) 505–514.
Cod: Rhet.

1683 **SOPHAENETUS** Hist.
5–4 B.C.: Stymphalicus
001 **Testimonia,** FGrH #109: 2B:523.
NQ: 39: Test.
002 **Fragmenta,** FGrH #109: 2B:523.
Q: 91: Hist.

1684 *SOPHIA JESU CHRISTI*
A.D. 2
001 **Fragmentum evangelii gnostici** (*P. Oxy.* 8.1081), ed. A.S. Hunt, *The Oxyrhynchus papyri,* pt. 8. London: Egypt Exploration Fund, 1911: 18.
Pap: Evangel., Apocryph.

0502 **SOPHILUS** Comic.
4 B.C.?
001 **Fragmenta,** ed. T. Kock, *Comicorum Atti-*

corum fragmenta, vol. 2. Leipzig: Teubner, 1884: 444–447.
frr. 3–8 + tituli.
Q: 101: Comic.

002 **Fragmenta**, ed. A. Meineke, *Fragmenta comicorum Graecorum*, vol. 3. Berlin: Reimer, 1840 (repr. De Gruyter, 1970): 581–583.
Q: 95: Comic.

x01 **Problema**.
App. Anth. 7.5: Cf. ANTHOLOGIAE GRAECAE APPENDIX (7052 007).
Dup. partim ARCHIMEDES Geom. (0552 012).

0011 **SOPHOCLES** Trag.
5 B.C.: Atheniensis
Scholia: Cf. SCHOLIA IN SOPHOCLEM (5037).

001 **Trachiniae**, ed. A. Dain and P. Mazon, *Sophocle*, vol. 1. Paris: Les Belles Lettres, 1955 (repr. 1967 (1st edn. rev.)): 14–60.
Cod: 7,679: Trag.

002 **Antigone**, ed. Dain and Mazon, *op. cit.*, vol. 1, 72–122.
Cod: 7,824: Trag.

003 **Ajax**, ed. Dain and Mazon, *op. cit.*, vol. 2 (1958; repr. 1968 (1st edn. rev.)): 10–59.
Cod: 8,332: Trag.

004 **Oedipus tyrannus**, ed. Dain and Mazon, *op. cit.*, vol. 2, 72–128.
Cod: 9,903: Trag.

005 **Electra**, ed. Dain and Mazon, *op. cit.*, vol. 2, 138–194.
Cod: 9,318: Trag.

006 **Philoctetes**, ed. Dain and Mazon, *op. cit.*, vol. 3 (1960; repr. 1967 (1st edn. rev.)): 10–66.
Cod: 9,379: Trag.

007 **Oedipus Coloneus**, ed. Dain and Mazon, *op. cit.*, vol. 3, 78–152.
Cod: 11,184: Trag.

008 **Fragmenta**, ed. S. Radt, *Tragicorum Graecorum fragmenta*, vol. 4. Göttingen: Vandenhoeck & Ruprecht, 1977: 99–120, 122–324, 326–338, 340–353, 355–380, 382–390, 392–435, 437–445, 447–484, 486–656.
frr. 1–25a, 28–72, 74–100a, 108–120, 122–141, 143–150, 152–159, 162–179, 180a–185, 187–190, 198a–203, 205–223b, 225–227, 235–289, 291–312, 314–314b, 316, 318–324, 326–334, 337–342, 345–360, 363–364, 367–371, 373–375, 377–412, 414–418, 420–445a, 447–450, 451a, 453–458, 460–469, 471–496, 498–527, 528a–546, 549–573, 576–644, 646–648, 650–655, 658–703, 706–730, 730a–g (ed. R. Kannicht), 732, 734–741, 743–747, 749–800, 803–804, 806–808, 811–829, 831–849, 851–881, 883–885a, 887–890, 892–898, 900–982, 984–985, 987–1027b, 1029–1032, 1034–1056, 1058–1063, 1065–1066, 1068, 1070, 1072–1079, 1081–1095, 1097–1112, 1114–1115, 1116a, 1117, 1119, 1122, 1124–1125, 1130–1133, 1135–1154.
Q, Pap: 16,027: Trag., Satyr.

009 **Fragmenta**, ed. M.L. West, *Iambi et elegi Graeci*, vol. 2. Oxford: Clarendon Press, 1972: 145–146.
frr. 1, 4–5.
Q: 46: Eleg., Epigr.

010 **Fragmenta**, ed. D.L. Page, *Poetae melici Graeci*. Oxford: Clarendon Press, 1962 (repr. 1967 (1st edn. corr.)): 380–381.
fr. 1.
Q, Epigr: 52: Lyr., Encom.

x01 **Epigrammata** (*App. Anth.*).
Epigramma exhortatorium et supplicatorium: 4.12.
Epigramma irrisorium: 5.5.
Dup. partim 0011 009 (fr. 4).
App. Anth. 4.12: Cf. ANTHOLOGIAE GRAECAE APPENDIX (7052 004).
App. Anth. 5.5: Cf. ANTHOLOGIAE GRAECAE APPENDIX (7052 005).

0326 **SOPHOCLES Junior** Trag.
4 B.C.

001 **Fragmentum**, ed. B. Snell, *Tragicorum Graecorum fragmenta*, vol. 1. Göttingen: Vandenhoeck & Ruprecht, 1971: 208.
fr. 1.
Q: 4: Trag.

4030 **SOPHONIAS** Phil.
A.D. 13–14

001 **In Aristotelis libros de anima paraphrasis**, ed. M. Hayduck, *Sophoniae in libros Aristotelis de anima paraphrasis* [*Commentaria in Aristotelem Graeca* 23.1. Berlin: Reimer, 1883]: 1–152.
Cod: 70,372: Phil., Comm.

x01 **In parva naturalia commentaria**.
CAG 5.6, pp. 1–44.
Cf. THEMISTIUS Phil. et Rhet. (2001 041).

0524 **SOPHRON** Mimogr.
5 B.C.

001 **Fragmenta**, ed. G. Kaibel, *Comicorum Graecorum fragmenta*, vol. 1.1 [*Poetarum Graecorum fragmenta*, vol. 6.1. Berlin: Weidmann, 1899]: 154–179.
frr. 1–3, 5–6, 10–12, 14–16, 18–30, 32–37, 39, 41–42, 46, 48–50, 52–64, 66–68, 70, 72–75, 81–92, 94–101, 104–106, 110, 117–118, 120–121, 123, 125–127, 129, 131, 134–135, 144, 149–150, 156–158, 163, 165–166, 168.
Q: 643: Comic.

002 **Fragmenta**, ed. J. Demiańczuk, *Supplementum comicum*. Krakau: Nakładem Akademii, 1912 (repr. Hildesheim: Olms, 1967): 125–126.
frr. 1–2.
Q: 34: Comic.

003 **Fragmentum**, ed. D.L. Page, *Select papyri*, vol. 3 [*Literary papyri*]. London: Heinemann, 1941 (repr. 1970): 330.
PSI 1214.
Pap: Mim.

004 **Titulus** (*P. Oxy.* 2.301), ed. B.P. Grenfell and A.S. Hunt, *The Oxyrhynchus papyri*, pt. 2. London: Egypt Exploration Fund, 1899: 303.
NQ: Mim.

4149 **SOPHRONIUS** Gramm.
A.D. 9: Alexandrinus
001 **Excerpta ex Joannis Characis commentariis in Theodosii Alexandrini canones**, ed. A. Hilgard, *Grammatici Graeci*, vol. 4.2. Leipzig: Teubner, 1894 (repr. Hildesheim: Olms, 1965): 375–434.
Cod: 22,006: Gramm.

4042 **SOPHRONIUS** Soph., Scr. Eccl. et Epigr.
A.D. 6–7: Damascenus, Hierosolymitanus
001 **Epistula Synodica**, MPG 87.3: 3148–3200.
Cod
002 **Orationes**, MPG 87.3: 3217–3364.
In sanctissimae deiparae annuntiationem (orat. 2): coll. 3217–3288.
In exaltationem sanctae crucis (orat. 4): coll. 3301–3309.
De festo sanctae crucis (orat. 5): coll. 3309–3316.
Encomium in sanctum Joannem Baptistam (orat. 7): coll. 3321–3354.
In sanctos apostolos Petrum et Paulum (orat. 8): coll. 3356–3364.
Encomium de sancto Joanne evangelista (orat. 9): col. 3364.
Cod
003 **De peccatorum confessione**, MPG 87.3: 3365–3372.
Cod
004 **Fragmentum de baptismate apostolorum**, MPG 87.3: 3372.
Cod
005 **Laudes in sanctos Cyrum et Joannem**, MPG 87.3: 3380–3424.
Cod
006 **Narratio miraculorum sanctorum Cyri et Joannis**, MPG 87.3: 3424–3676.
Cod
007 **De sanctis Cyro et Joanne**, MPG 87.3: 3677–3689.
Cod
008 **Alia vita acephala sanctorum martyrum Cyri et Joannis**, MPG 87.3: 3689–3696.
Cod
009 **Vita Mariae Aegyptiae**, MPG 87.3: 3697–3726.
Cod
010 **Anacreontica**, MPG 87.3: 3733–3838.
Cod
011 **Triodium**, MPG 87.3: 3840–3981.
Cod
012 **Commentarius**, MPG 87.3: 3981–4001.
Cod
013 **Oratio**, MPG 87.3: 4001–4004.
Cod
014 **Troparium horarum**, MPG 87.3: 4005–4009.
Cod

015 **Fragmentum dogmaticum**, MPG 87.3: 4009–4012.
Cod
016 **Epigrammata**, AG 1.90, 123; 7.679–680; 9.787.
Q: 211: Epigr.

0565 **SORANUS** Med.
A.D. 1–2: Ephesius
001 **Gynaeciorum libri iv**, ed. J. Ilberg, *Sorani Gynaeciorum libri iv, de signis fracturarum, de fasciis, vita Hippocratis secundum Soranum* [*Corpus medicorum Graecorum*, vol. 4. Leipzig: Teubner, 1927]: 3–152.
Cod: 42,426: Med.
002 **De signis fracturarum**, ed. Ilberg, *op. cit.*, 155–158.
Cod: 1,161: Med.
003 **De fasciis**, ed. Ilberg, *op. cit.*, 159–171.
Cod: 2,769: Med.
004 **Vita Hippocratis**, ed. Ilberg, *op. cit.*, 175–178.
Cod: 707: Biogr.

2481 **SOSANDER** Perieg.
ante 1 B.C.
001 **Testimonium**, FGrH #714: 3C:603.
NQ: 57: Test.

1076 **SOSANDRUS** Med.
ante A.D. 2
x01 **Fragmentum ap. Galenum.**
K12.733.
Cf. GALENUS Med. (0057 076).
x02 **Fragmentum ap. Aëtium** (lib. 7).
CMG, vol. 8.2, p. 328.
Cf. AËTIUS Med. (0718 007).

SOSIADES
Incertum
Cf. <SEPTEM SAPIENTES> (1667 005).

1686 **SOSIBIUS** Gramm.
fiq Sosibius Lacon
3 B.C.
x01 **Fragmentum.**
FGrH #595, fr. 26.
Cf. SOSIBIUS Gramm. (1685 002).

1685 **SOSIBIUS** Gramm.
fiq Sosibius ὁ λυτικός
3–2 B.C.: Lacon
001 **Testimonia**, FGrH #595: 3B:713–714.
NQ: 174: Test.
002 **Fragmenta**, FGrH #595: 3B:714–718.
frr. 1–25.
fr. 26: altero auctore Sosibio Gramm. (1686).
Q: 1,622: Hist.
003 **Fragmentum** (*P. Oxy.* 24.2389), ed. H.J. Mette, "Die 'Kleinen' griechischen Historiker heute," *Lustrum* 21 (1978) 32.
fr. 6 bis.
Pap: 45: Hist.

0503 **SOSICRATES** Comic.
3 B.C.?
001 **Fragmenta**, ed. T. Kock, *Comicorum Atticorum fragmenta*, vol. 3. Leipzig: Teubner, 1888: 391–392.
frr. 1–5, 7.
Q: 77: Comic.
002 **Fragmenta**, ed. A. Meineke, *Fragmenta comicorum Graecorum*, vol. 4. Berlin: Reimer, 1841 (repr. De Gruyter, 1970): 591–592.
Q: 67: Comic.

1687 **SOSICRATES** Hist.
2 B.C.: fort. Rhodius
001 **Testimonia**, FGrH #461: 3B:398–399.
NQ: 39: Test.
002 **Fragmenta**, FGrH #461: 3B:399–400.
Q: 454: Hist.

1077 **SOSICRATES** Med.
ante A.D. 1
x01 **Fragmentum ap. Galenum.**
K13.114.
Cf. GALENUS Med. (0057 076).

1748 **SOSIGENES** Phil.
2 B.C.: fort. Tarsensis
001 **Testimonium**, ed. J. von Arnim, *Stoicorum veterum fragmenta*, vol. 3. Leipzig: Teubner, 1903 (repr. Stuttgart: 1968): 258.
NQ: 64: Test.

0504 **SOSIPATER** Comic.
3 B.C.?
001 **Fragmentum**, ed. T. Kock, *Comicorum Atticorum fragmenta*, vol. 3. Leipzig: Teubner, 1888: 314–316.
fr. 1.
Cod: 378: Comic.
002 **Fragmentum**, ed. A. Meineke, *Fragmenta comicorum Graecorum*, vol. 4. Berlin: Reimer, 1841 (repr. De Gruyter, 1970): 482–484.
Cod: 381: Comic.

0338 **SOSIPHANES** Trag.
4 B.C.: Syracusanus
001 **Fragmenta**, ed. B. Snell, *Tragicorum Graecorum fragmenta*, vol. 1. Göttingen: Vandenhoeck & Ruprecht, 1971: 261–263.
frr. 1–5, 7.
Q: 92: Trag.

0340 **SOSITHEUS** Trag.
3 B.C.
001 **Fragmenta**, ed. B. Snell, *Tragicorum Graecorum fragmenta*, vol. 1. Göttingen: Vandenhoeck & Ruprecht, 1971: 270–272.
frr. 1, 2, 3–4.
Q: 166: Trag., Satyr.

2568 **[SOSTHENES]** Hist.
Incertum: Cnidius

001 **Fragmenta**, FGrH #846: 3C:931–932.
Q: 137: Hist.

1688 **SOSTRATUS** Gramm.
1 B.C.: Nyssensis
001 **Fragmenta**, FGrH #23: 1A:186–188, *11–*12 addenda.
fr. 4: Dup. partim 1688 002 (fr. 735).
fr. 7: Dup. partim SOSTRATUS Poeta (2694 001) (fr. 733).
Q: 810: Hist., Myth., Epic.
002 **Titulus**, ed. H. Lloyd-Jones and P. Parsons, *Supplementum Hellenisticum*. Berlin: De Gruyter, 1983: 353.
fr. 735.
Dup. partim 1688 001 (fr. 4).
NQ: 4: Epic.

2694 **SOSTRATUS** Poeta
vel Sosicrates
1 B.C.?: Phanagorita
001 **Tituli**, ed. H. Lloyd-Jones and P. Parsons, *Supplementum Hellenisticum*. Berlin: De Gruyter, 1983: 352.
fr. 732–733.
fr. 733: Dup. partim SOSTRATUS Gramm. (1688 001) (fr. 7).
NQ: 8: Epic., Eleg.

1689 **SOSYLUS** Hist.
3 B.C.: Lacedaemonius
001 **Testimonia**, FGrH #176: 2B:903.
NQ: 108: Test.
002 **Fragmenta**, FGrH #176: 2B:903–906.
fr. 1: *P. Würzburg.*
Q, Pap: 608: Hist.

1690 *SOTADEA*
Incertum
Cf. et SOTADES Iamb. (1691).
001 **Fragmenta**, ed. J.U. Powell, *Collectanea Alexandrina*. Oxford: Clarendon Press, 1925 (repr. 1970): 240–244.
frr. 6–23.
Q: 541: Iamb.

0505 **SOTADES** Comic.
4 B.C.
001 **Fragmenta**, ed. T. Kock, *Comicorum Atticorum fragmenta*, vol. 2. Leipzig: Teubner, 1884: 447–449.
frr. 1–3.
Q: 211: Comic.
002 **Fragmenta**, ed. A. Meineke, *Fragmenta comicorum Graecorum*, vol. 3. Berlin: Reimer, 1840 (repr. De Gruyter, 1970): 585–586, 588.
Q: 210: Comic.
003 **Fragmentum**, ed. J. Demiańczuk, *Supplementum comicum*. Krakau: Nakładem Akademii, 1912 (repr. Hildesheim: Olms, 1967): 83.
fr. 1.
Q: 33: Comic.

1691 **SOTADES** Iamb.
3 B.C.
Cf. et SOTADEA (1690).
001 **Fragmenta**, ed. J.U. Powell, *Collectanea Alexandrina*. Oxford: Clarendon Press, 1925 (repr. 1970): 238–239.
frr. 1–4.
Q: 75: Iamb.

2258 **SOTADES** Phil.
Incertum: Atheniensis
001 **Testimonium**, FGrH #358: 3B:218.
NQ: 12: Test.

2442 **SOTERICHUS** Epic. et Hist.
A.D. 3–4: Oasites
001 **Testimonia**, FGrH #641: 3C:187–188.
NQ: 68: Test.
002 **Fragmentum**, FGrH #641: 3C:188.
Q: 26: Hist.

1071 **SOTION** Biogr.
3–2 B.C.: Alexandrinus
001 **Fragmenta**, ed. F. Wehrli, *Sotion* [*Die Schule des Aristoteles*, suppl. 2. Basel: Schwabe, 1978]: 23–31.
Q

0587 **SOTION** <Paradox.>
A.D. 1
001 **Fragmenta**, ed. A. Westermann, *Scriptores rerum mirabilium Graeci*. Braunschweig: Westermann, 1839 (repr. Amsterdam: Hakkert, 1963): 183–191.
Cod: 1,294: Paradox.

2048 **Salaminius Hermias SOZOMENUS** Scr. Eccl.
A.D. 5: Gazaeus, Constantinopolitanus
001 **Historia ecclesiastica**, ed. J. Bidez and G.C. Hansen, *Sozomenus. Kirchengeschichte* [*Die griechischen christlichen Schriftsteller* 50. Berlin: Akademie-Verlag, 1960]: 1–408.
Cod: 110,642: Hist., Eccl.

1692 **SPEUSIPPUS** Phil.
4 B.C.: Atheniensis
001 **Epistulae** [Sp.], ed. R. Hercher, *Epistolographi Graeci*. Paris: Didot, 1873 (repr. Amsterdam: Hakkert, 1965): 632–634.
Cf. et 1692 002.
Cod: 496: Epist.
002 **Epistula ad Philippum regem** [Sp.], ed. E. Bickermann and J. Sykutris, *Speusipps Brief an König Philipp*. Leipzig: Hirzel, 1928: 7–12.
Cf. et 1692 001.
Cod: Epist.
004 **Epigramma**, AG 16.31.
Dup. partim 1692 005 (fr. 87b).
Q: 16: Epigr.
005 **Fragmenta**, ed. L. Tarán, *Speusippus of Athens* [*Philosophia Antiqua* 39. Leiden: Brill, 1981]: 135–168, 170–174.

frr. 1, 3–47, 49–55, 57–75, 77, 79–83, 85–87.
fr. 87a: Dup. ANONYMI EPIGRAMMATICI (AG) (0138 001) (AG 7.61).
fr. 87b: Dup. 1692 004.
Q, Pap: 10,815: Phil., Epigr.

1693 **SPHAERUS** Phil.
3 B.C.: Borysthenius
001 **Fragmenta**, ed. J. von Arnim, *Stoicorum veterum fragmenta*, vol. 1. Leipzig: Teubner, 1905 (repr. Stuttgart: 1968): 139–142.
Dup. partim 1693 003.
Q: 704: Phil.
002 **Testimonia**, FGrH #585: 3B:700–701.
NQ: 232: Test.
003 **Fragmenta**, FGrH #585: 3B:701.
Dup. partim 1693 001.
Q: 148: Hist., Phil.

1846 **SPINTHARUS** Trag.
5/4 B.C.: Heracleota
001 **Tituli**, ed. B. Snell, *Tragicorum Graecorum fragmenta*, vol. 1. Göttingen: Vandenhoeck & Ruprecht, 1971: 168.
NQ: 4: Trag.

4278 **SPORUS** Gramm.
vel Porus
A.D. 2–3: Nicaeensis
x01 **Fragmenta in Arati phaenomena** (in scholiis).
Martin, pp. 321, 431, 511.
Cf. SCHOLIA IN ARATUM (5013 001).
x02 **Fragmentum mathematicum in Archimedem**.
Heiberg & Stamatis, vol. 3, pp. 76–78.
Cf. EUTOCIUS Math. (4072 001).
x03 Κηρία Ἀριστοτελικά (fragmentum).
Heiberg & Stamatis, pp. 258.
Cf. EUTOCIUS Math. (4072 002).

STADIASMUS
Cf. PERIPLUS MARIS MAGNI (0077).

2998 **STAGIRIUS** Rhet. et Soph.
A.D. 4: Cappadox
x01 **Epistula ad Gregorium** [Sp.?].
Pasquali, *Epist.* 26, pp. 83–84.
Cf. GREGORIUS NYSSENUS Theol. (2017 033).

2182 **STAPHYLUS** Hist.
ante 2 B.C.: Naucratites
001 **Testimonium**, FGrH #269: 3A:80.
NQ: 26: Test.
002 **Fragmenta**, FGrH #269: 3A:80–82.
Q: 827: Hist.

STASINUS Epic.
Cf. CYPRIA (1296).

1694 **STATYLLIUS FLACCUS** Epigr.
fiq Tullius Flaccus
1 B.C.?

001 **Epigrammata**, AG **5**.5; **6**.193, 196; **7**.290, 542, 650; **9**.37, 44–45, 98, 117; **12**.12, 25–27; **16**.211.
AG 6.165: Cf. PHALAECUS Epigr. (1581 001).
AG 7.294: Cf. TULLIUS LAUREA Epigr. (1743 001).
Q: 557: Epigr.

9021 **STEPHANUS** Alchem.
fiq Stephanus Phil.
A.D. 7: Alexandrinus
Cf. et STEPHANUS Phil. (9019).
001 **De magna et sacra arte**, ed. J.L. Ideler, *Physici et medici Graeci minores*, vol. 2. Berlin: Reimer, 1842 (repr. Amsterdam: Hakkert, 1963): 199–253.
Cod

0506 **STEPHANUS** Comic.
4–3 B.C.
001 **Fragmentum**, ed. T. Kock, *Comicorum Atticorum fragmenta*, vol. 3. Leipzig: Teubner, 1888: 360.
fr. 1.
Q: 38: Comic.
002 **Fragmentum**, ed. A. Meineke, *Fragmenta comicorum Graecorum*, vol. 4. Berlin: Reimer, 1841 (repr. De Gruyter, 1970): 544.
Q: 37: Comic.

4028 **STEPHANUS** Gramm.
A.D. 6: Byzantius
001 **Ethnica** (epitome), ed. A. Meineke, *Stephan von Byzanz. Ethnika*. Berlin: Reimer, 1849 (repr. Graz: Akademische Druck- und Verlagsanstalt, 1958): 1–713.
Cod: 101,920: Lexicogr., Gramm., Geogr.
002 **Epigramma**, AG 9.385.
Q: 179: Epigr.

9020 **STEPHANUS** Gramm.
A.D. 12?: fort. Constantinopolitanus
001 **In artem rhetoricam commentaria**, ed. H. Rabe, *Stephani in artem rhetoricam commentarium* [*Commentaria in Aristotelem Graeca* 21.2. Berlin: Reimer, 1896]: 263–322.
Cod: 21,109: Rhet., Comm.

STEPHANUS Gramm.
Incertum
Cf. COMMENTARIA IN DIONYSII THRACIS ARTEM GRAMMATICAM (4175 004–005).

0736 **STEPHANUS** Med.
fiq Stephanus Atheniensis Med. et Phil.
A.D. 7: Alexandrinus
Cf. et STEPHANUS Med. et Phil. (0724).
001 **In Magni sophistae librum de urinis**, ed. U.C. Bussemaker, "In Magni sophistae librum de urinis," *Revue de Philologie* 1 (1845) 423–438, 543–560.
Cod: 8,356: Med.

0724 **STEPHANUS** Med. et Phil.
fiq Stephanus Alexandrinus Med.
A.D. 6/7: Atheniensis, Alexandrinus
Cf. et STEPHANUS Med. (0736).
Cf. et THEOPHILUS Protospatharius et STEPHANUS Atheniensis Med. (0746).
Cf. et THEOPHILUS Protospatharius, DAMASCIUS et STEPHANUS Atheniensis Med. (0728).
001 **Commentarii in priorem Galeni librum therapeuticum ad Glauconem**, ed. F.R. Dietz, *Scholia in Hippocratem et Galenum*, vol. 1. Königsberg: Borntraeger, 1834 (repr. Amsterdam: Hakkert, 1966): 233–344.
Cod: 29,913: Med., Comm.
002 **Scholia in Hippocratis prognosticon**, ed. J.M. Duffy, *Commentary on Hippocrates' Prognosticon* [*Diss. SUNY Buffalo* (1975)]: 1–243.
Cod: 51,436: Med., Comm.
003 **Collyrium ophthalmicum** (olim sub auctore Stephano Archiatro), ed. W. Studemund, *Index lectionum in universitate litterarum Vratislaviensi per hiemem anni 1888–1889*. Breslau: Breslau University Press, 1889: 12–14.
Cod: 1,062: Med.
004 **Scholia in Hippocratis de fracturis**, ed. D. Irmer, *Palladius. Kommentar zu Hippokrates 'De fracturis' und seine Parallelversion unter dem Namen des Stephanus von Alexandria* [*Hamburger philologische Studien* 45. Hamburg: Buske, 1977]: 17–89.
Cod: 6,587: Med., Comm.
005 **Scholia in Hippocratis aphorismos**, ed. L.G. Westerink, *Stephanus of Athens. Commentary on Hippocrates' aphorisms, sections 1–2* [*Corpus medicorum Graecorum* 11.1.3.1. Berlin: Akademie-Verlag, 1985]: 28–256.
Dup. partim THEOPHILUS Protospatharius, DAMASCIUS et STEPHANUS Atheniensis Med. (0728 001).
Cod: Med., Comm.
x01 **De pulsibus** (fragmentum e commentario in Galeni librum therapeuticum).
Dietz, p. 272.
Cf. 0724 001.

9019 **STEPHANUS** Phil.
fiq Stephanus Alchem.
A.D. 7: Alexandrinus, Constantinopolitanus
001 **In Aristotelis librum de interpretatione commentarium**, ed. M. Hayduck, *Stephani in librum Aristotelis de interpretatione commentarium* [*Commentaria in Aristotelem Graeca* 18.3. Berlin: Reimer, 1885]: 1–68.
Cod: 26,298: Phil., Comm.
002 **Commentarium in Ptolemaei canones** (excerpta e cod. Paris. gr. 2162), ed. H. Dodwell, *Dissertationes Cyprianicae*. Oxford, 1684: 128–141 (in appendice).
Cod: Astron., Comm.
003 **Commentarium in Ptolemaei canones** (ex-

cerpta e codd. Cantabr. Coll. Trin. 1043; Vat. Urbin. 80; Vat. gr. 304), ed. H. Usener, "De Stephano Alexandrino" in *Kleine Schriften*, vol. 3. Leipzig: Teubner, 1914 (repr. Osnabrück: Zeller, 1965): 295–317.
Cod: Astron., Comm.

005 **De magna et sacra arte**, ed. J.L. Ideler, *Physici et medici Graeci minores*, vol. 2. Berlin: Reimer, 1842 (repr. Amsterdam: Hakkert, 1963): 199–253.
Cod: Alchem.

x01 **In Aristotelis librum de anima.**
Hayduck, pp. 446–607 (liber 3).
Cf. JOANNES PHILOPONUS Phil. (4015 008).

4223 **STEPHANUS Archiatrus** Med.
A.D. 11: Constantinopolitanus

x01 **Collyrium ophthalmicum.**
Studemund, pp. 12–14.
Cf. STEPHANUS Med. et Phil. (0724 003).

0292 **STESICHORUS** Lyr.
vel Teisias
7–6 B.C.: Himeraeus

001 **Fragmenta**, ed. D.L. Page, *Poetae melici Graeci*. Oxford: Clarendon Press, 1962 (repr. 1967 (1st edn. corr.)): 97–102, 104, 106–109, 111–121, 123–132, 135–138.
frr. 1–2, 4, 7–8, 10–11, 15–16, 23, 32–35, 37, 40, 44–46, 51, 55–56, 58, 63, 65–68, 70, 72–73, 76–80, 82–84, 87, 89, 97, 101 + tituli.
Q, Pap: 735: Lyr.

002 **Fragmenta**, ed. D.L. Page, *Supplementum lyricis Graecis*. Oxford: Clarendon Press, 1974: 6–43.
fr. S7: e Strabone.
frr. S8–S16, S18, S20–84: *P. Oxy.* 32.2617.
frr. S17, S19: ex Athenaeo.
frr. S88–S105a, S106–S132: *P. Oxy.* 32.2619.
fr. S105b: *P. Oxy.* 32.2619 + 37.2803.
frr. S133–S147: *P. Oxy.* 37.2803.
frr. S148–S150: *P. Oxy.* 32.2618.
Dup. partim 0292 001.
Pap: 3,182: Lyr.

0981 **STESICHORUS II** Lyr.
4 B.C.: Himeraeus

001 **Titulus**, ed. D.L. Page, *Poetae melici Graeci*. Oxford: Clarendon Press, 1962 (repr. 1967 (1st edn. corr.)): 443.
NQ: 2: Lyr.

2171 **STESICLIDES** Hist.
vel Ctesicles
2–1 B.C.?: Atheniensis

001 **Fragmenta**, FGrH #245: 2B:1128–1129.
Q: 161: Hist., Chronogr.

1923 **STESIMBROTUS** Hist.
5 B.C.: Thasius

001 **Testimonia**, FGrH #107: 2B:515–516.
NQ: 142: Test.

002 **Fragmenta**, FGrH #107: **2B**:516–522; **3B**:742 addenda.
Q: 2,026: Hist.

0315 **STHENELUS** Trag.
5 B.C.

001 **Fragmentum**, ed. B. Snell, *Tragicorum Graecorum fragmenta*, vol. 1. Göttingen: Vandenhoeck & Ruprecht, 1971: 151.
fr. 1.
Q: 8: Trag.

002 **Fragmentum**, ed. H. Lloyd-Jones and P. Parsons, *Supplementum Hellenisticum*. Berlin: De Gruyter, 1983: 354.
fr. 736.
Q: 6: Hexametr.

1695 **<STHENIDAS>** Phil.
3 B.C./A.D. 2

001 **Fragmentum**, ed. H. Thesleff, *The Pythagorean texts of the Hellenistic period*. Åbo: Åbo Akademi, 1965: 187–188.
Q: 197: Phil.

4262 **STILPO** Phil.
4 B.C.: Megarensis, Atheniensis

001 **Testimonia**, ed. K. Döring, *Die Megariker* [*Studien zur antiken Philosophie* 2. Amsterdam: Grüner, 1972]: 10, 11, 20, 22, 24, 28–29, 30, 46–61, 62.
test. 27, 32a, 33, 69(?), 75, 83, 99, 106, 147–151e, 151i–157, 159–165, 167–194, 196–201, 204.
test. 27 (p. 10), 32a, 33 (p. 11) = Euclides (4247 001).
test. 69(?) (p. 20) = Euphantus (1912 003).
test. 75 (p. 22), 83 (p. 24) = Alexinus (2607 003).
test. 99 (pp. 28–29), 106 (p. 30) = Diodorus Cronus (0073 001).
test. 147–151e, 151i–157, 159–165, 167–194, 196–201 (pp. 46–61) = Stilpo.
test. 204 (p. 62) = Bryson (4276 001).
NQ: Test.

2037 **Joannes STOBAEUS**
A.D. 5: Macedonius

001 **Anthologium**, ed. C. Wachsmuth and O. Hense, *Ioannis Stobaei anthologium*, 5 vols. Berlin: Weidmann, 1–2:1884; 3:1894; 4:1909; 5:1912 (repr. 1958): 1:15–502; 2:3–264; 3:3–764; 4:1–675; 5:676–1143.
Cod: 392,249: Anthol., Phil., Rhet., Hist., Astron., Gnom., Doxogr., Poem.

0099 **STRABO** Geogr.
1 B.C.–A.D. 1: Amasiotes

001 **Geographica**, ed. A. Meineke, *Strabonis geographica*, 3 vols. Leipzig: Teubner, 1877 (repr. Graz: Akademische Druck- und Verlagsanstalt,

1969): 1:xiii–xv, 1–396; **2**:397–814; **3**:815–1173.
Cod: 299,833: Geogr.

002 **Testimonia**, FGrH #91: 2A:430.
NQ: 42: Test.

003 **Fragmenta**, FGrH #91: 2A:430–436.
Q: 1,748: Hist.

0507 **STRATON** Comic.
4–3 B.C.

001 **Fragmentum**, ed. T. Kock, *Comicorum Atticorum fragmenta*, vol. 3. Leipzig: Teubner, 1888: 361–362.
fr. 1.
Q: 302: Comic.

002 **Fragmentum**, ed. A. Meineke, *Fragmenta comicorum Graecorum*, vol. 4. Berlin: Reimer, 1841 (repr. De Gruyter, 1970): 545–546.
Q: 302: Comic.

003 **Fragmentum**, ed. C. Austin, *Comicorum Graecorum fragmenta in papyris reperta*. Berlin: De Gruyter, 1973: 205–206.
fr. 219.
Pap: 326: Comic.

1697 **STRATON** Epigr.
A.D. 2: Sardianus

001 **Epigrammata**, AG **11**.19, 21–22, 117, 225; **12**.1–11, 13, 15–16, 21, 175–229, 231, 234–255, 258; **16**.213.
AG 11.118–122: Cf. CALLICTER Epigr. (0148 001).
Q: 3,302: Epigr.

1963 **STRATON** Hist.
2 B.C.

001 **Testimonium**, FGrH #168: 2B:893.
NQ: 19: Test.

1080 **STRATON** Med.
3 B.C.: Alexandrinus

x01 **Fragmenta ap. Philumenum**.
CMG, vol. 10.1.1, pp. 9, 28, 30, 36, 40.
Cf. PHILUMENUS Med. (0671 001).

1081 **STRATON** Med.
A.D. 1: Berytensis

x01 **Fragmenta ap. Galenum**.
K13.290, 303.
Cf. GALENUS Med. (0057 076).

x02 **Fragmenta ap. Alexandrum Trallianum**.
Puschmann, vol. 1, pp. 563, 565, 571.
Cf. ALEXANDER Med. (0744 003).

1696 **STRATON** Phil.
3 B.C.: Lampsacenus

001 **Fragmenta**, ed. F. Wehrli, *Straton von Lampsakos* [*Die Schule des Aristoteles*, vol. 5, 2nd edn. Basel: Schwabe, 1969]: 12–42.
Scripta: fr. 18.

Logica et topica (testimonium): fr. 19.
Περὶ τοῦ προτέρου καὶ ὑστέρου: frr. 27–30.
Περὶ θεῶν: frr. 35–36.
Περὶ τοῦ ὄντος: frr. 40–41.2.
Περὶ ἀρχῶν τρία ἢ δύο (?). Περὶ αἰτιῶν. Περὶ δυνάμεως: frr. 42–43, 45, 48–49.
Περὶ κούφου καὶ βαρέος: frr. 50–52.
Περὶ τοῦ κενοῦ : frr. 54–57, 59–67.
Περὶ κινήσεως. Περὶ χρόνου: frr. 70–83.
Περὶ τοῦ οὐρανοῦ: frr. 84–88, 90–91.
Περὶ ζῳογονίας: frr. 95, 98–99.
Περὶ αἰσθήσεως. Περὶ ὄψεως. Περὶ χρωμάτων. Περὶ ὕπνου. Περὶ ἐνυπνίων: frr. 109–115, 118–119b, 121–128, 130–131.
Περὶ τἀγαθοῦ: fr. 134.
Εὑρημάτων ἔλεγχοι δύο: frr. 145–147.
Q: 7,984: Phil.

2645 **STRATONICUS** Poeta
5–4 B.C.: Atheniensis

001 **Fragmentum**, ed. H. Lloyd-Jones and P. Parsons, *Supplementum Hellenisticum*. Berlin: De Gruyter, 1983: 354.
fr. 737.
Q: 12: Poem.

0508 **STRATTIS** Comic.
5 B.C.: Atheniensis

001 **Fragmenta**, ed. T. Kock, *Comicorum Atticorum fragmenta*, vol. 1. Leipzig: Teubner, 1880: 711–715, 717–733.
frr. 1–4, 8–9, 11, 13–14, 22–48, 51–63, 66–67, 71–75, 77–80 + tituli.
Q: 627: Comic.

002 **Fragmenta**, ed. A. Meineke, *Fragmenta comicorum Graecorum*, vol. 2.2. Berlin: Reimer, 1840 (repr. De Gruyter, 1970): 763–764, 766–768, 771–776, 778–781, 783–788.
Q: 571: Comic.

003 **Fragmenta**, ed. J. Demiańczuk, *Supplementum comicum*. Krakau: Nakładem Akademii, 1912 (repr. Hildesheim: Olms, 1967): 84–86.
frr. 1–10.
Q: 40: Comic.

004 **Fragmenta**, ed. C. Austin, *Comicorum Graecorum fragmenta in papyris reperta*. Berlin: De Gruyter, 1973: 207–216.
fr. 220 + tituli.
Pap: 713: Comic.

005 **Fragmenta**, ed. Meineke, *FCG*, vol. 5.1 (1857; repr. 1970): cxvi.
Q: 8: Comic.

006 **Fragmentum**, ed. A. Bernabé and A. Ropero, "Un fragmento de Estratis," *Emerita* 51 (1983) 129.
Q: Comic.

1931 **STRATTIS** Hist.
post 4 B.C.: Olynthius

001 **Testimonium**, FGrH #118: 2B:622.
NQ: 21: Test.

STYLIANUS <Epigr.>
A.D. 9–10: Neocaesariensis
AG 16.387c.
Cf. ANONYMI EPIGRAMMATICI (AG) (0138 001).

9010 *SUDA*
vel *Suidas*
A.D. 10
001 **Lexicon**, ed. A. Adler, *Suidae lexicon*, 4 vols. [*Lexicographi Graeci* 1.1–1.4. Leipzig: Teubner, 1.1:1928; 1.2:1931; 1.3:1933; 1.4:1935 (repr. Stuttgart: 1.1:1971; 1.2:1967; 1.3:1967; 1.4:1971)]: **1.1**:1–549; **1.2**:1–740; **1.3**:1–632; **1.4**:1–854.
Cod: 627,192: Lexicogr.
002 **Onomasticon tacticon**, ed. Adler, *op. cit.*, vol. 1.4, 855–864.
Cod: 2,343: Lexicogr.

1760 **Gaius SUETONIUS TRANQUILLUS** Hist. et Gramm.
A.D. 1–2: Romanus
001 Περὶ βλασφημιῶν καὶ πόθεν ἑκάστη, ed. J. Taillardat, *Suétone. Περὶ βλασφημιῶν. Περὶ παιδιῶν.* Paris: Les Belles Lettres, 1967: 48–63.
Cod: 3,295: Rhet.
002 Περὶ τῶν παρ᾽ Ἕλλησι παιδιῶν, ed. Taillardat, *op. cit.*, 64–73.
Cod: 2,297: Rhet.

2416 **SUIDAS** Hist.
4/3 B.C.?: Thessalius
001 **Fragmenta**, FGrH #602: 3B:733–736.
Q: 882: Hist.

2660 **Lucius Cornelius SULLA FELIX** <Epigr.>
2–1 B.C.
x01 **Epigramma dedicatorium.**
App. Anth. 1.153: Cf. ANTHOLOGIAE GRAECAE APPENDIX (7052 001).

1920 **Gaius SULPICIUS GALBA** Hist.
1 B.C.
001 **Testimonia**, FGrH #92: 2A:436.
NQ: 107: Test.
002 **Fragmenta**, FGrH #92: 2A:436.
Q: 61: Hist.

1761 **SULPICIUS MAXIMUS** Epic.
A.D. 1
001 **Epigrammata**, ed. R. Cagnat, *Inscriptiones Graecae ad res Romanas pertinentes*, vol. 1. Rome: Bretschneider, 1964: 116–118.
Epigr: Epigr.
x01 **Epigramma sepulcrale.**
App. Anth. 2.267: Cf. ANTHOLOGIAE GRAECAE APPENDIX (7052 002).
Dup. 1761 001 (pp. 116–118).

1826 *SURONIS EPISTULA*
ante 2 B.C.
x01 **Epistula.**
FGrH #723, fr. 2.
Cf. EUPOLEMUS Judaeus Hist. (2486 002).

0264 **SUSARION** Comic.
6/5 B.C.: Megarensis
001 **Fragmentum**, ed. T. Kock, *Comicorum Atticorum fragmenta*, vol. 1. Leipzig: Teubner, 1880: 3.
fr. 1.
Dup. 0264 002–003.
Q: 31: Comic., Iamb.
002 **Fragmentum**, ed. M.L. West, *Iambi et elegi Graeci*, vol. 2. Oxford: Clarendon Press, 1972: 147.
Dup. 0264 001, 003.
Q: 32: Comic., Iamb.
003 **Fragmentum**, ed. A. Meineke, *Fragmenta comicorum Graecorum*, vol. 2.1. Berlin: Reimer, 1839 (repr. De Gruyter, 1970): 3.
Dup. 0264 001–002.
Q: 31: Comic., Iamb.

SYMEON Scr. Eccl.
A.D. 4: Mesopotamius
Cf. Pseudo-MACARIUS Scr. Eccl. (2109).

3115 **SYMEON METAPHRASTES** Biogr. et Hist.
vel Symeon Magister vel Symeon Logothetes
vel Pseudo-Symeon
A.D. 10: Constantinopolitanus
001 **Chronicon breve** (lib. 7–8) (redactio recentior), MPG 110: 1261–1285.
Cf. et GEORGIUS Monachus Chronogr. (3043 002).
Cod: 5,092: Hist., Chronogr.
x01 **Sermones de moribus** (a Symeone collecti).
MPG 32.1116–1381.
Cf. BASILIUS Theol. (2040 075).

3116 **SYMEON Neotheologus** Theol. et Poeta
vel Symeon Junior
A.D. 10–11: Constantinopolitanus
001 **Epistula de confessione** (olim sub auctore Joanne Damasceno), ed. K. Holl, *Enthusiasmus und Bussgewalt beim griechischen Mönchtum. Eine Studie zu Symeon dem Neuen Theologen.* Leipzig: Hinrichs, 1898 (repr. Hildesheim: Olms, 1969): 110–127.
Cod

1769 **SYMMACHUS** Int. Vet. Test.
A.D. 2
001 **Fragmenta**, ed. J. Reider, *An index to Aquila* (rev. N. Turner). Leiden: Brill, 1966: passim.
Q

1082 **SYNERUS** Med.
ante A.D. 2

x01 **Fragmentum ap. Galenum.**
K12.774-775.
Cf. GALENUS Med. (0057 076).

4043 **SYNESIUS** Epigr.
A.D. 6
001 **Epigramma**, AG 16.267.
Q: 49: Epigr.

2006 **SYNESIUS** Phil.
A.D. 4-5: Cyrenensis
001 **Epistulae**, ed. R. Hercher, *Epistolographi Graeci*. Paris: Didot, 1873 (repr. Amsterdam: Hakkert, 1965): 638-739.
Cod: 40,228: Epist.
002 **Oratio de regno**, ed. N. Terzaghi, *Synesii Cyrenensis opuscula*. Rome: Polygraphica, 1944: 5-62.
Cod: 9,343: Orat., Phil.
003 **Aegyptii sive de providentia**, ed. Terzaghi, *op. cit.*, 63-131.
Cod: 11,987: Phil.
004 **Ad Paeonium de dono astrolabii**, ed. Terzaghi, *op. cit.*, 132-142.
Cod: 1,787: Phil.
005 **De insomniis**, ed. Terzaghi, *op. cit.*, 143-189.
Cod: 7,697: Onir.
006 **Calvitii encomium**, ed. Terzaghi, *op. cit.*, 190-232.
Cod: 7,543: Encom., Satura
007 **Dion**, ed. Terzaghi, *op. cit.*, 233-278.
Cod: 8,316: Phil., Rhet.
008 **Homiliae**, ed. Terzaghi, *op. cit.*, 279-282.
Cod: 665: Homilet.
009 **Catastases**, ed. Terzaghi, *op. cit.*, 283-293.
Catastasis i: pp. 283-285.
Catastasis ii: pp. 285-293.
Cod: 1,871: Orat., Rhet.
010 **Hymni**, ed. A. Dell'Era, *Sinesio di Cirene. Inni*. Rome: Tumminelli, 1968: 33-167.
Cod: 4,228: Hymn.
011 **Epigrammata**, AG 16.76, 79.
Q: 18: Epigr.
x01 **Epigramma exhortatorium et supplicatorium.**
App. Anth. 4.74: Cf. ANTHOLOGIAE GRAECAE APPENDIX (7052 004).
Dup. partim 2006 004 (p. 142).

3118 *SYNTIPAS*
ante A.D. 11
001 **Syntipas** (translatio Michael Andreopuli), ed. A. Eberhard, *Fabulae romanenses Graece conscriptae*, vol. 1. Leipzig: Teubner, 1872: 1-135.
Cod: Narr. Fict.
002 **Syntipas** (recensio altera), ed. Eberhard, *op. cit.*, 136-196.
Cod: Narr. Fict.

2047 *SYRIANI, SOPATRI ET MARCELLINI SCHOLIA AD HERMOGENIS STATUS*
post A.D. 7

Cf. et MARCELLINUS Gramm. et Rhet. (4234).
Cf. et SOPATER Rhet. (2031).
Cf. et SYRIANUS Phil. (4017).
001 **Scholia ad Hermogenis librum** περὶ στάσεων, ed. C. Walz, *Rhetores Graeci*, vol. 4. Stuttgart: Cotta, 1833 (repr. Osnabrück: Zeller, 1968): 39-846.
Dup. partim SYRIANUS Phil. (4017 004).
Cod: 192,191: Rhet., Comm.

4017 **SYRIANUS** Phil.
A.D. 5: Atheniensis
Cf. et SYRIANI, SOPATRI ET MARCELLINI SCHOLIA AD HERMOGENIS STATUS (2047).
001 **In Aristotelis metaphysica commentaria**, ed. W. Kroll, *Syriani in metaphysica commentaria* [*Commentaria in Aristotelem Graeca* 6.1. Berlin: Reimer, 1902]: 1-195.
Cod: 77,033: Phil., Comm.
002 **Commentarium in Hermogenis librum** περὶ ἰδεῶν, ed. H. Rabe, *Syriani in Hermogenem commentaria*, vol. 1. Leipzig: Teubner, 1892: 1-95.
Cod: 16,725: Comm., Rhet.
003 **Praefatio in Hermogenis librum** περὶ ἰδεῶν [Sp.], ed. Rabe, *op. cit.*, vol. 1, 96-112.
Dup. partim PHOEBAMMON Soph. (2596 002).
Cod: 3,230: Comm., Rhet.
004 **Commentarium in Hermogenis librum** περὶ στάσεων, ed. Rabe, *op. cit.*, vol. 2 (1893): 1-203.
Dup. partim SYRIANI, SOPATRI ET MARCELLINI SCHOLIA AD HERMOGENIS STATUS (2047 001).
Cod: 39,801: Comm., Rhet.
x01 **Epigramma.**
AG 9.358.
Cf. et ANONYMI EPIGRAMMATICI (AG) (0138 001).

2540 **SYRISCUS** Hist.
3 B.C.: Cherronensis
001 **Testimonium**, FGrH #807: 3C:844.
test. 1: *Inscr. Cherronesos*.
NQ: 117: Test.

1827 **SYRUS** Astrol.
A.D. 2?
001 **Fragmenta**, ed. A. Olivieri, *Codices Florentini* [*Catalogus codicum astrologorum Graecorum*, vol. 1. Brussels: Lamertin, 1898]: 131-134, 171-172.
Cod

1766 **TATIANUS** Apol.
A.D. 2: Syrius
Scholia: Cf. ARETHAS Philol. et Scr. Eccl. (2130 015).
001 **Oratio ad Graecos**, ed. E.J. Goodspeed, *Die*

ältesten Apologeten. Göttingen: Vandenhoeck & Ruprecht, 1915: 268–305.
Cod: 10,694: Orat., Apol.

002 **Diatesseron**, ed. C.B. Welles, *The excavations at Dura-Europos: final report* 5, pt. 1. New Haven: Yale University Press, 1959: 74.
Pap: 86: Evangel.

2476 **TAURON** Hist.
4 B.C.?
001 **Testimonium**, FGrH #710: 3C:592.
NQ: 26: Test.
002 **Fragmentum**, FGrH #710: 3C:592.
Q: 36: Hist.

1084 **TELAMON** Med.
ante A.D. 2
x01 **Fragmentum ap. Galenum.**
K13.528.
Cf. GALENUS Med. (0057 077).

1597 **<TELAUGES>** Phil.
Incertum: Samius
001 **Titulus**, ed. H. Thesleff, *The Pythagorean texts of the Hellenistic period*. Åbo: Åbo Akademi, 1965: 189.
NQ: 3: Phil.

0510 **TELECLIDES** Comic.
5 B.C.
001 **Fragmenta**, ed. T. Kock, *Comicorum Atticorum fragmenta*, vol. 1. Leipzig: Teubner, 1880: 209–224.
frr. 1–5, 10, 13–14, 19–21, 23–28, 30–33, 35–45, 47–66.
Q: 428: Comic.
002 **Fragmenta**, ed. A. Meineke, *Fragmenta comicorum Graecorum*, vol. 2.1. Berlin: Reimer, 1839 (repr. De Gruyter, 1970): 361–366, 368–375.
p. 369: fr. 8 supplied from vol. 5.1, p. lx.
Q: 389: Comic.
003 **Fragmenta**, ed. J. Demiańczuk, *Supplementum comicum*. Krakau: Nakładem Akademii, 1912 (repr. Hildesheim: Olms, 1967): 86.
frr. 1–2.
Q: 6: Comic.
005 **Fragmentum**, ed. A. Guida, "Frammenti inediti di Eupoli, Teleclide, Teognide, Giuliano e Imerio da un nuovo codice del Lexicon Vindobonense," *Prometheus* 5 (1979) 202.
Q

2264 **TELEPHANES** Hist.
ante A.D. 3
001 **Fragmentum**, FGrH #371: 3B:233.
Q: 99: Hist., Perieg.

1049 **TELEPHANES** Med.
ante A.D. 2
x01 **Fragmentum ap. Galenum.**
K13.532.
Cf. GALENUS Med. (0057 077).

1698 **TELEPHUS** Gramm.
A.D. 2: Pergamenus
001 **Testimonia**, FGrH #505: 3B:482.
NQ: 154: Test.
002 **Fragmenta**, FGrH #505: 3B:483.
Q: 173: Hist.

1699 **TELES** Phil.
3 B.C.: fort. Megarensis
001 Περὶ τοῦ δοκεῖν καὶ τοῦ εἶναι, ed. O. Hense, *Teletis reliquiae*, 2nd edn. Tübingen: Mohr, 1909 (repr. Hildesheim: Olms, 1969): 3–4.
Q: 336: Phil.
002 Περὶ αὐταρκείας, ed. Hense, *op. cit.*, 5–20.
Q: 1,524: Phil.
003 Περὶ φυγῆς, ed. Hense, *op. cit.*, 21–32.
Q: 1,315: Phil.
004 Περὶ συγκρίσεως πενίας καὶ πλούτου (ap. Stobaeum), ed. Hense, *op. cit.*, 33–44.
Q: 1,229: Phil.
005 Περὶ συγκρίσεως πενίας καὶ πλούτου (ap. Stobaeum), ed. Hense, *op. cit.*, 45–48.
Q: 456: Phil.
006 Περὶ τοῦ μὴ εἶναι τέλος ἡδονήν, ed. Hense, *op. cit.*, 49–51.
Q: 227: Phil.
007 Περὶ περιστάσεων, ed. Hense, *op. cit.*, 52–54.
Q: 218: Phil.
008 Περὶ ἀπαθείας, ed. Hense, *op. cit.*, 55–62.
Q: 987: Phil.

2211 **TELESARCHUS** Hist.
3–2 B.C.?
001 **Fragmentum**, FGrH #308: 3B:15.
Q: 27: Hist.

0369 **TELESILLA** Lyr.
5 B.C.: Argiva
001 **Fragmenta**, ed. D.L. Page, *Poetae melici Graeci*. Oxford: Clarendon Press, 1962 (repr. 1967 (1st edn. corr.)): 372–374.
frr. 1–2, 6–8, 10.
Q: 17: Lyr.

0377 **TELESTES** Lyr.
5 B.C.: Selinuntius
001 **Fragmenta**, ed. D.L. Page, *Poetae melici Graeci*. Oxford: Clarendon Press, 1962 (repr. 1967 (1st edn. corr.)): 419–421.
frr. 1–2, 4, 6–7.
Q: 130: Lyr., Hymn.
002 **Titulus**, ed. Page, *op. cit.*, 421.
fr. 5.
NQ: 3: Lyr.

1903 **TELLIS** Hist.
3 B.C.
001 **Testimonium**, FGrH #61: 1A:298.
NQ: 24: Test.
002 **Fragmenta**, FGrH #61: 1A:299.
Q: 75: Hist., Myth.

0299 **TERPANDER** Lyr.
7 B.C.: Lesbius
001 **Fragmenta** (fort. auctore Terpandro), ed. D.L. Page, *Poetae melici Graeci*. Oxford: Clarendon Press, 1962 (repr. 1967 (1st edn. corr.)): 362. frr. 1–2.
Q: 19: Lyr., Hymn.
002 **Fragmentum** (fort. auctore Terpandro), ed. D.L. Page, *Supplementum lyricis Graecis*. Oxford: Clarendon Press, 1974: 4.
fr. S6: *P. Oxy.* 35.2737.
fr. S6: Dup. partim ALCMAN Lyr. (0291 002) (fr. S2).
fr. S6: Dup. partim ION Poeta et Phil. (0308 004) (fr. S316).
Pap: 4: Lyr.

1700 *TESTAMENTA XII PATRIARCHARUM*
2 B.C./A.D. 3
001 **Testamenta xii patriarcharum**, ed. M. de Jonge, *Testamenta xii patriarcharum*, 2nd edn. [*Pseudepigrapha veteris testamenti Graece* 1. Leiden: Brill, 1970]: 1–86.
Cod: 21,049: Pseudepigr., Hagiogr.

1701 *TESTAMENTUM ABRAHAE*
A.D. 1
001 **Testamentum Abrahae** (recensio A), ed. M.R. James, *The testament of Abraham* [*Texts and Studies* 2.2. Cambridge: Cambridge University Press, 1892]: 77–104.
Cod: 7,126: Hagiogr., Pseudepigr.
002 **Testamentum Abrahae** (recensio B), ed. James, *op. cit.*, 105–119.
Cod: 3,296: Hagiogr., Pseudepigr.

TESTAMENTUM ADAM
Cf. APOCALYPSIS ADAM (1153).

1702 *TESTAMENTUM JOBI*
A.D. 2/3
001 **Testamentum Jobi**, ed. S.P. Brock, *Testamentum Jobi* [*Pseudepigrapha veteris testamenti Graece* 2. Leiden: Brill, 1967]: 19–59.
Cod: 7,039: Hagiogr., Pseudepigr.

TESTAMENTUM MOSIS
Cf. ASSUMPTIO MOSIS (1201).

2679 *TESTAMENTUM SALOMONIS*
A.D. 3?
001 **Testamentum Salomonis** (recensiones A et B) (mss. HILPQ), ed. C.C. McCown, *The testament of Solomon*. Leipzig: Hinrichs, 1922: 8–75.
Cod: 8,634: Hagiogr.
002 **Testamentum Salomonis** (recensiones A et B) (mss. HIPQ), ed. McCown, *op. cit.*, 5–7.
Cod: 90: Hagiogr.
003 **Testamentum Salomonis** (recensio A) (mss. HI), ed. McCown, *op. cit.*, 5–6.
Cod: 102: Hagiogr.

004 **Testamentum Salomonis** (recensio A) (ms. L), ed. McCown, *op. cit.*, 5–7.
Cod: 145: Hagiogr.
005 **Testamentum Salomonis** (recensio C, I.1–3) (mss. VW), ed. McCown, *op. cit.*, 5–8.
Cod: 234: Hagiogr.
006 **Testamentum Salomonis** (recensio C) (mss. VWSTU), ed. McCown, *op. cit.*, 76–87.
Cod: 2,337: Hagiogr.
007 **Vita Salomonis** (cod. 132 Monasterii sancti Dionysii in Monte Atho), ed. McCown, *op. cit.*, 88–97.
Cod: 2,770: Hagiogr.
008 **Conspectus titulorum**, ed. McCown, *op. cit.*, 98–99.
Cod: 244: Hagiogr.
009 **Sigilla anuli Salomonis**, ed. McCown, *op. cit.*, 100–101.
Cod: 169: Hagiogr.
010 **Narratio de propheta et sapientissimo rege Salomone** (cod. Monasterii sancti Saba 290), ed. McCown, *op. cit.*, 102–120.
Cod: 6,185: Hagiogr.

2015 *TESTAMENTUM XL MARTYRUM*
post A.D. 4
001 **Testamentum xl martyrum**, ed. H. Musurillo, *The acts of the Christian martyrs*. Oxford: Clarendon Press, 1972: 354–360.
Cod: 1,015: Hagiogr.

1703 **TEUCER** Astrol.
A.D. 1: Babylonius
001 **Fragmenta**, ed. F. Boll, *Codices Germanici* [*Catalogus codicum astrologorum Graecorum* 7. Brussels: Lamertin, 1908]: 194–213.
Q
002 **Fragmenta**, ed. S. Weinstock, *Codices Britannici* [*Catalogus codicum astrologorum Graecorum* 9.2. Brussels: Academia, 1953]: 180–186.
Cod

1704 **TEUCER** Hist.
1 B.C.: Cyzicenus
001 **Testimonium**, FGrH #274: 3A:126.
NQ: 35: Test.
002 **Fragmenta**, FGrH #274: 3A:126–127.
Q: 220: Hist.

2288 **TEUPALUS** Hist.
Incertum: Eleus
001 **Testimonium**, FGrH #408: 3B:301.
NQ: 25: Test.

1705 **THALES** Phil.
6 B.C.: Milesius
Cf. et <SEPTEM SAPIENTES> (1667).
001 **Epistulae**, ed. R. Hercher, *Epistolographi Graeci*. Paris: Didot, 1873 (repr. Amsterdam: Hakkert, 1965): 740.
Q: 203: Epist.

002 **Testimonia**, ed. H. Diels and W. Kranz, *Die Fragmente der Vorsokratiker*, vol. 1, 6th edn. Berlin: Weidmann, 1951 (repr. Dublin: 1966): 67–79.
test. 1–23.
NQ: 4,583: Test.

003 **Fragmenta**, ed. Diels and Kranz, *op. cit.*, 80–81.
frr. 1–4.
Q: 279: Phil., Astron.

x01 **Epigramma dedicatorium.**
App. Anth. 1.21(?): Cf. ANTHOLOGIAE GRAECAE APPENDIX (7052 001).

1707 **Antonius THALLUS** Epigr.
fiq Antonius Argivus
A.D. 1: Milesius
Cf. et ANTONIUS Epigr. (0120).

001 **Epigrammata**, AG **6**.91, 235; **7**.188, 373; **9**.220.
Q: 203: Epigr.

1706 **THALLUS** Hist.
A.D. 1/2: fort. Samaritanus
001 **Testimonia**, FGrH #256: 2B:1157.
NQ: 84: Test.

002 **Fragmenta**, FGrH #256: 2B:1157–1158.
Q: 696: Hist., Chronogr.

0925 **THAMYRAS** Med.
ante A.D. 2
x01 **Fragmentum ap. Galenum.**
K13.300.
Cf. GALENUS Med. (0057 076).

1085 **THARSEUS** Med.
ante A.D. 1
x01 **Fragmentum ap. Galenum.**
K13.741–742.
Cf. GALENUS Med. (0057 077).

4044 **THEAETETUS** Epigr.
A.D. 6
001 **Epigrammata**, AG **6**.27; **9**.659; **10**.16; **16**.32b, 221, 233.
Q: 252: Epigr.

0123 **THEAETETUS** Phil. et Math.
5–4 B.C.: Atheniensis
001 **Testimonia**, ed. F. Lasserre, *De Léodamas de Thasos à Philippe d'Oponte*. Naples: Bibliopolis, 1987: 49–54.
test. 1c–10.
NQ: Test.

002 **Doctrina**, ed. Lasserre, *op. cit.*, 54–55, 57–66.
frr. 1–2, 5–42f.
NQ: Test.

1708 **THEAETETUS** Poeta
3 B.C.: Cyrenaeus
001 **Epigrammata**, AG **6**.357; **7**.444, 499, 727.
AG 13.29: Cf. NICAENETUS Epic. (0218 002).
Q: 151: Epigr.

x01 **Epigrammata** (*App. Anth.*).
Epigramma sepulcrale: 2.28.
Epigramma demonstrativum: 3.35.
App. Anth. 2.28: Cf. ANTHOLOGIAE GRAECAE APPENDIX (7052 002).
App. Anth. 3.35: Cf. ANTHOLOGIAE GRAECAE APPENDIX (7052 003).

1709 **THEAGENES** Hist.
3 B.C.?: Macedo
001 **Testimonium**, FGrH #774: 3C:768.
NQ: 66: Test.

002 **Fragmenta**, FGrH #774: 3C:768–770.
Q: 498: Hist.

2275 **THEAGENES** Phil.
6 B.C.: Rheginus
001 **Testimonia**, ed. H. Diels and W. Kranz, *Die Fragmente der Vorsokratiker*, vol. 1, 6th edn. Berlin: Weidmann, 1951 (repr. Dublin: 1966): 51–52.
test. 1–4.
NQ: 379: Test.

1710 **<THEAGES>** Phil.
3 B.C.?
001 **Fragmenta**, ed. H. Thesleff, *The Pythagorean texts of the Hellenistic period*. Åbo: Åbo Akademi, 1965: 190–193.
Q: 1,145: Phil.

0054 **<THEANO>** Phil.
post 4 B.C.?
001 **Fragmenta**, ed. H. Thesleff, *The Pythagorean texts of the Hellenistic period*. Åbo: Åbo Akademi, 1965: 195–201.
Q: 1,915: Phil., Epist.

1711 **<THEARIDAS>** Phil.
3 B.C.
001 **Fragmentum**, ed. H. Thesleff, *The Pythagorean texts of the Hellenistic period*. Åbo: Åbo Akademi, 1965: 201.
Q: 32: Phil.

1712 *THEBAÏS*
7/6 B.C.
001 **Fragmenta**, ed. T.W. Allen, *Homeri opera*, vol. 5. Oxford: Clarendon Press, 1912 (repr. 1969): 113–114.
frr. 1–5.
Q: Epic.

1713 **THEMISON** Hist.
ante 3 B.C.?
001 **Fragmenta**, FGrH #374: 3B:241.
Q: 124: Hist., Perieg.

1088 **THEMISON** Med.
1 B.C.–A.D. 1: Laodicensis

x01 **Fragmentum ap. Galenum.**
K13.158–159.
Cf. GALENUS Med. (0057 076).

x02 **Fragmenta ap. Soranum.**
CMG, vol. 4, pp. 10, 25.
Cf. SORANUS Med. (0565 001).

x03 Διάγνωσις περὶ τῶν ὀξέων καὶ χρονίων νοσημάτων [Dub.].
Fuchs, *RhM* 58, pp. 69–114.
Cf. ANONYMI MEDICI (0721 026).

2001 **THEMISTIUS** Phil. et Rhet.
A.D. 4: Constantinopolitanus

001 Περὶ φιλανθρωπίας ἢ Κωνστάντιος, ed. H. Schenkl and G. Downey, *Themistii orationes quae supersunt*, vol. 1. Leipzig: Teubner, 1965: 3–25.
Cod: 4,777: Orat.

002 Εἰς Κωνστάντιον τὸν αὐτοκράτορα, ὅτι μάλιστα φιλόσοφος ὁ βασιλεύς, ἢ χαριστήριος, ed. Schenkl and Downey, *op. cit.*, vol. 1, 27–56.
Cod: 4,688: Orat.

003 Πρεσβευτικὸς ὑπὲρ Κωνσταντινουπόλεως ῥηθεὶς ἐν Ῥώμῃ, ed. Schenkl and Downey, *op. cit.*, vol. 1, 57–68.
Cod: 2,345: Orat.

004 Εἰς τὸν αὐτοκράτορα Κωνστάντιον, ed. Schenkl and Downey, *op. cit.*, vol. 1, 69–89.
Cod: 3,969: Orat.

005 Ὑπατικὸς εἰς τὸν αὐτοκράτορα Ἰοβιανόν, ed. Schenkl and Downey, *op. cit.*, vol. 1, 91–104.
Cod: 2,205: Orat.

006 Φιλάδελφοι ἢ περὶ φιλανθρωπίας, ed. Schenkl and Downey, *op. cit.*, vol. 1, 105–125.
Cod: 3,681: Orat.

007 Περὶ τῶν ἠτυχηκότων ἐπὶ Οὐάλεντος, ed. Schenkl and Downey, *op. cit.*, vol. 1, 127–151.
Cod: 4,619: Orat.

008 Πενταετηρικός, ed. Schenkl and Downey, *op. cit.*, vol. 1, 153–180.
Cod: 5,474: Orat.

009 Προτρεπτικὸς Οὐαλεντινιανῷ νέῳ, ed. Schenkl and Downey, *op. cit.*, vol. 1, 181–194.
Cod: 2,350: Orat.

010 Ἐπὶ τῆς εἰρήνης Οὐάλεντι, ed. Schenkl and Downey, *op. cit.*, vol. 1, 195–214.
Cod: 3,560: Orat.

011 Δεκετηρικὸς ἢ περὶ τῶν πρεπόντων λόγων τῷ βασιλεῖ, ed. Schenkl and Downey, *op. cit.*, vol. 1, 215–230.
Cod: 3,648: Orat.

012 Ἐρωτικὸς ἢ περὶ κάλλους βασιλικοῦ, ed. Schenkl and Downey, *op. cit.*, vol. 1, 231–257.
Cod: 5,554: Orat.

014 Πρεσβευτικὸς εἰς Θεοδόσιον αὐτοκράτορα, ed. Schenkl and Downey, *op. cit.*, vol. 1, 259–265.
Cod: 976: Orat.

015 Εἰς Θεοδόσιον· τίς ἡ βασιλικωτάτη τῶν ἀρετῶν, ed. Schenkl and Downey, *op. cit.*, vol. 1, 267–286.
Cod: 4,266: Orat.

016 Χαριστήριος τῷ αὐτοκράτορι ὑπὲρ τῆς εἰρήνης καὶ τῆς ὑπατείας τοῦ στρατηγοῦ Σατορνίνου, ed. Schenkl and Downey, *op. cit.*, vol. 1, 287–304.
Cod: 3,803: Orat.

017 Ἐπὶ τῇ χειροτονίᾳ τῆς πολιαρχίας, ed. Schenkl and Downey, *op. cit.*, vol. 1, 305–309.
Cod: 841: Orat.

018 Περὶ τῆς τοῦ βασιλέως φιληκοΐας, ed. Schenkl and Downey, *op. cit.*, vol. 1, 311–325.
Cod: 2,524: Orat.

019 Ἐπὶ τῇ φιλανθρωπίᾳ τοῦ αὐτοκράτορος Θεοδοσίου, ed. Schenkl and Downey, *op. cit.*, vol. 1, 327–339.
Cod: 2,234: Orat.

020 Ἐπιτάφιος ἐπὶ τῷ πατρί, ed. Schenkl, Downey, and A.F. Norman, *op. cit.*, vol. 2 (1971): 1–15.
Cod: 2,312: Orat.

021 Βασανιστὴς ἢ φιλόσοφος, ed. Schenkl, Downey, and Norman, *op. cit.*, vol. 2, 17–49.
Cod: 6,336: Orat.

022 Περὶ φιλίας, ed. Schenkl, Downey, and Norman, *op. cit.*, vol. 2, 51–73.
Cod: 5,104: Orat.

023 Σοφιστής, ed. Schenkl, Downey, and Norman, *op. cit.*, vol. 2, 75–95.
Cod: 4,784: Orat.

024 Προτρεπτικὸς Νικομηδεῦσιν εἰς φιλοσοφίαν, ed. Schenkl, Downey, and Norman, *op. cit.*, vol. 2, 97–111.
Cod: 2,470: Orat., Rhet.

025 Πρὸς τὸν ἀξιώσαντα λέγειν ἐκ τοῦ παραχρῆμα, ed. Schenkl, Downey, and Norman, *op. cit.*, vol. 2, 113–115.
Cod: 373: Orat.

026 <Ὑπὲρ τοῦ λέγειν ἢ πῶς τῷ φιλοσόφῳ λεκτέον>, ed. Schenkl, Downey, and Norman, *op. cit.*, vol. 2, 117–151.
Cod: 5,792: Orat.

027 Περὶ τοῦ μὴ δεῖν τοῖς τόποις ἀλλὰ τοῖς ἀνδράσι προσέχειν, ed. Schenkl, Downey, and Norman, *op. cit.*, vol. 2, 153–167.
Cod: 2,816: Orat.

028 Ἡ ἐπὶ τῷ λόγῳ διάλεξις, ed. Schenkl, Downey, and Norman, *op. cit.*, vol. 2, 169–172.
Cod: 677: Orat.

029 Πρὸς τοὺς οὐκ ὀρθῶς ἐξηγουμένους τὸν σοφιστήν, ed. Schenkl, Downey, and Norman, *op. cit.*, vol. 2, 173–179.
Cod: 1,286: Orat.

030 Θέσις εἰ γεωργητέον, ed. Schenkl, Downey, and Norman, *op. cit.*, vol. 2, 181–186.
Cod: 1,022: Orat., Rhet.

031 Περὶ προεδρίας εἰς τὴν σύγκλητον, ed. Schenkl, Downey, and Norman, *op. cit.*, vol. 2, 187–192.
Cod: 992: Orat.

032 Μετριοπαθὴς ἢ φιλότεκνος, ed. Schenkl, Downey, and Norman, *op. cit.*, vol. 2, 193–204.
Cod: 2,480: Orat.

033 <Περὶ τῶν ὀνομάτων τοῦ βασιλέως καὶ τοῦ ὑπάτου>, ed. Schenkl, Downey, and Norman, *op. cit.*, vol. 2, 205–210.
Cod: 1,025: Orat.

034 Πρὸς τοὺς αἰτιασαμένους ἐπὶ τῷ δέξασθαι τὴν ἀρχήν, ed. Schenkl, Downey, and Norman, *op. cit.*, vol. 2, 211–232.
Cod: 4,259: Orat.

035 <Φ>ιλόπολις, ed. Schenkl, Downey, and Norman, *op. cit.*, vol. 3 (1974): 1.
Cod: 133: Orat., Rhet.

036 Περὶ ψυχῆς (fragmenta), ed. Schenkl, Downey, and Norman, *op. cit.*, vol. 3, 2–4.
Q: 240: Phil.

037 Περὶ φρονήσεως (fragmentum), ed. Schenkl, Downey, and Norman, *op. cit.*, vol. 3, 4–5.
Cod: 264: Phil.

038 **Analyticorum posteriorum paraphrasis**, ed. M. Wallies, *Themistii analyticorum posteriorum paraphrasis* [*Commentaria in Aristotelem Graeca* 5.1. Berlin: Reimer, 1900]: 1–66.
Cod: 23,690: Phil., Comm.

039 **In Aristotelis physica paraphrasis**, ed. H. Schenkl, *Themistii in Aristotelis physica paraphrasis* [*Commentaria in Aristotelem Graeca* 5.2. Berlin: Reimer, 1900]: 1–236.
Cod: 83,378: Phil., Comm.

040 **In Aristotelis libros de anima paraphrasis**, ed. R. Heinze, *Themistii in libros Aristotelis de anima paraphrasis* [*Commentaria in Aristotelem Graeca* 5.3. Berlin: Reimer, 1899]: 1–126.
Cod: 54,929: Phil., Comm.

041 **(Sophoniae) in parva naturalia commentarium**, ed. P. Wendland, *Themistii (Sophoniae) in parva naturalia commentarium* [*Commentaria in Aristotelem Graeca* 5.6. Berlin: Reimer, 1903]: 1–44.
Cod: 15,211: Phil., Comm.

042 **Quae fertur in Aristotelis analyticorum priorum librum i paraphrasis**, ed. M. Wallies, *Themistii quae fertur in Aristotelis analyticorum priorum librum i paraphrasis* [*Commentaria in Aristotelem Graeca* 23.3. Berlin: Reimer, 1884]: 1–164.
Cod: 74,437: Phil., Comm.

x01 **Epigramma**.
AG 11.292.
Cf. PALLADAS Epigr. (2123 001).

0055 *THEMISTOCLIS EPISTULAE*
Incertum
001 **Epistulae**, ed. R. Hercher, *Epistolographi Graeci*. Paris: Didot, 1873 (repr. Amsterdam: Hakkert, 1965): 741–762.
Cod: 8,862: Epist.

1924 **THEMISTOGENES** Hist.
4 B.C.?: Syracusanus
001 **Testimonia**, FGrH #108: 2B:522.
NQ: 136: Test.

2515 **THEOCHRESTUS** Hist.
post 4 B.C.?: fort. Cyrenaeus
001 **Testimonium**, FGrH #761: 3C:742.
NQ: 23: Test.
002 **Fragmenta**, FGrH #761: 3C:742–743.
Q: 165: Hist.

0206 **THEOCLES** Lyr.
3 B.C.?
001 **Ithyphalli**, ed. J.U. Powell, *Collectanea Alexandrina*. Oxford: Clarendon Press, 1925 (repr. 1970): 173.
Q: 18: Lyr.

1947 **THEOCLIUS** Hist.
vel Theocles vel Theoclus vel Theoclytus vel Theo Chius
A.D. 3–4?
001 **Fragmentum**, FGrH #214: 2B:945–946.
Q: 160: Hist.

0005 **THEOCRITUS** Bucol.
4–3 B.C.: Syracusanus
Scholia: Cf. SCHOLIA IN THEOCRITUM (5038).
001 **Idyllia**, ed. A.S.F. Gow, *Theocritus*, vol. 1, 2nd edn. Cambridge: Cambridge University Press, 1952 (repr. 1965): 4–236.
Cod, Pap: 20,502: Bucol.
002 **Epigrammata**, ed. Gow, *op. cit.*, 240–254.
Q: 972: Epigr.
003 **Syrinx**, ed. Gow, *op. cit.*, 256.
Cod: 80: Bucol.
004 **Fragmentum**, ed. Gow, *op. cit.*, 238.
fr. 3.
Q: 42: Bucol.
005 **Epigrammata**, AG **6**.336–340; **7**.262, 658; **9**.338, 432–435, 437, 598–600; **13**.3; **15**.21.
Dup. 0005 002–003.
AG 6.177: Cf. ANONYMI EPIGRAMMATICI (AG) (0138 001).
AG 7.534: Cf. AUTOMEDON Epigr. (0140 001).
AG 7.659–664: Cf. LEONIDAS Epigr. (1458 001).
Q: 751: Epigr.

1714 **THEOCRITUS** Soph.
4 B.C.: Chius
001 **Fragmentum**, ed. E. Diehl, *Anthologia lyrica Graeca*, fasc. 1, 3rd edn. Leipzig: Teubner, 1949: 127.
Dup. 1714 003, x01.
Q: 26: Epigr.
002 **Testimonium**, FGrH #760: 3C:742.
NQ: 34: Test.
003 **Fragmentum**, ed. H. Lloyd-Jones and P. Parsons, *Supplementum Hellenisticum*. Berlin: De Gruyter, 1983: 355.
fr. 738.
Dup. 1714 001, x01.
Q: 31: Epigr.

x01 **Epigramma sepulcrale.**
App. Anth. 2.46: Cf. ANTHOLOGIAE GRAE-
CAE APPENDIX (7052 002).
Dup. 1714 001, 003.

0329 **THEODECTAS** Trag.
4 B.C.: Phaselinus
001 **Fragmenta,** ed. B. Snell, *Tragicorum Graecorum fragmenta,* vol. 1. Göttingen: Vandenhoeck & Ruprecht, 1971: 230–237.
frr. 1–12, 13–20.
Q: 475: Trag., Satyr.
x01 **Aenigmata.**
App. Anth. 7.12–14: Cf. ANTHOLOGIAE
GRAECAE APPENDIX (7052 007).
Dup. partim 0329 001 (frr. 4, 18).

1928 **THEODECTES** Hist.
4 B.C.: Phaselinus
001 **Testimonium,** FGrH #113: 2B:525.
NQ: 28: Test.

2125 **THEODORETUS** Gramm.
A.D. 4
001 **Epigramma,** AG 16.34.
Q: 13: Epigr.

4089 **THEODORETUS** Scr. Eccl. et Theol.
A.D. 4–5: Cyrrhensis
001 **Graecarum affectionum curatio,** ed. P. Cani-
vet, *Théodoret de Cyr. Thérapeutique des mala-
dies helléniques,* 2 vols. [*Sources chrétiennes* 57.
Paris: Cerf, 1958]: **1**:100–287; **2**:296–446.
Cod: 68,875: Apol.
002 **Eranistes,** ed. G.H. Ettlinger, *Theodoret of
Cyrus. Eranistes.* Oxford: Clarendon Press,
1975: 61–266.
Cod: 56,357: Theol., Apol.
003 **Historia ecclesiastica,** ed. L. Parmentier and F.
Scheidweiler, *Theodoret. Kirchengeschichte,*
2nd edn. [*Die griechischen christlichen Schriftsteller* 44. Berlin: Akademie-Verlag, 1954]: 1–
349.
Cod: 70,201: Hist., Eccl.
004 **Historia religiosa** (= **Philotheus**), ed. P. Cani-
vet and A. Leroy-Molinghen, *Théodoret de Cyr.
L'histoire des moines de Syrie,* 2 vols. [*Sources
chrétiennes* 234, 257. Paris: Cerf, 1:1977;
2:1979]: **1**:124–144, 160–508; **2**:8–250, 254–
314.
Philotheus 31 = Oratio de divina et sancta
caritate.
Cod: 50,561: Hist., Eccl., Hagiogr., Orat.
005 **Epistulae:** *Collectio Patmensis* (epistulae 1–
52), ed. Y. Azéma, *Théodoret de Cyr. Correspondance I* [*Sources chrétiennes* 40. Paris: Cerf,
1955]: 74–121.
Cod: 8,907: Epist.
006 **Epistulae:** *Collectio Sirmondiana* (epistulae 1–
95), ed. Y. Azéma, *Théodoret de Cyr. Correspondance II* [*Sources chrétiennes* 98. Paris: Cerf,
1964]: 20–248.
Cod: 22,473: Epist.

007 **Epistulae:** *Collectio Sirmondiana* (epistulae
96–147), ed. Y. Azéma, *Théodoret de Cyr. Correspondance III* [*Sources chrétiennes* 111. Paris:
Cerf, 1965]: 10–232.
Cod: 24,352: Epist.
008 **Commentaria in Isaiam,** ed. J.-N. Guinot,
Théodoret de Cyr. Commentaire sur Isaïe, vols.
1–3 [*Sources chrétiennes* 276, 295, 315. Paris:
Cerf, 1:1980; 2:1982; 3:1984]: **1**:136–330;
2:12–478; **3**:12–350.
Cod: 101,155: Exeget.
010 **Ad quaesita magorum** (fragmentum) [Sp.], ed.
M. Brok, "Le livre contre les mages de Théodoret de Cyr," *Mélanges de science religieuse* 10
(1953) 183–184.
Cod: [724]: Apol.
016 **Quaestiones et responsiones ad orthodoxos**
[Dub.], ed. A. Papadopoulos-Kerameus, Θεο-
δωρήτου ἐπισκόπου πόλεως Κύρρου πρὸς τὰς
ἐπενεχθείσας αὐτῷ ἐπερωτήσεις παρά τινος
τὸν ἐξ Αἰγύπτου ἐπίσκοπον ἀποκρίσεις. St.
Petersburg: Kirschbaum, 1895: 1–150.
Cod: 37,003: Apol.
017 **Homilia in nativitate Joannis Baptistae** [Sp.],
ed. V. Latyšev, "Θεοδώρου τοῦ Δαφνοπάτου
λόγοι δύο," *Pravoslavnyj Palestinskij Sbornik*
59 (1910) 3–14.
Cod: [3,077]: Homilet., Exeget.
020 **De sancta trinitate,** MPG 75: 1148–1189.
Cod: 8,714: Theol., Apol.
021 **De incarnatione domini,** MPG 75: 1420–1477.
Cod: 11,879: Theol., Apol.
022 **Quaestiones in Octateuchum,** ed. N. Fernán-
dez Marcos and A. Sáenz-Badillos, *Theodoreti
Cyrensis quaestiones in Octateuchum* [*Textos y
Estudios* <<*Cardenal Cisneros*>> 17. Madrid:
Poliglota Matritense, 1979]: 3–318.
Quaestiones in Genesim: pp. 3–99.
Quaestiones in Exodum: pp. 100–152.
Quaestiones in Leviticum: pp. 153–189.
Quaestiones in Numeros: pp. 190–226.
Quaestiones in Deuteronomium: pp. 227–267.
Quaestiones in Josuam: pp. 268–288.
Quaestiones in Judices: pp. 289–311.
Quaestiones in Ruth: pp. 312–318.
Cod: 70,514: Exeget.
023 **Quaestiones in libros Regnorum et Paralipo-
menon,** MPG 80: 528–858.
Cod: 53,404: Exeget.
024 **Interpretatio in Psalmos,** MPG 80: 857–1997.
Cod: 194,286: Exeget.
025 **Explanatio in Canticum canticorum,** MPG 81:
28–213.
Cod: 36,753: Exeget.
026 **Interpretatio in Jeremiam,** MPG 81: 496–805.
Lib. 1–10 (In Jeremiam): coll. 496–760.
Lib. 11 (In Baruch): coll. 760–780.
Lib. 12 (In Lamentationes): coll. 780–805.
Cod: 52,534: Exeget.
027 **Interpretatio in Ezechielem,** MPG 81: 808–
1256.
Cod: 84,313: Exeget.

028 **Interpretatio in Danielem,** MPG 81: 1256–1546.
Cod: 54,851: Exeget.

029 **Interpretatio in xii prophetas minores,** MPG 81: 1545–1988.
Cod: 83,394: Exeget.

030 **Interpretatio in xiv epistulas sancti Pauli,** MPG 82: 36–877.
Cod: 160,697: Exeget.

031 **Haereticarum fabularum compendium,** MPG 83: 336–556.
Cod: 41,403: Hist., Eccl.

032 **De providentia orationes decem,** MPG 83: 556–773.
Cod: 43,555: Homilet., Theol.

033 **Libellus contra Nestorium ad Sporacium** [Sp.], MPG 83: 1153–1164.
Cod: 2,168: Theol., Apol.

034 **Ad eos qui in Euphratesia et Osrhoena regione, Syria, Phoenicia et Cilicia vitam monasticam degunt** (ex epistula 151), MPG 83: 1416–1433.
Cod: 3,659: Epist.

035 **Quod unicus filius sit dominus noster Jesus Christus** (ex epistula 151), MPG 83: 1433–1440.
Cod: 1,577: Epist., Theol.

036 **Libri v contra Cyrillum et concilium Ephesinum (Pentalogus)** (fragmenta Graeca), MPG 84: 65–88.
Cod: [4,163]: Apol.

037 **Contra Judaeos** (fragmentum) [Sp.], ed. M. Brok, "Un soi-disant fragment du 'Traité contre les Juifs' de Théodoret," *Revue d'histoire ecclésiastique* 45 (1950) 490–494.
Cod: [1,374]: Apol.

x01 **Expositio rectae fidei.**
Otto, vol. 4, pp. 2–66.
Cf. Pseudo-JUSTINUS MARTYR (0646 006).

x02 **Sermones quinque in Joannem Chrysostomum.**
Photius, *Bibliotheca* 273.
Cf. PHOTIUS Theol., Scr. Eccl. et Lexicogr. (4040 001).

x03 **Ex sermone Chalcedone, cum essent abituri, habito.**
ACO 1.1.7, pp. 82–83.
Cf. CONCILIA OECUMENICA (ACO) (5000 001).

x04 **Epistula ad Alexandrum Hierapolitanum** (= epistula 169 e collectione conciliari).
ACO 1.1.7, pp. 79–80.
Cf. CONCILIA OECUMENICA (ACO) (5000 001).

x05 **Epistula ad Joannem Antiochenum** (= epistula 150 e collectione conciliari).
ACO 1.1.6, pp. 107–108.
Cf. CONCILIA OECUMENICA (ACO) (5000 001).

x06 **Theodoreti impugnatio xii anathematismorum Cyrilli et Cyrilli apologia.**
ACO 1.1.6, pp. 108–144.

Cf. CONCILIA OECUMENICA (ACO) (5000 001).

x07 **Epistula ad Joannem Antiochenum** (= epistula 171 e collectione conciliari).
ACO 1.1.7, pp. 163–164.
Cf. CONCILIA OECUMENICA (ACO) (5000 001).

1715 **THEODORIDAS** Epigr.
3 B.C.: Syracusanus

001 **Epigrammata,** AG **6**.155–157, 222, 224; **7**.282, 406, 439, 479, 527–529, 722, 732, 738; **9**.743; **13**.8, 21; **16**.132.
Q: 525: Epigr.

002 **Fragmenta et tituli,** ed. H. Lloyd-Jones and P. Parsons, *Supplementum Hellenisticum.* Berlin: De Gruyter, 1983: 356–358.
frr. 739, 741–746, 748.
Q: 61: Epigr., Poem.

1094 **THEODORIDES** Trag.
4 B.C.

001 **Tituli,** ed. B. Snell, *Tragicorum Graecorum fragmenta,* vol. 1. Göttingen: Vandenhoeck & Ruprecht, 1971: 249.
NQ: 7: Trag.

1716 **THEODORUS** Epigr.
4–3 B.C.

001 **Epigramma,** AG 6.282.
Q: 37: Epigr.

2728 **THEODORUS** Epigr.
A.D. 4?

x01 **Epigramma.**
App. Anth. 2.705b addenda: Cf. ANTHOLOGIAE GRAECAE APPENDIX (7052 008).

4045 **THEODORUS** Epigr.
A.D. 6

001 **Epigramma,** AG 7.556.
Q: 16: Epigr.

3158 **THEODORUS** Epist.
A.D. 10: Cyzicenus

001 **Epistulae,** ed. J. Darrouzès, *Epistoliers byzantins du xe siècle* [*Archives de l'orient chrétien* 6. Paris: Institut Français d'Études Byzantines, 1960]: 317–341.
Epistulae Theodori ad Constantinum: pp. 319, 321, 322–323, 324–327, 328, 329–330, 331–332.
Epistulae Constantini ad Theodorum: pp. 317–318, 320, 321–322, 323–324, 327, 328–329, 330–331, 332.
Epistulae Theodori ad alios: pp. 333–341.
Cod: Epist.

1717 **THEODORUS** Gramm.
A.D. 2: Bithynius

001 **Epigramma,** AG 11.198.
Q: 12: Epigr.

2251 **THEODORUS** Hist.
5–4 B.C.?: Phocaeus
001 **Testimonium**, FGrH #406: 3B:300.
NQ: 26: Test.

1892 **THEODORUS** Hist.
post 4 B.C.: Iliensis
001 **Fragmenta**, FGrH #48: 1A:273.
Q: 89: Hist., Myth.

2161 **THEODORUS** Hist.
3 B.C.: fort. Rhodius
001 **Fragmentum**, FGrH #230: 2B:974.
Q: 48: Hist.

2551 **THEODORUS** Hist.
ante 2 B.C.
001 **Testimonium**, FGrH #822: 3C:896.
NQ: 12: Test.

2570 **THEODORUS** Hist.
1 B.C.: Gadarensis
001 **Testimonia**, FGrH #850: 3C:935–936.
NQ: 164: Test.
002 **Tituli**, FGrH #850: 3C:936.
NQ: Hist.

1904 **THEODORUS** Hist.
ante A.D. 2: Samothracenus
001 **Fragmenta**, FGrH #62: 1A:299.
Q: 106: Hist., Myth.

2150 **THEODORUS** Hist.
Incertum
001 **Testimonium**, FGrH #542: 3B:526.
NQ: 19: Test.

2237 **THEODORUS** Math.
5 B.C.: Cyrenaeus
001 **Testimonia**, ed. H. Diels and W. Kranz, *Die Fragmente der Vorsokratiker*, vol. 1, 6th edn. Berlin: Weidmann, 1951 (repr. Dublin: 1966): 397.
test. 1–5.
NQ: 200: Test.
002 **Testimonia et imitationes**, ed. M. Winiarczyk, *Diagorae Melii et Theodori Cyrenaei reliquiae*. Leipzig: Teubner, 1981: 31–46.
NQ: Test.

1090 **THEODORUS** Med.
A.D. 1: fort. Macedo
x01 **Fragmenta ap. Aëtium** (lib. 6, 8).
CMG, vol. 8.2, pp. 236, 476.
Cf. AËTIUS Med. (0718 006, 008).
x02 **Fragmentum ap. Aëtium** (lib. 16).
Zervos, *Gynaekologie des Aëtios*, p. 67.
Cf. AËTIUS Med. (0718 016).
x03 **Fragmenta ap. Philumenum**.
CMG, vol. 10.1.1, pp. 8–10, 39.
Cf. PHILUMENUS Med. (0671 001).

1028 **THEODORUS** Med.
fiq Theodorus Moschion vel Theodorus Priscianus
A.D. 4–5?
x01 **Fragmentum ap. Alexandrum Trallianum**.
Puschmann, vol. 1, p. 559.
Cf. ALEXANDER Med. (0744 003).

2947 **THEODORUS** Phil.
A.D. 3–4: Asinaeus
001 **Testimonia**, ed. W. Deuse, *Theodoros von Asine*. Wiesbaden: Steiner, 1973: 30–56.
NQ: Test.

2696 **THEODORUS** Poeta
ante 4 B.C.: Colophonius
001 **Titulus**, ed. H. Lloyd-Jones and P. Parsons, *Supplementum Hellenisticum*. Berlin: De Gruyter, 1983: 360.
fr. 753.
NQ: 4: Poem.

1987 **THEODORUS** Poeta
post 1 B.C.: fort. Smyrnaeus
001 **Testimonium**, FGrH #195: 2B:929.
NQ: 14: Test.
002 **Titulus**, ed. H. Lloyd-Jones and P. Parsons, *Supplementum Hellenisticum*. Berlin: De Gruyter, 1983: 359.
titul. 749.
NQ: 2: Epic.

4126 **THEODORUS** Scr. Eccl.
A.D. 4: Heracleensis
Cf. et THEODORUS Heracleensis vel THEODORUS Mopsuestenus Scr. Eccl. (2967).
002 **Fragmenta in Matthaeum** (in catenis), ed. J. Reuss, *Matthäus-Kommentare aus der griechischen Kirche* [Texte und Untersuchungen] 61. Berlin: Akademie-Verlag, 1957]: 55–95.
Q: 7,812: Exeget., Caten.
004 **Fragmenta in Joannem** (in catenis), ed. J. Reuss, *Johannes-Kommentare aus der griechischen Kirche* [Texte und Untersuchungen] 89. Berlin: Akademie-Verlag, 1966]: 67–176.
Q: 19,266: Exeget., Caten.

4135 **THEODORUS** Theol.
A.D. 4–5: Mopsuestenus
Cf. et THEODORUS Heracleensis vel THEODORUS Mopsuestenus Scr. Eccl. (2967).
009 **Fragmenta in Matthaeum** (in catenis), ed. J. Reuss, *Matthäus-Kommentare aus der griechischen Kirche* [Texte und Untersuchungen] 61. Berlin: Akademie-Verlag, 1957]: 96–135.
Q: 8,482: Exeget., Caten.
015 **Fragmenta in epistulam ad Romanos** (in catenis), ed. K. Staab, *Pauluskommentar aus der griechischen Kirche aus Katenenhandschriften gesammelt*. Münster: Aschendorff, 1933: 113–172.
Q: 19,618: Exeget., Caten.

016 **Fragmenta in epistulam i ad Corinthios** (in catenis), ed. Staab, *op. cit.*, 172–196.
Q: 6,000: Exeget., Caten.

017 **Fragmenta in epistulam ii ad Corinthios** (in catenis), ed. Staab, *op. cit.*, 196–200.
Q: 1,012: Exeget., Caten.

018 **Fragmenta in epistulam ad Hebraeos** (in catenis), ed. Staab, *op. cit.*, 200–212.
Q: 3,652: Exeget., Caten.

0611 **THEODORUS** Trag.
2 B.C.

001 **Tituli**, ed. B. Snell, *Tragicorum Graecorum fragmenta*, vol. 1. Göttingen: Vandenhoeck & Ruprecht, 1971: 304.
frr. 1–2.
NQ: 3: Trag., Satyr.

3123 **THEODORUS DAPHNOPATES** Scr. Eccl. et Hist.
fiq Theodorus Protosecretarius
A.D. 10: Constantinopolitanus
Cf. et THEODORUS Protosecretarius Biogr. (3154).

001 **Epistulae**, ed. J. Darrouzès and L.G. Westerink, *Théodore Daphnopatès. Correspondance.* Paris: Centre National de la Recherche Scientifique, 1978: 31–231.
Epist. 36–40 (pp. 199–231) dubia sunt.
Cod: Epist.

x01 **Theophanes Continuatus** (liber sextus fort. auctore Theodoro Daphnopate).
Bekker, pp. 353–481.
Cf. THEOPHANES CONTINUATUS (4153 001).

2967 **THEODORUS Heracleensis vel THEODORUS Mopsuestenus** Scr. Eccl.
A.D. 4–5
Cf. et THEODORUS Scr. Eccl. (4126).
Cf. et THEODORUS Theol. (4135).

001 **Fragmenta in Matthaeum** (in catenis), ed. J. Reuss, *Matthäus-Kommentare aus der griechischen Kirche* [*Texte und Untersuchungen* 61. Berlin: Akademie-Verlag, 1957]: 136–150.
Q: 2,421: Exeget., Caten.

1718 **THEODORUS ὁ παναγής** Gramm.
1 B.C.?: Atheniensis

001 **Fragmenta**, FGrH #346: 3B:208–209.
Q: 284: Hist., Gramm.

3154 **THEODORUS Protosecretarius** Biogr.
vel Theodorus Melodus
fiq Theodorus Daphnopates
A.D. 10
Cf. et THEODORUS DAPHNOPATES Scr. Eccl. et Hist. (3123).

001 **Dithyrambus in Theophanem**, ed. K. Krumbacher, "Dithyrambus auf Theophanes Confes-

sor," *Sitzungsberichte der bayerischen Akademie der Wissenschaften*, Philosoph.-philol. und hist. Kl., Heft 4. Munich, 1896: 608–618.
Cod: Biogr., Encom.

3157 **THEODORUS Scutariota** Hist.
A.D. 13: Cyzicenus

001 **Additamenta ad Georgii Acropolitae historiam**, ed. A. Heisenberg, *Georgii Acropolitae opera*, vol. 1. Leipzig: Teubner, 1903 (repr. Stuttgart: 1978 (1st edn. corr. P. Wirth)): 277–302.
Cod: 5,136: Hist., Chronogr.

2714 **THEODORUS STUDITES** Scr. Eccl. et Theol.
A.D. 8–9: Bithynius, Constantinopolitanus

001 **Homilia in nativitatem Mariae** (olim sub auctore Joanne Damasceno), MPG 96: 680–697.
Cod: 3,458: Homilet.

x01 **Epigramma exhortatorium et supplicatorium.**
App. Anth. 4.111: Cf. ANTHOLOGIAE GRAECAE APPENDIX (7052 004).

2020 **THEODOSIUS** Gramm.
A.D. 4–5: Alexandrinus

001 **Canones isagogici de flexione nominum**, ed. A. Hilgard, *Grammatici Graeci*, vol. 4.1. Leipzig: Teubner, 1894 (repr. Hildesheim: Olms, 1965): 3–42.
Cod: 7,078: Gramm.

002 **Canones isagogici de flexione verborum**, ed. Hilgard, *Gramm. Graec.* 4.1, 43–99.
Cod: 10,673: Gramm.

003 **Περὶ γραμματικῆς** [Sp.] (fort. auctore Theodoro Prodromo), ed. K. Göttling, *Theodosii Alexandrini grammatica*. Leipzig: Libraria Dykiana, 1822: 1–197.
Cod: 51,384: Gramm.

004 **Περὶ τόνου** [Sp.] (fort. auctore Theodoro Prodromo), ed. Göttling, *op. cit.*, 198–201.
Cod: 840: Gramm.

005 **Epitome catholicae Herodiani** [Sp.] (fort. auctore quodam Theodosio Byzantio), ed. Göttling, *op. cit.*, 202–205.
Cod: 935: Gramm.

006 **Περὶ κλίσεως τῶν εἰς ῶν βαρυτόνων** (e cod. Haun. 1965), ed. A. Hilgard, *Excerpta ex libris Herodiani technici*. Leipzig: Teubner, 1887: 16–22.
Cod: Gramm.

007 **Περὶ κλίσεως τῶν εἰς ῶν ὀξυτόνων** (e cod. Haun. 1965), ed. Hilgard, *Excerpta ex libris Herodiani technici*, 22–24.
Cod: Gramm.

THEODOSIUS Gramm.
A.D. 4–5?: fort. Byzantius
Cf. THEODOSIUS Gramm. (2020 005).

1719 **THEODOSIUS** Math. et Astron.
2–1 B.C.: Tripolites

001 **Sphaerica**, ed. J.L. Heiberg, *Theodosius Tripolites. Sphaerica* [*Abhandlungen der Gesellschaft der Wissenschaften zu Göttingen*, Philol.-
hist. Kl., N.F. 19.3. Berlin: Weidmann, 1927]:
2–164.
Cod: 27,146: Math.

002 **De habitationibus**, ed. R. Fecht, *Theodosii de
habitationibus liber, de diebus et noctibus libri
duo* [*Abhandlungen der Gesellschaft der Wissenschaften zu Göttingen*, Philol.-hist. Kl., N.F.
19.4. Berlin: Weidmann, 1927]: 14–42.
Cod: 4,294: Math., Astron.

003 **De diebus et noctibus**, ed. Fecht, *op. cit.*, 54–
154.
Cod: 18,499: Math., Astron.

1091 **THEODOSIUS** Med.
A.D. 2–3?

x01 **Fragmentum ap. Aëtium** (lib. 6).
CMG, vol. 8.2, p. 198.
Cf. AËTIUS Med. (0718 006).

x02 **Fragmentum ap. Alexandrum Trallianum.**
Puschmann, vol. 2, p. 565.
Cf. ALEXANDER Med. (0744 003).

1770 **THEODOTION** Int. Vet. Test.
A.D. 2

001 **Fragmenta**, ed. J. Reider, *An index to Aquila*
(rev. N. Turner). Leiden: Brill, 1966: passim.
Q

THEODOTUS Gnost.
A.D. 2
Cf. CLEMENS ALEXANDRINUS Theol. (0555
007).

1721 **THEODOTUS Coriarius Ebionites** Scr. Eccl.
A.D. 2–3

x01 **Fragmentum.**
Epiphanius, *Haer.* 54.
Cf. EPIPHANIUS Scr. Eccl. (2021 002).

1720 **THEODOTUS Judaeus** Epic.
ante 1 B.C.

002 **Fragmenta**, ed. H. Lloyd-Jones and P. Parsons,
Supplementum Hellenisticum. Berlin: De Gruy-
ter, 1983: 360–362.
frr. 757–764.
Dup. partim 1720 003.
Q: 341: Epic.

003 **Fragmenta**, FGrH #732: 3C:692–694.
Dup. partim 1720 002.
Q: 714: Hist., Epic.

1722 **THEOGENES** Hist.
ante 3 B.C.

001 **Fragmenta**, FGrH #300: 3B:3–4.
Q: 214: Hist.

0511 **THEOGNETUS** Comic.
3 B.C.?

001 **Fragmenta**, ed. T. Kock, *Comicorum Atti-*

corum fragmenta, vol. 3. Leipzig: Teubner,
1888: 364–365.
frr. 1–2 + titulus.
Q: 91: Comic.

002 **Fragmenta**, ed. A. Meineke, *Fragmenta comicorum Graecorum*, vol. 4. Berlin: Reimer, 1841
(repr. De Gruyter, 1970): 549–550.
Q: 90: Comic.

003 **Titulus**, ed. C. Austin, *Comicorum Graecorum
fragmenta in papyris reperta*. Berlin: De Gruyter, 1973: 216.
NQ: 4: Comic.

0002 **THEOGNIS** Eleg.
6 B.C.: Megarensis

001 **Elegiae**, ed. D. Young (post E. Diehl), *Theognis*, 2nd edn. Leipzig: Teubner, 1971: 1–83.
Cod: 9,928: Eleg.

002 **Fragmenta sedis incertae**, ed. Young, *op. cit.*,
83.
Cod: 50: Eleg.

003 **Fragmenta dubia**, ed. Young, *op. cit.*, 84–85.
frr. 1–10.
Q: 192: Eleg.

004 **Epigrammata**, AG 10.40, 113.
AG 10.40, 113: Dup. 0002 001 (vv. 527–528,
1151–1152, 1155–1156).
AG 9.118: Cf. BESANTINUS Poeta (0144 001).
Q: 29: Epigr.

2367 **THEOGNIS** Hist.
ante A.D. 3: Rhodius

001 **Fragmenta**, FGrH #526: 3B:503–504.
Dup. partim CARMINA POPULARIA (PMG)
(0295 001) (fr. 2).
Q: 213: Hist., Lyr.

0313 **THEOGNIS** Trag.
5 B.C.

001 **Fragmentum**, ed. B. Snell, *Tragicorum Graecorum fragmenta*, vol. 1. Göttingen: Vandenhoeck & Ruprecht, 1971: 146.
fr. 1.
Dup. 0207 001 (fr. 33).
Q: 3: Trag.

2964 **THEOGNOSTUS** Scr. Eccl.
A.D. 3: Alexandrinus

001 **Hypotyposes** (fragmenta), ed. A. von Harnack,
Die Hypotyposen des Theognostus [*Texte und
Untersuchungen* 24.3. Leipzig: Hinrichs, 1903]:
75–78.
Q, Cod

002 **Fragmentum** (Dub.), ed. J.A. Munitiz, "A frag-
ment attributed to Theognostus," *Journal of
Theological Studies*, n.s. 30 (1979) 56–66.
Q

1723 **THEOLYTUS** Epic.
ante 3 B.C.?: Methymnaeus

001 **Fragmentum**, ed. J.U. Powell, *Collectanea Al-*

exandrina. Oxford: Clarendon Press, 1925
(repr. 1970): 9.
Q: 22: Epic.

2332 **THEOLYTUS** Hist.
      4–3 B.C.?: fort. Methymnaeus
 001 **Fragmenta,** FGrH #478: 3B:442–443.
      Q: 205: Hist.

1838 **THEON** Gramm.
      1 B.C.–A.D. 1: Alexandrinus
 001 **Testimonia,** ed. K. Giese, *De Theone gramma-*
      tico eiusque reliquiis [*Diss.* Dresden (1867)]: 5–
      6, 12, 15, 18–19.
      NQ: 215: Test.
 002 **Fragmenta,** ed. Giese, *op. cit.,* 38–42, 44, 46–
      50, 53–55.
      Q: 1,057: Gramm., Comm.
 003 **Commentarium de Pythiis xii Pindari** (*P. Oxy.*
      31.2536), ed. E.G. Turner, *The Oxyrhynchus*
      papyri, pt. 31. London: Egypt Exploration So-
      ciety, 1966: 19–21.
      Pap: 271: Exeget.
 x01 **Arati genus** (olim sub auctore Theone Alexan-
      drino Gramm. vel Theone Alexandrino
      Math.).
      Martin, pp. 14–18.
      Cf. VITAE ARATI ET VARIA DE ARATO
      (4161 004).

2033 **THEON** Math.
      A.D. 4: Alexandrinus
      Cf. et EUCLIDES Geom. (1799 010, 011).
 001 **Commentaria in Ptolemaei syntaxin mathema-**
      ticam i–iv, ed. A. Rome, *Commentaires de*
      Pappus et de Théon d'Alexandrie sur l'Alma-
      geste, vols. 2–3 [*Studi e Testi* 72 & 106. Vatican
      City: Biblioteca Apostolica Vaticana, 2:1936;
      3:1943]: 2:317–804; 3:807–1085.
      Cf. et 2033 008.
      Cod: 149,939: Math., Comm.
 002 **Εἰς τοὺς προχείρους κανόνας** (commentarium
      parvum), ed. A. Tihon, *Le 'petit commentaire'*
      de Théon d'Alexandrie aux tables faciles de Pto-
      lémée [*Studi e Testi* 282. Vatican City: Bib-
      lioteca Apostolica Vaticana, 1978]: 199–298.
      Cod: 16,979: Math., Comm.
 006 **Testimonia,** FGrH #651: 3C:204.
      NQ: 75: Test.
 007 **Epigrammata,** AG 7.292; **9.**41, 491.
      Q: 63: Epigr.
 008 **Commentaria in Ptolemaei syntaxin mathema-**
      ticam v–xi, ed. J. Camerarius, *Theonis Alexan-*
      drini in Claudii Ptolemaei magnam construc-
      tionem commentariorum libri xi. Basel: Walder,
      1538.
      Cf. et 2033 001.
      Cod: Math., Comm.
 009 **Εἰς τοὺς προχείρους κανόνας** (liber 1) (com-
      mentarium magnum), ed. J. Mogenet and A.
      Tihon, *Le 'grand commentaire' de Théon d'Al-*
      exandrie aux tables faciles de Ptolémée [*Studi e*

Testi 315. Vatican City: Biblioteca Apostolica
Vaticana, 1985]: 93–158.
Cod: Math., Comm.

 x01 **Opticorum recensio Theonis.**
      Heiberg, vol. 7, pp. 144–246.
      Cf. EUCLIDES Geom. (1799 010).
 x02 **Scholia in opticorum recensionem Theonis.**
      Heiberg, vol. 7, pp. 251–284.
      Cf. SCHOLIA IN EUCLIDEM (5022 004).
 x03 **Epigrammata demonstrativa.**
      App. Anth. 3.146, 147(?): Cf. ANTHOLOGIAE
      GRAECAE APPENDIX (7052 003).
      App. Anth. 3.147: Cf. et HERMETICA (1286
      x01).
 x06 **Arati genus** (olim sub auctore Theone Alexan-
      drino Gramm. vel Theone Alexandrino
      Math.).
      Martin, pp. 14–18.
      Cf. VITAE ARATI ET VARIA DE ARATO
      (4161 004).
 x07 **Epistula ad Julianum quendam data** (olim sub
      auctore Theone Alexandrino Math.).
      Martin, pp. 533–534.
      Cf. VITAE ARATI ET VARIA DE ARATO
      (4161 009).

1092 **THEON** Med.
      A.D. 2: Alexandrinus
 x01 **Fragmentum ap. Galenum.**
      K6.96–97 in CMG, vol. 5.4.2, p. 44.
      Cf. GALENUS Med. (0057 036).

1724 **THEON** Phil.
      A.D. 2: Smyrnaeus
 001 **De utilitate mathematicae,** ed. E. Hiller, *Theo-*
      nis Smyrnaei philosophi Platonici expositio
      rerum mathematicarum ad legendum Platonem
      utilium. Leipzig: Teubner, 1878: 1–205.
      Cod: 38,866: Math., Phil.

0607 **Aelius THEON** Rhet.
      A.D. 1/2: Alexandrinus
      Scholia: Cf. SCHOLIA IN THEONEM RHE-
      TOREM (5046).
 001 **Progymnasmata,** ed. L. Spengel, *Rhetores*
      Graeci, vol. 2. Leipzig: Teubner, 1854 (repr.
      Frankfurt am Main: Minerva, 1966): 59–130.
      Cod: 19,034: Rhet.

4224 **THEON Archiatrus** Med.
      A.D. 4/6?: Alexandrinus
 x01 **Ἄνθρωπος** (fragmenta ap. Photium, *Bibl.* cod.
      220).
      Henry, vol. 3, pp. 139–140.
      Cf. PHOTIUS Theol., Scr. Eccl. et Lexicogr.
      (4040 001).

2965 **THEONAS** Scr. Eccl.
      A.D. 3–4: Alexandrinus
 001 **Epistula contra Manichaeos** (fragmenta) (*P.*
      Ryl. 3.469), ed. C.H. Roberts, *Catalogue of the*
      Greek and Latin papyri in the John Rylands

Library, vol. 3 [*Theological and literary texts*].
Manchester: Manchester University Press,
1938: 41–43.
Pap

THEOPHANES <Epigr.>
AG 7.537, 539.
Cf. PHANIAS Gramm. (1582 001).
Cf. PERSES Epigr. (1575 001).

1981 **THEOPHANES** Hist.
1 B.C.: Mytilenensis
001 **Testimonia**, FGrH #188: 2B:919–921.
NQ: 836: Test.
002 **Fragmenta**, FGrH #188: 2B:921–923.
Q: 611: Hist.

4046 **THEOPHANES CONFESSOR** Chronogr.
vel Theophanes Homologetes vel Theophanes
Megaloagrius vel Theophanes Isaacius
A.D. 8–9: Constantinopolitanus, Samothrace-
nus
Vita: Cf. NICEPHORUS Biogr. (3152).
Vitae: Cf. VITAE THEOPHANIS CONFESSO-
RIS (3153).
001 **Chronographia**, ed. C. de Boor, *Theophanis
chronographia*, vol. 1. Leipzig: Teubner, 1883
(repr. Hildesheim: Olms, 1963): 3–503.
Cod: 135,329: Hist., Chronogr.
002 **Epigrammata**, AG 15.14, 35.
Q: 57: Epigr.

4153 *THEOPHANES CONTINUATUS*
A.D. 10
001 **Chronographia** (lib. 1–6), ed. I. Bekker, *Theophanes Continuatus, Ioannes Cameniata, Symeon Magister, Georgius Monachus* [*Corpus scriptorum historiae Byzantinae*. Bonn: Weber,
1838]: 1–481.
Lib. 5 to be replaced by Ševčenko edition (in
TLG data bank).
Lib. 6: fort. auctore Theodoro Daphnopate.
Cod: 67,666: Hist., Chronogr.

2707 **THEOPHANES GRAPTOS** Poeta
A.D. 8–9: Hierosolymitanus
x01 **Epigramma demonstrativum**.
App. Anth. 3.309: Cf. ANTHOLOGIAE GRAE-
CAE APPENDIX (7052 003).

1725 **THEOPHILUS** Apol.
A.D. 2: Antiochenus
001 **Ad Autolycum**, ed. R.M. Grant, *Theophilus of
Antioch. Ad Autolycum*. Oxford: Clarendon
Press, 1970: 2–146.
Cod: 21,963: Apol.
002 **In Canticum canticorum** (fragmentum), ed. M.
Richard, "Les fragments exégétiques de Théo-
phile d'Alexandrie et de Théophile d'Anti-
oche," *Revue Biblique* 47 (1938) 392.
no. 11.
Q: Exeget.

0512 **THEOPHILUS** Comic.
4 B.C.
001 **Fragmenta**, ed. T. Kock, *Comicorum Atticorum fragmenta*, vol. 2. Leipzig: Teubner,
1884: 473–477.
frr. 1–12.
Q: 308: Comic.
002 **Fragmenta**, ed. A. Meineke, *Fragmenta comicorum Graecorum*, vol. 3. Berlin: Reimer, 1840
(repr. De Gruyter, 1970): 626–631.
Q: 309: Comic.

4250 **THEOPHILUS** Gramm.
3 B.C.: fort. Alexandrinus
001 **Fragmentum**, ed. F. Montanari, *I frammenti
dei grammatici Agathokles, Hellanikos, Ptolemaios Epithetes* [*Sammlung griechischer und
lateinischer Grammatiker* 7. Berlin: De Gruyter, 1988]: 114.
Q: Gramm.

2496 **THEOPHILUS** Hist.
ante 2 B.C.?
001 **Fragmentum**, FGrH #733: 3C:695.
Q: 33: Hist.

2203 **[THEOPHILUS]** Hist.
Incertum
001 **Fragmenta**, FGrH #296: 3A:179–180.
Q: 262: Hist., Nat. Hist.

2394 **THEOPHILUS** Hist.
Incertum
001 **Fragmentum**, FGrH #573: 3B:674.
Q: 72: Hist., Perieg.

1093 **THEOPHILUS** Med.
ante A.D. 6
x01 **Fragmentum ap. Aëtium** (lib. 7).
CMG, vol. 8.2, p. 382.
Cf. AËTIUS Med. (0718 007).
x02 **Fragmentum ap. Alexandrum Trallianum**.
Puschmann, vol. 2, p. 19.
Cf. ALEXANDER Med. (0744 003).

4115 **THEOPHILUS** Scr. Eccl.
A.D. 4: Alexandrinus
029 **Fragmenta in Matthaeum** (in catenis), ed. J.
Reuss, *Matthäus-Kommentare aus der griech-
ischen Kirche* [*Texte und Untersuchungen* 61.
Berlin: Akademie-Verlag, 1957]: 151–152.
Q: 231: Exeget., Caten.
030 **Fragmenta in Joannem** (in catenis), ed. J.
Reuss, *Johannes-Kommentare aus der griech-
ischen Kirche* [*Texte und Untersuchungen* 89.
Berlin: Akademie-Verlag, 1966]: 187.
Q: 77: Exeget., Caten.

1050 **THEOPHILUS et NARCISSUS** Scr. Eccl.
A.D. 2: Caesariensis (Theophilus), Hierosolymitanus (Narcissus)
001 **Epistula de pascha** (fragmentum), ed. P. Nau-

tin, *Lettres et écrivains chrétiens des 2ᵉ et 3ᵉ siècles* [*Patristica* 2. Paris: Cerf, 1961]: 85–87.
Q

2706 THEOPHILUS Imperator
A.D. 9: Constantinopolitanus
x01 **Epigramma demonstrativum.**
App. Anth. 3.308: Cf. ANTHOLOGIAE GRAECAE APPENDIX (7052 003).

0729 THEOPHILUS Protospatharius Med.
A.D. 9/10: Constantinopolitanus
Cf. et THEOPHILUS Protospatharius, DAMASCIUS et STEPHANUS Atheniensis Med. (0728).
Cf. et THEOPHILUS Protospatharius et STEPHANUS Atheniensis Med. (0746).
002 **De urinis**, ed. J.L. Ideler, *Physici et medici Graeci minores*, vol. 1. Berlin: Reimer, 1841 (repr. Amsterdam: Hakkert, 1963): 261–283.
Cod: 6,527: Med.
003 **De excrementis**, ed. Ideler, *op. cit.*, 397–408.
Cod: 3,352: Med.
004 **De pulsibus**, ed. F.Z. Ermerins, *Anecdota medica Graeca*. Leiden: Luchtmans, 1840 (repr. Amsterdam: Hakkert, 1963): 3–77.
Cod: 7,012: Med.
005 **De corporis humani fabrica libri quinque**, ed. G.A. Greenhill, *Theophili Protospatharii de corporis humani fabrica libri v.* Oxford: Oxford University Press, 1842: 1–272.
Cod: 30,583: Med.
006 **Apotherapeutica** (excerpta e cod. Laur. plut. 75.19), ed. A.P. Kousis, "The apotherapeutic of Theophilos according [to] the Laurentian codex, plut. 75, 19," Πρακτικὰ τῆς ᾽Ακαδημίας ᾽Αθηνῶν 19 (1948) 37–45.
Cod: Med.

0728 THEOPHILUS Protospatharius, DAMASCIUS et STEPHANUS Atheniensis Med.
post A.D. 9/10
Cf. et STEPHANUS Med. et Phil. (0724).
Cf. et THEOPHILUS Protospatharius Med. (0729).
Cf. et DAMASCIUS Phil. (4066).
Cf. et THEOPHILUS Protospatharius et STEPHANUS Atheniensis Med. (0746).
001 **Commentarii in Hippocratis aphorismos**, ed. F.R. Dietz, *Scholia in Hippocratem et Galenum*, vol. 2. Königsberg: Borntraeger, 1834 (repr. Amsterdam: Hakkert, 1966): 236, 238–240, 244–544.
Cod: 72,602: Med., Comm.

0746 THEOPHILUS Protospatharius et STEPHANUS Atheniensis Med.
post A.D. 9/10
Cf. et STEPHANUS Med. et Phil. (0724).
Cf. et THEOPHILUS Protospatharius Med. (0729).
Cf. et THEOPHILUS Protospatharius, DAMAS-

CIUS et STEPHANUS Atheniensis Med. (0728).
001 **De febrium differentia**, ed. D. Sicurus, *Theophili et Stephani Atheniensis de febrium differentia ex Hippocrate et Galeno*. Florence: Bengini, 1862: 5–46.
Cf. et PALLADIUS Med. (0726 002).
Cod: 12,888: Med.

0093 THEOPHRASTUS Phil.
4–3 B.C.: Eresius
001 **Historia plantarum**, ed. A. Hort, *Theophrastus. Enquiry into plants*, 2 vols. Cambridge, Mass.: Harvard University Press, 1916 (repr. 1:1968; 2:1961): 1:2–474; 2:2–320.
Cod: 73,980: Nat. Hist.
002 **De causis plantarum** (lib. 1), ed. R.E. Dengler, *Theophrastus. De causis plantarum, book one*. Philadelphia: University of Pennsylvania Press, 1927: 12–138.
Cf. et 0093 014.
Cod: 12,284: Nat. Hist.
003 **De sensu et sensibilibus** (= fr. 1, Wimmer), ed. H. Diels, *Doxographi Graeci*. Berlin: Reimer, 1879 (repr. De Gruyter, 1965): 499–527.
Cod: 9,212: Phil., Doxogr.
004 **De lapidibus** (= fr. 2, Wimmer), ed. D.E. Eichholz, *Theophrastus. De lapidibus*. Oxford: Clarendon Press, 1965: 56–84.
Cod: 4,379: Nat. Hist.
005 **De igne** (= fr. 3, Wimmer), ed. V. Coutant, *Theophrastus. De igne*. Assen: Royal Vangorcum, 1971: 3–51.
Cod: 6,390: Nat. Hist.
006 **Metaphysica** (= fr. 12, Wimmer), ed. W.D. Ross and F.H. Fobes, *Theophrastus. Metaphysics*. Oxford: Clarendon Press, 1929 (repr. Hildesheim: Olms, 1967): 2–38.
Cod: 3,559: Phil.
007 **De pietate**, ed. W. Pötscher, *Theophrastos. Περὶ εὐσεβείας* [*Philosophia antiqua* 11. Leiden: Brill, 1964]: 146–184.
Cod: 4,526: Phil.
008 **Physicorum opiniones**, ed. Diels, *op. cit.*, 475–495.
Dup. partim 0093 010 (pp. 417–462 passim).
Q: 4,897: Doxogr.
009 **Characteres**, ed. P. Steinmetz, *Theophrast. Charaktere*, vol. 1 [*Das Wort der Antike* 7. Munich: Hueber, 1960]: 62–106.
Cod: 6,876: Rhet.
010 **Fragmenta**, ed. F. Wimmer, *Theophrasti Eresii opera, quae supersunt, omnia*. Paris: Didot, 1866 (repr. Frankfurt am Main: Minerva, 1964): 364–410, 417–462.
De odoribus (fr. 4): pp. 364–376.
De ventis (fr. 5): pp. 376–389.
De signis tempestatum (fr. 6): pp. 389–398.
De lassitudine (fr. 7): pp. 398–401.
De vertigine (fr. 8): pp. 401–403.
De sudore (fr. 9): pp. 403–408.

De animi defectione (fr. 10): p. 409.
De nervorum resolutione (fr. 11): pp. 409–410.
Fragmenta varia (frr. 13–190): pp. 417–462.
Q, Cod: 36,234: Phil., Nat. Hist.
011 Περὶ λέξεως (P. Hamb. 128), ed. B.
Snell, Griechische Papyri der Hamburger Staats- und Universitätsbibliothek mit einigen Stücken aus der Sammlung Hugo Ibscher [Veröffentlichungen aus der Hamburger Staats- und Universitätsbibliothek 4. Hamburg: Augustin, 1954]: 38.
Pap
012 De aqua (P. Hibeh 1.16), ed. B.P. Grenfell and A.S. Hunt, The Hibeh papyri, pt. 1. London: Egypt Exploration Fund, 1906: 62–63.
Pap
013 De animalibus (P. Lit. Lond. 164 [Brit. mus. inv. 2242]), ed. H.J.M. Milne, "A new fragment of Theophrastus," Classical review 36 (1922) 67.
Pap: Nat. Hist.
014 De causis plantarum (lib. 2–6), ed. Wimmer, op. cit., 192–319.
Cf. et 0093 002.
Cod: 59,608: Nat. Hist.
015 De eligendis magistratibus (fragmenta), ed. W. Aly, Fragmentum Vaticanum de eligendis magistratibus e codice bis rescripto Vat. gr. 2306 [Studi e Testi 104. Vatican City: Biblioteca Apostolica Vaticana, 1943]: 13–28.
Cod: 1,001: Phil., Hist.

3130 **THEOPHYLACTUS SIMOCATTA** Hist. et Epist.
A.D. 7: Aegyptius, Constantinopolitanus
001 **Epistulae**, ed. G. Zanetto, Theophylacti Simocatae epistulae. Leipzig: Teubner, 1985: 1–44.
Cod: 7,631: Epist.
003 **Historiae**, ed. C. de Boor, Theophylacti Simocattae historiae. Leipzig: Teubner, 1887 (repr. Stuttgart: 1972 (1st edn. corr. P. Wirth)): 20–314.
Dialogus: pp. 20–22.
Index: pp. 22–36.
Prooemium: pp. 36–38.
Historiae (lib. 1–8): pp. 38–314.
Cod: 65,489: Hist., Dialog.
007 **Quaestiones physicae**, ed. L. Massa Positano, Teofilatto Simocata. Questioni naturali, 2nd edn. Naples: Libreria Scientifica Editrice, 1965: 7–38.
Cod: 4,293: Nat. Hist., Dialog.
009 **De vitae termino**, ed. G. Zanetto, Teofilatto Simocatta. De vitae termino [Κοινωνία 3. Naples: d'Auria, 1979]: 37–52.
Cod: 3,491: Nat. Hist.

0513 **THEOPOMPUS** Comic.
5–4 B.C.
001 **Fragmenta**, ed. T. Kock, Comicorum Atticorum fragmenta, vol. 1. Leipzig: Teubner, 1880: 733–756.

frr. 2–15, 17, 19–27, 29–30, 32–38, 40–44, 46–48, 50–56, 58–64, 66–77, 79–99 + tituli.
Q: 674: Comic.
002 **Fragmenta**, ed. A. Meineke, Fragmenta comicorum Graecorum, vol. 2.2. Berlin: Reimer, 1840 (repr. De Gruyter, 1970): 792–813, 815–819.
Q: 637: Comic.
003 **Fragmenta**, ed. J. Demiańczuk, Supplementum comicum. Krakau: Nakładem Akademii, 1912 (repr. Hildesheim: Olms, 1967): 86–87.
frr. 1–3.
Q: 28: Comic.
004 **Titulus**, ed. C. Austin, Comicorum Graecorum fragmenta in papyris reperta. Berlin: De Gruyter, 1973: 217.
NQ: 2: Comic.

1726 **THEOPOMPUS** Epic.
post 4 B.C.: Colophonius
001 **Fragmentum**, ed. J.U. Powell, Collectanea Alexandrina. Oxford: Clarendon Press, 1925 (repr. 1970): 28.
Dup. 1726 002.
Q: 10: Epic.
002 **Fragmentum**, ed. H. Lloyd-Jones and P. Parsons, Supplementum Hellenisticum. Berlin: De Gruyter, 1983: 365.
fr. 765.
Dup. 1726 001.
Q: 12: Epic.

0566 **THEOPOMPUS** Hist.
4 B.C.: Chius
001 **Testimonia**, FGrH #115: 2B:526–536; 3B:742 addenda.
NQ: 3,150: Test.
002 **Fragmenta**, FGrH #115: 2B:536–617; 3B:742 addenda.
fr. 165: P. Oxy. 7.1012.
fr. 305: Inscr. Priene 37.
Q, Pap, Epigr: 23,521: Hist., Epist., Encom.
003 **Fragmentum** (P. Colon. 5861), ed. H.J. Mette, "Die 'Kleinen' griechischen Historiker heute," Lustrum 21 (1978) 17.
fr. 382 bis.
Pap: 68: Hist.
x01 **Fragmenta**.
FGrH #105, frr. 3, 4, 6.
Cf. ANONYMI HISTORICI (FGrH) (1139 004).

1874 **Gaius Julius THEOPOMPUS** Myth.
1 B.C.: Cnidius
001 **Testimonia**, FGrH #21: 1A:185–186.
NQ: 99: Test.

4047 **THEOSEBEIA** Epigr.
A.D. 5
001 **Epigramma**, AG 7.559.
Q: 27: Epigr.

1727 **THEOTIMUS** Hist.
2 B.C.?
001 **Fragmenta**, FGrH #470: 3B:425–427.
Q: 394: Hist.

2561 **THEOTIMUS** Hist.
Incertum
001 **Fragmenta**, FGrH #834: 3C:902–903.
Q: 86: Hist.

1728 **THESEUS** Hist.
A.D. 1?
001 **Testimonium**, FGrH #453: 3B:381.
NQ: 23: Test.
002 **Fragmenta**, FGrH #453: 3B:381–382.
Q: 239: Hist.

0301 **THESPIS** Trag.
6 B.C.: Atheniensis
001 **Fragmenta**, ed. B. Snell, *Tragicorum Graecorum fragmenta*, vol. 1. Göttingen: Vandenhoeck & Ruprecht, 1971: 65–66.
frr. 1–5.
Q: 75: Trag.

1004 **THESSALUS** Med. et Astrol.
A.D. 1: Trallianus
001 **De virtutibus herbarum** (cod. Paris. gr. 2502 et cod. Vindobonensis med. gr. 23), ed. H.-V. Friedrich, *Thessalos von Tralles [Beiträge zur klassischen Philologie* 28. Meisenheim am Glan: Hain, 1968]: 43–44, 56, 59, 62, 65, 137, 142, 147, 175, 179, 183, 187, 219, 223, 227, 231, 235, 239, 243, 247, 251, 255, 259, 263, 267.
Cod
002 **De virtutibus herbarum** (cod. Matritensis bibl. nat. 4631 [olim 110]), ed. Friedrich, *op. cit.*, 45, 47, 49, 51, 53, 55, 58, 61, 64, 68, 73, 78, 83, 88, 93, 98, 103.
Cod
003 **De virtutibus herbarum** (cod. Monacensis 542), ed. Friedrich, *op. cit.*, 69, 74, 79, 84, 89, 94, 99, 104, 108, 112, 116, 120, 124, 128, 132, 136, 141, 146, 151, 155, 159, 163, 167, 171.
Cod
004 **De virtutibus herbarum** (codd. BHL), ed. Friedrich, *op. cit.*, 195, 199, 203, 207, 211, 215.
Cod
005 **De virtutibus herbarum** (codd. ADE), ed. Friedrich, *op. cit.*, 195, 196, 268.
Cod
x01 **Fragmenta ap. Galenum.**
K1.176; **10.**7–8, 73, 250–252.
Cf. GALENUS Med. (0057 066) et Pseudo-GALENUS Med. (0530 043).

1095 **THEUDAS** Med.
ante A.D. 1

x01 **Fragmentum ap. Galenum.**
K13.925.
Cf. GALENUS Med. (0057 077).

2198 **THEUDIUS** Math. et Phil.
4 B.C.: Magnes
001 **Testimonium**, ed. F. Lasserre, *De Léodamas de Thasos à Philippe d'Oponte.* Naples: Bibliopolis, 1987: 133.
NQ: Test.
002 **Fragmenta**, ed. Lasserre, *op. cit.*, 133.
frr. 1–2b.
Q, Pap: Phil.

0816 **THEUDO[TUS]** Trag.
1 B.C.
001 **Titulus**, ed. B. Snell, *Tragicorum Graecorum fragmenta*, vol. 1. Göttingen: Vandenhoeck & Ruprecht, 1971: 310.
NQ: 2: Satyr.

2400 **THIBRON** Hist.
5/4 B.C.?: Lacedaemonius
001 **Testimonium**, FGrH #581: 3B:692–693.
NQ: 169: Test.

4048 **THOMAS** Epigr.
A.D. 6
001 **Epigramma**, AG 16.379.
Q: 25: Epigr.

4049 **THOMAS** Epigr.
A.D. 6
001 **Epigramma**, AG 16.315.
Q: 23: Epigr.

9023 **THOMAS MAGISTER** Philol.
vel Theodulus
A.D. 13–14: Thessalonicensis, Constantinopolitanus
002 **Poemata de Arato** [Dub.], ed. J. Martin, *Scholia in Aratum vetera.* Stuttgart: Teubner, 1974: 558–559.
Cod: 285: Iamb.
x01 **Vitae Aristophanis.**
Koster, vol. 1.1A, pp. 146–147, 149.
Cf. VITAE ARISTOPHANIS (4158 009–010).
x02 **Scholia et argumenta in Aristophanem.**
Cf. SCHOLIA IN ARISTOPHANEM (5014 005, 012).
x03 **Scholia in Pindarum.**
Cf. SCHOLIA IN PINDARUM (5034 003–005, 007).
x04 **Scholia in Aeschylum.**
Cf. SCHOLIA IN AESCHYLUM (5010 006–007, 010).
x05 **Scholia in Sophoclis Oedipum tyrannum.**
Longo, pp. 167–265.
Cf. SCHOLIA IN SOPHOCLEM (5037 005).

2231 **THRASYALCES** Phil.
5/4 B.C.: Thasius

001 **Testimonia**, ed. H. Diels and W. Kranz, *Die Fragmente der Vorsokratiker*, vol. 1, 6th edn. Berlin: Weidmann, 1951 (repr. Dublin: 1966): 377.
test. 1–2.
NQ: 126: Test.

0056 ***THRASYBULI EPISTULA***
Incertum
001 **Epistula**, ed. R. Hercher, *Epistolographi Graeci*. Paris: Didot, 1873 (repr. Amsterdam: Hakkert, 1965): 787.
Q: 67: Epist.

1762 **THRASYLLUS** Astrol.
fiq Thrasyllus Hist.
A.D. 1: Alexandrinus
Cf. et THRASYLLUS Hist. (2428).
001 **Fragmenta**, ed. W. Kroll and A. Olivieri, *Codices Parisini* [*Catalogus codicum astrologorum Graecorum* 8.3. Brussels: Lamertin, 1912]: 99–101.
Cod

2176 **THRASYLLUS** Hist.
1 B.C.–A.D. 1: Rhodius
001 **Fragmentum**, FGrH #253: 2B:1152–1153.
Q: 272: Hist., Chronogr.

2428 **THRASYLLUS** Hist.
fiq Thrasyllus Astrol.
A.D. 1?: Mendesicus
Cf. et THRASYLLUS Astrol. (1762).
001 **Fragmenta**, FGrH #622: 3C:156–157.
Q: 356: Hist., Nat. Hist.

4264 **THRASYMACHUS** Phil.
4 B.C.: Corinthius, Atheniensis
001 **Testimonium**, ed. K. Döring, *Die Megariker* [*Studien zur antiken Philosophie* 2. Amsterdam: Grüner, 1972]: 46.
test. 147 = Stilpo (4262 001).
NQ: Test.

1729 **THRASYMACHUS** Rhet. et Soph.
5 B.C.: Chalcedonius
001 **Testimonia**, ed. H. Diels and W. Kranz, *Die Fragmente der Vorsokratiker*, vol. 2, 6th edn. Berlin: Weidmann, 1952 (repr. Dublin: 1966): 319–321.
test. 1–14.
NQ: 605: Test.
002 **Fragmenta**, ed. Diels and Kranz, *op. cit.*, 321–326.
frr. 1–8.
Q: 882: Phil., Rhet.

1097 **THREPTUS** Med.
ante A.D. 2
x01 **Fragmentum ap. Galenum**.
K13.828.
Cf. GALENUS Med. (0057 077).

0003 **THUCYDIDES** Hist.
5 B.C.: Atheniensis
Scholia: Cf. SCHOLIA IN THUCYDIDEM (5039).
001 **Historiae**, ed. H.S. Jones and J.E. Powell, *Thucydidis historiae*, 2 vols. Oxford: Clarendon Press, 1:1942 (repr. 1970 (1st edn. rev.)); 2:1942 (repr. 1967 (2nd edn. rev.)).
Cod: 153,260: Hist.
002 **Epigramma**, AG 7.45.
Q: 32: Epigr.

0514 **THUGENIDES** Comic.
5 B.C.
001 **Fragmenta**, ed. T. Kock, *Comicorum Atticorum fragmenta*, vol. 3. Leipzig: Teubner, 1888: 377–378.
frr. 1–5.
Q: 16: Comic.
002 **Fragmenta**, ed. A. Meineke, *Fragmenta comicorum Graecorum*, vol. 4. Berlin: Reimer, 1841 (repr. De Gruyter, 1970): 593.
Q: 9: Comic.
003 **Fragmentum**, ed. J. Demiańczuk, *Supplementum comicum*. Krakau: Nakładem Akademii, 1912 (repr. Hildesheim: Olms, 1967): 87.
fr. 1.
Q: 6: Comic.

1730 **THYILLUS** Epigr.
1 B.C.
001 **Epigrammata**, AG **6**.170; 7.223; **10**.5.
Q: 121: Epigr.

1731 **THYMOCLES** Epigr.
3 B.C.?
001 **Epigramma**, AG 12.32.
Q: 30: Epigr.

2126 **TIBERIUS** Epigr.
A.D. 4/5
001 **Epigrammata**, AG 9.2, 370.
AG 9.371: Cf. ANONYMI EPIGRAMMATICI (AG) (0138 001).
Q: 83: Epigr.

2601 **TIBERIUS** Rhet.
A.D. 3/4
001 **De figuris Demosthenicis**, ed. G. Ballaira, *Tiberii de figuris Demosthenicis*. Rome: Ateneo, 1968: 7–45.
Cod
002 **Fragmenta**, ed. Ballaira, *op. cit.*, 55–57.
Q

1098 **TIBERIUS Imperator**
A.D. 1: Romanus
x01 **Fragmentum ap. Galenum**.
K13.836.
Cf. GALENUS Med. (0057 077).
x02 **Epigramma**.

AG 9.387: Cf. HADRIANUS Imperator (0195 001).

1732 **TIMACHIDAS** Hist.
1 B.C.: Rhodius
001 **Anagraphe Lindia**, FGrH #532: 3B:506–514.
Epigr: 2,924: Hist.
002 **Fragmenta et tituli**, ed. H. Lloyd-Jones and P. Parsons, *Supplementum Hellenisticum*. Berlin: De Gruyter, 1983: 366–367.
frr. (+ titul.) 769–773.
Q: 32: Hexametr.

1105 **TIMAEUS** Astrol.
ante 2 B.C.
001 **Fragmentum**, ed. A. Olivieri, *Codices Florentini [Catalogus codicum astrologorum Graecorum* 1. Brussels: Lamertin, 1898]: 97–99.
Cod

2602 **TIMAEUS** Gramm.
A.D. 1/4
001 **Lexicon Platonicum**, ed. K.F. Hermann, *Platonis dialogi secundum Thrasylli tetralogias dispositi*, vol. 6. Leipzig: Teubner, 1853: 397–408.
Cod

1733 **TIMAEUS** Hist.
4–3 B.C.: Tauromenitanus
001 **Testimonia**, FGrH #566: 3B:581–591.
NQ: 3,635: Test.
002 **Fragmenta**, FGrH #566: 3B:592–658.
Q: 23,787: Hist.
003 **Fragmenta**, ed. H.J. Mette, "Die 'Kleinen' griechischen Historiker heute," *Lustrum* 21 (1978) 31.
fr. 88 bis a–b.
fr. 88 bis a: *P. Oxy.* 32.2637.
Q, Pap: 154: Hist.

2569 **<TIMAEUS>** Hist.
post 4 B.C.?
001 **Testimonium**, FGrH #848: 3C:935.
NQ: 24: Test.
002 **Titulus**, FGrH #848: 3C:935.
NQ: Hist.

1734 **TIMAEUS** Phil.
3/2 B.C.?: Locrus
001 **Fragmenta et titulus** [Sp.], ed. W. Marg, *The Pythagorean texts of the Hellenistic period* (ed. H. Thesleff). Åbo: Åbo Akademi, 1965: 203, 205–225.
Cod: 4,582: Phil., Math.
002 **Testimonia**, ed. H. Diels and W. Kranz, *Die Fragmente der Vorsokratiker*, vol. 1, 6th edn. Berlin: Weidmann, 1951 (repr. Dublin: 1966): 441.
test. 1–4.
NQ: 145: Test.

1918 **TIMAGENES** Hist.
1 B.C.: Alexandrinus
001 **Testimonia**, FGrH #88: 2A:318–319.
NQ: 511: Test.
002 **Fragmenta**, FGrH #88: 2A:319–323.
Q: 1,290: Hist.

2268 **TIMAGORAS** Hist.
Incertum
001 **Fragmenta**, FGrH #381: 3B:250.
Q: 91: Hist.

4275 **TIMAGORAS** Phil.
4 B.C.: Gelous, Atheniensis
001 **Testimonium**, ed. K. Döring, *Die Megariker [Studien zur antiken Philosophie* 2. Amsterdam: Grüner, 1972]: 52, 61.
test. 164a = Stilpo (4262 001).
NQ: Test.

0889 **TIMESITHEUS** Trag.
Incertum
001 **Tituli**, ed. B. Snell, *Tragicorum Graecorum fragmenta*, vol. 1. Göttingen: Vandenhoeck & Ruprecht, 1971: 324–325.
NQ: 20: Trag., Satyr.

1960 **TIMOCHARES** Hist.
2 B.C.
001 **Fragmentum**, FGrH #165: 2B:891.
Q: 67: Hist.

0515 **TIMOCLES** Comic.
fiq Timocles Trag.
4 B.C.
Cf. et TIMOCLES Trag. (0333).
001 **Fragmenta**, ed. T. Kock, *Comicorum Atticorum fragmenta*, vol. 2. Leipzig: Teubner, 1884: 451–466.
frr. 1–16, 18–25, 27–38 + tituli.
Q: 1,093: Comic.
002 **Fragmenta**, ed. A. Meineke, *Fragmenta comicorum Graecorum*, vol. 3. Berlin: Reimer, 1840 (repr. De Gruyter, 1970): 590–600, 602–613.
p. 613, fr. 5: line 2 supplied from vol. 5.1, p. 96.
Q: 1,119: Comic.
003 **Fragmenta**, ed. J. Demiańczuk, *Supplementum comicum*. Krakau: Nakładem Akademii, 1912 (repr. Hildesheim: Olms, 1967): 88–89.
frr. 1–3.
Q: 79: Comic.
004 **Fragmentum**, ed. C. Austin, *Comicorum Graecorum fragmenta in papyris reperta*. Berlin: De Gruyter, 1973: 217–218.
fr. 222.
Pap: 104: Comic.

0333 **TIMOCLES** Trag.
fiq Timocles Comic.
4 B.C.
Cf. et TIMOCLES Comic. (0515).

001 **Fragmentum**, ed. B. Snell, *Tragicorum Grae-*
corum fragmenta, vol. 1. Göttingen: Vandenhoeck & Ruprecht, 1971: 252.
frr. 1–2.
Q: 35: Trag., Satyr.

1099 **TIMOCLIANUS** Med.
ante A.D. 4
x01 **Fragmentum ap. Oribasium**.
CMG, vol. 6.2.2, p. 240.
Cf. ORIBASIUS Med. (0722 003).

2388 **TIMOCRATES** Hist.
A.D. 1?
001 **Fragmentum**, FGrH #563: 3B:577.
Q: 27: Hist.

2459 **TIMOCRATES** Hist.
Incertum: Adramyttenus
001 **Testimonium**, FGrH #672: 3C:284.
NQ: 13: Test.

1100 **TIMOCRATES** Med.
ante A.D. 2
x01 **Fragmentum ap. Galenum**.
K12.887.
Cf. GALENUS Med. (0057 076).

0265 **TIMOCREON** Lyr.
5 B.C.: Rhodius
001 **Fragmenta**, ed. M.L. West, *Iambi et elegi*
Graeci, vol. 2. Oxford: Clarendon Press, 1972:
149.
frr. 7, 9, 10.
Q: 25: Iamb., Epigr.
002 **Fragmenta**, ed. D.L. Page, *Poetae melici*
Graeci. Oxford: Clarendon Press, 1962 (repr.
1967 (1st edn. corr.)): 375–378.
frr. 1–6.
Q: 169: Lyr.
003 **Epigramma**, AG 13.31.
AG 16.11: Cf. HERMOCREON Epigr. (1422
001).
Q: 15: Epigr.

2363 **TIMOCRITUS** Hist.
Incertum
001 **Titulus**, FGrH #522: 3B:494.
NQ: Hist.

2301 **TIMOGENES** Hist. et Rhet.
vel Timagenes
A.D. 1: Milesius
001 **Testimonium**, FGrH #435: 3B:368.
NQ: 26: Test.

2533 **TIMOLAUS** Hist.
Incertum
001 **Fragmentum**, FGrH #798: 3C:836.
Q: 129: Hist.

2697 **TIMOLAUS** Rhet.
4 B.C.: Macedo, Larissaeus
001 **Fragmentum**, ed. H. Lloyd-Jones and P. Parsons, *Supplementum Hellenisticum*. Berlin: De
Gruyter, 1983: 395.
fr. 849.
Dup. partim 2697 002.
Q: 37: Hexametr., Comm.
002 **Fragmenta**, FHG 4: 521.
Dup. partim 2697 001.
Q: Hist., Hexametr., Comm.

2509 **TIMOMACHUS** Hist.
4/3 B.C.?
001 **Fragmenta**, FGrH #754: 3C:736.
Q: 159: Hist.

1735 **TIMON** Phil.
4–3 B.C.: Phliasius
002 **Epigrammata**, AG 10.38; 11.296.
Dup. partim 1735 003 (frr. 791, v. 2; 815).
AG 7.313: Cf. ANONYMI EPIGRAMMATICI
(AG) (0138 001).
Q: 24: Epigr.
003 **Fragmenta et tituli**, ed. H. Lloyd-Jones and P.
Parsons, *Supplementum Hellenisticum*. Berlin:
De Gruyter, 1983: 368–394.
frr. (+ titul.) 775–846.
fr. 791, v. 2: Dup. partim 1735 002 (AG 10.38).
fr. 815: Dup. partim 1735 002 (AG 11.296).
Q: 1,053: Hexametr., Eleg., Epigr.

1736 **TIMONAX** Hist.
4/3 B.C.?
001 **Fragmenta**, FGrH #842: 3C:928–929.
Q: 108: Hist.

2386 **TIMONIDES** Hist.
4 B.C.: Leucadius
001 **Testimonia**, FGrH #561: 3B:574.
NQ: 164: Test.
002 **Fragmenta**, FGrH #561: 3B:574–576.
Q: 369: Hist.

1002 **TIMOSTHENES** Geogr.
3 B.C.: Rhodius
001 **Fragmenta**, ed. E.A. Wagner, *Die Erdbeschreib-*
ung des Timosthenes von Rhodus [*Diss. Leipzig*
(1888)]: 10–11, 64–73.
Dup. partim 1002 002.
Q: Geogr., Myth.
002 **Fragmentum**, FGrH #354: 3B:217.
Dup. partim 1002 001.
Q: 32: Hist., Myth.

0516 **TIMOSTRATUS** Comic.
2 B.C.: Atheniensis
001 **Fragmenta**, ed. T. Kock, *Comicorum Atti-*
corum fragmenta, vol. 3. Leipzig: Teubner,
1888: 355–357.
frr. 1–7 + tituli.
Q: 44: Comic.

002 **Tituli**, ed. A. Meineke, *Fragmenta comicorum Graecorum*, vol. 4. Berlin: Reimer, 1841 (repr. De Gruyter, 1970): 595.
NQ: 5: Comic.

003 **Fragmenta**, ed. Meineke, *FCG*, vol. 5.1 (1857; repr. 1970): cccxxvii–cccxxviii.
Dup. partim COMICA ADESPOTA (FCG) 0602 001 (vol. 4, p. 692, fr. 351).
Q: 25: Comic.

0517 **TIMOTHEUS** Comic.
4/3 B.C.?: Atheniensis

001 **Fragmenta**, ed. T. Kock, *Comicorum Atticorum fragmenta*, vol. 2. Leipzig: Teubner, 1884: 450.
frr. 1–2 + titulus.
Q: 45: Comic.

002 **Fragmenta**, ed. A. Meineke, *Fragmenta comicorum Graecorum*, vol. 3. Berlin: Reimer, 1840 (repr. De Gruyter, 1970): 589.
Q: 41: Comic.

2449 **TIMOTHEUS** Gramm.
A.D. 6: Gazaeus

001 **Testimonia**, FGrH #652: 3C:204–205.
NQ: 100: Test.

002 Κανόνες καθολικοὶ περὶ συντάξεως (e cod. Coislin. 387), ed. J.A. Cramer, *Anecdota Graeca e codd. manuscriptis bibliothecae regiae Parisiensis*, vol. 4. Oxford: Oxford University Press, 1841 (repr. Hildesheim: Olms, 1967): 239–244.
Cod: Gramm.

003 **Excerpta ex libris de animalibus** (e cod. Paris. gr. 2422), ed. M. Haupt, "Excerpta ex Timothei Gazaei libris de animalibus," *Hermes* 3 (1869) 1–30, 174.
Cod: Nat. Hist., Paradox.

x01 **Eclogae de animalibus**.
CAG, suppl. 1.1, pp. 1–154 (passim).
Cf. ARISTOPHANES Gramm. (0644 001).

2213 **[TIMOTHEUS]** Hist.
Incertum

001 **Fragmenta**, FGrH #313: 3B:22.
Q: 179: Hist.

0376 **TIMOTHEUS** Lyr.
5–4 B.C.: Milesius

001 **Fragmenta**, ed. D.L. Page, *Poetae melici Graeci*. Oxford: Clarendon Press, 1962 (repr. 1967 (1st edn. corr.)): 400–413, 415–418.
frr. 2, 4–5, 10–15, 18, 20–28.
fr. 15 = *Persae* (*P. Berol.* 9865).
Q, Pap: 1,089: Lyr.

002 **Tituli**, ed. Page, *op. cit.*, 399–400, 402, 414–415.
frr. 1–3, 8–9, 16–17, 19.
NQ: 15: Lyr.

x01 **Epigramma**.
AG 7.45.
Cf. THUCYDIDES Hist. (0003 002).

1101 **TIMOTHEUS** Med.
4/3 B.C.?: Metapontinus

x01 **Fragmentum ap. Anonymum Londinensem**.
Iatrica 8.10–32.
Cf. ANONYMUS LONDINENSIS Med. (0643 001).

0467 **TIMOTHEUS** Trag.
4 B.C.

001 **Tituli**, ed. B. Snell, *Tragicorum Graecorum fragmenta*, vol. 1. Göttingen: Vandenhoeck & Ruprecht, 1971: 196.
fr. 1.
NQ: 2: Trag.

2719 **TIMOTHEUS AELURUS** Scr. Eccl.
A.D. 5: Alexandrinus

x01 **Ad Leonem imperatorem petitio** (in *Doctrina patrum*).
Diekamp, p. 165 (fr. 9).
Cf. DOCTRINA PATRUM (7051 001).

x02 **Contra eos qui dicunt duas naturas** (fragmenta ap. Justinianum, *Contra monophysitas*).
Amelotti, Albertella & Migliardi (post Schwartz), pp. 42, 44.
Cf. Flavius JUSTINIANUS Imperator Theol. (2734 001).

x03 **Contra eos qui dicunt duas naturas** (fragmenta ap. Eustathium, *Epistula de duabus naturis*).
MPG 86.1.904.
Cf. EUSTATHIUS Theol. (2810 001).

x04 **Dialogus cum Calonymo** (fragmentum ap. Leontium, *Contra monophysitas*) [Sp.].
MPG 86.2.1850.
Cf. LEONTIUS Theol. (2819 001).

1793 **TIMOXENUS** Comic.
Incertum

001 **Titulus**, ed. T. Kock, *Comicorum Atticorum fragmenta*, vol. 3. Leipzig: Teubner, 1888: 366.
NQ: 2: Comic.

1737 ***TITANOMACHIA***
fort. auctore Arctino Milesio vel Eumelo Corinthio
post 7 B.C.

001 **Fragmenta**, ed. T.W. Allen, *Homeri opera*, vol. 5. Oxford: Clarendon Press, 1912 (repr. 1969): 111.
frr. 4–6.
Q: Epic.

1102 **TITUS Imperator**
A.D. 1: Romanus

x01 **Fragmentum ap. Galenum**.
K13.360.
Cf. GALENUS Med. (0057 076).

3002 ***TRACTATUS DE COMOEDIA***
Varia

001 **De comoedia**, ed. W.J.W. Koster, *Prolegomena de comoedia. Scholia in Acharnenses, Equites,*

Nubes [*Scholia in Aristophanem* 1.1A. Groningen: Bouma, 1975]: 7–10.
Cod: Gramm.

002 **De comoedia**, ed. Koster, *op. cit.*, 11–12.
Cod: Gramm.

003 **De comoedia**, ed. Koster, *op. cit.*, 13–15.
Cod: Gramm.

004 **De comoedia**, ed. Koster, *op. cit.*, 15–16.
Cod: Gramm.

005 **De choro**, ed. Koster, *op. cit.*, 17–18.
Cod: Gramm.

006 **Nomina comoediae veterae poetarum et dramata**, ed. Koster, *op. cit.*, 18.
Cod: Gramm.

007 **De Hellenismo et Atticismo**, ed. Koster, *op. cit.*, 19.
Cod: Gramm.

008 **De choro**, ed. Koster, *op. cit.*, 19–20.
Cod: Gramm.

009 **De scoliis**, ed. Koster, *op. cit.*, 20–21.
Cod: Gramm.

010 **De histrionibus**, ed. Koster, *op. cit.*, 21.
Cod: Gramm.

011 **De partibus comoediae**, ed. Koster, *op. cit.*, 21.
Cod: Gramm.

012 **De metro comico**, ed. Koster, *op. cit.*, 22.
Cod: Gramm.

013 Ἐκ ποίας αἰτίας συνέστη ἡ κωμῳδία sive Περὶ κωμῳδίας (Anonymus Crameri 1), ed. Koster, *op. cit.*, 39–42.
Cod: Gramm.

014 **De comoedia** (Anonymus Crameri 2), ed. Koster, *op. cit.*, 43–48.
Cod: Gramm.

015 **De poeticae generibus** (fort. auctore Joanne Tzetza), ed. Koster, *op. cit.*, 50.
Cod: Gramm.

016 **De comoedia**, ed. Koster, *op. cit.*, 50.
Cod

017 **Tractatus Coislinianus** (e cod. Paris. Coisl. 120), ed. Koster, *op. cit.*, 63–67.
Cod: Gramm.

1738 ***TRAGICA ADESPOTA***
Varia

001 **Fragmenta**, ed. A. Nauck, *Tragicorum Graecorum fragmenta.* Leipzig: Teubner, 1889 (repr. Hildesheim: Olms, 1964): 837–958.
frr. 1–2, 4–12, 14, 16–18, 20, 22–48, 51–53, 55–144, 147–155, 157–249, 251–289, 291–431, 433–460, 462–577, 579–602.
Q, Pap, Epigr: 4,522: Trag., Satyr.

002 **Fragmenta**, ed. B. Snell, *Tragicorum Graecorum fragmenta. Supplementum.* Hildesheim: Olms, 1964: 21–41.
frr. 1a–1b, 5a–5c, 12a, 14a–14b, 21a, 27a, 34a–34e, 37a–37b, 40a, 59a, 76a, 83a, 84a, 86 app, 88a, 89a, 97a, 103a, 109a, 116.1, 123a, 126a, 144a, 145a, 146a, 151a, 197a–197d, 198a, 204a, 210a, 225a, 226a, 228a–228c, 233a, 234a, 239a, 242a, 270a, 279a–279b, 279d–279g, 287a, 290a, 295a, 302a, 307a–307b,

323a–323h, 327a, 328a–328d, 336a–336b, 337a, 339a, 340a, 348a–348e, 365a, 369a, 374.3–4, 384a, 416a, 427a, 437a, 438a, 443a–443d, 445a, 456a, 546a, 561b, 562a, 564a–564d, 566a–566e, 581a, 583a, 584, 587a–587c, 593a, 594a–594b, 605, 606, [608], 609, 611, 616.
Q, Pap, Epigr: 729: Trag., Satyr.

003 **Fragmenta**, ed. R. Kannicht and B. Snell, *Tragicorum Graecorum fragmenta*, vol. 2. Göttingen: Vandenhoeck & Ruprecht, 1981: 3–173, 177–218, 220–319.
frr. 1–3f, 5–8m, 9a–11, 12a, 13a–14c, 16–18, 20–21a, 26, 27a, 33, 34a–34c, 34e–43, 45–48, 51–51a, 53, 55–57, 59–61c, 63–63a, 67–67a, 69–71, 73, 75a–83b, 84a–89a, 90–93, 95–97, 99–101, 102a, 103a–103d, 105, 107a–110a, 114–115, 117, 118a–118b, 120a–120b, 122, 123a–130, 137–138, 144a–145c, 146a–151a, 152a–153, 155, 158–168, 170–178, 181, 182a–186, 188–197, 197b–197d, 198a–204a, 206, 207a–208, 210a–211, 213–216, 218–228c, 230–240, 242a, 244–248, 250–270, 271–276, 278, 279a–279u, 281–283, 285–286, 288–289, 290a–295a, 296–297, 302a–306, 307a–307b, 323–323a, 323h–327s, 328c–347a, 348a–348h, 349, 351–357, 359–361, 363, 365–372, 375–376, 378a–384a, 386, 388, 391–393, 397–402, 404–410a, 412–413, 415–416b, 418a–427, 428–429, 430a–430b, 432a, 433, 438a, 439, 440a–442, 443a–443d, 445–445a, 447–450a, 451–456, 457–458, 460–460a, 462–469, 471, 473–504, 506–514, 515a, 516a–521, 523, 525a–537, 539–540, 543–544, 546a, 548–549, 551–553, 556–560, 561, 562–563, 564a–566a, 566c–573, 579–581a, 583a, 585–585b, 586a, 587, 587b–597, 599, 601–602a, 617–710, 712–734b.
Q, Pap: 13,797: Trag., Satyr.

1739 **TRAJANUS Imperator**
A.D. 1–2 : Romanus

001 **Epigrammata**, AG 9.388/389; **11.418.**
AG 6.332: Cf. HADRIANUS Imperator (0195 001).
AG 9.388/389: Cf. et ANONYMI EPIGRAMMATICI (AG) (0138 001).
Q: 56: Epigr.

2999 **Demetrius TRICLINIUS** Philol.
A.D. 13–14: Thessalonicensis, Constantinopolitanus

001 **De comoedia**, ed. W.J.W. Koster, *Prolegomena de comoedia. Scholia in Acharnenses, Equites, Nubes* [*Scholia in Aristophanem* 1.1A. Groningen: Bouma, 1975]: 55–56.
Cod: Gramm.

002 Περὶ σημείων τῆς κοινῆς συλλαβῆς τῶν ἐντὸς κειμένων τῆς βίβλου, ed. Koster, *op. cit.*, 57–59.
Cod: Gramm.

x01 **Scholia in Aeschylum.**

Cf. SCHOLIA IN AESCHYLUM (5010 002–003, 006–008, 010, 019, 023).

x02 **Scholia in Aristophanem.**
Cf. SCHOLIA IN ARISTOPHANEM (5014 001–002, 005, 007–008).

x03 **Scholia in Pindarum.**
Cf. SCHOLIA IN PINDARUM (5034 003–004, 007).

x04 **Scholia metrica in Euripidem.**
Wagenvoort, pp. 314–332.
Cf. SCHOLIA IN EURIPIDEM (5023 007).

x05 **Scholia in Sophoclem.**
Longo, pp. 269–297.
Cf. SCHOLIA IN SOPHOCLEM (5037 005).

0647 **TRIPHIODORUS** Epic. et Gramm.
vel Tryphiodorus
A.D. 3/5: Aegyptius

001 ″Αλωσις Ἰλίου, ed. A.W. Mair, *Oppian, Colluthus, Tryphiodorus.* Cambridge, Mass.: Harvard University Press, 1928 (repr. 1963): 580–632.
Cod: 4,257: Epic.

TROILUS Gramm.
fiq Troilus Soph.
A.D. 4–5?
Cf. TROILUS Soph. (2127).

2127 **TROILUS** Soph.
fiq Troilus Gramm.
A.D. 4–5: Sidonius, Constantinopolitanus

001 **Prolegomena in Hermogenis artem rhetoricam,** ed. C. Walz, *Rhetores Graeci,* vol. 6. Stuttgart: Cotta, 1834 (repr. Osnabrück: Zeller, 1968): 42–55.
Prolegomena: pp. 42–54.
Apospasma [Sp.]: pp. 54–55.
Cod: 3,379: Rhet.

002 **Epigramma** (auctore Troilo Grammatico), AG 16.55.
Q: 17: Epigr.

0588 **TROPHILUS** <Paradox.>
vel Herophilus vel Pamphilus
fiq Herophilus Med.
A.D. 1
Cf. et HEROPHILUS Med. (0928).

001 **Fragmenta,** ed. A. Giannini, *Paradoxographorum Graecorum reliquiae.* Milan: Istituto Editoriale Italiano, 1965: 392–393.
Q

4236 **TROPHONIUS** Rhet.
A.D. 6

001 **Prolegomena in artem rhetoricam,** ed. H. Rabe, *Prolegomenon sylloge [Rhetores Graeci* 14. Leipzig: Teubner, 1931]: 1–14.
Cod: Rhet., Comm.

1740 **TRYPHON** Epigr.
1 B.C./A.D. 1?

001 **Epigramma,** AG 9.488.
Q: 25: Epigr.

1104 **TRYPHON** Med.
1 B.C.–A.D. 1: Creticus

x01 **Fragmentum ap. Galenum.**
K13.253.
Cf. GALENUS Med. (0057 076).

0609 **TRYPHON I** Gramm.
1 B.C.: Alexandrinus, Romanus

001 Περὶ τρόπων, ed. L. Spengel, *Rhetores Graeci,* vol. 3. Leipzig: Teubner, 1856 (repr. Frankfurt am Main: Minerva, 1966): 191–206.
Cod: 3,062: Rhet.

002 Περὶ παθῶν, ed. R. Schneider, *Excerpta περὶ παθῶν [Programm Gymnasium Duisburg* (1895)]: 4–21.
Cod: 2,749: Rhet.

003 **Fragmenta,** ed. A. von Velsen, *Tryphonis grammatici Alexandrini fragmenta.* Berlin: Nikolaus, 1853 (repr. Amsterdam: Hakkert, 1965): 5, 7–71, 73–78, 80–82, 84, 86, 88–102.
Q: 8,706: Gramm.

004 Περὶ μέτρων, ed. H. zur Jacobsmühlen, *Pseudo-Hephaestion. De metris [Dissertationes philologicae Argentoratenses selectae* 10. Strassburg: Trübner, 1886].
Q

006 **De dialecto Lacedaemonia** (titulus) (*P. Oxy.* 24.2396), ed. E. Lobel, *The Oxyrhynchus papyri,* pt. 24. London: Egypt Exploration Society, 1957: 90.
Pap

007 Περὶ πνευμάτων, ed. L.C. Valckenaer, *Joannis Scapulae lexicon Graeco-Latinum.* Oxford: Clarendon Press, 1820.
Cod

x01 **Ars grammatica** (fragmentum) (*P. Lit. Lond.* 182 = *P. Lond.* 126).
Wouters, pp. 67–73.
Cf. ANONYMI GRAMMATICI (0072 004).

1763 **TRYPHON II** Gramm.
1 B.C.?

001 **De tropis** (olim sub auctore Gregorio Corinthio), ed. M.L. West, "Tryphon. De tropis," *Classical Quarterly* n.s. 15 (1965) 236–248.
Dup. partim COMMENTARIA IN DIONYSII THRACIS ARTEM GRAMMATICAM (4175 005).
Cod: 2,340: Rhet.

1103 **TRYPHON** ὁ ἀρχαῖος Med.
1 B.C.–A.D. 1

x01 **Fragmenta ap. Galenum.**
K12.784, 843.
Cf. GALENUS Med. (0057 076).

1741 **<TUDICIUS GALLUS>** Epigr.
Incertum

001 **Epigramma**, AG 5.49.
Q: 31 : Epigr.

TULLIUS BASSUS Med.
Cf. Julius BASSUS Med. (0941).

TULLIUS FLACCUS Epigr.
fiq Statyllius Flaccus
AG 9.37.
Cf. STATYLLIUS FLACCUS Epigr. (1694
001).

1742 **TULLIUS GEMINUS** Epigr.
A.D. 1?
001 **Epigrammata**, AG **6**.260; **7**.73; **9**.288, 414, 707,
740; **16**.30, 103, 205.
AG 7.72: Cf. MENANDER Comic. (0541 044).
AG 7.746: Cf. <PYTHAGORAS> Phil. (0632
005).
AG 9.410: Cf. TULLIUS SABINUS Gramm.
(1745 001).
Q: 343 : Epigr.

1743 **TULLIUS LAUREA** Epigr.
1 B.C.
001 **Epigrammata**, AG **7**.17, 294; **12**.24.
Q: 154 : Epigr.

1745 **TULLIUS SABINUS** Gramm.
A.D. 1?: Sabinus
001 **Epigrammata**, AG **6**.158; **9**.410.
Q: 68 : Epigr.

1106 **TURPILIANUS** Med.
ante A.D. 1
x01 **Fragmentum ap. Galenum**.
K13.736.
Cf. GALENUS Med. (0057 077).

1744 **TYMNES** Epigr.
3 B.C.
001 **Epigrammata**, AG **6**.151; **7**.199, 211, 433, 477,
729; **16**.237.
Q: 205 : Epigr.

0367 **TYNNICHUS** Lyr.
6/5 B.C.: Chalcidensis
001 **Fragmentum**, ed. D.L. Page, *Poetae melici
Graeci*. Oxford: Clarendon Press, 1962 (repr.
1967 (1st edn. corr.)): 366.
fr. 1.
Q: 4 : Lyr., Hymn.

1266 **TYRANNION** Gramm.
1 B.C.: Amisenus
001 **Fragmenta**, ed. W. Haas, *Die Fragmente des
Grammatikers Dionysios Thrax* [*Sammlung
griechischer und lateinischer Grammatiker* 3.
Berlin: De Gruyter, 1977]: 101–125, 127–131,

133–137, 139–140, 142–162, 164–166, 168–
169, 172–174, 176.
frr. 1–63.
Q, Pap: 5,497: Gramm.

1611 **TYRANNION Junior** Gramm.
vel Diocles Gramm.
1 B.C.–A.D. 1: Romanus
001 **Fragmenta**, ed. W. Haas, *Die Fragmente des
Grammatikers Dionysios Thrax* [*Sammlung
griechischer und lateinischer Grammatiker* 3.
Berlin: De Gruyter, 1977]: 178–180.
frr. 64–67.
Q, Pap: 261 : Gramm.

0266 **TYRTAEUS** Eleg.
7 B.C.: Lacedaemonius
001 **Fragmenta**, ed. M.L. West, *Iambi et elegi
Graeci*, vol. 2. Oxford: Clarendon Press, 1972:
150–163.
frr. 2, 4–7, 10–14, 17–24.
fr. 2: *P. Oxy.* 38.2824.
frr. 18–23: *P. Berol.* 11675.
Q, Pap: 1,201 : Eleg.
002 **Fragmenta**, FGrH #580: 3B:690–692.
Q: 823 : Hist., Eleg.

9024 **Isaac TZETZES** Gramm.
A.D. 12: Constantinopolitanus
001 **De metris Pindaricis**, ed. A.B. Drachmann,
*Isaac Tzetzae de metris Pindaricis commentar-
ius* [*Danske Videnskabernes Selskabs*, Hist.-filol.
Meddelelser 9.3. Copenhagen: Höst, 1925].
Cod: Gramm.
x01 **Introductio in Lycophronem** (olim sub auctore
Isaac Tzetza, nunc auctore Joanne Tzetza).
Scheer, pp. 1–4.
Cf. SCHOLIA IN LYCOPHRONEM (5030 001).
x02 **Scholia in Lycophronem**.
Scheer, pp. 8–397 passim.
Cf. SCHOLIA IN LYCOPHRONEM (5030 001).

9022 **Joannes TZETZES** Gramm. et Poeta
A.D. 12: Constantinopolitanus
001 **Chiliades**, ed. P.A.M. Leone, *Ioannis Tzetzae
historiae*. Naples: Libreria Scientifica Editrice,
1968.
Cod: Gramm., Poem.
003 **Prolegomena de comoedia Aristophanis**, ed.
W.J.W. Koster, *Prolegomena de comoedia. Scholia in Acharnenses, Equites, Nubes* [*Scholia in
Aristophanem* 1.1A. Groningen: Bouma, 1975]:
22–38.
Ἀλέξανδρος ὁ Αἰτωλὸς καὶ Λυκόφρων ὁ Χαλι-
δεὺς μεγαλοδωρίαις (prooemium 1): pp. 22–31.
Ἀλέξανδρος ὁ Αἰτωλὸς καὶ Λυκόφρων ὁ Χαλι-
δεύς, ἀλλὰ (prooemium 2): pp. 31–38.
Cod: Gramm.
004 **Versus de differentiis poematorum**, ed. Koster,
op. cit., 84–109.
Introductio: pp. 84–94.

De comoedia: pp. 94–98.
De tragoedia: pp. 99–109.
Cod: Gramm., Iamb.

005 **Epistulae**, ed. P.A.M. Leone, *Ioannis Tzetzae epistulae*. Leipzig: Teubner, 1972: 1–157.
Cod: Epist.

006 **De Pleiadibus** (excerptum), ed. J. Martin, *Scholia in Aratum vetera*. Stuttgart: Teubner, 1974: 547–551.
Cod: 956: Astron., Comm.

007 **Scholia in Anthologiam Graecam** (e cod. Paris. suppl. gr. 316), ed. A.C. Lolos, "Antike Scholien zu Anthologia Graeca-Palatina," *Hellenika* 33 (1981) 376–381.
Cod: Schol.

x01 **Exegesis in scutum Hesiodi.**
Gaisford, pp. 609–654.
Cf. Joannes PEDIASIMUS Gramm. (2592 003).

x02 **Commentarium in Ptolemaei canones** (olim sub auctore Tzetza).
Dodwell, pp. 128–141; Usener, pp. 38–84.
Cf. STEPHANUS Phil. (9019 002–003).

x03 **De poeticae generibus** (fort. auctore Joanne Tzetza).
Koster, vol. 1.1A, p. 50.
Cf. TRACTATUS DE COMOEDIA (3002 015).

x04 **Vitae Aristophanis.**
Koster, vol. 1.1A, pp. 144–145.
Cf. VITAE ARISTOPHANIS (4158 007–008).

x05 **Vita Oppiani.**
Colonna, p. 40.
Cf. VITAE OPPIANI (4172 006).

x06 **Scholia et argumenta in Aristophanem.**
Cf. SCHOLIA IN ARISTOPHANEM (5014 015–021, 023).

x07 **Epigrammata in Oppianum.**
Bussemaker, pp. 260, 276.
Cf. SCHOLIA IN OPPIANUM (5032 002).

x08 **Interpretatio et scholia in Hesiodi opera et dies.**
Gaisford, pp. 10–22, 23–447 passim.
Cf. SCHOLIA IN HESIODUM (5025 002).

x09 **Introductio et scholia in Lycophronem.**
Scheer, pp. 1–4, 8–398 passim.
Introductio: olim sub auctore Isaac Tzetza.
Cf. SCHOLIA IN LYCOPHRONEM (5030 001).

1824 *UAPHRIS EPISTULA*
ante 2 B.C.
x01 **Epistula.**
FGrH #723, fr. 2.
Cf. EUPOLEMUS Judaeus Hist. (2486 002).

2604 **ULPIANUS** Gramm. et Rhet.
fiq Ulpianus Antiochenus
A.D. 4
001 **Prolegomena in Demosthenis orationes Olynthiacas et Philippicas**, ed. M. Dilts, *Scholia Demosthenica*, vol. 1. Leipzig: Teubner, 1983: 1–13.
Cod: 4,187: Schol.

4229 **ULPIANUS** Soph.
fiq Ulpianus Emesenus
A.D. 4: Antiochenus, Ascalonius, Emesenus
x01 **Scholia in Demosthenem** (fort. auctore Ulpiano).
Dilts, vol. 1, pp. 14–235; vol. 2, pp. 1–384.
Cf. SCHOLIA IN DEMOSTHENEM (5017 001).

2462 **ULPIANUS** Soph.
fiq Ulpianus Antiochenus
A.D. 4?: fort. Emesenus
001 **Testimonium**, FGrH #676: 3C:344.
NQ: 38: Test.
002 **Fragmenta**, FGrH #676: 3C:344.
Arabica (fr. 1): fort. auctore Ulpiano Emeseno.
Q: 56: Hist.

2670 **URANIUS** Epigr.
A.D. 2?
x01 **Epigramma dedicatorium.**
App. Anth. 1.194: Cf. ANTHOLOGIAE GRAECAE APPENDIX (7052 001).

2461 **URANIUS** Hist.
A.D. 6?: Syrius
001 **Testimonia**, FGrH #675: 3C:339–340.
NQ: 201: Test.
002 **Fragmenta**, FGrH #675: 3C:340–344.
Q: 888: Hist.

1089 **URBANUS** Med.
vel Orbanus
ante A.D. 2: Indus
x01 **Fragmentum ap. Galenum.**
K14.109–111.
Cf. GALENUS Med. (0057 078).

URBICIUS Tact.
A.D. 5–6: Constantinopolitanus
Cf. Pseudo-MAURICIUS Tact. (3075).

1107 **Terentius VALENS** Med.
ante A.D. 2
x01 **Fragmenta ap. Galenum.**
K12.766; 13.115, 279, 292, 827.
Cf. GALENUS Med. (0057 076–077).

1746 **VALENTINUS** Gnost.
A.D. 2
001 **Valentini hymnus**, ed. E. Heitsch, *Die griechischen Dichterfragmente der römischen Kaiserzeit*, vol. 1, 2nd edn. Göttingen: Vandenhoeck & Ruprecht, 1963: 155.
Q: 35: Hymn.
002 **Fragmenta**, ed. W. Völker, *Quellen zur Geschichte der christlichen Gnosis*. Tübingen: Mohr, 1932: 57–60.
frr. 1–9.
Q

1950 **VARRO** Hist.
post 4 B.C.
001 **Testimonium**, FGrH #149: 2B:818.
NQ: 11: Test.

1802 *VERSUS HEROICI*
Varia
Cf. et HOMERUS Epic. (0012).
Cf. et HYMNI HOMERICI (0013).
001 **Fragmenta**, ed. T.W. Allen, *Homeri opera*, vol.
5. Oxford: Clarendon Press, 1912 (repr. 1969):
148–151.
frr. 1–2, 4–23, 25.
Q

1764 **VETTIUS VALENS** Astrol.
A.D. 2: Antiochenus
001 **Anthologiarum libri ix**, ed. W. Kroll, *Vettii Valentis anthologiarum libri*. Berlin: Weidmann,
1908 (repr. 1973): 1–363.
Cod: 110,961: Astrol.
002 **Additamenta vetusta**, ed. Kroll, *op. cit.*, 364–
372.
Cod: [3,500]: Astrol.
003 **Fragmenta**, ed. W. Kroll and A. Olivieri,
*Codices Veneti [Catalogus codicum astrologorum
Graecorum 2*. Brussels: Lamertin, 1900]: 161–
163, 170, 174.
Q: Astrol.
004 **Fragmenta**, ed. D. Bassi, F. Cumont, A. Martini and A. Olivieri, *Codices Italici [Catalogus
codicum astrologorum Graecorum*, vol. 4. Brussels: Lamertin, 1903]: 146–149.
Cod
005 **Fragmenta**, ed. W. Kroll, *Codices Romani
[Catalogus codicum astrologorum Graecorum*,
vol. 5.2. Brussels: Lamertin, 1906]: 52–53,
113, 120–121.
Cod
006 **Fragmenta**, ed. J. Heeg, *Codices Romani [Cata-
logus codicum astrologorum Graecorum*, vol.
5.3. Brussels: Lamertin, 1910]: 112, 117–118.
Q
007 **Fragmenta**, ed. F. Cumont, *Codices Parisini
[Catalogus codicum astrologorum Graecorum*,
vol. 8.1. Brussels: Lamertin, 1929]: 163–171,
240, 249.
Q, Cod

VETUS TESTAMENTUM
Cf. SEPTUAGINTA (0527).

1747 *VITA ADAM ET EVAE*
vel *Apocalypsis Mosis*
1 B.C./A.D. 1
001 **Vita Adam et Evae** (*sub titulo* **Apocalypsis
Mosis**), ed. C. Tischendorf, *Apocalypses apocryphae*. Leipzig: Mendelssohn, 1866: 1–23.
Cod: 4,613: Apocalyp., Hagiogr., Apocryph.

1521 *VITA ET SENTENTIAE SECUNDI*
A.D. 2

001 **Vita Secundi**, ed. B.E. Perry, *Secundus the
silent philosopher [American Philological Association Philological Monographs* 22. Ithaca, New
York: American Philological Association,
1964]: 68–78.
Cod: 1,167: Biogr.
002 **Sententiae**, ed. Perry, *op. cit.*, 78–90.
Cod: 587: Gnom.

VITA PHILONIDIS
ante A.D. 1
Cf. ANONYMUS EPICUREUS Phil. (1779
003).

4166 *VITAE AESCHINIS*
Varia
001 **Vitae Aeschinis**, ed. W. Dindorf, *Scholia
Graeca in Aeschinem et Isocratem*: Oxford Uni-
versity Press, 1852: 166–296, 297–414, 415–
503, 504–510, 511–512., 1–6.
Apollonii vita: pp. 1–3.
Vitae anonymae: pp. 4–6.
Apollonii vita: Dup. APOLLONIUS Biogr.
(1167 001).
Cod: 1,175: Biogr.

1765 *VITAE AESOPI*
A.D. 1
Cf. et AESOPUS Scr. Fab. et AESOPICA
(0096).
001 **Vita G** (e cod. 397 Bibliothecae Pierponti Mor-
gan) (recensio 3), ed. B.E. Perry, *Aesopica*, vol.
1. Urbana: University of Illinois Press, 1952:
35–77.
Cod: 17,247: Narr. Fict.
002 **Vita W** (vita Aesopi Westermanniana) (recensio
2), ed. Perry, *op. cit.*, 81–107.
Cod: 13,785: Narr. Fict.
003 **Vita Pl vel Accursiana** (sub auctore Maximo
Planude) (recensio 1), ed. A. Eberhard, *Fabulae romanenses Graece conscriptae*, vol. 1. Leipzig: Teubner, 1872: 226–305.
Cod: Narr. Fict.
004 **Vita** (auctore Aphthonio), ed. Eberhard, *op.
cit.*, 306–308.
Cod: Narr. Fict.
005 Βιβλίον μυθικὸν τοῦ Αἰσώπου, εἰκονίζον ἀπὸ
τῶν ἀλόγων ζῴων πρὸς τὰς τῆς ἀνθρωπίνης
φύσεως πράξεις, ed. Eberhard, *op. cit.*, 309–
310.
Cod: Narr. Fict.

4161 *VITAE ARATI ET VARIA DE ARATO*
Varia
001 **Excerptum praefationis in phaenomena** (=
Anonymus II.3), ed. J. Martin, *Scholia in Ara-
tum vetera*. Stuttgart: Teubner, 1974: 1–4.
Cod: 241: Astron., Comm.
002 **Vita Arati** (= Vita 1) (olim sub auctore Achille
Tatio) (e cod. Vat. gr. 191), ed. Martin, *op. cit.*,
6–10.
Cod: 888: Biogr.

003 **Vita Arati** (= Vita 2) (e codd. Matrit. 4691 + 4629), ed. Martin, *op. cit.*, 11–13.
Cod: 403: Biogr.

004 **Arati genus** (= Vita 3) (olim sub auctore Theone Alexandrino Gramm. vel Theone Alexandrino Math.) (e codd. Edimburg. + Ambros. C263), ed. Martin, *op. cit.*, 14–18.
Cod: 421: Biogr.

005 **Vita Arati** (= Vita 4) (e codd. Matrit. 4691 + 4629; Vat. gr. 1910; Paris. gr. 2403; Scorial. Σ III 3; Palat. 40; Estensi II B 14), ed. Martin, *op. cit.*, 19–21.
Cod: 244: Biogr.

006 **Prolegomena in Aratum** (e cod. Paris. suppl. gr. 607A), ed. Martin, *op. cit.*, 23–31.
Cod: 1,518: Astron.

007 **Prolegomena in Aratum** (= Περὶ ἐξηγήσεως) (olim sub auctore Achille Tatio) (e cod. Vat. gr. 191), ed. Martin, *op. cit.*, 32–34.
Cod: 534: Astron., Comm.

008 **De zodiaco** (olim sub auctore Leontio Mechanico), ed. Martin, *op. cit.*, 529–532.
Cod: 525: Astron.

009 **Epistula ad Julianum quendam data** (olim sub auctore Theone Alexandrino Math.), ed. Martin, *op. cit.*, 533–534.
Cod: 158: Epist., Astron.

010 **Excerpta varia de phaenomenis Arati**, ed. Martin, *op. cit.*, 535–544.
Cod: 1,104: Astron., Comm.

011 **Astronomica** (in appendice cod. Scorialensis Σ III 3), ed. Martin, *op. cit.*, 556–557.
Cod: 226: Astron.

012 **Ἐξ ἑτέρων σχολίων εἰσαγωγή** (= Anonymus I) (e cod. Vat. gr. 191), ed. E. Maass, *Commentariorum in Aratum reliquiae*. Berlin: Weidmann, 1898 (repr. 1958): 89–98.
Cod: 2,775: Astron.

013 **Prooemium in Arati phaenomena**, ed. Maass, *op. cit.*, 102–104, 106, 108, 110, 112, 114, 116, 118, 120, 122, 124–133.
Cod: 3,428: Astron., Comm.

014 **Sphaera** (olim sub auctore Empedocle), ed. Maass, *op. cit.*, 154–170.
Cod: 1,080: Astron.

4158 *VITAE ARISTOPHANIS*
Varia

001 **Vita**, ed. W.J.W. Koster, *Prolegomena de comoedia. Scholia in Acharnenses, Equites, Nubes* [*Scholia in Aristophanem* 1.1A. Groningen: Bouma, 1975]: 133–136.
Cod: Biogr.

002 **Vita**, ed. Koster, *op. cit.*, 136–140.
Cod: Biogr.

003 **Epigramma in Aristophanem**, ed. Koster, *op. cit.*, 141.
Cod: Epigr.

004 **Vita dramatumque catalogus**, ed. Koster, *op. cit.*, 141–142.
Cod: Biogr.

005 **Vita**, ed. Koster, *op. cit.*, 143.
Cod: Biogr.

006 **Vita**, ed. Koster, *op. cit.*, 143–144.
Cod: Biogr.

007 **Vita Tzetziana 1**, ed. Koster, *op. cit.*, 144.
Cod: Biogr.

008 **Vita Tzetziana 2**, ed. Koster, *op. cit.*, 144–145.
Cod: Biogr.

009 **Vita Thomana 1**, ed. Koster, *op. cit.*, 146–147.
Cod: Biogr.

010 **Vita Thomana 2**, ed. Koster, *op. cit.*, 149.
Cod: Biogr.

4173 *VITAE DIONYSII PERIEGETAE*
Varia

001 **Vita Dionysii**, ed. R. Kassel, "Antimachos in der Vita Chisiana des Dionysios Periegetes," *Catalepton. Festschrift für Bernhard Wyss*. Basel: Seminar für klassische Philologie, 1985: 70–73.
Cod: Biogr.

x01 **Vita Dionysii**.
Müller, pp. 427–428.
Cf. SCHOLIA IN DIONYSIUM PERIEGETAM (5019 001).

x02 **Vita Dionysii**.
Ludwich, pp. 575–576.
Cf. SCHOLIA IN DIONYSIUM PERIEGETAM (5019 002).

1749 *VITAE HESIODI PARTICULA*
Incertum
Cf. et HESIODUS Epic. (0020).

001 **Vitae Hesiodi particula**, ed. T.W. Allen, *Homeri opera*, vol. 5. Oxford: Clarendon Press, 1912 (repr. 1969): 222–224.
Cod: 441: Biogr.

1805 *VITAE HOMERI*
Varia
Cf. et CERTAMEN HOMERI ET HESIODI (1252).

001 **Vita Herodotea**, ed. T.W. Allen, *Homeri opera*, vol. 5. Oxford: Clarendon Press, 1912 (repr. 1969): 192–218.
Cod: 4,479: Biogr.

002 **<Plutarchi> vita**, ed. Allen, *op. cit.*, 239–245.
Cod: 978: Biogr.

003 **Vita Proculea** (e *Chrestomathia*), ed. Allen, *op. cit.*, 99–102.
Dup. partim PROCLUS Phil. (4036 023).
Cod: 589: Biogr.

004 **Vita quarta**, ed. Allen, *op. cit.*, 245–246.
Cod: 188: Biogr.

005 **Vita quinta**, ed. Allen, *op. cit.*, 247–250.
Cod: 408: Biogr.

006 **Vita sexta**, ed. Allen, *op. cit.*, 250–253.
Cod: 555: Biogr.

007 **Vita septima** (Eustathii vita, *Od.* 1713.17), ed. Allen, *op. cit.*, 253–254.
Cod: 129: Biogr.

008 **Tzetzae vita** (*Chil.* 13.626–665), ed. Allen, *op. cit.*, 254–255.
Cod: 277: Biogr.

009 **Eustathii vita** (*Il.* 4.17), ed. Allen, *op. cit.*, 255.
Cod: 95: Biogr.

010 **Sudae vita**, ed. Allen, *op. cit.*, 256–267.
Cod: 1,725: Biogr.

4172 *VITAE OPPIANI*
Varia

002 **Vita Oppiani Anazarbensis** (e cod. phil. gr. 135 in Bibl. nat. in Vindob.), ed. O. Mazal, "Eine neue Rezension der Biographie Oppians," *Wiener Studien* 80 (1967) 118.
Cod: Biogr.

003 **Vita Oppiani** (e cod. Matr. XX), ed. J. Iriarte, *Regiae Bibliothecae Matritensis codices Graeci mss.*, vol. 1. Madrid: Perez de Soto, 1769: 82.
Cod: Biogr.

004 **Vita Oppiani** (Vita α), ed. A. Westermann, Βιογράφοι. *Vitarum scriptores Graeci minores.* Braunschweig: Westermann, 1845 (repr. Amsterdam: Hakkert, 1964): 63–65.
Cod: Biogr.

005 **Vita Oppiani** (Vita β), ed. Westermann, *op. cit.*, 65–66.
Cod: Biogr.

006 **Vita Tzetziana** (e codd. Laur. gr. 31.3, Ambros. gr. C 222 inf., Vat. gr. 1345), ed. A. Colonna, "De vita Oppiani antiquissima," *Bollettino del comitato per la preparazione dell'edizione nazionale dei classici greci e latini* 12 (1964) 40.
Cod: Biogr.

x01 **Vita Oppiani**.
Adler, vol. 1.3, p. 547.
Cf. SUDA (9010 001).

x02 **Vita Oppiani** (auctore Constantino Manasse).
Colonna, pp. 38–39.
Cf. Constantinus MANASSES Poeta et Hist. (3074 002).

4170 *VITAE PINDARI ET VARIA DE PINDARO*
Varia
Cf. et PINDARUS Lyr. (0033).

001 **Vitae et varia de Pindaro**, ed. A.B. Drachmann, *Scholia vetera in Pindari carmina*, vol. 1. Leipzig: Teubner, 1903 (repr. Amsterdam: Hakkert, 1969): 1–11.
Vita Ambrosiana: vol. 1, pp. 1–4.
Vita Thomana et hypothesis Olympiorum: vol. 1, pp. 4–8.
Vita metrica: vol. 1, pp. 8–9.
Pentathlon et de novem lyricis: vol. 1, pp. 10–11.
Cod: 1,524: Biogr., Gramm.

1750 *VITAE PROPHETARUM*
Varia

001 **Enumeratio lxxii prophetarum et prophetissa-** **rum** (Epiphanii textus), ed. T. Schermann, *Prophetarum vitae fabulosae.* Leipzig: Teubner, 1907: 1–3.
Dup. EPIPHANIUS Scr. Eccl. (2021 020).
Cod

002 **De prophetarum vita et obitu** (Epiphanii recensio prior), ed. Schermann, *op. cit.*, 4–25.
Dup. EPIPHANIUS Scr. Eccl. (2021 021).
Cod

003 **De prophetarum vita et obitu** (Dorothei recensio), ed. Schermann, *op. cit.*, 26–55.
Cod

004 **De prophetarum vita et obitu** (Epiphanii recensio altera), ed. Schermann, *op. cit.*, 55–67.
Dup. EPIPHANIUS Scr. Eccl. (2021 022).
Cod

005 **De prophetarum vita et obitu** (recensio anonyma), ed. Schermann, *op. cit.*, 68–98.
Cod

006 **De prophetarum vita et obitu** (recensio scholiis Hesychii aliorumque patrum in prophetas adjecta), ed. Schermann, *op. cit.*, 99–104.
Cod

007 **Index apostolorum** (Epiphanii textus), ed. Schermann, *op. cit.*, 107–117.
Dup. EPIPHANIUS Scr. Eccl. (2021 023).
Cod

008 **Index discipulorum** (Epiphanii textus), ed. Schermann, *op. cit.*, 118–126.
Dup. EPIPHANIUS Scr. Eccl. (2021 024).
Cod

009 **Appendices ad indices apostolorum discipulorumque** (Epiphanii textus), ed. Schermann, *op. cit.*, 126–131.
Dup. EPIPHANIUS Scr. Eccl. (2021 043).
Cod

010 **Index apostolorum discipulorumque Domini** (textus Pseudo-Dorothei), ed. Schermann, *op. cit.*, 132–160.
Cod

011 **De baptismate apostolorum et beatae Mariae virginis**, ed. Schermann, *op. cit.*, 160–163.
Cod

012 **Index apostolorum discipulorumque Domini** (textus Pseudo-Hippolyti), ed. Schermann, *op. cit.*, 164–170.
Cod

013 **Index anonymus Graeco-Syrus**, ed. Schermann, *op. cit.*, 171–177.
Cod

014 **Index apostolorum discipulorumque Domini** (textus Pseudo-Symeonis logothetae), ed. Schermann, *op. cit.*, 177–183.
Q

015 **Index apostolorum discipulorumque** (in menologio Basilii II imperatoris) (forma brevior), ed. Schermann, *op. cit.*, 184–185.
Q

016 **Index apostolorum discipulorumque** (in synaxariis Graecis) (forma longior), ed. Schermann, *op. cit.*, 185–194.
Q

017 **Index apostolorum discipulorumque** (forma abbreviata), ed. Schermann, *op. cit.*, 194–197.
Cod

018 **Textus mixtus apostolorum indicum** (inter recensionem Hippolyti et Dorothei), ed. Schermann, *op. cit.*, 197–200.
Cod

019 **Textus mixtus apostolorum indicum** (inter recensionem Hippolyti et Dorothei et textum Epiphanii), ed. Schermann, *op. cit.*, 200–202.
Cod

020 **De apostolorum parentibus** (textus anonymus), ed. Schermann, *op. cit.*, 203–204.
Cod

021 **Versus in duodecim apostolos** (textus Joannis Euchaitensis), ed. Schermann, *op. cit.*, 204–205.
Cod

022 **Index apostolorum** (homilia Pseudo-Chrysostomi in xii apostolos), ed. Schermann, *op. cit.*, 206.
Dup. partim JOANNES CHRYSOSTOMUS Scr. Eccl. (2062 227).
Cod

3153 *VITAE THEOPHANIS CONFESSORIS*
post A.D. 10
Cf. et NICEPHORUS Biogr. (3152).
Cf. et THEODORUS Protosecretarius Biogr. (3154).

001 **Anonymi vita Theophanis**, ed. C. de Boor, *Theophanis chronographia*, vol. 2. Leipzig: Teubner, 1885 (repr. Hildesheim: Olms, 1963): 3–12.
Cod: Biogr.

002 **Vita Theophanis** (ex officio festi eius diei desumpta in editione Parisina), ed. de Boor, *op. cit.*, 3–12, 28–30.
Cod: Biogr.

003 **Vita Theophanis** (ex menologio codicis bibliothecae Messinensis), ed. de Boor, *op. cit.*, 30.
Cod: Biogr.

004 **Officium Theophanis**, MPG 108: 45–53.
Cod: Biogr.

x01 **Vita Theophanis** (sub auctore Nicephoro).
de Boor, pp. 13–27.
Cf. NICEPHORUS Biogr. (3152 001).

x02 **Encomium in Theophanem** (sub auctore Theodoro).
Krumbacher, pp. 608–618.
Cf. THEODORUS Protosecretarius Biogr. (3154 001).

x03 **Encomium et vita Theophanis** (sub auctore Methodio).
Spyridonov, pp. 95–96, 113–165.
Cf. METHODIUS I Scr. Eccl. (2708 001).

1751 **XANTHUS** Hist.
5 B.C.: Lydius
001 **Testimonia**, FGrH #765: 3C:750–751.
NQ: 319: Test.

002 **Fragmenta**, FGrH #765: 3C:751–758.
Q: 2,123: Hist.

003 **Fragmentum**, ed. H.J. Mette, "Die 'Kleinen' griechischen Historiker heute," *Lustrum* 21 (1978) 38.
fr. 2 bis.
Q: 50: Hist.

1752 **XENAGORAS** Hist. et Geogr.
4/1 B.C.: fort. Heracleensis
001 **Testimonia**, FGrH #240: 2B:1005.
NQ: 66: Test.

002 **Fragmenta**, FGrH #240: 2B:1005–1010; 3B:744 addenda.
Q: 1,537: Hist., Chronogr.

0518 **XENARCHUS** Comic.
4 B.C.
001 **Fragmenta**, ed. T. Kock, *Comicorum Atticorum fragmenta*, vol. 2. Leipzig: Teubner, 1884: 467–473.
frr. 1–14.
Q: 464: Comic.

002 **Fragmenta**, ed. A. Meineke, *Fragmenta comicorum Graecorum*, vol. 3. Berlin: Reimer, 1840 (repr. De Gruyter, 1970): 614, 616–617, 620–625.
Q: 469: Comic.

1830 **XENARCHUS** Phil.
1 B.C.–A.D. 1: Seleuciensis
x01 **Fragmenta ap. Simplicium.**
CAG 7, pp. 13, 14, 21–22, 23–24, 50, 55, 56, 70, 286.
Cf. SIMPLICIUS Phil. (4013 001).

2355 **XENIADES** Soph.
5 B.C.?: Corinthius
001 **Testimonium**, ed. H. Diels and W. Kranz, *Die Fragmente der Vorsokratiker*, vol. 2, 6th edn. Berlin: Weidmann, 1952 (repr. Dublin: 1966): 271.
NQ: 51: Test.

1753 **XENION** Hist.
post 4 B.C.?
001 **Fragmenta**, FGrH #460: 3B:397–398.
Q: 419: Hist.

0519 **XENO** Comic.
3 B.C.
001 **Fragmentum**, ed. T. Kock, *Comicorum Atticorum fragmenta*, vol. 3. Leipzig: Teubner, 1888: 390.
fr. 1.
Q: 13: Comic.

002 **Fragmentum**, ed. A. Meineke, *Fragmenta comicorum Graecorum*, vol. 4. Berlin: Reimer, 1841 (repr. De Gruyter, 1970): 596.
Q: 11: Comic.

4252 **XENO** Gramm.
3/2 B.C. : Alexandrinus
001 **Testimonia**, ed. F. Montanari, *I frammenti dei grammatici Agathokles, Hellanikos, Ptolemaios Epithetes* [*Sammlung griechischer und lateinischer Grammatiker* 7. Berlin: De Gruyter, 1988]: 120.
test. 2: Πρὸς τὸ παράδοξον.
NQ: Test.

2558 **XENO** Hist.
Incertum
001 **Testimonium**, FGrH #824: 3C:898.
NQ: 29: Test.

0316 **XENOCLES** Trag.
5 B.C.
001 **Fragmentum**, ed. B. Snell, *Tragicorum Graecorum fragmenta*, vol. 1. Göttingen: Vandenhoeck & Ruprecht, 1971: 153.
fr. 1-3.
Q: 30: Trag., Satyr.

XENOCRATES Epigr.
AG 7.291; 16.186.
Cf. XENOCRITUS Epigr. (0091 001).

2174 **XENOCRATES** Hist.
Incertum
001 **Fragmentum**, FGrH #248: 2B:1130.
Q: 28: Hist., Chronogr.

1009 **XENOCRATES** Med.
A.D. 1: Aphrodisiensis
001 **De lapidibus**, ed. M. Wellmann, "Die Stein- und Gemmenbücher der Antike," *Quellen und Studien zur Geschichte der Naturwissenschaften und Medizin* 4.4 (1935) 86-149 (passim).
Q
x01 **Fragmenta ap. Galenum**.
K12.261; 13.90-91, 846, 931.
Cf. GALENUS Med. (0057 076-077).
x02 **Fragmenta ap. Oribasium**.
CMG, vol. 6.1.1, pp. 47-57; 6.1.2, p. 296.
Cf. ORIBASIUS Med. (0722 001).

0634 **XENOCRATES** Phil.
4 B.C.: Chalcedonius
001 **Testimonia, doctrina et fragmenta**, ed. M.I. Parente, *Senocrate-Ermodoro. Frammenti.* Naples: Bibliopolis, 1982: 51-78, 80-138, 141-142, 144-153.
frr. 1-8, 10-12, 14-23, 25, 27-43, 46, 47a, 49-50, 52-60, 62-72, 77-79, 81-85, 87-120, 122-163, 165-175, 178-198, 203, 205-206, 209-213, 215-217, 219-233, 236-240, 249, 251-255, 258-262, 264-268.
Epistula [Sp.] (pp. 152-153): Dup. SOCRATICORUM EPISTULAE (0637 001, p. 634, epist. 34).
Q, Pap: Phil., Epist.

0091 **XENOCRITUS** Epigr.
ante 1 B.C.: Rhodius
001 **Epigrammata**, AG 7.291; 16.186.
Q: 81: Epigr.

2306 **XENOMEDES** Hist.
5 B.C.?: Ceus
001 **Testimonia**, FGrH #442: 3B:372.
NQ: 73: Test.
002 **Fragmenta**, FGrH #442: 3B:372-374.
Q: 351: Hist.

0267 **XENOPHANES** Poet. Phil.
6-5 B.C.: Colophonius
001 **Fragmenta**, ed. M.L. West, *Iambi et elegi Graeci*, vol. 2. Oxford: Clarendon Press, 1972: 164-170.
frr. B1-3, 5-9, A14, B14, 45.
Q: 486: Eleg.
002 **Fragmenta** (Silli et De natura), ed. E. Diehl, *Anthologia lyrica Graeca*, fasc. 1, 3rd edn. Leipzig: Teubner, 1949: 68-74.
frr. 9-11, 13-34.
Q: 377: Hexametr.
003 **Epigramma**, AG 7.120.
AG 7.119: Cf. ANONYMI EPIGRAMMATICI (AG) (0138 001).
Q: 26: Epigr.
004 **Testimonium**, FGrH #450: 3B:378.
NQ: 18: Test.
005 **Testimonia**, ed. H. Diels and W. Kranz, *Die Fragmente der Vorsokratiker*, vol. 1, 6th edn. Berlin: Weidmann, 1951 (repr. Dublin: 1966): 113-126.
test. 1-52.
NQ: 5,242: Test.
006 **Fragmenta**, ed. Diels and Kranz, *op. cit.*, 126-138.
frr. 1-42, 45.
Q: 1,596: Phil., Eleg., Hexametr.

2518 **XENOPHILUS** Hist.
post 4 B.C.?
001 **Fragmentum**, FGrH #767: 3C:758.
Q: 104: Hist.

2241 **XENOPHILUS** Phil. et Mus.
4 B.C.: Chalcidensis
001 **Testimonia**, ed. H. Diels and W. Kranz, *Die Fragmente der Vorsokratiker*, vol. 1, 6th edn. Berlin: Weidmann, 1951 (repr. Dublin: 1966): 442-443.
test. 1-3.
NQ: 164: Test.

0032 **XENOPHON** Hist.
5-4 B.C.: Atheniensis
Cf. et XENOPHONTIS EPISTULAE (1754).
Scholia: Cf. SCHOLIA IN XENOPHONTEM (5040).
001 **Hellenica**, ed. E.C. Marchant, *Xenophontis*

opera omnia, vol. 1. Oxford: Clarendon Press, 1900 (repr. 1968).
Cod: 67,939: Hist.

002 **Memorabilia**, ed. Marchant, *op. cit.*, vol. 2, 2nd edn. (1921; repr. 1971).
Cod: 36,436: Phil., Dialog., Biogr.

003 **Oeconomicus**, ed. Marchant, *op. cit.*, vol. 2.
Cod: 18,124: Phil., Dialog.

004 **Symposium**, ed. Marchant, *op. cit.*, vol. 2.
Cod: 9,657: Phil., Dialog.

005 **Apologia Socratis**, ed. Marchant, *op. cit.*, vol. 2.
Cod: 2,032: Phil.

006 **Anabasis**, ed. Marchant, *op. cit.*, vol. 3 (1904; repr. 1961).
Cod: 58,307: Hist.

007 **Cyropaedia**, ed. Marchant, *op. cit.*, vol. 4 (1910; repr. 1970).
Cod: 80,710: Narr. Fict., Biogr.

008 **Hiero**, ed. Marchant, *op. cit.*, vol. 5 (1920; repr. 1969).
Cod: 6,071: Phil., Dialog.

009 **Agesilaus**, ed. Marchant, *op. cit.*, vol. 5.
Cod: 7,559: Hist., Encom.

010 **De republica Lacedaemoniorum**, ed. Marchant, *op. cit.*, vol. 5.
Cod: 5,026: Hist., Phil.

011 **De vectigalibus**, ed. Marchant, *op. cit.*, vol. 5.
Cod: 3,935: Phil., Hist.

012 **Hipparchicus**, ed. Marchant, *op. cit.*, vol. 5.
Cod: 5,895: Hist., Tact.

013 **De re equestri**, ed. Marchant, *op. cit.*, vol. 5.
Cod: 7,105: Nat. Hist.

014 **Cynegeticus**, ed. Marchant, *op. cit.*, vol. 5.
Cod: 9,257: Phil., Nat. Hist.

015 **Atheniensium respublica** [Sp.], ed. Marchant, *op. cit.*, vol. 5.
Cod: 3,252: Phil., Hist.

1926 **XENOPHON** Hist.
post 4 B.C.: Atheniensis
001 **Testimonium**, FGrH #111: 2B:524.
NQ: 27: Test.

1973 **XENOPHON** Hist.
3–2 B.C.
001 **Testimonium**, FGrH #179: 2B:906.
NQ: 16: Test.

2376 **XENOPHON** Hist.
A.D. 2: fort. Samius
001 **Testimonium**, FGrH #540a: 3B:523.
test. 1: *Inscr. Samos* (Heraion inv. 183).
NQ: 20: Test.

1876 **XENOPHON** Hist.
ante A.D. 3
001 **Testimonium**, FGrH #24: 1A:188.
NQ: 14: Test.

2510 **XENOPHON** Hist.
Incertum: Cyprius

001 **Testimonium**, FGrH #755: 3C:736.
NQ: 20: Test.

1108 **XENOPHON** Med.
4/3 B.C.: Cous
x01 **Fragmentum ap. Oribasium**.
CMG, vol. 6.2.1, p. 166.
Cf. ORIBASIUS Med. (0722 001).

x02 **Fragmentum ap. Erotianum**.
Nachmanson, p. 108.
Cf. EROTIANUS Gramm. et Med. (0716 002).

0641 **XENOPHON** Scr. Erot.
A.D. 2/3: Ephesius
001 **Ephesiaca**, ed. G. Dalmeyda, *Xénophon d'Éphèse. Les Éphésiaques ou le roman d'Habrocomès et d'Anthia*. Paris: Les Belles Lettres, 1926 (repr. 1962): 3–77.
Cod: 17,197: Narr. Fict.

002 **Testimonium**, FGrH #419: 3B:316.
NQ: 22: Test.

1754 ***XENOPHONTIS EPISTULAE***
Incertum
Cf. et XENOPHON Hist. (0032).
001 **Epistulae**, ed. R. Hercher, *Epistolographi Graeci*. Paris: Didot, 1873 (repr. Amsterdam: Hakkert, 1965): 788–791.
Q: 1,201: Epist.

x01 **Epistulae ad Socraticos**.
Epist. Graec., pp. 621–622, 623–625.
Cf. SOCRATICORUM EPISTULAE (0637 001).

2229 **XUTHUS** Phil.
5 B.C.: Crotoniensis
001 **Testimonium**, ed. H. Diels and W. Kranz, *Die Fragmente der Vorsokratiker*, vol. 1, 6th edn. Berlin: Weidmann, 1951 (repr. Dublin: 1966): 376.
NQ: 79: Test.

0601 **<ZALEUCUS Nomographus> <Phil.>**
4/2 B.C.?: Locrus
001 **Fragmenta**, ed. H. Thesleff, *The Pythagorean texts of the Hellenistic period*. Åbo: Åbo Akademi, 1965: 225–229.
Q: 698: Phil.

0076 **ZELOTUS** Epigr.
Incertum
001 **Epigramma**, AG 9.30.
AG 9.31: Cf. ANONYMI EPIGRAMMATICI (AG) (0138 001).
Q: 19: Epigr.

2276 **ZENIS** Hist.
4 B.C.?: Chius
001 **Fragmentum**, FGrH #393: 3B:284.
Q: 41: Hist.

2528 **ZENO** Hist.
3 B.C.: Sidonius

001 **Testimonium,** FGrH #791: 3C:824–825.
NQ: 27: Test.

002 **Titulus,** FGrH #791: 3C:825.
NQ: Hist.

1956 **ZENO** Hist.
3 B.C.?

001 **Testimonium,** FGrH #158: 2B:883.
NQ: 29: Test.

2364 **ZENO** Hist.
2 B.C.: Rhodius

001 **Testimonia,** FGrH #523: 3B:494–495.
NQ: 360: Test.

002 **Fragmenta,** FGrH #523: 3B:495–502.
Q: 2,516: Hist.

1109 **ZENO** Med.
2 B.C.

x01 **Fragmentum ap. Pseudo-Galenum.**
K19.409.
Cf. Pseudo-GALENUS Med. (0530 041).

1110 **ZENO** Med.
1 B.C.: Laodicensis

x01 **Fragmenta ap. Galenum.**
K14.163, 171.
Cf. GALENUS Med. (0057 078).

x02 **Fragmentum ap. Philumenum.**
CMG, vol. 10.1.1, p. 14.
Cf. PHILUMENUS Med. (0671 001).

0595 **ZENO** Phil.
5 B.C.: Eleaticus

001 **Testimonia,** ed. H. Diels and W. Kranz, *Die Fragmente der Vorsokratiker,* vol. 1, 6th edn. Berlin: Weidmann, 1951 (repr. Dublin: 1966): 247–255.
test. 1–30.
NQ: 3,579: Test.

002 **Fragmenta,** ed. Diels and Kranz, *op. cit.,* 255–258.
frr. 1–4.
Q: 427: Phil.

0635 **ZENO** Phil.
4–3 B.C.: Citieus
Cf. et ZENONIS EPISTULA (0125).

001 **Testimonia et fragmenta,** ed. J. von Arnim, *Stoicorum veterum fragmenta,* vol. 1. Leipzig: Teubner, 1905 (repr. Stuttgart: 1968): 3–71.
Testimonia (frr. 1–46): pp. 3–16.
Logica (frr. 47–51): p. 16.
De ratione cognitionis (frr. 52–73): pp. 16–21.
Rhetorica (frr. 74–84): pp. 21–23.
Physica (frr. 85–177): pp. 24–45.
Ethica (fr. 178): p. 45.
De fine bonorum (frr. 179–189): pp. 45–47.
De bonis et malis (fr. 190): p. 47.
De indifferentibus (frr. 191–196): pp. 47–48.
De prima conciliatione (frr. 197–198): pp. 48–49.

De virtute (frr. 199–204): pp. 49–50.
De affectibus (frr. 205–215): pp. 50–52.
De sapiente et insipiente (frr. 216–229): pp. 52–55.
De mediis officiis (frr. 230–232): pp. 55–56.
Vitae agendae praecepta (frr. 233–271): pp. 56–62.
De Cratete, De Homero, De Hesiodo (frr. 272–276): pp. 62–63.
Apophthegmata (frr. 277–332): pp. 63–71.
fr. 219: Dup. partim 0635 002 (fr. 852a).
fr. 237: Dup. partim 0635 002 (fr. 852).
Q: 21,085: Phil., Rhet., Gnom., Iamb.

002 **Fragmenta,** ed. H. Lloyd-Jones and P. Parsons, *Supplementum Hellenisticum.* Berlin: De Gruyter, 1983: 396.
frr. 852–852a.
Dup. partim 0635 001 (frr. 219, 237).
Q: 24: Phil., Iamb.

2294 **ZENO** Phil.
3–2 B.C.: Tarsensis

001 **Fragmenta,** ed. J. von Arnim, *Stoicorum veterum fragmenta,* vol. 3. Leipzig: Teubner, 1903 (repr. Stuttgart: 1968): 209.
Q: 217: Phil.

2134 **ZENO** Phil.
2–1 B.C.: Sidonius

001 **Fragmenta,** ed. A. Angeli and M. Colaizzo, "I frammenti di Zenone Sidonio," *Cronache Ercolanesi* 9 (1979) 72, 75–82, 85.
frr. 1–4, 11–28.
Pap

002 **Fragmenta incerta,** ed. Angeli and Colaizzo, *op. cit.,* 85–86.
frr. 1–7.
Pap

2167 **ZENOBIA Regina Palmyrae** <Hist.>
A.D. 3: Palmyrena

001 **Testimonium,** FGrH #626: 3C:161.
NQ: 53: Test.

0596 **ZENOBIUS** Gramm.
fiq Zenobius Sophista
A.D. 2?
Cf. et ZENOBIUS Sophista <Paroemiogr.> (0098).

001 **Epigramma,** AG 9.711.
Q: 16: Epigr.

0098 **ZENOBIUS Sophista** <Paroemiogr.>
fiq Zenobius Gramm.
A.D. 2
Cf. et ZENOBIUS Gramm. (0596).

001 **Epitome collectionum Lucilli Tarrhaei et Didymi,** ed. E.L. von Leutsch and F.G. Schneidewin, *Corpus paroemiographorum Graecorum,* vol. 1. Göttingen: Vandenhoeck & Ruprecht, 1839 (repr. Hildesheim: Olms, 1965): 1–175.
Cod: 21,273: Paroem.

0597 **ZENODORUS** Gramm.
fiq Zenodotus Ephesius
2-1 B.C.?
Cf. et ZENODOTUS Gramm. (0590).
001 Περὶ συνηθείας, ed. E. Miller, "Opuscles
divers," *Lexica Graeca minora* (ed. K. Latte &
H. Erbse). Hildesheim: Olms, 1965: 253-258.
Cod: 1,248: Lexicogr.

0599 **ZENODORUS** Math.
3 B.C.?
x01 **Fragmenta ap. Theonem Alexandrinum.**
Rome, pp. 355-600 (passim).
Cf. THEON Math. (2033 001).

0600 **ZENODOTUS** <Epigr.>
2 B.C.
001 **Epigramma,** AG 7.117.
Q: 40: Epigr.

0590 **ZENODOTUS** Gramm.
4-3 B.C.: Ephesius
Cf. et ZENODORUS Gramm. (0597).
001 **Fragmenta,** ed. H. Duentzer, *De Zenodoti studiis Homericis.* Göttingen: Dieterich, 1848:
passim.
Q
002 **Fragmenta,** ed. A. Römer, "Über die Homerre-
cension des Zenodot," *Abhandlungen der
königlich bayerischen Akademie der Wissenschaften,* Philosoph.-philol. Kl., Bd. 17 (Munich: Franz, 1886): passim.
Q
003 **Fragmenta,** FGrH #19: 1A:183-184.
Q: 288: Hist., Myth.
004 **Epigrammata,** AG 7.315; **16**.14.
Q: 59: Epigr.

2550 **ZENODOTUS** Hist.
2 B.C.: Troezenius
001 **Fragmenta,** FGrH #821: 3C:895-896.
Q: 337: Hist.

0354 **ZENODOTUS** Trag.
Incertum
001 **Fragmentum,** ed. B. Snell, *Tragicorum Graecorum fragmenta,* vol. 1. Göttingen: Vandenhoeck & Ruprecht, 1971: 325.
Q: 14: Trag.

0125 ***ZENONIS EPISTULA***
Incertum
Cf. et ZENO Phil. (0635).
001 **Epistula,** ed. R. Hercher, *Epistolographi Graeci.*
Paris: Didot, 1873 (repr. Amsterdam: Hakkert,
1965): 792.
Q: 123: Epist.

1111 **ZENOPHILUS** Med.
ante A.D. 4
x01 **Fragmentum ap. Oribasium.**
CMG, 6.3, p. 116.

Cf. ORIBASIUS Med. (0722 005).
x02 **Fragmentum ap. Aëtium** (lib. 11).
Daremberg-Ruelle, p. 574.
Cf. AËTIUS Med. (0718 011).

2647 **ZENOTHEMIS** Geogr.
2 B.C.?
001 **Fragmentum,** ed. H. Lloyd-Jones and P. Parsons, *Supplementum Hellenisticum.* Berlin: De
Gruyter, 1983: 397.
fr. 855.
Q: 15: Geogr., Eleg.

1113 **ZEUXIS** Med.
ante A.D. 1
x01 **Fragmentum ap. Galenum.**
K12.834.
Cf. GALENUS Med. (0057 076).

1112 **ZEUXIS Major** Med.
2 B.C.: Tarentinus
x01 **Fragmentum ap. Galenum.**
K17.2.165-166 in CMG, vol. 5.10.2.2, p. 217.
Cf. GALENUS Med. (0057 091).

1114 **ZOILUS** Med.
ante A.D. 1
x01 **Fragmenta ap. Galenum.**
K**12**.632, 763-764, 771-772; **14**.178.
Cf. GALENUS Med. (0057 076, 078).
x02 **Fragmentum ap. Aëtium** (lib. 7).
CMG, vol. 8.2, p. 392.
Cf. AËTIUS Med. (0718 007).
x03 **Fragmentum ap. Alexandrum Trallianum.**
Puschmann, vol. 2, p. 39.
Cf. ALEXANDER Med. (0744 003).

0128 **ZOILUS** Phil. et Rhet.
4 B.C.: Amphipolitanus
001 **Testimonia,** FGrH #71: **2A**:109-110; **3B**:741
addenda.
NQ: 323: Test.
002 **Fragmenta,** FGrH #71: **2A**:110-112.
Q: 756: Hist., Rhet., Encom.

4243 **ZONAEUS** Soph.
A.D. 5-6
001 **De figuris** [Sp.], ed. L. Spengel, *Rhetores
Graeci,* vol. 3. Leipzig: Teubner, 1856 (repr.
Frankfurt am Main: Minerva, 1966): 161-170.
Cod: Rhet.

0130 **ZOPYRUS** Hist.
4-3 B.C.?: fort. Magnes
001 **Fragmenta,** FGrH #494: 3B:465-466.
Q: 272: Hist.

0129 **ZOPYRUS** Hist.
Incertum
001 **Fragmenta,** FGrH #336: 3B:187-188.
Q: 177: Hist.

1116 **ZOPYRUS** Med.
2–1 B.C.: Alexandrinus
x01 **Fragmenta ap. Galenum.**
K14.115, 150–151.
Cf. GALENUS Med. (0057 078).
x02 **Fragmenta ap. Oribasium.**
CMG, vol. 6.1.2, pp. 217, 222, 223, 226, 228,
231, 235.
Cf. ORIBASIUS Med. (0722 001).

0355 **ZOPYRUS** Trag.
3 B.C.?
001 **Fragmentum**, ed. B. Snell, *Tragicorum Graecorum fragmenta*, vol. 1. Göttingen: Vandenhoeck & Ruprecht, 1971: 325.
Q: 13: Trag.

1829 **<ZOROASTER Magus>**
Incertum
001 **Fragmenta**, ed. J. Bidez and F. Cumont, *Les
mages hellénisés*, vol. 2. Paris: Les Belles
Lettres, 1938: 59–60, 157, 158, 159, 161–162,
174–175, 179–187, 188–195, 209–218, 220–
226, 232–233.
Q, Cod

1755 **ZOSIMUS** Epigr.
1 B.C.?: Thasius
001 **Epigrammata**, AG **6**.15, 183–185; **9**.40.
Q: 195: Epigr.

2687 **ZOSIMUS** Epigr.
A.D. 3/4
x01 **Epigrammata sepulcralia.**
App. Anth. 2.497–498: Cf. ANTHOLOGIAE
GRAECAE APPENDIX (7052 002).

4084 **ZOSIMUS** Hist.
A.D. 5?: Constantinopolitanus
001 **Historia nova**, ed. F. Paschoud, *Zosime. His-
toire nouvelle*, vols. 1–3.1. Paris: Les Belles
Lettres, 1:1971; 2.1–2.2:1979; 3.1:1986: **1**:8–
64, 70–128; **2.1**:8–58; **2.2**:262–330; **3.1**:6–74.
Lib. 1–2: vol. 1.
Lib. 3: vol. 2.1.
Lib. 4: vol. 2.2.
Lib. 5: vol. 3.1.
Cod: 62,429: Hist.

1117 **ZOSIMUS** Med.
ante A.D. 2
x01 **Fragmentum ap. Galenum.**
K12.753.
Cf. GALENUS Med. (0057 076).
x02 **Fragmentum ap. Oribasium.**
CMG, vol. 6.2.2, p. 232.
Cf. ORIBASIUS Med. (0722 003).
x03 **Fragmentum ap. Paulum.**
CMG, vol. 9.2, p. 378.
Cf. PAULUS Med. (0715 001).

INDEX OF TLG AUTHOR NUMBERS

The authors in this index are listed in order of their TLG author numbers. This arrangement is intended primarily for those who consult TLG machine-readable texts and require a reference system that translates author numbers into author names.

0149 **CAPITO** Epigr.
0150 **CARPHYLLIDES** Epigr.
0151 **CEREALIUS** Epigr.
0152 **CHAEREMON** Epigr.
0153 **CORNELIUS LONG(IN)US**
Epigr.
0154 **CRINAGORAS** Epigr.
0156 **CYLLENIUS** Epigr.
0157 **CYRILLUS** Epigr.
0158 **DAMAGETUS** Epigr.
0159 **DEMETRIUS** Epigr.
0160 **DEMIURGUS** Epigr.
0161 **DEMOCRITUS** Epigr.
0162 Julius **DIOCLES** Rhet.
0163 **DIODORUS** Epigr.
0164 **DIODORUS ZONAS** Rhet.
0165 **DIODORUS** Rhet.
0166 **DIODORUS** Gramm.
0167 **DIONYSIUS** Epigr.
0168 **DIONYSIUS** Epigr.
0169 **DIONYSIUS** Epigr.
0170 **DIONYSIUS** Epigr.
0171 **DIONYSIUS Sophista** <Epigr.>
0172 **DIOPHANES** Epigr.
0173 **DIOSCORIDES** Epigr.
0174 **DIOTIMUS** Epic.
0175 **DIOTIMUS** Epigr.
0176 **DIOTIMUS** Epigr.
0177 **DIPHILUS** Epigr.
0178 **DURIS** Epigr.
0179 **EPIGONUS** Epigr.
0180 **ERYCIUS** Epigr.
0181 **ETRUSCUS** Epigr.
0182 **EUENUS** Gramm.
0183 **EUENUS** Epigr.
0184 **EUGENES** Epigr.
0185 **EUODUS** Epigr.
0186 Marcus Cornelius **FRONTO** Rhet.
0187 **GAETULICUS II** Epigr.
0188 **GAETULICUS I** Epigr.
0189 Gaius Cornelius **GALLUS**
<Epigr.>
0190 **GAURADAS** Epigr.
0191 **GERMANICUS CAESAR**
<Epigr.>
0192 **GLAUCUS** Epigr.
0193 **GLAUCUS** Epigr.
0194 **GLYCON** Epigr.
0195 **HADRIANUS Imperator**
0196 **HECATAEUS** Epigr.
0197 **HEDYLE** Epigr.
0198 **HEDYLUS** Epigr.
0199 **BACCHYLIDES** Lyr.
0200 *MANTISSA PROVERBIORUM*
0201 **ISYLLUS** Lyr.
0202 **MACE(DONIUS)** Lyr.
0203 **LIMENIUS** Lyr.
0204 **ARISTONOUS** Lyr.
0205 **PHILODAMUS** Lyr.
0206 **THEOCLES** Lyr.
0207 **HERMOCLES** Lyr.
0208 **DOSIADAS** Lyr.
0209 **SELEUCUS** Lyr.
0210 **EUPHRONIUS** Lyr.
0211 **SIMIAS** Gramm.
0212 **PHILETAS** Eleg. et Gramm.
0213 **HERMESIANAX** Eleg.
0214 **PHANOCLES** Eleg.
0215 **ANTAGORAS** Epic.
0216 **ALEXANDER** Trag. et Lyr.

0217 **ANACREON Junior** Eleg.
0218 **NICAENETUS** Epic.
0219 **RHIANUS** Epic.
0220 **MOERO** Epic.
0221 **EUPHORION** Epic.
0222 **ERATOSTHENES** Philol. et
ERATOSTHENICA
0223 **AMYCLAS** Phil.
0224 **MENEDEMUS** Phil.
0225 **HESTIAEUS** Phil.
0226 **ERASTUS et CORISCUS** Phil.
0227 *ANONYMI CURETUM HYM-
NUS*
0228 *ANONYMI HYMNUS IN DAC-
TYLOS IDAEOS*
0229 **ASCLEPIADES** Phil.
0230 *LYRICA ADESPOTA* (CA)
0231 *ELEGIACA ADESPOTA* (CA)
0232 **ARCHILOCHUS** Iamb. et Eleg.
0233 **HIPPONAX** Iamb.
0234 *ELEGIACA ADESPOTA* (IEG)
0235 *IAMBICA ADESPOTA* (IEG)
0236 **ALCIBIADES** <Eleg.>
0237 **ANACREON** Lyr.
0238 **ANANIUS** Iamb.
0239 **ANTIMACHUS** Eleg. et Epic.
0240 **HERMOLOCHUS** Lyr.
0241 **ARISTOXENUS** <Comic.>
0242 **ASIUS** Epic. et Eleg.
0243 **CALLINUS** Eleg.
0244 **CLEOBULINA** Scriptor Aenigmatum
0245 **DEMODOCUS** Eleg.
0246 **DIONYSIUS** Eleg.
0247 **DIONYSIUS II** <Eleg.>
0248 **DIPHILUS** Epic. et Iamb.
0249 **ECHEMBROTUS** Lyr. et Eleg.
0250 **EUCLIDES** Comic. vel Iamb.
0251 **EUENUS** Eleg.
0252 **HERMIPPUS** Comic.
0253 **[HOMERUS]** <Epic.>
0254 **MELANTHIUS** Trag. et Eleg.
0255 **MIMNERMUS** Eleg.
0256 **PANARCES** Scriptor Aenigmatum
0257 **PHILISCUS** Rhet.
0258 **PIGRES** Eleg.
0259 **SCYTHINUS** Poet. Phil.
0260 **SEMONIDES** Eleg. et Iamb.
0261 **SIMONIDES** Lyr.
0262 **SOCRATES** Phil.
0263 **SOLON** Nomographus et Poeta
0264 **SUSARION** Comic.
0265 **TIMOCREON** Lyr.
0266 **TYRTAEUS** Eleg.
0267 **XENOPHANES** Poet. Phil.
0268 **MESOMEDES** Lyr.
0269 *NAUTARUM CANTIUNCULAE*
0270 **MENAECHMUS** Math. et Phil.
0271 *CONVENTUS AVIUM*
0272 *DE ARBORIBUS AVIBUSQUE
FABULAE*
0273 *SCOLIA ALPHABETICA*
0274 **SECUNDUS** Epigr.
0275 *PEIRAZOMENE*
0276 *CANTUS LUGUBRIS*
0277 *MONODIA*
0278 *PRAELUSIO MIMI*
0279 *DISCIPULORUM CANTIUN-
CULA*
0280 **ANDROMACHUS** Poet. Med.

0281 **MARCELLUS** Poet. Med.
0282 **ANONYMUS DE VIRIBUS HER-
BARUM**
0283 **HERACLIDES PONTICUS Junior** Gramm.
0284 Aelius **ARISTIDES** Rhet.
0285 **DINOSTRATUS** Math. et Phil.
0286 *CARMEN ASTROLOGICUM*
0288 **PISANDER** Epic.
0289 **AMMONIUS** Epigr.
0290 *ENCOMIUM DUCIS THEBAI-
DOS*
0291 **ALCMAN** Lyr.
0292 **STESICHORUS** Lyr.
0293 **IBYCUS** Lyr.
0294 **CORINNA** Lyr.
0295 *CARMINA POPULARIA* (PMG)
0296 *CARMINA CONVIVIALIA*
(PMG)
0297 *LYRICA ADESPOTA* (PMG)
0298 **EUMELUS** Epic.
0299 **TERPANDER** Lyr.
0300 *ACTA ALEXANDRINORUM*
0301 **THESPIS** Trag.
0302 **CHOERILUS** Trag.
0303 **PHRYNICHUS** Trag.
0304 *ACTA ET MARTYRIUM APOL-
LONII*
0305 **ARISTIAS** Trag.
0306 **ARISTARCHUS** Trag.
0307 **NEOPHRON** Trag.
0308 **ION** Poeta et Phil.
0309 **ACHAEUS** Trag.
0310 **CARCINUS** Trag.
0311 **IOPHON** Trag.
0312 **PHILOCLES** Trag.
0313 **THEOGNIS** Trag.
0314 **MORSIMUS** Trag.
0315 **STHENELUS** Trag.
0316 **XENOCLES** Trag.
0317 *ACTA JOANNIS*
0318 **AGATHON** Trag.
0319 **CRITIAS** Phil., Trag. et Eleg.
0320 **DIOGENES** Trag.
0321 **AESCHYLUS** Trag.
0322 **DICAEOGENES** Trag.
0323 **ANTIPHON** Trag.
0324 **PATROCLES** Trag.
0325 **ASTYDAMAS** Trag.
0326 **SOPHOCLES Junior** Trag.
0327 **CARCINUS Junior** Trag.
0328 **CHAEREMON** Trag.
0329 **THEODECTAS** Trag.
0330 **DIONYSIUS I** <Trag.>
0331 **<POLYIDUS>** Trag.
0332 **CLEAENETUS** Trag.
0333 **TIMOCLES** Trag.
0334 **DIOGENES** Phil. et Trag.
0335 **PHILISCUS** Trag.
0336 **CRATES** Poet. Phil.
0337 **PYTHON** Trag.
0338 **SOSIPHANES** Trag.
0339 **MOSCHION** Trag.
0340 **SOSITHEUS** Trag.
0341 **LYCOPHRON** Trag.
0342 **NICOMACHUS** Trag.
0343 **EZECHIEL** Trag.
0344 **MELANTHIUS** Trag.
0345 **APOLLONIDES** Trag.
0346 **POMPEIUS MACER** <Trag.>

0347 **SERAPION** Trag.
0348 **BIOTUS** Trag.
0349 **DEMONAX** <Trag.>
0350 <**DIONYSIUS**> Trag. vel Comic.
0351 **[HIPPOTHOON]** Trag.
0352 **ISIDORUS** Trag.
0353 <**SCLERIAS**> Trag.
0354 **ZENODOTUS** Trag.
0355 **ZOPYRUS** Trag.
0356 **EPAPHRODITUS** Gramm.
0357 **DIDYMUS** Scriptor De Mensuris
0358 **NICOMACHUS** Math.
0359 **ISIDORUS** Scriptor Hymnorum
0360 **ARMENIDAS** Hist.
0361 **CLEONIDES** Mus.
0362 *CARMINA DELPHIS INVENTA*
0363 Claudius **PTOLEMAEUS** Math.
0364 *DANAIS*
0365 **APOLLODORUS** Lyr.
0366 **LASUS** Lyr.
0367 **TYNNICHUS** Lyr.
0368 **CYDIAS** Lyr.
0369 **TELESILLA** Lyr.
0370 **LAMPROCLES** Lyr.
0371 **DIAGORAS** Lyr.
0372 **PRAXILLA** Lyr.
0373 **MELANIPPIDES** Lyr.
0374 **LICYMNIUS** Lyr.
0375 **CINESIAS** Lyr.
0376 **TIMOTHEUS** Lyr.
0377 **TELESTES** Lyr.
0378 **ARIPHRON** Lyr.
0379 **PHILOXENUS** Lyr.
0380 **PHILOXENUS** Lyr.
0381 **LYCOPHRONIDES** Lyr.
0382 **CASTORION** Lyr.
0383 **ALCAEUS** Lyr.
0384 *ACTA JUSTINI ET SEPTEM SODALIUM*
0385 **CASSIUS DIO** Hist.
0386 *CHILONIS EPISTULA*
0387 *SAPPHUS vel ALCAEI FRAGMENTA*
0388 *ACTA PAULI*
0389 *ACTA PETRI*
0390 *MARTYRIUM CARPI, PAPYLI ET AGATHONICAE*
0391 *ACTA SCILLITANORUM MARTYRUM*
0392 **ACUSILAUS** Hist.
0393 **PISANDER** Myth.
0394 **APOLLONIUS** Comic.
0395 **DIOPHANTUS** Comic.
0396 **EUPHANES** Comic.
0397 **PRONOMUS** Lyr.
0398 **SIMYLUS** Comic.
0399 **EUDOXUS** Comic.
0400 **ALCAEUS** Comic.
0401 **ALEXANDER** Comic.
0402 **ALEXIS** Comic.
0403 **AMIPSIAS** Comic.
0404 **AMPHIS** Comic.
0405 **ANAXANDRIDES** Comic.
0406 **ANAXILAS** Comic.
0407 **ANAXIPPUS** Comic.
0408 *COMICA ADESPOTA* (CAF)
0409 **ANTIDOTUS** Comic.
0410 **ANTIPHANES** Comic.
0411 **APOLLODORUS** Comic.

0412 **APOLLODORUS Carystius vel APOLLODORUS Gelous** Comic.
0413 **APOLLODORUS** Comic.
0414 **APOLLOPHANES** Comic.
0415 **ARAROS** Comic.
0416 **ARCHEDICUS** Comic.
0417 **ARCHIPPUS** Comic.
0418 **ARISTAGORAS** Comic.
0419 **ARISTOMENES** Comic.
0420 **ARISTONYMUS** Comic.
0421 **ARISTOPHON** Comic.
0422 **ATHENIO** Comic.
0423 **AUTOCRATES** Comic.
0424 **AXIONICUS** Comic.
0425 **BATO** Comic.
0426 **CALLIAS** Comic.
0427 <**CALLIPPUS**> Comic.
0428 **CANTHARUS** Comic.
0429 **CEPHISODORUS** Comic.
0430 **CHARICLIDES** Comic.
0431 **CHIONIDES** Comic.
0432 **CLEARCHUS** Comic.
0433 **CRATES** Comic.
0434 **CRATINUS** Comic.
0435 **CRATINUS Junior** Comic.
0436 **CRITO** Comic.
0437 **CROBYLUS** Comic.
0438 **DAMOXENUS** Comic.
0439 **DEMETRIUS** Comic.
0440 **DEMETRIUS Junior** Comic.
0441 **DEMONICUS** Comic.
0442 **DEXICRATES** Comic.
0443 **DIOCLES** Comic.
0444 **DIODORUS** Comic.
0445 **DIONYSIUS** Comic.
0446 **DIOXIPPUS** Comic.
0447 **DIPHILUS** Comic.
0448 **DROMO** Comic.
0449 **ECPHANTIDES** Comic.
0450 **EPHIPPUS** Comic.
0451 **EPICRATES** Comic.
0452 **EPIGENES** Comic.
0453 **EPILYCUS** Comic.
0454 **EPINICUS** Comic.
0455 **ERIPHUS** Comic.
0456 **EUANGELUS** Comic.
0457 **EUBULIDES** Comic.
0458 **EUBULUS** Comic.
0459 **EUNICUS** Comic.
0460 **EUPHRO** Comic.
0461 **EUPOLIS** Comic.
0462 **EUTHYCLES** Comic.
0463 **HEGEMON** Parodius
0464 **HEGESIPPUS** Comic.
0465 **HENIOCHUS** Comic.
0466 **HERACLIDES** Comic.
0467 **TIMOTHEUS** Trag.
0468 **HIPPARCHUS** Comic.
0469 **LAON** Comic.
0470 **LEUCO** Comic.
0471 **LYNCEUS** Comic.
0472 **LYSIPPUS** Comic.
0473 **MACHON** Comic.
0474 **MAGNES** Comic.
0475 **METAGENES** Comic.
0476 **MNESIMACHUS** Comic.
0477 **MYRTILUS** Comic.
0478 **NAUSICRATES** Comic.
0479 **NICO** Comic.

0480 **NICOCHARES** Comic.
0481 **NICOLAUS** Comic.
0482 **NICOMACHUS** Comic.
0483 **NICOPHON** Comic.
0484 **NICOSTRATUS** Comic.
0485 **OPHELIO** Comic.
0486 **PHERECRATES** Comic.
0487 **PHILEMON** Comic.
0488 **PHILEMON Junior** Comic.
0489 **PHILETAERUS** Comic.
0490 **PHILIPPIDES** Comic.
0491 **PHILISCUS** Comic.
0492 **PHILONIDES** Comic.
0493 **PHILOSTEPHANUS** Comic.
0494 **PHILYLLIUS** Comic.
0495 **PHOENICIDES** Comic.
0496 **PHRYNICHUS** Comic.
0497 **PLATO** Comic.
0498 **POLIOCHUS** Comic.
0499 **POLYZELUS** Comic.
0500 **POSIDIPPUS** Comic.
0501 **SANNYRION** Comic.
0502 **SOPHILUS** Comic.
0503 **SOSICRATES** Comic.
0504 **SOSIPATER** Comic.
0505 **SOTADES** Comic.
0506 **STEPHANUS** Comic.
0507 **STRATON** Comic.
0508 **STRATTIS** Comic.
0509 <**MYIA**> Phil.
0510 **TELECLIDES** Comic.
0511 **THEOGNETUS** Comic.
0512 **THEOPHILUS** Comic.
0513 **THEOPOMPUS** Comic.
0514 **THUGENIDES** Comic.
0515 **TIMOCLES** Comic.
0516 **TIMOSTRATUS** Comic.
0517 **TIMOTHEUS** Comic.
0518 **XENARCHUS** Comic.
0519 **XENO** Comic.
0520 **ARCESILAUS** Comic.
0521 **EPICHARMUS** Comic. et *PSEUDEPICHARMEA*
0522 **PISANDER** Epic.
0523 **MENECRATES** Comic.
0524 **SOPHRON** Mimogr.
0525 **PAUSANIAS** Perieg.
0526 Flavius **JOSEPHUS** Hist.
0527 *SEPTUAGINTA*
0528 **AËTIUS** Doxogr.
0529 **ARIUS DIDYMUS** Doxogr.
0530 **Pseudo-GALENUS** Med.
0531 **HERMIAS** Phil.
0532 **ACHILLES TATIUS** Scr. Erot.
0533 **CALLIMACHUS** Philol.
0534 **CALLISTHENES** Hist.
0535 **DEMADES** Orat. et Rhet.
0536 **EPHORUS** Hist.
0537 **EPICURUS** Phil.
0538 **HECATAEUS** Hist.
0539 **HELLANICUS** Hist.
0540 **LYSIAS** Orat.
0541 **MENANDER** Comic.
0542 Julius **POLLUX** Gramm.
0543 **POLYBIUS** Hist.
0544 **SEXTUS EMPIRICUS** Phil.
0545 Claudius **AELIANUS** Soph.
0546 **AELIANUS** Tact.
0547 **ANAXIMENES** Hist. et Rhet.

0548 **APOLLODORUS** Myth.
0549 **APOLLODORUS** Gramm.
0550 **APOLLONIUS** Geom.
0551 **APPIANUS** Hist.
0552 **ARCHIMEDES** Geom.
0553 **ARTEMIDORUS** Onir.
0554 **CHARITON** Scr. Erot.
0555 **CLEMENS ALEXANDRINUS** Theol.
0556 **ASCLEPIODOTUS** Tact.
0557 **EPICTETUS** Phil.
0558 *HELLENICA*
0559 **HERON** Mech.
0560 **[LONGINUS]** Rhet.
0561 **LONGUS** Scr. Erot.
0562 **MARCUS AURELIUS ANTONINUS Imperator** Phil.
0563 **MAXIMUS** Soph.
0564 **RUFUS** Med.
0565 **SORANUS** Med.
0566 **THEOPOMPUS** Hist.
0567 **HERACLEON** Gramm.
0568 **ANTIGONUS** Paradox.
0569 **APOLLONIUS** Paradox.
0570 **ARCHELAUS** Paradox.
0571 **ARISTOCLES** Paradox.
0572 **GAIUS** Scr. Eccl.
0574 **LYSIMACHUS** Hist.
0575 **<MOSCHION>** Gnom.
0576 **MUSAEUS** Epic.
0577 **NICOLAUS** Hist.
0578 **NYMPHODORUS** Hist.
0579 *ORPHICA*
0580 *PARADOXOGRAPHUS FLORENTINUS*
0581 *PARADOXOGRAPHUS PALATINUS*
0582 *PARADOXOGRAPHUS VATICANUS*
0583 **PHILOCHORUS** Hist.
0584 **PHILOSTEPHANUS** Hist.
0585 **Publius Aelius PHLEGON** Paradox.
0586 **POLEMON** Perieg.
0587 **SOTION** <Paradox.>
0588 **TROPHILUS** <Paradox.>
0589 *EPISTULAE PRIVATAE*
0590 **ZENODOTUS** Gramm.
0591 **ANTISTHENES** Rhet. et Phil.
0592 **HERMOGENES** Rhet.
0593 **GORGIAS** Rhet. et Soph.
0594 **ALEXANDER** Rhet. et Soph.
0595 **ZENO** Phil.
0596 **ZENOBIUS** Gramm.
0597 **ZENODORUS** Gramm.
0598 *RHETORICA ANONYMA*
0599 **ZENODORUS** Math.
0600 **ZENODOTUS** <Epigr.>
0601 **<ZALEUCUS Nomographus>** <Phil.>
0602 *COMICA ADESPOTA* (FCG)
0603 **SILENUS** Trag.
0604 **PTOLEMAEUS IV PHILOPATOR** Trag.
0605 **POLYBIUS** Rhet.
0606 **RUFUS** Soph.
0607 **Aelius THEON** Rhet.
0608 **SATYRUS** Biogr.
0609 **TRYPHON I** Gramm.
0610 **ALCIDAMAS** Rhet.

0611 **THEODORUS** Trag.
0612 **DIO CHRYSOSTOMUS** Soph.
0613 **<DEMETRIUS>** Rhet.
0614 **Valerius BABRIUS** Scr. Fab.
0615 **ASPASIUS** Phil.
0616 **POLYAENUS** Rhet.
0617 **ANAXIMENES** Phil.
0618 *ANTIGONI EPISTULA*
0619 **APOLLONIUS** Phil.
0620 **ARCHYTAS** Phil.
0621 **[ATH]ENODORUS** Trag.
0622 *CLEOBULI EPISTULA*
0623 *CRATETIS EPISTULAE*
0624 **DEMETRIUS** Phil. et Hist.
0625 **POLEMAEUS** Trag.
0626 **HERACLITUS** Phil.
0627 **HIPPOCRATES** Med. et *CORPUS HIPPOCRATICUM*
0628 **Gaius MUSONIUS RUFUS** Phil.
0629 **PERIANDER** <Phil.>
0630 **PHERECYDES** Phil. et Myth.
0631 **PITTACUS** <Lyr.>
0632 **<PYTHAGORAS>** Phil.
0633 **<LYSIS>** Phil.
0634 **XENOCRATES** Phil.
0635 **ZENO** Phil.
0636 *SOCRATIS EPISTULAE*
0637 *SOCRATICORUM EPISTULAE*
0638 **Flavius PHILOSTRATUS** Soph.
0639 **MENECRATES** Med.
0640 **ALCIPHRON** Rhet. et Soph.
0641 **XENOPHON** Scr. Erot.
0643 **ANONYMUS LONDINENSIS** Med.
0644 **ARISTOPHANES** Gramm.
0645 **JUSTINUS MARTYR** Apol.
0646 **Pseudo-JUSTINUS MARTYR**
0647 **TRIPHIODORUS** Epic. et Gramm.
0648 **ONASANDER** Tact.
0649 **LESBONAX** Rhet.
0650 **HERODAS** Mimogr.
0651 **ANTONINUS LIBERALIS** Myth.
0652 **PHILOSTRATUS Junior** Soph.
0653 **ARATUS** Epic. et Astron.
0654 **Lucius Annaeus CORNUTUS** Phil.
0655 **PARTHENIUS** Myth.
0656 **DIOSCORIDES PEDANIUS** Med.
0657 **CRATEUAS** Med.
0658 **HELIODORUS** Scr. Erot.
0659 *COMICA ADESPOTA* (Suppl. Com.)
0660 **APOLLONIUS** Med.
0661 **ARCHIGENES** Med.
0662 *COMICA ADESPOTA* (CGFPR)
0663 *PRAECEPTA SALUBRIA*
0664 **DIOCLES** Med.
0665 **ADRIANUS** Hist.
0666 **ADRIANUS** Rhet. et Soph.
0667 **MARCELLINUS I** Med.
0668 *AEGIMIUS*
0669 **ANTONIUS MUSA** Med.
0670 **AELIUS PUBLIUS JULIUS** Scr. Eccl.
0671 **PHILUMENUS** Med.
0672 **PRAXAGORAS** Med.
0673 **AESCHINES SOCRATICUS** Phil.
0674 **AELIUS PROMOTUS** Med.
0675 **AGATHINUS** Med.

0676 **AGLAÏS** Poet. Med.
0677 **ANDREAS** Med.
0678 **ANDRON** Med.
0679 **AESCHRION** Lyr.
0680 **APOLLONIUS** Med.
0681 **ASCLEPIADES Pharmacion** Med.
0682 **ATHENAEUS** Med.
0683 *AETHIOPIS*
0684 **CLEOPATRA VII PHILOPATOR** <Med.>
0685 **Titus Statilius CRITO** Med.
0686 **AETHLIUS** Hist.
0687 **AGACLYTUS** Hist.
0688 **AGATHOCLES** Hist.
0689 **DEMOSTHENES Philalethes** Med.
0690 **ERASISTRATUS** Med.
0691 *HARPOCRATIONIS EPISTULA*
0692 **HELIODORUS** Med.
0693 **ALBINUS** Phil.
0694 **HERACLIDES** Med.
0695 **ALCIMUS** Hist.
0696 *ALCMAEONIS*
0697 **Cornelius ALEXANDER** Polyhist.
0698 **ALEXANDER** Rhet.
0699 **ALEXION** Gramm.
0700 **APOLLODORUS** Trag.
0701 **MNESITHEUS** Med.
0702 **MNESITHEUS** Med.
0703 **NUMENIUS** Poet. Didac.
0704 **NUMENIUS** Med.
0705 **ANONYMUS SENEX** Med.
0706 **PHILO** Med.
0707 **ALEXIS** Hist.
0708 **<AMMONIUS>** Gramm.
0709 **AMMONIUS** Hist.
0710 *AMPHIARAI EXILIUM* (?)
0711 **AMPHITHEUS** (?) Hist.
0712 **AMYNTAS** Hist.
0713 **ANAXAGORAS** Phil.
0714 **ANAXARCHUS** Phil.
0715 **PAULUS** Med.
0716 **EROTIANUS** Gramm. et Med.
0717 **HYPSICLES** Math. et Astron.
0718 **AËTIUS** Med.
0719 **ARETAEUS** Med.
0720 **HARMODIUS** Trag.
0721 **ANONYMI MEDICI**
0722 **ORIBASIUS** Med.
0723 **LEO** Phil.
0724 **STEPHANUS** Med. et Phil.
0725 **ANAXIMANDER** Phil.
0726 **PALLADIUS** Med.
0727 **JOANNES** Med.
0728 **THEOPHILUS Protospatharius, DAMASCIUS et STEPHANUS Atheniensis** Med.
0729 **THEOPHILUS Protospatharius** Med.
0730 **MELETIUS** Med.
0731 **ADAMANTIUS Judaeus** Med.
0732 **ALEXANDER** Phil.
0733 **CASSIUS Iatrosophista** Med.
0734 **<LUCAS Apostolus>** Med.
0735 **EUDEMUS** Med.
0736 **STEPHANUS** Med.
0737 **JULIANUS** Scriptor Legis De Medicis
0738 *HIPPIATRICA*
0739 **APOLLONIUS** Med.

0740 *JUSJURANDUM MEDICUM*
0741 APOLLONIUS Med.
0742 *HYMNI ANONYMI*
0743 NEMESIUS Theol.
0744 ALEXANDER Med.
0745 HIEROPHILUS Soph. et Phil.
0746 THEOPHILUS Protospatharius et STEPHANUS Atheniensis Med.
0747 APOLLONIUS Archistrator Med.
0748 SEVERUS Iatrosophista Med.
0749 ANTYLLUS Med.
0750 HELIODORUS Trag.
0751 Pseudo-HIPPOCRATES Med.
0752 EUTECNIUS Soph.
0753 AENEAS Med.
0754 ABASCANTUS Med.
0755 ACACIUS Med.
0756 ACHILLAS Med.
0757 ACHOLIUS Med.
0758 AMARANTUS Gramm.
0759 ANTHUS Med.
0760 APHRODISEUS Med.
0761 AGAPETUS Med.
0762 AGATHOCLES Med.
0763 Julius AGRIPPA Med.
0764 ALCAMENES Med.
0765 ALCIMION Med.
0766 ALCMAEON Phil.
0767 ALEXANDER Philalethes Med.
0768 AMMONIUS Lithotomus Med.
0769 APION Med.
0770 AMYTHAON Med.
0771 AMPHION Med.
0772 ANDROMACHUS Minor Med.
0773 ANDRONICUS Med.
0774 AXIORIUS Med.
0775 ANTHAEUS Med.
0776 ANTIGONUS Med.
0777 ANTIOCHUS Philometor <Med.>
0778 ANTIOCHUS Med.
0779 ANTIPATER Med.
0780 ANTIPHANES Med.
0781 Pomponius BASSUS <Med.>
0782 APOLLONIUS Med.
0783 APHRODAS Med.
0784 APHTHONIUS Soph.
0785 APOLLINARIUS Med.
0786 APOLLODORUS Med.
0787 BLASTUS Med.
0788 CHARICLES Med.
0789 Claudius APOLLONIUS Med.
0790 APOLLONIUS MYS Med.
0791 APOLLONIUS Ther Med.
0792 APOLLONIUS Med.
0793 DIONYSIUS Med.
0794 APOLLOPHANES Med.
0795 AQUILA SECUNDILLA Med.
0796 ARCHIBIUS Med.
0797 GALLUS Med.
0798 ARISTARCHUS Med.
0799 ANONYMUS NAUCRATITES Med.
0800 ANONYMUS OLYMPIONICES Med.
0801 ARISTION Med.
0802 ARISTOCLES Med.
0803 ARISTOCRATES Gramm.
0804 Marcus GALLUS Med.
0805 MNESITHEUS Med.

0806 ARISTOXENUS Med.
0807 ARRHABIANUS Med.
0808 MUSA Med.
0809 ARTEMIDORUS CAPITO Med.
0810 APOLLONIUS et ALCIMION Med.
0811 ASCLEPIADES Med.
0812 ASCLEPIUS Med.
0813 ASPASIUS Med.
0814 ASTERIUS Med.
0815 ATIMETRUS Med.
0816 THEUDO[TUS] Trag.
0817 APOLLONIUS Organicus Med.
0818 AZANITES Med.
0819 BACCHIUS Med.
0820 BAPHULLUS vel HERAS Med.
0821 CLEOPHANTUS Med.
0822 GAIUS Med.
0823 ALCIMION vel NICOMACHUS Med.
0824 CALLINICUS Med.
0825 MELITO Trag.
0826 CASTUS Med.
0827 CEPHISOPHON Med.
0828 CHARITON Med.
0829 CHARIXENES Med.
0830 CHRYSERMUS Med.
0831 CHRYSIPPUS Med.
0832 ANTIPATER et CLEOPHAN-TUS Med.
0833 ANAXION Trag.
0834 Flavius CLEMENS <Med.>
0835 CLEOBULUS Med.
0836 CLEON Med.
0837 CLEONIACUS Med.
0838 CODAMUS vel NICOMEDES Rex Bithyniae <Med.>
0839 CODIUS TUCUS Med.
0840 CONSTANTINUS Med.
0841 CORNELIUS Med.
0842 CRATERUS Med.
0843 CRATIPPUS Med.
0844 CRISPUS Med.
0845 CTESIAS Hist. et Med.
0846 CTESIPHON Med.
0847 CYRUS Med.
0848 Servilius DAMOCRATES Poet. Med.
0849 Claudius DAMONICUS Med.
0850 ANTONIUS Med.
0851 DARIUS Med.
0852 ANTYLLUS et HELIODORUS Med.
0853 ANTYLLUS et POSIDONIUS Med.
0854 DIAGORAS Med.
0855 DIDYMUS Med.
0856 DIEUCHES Med.
0857 DIODORUS Med.
0858 APELLES Med.
0859 DIOGENES Med.
0860 DIOMEDES Med.
0861 DION Med.
0862 DIONYSIUS CYRTUS Med.
0863 DIONYSIUS Empiricus Med.
0864 DIONYSIUS Med.
0865 DIONYSIUS Med.
0866 APHRODAS et MOSCHION Med.
0867 DIOPHANTUS Med.

0868 DIOSCORUS Med.
0869 ARCHIGENES et POSIDONIUS Med.
0870 DIOSCORIDES Phacas Med.
0871 ARISTARCHUS Med.
0872 DIPHILUS Med.
0873 DOMITIUS NIGRINUS Med.
0874 DOROTHEUS Med.
0875 DOSITHEUS Med.
0876 PHRYNICHUS II Trag.
0877 DELETIUS Med.
0878 Aristus ARISTARCHUS Med.
0879 ASCLEPIUS et MACHAON Med.
0880 EPIDAURUS Med.
0881 EPIGONUS Med.
0882 CRITO et HERODOTUS Med.
0883 HERACLAS Med.
0884 DIOCLES Med.
0885 Pseudo-ESDRAS
0886 EUANGELUS Med.
0887 EUBULUS Med.
0888 EUDEMUS Poet. Med.
0889 TIMESITHEUS Trag.
0890 EUMERUS Med.
0891 EUGENIUS Med.
0892 EUGERASIA Med.
0893 EUNOMUS Med.
0894 EUPHRANOR Med.
0895 EURYPHON Med.
0896 EUSCHEMUS Med.
0897 EUTHYDEMUS Med.
0898 EUTONIUS Med.
0899 EUTYCHIANUS Med.
0900 CLEOMENES Lyr.
0901 FLAVIANUS Med.
0902 FLAVIUS Med.
0903 EUDEMUS Senior Med.
0904 GAIUS Med.
0905 Aelius GALLUS Med.
0906 GEMELLUS Med.
0907 GENNADIUS Med.
0908 GLAUCIAS Med.
0909 HALIEUS Med.
0910 HERODOTUS et PHILUMENUS Med.
0911 GLYTUS Med.
0912 HARPALUS Med.
0913 HARPOCRATION Med.
0914 HARPOCRAS Med.
0915 HERACLIDES Med.
0916 HERACLIDES Med.
0917 HERAS Med.
0918 LAMYNTHIUS Lyr.
0919 HERMIAS Med.
0920 [MAIA] Med.
0921 HERMOGENES Med.
0922 EPIGONUS vel HERMON Med.
0923 HERMOPHILUS Med.
0924 ORIGENIA Med.
0925 THAMYRAS Med.
0926 HERODOTUS Med.
0927 HERON Med.
0928 HEROPHILUS Med.
0929 HICESIUS Med.
0930 HIERAX Med.
0931 ANTONINUS Med.
0932 HYBRISTUS Med.
0933 HYGIENUS Med.
0934 JACOBUS Psychrestus Med.

1132 **ANONYMUS ALEXANDRI** Phil.
1133 **ANONYMUS DIODORI** Phil.
1134 **ANONYMUS IAMBLICHI** Phil.
1135 **ANONYMUS PHOTII** Phil.
1136 **ANONYMUS PRESBYTER** Scr. Eccl.
1137 **ANONYMUS PYTHAGOREUS** Astrol.
1138 **LYCON** Phil.
1139 **ANONYMI HISTORICI** (FGrH)
1140 **ANTICLIDES** Hist.
1141 **ANTIMACHUS** Epic.
1142 **ANTIGONUS** Astrol.
1143 **ANTIOCHUS** Phil.
1144 **ANTIOCHUS** Astrol.
1145 **ANTIOCHUS** Hist.
1146 **ANTIPATER** Phil.
1147 **ANTIPHON** Soph.
1148 **ANTONIUS DIOGENES** Scr. Erot.
1149 *ANTONINI PII IMPERATORIS EPISTULA*
1150 **APHAREUS** Rhet.
1151 **APHRODISIUS-EUPHEMIUS** Hist.
1152 **APION** Gramm.
1153 *APOCALYPSIS ADAM*
1154 *APOCALYPSIS BARUCH*
1155 *APOCALYPSIS SYRIACA BARUCHI*
1156 *APOCALYPSIS ELIAE*
1157 *APOCALYPSIS ESDRAE*
1158 *APOCALYPSIS JOANNIS*
1159 *APOCALYPSIS PETRI*
1160 *APOCALYPSIS SOPHONIAE*
1161 *APOCRYPHON EZECHIEL*
1162 **APOLLAS** Hist.
1163 Claudius **APOLLINARIUS** Apol.
1164 **APOLLODORUS** Hist.
1165 **APOLLODORUS** Mech.
1166 **APOLLODORUS** Phil.
1167 **APOLLONIUS** Biogr.
1168 **APOLLONIUS** Soph.
1169 **APOLLONIUS** Hist.
1170 **APOLLONIUS** Hist.
1171 **APOLLONIUS** Scr. Eccl.
1172 **ARCESILAUS** Phil.
1173 **ARCHEDEMUS** Phil.
1174 **ARCHEMACHUS** Hist.
1175 **ARCHESTRATUS** Parodius
1176 **ARCHYTAS** Epic.
1177 Pseudo-**ARCHYTAS** Phil.
1178 <**ARESAS**> Phil.
1179 <**ARIMNESTUS**> Phil.
1180 <**ARISTAEUS**> Phil.
1181 **ARISTARCHUS** Astron.
1182 [**ARISTEAS**] Epic.
1183 *ARISTEAE EPISTULA*
1184 **ARISTIDES** Apol.
1185 **ARISTIDES** Hist.
1186 **ARISTOBULUS Judaeus** Phil.
1187 **ARISTOBULUS** Hist.
1188 **ARISTOCLES** Phil.
1189 **ARISTOCRATES** Hist.
1190 **ARISTAGORAS** Hist.
1191 <**ARISTOMBROTUS**> Phil.
1192 **ARISTON** Phil.
1193 **ARISTON** Phil.
1194 **ARISTONICUS** Gramm.

1195 **ARISTONYMUS** Gnom.
1196 **ARISTOPHANES** Hist.
1197 **ARTEMON** Gramm.
1198 **ASCLEPIADES** Hist.
1199 **ASCLEPIADES** Hist. et Gramm.
1200 **ASCLEPIADES** Myth.
1201 *ASSUMPTIO MOSIS*
1202 <**ATHAMAS**> Phil.
1203 *PAEANES* (CA)
1204 **ATHENAEUS** Mech.
1205 **ATHENAGORAS** Apol.
1206 **ATHENODORUS** Phil.
1207 **ATTALUS** Math. et Astron.
1208 **ATTICUS** Phil.
1209 **AUTOCLIDES** Hist.
1210 **AUTOLYCUS** Astron.
1211 **BALAGRUS** Hist.
1212 *ATRIDARUM REDITUS*
1213 **Julia BALBILLA** Lyr.
1214 **BARDESANES** Gnost.
1215 **BALBILLUS** Astrol.
1216 *BARNABAE EPISTULA*
1217 **BASILIDES** Gnost.
1218 **BASILIS** Hist.
1219 **BATO** Hist. et Rhet.
1220 *BATRACHOMYOMACHIA*
1221 **APOLLINARIUS** Astrol.
1222 **BEROS(S)US** Hist. et Astrol.
1223 **BIAS** <Phil.>
1224 **BION** Phil.
1225 **BION** Hist.
1226 **BITON** Mech.
1227 **BLAESUS** Comic.
1228 [**BOEO**] Epic.
1229 [**BOEUS**] Epic.
1230 <**BROTINUS**> Phil.
1231 <**BRYSON**> Phil.
1232 <**BUTHERUS**> Phil.
1233 **CAECILIUS** Rhet.
1234 Pseudo-**CAECILIUS** Rhet.
1235 **CALLIAS** Hist.
1236 **CALLICRATES-MENECLES** Perieg.
1237 <**CALLICRATIDAS**> Phil.
1238 **CALLICRATES** Astrol.
1239 **Domitius CALLISTRATUS** Hist.
1240 **CALLIXENUS** Hist.
1241 *CARMEN NAUPACTIUM*
1242 *CANON LIBRORUM*
1243 *ODAE SALOMONIS*
1244 **CARNEISCUS** Phil.
1245 **CARYSTIUS** Hist.
1246 **CASTOR** Rhet.
1247 <**CEBES**> Phil.
1248 **CELSUS** Phil.
1249 **CEPHALION** Hist. et Rhet.
1250 **CERCIDAS** Iamb.
1251 **CHAMAELEON** Phil.
1252 *CERTAMEN HOMERI ET HESIODI*
1253 **CHAERIS** Gramm.
1254 **CHARAX** Hist.
1255 **CHARES** Hist.
1256 **CHARES** Gnom.
1257 **CHARINUS** Choliamb.
1258 **CHARON** Hist.
1259 <**CHARONDAS Nomographus**> <Phil.>
1260 **CHERSIAS** Epic.

1261 **CHILON** <Phil.>
1262 **CHOERILUS** Epic.
1263 **CHOERILUS** Epic.
1264 **CHRYSIPPUS** Phil.
1265 **CHRYSIPPUS** Scriptor Rei Coquinariae
1266 **TYRANNION** Gramm.
1267 *CHRISTI EPISTULA*
1268 **CLAUDIUS** Hist.
1269 **CLEANTHES** Phil.
1270 **CLEARCHUS** Phil.
1271 **CLEMENS ROMANUS** Theol. et *CLEMENTINA*
1272 **CLEOMEDES** Astron.
1273 **CLEON** Eleg.
1274 **CLEOBULUS** Lyr. et Epigr.
1275 **CLEOSTRATUS** Poet. Phil.
1276 **CLIDEMUS** Hist.
1277 <**CLINIAS**> Phil.
1278 **CLITARCHUS** Gnom.
1279 **CLITARCHUS** Hist.
1280 **CLITOMACHUS** Phil.
1281 [**CLITOPHON**] Hist.
1282 **CLYTUS** Hist.
1283 **COLOTES** Phil.
1284 **COMARCHUS** Hist.
1285 **CONON** Hist.
1286 *CORPUS HERMETICUM*
1287 **CRANTOR** Phil.
1288 **CRATERUS** Hist.
1289 **CRATES** Hist.
1290 **CRATES** Gramm.
1291 **CREOPHYLUS** Hist.
1292 **CRITO** Phil.
1293 **CRINIS** Phil.
1294 **CRITOLAUS** Phil.
1295 **CRITODEMUS** Astrol.
1296 *CYPRIA*
1297 **DAMIPPUS** Phil.
1298 *DEMETRII PHALEREI EPISTULA*
1299 **DEMETRIUS** Hist.
1300 **DEMETRIUS LACON** Phil.
1301 **DEMETRIUS** Poet. Phil.
1302 **DEMETRIUS** Rhet.
1303 **DEMOCHARES** Orat. et Hist.
1304 **DEMOCRITUS** Phil.
1305 **DEMOCRITUS** Hist.
1306 **BOLUS** Phil.
1307 **DEMON** Hist.
1308 **DEMOSTHENES** Epic.
1309 *DIALEXEIS* (Δισσοὶ λόγοι)
1310 **DICTYS** Hist.
1311 *DIDACHE XII APOSTOLORUM*
1312 **DIDYMUS** Gramm.
1313 **DIEUCHIDAS** Hist.
1314 **DINIAS** Hist.
1315 **DINOLOCHUS** Comic.
1316 **DINON** Hist.
1317 **DIOCLES** Math.
1318 **DIODORUS** Rhet.
1319 **DIOGENES** Phil.
1320 **DIOGENES** Phil.
1321 **DIOGENES** Phil.
1322 **DIOGENIANUS** Phil.
1323 **Aelius DIONYSIUS** Attic.
1324 **DIONYSIUS** Hist.
1325 *DIOGENIS SINOPENSIS EPISTULAE*

1326 **DIONYSIUS** Epic.
1327 *DIONIS EPISTULAE*
1328 **DIONYSIUS** Hist.
1329 **DIONYSIUS** Scr. Eccl.
1330 **DIUS** Hist.
1331 **DIONYSIUS** ὁ Κυκλογράφος Hist.
1332 <**DIOTOGENES**> Phil.
1333 **CARNEADES** Phil.
1334 **DIUS** Phil.
1335 **DORION** Scr. Rerum Nat.
1336 **DOROTHEUS** Hist.
1337 **DOROTHEUS** Astrol.
1338 **DOSIADAS** Hist.
1339 **DURIS** Hist.
1340 <**ECCELUS**> Phil.
1341 <**ECPHANTUS**> Phil.
1342 **EMPEDOCLES** Poet. Phil.
1343 **EPARCHIDES** Hist.
1344 *EPICA ADESPOTA* (CA)
1345 *EPICA INCERTA* (CA)
1346 **EPHRAEM** Scr. Eccl.
1347 **EPIMENIDES** Phil.
1348 **EPIPHANES** Gnost.
1349 *EPISTULA A MARTYRIBUS LUGDUNENSIBUS*
1350 *EPISTULA AD DIOGNETUM*
1351 *EPIGONI*
1352 *EPISTULA ECCLESIARUM APUD LUGDUNUM ET VIENNAM*
1353 *EPITAPHIUM ABERCII*
1354 **ERGIAS** Hist.
1355 **ERINNA** Lyr.
1356 *ESDRAS V/VI*
1357 **EUDEMUS** Phil.
1358 **EUDOXUS** Astron.
1359 **PANAETIUS** Phil.
1360 <**EURYPHAMUS**> Phil.
1361 **EUMEDES** Comic.
1362 <**EURYTUS**> Phil.
1363 **EURYTUS** Lyr.
1364 *EVANGELIUM AEGYPTIUM*
1365 **MELAMPUS** Scriptor De Divinatione
1366 *EVANGELIUM BARTHOLOMAEI*
1367 *EURIPIDIS EPISTULAE*
1368 *EVANGELIUM EBIONITUM*
1369 *EVANGELIUM MARIAE*
1370 *EVANGELIUM NAASSENUM*
1371 *EVANGELIUM PETRI*
1372 *EVANGELIUM EVAE*
1373 *EVANGELIUM PHILIPPI*
1374 *EVANGELIUM SECUNDUM HEBRAEOS*
1375 *EVANGELIUM THOMAE*
1376 **EUDEMUS** Rhet.
1377 **FAVORINUS** Phil. et Rhet.
1378 *FRAGMENTA EVANGELIORUM INCERTORUM*
1379 *FRAGMENTUM ALCHEMICUM*
1380 **HERMAGORAS Minor** Rhet.
1381 *FRAGMENTUM SYNODICAE EPISTULAE CONCILII CAESARIENSIS*
1382 *FRAGMENTUM TELIAMBICUM*
1383 **GEMINUS** Astron.
1384 **PHILEMON III** Comic.

1385 **GLAUCUS** Hist.
1386 *HISTORIA ALEXANDRI MAGNI*
1387 **(H)AGIAS-DERCYLUS** Hist.
1388 **HARMODIUS** Hist.
1389 **HARPOCRATION** Gramm.
1390 **HECATAEUS** Hist.
1391 **HEGEMON** Epic.
1392 **HEGESANDER** Hist.
1393 **HEGESIANAX** Epic. et Astron.
1394 **HEGESIAS** Hist. et Orat.
1395 **HEGESINUS** Epic.
1396 **HEGESIPPUS** Epigr.
1397 **HEGESIPPUS** Hist.
1398 **HEGESIPPUS** Scr. Eccl.
1399 **PAMPHILUS** Trag.
1400 **HELIODORUS** Perieg.
1401 **HELLADIUS** Epigr.
1402 **HEPHAESTION** Gramm.
1403 **HERACLEON** Gnost.
1404 **APOLLONIUS** Gramm.
1405 **HERACLIDES Criticus** Perieg.
1406 **HERACLIDES** Hist.
1407 **HERACLIDES LEMBUS** Hist.
1408 **HERACLIDES** Gramm.
1409 **HERACLIDES PONTICUS** Phil.
1410 **HERACLIDES** Epigr.
1411 *HERACLITI EPHESII EPISTULAE*
1412 *Pseudo-HERACLITI EPISTULAE*
1413 **HERACLITUS** Paradox.
1414 **HERACLITUS** Phil.
1415 **HERACLITUS** Epigr.
1416 **(H)EREN(N)IUS PHILO** Hist. et Gramm.
1417 **HERMAGORAS** Rhet.
1418 **HERMAPION** Hist.
1419 **HERMAS** Scr. Eccl.
1420 **HERMIAS** Iamb.
1421 **HERMIPPUS** Gramm. et Hist.
1422 **HERMOCREON** Epigr.
1423 **HERMODORUS** Epigr.
1424 **HERMOGENES** Hist.
1425 **HERMONAX** Epic.
1426 **HERODES ATTICUS** Soph.
1427 **HERODORUS** Hist.
1428 **HESTIAEUS** Hist.
1429 **HIEROCLES** Phil.
1430 **HIERONYMUS** Phil.
1431 **HIPPARCHUS** Astron. et Geogr.
1432 <**HIPPARCHUS**> Phil.
1433 **HIPPARCHUS** <Epigr.>
1434 **HIPPIAS** Soph.
1435 **HIPPIAS** Hist.
1436 <**HIPPODAMUS**> Phil.
1437 **HIPPON** Phil.
1438 **HIPPYS** Hist.
1439 **HERMARCHUS** Phil.
1440 **HONESTUS** Epigr.
1441 **IAMBLICHUS** Scr. Erot.
1442 **IDOMENEUS** Hist.
1443 **IGNATIUS** Scr. Eccl.
1444 *ILIAS PARVA*
1445 *ILIU PERSIS*
1446 **ION** Eleg.
1447 **IRENAEUS** Theol.
1448 **ISIDORUS** Gnost.
1449 **ISIDORUS** Epigr.

1450 **ISTER** Hist.
1451 *JOSEPHUS ET ASENETH*
1452 **JUBA II Rex Mauretaniae** <Hist.>
1453 **JUNCUS** Phil.
1454 **JUSTINUS** Gnost.
1455 *KERYGMA PETRI*
1456 **LACO** Epigr.
1457 **Julius LEONIDAS** Math. et Astrol.
1458 **LEONIDAS** Epigr.
1459 **LEPIDUS** Hist.
1460 **LESBONAX** Gramm.
1461 **LEUCIPPUS** Phil.
1462 *LIBER ELDAD ET MODAD*
1463 *LIBER ENOCH*
1464 *LIBER JUBILAEORUM*
1465 [**LINUS**] Epic.
1466 **LOLLIANUS** Scr. Erot.
1467 **LOLLIANUS** Soph.
1468 **LUCILLIUS** Epigr.
1469 **LYCEAS** Hist.
1470 **LYCUS** Hist.
1471 *LYRICA ADESPOTA* (SLG)
1472 **LYSISTRATUS** Epigr.
1473 **MACEDONIUS I** Epigr.
1474 **Quintus MAECIUS** Epigr.
1475 **MAIISTAS** Epic.
1476 **MAMERCUS** Eleg.
1477 **MANETHO** Hist.
1478 **Pseudo-MANETHO** Hist.
1479 *MARCI AURELII EPISTULA*
1480 **MARIA JUDAEA** Alchem.
1481 **MARSYAS Pellaeus et MARSYAS Philippeus** Hist.
1482 *CYRANIDES*
1483 *MARTYRIUM ET ASCENSIO ISAIAE*
1484 *MARTYRIUM POLYCARPI*
1485 *MARTYRIUM PTOLEMAEI ET LUCII*
1486 **MATRON** Parodius
1487 **MAXIMUS** Astrol.
1488 **MAXIMUS** Theol.
1489 **MEGASTHENES** Hist.
1490 <**MEGILLUS**> Phil.
1491 **MELANTHIUS** Hist.
1492 **MELEAGER** Epigr.
1493 **MELINNO** Lyr.
1494 **MELISSUS** Phil.
1495 **MELITO** Apol.
1496 **MEMNON** Hist.
1497 **MENAECHMUS** Hist.
1498 **MENANDER** Hist.
1499 **MENECLES** Hist.
1500 **MENECRATES** Poet. Phil.
1501 **MENECRATES** Epigr.
1502 **MENECRATES** Epigr.
1503 **MENECRATES** Hist.
1504 **MENELAUS** Epic.
1505 **MENESTHENES** Hist.
1506 **MENODOTUS** Hist.
1507 <**METOPUS**> Phil.
1508 **METRODORUS** Phil.
1509 <**MILON**> <Phil.>
1510 *MIMI ANONYMI*
1511 **MIMNERMUS** Trag.
1512 *MINYAS*
1513 **MNASALCES** Epigr.
1514 **MNASEAS** Perieg.
1515 **MOERIS** Attic.

1516 **MOLPIS** Hist.
1517 **MOSCHION** Hist. et Paradox.
1518 Quintus Mucius **SCAEVOLA**
Epigr.
1519 **MUNDUS MUNATIUS** Epigr.
1520 **MUSICIUS** Epigr.
1521 *VITA ET SENTENTIAE SE-*
CUNDI
1522 **MYRINUS** Epigr.
1523 **MYRON** Hist.
1524 **NAUMACHIUS** Epic.
1525 **NEANTHES** Hist.
1526 **NEOPTOLEMUS** Gramm.
1527 **NEPUALIUS** Phil.
1528 **NESTOR** Epic.
1529 **NICANDER** Gramm.
1530 **NICANOR** Gramm.
1531 **NICARCHUS I** Epigr.
1532 **NICARCHUS II** Epigr.
1533 **NICIAS** Epigr.
1534 **NICOCLES** Hist.
1535 **NICOCRATES** Hist.
1536 **NICODEMUS** Epigr.
1537 **NICOMACHUS** Epigr.
1538 **NICOMACHUS** Hist.
1539 **NICOSTRATUS** Soph.
1540 **NOSSIS** Epigr.
1541 *NOSTOI*
1542 **NUMENIUS** Phil.
1543 **NUMENIUS** Epigr.
1544 **NYMPHIS** Hist.
1545 **OCELLUS** Phil.
1546 *OECHALIAE HALOSIS*
1547 *OEDIPODEA*
1548 **OENOMAUS** Phil.
1549 **<ONATAS>** Phil.
1550 *ORACULA CHALDAICA*
1551 *ORACULA SIBYLLINA*
1552 *ORATIO JOSEPHI*
1553 **<PALAEPHATUS>** Myth.
1554 **PAMPHILUS** Epigr.
1555 **PANCRATES** Epic.
1556 **PANCRATES** Epigr.
1557 **PANYASSIS** Epic.
1558 **PAPIAS** Scr. Eccl.
1559 *BUCOLICUM*
1560 *MATTHIAE TRADITIONES*
1561 **PARDALAS** Epigr.
1562 **PARMENIDES** Poet. Phil.
1563 **PARMENION** Epigr.
1564 **PARMENISCUS** Gramm.
1565 **[PARMENO]** Epigr.
1566 **PARMENO** Iamb.
1567 **PARRHASIUS** Epigr.
1568 **PARTHAX** Hist.
1569 **PAUSANIAS** Attic.
1570 *EPITAPHIUM PECTORII*
1571 **<PEMPELUS>** Phil.
1572 **<PERICTIONE>** Phil.
1573 **PERITAS** Epigr.
1574 **PERSAEUS** Phil.
1575 **PERSES** Epigr.
1576 **PHAEDIMUS** <Epic.>
1577 **PHAEDIMUS** Epigr.
1578 **PHAENIAS** Phil.
1579 **PHAËNNUS** Epigr.
1580 **PHAESTUS** Epic.
1581 **PHALAECUS** Epigr.
1582 **PHANIAS** Gramm.

1583 **PHANODEMUS** Hist.
1584 **PHERECYDES** Hist.
1585 *PHERECYDIS EPISTULA*
1586 **PHILAENIS** Scriptor De Aphrodisiis
1587 **PHILIADES** Eleg.
1588 **PHILICUS** Lyr.
1589 **PHILIPPUS** Epigr.
1590 **PHILIPPUS** Hist.
1591 **PHILISTUS** Hist.
1592 **PHILITAS** Epigr.
1593 **PHILO** <Epigr.>
1594 **PHILO Judaeus Senior** Epic.
1595 **PHILODEMUS** Phil.
1596 **PHILOLAUS** Phil.
1597 **<TELAUGES>** Phil.
1598 **PHILOMNESTUS** Hist.
1599 **PHILO** Mech.
1600 **PHILOSTRATUS Major** Soph.
1601 **PHILOXENUS** Epigr.
1602 **PHILOXENUS** Gramm.
1603 **<PHINTYS>** Phil.
1604 **PHOCYLIDES** Eleg. et Gnom.
1605 **Pseudo-PHOCYLIDES** Gnom.
1606 **PHOENIX** Iamb.
1607 *PHORONIS*
1608 **PHRYNICHUS** Attic.
1609 **PHYLARCHUS** Hist.
1610 **PINYTUS** Epigr.
1611 **TYRANNION Junior** Gramm.
1612 **PISO** Epigr.
1613 *PITTACI EPISTULA*
1614 **PLATO Junior** Epigr.
1615 **PLATONIUS** Gramm.
1616 **POLEMON I** <Epigr.>
1617 **Marcus Antonius POLEMON**
Soph.
1618 **POLLIANUS** Epigr.
1619 **POLUS LUCANUS** Phil.
1620 **Julius POLYAENUS** Epigr.
1621 **POLYAENUS** Epigr.
1622 **POLYCARPUS** Scr. Eccl.
1623 **POLYCHARMUS** Hist.
1624 **POLYCHARMUS** Hist.
1625 **POLYCLITUS** Phil.
1626 **POLYCRATES** Scr. Eccl.
1627 **POLYCRATES** Hist.
1628 **POLYSTRATUS** Epigr.
1629 **POLYSTRATUS** Phil.
1630 **POLYZELUS** Hist.
1631 **POMPEIUS MACER Junior** Epigr.
1632 **POSIDIPPUS** Epigr.
1633 **PRAXITELES** <Epigr.>
1634 **PRODICUS** Soph.
1635 **PROTAGORAS** Soph.
1636 **PROTAGORIDES** Hist.
1637 *PROTEVANGELIUM JACOBI*
1638 **PROXENUS** Hist.
1639 **PSEUDO-AUCTORES HEL-**
LENISTAE (PsVTGr)
1640 **PTOLEMAEUS** Epigr.
1641 **PTOLEMAEUS** Gnost.
1642 **Pseudo-PTOLEMAEUS**
1643 **PTOLEMAEUS** Gramm.
1644 **PTOLEMAEUS** Phil. et Gramm.
1645 **PTOLEMAEUS VIII EUERGE-**
TES II <Hist.>
1646 **PTOLEMAEUS** Hist.
1647 **PTOLEMAEUS** Hist.

1648 **PYRGION** Hist.
1649 **PYTHAENETUS** Hist.
1650 **PYTHEAS** Perieg.
1651 **PYTHERMUS** Hist.
1652 **QUADRATUS** Apol.
1653 **RARUS** Epigr.
1654 **RHINTHON** Comic.
1655 **RHODO** Scr. Eccl.
1656 **RUFINUS** Epigr.
1657 *SAMIORUM ANNALES*
1658 **SAMUS** Epigr.
1659 **SATRIUS** Epigr.
1660 **SATYRUS** Epigr.
1661 **SATYRUS** Hist.
1662 **SCIRAS** Comic.
1663 **SEMUS** Gramm.
1664 **SENIORES ALEXANDRINI** Scr.
Eccl.
1665 **SENIORES APUD IRENAEUM**
Scr. Eccl.
1666 *SENTENTIAE SEXTI*
1667 **<SEPTEM SAPIENTES>** Phil.
1668 **SERAPION** Epigr.
1669 **SERAPION** Astrol.
1670 **SERAPION** Scr. Eccl.
1671 **SERENUS** Gnom.
1672 **SERVIUS** Hist.
1673 **SIMMIAS** Epigr.
1674 **<SIMON MAGUS>** Gnost.
1675 **SIMYLUS** Eleg.
1676 **SIMYLUS** Iamb.
1677 **SOCRATES** Epigr.
1678 **SOCRATES** Hist.
1679 **SOCRATES** Hist.
1680 **<SODAMUS>** Eleg.
1681 *SOLONIS EPISTULAE*
1682 **SOPATER** Comic.
1683 **SOPHAENETUS** Hist.
1684 *SOPHIA JESU CHRISTI*
1685 **SOSIBIUS** Gramm.
1686 **SOSIBIUS** Gramm.
1687 **SOSICRATES** Hist.
1688 **SOSTRATUS** Gramm.
1689 **SOSYLUS** Hist.
1690 *SOTADEA*
1691 **SOTADES** Iamb.
1692 **SPEUSIPPUS** Phil.
1693 **SPHAERUS** Phil.
1694 **STATYLLIUS FLACCUS** Epigr.
1695 **<STHENIDAS>** Phil.
1696 **STRATON** Phil.
1697 **STRATON** Epigr.
1698 **TELEPHUS** Gramm.
1699 **TELES** Phil.
1700 *TESTAMENTA XII PATRI-*
ARCHARUM
1701 *TESTAMENTUM ABRAHAE*
1702 *TESTAMENTUM JOBI*
1703 **TEUCER** Astrol.
1704 **TEUCER** Hist.
1705 **THALES** Phil.
1706 **THALLUS** Hist.
1707 **Antonius THALLUS** Epigr.
1708 **THEAETETUS** Poeta
1709 **THEAGENES** Hist.
1710 **<THEAGES>** Phil.
1711 **<THEARIDAS>** Phil.
1712 *THEBAÏS*
1713 **THEMISON** Hist.

1920 Gaius SULPICIUS GALBA Hist.
1921 JASON Hist. et Gramm.
1922 CHRYSERUS Hist.
1923 STESIMBROTUS Hist.
1924 THEMISTOGENES Hist.
1925 HEGEMON Epigr.
1926 XENOPHON Hist.
1927 CEPHISODORUS Hist.
1928 THEODECTES Hist.
1929 ANTIPATER Hist.
1930 LAMACHUS Hist.
1931 STRATTIS Hist.
1932 BAETO Hist.
1933 NICANDER Hist.
1934 PHILONIDES Hist.
1935 ARCHELAUS Hist.
1936 EPHIPPUS Hist.
1937 NICOBULE Hist.
1938 POLYCLITUS Hist.
1939 MEDIUS Hist.
1940 CALLICRATES Hist.
1941 LEO Hist.
1942 NEARCHUS Hist.
1943 ONESICRITUS Hist.
1944 PTOLEMAEUS I SOTER Hist.
1945 ANTIGENES Hist.
1946 ARISTUS Hist.
1947 THEOCLIUS Hist.
1948 NICANOR Hist.
1949 POTAMON Hist.
1950 VARRO Hist.
1951 AMYNTIANUS Hist.
1952 DIOGNETUS Hist.
1953 HIERONYMUS Hist.
1954 HERACLIDES Phil.
1955 ASCLEPIADES Hist.
1956 ZENO Hist.
1957 DEMETRIUS Hist.
1958 SIMONIDES Hist.
1959 MNESIPTOLEMUS Hist.
1960 TIMOCHARES Hist.
1961 NICOMACHUS Hist.
1962 HERACLITUS Hist.
1963 STRATON Hist.
1964 POSIDONIUS Hist.
1965 LYSIMACHUS Hist.
1966 NEANTHES Junior Hist.
1967 LESCHIDES Hist.
1968 FABIUS CERYLLIANUS Hist.
1969 PHILINUS Hist.
1970 SILENUS Hist.
1971 CLAUDIUS EUSTHENIUS Hist.
1972 EUMACHUS Hist.
1973 XENOPHON Hist.
1974 HANNIBAL Rex Carthaginien-
     sium Hist.
1975 JASON Hist.
1976 METRODORUS Hist.
1977 Lucius Licinius LUCULLUS Hist.
1978 LEO Hist.
1979 HERACLIDES Hist.
1980 AESOPUS Hist.
1981 THEOPHANES Hist.
1982 Titus Pomponius ATTICUS Hist.
1983 HYPSICRATES Hist.
1984 EMPYLUS Hist.
1985 Asinius POLLIO Hist.
1986 BOETHUS Hist.
1987 THEODORUS Poeta

1988 Gaius Julius POLYAENUS Soph.
     et Hist.
1989 Quintus DELLIUS Hist.
1990 OLYMPUS Hist.
1991 PTOLEMAEUS Hist.
1992 ARISTON Apol.
1993 ANTIOCHIANUS Hist.
1994 CREPEREIUS CALPURNIANUS
     Hist.
1995 DEMETRIUS Hist.
1996 CALLIMORPHUS Med.
1997 ANTIPATER Hist.
1998 EPHORUS Junior Hist.
1999 ONASIMUS Hist.
2000 PLOTINUS Phil.
2001 THEMISTIUS Phil. et Rhet.
2002 ANONYMUS SEGUERIANUS
     Rhet.
2003 Flavius Claudius JULIANUS
     Imperator Phil.
2004 *AMELII EPISTULA*
2005 *MARTYRIUM PIONII*
2006 SYNESIUS Phil.
2007 *MARTYRIUM POTAMIAENAE
     ET BASILIDIS*
2008 *MARTYRIUM CONONIS*
2009 *MARTYRIUM MARINI*
2010 *MARTYRIUM DASII*
2011 *MARTYRIUM AGAPAE, IRE-
     NAE, CHIONAE ET SODALIUM*
2012 *ACTA EUPLI*
2013 PHILO Phil.
2014 *ACTA PHILEAE*
2015 *TESTAMENTUM XL MAR-
     TYRUM*
2016 *PASSIO PERPETUAE ET FELI-
     CITATIS*
2017 GREGORIUS NYSSENUS Theol.
2018 EUSEBIUS Scr. Eccl. et Theol.
2019 PELAGIUS Alchem.
2020 THEODOSIUS Gramm.
2021 EPIPHANIUS Scr. Eccl.
2022 GREGORIUS NAZIANZENUS
     Theol.
2023 IAMBLICHUS Phil.
2025 MAXIMUS Rhet.
2027 Valerius APSINES Rhet.
2029 *ANONYMI GEOGRAPHIA IN
     SPHAERA INTELLIGENDA*
2030 *GEOGRAPHICA ADESPOTA*
     (GGM)
2031 SOPATER Rhet.
2032 PAPPUS Math.
2033 THEON Math.
2034 PORPHYRIUS Phil.
2035 ATHANASIUS Theol.
2036 DEXIPPUS Phil.
2037 Joannes STOBAEUS
2038 *ACTA THOMAE*
2039 DIOPHANTUS Math.
2040 BASILIUS Theol.
2041 MARCELLUS Theol.
2042 ORIGENES Theol.
2043 HEPHAESTION Astrol.
2045 NONNUS Epic.
2046 QUINTUS Epic.
2047 *SYRIANI, SOPATRI ET MAR-
     CELLINI SCHOLIA AD HER-
     MOGENIS STATUS*

2048 Salaminius Hermias SOZOME-
     NUS Scr. Eccl.
2049 SALLUSTIUS Phil.
2050 EUNAPIUS Hist. et Soph.
2051 HIMERIUS Soph.
2052 HORAPOLLO Gramm.
2053 PAULUS Astrol.
2054 ARISTIDES QUINTILIANUS
     Mus.
2055 SERENUS Geom.
2057 SOCRATES Scholasticus Hist.
2058 PHILOSTORGIUS Scr. Eccl.
2059 ALEXANDER Theol.
2060 ASTERIUS Scr. Eccl.
2061 ASTERIUS Sophista Scr. Eccl.
2062 JOANNES CHRYSOSTOMUS
     Scr. Eccl.
2063 GREGORIUS THAUMA-
     TURGUS Scr. Eccl.
2064 ACACIUS Theol.
2074 APOLLINARIS Theol.
2084 BASILIUS Scr. Eccl.
2102 DIDYMUS CAECUS Scr. Eccl.
2109 Pseudo-MACARIUS Scr. Eccl.
2110 CYRILLUS Scr. Eccl.
2111 PALLADIUS Scr. Eccl.
2112 AMPHILOCHIUS Scr. Eccl.
2115 HIPPOLYTUS Scr. Eccl.
2116 ARCADIUS Gramm.
2117 ANONYMUS DE METRORUM
     RATIONE
2118 *GRYLLUS*
2119 CHRISTODORUS Epic.
2120 PANTELEIUS Epic.
2121 DIOSCORUS Epic.
2122 Gaius ASINIUS QUADRATUS
     Hist.
2123 PALLADAS Epigr.
2124 PHOCAS Diaconus Epigr.
2125 THEODORETUS Gramm.
2126 TIBERIUS Epigr.
2127 TROILUS Soph.
2128 DIOGENES Epigr.
2129 EUPITHIUS Epigr.
2130 ARETHAS Philol. et Scr. Eccl.
2131 PHILISCUS Epigr.
2133 ACHILLES TATIUS Astron.
2134 ZENO Phil.
2135 ALYPIUS Mus.
2136 BACCHIUS GERON Mus.
2137 GAUDENTIUS Phil. et Mus.
2138 *CANTICUM EURIPIDIS*
2139 *EPITAPHIUM SICILI*
2140 IAMBLICHUS Alchem.
2141 Publius Herennius DEXIPPUS
     Hist.
2142 PHILIPPUS Hist.
2143 HERMOGENES Hist.
2144 NICOSTRATUS Hist.
2145 PHILOSTRATUS Hist.
2146 EUSEBIUS Hist.
2147 CLEMENS Hist.
2148 ARISTODEMUS Hist.
2149 ERETES Hist.
2150 THEODORUS Hist.
2151 PRAXAGORAS Hist.
2152 BEMARCHIUS Hist.
2153 BION Phil. et Math.
2154 CYLLENIUS Hist.

2155 **CALLISTION** Hist.
2156 **ELEAZAR** Hist.
2157 **MAGNUS** Hist.
2158 **EUTYCHIANUS** Hist.
2159 **LEANDR(I)US** Hist.
2160 **PYRRHUS** Hist.
2161 **THEODORUS** Hist.
2162 **ARATUS** Hist.
2163 Publius Cornelius **SCIPIO Major** Hist.
2164 Publius Cornelius **SCIPIO NA-SICA CORCULUM** Hist.
2165 Marcus Tullius **CICERO** Orat.
2166 **HERODES I Rex Judaeorum** Hist.
2167 **ZENOBIA Regina Palmyrae** <Hist.>
2168 **APOLLOPHANES** Phil.
2169 **HERILLUS** Phil.
2170 **EUTHYMENES** Hist.
2171 **STESICLIDES** Hist.
2172 **ANDRON** Hist.
2173 **ANTILEON** Hist.
2174 **XENOCRATES** Hist.
2175 **<AUTOCHARIS>** Hist.
2176 **THRASYLLUS** Hist.
2177 Tiberius Claudius **POLYBIUS** Hist.
2178 Cassius **LONGINUS** Phil. et Rhet.
2179 **PYTHEUS-SATYRUS** Hist.
2180 **JUDAS** Hist.
2181 **MOSES** Alchem.
2182 **STAPHYLUS** Hist.
2183 **JASON** Hist.
2184 **CLAUDIUS Imperator**
2185 **DIONYSIUS** Μεταθέμενος Phil.
2186 **LEO** Hist.
2187 **POSIDONIUS** Hist.
2188 **PHILIPPUS** Hist.
2189 **CALLINICUS** Soph.
2190 **[CLITONYMUS]** Hist.
2191 **GLAUCIPPUS** Hist.
2192 **[AGATHARCHIDES]** Hist.
2193 **[ARETADES]** Hist.
2194 **[ARISTIDES]** Hist.
2195 **[CHRYSERMUS]** Hist.
2196 **[DERCYLLUS]** Hist.
2197 **[DOROTHEUS]** Hist.
2198 **THEUDIUS** Math. et Phil.
2199 **[CALLISTHENES]** Hist.
2200 **LIBANIUS** Rhet. et Soph.
2201 **[CTESIPHON]** Hist.
2202 **[MENYLLUS]** Hist.
2203 **[THEOPHILUS]** Hist.
2204 **AUTOCRATES** Hist.
2205 **AUTESION** Hist.
2206 **[DIOCLES]** Hist.
2207 **ATHANIDAS** Hist.
2208 **DEMETRIUS** Hist.
2209 **CHERSIPHRON-METAGENES** Hist.
2210 **ANAXICRATES** Hist.
2211 **TELESARCHUS** Hist.
2212 **LYCEAS** Hist.
2213 **[TIMOTHEUS]** Hist.
2214 **ARCHITIMUS** Hist.
2215 **AR(I)AETHUS** Hist.
2216 **ARISTIPPUS** Hist.
2217 **NICIAS** Hist.
2218 **CALLIPHON et DEMOCEDES** Med. et Phil.

2219 **AMELESAGORAS** Hist.
2220 **ATHENAEUS** Math. et Phil.
2221 **ANTIOCHUS-PHERECYDES** Hist.
2222 **CADMUS Junior** Hist.
2223 **ARISTON** Hist.
2224 **ASCLEPIADES** Gramm.
2225 **PARM(EN)ISCUS** Phil.
2226 **ICCUS** Phil.
2227 **PARON** Phil.
2228 **MENESTOR** Phil.
2229 **XUTHUS** Phil.
2230 **BOÏDAS** Phil.
2231 **THRASYALCES** Phil.
2232 **DAMON** Mus.
2233 Pseudo-**POLEMON**
2234 **OENOPIDES** Phil.
2235 **HIPPOCRATES** Math.
2236 **EUTROPIUS** Hist.
2237 **THEODORUS** Math.
2238 **SCOPAS** (?) Hist.
2239 **PYTHAGORISTAE** (D-K) Phil.
2240 **HICETAS** Phil.
2241 **XENOPHILUS** Phil. et Mus.
2242 **ECHECRATES** Phil.
2243 *APOCALYPSIS SEDRACH*
2244 **DAMON et PHINTIAS** Phil.
2245 **SIMUS** Phil.
2246 **LYCON** Phil.
2247 **PETRON** Phil.
2248 *ACTA XANTHIPPAE ET POLY-XENAE*
2249 **DRACO** Hist.
2250 **MELITO** Hist.
2251 **THEODORUS** Hist.
2252 **CALLISTRATUS** Gramm.
2253 **ANTIPHANES Junior** Hist.
2254 **AMMONIUS** Hist.
2255 **GORGIAS** Hist.
2256 **HELICON** Math., Astron. et Phil.
2257 **DIONYSIUS** Hist.
2258 **SOTADES** Phil.
2259 **HABRON** Hist.
2260 **HIPPASUS** Phil.
2261 **ARISTOMENES** Hist.
2262 **LYSIMACHIDES** Hist.
2263 **CHARICLES** Hist.
2264 **TELEPHANES** Hist.
2265 **DIODORUS** Perieg.
2266 **PAXAMUS** Hist. et Scr. Rerum Nat.
2267 **LYCUS** Hist.
2268 **TIMAGORAS** Hist.
2269 **ARISTODEMUS** Hist. et Gramm.
2270 **CALLIPPUS** Hist.
2271 **AMPHION** Hist.
2272 **PHOCUS** Phil.
2273 **DAMON** Hist.
2274 **HESYCHIUS Illustrius** Hist.
2275 **THEAGENES** Phil.
2276 **ZENIS** Hist.
2277 **HYPERMENES** Hist.
2278 **PHANODICUS** Hist.
2279 **NICOCHARES** Hist.
2280 **DINARCHUS** Hist.
2281 **DEMOTELES** Hist.
2282 **MELISSEUS** Hist.
2283 **APOLLONIUS** Hist.
2284 **ANAXANDRIDAS** Hist.

2285 **ALCETAS** Hist.
2286 **CERCOPS** Phil.
2287 *FRAGMENTUM STOICUM*
2288 **TEUPALUS** Hist.
2289 **ECHEPHYLIDAS** Hist.
2290 **ARISTARCHUS** Hist.
2291 **CRATYLUS** Phil.
2292 **ARISTODEMUS** Hist.
2293 **EUALCES** Hist.
2294 **ZENO** Phil.
2295 **APOLLODORUS** Hist.
2296 **ARISTOTELES** Hist.
2297 **PROXENUS** Hist.
2298 **LYSANIAS** Hist.
2299 **DEMODAMAS** Hist.
2300 **PROMATHIDAS** Hist.
2301 **TIMOGENES** Hist. et Rhet.
2302 **ARISTOCLES** Hist.
2303 **ARCHELAUS** Phil.
2304 **IDAEUS** Phil.
2305 **CLIDEMUS** Phil.
2306 **XENOMEDES** Hist.
2307 **ARTEMON** Hist.
2308 **DEMOGNETUS** Hist.
2309 **JASON** Hist.
2310 **POSIDIPPUS** Hist.
2311 **HEROPYTHUS** Hist.
2312 **ERXIAS** Hist.
2313 **ANTISTHENES** Phil.
2314 **DIOGENES** Phil.
2315 **DIODORUS** Hist.
2316 **DIOXIPPUS** Hist.
2317 **HERMIAS** Phil.
2318 **MACARIUS** Hist.
2319 **APOLLODORUS** Phil.
2320 **ECHEMENES** Hist.
2321 **LAOSTHENIDAS** Hist.
2322 **ANTENOR** Hist.
2323 **PETELLIDAS** Hist.
2324 **DINARCHUS** Hist.
2325 **MENECLES** Hist.
2326 **DEI(L)OCHUS** Hist.
2327 **POLYGNOSTUS** Hist.
2328 **DIOGENES** Hist.
2329 **PHERECYDES** Hist.
2330 **SCAMON** Hist.
2331 **MYRSILUS** Hist.
2332 **THEOLYTUS** Hist.
2333 **POSSIS** Hist.
2334 **NAUSIPHANES** Phil.
2335 **PRAXION** Hist.
2336 **HEREAS** Hist.
2337 (not present)
2338 **CADMUS** Hist.
2339 **MAEANDRIUS** Hist.
2340 **DIOTIMUS** Phil.
2341 **ARISTOCRITUS** Hist.
2342 **ARISTIDES** Hist.
2343 **EUDEMUS** Hist.
2344 **PHILTEAS** Hist.
2345 **AGL(A)OSTHENES** Hist.
2346 **ANDRISCUS** Hist.
2347 **DEMEAS** Hist.
2348 **DIOGENES** Hist.
2349 **[PYRANDER]** Hist.
2350 **ANTIPATER** Hist.
2351 **ANTISTHENES** Hist.
2352 **ARISTION** Hist.
2353 **ARISTONYMUS** Hist.
2354 **DIONYSIUS** Hist.

2355 **XENIADES** Soph.
2356 **EUCRATES** Hist.
2357 **GORGON** Hist.
2358 **HAGELOCHUS** Hist.
2359 **HAGESTRATUS** Hist.
2360 **HIERON** Hist.
2361 **NICASYLUS** Hist.
2362 **ONOMASTUS** Hist.
2363 **TIMOCRITUS** Hist.
2364 **ZENO** Hist.
2365 **EUDEMUS** Hist.
2366 **PHAENNUS** Hist.
2367 **THEOGNIS** Hist.
2368 **AELURUS** Hist.
2369 **GORGOSTHENES** Hist.
2370 **HIEROBOLUS** Hist.
2371 *CHRONICON PASCHALE*
2372 **EUAGON** Hist.
2373 **OLYMPICHUS** Hist.
2375 **LEO** Hist.
2376 **XENOPHON** Hist.
2377 **AESCHRION** Epic.
2378 **AENEAS** Hist.
2379 **ATHENACON** Hist.
2380 **IDOMENEUS** Hist.
2381 **DEMETRIUS** Hist.
2382 **MALACUS** Hist.
2383 **DIODORUS** Phil.
2384 **HERMIAS** Hist.
2385 **POLYCRITUS** Hist.
2386 **TIMONIDES** Hist.
2387 **ATHANIS** Hist.
2388 **TIMOCRATES** Hist.
2389 **ANTANDER** Hist.
2390 **[DIONYSIUS]** Hist.
2391 **HIPPOSTRATUS** Hist.
2392 **ARTEMON** Hist.
2393 **ANDREAS** Hist.
2394 **THEOPHILUS** Hist.
2395 **PISISTRATUS** Hist.
2396 **HYPEROCHUS** Hist.
2397 **BOETHUS** Phil.
2398 **BASILIDES** Phil.
2399 **EUDROMUS** Phil.
2400 **THIBRON** Hist.
2401 **PAUSANIAS II Rex Lace-**
daemonis Hist.
2402 **LYSANDER** Hist.
2403 **PERSAEUS** Hist.
2404 **HIEROCLES et PHILAGRIUS**
Scriptores Facetiarum
2405 **ARISTOCLES** Hist.
2406 **HIPPASUS** Hist.
2407 **PAUSANIAS** Hist.
2408 **HIEROCLES** Hist.
2409 **DIOSCURIDES** Hist.
2410 **POLYCRATES** Hist.
2411 **CLEOMENES III Rex Lace-**
daemonis Hist.
2412 **ANDROETAS** Hist.
2413 **AENESIDEMUS** Hist.
2414 **MOSMES** (?) Hist.
2415 **PHILOCRATES** Hist.
2416 **SUIDAS** Hist.
2417 **CINEAS** Rhet.
2418 **ARCHINUS** Hist.
2419 **HEROPHANES** Hist.
2420 **HEGIAS** Hist.
2421 **CHARON** Hist.
2422 **PHILISTUS** Hist.

2423 **ASCLEPIADES** Hist. et Gramm.
2424 **CHAEREMON** Hist. et Phil.
2425 **EUAGORAS** Hist.
2426 **HERMAEUS** Hist.
2427 **LYSIMACHUS** Hist.
2428 **THRASYLLUS** Hist.
2429 **ARISTAENETUS** Hist.
2430 **ASCLEPIADES** Hist.
2431 **Lucius Annaeus SENECA** Phil.
2432 *MARMOR PARIUM*
2433 *ADDITAMENTA* (FGrH)
2434 **AELIUS DIUS** Hist.
2435 **ANTISTHENES** Hist.
2436 *EPHEMERIDES*
2437 **HERMATELES** Hist.
2438 **HELLADIUS** Hist.
2439 **LUPERCUS** Gramm.
2440 **HERMIAS** Hist.
2441 **CLINIAS** Hist.
2442 **SOTERICHUS** Epic. et Hist.
2443 **ARATUS** Hist.
2444 **LYCOPHRON** Soph.
2445 **AMOMETUS** Hist.
2446 **DIONYSIUS** Hist.
2447 **ARISTON** Phil.
2448 **BUTORIDAS** Hist.
2449 **TIMOTHEUS** Gramm.
2450 **PALAEPHATUS** Gramm.
2451 **APOLLONIDES HORAPIUS**
Hist.
2452 **GALITAS** (?) Hist.
2453 **ARISTOCLES** Hist.
2454 **DALION** Hist.
2455 **ARISTOCREON** Hist.
2456 **NESSAS** Phil.
2457 **PHILO** Hist.
2458 **MARCELLUS** Hist.
2459 **TIMOCRATES** Hist.
2460 **GLAUCUS** Hist.
2461 **URANIUS** Hist.
2462 **ULPIANUS** Soph.
2463 **ARTAVASDES** Hist.
2464 **SEMERONIUS** Hist.
2465 **ATHENAEUS** Hist.
2466 **DIONYSIUS** Hist.
2468 **HERMOTIMUS** Math.
2469 **DIOGENES** Hist.
2470 **DIOCLES** Hist.
2471 **PHARNUCHUS** Hist.
2472 **ARTEMIDORUS** Hist.
2473 **ABLABIUS** Hist.
2474 **NICANDER** Hist.
2475 **MENECRATES** Hist.
2476 **TAURON** Hist.
2477 **POLLES** Hist.
2478 **ANTONIUS JULIANUS** Hist.
2479 **PATROCLES** Hist.
2480 **ORTHAGORAS** Hist.
2481 **SOSANDER** Perieg.
2482 **DAIMACHUS** Hist.
2483 **DIONYSIUS** Hist.
2484 **[CAEMARON]** Hist.
2485 **DEMETRIUS Judaeus** Hist.
2486 **EUPOLEMUS Judaeus** Hist.
2487 **Pseudo-EUPOLEMUS Judaeus**
Hist.
2488 **ARISTEAS Judaeus** Hist.
2489 **ARTAPANUS Judaeus** Hist.
2490 **CLEODEMUS-MALCHUS** Hist.
2491 **APOLLONIUS MOLO** Hist.

2492 **AMPHINOMUS** Math.
2493 **DAMOCRITUS** Hist.
2494 **NICARCHUS** Hist.
2495 **PAMPHILUS** Phil.
2496 **THEOPHILUS** Hist.
2497 **JUSTUS Judaeus** Hist.
2498 **JOANNES I** Hist.
2499 **EUSTOCHIUS** Soph.
2500 **ALEXANDER** Hist.
2501 **HIPPAGORAS** Hist.
2502 **ERATOSTHENES** Hist.
2503 **Publius Anteius ANTIOCHUS**
Soph.
2504 **CANDIDUS** Hist.
2505 **Cnaeus AUFIDIUS** Hist.
2506 **CAPITO** Hist.
2507 **ANDROCLES** Hist.
2508 **CREON** Hist.
2509 **TIMOMACHUS** Hist.
2510 **XENOPHON** Hist.
2511 **DEMETRIUS** Hist.
2512 **PAEON** Hist.
2513 **ARISTIPPUS** Hist.
2514 **Publius Cornelius SCIPIO** Hist.
2515 **THEOCHRESTUS** Hist.
2516 **HESIANAX** Hist.
2517 **MENIPPUS** Hist.
2518 **XENOPHILUS** Hist.
2519 **ARISTAENETUS** Hist.
2520 **NICOMEDES** Hist.
2521 **ANTIGONUS** Hist.
2522 **DEMETRIUS** Hist.
2523 **NICOSTRATUS** Hist.
2524 **SELEUCUS** Gramm.
2525 **LAETUS** Hist.
2526 **HIERONYMUS** Hist.
2527 **PHILOSTRATUS** Hist.
2528 **ZENO** Hist.
2529 **ASPASIUS** Hist.
2530 **ASPASIUS** Hist.
2531 **METROPHANES** Hist.
2532 **[HERMESIANAX]** Hist.
2533 **TIMOLAUS** Hist.
2534 **AGATHOCLES** Hist.
2535 **AGATHON** Hist.
2536 **ANDRON** Geogr.
2537 **APOLLODORUS** Hist.
2538 **DIONYSIUS** Hist.
2539 **DIOPHANTUS** Hist.
2540 **SYRISCUS** Hist.
2541 **DEMETRIUS** Hist.
2542 **Quintus FABIUS PICTOR** Hist.
2543 **Lucius CINCIUS ALIMENTUS**
Hist.
2544 **Aelius POSTUMIUS ALBINUS**
Hist.
2545 **Gaius ACILIUS** Phil. et Hist.
2546 **Publius RUTILIUS RUFUS** Hist.
2547 **ANTIGONUS** Hist.
2548 **PROMATHION** Hist.
2549 **DIOCLES** Hist.
2550 **ZENODOTUS** Hist.
2551 **THEODORUS** Hist.
2552 **CRITOLAUS** Hist.
2553 **RUFUS** Hist.
2554 **LEONIDES** Hist.
2555 **AGESILAUS** Hist.
2556 **[ALEXARCHUS]** Hist.
2557 **[ARISTOBULUS]** Hist.
2558 **XENO** Hist.

2559 **[CHRYSIPPUS]** Hist.
2560 **PYTHOCLES** Hist.
2561 **THEOTIMUS** Hist.
2562 **ARISTOTHEUS** Hist.
2563 **PYRRHO** Hist.
2564 **PALLADIUS** Hist.
2565 **MNESIMACHUS** Hist.
2566 **[AGATHON]** Hist.
2567 **CTESIPPUS** Hist.
2568 **[SOSTHENES]** Hist.
2569 **<TIMAEUS>** Hist.
2570 **THEODORUS** Hist.
2571 **HIEROCLES** Phil.
2572 **DEMETRIUS** Hist.
2573 **PAUSANIAS** Hist.
2574 **DIONYSOPHANES** Hist.
2575 **JASON** Hist.
2576 **JOANNES** Gramm.
2577 **ANATOLIUS** Phil. et Math.
2578 **JOANNES** Gramm. et Poeta
2580 **Joannes Laurentius LYDUS** Hist.
2582 **MALCHUS** Hist.
2583 **MANETHO** Astrol.
2584 *ANONYMI DE COMOEDIA*
2585 **MARCELLINUS** Biogr.
2586 **MENANDER** Rhet.
2587 **ARISTON** Phil.
2589 **OLYMPIODORUS** Alchem.
2590 **OLYMPIODORUS** Hist.
2591 **ORION** Gramm.
2592 **Joannes PEDIASIMUS** Gramm.
2593 **PETRUS PATRICIUS** Hist.
2594 **PHILLIS** Hist.
2595 **PHILO** Paradox.
2596 **PHOEBAMMON** Soph.
2597 **PAMPHOS** Poeta
2598 **PROCOPIUS** Rhet. et Scr. Eccl.
2600 **SIMON** Scriptor De Re Equestri
2601 **TIBERIUS** Rhet.
2602 **TIMAEUS** Gramm.
2604 **ULPIANUS** Gramm. et Rhet.
2605 **AGAMESTOR** Eleg.
2606 **AGATHYLLUS** Eleg.
2607 **ALEXINUS** Phil.
2608 **ARCHEBULUS** Poeta
2609 **ASOPODORUS** Iamb.
2610 **BOISCUS** Iamb.
2611 **BUTAS** Eleg.
2612 **CAECALUS** (?) Epic.
2613 **CALLIMACHUS Junior** Epic.
2614 **CLEOMACHUS** Poeta
2615 **DAPHITAS** Gramm. vel Soph.
2616 **DEMARETA** Poeta
2617 **DEMETRIUS** Poeta
2618 **DIDYMARCHUS** Poeta
2619 **DIONYSIUS** Epic.
2620 **DIONYSIUS IAMBUS** Gramm. et
     Poeta
2621 **DIOPHILUS vel DIOPHILA**
     Poeta
2622 **DORIEUS** Poeta
2623 **EUANTHES** Epic.
2624 **HERMIAS** Poeta
2625 **HERODICUS** Gramm.
2626 **HIPPARCHUS** Parodius
2627 **DAMIANUS** Scriptor De Opticis
2628 **IDAEUS** Epic.
2630 **LOBO** Poeta
2631 **MENOPHILUS** Poeta
2632 **COMARIUS** Alchem.

2633 **NICERATUS** Epic.
2634 **PAMPHILUS** Poeta
2635 **PERSINUS** Poeta
2636 **PHERENICUS** Epic.
2637 **EUSTATHIUS** Hist.
2638 **PHILO** Poeta
2639 **POSIDONIUS** Epic.
2640 **EUSEBIUS** Phil.
2641 **PRISCUS** Epic.
2642 **<ASTRAMPSYCHUS Magus>**
     Onir.
2643 **Decimus Magnus AUSONIUS**
     Gramm. et Rhet.
2644 **SMINTHES** Astron.
2645 **STRATONICUS** Poeta
2646 *FRAGMENTA ADESPOTA* (SH)
2647 **ZENOTHEMIS** Geogr.
2648 *ADESPOTA PAPYRACEA* (SH)
2649 **AMYNTAS** Epigr.
2650 **ARRIANUS** Epic.
2651 **ARTEMIDORUS** Eleg.
2652 **DIODORUS** Eleg.
2653 **ERYCIUS** Poeta
2654 *PHYSIOLOGUS GRAECUS*
2655 **<DAMIGERON Magus>**
2657 *MARTYRIUM IGNATII*
2658 **ARION** Lyr.
2659 **ARISTOCREON** Epigr.
2660 **Lucius Cornelius SULLA FELIX**
     <Epigr.>
2661 **CATILIUS** Epigr.
2662 **CELSUS** Epigr.
2663 **GEMELLUS** Epigr.
2664 **CAECILIA** Epigr.
2665 **Mettius PAEON** Epigr.
2666 **CATULUS** Epigr.
2667 **PHALERNUS** Poeta et Soph.
2668 **ARIUS** Epic.
2669 **ARRIANUS** Epigr.
2670 **URANIUS** Epigr.
2671 **HERACLIUS** Epigr.
2672 **CATULLINUS** Epigr.
2673 **JUNIOR** Poeta
2674 **NICOMEDES** Med.
2675 **MAXIMUS** Epigr.
2676 **MARCELLUS** Epigr.
2677 **PIUS** Gramm.
2678 **<PETRONIUS APOLLO-**
     DORUS> Epigr.
2679 *TESTAMENTUM SALOMONIS*
2681 **DIODORUS** Phil.
2682 **PYTHEAS** Epigr.
2683 **DIONYSIUS** Poeta
2684 **MENECLES** Phil.
2685 **ENNOEUS** Poeta
2686 **LUCULLUS** Epigr.
2687 **ZOSIMUS** Epigr.
2688 **RUFUS** Epigr.
2689 **CHIRISOPHUS** Epigr.
2690 **GEORGIUS <Epigr.>**
2691 **[MUSAEUS]** Phil.
2692 **PHILINNA** Poeta
2693 **PTOLEMAEUS III EUERGETES**
     I **<Epigr.>**
2694 **SOSTRATUS** Poeta
2696 **THEODORUS** Poeta
2697 **TIMOLAUS** Rhet.
2698 **HIPPODAMAS** Epigr.
2699 **AMPHICRATES** Rhet.
2700 **AELIANUS** Epigr.

2701 **GEORGIUS PISIDES** Poeta
2702 **Michael PSELLUS** Polyhist.
2703 **ANNA COMNENA** Hist.
2704 **MICHAEL** Epigr.
2705 **NICETAS DAVID** Gramm., Phil.
     et Scr. Eccl.
2706 **THEOPHILUS Imperator**
2707 **THEOPHANES GRAPTOS** Poeta
2708 **METHODIUS I** Scr. Eccl.
2709 **Joannes MAUROPUS** Rhet. et
     Poeta
2710 **LEO BARDALAS** Epigr.
2711 **ASPASIA <Epigr.>**
2712 **DIOPHANTUS** Epigr.
2713 **NICOLAUS** Epigr.
2714 **THEODORUS STUDITES** Scr.
     Eccl. et Theol.
2715 **ANDREAS Libadinarius** Epigr.
2716 **MANUEL** Epigr.
2717 **EUSTATHIUS** Epigr.
2718 **Manuel PHILES** Poeta
2719 **TIMOTHEUS AELURUS** Scr.
     Eccl.
2720 **Pseudo-EUSEBIUS** Scr. Eccl.
2721 **Theodorus PRODROMUS** Poly-
     hist. et Poeta
2722 **PERSEUS** Epigr.
2723 **EUMETIS** Epigr.
2724 **AMMONIUS** Scr. Eccl.
2725 **DIOSCORUS I** Theol.
2726 **BASILIUS Megalomytes** Epigr.
2727 **AULICALAMUS** Epigr.
2728 **THEODORUS** Epigr.
2729 **PRORUS** Phil.
2730 **CLEARCHUS** Epigr.
2731 **IOMEDES** Epigr.
2732 **PETRUS MONGUS** Scr. Eccl.
2733 **EVAGRIUS Scholasticus** Scr. Eccl.
2734 **Flavius JUSTINIANUS Imperator**
     Theol.
2736 **CONSTANTINUS I Imperator**
2744 *HISTORIA MONACHORUM IN*
     AEGYPTO
2762 **GENNADIUS I** Scr. Eccl.
2798 **Pseudo-DIONYSIUS AREOPA-**
     GITA Theol. et Scr. Eccl.
2800 **BASILIUS** Scr. Eccl.
2810 **EUSTATHIUS** Theol.
2819 **LEONTIUS** Theol.
2824 **EULOGIUS** Theol.
2856 **Joannes MOSCHUS** Scr. Eccl.
2866 **OECUMENIUS** Rhet. et Phil.
2867 **Pseudo-ANDRONICUS** Scriptor
     Catalogi Poetarum
2871 **JOANNES MALALAS** Chronogr.
2877 **CYRILLUS** Biogr.
2881 **ROMANUS MELODUS** Hym-
     nogr.
2890 **MINUCIANUS** Rhet.
2892 **MAXIMUS CONFESSOR** Theol.
     et Poeta
2903 **MINUCIANUS Junior** Rhet.
2904 **NICOLAUS** Rhet. et Soph.
2934 **JOANNES DAMASCENUS**
     Theol. et Scr. Eccl.
2937 **LACHARES** Soph.
2944 **LEO VI SAPIENS Imperator**
     Phil., Scr. Eccl. et Poeta
2945 *GNOMOLOGIUM VATICANUM*
2947 **THEODORUS** Phil.

4139 SEVERIANUS Scr. Eccl.
4143 JOANNES Diaconus Rhet.
4144 NICOLAUS CALLICLES Med. et
   Poeta
4145 NICEPHORUS GREGORAS
   Polyhist.
4146 Maximus PLANUDES Polyhist.
4147 *FLORILEGIUM CYRILLIANUM*
4148 *FLORILEGIUM ANTICHALCE-*
   DONIUM
4149 SOPHRONIUS Gramm.
4150 *ANACREONTEA*
4153 *THEOPHANES CONTINUATUS*
4154 Pseudo-OECUMENIUS Scr. Eccl.
4155 *NAUTICUS LAPIDARIUS*
4156 *ECCLESIASTICA ADESPOTA*
4157 JOANNES Rhet.
4158 *VITAE ARISTOPHANIS*
4159 GERMANUS Gramm.
4161 *VITAE ARATI ET VARIA DE*
   ARATO
4165 ANONYMI IN ARISTOTELIS
   LIBRUM DE INTERPRETATI-
   ONE
4166 *VITAE AESCHINIS*
4167 LEONTIUS Mech.
4168 ANONYMUS BYZANTINUS IN
   PORPHYRII ISAGOGEN Phil.
4170 *VITAE PINDARI ET VARIA DE*
   PINDARO
4171 ANONYMI IN OPPIANI OPERA
4172 *VITAE OPPIANI*
4173 *VITAE DIONYSII PERIEGE-*
   TAE
4174 *PARAPHRASES IN DIONY-*
   SIUM PERIEGETAM
4175 *COMMENTARIA IN DIONYSII*
   THRACIS ARTEM GRAMMA-
   TICAM
4176 PHILIPPUS Math., Astron. et
   Phil.
4177 DIONYSIUS Gramm.
4178 DIONYSIUS Gramm.
4179 DIONYSIUS Gramm.
4180 DIONYSIUS Gramm.
4181 DIONYSIUS Gramm. et Mus.
4182 DIONYSIUS Onir.
4184 DIONYSIUS Soph.
4185 DIONYSIUS LEPTUS Gramm. et
   Rhet.
4186 DIONYSIUS Gramm.
4187 LEO MAGENTINUS Phil.
4190 ANONYMI IN ARISTOTELIS
   ANALYTICA PRIORA
4191 ANONYMI IN ARISTOTELIS
   ANALYTICA POSTERIORA
4192 ANONYMI IN ARISTOTELIS
   TOPICA
4193 ANONYMI IN ARISTOTELIS
   SOPHISTICOS ELENCHOS
4194 ANONYMI IN ARISTOTELIS
   PHYSICA
4195 ANONYMI IN ARISTOTELIS
   LIBRUM DE CAELO
4196 ANONYMI IN ARISTOTELIS
   METAPHYSICA
4201 JOANNES CHORTASMENUS
   Gramm.

4210 *ANONYMI DE VENTIS*
4223 STEPHANUS Archiatrus Med.
4224 THEON Archiatrus Med.
4227 ANONYMUS DE PHILOSOPHIA
   PLATONICA Phil.
4228 ANONYMUS IN INTRODUCTI-
   ONEM ARITHMETICAM NICO-
   MACHI Math.
4229 ULPIANUS Soph.
4230 DIONYSIUS Soph.
4231 Demetrius MOSCHUS Philol.
4234 MARCELLINUS Gramm. et Rhet.
4235 JOANNES Rhet.
4236 TROPHONIUS Rhet.
4237 Joannes ARGYROPULUS
   Gramm.
4239 SEVERUS Soph.
4240 GEORGIUS MONUS Soph.
4241 GEORGIUS Diaereta Soph.
4242 CYRUS Rhet.
4243 ZONAEUS Soph.
4244 COCONDRIUS Rhet.
4245 HELLANICUS Gramm.
4246 PTOLEMAEUS ὁ ʼΕπιθέτης
   Gramm.
4247 EUCLIDES Phil.
4248 AGATHOCLES Gramm.
4249 BACCHIADAS Epigr.
4250 THEOPHILUS Gramm.
4251 ANAXAGORAS Gramm.
4252 XENO Gramm.
4253 DIOCLIDES Phil.
4254 DIONYSIUS Phil.
4255 ICHTHYAS Phil.
4256 CLINOMACHUS Phil.
4257 EUBULIDES Phil.
4258 MEMNON <Phil.>
4259 APOLLONIUS CRONUS Phil.
4260 PHILO Phil.
4261 PANTHOIDES Phil.
4262 STILPO Phil.
4263 PASICLES Phil.
4264 THRASYMACHUS Phil.
4265 PHILIPPUS Phil.
4266 SIMMIAS Phil.
4267 ALCIMUS Rhet.
4268 ARISTIDES Phil.
4269 DIPHILUS Phil.
4270 METRODORUS Theorematicus
   Phil.
4271 MYRMEX Phil.
4272 PAEONIUS Phil.
4273 CLITARCHUS Phil.
4274 PHRASIDEMUS Phil.
4275 TIMAGORAS Phil.
4276 BRYSON Phil. et Soph.
4277 POLYXENUS Soph.
4278 SPORUS Gramm.
4279 *PARAPHRASES IN HOMERI*
   OPERA
4280 Theodorus MELITENIOTES
   Gramm.
4282 ANONYMUS MANICHAEUS
   Biogr.
5000 *CONCILIA OECUMENICA*
   (ACO)
5001 *ORACULA*

5002 *MAGICA*
5003 *EROTICA ADESPOTA*
5005 *HYPOTHESES* (in papyris)
5008 *SCHOLIA IN AELIUM ARISTI-*
   DEM
5009 *SCHOLIA IN AESCHINEM*
5010 *SCHOLIA IN AESCHYLUM*
5011 *SCHOLIA IN ANTHOLOGIAM*
   GRAECAM
5012 *SCHOLIA IN APOLLONIUM*
   RHODIUM
5013 *SCHOLIA IN ARATUM*
5014 *SCHOLIA IN ARISTOPHANEM*
5015 *SCHOLIA IN ARISTOTELEM*
5016 *SCHOLIA IN CALLIMACHUM*
5017 *SCHOLIA IN DEMOSTHENEM*
5018 *SCHOLIA IN DIONYSIUM*
   BYZANTIUM
5019 *SCHOLIA IN DIONYSIUM*
   PERIEGETAM
5020 *SCHOLIA IN DIONYSIUM*
   THRACEM
5021 *SCHOLIA IN DIOPHANTUM*
5022 *SCHOLIA IN EUCLIDEM*
5023 *SCHOLIA IN EURIPIDEM*
5024 *ANONYMI IN HERMOGENEM*
5025 *SCHOLIA IN HESIODUM*
5026 *SCHOLIA IN HOMERUM*
5027 *SCHOLIA IN IAMBLICHUM*
   PHILOSOPHUM
5028 *SCHOLIA IN ISOCRATEM*
5029 *SCHOLIA IN LUCIANUM*
5030 *SCHOLIA IN LYCOPHRONEM*
5031 *SCHOLIA IN NICANDRUM*
5032 *SCHOLIA IN OPPIANUM*
5033 *SCHOLIA IN PAUSANIAM*
5034 *SCHOLIA IN PINDARUM*
5035 *SCHOLIA IN PLATONEM*
5036 *SCHOLIA IN PORPHYRIUM*
5037 *SCHOLIA IN SOPHOCLEM*
5038 *SCHOLIA IN THEOCRITUM*
5039 *SCHOLIA IN THUCYDIDEM*
5040 *SCHOLIA IN XENOPHONTEM*
5041 *SCHOLIA IN TATIANUM*
5043 *SCHOLIA IN HERMOGENEM*
5044 *SCHOLIA IN ALCMANEM*
5045 *ANONYMI IN APHTHONIUM*
5046 *SCHOLIA IN THEONEM*
   RHETOREM
5047 *SCHOLIA IN ARISTIDEM*
   QUINTILIANUM
5048 *SCHOLIA IN CLEMENTEM AL-*
   EXANDRINUM
5049 *SCHOLIA IN EUSEBIUM*
7000 *ANTHOLOGIA GRAECA*
7051 *DOCTRINA PATRUM*
7052 *ANTHOLOGIAE GRAECAE*
   APPENDIX
7056 ANONYMI EPIGRAMMATICI
   (App. Anth.)
9003 ANONYMUS LEXICO-
   GRAPHUS
9004 *ANONYMI IN ARISTOTELIS*
   LIBRUM ALTERUM ANALYT-
   ICORUM POSTERIORUM COM-
   MENTARIUM
9005 ANASTASIUS TRAULUS Epigr.

9006 **GREGORIUS** Paroemiogr.
9007 ***APPENDIX PROVERBIORUM***
9008 **Macarius CHRYSOCEPHALUS**
Paroemiogr.
9009 **Michael APOSTOLIUS** Paroemiogr.
9010 ***SUDA***
9011 **IGNATIUS** Epigr.
9012 **IGNATIUS** Biogr. et Poeta

9013 **CONSTANTINUS CEPHALAS**
<Epigr.>
9014 **CONSTANTINUS** <Epigr.>
9015 **CONSTANTINUS** Gramm.
9016 **LEO Philosophus** Gramm.
9017 **MICHAEL** Epigr.
9018 **ARSENIUS** Paroemiogr.
9019 **STEPHANUS** Phil.
9020 **STEPHANUS** Gramm.

9021 **STEPHANUS** Alchem.
9022 **Joannes TZETZES** Gramm. et
Poeta
9023 **THOMAS MAGISTER** Philol.
9024 **Isaac TZETZES** Gramm.
9025 **Manuel MOSCHOPULUS**
Gramm.
9026 ***IAMBICA ADESPOTA***

INDEX TO OUT-OF-ORDER WORKS IN LARGE BIBLIOGRAPHIES

In this *Canon,* discrete works under a given author's name are generally presented in sequential order of work numbers. Occasionally, however, works are arranged according to other principles that necessarily distort the sequence of work numbers. In certain cases, it seemed logical to group thematically related works together. In other instances, arrangement was dictated by the order of works within a single edition, even though the works in question were otherwise unrelated.

The purpose of this index is to facilitate the task of locating bibliographic information for specific works that are not listed in ascending numerical order. The information provided here applies only to bibliographies that exceed one page and only for the following authors: Aristoteles Phil. et *Corpus Aristotelicum;* Didymus Caecus Scr. Eccl.; Galenus Med.; Gregorius Nyssenus Theol; Joannes Chrysostomus Scr. Eccl.; Origenes Theol.; Plutarchus Biogr. et Phil. Below, work numbers are listed sequentially for these authors. Each work is accompanied by a reference to the precise page and column in which the bibliographic details for that work are given. Works numbered with the prefix *x*- are not included in this index.

ARISTOTELES Phil. et
CORPUS ARISTOTEL-
ICUM (0086)
001 p. 64, col. 1
002 p. 64, col. 1
003 p. 64, col. 1
004 p. 64, col. 1
005 p. 64, col. 1
006 p. 64, col. 2
007 p. 64, col. 2
008 p. 64, col. 2
009 p. 64, col. 2
010 p. 64, col. 2
011 p. 64, col. 2
012 p. 64, col. 2
013 p. 64, col. 2
014 p. 64, col. 2
015 p. 64, col. 2
016 p. 64, col. 2
017 p. 64, col. 2
018 p. 64, col. 2
019 p. 65, col. 1
020 p. 65, col. 1
021 p. 65, col. 1
022 p. 65, col. 1
023 p. 65, col. 1
024 p. 65, col. 1
025 p. 65, col. 1
026 p. 65, col. 1
027 p. 65, col. 1
028 p. 65, col. 1
029 p. 65, col. 1
030 p. 65, col. 1
031 p. 65, col. 1
032 p. 65, col. 1
033 p. 65, col. 2
034 p. 65, col. 1

035 p. 65, col. 2
036 p. 65, col. 2
037 p. 65, col. 2
038 p. 65, col. 2
040 p. 65, col. 2
041 p. 65, col. 2
042 p. 65, col. 2
043 p. 65, col. 2
044 p. 65, col. 2
045 p. 65, col. 2
046 p. 65, col. 2
047 p. 65, col. 2
048 p. 65, col. 2
049 p. 65, col. 2
050 p. 65, col. 2
051 p. 66, col. 1
052 p. 64, col. 1
053 p. 64, col. 1
054 p. 65, col. 1
055 p. 66, col. 1
056 p. 66, col. 1

DIDYMUS CAECUS Scr.
Eccl. (2102)
001 p. 129, col. 1
002 p. 129, col. 1
003 p. 129, col. 1
004 p. 129, col. 1
005 p. 129, col. 2
006 p. 129, col. 2
007 p. 129, col. 2
008 p. 130, col. 1
009 p. 130, col. 1
010 p. 129, col. 2
011 p. 129, col. 2
012 p. 130, col. 1
013 p. 129, col. 1

014 p. 129, col. 1
015 p. 129, col. 2
016 p. 129, col. 1
017 p. 129, col. 1
018 p. 129, col. 1
019 p. 129, col. 1
020 p. 129, col. 1
021 p. 129, col. 2
022 p. 129, col. 2
023 p. 129, col. 2
025 p. 129, col. 2
026 p. 130, col. 1
027 p. 130, col. 1
028 p. 130, col. 1
030 p. 130, col. 1
032 p. 130, col. 1
033 p. 130, col. 1
035 p. 130, col. 1
037 p. 130, col. 1
040 p. 130, col. 1
041 p. 128, col. 2
042 p. 130, col. 1
043 p. 130, col. 1
046 p. 130, col. 1
047 p. 129, col. 2
048 p. 129, col. 2
049 p. 129, col. 1

GALENUS Med. (0057)
001 p. 174, col. 2
002 p. 172, col. 2
003 p. 174, col. 2
004 p. 173, col. 1
005 p. 174, col. 1
006 p. 171, col. 1
007 p. 171, col. 2
008 p. 174, col. 2

009 p. 173, col. 1
010 p. 173, col. 1
011 p. 171, col. 2
012 p. 171, col. 2
013 p. 171, col. 2
014 p. 171, col. 2
015 p. 174, col. 1
016 p. 173, col. 1
017 p. 173, col. 1
018 p. 171, col. 2
019 p. 173, col. 2
020 p. 174, col. 2
021 p. 171, col. 2
022 p. 171, col. 2
023 p. 174, col. 2
024 p. 174, col. 2
025 p. 174, col. 2
026 p. 174, col. 2
027 p. 172, col. 2
028 p. 173, col. 1
029 p. 173, col. 1
030 p. 173, col. 1
031 p. 171, col. 2
032 p. 173, col. 1
033 p. 173, col. 1
034 p. 174, col. 2
035 p. 174, col. 1
036 p. 173, col. 2
037 p. 173, col. 2
038 p. 173, col. 2
039 p. 173, col. 2
040 p. 171, col. 2
041 p. 171, col. 2
042 p. 171, col. 2
043 p. 171, col. 2
044 p. 171, col. 2
045 p. 171, col. 2

INDEX OF CLASSIFICATION TAGS

The following information is intended to assist those who wish to consider TLG machine-readable texts according to specific categories identified in this *Canon*. The arrangement of this index is determined by alphabetical order of classification tags, under which author-work numbers are listed sequentially. Author numbers may be translated into author names by referring to the index of TLG author numbers on pages 407–423. Work numbers may then be resolved into work titles by consulting the bibliography to a given author in the *Canon* proper.

Although classification tags are affixed to all works deposited in the TLG data bank, many works awaiting the data entry process also are accompanied by one or more labels. Nevertheless, there has been no systematic effort to tag all works before they have been added to the data bank.

Since the character of certain works requires more than one classification, some author-work numbers are necessarily repeated under the appropriate classification label.

Acta (21 works)
0031 005; **0300** 001; **0317** 001–002; **0388** 001–002, 004–005; **0389** 001; **2038** 001–006; **2248** 001; **2948** 001–004; **2949** 001.

Alchemica (6 works)
1304 002; **1379** 001; **1480** 001; **2632** 001; **4086** 001; **9019** 005.

Anthologia (7 works)
2037 001; **2040** 075; **2591** 004; **4147** 001; **4148** 001; **7000** 001; **7051** 001.

Apocalypsis (22 works)
0031 027; **0527** 056–057; **1153** 001; **1154** 001; **1155** 001; **1156** 001; **1157** 001–002; **1158** 001–003; **1159** 001; **1201** 001; **1419** 001–004; **1463** 001–002; **1747** 001; **2243** 001.

Apocrypha (70 works)
0317 001–002; **0388** 001–005; **0389** 001; **0527** 017, 020–026, 034, 050, 052, 054–055, 058–059; **1153** 001; **1158** 001–003; **1159** 001–002; **1364** 001; **1366** 001–002; **1368** 001; **1369** 001–002; **1370** 001; **1371** 001; **1372** 001; **1373** 001; **1374** 001; **1375** 001; **1378** 001–009; **1455** 001; **1560** 001; **1637** 001; **1684** 001; **1747** 001; **1774** 001; **1776** 001–003; **2038** 001–002, 004–006; **2243** 001; **2948** 001–004; **2949** 001.

Apologetica (78 works)
0018 030–032, 039; **0526** 002–003; **0645** 001–004; **0646** 001–005, 008–012; **1163** 001; **1184** 001–003; **1205** 001; **1350** 001; **1495** 001, 003; **1725**

001; **1766** 001; **2017** 030–031, 046, 078; **2018** 001, 005–006, 010, 017, 021–024; **2022** 016, 022–024, 044; **2035** 001, 011–012, 030, 032; **2042** 001; **2062** 372–373; **2130** 033; **4089** 001–002, 010, 016, 020–021, 033, 036–037; **4090** 014–016, 111, 139–142, 144, 170, 175–176.

Astrologica (38 works)
0286 001; **0363** 007; **0530** 024; **0653** 002, 004; **0691** 001; **1126** 002–003; **1137** 001; **1142** 001; **1144** 001–005; **1215** 001–002; **1221** 001; **1238** 001; **1337** 001–003; **1421** 001, 003; **1487** 001–002; **1642** 001; **1764** 001–003; **2043** 001–005; **2053** 001–002; **4036** 022.

Astronomica (51 works)
0007 126; **0020** 006; **0222** 001, 015; **0363** 002–006; **0653** 001, 005; **0698** 002; **0717** 002; **1181** 001; **1207** 001; **1210** 001–002; **1272** 001; **1275** 002; **1358** 001, 003; **1383** 001–002; **1393** 001, 004; **1705** 003; **1719** 002–003; **1799** 012–014; **2133** 001; **2644** 001; **2651** 001; **3074** 003; **4036** 002; **4161** 001, 006–014; **4167** 001; **4176** 002; **9019** 002–003; **9022** 006.

Biographa (155 works)
0004 001; **0007** 001–066, 121, 145; **0018** 022; **0032** 002, 007; **0062** 008; **0066** 001; **0088** 006; **0095** 002; **0284** 023–028; **0526** 002; **0565** 004; **0577** 002; **0608** 001; **0610** 004; **0638** 001, 003; **1421** 001; **1521** 001; **1749** 001; **1779** 003; **1805** 001–010; **2018** 020; **2022** 004, 061; **2023** 001; **2034** 001–

002; **2050** 001; **2274** 003, 007; **2585** 001; **2708** 001; **3074** 002; **3152** 001; **3153** 001–004; **3154** 001; **3167** 001; **4066** 002, 007; **4075** 003; **4158** 001–002, 004–010; **4161** 002–005; **4166** 001; **4170** 001; **4172** 002–006; **4173** 001; **4282** 001; **5010** 005; **5012** 001; **5019** 001; **5023** 001; **5028** 001; **5030** 001; **5038** 001; **9012** 002.

Bucolica (12 works)
0005 001, 003–004; **0035** 001–005; **0036** 001–003; **1559** 001.

Catena (201 works)
2040 083–084, 086–088, 090; **2042** 006, 010–012, 014–015, 017, 022, 025, 034–036, 085; **2061** 001; **2062** 184–186; **2063** 013, 016, 025–026; **2064** 002; **2074** 037–045; **2102** 004, 013–015, 023, 025–028, 030, 046; **2115** 027; **2130** 002–008; **2598** 001–004, 015; **2724** 001–003, 005, 007–009; **2762** 004–009; **2866** 002–015; **2892** 093–094, 097–099; **2934** 045, 064; **2959** 007, 011; **2961** 001; **2967** 001; **4040** 014–028; **4090** 029, 104–108, 171–172; **4102** 001–008, 010–046; **4115** 029–030; **4124** 004–009, 012–013; **4126** 002, 004; **4134** 005; **4135** 009, 015–018; **4139** 039–052; **4154** 001–002.

Chronographa (51 works)
0081 018; **0222** 008, 012; **0549** 002; **0585** 003; **1139** 017–020, 027; **1246** 002; **1477** 002; **1478** 001; **1647** 002; **1706** 002; **1752** 002; **2018** 040; **2034** 010; **2115** 036–037; **2149** 001; **2170** 001; **2171** 001; **2172** 001; **2173** 001; **2174** 001; **2175** 001; **2176** 001; **2177**

001; **2371** 001; **2432** 001; **2573** 002; **2871** 001–003; **3043** 001–002; **3045** 001; **3051** 001–002; **3063** 001; **3064** 002; **3074** 001; **3086** 001–002; **3115** 001; **3141** 002–003; **3157** 001; **4046** 001; **4153** 001.

Comica (493 works)
0019 001–018; **0241** 002–003; **0252** 001–003, 005; **0264** 001–003; **0303** 001; **0394** 001; **0395** 001–002; **0396** 001; **0398** 001–002; **0399** 001–002; **0400** 001–004; **0401** 001–002; **0402** 001–006; **0403** 001–004; **0404** 001–002; **0405** 001–004; **0406** 001–002; **0407** 001–002; **0408** 001–002; **0409** 001–002; **0410** 001–005; **0411** 001–004; **0412** 001–002; **0413** 001–002; **0414** 001–004; **0415** 001–004; **0416** 001–002; **0417** 001–004; **0418** 001–002; **0419** 001–003; **0420** 001–002; **0421** 001–003; **0422** 001–002; **0423** 001–003; **0424** 001–003; **0425** 001–002; **0426** 001–005; **0427** 001–002; **0428** 001–004; **0429** 001–002; **0430** 001–002; **0431** 001–003; **0432** 001–002; **0433** 001–005; **0434** 001–006; **0435** 001–002; **0436** 001–002; **0437** 001–002; **0438** 001–002; **0439** 001–003; **0440** 001–002; **0441** 001–002; **0442** 001–002; **0443** 001–004; **0444** 001–002; **0445** 001–003; **0446** 001–002; **0447** 001–003; **0448** 001–002; **0449** 001–003; **0450** 001–003; **0451** 001–002; **0452** 001–002; **0453** 001–003; **0454** 001–002; **0455** 001–002; **0456** 001–002; **0457** 001–002; **0458** 001–006; **0459** 001–002; **0460** 001–002; **0461** 001–005; **0462** 001–002; **0463** 001–002; **0464** 001–002; **0465** 001–002; **0466** 001–002; **0468** 001–002; **0469** 001–002; **0470** 001–003; **0471** 001–002; **0472** 001–003; **0473** 001–003; **0474** 001–003; **0475** 001–002; **0476** 001–002; **0477** 001–003; **0478** 001–003; **0479** 001–002; **0480** 001–003; **0481** 001–002; **0482** 001–002; **0483** 001–002; **0484** 001–005; **0485** 001–002; **0486** 001–006; **0487** 001–004, 006–007, 009; **0488** 001–004; **0489** 001–003; **0490** 001–002; **0491** 001–003; **0492** 001–003; **0493** 001–002; **0494** 001–004; **0495** 001–003; **0496** 001–005; **0497** 001–004, 006–007; **0498** 001–002; **0499** 001–003; **0500** 001–003; **0501** 001–005; **0502** 001–002; **0503** 001–002; **0504** 001–002; **0505** 001–003; **0506** 001–002; **0507** 001–003; **0508** 001–006; **0510** 001–003; **0511** 001–003; **0512** 001–002; **0513** 001–004; **0514** 001–003; **0515** 001–004; **0516** 001–003; **0517** 001–002; **0518** 001–002; **0519** 001–002; **0520** 001; **0521** 001–006, 008; **0523** 001–003; **0524** 001–002; **0541** 001–041, 045, 049; **0602** 001–002; **0659** 001–005; **0662** 001–009; **1227** 001; **1315** 001–002; **1361** 001; **1384**

001; **1639** 001; **1654** 001–002; **1662** 001; **1676** 001; **1682** 001; **1780** 001–002; **1781** 001–002; **1782** 001–002; **1783** 001–002; **1784** 001–002; **1785** 001; **1786** 001; **1787** 001–002; **1788** 001–002; **1792** 001; **1793** 001; **1794** 001; **1795** 001; **2239** 001; **5005** 001–008, 050–052, 054–055.

Commentarius (290 works)
0022 005; **0057** 005, 008, 032, 092, 095, 100–101; **0084** 003; **0199** 007–008; **0552** 012; **0598** 010; **0615** 001; **0624** 001; **0660** 001; **0716** 002; **0724** 001–002, 004–005; **0726** 001, 004–005; **0727** 001; **0728** 001; **0732** 004–008, 010–011, 015, 018; **0752** 001–003, 005; **1207** 001; **1264** 003; **1273** 002; **1312** 003; **1409** 001; **1414** 001; **1431** 003; **1838** 002; **2001** 038–042; **2023** 004; **2031** 002; **2032** 002; **2033** 001–002, 008–009; **2034** 004, 006–007, 009, 014–022, 029; **2036** 001; **2047** 001; **2052** 001; **2571** 001; **2596** 002; **2697** 001–002; **2892** 084, 103; **3027** 001–005; **3062** 001; **3141** 012; **3151** 002; **3159** 001; **4007** 001; **4013** 001–006; **4014** 001; **4015** 001–009; **4016** 001–005; **4017** 001–004; **4018** 001; **4019** 001–006, 008; **4020** 001–003; **4021** 001–002; **4022** 001; **4026** 001–003; **4027** 001–004; **4030** 001; **4031** 001–003; **4032** 001; **4033** 001–003; **4034** 001–009; **4036** 001, 007–011, 021–022; **4065** 002; **4066** 004–006, 008; **4072** 001–004; **4075** 002; **4083** 001–003, 005–006; **4092** 002; **4093** 001–002; **4143** 001; **4146** 001–010; **4157** 001–002, 004; **4161** 001, 007, 010, 013; **4165** 001–002; **4168** 001; **4171** 001; **4174** 001–002; **4175** 001–007; **4187** 001–003, 006–010; **4190** 001–005; **4191** 001–002; **4192** 001–005; **4193** 003–005, 009–010, 012; **4194** 001–003, 007; **4195** 001–004; **4196** 001–002; **4201** 001; **4227** 001; **4228** 001; **4235** 001–002; **4236** 001; **4237** 001; **4240** 002–003; **4279** 001; **5024** 001–022; **5045** 001–004; **9004** 001; **9019** 001–003; **9020** 001; **9022** 006.

Concilia (6 works)
2035 003, 005; **5000** 001–004.

Coquinaria (3 works)
0521 002, 008; **0897** 001.

Dialogus (128 works)
0007 077, 079, 090–092, 095, 107, 109, 112–113, 126, 129–130, 138–139; **0032** 002–004, 008; **0059** 001, 003–035, 038; **0061** 002–004, 006–008; **0062** 015–026, 030–032, 034–035, 039–040, 043–047, 050, 055, 061, 063, 065–070; **0086** 051; **0094** 002; **0572** 001; **0591** 002; **0638** 004–005; **0645** 003; **0673** 001–003; **1286** 002, 017; **2017** 056; **2035** 027, 034, 099, 109; **2042** 018; **2074**

018; **2111** 004; **2892** 007, 042; **2934** 012, 014, 032; **2950** 001; **3130** 003, 007; **4001** 001; **4090** 023, 026–027, 110; **4156** 001.

Doxographa (12 works)
0004 001; **0093** 003, 008; **0094** 003; **0528** 001–002; **0529** 001; **0530** 042; **0531** 001; **1193** 001; **1269** 002; **2037** 001.

Ecclesiastica (124 works)
0572 001; **1171** 001; **1311** 001; **1353** 001; **1570** 001; **1665** 001; **2017** 076; **2018** 002; **2021** 004–006, 018–019, 025–028; **2035** 005, 009, 016, 029, 034–035, 046, 058, 084, 102, 118, 126–127; **2040** 002, 040–052, 065–067, 070, 072, 074, 076, 078–082; **2042** 007; **2048** 001; **2057** 001; **2058** 001–003; **2062** 001–011, 085–088, 116, 119, 281, 346, 378, 429, 499; **2102** 032–033, 035, 037; **2109** 011–012; **2110** 010; **2111** 002; **2112** 002, 011, 015; **2115** 047, 055, 057, 059; **2130** 014–015, 018–019, 033; **2733** 001; **2734** 008, 024–025; **2892** 008, 053, 087–088, 091–092; **2934** 021; **3023** 013; **3079** 005; **3147** 001; **4089** 003–004, 031; **5048** 001; **5049** 001; **7051** 001.

Elegiaca (78 works)
0002 001–003; **0011** 009; **0085** 009; **0086** 049; **0198** 002; **0212** 001–002, 004; **0213** 001; **0214** 001; **0216** 001; **0217** 001; **0231** 001; **0232** 001; **0234** 001; **0236** 001; **0237** 001; **0239** 001–002; **0242** 001; **0243** 001; **0244** 001; **0245** 001; **0246** 001; **0247** 001; **0251** 001; **0254** 001; **0255** 001, 003; **0257** 001; **0258** 001; **0261** 001; **0262** 001; **0263** 001; **0266** 001–002; **0267** 001, 006; **0280** 001; **0284** 057; **0308** 002, 009; **0319** 002, 004; **0336** 002, 004; **0533** 001, 005; **0653** 005; **0655** 002–003; **0676** 002; **0706** 001; **0888** 001; **1273** 001–002; **1570** 001; **1604** 001; **1632** 004; **1675** 002; **1735** 003; **2022** 059–062; **2433** 005; **2605** 001; **2606** 001; **2611** 001; **2646** 001; **2647** 001; **2648** 002; **2651** 001; **2694** 001; **2934** 072.

Encomiastica (149 works)
0006 022; **0010** 009–010; **0011** 010; **0032** 009; **0033** 001–005; **0061** 003, 008; **0062** 006, 010, 045; **0086** 051; **0128** 002; **0199** 001, 003–004; **0230** 001; **0261** 002; **0284** 013–014, 016, 055; **0290** 001; **0295** 001; **0308** 005; **0378** 001; **0566** 002; **0577** 002; **0593** 003; **0612** 002; **1139** 029; **1394** 002; **1816** 002, 005–006, 009, 011–012, 014–016; **1887** 001; **1888** 002; **2003** 001–002; **2006** 006; **2017** 021–023, 040, 048, 051, 064–069, 075; **2018** 020, 022; **2022** 005–006, 021, 028, 031, 034, 037–038; **2040** 023, 033–035, 038;

2060 001–002; **2062** 014, 039–048, 050, 052–058, 072, 098, 124, 126, 128–129, 132, 135, 226–229, 247, 254, 267, 298–299, 311, 338, 383, 402, 418, 437, 445–446, 465, 486, 488; **2063** 001; **2112** 014, 031; **2121** 001; **2130** 033; **2598** 011; **2607** 001; **2621** 001; **2650** 001; **2708** 001; **2721** 001; **2800** 006; **2934** 059–060; **3000** 001; **3023** 014; **3141** 005, 009, 013; **3154** 001; **4038** 001; **4090** 117.

Epica (142 works)

0001 001–002, 004; **0012** 001–002; **0020** 001–004, 007; **0022** 001–003; **0023** 001; **0024** 001; **0174** 002–003; **0216** 001; **0218** 001; **0219** 001, 003, 005; **0220** 001; **0221** 001–002; **0222** 003, 009, 013; **0239** 002, 004; **0242** 002; **0288** 002; **0298** 002, 004; **0302** 001; **0321** 003; **0336** 004; **0364** 001; **0533** 001, 005; **0576** 003; **0579** 002; **0647** 001; **0653** 001, 005; **0668** 001; **0683** 001; **0696** 001; **0710** 001; **1139** 007; **1141** 001–002; **1176** 001; **1182** 001; **1212** 001; **1228** 001; **1229** 001; **1241** 001; **1260** 001; **1263** 001–004; **1273** 002; **1296** 001; **1308** 001–002; **1326** 001; **1344** 001; **1345** 001–002; **1351** 001; **1391** 002, 004; **1393** 001, 004; **1395** 001, 003; **1425** 001; **1444** 001; **1445** 001; **1475** 001; **1504** 002–003; **1512** 001; **1524** 001; **1526** 001, 003; **1541** 001; **1546** 001; **1547** 001; **1557** 001; **1576** 001; **1580** 001–003; **1594** 002, 004; **1607** 001; **1639** 001; **1688** 001–002; **1712** 001; **1720** 002–003; **1723** 001; **1726** 001–002; **1737** 001; **1757** 001; **1816** 003–005, 008, 013, 017, 019–020; **1906** 002; **1967** 002; **1987** 002; **2045** 001; **2046** 001; **2119** 001, 004; **2120** 001; **2121** 001; **2212** 002; **2333** 002; **2385** 003; **2612** 001; **2613** 001; **2628** 001; **2633** 001; **2636** 001; **2639** 001; **2641** 001; **2650** 001; **2694** 001; **4038** 001; **4081** 001; **4082** 001.

Epigrammatica (438 works)

0001 002–003; **0002** 004; **0003** 002; **0004** 002; **0005** 002, 005; **0006** 031; **0009** 002; **0011** 009; **0012** 003; **0022** 003, 006; **0035** 005–006; **0059** 039, 041; **0061** 009–010; **0076** 001; **0085** 010; **0091** 001; **0096** 014; **0101** 001; **0102** 001; **0103** 001; **0104** 001; **0105** 001; **0106** 001; **0107** 001; **0108** 001; **0109** 001; **0110** 001; **0111** 001; **0112** 001; **0113** 001; **0114** 001; **0117** 001; **0118** 001; **0119** 001; **0120** 001; **0121** 001; **0122** 001; **0124** 001; **0126** 001; **0127** 001; **0131** 001–002; **0132** 001; **0133** 001; **0134** 001; **0135** 002; **0136** 001; **0137** 001; **0138** 001; **0140** 001; **0141** 002–003; **0142** 001; **0143** 001; **0144** 001; **0145** 001; **0146** 001–002; **0147** 001; **0148** 001; **0149** 001; **0150** 001; **0151** 001; **0152** 001; **0153** 001;

0154 001; **0156** 001; **0157** 001; **0158** 001; **0159** 001; **0160** 001; **0161** 001; **0162** 001; **0163** 001; **0164** 001; **0165** 001; **0166** 001; **0167** 001; **0168** 001; **0169** 001; **0170** 001; **0171** 001; **0172** 001; **0173** 001; **0174** 001; **0175** 001; **0176** 001; **0177** 001; **0178** 001; **0179** 001; **0180** 001; **0181** 001; **0182** 001; **0183** 001; **0184** 001; **0185** 001; **0186** 005; **0187** 001; **0188** 001; **0189** 001; **0190** 001; **0191** 001; **0192** 001; **0193** 001; **0194** 001; **0195** 001; **0196** 001; **0197** 001; **0198** 001–002; **0199** 006, 009; **0208** 001–002; **0211** 001–002; **0212** 001–002; **0215** 001–002; **0216** 001–002; **0218** 001–002; **0219** 001–002; **0220** 001–002; **0221** 001, 004; **0222** 005, 009; **0232** 001, 003; **0237** 004; **0239** 002–003; **0245** 001–002; **0249** 001; **0255** 002; **0259** 003; **0261** 001, 003; **0265** 001, 003; **0267** 003; **0268** 002; **0274** 001; **0288** 003; **0289** 001–002; **0308** 009; **0336** 003–004; **0363** 013; **0487** 008; **0497** 005; **0521** 002, 008; **0533** 001, 003–004; **0541** 044, 046; **0552** 012, 014; **0568** 002, 004; **0570** 002–003; **0571** 002, 004; **0584** 001–003; **0590** 004; **0596** 001; **0600** 001; **0631** 002; **0632** 002, 005; **0638** 009; **0653** 003, 005; **0658** 002; **0679** 001–002; **0959** 001; **1150** 001; **1172** 001; **1213** 001; **1262** 001–002; **1264** 004–005; **1274** 001–002; **1290** 001; **1342** 002, 004; **1353** 001; **1355** 001–002; **1391** 001; **1396** 001; **1401** 001; **1410** 001; **1415** 001; **1422** 001; **1423** 001; **1433** 001; **1440** 001; **1446** 001–002; **1449** 001; **1456** 001; **1457** 001; **1458** 001; **1468** 001; **1472** 001; **1473** 001; **1474** 001; **1476** 001; **1492** 001; **1501** 001; **1502** 001; **1513** 001; **1518** 001; **1519** 001; **1520** 001; **1522** 001; **1526** 003; **1528** 001; **1531** 001; **1532** 001; **1533** 001; **1536** 001; **1537** 001; **1540** 001; **1543** 001; **1548** 002; **1554** 001; **1555** 001, 003; **1556** 001–002; **1563** 001; **1565** 001; **1566** 001; **1567** 001; **1573** 001; **1575** 001; **1577** 001; **1579** 001; **1581** 001; **1582** 001; **1587** 001; **1589** 001; **1592** 001; **1593** 001; **1595** 730; **1601** 001; **1604** 002; **1610** 001; **1612** 001; **1614** 001; **1616** 001; **1618** 001; **1620** 001; **1621** 001; **1628** 001; **1631** 001; **1632** 001–002, 004; **1633** 001; **1640** 001; **1653** 001; **1656** 001; **1658** 001; **1659** 001; **1660** 001; **1667** 006; **1668** 001; **1673** 001; **1677** 001; **1680** 001; **1692** 004–005; **1694** 001; **1697** 001; **1707** 001; **1708** 001; **1714** 001, 003; **1715** 001–002; **1716** 001; **1717** 001; **1730** 001; **1731** 001; **1735** 002–003; **1739** 001; **1740** 001; **1741** 001; **1742** 001; **1743** 001; **1744** 001; **1745** 001; **1755** 001; **1761** 001; **1775** 001; **1799** 017; **1819** 001; **1865** 001; **2003** 014, 018; **2006** 011; **2022** 057, 059, 061, 063–064; **2033** 007; **2045** 003; **2058** 006; **2119** 002;

2122 001; **2123** 001; **2124** 001; **2125** 001; **2126** 001; **2127** 002; **2128** 001; **2129** 001; **2130** 001, 034; **2131** 001; **2200** 011; **2302** 001; **2409** 002; **2610** 001; **2615** 001; **2622** 001; **2625** 001; **2630** 001–002; **2643** 002; **2648** 003; **2649** 001; **2693** 001; **2892** 082; **2988** 001; **3079** 002; **4023** 001; **4024** 002; **4028** 002; **4035** 001; **4036** 003, 017; **4039** 004; **4040** 011; **4041** 001; **4042** 016; **4043** 001; **4044** 001; **4045** 001; **4046** 002; **4047** 001; **4048** 001; **4049** 001; **4050** 001; **4051** 001; **4052** 001; **4053** 001; **4054** 001; **4055** 001; **4056** 001; **4057** 001; **4058** 001; **4059** 001; **4060** 001; **4061** 001; **4062** 001; **4063** 001; **4064** 001; **4066** 001; **4067** 001; **4068** 001; **4069** 001; **4070** 001; **4071** 001; **4073** 001; **4074** 001; **4075** 001; **4076** 001; **4077** 001; **4078** 001; **4079** 001; **4158** 003; **5008** 001; **5014** 002, 007–010, 012–014; **5032** 002; **5037** 006; **5039** 001; **7000** 001; **7052** 001–008; **9005** 001; **9011** 001; **9012** 001; **9013** 001; **9014** 001; **9015** 001; **9016** 001; **9017** 001.

Epistolographa (329 works)

0007 076, 111, 145; **0010** 022–030; **0014** 012, 063; **0026** 004; **0031** 006–026; **0037** 001; **0038** 001; **0039** 001; **0040** 001; **0041** 001–002; **0042** 001; **0043** 001; **0044** 001; **0045** 001; **0046** 001; **0047** 001; **0048** 001; **0049** 001; **0050** 001; **0051** 001; **0052** 001; **0053** 001; **0054** 001; **0055** 001; **0056** 001; **0059** 036; **0062** 007; **0074** 008; **0081** 008, 011, 015; **0086** 011, 051; **0125** 001; **0186** 001–004; **0284** 041; **0386** 001; **0388** 003; **0509** 001; **0527** 052; **0537** 004, 006–008; **0540** 036; **0542** 001; **0545** 003; **0551** 016; **0555** 008; **0557** 006; **0566** 002; **0583** 002; **0589** 001; **0618** 001; **0622** 001; **0623** 001; **0627** 055; **0628** 003; **0629** 001; **0632** 002; **0633** 001; **0634** 001; **0636** 001; **0637** 001; **0638** 002, 006; **0639** 001; **0640** 001; **0646** 004, 007; **0653** 005; **0691** 001; **0744** 001, 004; **0751** 001–002; **1121** 001; **1130** 001; **1139** 007; **1149** 001; **1177** 001; **1183** 001; **1216** 001; **1271** 001–003, 005, 010; **1298** 001; **1325** 001; **1327** 001; **1329** 001; **1349** 001; **1350** 001; **1352** 001; **1367** 001; **1381** 001; **1411** 001; **1412** 001; **1443** 001–002; **1477** 002; **1479** 001; **1484** 001; **1585** 001; **1613** 001; **1622** 001; **1626** 001; **1641** 001; **1670** 001; **1681** 001; **1692** 001–002; **1705** 001; **1754** 001; **1803** 001; **1978** 002; **2003** 005–006, 013, 015–016; **2004** 001; **2006** 001; **2017** 033, 041, 070, 076, 080, 084; **2018** 008, 013–016, 027; **2021** 002, 007, 009, 011; **2022** 001–002; **2034** 005, 013; **2035** 003–011, 013–015, 028, 033, 040–041, 043, 045, 049–055, 059, 065, 085, 105, 110, 112–113, 119–121, 123; **2040** 004–005;

2041 001; **2042** 033, 040–041, 045; **2061** 004; **2062** 001, 007–008, 086, 088, 094–097, 281, 344, 367, 376, 383, 421, 499; **2063** 005; **2074** 024–025, 030; **2109** 005; **2110** 010, 013; **2111** 003; **2112** 002, 015–016, 018; **2115** 024, 048, 059; **2130** 033–034; **2163** 001; **2200** 001–003; **2486** 002; **2598** 005–006, 019; **2643** 001; **2734** 004, 019, 021–022; **2798** 006–015; **2810** 001; **2892** 020, 022–023, 044–046, 072, 078, 080, 089, 107–108; **2934** 011, 047, 050; **2952** 001; **2953** 001; **2966** 002; **2991** 016; **3123** 001; **3130** 001; **3141** 011; **3147** 003; **3158** 001; **4000** 001; **4001** 002; **4040** 009, 029; **4085** 001; **4089** 005–007, 034–035; **4090** 022, 114–115, 162–163, 165–167; **4161** 009; **4184** 001; **4193** 005; **5000** 001, 003–004; **9022** 005.

Evangelica (30 works)
0031 001–004; **1364** 001; **1366** 001–002; **1368** 001; **1369** 001–002; **1370** 001; **1371** 001; **1372** 001; **1373** 001; **1374** 001; **1375** 001; **1378** 001–009; **1560** 001; **1637** 001; **1684** 001; **1766** 002; **2045** 002.

Exegetica (574 works)
0018 001–024, 034–035, 040; **0555** 008; **1130** 001; **1136** 001; **1186** 001; **1398** 001; **1447** 005; **1495** 003; **1558** 001; **1664** 001; **1725** 002; **1838** 003; **2017** 011, 027–029, 032, 042, 047, 053, 055, 071, 078–079, 081, 084; **2018** 012, 019, 021, 028–032, 034–038; **2021** 004–006; **2022** 045, 053; **2034** 009; **2035** 017–019, 039, 044, 054, 057, 059, 061–063, 068, 071, 074, 078, 080, 115–116, 122; **2038** 003; **2040** 001, 009, 028, 032, 062, 083–084, 086–088, 090; **2042** 005–006, 009–017, 019–024, 026–032, 034–039, 042–044, 047–079, 081, 084–087; **2045** 002; **2061** 001–002; **2062** 061–071, 073–074, 076–080, 084, 112–115, 122, 134, 137, 141, 143–145, 148–149, 151–168, 178–180, 183–187, 196–201, 203–209, 213, 215–216, 230–236, 239, 241–242, 244, 248–250, 283–284, 290, 294, 305, 308–309, 312, 314–315, 317–318, 323, 328, 347, 352, 358–359, 379, 383, 412, 425, 430, 432, 443, 447, 464, 495, 497–498, 500; **2063** 006, 013, 016, 025–026; **2064** 002; **2074** 031–046; **2102** 001–007, 010–011, 013–023, 025–028, 030, 041, 046–049; **2110** 009; **2112** 007, 010, 016, 018–027; **2115** 003–023, 026–035, 038, 044–046, 049–053; **2130** 002–008, 033; **2598** 014–015; **2720** 012; **2724** 001–003, 005, 007–009; **2762** 004–009; **2800** 017; **2824** 001–003; **2866** 001–015; **2892** 001–002, 005–006, 012, 018, 051, 054–060, 062, 093–094, 097–099, 102–103; **2934** 007, 045, 053, 064; **2957** 002; **2959** 007, 011; **2961** 001; **2967** 001; **4040** 014–028; **4089** 008,

017, 022–030; **4090** 001–006, 029–031, 095–108, 112, 115–116, 118, 120, 124–127, 129, 171–172; **4115** 029–030; **4124** 004–009, 012–013; **4126** 002, 004; **4134** 005; **4135** 009, 015–018; **4139** 039–052; **4147** 001; **4148** 001; **4154** 001–002; **5000** 002; **7051** 001.

Fabula (14 works)
0096 002–013, 015; **0614** 001.

Geographa (38 works)
0067 001, 004–005; **0074** 004; **0079** 002; **0090** 001; **0092** 001; **0094** 001; **0099** 001; **0222** 002; **0363** 009, 014; **0525** 001; **0686** 002; **0698** 002; **1002** 001; **1052** 001, 003; **1139** 025; **1358** 001; **1409** 001; **1427** 002; **1431** 002; **1434** 002, 004; **1650** 001; **1864** 001; **1917** 002; **2018** 011; **2029** 001; **2030** 001; **2307** 001; **2647** 001; **4003** 003; **4028** 001; **4061** 002; **4174** 001–002.

Gnomica (46 works)
0007 081–082; **0096** 016–017; **0319** 004; **0521** 002, 008; **0534** 002; **0537** 002; **0541** 042, 047–048; **0557** 004–005; **0624** 001; **0628** 002; **0635** 001; **0662** 004; **1139** 030; **1234** 001; **1256** 001–002; **1269** 002; **1278** 001; **1304** 002; **1521** 002; **1604** 001; **1605** 001; **1666** 001; **1667** 002, 004–006; **1759** 001–002; **1791** 001–002; **2021** 028; **2022** 014, 060; **2034** 008; **2037** 001; **2063** 021; **2109** 011; **2591** 004; **7051** 001.

Grammatica (176 works)
0062 014; **0063** 001, 004; **0066** 001; **0072** 001, 003–023; **0082** 001–005; **0086** 036; **0087** 001–034, 036–040, 042–043, 045–050; **0089** 001; **0212** 003; **0222** 007; **0356** 001; **0533** 001, 005; **0549** 002; **0567** 001; **0609** 003; **0644** 002–003, 005–007, 012; **0662** 004, 008; **0688** 004; **0708** 002; **0958** 001; **1047** 001; **1194** 001–002; **1251** 001; **1253** 001; **1266** 001; **1312** 002–003; **1402** 001–005; **1408** 001–002; **1460** 001; **1611** 001; **1615** 001; **1718** 001; **1756** 001; **1758** 001; **1809** 001; **1838** 002; **1841** 001; **1850** 001; **1983** 002; **2020** 001–007; **2116** 001; **2130** 037; **2178** 004; **2255** 002; **2269** 001; **2449** 002; **2867** 001; **2999** 001–002; **3002** 001–015, 017; **4028** 001; **4093** 001–002; **4149** 001; **4170** 001; **4175** 001–007; **4245** 001; **4246** 001; **4250** 001; **9022** 001, 003–004; **9024** 001.

Hagiographa (162 works)
0304 001; **0384** 001–003; **0388** 002; **0389** 001; **0390** 001; **0391** 001; **0527** 026; **1349** 001; **1352** 001; **1398** 001; **1451** 001; **1483** 001; **1484** 001; **1485** 001; **1700** 001; **1701** 001–002; **1702** 001; **1747** 001; **2005** 001; **2007** 001; **2008** 001; **2009** 001; **2010** 001; **2011**

001; **2012** 001; **2014** 001; **2015** 001; **2016** 001; **2017** 040–042, 048, 051–052, 064–069, 073, 075; **2018** 003–004, 025–026, 033; **2021** 020–024, 043; **2022** 028, 034, 037; **2035** 047, 104; **2038** 001, 004–006; **2040** 023, 033–035, 038; **2062** 014, 039–048, 050, 052–058, 124, 126, 135, 224–229, 232, 254, 282, 293, 298–299, 304, 348–350, 362, 383, 402, 418, 423, 436–437, 445–446, 459, 486, 489; **2111** 001, 004; **2112** 030; **2248** 001; **2657** 001–002; **2679** 001–010; **2744** 001; **2800** 006, 018; **2856** 001–003; **2877** 001–008; **2934** 059–060, 062, 066; **2948** 001–004; **2949** 001; **2966** 002; **4089** 004; **4090** 121.

Hexametrica (96 works)
0020 006; **0022** 005; **0084** 001; **0211** 001; **0212** 001; **0230** 001; **0233** 001; **0251** 001; **0253** 001; **0262** 001; **0263** 001; **0267** 002, 006; **0273** 001–002; **0281** 001; **0282** 001; **0284** 057; **0286** 001; **0290** 001; **0315** 002; **0319** 004; **0336** 002, 004; **0522** 001; **0579** 001, 003, 011; **0598** 005; **0627** 057; **0632** 001–002; **0698** 002; **0703** 001; **0740** 001; **0750** 001–002; **0856** 001; **0897** 001; **1139** 029; **1193** 001–002; **1264** 005; **1269** 001; **1275** 002; **1301** 002; **1342** 004; **1355** 001, 003; **1382** 001; **1442** 002; **1487** 001; **1500** 001; **1533** 002; **1555** 001; **1556** 001; **1562** 002; **1577** 002; **1604** 001; **1605** 001; **1609** 002–003; **1732** 002; **1735** 003; **1813** 001; **1816** 001–002, 006–007, 010, 014–016, 018, 021; **1836** 001; **1933** 002; **2018** 021; **2022** 013, 059–062; **2045** 002; **2074** 046; **2318** 001; **2617** 001; **2620** 001; **2621** 001; **2625** 001; **2631** 001; **2646** 001; **2648** 001; **2653** 001; **2697** 001–002.

Historica (1035 works)
0003 001; **0007** 083, 085, 125, 127, 129–130, 145, 148; **0008** 002; **0015** 001; **0016** 001; **0022** 001–003; **0023** 001; **0024** 001; **0032** 001, 006, 009–015; **0060** 001–003; **0062** 053; **0063** 003; **0065** 003; **0066** 001; **0067** 004; **0070** 002; **0074** 001–004, 006–007, 009–016, 018; **0080** 002; **0081** 001, 018; **0084** 002–003; **0086** 003–005, 007, 012–015, 018, 020–021, 026, 030–031, 036–037, 043, 046, 051, 054, 056; **0093** 001–002, 004–005, 010, 013–015; **0099** 003; **0116** 001; **0128** 002; **0129** 001; **0130** 001; **0213** 003; **0219** 005–006; **0222** 008, 012, 014; **0255** 003; **0257** 002; **0259** 004; **0261** 005; **0266** 002; **0281** 001; **0282** 001; **0298** 004; **0308** 007; **0360** 001; **0385** 001–016, 018; **0392** 002; **0393** 002; **0526** 001, 004; **0527** 001–009, 011–018, 023–024; **0534** 002–003; **0535** 003; **0536** 001, 003–004; **0538** 002–003; **0539** 002–003; **0543** 001–002; **0545** 001–002,

4040 001; **4046** 001; **4076** 003–006; **4080** 001; **4084** 001; **4089** 003–004, 031; **4145** 001; **4153** 001; **4155** 001; **4210** 001.

Homiletica (668 works)

0555 006, 008; **1495** 001, 003; **2006** 008; **2017** 009–023, 029, 032, 034–039, 047, 049, 053, 059–060, 062–063, 071–073, 075; **2021** 012–017, 042; **2022** 066; **2035** 017–021, 023, 031, 036–039, 056, 063, 069–070, 076, 079, 082–083, 086–091, 094, 101, 122, 125; **2040** 001, 006–008, 011–012, 018, 020–042, 044, 046, 053–063, 068–069, 075; **2042** 009, 013, 016–017, 021–025, 027, 064–065, 080, 082, 084, 086; **2060** 001–007; **2061** 001; **2062** 012, 014–037, 039–084, 089–093, 098–101, 103–108, 110–115, 117–118, 120–142, 144–145, 148–157, 159–182, 196–208, 210–212, 214–222, 224–280, 282–338, 347–366, 374–375, 379–386, 388–390, 402–415, 417, 419–420, 422–425, 427, 430–432, 434–438, 440–445, 447–449, 452, 455, 459, 463–465, 473, 484, 486, 488–494, 496, 498, 500, 502–504; **2063** 009–010; **2074** 017; **2109** 001–004, 006–009, 013; **2110** 001–009, 011–012; **2112** 001, 003–010, 012–013, 017, 026, 031; **2115** 002, 006, 010, 026–028, 033–034, 039, 046; **2130** 034; **2274** 004; **2714** 001; **2720** 001–023, 026–032, 034–038; **2800** 003–012; **2892** 081; **2934** 022–031, 054–057, 075; **4055** 002; **4089** 017, 032; **4090** 008–013, 017, 030, 095, 116–122, 148–149; **4124** 001, 003; **4138** 001; **4156** 002.

Hymnus (132 works)

0013 001–034; **0022** 003; **0033** 005; **0086** 050; **0199** 004; **0201** 001; **0202** 001; **0203** 001; **0204** 001–002; **0205** 001–002; **0227** 001; **0228** 001; **0230** 001; **0268** 001; **0284** 001–008, 017–018, 057; **0298** 001–002; **0299** 001; **0308** 005; **0359** 001; **0366** 001; **0367** 001; **0370** 001; **0372** 001; **0373** 001; **0374** 001–002; **0377** 001; **0380** 001; **0382** 002; **0397** 001; **0527** 027–028, 050; **0533** 002; **0555** 003; **0579** 001; **0653** 005; **0742** 001–014, 016–020; **0900** 001; **1203** 001–006; **1269** 001; **1286** 022; **1495** 001; **1588** 001; **1746** 001; **2006** 010; **2022** 059; **2038** 002–003; **2623** 001; **2648** 004; **2734** 017; **2881** 001–003, 005; **2892** 104; **2971** 001; **3023** 016–017; **3141** 008; **4036** 015–016.

Hypothesis (108 works)

0662 005–006; **2035** 060; **2062** 155–156, 159–160, 163–164, 167–168, 197; **2200** 007; **5005** 001–016, 018–040, 042–045, 047, 049–055; **5008** 001; **5010** 001, 003–007, 009, 020–021; **5012** 001; **5014** 001–003, 005–010, 012–015, 017–021; **5016** 001; **5017** 001; **5023** 001, 007; **5026** 007, 009, 011–012; **5028** 001; **5030** 001; **5034** 001; **5037** 001, 003, 006; **5038** 001.

Iambica (82 works)

0068 001–002; **0069** 001; **0137** 002; **0232** 001; **0233** 001; **0235** 001; **0237** 001; **0238** 001; **0245** 001; **0248** 001; **0250** 001; **0251** 001; **0252** 004; **0253** 001; **0255** 001; **0256** 001; **0259** 001; **0260** 001; **0263** 001; **0264** 001–003; **0265** 001; **0336** 004; **0533** 001, 005; **0541** 042; **0635** 001–002; **0679** 002; **1250** 001; **1256** 001–002; **1257** 002; **1264** 005; **1269** 001–002; **1287** 001–002; **1358** 001; **1386** 018–019; **1420** 001; **1566** 001–002; **1606** 001; **1676** 001–002; **1690** 001; **1691** 001; **1797** 001–002; **1816** 009, 011–012; **1821** 001–002; **1906** 002; **2022** 004, 012, 014, 059–061; **2112** 002; **2300** 003; **2609** 001; **2634** 001; **2646** 001; **2648** 004; **2721** 002; **2934** 072, 074; **3141** 005–007; **3151** 002; **4150** 001; **9022** 004; **9023** 002; **9026** 001.

Invectiva (8 works)

0062 028, 038, 042, 049; **1171** 001; **2022** 018–019; **2112** 011.

Jurisprudentia (12 works)

2062 429; **2734** 010–014, 026–027; **3023** 025–026; **3063** 003; **3079** 002.

Lexicographa (63 works)

0057 106; **0087** 041; **0530** 003; **0542** 001; **0597** 001; **0644** 002–003, 010–011; **0662** 007; **0708** 001; **0716** 001; **0751** 005; **1152** 003–004; **1168** 001; **1312** 004; **1323** 001; **1376** 001; **1389** 001; **1416** 002; **1515** 001; **1569** 001; **1608** 001–005; **2018** 011; **2274** 002; **2591** 001–003, 005–006; **2991** 001–016; **2995** 001–002; **4015** 012; **4028** 001; **4040** 001, 029; **4085** 002–003; **4099** 001; **9003** 001; **9010** 001–002.

Liturgica (24 works)

2021 032; **2022** 055; **2040** 064, 070–071, 073, 076–077; **2062** 339–343, 345, 368–371, 426, 428, 487; **2109** 010; **2892** 050; **2934** 061.

Lyrica (126 works)

0006 022; **0009** 001, 003–004; **0011** 010; **0033** 001–005; **0083** 002; **0086** 050; **0165** 002; **0199** 001–005; **0201** 001; **0202** 001; **0203** 001; **0204** 001–002; **0205** 001–002; **0206** 001; **0207** 001; **0209** 001; **0210** 001; **0227** 001; **0230** 001; **0232** 002; **0237** 002–003; **0240** 001; **0261** 001; **0265** 002; **0269** 001–002; **0271** 001; **0272** 001; **0273** 001–002; **0275** 001; **0276** 001; **0277** 001; **0278** 001; **0279** 001; **0283** 001–002; **0291** 001–002; **0292** 001–002; **0293** 001–002; **0294** 001; **0295** 001; **0296** 001; **0297** 001; **0298** 001–002; **0299** 001–002; **0308** 003–005; **0365** 001; **0366** 001–002; **0367** 001; **0368** 001; **0369** 001; **0370** 001; **0371** 001–002; **0372** 001; **0373** 001; **0374** 001–002; **0375** 001–002; **0376** 001–002; **0377** 001–002; **0378** 001; **0379** 001–002; **0380** 001; **0381** 001; **0382** 001–002; **0383** 001–003; **0387** 001–002; **0397** 001; **0533** 001; **0631** 001; **0900** 001; **0918** 001; **0971** 001; **0981** 001; **1203** 001–006; **1223** 001; **1261** 001; **1274** 001; **1363** 001; **1382** 001; **1471** 001; **1493** 001; **1815** 001; **1833** 001; **1836** 001; **2022** 059–060; **2118** 001; **2367** 001; **2607** 001.

Magica (6 works)

0742 016; **1482** 001; **5002** 001–004.

Mathematica (85 works)

0018 038; **0078** 002; **0086** 019, 036; **0222** 004–005; **0358** 001, 003; **0363** 001, 012; **0550** 001–002; **0552** 001–014; **0559** 006, 008–010; **0717** 001; **1052** 001; **1147** 003; **1277** 001; **1317** 001; **1357** 001; **1358** 001; **1719** 001–003; **1724** 001; **1734** 001; **1799** 001–011, 016; **2023** 003–005; **2032** 001–002; **2033** 001–002, 008–009; **2039** 001–005; **2055** 001–002; **2577** 001–002; **3159** 001; **4005** 001; **4013** 004; **4036** 011; **4072** 001–004; **4088** 003, 005; **4146** 001; **4176** 002; **4228** 001.

Mechanica (19 works)

0086 023; **0363** 012; **0552** 013; **0559** 001–002, 004–005, 007, 012–013; **1165** 001; **1177** 001; **1204** 001; **1226** 001; **1599** 001–002; **4015** 017; **4088** 003; **4167** 001.

Medica (344 works)

0007 077; **0022** 001–003; **0057** 001–004, 006–080, 083–096, 099–107, 111, 114–115, 121; **0086** 036; **0280** 001; **0281** 001; **0284** 023–028; **0530** 001–002, 005–006, 009, 012, 023–024, 026, 029, 031–037, 041, 043, 045–046; **0564** 001–007; **0565** 001–003; **0627** 001–054, 056–057; **0643** 001–002; **0653** 005; **0656** 001–002; **0657** 001; **0660** 001; **0661** 001–002; **0663** 001; **0667** 001; **0671** 001; **0676** 001–002; **0691** 001; **0706** 001; **0715** 001; **0716** 001–002; **0718** 001–009, 011–013, 015–016; **0719** 001–004; **0721** 001–017, 020–028; **0722** 001–005; **0723** 001–002; **0724** 001–005; **0726** 001–004; **0727** 001; **0728** 001; **0729** 002–006; **0730** 001–002; **0731** 001; **0732** 001–003, 017; **0733** 001; **0734** 001; **0736** 001; **0737** 001; **0738** 001–010; **0740** 001; **0743** 001; **0744** 001–005; **0745** 001–002; **0746** 001; **0748** 001; **0749** 001; **0750** 001–002; **0751** 002–004, 007; **0752** 001–002; **0790** 001; **0845** 002; **0888** 001; **0926** 001; **1118** 001–002; **2021** 004–006; **2022** 056; **4040** 001.

Metrologica (20 works)

0018 038; **0357** 001; **0530** 022; **0552**

002; **0559** 003, 006–007, 010–011, 014–016; **2018** 018; **2021** 033, 036–041.

Mimus (9 works)
0230 001; **0278** 001; **0524** 003–004; **0650** 001; **1510** 001–004.

Musica (32 works)
0086 036; **0088** 001–006; **0094** 002; **0222** 004; **0358** 002, 004; **0361** 001; **0362** 001; **0363** 010–011; **0620** 002; **1127** 001; **1320** 001; **1595** 221–222, 230; **1799** 015; **1814** 001; **2034** 021; **2054** 001; **2135** 001; **2136** 001; **2137** 001; **2138** 001; **2139** 001; **2232** 002; **4181** 001.

Mythographa (73 works)
0007 085, 145, 148; **0222** 001; **0259** 004; **0261** 005; **0392** 002; **0393** 002; **0538** 002; **0539** 002; **0548** 001; **0549** 002; **0590** 003; **0638** 004; **0651** 001; **0655** 001; **1002** 001–002; **1120** 002; **1123** 001; **1139** 001–002; **1200** 002; **1285** 002; **1310** 003; **1331** 002; **1390** 002; **1393** 003; **1414** 001; **1427** 002; **1508** 001, 003; **1553** 001, 003; **1584** 002; **1672** 001; **1688** 001; **1812** 001; **1864** 001; **1870** 002; **1871** 002; **1873** 001; **1875** 001; **1877** 001; **1879** 001; **1880** 001; **1881** 002; **1882** 002; **1883** 002; **1885** 001; **1886** 001; **1887** 001; **1888** 002; **1889** 001; **1891** 001; **1892** 001; **1893** 002; **1895** 001; **1896** 001; **1897** 001; **1898** 001; **1899** 001; **1900** 001; **1901** 001; **1902** 001; **1903** 002; **1904** 001; **1905** 002; **2433** 001; **2592** 001; **2618** 001; **5005** 047, 049.

Narratio Ficta (95 works)
0007 114; **0032** 007; **0041** 001–002; **0061** 001; **0062** 012, 044; **0527** 010, 019–022, 025, 032, 041, 054–059; **0532** 001; **0554** 001; **0561** 001; **0638** 001; **0641** 001; **0655** 001; **0658** 001; **1148** 001–003; **1252** 001–002; **1271** 004, 006–009, 011–012; **1386** 001–016, 018–020; **1441** 001; **1451** 001; **1466** 001; **1765** 001–005; **1804** 001–002; **1943** 002; **2111** 005; **2433** 029, 033; **2934** 066; **3001** 001–003; **3118** 001–002; **4040** 001; **5003** 001–004, 006–010, 013–018.

Naturalis Historia (114 works)
0007 125, 127, 129–130, 145; **0022** 001–003; **0023** 001; **0024** 001; **0032** 013–014; **0074** 007; **0084** 002–003; **0086** 004–005, 007, 012–015, 018, 020–021, 026, 030–031, 036–037, 043, 046, 051, 054, 056; **0093** 001–002, 004–005, 010, 013–014; **0281** 001; **0282** 001; **0545** 001–002, 004; **0571** 003; **0579** 003–004, 011–012; **0644** 001; **0721** 008; **0731** 002; **0732** 002, 008; **0733** 001; **0751** 005; **0752** 001–003, 005; **0845** 002; **1052** 001, 003; **1118** 003; **1139** 035; **1264** 001; **1270**

001; **1281** 001; **1336** 002; **1357** 001; **1421** 001; **1452** 002; **1482** 001; **1578** 001; **1665** 001; **1678** 002; **1902** 001; **1951** 002; **2021** 004–006; **2190** 001; **2195** 001; **2196** 001; **2197** 001; **2201** 001; **2203** 001; **2428** 001; **2449** 003; **2566** 001; **2575** 001; **2600** 001–002; **2972** 001; **3130** 007, 009; **4013** 001–002, 004; **4015** 005–007, 009; **4019** 003; **4034** 002–005; **4080** 001; **4155** 001; **4210** 001.

Onirocritica (12 works)
0018 019, 039; **0086** 008; **0284** 023–028; **0553** 001; **1147** 003; **2006** 005.

Oraculum (7 works)
1550 001; **1551** 001–003; **1771** 001; **2034** 011; **2960** 001.

Oratio (291 works)
0010 001–021; **0014** 001–011, 013–062, 064; **0017** 001–013; **0026** 001–003; **0027** 001–005; **0028** 001–007; **0029** 004–008; **0030** 001–007; **0034** 001–002; **0086** 051; **0284** 009–016, 019–022, 040, 042–044, 047–048, 050–051, 055; **0535** 001; **0540** 001–036; **0612** 001, 003; **0646** 001; **1426** 001; **1766** 001; **2001** 001–011, 013–035; **2003** 007–009, 011, 014, 020; **2006** 002, 009; **2022** 005–011, 015–052, 054; **2035** 042, 117; **2051** 001–003; **2063** 001; **2130** 033–034; **2200** 004; **3023** 014, 019; **3141** 010; **4040** 001; **4089** 004.

Paradoxographa (43 works)
0062 011; **0067** 002; **0086** 027; **0094** 004; **0545** 001–002, 004–005; **0568** 001, 003; **0569** 001; **0570** 001; **0571** 002–003; **0574** 001; **0580** 001; **0581** 001; **0582** 001; **0584** 001; **0585** 001, 003; **0587** 001; **0644** 001; **0697** 002; **1192** 001; **1413** 001; **1416** 006; **1517** 001; **1578** 001; **1644** 004; **1864** 001–002; **1882** 002; **2331** 002; **2449** 003; **4037** 001–008.

Parodica (16 works)
0463 003; **1175** 001–002; **1220** 001–002; **1224** 001–002; **1486** 001–003; **1800** 001–002; **1801** 001–003; **2626** 001.

Paroemiographa (21 works)
0007 146–147, 149; **0066** 001; **0096** 001; **0097** 001–002; **0098** 001; **0200** 001; **0527** 029; **0644** 004; **1270** 001; **1307** 002; **9006** 001–004; **9007** 001; **9008** 001; **9009** 001; **9018** 001.

Periegesis (34 works)
0064 001; **0065** 001, 003; **0068** 001–002; **0069** 001; **0070** 002; **0071** 001; **0075** 001; **0077** 001; **0083** 001; **0084** 001; **0525** 001; **0534** 002; **0538** 002; **0578** 002; **0845** 002; **1139** 024; **1199** 002; **1236** 001; **1400** 002; **1405** 001;

1650 001; **1713** 001; **1778** 002; **1942** 002; **2264** 001; **2265** 001; **2394** 001; **2521** 001; **2535** 001; **2536** 002; **4003** 001–002.

Philosophica (829 works)
0007 067–083, 089–113, 115–120, 126–127, 129–141, 143–145; **0018** 001, 003, 006–013, 015–016, 020–031, 036, 038–040, 047; **0020** 006; **0032** 002–005, 008, 010–011, 014–015; **0051** 001; **0054** 001; **0057** 003, 005, 010, 026, 032–033, 081, 084, 104–105; **0059** 001–035, 037–038; **0062** 007; **0066** 001; **0078** 002; **0086** 001–003, 005–006, 008–010, 012–013, 016–018, 020, 022, 024–026, 028–031, 033–038, 040–045, 047–048, 051–054; **0088** 006; **0089** 001; **0093** 003, 006–007, 010, 015; **0095** 001–002; **0222** 006; **0224** 002; **0225** 002; **0226** 002; **0229** 002; **0267** 006; **0270** 002; **0308** 009; **0319** 004; **0363** 008; **0392** 004; **0509** 001; **0521** 001–002, 008; **0529** 002; **0530** 012, 020, 041–042; **0537** 001, 003, 005, 009; **0544** 001; **0545** 004; **0555** 001–002, 004–005; **0557** 001–003; **0562** 001; **0579** 010; **0591** 002; **0593** 003; **0595** 002; **0601** 001; **0615** 001; **0617** 002; **0620** 002; **0624** 001; **0626** 002; **0628** 001–002, 004; **0630** 002; **0632** 001–002; **0633** 001; **0634** 001; **0635** 001–002; **0643** 001–002; **0654** 002; **0673** 001–003; **0693** 001–002; **0713** 002; **0714** 002; **0723** 001; **0725** 002; **0732** 001, 004–008, 010–018; **0743** 001; **0766** 002; **1052** 001–002; **1128** 001; **1132** 001; **1133** 001; **1134** 001; **1135** 001; **1138** 001; **1143** 001; **1146** 001; **1147** 001, 003; **1166** 001; **1173** 001; **1177** 001; **1178** 001; **1179** 001; **1180** 001; **1186** 001; **1188** 001; **1191** 001; **1192** 001; **1193** 001; **1202** 001; **1205** 002; **1208** 001; **1224** 001; **1230** 001; **1231** 001; **1232** 001; **1237** 001; **1247** 001; **1248** 001; **1251** 001; **1259** 001; **1264** 001–002, 004, 006–007; **1269** 002; **1270** 001; **1275** 002; **1277** 001; **1283** 001; **1286** 001–014, 016–023; **1287** 001; **1292** 001; **1293** 001; **1294** 001; **1297** 001; **1300** 001–006; **1301** 001; **1304** 002; **1309** 001; **1319** 002; **1320** 001; **1321** 001–010; **1322** 001; **1332** 001; **1333** 001; **1334** 001; **1340** 001; **1341** 001; **1342** 001; **1347** 002, 004; **1357** 001; **1360** 001; **1362** 001; **1377** 002–003; **1390** 004; **1407** 001; **1409** 001; **1429** 001–003; **1432** 001; **1434** 004; **1436** 001; **1437** 002; **1461** 002; **1490** 001; **1494** 002; **1507** 001; **1508** 003; **1509** 001; **1542** 001; **1545** 001–002; **1548** 001; **1549** 001; **1562** 002; **1571** 001; **1572** 001; **1574** 001; **1578** 001; **1595** 001, 010, 020, 030–031, 040, 053, 055, 060, 070, 080–082, 088–089, 091, 095–096, 098–102, 113, 115–119, 132, 135, 138–139, 141, 143, 150–151, 164, 168, 172–173, 175, 179, 181–182, 185, 190,

001; **0324** 001; **0325** 001; **0326** 001; **0327** 001; **0328** 001; **0329** 001; **0330** 001; **0331** 001; **0332** 001; **0333** 001; **0334** 001; **0335** 001; **0336** 001–002, 004; **0338** 001; **0339** 001; **0340** 001; **0341** 001–002; **0342** 001; **0343** 001; **0344** 001; **0345** 001; **0346** 001; **0347** 001; **0348** 001; **0349** 001; **0350** 001;

0351 001; **0352** 001; **0353** 001; **0354** 001; **0355** 001; **0467** 001; **0603** 001; **0604** 001; **0611** 001; **0621** 001; **0625** 001; **0700** 001; **0825** 001; **0876** 001; **0889** 001; **1087** 001; **1094** 001; **1096** 001; **1115** 001; **1150** 002; **1399** 001; **1511** 001; **1639** 001; **1738** 001–003;

1833 001–002; **1839** 001; **1840** 001; **1843** 001; **1844** 001; **1845** 001; **1846** 001; **1848** 001; **2022** 003; **5005** 009–014, 018–040, 042–045, 053.

Zoologica (4 works)
    0086 012, 014–015, 021.

INDEX OF CITATION SYSTEMS IN TLG TEXTS

The following index identifies the precise form of citation adopted for each text deposited in the TLG data bank. The purpose of this information is to facilitate consultation of TLG machine-readable texts. Citation information is not provided, however, for texts that have not yet been added to the data bank.

For ease of reference, citation information is given in sequential work number order under author names listed alphabetically. Where a specific citation system applies to several works in numerical order, these works are listed inclusively rather than seriatim.

Levels of citation are set off by raised periods, with the highest level indicated first, For example, the notation *Book • chapter • section • line* signifies the four levels used to cite passages in Thucydides' *Historiae* (0003 001), whereas Isocrates' *Fragmenta* (0010 031) are cited according to a two-level system, i.e., *Fragment • line*. Within a particular level, a hyphen may be used to indicate more than one possible component. For instance, under *Scholia in Aristophanem* (5014 018), the citation system is given as *Argumentum-dramatis personae-scholion • line*. This is actually a two-level citation system capable of yielding three different configurations: *argumentum* and *line, dramatis personae* and *line*, or *scholion* and *line*.

A plus (+) within a citation level indicates that both components are found at that level. In the case of the *Anonymi in Aristotelis sophisticos elenchos* (4193), the citation system for work 002 (*Scholia in sophisticos elenchos*) consists of two levels, *Bekker page + line • line of scholion*.

1883 **ABARIS** Hist.
  001 Volume–Jacoby#–T • fragment • line
  002 Volume–Jacoby#–F • fragment • line
1891 **ABAS** Hist.
  001 Volume–Jacoby#–F • fragment • line
2473 **ABLABIUS** Hist.
  001 Volume–Jacoby#–T • fragment • line
  002 Volume–Jacoby#–F • fragment • line
4023 **ABLABIUS** Rhet.
  001 Book • epigram • line
0116 **ABYDENUS** Hist.
  001 Volume–Jacoby#–F • fragment • line
2064 **ACACIUS** Theol.
  002 Page • line
0101 **ACERATUS** Gramm.
  001 Book • epigram • line
1832 **ACESANDER** Hist.
  001 Volume–Jacoby#–F • fragment • line
  002 FGrH fragment • line
1878 **ACESTORIDES** Hist.
  001 Volume–Jacoby#–T • fragment • line
0309 **ACHAEUS** Trag.
  001 Fragment • line
2133 **ACHILLES TATIUS** Astron.
  001 Section • line
0532 **ACHILLES TATIUS** Scr. Erot.
  001 Book • chapter • section • line
2545 **Gaius ACILIUS** Phil. et Hist.
  001 Volume–Jacoby#–T • fragment • line
  002 Volume–Jacoby#–F • fragment • line
3141 **Georgius ACROPOLITES** Hist.

  002–003 Section • line
  005–008 Line
  009 Section • line
  010 Oration • section • line
  011 Page • line
  012–013 Section • line
0300 *ACTA ALEXANDRINORUM*
  001 Chapter • column or fragment • line
2949 *ACTA BARNABAE*
  001 Section • line
0304 *ACTA ET MARTYRIUM APOL-LONII*
  001 Section • line
2012 *ACTA EUPLI*
  001 Chapter • section • line
0317 *ACTA JOANNIS*
  001–002 Section • line
0384 *ACTA JUSTINI ET SEPTEM SODALIUM*
  001–003 Chapter • section • line
0388 *ACTA PAULI*
  001 Fragment • line
  002 Section • line
  003 Codex page • line
  004 Section • line
  005 Line
0389 *ACTA PETRI*
  001 Section • line
2014 *ACTA PHILEAE*
  001 Column • line
2948 *ACTA PHILIPPI*

  001–004 Section • line
0391 *ACTA SCILLITANORUM MAR-TYRUM*
  001 Page • line
2038 *ACTA THOMAE*
  001 Section • line
  002–003 Line
  004 Section • line
  005 Page • line
0392 **ACUSILAUS** Hist.
  001 Volume–Jacoby#–T • fragment • line
  002 Volume–Jacoby#–F • fragment • line
  003–004 Fragment • line
0102 **ADAEUS** Epigr.
  001 Book • epigram • line
0731 **ADAMANTIUS Judaeus** Med.
  001 Book • section • line
  002 Page • line
2433 *ADDITAMENTA* (FGrH)
  001–002 Volume–Jacoby#–F • fragment • line
  003 Volume–Jacoby#–T+F • fragment • line
  004–006 Volume–Jacoby#–F • fragment • line
  007 Volume–Jacoby#–T • fragment • line
  008 Volume–Jacoby#–F • fragment • line
  010–011 Volume–Jacoby#–T+F • fragment • line
  012–014 Volume–Jacoby#–F • fragment • line

016–050 Volume–Jacoby#–F • fragment •
line
051–053 FGrH fragment • line
2648 *ADESPOTA PAPYRACEA* (SH)
001–004 Fragment • line
0666 **ADRIANUS** Rhet. et Soph.
001 Page • line
0668 *AEGIMIUS*
001 Fragment • line
0545 **Claudius AELIANUS** Soph.
001–002 Book • section • line
003 Epistle • line
004 Fragment • line
005 Line
0546 **AELIANUS** Tact.
001 Chapter • section • line
2434 **AELIUS DIUS** Hist.
001 Volume–Jacoby#–T • fragment • line
002 Volume–Jacoby#–F • fragment • line
0103 **AEMILIANUS** Rhet.
001 Book • epigram • line
2378 **AENEAS** Hist.
001 Volume–Jacoby#–F • fragment • line
0058 **AENEAS** Tact.
001 Chapter • section • line
2413 **AENESIDEMUS** Hist.
001 Volume–Jacoby#–F • fragment • line
0026 **AESCHINES** Orat.
001–003 Section • line
004 Epistle • section • line
0104 **AESCHINES** Rhet.
001 Book • epigram • line
0673 **AESCHINES SOCRATICUS** Phil.
001 Fragment • line
2377 **AESCHRION** Epic.
001 Volume–Jacoby#–T • fragment • line
002 Volume–Jacoby#–F • fragment • line
0679 **AESCHRION** Lyr.
001 Book • epigram • line
002 Fragment • line
0085 **AESCHYLUS** Trag.
001–007 Line
008 Tetralogy • play • fragment • line
009 Fragment • line
010 Book • epigram • line
011 Fragment • line
0321 **AESCHYLUS** Trag.
001 Fragment • line
002 Volume–Jacoby#–T • fragment • line
003 Fragment • line
1980 **AESOPUS** Hist.
001 Volume–Jacoby#–T • fragment • line
002 Volume–Jacoby#–F • fragment • line
0096 **AESOPUS** Scr. Fab. et *AESOPICA*
001 Section • line
002 Fable • version • line
003 Fable • line
004 Fable • version • line
005–010 Fable • line
011 Line
012–013 Fable • line
014 Book • epigram • line
015 Fable • line
016 Sententia • line
017 Proverb • line
0683 *AETHIOPIS*
001 Fragment • line
0686 **AETHLIUS** Hist.
001 Volume–Jacoby#–T • fragment • line

002 Volume–Jacoby#–F • fragment • line
0528 **AËTIUS** Doxogr.
001–002 Page • line
0718 **AËTIUS** Med.
001–009 Chapter • line
011–013 Chapter • line
015–016 Chapter • line
0687 **AGACLYTUS** Hist.
001 Volume–Jacoby#–F • fragment • line
2605 **AGAMESTOR** Eleg.
001 Fragment • line
0067 **AGATHARCHIDES** Geogr.
001 Section • line
003 Volume–Jacoby#–T • fragment • line
004 Volume–Jacoby#–F • fragment • line
005 Fragment • line
2192 **[AGATHARCHIDES]** Hist.
001 Volume–Jacoby#–F • fragment • line
0090 **AGATHEMERUS** Geogr.
001 Section • line
4024 **AGATHIAS Scholasticus** Hist. et
Epigr.
001 Page • line
002 Book • epigram • line
0688 **AGATHOCLES** Hist.
001 Volume–Jacoby#–T • fragment • line
002 Volume–Jacoby#–F • fragment • line
003 FGrH fragment • line
1775 **Pseudo-AGATHON** Epigr.
001 Epigram • line
2535 **AGATHON** Hist.
001 Volume–Jacoby#–F • fragment • line
2566 **[AGATHON]** Hist.
001 Volume–Jacoby#–F • fragment • line
0318 **AGATHON** Trag.
001 Fragment • line
2606 **AGATHYLLUS** Eleg.
001 Fragment • line
2555 **AGESILAUS** Hist.
001 Volume–Jacoby#–F • fragment • line
0105 **AGIS** Epigr.
001 Book • epigram • line
0676 **AGLAÏS** Poet. Med.
001 Line
002 Fragment • line
2345 **AGL(A)OSTHENES** Hist.
001 Volume–Jacoby#–T • fragment • line
002 Volume–Jacoby#–F • fragment • line
1835 **AGROETAS** Hist.
001 Volume–Jacoby#–F • fragment • line
0693 **ALBINUS** Phil.
001 Chapter • section • line
002 Section • line
0400 **ALCAEUS** Comic.
001 Fragment • line
002 Play • fragment • line
003 Fragment • line
004 Play • fragment • line
0106 **ALCAEUS** Epigr.
001 Book • epigram • line
0383 **ALCAEUS** Lyr.
001–003 Fragment • line
2285 **ALCETAS** Hist.
001 Volume–Jacoby#–F • fragment • line
0236 **ALCIBIADES** <Eleg.>
001 Line
0610 **ALCIDAMAS** Rhet.
001 Fragment • section • line
1780 **ALCIMENES** Comic.

001 Fragment • line
002 Page • line
0695 **ALCIMUS** Hist.
001 Volume–Jacoby#–T • fragment • line
002 Volume–Jacoby#–F • fragment • line
0640 **ALCIPHRON** Rhet. et Soph.
001 Book • epistle • section • line
0766 **ALCMAEON** Phil.
001–002 Fragment • line
0696 *ALCMAEONIS*
001 Fragment • line
0291 **ALCMAN** Lyr.
001 Fragment • subfragment • line
002 Fragment • line
0401 **ALEXANDER** Comic.
001 Fragment • line
002 Play • fragment • line
0107 **ALEXANDER** Epigr.
001 Book • epigram • line
2500 **ALEXANDER** Hist.
001 Volume–Jacoby#–T • fragment • line
1864 **ALEXANDER** Hist.
001 Volume–Jacoby#–F • fragment • line
0744 **ALEXANDER** Med.
001–004 Volume • page • line
005 Page • line
0732 **ALEXANDER** Phil.
001 Page • line
002 Book • section • line
003 Chapter • section • line
004–008 Page • line
010–015 Page • line
016 Fragment • line
017 Book • section • line
0697 **Cornelius ALEXANDER** Polyhist.
001 Volume–Jacoby#–T • fragment • line
002 Volume–Jacoby#–F • fragment • line
0698 **ALEXANDER** Rhet.
002 Fragment • line
0594 **ALEXANDER** Rhet. et Soph.
001–002 Page • line
2059 **ALEXANDER** Theol.
001 Section • line
0216 **ALEXANDER** Trag. et Lyr.
001 Fragment • line
002 Book • epigram • line
003 Fragment • line
0042 *ALEXANDRI MAGNI EPISTU-
LAE*
001 Epistle • line
2556 **[ALEXARCHUS]** Hist.
001 Volume–Jacoby#–F • fragment • line
2607 **ALEXINUS** Phil.
001 Fragment • line
0402 **ALEXIS** Comic.
001 Fragment • line
002 Play • fragment • line
003–005 Fragment • line
006 Play • fragment • line
0707 **ALEXIS** Hist.
001 Volume–Jacoby#–F • fragment • line
0108 **ALPHEUS** Epigr.
001 Book • epigram • line
0043 *AMASIS EPISTULAE*
001 Epistle • line
2219 **AMELESAGORAS** Hist.
001 Volume–Jacoby#–T • fragment • line
002 Volume–Jacoby#–F • fragment • line
2004 *AMELII EPISTULA*

001 Line
0403 **AMIPSIAS** Comic.
001 Fragment • line
002 Play • fragment • line
003–004 Fragment • line
0109 **AMMIANUS** Epigr.
001 Book • epigram • line
0110 **AMMONIDES** Epigr.
001 Book • epigram • line
0289 **AMMONIUS** Epigr.
001 Line
002 Book • epigram • line
0708 <**AMMONIUS**> Gramm.
001 Lexical entry • line
002 Section • line
2254 **AMMONIUS** Hist.
001 Volume–Jacoby#–T • fragment • line
002 Volume–Jacoby#–F • fragment • line
0709 **AMMONIUS** Hist.
001 Volume–Jacoby#–F • fragment • line
4016 **AMMONIUS** Phil.
001–005 Page • line
2724 **AMMONIUS** Scr. Eccl.
003 Fragment • line
2445 **AMOMETUS** Hist.
001 Volume–Jacoby#–T • fragment • line
002 Volume–Jacoby#–F • fragment • line
0710 *AMPHIARAI EXILIUM* (?)
001 Line
2112 **AMPHILOCHIUS** Scr. Eccl.
001–011 Line
012 Page • line
013–015 Line
016 Fragment • line
017 Line
018 Fragment • line
019–025 Volume • page • line
026 Fragment • line
2271 **AMPHION** Hist.
001 Volume–Jacoby#–F • fragment • line
0404 **AMPHIS** Comic.
001 Fragment • line
002 Play • fragment • line
0711 **AMPHITHEUS** (?) Hist.
001 Volume–Jacoby#–F • fragment • line
2649 **AMYNTAS** Epigr.
001 Fragment • line
0712 **AMYNTAS** Hist.
001 Volume–Jacoby#–F • fragment • line
1951 **AMYNTIANUS** Hist.
001 Volume–Jacoby#–T • fragment • line
002 Volume–Jacoby#–F • fragment • line
0037 *ANACHARSIDIS EPISTULAE*
001 Epistle • line
0237 **ANACREON** Lyr.
001–003 Fragment • line
004 Book • epigram • line
0217 **ANACREON Junior** Eleg.
001 Line
4150 *ANACREONTEA*
001 Fragment • line
0238 **ANANIUS** Iamb.
001 Fragment • line
9005 **ANASTASIUS TRAULUS** Epigr.
001 Book • epigram • line
0713 **ANAXAGORAS** Phil.
001–002 Fragment • line
2284 **ANAXANDRIDAS** Hist.
001 Volume–Jacoby#–T • fragment • line
002 Volume–Jacoby#–F • fragment • line

0405 **ANAXANDRIDES** Comic.
001 Fragment • line
002 Play • fragment • line
003–004 Fragment • line
0714 **ANAXARCHUS** Phil.
001–002 Fragment • line
2210 **ANAXICRATES** Hist.
001 Volume–Jacoby#–F • fragment • line
0406 **ANAXILAS** Comic.
001 Fragment • line
002 Play • fragment • line
0725 **ANAXIMANDER** Phil.
001–002 Fragment • line
1120 **ANAXIMANDER Junior** Hist.
001 Volume–Jacoby#–T • fragment • line
002 Volume–Jacoby#–F • fragment • line
0547 **ANAXIMENES** Hist. et Rhet.
001 Chapter • section • line
002 Volume–Jacoby#–T • fragment • line
003 Volume–Jacoby#–F • fragment • line
0617 **ANAXIMENES** Phil.
001–002 Fragment • line
1121 *ANAXIMENIS MILESII EPIS-
TULAE*
001 Epistle • line
0833 **ANAXION** Trag.
001 Line
0407 **ANAXIPPUS** Comic.
001 Fragment • line
002 Play • fragment • line
0027 **ANDOCIDES** Orat.
001–004 Section • line
005 Fragment • section • line
2393 **ANDREAS** Hist.
001 Volume–Jacoby#–F • fragment • line
2346 **ANDRISCUS** Hist.
001 Volume–Jacoby#–F • fragment • line
2507 **ANDROCLES** Hist.
001 Volume–Jacoby#–F • fragment • line
2412 **ANDROETAS** Hist.
001 Volume–Jacoby#–F • fragment • line
0280 **ANDROMACHUS** Poet. Med.
001 Line
2536 **ANDRON** Geogr.
001 Volume–Jacoby#–T • fragment • line
002 Volume–Jacoby#–F • fragment • line
1123 **ANDRON** Hist.
001 Volume–Jacoby#–F • fragment • line
2172 **ANDRON** Hist.
001 Volume–Jacoby#–F • fragment • line
1122 **ANDRON** Paradox.
001 Volume–Jacoby#–F • fragment • line
0111 **ANDRONICUS** Epigr.
001 Book • epigram • line
1124 **ANDRONICUS RHODIUS** Phil.
001–002 Chapter • section • line
1778 **ANDROSTHENES** Perieg.
001 Volume–Jacoby#–T • fragment • line
002 Volume–Jacoby#–F • fragment • line
1125 **ANDROTION** Hist.
001 Volume–Jacoby#–T • fragment • line
002 Volume–Jacoby#–F • fragment • line
2703 **ANNA COMNENA** Hist.
001 Book • chapter • section • line
1127 *ANONYMA DE MUSICA
SCRIPTA BELLERMANNIANA*
001 Section • line
1836 *ANONYMI AULODIA*
001 Fragment • line
1128 *ANONYMI COMMENTARIUS*

IN PLATONIS THEAETETUM
001 Section • line
0227 *ANONYMI CURETUM HYM-
NUS*
001 Line
1129 **ANONYMI DE BARBARISMO
ET SOLOECISMO** Gramm.
001–002 Page • line
2972 *ANONYMI DE TERRAE MOTI-
BUS*
001 Page • line
0138 **ANONYMI EPIGRAMMATICI**
(AG)
001 Book • epigram • line
3156 *ANONYMI EXEGESIS IN HESI-
ODI THEOGONIAM*
001 Page • line
2029 *ANONYMI GEOGRAPHIA IN
SPHAERA INTELLIGENDA*
001 Section • line
0092 *ANONYMI GEOGRAPHIAE
EXPOSITIO COMPENDIARIA*
001 Section • line
0072 **ANONYMI GRAMMATICI**
001 Part • volume • page • line
003–023 Line
1139 **ANONYMI HISTORICI** (FGrH)
001–002 Volume–Jacoby#–F • fragment •
line
003 Volume–Jacoby#–T+F • fragment •
line
004–006 Volume–Jacoby#–F • fragment •
line
007 Volume–Jacoby#–T+F • fragment •
line
008 Volume–Jacoby#–F • fragment • line
009 Volume–Jacoby#–T • fragment • line
010–011 Volume–Jacoby#–F • fragment •
line
012 Volume–Jacoby#–T • fragment • line
013 Volume–Jacoby#–T+F • fragment •
line
014–020 Volume–Jacoby#–F • fragment •
line
021 Volume–Jacoby#–T • fragment • line
022–031 Volume–Jacoby#–F • fragment •
line
032 Volume–Jacoby#–T+F • fragment •
line
033–035 Volume–Jacoby#–F • fragment •
line
036 Volume–Jacoby#–T+F • fragment •
line
037–038 Line
039 FGrH fragment • line
040 Line
041 FGrH fragment • line
0228 *ANONYMI HYMNUS IN DAC-
TYLOS IDAEOS*
001 Line
4026 **ANONYMI IN ARISTOTELIS
ARTEM RHETORICAM**
001–003 Page • line
4027 **ANONYMI IN ARISTOTELIS
CATEGORIAS**
001 Page • line
4033 **ANONYMI IN ARISTOTELIS
ETHICA NICOMACHEA**
001–003 Page • line
9004 *ANONYMI IN ARISTOTELIS*

LIBRUM ALTERUM ANALYT-
ICORUM POSTERIORUM
COMMENTARIUM
001 Volume • page • line
4165 **ANONYMI IN ARISTOTELIS**
LIBRUM DE INTERPRETA-
TIONE
001 Page • line
4032 *ANONYMI IN ARISTOTELIS*
LIBRUM PRIMUM ANALYT-
ICORUM POSTERIORUM
COMMENTARIUM
001 Page • line
4193 **ANONYMI IN ARISTOTELIS**
SOPHISTICOS ELENCHOS
002 Bekker page+line • line of scholion
003–004 Scholion • line
005 Line
010 Bekker page+line • line of scholion
012 Section • line
5024 **ANONYMI IN HERMOGENEM**
001 Volume • page • line
4171 **ANONYMI IN OPPIANI OPERA**
001 Page • line
0721 **ANONYMI MEDICI**
001 Section • line
002 Page • line
003–005 Section • line
006 Chapter • section • line
007 Line
008–009 Chapter • section • line
010 Chapter • line
011 Line
012 Section • line
013 Line
014 Page • line
015 Line
016 Page • line
017 Chapter • line
020–021 Page • line
022 Line
023 Section • line
024 Page • line
025–026 Section • line
4037 **ANONYMI PARADOXO-**
GRAPHI
001–002 Section • line
003–006 Line
007–008 Page • line
1131 **ANONYMUS AD AVIRCIUM**
MARCELLUM CONTRA CATA-
PHRYGAS
001 Fragment • line
1132 **ANONYMUS ALEXANDRI** Phil.
001 Page • line
2117 **ANONYMUS DE METRORUM**
RATIONE
001 Line
4227 **ANONYMUS DE PHILOSOPHIA**
PLATONICA Phil.
001 Section • line
1813 **ANONYMUS DE PLANTIS AE-**
GYPTIIS
001 Column • line
0282 **ANONYMUS DE VIRIBUS HER-**
BARUM
001 Line
1133 **ANONYMUS DIODORI** Phil.
001 Page • line

4005 **ANONYMUS Discipulus Isidori**
Milesii Mech.
001 Section • line
1779 **ANONYMUS EPICUREUS** Phil.
001–002 Fragment • line
1134 **ANONYMUS IAMBLICHI** Phil.
001 Fragment • line
9003 **ANONYMUS LEXICO-**
GRAPHUS
001 Lexical entry • line
0643 **ANONYMUS LONDINENSIS**
Med.
001 Section • line
002 Fragment • section • line
1135 **ANONYMUS PHOTII** Phil.
001 Page • line
1136 **ANONYMUS PRESBYTER** Scr.
Eccl.
001 Page • line
2002 **ANONYMUS SEGUERIANUS**
Rhet.
001 Section • line
0215 **ANTAGORAS** Epic.
001 Epigram • line
002 Book • epigram • line
2389 **ANTANDER** Hist.
001 Volume–Jacoby#–T • fragment • line
2322 **ANTENOR** Hist.
001 Volume–Jacoby#–T • fragment • line
002 Volume–Jacoby#–F • fragment • line
4088 **ANTHEMIUS** Mech. et Math.
003 Page • line
005 Page • line
7000 *ANTHOLOGIA GRAECA*
001 Book • epigram • line
7052 *ANTHOLOGIAE GRAECAE*
APPENDIX
001–008 Section • epigram • line
1140 **ANTICLIDES** Hist.
001 Volume–Jacoby#–T • fragment • line
002 Volume–Jacoby#–F • fragment • line
1884 **ANTIDAMAS** Hist.
001 Volume–Jacoby#–F • fragment • line
0409 **ANTIDOTUS** Comic.
001 Fragment • line
002 Play • fragment • line
1945 **ANTIGENES** Hist.
001 Volume–Jacoby#–T • fragment • line
002 Volume–Jacoby#–F • fragment • line
003 FGrH fragment • line
0618 *ANTIGONI EPISTULA*
001 Line
2547 **ANTIGONUS** Hist.
001 Volume–Jacoby#–T • fragment • line
002 Volume–Jacoby#–F • fragment • line
2521 **ANTIGONUS** Hist.
001 Volume–Jacoby#–F • fragment • line
0568 **ANTIGONUS** Paradox.
001 Chapter • section • line
002 Book • epigram • line
003–004 Fragment • line
2173 **ANTILEON** Hist.
001 Volume–Jacoby#–F • fragment • line
0239 **ANTIMACHUS** Eleg. et Epic.
001–002 Fragment • line
003 Book • epigram • line
004 Fragment • line
1141 **ANTIMACHUS** Epic.
001–002 Fragment • line

0044 *ANTIOCHI REGIS EPISTULAE*
001 Epistle • line
1993 **ANTIOCHIANUS** Hist.
001 Volume–Jacoby#–F • fragment • line
0112 **ANTIOCHUS** Epigr.
001 Book • epigram • line
1145 **ANTIOCHUS** Hist.
001 Volume–Jacoby#–T • fragment • line
002 Volume–Jacoby#–F • fragment • line
1879 **ANTIOCHUS** Hist.
001 Volume–Jacoby#–F • fragment • line
1143 **ANTIOCHUS** Phil.
001 Fragment • line
2503 **Publius Anteius ANTIOCHUS**
Soph.
001 Volume–Jacoby#–T • fragment • line
2221 **ANTIOCHUS-PHERECYDES**
Hist.
001 Volume–Jacoby#–T • fragment • line
002 Volume–Jacoby#–F • fragment • line
0113 **ANTIPATER** Epigr.
001 Book • epigram • line
1865 **ANTIPATER** Epigr.
001 Book • epigram • line
0114 **ANTIPATER** Epigr.
001 Book • epigram • line
1910 **ANTIPATER** Hist.
001 Volume–Jacoby#–T • fragment • line
002 Volume–Jacoby#–F • fragment • line
1929 **ANTIPATER** Hist.
001 Volume–Jacoby#–T • fragment • line
2350 **ANTIPATER** Hist.
001 Volume–Jacoby#–T • fragment • line
002 Volume–Jacoby#–F • fragment • line
1997 **ANTIPATER** Hist.
001 Volume–Jacoby#–T • fragment • line
1898 **ANTIPATER** Hist.
001 Volume–Jacoby#–F • fragment • line
1146 **ANTIPATER** Phil.
001 Fragment • line
0410 **ANTIPHANES** Comic.
001 Fragment • line
002 Play • fragment • line
003–004 Fragment • line
005 Play • fragment • line
0117 **ANTIPHANES** Epigr.
001 Book • epigram • line
2253 **ANTIPHANES Junior** Hist.
001 Volume–Jacoby#–T • fragment • line
002 Volume–Jacoby#–F • fragment • line
0118 **ANTIPHILUS** Epigr.
001 Book • epigram • line
0028 **ANTIPHON** Orat.
001 Section • line
002–004 Tetralogy • section • line
005–006 Section • line
007 Oration or treatise • fragment • line
1147 **ANTIPHON** Soph.
001–003 Fragment • line
0323 **ANTIPHON** Trag.
001 Fragment • line
2351 **ANTISTHENES** Hist.
001 Volume–Jacoby#–T • fragment • line
002 Volume–Jacoby#–F • fragment • line
2313 **ANTISTHENES** Phil.
001 Fragment • line
0591 **ANTISTHENES** Rhet. et Phil.
001–002 Fragment • line
0119 **ANTISTIUS** <Epigr.>

001 Book • epigram • line
1149 *ANTONINI PII IMPERATORIS*
EPISTULA
001 Line
0651 ANTONINUS LIBERALIS Myth.
001 Chapter • section • line
0120 ANTONIUS Epigr.
001 Book • epigram • line
2478 ANTONIUS JULIANUS Hist.
001 Volume–Jacoby#–T • fragment • line
0749 ANTYLLUS Med.
001 Page • line
0121 ANYTE Epigr.
001 Book • epigram • line
1150 APHAREUS Rhet.
001 Epigram • line
002 Line
1151 APHRODISIUS-EUPHEMIUS
Hist.
001 Volume–Jacoby#–F • fragment • line
1152 APION Gramm.
001 Volume–Jacoby#–T • fragment • line
002 Volume–Jacoby#–F • fragment • line
003 Volume • page • line
004 Fragment • line
1153 *APOCALYPSIS ADAM*
001 Fragment • section • line
1154 *APOCALYPSIS BARUCH*
001 Chapter • section • line
1156 *APOCALYPSIS ELIAE*
001 Page • line
1157 *APOCALYPSIS ESDRAE*
001–002 Page • line
1158 *APOCALYPSIS JOANNIS*
001–002 Section • line
003 Page • line
1160 *APOCALYPSIS SOPHONIAE*
001 Page • line
1155 *APOCALYPSIS SYRIACA*
BARUCHI
001 Page • line
1161 *APOCRYPHON EZECHIEL*
001 Page • line
1162 APOLLAS Hist.
001 Volume–Jacoby#–F • fragment • line
2074 APOLLINARIS Theol.
037–038 Fragment • line
039 Page • line
041 Fragment • line
1163 Claudius APOLLINARIUS Apol.
001 Fragment • line
0122 APOLLINARIUS Epigr.
001 Book • epigram • line
0411 APOLLODORUS Comic.
001 Fragment • line
002 Play • fragment • line
003–004 Fragment • line
0413 APOLLODORUS Comic.
001 Fragment • line
002 Play • fragment • line
0549 APOLLODORUS Gramm.
001 Volume–Jacoby#–T • fragment • line
002 Volume–Jacoby#–F • fragment • line
003 FGrH fragment • line
2537 APOLLODORUS Hist.
001 Volume–Jacoby#–T • fragment • line
2295 APOLLODORUS Hist.
001 Volume–Jacoby#–F • fragment • line
1164 APOLLODORUS Hist.

001 Volume–Jacoby#–F • fragment • line
0365 APOLLODORUS Lyr.
001 Line
1165 APOLLODORUS Mech.
001 Wescher page • line
0548 APOLLODORUS Myth.
001 Chapter • section • line
2319 APOLLODORUS Phil.
001 Fragment • line
1166 APOLLODORUS Phil.
001 Fragment • line
0700 APOLLODORUS Trag.
001 Line
0412 APOLLODORUS Carystius vel
APOLLODORUS Gelous Comic.
001 Fragment • line
002 Play • fragment • line
0124 APOLLONIDES Epigr.
001 Book • epigram • line
0345 APOLLONIDES Trag.
001 Fragment • line
2451 APOLLONIDES HORAPIUS
Hist.
001 Volume–Jacoby#–F • fragment • line
0394 APOLLONIUS Comic.
001 Fragment • line
0550 APOLLONIUS Geom.
001 Book • section • line
1170 APOLLONIUS Hist.
001 Volume–Jacoby#–T • fragment • line
002 Volume–Jacoby#–F • fragment • line
1169 APOLLONIUS Hist.
001 Volume–Jacoby#–T • fragment • line
002 Volume–Jacoby#–F • fragment • line
2283 APOLLONIUS Hist.
001 Volume–Jacoby#–F • fragment • line
0660 APOLLONIUS Med.
001 Section • line
0569 APOLLONIUS Paradox.
001 Chapter • section • line
1171 APOLLONIUS Scr. Eccl.
001 Fragment • line
1168 APOLLONIUS Soph.
001 Page • line
0082 APOLLONIUS DYSCOLUS
Gramm.
001–003 Part • volume+fascicle • page •
line
004 Part • volume • page • line
2491 APOLLONIUS MOLO Hist.
001 Volume–Jacoby#–T • fragment • line
002 Volume–Jacoby#–F • fragment • line
0001 APOLLONIUS RHODIUS Epic.
001 Book • line
002 Fragment • line
003 Book • epigram • line
0414 APOLLOPHANES Comic.
001 Fragment • line
002 Play • fragment • line
003–004 Fragment • line
2168 APOLLOPHANES Phil.
001 Fragment • line
9009 Michael APOSTOLIUS Paroemiogr.
001 Centuria • section • line
9007 *APPENDIX PROVERBIORUM*
001 Centuria • section • line
0551 APPIANUS Hist.
001 Section • line

001 Volume–Jacoby#–F • fragment • line
002–006 Chapter • section • line
007–009 Section • line
010–011 Chapter • section • line
012–014 Section • line
015 Fragment • section • line
016 Section • line
017 Book • chapter • section • line
018 Volume–Jacoby#–T • fragment • line
2027 Valerius APSINES Rhet.
001–002 Page • line
4035 ARABIUS Epigr.
001 Book • epigram • line
0415 ARAROS Comic.
001 Fragment • line
002 Play • fragment • line
003 Fragment • line
0653 ARATUS Epic. et Astron.
001 Line
003 Book • epigram • line
005 Fragment • line
2443 ARATUS Hist.
001 Volume–Jacoby#–T • fragment • line
2162 ARATUS Hist.
001 Volume–Jacoby#–T • fragment • line
002 Volume–Jacoby#–F • fragment • line
0038 *ARCESILAI EPISTULA*
001 Line
0520 ARCESILAUS Comic.
001 Fragment • line
1172 ARCESILAUS Phil.
001 Fragment • line
2608 ARCHEBULUS Poeta
001 Fragment • line
1173 ARCHEDEMUS Phil.
001 Fragment • line
0416 ARCHEDICUS Comic.
001 Fragment • line
002 Play • fragment • line
1935 ARCHELAUS Hist.
001 Volume–Jacoby#–T • fragment • line
002 Volume–Jacoby#–F • fragment • line
0570 ARCHELAUS Paradox.
002 Book • epigram • line
003 Fragment • line
2303 ARCHELAUS Phil.
001–002 Fragment • line
1174 ARCHEMACHUS Hist.
001 Volume–Jacoby#–F • fragment • line
1175 ARCHESTRATUS Parodius
001–002 Fragment • line
1115 ARCHESTRATUS Trag.
001 Line
0127 Aulus Licinius ARCHIAS Epigr.
001 Epigram • line
0126 ARCHIAS Epigr.
001 Book • epigram • line
002 Volume–Jacoby#–T • fragment • line
0661 ARCHIGENES Med.
001–002 Page • line
0232 ARCHILOCHUS Iamb. et Eleg.
001–002 Fragment • line
003 Book • epigram • line
0552 ARCHIMEDES Geom.
001–012 Volume • page • line
013–014 Fragment • line
0131 ARCHIMELUS Epigr.
001 Book • epigram • line
002 Fragment • line
2418 ARCHINUS Hist.

2562 **ARISTOTHEUS** Hist.
001 Volume–Jacoby#–T • fragment • line
0241 **ARISTOXENUS** <Comic.>
002 Line
003 Fragment • line
0088 **ARISTOXENUS** Mus.
001 Page • line
002 Fragment • line
003–004 Page • line
005 Column • line
006 Fragment • line
1946 **ARISTUS** Hist.
001 Volume–Jacoby#–T • fragment • line
002 Volume–Jacoby#–F • fragment • line
0529 **ARIUS DIDYMUS** Doxogr.
001 Fragment • line
002 Page+column • line
0360 **ARMENIDAS** Hist.
001 Volume–Jacoby#–F • fragment • line
2650 **ARRIANUS** Epic.
001 Fragment • line
0074 **Flavius ARRIANUS** Hist. et Phil.
001 Book • chapter • section • line
002–005 Chapter • section • line
006–008 Section • line
009–011 Fragment • line
012 Line
013 Fragment • line
014 Column • line
015 Line
016 Section • line
017 Volume–Jacoby#–T • fragment • line
018 Volume–Jacoby#–F • fragment • line
9018 **ARSENIUS** Paroemiogr.
001 Centuria • section • line
2489 **ARTAPANUS Judaeus** Hist.
001 Volume–Jacoby#–F • fragment • line
2463 **ARTAVASDES** Hist.
001 Volume–Jacoby#–T • fragment • line
0045 *ARTAXERXIS EPISTULAE*
001 Epistle • line
2651 **ARTEMIDORUS** Eleg.
001 Fragment • line
0080 **ARTEMIDORUS** Geogr.
002 Volume–Jacoby#–F • fragment • line
0135 **ARTEMIDORUS** Gramm.
002 Book • epigram • line
2472 **ARTEMIDORUS** Hist.
001 Volume–Jacoby#–T • fragment • line
0553 **ARTEMIDORUS** Onir.
001 Book • chapter • line
0136 **ARTEMON** Epigr.
001 Book • epigram • line
2307 **ARTEMON** Hist.
001 Volume–Jacoby#–F • fragment • line
2392 **ARTEMON** Hist.
001 Volume–Jacoby#–T • fragment • line
002 Volume–Jacoby#–F • fragment • line
0137 **ASCLEPIADES** Epigr.
001 Book • epigram • line
002 Fragment • line
2224 **ASCLEPIADES** Gramm.
001 Volume–Jacoby#–T • fragment • line
002 Volume–Jacoby#–F • fragment • line
1955 **ASCLEPIADES** Hist.
001 Volume–Jacoby#–F • fragment • line
1198 **ASCLEPIADES** Hist.
001 Volume–Jacoby#–F • fragment • line
2430 **ASCLEPIADES** Hist.

001 Volume–Jacoby#–T • fragment • line
002 Volume–Jacoby#–F • fragment • line
1199 **ASCLEPIADES** Hist. et Gramm.
001 Volume–Jacoby#–T • fragment • line
002 Volume–Jacoby#–F • fragment • line
2423 **ASCLEPIADES** Hist. et Gramm.
001 Volume–Jacoby#–F • fragment • line
1200 **ASCLEPIADES** Myth.
001 Volume–Jacoby#–T • fragment • line
002 Volume–Jacoby#–F • fragment • line
0556 **ASCLEPIODOTUS** Tact.
001 Chapter • section • line
4018 **ASCLEPIUS** Phil.
001 Page • line
2122 **Gaius ASINIUS QUADRATUS** Hist.
001 Book • epigram • line
002 Volume–Jacoby#–T • fragment • line
003 Volume–Jacoby#–F • fragment • line
0242 **ASIUS** Epic. et Eleg.
001 Line
002 Fragment • line
2609 **ASOPODORUS** Iamb.
001 Fragment • line
2529 **ASPASIUS** Hist.
001 Volume–Jacoby#–T • fragment • line
2530 **ASPASIUS** Hist.
001 Volume–Jacoby#–T • fragment • line
0615 **ASPASIUS** Phil.
001 Page • line
1201 *ASSUMPTIO MOSIS*
001 Page • line
2060 **ASTERIUS** Scr. Eccl.
001 Homily • chapter • section • line
002 Homily • page • line
2061 **ASTERIUS Sophista** Scr. Eccl.
001 Homily • section • line
002 Fragment • line
0325 **ASTYDAMAS** Trag.
001 Fragment • line
1202 <**ATHAMAS**> Phil.
001 Page • line
2035 **ATHANASIUS** Theol.
001 Section • line
002–010 Chapter • section • line
011–012 Section • line
013–016 Page • line
017–020 Chapter • section • line
021 Page • line
023 Fragment • line
024–025 Page • line
026 Chapter • section • line
027–028 Volume • page • line
029 Section • line
030 Page • line
031 Fragment • line
032 Folio • line
033 Line
034 Section • line
035 Page • line
036–038 Section • line
039–047 Volume • page • line
049–091 Volume • page • line
094 Volume • page • line
099–107 Volume • page • line
109 Volume • page • line
110 Section • line
111 Page • line
115 Volume • page • line

116 Page • line
117 Section • line
118 Chapter • section • line
119 Volume • page • line
120 Line
121–126 Volume • page • line
127 Chapter • section • line
2207 **ATHANIDAS** Hist.
001 Volume–Jacoby#–F • fragment • line
2387 **ATHANIS** Hist.
001 Volume–Jacoby#–T • fragment • line
002 Volume–Jacoby#–F • fragment • line
2379 **ATHENACON** Hist.
001 Volume–Jacoby#–T • fragment • line
002 Volume–Jacoby#–F • fragment • line
0141 **ATHENAEUS** Epigr.
002 Book • epigram • line
003 Fragment • line
2465 **ATHENAEUS** Hist.
001 Volume–Jacoby#–F • fragment • line
1204 **ATHENAEUS** Mech.
001 Section • line
0008 **ATHENAEUS** Soph.
001 Book • Kaibel paragraph • line
002 Volume–Jacoby#–F • fragment • line
003–005 Volume • page • line
1205 **ATHENAGORAS** Apol.
001–002 Chapter • section • line
0422 **ATHENIO** Comic.
001 Fragment • line
002 Play • fragment • line
1206 **ATHENODORUS** Phil.
001 Volume–Jacoby#–T • fragment • line
002 Volume–Jacoby#–F • fragment • line
0621 [**ATH**]**ENODORUS** Trag.
001 Line
1212 *ATRIDARUM REDITUS*
001 Line
1207 **ATTALUS** Math. et Astron.
001 Fragment • line
1982 **Titus Pomponius ATTICUS** Hist.
001 Volume–Jacoby#–T • fragment • line
1208 **ATTICUS** Phil.
001 Fragment • section • line
2505 **Cnaeus AUFIDIUS** Hist.
001 Volume–Jacoby#–T • fragment • line
002 Volume–Jacoby#–F • fragment • line
1782 **AUGEAS** Comic.
001–002 Page • line
2205 **AUTESION** Hist.
001 Volume–Jacoby#–F • fragment • line
002 FGrH fragment • line
2175 <**AUTOCHARIS**> Hist.
001 Volume–Jacoby#–F • fragment • line
1209 **AUTOCLIDES** Hist.
001 Volume–Jacoby#–F • fragment • line
0423 **AUTOCRATES** Comic.
001 Fragment • line
002 Play • fragment • line
003 Fragment • line
2204 **AUTOCRATES** Hist.
001 Volume–Jacoby#–F • fragment • line
1210 **AUTOLYCUS** Astron.
001 Section • line
002 Chapter • section • line
0140 **AUTOMEDON** Epigr.
001 Book • epigram • line
0424 **AXIONICUS** Comic.
001 Fragment • line

002–003 Play • fragment • line
0614 **Valerius BABRIUS** Scr. Fab.
001 Section • fable • line
0199 **BACCHYLIDES** Lyr.
001 Ode • line
002 Dithyramb • line
003–005 Fragment • line
006 Epigram • line
007–008 Fragment • line
009 Book • epigram • line
0142 **[BACIS]**
001 Book • epigram • line
1932 **BAETO** Hist.
001 Volume–Jacoby#–T • fragment • line
002 Volume–Jacoby#–F • fragment • line
1211 **BALAGRUS** Hist.
001 Volume–Jacoby#–T • fragment • line
002 Volume–Jacoby#–F • fragment • line
1213 **Julia BALBILLA** Lyr.
001 Epigram • line
4051 **Joannes BARBUCALLUS**
Gramm.
001 Book • epigram • line
1214 **BARDESANES** Gnost.
001 Volume–Jacoby#–F • fragment • line
3159 **BARLAAM** Theol. et Math.
001 Page • line
1216 ***BARNABAE EPISTULA***
001 Chapter • section • line
2398 **BASILIDES** Phil.
001 Fragment • line
1218 **BASILIS** Hist.
001 Volume–Jacoby#–T • fragment • line
002 Volume–Jacoby#–F • fragment • line
2800 **BASILIUS** Scr. Eccl.
003–008 Volume • page • line
012 Volume • page • line
2040 **BASILIUS** Theol.
001 Homily • section • line
002 Section • line
003 Chapter • section • line
004 Epistle • section • line
005 Epistle • line
006 Page • line
007–008 Section • line
009 Chapter • section • line
010–011 Line
012 Section • line
013 Page • line
018–075 Volume • page • line
0425 **BATO** Comic.
001 Fragment • line
002 Play • fragment • line
1219 **BATO** Hist. et Rhet.
001 Volume–Jacoby#–T • fragment • line
002 Volume–Jacoby#–F • fragment • line
1220 ***BATRACHOMYOMACHIA***
001–002 Line
2152 **BEMARCHIUS** Hist.
001 Volume–Jacoby#–T • fragment • line
1222 **BEROS(S)US** Hist. et Astrol.
001 Volume–Jacoby#–T • fragment • line
002 Volume–Jacoby#–F • fragment • line
0144 **BESANTINUS** Poeta
001 Book • epigram • line
0145 **BIANOR** Epigr.
001 Book • epigram • line
1223 **BIAS** <Phil.>
001 Line

002 Volume–Jacoby#–T • fragment • line
0036 **BION** Bucol.
001–002 Line
003 Fragment • line
1871 **BION** Hist.
001 Volume–Jacoby#–T • fragment • line
002 Volume–Jacoby#–F • fragment • line
1225 **BION** Hist.
001 Volume–Jacoby#–T • fragment • line
002 Volume–Jacoby#–F • fragment • line
1224 **BION** Phil.
001–002 Fragment • line
2153 **BION** Phil. et Math.
001 Fragment • line
1919 **BION** Rhet.
001 Volume–Jacoby#–T • fragment • line
002 Volume–Jacoby#–F • fragment • line
1792 **BIOTTUS** Comic.
001 Fragment • line
0348 **BIOTUS** Trag.
001 Fragment • line
1226 **BITON** Mech.
001 Section • line
1227 **BLAESUS** Comic.
001 Fragment • line
1228 **[BOEO]** Epic.
001 Fragment • line
0146 **BOETHUS** Epigr.
001 Book • epigram • line
002 Fragment • line
1986 **BOETHUS** Hist.
001 Volume–Jacoby#–T • fragment • line
2397 **BOETHUS** Phil.
001 Fragment • line
1229 **[BOEUS]** Epic.
001 Line
2230 **BOÏDAS** Phil.
001 Fragment • line
2610 **BOISCUS** Iamb.
001 Fragment • line
1306 **BOLUS** Phil.
004 Volume–Jacoby#–T • fragment • line
005 Volume–Jacoby#–F • fragment • line
006 Fragment • line
1900 **BOTRYAS** Hist.
001 Volume–Jacoby#–F • fragment • line
1230 **<BROTINUS>** Phil.
001 Page • line
002 Fragment • line
1803 ***BRUTI EPISTULAE***
001 Epistle • line
1231 **<BRYSON>** Phil.
001 Page • line
1559 ***BUCOLICUM***
001 Fragment • line
2611 **BUTAS** Eleg.
001 Fragment • line
1232 **<BUTHERUS>** Phil.
001 Page • line
2338 **CADMUS** Hist.
001 Volume–Jacoby#–T • fragment • line
002 Volume–Jacoby#–F • fragment • line
2222 **CADMUS Junior** Hist.
001 Volume–Jacoby#–T • fragment • line
2612 **CAECALUS** (?) Epic.
001 Fragment • line
1233 **CAECILIUS** Rhet.
002 Volume–Jacoby#–T • fragment • line
003 Volume–Jacoby#–F • fragment • line

2484 **[CAEMARON]** Hist.
001 Volume–Jacoby#–F • fragment • line
0040 ***CALANI EPISTULA***
001 Line
0147 **CALLEAS** Epigr.
001 Book • epigram • line
0426 **CALLIAS** Comic.
001 Fragment • line
002 Play • fragment • line
003–004 Fragment • line
005 Play • fragment • line
1235 **CALLIAS** Hist.
001 Volume–Jacoby#–T • fragment • line
002 Volume–Jacoby#–F • fragment • line
1783 **CALLICRATES** Comic.
001 Fragment • line
002 Page • line
1940 **CALLICRATES** Hist.
001 Volume–Jacoby#–F • fragment • line
1236 **CALLICRATES-MENECLES**
Perieg.
001 Volume–Jacoby#–F • fragment • line
1237 **<CALLICRATIDAS>** Phil.
001 Page • line
0148 **CALLICTER** Epigr.
001 Book • epigram • line
0533 **CALLIMACHUS** Philol.
001 Fragment • line
002 Hymn • line
003 Epigram • line
004 Book • epigram • line
005 Fragment • line
2613 **CALLIMACHUS Junior** Epic.
001 Fragment • line
1996 **CALLIMORPHUS** Med.
001 Volume–Jacoby#–F • fragment • line
2189 **CALLINICUS** Soph.
001 Volume–Jacoby#–T • fragment • line
002 Volume–Jacoby#–F • fragment • line
0243 **CALLINUS** Eleg.
001 Fragment • line
2218 **CALLIPHON et DEMOCEDES**
Med. et Phil.
001 Fragment • line
0427 **<CALLIPPUS>** Comic.
001 Fragment • line
002 Play • fragment • line
2270 **CALLIPPUS** Hist.
001 Volume–Jacoby#–F • fragment • line
0534 **CALLISTHENES** Hist.
001 Volume–Jacoby#–T • fragment • line
002 Volume–Jacoby#–F • fragment • line
003 FGrH fragment • line
2199 **[CALLISTHENES]** Hist.
001 Volume–Jacoby#–F • fragment • line
2155 **CALLISTION** Hist.
001 Volume–Jacoby#–T • fragment • line
002 Volume–Jacoby#–F • fragment • line
2252 **CALLISTRATUS** Gramm.
001 Volume–Jacoby#–F • fragment • line
1239 **Domitius CALLISTRATUS** Hist.
001 Volume–Jacoby#–F • fragment • line
1845 **CALLISTRATUS** Trag.
001 Line
1240 **CALLIXENUS** Hist.
001 Volume–Jacoby#–T • fragment • line
002 Volume–Jacoby#–F • fragment • line
3015 **Joannes CAMENIATES** Hist.
001 Chapter • section • line

2504 **CANDIDUS** Hist.
001 Volume-Jacoby#-T • fragment • line
0428 **CANTHARUS** Comic.
001 Fragment • line
002 Play • fragment • line
003–004 Fragment • line
0276 *CANTUS LUGUBRIS*
001 Line
0149 **CAPITO** Epigr.
001 Book • epigram • line
2506 **CAPITO** Hist.
001 Volume-Jacoby#-T • fragment • line
002 Volume-Jacoby#-F • fragment • line
0310 **CARCINUS** Trag.
001 Fragment • line
0327 **CARCINUS Junior** Trag.
001 Fragment • line
0286 *CARMEN ASTROLOGICUM*
001 Line
1241 *CARMEN NAUPACTIUM*
001 Fragment • line
0296 *CARMINA CONVIVIALIA*
(PMG)
001 Fragment • line
0295 *CARMINA POPULARIA* (PMG)
001 Fragment • line
0150 **CARPHYLLIDES** Epigr.
001 Book • epigram • line
0385 **CASSIUS DIO** Hist.
001 Book • chapter • section • line
002 Page • line
003–004 Book • chapter • section • line
005 Page • line
006–007 Book • chapter • section • line
008 Page • line
009 Fragment • section • line
010 Dindorf-Stephanus page • line
011–012 Excerpt • line
013–014 Page • line
015 Fragment • line
016 Line
017 Volume-Jacoby#-T • fragment • line
018 Volume-Jacoby#-F • fragment • line
0733 **CASSIUS Iatrosophista** Med.
001 Section • line
1246 **CASTOR** Rhet.
001 Volume-Jacoby#-T • fragment • line
002 Volume-Jacoby#-F • fragment • line
0382 **CASTORION** Lyr.
001 Line
002 Fragment • line
4102 *CATENAE (Novum Testamentum)*
001–008 Page • line
010–046 Page • line
1887 **CAUCALUS** Rhet.
001 Volume-Jacoby#-F • fragment • line
1247 <**CEBES**> Phil.
001 Chapter • section • line
1248 **CELSUS** Phil.
001 Chapter • section • line
1249 **CEPHALION** Hist. et Rhet.
001 Volume-Jacoby#-T • fragment • line
002 Volume-Jacoby#-F • fragment • line
0429 **CEPHISODORUS** Comic.
001 Fragment • line
002 Play • fragment • line
1927 **CEPHISODORUS** Hist.
001 Volume-Jacoby#-F • fragment • line
1250 **CERCIDAS** Iamb.

001 Fragment • line
2286 **CERCOPS** Phil.
001 Fragment • line
0151 **CEREALIUS** Epigr.
001 Book • epigram • line
1252 *CERTAMEN HOMERI ET HE-
SIODI*
001–002 Line
0152 **CHAEREMON** Epigr.
001 Book • epigram • line
2424 **CHAEREMON** Hist. et Phil.
001 Volume-Jacoby#-T • fragment • line
002 Volume-Jacoby#-F • fragment • line
0328 **CHAEREMON** Trag.
001 Fragment • line
1795 **CHAERION** Comic.
001 Fragment • line
1251 **CHAMAELEON** Phil.
001 Fragment • line
002 Wehrli fragment • line
1254 **CHARAX** Hist.
001 Volume-Jacoby#-T • fragment • line
002 Volume-Jacoby#-F • fragment • line
1256 **CHARES** Gnom.
001 Sententia • line
002 Line
1255 **CHARES** Hist.
001 Volume-Jacoby#-T • fragment • line
002 Volume-Jacoby#-F • fragment • line
2263 **CHARICLES** Hist.
001 Volume-Jacoby#-F • fragment • line
0430 **CHARICLIDES** Comic.
001 Fragment • line
002 Play • fragment • line
1257 **CHARINUS** Choliamb.
002 Fragment • line
0554 **CHARITON** Scr. Erot.
001 Book • chapter • section • line
1258 **CHARON** Hist.
001 Volume-Jacoby#-T • fragment • line
002 Volume-Jacoby#-F • fragment • line
2421 **CHARON** Hist.
001 Volume-Jacoby#-T • fragment • line
1259 <**CHARONDAS Nomographus**>
<Phil.>
001 Page • line
1260 **CHERSIAS** Epic.
001 Line
2209 **CHERSIPHRON-METAGENES**
Hist.
001 Volume-Jacoby#-T • fragment • line
0386 *CHILONIS EPISTULA*
001 Line
0431 **CHIONIDES** Comic.
001 Fragment • line
002 Play • fragment • line
003 Page • line
0041 *CHIONIS EPISTULAE*
001 Epistle • section • line
1263 **CHOERILUS** Epic.
001 Line
002–004 Fragment • line
1262 **CHOERILUS** Epic.
001 Line
002 Fragment • line
0302 **CHOERILUS** Trag.
001 Fragment • line
4093 **Georgius CHOEROBOSCUS**
Gramm.

001–002 Page • line
1797 *CHOLIAMBICA ADESPOTA*
(ALG)
001 Line
002 Fragment • line
2119 **CHRISTODORUS** Epic.
001 Fragment • line
002 Book • epigram • line
003 Volume-Jacoby#-T • fragment • line
004 Volume-Jacoby#-F • fragment • line
2371 *CHRONICON PASCHALE*
001 Page • line
2195 **[CHRYSERMUS]** Hist.
001 Volume-Jacoby#-F • fragment • line
1922 **CHRYSERUS** Hist.
001 Volume-Jacoby#-T • fragment • line
002 Volume-Jacoby#-F • fragment • line
2559 **[CHRYSIPPUS]** Hist.
001 Volume-Jacoby#-F • fragment • line
1264 **CHRYSIPPUS** Phil.
001–003 Fragment • line
004 Treatise • fragment • line
005 Fragment • line
9008 **Macarius CHRYSOCEPHALUS**
Paroemiogr.
001 Centuria • section • line
2165 **Marcus Tullius CICERO** Orat.
001 Volume-Jacoby#-T • fragment • line
002 Volume-Jacoby#-F • fragment • line
2543 **Lucius CINCIUS ALIMENTUS**
Hist.
001 Volume-Jacoby#-T • fragment • line
002 Volume-Jacoby#-F • fragment • line
2417 **CINEAS** Rhet.
001 Volume-Jacoby#-T • fragment • line
002 Volume-Jacoby#-F • fragment • line
0375 **CINESIAS** Lyr.
001–002 Fragment • line
4057 **CLAUDIANUS** Epigr.
001 Book • epigram • line
4056 **Claudius CLAUDIANUS** Poeta
001 Book • epigram • line
002 Volume-Jacoby#-T • fragment • line
1268 **CLAUDIUS** Hist.
001 Volume-Jacoby#-F • fragment • line
1971 **CLAUDIUS EUSTHENIUS** Hist.
001 Volume-Jacoby#-T • fragment • line
2184 **CLAUDIUS Imperator**
001 Volume-Jacoby#-T • fragment • line
002 Volume-Jacoby#-F • fragment • line
0332 **CLEAENETUS** Trag.
001 Fragment • line
1269 **CLEANTHES** Phil.
001–002 Fragment • line
0432 **CLEARCHUS** Comic.
001 Fragment • line
002 Play • fragment • line
1270 **CLEARCHUS** Phil.
001 Fragment • line
2147 **CLEMENS** Hist.
001 Volume-Jacoby#-T • fragment • line
0555 **CLEMENS ALEXANDRINUS**
Theol.
001 Chapter • section • subsection • line
002 Book • chapter • subchapter • section •
line
003 Line
004 Book • chapter • section • subsection •
line

005–006 Chapter • section • line
007 Section • extract • excerpt • line
008 Fragment • line
1271 **CLEMENS ROMANUS** Theol. et
CLEMENTINA
001–005 Chapter • section • line
006 Homily • chapter • section • line
007 Book • chapter • section • line
008–009 Book • chapter • line
010 Book • chapter • section • line
011–012 Section • line
0622 *CLEOBULI EPISTULA*
001 Line
0244 **CLEOBULINA** Scriptor Aenigmatum
001 Fragment • line
1274 **CLEOBULUS** Lyr. et Epigr.
001 Fragment • line
002 Book • epigram • line
2490 **CLEODEMUS-MALCHUS** Hist.
001 Volume-Jacoby#–F • fragment • line
2614 **CLEOMACHUS** Poeta
001 Fragment • line
1272 **CLEOMEDES** Astron.
001 Page • line
0900 **CLEOMENES** Lyr.
001 Fragment • line
2411 **CLEOMENES III Rex Lacedae-**
monis Hist.
001 Volume-Jacoby#–F • fragment • line
1273 **CLEON** Eleg.
001–002 Fragment • line
0361 **CLEONIDES** Mus.
001 Section • line
1087 **CLEOPHON** Trag.
001 Line
1275 **CLEOSTRATUS** Poet. Phil.
001–002 Fragment • line
1276 **CLIDEMUS** Hist.
001 Volume-Jacoby#–T • fragment • line
002 Volume-Jacoby#–F • fragment • line
2305 **CLIDEMUS** Phil.
001 Fragment • line
2441 **CLINIAS** Hist.
001 Volume-Jacoby#–T • fragment • line
1277 <**CLINIAS**> Phil.
001 Page • line
002 Fragment • line
1278 **CLITARCHUS** Gnom.
001 Sententia • line
1279 **CLITARCHUS** Hist.
001 Volume-Jacoby#–T • fragment • line
002 Volume-Jacoby#–F • fragment • line
2190 **[CLITONYMUS]** Hist.
001 Volume-Jacoby#–F • fragment • line
1281 **[CLITOPHON]** Hist.
001 Volume-Jacoby#–F • fragment • line
1282 **CLYTUS** Hist.
001 Volume-Jacoby#–F • fragment • line
4081 **COLLUTHUS** Epic.
001 Line
1284 **COMARCHUS** Hist.
001 Volume-Jacoby#–F • fragment • line
4058 **COMETAS Chartularius** Epigr.
001 Book • epigram • line
4059 **COMETAS Grammaticus** Epigr.
001 Book • epigram • line
4060 **COMETAS Scholasticus** Epigr.
001 Book • epigram • line

0408 *COMICA ADESPOTA* (CAF)
001–002 Fragment • line
0662 *COMICA ADESPOTA* (CGFPR)
001–009 Fragment • line
0602 *COMICA ADESPOTA* (FCG)
001–002 Play • fragment • line
0659 *COMICA ADESPOTA* (Suppl.
Com.)
001–005 Fragment • line
4175 *COMMENTARIA IN DIONYSII*
THRACIS ARTEM GRAM-
MATICAM
001–007 Page • line
5000 *CONCILIA OECUMENICA*
(ACO)
001–003 Tome+volume+part • page • line
004 Tome • page • line
1285 **CONON** Hist.
001 Volume-Jacoby#–T • fragment • line
002 Volume-Jacoby#–F • fragment • line
9014 **CONSTANTINUS** <Epigr.>
001 Book • epigram • line
9015 **CONSTANTINUS** Gramm.
001 Book • epigram • line
3023 **CONSTANTINUS VII POR-**
PHYROGENITUS Imperator
001 Page • line
002 Volume • page • line
003–004 Page • line
008 Chapter • line
009 Asia–Europe • chapter • line
010 Page • line
011 Volume • page • line
019 Line
9013 **CONSTANTINUS CEPHALAS**
<Epigr.>
001 Book • epigram • line
0271 *CONVENTUS AVIUM*
001 Line
0294 **CORINNA** Lyr.
001 Fragment • column or subfragment •
line
0153 **CORNELIUS LONG(IN)US**
Epigr.
001 Book • epigram • line
0654 **Lucius Annaeus CORNUTUS**
Phil.
002 Page • line
1286 *CORPUS HERMETICUM*
001–014 Section • line
016–019 Section • line
020 Fragment • section • line
021 Fragment • line
022 Line
4061 **COSMAS INDICOPLEUSTES**
Geogr.
001 Book • epigram • line
002 Book • section • line
1287 **CRANTOR** Phil.
001–002 Fragment • line
1288 **CRATERUS** Hist.
001 Volume-Jacoby#–T • fragment • line
002 Volume-Jacoby#–F • fragment • line
0433 **CRATES** Comic.
001 Fragment • line
002 Play • fragment • line
003–004 Fragment • line
005 Play • fragment • line
1290 **CRATES** Gramm.

001 Book • epigram • line
1289 **CRATES** Hist.
001 Volume-Jacoby#–F • fragment • line
0336 **CRATES** Poet. Phil.
001–002 Fragment • line
003 Book • epigram • line
004 Fragment • line
0623 *CRATETIS EPISTULAE*
001 Epistle • section • line
0657 **CRATEUAS** Med.
001 Fragment • line
0434 **CRATINUS** Comic.
001 Fragment • line
002 Play • fragment • line
003–005 Fragment • line
006 Play • fragment • line
0435 **CRATINUS Junior** Comic.
001 Fragment • line
002 Play • fragment • line
1907 **CRATIPPUS** Hist.
001 Volume-Jacoby#–T • fragment • line
002 Volume-Jacoby#–F • fragment • line
2291 **CRATYLUS** Phil.
001 Fragment • line
2508 **CREON** Hist.
001 Volume-Jacoby#–F • fragment • line
1291 **CREOPHYLUS** Hist.
001 Volume-Jacoby#–F • fragment • line
1994 **CREPEREIUS CALPURNIANUS**
Hist.
001 Volume-Jacoby#–F • fragment • line
0154 **CRINAGORAS** Epigr.
001 Book • epigram • line
1293 **CRINIS** Phil.
001 Fragment • line
0319 **CRITIAS** Phil., Trag. et Eleg.
001–004 Fragment • line
0436 **CRITO** Comic.
001 Fragment • line
002 Play • fragment • line
1867 **CRITO** Hist.
001 Volume-Jacoby#–T • fragment • line
002 Volume-Jacoby#–F • fragment • line
1292 **CRITO** Phil.
001 Page • line
3147 **Michael CRITOBULUS** Hist.
001 Page • line
002 Line
003 Codex • section • line
004 Book • chapter • section • line
2552 **CRITOLAUS** Hist.
001 Volume-Jacoby#–F • fragment • line
1294 **CRITOLAUS** Phil.
001 Fragment • line
0437 **CROBYLUS** Comic.
001 Fragment • line
002 Play • fragment • line
0845 **CTESIAS** Hist. et Med.
001 Volume-Jacoby#–T • fragment • line
002 Volume-Jacoby#–F • fragment • line
003 FGrH fragment • line
2201 **[CTESIPHON]** Hist.
001 Volume-Jacoby#–F • fragment • line
2567 **CTESIPPUS** Hist.
001 Volume-Jacoby#–F • fragment • line
0368 **CYDIAS** Lyr.
001 Fragment • line
0156 **CYLLENIUS** Epigr.
001 Book • epigram • line

2154 **CYLLENIUS** Hist.
001 Volume–Jacoby#–T • fragment • line
1482 *CYRANIDES*
001 Book • section • line
2877 **CYRILLUS** Biogr.
001–008 Page • line
0157 **CYRILLUS** Epigr.
001 Book • epigram • line
2110 **CYRILLUS** Scr. Eccl.
001 Section • line
002–004 Catechesis • chapter • line
005 Section • subsection • line
006–007 Section • line
008–009 Page • line
010 Volume • chapter • line
011 Volume • page • line
4090 **CYRILLUS** Theol.
001–002 Volume • page • line
003–006 Page • line
008–022 Page • line
023 Aubert page • line
026–027 Aubert page • line
029 Fragment • line
031 Fragment • line
096–112 Volume • page • line
114–124 Volume • page • line
4055 **Flavius CYRUS** Epic.
001 Book • epigram • line
1908 **DAIMACHUS** Hist.
001 Volume–Jacoby#–T • fragment • line
002 Volume–Jacoby#–F • fragment • line
2482 **DAIMACHUS** Hist.
001 Volume–Jacoby#–T • fragment • line
002 Volume–Jacoby#–F • fragment • line
2454 **DALION** Hist.
001 Volume–Jacoby#–T • fragment • line
002 Volume–Jacoby#–F • fragment • line
0158 **DAMAGETUS** Epigr.
001 Book • epigram • line
4066 **DAMASCIUS** Phil.
001 Book • epigram • line
002 Fragment • line
003 Volume • page • line
004 Page • line
005–006 Section • line
007 Fragment • line
008 Section • line
1868 **DAMASTES** Hist.
001 Volume–Jacoby#–T • fragment • line
002 Volume–Jacoby#–F • fragment • line
1297 **DAMIPPUS** Phil.
001 Page • line
4067 **DAMOCHARIS** Gramm.
001 Book • epigram • line
2493 **DAMOCRITUS** Hist.
001 Volume–Jacoby#–F • fragment • line
2273 **DAMON** Hist.
001 Volume–Jacoby#–F • fragment • line
2232 **DAMON** Mus.
001–002 Fragment • line
2244 **DAMON et PHINTIAS** Phil.
001 Fragment • line
0438 **DAMOXENUS** Comic.
001 Fragment • line
002 Play • fragment • line
2615 **DAPHITAS** Gramm. vel Soph.
001 Fragment • line
1894 <**DARES**> Hist.
001 Volume–Jacoby#–T • fragment • line

4021 **DAVID** Phil.
001–002 Page • line
0272 *DE ARBORIBUS AVIBUSQUE*
FABULAE
001 Fragment • column • line
2326 **DEI(L)OCHUS** Hist.
001 Volume–Jacoby#–T • fragment • line
002 Volume–Jacoby#–F • fragment • line
003 FGrH fragment • line
1989 **Quintus DELLIUS** Hist.
001 Volume–Jacoby#–F • fragment • line
0535 **DEMADES** Orat. et Rhet.
001 Fragment • line
002 Volume–Jacoby#–T • fragment • line
003 Volume–Jacoby#–F • fragment • line
1812 **DEMARATUS** Hist.
001 Volume–Jacoby#–F • fragment • line
2616 **DEMARETA** Poeta
001 Fragment • line
2347 **DEMEAS** Hist.
001 Volume–Jacoby#–F • fragment • line
1298 *DEMETRII PHALEREI EPIS-*
TULA
001 Line
0439 **DEMETRIUS** Comic.
001 Fragment • line
002 Play • fragment • line
003 Fragment • line
0159 **DEMETRIUS** Epigr.
001 Book • epigram • line
1756 **DEMETRIUS** Gramm.
001 Fragment • line
2208 **DEMETRIUS** Hist.
001 Volume–Jacoby#–T • fragment • line
002 Volume–Jacoby#–F • fragment • line
1957 **DEMETRIUS** Hist.
001 Volume–Jacoby#–T • fragment • line
1299 **DEMETRIUS** Hist.
001 Volume–Jacoby#–T • fragment • line
002 Volume–Jacoby#–F • fragment • line
2381 **DEMETRIUS** Hist.
001 Volume–Jacoby#–F • fragment • line
1917 **DEMETRIUS** Hist.
001 Volume–Jacoby#–T • fragment • line
002 Volume–Jacoby#–F • fragment • line
2522 **DEMETRIUS** Hist.
001 Volume–Jacoby#–F • fragment • line
1901 **DEMETRIUS** Hist.
001 Volume–Jacoby#–F • fragment • line
1995 **DEMETRIUS** Hist.
001 Volume–Jacoby#–F • fragment • line
2511 **DEMETRIUS** Hist.
001 Volume–Jacoby#–F • fragment • line
2541 **DEMETRIUS** Hist.
001 Volume–Jacoby#–T • fragment • line
2572 **DEMETRIUS** Hist.
001 Volume–Jacoby#–F • fragment • line
0624 **DEMETRIUS** Phil. et Hist.
001 Fragment • line
002 Volume–Jacoby#–T • fragment • line
003 Volume–Jacoby#–F • fragment • line
1301 **DEMETRIUS** Poet. Phil.
002 Fragment • line
2617 **DEMETRIUS** Poeta
001 Fragment • line
1302 **DEMETRIUS** Rhet.
001–002 Section • line
0613 <**DEMETRIUS**> Rhet.
001 Section • line

1849 **DEMETRIUS** Trag.
001 Line
2485 **DEMETRIUS Judaeus** Hist.
001 Volume–Jacoby#–F • fragment • line
0440 **DEMETRIUS Junior** Comic.
001 Fragment • line
002 Play • fragment • line
0160 **DEMIURGUS** Epigr.
001 Book • epigram • line
1303 **DEMOCHARES** Orat. et Hist.
001 Volume–Jacoby#–T • fragment • line
002 Volume–Jacoby#–F • fragment • line
0161 **DEMOCRITUS** Epigr.
001 Book • epigram • line
1305 **DEMOCRITUS** Hist.
001 Volume–Jacoby#–T • fragment • line
002 Volume–Jacoby#–F • fragment • line
1304 **DEMOCRITUS** Phil.
001–002 Fragment • line
2299 **DEMODAMAS** Hist.
001 Volume–Jacoby#–T • fragment • line
002 Volume–Jacoby#–F • fragment • line
0245 **DEMODOCUS** Eleg.
001 Fragment • line
002 Book • epigram • line
2308 **DEMOGNETUS** Hist.
001 Volume–Jacoby#–F • fragment • line
1307 **DEMON** Hist.
001 Volume–Jacoby#–T • fragment • line
002 Volume–Jacoby#–F • fragment • line
2969 **DEMONAX** Phil.
001 Fragment • line
0349 **DEMONAX** <Trag.>
001 Fragment • line
0441 **DEMONICUS** Comic.
001 Fragment • line
002 Play • fragment • line
1308 **DEMOSTHENES** Epic.
001 Fragment • line
002 Volume–Jacoby#–F • fragment • line
1819 **Pseudo-DEMOSTHENES** Epigr.
001 Epigram • line
0014 **DEMOSTHENES** Orat.
001–061 Section • line
062 Exordium • section • line
063 Epistle • section • line
064 Oration • fragment • line
2281 **DEMOTELES** Hist.
001 Volume–Jacoby#–T • fragment • line
2196 **[DERCYLLUS]** Hist.
001 Volume–Jacoby#–F • fragment • line
0442 **DEXICRATES** Comic.
001 Fragment • line
002 Play • fragment • line
2141 **Publius Herennius DEXIPPUS**
Hist.
001 Volume–Jacoby#–T • fragment • line
002 Volume–Jacoby#–F • fragment • line
2036 **DEXIPPUS** Phil.
001 Page • line
0371 **DIAGORAS** Lyr.
001 Fragment • line
1309 *DIALEXEIS* (Δισσοὶ λόγοι)
001 Fragment • line
0066 **DICAEARCHUS** Phil.
001 Fragment • line
0322 **DICAEOGENES** Trag.
001 Fragment • line
1310 **DICTYS** Hist.

002 Volume-Jacoby#–T • fragment • line
003 Volume-Jacoby#–F • fragment • line
1311 **DIDACHE XII APOSTOLORUM**
001 Chapter • section • line
2618 **DIDYMARCHUS** Poeta
001 Fragment • line
1312 **DIDYMUS** Gramm.
001 Volume-Jacoby#–F • fragment • line
003 Column • line
004 Page • line
2102 **DIDYMUS CAECUS** Scr. Eccl.
001–003 Codex page • line
004 Papyrus page or catena fragment • line
005–007 Codex page • line
008–009 Chapter • section • line
010 Book • section • line
011 Codex page • line
012–014 Volume • page • line
021 Fragment • line
022 Volume • page • line
025 Fragment • line
026–028 Page • line
030 Page • line
032–033 Volume • page • line
035 Volume • page • line
037 Volume • page • line
040 Page • line
041 Codex page • line
042–043 Volume • page • line
046 Page • line
047–049 Codex page • line
0357 **DIDYMUS** Scriptor De Mensuris
001 Section • line
0856 **DIEUCHES** Med.
001 Fragment • line
1313 **DIEUCHIDAS** Hist.
001 Volume-Jacoby#–T • fragment • line
002 Volume-Jacoby#–F • fragment • line
2324 **DINARCHUS** Hist.
001 Volume-Jacoby#–T • fragment • line
2280 **DINARCHUS** Hist.
001 Volume-Jacoby#–T • fragment • line
002 Volume-Jacoby#–F • fragment • line
0029 **DINARCHUS** Orat.
004–006 Section • line
007 Oration • fragment • line
008 Fragment • line
1314 **DINIAS** Hist.
001 Volume-Jacoby#–T • fragment • line
002 Volume-Jacoby#–F • fragment • line
003 FGrH fragment • line
1315 **DINOLOCHUS** Comic.
001–002 Fragment • line
1316 **DINON** Hist.
001 Volume-Jacoby#–T • fragment • line
002 Volume-Jacoby#–F • fragment • line
0612 **DIO CHRYSOSTOMUS** Soph.
001 Oration • section • line
002 Line
003 Fragment • line
0443 **DIOCLES** Comic.
001 Fragment • line
002–003 Play • fragment • line
004 Fragment • line
2549 **DIOCLES** Hist.
001 Volume-Jacoby#–T • fragment • line
2470 **DIOCLES** Hist.

001 Volume-Jacoby#–F • fragment • line
2206 **[DIOCLES]** Hist.
001 Volume-Jacoby#–F • fragment • line
0162 **Julius DIOCLES** Rhet.
001 Book • epigram • line
0444 **DIODORUS** Comic.
001 Fragment • line
002 Play • fragment • line
2652 **DIODORUS** Eleg.
001 Fragment • line
0163 **DIODORUS** Epigr.
001 Book • epigram • line
0166 **DIODORUS** Gramm.
001 Book • epigram • line
2315 **DIODORUS** Hist.
001 Volume-Jacoby#–F • fragment • line
2265 **DIODORUS** Perieg.
001 Volume-Jacoby#–F • fragment • line
2681 **DIODORUS** Phil.
001 Line
2383 **DIODORUS** Phil.
001 Fragment • line
0165 **DIODORUS** Rhet.
001 Book • epigram • line
002 Fragment • line
1318 **DIODORUS** Rhet.
001 Page • line
4134 **DIODORUS** Scr. Eccl.
005 Page • line
0060 **DIODORUS SICULUS** Hist.
001 Book • chapter • section • line
002 Fragment • line
003 Book • chapter • section • line
0164 **DIODORUS ZONAS** Rhet.
001 Book • epigram • line
2128 **DIOGENES** Epigr.
001 Book • epigram • line
2348 **DIOGENES** Hist.
001 Volume-Jacoby#–T • fragment • line
2469 **DIOGENES** Hist.
001 Volume-Jacoby#–F • fragment • line
2328 **DIOGENES** Hist.
001 Volume-Jacoby#–T • fragment • line
002 Volume-Jacoby#–F • fragment • line
1319 **DIOGENES** Phil.
001–002 Fragment • line
2314 **DIOGENES** Phil.
001 Fragment • line
1320 **DIOGENES** Phil.
001 Fragment • line
1321 **DIOGENES** Phil.
001–008 Fragment • line
0334 **DIOGENES** Phil. et Trag.
001 Fragment • line
0320 **DIOGENES** Trag.
001 Fragment • line
0004 **DIOGENES LAERTIUS** Biogr.
001 Book • section • line
002 Book • epigram • line
0097 **<DIOGENIANUS>** Paroemiogr.
001–002 Centuria • section • line
1322 **DIOGENIANUS** Phil.
001 Fragment • line
1325 **DIOGENIS SINOPENSIS EPIS-**
TULAE
001 Epistle • section • line
1952 **DIOGNETUS** Hist.
001 Volume-Jacoby#–T • fragment • line
002 Volume-Jacoby#–F • fragment • line

1327 **DIONIS EPISTULAE**
001 Epistle • line
1323 **Aelius DIONYSIUS** Attic.
001 Alphabetic letter • entry • line
0445 **DIONYSIUS** Comic.
001 Fragment • line
002–003 Play • fragment • line
0246 **DIONYSIUS** Eleg.
001 Fragment • line
1326 **DIONYSIUS** Epic.
001 Fragment • line
2619 **DIONYSIUS** Epic.
001 Fragment • line
0169 **DIONYSIUS** Epigr.
001 Book • epigram • line
0170 **DIONYSIUS** Epigr.
001 Book • epigram • line
0168 **DIONYSIUS** Epigr.
001 Book • epigram • line
0167 **DIONYSIUS** Epigr.
001 Book • epigram • line
0083 **DIONYSIUS** Geogr.
002 Fragment • line
003 Section • line
0069 **DIONYSIUS** Geogr.
001 Line
2466 **DIONYSIUS** Hist.
001 Volume-Jacoby#–T • fragment • line
002 Volume-Jacoby#–F • fragment • line
2257 **DIONYSIUS** Hist.
001 Volume-Jacoby#–T • fragment • line
1324 **DIONYSIUS** Hist.
001 Volume-Jacoby#–F • fragment • line
2538 **DIONYSIUS** Hist.
001 Volume-Jacoby#–F • fragment • line
2483 **DIONYSIUS** Hist.
001 Volume-Jacoby#–T • fragment • line
002 Volume-Jacoby#–F • fragment • line
2446 **DIONYSIUS** Hist.
001 Volume-Jacoby#–F • fragment • line
2354 **DIONYSIUS** Hist.
001 Volume-Jacoby#–T • fragment • line
2390 **[DIONYSIUS]** Hist.
001 Volume-Jacoby#–F • fragment • line
0084 **DIONYSIUS** Perieg.
001–002 Line
003 Chapter • section • line
1329 **DIONYSIUS** Scr. Eccl.
001 Page • line
0350 **<DIONYSIUS>** Trag. vel Comic.
001 Fragment • line
0330 **DIONYSIUS I <Trag.>**
001 Fragment • line
002 Volume-Jacoby#–T • fragment • line
0247 **DIONYSIUS II <Eleg.>**
001 Fragment • line
0081 **DIONYSIUS HALICARNAS-**
SENSIS Rhet. et Hist.
001 Book • chapter • section • line
002–014 Section • line
015–016 Chapter • section • line
017 Volume-Jacoby#–T • fragment • line
018 Volume-Jacoby#–F • fragment • line
2620 **DIONYSIUS IAMBUS** Gramm. et
Poeta
001 Fragment • line
2185 **DIONYSIUS** Μεταθέμενος Phil.
001 Fragment • line
1331 **DIONYSIUS** ὁ Κυκλογράφος Hist.

001 Volume–Jacoby#–T • fragment • line
002 Volume–Jacoby#–F • fragment • line
1881 **DIONYSIUS SCYTOBRACHION** Gramm.
001 Volume–Jacoby#–T • fragment • line
002 Volume–Jacoby#–F • fragment • line
003 FGrH fragment • line
0171 **DIONYSIUS Sophista** <Epigr.>
001 Book • epigram • line
0063 **DIONYSIUS THRAX** Gramm.
001 Part • volume • page • line
002 Volume–Jacoby#–T • fragment • line
003 Volume–Jacoby#–F • fragment • line
004 Fragment • line
1909 **DIONYSODORUS** Hist.
001 Volume–Jacoby#–T • fragment • line
002 Volume–Jacoby#–F • fragment • line
2574 **DIONYSOPHANES** Hist.
001 Volume–Jacoby#–F • fragment • line
0172 **DIOPHANES** Epigr.
001 Book • epigram • line
0395 **DIOPHANTUS** Comic.
001 Fragment • line
002 Page • line
2539 **DIOPHANTUS** Hist.
001 Volume–Jacoby#–T • fragment • line
002 Volume–Jacoby#–F • fragment • line
2039 **DIOPHANTUS** Math.
001 Page • line
002–005 Volume • page • line
2621 **DIOPHILUS vel DIOPHILA** Poeta
001 Fragment • line
0173 **DIOSCORIDES** Epigr.
001 Book • epigram • line
0656 **DIOSCORIDES PEDANIUS** Med.
001 Book • chapter • section • line
002 Chapter • section • line
1118 **Pseudo-DIOSCORIDES** Med.
001–003 Section • line
2121 **DIOSCORUS** Epic.
001 Fragment • line
2409 **DIOSCURIDES** Hist.
001 Volume–Jacoby#–T • fragment • line
002 Volume–Jacoby#–F • fragment • line
003 FGrH fragment • line
0174 **DIOTIMUS** Epic.
001 Book • epigram • line
002–003 Fragment • line
0175 **DIOTIMUS** Epigr.
001 Book • epigram • line
0176 **DIOTIMUS** Epigr.
001 Book • epigram • line
2340 **DIOTIMUS** Phil.
001 Fragment • line
1332 <**DIOTOGENES**> Phil.
001 Page • line
0446 **DIOXIPPUS** Comic.
001 Fragment • line
002 Play • fragment • line
2316 **DIOXIPPUS** Hist.
001 Volume–Jacoby#–F • fragment • line
0447 **DIPHILUS** Comic.
001 Fragment • line
002–003 Play • fragment • line
0248 **DIPHILUS** Epic. et Iamb.
001 Line
0177 **DIPHILUS** Epigr.
001 Book • epigram • line

0279 ***DISCIPULORUM CANTIUN-CULA***
001 Line
1330 **DIUS** Hist.
001 Volume–Jacoby#–T • fragment • line
002 Volume–Jacoby#–F • fragment • line
1334 **DIUS** Phil.
001 Page • line
1911 **DIYLLUS** Hist.
001 Volume–Jacoby#–T • fragment • line
002 Volume–Jacoby#–F • fragment • line
7051 ***DOCTRINA PATRUM***
001 Page • line
2622 **DORIEUS** Poeta
001 Fragment • line
1337 **DOROTHEUS** Astrol.
001 Page • line
002 Fragment • section • line
003 Fragment • line
1336 **DOROTHEUS** Hist.
001 Volume–Jacoby#–T • fragment • line
002 Volume–Jacoby#–F • fragment • line
2197 **[DOROTHEUS]** Hist.
001 Volume–Jacoby#–F • fragment • line
1338 **DOSIADAS** Hist.
001 Volume–Jacoby#–T • fragment • line
002 Volume–Jacoby#–F • fragment • line
0208 **DOSIADAS** Lyr.
001 Line
002 Book • epigram • line
1896 **[DOSITHEUS]** Hist.
001 Volume–Jacoby#–F • fragment • line
2249 **DRACO** Hist.
001 Volume–Jacoby#–F • fragment • line
0448 **DROMO** Comic.
001 Fragment • line
002 Play • fragment • line
0178 **DURIS** Epigr.
001 Book • epigram • line
1339 **DURIS** Hist.
001 Volume–Jacoby#–T • fragment • line
002 Volume–Jacoby#–F • fragment • line
003 FGrH fragment • line
1340 <**ECCELUS**> Phil.
001 Page • line
2242 **ECHECRATES** Phil.
001 Fragment • line
0249 **ECHEMBROTUS** Lyr. et Eleg.
001 Line
2320 **ECHEMENES** Hist.
001 Volume–Jacoby#–F • fragment • line
2289 **ECHEPHYLIDAS** Hist.
001 Volume–Jacoby#–F • fragment • line
002 FGrH fragment • line
0449 **ECPHANTIDES** Comic.
001 Fragment • line
002 Play • fragment • line
003 Fragment • line
1341 <**ECPHANTUS**> Phil.
001 Page • line
002 Fragment • line
2156 **ELEAZAR** Hist.
001 Volume–Jacoby#–T • fragment • line
0231 ***ELEGIACA ADESPOTA*** (CA)
001 Fragment • line
0234 ***ELEGIACA ADESPOTA*** (IEG)
001 Fragment • line
1897 **ELEUSIS** Hist.
001 Volume–Jacoby#–F • fragment • line

4020 **ELIAS** Phil.
001–002 Page • line
1342 **EMPEDOCLES** Poet. Phil.
002 Book • epigram • line
003–004 Fragment • line
1984 **EMPYLUS** Hist.
001 Volume–Jacoby#–T • fragment • line
0290 ***ENCOMIUM DUCIS THEBAI-DOS***
001 Line
1343 **EPARCHIDES** Hist.
001 Volume–Jacoby#–F • fragment • line
2436 ***EPHEMERIDES***
001 Volume–Jacoby#–T • fragment • line
002 Volume–Jacoby#–F • fragment • line
0450 **EPHIPPUS** Comic.
001 Fragment • line
002–003 Play • fragment • line
1936 **EPHIPPUS** Hist.
001 Volume–Jacoby#–T • fragment • line
002 Volume–Jacoby#–F • fragment • line
0536 **EPHORUS** Hist.
002 Volume–Jacoby#–T • fragment • line
003 Volume–Jacoby#–F • fragment • line
004 FGrH fragment • line
1998 **EPHORUS Junior** Hist.
001 Volume–Jacoby#–T • fragment • line
4138 **EPHRAEM SYRUS** Theol.
001 Page • line
1344 ***EPICA ADESPOTA*** (CA)
001 Fragment • line
1816 ***EPICA ADESPOTA*** (GDRK)
001–002 Line
003 Fragment • line
004 Line
005–006 Fragment • line
007 Line
008–009 Fragment • line
010–015 Line
016 Fragment • line
017–021 Line
1345 ***EPICA INCERTA*** (CA)
001 Fragment • line
002 Line
0521 **EPICHARMUS** Comic. et ***PSEUDEPICHARMEA***
001–008 Fragment • line
0451 **EPICRATES** Comic.
001 Fragment • line
002 Play • fragment • line
0557 **EPICTETUS** Phil.
001 Book • chapter • section • line
002 Chapter • section • line
003 Fragment • line
004–005 Sententia • line
006 Section • line
0537 **EPICURUS** Phil.
001–002 Fragment • line
003 Treatise • fragment • line
004–005 Fragment • line
006–008 Section • line
0452 **EPIGENES** Comic.
001 Fragment • line
002 Play • fragment • line
0179 **EPIGONUS** Epigr.
001 Book • epigram • line
0453 **EPILYCUS** Comic.
001 Fragment • line
002 Play • fragment • line

003 Fragment • line
1347 **EPIMENIDES** Phil.
001 Volume–Jacoby#–T • fragment • line
002 Volume–Jacoby#–F • fragment • line
003–004 Fragment • line
005 FGrH fragment • line
0454 **EPINICUS** Comic.
001 Fragment • line
002 Play • fragment • line
2021 **EPIPHANIUS** Scr. Eccl.
001 Chapter • section • line
002–003 Volume • page • line
004 Chapter • section • line
005–006 Volume • page • line
007 Page • line
008–010 Fragment • line
011 Page • line
012–019 Volume • page • line
020–024 Page • line
025 Line
026 Section • subsection • line
027 Line
028 Volume • page • line
029–030 Page • line
032 Page • line
033 Line
036 Line
037 Page • line
038 Excerpt • section • line
039 Section • line
040 Volume • page • line
041 Line
042 Section • line
043 Page • line
1349 *EPISTULA A MARTYRIBUS LUGDUNENSIBUS*
001 Page • line
1350 *EPISTULA AD DIOGNETUM*
001 Chapter • section • line
1352 *EPISTULA ECCLESIARUM APUD LUGDUNUM ET VIENNAM*
001 Chapter • section • line
1353 *EPITAPHIUM ABERCII*
001 Line
1570 *EPITAPHIUM PECTORII*
001 Line
2502 **ERATOSTHENES** Hist.
001 Volume–Jacoby#–T • fragment • line
002 Volume–Jacoby#–F • fragment • line
0222 **ERATOSTHENES** Philol. et *ERATOSTHENICA*
001 Chapter • section • line
009 Fragment • line
010 Line
011 Volume–Jacoby#–T • fragment • line
012 Volume–Jacoby#–F • fragment • line
013 Fragment • line
015 Page • line
4063 **ERATOSTHENES Scholasticus** Epigr.
001 Book • epigram • line
2149 **ERETES** Hist.
001 Volume–Jacoby#–F • fragment • line
1354 **ERGIAS** Hist.
001 Volume–Jacoby#–F • fragment • line
1355 **ERINNA** Lyr.
001 Fragment • line
002 Book • epigram • line

003 Fragment • line
0455 **ERIPHUS** Comic.
001 Fragment • line
002 Play • fragment • line
0716 **EROTIANUS** Gramm. et Med.
001 Klein page • line
002 Fragment • line
2312 **ERXIAS** Hist.
001 Volume–Jacoby#–F • fragment • line
0180 **ERYCIUS** Epigr.
001 Book • epigram • line
2653 **ERYCIUS** Poeta
001 Fragment • line
0181 **ETRUSCUS** Epigr.
001 Book • epigram • line
4099 *ETYMOLOGICUM MAGNUM*
001 Kallierges page • line
2372 **EUAGON** Hist.
001 Volume–Jacoby#–T • fragment • line
002 Volume–Jacoby#–F • fragment • line
2425 **EUAGORAS** Hist.
001 Volume–Jacoby#–T • fragment • line
2293 **EUALCES** Hist.
001 Volume–Jacoby#–F • fragment • line
0456 **EUANGELUS** Comic.
001 Fragment • line
002 Play • fragment • line
2623 **EUANTHES** Epic.
001 Fragment • line
1096 **EUARETUS** Trag.
001 Fragment • line
1800 **EUBOEUS** Parodius
001–002 Fragment • line
0457 **EUBULIDES** Comic.
001 Fragment • line
002 Play • fragment • line
0458 **EUBULUS** Comic.
001 Fragment • line
002 Play • fragment • line
003–005 Fragment • line
006 Play • fragment • line
0250 **EUCLIDES** Comic. vel Iamb.
001 Fragment • line
1799 **EUCLIDES** Geom.
001 Book • demonstratio • line
002 Demonstratio • line
003 Page • line
004–005 Demonstratio • line
006 Book • demonstratio • line
007–009 Section • line
010 Page • line
011–015 Section • line
016 Page • line
017 Line
2356 **EUCRATES** Hist.
001 Volume–Jacoby#–F • fragment • line
2343 **EUDEMUS** Hist.
001 Volume–Jacoby#–T • fragment • line
1357 **EUDEMUS** Phil.
001 Fragment • line
0888 **EUDEMUS** Poet. Med.
001 Fragment • line
1376 **EUDEMUS** Rhet.
001 Folio • line
1358 **EUDOXUS** Astron.
001 Fragment • line
003 Column • line
0399 **EUDOXUS** Comic.
001 Fragment • line

002 Play • fragment • line
1915 **EUDOXUS** Hist.
001 Volume–Jacoby#–T • fragment • line
002 Volume–Jacoby#–F • fragment • line
2399 **EUDROMUS** Phil.
001 Fragment • line
0251 **EUENUS** Eleg.
001 Fragment • line
0183 **EUENUS** Epigr.
001 Book • epigram • line
0182 **EUENUS** Gramm.
001 Book • epigram • line
0184 **EUGENES** Epigr.
001 Book • epigram • line
1905 **EUHEMERUS** Scriptor De Sacra Historia
001 Volume–Jacoby#–T • fragment • line
002 Volume–Jacoby#–F • fragment • line
1972 **EUMACHUS** Hist.
001 Volume–Jacoby#–F • fragment • line
1361 **EUMEDES** Comic.
001 Fragment • line
0298 **EUMELUS** Epic.
001–002 Fragment • line
003 Volume–Jacoby#–T • fragment • line
004 Volume–Jacoby#–F • fragment • line
1913 **EUMELUS** Hist.
001 Volume–Jacoby#–F • fragment • line
2050 **EUNAPIUS** Hist. et Soph.
001 Book • chapter • section • line
002 Volume • page • line
0459 **EUNICUS** Comic.
001 Fragment • line
002 Play • fragment • line
0185 **EUODUS** Epigr.
001 Book • epigram • line
0396 **EUPHANES** Comic.
001 Fragment • line
1912 **EUPHANTUS** Phil.
001 Volume–Jacoby#–T • fragment • line
002 Volume–Jacoby#–F • fragment • line
0221 **EUPHORION** Epic.
001–002 Fragment • line
004 Book • epigram • line
0460 **EUPHRO** Comic.
001 Fragment • line
002 Play • fragment • line
0210 **EUPHRONIUS** Lyr.
001 Line
2129 **EUPITHIUS** Epigr.
001 Book • epigram • line
2486 **EUPOLEMUS Judaeus** Hist.
001 Volume–Jacoby#–T • fragment • line
002 Volume–Jacoby#–F • fragment • line
2487 **Pseudo-EUPOLEMUS Judaeus** Hist.
001 Volume–Jacoby#–F • fragment • line
0461 **EUPOLIS** Comic.
001 Fragment • line
002 Play • fragment • line
003–004 Fragment • line
005 Play • fragment • line
0006 **EURIPIDES** Trag.
001–019 Line
020–022 Fragment • line
023 Line
024–027 Fragment • line
028 Column • line
029 Fragment • line

030 Page • fragment • line
031 Book • epigram • line
032–033 Fragment • line
1840 **EURIPIDES II** Trag.
001 Line
1367 *EURIPIDIS EPISTULAE*
001 Epistle • section • line
1360 <EURYPHAMUS> Phil.
001 Page • line
1362 <EURYTUS> Phil.
001 Page • line
002 Fragment • line
2146 **EUSEBIUS** Hist.
001 Volume-Jacoby#–T • fragment • line
002 Volume-Jacoby#–F • fragment • line
2640 **EUSEBIUS** Phil.
001 Fragment • line
4124 **EUSEBIUS** Scr. Eccl.
007–009 Page • line
2018 **EUSEBIUS** Scr. Eccl. et Theol.
001–002 Book • chapter • section • line
003–004 Chapter • section • line
005 Book • chapter • section • line
006 Fragment • line
007 Chapter • section • line
008 Line
009 Chapter • section • line
010 Fragment • line
011 Page • line
012 Volume • page • line
013 Line
014–016 Section • line
017 Page • line
018 Section • line
019 Book • section • line
020 Book • chapter • section • line
021–022 Chapter • section • line
023 Page • line
024 Fragment • line
025–039 Volume • page • line
4083 **EUSTATHIUS** Philol. et Scr. Eccl.
001–003 Volume • page • line
2499 **EUSTOCHIUS** Soph.
001 Volume-Jacoby#–T • fragment • line
002 Volume-Jacoby#–F • fragment • line
4031 **EUSTRATIUS** Phil.
001–003 Page • line
0752 **EUTECNIUS** Soph.
001 Page • line
003 Page • line
005 Book • section • line
0462 **EUTHYCLES** Comic.
001 Fragment • line
002 Play • fragment • line
0897 **EUTHYDEMUS** Med.
001 Fragment • line
2170 **EUTHYMENES** Hist.
001 Volume-Jacoby#–F • fragment • line
4068 **EUTOLMIUS** Epigr.
001 Book • epigram • line
2236 **EUTROPIUS** Hist.
001 Book • chapter • line
2158 **EUTYCHIANUS** Hist.
001 Volume-Jacoby#–F • fragment • line
2733 **EVAGRIUS Scholasticus** Scr. Eccl.
001 Page • line
1364 *EVANGELIUM AEGYPTIUM*
001 Fragment • line

1366 *EVANGELIUM BARTHOLO-MAEI*
001 Chapter • section • line
002 Fragment • section • line
1368 *EVANGELIUM EBIONITUM*
001 Fragment • line
1372 *EVANGELIUM EVAE*
001 Line
1369 *EVANGELIUM MARIAE*
001 Section • line
1373 *EVANGELIUM PHILIPPI*
001 Line
1374 *EVANGELIUM SECUNDUM HEBRAEOS*
001 Fragment • line
1375 *EVANGELIUM THOMAE*
001 Line
0343 **EZECHIEL** Trag.
001 Line
1968 **FABIUS CERYLLIANUS** Hist.
001 Volume-Jacoby#–F • fragment • line
2542 **Quintus FABIUS PICTOR** Hist.
001 Volume-Jacoby#–T • fragment • line
002 Volume-Jacoby#–F • fragment • line
1377 **FAVORINUS** Phil. et Rhet.
001 Fragment • line
002 Section • line
003 Fragment • line
4147 *FLORILEGIUM CYRILLIANUM*
001 Page • line
2646 *FRAGMENTA ADESPOTA* (SH)
001 Fragment • line
1817 *FRAGMENTA ANONYMA* (PsVTGr)
001 Page • line
2287 *FRAGMENTUM STOICUM*
001 Fragment • line
1381 *FRAGMENTUM SYNODICAE EPISTULAE CONCILII CAE-SARIENSIS*
001 Page • line
1382 *FRAGMENTUM TELIAMBI-CUM*
001 Column • line
0186 **Marcus Cornelius FRONTO** Rhet.
001–004 Epistle • section • line
005 Book • epigram • line
4069 **GABRIELIUS** Epigr.
001 Book • epigram • line
0188 **GAETULICUS I** Epigr.
001 Book • epigram • line
0187 **GAETULICUS II** Epigr.
001 Book • epigram • line
0572 **GAIUS** Scr. Eccl.
001 Page • line
3039 **Joannes GALENUS** Gramm.
001–002 Page • line
0057 **GALENUS** Med.
001 Section • line
002–004 Kühn volume • page • line
005 Fragment • line
006–007 Volume • page • line
008–010 Kühn volume • page • line
011–014 Volume • page • line
015 Chapter • section • line
016–017 Kühn volume • page • line
018 Volume • page • line
019 Section • line
020 Kühn volume • page • line

021–022 Volume • page • line
023–025 Kühn volume • page • line
026 Fragment • line
027–030 Kühn volume • page • line
031 Volume • page • line
032 Book • chapter • section • line
033–034 Kühn volume • page • line
035 Book • chapter • section • line
036–039 Kühn volume • page • line
040–045 Volume • page • line
046–047 Page • line
048–051 Volume • page • line
052 Kühn volume • page • line
053 Volume • page • line
054 Kühn volume • page • line
055–063 Volume • page • line
064 Kühn volume • page • line
065–071 Volume • page • line
072 Kühn volume • page • line
073 Book • chapter • section • line
074 Kühn volume • page • line
075–079 Volume • page • line
080 Line
081 Chapter • section • line
082 Kühn volume • page • line
083–084 Volume • page • line
085–091 Kühn volume • page • line
092 Volume • page • line
093–094 Kühn volume • page • line
095–096 Volume • page • line
099 Kühn volume • page • line
100–102 Volume • page • line
103 Dietz page • line
104–105 Kühn volume • page • line
106 Volume • page • line
107 Chapter • section • line
111 Kühn volume • page • line
114 Volume • page • line
115 Kühn volume • page • line
121 Book • chapter • line
0530 **Pseudo-GALENUS** Med.
001 Page • line
002 Kühn volume • page • line
003 Page • line
005 Volume • page • line
006 Chapter • section • line
009 Volume • page • line
012 Volume • page • line
020 Section • line
022 Fragment • section • line
023–024 Volume • page • line
026 Volume • page • line
029 Volume • page • line
031–036 Volume • page • line
037 Kühn volume • page • line
041 Volume • page • line
042 Section • line
043 Volume • page • line
045 Volume • page • line
046 Line
2452 **GALITAS** (?) Hist.
001 Volume-Jacoby#–T • fragment • line
0189 **Gaius Cornelius GALLUS** <Epigr.>
001 Book • epigram • line
0190 **GAURADAS** Epigr.
001 Book • epigram • line
1383 **GEMINUS** Astron.
001 Chapter • section • line

002   Page • line
2762   GENNADIUS I Scr. Eccl.
004–009 Page • line
2030   *GEOGRAPHICA ADESPOTA*
(GGM)
001   Fragment • line
4080   *GEOPONICA*
001   Book • chapter • section • line
3043   GEORGIUS Monachus Chronogr.
001   Page • line
002   Volume • page • line
**3051   *GEORGIUS MONACHUS CON-*
*TINUATUS***
001   Page • line
2971   GEORGIUS PECCATOR Poeta
001   Line
0191   GERMANICUS CAESAR
<Epigr.>
001   Book • epigram • line
4070   GERMANUS Epigr.
001   Book • epigram • line
2191   GLAUCIPPUS Hist.
001   Volume–Jacoby#–F • fragment • line
0192   GLAUCUS Epigr.
001   Book • epigram • line
0193   GLAUCUS Epigr.
001   Book • epigram • line
2460   GLAUCUS Hist.
001   Volume–Jacoby#–F • fragment • line
1385   GLAUCUS Hist.
001   Volume–Jacoby#–F • fragment • line
0194   GLYCON Epigr.
001   Book • epigram • line
2255   GORGIAS Hist.
001   Volume–Jacoby#–T • fragment • line
002   Volume–Jacoby#–F • fragment • line
0593   GORGIAS Rhet. et Soph.
001   Volume–Jacoby#–T • fragment • line
002–003 Fragment • line
2357   GORGON Hist.
001   Volume–Jacoby#–F • fragment • line
2369   GORGOSTHENES Hist.
001   Volume–Jacoby#–T • fragment • line
1872   GORGUS Epigr.
001   Volume–Jacoby#–T • fragment • line
9006   GREGORIUS Paroemiogr.
001–004 Centuria • section • line
2022   GREGORIUS NAZIANZENUS
Theol.
001–002 Epistle • section • line
003–004 Line
005–006 Chapter • section • line
007–011 Section • line
012–014 Line
015–055 Volume • page • line
056   Section • line
057   Book • epigram • line
059–062 Volume • page • line
2017   GREGORIUS NYSSENUS Theol.
001–029 Volume • page • line
030   Book • chapter • section • line
031   Section • line
032   Volume • page • line
033   Epistle • section • line
034–040 Page • line
041   Section • line
042–044 Chapter • section • line
046   Section • line
047   Page • line

048   Section • line
049   MPG page • line
051   Line
052   Section • line
053   Volume • page • line
055–056 Volume • page • line
058–073 Volume • page • line
074   Line
075–080 Volume • page • line
081–084 Page • line
2063   GREGORIUS THAUMATUR-
GUS Scr. Eccl.
001   Section • line
005   Section • line
006   Volume • page • line
008–010 Volume • page • line
013   Volume • page • line
016   Page • line
021–022 Fragment • line
025   Page • line
028   Line
2118   *GRYLLUS*
001   Line
2259   HABRON Hist.
001   Volume–Jacoby#–T • fragment • line
0195   HADRIANUS Imperator
001   Book • epigram • line
1387   (H)AGIAS-DERCYLUS Hist.
001   Volume–Jacoby#–T • fragment • line
002   Volume–Jacoby#–F • fragment • line
1974   HANNIBAL Rex Carthaginien-
sium Hist.
001   Volume–Jacoby#–T • fragment • line
1388   HARMODIUS Hist.
001   Volume–Jacoby#–F • fragment • line
0720   HARMODIUS Trag.
001   Line
1389   HARPOCRATION Gramm.
001   Page • line
0691   *HARPOCRATIONIS EPISTULA*
001   Section • line
0196   HECATAEUS Epigr.
001   Book • epigram • line
0538   HECATAEUS Hist.
001   Volume–Jacoby#–T • fragment • line
002   Volume–Jacoby#–F • fragment • line
003   FGrH fragment • line
1390   HECATAEUS Hist.
001   Volume–Jacoby#–T • fragment • line
002   Volume–Jacoby#–F • fragment • line
003–004 Fragment • line
0197   HEDYLE Epigr.
001   Fragment • line
0198   HEDYLUS Epigr.
001   Book • epigram • line
002   Fragment • line
1391   HEGEMON Epic.
001   Book • epigram • line
002   Fragment • line
003   Volume–Jacoby#–T • fragment • line
004   Volume–Jacoby#–F • fragment • line
0463   HEGEMON Parodius
001   Fragment • line
002   Play • fragment • line
003   Line
1393   HEGESIANAX Epic. et Astron.
001   Fragment • line
002   Volume–Jacoby#–T • fragment • line
003   Volume–Jacoby#–F • fragment • line

004   Fragment • line
1394   HEGESIAS Hist. et Orat.
001   Volume–Jacoby#–T • fragment • line
002   Volume–Jacoby#–F • fragment • line
1395   HEGESINUS Epic.
001   Line
002   Volume–Jacoby#–T • fragment • line
003   Volume–Jacoby#–F • fragment • line
0464   HEGESIPPUS Comic.
001   Fragment • line
002   Play • fragment • line
1396   HEGESIPPUS Epigr.
001   Book • epigram • line
1397   HEGESIPPUS Hist.
001   Volume–Jacoby#–T • fragment • line
002   Volume–Jacoby#–F • fragment • line
1398   HEGESIPPUS Scr. Eccl.
001   Page • line
2420   HEGIAS Hist.
001   Volume–Jacoby#–F • fragment • line
1400   HELIODORUS Perieg.
001   Volume–Jacoby#–T • fragment • line
002   Volume–Jacoby#–F • fragment • line
0658   HELIODORUS Scr. Erot.
001   Book • chapter • section • line
002   Book • epigram • line
0750   HELIODORUS Trag.
001   Line
002   Fragment • line
1401   HELLADIUS Epigr.
001   Book • epigram • line
2438   HELLADIUS Hist.
001   Volume–Jacoby#–T • fragment • line
0539   HELLANICUS Hist.
001   Volume–Jacoby#–T • fragment • line
002   Volume–Jacoby#–F • fragment • line
003   FGrH fragment • line
0558   *HELLENICA*
001–002 Fragment • column • section •
line
003   Fragment • line
004   Volume–Jacoby#–F • fragment • line
005   Line
0465   HENIOCHUS Comic.
001   Fragment • line
002   Play • fragment • line
2043   HEPHAESTION Astrol.
001–005 Page • line
1402   HEPHAESTION Gramm.
001–005 Page • line
0466   HERACLIDES Comic.
001   Fragment • line
002   Play • fragment • line
1410   HERACLIDES Epigr.
001   Book • epigram • line
1408   HERACLIDES Gramm.
001   Fragment • line
002   Line
1406   HERACLIDES Hist.
001   Volume–Jacoby#–T • fragment • line
002   Volume–Jacoby#–F • fragment • line
1979   HERACLIDES Hist.
001   Volume–Jacoby#–T • fragment • line
1954   HERACLIDES Phil.
001   Fragment • line
1844   HERA[CLIDES] Trag.
001   Line
1405   HERACLIDES Criticus Perieg.
001   Fragment • section • line

1407 **HERACLIDES LEMBUS** Hist.
001 Section • line

1409 **HERACLIDES PONTICUS** Phil.
001 Fragment • line

0283 **HERACLIDES PONTICUS Junior** Gramm.
001–002 Fragment • line

1411 *HERACLITI EPHESII EPISTULAE*
001 Epistle • section • line

1412 *Pseudo-HERACLITI EPISTULAE*
001 Page • line

1784 **<HERACLITUS>** Comic.
001 Fragment • line
002 Page • line

1415 **HERACLITUS** Epigr.
001 Book • epigram • line

1962 **HERACLITUS** Hist.
001 Volume–Jacoby#–T • fragment • line

1413 **HERACLITUS** Paradox.
001 Section • line

0626 **HERACLITUS** Phil.
001–002 Fragment • line

1414 **HERACLITUS** Phil.
001 Chapter • section • line

2336 **HEREAS** Hist.
001 Volume–Jacoby#–F • fragment • line

1416 **(H)EREN(N)IUS PHILO** Hist. et Gramm.
002 Lexical entry • line
005 Volume–Jacoby#–T • fragment • line
006 Volume–Jacoby#–F • fragment • line

2169 **HERILLUS** Phil.
001 Fragment • line

2426 **HERMAEUS** Hist.
001 Volume–Jacoby#–F • fragment • line

1418 **HERMAPION** Hist.
001 Volume–Jacoby#–F • fragment • line

1419 **HERMAS** Scr. Eccl.
001–004 Chapter • section • line

2437 **HERMATELES** Hist.
001 Volume–Jacoby#–T • fragment • line

0213 **HERMESIANAX** Eleg.
001 Fragment • line
002 Volume–Jacoby#–T • fragment • line
003 Volume–Jacoby#–F • fragment • line

2532 **[HERMESIANAX]** Hist.
001 Volume–Jacoby#–F • fragment • line

2384 **HERMIAS** Hist.
001 Volume–Jacoby#–T • fragment • line
002 Volume–Jacoby#–F • fragment • line

2440 **HERMIAS** Hist.
001 Volume–Jacoby#–T • fragment • line

1420 **HERMIAS** Iamb.
001 Line

0531 **HERMIAS** Phil.
001 Section • line

2624 **HERMIAS** Poeta
001 Fragment • line

0252 **HERMIPPUS** Comic.
001 Fragment • line
002 Play • fragment • line
003–005 Fragment • line

1421 **HERMIPPUS** Gramm. et Hist.
001 Fragment • line
003 Fragment • line

0207 **HERMOCLES** Lyr.
001 Line

1422 **HERMOCREON** Epigr.
001 Book • epigram • line

1423 **HERMODORUS** Epigr.
001 Book • epigram • line

1424 **HERMOGENES** Hist.
001 Volume–Jacoby#–F • fragment • line

2143 **HERMOGENES** Hist.
001 Volume–Jacoby#–T • fragment • line

0921 **HERMOGENES** Med.
001 Volume–Jacoby#–T • fragment • line

0592 **HERMOGENES** Rhet.
001–002 Section • line
003–004 Chapter • section • line
005 Section • line
006 Volume–Jacoby#–T • fragment • line

0240 **HERMOLOCHUS** Lyr.
001 Line

1425 **HERMONAX** Epic.
001 Fragment • line

0650 **HERODAS** Mimogr.
001 Mime • line

2166 **HERODES I Rex Judaeorum** Hist.
001 Volume–Jacoby#–F • fragment • line

1426 **HERODES ATTICUS** Soph.
001 Section • line

0015 **HERODIANUS** Hist.
001 Book • chapter • section • line

0087 **Aelius HERODIANUS et Pseudo-HERODIANUS** Gramm. et Rhet.
001–002 Part • volume • page • line
003–034 Part+volume • page • line
035–036 Page • line
037 Section • line
038 Page • line
039 Fragment • line
040 Line
041 Section • line
042 Line
043–048 Page • line
049 Line
050 Page • line

2625 **HERODICUS** Gramm.
001 Fragment • line

1427 **HERODORUS** Hist.
001 Volume–Jacoby#–T • fragment • line
002 Volume–Jacoby#–F • fragment • line

0016 **HERODOTUS** Hist.
001 Book • section • line

0559 **HERON** Mech.
001 Book • chapter • line
002 Chapter • section • line
003 Fragment • line
004 Book • fragment • line
005 Line
006 Book • chapter • line
007 Section • line
008–009 Chapter • section • line
010 Chapter • subchapter • section • line
011 Chapter • section • line
012 Section • line
013 Chapter • section • line
014 Fragment • section • line
015 Chapter • section • line
016 Section • line

2419 **HEROPHANES** Hist.
001 Volume–Jacoby#–F • fragment • line

2311 **HEROPYTHUS** Hist.
001 Volume–Jacoby#–F • fragment • line

2516 **HESIANAX** Hist.

001 Volume–Jacoby#–F • fragment • line

0020 **HESIODUS** Epic.
001–003 Line
004–007 Fragment • line

1428 **HESTIAEUS** Hist.
001 Volume–Jacoby#–F • fragment • line

4085 **HESYCHIUS** Lexicogr.
001 Line
002–003 Alphabetic letter • entry • line

2274 **HESYCHIUS Illustrius** Hist.
001 Volume–Jacoby#–F • fragment • line

2240 **HICETAS** Phil.
001 Fragment • line

2370 **HIEROBOLUS** Hist.
001 Volume–Jacoby#–T • fragment • line

1429 **HIEROCLES** Phil.
001 Column • line
002 Page • line
003 Fragment • line

2571 **HIEROCLES** Phil.
001 Chapter • section • line

1953 **HIERONYMUS** Hist.
001 Volume–Jacoby#–T • fragment • line
002 Volume–Jacoby#–F • fragment • line

2526 **HIERONYMUS** Hist.
001 Volume–Jacoby#–F • fragment • line

1430 **HIERONYMUS** Phil.
001 Fragment • line

0745 **HIEROPHILUS** Soph. et Phil.
001 Chapter • section • line
002 Page • line

2051 **HIMERIUS** Soph.
001 Oration • line
002–003 Fragment • line

2501 **HIPPAGORAS** Hist.
001 Volume–Jacoby#–F • fragment • line

1431 **HIPPARCHUS** Astron. et Geogr.
002 Fragment • line
003 Book • chapter • section • line

0468 **HIPPARCHUS** Comic.
001 Fragment • line
002 Play • fragment • line

1433 **HIPPARCHUS <Epigr.>**
001 Fragment • line

2626 **HIPPARCHUS** Parodius
001 Fragment • line

1432 **<HIPPARCHUS>** Phil.
001 Page • line

2406 **HIPPASUS** Hist.
001 Volume–Jacoby#–T • fragment • line
002 Volume–Jacoby#–F • fragment • line

2260 **HIPPASUS** Phil.
001 Fragment • line
002 Page • line

1435 **HIPPIAS** Hist.
001 Volume–Jacoby#–F • fragment • line

1434 **HIPPIAS** Soph.
001 Volume–Jacoby#–T • fragment • line
002 Volume–Jacoby#–F • fragment • line
003–004 Fragment • line

0738 *HIPPIATRICA*
001 Chapter • section • line
002 Appendix • line
003–005 Section • line
006 Chapter • section • line
007–008 Section • line
009–010 Chapter • section • line

2235 **HIPPOCRATES** Math.
001 Fragment • line

0627 **HIPPOCRATES** Med. et *COR-PUS HIPPOCRATICUM*
001–005 Section • line
006 Book • chapter • section • line
007–012 Section • line
013 Line
014–015 Section • line
016 Book • section • line
017–022 Section • line
023 Book • section • line
024–053 Section • line
054 Line
055 Epistle • line
056 Page • line
057 Line
0751 **Pseudo-HIPPOCRATES** Med.
001–004 Page • line
005 Lexical entry • line
1436 **<HIPPODAMUS>** Phil.
001 Page • line
002 Fragment • line
2115 **HIPPOLYTUS** Scr. Eccl.
002 Chapter • section • line
003 Section • line
004–005 Fragment • line
006 Line
007 Fragment • line
008 Line
009 Fragment • line
010 Line
011–018 Fragment • line
019 Volume • page • line
020–022 Fragment • line
023 Page • line
024 Fragment • line
025 Line
026 Section • line
027 Fragment • line
028 Page • line
029 Section • line
030 Book • chapter • section • line
031 Line
032 Section • line
033 Page • line
034 Fragment • line
035 Line
036 Section • line
037 Verso–recto+column • line
038–039 Page • line
042 Line
043–046 Fragment • line
047–048 Line
049 Chapter • section • line
050 Fragment • line
051 Line
052 Section • line
053 Fragment • section • line
055–056 Page • line
057 Line
058 Fragment • line
059 Volume • page • line
060 Book • chapter • section • line
1437 **HIPPON** Phil.
001–002 Fragment • line
0233 **HIPPONAX** Iamb.
001 Fragment • line
2391 **HIPPOSTRATUS** Hist.
001 Volume–Jacoby#–T • fragment • line
002 Volume–Jacoby#–F • fragment • line

0351 **[HIPPOTHOON]** Trag.
001 Fragment • line
1438 **HIPPYS** Hist.
001 Volume–Jacoby#–T • fragment • line
002 Volume–Jacoby#–F • fragment • line
1386 *HISTORIA ALEXANDRI MAGNI*
001 Book • chapter • section • line
002 Book • section • line
003 Section • line
004 Chapter • section • line
005 Section • line
006 Chapter • section • line
007–009 Page • line
010–011 Book • section • line
012–013 Chapter • section • line
014–015 Page • line
016 Section • line
018–020 Line
2744 *HISTORIA MONACHORUM IN AEGYPTO*
001 Vita • line
0012 **HOMERUS** Epic.
001–002 Book • line
003 Book • epigram • line
0253 **[HOMERUS]** <Epic.>
001 Fragment • line
1440 **HONESTUS** Epigr.
001 Book • epigram • line
2052 **HORAPOLLO** Gramm.
001 Book • section • line
002 Volume–Jacoby#–T • fragment • line
0742 *HYMNI ANONYMI*
001–002 Fragment • line
003–004 Line
005 Fragment • line
006–015 Line
016 Fragment • line
017–018 Line
0013 *HYMNI HOMERICI*
001–034 Line
0030 **HYPERIDES** Orat.
001–003 Fragment • column • line
004 Fragment • line
005–006 Column • line
007 Fragment • line
2277 **HYPERMENES** Hist.
001 Volume–Jacoby#–F • fragment • line
2396 **HYPEROCHUS** Hist.
001 Volume–Jacoby#–F • fragment • line
002 Fragment • line
0717 **HYPSICLES** Math. et Astron.
001 Section • line
002 Line
1983 **HYPSICRATES** Hist.
001 Volume–Jacoby#–T • fragment • line
002 Volume–Jacoby#–F • fragment • line
9026 *IAMBICA ADESPOTA*
001 Line
1821 *IAMBICA ADESPOTA* (ALG)
001–002 Fragment • line
0235 *IAMBICA ADESPOTA* (IEG)
001 Fragment • line
2023 **IAMBLICHUS** Phil.
001 Chapter • section • line
002 Page • line
003 Section • line
004–005 Page • line
006 Chapter • section • line

1441 **IAMBLICHUS** Scr. Erot.
001 Fragment • line
0293 **IBYCUS** Lyr.
001–002 Fragment • line
2226 **ICCUS** Phil.
001 Fragment • line
2628 **IDAEUS** Epic.
001 Fragment • line
2304 **IDAEUS** Phil.
001 Fragment • line
1442 **IDOMENEUS** Hist.
001 Volume–Jacoby#–T • fragment • line
002 Volume–Jacoby#–F • fragment • line
2380 **IDOMENEUS** Hist.
001 Volume–Jacoby#–T • fragment • line
9012 **IGNATIUS** Biogr. et Poeta
001 Book • epigram • line
9011 **IGNATIUS** Epigr.
001 Book • epigram • line
1443 **IGNATIUS** Scr. Eccl.
001–002 Epistle • chapter • section • line
1446 **ION** Eleg.
001 Fragment • line
002 Book • epigram • line
0308 **ION** Poeta et Phil.
001–005 Fragment • line
006 Volume–Jacoby#–T • fragment • line
007 Volume–Jacoby#–F • fragment • line
008–009 Fragment • line
0311 **IOPHON** Trag.
001 Fragment • line
4071 **IRENAEUS** Epigr.
001 Book • epigram • line
1447 **IRENAEUS** Theol.
001 Book • chapter • section • line
002 Section • line
003 Fragment • section • line
004 Section • line
005 Fragment • line
007–008 Fragment • line
0017 **ISAEUS** Orat.
001–012 Section • line
013 Oration • fragment • section • line
1449 **ISIDORUS** Epigr.
001 Book • epigram • line
4052 **ISIDORUS** Epigr.
001 Book • epigram • line
0070 **ISIDORUS** Geogr.
001 Volume–Jacoby#–T • fragment • line
002 Volume–Jacoby#–F • fragment • line
0359 **ISIDORUS** Scriptor Hymnorum
001 Hymn • line
0352 **ISIDORUS** Trag.
001 Fragment • line
0010 **ISOCRATES** Orat.
001–030 Section • line
031 Fragment • line
1450 **ISTER** Hist.
001 Volume–Jacoby#–T • fragment • line
002 Volume–Jacoby#–F • fragment • line
003 FGrH fragment • line
0201 **ISYLLUS** Lyr.
001 Line
2183 **JASON** Hist.
001 Volume–Jacoby#–F • fragment • line
1975 **JASON** Hist.
001 Volume–Jacoby#–T • fragment • line
2575 **JASON** Hist.
001 Volume–Jacoby#–F • fragment • line

1921 **JASON** Hist. et Gramm.
001 Volume–Jacoby#–T • fragment • line
0727 **JOANNES** Med.
001 Volume • page • line
3173 **JOANNES** Scr. Eccl.
001–002 Volume • page • line
2498 **JOANNES I** Hist.
001 Volume–Jacoby#–T • fragment • line
4201 **JOANNES CHORTASMENUS**
Gramm.
001 Page • line
2062 **JOANNES CHRYSOSTOMUS**
Scr. Eccl.
001–002 Section • line
003–006 Volume • page • line
007–009 Section • line
010–011 Line
012 Homily • line
014–037 Volume • page • line
039–084 Volume • page • line
085 Chapter • section • line
086 Section • line
087 Chapter • section • line
088 Epistle • section • line
089–101 Volume • page • line
103–108 Volume • page • line
110–145 Volume • page • line
148–187 Volume • page • line
196–211 Volume • page • line
212 Page • line
213–222 Volume • page • line
224–259 Volume • page • line
260–262 Section • line
263–264 Volume • page • line
265 Chapter • section • line
266 Section • line
267–280 Volume • page • line
281 Line
282–338 Volume • page • line
344 Line
345–366 Volume • page • line
367 Page • line
368–371 Volume • page • line
373–374 Section • line
376 Version or recension • line
378 Line
379 Section • line
380–381 Page • line
382 Catechesis • section • line
384 Fragment • line
402 Line
413 Section • line
414 Page • line
415 Section • line
417–420 Page • line
421 Line
423 Section • line
424 Line
425 Section • line
426 Line
427 Section • line
428 Line
429 Section • line
430 Page • line
432 Section • line
433 Line
434–435 Page • line
436 Section • line

437 Page • line
438 Line
442–443 Page • line
444–445 Line
446 Section • line
447 Page • line
452 Section • line
463 Line
473 Fragment • line
484 Page • line
486 Homily • section • line
488 Line
489 Section • line
491–494 Line
495 Chapter • section • line
496 Line
497 Chapter • section • line
498 Homily • section • line
499 Version • fragment • line
500 Section • line
502 Line
2934 **JOANNES DAMASCENUS**
Theol. et Scr. Eccl.
001–014 Section • line
018–019 Volume • page • line
021 Volume • page • line
035–048 Volume • page • line
050–057 Volume • page • line
059–062 Volume • page • line
064 Volume • page • line
066 Page • line
067–068 Section • line
2871 **JOANNES MALALAS** Chronogr.
001–003 Page • line
4015 **JOANNES PHILOPONUS** Phil.
001–009 Volume • page • line
010–011 Page • line
017 Page • line
3155 **JOANNES Protospatharius**
Gramm.
001 Page • line
3063 **JOANNES SCYLITZES** Hist.
001 Page • line
0526 **Flavius JOSEPHUS** Hist.
001 Book • chapter • section • line
002 Section • line
003–004 Book • section • line
1451 *JOSEPHUS ET ASENETH*
001 Chapter • section • line
1452 **JUBA II Rex Mauretaniae** <Hist.>
001 Volume–Jacoby#–T • fragment • line
002 Volume–Jacoby#–F • fragment • line
2180 **JUDAS** Hist.
001 Volume–Jacoby#–T • fragment • line
4050 **JULIANUS** <Epigr.>
001 Book • epigram • line
4053 **JULIANUS** <Epigr.>
001 Book • epigram • line
4054 **JULIANUS** <Epigr.>
001 Book • epigram • line
2003 **Flavius Claudius JULIANUS**
Imperator Phil.
001–012 Section • line
013 Epistle • line
014 Fragment • line
015–016 Epistle • line
018 Book • epigram • line
019 Volume–Jacoby#–T • fragment • line

020 Line
0737 **JULIANUS** Scriptor Legis De
Medicis
001 Line
1757 **JULIUS** Epic.
001 Fragment • line
0740 *JUSJURANDUM MEDICUM*
001 Line
2734 **Flavius JUSTINIANUS Imperator**
Theol.
013–014 Page • line
0645 **JUSTINUS MARTYR** Apol.
001–003 Chapter • section • line
004 Fragment • line
0646 **Pseudo-JUSTINUS MARTYR**
001–011 Morel page • section • line
012 Fragment • line
2497 **JUSTUS Judaeus** Hist.
001 Volume–Jacoby#–T • fragment • line
002 Volume–Jacoby#–F • fragment • line
1456 **LACO** Epigr.
001 Book • epigram • line
2525 **LAETUS** Hist.
001 Volume–Jacoby#–T • fragment • line
002 Volume–Jacoby#–F • fragment • line
1930 **LAMACHUS** Hist.
001 Volume–Jacoby#–T • fragment • line
0370 **LAMPROCLES** Lyr.
001 Fragment • line
0918 **LAMYNTHIUS** Lyr.
001 Fragment • line
0469 **LAON** Comic.
001 Fragment • line
002 Play • fragment • line
0366 **LASUS** Lyr.
001–002 Fragment • line
2159 **LEANDR(I)US** Hist.
001 Volume–Jacoby#–F • fragment • line
1941 **LEO** Hist.
001 Volume–Jacoby#–T • fragment • line
002 Volume–Jacoby#–F • fragment • line
1978 **LEO** Hist.
001 Volume–Jacoby#–T • fragment • line
002 Volume–Jacoby#–F • fragment • line
2375 **LEO** Hist.
001 Volume–Jacoby#–T • fragment • line
2186 **LEO** Hist.
001 Volume–Jacoby#–T • fragment • line
002 Volume–Jacoby#–F • fragment • line
0723 **LEO** Phil.
001 Section • line
002 Chapter • section • line
4187 **LEO MAGENTINUS** Phil.
006 Bekker page+line • line of scholion
008 Scholion • line
009 Line
9016 **LEO Philosophus** Gramm.
001 Book • epigram • line
1458 **LEONIDAS** Epigr.
001 Book • epigram • line
1457 **Julius LEONIDAS** Math. et Astrol.
001 Book • epigram • line
2554 **LEONIDES** Hist.
001 Volume–Jacoby#–F • fragment • line
4167 **LEONTIUS** Mech.
001 Section • line
4062 **LEONTIUS Minotaurus** Epigr.
001 Book • epigram • line

1459 **LEPIDUS** Hist.
001 Volume–Jacoby#–F • fragment • line
0649 **LESBONAX** Rhet.
001–003 Section • line
1967 **LESCHIDES** Hist.
001 Volume–Jacoby#–T • fragment • line
002 Fragment • line
1461 **LEUCIPPUS** Phil.
001–002 Fragment • line
0470 **LEUCO** Comic.
001 Fragment • line
002 Play • fragment • line
003 Fragment • line
2200 **LIBANIUS** Rhet. et Soph.
001–003 Epistle • section • line
004 Oration • section • line
005 Declamation • (subdivision) •
section • line
006 Progymnasma • section • subsection •
line
007 Oration • section • line
008 Section • line
009 Fragment • section • line
011 Book • epigram • line
012 Section • line
013 Fragment • line
1462 ***LIBER ELDAD ET MODAD***
001 Page • line
1463 ***LIBER ENOCH***
001–002 Chapter • section • line
1859 ***LIBER JANNES ET MAMBRES***
001 Page • line
1464 ***LIBER JUBILAEORUM***
001 Page • line
0374 **LICYMNIUS** Lyr.
001–002 Fragment • line
0203 **LIMENIUS** Lyr.
001 Line
2630 **LOBO** Poeta
001 Fragment • line
002 Page • line
1466 **LOLLIANUS** Scr. Erot.
001 Fragment • line
0143 **LOLLIUS BASSUS** Epigr.
001 Book • epigram • line
2178 **Cassius LONGINUS** Phil. et Rhet.
001 Walz page • line
002 Section • line
0560 **[LONGINUS]** Rhet.
001 Chapter • section • line
0561 **LONGUS** Scr. Erot.
001 Book • chapter • section • line
0734 **<LUCAS Apostolus>** Med.
001 Section • line
0062 **LUCIANUS** Soph.
001 Chapter • section • line
002–065 Section • line
066–069 Dialogue • section • line
070 Section • line
071 Line
0061 **Pseudo-LUCIANUS** Soph.
001–004 Section • line
005 Line
006–008 Section • line
009 Line
010 Book • epigram • line
1468 **LUCILLIUS** Epigr.
001 Book • epigram • line
1977 **Lucius Licinius LUCULLUS** Hist.

001 Volume–Jacoby#–T • fragment • line
2439 **LUPERCUS** Gramm.
001 Volume–Jacoby#–T • fragment • line
1469 **LYCEAS** Hist.
001 Volume–Jacoby#–F • fragment • line
2212 **LYCEAS** Hist.
001 Volume–Jacoby#–F • fragment • line
002 Fragment • line
2246 **LYCON** Phil.
001 Fragment • line
1138 **LYCON** Phil.
001 Fragment • line
2444 **LYCOPHRON** Soph.
001 Fragment • line
0341 **LYCOPHRON** Trag.
001 Fragment • line
002 Line
0381 **LYCOPHRONIDES** Lyr.
001 Fragment • line
0034 **LYCURGUS** Orat.
001 Section • line
002 Oration • fragment • line
1470 **LYCUS** Hist.
001 Volume–Jacoby#–T • fragment • line
002 Volume–Jacoby#–F • fragment • line
003 FGrH fragment • line
2267 **LYCUS** Hist.
001 Volume–Jacoby#–F • fragment • line
2580 **Joannes Laurentius LYDUS** Hist.
001 Page • line
002 Book • section • line
003 Section • line
0471 **LYNCEUS** Comic.
001 Fragment • line
002 Play • fragment • line
0230 ***LYRICA ADESPOTA*** (CA)
001 Fragment • line
0297 ***LYRICA ADESPOTA*** (PMG)
001 Fragment • subfragment • line
1471 ***LYRICA ADESPOTA*** (SLG)
001 Fragment • line
2402 **LYSANDER** Hist.
001 Volume–Jacoby#–T • fragment • line
2298 **LYSANIAS** Hist.
001 Volume–Jacoby#–F • fragment • line
0540 **LYSIAS** Orat.
001–034 Section • line
035 Oration • section • line
036 Page • line
2262 **LYSIMACHIDES** Hist.
001 Volume–Jacoby#–F • fragment • line
0574 **LYSIMACHUS** Hist.
001 Volume–Jacoby#–F • fragment • line
002 FGrH fragment • line
1965 **LYSIMACHUS** Hist.
001 Volume–Jacoby#–T • fragment • line
2427 **LYSIMACHUS** Hist.
001 Volume–Jacoby#–T • fragment • line
002 Volume–Jacoby#–F • fragment • line
0472 **LYSIPPUS** Comic.
001 Fragment • line
002 Play • fragment • line
003 Fragment • line
0633 **<LYSIS>** Phil.
001 Page • line
002 Fragment • line
1472 **LYSISTRATUS** Epigr.
001 Book • epigram • line
2318 **MACARIUS** Hist.

001 Volume–Jacoby#–F • fragment • line
2109 **Pseudo-MACARIUS** Scr. Eccl.
001 Homily • chapter • section • line
002 Homily • line
003–004 Homily • section • line
005–009 Page • line
010–012 Volume • page • line
013 Page • line
0202 **MACE(DONIUS)** Lyr.
001 Line
1473 **MACEDONIUS I** Epigr.
001 Book • epigram • line
4064 **MACEDONIUS II** Epigr.
001 Book • epigram • line
0473 **MACHON** Comic.
001–002 Fragment • line
003 Play • fragment • line
2339 **MAEANDRIUS** Hist.
001 Volume–Jacoby#–F • fragment • line
1474 **Quintus MAECIUS** Epigr.
001 Book • epigram • line
5002 ***MAGICA***
001–004 Preisendanz number • line
0474 **MAGNES** Comic.
001 Fragment • line
002 Play • fragment • line
003 Fragment • line
2157 **MAGNUS** Hist.
001 Volume–Jacoby#–T • fragment • line
002 Volume–Jacoby#–F • fragment • line
0959 **MAGNUS** Med.
001 Book • epigram • line
1475 **MAIISTAS** Epic.
001 Line
2382 **MALACUS** Hist.
001 Volume–Jacoby#–F • fragment • line
1476 **MAMERCUS** Eleg.
001 Epigram • line
3074 **Constantinus MANASSES** Poeta et
Hist.
002 Line
1477 **MANETHO** Hist.
001 Volume–Jacoby#–T • fragment • line
002 Volume–Jacoby#–F • fragment • line
1478 **Pseudo-MANETHO** Hist.
001 Volume–Jacoby#–F • fragment • line
0200 ***MANTISSA PROVERBIORUM***
001 Centuria • section • line
0667 **MARCELLINUS I** Med.
001 Line
2458 **MARCELLUS** Hist.
001 Volume–Jacoby#–F • fragment • line
0281 **MARCELLUS** Poet. Med.
001 Line
2041 **MARCELLUS** Theol.
001 Fragment • line
004 Chapter • section • line
005 Page • line
1479 ***MARCI AURELII EPISTULA***
001 Page • line
4003 **MARCIANUS** Geogr.
001–002 Section • line
003 Fragment • line
0562 **MARCUS AURELIUS ANTO-
NINUS Imperator** Phil.
001 Book • chapter • section • line
4073 **MARIANUS** Epigr.
001 Book • epigram • line
4074 **MARINUS** Epigr.

001 Book • epigram • line
4075 **MARINUS** Phil.
001 Book • epigram • line
002 Page • line
2432 *MARMOR PARIUM*
001 Volume-Jacoby#-F • fragment • line
1481 **MARSYAS Pellaeus et MARSYAS Philippeus** Hist.
001 Volume-Jacoby#-T • fragment • line
002–004 Volume-Jacoby#-F • fragment • line
2011 *MARTYRIUM AGAPAE, IRE-NAE, CHIONAE ET SODALIUM*
001 Chapter • section • line
0390 *MARTYRIUM CARPI, PAPYLI ET AGATHONICAE*
001 Section • line
2008 *MARTYRIUM CONONIS*
001 Chapter • section • line
2010 *MARTYRIUM DASII*
001 Chapter • section • line
1483 *MARTYRIUM ET ASCENSIO ISAIAE*
001 Page • line
2009 *MARTYRIUM MARINI*
001 Section • line
2005 *MARTYRIUM PIONII*
001 Chapter • section • line
1484 *MARTYRIUM POLYCARPI*
001 Chapter • section • line
2007 *MARTYRIUM POTAMIAENAE ET BASILIDIS*
001 Section • line
1485 *MARTYRIUM PTOLEMAEI ET LUCII*
001 Section • line
1888 **MATRIS** Hist.
001 Volume-Jacoby#-T • fragment • line
002 Volume-Jacoby#-F • fragment • line
1486 **MATRON** Parodius
001 Line
002–003 Fragment • line
1560 *MATTHIAE TRADITIONES*
001 Fragment • line
1487 **MAXIMUS** Astrol.
001–002 Section • line
2025 **MAXIMUS** Rhet.
001 Volume • page • line
0563 **MAXIMUS** Soph.
001 Lecture • chapter • section • line
1488 **MAXIMUS** Theol.
001 Page • line
1939 **MEDIUS** Hist.
001 Volume-Jacoby#-T • fragment • line
002 Volume-Jacoby#-F • fragment • line
1489 **MEGASTHENES** Hist.
001 Volume-Jacoby#-T • fragment • line
002 Volume-Jacoby#-F • fragment • line
1490 **<MEGILLUS>** Phil.
001 Page • line
0373 **MELANIPPIDES** Lyr.
001 Fragment • line
1491 **MELANTHIUS** Hist.
001 Volume-Jacoby#-F • fragment • line
0344 **MELANTHIUS** Trag.
001 Fragment • line
0254 **MELANTHIUS** Trag. et Eleg.
001 Line
002 Fragment • line

1492 **MELEAGER** Epigr.
001 Book • epigram • line
0730 **MELETIUS** Med.
001–002 Page • line
1848 **MELETUS Junior** Trag.
001 Line
1493 **MELINNO** Lyr.
001 Fragment • line
0051 **<MELISSA>** Phil.
001 Page • line
2282 **MELISSEUS** Hist.
001 Volume-Jacoby#-F • fragment • line
1494 **MELISSUS** Phil.
001–002 Fragment • line
1495 **MELITO** Apol.
001–002 Line
003 Fragment • section • line
2250 **MELITO** Hist.
001 Volume-Jacoby#-F • fragment • line
0825 **MELITO** Trag.
001 Line
1496 **MEMNON** Hist.
001 Volume-Jacoby#-T • fragment • line
002 Volume-Jacoby#-F • fragment • line
1497 **MENAECHMUS** Hist.
001 Volume-Jacoby#-T • fragment • line
002 Volume-Jacoby#-F • fragment • line
0541 **MENANDER** Comic.
001 Line
002 Fragment • line
003 Line
004 Fragment • line
005 Line
006 Fragment • line
007 Line
008 Fragment • line
009–010 Line
011 Fragment • line
012–013 Line
014 Fragment • line
015 Line
016 Fragment • line
017 Line
018 Fragment • line
019 Line
020 Fragment • line
021 Line
022 Fragment • line
023 Line
024 Fragment • line
025 Line
026 Fragment • line
027 Line
028 Fragment • line
029–031 Line
032 Fragment • line
033–035 Line
036–037 Fragment • line
038 Fragment • column • line
039 Fragment • line
040 Play • fragment • line
041 Fragment • line
042 Line
044 Book • epigram • line
045 Fragment • line
046 Epigram • fragment • line
047 Sententia • section • line
048 Sententia • line
049 Play • fragment • line

1498 **MENANDER** Hist.
001 Volume-Jacoby#-T • fragment • line
002 Volume-Jacoby#-F • fragment • line
2586 **MENANDER** Rhet.
001–002 Spengel page • line
4076 **MENANDER Protector** Hist.
001 Book • epigram • line
003–005 Section • line
006 Page • line
1791 *MENANDRI ET PHILISTIONIS SENTENTIAE*
001 Section • line
002 Sententia • section • line
1499 **MENECLES** Hist.
001 Volume-Jacoby#-F • fragment • line
2325 **MENECLES** Hist.
001 Volume-Jacoby#-T • fragment • line
0523 **MENECRATES** Comic.
001 Fragment • line
002 Page • line
003 Fragment • line
1501 **MENECRATES** Epigr.
001 Book • epigram • line
1502 **MENECRATES** Epigr.
001 Book • epigram • line
1503 **MENECRATES** Hist.
001 Volume-Jacoby#-F • fragment • line
2475 **MENECRATES** Hist.
001 Volume-Jacoby#-F • fragment • line
0639 **MENECRATES** Med.
001 Line
1500 **MENECRATES** Poet. Phil.
001 Fragment • line
1504 **MENELAUS** Epic.
001 Volume-Jacoby#-T • fragment • line
002 Volume-Jacoby#-F • fragment • line
003 Fragment • line
2228 **MENESTOR** Phil.
001 Fragment • line
1787 **[MENIPPUS]** Comic.
001 Fragment • line
002 Page • line
0079 **MENIPPUS** Geogr.
002 Fragment • line
0052 **MENIPPUS** Phil.
001 Line
1506 **MENODOTUS** Hist.
001 Volume-Jacoby#-F • fragment • line
1916 **MENODOTUS** Hist.
001 Volume-Jacoby#-T • fragment • line
2631 **MENOPHILUS** Poeta
001 Fragment • line
2202 **[MENYLLUS]** Hist.
001 Volume-Jacoby#-T • fragment • line
0268 **MESOMEDES** Lyr.
001 Fragment • line
002 Book • epigram • line
0475 **METAGENES** Comic.
001 Fragment • line
002 Play • fragment • line
1507 **<METOPUS>** Phil.
001 Page • line
4077 **METRODORUS** Epigr.
001 Book • epigram • line
1976 **METRODORUS** Hist.
001 Volume-Jacoby#-T • fragment • line
002 Volume-Jacoby#-F • fragment • line
1508 **METRODORUS** Phil.
001 Volume-Jacoby#-F • fragment • line

002–003 Fragment • line
1811 **METRODORUS Major** Phil.
001 Fragment • line
2531 **METROPHANES** Hist.
001 Volume–Jacoby#–T • fragment • line
002 Volume–Jacoby#–F • fragment • line
9017 **MICHAEL** Epigr.
001 Book • epigram • line
4034 **MICHAEL** Phil.
001–006 Page • line
008 Page • line
009 Scholion • line
4078 **MICHAELIUS** Gramm.
001 Book • epigram • line
1509 <**MILON**> <Phil.>
001 Page • line
0255 **MIMNERMUS** Eleg.
001 Fragment • line
002 Book • epigram • line
003 Volume–Jacoby#–F • fragment • line
1511 **MIMNERMUS** Trag.
001 Fragment • line
1512 *MINYAS*
001 Fragment • line
0039 *MITHRIDATIS EPISTULA*
001 Section • line
1513 **MNASALCES** Epigr.
001 Book • epigram • line
1514 **MNASEAS** Perieg.
002 FHG fragment • line
0476 **MNESIMACHUS** Comic.
001 Fragment • line
002 Play • fragment • line
2565 **MNESIMACHUS** Hist.
001 Volume–Jacoby#–F • fragment • line
1959 **MNESIPTOLEMUS** Hist.
001 Volume–Jacoby#–T • fragment • line
1890 **MODERATUS** Phil.
001 Fragment • line
0220 **MOERO** Epic.
001 Fragment • line
002 Book • epigram • line
1516 **MOLPIS** Hist.
001 Volume–Jacoby#–T • fragment • line
002 Volume–Jacoby#–F • fragment • line
2968 **MONIMUS** Phil.
001 Fragment • line
0277 *MONODIA*
001 Line
1771 **MONTANUS et MONTANIS-
TAE** Theol.
001 Oracle number • line
0314 **MORSIMUS** Trag.
001 Fragment • line
1517 **MOSCHION** Hist. et Paradox.
001 Volume–Jacoby#–F • fragment • line
0339 **MOSCHION** Trag.
001 Fragment • line
0035 **MOSCHUS** Bucol.
001–004 Line
005 Fragment • line
006 Book • epigram • line
2414 **MOSMES** (?) Hist.
001 Volume–Jacoby#–F • fragment • line
1519 **MUNDUS MUNATIUS** Epigr.
001 Book • epigram • line
0576 **MUSAEUS** Epic.
001 Volume–Jacoby#–T • fragment • line
002 Volume–Jacoby#–F • fragment • line

003 Fragment • line
2691 **[MUSAEUS]** Phil.
001–002 Fragment • line
4082 **MUSAEUS Grammaticus** Epic.
001 Line
1520 **MUSICIUS** Epigr.
001 Book • epigram • line
0628 **Gaius MUSONIUS RUFUS** Phil.
001 Discourse • line
002 Fragment • line
003 Epistle • line
004 Line
0509 <**MYIA**> Phil.
001 Page • line
1522 **MYRINUS** Epigr.
001 Book • epigram • line
1523 **MYRON** Hist.
001 Volume–Jacoby#–T • fragment • line
002 Volume–Jacoby#–F • fragment • line
2331 **MYRSILUS** Hist.
001 Volume–Jacoby#–T • fragment • line
002 Volume–Jacoby#–F • fragment • line
0477 **MYRTILUS** Comic.
001 Fragment • line
002 Play • fragment • line
003 Fragment • line
1524 **NAUMACHIUS** Epic.
001 Line
0478 **NAUSICRATES** Comic.
001 Fragment • line
002 Play • fragment • line
003 Fragment • line
2334 **NAUSIPHANES** Phil.
001–002 Fragment • line
0269 *NAUTARUM CANTIUNCULAE*
001–002 Line
1525 **NEANTHES** Hist.
001 Volume–Jacoby#–T • fragment • line
002 Volume–Jacoby#–F • fragment • line
1966 **NEANTHES Junior** Hist.
001 Volume–Jacoby#–F • fragment • line
1942 **NEARCHUS** Hist.
001 Volume–Jacoby#–T • fragment • line
002 Volume–Jacoby#–F • fragment • line
0995 **[NECHEPSO et PETOSIRIS]**
Astrol.
002 Volume–Jacoby#–T • fragment • line
4079 **NEILUS** Epigr.
001 Book • epigram • line
0743 **NEMESIUS** Theol.
001 Section • line
0307 **NEOPHRON** Trag.
001 Fragment • line
1526 **NEOPTOLEMUS** Gramm.
001 Fragment • line
002 Volume–Jacoby#–T • fragment • line
003 Volume–Jacoby#–F • fragment • line
2456 **NESSAS** Phil.
001–002 Fragment • line
1528 **NESTOR** Epic.
001 Book • epigram • line
0218 **NICAENETUS** Epic.
001 Fragment • line
002 Book • epigram • line
0022 **NICANDER** Epic.
001–002 Line
003 Fragment • line
005 Fragment • line
006 Book • epigram • line

1529 **NICANDER** Gramm.
001 Volume–Jacoby#–T • fragment • line
002 Volume–Jacoby#–F • fragment • line
1933 **NICANDER** Hist.
001 Volume–Jacoby#–T • fragment • line
002 Volume–Jacoby#–F • fragment • line
2474 **NICANDER** Hist.
001 Volume–Jacoby#–F • fragment • line
1530 **NICANOR** Gramm.
001 Volume–Jacoby#–T • fragment • line
002 Volume–Jacoby#–F • fragment • line
1948 **NICANOR** Hist.
001 Volume–Jacoby#–F • fragment • line
2494 **NICARCHUS** Hist.
001 Volume–Jacoby#–F • fragment • line
1531 **NICARCHUS I** Epigr.
001 Book • epigram • line
1532 **NICARCHUS II** Epigr.
001 Book • epigram • line
2633 **NICERATUS** Epic.
001 Fragment • line
0046 *NICIAE EPISTULA*
001 Line
1533 **NICIAS** Epigr.
001 Book • epigram • line
002 Fragment • line
2217 **NICIAS** Hist.
001 Volume–Jacoby#–F • fragment • line
1902 <**NICIAS**> Hist.
001 Volume–Jacoby#–F • fragment • line
0479 **NICO** Comic.
001 Fragment • line
002 Play • fragment • line
1937 **NICOBULE** Hist.
001 Volume–Jacoby#–T • fragment • line
002 Volume–Jacoby#–F • fragment • line
0480 **NICOCHARES** Comic.
001 Fragment • line
002 Play • fragment • line
003 Fragment • line
2279 **NICOCHARES** Hist.
001 Volume–Jacoby#–T • fragment • line
1534 **NICOCLES** Hist.
001 Volume–Jacoby#–F • fragment • line
1535 **NICOCRATES** Hist.
001 Volume–Jacoby#–F • fragment • line
1536 **NICODEMUS** Epigr.
001 Book • epigram • line
0481 **NICOLAUS** Comic.
001 Fragment • line
002 Play • fragment • line
0577 **NICOLAUS** Hist.
001 Volume–Jacoby#–T • fragment • line
002 Volume–Jacoby#–F • fragment • line
0482 **NICOMACHUS** Comic.
001 Fragment • line
002 Play • fragment • line
1537 **NICOMACHUS** Epigr.
001 Book • epigram • line
1538 **NICOMACHUS** Hist.
001 Volume–Jacoby#–F • fragment • line
1961 **NICOMACHUS** Hist.
001 Volume–Jacoby#–F • fragment • line
0358 **NICOMACHUS** Math.
001 Book • chapter • section • line
002 Chapter • section • line
003 Page • line
004 Section • line
1843 **NICOMACHUS** Trag.

001 Line
0342 **NICOMACHUS** Trag.
    001 Fragment • line
2520 **NICOMEDES** Hist.
    001 Volume–Jacoby#–F • fragment • line
0483 **NICOPHON** Comic.
    001 Fragment • line
    002 Play • fragment • line
0484 **NICOSTRATUS** Comic.
    001 Fragment • line
    002 Play • fragment • line
    003–004 Fragment • line
    005 Play • fragment • line
2523 **NICOSTRATUS** Hist.
    001 Volume–Jacoby#–F • fragment • line
2144 **NICOSTRATUS** Hist.
    001 Volume–Jacoby#–T • fragment • line
1804 *NINUS*
    001 Fragment • line
2045 **NONNUS** Epic.
    001 Book • line
    002 Demonstratio • line
    003 Book • epigram • line
1540 **NOSSIS** Epigr.
    001 Book • epigram • line
0031 *NOVUM TESTAMENTUM*
    001–017 Chapter • section • line
    018 Section • line
    019–023 Chapter • section • line
    024 Section • line
    025 Chapter • section • line
    026 Section • line
    027 Chapter • section • line
1543 **NUMENIUS** Epigr.
    001 Book • epigram • line
1542 **NUMENIUS** Phil.
    001 Fragment • line
0703 **NUMENIUS** Poet. Didac.
    001 Fragment • line
1544 **NYMPHIS** Hist.
    001 Volume–Jacoby#–T • fragment • line
    002 Volume–Jacoby#–F • fragment • line
0578 **NYMPHODORUS** Hist.
    001 Volume–Jacoby#–T • fragment • line
    002 Volume–Jacoby#–F • fragment • line
1545 **OCELLUS** Phil.
    001 Chapter • section • line
    002–003 Fragment • line
2866 **OECUMENIUS** Rhet. et Phil.
    001–015 Page • line
4154 **Pseudo-OECUMENIUS** Scr. Eccl.
    001–002 Page • line
0971 **OENIADES** Lyr.
    001 Line
1548 **OENOMAUS** Phil.
    001 Fragment • line
    002 Book • epigram • line
2234 **OENOPIDES** Phil.
    001 Fragment • line
2373 **OLYMPICHUS** Hist.
    001 Volume–Jacoby#–F • fragment • line
4019 **OLYMPIODORUS** Phil.
    001–003 Page • line
    004 Section • line
    005–006 Chapter • section • line
    008 Page • line
1990 **OLYMPUS** Hist.
    001 Volume–Jacoby#–F • fragment • line
0648 **ONASANDER** Tact.

001 Chapter • section • line
1999 **ONASIMUS** Hist.
    001 Volume–Jacoby#–T • fragment • line
    002 Volume–Jacoby#–F • fragment • line
1889 **ONASUS** Hist.
    001 Volume–Jacoby#–F • fragment • line
1549 **<ONATAS>** Phil.
    001 Page • line
1943 **ONESICRITUS** Hist.
    001 Volume–Jacoby#–T • fragment • line
    002 Volume–Jacoby#–F • fragment • line
0485 **OPHELIO** Comic.
    001 Fragment • line
    002 Play • fragment • line
0023 **OPPIANUS** Epic.
    001 Book • line
0024 **OPPIANUS** Epic.
    001 Book • line
1550 *ORACULA CHALDAICA*
    001 Oracle • line
1551 *ORACULA SIBYLLINA*
    001 Section • line
    002 Fragment • line
1552 *ORATIO JOSEPHI*
    001 Page • line
1858 *ORATIO MANASSIS*
    001 Page • line
0722 **ORIBASIUS** Med.
    001 Book • chapter • section • line
    002–003 Chapter • section • line
    004–005 Book • chapter • section • line
    010 Volume–Jacoby#–T • fragment • line
2042 **ORIGENES** Theol.
    001 Book • section • line
    002 Book • chapter • section • line
    003–004 Fragment • line
    005 Book • chapter • section • line
    006 Fragment • line
    007 Section • line
    008 Chapter • section • line
    009 Homily • section • line
    010–011 Fragment • line
    012 Line
    013 Section • line
    014 Fragment • line
    015 Line
    016 Homily • page • line
    017 Fragment • line
    018 Section • line
    019–020 Chapter • section • line
    021 Homily • section • line
    022–028 Page • line
    029 Book • section • line
    030 Book • chapter • section • line
    031 Fragment • line
    032 Page • line
    033–036 Section • line
    037 Fragment • line
    038 Page • line
    039 Chapter • section • line
    040–041 Line
    042–043 Scholion • line
    044 Psalm • verse • line
    045–078 Volume • page • line
    079 Book • chapter • section • line
    084 Fragment • section • line
0579 *ORPHICA*
    001 Hymn • line
    002–003 Line

    004 Page • line
    009–010 Fragment • line
2480 **ORTHAGORAS** Hist.
    001 Volume–Jacoby#–F • fragment • line
1203 *PAEANES* (CA)
    001–004 Line
    005 Fragment • line
    006 Line
2512 **PAEON** Hist.
    001 Volume–Jacoby#–F • fragment • line
2450 **PALAEPHATUS** Gramm.
    001 Volume–Jacoby#–T • fragment • line
    002 Volume–Jacoby#–F • fragment • line
1553 **<PALAEPHATUS>** Myth.
    001 Section • line
    002 Volume–Jacoby#–T • fragment • line
    003 Volume–Jacoby#–F • fragment • line
2123 **PALLADAS** Epigr.
    001 Book • epigram • line
2564 **PALLADIUS** Hist.
    001 Volume–Jacoby#–T • fragment • line
0726 **PALLADIUS** Med.
    001 Volume • page • line
    002 Chapter • section • line
    003 Line
    004 Page • line
2111 **PALLADIUS** Scr. Eccl.
    001 Vita • section • line
    002–004 Page • line
    005 Chapter • section • line
1554 **PAMPHILUS** Epigr.
    001 Book • epigram • line
2634 **PAMPHILUS** Poeta
    001 Fragment • line
1399 **PAMPHILUS** Trag.
    001 Line
4038 **PAMPREPIUS** Epic.
    001 Fragment • line
    002 Volume–Jacoby#–T • fragment • line
0256 **PANARCES** Scriptor Aenigmatum
    001 Fragment • line
1555 **PANCRATES** Epic.
    001 Fragment+column • line
    002 Volume–Jacoby#–T • fragment • line
    003 Volume–Jacoby#–F • fragment • line
1556 **PANCRATES** Epigr.
    001 Fragment • line
    002 Book • epigram • line
2120 **PANTELEIUS** Epic.
    001 Line
1557 **PANYASSIS** Epic.
    001 Fragment • line
    002 Volume–Jacoby#–T • fragment • line
1558 **PAPIAS** Scr. Eccl.
    001 Fragment • section • line
2032 **PAPPUS** Math.
    001–002 Page • line
0580 *PARADOXOGRAPHUS FLO-RENTINUS*
    001 Section • line
0581 *PARADOXOGRAPHUS PALA-TINUS*
    001 Section • line
0582 *PARADOXOGRAPHUS VATI-CANUS*
    001 Section • line
1772 *PARALEIPOMENA JEREMIOU*
    001 Chapter • section • line
1785 **PARAMONUS** Comic.

001 Fragment • line
4174 *PARAPHRASES IN DIONY-SIUM PERIEGETAM*
001–002 Section • line
1562 PARMENIDES Poet. Phil.
001–002 Fragment • line
1563 PARMENION Epigr.
001 Book • epigram • line
2225 PARM(EN)ISCUS Phil.
001 Fragment • line
1565 [PARMENO] Epigr.
001 Book • epigram • line
1566 PARMENO Iamb.
001–002 Fragment • line
1801 *PARODICA ANONYMA*
001–002 Fragment • line
2227 PARON Phil.
001 Fragment • line
1567 PARRHASIUS Epigr.
001 Epigram • line
1568 PARTHAX Hist.
001 Volume–Jacoby#–F • fragment • line
0655 PARTHENIUS Myth.
001 Chapter • section • line
002–003 Fragment • line
2016 *PASSIO PERPETUAE ET FELI-CITATIS*
001 Section • line
2479 PATROCLES Hist.
001 Volume–Jacoby#–T • fragment • line
002 Volume–Jacoby#–F • fragment • line
0324 PATROCLES Trag.
001 Fragment • line
2053 PAULUS Astrol.
001–002 Page • line
0715 PAULUS Med.
001 Book • chapter • section • line
4039 PAULUS Silentiarius Poet. Christ.
004 Book • epigram • line
0047 *PAUSANIAE I ET XERXIS EPISTULAE*
001 Epistle • line
1569 PAUSANIAS Attic.
001 Alphabetic letter • entry • line
2407 PAUSANIAS Hist.
001 Volume–Jacoby#–T • fragment • line
2573 PAUSANIAS Hist.
001 Volume–Jacoby#–T • fragment • line
002 Volume–Jacoby#–F • fragment • line
0525 PAUSANIAS Perieg.
001 Book • chapter • section • line
2401 PAUSANIAS II Rex Lacedae-monis Hist.
001 Volume–Jacoby#–T • fragment • line
2266 PAXAMUS Hist. et Scr. Rerum Nat.
001 Volume–Jacoby#–T • fragment • line
2592 Joannes PEDIASIMUS Gramm.
003 Page • line
0275 *PEIRAZOMENE*
001 Line
1571 <PEMPELUS> Phil.
001 Page • line
0629 PERIANDER <Phil.>
001 Epistle • line
1572 <PERICTIONE> Phil.
001 Page • line
0064 *PERIPLUS HANNONIS*
001 Section • line

0071 *PERIPLUS MARIS ERYTH-RAEI*
001 Section • line
0077 *PERIPLUS MARIS MAGNI*
001 Section • line
0075 *PERIPLUS PONTI EUXINI*
001 Section • line
1573 PERITAS Epigr.
001 Book • epigram • line
2403 PERSAEUS Hist.
001 Volume–Jacoby#–T • fragment • line
002 Volume–Jacoby#–F • fragment • line
1574 PERSAEUS Phil.
001 Fragment • line
1575 PERSES Epigr.
001 Book • epigram • line
2635 PERSINUS Poeta
001 Fragment • line
2323 PETELLIDAS Hist.
001 Volume–Jacoby#–F • fragment • line
2247 PETRON Phil.
001 Fragment • line
1576 PHAEDIMUS <Epic.>
001 Line
1577 PHAEDIMUS Epigr.
001 Book • epigram • line
002 Fragment • line
1578 PHAENIAS Phil.
001 Fragment • line
1579 PHAËNNUS Epigr.
001 Book • epigram • line
1580 PHAESTUS Epic.
001 Line
002 Volume–Jacoby#–F • fragment • line
003 Fragment • line
1581 PHALAECUS Epigr.
001 Book • epigram • line
0053 *PHALARIDIS EPISTULAE*
001 Epistle • section • line
1582 PHANIAS Gramm.
001 Book • epigram • line
0214 PHANOCLES Eleg.
001 Fragment • line
1583 PHANODEMUS Hist.
001 Volume–Jacoby#–T • fragment • line
002 Volume–Jacoby#–F • fragment • line
2278 PHANODICUS Hist.
001 Volume–Jacoby#–F • fragment • line
2471 PHARNUCHUS Hist.
001 Volume–Jacoby#–T • fragment • line
0486 PHERECRATES Comic.
001 Fragment • line
002 Play • fragment • line
003–005 Fragment • line
006 Play • fragment • line
1584 PHERECYDES Hist.
001 Volume–Jacoby#–T • fragment • line
002 Volume–Jacoby#–F • fragment • line
2329 PHERECYDES Hist.
001 Volume–Jacoby#–T • fragment • line
002 Volume–Jacoby#–F • fragment • line
0630 PHERECYDES Phil. et Myth.
001–002 Fragment • line
1585 *PHERECYDIS EPISTULA*
001 Line
2636 PHERENICUS Epic.
001 Fragment • line
1880 PHIDALIUS Hist.
001 Volume–Jacoby#–F • fragment • line

2966 PHILEAS Scr. Eccl.
002 Section • line
0487 PHILEMON Comic.
001 Fragment • line
002 Play • fragment • line
003–004 Fragment • line
006–007 Fragment • line
008 Book • epigram • line
009 Play • fragment • line
0488 PHILEMON Junior Comic.
001 Fragment • line
002 Play • fragment • line
0489 PHILETAERUS Comic.
001 Fragment • line
002 Play • fragment • line
003 Fragment • line
0212 PHILETAS Eleg. et Gramm.
001 Fragment • line
002 Title • fragment • line
003–004 Fragment • line
1587 PHILIADES Eleg.
001 Fragment • line
1588 PHILICUS Lyr.
001 Fragment • line
1969 PHILINUS Hist.
001 Volume–Jacoby#–T • fragment • line
002 Volume–Jacoby#–F • fragment • line
0490 PHILIPPIDES Comic.
001 Fragment • line
002 Play • fragment • line
1781 PHILIPPUS Comic.
001 Fragment • line
002 Page • line
1589 PHILIPPUS Epigr.
001 Book • epigram • line
1590 PHILIPPUS Hist.
001 Volume–Jacoby#–F • fragment • line
2142 PHILIPPUS Hist.
001 Volume–Jacoby#–T • fragment • line
002 Volume–Jacoby#–F • fragment • line
2188 PHILIPPUS Hist.
001 Volume–Jacoby#–T • fragment • line
002 Volume–Jacoby#–F • fragment • line
0048 PHILIPPUS II Rex Macedonum <Epist.>
001 Epistle • section • line
0491 PHILISCUS Comic.
001 Fragment • line
002 Play • fragment • line
003 Fragment • line
2131 PHILISCUS Epigr.
001 Book • epigram • line
0257 PHILISCUS Rhet.
001 Line
002 Volume–Jacoby#–F • fragment • line
0335 PHILISCUS Trag.
001 Fragment • line
1870 PHILISTIDES Hist.
001 Volume–Jacoby#–T • fragment • line
002 Volume–Jacoby#–F • fragment • line
1591 PHILISTUS Hist.
001 Volume–Jacoby#–T • fragment • line
002 Volume–Jacoby#–F • fragment • line
2422 PHILISTUS Hist.
001 Volume–Jacoby#–T • fragment • line
1592 PHILITAS Epigr.
001 Book • epigram • line
1593 PHILO <Epigr.>
001 Book • epigram • line

2457 PHILO Hist.
001 Volume-Jacoby#–T • fragment • line
002 Volume-Jacoby#–F • fragment • line
1599 PHILO Mech.
001–002 Thevenot page • line
0706 PHILO Med.
001 Fragment • line
2638 PHILO Poeta
001 Fragment • line
0018 PHILO JUDAEUS Phil.
001 Section • line
002 Book • section • line
003–018 Section • line
019 Book • section • line
020–021 Section • line
022 Book • section • line
023 Section • line
024 Book • section • line
025–031 Section • line
032 Page • line
033 Fragment • section • line
034–035 Book • fragment • line
036 Fragment • line
038–039 Fragment • line
041–042 Line
1594 PHILO Judaeus Senior Epic.
002 Fragment • line
003 Volume-Jacoby#–T • fragment • line
004 Volume-Jacoby#–F • fragment • line
0583 PHILOCHORUS Hist.
001 Volume-Jacoby#–T • fragment • line
002 Volume-Jacoby#–F • fragment • line
003 FGrH fragment • line
1794 PHILOCLES Comic.
001 Fragment • line
0312 PHILOCLES Trag.
001 Fragment • line
2415 PHILOCRATES Hist.
001 Volume-Jacoby#–F • fragment • line
0205 PHILODAMUS Lyr.
001 Line
002 Fragment • line
1595 PHILODEMUS Phil.
001 Line
010 Column • line
020 Column • line
030–031 Column • line
053 Fragment+column • line
055 Fragment+column • line
060 Text-note • fragment • line
070 Papyrus number • line
115–116 Column • line
117 Line
118–119 Column • line
132 Column • line
138 Fragment or column • line
139 Diels column or fragment • line
199 Column • line
200 Fragment or column • line
221 Book or papyrus number • fragment or column • line
222 Fragment • line
230 Column • line
241 Fragment or column • line
261 Fragment or column • line
264 Fragment or column • line
271 Fragment or column • line
294 Fragment or column • line
301 Fragment • line

304 VH volume • line
310 Line
316 Fragment+column • line
317 Fragment • line
319 Page • line
326 Fragment or column • line
330 Fragment • line
336 Column • line
344 Fragment • line
346 Fragment+column • line
348 Line
362 Fragment or Oxford papyrus number • line
370 Book • fragment or fragment+column • line
370 Book • fragment or fragment+column • line
374–376 Fragment • line
380 Fragment • line
382 Fragment • line
386 Fragment • line
388 Fragment • line
400 Fragment • line
402 Fragment • line
410 Fragment • line
412 Fragment • line
414 Fragment • line
416 Fragment • line
418 Fragment • line
424 Papyrus number • fragment+column • line
472 Column–subscriptio–fragment • line
595 Fragment+column • line
674 Fragment • line
678 Line
730 Book • epigram • line
1596 PHILOLAUS Phil.
001–002 Fragment • line
003 Page • line
1598 PHILOMNESTUS Hist.
001 Volume-Jacoby#–F • fragment • line
0492 PHILONIDES Comic.
001 Fragment • line
002 Play • fragment • line
003 Fragment • line
1934 PHILONIDES Hist.
001 Volume-Jacoby#–T • fragment • line
002 Volume-Jacoby#–F • fragment • line
0493 PHILOSTEPHANUS Comic.
001 Fragment • line
002 Play • fragment • line
0584 PHILOSTEPHANUS Hist.
003 Fragment • line
2058 PHILOSTORGIUS Scr. Eccl.
006 Book • epigram • line
2527 PHILOSTRATUS Hist.
001 Volume-Jacoby#–F • fragment • line
2145 PHILOSTRATUS Hist.
001 Volume-Jacoby#–T • fragment • line
002 Volume-Jacoby#–F • fragment • line
0638 Fiavius PHILOSTRATUS Soph.
001 Chapter • section • line
002 Epistle • line
003 Chapter • Olearius page • line
004–005 Olearius page • line
006 Section • epistle or discourse • line
007 Section • line
009 Book • epigram • line
0652 PHILOSTRATUS Junior Soph.

001 Olearius page • line
1600 PHILOSTRATUS Major Soph.
001 Book • chapter • section • line
1601 PHILOXENUS Epigr.
001 Book • epigram • line
0379 PHILOXENUS Lyr.
001–002 Fragment • line
0380 PHILOXENUS Lyr.
001 Fragment • line
002 Line
2344 PHILTEAS Hist.
001 Volume-Jacoby#–T • fragment • line
002 Volume-Jacoby#–F • fragment • line
0671 PHILUMENUS Med.
001 Chapter • section • line
0494 PHILYLLIUS Comic.
001 Fragment • line
002 Play • fragment • line
003–004 Fragment • line
1603 <PHINTYS> Phil.
001 Page • line
0585 Publius Aelius PHLEGON Paradox.
001 Chapter • section • line
002 Volume-Jacoby#–T • fragment • line
003 Volume-Jacoby#–F • fragment • line
2124 PHOCAS Diaconus Epigr.
001 Book • epigram • line
1604 PHOCYLIDES Eleg. et Gnom.
001 Fragment • line
002 Book • epigram • line
1605 Pseudo-PHOCYLIDES Gnom.
001 Line
0495 PHOENICIDES Comic.
001 Fragment • line
002 Play • fragment • line
003 Fragment • line
1606 PHOENIX Iamb.
001 Fragment • line
1788 PHORMIS Comic.
001–002 Fragment • line
1607 *PHORONIS*
001 Fragment • line
4040 PHOTIUS Theol., Scr. Eccl. et Lexicogr.
001 Codex • Bekker page • line
011 Book • epigram • line
014–026 Page • line
027–028 Fragment • line
1608 PHRYNICHUS Attic.
001 Page • line
002–004 Lexical entry • line
005 Fragment • line
0496 PHRYNICHUS Comic.
001 Fragment • line
002 Play • fragment • line
003–004 Fragment • line
005 Play • fragment • line
0303 PHRYNICHUS Trag.
001 Fragment • line
0876 PHRYNICHUS II Trag.
001 Line
1609 PHYLARCHUS Hist.
001 Volume-Jacoby#–T • fragment • line
002 Volume-Jacoby#–F • fragment • line
003 Fragment • line
0258 PIGRES Eleg.
001 Line
0033 PINDARUS Lyr.

001–004 Ode • line
005 Type of poem • fragment • line
1610 **PINYTUS** Epigr.
001 Book • epigram • line
0288 **PISANDER** Epic.
002 Fragment • line
003 Book • epigram • line
0522 **PISANDER** Epic.
001 Fragment • line
0393 **PISANDER** Myth.
001 Volume–Jacoby#–T • fragment • line
002 Volume–Jacoby#–F • fragment • line
0049 *PISISTRATI EPISTULA*
001 Line
2395 **PISISTRATUS** Hist.
001 Volume–Jacoby#–F • fragment • line
1612 **PISO** Epigr.
001 Book • epigram • line
1613 *PITTACI EPISTULA*
001 Line
0631 **PITTACUS** <Lyr.>
001 Line
002 Book • epigram • line
0497 **PLATO** Comic.
001 Fragment • line
002 Play • fragment • line
003–004 Fragment • line
005 Book • epigram • line
006 Fragment • line
007 Play • fragment • line
0059 **PLATO** Phil.
001–038 Stephanus page • section • line
039 Book • epigram • line
040 Fragment • line
041 Epigram • line
1614 **PLATO Junior** Epigr.
001 Book • epigram • line
1615 **PLATONIUS** Gramm.
001 Line
1895 **PLESIMACHUS** Hist.
001 Volume–Jacoby#–F • fragment • line
2000 **PLOTINUS** Phil.
001 Ennead • chapter • section • line
0007 **PLUTARCHUS** Biogr. et Phil.
001–066 Chapter • section • line
067–123 Stephanus page • section • line
125–141 Stephanus page • section • line
143–144 Section • line
145 Fragment • line
146 Centuria • section • line
147 Line
148 Volume–Jacoby#–F • fragment • line
0094 **Pseudo-PLUTARCHUS**
001 Chapter • section • line
002–003 Stephanus page • section • line
0625 **POLEMAEUS** Trag.
001 Line
0586 **POLEMON** Perieg.
002 FHG fragment • line
1617 **Marcus Antonius POLEMON**
Soph.
001 Declamation • section • line
002 Page • line
1616 **POLEMON I** <Epigr.>
001 Book • epigram • line
0498 **POLIOCHUS** Comic.
001 Fragment • line
002 Play • fragment • line
2477 **POLLES** Hist.

001 Volume–Jacoby#–T • fragment • line
1618 **POLLIANUS** Epigr.
001 Book • epigram • line
1985 **Asinius POLLIO** Hist.
001 Volume–Jacoby#–T • fragment • line
0542 **Julius POLLUX** Gramm.
001 Book • section • line
1869 **POLUS** Rhet. et Hist.
001 Volume–Jacoby#–T • fragment • line
1620 **Julius POLYAENUS** Epigr.
001 Book • epigram • line
1621 **POLYAENUS** Epigr.
001 Book • epigram • line
0616 **POLYAENUS** Rhet.
001 Book • chapter • section • line
002 Excerpt • section • line
003 Volume–Jacoby#–T • fragment • line
004 Volume–Jacoby#–F • fragment • line
1988 **Gaius Julius POLYAENUS** Soph.
et Hist.
001 Volume–Jacoby#–T • fragment • line
1886 **POLYARCHUS** Hist.
001 Volume–Jacoby#–F • fragment • line
0543 **POLYBIUS** Hist.
001 Book • chapter • section • line
002 Fragment • line
003 Volume–Jacoby#–T • fragment • line
2177 **Tiberius Claudius POLYBIUS**
Hist.
001 Volume–Jacoby#–F • fragment • line
0605 **POLYBIUS** Rhet.
001–002 Page • line
1622 **POLYCARPUS** Scr. Eccl.
001 Chapter • section • line
1624 **POLYCHARMUS** Hist.
001 Volume–Jacoby#–F • fragment • line
1623 **POLYCHARMUS** Hist.
001 Volume–Jacoby#–F • fragment • line
1938 **POLYCLITUS** Hist.
001 Volume–Jacoby#–T • fragment • line
002 Volume–Jacoby#–F • fragment • line
1625 **POLYCLITUS** Phil.
001–002 Fragment • line
2410 **POLYCRATES** Hist.
001 Volume–Jacoby#–T • fragment • line
1627 **POLYCRATES** Hist.
001 Volume–Jacoby#–F • fragment • line
1626 **POLYCRATES** Scr. Eccl.
001 Page • line
2385 **POLYCRITUS** Hist.
001 Volume–Jacoby#–T • fragment • line
002 Volume–Jacoby#–F • fragment • line
003 Fragment • line
0331 <**POLYIDUS**> Trag.
001 Fragment • line
1839 **POLYPHRASMON** Trag.
001 Line
1628 **POLYSTRATUS** Epigr.
001 Book • epigram • line
1629 **POLYSTRATUS** Phil.
001 Fragment or column • line
002 Fragment • column • line
0499 **POLYZELUS** Comic.
001 Fragment • line
002 Play • fragment • line
003 Fragment • line
1630 **POLYZELUS** Hist.
001 Volume–Jacoby#–F • fragment • line
0346 **POMPEIUS MACER** <Trag.>

001 Fragment • line
1631 **POMPEIUS MACER Junior** Epigr.
001 Book • epigram • line
2034 **PORPHYRIUS** Phil.
001–002 Section • line
003 Book • section • line
004–005 Section • line
006–007 Volume • page • line
008 Sententia • line
009 Book • fragment • line
010 Fragment • section • line
011 Page • line
012 Section • line
013 Chapter • section • line
014 Iliad book • section • line
015 Page • line
016 Odyssey book • section • line
017–018 Section • line
019–021 Page • line
022 Book • fragment • line
023 Fragment • line
024 Volume–Jacoby#–T • fragment • line
025 Volume–Jacoby#–F • fragment • line
027 Fragment • line
029 Section • line
0500 **POSIDIPPUS** Comic.
001 Fragment • line
002 Play • fragment • line
003 Fragment • line
1632 **POSIDIPPUS** Epigr.
001 Book • epigram • line
004 Fragment • line
2310 **POSIDIPPUS** Hist.
001 Volume–Jacoby#–F • fragment • line
2639 **POSIDONIUS** Epic.
001 Fragment • line
1964 **POSIDONIUS** Hist.
001 Volume–Jacoby#–F • fragment • line
2187 **POSIDONIUS** Hist.
001 Volume–Jacoby#–T • fragment • line
1052 **POSIDONIUS** Phil.
001 Fragment • line
002 Volume–Jacoby#–T • fragment • line
003 Volume–Jacoby#–F • fragment • line
2333 **POSSIS** Hist.
001 Volume–Jacoby#–F • fragment • line
002 Fragment • line
2544 **Aelius POSTUMIUS ALBINUS**
Hist.
001 Volume–Jacoby#–T • fragment • line
002 Volume–Jacoby#–F • fragment • line
1949 **POTAMON** Hist.
001 Volume–Jacoby#–T • fragment • line
002 Volume–Jacoby#–F • fragment • line
0663 *PRAECEPTA SALUBRIA*
001 Line
0278 *PRAELUSIO MIMI*
001 Line
1833 **PRATINAS** Trag.
001–002 Fragment • line
2151 **PRAXAGORAS** Hist.
001 Volume–Jacoby#–T • fragment • line
0372 **PRAXILLA** Lyr.
001 Fragment • line
2335 **PRAXION** Hist.
001 Volume–Jacoby#–F • fragment • line
0089 **PRAXIPHANES** Phil.
001 Fragment • line
1633 **PRAXITELES** <Epigr.>

001 Epigram • line
4014 **PRISCIANUS** Phil.
001 Page • line
2641 **PRISCUS** Epic.
001 Fragment • line
4036 **PROCLUS** Phil.
001 Volume • page • line
002 Chapter • section • line
003 Book • epigram • line
004 Volume • page • line
005 Section • line
006 Book • section • line
007 Section • line
008 Page • line
009 Section • line
010 Volume • page • line
011 Page • line
012–014 Section • line
015 Hymn • line
016 Fragment • line
017 Epigram • line
018 Page • line
020 Page • line
021 Fragment • line
4029 **PROCOPIUS** Hist.
001 Book • chapter • section • line
002 Chapter • section • line
003 Book • chapter • section • line
1634 **PRODICUS** Soph.
001–002 Fragment • line
2300 **PROMATHIDAS** Hist.
001 Volume–Jacoby#–T • fragment • line
002 Volume–Jacoby#–F • fragment • line
003 Fragment • line
2548 **PROMATHION** Hist.
001 Volume–Jacoby#–F • fragment • line
0397 **PRONOMUS** Lyr.
001 Line
2729 **PRORUS** Phil.
001 Page • line
1635 **PROTAGORAS** Soph.
001–002 Fragment • line
003 Line
1636 **PROTAGORIDES** Hist.
001 Volume–Jacoby#–T • fragment • line
002 Volume–Jacoby#–F • fragment • line
1637 *PROTEVANGELIUM JACOBI*
001 Section • line
1638 **PROXENUS** Hist.
001 Volume–Jacoby#–F • fragment • line
2297 **PROXENUS** Hist.
001 Volume–Jacoby#–F • fragment • line
1914 **PSAON** Hist.
001 Volume–Jacoby#–T • fragment • line
2702 **Michael PSELLUS** Polyhist.
001 Chapter • section • line
1639 **PSEUDO-AUCTORES HELLE-NISTAE** (PsVTGr)
001 Page • line
0050 *PTOLEMAEI II PHILADELPHI ET ELEAZARI EPISTULAE*
001 Epistle • line
1640 **PTOLEMAEUS** Epigr.
001 Book • epigram • line
1641 **PTOLEMAEUS** Gnost.
001 Chapter • section • line
1646 **PTOLEMAEUS** Hist.
001 Volume–Jacoby#–T • fragment • line

002 Volume–Jacoby#–F • fragment • line
1991 **PTOLEMAEUS** Hist.
001 Volume–Jacoby#–F • fragment • line
1647 **PTOLEMAEUS** Hist.
001 Volume–Jacoby#–T • fragment • line
002 Volume–Jacoby#–F • fragment • line
0363 **Claudius PTOLEMAEUS** Math.
001–006 Volume • page • line
007 Book • chapter • section • line
008 Volume • page • line
009 Book • chapter • section • line
010 Chapter • section • line
011 Section • line
012 Fragment • line
013 Book • epigram • line
014 Book • chapter • section • line
1642 **Pseudo-PTOLEMAEUS**
001 Section • line
1944 **PTOLEMAEUS I SOTER** Hist.
001 Volume–Jacoby#–T • fragment • line
002 Volume–Jacoby#–F • fragment • line
2693 **PTOLEMAEUS III EUERGETES I** <Epigr.>
001 Fragment • line
0604 **PTOLEMAEUS IV PHILOPA-TOR** Trag.
001 Line
1645 **PTOLEMAEUS VIII EUERGE-TES II** <Hist.>
001 Volume–Jacoby#–T • fragment • line
002 Volume–Jacoby#–F • fragment • line
1814 **PTOLEMAIS** Phil.
001 Page • line
2349 **[PYRANDER]** Hist.
001 Volume–Jacoby#–F • fragment • line
1648 **PYRGION** Hist.
001 Volume–Jacoby#–F • fragment • line
2563 **PYRRHO** Hist.
001 Volume–Jacoby#–F • fragment • line
2160 **PYRRHUS** Hist.
001 Volume–Jacoby#–F • fragment • line
1649 **PYTHAENETUS** Hist.
001 Volume–Jacoby#–F • fragment • line
0632 **<PYTHAGORAS>** Phil.
001 Line
002 Page • line
005 Book • epigram • line
006 Fragment • line
2239 **PYTHAGORISTAE** (D-K) Phil.
001 Fragment • line
1650 **PYTHEAS** Perieg.
001 Fragment • line
1651 **PYTHERMUS** Hist.
001 Volume–Jacoby#–F • fragment • line
2179 **PYTHEUS-SATYRUS** Hist.
001 Volume–Jacoby#–T • fragment • line
002 Volume–Jacoby#–F • fragment • line
2560 **PYTHOCLES** Hist.
001 Volume–Jacoby#–F • fragment • line
0337 **PYTHON** Trag.
001 Fragment • line
2046 **QUINTUS** Epic.
001 Book • line
1653 **RARUS** Epigr.
001 Book • epigram • line
0598 *RHETORICA ANONYMA*
001 Fragment • line
002 Page • line

0219 **RHIANUS** Epic.
001 Fragment • line
002 Book • epigram • line
003 Fragment • line
004 Volume–Jacoby#–T • fragment • line
005 Volume–Jacoby#–F • fragment • line
006 FGrH fragment • line
1654 **RHINTHON** Comic.
001–002 Fragment • line
2881 **ROMANUS MELODUS** Hym-nogr.
001 Hymn • section • line
002–003 Hymn • proem-strophe • section • line
005 Hymn • proem-strophe • section • line
1656 **RUFINUS** Epigr.
001 Book • epigram • line
4041 **RUF(IN)US** Epigr.
001 Book • epigram • line
2553 **RUFUS** Hist.
001 Volume–Jacoby#–T • fragment • line
002 Volume–Jacoby#–F • fragment • line
0564 **RUFUS** Med.
001 Chapter • section • line
002–006 Section • line
007 Chapter • section • line
0606 **RUFUS** Soph.
001 Page • line
2546 **Publius RUTILIUS RUFUS** Hist.
001 Volume–Jacoby#–T • fragment • line
002 Volume–Jacoby#–F • fragment • line
2049 **SALLUSTIUS** Phil.
001 Chapter • section • line
1657 *SAMIORUM ANNALES*
001 Volume–Jacoby#–F • fragment • line
1658 **SAMUS** Epigr.
001 Book • epigram • line
0501 **SANNYRION** Comic.
001 Fragment • line
002 Play • fragment • line
003–004 Fragment • line
0009 **SAPPHO** Lyr.
001 Fragment • line
002 Book • epigram • line
003–004 Fragment • line
1815 **SAPPHO et ALCAEUS** Lyr.
001 Fragment • line
0387 *SAPPHUS vel ALCAEI FRAG-MENTA*
001–002 Fragment • line
1659 **SATRIUS** Epigr.
001 Book • epigram • line
0608 **SATYRUS** Biogr.
001 Fragment • line
1660 **SATYRUS** Epigr.
001 Book • epigram • line
1661 **SATYRUS** Hist.
001 FGrH fragment+papyrus fragment or column • line
002 Volume–Jacoby#–F • fragment • line
1873 **SATYRUS "Zeta"** Hist.
001 Volume–Jacoby#–F • fragment • line
1518 **Quintus Mucius SCAEVOLA** Epigr.
001 Book • epigram • line
2330 **SCAMON** Hist.
001 Volume–Jacoby#–T • fragment • line
002 Volume–Jacoby#–F • fragment • line

0527 SEPTUAGINTA
001–026 Chapter • section • line
027 Psalm • section • line
028 Ode • section • line
029 Proverb • section • line
030–034 Chapter • section • line
035 Psalm • section • line
036–039 Chapter • section • line
040 Section • line
041–051 Chapter • section • line
052 Section • line
053 Chapter • section • line
054–055 Section • line
056–057 Chapter • section • line
058–059 Section • line
1668 SERAPION Epigr.
001 Book • epigram • line
1670 SERAPION Scr. Eccl.
001 Page • line
0347 SERAPION Trag.
001 Fragment • line
2055 SERENUS Geom.
001–002 Page • line
1672 SERVIUS Hist.
001 Volume-Jacoby#–F • fragment • line
4139 SEVERIANUS Scr. Eccl.
039–052 Page • line
2970 SEVERUS Phil.
001 Page+column • line
0748 SEVERUS Iatrosophista Med.
001 Page • line
0544 SEXTUS EMPIRICUS Phil.
001–002 Book • section • line
1970 SILENUS Hist.
001 Volume-Jacoby#–T • fragment • line
002 Volume-Jacoby#–F • fragment • line
1877 SILENUS Hist.
001 Volume-Jacoby#–T • fragment • line
0603 SILENUS Trag.
001 Line
0211 SIMIAS Gramm.
001 Fragment • line
002 Book • epigram • line
1673 SIMMIAS Epigr.
001 Book • epigram • line
2600 SIMON Scriptor De Re Equestri
001 Section • line
002 Fragment • line
1906 SIMONIDES Epic.
001 Volume-Jacoby#–T • fragment • line
002 Fragment • line
1958 SIMONIDES Hist.
001 Volume-Jacoby#–T • fragment • line
0261 SIMONIDES Lyr.
001 Fragment • line
002 Fragment • subfragment • line
003 Book • epigram • line
004 Volume-Jacoby#–T • fragment • line
005 Volume-Jacoby#–F • fragment • line
4013 SIMPLICIUS Phil.
001–005 Volume • page • line
006 Page • line
2245 SIMUS Phil.
001 Fragment • line
0398 SIMYLUS Comic.
001 Fragment • line
002 Page • line
1675 SIMYLUS Eleg.
002 Fragment • line

1676 SIMYLUS Iamb.
001 Page • line
002 Fragment • line
1893 SISYPHUS Hist.
001 Volume-Jacoby#–T • fragment • line
002 Volume-Jacoby#–F • fragment • line
2644 SMINTHES Astron.
001 Fragment • line
1677 SOCRATES Epigr.
001 Book • epigram • line
1678 SOCRATES Hist.
001 Volume-Jacoby#–T • fragment • line
002 Volume-Jacoby#–F • fragment • line
1679 SOCRATES Hist.
001 Volume-Jacoby#–F • fragment • line
0262 SOCRATES Phil.
001 Fragment • line
2057 SOCRATES Scholasticus Hist.
001 Book • chapter • line
0637 SOCRATICORUM EPISTULAE
001 Epistle • section • line
0636 SOCRATIS EPISTULAE
001 Epistle • section • line
1680 <SODAMUS> Eleg.
001 Fragment • line
1786 SOGENES Comic.
001 Fragment • line
0263 SOLON Nomographus et Poeta
001 Fragment • line
1681 SOLONIS EPISTULAE
001 Epistle • line
1682 SOPATER Comic.
001 Fragment • line
2031 SOPATER Rhet.
001–003 Volume • page • line
1683 SOPHAENETUS Hist.
001 Volume-Jacoby#–T • fragment • line
002 Volume-Jacoby#–F • fragment • line
0502 SOPHILUS Comic.
001 Fragment • line
002 Play • fragment • line
0011 SOPHOCLES Trag.
001–007 Line
008–010 Fragment • line
0326 SOPHOCLES Junior Trag.
001 Fragment • line
4030 SOPHONIAS Phil.
001 Page • line
0524 SOPHRON Mimogr.
001–002 Fragment • line
4149 SOPHRONIUS Gramm.
001 Page • line
4042 SOPHRONIUS Soph., Scr. Eccl. et Epigr.
016 Book • epigram • line
0565 SORANUS Med.
001 Book • chapter • section • line
002–004 Section • line
2481 SOSANDER Perieg.
001 Volume-Jacoby#–T • fragment • line
1685 SOSIBIUS Gramm.
001 Volume-Jacoby#–T • fragment • line
002 Volume-Jacoby#–F • fragment • line
003 FGrH fragment • line
0503 SOSICRATES Comic.
001 Fragment • line
002 Play • fragment • line
1687 SOSICRATES Hist.
001 Volume-Jacoby#–T • fragment • line

002 Volume-Jacoby#–F • fragment • line
1748 SOSIGENES Phil.
001 Fragment • line
0504 SOSIPATER Comic.
001 Fragment • line
002 Play • fragment • line
0338 SOSIPHANES Trag.
001 Fragment • line
0340 SOSITHEUS Trag.
001 Fragment • line
2568 [SOSTHENES] Hist.
001 Volume-Jacoby#–F • fragment • line
1688 SOSTRATUS Gramm.
001 Volume-Jacoby#–F • fragment • line
002 Fragment • line
2694 SOSTRATUS Poeta
001 Fragment • line
1689 SOSYLUS Hist.
001 Volume-Jacoby#–T • fragment • line
002 Volume-Jacoby#–F • fragment • line
1690 SOTADEA
001 Fragment • line
0505 SOTADES Comic.
001 Fragment • line
002–003 Play • fragment • line
1691 SOTADES Iamb.
001 Fragment • line
2258 SOTADES Phil.
001 Volume-Jacoby#–T • fragment • line
2442 SOTERICHUS Epic. et Hist.
001 Volume-Jacoby#–T • fragment • line
002 Volume-Jacoby#–F • fragment • line
0587 SOTION <Paradox.>
001 Section • line
2048 Salaminius Hermias SOZOMENUS Scr. Eccl.
001 Book • chapter • section • line
1692 SPEUSIPPUS Phil.
001 Epistle • section • line
004 Book • epigram • line
005 Fragment • line
1693 SPHAERUS Phil.
001 Fragment • line
002 Volume-Jacoby#–T • fragment • line
003 Volume-Jacoby#–F • fragment • line
1846 SPINTHARUS Trag.
001 Line
2182 STAPHYLUS Hist.
001 Volume-Jacoby#–T • fragment • line
002 Volume-Jacoby#–F • fragment • line
1694 STATYLLIUS FLACCUS Epigr.
001 Book • epigram • line
0506 STEPHANUS Comic.
001 Fragment • line
002 Play • fragment • line
4028 STEPHANUS Gramm.
001 Page • line
002 Book • epigram • line
9020 STEPHANUS Gramm.
001 Page • line
0736 STEPHANUS Med.
001 Section • line
0724 STEPHANUS Med. et Phil.
001 Volume • page • line
002 Chapter • section • line
003–004 Page • line
9019 STEPHANUS Phil.
001 Page • line
0292 STESICHORUS Lyr.

001–002 Fragment • line
0981 **STESICHORUS II** Lyr.
001 Line
2171 **STESICLIDES** Hist.
001 Volume–Jacoby#–F • fragment • line
1923 **STESIMBROTUS** Hist.
001 Volume–Jacoby#–T • fragment • line
002 Volume–Jacoby#–F • fragment • line
0315 **STHENELUS** Trag.
001–002 Fragment • line
1695 **<STHENIDAS>** Phil.
001 Page • line
2037 **Joannes STOBAEUS**
001 Book • chapter • section • line
0099 **STRABO** Geogr.
001 Book • chapter • section • line
002 Volume–Jacoby#–T • fragment • line
003 Volume–Jacoby#–F • fragment • line
0507 **STRATON** Comic.
001 Fragment • line
002 Play • fragment • line
003 Fragment • line
1697 **STRATON** Epigr.
001 Book • epigram • line
1963 **STRATON** Hist.
001 Volume–Jacoby#–T • fragment • line
1696 **STRATON** Phil.
001 Fragment • line
2645 **STRATONICUS** Poeta
001 Fragment • line
0508 **STRATTIS** Comic.
001 Fragment • line
002 Play • fragment • line
003–004 Fragment • line
005 Play • fragment • line
1931 **STRATTIS** Hist.
001 Volume–Jacoby#–T • fragment • line
9010 *SUDA*
001 Alphabetic letter • entry • line
002 Section • line
1760 **Gaius SUETONIUS TRAN-
    QUILLUS** Hist. et Gramm.
001–002 Section • line
2416 **SUIDAS** Hist.
001 Volume–Jacoby#–F • fragment • line
1920 **Gaius SULPICIUS GALBA** Hist.
001 Volume–Jacoby#–T • fragment • line
002 Volume–Jacoby#–F • fragment • line
0264 **SUSARION** Comic.
001 Fragment • line
002 Line
003 Fragment • line
3115 **SYMEON METAPHRASTES**
    Biogr. et Hist.
001 Volume • page • line
4043 **SYNESIUS** Epigr.
001 Book • epigram • line
2006 **SYNESIUS** Phil.
001 Epistle • line
002 Section • line
003 Chapter • section • line
004–007 Section • line
008 Homily • line
009 Oration • section • line
010 Hymn • line
011 Book • epigram • line
2047 *SYRIANI, SOPATRI ET MAR-
    CELLINI SCHOLIA AD HER-
    MOGENIS STATUS*

001 Volume • page • line
4017 **SYRIANUS** Phil.
001–004 Page • line
2540 **SYRISCUS** Hist.
001 Volume–Jacoby#–T • fragment • line
1766 **TATIANUS** Apol.
001 Chapter • section • line
002 Line
2476 **TAURON** Hist.
001 Volume–Jacoby#–T • fragment • line
002 Volume–Jacoby#–F • fragment • line
1597 **<TELAUGES>** Phil.
001 Page • line
0510 **TELECLIDES** Comic.
001 Fragment • line
002 Play • fragment • line
003 Fragment • line
2264 **TELEPHANES** Hist.
001 Volume–Jacoby#–F • fragment • line
1698 **TELEPHUS** Gramm.
001 Volume–Jacoby#–T • fragment • line
002 Volume–Jacoby#–F • fragment • line
1699 **TELES** Phil.
001–008 Page • line
2211 **TELESARCHUS** Hist.
001 Volume–Jacoby#–F • fragment • line
0369 **TELESILLA** Lyr.
001 Fragment • line
0377 **TELESTES** Lyr.
001–002 Fragment • line
1903 **TELLIS** Hist.
001 Volume–Jacoby#–T • fragment • line
002 Volume–Jacoby#–F • fragment • line
0299 **TERPANDER** Lyr.
001–002 Fragment • line
1700 *TESTAMENTA XII PATRI-
    ARCHARUM*
001 Testamentum • chapter • section •
    line
1701 *TESTAMENTUM ABRAHAE*
001–002 Section • line
1702 *TESTAMENTUM JOBI*
001 Chapter • section • line
2679 *TESTAMENTUM SALOMONIS*
001–010 Page • line
2015 *TESTAMENTUM XL MAR-
    TYRUM*
001 Chapter • section • line
1704 **TEUCER** Hist.
001 Volume–Jacoby#–T • fragment • line
002 Volume–Jacoby#–F • fragment • line
2288 **TEUPALUS** Hist.
001 Volume–Jacoby#–T • fragment • line
1705 **THALES** Phil.
001 Epistle • line
002–003 Fragment • line
1707 **Antonius THALLUS** Epigr.
001 Book • epigram • line
1706 **THALLUS** Hist.
001 Volume–Jacoby#–T • fragment • line
002 Volume–Jacoby#–F • fragment • line
4044 **THEAETETUS** Epigr.
001 Book • epigram • line
1708 **THEAETETUS** Poeta
001 Book • epigram • line
1709 **THEAGENES** Hist.
001 Volume–Jacoby#–T • fragment • line
002 Volume–Jacoby#–F • fragment • line
2275 **THEAGENES** Phil.

001 Fragment • line
1710 **<THEAGES>** Phil.
001 Page • line
0054 **<THEANO>** Phil.
001 Page • line
1711 **<THEARIDAS>** Phil.
001 Page • line
1713 **THEMISON** Hist.
001 Volume–Jacoby#–F • fragment • line
2001 **THEMISTIUS** Phil. et Rhet.
001–011 Harduin page • section • line
013–034 Harduin page • section • line
035 Line
036 Fragment • line
037 Dindorf page • section • line
038–042 Volume • page • line
0055 *THEMISTOCLIS EPISTULAE*
001 Epistle • line
1924 **THEMISTOGENES** Hist.
001 Volume–Jacoby#–T • fragment • line
2515 **THEOCHRESTUS** Hist.
001 Volume–Jacoby#–T • fragment • line
002 Volume–Jacoby#–F • fragment • line
0206 **THEOCLES** Lyr.
001 Line
1947 **THEOCLIUS** Hist.
001 Volume–Jacoby#–F • fragment • line
0005 **THEOCRITUS** Bucol.
001 Idyll • line
002 Epigram • line
003 Line
004 Fragment • line
005 Book • epigram • line
1714 **THEOCRITUS** Soph.
001 Fragment • line
002 Volume–Jacoby#–T • fragment • line
003 Fragment • line
0329 **THEODECTAS** Trag.
001 Fragment • line
1928 **THEODECTES** Hist.
001 Volume–Jacoby#–T • fragment • line
2125 **THEODORETUS** Gramm.
001 Book • epigram • line
4089 **THEODORETUS** Scr. Eccl. et
    Theol.
001 Book • section • line
002–003 Page • line
004 Vita • section • line
005–007 Epistle • line
008 Section • line
016 Page • line
020–021 Volume • page • line
022 Page • line
023–035 Volume • page • line
1715 **THEODORIDAS** Epigr.
001 Book • epigram • line
002 Fragment • line
1094 **THEODORIDES** Trag.
001 Line
1716 **THEODORUS** Epigr.
001 Book • epigram • line
4045 **THEODORUS** Epigr.
001 Book • epigram • line
3158 **THEODORUS** Epist.
001 Epistle • line
1717 **THEODORUS** Gramm.
001 Book • epigram • line
2251 **THEODORUS** Hist.
001 Volume–Jacoby#–T • fragment • line

1892 **THEODORUS** Hist.
001 Volume–Jacoby#–F • fragment • line
2161 **THEODORUS** Hist.
001 Volume–Jacoby#–F • fragment • line
2551 **THEODORUS** Hist.
001 Volume–Jacoby#–T • fragment • line
2570 **THEODORUS** Hist.
001 Volume–Jacoby#–T • fragment • line
1904 **THEODORUS** Hist.
001 Volume–Jacoby#–F • fragment • line
2150 **THEODORUS** Hist.
001 Volume–Jacoby#–T • fragment • line
2237 **THEODORUS** Math.
001 Fragment • line
2696 **THEODORUS** Poeta
001 Fragment • line
1987 **THEODORUS** Poeta
001 Volume–Jacoby#–T • fragment • line
002 Fragment • line
4126 **THEODORUS** Scr. Eccl.
002 Fragment • line
004 Fragment • line
4135 **THEODORUS** Theol.
009 Fragment • line
015–018 Page • line
0611 **THEODORUS** Trag.
001 Line
2967 **THEODORUS Heracleensis vel**
THEODORUS Mopsuestenus Scr.
Eccl.
001 Fragment • line
1718 **THEODORUS** ὁ παναγής Gramm.
001 Volume–Jacoby#–F • fragment • line
3157 **THEODORUS Scutariota** Hist.
001 Fragment • line
2714 **THEODORUS STUDITES** Scr.
Eccl. et Theol.
001 Volume • page • line
2020 **THEODOSIUS** Gramm.
001–002 Part • volume • page • line
003–005 Page • line
1719 **THEODOSIUS** Math. et Astron.
001 Chapter • section • line
002 Section • line
003 Page • line
1720 **THEODOTUS Judaeus** Epic.
002 Fragment • line
003 Volume–Jacoby#–F • fragment • line
1722 **THEOGENES** Hist.
001 Volume–Jacoby#–F • fragment • line
0511 **THEOGNETUS** Comic.
001 Fragment • line
002 Play • fragment • line
003 Fragment • line
0002 **THEOGNIS** Eleg.
001–002 Line
003 Fragment • line
004 Book • epigram • line
2367 **THEOGNIS** Hist.
001 Volume–Jacoby#–F • fragment • line
0313 **THEOGNIS** Trag.
001 Fragment • line
1723 **THEOLYTUS** Epic.
001 Fragment • line
2332 **THEOLYTUS** Hist.
001 Volume–Jacoby#–F • fragment • line
1838 **THEON** Gramm.
001 Fragment • line
002 Page • line

003 Column • line
2033 **THEON** Math.
001–002 Page • line
006 Volume–Jacoby#–T • fragment • line
007 Book • epigram • line
1724 **THEON** Phil.
001 Page • line
0607 **Aelius THEON** Rhet.
001 Page • line
1981 **THEOPHANES** Hist.
001 Volume–Jacoby#–T • fragment • line
002 Volume–Jacoby#–F • fragment • line
4046 **THEOPHANES CONFESSOR**
Chronogr.
001 Page • line
002 Book • epigram • line
4153 *THEOPHANES CONTINUATUS*
001 Page • line
1725 **THEOPHILUS** Apol.
001 Book • section • line
0512 **THEOPHILUS** Comic.
001 Fragment • line
002 Play • fragment • line
2496 **THEOPHILUS** Hist.
001 Volume–Jacoby#–F • fragment • line
2203 **[THEOPHILUS]** Hist.
001 Volume–Jacoby#–F • fragment • line
2394 **THEOPHILUS** Hist.
001 Volume–Jacoby#–F • fragment • line
4115 **THEOPHILUS** Scr. Eccl.
029–030 Fragment • line
0729 **THEOPHILUS Protospatharius**
Med.
002–003 Chapter • section • line
004 Page • line
005 Book • section • line
0728 **THEOPHILUS Protospatharius,**
DAMASCIUS et STEPHANUS
Atheniensis Med.
001 Volume • page • line
0746 **THEOPHILUS Protospatharius et**
STEPHANUS Atheniensis Med.
001 Page • line
0093 **THEOPHRASTUS** Phil.
001–002 Book • chapter • section • line
003–004 Section • line
005 Fragment • line
006 Usener page • line
007 Fragment • line
008 Section • line
009 Chapter • section • line
010 Fragment • section • line
014 Book • chapter • section • line
015 Folio • line
3130 **THEOPHYLACTUS SIMO-**
CATTA Hist. et Epist.
001 Epistle • line
003 Book–dialogue–index • chapter •
section • line
007 Page • line
009 Section • line
0513 **THEOPOMPUS** Comic.
001 Fragment • line
002 Play • fragment • line
003–004 Fragment • line
1726 **THEOPOMPUS** Epic.
001 Line
002 Fragment • line
0566 **THEOPOMPUS** Hist.

001 Volume–Jacoby#–T • fragment • line
002 Volume–Jacoby#–F • fragment • line
003 FGrH fragment • line
1874 **Gaius Julius THEOPOMPUS**
Myth.
001 Volume–Jacoby#–T • fragment • line
4047 **THEOSEBEIA** Epigr.
001 Book • epigram • line
1727 **THEOTIMUS** Hist.
001 Volume–Jacoby#–F • fragment • line
2561 **THEOTIMUS** Hist.
001 Volume–Jacoby#–F • fragment • line
1728 **THESEUS** Hist.
001 Volume–Jacoby#–T • fragment • line
002 Volume–Jacoby#–F • fragment • line
0301 **THESPIS** Trag.
001 Fragment • line
0816 **THEUDO[TUS]** Trag.
001 Line
2400 **THIBRON** Hist.
001 Volume–Jacoby#–T • fragment • line
4048 **THOMAS** Epigr.
001 Book • epigram • line
4049 **THOMAS** Epigr.
001 Book • epigram • line
9023 **THOMAS MAGISTER** Philol.
002 Poem • line
2231 **THRASYALCES** Phil.
001 Fragment • line
0056 *THRASYBULI EPISTULA*
001 Line
2176 **THRASYLLUS** Hist.
001 Volume–Jacoby#–F • fragment • line
2428 **THRASYLLUS** Hist.
001 Volume–Jacoby#–T • fragment • line
1729 **THRASYMACHUS** Rhet. et Soph.
001–002 Fragment • line
0003 **THUCYDIDES** Hist.
001 Book • chapter • section • line
002 Book • epigram • line
0514 **THUGENIDES** Comic.
001 Fragment • line
002 Play • fragment • line
003 Fragment • line
1730 **THYILLUS** Epigr.
001 Book • epigram • line
1731 **THYMOCLES** Epigr.
001 Book • epigram • line
2126 **TIBERIUS** Epigr.
001 Book • epigram • line
1732 **TIMACHIDAS** Hist.
001 Volume–Jacoby#–F • fragment • line
002 Fragment • line
1733 **TIMAEUS** Hist.
001 Volume–Jacoby#–T • fragment • line
002 Volume–Jacoby#–F • fragment • line
003 FGrH fragment • line
2569 **<TIMAEUS>** Hist.
001 Volume–Jacoby#–T • fragment • line
1734 **TIMAEUS** Phil.
001 Page • line
002 Fragment • line
1918 **TIMAGENES** Hist.
001 Volume–Jacoby#–T • fragment • line
002 Volume–Jacoby#–F • fragment • line
2268 **TIMAGORAS** Hist.
001 Volume–Jacoby#–F • fragment • line
0889 **TIMESITHEUS** Trag.
001 Line

1960 **TIMOCHARES** Hist.
001 Volume-Jacoby#-F • fragment • line
0515 **TIMOCLES** Comic.
001 Fragment • line
002 Play • fragment • line
003-004 Fragment • line
0333 **TIMOCLES** Trag.
001 Fragment • line
2388 **TIMOCRATES** Hist.
001 Volume-Jacoby#-F • fragment • line
2459 **TIMOCRATES** Hist.
001 Volume-Jacoby#-T • fragment • line
0265 **TIMOCREON** Lyr.
001-002 Fragment • line
003 Book • epigram • line
2301 **TIMOGENES** Hist. et Rhet.
001 Volume-Jacoby#-T • fragment • line
2533 **TIMOLAUS** Hist.
001 Volume-Jacoby#-F • fragment • line
2697 **TIMOLAUS** Rhet.
001 Fragment • line
2509 **TIMOMACHUS** Hist.
001 Volume-Jacoby#-F • fragment • line
1735 **TIMON** Phil.
002 Book • epigram • line
003 Fragment • line
1736 **TIMONAX** Hist.
001 Volume-Jacoby#-F • fragment • line
2386 **TIMONIDES** Hist.
001 Volume-Jacoby#-T • fragment • line
002 Volume-Jacoby#-F • fragment • line
1002 **TIMOSTHENES** Geogr.
002 Volume-Jacoby#-F • fragment • line
0516 **TIMOSTRATUS** Comic.
001 Fragment • line
002-003 Play • fragment • line
0517 **TIMOTHEUS** Comic.
001 Fragment • line
002 Play • fragment • line
2449 **TIMOTHEUS** Gramm.
001 Volume-Jacoby#-T • fragment • line
2213 **[TIMOTHEUS]** Hist.
001 Volume-Jacoby#-F • fragment • line
0376 **TIMOTHEUS** Lyr.
001-002 Fragment • line
0467 **TIMOTHEUS** Trag.
001 Line
1793 **TIMOXENUS** Comic.
001 Fragment • line
1738 *TRAGICA ADESPOTA*
001-003 Fragment • line
1739 *TRAJANUS* **Imperator**
001 Book • epigram • line
0647 **TRIPHIODORUS** Epic. et Gramm.
001 Line
2127 **TROILUS** Soph.
001 Page • line
002 Book • epigram • line
1740 **TRYPHON** Epigr.
001 Book • epigram • line
0609 **TRYPHON I** Gramm.
001-002 Page • line
003 Treatise • fragment • line
1763 **TRYPHON II** Gramm.
001 Chapter • section • line
1741 **<TUDICIUS GALLUS>** Epigr.
001 Book • epigram • line

1742 **TULLIUS GEMINUS** Epigr.
001 Book • epigram • line
1743 **TULLIUS LAUREA** Epigr.
001 Book • epigram • line
1745 **TULLIUS SABINUS** Gramm.
001 Book • epigram • line
1744 **TYMNES** Epigr.
001 Book • epigram • line
0367 **TYNNICHUS** Lyr.
001 Line
1266 **TYRANNION** Gramm.
001 Fragment • line
1611 **TYRANNION Junior** Gramm.
001 Fragment • line
0266 **TYRTAEUS** Eleg.
001 Fragment • line
002 Volume-Jacoby#-F • fragment • line
9022 **Joannes TZETZES** Gramm. et Poeta
006 Page • line
2604 **ULPIANUS** Gramm. et Rhet.
001 Page • line
2462 **ULPIANUS** Soph.
001 Volume-Jacoby#-T • fragment • line
002 Volume-Jacoby#-F • fragment • line
2461 **URANIUS** Hist.
001 Volume-Jacoby#-T • fragment • line
002 Volume-Jacoby#-F • fragment • line
1746 **VALENTINUS** Gnost.
001 Line
1950 **VARRO** Hist.
001 Volume-Jacoby#-T • fragment • line
1764 **VETTIUS VALENS** Astrol.
001 Page • line
1747 *VITA ADAM ET EVAE*
001 Section • line
1521 *VITA ET SENTENTIAE SE-CUNDI*
001 Page • line
002 Sententia • line
4166 *VITAE AESCHINIS*
001 Vita • line
1765 *VITAE AESOPI*
001-002 Section • line
4161 *VITAE ARATI ET VARIA DE ARATO*
001-005 Page • line
006 Section • line
007-009 Page • line
010-014 Section • line
4173 *VITAE DIONYSII PERI-EGETAE*
001 Line
1749 *VITAE HESIODI PARTICULA*
001 Line
1805 *VITAE HOMERI*
001 Line
002 Part • line
003 Page • line
004-007 Line
008 Chiliad • line
009-010 Line
4172 *VITAE OPPIANI*
002 Line
004-006 Line
4170 *VITAE PINDARI ET VARIA DE PINDARO*
001 Page • line

1751 **XANTHUS** Hist.
001 Volume-Jacoby#-T • fragment • line
002 Volume-Jacoby#-F • fragment • line
003 FGrH fragment • line
1752 **XENAGORAS** Hist. et Geogr.
001 Volume-Jacoby#-T • fragment • line
002 Volume-Jacoby#-F • fragment • line
0518 **XENARCHUS** Comic.
001 Fragment • line
002 Play • fragment • line
2355 **XENIADES** Soph.
001 Fragment • line
1753 **XENION** Hist.
001 Volume-Jacoby#-F • fragment • line
0519 **XENO** Comic.
001 Fragment • line
002 Play • fragment • line
2558 **XENO** Hist.
001 Volume-Jacoby#-T • fragment • line
0316 **XENOCLES** Trag.
001 Fragment • line
2174 **XENOCRATES** Hist.
001 Volume-Jacoby#-F • fragment • line
0091 **XENOCRITUS** Epigr.
001 Book • epigram • line
2306 **XENOMEDES** Hist.
001 Volume-Jacoby#-T • fragment • line
002 Volume-Jacoby#-F • fragment • line
0267 **XENOPHANES** Poet. Phil.
001-002 Fragment • line
003 Book • epigram • line
004 Volume-Jacoby#-T • fragment • line
005-006 Fragment • line
2518 **XENOPHILUS** Hist.
001 Volume-Jacoby#-F • fragment • line
2241 **XENOPHILUS** Phil. et Mus.
001 Fragment • line
0032 **XENOPHON** Hist.
001-002 Book • chapter • section • line
003-004 Chapter • section • line
005 Section • line
006-007 Book • chapter • section • line
008-015 Chapter • section • line
1926 **XENOPHON** Hist.
001 Volume-Jacoby#-T • fragment • line
1973 **XENOPHON** Hist.
001 Volume-Jacoby#-T • fragment • line
2376 **XENOPHON** Hist.
001 Volume-Jacoby#-T • fragment • line
1876 **XENOPHON** Hist.
001 Volume-Jacoby#-T • fragment • line
2510 **XENOPHON** Hist.
001 Volume-Jacoby#-T • fragment • line
0641 **XENOPHON** Scr. Erot.
001 Book • chapter • section • line
002 Volume-Jacoby#-T • fragment • line
1754 *XENOPHONTIS EPISTULAE*
001 Epistle • line
2229 **XUTHUS** Phil.
001 Fragment • line
0601 **<ZALEUCUS Nomographus>** <Phil.>
001 Page • line
0076 **ZELOTUS** Epigr.
001 Book • epigram • line
2276 **ZENIS** Hist.
001 Volume-Jacoby#-F • fragment • line
2528 **ZENO** Hist.

001 Volume–Jacoby#–T • fragment • line
1956 **ZENO** Hist.
001 Volume–Jacoby#–T • fragment • line
2364 **ZENO** Hist.
001 Volume–Jacoby#–T • fragment • line
002 Volume–Jacoby#–F • fragment • line
0595 **ZENO** Phil.
001–002 Fragment • line
0635 **ZENO** Phil.
001–002 Fragment • line
2294 **ZENO** Phil.
001 Fragment • line
2167 **ZENOBIA Regina Palmyrae**
     <Hist.>
001 Volume–Jacoby#–T • fragment • line
0596 **ZENOBIUS** Gramm.

001 Book • epigram • line
0098 **ZENOBIUS Sophista** <Paroemi-
     ogr.>
001 Centuria • section • line
0597 **ZENODORUS** Gramm.
001 Page • line
0600 **ZENODOTUS** <Epigr.>
001 Book • epigram • line
0590 **ZENODOTUS** Gramm.
003 Volume–Jacoby#–F • fragment • line
004 Book • epigram • line
2550 **ZENODOTUS** Hist.
001 Volume–Jacoby#–F • fragment • line
0354 **ZENODOTUS** Trag.
001 Fragment • line
0125 ***ZENONIS EPISTULA***

001 Line
2647 **ZENOTHEMIS** Geogr.
001 Fragment • line
0128 **ZOILUS** Phil. et Rhet.
001 Volume–Jacoby#–T • fragment • line
002 Volume–Jacoby#–F • fragment • line
0130 **ZOPYRUS** Hist.
001 Volume–Jacoby#–F • fragment • line
0129 **ZOPYRUS** Hist.
001 Volume–Jacoby#–F • fragment • line
0355 **ZOPYRUS** Trag.
001 Fragment • line
1755 **ZOSIMUS** Epigr.
001 Book • epigram • line
4084 **ZOSIMUS** Hist.
001 Book • chapter • section • line